Jonathan M. Scott
Frank Martin

seventh edition

Strategic Management
Awareness and Change

CENGAGE
Learning®

Australia • Brazil • Japan • Korea • Mexico • Singapore • Spain • United Kingdom • United States

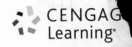

Strategic Management: Awareness & Change, 7th Edition
John Thompson, Jonathan M. Scott and Frank Martin

Publishing Director: Linden Harris

Publisher: Andrew Ashwin

Development Editor: Felix Rowe

Production Editor: Beverley Copland

Manufacturing Buyer: Elaine Willis

Marketing Manager: Amanda Cheung

Typesetter: MPS Limited

Cover design: Adam Renvoize

For product information and technology assistance,
contact **emea.info@cengage.com**.
For permission to use material from this text or product,
and for permission queries,
email **emea.permissions@cengage.com**.

British Library Cataloguing-in-Publication Data
A catalogue record for this book is available from the British Library.

ISBN: 978-1-4080-6402-3

Cengage Learning EMEA
Cheriton House, North Way, Andover, Hampshire, SP10 5BE
United Kingdom

Cengage Learning products are represented in Canada by Nelson Education Ltd.

For your lifelong learning solutions, visit **www.cengage.co.uk**

Purchase your next print book, e-book or e-chapter at
www.cengagebrain.com

Printed by China by RR Donnelley
1 2 3 4 5 6 7 8 9 10 – 15 14 13

Brief contents

Part 1   Understanding strategy and strategic management 1

Part 2   Analysis and positioning 109

Part 3   Strategy development 259

Part 4   Strategic growth issues 379

Part 5   Strategy implementation and strategic management 485

Contents

Part 1 Understanding strategy and strategic management 1

Part 3   Strategy development 259

Part 4   Strategic growth issues   379

List of cases

Online Cases

A range of additional cases can be found on the associated online platform. See the list provided at the end of each chapter.

Preface

About this book

This book is about strategic awareness, strategic analysis, strategy development, strategic decision making and the management of strategic change. It is designed for use by students who will become future managers and for managers in practice; after all, in some way or another, *all managers are strategy makers*. It looks at how managers become strategically aware of their company's position and potential opportunities for change, at how changes often happen in reality, and at how the process might be managed more effectively.

Strategic management is concerned with the actions that organizations take to deal with the changes, opportunities, threats, challenges and surprises in their external and internal environments. Put simply, strategies are means to ends. How, then, do organizations:

- determine desired outcomes?
- understand the circumstances and events affecting these outcomes and the means of attaining them?
- decide upon actions that they intend to take?
- implement these desired strategies through a series of tactical moves and changes?
- evaluate progress and relative success?

These are the broad themes addressed in this book.

Since the first edition was written over 20 years ago, the subject of strategic management has been developed and our understanding of certain aspects has changed. In addition, the world of business has been transformed by the rapid growth of the Internet and the emergence of the new and entrepreneurial dot.com organizations, and more recently a protracted recession fuelled in part by a banking crisis. At the same time, entrepreneurship as a subject has also increased in popularity and significance and it is not realistic to treat it as completely divorced from strategy as the two are very clearly related. While some of these changes were reflected in earlier editions of this book, this seventh edition sees further revisions to both the structure and content to bring both the text and the case material fully up-to-date. For this edition, we have edited every chapter and reduced the overall extent by removing material that had become somewhat dated. We have introduced some new content and figures; in particular, we have strengthened our treatment of innovation and entrepreneurship. Research Snapshots (explained later in this Preface) have been introduced at the end of most chapters. Further discernible changes have also been made to the structure of the book, especially to the running order of chapters, so as to make the book easier to navigate. The business model has been extended and given a chapter of its own; international strategy has been incorporated into the chapter on strategic (and international) growth rather than separated out. The case collection has been revised. The scope and variety of short cases has been increased, although the total number has been reduced to 81. All the retained cases have been checked for relevance and, where appropriate, revised. For this edition, John Thompson has continued his collaboration with Frank Martin from the University of Stirling; and Dr Jonathan M. Scott from University Teesside has joined and strengthened the author team.

Thinking strategically

Strategy is about how an organization sets about getting to where it wants to get. It is about setting, pursuing and achieving its mission and objectives. In the early stages of a company's development, this aspect is usually straightforward. It is not difficult for everyone concerned to appreciate the desired end points and the routes forward. As the business grows and diversifies then it separates into different parts and these have to be co-ordinated. Strategy takes on a different complexity. The ideal outcome is synergistic – the sum of the achievements of the various parts exceeds what they might be expected to achieve individually and independently. At this stage, issues of strategy and structure (including managing and controlling within the structure) have to be dealt with together. The ability to implement strategic ideas holds the key to prosperity.

If something goes wrong, it could be that the organization has made a strategic misjudgement – it has attempted to do something for which it is inadequately or inappropriately resourced, for example – or it could be that it makes mistakes in implementation – it underestimates the reaction of its competitors, perhaps.

Uncertainty (and, therefore, risk) is always prevalent in strategy. Organizations will plan to some extent, and they will vary in the extent to which they do plan. But managers can never plan for every eventuality and possibility. Strategies emerge as managers and organizations react to the world around them. They attempt to counter threats and seize opportunities. Flexibility is essential. How they do this comes down to the style and approach of the person in ultimate charge – the strategic leader. But in some way or other every manager is (potentially) a 'strategy maker'.

We might here draw a parallel with the 2012 London Olympic Games. Thousands of volunteers performing a wide range of modest support roles were seen as both essential and valuable for making sure 'everything worked' and enhancing the visitor experience. Although working to instruction, many of them made individual contributions and developed their own particular ways of doing things. They were called Games Makers.

Strategy may involve planning, plans and even formal documentation, but fundamentally it is a way of thinking and behaving.

In the end, it is probably true that 'everything in strategy is simple, but nothing in strategy is very easy'. It is a mistake to over-complicate things. It is also a mistake to underestimate competition – in part because new competitors can enter an industry quickly and surprisingly – or to ignore change pressures and become complacent.

It has to be tempting, though, to sit back and enjoy the fruits of success once an organization has become an industry leader and maybe a global organization in the process. But size and success is no guarantee of permanency, especially in the uncertain and turbulent economic conditions we have witnessed all round the world in the recent past. Corporate history (like military history) contains numerous stories of once-great, once-dominant corporations that have fallen by the wayside. It is vital that stasis and inertia are avoided. Again, it is an attitude of mind.

Prolonged success, then, in part, depends upon how organizations deal with setbacks and crises when they occur. Astute companies will have made preparations for dealing with possible crises, but they will still have to be dealt with when they happen. Yet again, this comes down to an ability to think things through and to stay vigilant and flexible. As always happens, some organizations will emerge intact from the recession we are still experiencing as we write these comments and be in a position to exploit the opportunities that are there. But other organizations will have fared less well. We need to understand why this is the case.

Of course, from time to time there will be changes of strategic leadership. When these changes happen, it is likely that newcomers will want to change strategies and/or structures. There is always the potential to improve things but it is equally possible to destroy something that works well.

From this short and cryptic explanation of strategy, you will see why we subtitle our book 'Awareness & Change'!

How to use this book

Structure and content

The content generally follows the established Analysis, Choice, Implementation model that is used in most strategy texts, and is structured in five parts, which systematically deal with a series of key questions and issues.

Part 1: *Understanding Strategy and Strategic Management* looks at the strategy process as a whole and includes a comprehensive explanation and framework of the process around which the book is structured. Part 1 introduces a mindmap summary of the book as a whole. Material on the business model is developed in a short dedicated chapter to stress its significance for understanding the strategy of an organization.

Content:

Chapter 1 What is strategy and who is involved?
Chapter 2 The business model and the revenue model
Chapter 3 Strategic purpose

Appended to Part 1 is a supplement on using frameworks to analyze strategy cases which lists the various tools and techniques that can be used to carry out a strategic analysis of any organization. These are then developed throughout the book, but this supplement is particularly useful for assignments and case analyses.

Part 2: *Analysis and Positioning* looks at three distinct but clearly related approaches to strategy: market- or opportunity-driven; resource-based; and competitor-influenced strategic management. It is crafted around the Environment–Values–Resources (E–V–R) model introduced in Chapter 1. Part 2 includes a number of tools and techniques which help us to understand the current competitive situation. This part also looks at strategic positioning and competitive advantage. Culture is a vital element of our study as it determines how strategies and changes are both determined and implemented.

Content:

Chapter 4 The business environment and strategy
Chapter 5 Resource-led strategy
Chapter 6 The dynamics of competition
Chapter 7 Introducing culture and values.

Part 3: *Strategy Development* describes and evaluates the different ways in which strategies are formulated and created. Several valuable planning models and techniques are discussed. We also look at both entrepreneurship and intrapreneurship in the chapter on strategic leadership; and we also explore the role and value of strategic planning. The part opens with a study of the various strategic alternatives that a firm might consider and with the determinants of a good choice.

Content:

Chapter 8 Creating and formulating strategy: alternatives, evaluation and choice
Chapter 9 Strategic planning
Chapter 10 Strategic leadership and intrapreneurship: towards visionary leadership?

Part Four: *Strategic Growth Issues* deals with both growth and retrenchment issues, which includes material on international strategy. There is also a discussion of business failure. This part opens with a chapter on evaluating strategic success.

Content:

Chapter 11 Strategic control and measuring success
Chapter 12 Issues in strategic and international growth
Chapter 13 Failure, consolidation and recovery strategies

Part Five: *Strategy Implementation and Strategic Management* evaluates the issues involved in strategy implementation. Organization structures, resource management and the complexities of managing change are included, as are issues of risk and crisis management.

Content:

Chapter 14 Strategy implementation and structure
Chapter 15 Leading change
Chapter 16 Managing strategy in the organization
Chapter 17 Final thoughts and reflections: the practice of strategy

Strategic management is a complex and dynamic subject and, as we said at the beginning of this Preface, since the first six editions of this book were published a number of new ideas and views have emerged. In addition, certain practices and priorities have changed to reflect developments around the world. Consequently, the whole text has once again been reviewed and, where appropriate, restructured. Every chapter has been edited and rewritten – although there are few radical changes – and some have been consolidated. Inevitably, new material has been added and some taken out. Many of the short cases are new.

Key themes

Strategy in practice

This new book contains a total of 81 short cases within the various chapters, which is fewer than the previous edition. We reviewed every case in the sixth edition and concluded that some, whilst still having value as a story illustrating a key theme, situation or decision, were best used as supplementary material. Consequently, they have been moved to become online learning materials, easily accessible on the online platform. They are listed at the end of every chapter for you to follow up as you wish. A number of new cases have been written for this edition and in this task we were keen to make sure there is a wide variety of organizations and countries. Clearly, then, we believe there is 'something here for everyone'. Lecturers who use the book will choose the ones that work best for their teaching and their students. Some 50 of the cases feature what we might call Western businesses – here organizations from the UK, USA and Europe all feature. The remaining cases are split roughly 50:50 between cases written about Far Eastern organizations, mainly Chinese and Indian companies, and cases written about organizations in the Southern Hemisphere: the African continent, Australia, New Zealand and South America.

All the cases cover large and small businesses, both national and international in scope, manufacturing and service, and the private, public and non-profit sectors, including social enterprises. The retail, leisure, financial and transport service industries are included, as are several non-profit and charity organizations. We have included a reasonable number of retail examples for several reasons. First, they are mostly recognizable companies that students can readily visit and experience at first hand. Second, they sell products that many readers will buy regularly. Third, they are in an industry that is subject to fashion and innovation; strategies change frequently. We have also determinedly included cases from industries that place a heavy reliance on the Internet. In part this is because they are typically very contemporary, but again it is because students can easily access them for follow-up material. A few of the cases have been included in earlier editions of this book, but where this is so they have been either updated or rewritten for this new edition.

Differing perspectives

It must be emphasized that no single approach, model or theory can explain the realities of strategic change in practice for all organizations; different organizations and managers will find certain approaches much more relevant to their circumstances and style. All approaches will have both supporters and critics. It is, therefore, important to study the various approaches within a sound intellectual framework so that they can be evaluated by students and other readers.

Students of business and management and practising managers must work out for themselves the intricacies and difficulties of managing organizations at the corporate level and of managing strategic change at all levels of the organization. It is no good being told how to be prescriptive when it is patently obvious that there is no universal model. Observations of practice in isolation are equally limited in their usefulness.

However, an attempt to find explanations that can be utilized does make sense. Testing and evaluating reality against a theoretical framework helps this process.

Key features

Cases and examples In addition to numerous references in the main text to organizations and events, as we mentioned above, some 80 short case examples are included. The cases are all designed to illustrate points in the main text. They are also intended to supplement the reader's own experiences and investigation. There are specific questions at the end of every case and relevant website addresses are provided to enable easy follow-up. Inevitably, some of the cases will date during the life of the text, in the sense that the strategies and fortunes of the companies featured in the examples will change. Strategies have life cycles, and strategies that prove effective at certain times will not always remain so. Companies that fail to change their strategies at the right time are likely to experience declining fortunes. Questions are included at the ends of chapters to encourage the reader to research and analyze the subsequent fortunes of companies included as cases.

As teachers and examiners ourselves, we are aware of the value of longer and more analytical cases that can be particularly useful for examination purposes. We also recognize that a number of competing books feature a selection of such cases. Instead we recommend that lecturers visit the Case Centre website – www.thecasecentre.org – where they will be able to search through abstracts for literally thousands of cases written by case writers from around the world – many of whom have enjoyed direct access to the organizations involved. In fact, longer cases on many of the organizations we feature in our 80 cases are there to be found if you are attracted to a particular business.

Learning objectives These appear at the start of every chapter to help you monitor your understanding and progress through the chapter. You will see we have adopted a principle of one learning objective for each major section in a chapter.

Boxes These are used in the text and featured separately within the relevant chapter for special emphasis and easy reference. They cover five tasks:

1 Boxes define Key Concepts in strategy and also explain significant contributions which underpin an understanding of strategic management.

2 Critical Reflections feature debates and discussions where there are differing opinions.

3 Strategy in Action boxes provide annotated applications of particular ideas and concepts.

4 Strategy in Practice boxes are new and they put strategy decisions and actions into an everyday setting to help provide insight into how we might interpret behaviours and events.

Research Snapshots are also new and appear at the end of most chapters. We believe that some, but not all, readers will be keen to access up-to-date and relevant journal articles and follow up on the current and recent strategy research agenda. Rather than attempt to capture this level of detail in the main text, and to keep the book easy-to-read, we have developed and separated these summaries and recommended reading lists. Where Research Snapshots are inappropriate to a chapter (for example, due to the 'generic' or introductory nature of its material), within the chapter the rationale for its exclusion is given.

Finance in Action Linked directly to certain chapters, and in the form of online appendices, there are Finance in Action supplements which expand upon points introduced in the text. They provide more detail than some readers will require; for others they enhance key aspects of strategic analysis.

Figures A comprehensive set of figures, which are either new or redrawn, illustrate and explain the issues covered in the text.

Quotations Short and pithy quotations from a variety of senior managers in the private and the public sectors are sprinkled throughout the text to illustrate a spectrum of opinions. These are useful for provoking class discussion and examination questions.

Chapter summaries An outline summary of the content and main points is given at the end of every chapter. This can help readers to check that they appreciate the main points and issues before reading on.

Questions and research assignments These are included at the end of each chapter. Some questions relate to the ideas contained in the text and the illustrative cases, and some are examples of the type that feature in non-case study examinations of this subject.

Several research projects, both library- and Internet-based, are included to encourage the reader to develop their knowledge and understanding further. The website provides a gateway of links to sites that are helpful in researching the Internet projects.

In addition we have included one extra short case at the ends of chapters 1–16 to allow further exploration of strategy in action.

Further reading There are also three different types of listings of books, chapters, journal articles and other sources of literature at the end of each chapter: (i) **Bibliography** are works that are not cited directly in the text but would be useful for students to follow up (compiled at the back of the book), (ii) **References** are those pieces of literature which are directly cited in the text and (iii) **Further reading** are the full list of references for each Research Snapshot, but which have not been called references, but instead 'further reading', to distinguish them from the reference list at the end of each chapter.

It should be appreciated that, although fresh articles are being published all the time, only a very small number add anything really new to our understanding of strategy and strategic management.

Glossary The book also includes a glossary, including definitions of well over 100 key terms. For ease of reference, words that are included in the glossary are highlighted in purple in the text.

Online resources

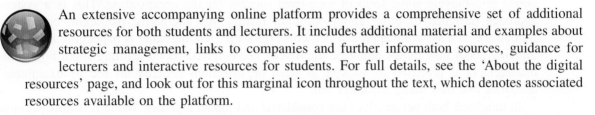 An extensive accompanying online platform provides a comprehensive set of additional resources for both students and lecturers. It includes additional material and examples about strategic management, links to companies and further information sources, guidance for lecturers and interactive resources for students. For full details, see the 'About the digital resources' page, and look out for this marginal icon throughout the text, which denotes associated resources available on the platform.

Advice for lecturers

Teaching aims

The main purpose of the book is to help students who aim to become managers, and managers in practice, to:

- develop their strategic awareness
- increase their understanding of how the functional areas of management (in which they are most likely to work) contribute to strategic management and to strategic changes within organizations
- appreciate how strategic change is managed in organizations.

The content is broad and the treatment is both academic and practical, in order to provide value for practising managers as well as full- and part-time students. The subject matter included is taught in a wide variety of courses, including undergraduate courses in business studies and related areas, MBA and other postgraduate Master's degrees, post-experience management courses and courses for a number of professional qualifications. The subject can be entitled strategic management, business policy, corporate strategy or business planning, although strategic management now seems the most popular.

The material is relevant for all types of organization: large and small businesses, manufacturing and service organizations, social enterprises and both the public and private sectors. The examples included relate to all of these. Although the topics discussed are broadly applicable, certain issues are sector specific, and these are discussed individually.

This edition has been written and structured into 16 main chapters to support courses that last up to a full academic year. Clearly, some lecturers will opt to spend longer than a single week or session on some topics or possibly switch the order of the chapters marginally. Neither of these should present any problems and suggested course outlines are provided on the website for different types of course. Some courses in strategy run for only a single semester, focusing more on the analytical aspects of the subject. A careful selection of chapters, in a logical sequence, can underpin such courses quite readily and a suggested outline is provided on the companion website.

Advice for students

Studying strategy

Strategic management is concerned with understanding, as well as choosing and implementing, the strategy or strategies that an organization follows. It is a complex process that can be considered from a number of different perspectives. For example, one can design prescriptive models based on a series of logical stages that look at how to choose and implement strategies aimed at achieving some form of long-term success for the organization. This is a systematic approach designed to bring about optimum results. An alternative paradigm, or conceptual framework, is a systemic approach that concerns understanding what is happening in reality and thinking about how things might be improved. The emphasis is on learning about how strategic management is practised by looking at what organizations actually do and by examining the decisions that they make and carry out.

In this book both perspectives are considered and linked together. While it is always useful to develop models that attempt to provide optimizing solutions, this approach is inadequate if it fails to explain reality. Strategic management and strategic change are dynamic, often the result of responses to environmental pressures, and frequently not the product of extensive deliberations involving all affected managers.

Managers should be aware of the issues and questions that must be addressed if changes in strategy are to be formulated and implemented effectively. At the same time, they should be aware of the managerial and behavioural processes taking place within organizations in order that they can understand how changes actually come about.

Prescriptive models are found quite frequently in business and management teaching. For example, there are models for rational decision-making built around the clear recognition and definition of a problem and the careful and objective analysis and evaluation of the alternative solutions. There are economic models of various market structures showing how an organization can maximize profit. However, decision-making invariably involves subjectivity and short cuts, and organizations do not always seek profit maximization as their top priority. Although organizations and individuals rarely follow these models slavishly – quite often they cannot, and sometimes they choose not to – this does not render them worthless. Far from it: they provide an excellent framework or yardstick for evaluating how people reach their decisions, what objectives are being pursued and how situations might be improved. The argument is that if managers observe what is happening and seek to explain it and evaluate it against some more ideal state then they will see ways of managing things more effectively. In this way, managerial performance can be improved. Note the use of the expression 'more effectively'. For a whole variety of reasons, situations cannot be managed *perfectly*.

The reader with personal experience of organizations, management and change (whether it is limited or extensive, broad or specialized) should use this experience to complement the examples and cases described in the book. Ideally, the experience and the cases will be used jointly to evaluate the theories and concepts discussed. There is no universal approach to the management of strategy and strategic change. An individual must establish what approaches and decisions are likely to prove most effective in particular circumstances, and why. This learning experience can be enhanced by:

- evaluating the theoretical and conceptual contributions of various authors
- considering practical examples of what has proved successful and unsuccessful for organizations

- examining these two aspects in combination to see which theories and concepts best help an understanding of reality.

The manager's job is change. It is what we live with. It is what we are here to create. If we cannot do that, then we are not good at the job. It is our basic job to have the nerve to keep changing and changing and changing again.

SIR PETER PARKER

Pressures to change are always present in the form of opportunities and threats. At any point in time, the significance of these pressures will vary markedly from industry to industry and from organization to organization. Managers may be aware of them and seek to respond positively; they may recognize opportunities and threats and choose to do little about them other than perhaps to avert crises; or they may be totally unaware of them. A lack of awareness can mean that potentially good opportunities are also lost; it may mean that businesses fail if they are not able to react and respond to the threats and problems when they arise. All businesses must react to pressures from the environment such as supply shortages, new products from competitors or new retailing opportunities, but some will be very proactive and thereby seek to manage their environment.

It is important to point out that students of strategic management may not be, or may not become, key strategic decision-makers in their organizations but instead may specialize in one particular function, such as marketing, production or finance. Similarly, their experience may be with only one product or one division if their employer is a multi-product or multi-divisional organization. Nevertheless, the decisions that they make or to which they contribute can affect the strategy for a particular product or service and in turn affect the organization. It is vital that they appreciate exactly how their function operates within an organizational context, and how decisions made in their area of interest can affect both other functions and the organization as a whole.

Finally, and to reinforce this last point, students occasionally ask whether 'strategic management' is about the management of strategy in organizations or about how people can manage strategically – an interesting point! The focus here is on the management of strategy in organizations but, by studying and applying the theory, and reflecting on its relevance in the context of personal observations and experience, readers should be able to improve their strategic effectiveness as managers. In essence they will benefit – as will any organization in which they work – by being better placed to take a strategic perspective and to use it to inform decisions and actions. Remember, there are no finite answers to the decisions and actions that should be taken. Organizations, and many of the problem issues they have to deal with, are complex and ill-defined. After all, if strategy were straightforward, the relative success rate of organizations of every type and size would be much greater than it is.

Experience is a wonderful thing, but not a useful one. When you are young, you don't trust others' experience – for if you do, this can paralyze you. When you get old, it is too late to use it – and you cannot transmit it for the reasons outlined.

JACQUES CALVET, WHEN LE PRESIDENT DU DIRECTOIRE, PSA PEUGEOT CITROËN

Acknowledgements

The publisher would like to thank the following reviewers for their contribution:

Dr Celine Chew,
Lecturer in Marketing and Strategy, Cardiff Business School, UK

Dr Rose Quan,
Senior Lecturer, Newcastle Business School, UK

Dr Stephen Henderson,
Senior Lecturer, Leeds Metropolitan University, UK

Mike Holland,
Director of Research, PriceMetrics, South Africa

Winnet Sami,
UNISA, South Africa

The publisher also thanks the various copyright holders for granting permission to reproduce material throughout the text. A credits page is provided at the back of the book. Every effort has been made to trace all copyright holders, but if any issues remain outstanding the publisher will be pleased to make the necessary arrangements at the first opportunity. Please contact the publisher directly.

Walk-through tour

Learning Objectives appear at the start of every chapter to help you monitor your understanding and progress through the chapter.

Quotes from senior managers in the private and public sectors are used throughout the text to illustrate a spectrum of opinions; these are ideal for provoking class discussion and examination questions.

Cases appear throughout the book to show how each chapter's main issues are applied in real-life business situations in different types of international and national companies. Each case is accompanied by questions to help test your understanding of the issues.

Glossary Terms are highlighted in colour throughout and explained in full in a glossary at the end of the book, enabling you to find explanations of key terms quickly.

Summaries end each chapter comprehensively by providing a thorough recap of the key issues in each chapter, helping you to assess your understanding and revise key content.

Research Snapshots provide insight into the latest research in the field of strategic management.

Strategy activities appear at the end of each chapter to aid and promote strategic thinking and analysis.

Bibliography and References include comprehensive references and often annotated further reading that allow you to explore the subject further, and acts as a starting point for projects and assignments.

Questions and Research Assignments and Internet and Library Projects provided at the end of each chapter help reinforce and test your knowledge and understanding, and provide a basis for group discussions and activities.

DIGITAL RESOURCES

Dedicated Instructor Resources

To discover the dedicated instructor online support resources accompanying this textbook, instructors should register here for access:
http://login.cengage.com

Resources include:

- Instructor's Manual
- ExamView Testbank
- PowerPoint slides

Instructor access

Instructors can access the online student platform by registering at **http://login.cengage.com** or by speaking to their local Cengage Learning EMEA representative.

Instructor resources

Instructors can use the integrated Engagement Tracker to track students' preparation and engagement. The tracking tool can be used to monitor progress of the class as a whole, or for individual students.

Student access

Students can access the online platform using the unique personal access card included in the front of the book.

Student resources

The platform offers a range of interactive learning tools tailored to the seventh edition of Strategic Management: Awareness and Change, including:

- Quizzes and self-test questions
- Interactive eBook
- Games
- Online Cases
- Web supplements referred to in the text
- Glossary, flashcards and crossword puzzles
- Links to useful websites

Look out for this symbol throughout the text to denote accompanying digital resources.

Understanding strategy and strategic management

Organizations, their strategies, their structures and how they are managed become ever more complex. Among the reasons for such complexity are the increasing turbulence and propensity to change in the **business environment**, and the tendency for multi-product, multinational organizations to become commonplace. Organizations need to know where they are, where they are going and how to manage the changes. Managers in these organizations need to know where their roles fit in relation to the whole and how they can contribute to strategic developments and changes. These are the issues addressed by a study of **strategic management**.

The first part of this book is designed to provide a broad appreciation of strategic management and to develop the framework used in the book in order to:

- outline the scope and complexity of the study area
- provide an initial overview of some major contributors to the subject in order to illustrate what is meant by, and included in the definition of, strategic management and to demonstrate that there is no single universally accepted approach
- provide a framework for the structure and content of the book
- explain the significance of a robust business model
- examine what is meant by purpose, direction and **objectives**, and consider how these might be set and used
- help you to think and act in a strategic way.

In Chapter 1 we introduce the subject of **strategy** and create the framework for this book. We examine and discuss what strategy is, who is involved in strategic decisions and how and when they are involved.

Chapter 2 is a relatively short chapter on the business and revenue models. These topics could have been included in Chapter 1 but we believe they are of significant importance and deserve special treatment.

Chapter 3 sets strategic decision-making into the context of strategic purpose; it helps us to understand why organizations pursue particular routes and what they are hoping to achieve.

There is a supplement to Part 1 which lists a variety of different frameworks that can be used for carrying out the strategic analysis of both an organization with which you are directly familiar and a strategy case study. It is written as a reference chapter and the various frameworks are then explored in greater depth as we progress through the book.

Chapter 1

What is strategy and who is involved?

PART 1
Understanding strategy

1 What is strategy and who is involved?
- Appendix

2 The business model and the revenue model

3 Strategic purpose
- Supplement:
  Using frameworks to analyze strategy cases

PART 5
Strategy implementation

14 Strategy implementation and structure

15 Leading change

16 Managing strategy in the organization

17 Final thoughts and reflections: the practice of strategy

STRATEGIC MANAGEMENT: AWARENESS AND CHANGE

PART 2
Analysis and positioning

4 The business environment and strategy

5 Resource-led strategy

6 The dynamics of competition

7 Introducing culture and values

PART 4
Strategic growth issues

11 Strategic control and measuring success

12 Issues in strategic and international growth

13 Failure, consolidation and recovery strategies

PART 3
Strategy development

8 Creating and formulating strategy: alternatives, evaluation and choice

9 Strategic planning

10 Strategic leadership and intrapreneurship: towards visionary leadership?

Learning objectives

Having read to the end of this chapter, you should be able to:

- define strategic management and strategic change, distinguishing between different types of, and perspectives on, strategy **(Section 1.1)**

- comprehend the importance of strategy as practice **(Section 1.2)**

- apply Thompson's E–V–R (Environment–Values–Resources) congruence model to organizations and their strategies **(Section 1.3)**

- clarify the three broad approaches to **strategy creation**, namely visionary ideas, planning and emergence **(Section 1.4)**

- appreciate how different views of strategy have developed **(Secton 1.5)**.

Strategies are means to ends. All organizations, large and small, profit-seeking and not-for-profit, private and public sector, have a purpose, which may or may not be articulated in the form of a mission and/or **vision** statement. Strategies relate to the pursuit of this purpose. Strategies must be created and implemented, and these issues are addressed by our study of strategic management.

1.1 Strategy explained

Organizations that succeed and sustain that success over a period of time will be able to demonstrate a number of achievements.

First – there is a clear purpose for what they are doing. This gives a degree of focus and directs the key decisions that need to be made. The purpose thus provides direction against which alternative choices and actions can be evaluated. We might also describe having a clear purpose and direction – together with the choice of actions designed to help fulfil that purpose – as having mastery of the so-called 'big picture'.

Working towards this big picture requires (co-ordinated) activities which cut across the various functional areas of the business – and sometimes a number of different individual businesses within the corporate whole. This more detailed level might be described as the 'little picture'. It is at this level that limited but critical competitive gains might be made. If we take a sporting analogy, then single goals can determine matches and sprinters beat their rivals by fractions of a second. The extent of the difference might not be great but it still matters.

As well as mastery of the big picture, strategic success requires getting the details right. Sustaining success requires continuous improvement and innovation at the activity level – but always with the big picture in mind. In summary, strategic success requires both a clear big picture and mastery of the details. Both are required; one alone is not enough.

Whilst we talk about organizations, they comprise people working individually and in teams (both formal and informal teams) who make decisions, and carry out (and improve) all the activities in which the organization engages. Clear understanding of the purpose and the overall strategy, commitment towards these and consistent **values** are, therefore, important in making serious progress. An additional argument might be made that an ethical approach is also of great significance.

In turn, these are affected by the way the organization is led and directed. Understanding strategic **leadership** is, therefore, at the core of strategic management.

Strategy in a nutshell

Adding some detail to this description, but still keeping the message simple, is a very important task. Strategy is about how organizations cope with the world, which is dynamic and emergent. Technologies, fashion and competitors all change constantly and simultaneously. Organizations have to harness all their strategic resources (including, in particular, their employees), deal with other **stakeholders** (such as funders and suppliers) and meet the expectations of their customers or clients. They sometimes have to deal with legislative and other constraints and often they have to out-manoeuvre competitors.

Strategies are means to ends; the process of strategic management involves:

- clarifying the desired ends
- mapping out a route for achieving them (*creating strategies*)
- putting those strategies into practice (**implementation**)
- changing what you are doing tactically in the face of competition and unexpected issues that arise
- evaluating progress and performance.

To do this effectively, organizations need a clear, if broad, vision and a willingness to be flexible in its pursuit. Strategies are sometimes determinedly intentional but on occasions they emerge from the choices that organizations make in the face of dynamic uncertainty. Intention can come from the personal insight of individuals and from a more analytical process.

Organizations thus need to be able to harness and deploy the necessary resources and to respond to both opportunities and competition. It is here that any distinctive **competitive advantage** (a real edge over rivals) is created.

To thrive and grow, organizations must be able to meet the expectations of their customers or clients and to do what they do at least as well as, and ideally better than, any rivals. Competitiveness is based on many things, but being different (in both a distinctive and a meaningful way), cost management and speed are all critical.

We can, therefore, think of strategy from three distinct, but clearly linked, perspectives – opportunity, capability and competitiveness. These three themes, together with aspirations and values, are the five key strategy drivers. They affect both the choices organizations make and how well they perform.

Strategy involves creation and ideas and also delivery – implementation. Implementation depends upon people who work together in organizations which can be cohesive and effective or more disjointed.

When organizations succeed, it is highly likely that they are doing the right things well. But if things go wrong, was the real problem what they were doing (the strategies) or how they were doing it (implementation)? It can be either – or both!

Put another way, successful organizations have a clear business model, which they implement well. They are clear what their product (or service) is, for whom it is intended, and why these target customers (clients) have a compelling reason to do business with them. And they produce and deliver the right **quality** both on time and consistently. Their customers are satisfied.

A number of important themes emerge from this. It is people who produce and deliver the products and services and so their skills, capabilities and motivation are critical. In turn, people work in organizations – in which their roles need to be clear but where they have some freedom to influence what goes on. In a competitive and uncertain environment it will be necessary for organizations to change from time to time, and sometimes quite frequently. Organizations must react to what happens in the world and in their industry; and they should look to innovate proactively to get and stay one step ahead of their rivals.

The ability to match resources and opportunities effectively, to harness resources and satisfy customer expectations, meeting performance targets in the process, and to change things as and when necessary, are very dependent upon the strategic leadership of the organization and the culture and values prevalent within the organization. The congruence (or relative incongruence) of environment, resources and values is, therefore, a good test of strategic **effectiveness**.

Above all, strategy is about choices: choosing what to do and choosing what not to do. The secret is to keep things focused and straightforward and to 'deliver' **through the implementation stage**.

What are strategies?

At their simplest, strategies help to explain the things that managers and organizations do. These actions or **activities** are designed and carried out in order to fulfil certain designated purposes, some of them short term in nature, others longer term. The organization has a direction and broad purpose, which should always be clear, articulated and understood, and which sometimes will be summarized in the form of a **mission statement**. More specific **milestones** and targets (objectives) can help to guide specific actions and measure progress.

Strategies, then, are means to ends

They are relevant for the organization as a whole, and for the individual businesses and/or functions that comprise the organization. They are created and changed in a variety of ways. They have, however, one common feature: they all have **life cycles** and need changing, either marginally or dramatically, at certain times.

To some extent all managers are strategy makers

While strategic management incorporates major changes of direction for the whole business, such as **diversification** and growth overseas, it also involves smaller changes in strategies for individual products and services and in particular functions such as marketing and operations. Decisions by managers in relation to their particular areas of product or functional responsibility have a strategic impact and contribute to **strategic change**.

Strategic management is a complex and fascinating subject with straightforward underlying principles but no 'right answers'. Strategy is about issues and perspectives on problems – there is no single, *prescriptive* doctrine which satisfies everyone's views.

Companies succeed if their strategies are appropriate for the circumstances they face, feasible in respect of their resources, skills and capabilities, and desirable to their important stakeholders – those individuals and groups, both internal and external, who have a stake in, and an influence over, the business. Simply, strategy is fundamentally about a fit between the organization's resources and the markets it targets – plus, of course, the ability to sustain fit over time and in changing circumstances.

Companies fail when their strategies fail to meet the expectations of these stakeholders or produce outcomes which are undesirable to them. To succeed long-term, companies must compete effectively and outperform their rivals in a dynamic, and often turbulent, **environment**. To accomplish such *strategic success*, they must find suitable ways for creating and **adding value** for their customers. A **culture** of internal co-operation and customer orientation, together with a willingness to learn, adapt and change, is ideal. **Alliances** and good working relationships with suppliers, distributors and customers are often critically important as well.

Some 35 years ago Morrison and Lee (1979) concluded that successful companies seem to be distinguished from their less successful competitors by a common pattern of management practices and these still hold:

- First, they identify more effectively than their competitors the **key success factors** inherent in the economics of each business. For example, in the airline industry, with its high fixed costs and relatively inflexible route allocations, a high load factor is critical to success. It is important, though, that high load factors are not at the expense of healthy sales of more expensive seats, and this requires skilful marketing.

- Second, they segment their markets so as to gain decisive competitive advantage, basing the segmentation on competitive analysis and often separating segments according to the strengths and weaknesses of different competitors – which enables them to concentrate on segments where they can both maximize their competitive advantage and avoid head-on competition with stronger competitors.

- Third, they carefully measure and analyze any competitive advantage. This requires a sound basis for assessing a company's advantages relative to its competitors.

- Fourth, they anticipate their competitors' responses. Good **strategic thinking** also implies an understanding of how situations will change over time. Business strategy, like **military strategy**, is a matter of manoeuvring for superior position and anticipating how competitors will respond, and with what measure of success.

- Fifth, they exploit more, or different, degrees of freedom than their competitors. Specifically, they seek to stay ahead of their rivals by looking for new competitive opportunities. Whilst innovation and constant improvement are essential, there are also potentially huge rewards for organizations which are first to reach the new competitive high ground by changing the currently practised rules of competition.

- Finally, they give investment priority to businesses or areas that promise a competitive advantage.

Because there are many views on strategy and strategic management and no single, universally accepted approach, a study of **strategic changes** in a variety of different organizations is valuable. An examination of outcomes, followed by an analysis of the decisions which led to these relative successes and failures, is rich in learning potential. Examples should not be confined to just one sector. Manufacturing and service businesses, the private and public sectors and **not-for-profit organizations** are all relevant.

Everyone who can make or influence decisions which impact on the strategic effectiveness of the business should have at least a basic understanding of the concepts and processes of strategy. The processes will often be informal, and the outcomes not documented clearly. But they still exist, and managing the processes effectively determines the organization's future. Without this understanding, people often fail to appreciate the impact of their decisions and actions for other people within the business. They are less likely to be able to learn from observing and reflecting upon the actions of others. They are also more likely to miss or misjudge new opportunities and growing threats in the organization's environment.

As a starting point, key terms used in this book are defined in Key Terms 1.1 and examples of strategic changes over time in three familiar organizations are illustrated in Strategy in Action 1.1.

Key Terms 1.1

Mission and Vision both relate to the essential purpose of the organization. The **vision** concerns why it is in existence and what it aims to become; the **mission** reflects what it needs to be if it is to pursue its purpose. It embraces the nature of the business(es) it is in, and the customers it seeks to serve and satisfy.

Values statements represent word pictures which reflect the future standing of the organization and how it will behave and feel. They will typically comprise a set of behaviours and key values to which employees should subscribe. They are linked to the mission, but there is a subtle difference.

Objectives (or goals) are desired states or results linked to particular time-scales and concerning such things as size or type of organization, the nature and variety of the areas of interest and levels of success. Taken to a particular level of detail they can become targets and milestones.

Strategies are means to ends, and these ends concern the purpose and objectives of the organization. They are the things that businesses do, the paths they follow and the decisions they take, in order to reach certain points and levels of success.

Tactics are the specific activities which deliver and implement the strategies in order to fulfil objectives and pursue the mission. Often short term, they can be changed frequently if necessary.

Strategic thinking is the ability of the organization (and its managers) to synthesize and share the learning from the organization's history, understand its present competencies and position and clarify ways forward.

Strategic awareness is the understanding of managers within the organization about: (a) the strategies being followed by the organization and its competitors, (b) how the effectiveness of these strategies might be improved and (c) the need for, and suitability of, opportunities for change.

Strategic management is a process or processes which need to be understood more than it is a discipline which can be taught. It is the process by which organizations determine their purpose, objectives and desired levels of attainment; decide on actions for achieving these objectives in an appropriate time-scale, and frequently in a changing environment; implement the actions; and assess progress and results. Whenever and wherever necessary, the actions may be changed or modified. The magnitude of these changes can be dramatic and revolutionary, or more gradual and evolutionary.

Strategic change concerns changes which take place over time to the strategies and objectives of the organization. Change can be gradual or evolutionary; or more dramatic, even revolutionary.

Synergy is the term used for the added value or additional benefits which ideally accrue from the linkage or fusion of two businesses, or from increased co-operation either between different parts of the same organization or between a company and its suppliers, distributors and customers. Internal co-operation may represent linkages between either different divisions or different functions.

Strategy in Action 1.1   Examples of Historic Strategy Changes

WH Smith, desiring growth beyond the scope offered from its (then) current business lines (wholesaling and retailing newspapers and magazines, stationery, books and sounds), diversified into do-it-yourself with a chain of Do-It-All stores, introduced travel agencies into a number of its existing stores and acquired related interests in Canada and America. Travel was later divested, along with investments in cable television, to enable greater concentration on sounds, videos and consumer and office stationery. Important acquisitions included the Our Price and Virgin music stores and the Waterstones chain of specialist booksellers. Do-It-All became a joint venture with Boots, but it struggled to be profitable with strong competition from B&Q and Texas, acquired by Sainsbury's in the mid-1990s. In 1996 WH Smith divested Do-It-All and its office stationery businesses. Later in the 1990s both Waterstones and Our Price were also divested, and the book publisher, Hodder Headline, was acquired – and later also divested.

In the last few years the Group has split into two separately listed companies: WH Smith now incorporates the retail stores in town and city centres and at airports and railway stations, whilst WH Smith News is the newspaper and magazine wholesale and distribution business. The retail stores have reduced their interest in music (because of the low margins and serious competition from other retailers, especially on-line retailers) and instead they focus on books, magazines, newspapers, cards and stationery. Other products – including chocolate – have been added as impulse purchase opportunities. Customers who have bought from WH Smith over the years generally now comment that the stores feel different from in the past,

that they are cluttered as the company attempts to achieve as much revenue as possible from every square foot of floor space. As a bookshop, for example, WH Smith is very different from a specialist bookseller such as Waterstones – although this company too has been subject to major changes. The highest growth in recent years has come from the shops at airports and railway stations.

The Burton Group is another UK high street retailer whose name has 'always seemed to be around'. Unlike WH Smith, Burton originally manufactured the men's suits that it sold. At one time made-to-measure bespoke suits were far more popular than off-the-peg clothes. But technology changed this as sizing became easier. Burton closed the last of its manufacturing interests in 1988. Once one of the leading men's clothing manufacturers in Europe, the group, by a series of related acquisitions and divestments, became essentially a major retailer of fashion goods for both men and women, changing the group name to Arcadia. In recent years Burton acquired – and later divested – Debenham's. Arcadia is now owned by the entrepreneur and specialist in corporate turnarounds, Philip Green. In part because of the opportunities offered by IT – and also faster transportation – bespoke clothing, often manufactured in the Far East but using European cloths – has been resurgent.

Oxfam is a UK based international charity that lobbies, campaigns, raises funds and carries out relief work related to famines and natural disasters such as the devastating tsunami in Indonesia back in 2004. One of its fund raising activities is Oxfam shops which are visible on high streets in most towns and cities and which rely extensively on volunteers and donated items. They have been described somewhat tongue-in-cheek as shops where middle class ladies sell their own mothers' cast-offs to their friends' daughters. In recent years Oxfam has opened specialist second-hand bookshops and in 2008 it announced a new venture in London. It was to open a fashion boutique in a deliberate attempt to move more up-market. The clothes would be new, remades or donations from designers. Oxfam is typical of many charities which have, on the one hand, to be aggressive fund raisers whilst, on the other hand, doing good and being seen to be doing good. In 2008 the shops were realizing that as the economy tightened many people were buying fewer new clothes and as a consequence discarding fewer clothes.

Explaining strategic management

Key Terms 1.1 defines strategic management as a process involving creation, implementation and change; and there are a number of components.

Obviously, first, the *strategy* itself. This is concerned with the establishment of a clear direction for the organization and for every business, product and service, and a means for getting there which requires the creation of strong competitive positions.

The second requirement is excellence in the **implementation** of strategies in order to yield effective performance.

Third, *creativity and* **innovation** to ensure that the organization is responsive to pressures for change and that strategies are improved and renewed.

Fourth, the ability to manage *strategic change*, both continuous, gradual, incremental changes and more dramatic, discontinuous changes. Innovation and change concern the strategy process in an organization.

Sound implementation and innovation should enable an organization to thrive and prosper in a dynamic, global environment, but in turn they depend on competencies in **strategic awareness** and learning. Organizations must be able to make sense of the world in which they operate and compete – spotting key opportunities and threats from the various signals is critically important and some do it better than others. Organizations must understand the strategic value of the resources that they employ and deploy, and how they can be used to satisfy the needs and expectations of customers and other stakeholders while outperforming competitors.

Strategy is about actions, not **plans** *– specifically the commitment of resources to achieving strategic ends ... concrete steps that immediately affect people's lives, not abstract intentions.*

ANDREW S. GROVE, CEO, INTEL

Many of these points are evident in the story of the now ubiquitous low-price, no-frills airlines, such as Ryanair and easyJet (See Case 1.1) which shows that:

- newcomers can change an industry – by being creative, innovative and different
- new competitors can, and will, find ways of breaking down apparent barriers to entry
- companies need to find some clear and distinct competitive advantage, something which is both attractive to customers and profitable
- this advantage will come from what organizations do, their distinctive competencies and capabilities
- charismatic and visible **strategic leaders** often have a major impact on the choice and implementation of key strategies
- people are critically important if strategies are to be implemented effectively
- the Internet is becoming increasingly important, and
- business can be fun!

It is, however, also important to realize that in many organizations certain parts may be 'world class' and highly profitable while other businesses are not. Good practices in the strong businesses can be discerned, transferred and learned, but this may not be enough. Some industries and competitive environments are

Case 1.1   The Low-Price, No-Frills Airlines   US, UK

This case features the three best known airlines in this sector of the industry. They have all been growing in recent years and their success has been earned at a time when the world's leading full-service carriers have all experienced problems. Their strategies may all be similar, but their stories, and the strategic leaders behind them, are quite different.

Herb Kelleher began **Southwest Air** in 1971 with a simple intention – 'fly people safely, cheaply and conveniently between Dallas, Houston and San Antonio', three key cities in Texas. Kelleher set out to compete against coach and car travel rather than the other airlines. He had been a champion college athlete and a successful Texas lawyer before he started the airline when he was 40 years old. The idea for Southwest, however, had come from a client (and co-founder of the business) who spotted the gap in the market.

Southwest has prospered and grown to become one of the largest carriers in the USA. After 30 successful years it served over 50 cities in 27 states and had some 2500 flights every day. Kelleher's strategy, competitive advantage and success has always been based on a number of factors:

- frequent and reliable departures
- relatively short journeys by American standards, now averaging 450 miles but with the average having increased as the airline has grown in size and destinations
- the choice of smaller airports nearer to city centres where relevant, in preference to international airports which are further away from the centre
- very low prices
- automated ticketing and direct bookings (without travel agents), and now using the Internet extensively
- limited *frills*, limited refreshments, no videos and just one class of seating – if airlines serve only soft drinks rather than coffee and tea (with the inevitable milk, sugar and stirrer) it is easier to collect passenger rubbish and thus speed up cabin cleaning between flights
- no seat assignments – which encourages passengers to turn up early so they can be towards the front of the boarding line, which in turn means planes are likely to take off on time. Now people who check-in online the day before they fly get boarding priority
- fast gate turnarounds, to maximize the time the planes are in the air

- a standardized fleet of Boeing 737s, to simplify maintenance.

Southwest is clearly America's leading short-distance, point-to-point carrier. Others have preceded it and others have joined the industry, but none of these has been able to make the equivalent impact. Southwest has won the US Department of Transport's coveted 'Triple Crown' award of best on-time record, best baggage handling and fewest customer complaints on several occasions. Every new route and destination is immediately popular and, as a result, Southwest has been consistently profitable for over 40 years, a unique record for an airline anywhere in the world.

Kelleher is a renowned 'people person'. Through profit-sharing schemes, employees own over 10 per cent of the company's stock, and he has made 'working in the airline industry an adventure'. Southwest is dynamic and responsive; employees accept empowerment and are motivated to work hard and deliver high levels of service consistently. Rules and regulations are minimized to allow staff the freedom to deal with issues as they arise. 'Ask employees what's important to them. Ask customers what's important to them. Then do it. It's that simple,' says Kelleher. The frequent flyer programme, unusually, rewards passengers for the number of individual flights, not the miles flown.

But it is never that simple! Southwest is also renowned as 'one of the zaniest companies in history'. From the very beginning, Kelleher encouraged flight attendants to crack jokes during in-flight emergency briefings, but, at the same time, operate with very high safety standards. He was determined that passengers would enjoy their flights. Some of the planes are decorated externally to reinforce the fun image. Three of them, promoting major sponsor Sea World, are flying killer whales; one is painted with the Texas flag; another is christened Arizona One, a spoof of Air Force One. Flight attendants have been known to hide in the overhead lockers as passengers come on board, startling them as they open up the lockers. Kelleher often appears in fancy dress for certain flights and special occasions. A special prize for the passenger with the biggest hole in their sock is quite typical.

Consequently, a sense of humour has become a key element in the recruitment process. During their training, employees are given a book with sections on jokes, games and songs – but they are all encouraged to develop an individual style. 'At Southwest we don't want clones – everyone is expected to colour outside the lines.' Kelleher is dedicated and focused and in possession of a strong ego. He is creative and innovative and he understands the contribution that people can make. He has always had the courage to be different. When he was introduced to an idea he appreciated the opportunity and activated it. Truly profit orientated, he has been extremely successful in a dynamic and cruel industry, where many competing airlines have failed.

Southwest has become a hugely popular airline and an iconic brand in America, it has flown over one billion passengers wihout a single fatal accident, but in 2008 it was fined for security breaches and criticized by the Federal Aviation Authority. Staff had been skimping on-board inspections – which all take up time between flights. Higher security vigilance is not an easy issue for airlines which want their planes to be on the ground for as short a time as possible. Presidential hopeful, Hillary Clinton, even commented that 'Southwest had a lot to answer for.'

easyJet, begun in 1995 by a 28-year-old Greek entrepreneur, Stelios Haji-Ioannou, the son of a wealthy shipping magnate, was a pioneer of no-frills flying in Europe. He intended to 'make flying in Europe affordable for more and more people'. Parodying British Airways' claim to be 'The World's Favourite Airline', easyJet began to call itself 'The Web's Favourite Airline.' The majority of its bookings come via the Internet; the rest are direct over the telephone. There are no commissioned travel agency bookings, no tickets and no on-board meals. Originally, when passengers with a reservation checked-in at the airport, they were allocated a number, based on their time of check-in, not when they prebooked, and this determined the order in which they boarded the aircraft. There were no seat reservations. easyJet's first hub airports in the UK were the relatively uncongested and quick turnaround Luton and Liverpool; and destinations are concentrated in Scotland and continental Europe, including Athens, Barcelona, Geneva and Nice. All the aeroplanes are relatively new Airbuses, painted white and orange and featuring easyJet's telephone number on the side. The airline became profitable for the first time in 1998. easyJet acquired Go, the no-frills competitor set up by British Airways. This meant a new hub at Stansted, the UK base of rival Ryanair, and rapid expansion. Early problems in co-ordinating the operations of the two carriers affected profitability.

Stelios had studied in the UK, at the London School of Economics and City University, and then worked for his father for a short while. He began his first business,

Stelmar Tankers, in 1992. easyJet's strategy was modelled on Southwest Air, but Stelios claimed he had been inspired by Richard Branson and Virgin Atlantic. His approach to customers and people mirrors that of Branson. Commuting from Nice – his main home is in Monte Carlo – initially he flew on his own planes several times a week and talked to the passengers. A television 'docusoap' on easyJet which began in 1998 showed that Stelios was regularly present at Luton (his headquarters) and willing to help resolve passenger problems.

I lead by example. I believe that people will do things if they see their boss doing exactly the same things … the best way to motivate a team is to convince them they're always under attack … having an external enemy is the best way of focusing their mind on results, rather than fighting each other and becoming complacent … I'm keen that important information is available to everybody in the company … there are no secrets.

The easyJet product is, in reality, a package of services, many subcontracted in. easyJet provides the planes and their crews, and markets and sells the flights. As a company, it is focused. Check-in and information services, snacks (for passengers to buy before they board the aeroplane), baggage handling and fleet maintenance are all bought in from specialists.

Stelios recruited Ray Webster, a senior executive from Air New Zealand, to be the chief executive of easyJet – and in 2002 he announced that he would relinquish the chairman's role so he could focus his energy and efforts on his other businesses. Sir Colin Chandler, who had been the strategic leader at defence giant, Vickers, replaced him. easyJet had planes on order from both Boeing (more 737s) and Airbus Industrie; when its fleet comprised two different aircraft easyJet had a different business model from that of Southwest Air and its main rival, Ryanair, the European market leader.

Stelios is a serial entrepreneur and he has begun a number of other businesses since the lauch of easyJet. None of them has been consistently profitable though. They include:

easyInternet café
easyCar – low cost car rental, mainly at airports
easyInternetdotcom – providing free web access
easyValue – a price comparison site on the web
easyMoney – an Internet bank
easyCinema – a cut-price cinema seat business.

In 2010 and 2011 easyJet's profits were hit by rising fuel costs and they recorded growing losses. Stelios, still the leading shareholder, was openly critical of certain Board members and Board decisions. In 2011 he also announced he planned to start another, new lost cost airline which he would call Fastjet.

easyJet's main rival is **Ryanair**, which was started by the Ryan family in Dublin in 1985 as a direct rival to Aer Lingus. A full-service carrier, it failed to grow into a profitable business. Michael O'Leary, a tax accountant, joined the business in 1991 and he soon became the strategic leader. O'Leary went to America to learn about Southwest Air and re-launched Ryanair as a no-frills, low-cost carrier. Again he has only used Boeing 737s; and Ryanair always looks for airports with relatively low charges even if they are several miles outside the city they serve. For example, the one serving Brussels (Charleroi) is 40km to the south of the city; the commute to Stockholm is 100km; and the one designated Copenhagen is actually over the border in Sweden. This provides a cost saving when compared with easyJet. Ryanair acquired Buzz, a rival low-cost carrier started by the Dutch airline, KLM. Whereas Stelios retained most of the Go operations when he acquired that business, O'Leary has retained only certain Buzz routes and very few of the staff.

Michael O'Leary has been described as 'bullying, foul-mouthed, charming and humorous'. He is invariably the public face of Ryanair and keen to defend the airline against any criticism of its strategies. His very successful strategy is based on defining a rival-beating price for a route, undercutting easyJet wherever they compete for a route, and then making sure costs are driven down to allow that route to be profitable. 'Everything we do is designed to pass on lower fares.' Like easyJet most promotions feature low fares. Ryanair claim the first 70 per cent of seats on every flight are available at the two lowest fares – for later bookings the prices can rise substantially.

Ryanair is the cost leader in the European industry. O'Leary generally manages to keep the costs at two-thirds of easyJet's, which means Ryanair's costs are 60 per cent of those incurred by UK holiday charter airlines and 50 per cent of those attributable to the leading full-service domestic carriers. O'Leary achieves savings in a number of ways, in particular:

- Buying aircraft when the manufacturers are experiencing trading problems, thus driving down the price.
- Selling costs – there are only direct sales. Outlawing travel agents can mean a saving of up to 15 per cent.

- Passenger services provided – there are no tickets in the normal sense and no air bridges – passengers have to walk out to the aircraft. There is a charge for any soft drinks served on board.
- Crew costs – pay rates are lower than rivals, and there are just three cabin crew on every flight, low for an aircraft of this size, but they are not there to serve food and drinks but to look after passenger safety.
- Ground handling – in part by not worrying how far away from cities airports are, and obtaining huge discounts by using airports which are chasing business.
- Seat density – Ryanair packs 15 per cent more passengers in its Boeings.
- Ryanair has begun charging for every case put into the hold and even experimented with flights where no hold bags are allowed – everything must be carried on, but with normal size restrictions applying.
- The airline charges people who need manual help to check in; instead customers are expected to use the self-service booths.
- Ryanair designs its own advertisements, ignoring specialist agencies. One irreverent ad featured the Pope and the phrase *Psst … want to know the 4th secret of Fatima*? which upset the Catholic Church but earned a huge amount of free publicity. By allowing other brands to be advertised on the outside of its planes Ryanair earns additional revenue.

By striking alliances with local hotels and transport providers (such as car hire firms) Ryanair earns commissions, which constitute some 15 per cent of its net profits. The airline has also started allowing passengers to use mobile phones and Blackberry's in the air – because it can earn a commission.

There are other less obvious reductions in the services provided by the no-frills airlines. Ryanair, for example, only have a relatively small customer services activity. The low-cost model means they are likely to be less sympathetic than the full-service carriers if passengers miss their flight or the flight has to be cancelled.

Ryanair has had to face its critics. It has been fined for charging a passenger for the provision of a wheelchair, a practice it vigorously defended and it has been accused of low service and a lack of responsibility when cases are damaged. A television documentary suggested the cost cutting and time saving had gone too far because when things were tight passenger passports were not being inspected properly before they boarded the plane. In addition its pilots were flying the maximum number of hours allowed on a routine rather than an exceptional basis.

In 2007 O'Leary gambled on oil prices falling, rather than rising, and he did not hedge. Ryanair profits were badly affected as fuel costs doubled to become 50 per cent of operating costs.

The no-frills carriers have certainly had a major impact upon the airline industry and their success has in part been at the expense of the full-service carriers, such as British Airways in the UK, who have had to respond. There are a proportion of passengers who will always opt for the lowest price; others will never compromise on service. In-between people have a choice to make and BA for one has worked hard to trim its costs and reduce its fares in order to narrow the price gap.

There are some interesting paradoxes. Customers confirm they do not enjoy the low levels of service, but they accept it on short-haul flights if the prices stay low. There is, therefore, potentially resistance against fare increases and so Ryanair has been reluctant to increase posted fare prices even though its costs have been escalating. But it has been more willing to increase its 'optional' supplementary charges, including charges for using certain credit cards. Realistically Ryanair needs to persuade more people to fly, maybe with new routes, or to switch from other airlines – and in this context it continues with its programme of buying new aircraft.

Some would say its staff are partially exploited with long hours and relatively low wages for the industry, but there is no shortage of recruits. Enough people seem to like and want this type of work.

There are even those who claim the low-cost airline business model is broken and needs fixing, but this is denied by the airlines themselves. Moreover, evidence suggests it is not broken.

Question/Task

This Minicase introduces a number of important issues. Amongst them are:

1 New competitors can dramatically change an industry.
2 Rivals compete to establish and maintain a competitive edge.
3 The role of a strategic leader is critical.
4 The Internet has offered new strategic opportunities.

Either think about or discuss with colleagues what you think the key messages are in relation to these issues.

The quotations from Stelios Haji-Ioannou are extracted from: Maitland, A. (1998) No frills and lots of feedback, *Financial Times*, 17 September.

simply less friendly and *premium* profits are unlikely. The real danger occurs if the weaker businesses threaten to bring down the strong ones that are forced to subsidize them. It is an irony that companies in real difficulty, possibly through strategic weaknesses, need to turn in an excellent performance if they are to survive.

Finally, it must be realized that past and current success is no guarantee of success in the future. Companies are not guaranteed, or entitled to, continued prosperity. They must adapt and change in a dynamic environment. Many fail to do this, for all sorts of reasons, and disappear. Some close down; others are acquired. Another featured chapter case, Marks and Spencer plc, is an excellent example of a previously outstanding company that has lost its way in recent years but which appears to have recovered (Case 1.2).

Case 1.2   Marks and Spencer plc   UK

Marks and Spencer (M&S) is a well-known and revered high-street retailer in the UK. The early growth of M&S was built around clothing, and its reputation owes much to the popularity of its underwear! M&S introduced us to lycra and Y-fronts. It built a second reputation for foods, pioneering chilled fresh varieties and bringing the avocado pear to the UK mass market. Always gradually, other ranges such as cosmetics, homewear, gifts and furniture have been added systematically. A home-delivery service for furniture has been expanded to include other items. Every shopping centre developer wants M&S to open a store, as they always attract customers.

The original foundations of the business lay with a young, Jewish immigrant and his Leeds market stall. Michael Marks had a poor grasp of English, a clear disadvantage for a trader in a noisy street market! Opportunistically, he turned his disadvantage into a strength. He had a sign on his stall: *Don't Ask The Price – It's a Penny*, and for a penny he provided the widest range and best-quality items he could find. This philosophy of *value for money* has pervaded through the generations and been sustained with innovation and change – but the focus on value has never been lost. The market stall led to a store, and then to stores on most high streets in Britain. The Spencer in the name came from Marks' first business partner, an accountant. However the Marks family became related to the Sieff family through marriage, and it is these two families together who have controlled the business through most of its history. Indeed Simon Marks (strategic leader from 1916 to 1964 and the man who really established and cemented in place Marks and Spencer's high street dominance), and his successor Marcus Sieff, have both been described as 'retail geniuses'.

The strategy of M&S then, is concerned with diversification of their product ranges within these broad product groups, but at the same time seeking to specialize where their own St Michael label could be used effectively. All M&S products have traditionally carried the M&S name and quite often the St Michael brand. At the beginning of the new millennium a decision was made to reduce the emphasis on using the St Michael brand name and emphasize the company name more prominently. M&S seeks to innovate whilst upgrading and adding value to its existing ranges. Over the years, M&S has found that many of its long-established stores in town and city centres are simply too small. An expansion programme has therefore developed along several lines. Adjacent units have been acquired when practical and new larger stores created, especially in new out-of-town shopping centres; if land has been available, buildings have been extended; and new sales floors have been opened up by converting stockrooms and moving stock to outside warehouses. This brings its own logistics problems. Satellite stores – smaller branches some distance away from the main branch – have been opened in certain towns. These satellites typically carry complete ranges – it might be men's fashions, ladies' clothes or children's items. The choice depends on the square footage available and the local prospects for particular lines. In a similar vein, in towns considered too small to support a full branch, specialist stores, perhaps just for food, have been opened. M&S Simply Food stores at railway stations and motorway services are very popular. The selection of products within the whole M&S range varies between stores.

Other strategic changes are:

- Constant improvements in displays, partly to present products better, and also to get more items into the stores. 'Sales per square foot' is a vital measure of success.
- Electronic point-of-sale (EPOS). Information technology has been harnessed to improve productivity and to enable M&S to respond more quickly to market changes, particularly relevant for fashion items. Thanks in part to technology, M&S staff costs as a percentage of their turnover are less than those of many competitors, but the quality of service has remained high.
- The development of support financial services, such as unit trusts, building upon the success of the M&S Chargecard, the third most popular credit card in the UK. This business has now been divested.
- International growth in, for example, France, Belgium, Canada, USA and Hong Kong. The development has been gradual, with one of the objectives being to introduce new types of competition. Some mistakes have been made as part of the learning process, and sales in some countries have been disappointing, but the risks have been contained in order not to threaten UK interests. China has been added to the list in 2008. Recently there have been some withdrawals and attempted withdrawals.

In the 1930s M&S pioneered a new form of inventory control when it designed perforated tags in two identical halves. Half was torn off at the point-of-sale, dropped in a box and then sent to the Baker Street (London) head office, where it was used to direct store replenishment. Over time this enabled M&S to introduce sophisticated replenishment from out-of-town warehouses and reduce the in-store stockrooms in favour of more direct selling space.

M&S possesses a number of identifiable strategic resources which have been instrumental in meeting customer key success factors, and thereby providing long-term profitable returns for shareholders. They include:

Physical resources	The wide range of value-for-money, own-brand products
	The sites and store displays
Intangible resources	Image and reputation
	Staff knowledge, expertise and commitment to service
Capabilities/ processes	Supply-chain management.

While there have been, and continue to be, strategic changes, the fundamental principles or values upon which the business grew and prospered have remained constant until the last few years. These are:

- High-quality, dependable products, styled conservatively and offering good value for money.
- Good relations with employees, customers, suppliers and other stakeholders.
- Simple operations.
- Comfortable stores.
- Financial prudence (most properties, for example, are freehold – they have not been sold and leased back to fund the expansion).

The foundation for the unique (St Michael) products and competitive prices was the M&S system of supply-chain relationships, a considerable proportion of these being with UK manufacturers for much of its history. In recent years M&S has, somewhat controversially, included more and more goods sourced overseas, sometimes for particular quality issues, but mostly for lower costs. In general, where they have been successful, the arrangements with suppliers have been long-term and non-contractual. They are based on mutual trust and common understanding. M&S is actively involved in product specification, input management (to their suppliers), quality control and production scheduling. M&S is frequently the supplier's most important customer. Why has it worked so effectively? The M&S reputation for fair dealing – with its suppliers, customers and employees – has for many years been seen as too valuable to put at risk.

But, at the end of the 1990s, this long-established business was suffering declines in sales and profits. Critics argued that too many product ranges were no longer the winners that people associated with the company, and its management needed strengthening at all levels. Interestingly, this setback occurred in the decade when the company had, for the first time in its history, a chief executive who was not a descendant of one of the Marks or Sieff families.

Simply, Marks and Spencer had:

- 'Taken its eye off' its customers and become over-reliant on its image and reputation.
- Become too reliant on (typically UK based) suppliers whose costs were relatively uncompetitive in global terms and at the same time.
- Allowed margins to increase gradually, tarnishing the longstanding value-for-money image.
- Lost some of the fashion element in its key clothing ranges.

Peter Drucker (1985) had earlier summarized M&S as 'probably more entrepreneurial and innovative than any other company in Western Europe these last 50 years … may have had a greater impact on the British economy, and even on British society, than any other change agent in Britain, and arguably more than government or laws'.

Was it conceivable that this visible and successful business was under real threat for the first time? Clara Freeman (2000), at that time an M&S executive, admitted that M&S 'lost the pace, lost the focus … no-one saw it coming. It was the classic management story – everything is going swimmingly and you don't tinker with a successful formula. After sales and profits declined, M&S put the magnifying lens on the business and asked what was wrong. Staff and customers told us that the quality was not as consistent as it used to be, and the service needs to be better than it is'.

In 1999 the current Chairman and Chief Executive, Richard Greenbury, announced he would retire early and, after a very visible and acrimonious internal wrangle, a new Chief Executive (Peter Salsbury) was appointed from inside the business. Later, a new Executive Chairman, Luc Vandevelde, previously the head of a major French supermarket chain, was recruited. Several ranges were quickly revamped and successful stock trials accelerated. M&S began to use more demographic and customer data to determine the product ranges for each store – previously stores of roughly the same size had carried similar ranges, regardless of their location. Sales did not pick up as rapidly as had been hoped, and rumours of possible takeover bids appeared in the press. Salsbury resigned as Chief Executive, to be replaced by Roger Holmes, recruited from Kingfisher.

Under Holmes, product ranges were changed again. Clothing was to be designed for people who prefer classic styles and for those who prefer the latest fashions. Lesiure clothing has become more prominent. At the same time the branded Per Una range, designed and sourced by George Davies, the entrepreneur responsible for the growth of the Next chain and the introduction of the George clothing range to Asda, has been added. This was a joint venture deal with Davies, an unusual approach for M&S, but it secured the services of a leading designer and it has been very successful. David Beckham has endorsed a range of children's clothing. A number of stores have been sold and leased back to raise cash. A new format for furniture and furnishings, designed by Victor Radice, recruited from Selfridges, was trialled. More and more products are sourced overseas. Staffing levels are tighter than in the past. Sales and profits – and the share price – all improved but not dramatically. Holmes vowed that the company would never be complacent again.

In 2004 the entrepreneur Philip Green (owner of Arcadia and BhS – made a bid for the company, but the M&S Board rejected his offer. Some institutional shareholders were willing to accept it, though. The Board was provoked, however, to make changes. Van de Velde left, along with Holmes and Radice. The new CEO was Stuart Rose, who had previously been responsible for the turnaround at Arcadia before its sale to Philip Green. Radice's new home store format was dropped and Rose negotiated to sell M&S' financial services business.

Stuart Rose described his approach in an article published in the *Harvard Business Review* in 2007.

- He had seen his immediate priority to be improved stock control – and in turn the supply chain – an increasing number of sub-brands had led to a growth in inventory.
- The new store format pioneered by Radice was quickly abandoned but generally store layouts were improved up and down the country.

- Financial services were divested and a new deal was struck with George Davies.
- It was apparent that he needed to improve the product, improve the stores and improve the service – really the challenge for every retailer all the time! But first it was necessary to be clear just why M&S was as successful as it was – there was complacency about a number of things.
- In the past M&S had come to rely on consultants, arguably an over-reliance, and there was now to be more emphasis on in-house solutions.
- The senior management team was to be strengthened, although some would be leaving, and more decisions would be devolved to the store management teams, albeit within clear parameters.
- Service quality would be pushed with stronger HR policies for staff in the stores.
- The company needed to become more demand-led and less supply-driven than it had traditionally been.
- With clothing there would be three distinct price and quality bands – good, better and best – to give a different market position and appeal. In addition there are autograph designer brands, especially with male fashion. *This proved successful as clothing market shares improved.*
- New brand advertising featured recognizable models such as Twiggy and Myleene Klass.
- There was continuing innovation including, for example, machine washable men's suits and branded electronics products.
- Energy efficiency and organic foods were targeted.

Had he succeeded? The decline was definitely halted and turnaround begun. One prescient headline proclaimed 'out of intensive care but not yet fighting fit'. Profits and market shares, especially for clothing, were improved. In 2007/8 pre-tax profits exceeded the £1 billion threshold for the first time in 10 years. The shares had performed well. Rose was something of a hero; Philip Green was almost forgotten.

But then the 2008 economic squeeze began to hit the high streets; many retailers were affected to varying degrees. M&S was robustly honest about anticipated profit fall-backs in the future and this became headline news. Food sales were most at risk as M&S was still seen by many as treat food rather than the main weekly shop. The Head of Food left. A year later M&S introduced mainstream branded products, such as Bovril, Coca-Cola and Kellogg's for the first time in its history in order to broaden its offer and appeal. Generally this has worked with foods but sales of electronic products (including brands such as Sony) have not been stunning. Rose himself did not escape without criticism – many shareholders were unhappy that he had been made Executive Chairman as well as CEO and would have preferred that the two roles remained split.

In 2010 it was announced that Marc Bolland had been recruited from Morrisons to replace Rose as CEO – many had assumed there would be an internal promotion this time. A new Chairman was also appointed and Rose finally left M&S stronger than when he found it in 2011. At this time the business was doing better than many other big high street names but it was capable of further improvement. Fashion ranges had changed – to separate smart from casual, traditional from designer and budget from more expensive offerings. M&S was still, though, perceived as a 'UK retailer that exports' rather than an international retailer. It had around 350 stores in 40 countries and a programme of expansion overseas was ongoing.

References

Drucker, PF (1985) *Innovation and Entrepreneurship*, Heinemann.

Freeman, C (2000) Interview, *Management Today*, January.

Rose, S (2007) Back in Fashion – How We're Reviving a Business Icon, *Harvard Business Review*, May.

Questions

1 Why do you think Marks and Spencer's fortunes changed as quickly as they did? How might such a decline have been avoided?

2 Is it realistic to claim they will 'never be complacent again'? If so, what is required to engineer this?

3 *(If you are an M&S customer …)* Did you notice many changes during recent years?

Task

Research the attempted bid by Philip Green for Marks and Spencer. Do you feel the outcome was 'the best all-round'?

SOURCE: THIS CASE STUDY WAS PREPARED USING PRIMARILY PUBLICLY AVAILABLE SOURCES OF INFORMATION FOR THE PURPOSES OF CLASSROOM DISCUSSION; IT DOES NOT INTEND TO ILLUSTRATE EITHER EFFECTIVE OR INEFFECTIVE HANDLING OF A MANAGERIAL SITUATION.

Five perspectives on strategy

The best way to predict the future is to invent it.

JOHN SCULLEY, WHEN CHAIRMAN, APPLE COMPUTERS

More than anyone else, Henry Mintzberg has been responsible for drawing attention to alternative views and perspectives on strategy, all of them legitimate. Mintzberg *et al.* (1998) provide an excellent summary of his work on this topic.

Figure 1.1 illustrates the five:

● **Perspective** – this is the 'big picture' discussed above
● **Pattern** – making sense of the past, bringing the organization to its
● **Position** – a clear understanding of the present
● **Plan** – looking ahead and trying to discern a clear picture of possible courses of action
● **Tactic** – activities at the 'little picture' level in a dynamic and competitive world.

The top oval, then, suggests that strategies can be seen in a *visionary* context. Here it is implied that strategy can be considered as a clear strategic purpose, intent and direction for the organization, but without the detail worked out. In a dynamic environment, managers would then determine more detailed and specific strategies in 'real-time' rather than exclusively in advance. However, they would always have a framework of direction to guide their decision-making and help them to determine what is appropriate. In addition, some strategies come from a visionary input from an entrepreneurial manager, or strategic leader, who spots an opportunity and is minded to act on it.

Figure 1.1   Five views of strategy

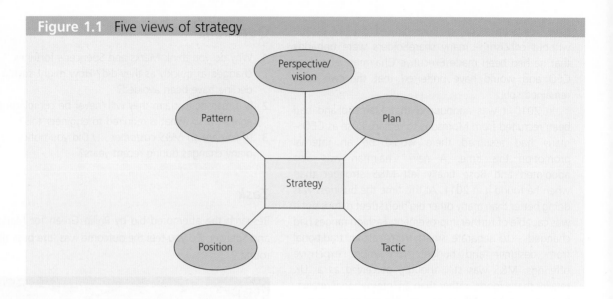

This perspective contrasts with some people's thinking that strategy and *planning* are synonymous. Certainly, as we shall see later in this chapter, **strategic planning** has a crucial role in strategy creation, but it does not fully explain how strategies are changed. Both the visionary and planning perspective are concerned with thinking ahead as far as it might be sensible to think and plan. While the *tactical* view is also about the future, it is really about the immediate future. The assumption being made here is that competitors in a dynamic market will constantly adopt new ploys in an attempt to steal a short-term gain or advantage. Their **tactics** may be easily copied, but there can be some temporary advantage when rivals are caught by surprise and need time to react.

Metaphorically, we can relate these ideas to a game of competitive football. There will be a broad purpose concerned with finishing at a certain level in a league or winning a cup competition, and this will influence the fundamental approach to every game. Sometimes a win would be seen as essential; on other occasions a 'clean sheet' would be more desirable or a draw could be perfectly satisfactory. From this, more detailed game plans will be devised for every match. But, inevitably, 'the best laid schemes o' mice and men gang aft a gley' (Burns). Early goals by the opposition can imply a setback and demand that plans are quickly revised and tactics changed. This is always possible at half-time, but during the match the team will have to rely on shouted instructions from the touchline and leadership from the team captain as play continues. Individual players will always be allowed some freedom of movement and the opportunity to show off their particular skills. New tactics will emerge as players regroup and adapt to the circumstances, but quite often games will be turned around by the individual vision, inspiration and brilliance of key players.

These three views all concern the future and imply change; the notion of *position* is akin to the idea of freezing time momentarily. It relates to strategic fit and the organization's competitive position at the present time. It is, in effect, a statement of what is happening; and it can be vital for 'taking stock', realizing and clarifying a situation so that future changes are based on clear **knowledge** rather than assumption.

Of course, organizations come to their present position as a result of decisions taken previously; plans have been implemented and tactics adjusted as events have unfolded. It is again crucial to analyze and understand this evolving *pattern*, appreciating just what has happened, why and how. This can be a valuable foundation for future decisions, plans and actions but, although history can be a guide to the future, rarely in strategy are events repeated without some amendment. The importance of clarifying the pattern from the various decisions and changes also explains why strategy has irreverently been described as a 'series of, mindless, random events, rationalized in retrospect'!

Our understanding of these alternative perspectives will be strengthened when we look at how strategies are created and changed.

Strategic thinking

Strategic thinking embraces the past, present and future. Understanding patterns and lessons from the past will certainly inform the future – but given the dynamic, turbulent and uncertain business environments that affect many industries and organizations, it would be dangerous to assume that the future will reflect the past and be a continuation of either past or existing trends.

Figure 1.2 shows (bottom triangle) how strategies which link competencies with a strategic vision for the future embrace learning from the past, an awareness of existing competencies and some insight into likely future trends. The top part of the figure highlights that *organizational learning* is required to build the future and that it encompasses:

- a reflection on how present strategies have emerged over time
- an understanding of current competencies and the strategic value of particular resources and the linkages between them
- knowledge of existing competitors and what they are doing at the moment – and preparing to do in the future
- an appreciation of possible new sources of competition
- an awareness of wider environmental opportunities and threats
- an ability to share information with, and thus learn from, external partners and contacts, including suppliers, distributors and customers.

Figure 1.2 Organizational learning

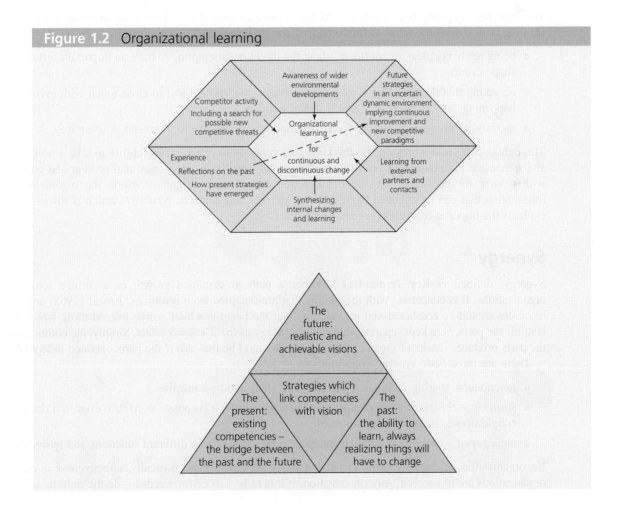

The effective organization will synthesize this learning into insightful strategies for dealing with future uncertainties.

Campbell and Alexander (1997) offer a different, but clearly related, approach to strategic thinking. They delineate three elements. First, insight into operating issues: with **benchmarking** other organizations (searching for good practices), process re-engineering and total quality management, organizations should look for opportunities to improve continuously the way they do things. Second, future-gazing: exponents of chaos theory warn of the need always to be ready for the unexpected and unpredictable; and so here the emphasis is on discontinuous change, and the idea of reinventing and thus controlling developments in the industry. Put another way, establishing new rules of competition and seizing the high ground ahead of any rivals. Scenario building plays an important role. The third element is behaviour and culture. Without a clear and communicated vision and direction, and with an absence of employees who are willing to engage the future and look for change opportunities, strategic thinking will be very limited and unimaginative. Simply, the organization must become more entrepreneurial in a dynamic environment.

Courtney *et al.* (1997) distinguish four alternative future patterns and three broad approaches, which have different degrees of relevance for different situations.

The four futures are:

- a clear and definable future, which implies a continuation of present trends
- a limited and definable number of discrete alternatives which can be evaluated and judged
- a known range of possibilities, which can be defined only in more general terms
- real uncertainty, and with the possibility of major disruption and change.

The three broad approaches, which should not be seen as mutually exclusive, for utilizing organizational learning to deal with the relevant future pattern are:

- being relatively clear, or confident, about the direction, attempting to have an important influence and shape events
- accepting that there will be some uncertainty, staying vigilant and in close touch with events and happenings and adapting to retain a strong position
- monitoring events and waiting for an appropriate opportunity to intervene in some way.

Throughout this section on strategic thinking, the emphasis has been on the ability to take a holistic view and synthesize information. We need to synthesize information from the past and present and combine it with a view of the future. This embraces information which originates inside the organization and information that can be obtained from external partners and contacts. **Synergy**, which is discussed next, explains the importance of linkages and synthesis.

Synergy

Synergy (defined in Key Terms 1.1) is either a path to sustained growth or a 'bridge too far' for organizations. It is concerned with the returns that are obtained from resources. Ansoff (1968) argues that resources should be combined and managed so that the benefits which accrue exceed those which would result if the parts were kept separate, describing synergy as the $2 + 2 = 5$ effect. Simply, the combination of the parts produces results of greater magnitude than would be the case if the parts operated independently.

There are three basic synergy opportunities:

- *functional* – sharing facilities, competencies, ideas and best practice
- *strategic* – complementary competitive strategies across a corporate portfolio: even in a diversified conglomerate, some sharing is possible
- *managerial* – compatible styles of management and values in different functions and businesses.

No organization deliberately plans to fail but many do fail to plan. Basically, effectiveness is crucial if organizations are to succeed. Any organization, if it is to be successful, needs to 'do the right thing'. It can only do this through strategic thinking. This book provides the strategist with a range of strategic tools with which to guide their thinking. In a forthcoming chapter we examine how strategy can be influenced by external environmental forces. Strategic thinking, then, relates to an organization's ability to gather, harness and utilize relevant information from inside the organization and from the (changing) external environment. The desired outcome is strong competitive strategies. Strategic thinking demands an ability to learn from the past, to understand the present and to think ahead. Effective thinking can be used to generate synergy, where the total achievements of the whole organization exceed what would be achieved if the various parts were working independently.

Functional, competitive and corporate strategies

Figure 1.3 reflects the three distinct perspectives of strategic analysis:

1 the strategic environment
2 the business as a competing organization
3 the individual strategist.

The diagram summarizes three distinct, but interrelated and interdependent, levels of strategy: corporate (the whole organization), competitive (the distinct strategy for each constituent business, product or service in the organization) and functional (the activities which underpin the competitive strategies).

Simply, most organizations choose to produce one or more related or unrelated product or service for one or more market or market segment. Consequently, the organization should be structured to encompass this range of product markets or service markets. As the number and diversity of products increases, the structure is likely to be centred on divisions which are sometimes referred to as **strategic business units** (SBUs). Such SBUs are responsible individually for developing, manufacturing and marketing their own product or group of products. Each SBU will, therefore, have a strategy, which Porter (1980) calls a **competitive strategy**. Competitive strategy is concerned with 'creating and maintaining a competitive advantage in each and every area of business' (Porter, 1980). It can be achieved through any one function, although it is likely to be achieved through a unique and distinctive combination of functional activities.

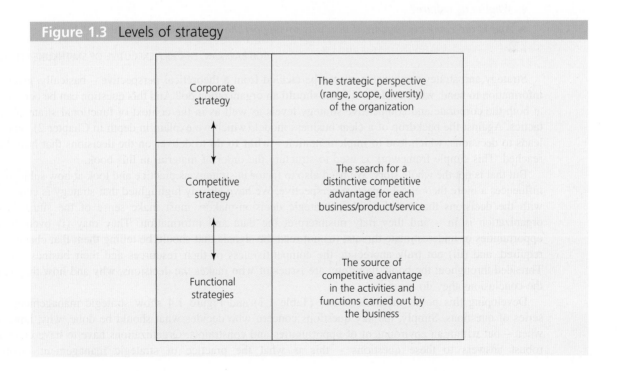

Figure 1.3   Levels of strategy

Corporate strategy	The strategic perspective (range, scope, diversity) of the organization
Competitive strategy	The search for a distinctive competitive advantage for each business/product/service
Functional strategies	The source of competitive advantage in the activities and functions carried out by the business

For each functional area of the business, such as production, marketing and human resources, the company will have a functional strategy. It is important that **functional strategies** are designed and managed in a co-ordinated way so that they interrelate with each other and at the same time collectively allow the competitive strategy to be implemented properly.

Successful competitive and functional strategies add value in ways which are perceived to be important by the company's stakeholders, especially its customers, and which help to distinguish the company from its competitors. Mathur and Kenyon (1998) reinforce these points and contend that competitive advantage is fundamentally about the positioning and fit of an organization in its industry or market, and that success is based on distinct differences and sound cost management.

Corporate strategy, essentially and simply, is deciding what businesses the organization should be in and how the overall group of activities should be structured and managed. It has been described by Porter as 'the overall plan for a diversified business', although it is perfectly acceptable for a business to elect to stay focused on only one product or service range. This does happen in many companies, especially small businesses. In this case, the corporate and competitive strategies are synonymous. Corporate strategy for a multi-business group is concerned with maintaining or improving overall growth and profit performance through **acquisition**, organic investment (internally funded growth), **divestment** and closure. The term strategic perspective is often used to describe the range and diversity of activities, in other words the corporate strategy. Each activity then has a competitive position or strategy. The management of corporate strategy concerns the creation and safeguarding of *synergies* from the portfolio of businesses and activities.

1.2 Strategy as practice

All newly appointed chief executives should ask five key questions:

- *What are the basic goals of the company?*
- *What is the strategy for achieving these goals?*
- *What are the fundamental issues facing the company?*
- *What is its culture?*
- *And is the company organized in a way to support the goals, issues and culture?*

BOB BAUMAN, EX-CHIEF EXECUTIVE OF SMITHKLINE BEECHAM

Strategy and strategic management can be tackled from a theoretical perspective – basically, given the information to hand, **what could** and **what should** an organization do? And this question can be considered at both the corporate and competitive strategy levels as well as in the context of functional strategies and tactics. Against the backdrop of a clear business model (which we explain in depth in Chapter 2), analysis leads to decisions, which lead to implementation – **what to do** to deliver on the decisions that have been reached. This simple framework is used to structure the order of material in this book.

But that is not the whole story. We need also to factor in strategy as practice and look at how subjectivity influences a more theoretical objective perspective. We have already highlighted that strategy is concerned with the decisions that people make. Strategic decision-makers must make sense of the situation the organization is in – and they may misinterpret the data and information. They may (i) overestimate opportunities or underestimate threats, (ii) not read the signals that should be telling them that changes are required, and (iii) not truly appreciate the competitiveness of their resources and their business model. Threaded throughout the book, therefore, are issues of **who** makes the decisions, **why** and **how** they reach the conclusions they do reach.

Developing this point, the table below (Table 1.1) and Figure 1.4 show strategic management as a series of questions. Simply, the key questions concern who decides what should be done, why, how, and when – but within an environment of opportunities and constraints. Organizations have to have clear and robust answers to these questions – this is what the practice of strategic management involves.

Table 1.1   Strategic management

Key strategy question	Relevant chapter	Strategic theme
Who decides	10	Leadership/entrepreneurship
	7	Culture
	14	Organization structure
What to do	2 and 8	Business and revenue model, alternatives and choices
	12 and 13	Growth issues to consider
Why (do they make the choices they do)	3	Objectives and purpose
(What might they have in mind)	16	Level of ambition/desire to avoid risk
How (do they decide)	9 and 10	Strategy creation
and **When**	15	Change issues
using what information	4	Strategic awareness and knowledge
and what resources	5	Resources and capability
and, in turn, affected by (which factors)	4	Environmental forces
	6	Competition
with what **outcomes**	11	Performance

Figure 1.4   Strategic management questions framework

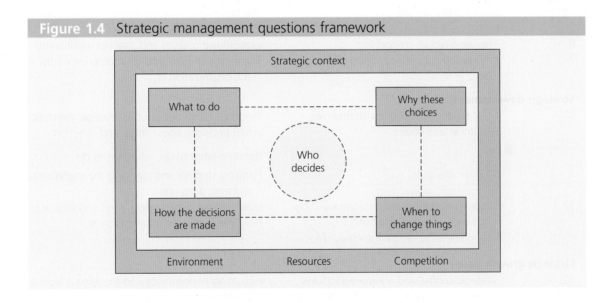

Sound answers will result in a clear and defensible **business model** – a topic we explore in more depth in Chapter 2. In the table, the *more* theoretical (but not exclusively theoretical) elements are shown in blue. The black print flags the more subjective – strategy as practice – elements of strategy.

Alongside the questions in the table are the relevant chapters in this book. Reading from top to bottom, the questions are presented in a logical flow in respect of how someone might 'tell the story' and, in this context, with the contextual constraints coming at the end rather than the beginning – but there is no requirement that organizations will have sought to answer the questions, or would expect to answer them, in any particular order. Until sense can be made of the environment and the context, for example, the specific questions cannot be tackled seriously. Hence the order the material is presented in this book allows for a build up of the issues step by step to allow the questions to be answered – starting with the contextual variables.

The core framework for this book, therefore, is as follows:

- The Business Model (what we are offering the marketplace)
- Strategic Analysis – environment, resources, competition, culture and values (*background and contextual themes*)
- Strategy Creation and Strategic Choice (*strategic decision-making*)
- Strategy Implementation (*managing strategy and strategic change*).

Table 1.2   Strategic management: awareness and change topics

Chapter	Part and chapter title	Themes, issues, questions
Understanding strategy and strategic management		
1	What is strategy and who is Involved?	
2	The business model and the revenue model	The big picture
		What the organization is all about and how it is seen by others
3	Strategic purpose *Using Frameworks to Analyze Strategy Cases*	Why the organization exists and what it aspires to be
Analysis and positioning		
4	The Business Environment and Strategy	General external opportunities and constraints
5	Resource-led strategy	The building blocks that enable the organization to function
6	The Dynamics of competition	Competitive realities and strategic positioning
7	Introducing culture and values	The essential 'lubricants' that determine how effective the organization is
Strategic development		
8	Creating and formulating: alternatives, evaluation and choice	Processes for deciding what strategic direction to take actual decisions about focus and direction. Deciding what to do; what not to do
9	Strategic planning	Planning strategy and planning the implementation of strategic decisions
10	Strategic leadershipand intrapreneurship: towards visionary leadership? Entrepreneurship and Intrapreneurship	How well the organization is led and directed How innovative the organization is
Strategic growth Issues		
11	Strategic control and measuring success	Evaluating performance and the impact from activities
12	Issues in strategic and international growth	Contextual issues affecting the directional choices the organization makes
13	Failure, consolidation and recovery strategies	
Strategy implementation and strategic management		
14	Strategy implementation and structure	Structuring the organization to co-ordinate activities and to enable strategic choices to be put into practice and carried through
15	Leading change	Innovating and changing in an uncertain and complex world
16	Managing strategy in the organization	Staying focused and dealing with crises
17	Final Thoughts and Reflections: The Practice of Strategy	A reprise of how the 'big picture' and the 'little picture' detail must all come together

… and this framework has been expanded in Table 1.2 to illustrate the key theme and issue being tackled in each chapter. The core framework has also been extended into the mindmap which appears at the beginning of every chapter.

We return to this framework towards the end of the book when we reprise strategy as practice.

1.3 E–V–R congruence

If one wished to claim that an organization was being managed effectively from a strategic point of view, one would have to show, first, that its managers appreciated fully the dynamics, opportunities and threats present in their competitive environment, and that they were paying due regard to wider societal issues; and, secondly, that the organization's resources (inputs) were being managed strategically, taking into account its strengths and weaknesses, and that the organization was taking advantage of its opportunities. Key success factors and **core competencies** would be matched.

The factors behind these matching issues are ubiquitously listed in the form of a **SWOT Analysis**, a simple framework that most readers will already be familiar with. SWOT stands for:

Strengths	)
Weaknesses	) the (internal) resource themes
Opportunities	)
Threats	) the (external) environmental themes.

Effective matching will not just happen, though. It needs to be managed. Moreover, potential new opportunities need to be sought and resources developed. It is also important, therefore, that the values of the organization match the needs of the environment and the key success factors. It is the values and culture that determine whether the environment and resources are currently matched, and whether they stay congruent in changing circumstances.

Values are traditionally subsumed as a resource in a SWOT (strengths, weaknesses, opportunities, threats) analysis, but it is useful to separate them out. The notion of **E–V–R (environment–values–resources) congruence** then is an integration of these issues. Basically, there is an overlap between the environment (key success factors) and resources (competencies and capabilities), and the organization is committed to sustaining this overlap with effective strategic change initiatives. This notion of E–V–R congruence is illustrated in the top left diagram in Figure 1.5.

The value of E–V–R analysis is that it provides a straightforward framework for assessing the organization's existing strategies and strategic needs. It is crystal clear at a conceptual level what organizations have to achieve and sustain strategically; the challenge then is to use the logic to explore and create opportunities and ways for achieving and sustaining congruence by dealing with the various, but different, risks that organizations have to manage if they are to avoid crises in the face of uncertainty.

If we conclude that an organization does enjoy E–V–R congruence, it is important to test its robustness. Conceptually the three circles can merely overlay each other, and be easily pulled apart. Alternatively, like the old magician's trick, they can seem like interlocking circles which seem difficult to separate.

The other four illustrations in Figure 1.5 illustrate alternative instances of incongruence. E–V–R analysis can be applied at more than one level; and consequently different managers should be in positions where they can address which of the alternatives in Figure 1.5 best represents their organization and their individual business. Having selected the one that they feel best sums up the present situation, they can immediately see the direction and thrust of the changes that are needed to create or restore congruency.

Managers at the individual business level might find it more expedient to recast the mnemonic E–V–R with three Cs – *C*ustomer expectations (for E); *C*ompetencies and capabilities (for R) and *C*ulture (for V). Working downwards from the top left in the figure, a 'lost organization' is seen next. Possibly there was congruency at some time, but now products, services and markets are out of alignment and the values inappropriate. Without major changes to strategy, structure and style, almost certainly involving a change of strategic leader, an organization in this situation has no future. This degree of incongruence would be relatively unusual, but the other three possibilities are not.

Figure 1.5   E–V–R congruence

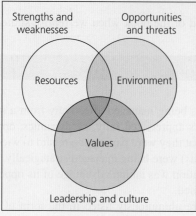

E–V–R congruence

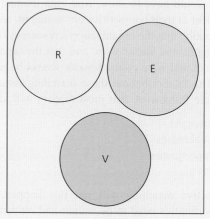

The lost organization

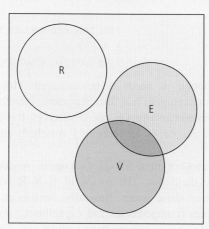

The consciously incompetent
organization

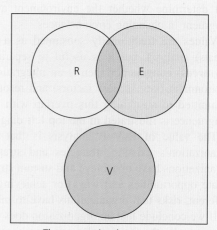

The unconsciously competent
organization

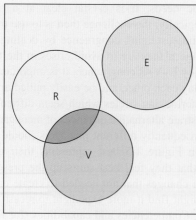

Strategic drift

The 'consciously incompetent' organization is aware of the needs for success in its marketplace, and managers appreciate the importance of satisfying its customers, but it is simply not achieving the desired level of service and quality. Managers may well have some insight into what might be improved but not be in a position to achieve this improvement. Maybe there is a key resource shortage of some form or a lack of investment, or a person or people with key skills have left and not been replaced. Possibly too many managers are unwilling to grasp the changes that are needed and accept **empowerment** and responsibility. It is typical for a company in this situation to be constantly fighting crises and problems. Because of the customer orientation, there will be a commitment to resolve the problems and difficulties and, for this reason, some customers may be somewhat tolerant. However, the organization is likely to be highly reactive and, consequently, again the position cannot be sustained indefinitely. A more proactive and entrepreneurial approach will be required to strengthen the resource base and restore congruency with a fresh strategic position.

In contrast, the 'unconsciously competent' organization enjoys **strategic positioning** without any real commitment, especially to improvement and change. Things are working, at a surface level and possibly with some element of luck. Any success is taken for granted. The organization is unable to exploit its strengths and, if it fails to address this, then E and R will drift apart over time, possibly sooner rather than later, to create a lost organization. The required change in culture and values probably implies a change of leadership, certainly of leadership style, to increase **decentralization** and empowerment.

'Strategic drift' is commonplace. An organization which is internally cohesive simply loses touch with its environment. Demands may change, and fresh competition may make the company's products and services less attractive than in the past. The challenge then concerns realignment in a dynamic environment, which certainly requires a change in management style and, possibly again, leadership. This organization desperately needs new ideas, which may already be available inside the organization, but have not been captured.

An article by Drucker (1994) complements both this model and these arguments when he states that all organizations have implicit or explicit 'theories' for their business, incorporating:

- assumptions about the environment, specifically markets, customers and important technologies
- assumptions about its mission or purpose, and
- assumptions about the core (content) competencies required to fulfil the mission.

These assumptions, at any time, must be realistic, congruent, communicated and understood; to achieve this they must be evaluated regularly and rigorously.

Pümpin (1987) uses the term strategic excellence positions (SEPs) to describe 'capabilities which enable an organization to produce better-than-average results over the longer term compared with its competitors'. SEPs imply that organizations appreciate the views of customers and develop the capabilities required to satisfy these needs. Moreover, they are perceived by their customers to be a superior competitor because of their skills and accomplishments.

It is important to deploy resources and to focus the drive for excellence (an aspect of the organization's culture) on issues which matter to customers. IBM, for example, have succeeded historically by concentrating on service, Rolls Royce motor cars on image and quality and Procter & Gamble on advertising and **branding**.

Businesses should seek to develop competitive advantage and a strategic excellence position for each product and service. Overall E–V–R congruence then depends on these SEPs together with any corporate benefits from linkages and interrelationships.

The development of SEPs and E–V–R congruence takes time, and requires that all functional areas of the business appreciate which factors are most significant to customers. Once achieved, however, it cannot be assumed that long-term success is guaranteed. Situations change and new windows of opportunity open (Abell, 1978). The demand for guaranteed overnight parcel deliveries anywhere in the country, and immediate services within cities, opened up the opportunity for couriers; new technologies used in laptop computers, facsimile machines and the Internet have created demand and behaviour changes. Competitors may behave unexpectedly, and consequently there is a need for strategic awareness and for monitoring potential change situations.

Bettis and Prahalad (1995) argue that business decisions are affected by a 'dominant logic', championed by the strategic leader and communicated through the organization. This could be an articulated vision or a culturally integrated **paradigm** concerning 'what the business is about and how things get done'. It is shown next how **strategic regeneration** implies that this logic needs to be changed. IBM's growth and early industry dominance was built on a belief that mainframe computers were essential for organizations. Competitors such as Microsoft, which concentrated on software, highlighted that IBM's logic was outdated and it needed to be 'unlearned'. New products and new processes alone would prove inadequate. The new logic is one of decentralized personal computers in the hands of knowledgeable workers.

Organizations, therefore, should build on their past successes while always realizing that the past may not be the best guide to the future.

An alternative presentation

E–V–R Congruence provides a framework for evaluating how strategically robust an organization is at a point in time – and also for tracking changes over time. The same idea can be used to look at just what an organization is doing and its strategic position. In this case the variables are:

- products and services
- actions and activities
- values

and these are illustrated in Figure 1.6.

It needs pointing out here – and we will expand on the point later in the book – that here we are concerned with the *value* (for the customer) that is provided by products and services, not simply what they are. This value is critical in a competitive context but it is not the same as the *values* shown in the bottom circle that help explain how the organization and its decision-makers behave.

Case 1.3 on McDonald's picks up on these arguments and explores innovation in the context of a core business model, losing and regaining E–V–R congruence in much the same way as Marks and Spencer arguably has, and the impact of changes of strategic leader.

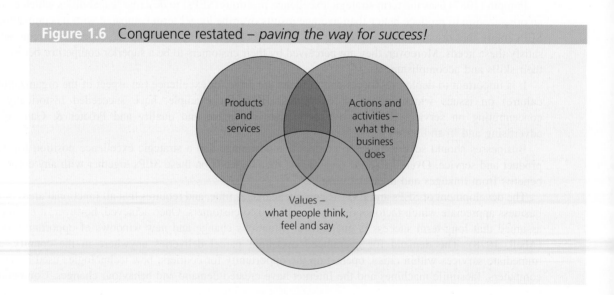

Figure 1.6   Congruence restated – *paving the way for success!*

Products and services

Actions and activities – what the business does

Values – what people think, feel and say

Case 1.3   McDonald's   US

McDonald's, built by a visionary, the late Ray Kroc, has become a very successful international company, with outlets in over 120 countries. Its products are popular with large numbers of customers, and certainly not just children. In 1996, according to Interbrand consultants, McDonald's ousted Coca-Cola as the world's best-known brand. But later the company would record its first ever trading loss.

Ray Kroc has been described by *Time Magazine* as 'one of the most influential builders of the twentieth century'. Few children refuse a McDonald's burger – and its golden arches logo became a symbol of American enterprise. Kroc was a truly opportunistic and focused entrepreneur who built an organizational network of dedicated franchisees. Yet his entrepreneurial contribution began late in life and the McDonald's chain of hamburger restaurants was certainly not his own invention. Instead he saw – really he stumbled on – an opportunity where others missed the true potential for an idea. Once he had seen the opportunity he rigorously applied business acumen and techniques to focus on providing value for his customers. By standardizing his product and restaurants he was able to guarantee high and consistent quality at relatively low cost. Kroc was also wise enough to use the expertise that his franchisees were developing. The golden arches brand and the Ronald McDonald character became ubiquitous.

In 1955, at the age of 52, Ray Kroc completed 30 years as a salesman, mainly selling milkshake machines to various types of restaurant across America, including hamburger joints. His customers included the McDonald brothers who, having moved from New Hampshire to Hollywood, but failing to make any headway in the movie business, had opened a small drive-through restaurant in San Bernadino, California. They offered a limited menu, paper plates and plastic cups, and guaranteed the food in 60 seconds. When their success drove them to buy eight milkshake machines, instead of the two their small size would logically suggest, Ray Kroc's interest was alerted and he set off to see the restaurant. Kroc's vision was for a national chain which could benefit from organization and business techniques. He bought out the McDonald brothers and set about building a global empire. After he officially retired from running the business, and until his death in 1984, Ray Kroc stayed on as President and visited two or three different restaurants every week. He saw himself as the 'company's conscience', checking standards against his QSCV vision – quality food, fast and friendly service, clean restaurants and value for money.

The McDonald's empire grew to exceed 30000 restaurants worldwide serving 40 million people everyday; America always remained the biggest market. At one stage up to 3000 new ones were being opened in a single year. Although the number of Subway branches surpassed McDonalds (34000 against 33000) – Kentucky Fried Chicken is third with 20000 branches – Subway's global revenues of US$15 billion was US$9 billion behind McDonald's income. The basic formula has worked as well in Moscow and Beijing as it has in the USA. Although the products available are broadly similar in the USA and Europe, menus are seen as flexible in various parts of the world. Japanese stores, for example, feature Teriyaki Burgers, sausage patties with teriyaki sauce. Indian restaurants offer McCurry Pans, Egypt McFalafels, China chicken wings and chicken sandwiches, using the preferred dark meat, and the Eastern Provinces of Canada have McLobster Rolls. Many of the stores are franchises; the rest are mainly joint ventures. Eight thousand are company operated, and the recent trend has been for this proportion to decline in favour of more franchises. An 'ideal' franchise partner runs between ten and 15 restaurants.

The growth and success in an industry where 'fast food is a by-word for low wages and an unskilled temporary workforce' is not accidental. It has been very carefully planned and managed, although McDonald's relies a lot on the people at the sharp end. Employees are often young; they work a closely prescribed system, operating internationally established rules and procedures for preparing, storing and selling food. Various incentive schemes are practised. Labour turnover is high, however, and consequently McDonald's has its critics as well as its supporters. Nevertheless, it is obvious that some competitors seek to emulate McDonald's in a number of ways: products, systems and employee attitudes.

Our competitors can copy many of our secrets, but they cannot duplicate our pride, our enthusiasm and our dedication for this business.

McDonald's has been profitable because it is efficient and productive; and it has stayed ahead of its competitors by being innovative and looking for new opportunities.

A lot of the developments are planned and imaginative. McDonald's does not move into new countries without thorough investigation of the potential; the same is true for new locations. There are now McDonald's branches in American hospitals, military bases and zoos; worldwide they can be found in airport terminals, motorway service stations, supermarkets (Tesco) and on board cruise ships and Swiss trains.

McDonald's relies heavily on its suppliers for fresh food; again, arrangements are carefully planned, monitored and controlled. The in-store systems for cooking and running branches are very tight, to ensure that products and service standards are the same worldwide. New product development has utilized all of the group's resources. The Big Mac, which was introduced nationally in the USA in 1968, was the idea of a Pittsburgh franchisee who had seen a similar product elsewhere. The aim was to broaden the customer base and make McDonald's more adult orientated. The company allowed the franchisee to try the product in his restaurant in 1967, although there was some initial resistance amongst executives who wished to retain a narrow product line, and it proved highly successful.

Egg McMuffins in the early 1970s were a response to a perceived opportunity – a breakfast menu and earlier opening times. Previously the restaurants opened at 11.00 am. Although the opportunity was appreciated the development of the product took place over 4 years, and the final launch version was created by a Santa Barbara franchisee who had to invent a new cooking utensil.

When Chicken McNuggets were launched in 1982 it was the first time that small boneless pieces of chicken had been mass produced. The difficult development of the product was carried out in conjunction with a supplier and there was immediate competitive advantage. The product was not readily copied. From being essentially a hamburger chain McDonald's quickly became number two to Kentucky Fried Chicken for fastfood chicken meals.

McDonald's continually tries out new menus, such as pizzas, in order to extend its share of the overall fastfood market, but for many years it avoided any diversification, nor did it offer any different 'food concept'. To enhance its image of good value, and to compete in a very dynamic industry, McDonald's offers 'extra-value meals', special combinations at low prices. However McDonald's has been criticized for increasing portion sizes as a marketing tool – which might seem like extra value but is, at the same time, encouraging greater consumption of fast food at any one time.

In addition, McDonald's is a 'penny profit' business. It takes hard work and attention to detail to be financially successful. Store managers must do two things well: control costs and increase sales. Increased sales come from the products, certainly, but also from service. Cost control is vital, but it must not be achieved by compromising product quality, customer service or restaurant appearance. Instead, it requires a focus on productivity and attention to detail. Success with these strategies has been achieved partly through serious attempts to share learning and best practice throughout the global network.

The company became an industry leader and contends there were six main reasons behind this:

- Visibility: to this end substantial resources are devoted to marketing. The golden arches symbol is instantly recognizable.
- Ownership or control of real-estate sites: McDonald's argues that this factor differentiates it from its competitors who lease more.
- Its commitment to franchising and supplier partnerships.
- It is worldwide, with restaurants in over 120 countries, and uses local managers and employees.
- The structure is very decentralized but lines of responsibility and accountability are clear.
- It is a growth company – or at least it has been for most of its existence.

Setbacks and renewal

By the mid-1990s, with the company still growing rapidly, the 'early warning signs' began to appear for the first time. The company held 40 per cent of the US market for its products, and yet its burgers were not coming out as superior to Wendy's and Burger King in taste tests. In addition, a special promotion in America, based around burgers for 55 cents each, did not prove successful because of the conditions attached to the offer. A new spicier – and premium price – burger for adults, the Arch Deluxe, had not taken off. New restaurants in the USA were beginning to take sales away from existing ones, rather than generating new business. Established franchisees were hardly delighted! One complained, sued and won $16 million in damages. A leading franchisee pressure group expressed the view that the entrepreneurial drive of founder Ray Kroc (who died in 1984) had been lost and replaced by a non-entrepreneurial bureaucracy. This change of culture was one reason why McDonald's recently pursued a libel action in the UK against two environmentalists: a case where McDonald's won the legal argument but lost the accompanying public relations battle.

After a period of criticism and disappointing results McDonald's began to fight back. With franchisees paying half the costs, new computerized kitchen equipment has been systematically installed in its 30000 restaurants, allowing fast cooking to order. Ready-to-serve meals no longer have to stand for a few minutes on heated trays. In addition, McDonald's began to experiment with new low-risk opportunities for its competencies in supply-chain management, franchising, promotion and merchandising by acquiring new restaurant chains. Included were a group of Mexican restaurants in Colorado, a chain of pizza outlets in Ohio, 23 Aroma coffee shops in London and the Boston Market chain of chicken restaurants. The US operations were split into five independent geographical regions.

But all of these initiatives failed to stop McDonald's starting to trade at a loss for the first time in 2002. Also for the first time, restaurants were closed down – some 700 in all, especially where there was unnecessary duplication – as a response to falling sales. The share price tumbled. Jim Cantalupo, a retired strategic leader, was tempted back to try to restore the past glory. Was this possible – or was the brand at the beginning of the end of its life cycle? Interestingly McDonald's fastest growing competitor was Subway which markets fresh sandwiches and is perceived to be offering a far healthier alternative.

Cantalupo's strategy had a number of important elements:

- The focus was to be on new customers rather than new restaurants.
- In part this was to be achieved through healthier food options. Some of this would be achieved in the content and the preparation; at the same time people would be encouraged to eat more healthily.
- Existing customers would be encouraged to visit the restaurants more often – and to support this, service must get better. Fresh, hot food must be available within a 3 minute promise. The toilets must be spotless at all times, however busy the restaurant is. Underpinning this was to be a renewed emphasis on staff training.
- New products feature more imagination and innova-tion. There is now (rolled out from trials in America) a wider range of salads and new desserts, including

bagged fresh fruit. Vegetables such as carrot sticks are available. For the adult taste, Mexican burgers are beginning to make inroads in America where there is a large Hispanic-speaking population.

Both sales and profitability rose again, but was McDonalds truly turned around?

A major setback was the sudden death (from a heart attack) of Jim Cantalupo in 2004 – he was 60 years old – and another strategic leader had to be found. Australian Charlie Bell, aged 43, who had worked closely with Cantalupo, seemed an ideal choice. Together they had introduced the slogan 'I'm Lovin' It' and adopted the mantra: 'attract more customers by being better rather than bigger'. But in 2005 Bell also died suddenly and unexpectedly, from cancer.

His replacement was Jim Skinner who opted to increase the company's presence in China ahead of the 2008 Olympic Games. The number of outlets was to double from 500 to 1000, with, for the first time, drive-throughs. The menus would feature both American and Chinese influences.

Range enhancements in the USA included breakfast cereals and there was a deliberate drive to provide more nutritional information. But success around the world was uneven, with Europe showing a decline in sales.

Limited changes continued. The McCafé concept, pioneered successfully in Australia and New Zealand, was introduced to the USA. McCafés are situated alongside McDonald's restaurants and they mimic Starbucks – at a lower price point. They sell light (cold) snacks and treats as well as a range of coffee products and soft drinks. This is an important expansion as drinks generally are very high margin and very profitable.

A major store revamp programme, already begun, intensified. There were 'too many tired stores'. New designs, new colours, new layouts, touch-activated self-service screen ordering points, piped smells and sounds all featured. Sofa areas, much like those found in some Starbucks outlets, were trialled in selected locations. Opening hours were generally increased.

In 2007 McDonald's posted its 'best financial results for 30 years'. There had been 4 years of continuous monthly sales increases with 4 million more customers using basically the same number of restaurants.

McDonald's then had to face the challenge of the global recession. Allowing a perception that it was in part a reaction to adverse comments, the size of some of its products was trimmed. A budget range of 'dollar hamburgers and cheeseburgers' was tweaked. When cheese prices increased the number of cheese slices in a double cheeseburger was reduced from two to one and a new 'McDouble' created. Customers could have a second cheese slice but at an slightly increased price.

Yet controversy continues to stalk McDonalds – and also gives it valuable publicity. Some people in France, for example, where the company is very successful, were incensed when a branch was opened in the Louvre!

In 2011 the company recorded 100 months of consecutive same-store sales growth.

Questions

1 How does McDonald's create value for its customers?

2 How might it create new values in the future?

3 What are its important competencies and capabilities?

4 To what extent do you think issues of strategic leadership and culture have influenced its growth and prosperity?

1.4 Strategy creation

This section looks in greater detail at *how* strategies are changed and *by whom* and how new strategies are created. Until we appreciate this we will not understand the practice of strategy in different organizations.

Opportunities for change

> *A wise man will make more opportunities than he finds.*
>
> FRANCIS BACON

It is vital that managers are strategically aware both of potentially threatening developments and of opportunities for profitable change, and that they seek to match and improve the fit between the environment and the organization's resources.

There is, however, no single recommended approach for seeking out and pursuing new opportunities. There is a broad spectrum ranging from what might be termed entrepreneurial opportunism to what Quinn (1980) calls '**logical incrementalism**'.

Strategic change can be relatively evolutionary or gradual, or much more dramatic or revolutionary. The nature of the opportunities (and threats) is directly related to both the general and the specific industry environments; and the approach that particular organizations take in seeking to match resources to the environment is dependent on the basic values of the organization and the style of the strategic leader. However, as will be seen, it does not follow that the strategic leader is the sole manager of strategic change.

Effectively managed change requires a vision of the future – where the organization is heading or wants to go – together with the means for creating and reaching this future. Planning a way forward from where the organization is now may not be enough to create the future vision; at the same time, when there is a vision, it is illogical to set off in pursuit without the appropriate 'equipment'. There must be a clear vision of a route, and this requires planning; on the way, managers should stay alert for dangers and opportunity (see Figure 1.7). Well-tracked routes (strategies that have proved successful in the past) and experience can both be beneficial, but in a dynamic environment there will always be an element of the unknown.

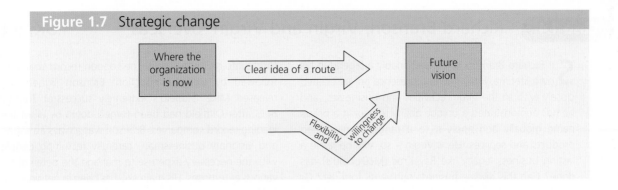

Figure 1.7 Strategic change

Planning and strategy creation

Businesses do not plan to fail – rather they fail to plan.

CHRIS GORMAN, ENTREPRENEUR

All managers plan. They plan how they might achieve objectives.

In essence, planning is essential to provide direction and to ensure that the appropriate resources are available where and when they are needed for the pursuit of objectives. Sometimes the planning process is detailed and formal; on other occasions planning may be informal, unstructured and essentially 'in the mind'. In the context of strategy formulation a clear distinction needs to be made between the cerebral activity of informal planning ('planning strategy') and formalized planning systems ('strategic planning').

Formal strategic planning systems are most useful in stable conditions. Environmental opportunities and threats are forecast, and then, as we saw earlier, strategies are planned and implemented. Strategies which are appropriate, feasible and desirable are most likely to help the organization to achieve its mission and objectives.

Where the environment is more turbulent and less predictable, strategic success requires flexibility, and the ability to learn about new opportunities and introduce appropriate changes continuously. Planning systems can still make a valuable contribution but the plans must not be inflexible.

In addition, it is important not to discount the contribution of visionary strategic leaders who become aware of opportunities – and, on occasions, create new opportunities – and take risks based on their awareness and insight of markets and customers.

Visionary and entrepreneurial leadership

Strategic planning systems imply that strategies are selected carefully and systematically from an analytical process. In other instances, major strategic changes will be decided upon without lengthy formal analysis. Typically such changes will reflect strong, entrepreneurial leadership and be visionary and discontinuous: I have seen the future and this is it! **Let us go and make it happen.** A good example is provided by Richard Branson and Virgin – see Case 1.4.

To an outsider it can often appear that the organization is pursuing growth with high-risk strategies, which are more reliant on luck than serious thought. This can underestimate the thinking that is involved, because quite often these **entrepreneurs** and visionary leaders have an instinctive feel for the products, services and markets involved, and enjoy a clear awareness and insight of the opportunities and risks.

This mode of strategy creation is most viable when the strategic leader has the full confidence of the organization, and he or she can persuade others to follow his or her ideas and implement the strategies successfully. Implementation requires more detailed planning and incremental changes with learning: initially it is the broad strategic idea that is formulated entrepreneurially.

Formal planning and/or visionary leadership will invariably determine important changes to corporate strategies; competitive and functional level changes are more likely to involve **emergent strategy** in the form of adaptive and incremental changes. The actual implementation of corporate level decisions is also likely to be incremental.

Case 1.4   Richard Branson, Virgin and Virgin 'overseas'   UK, Int

Sir Richard Branson is unquestionably a legend in his own lifetime. His name and presence are associated closely with all the Virgin activities and businesses, and he has demonstrated a unique ability to exploit a brand name globally and apply it to a range of diversified products and services. He *is* Virgin – so, will he leave a lasting business legacy like Ray Kroc (McDonald's) has done? Can this diverse business outlive its founder? Or would Virgin be split up into its many constituent businesses without Branson to lead it? Will the legacy be different in different parts of the world?

Branson is creative, opportunistic and dedicated to those activities in which he engages. Possessed of a strong ego, he is an excellent self-publicist. Popular with customers and employees, he has created a hugely successful people-driven business. His determination to succeed and his willingness to take risks are manifest in his (past) trans-Atlantic power boating and round-the-world ballooning exploits. Although he has said that he 'wouldn't do this if I didn't think I'd survive', the *Financial Times* has commented that 'all those associated with Mr Branson have to accept that he is an adventurer … he takes risks few of us would contemplate'. He has chosen to enter and compete in industries dominated by large and powerful corporations. Having challenged British Airways very visibly, for example, Coca-Cola has also been a target. He is now offering pioneering short passenger flights into space. Significantly, and not unexpectedly, his name comes up frequently when other business people are asked to name the person they most admire.

Now nearly 60 years old, Branson has been running businesses for some 40 years; and from nothing he has built a personal fortune of £3 billion. He began *Student* magazine when he was a 16-year-old public schoolboy, selling advertising from a public telephone booth. Ever opportunistic, he incorporated a mail order record business, buying the records from wholesalers once he had a firm order and cash in advance. Thwarted by a 2-month postal strike, Branson decided to enter retailing. Realizing the importance of location, he started looking for something along Oxford Street in London. Spotting an unused first floor above a shoe shop, he persuaded the owner to let him use it rent free until a paying tenant came along, on the grounds that if he was successful he would generate extra business for the shoe shop! He had a queue stretching 100 yards when it opened and never looked back – characteristically, he had turned a threat into an opportunity. The London record shop was followed by record production: Branson signed and released Mike Oldfield's extremely successful *Tubular Bells* after Oldfield had been turned down by all of the leading record companies. Branson was always an astute and visionary businessman, carefully recruiting people with the necessary expertise to manage the detail of his various enterprises. His main skill has been in networking, finding opportunities and securing the resources necessary for their exploitation. In this he has had to show courage and flexibility.

He decided to begin a trans-Atlantic airline in 1984. The move had been prompted by an American who approached him with a proposal for an all-business-class trans-Atlantic service. Although Branson rejected this particular focus, he took just a few weeks to make his decision. In this short period Branson analyzed why small airlines had previously failed with similar ventures. In particular he focused on Freddie Laker's Skytrain which had competed with a basic service and low prices. When the major airlines reduced their prices Skytrain was driven from the market as it had no other competitive advantage. Branson saw an opportunity: Virgin Atlantic Airways would offer added value and superior service at competitive prices, and concentrate on a limited number of the most lucrative routes. Branson had both a vision and many critics, who argued that he lacked the requisite skills.

He set about implementing his vision, initially leasing two Boeing 747 jumbo jets, and ensured that he generated publicity and notoriety for his initiative. More detailed planning came later after he began recruiting people with expertise in the industry. In this case the planning concentrated on the implementation of a visionary strategy. The airline has grown steadily since its creation and has won a number of awards for the quality of its service. It was the business that gave him a global presence. Additional aircraft have been leased and bought, and new routes such as Hong Kong, the Caribbean and South Africa have been added. The growth has been in limited, incremental steps as Virgin Atlantic has learnt from experience in a very dynamic environment. The major carriers such as British Airways have clearly seen Virgin as a threat – but realistically only after Branson's early successes – and have been forced to respond. Simply, when Virgin broke into the trans-Atlantic market with its innovative new service, it took the existing carriers by surprise; this was competition from an unexpected source. A successful holiday business has also been developed alongside the airline.

Over many years Branson has successfully marketed a range of products and services by systematically applying the Virgin brand name. The products and services may have been diversified – holidays, consumer products such as Virgin Vodka and Virgin Cola, cinemas, a radio station, mobile phones, financial services and Virgin Railways are examples – but the customer-focused brand image has remained constant.

Virgin was floated in 1986 but later reprivatized; Branson had been uncomfortable with the accountability expectations of institutional shareholders. Since then he has used joint ventures, minority partners and divestments (such as the sales of his music business and record shops) to raise money for new ventures and changes of direction. In 1999 Branson sold a 49 per cent stake in the airline to Singapore Airlines, partly to strengthen its competitiveness, but also to raise money for investment in further new ventures. A similar percentage of Virgin Trains was sold to the bus and train operator, Stagecoach. When Virgin Music was sold to Thorn EMI the general belief was that the money was required to subsidize the growing airline. More recently profits from the successful airline have allegedly been used to shore up other Virgin businesses. Another major sale was Virgin Mobile to NTL/Telewest for £1 billion, plus £8.5 million a year for use of the name Virgin Media for the new group, of which he retains a 15 per cent shareholding.

Describing itself as a 'branded venture capital company', Virgin has created over 300 businesses; and a few years ago Branson decided to increase his presence in electronic commerce and the Internet, believing that a vast range of products and services can be sold this way under the Virgin umbrella. A typical success story has been Virgin Wine. When BA and Air France decided, in 2003, to stop all Concorde flights, Branson was interested in continuing them with the Virgin brand. It is natural that there have been setbacks, one of the most notable being his failure to secure the National Lottery franchise from Camelot with his People's Lottery. When the Northern Rock Building Society was in real difficulties – and before it was eventually nationalized – Branson tried to piece together a rescue package. He failed at the time but never lost interest. In November 2011 Virgin Money absorbed what was left of Northern Rock. He struck a good deal and arguably the UK taxpayer is a loser.

Branson has moved into animation with Virgin Comics and healthcare with clinics that offer a package of conventional, homeopathic and complementary medicines together. He has also taken a lead with the 'green agenda'. Virgin Fuels is developing biofuels and he has dedicated some of the profits from Virgin Atlantic and Virgin Trains for research. He is also funding the Virgin Earth Challenge, whereby a prize of US$25 million is available for anyone who can invent a safe and effective way of removing greenhouse gases from the atmosphere. He also established global think tanks to deal with such challenges as the carbon footprint and the way we use our oceans.

In 2004 Branson licensed the technology behind SpaceshipOne – a private manned spacecraft. The technology was owned and developed by a business owned by Microsoft co-founder Paul Allen. Virgin Galactic was going to build five spacecraft to provide short trips into space for wealthy space tourists. Customers would be flown outside the earth's atmosphere and back – not to a space station. Each craft would have five seats. Those interested will not need to be young or especially fit, but they will have to be willing to commit 3 days to training ahead of their journey.

Branson's business philosophy is built around quality products and services, value for money, innovation and an element of fun. 'I never let accountants get in the way of business. You only live once and you might as well have a fun time while you're living.' In 2009 he invested in Formula One with a Virgin Racing Team.

By focusing on customers and service he has frequently been able to add value where larger competitors have developed a degree of complacency. 'The challenge of learning and trying to do something better than in the past is irresistible.' Branson always realized that this would be impossible without the appropriate people and created an organization with a devolved and informal culture. Business ideas can, and do, come from anywhere in Virgin. And from people outside the organization. Branson has always made sure he is approachable. Employees with ideas that Branson likes will be given encouragement and development capital. Once a venture reaches a certain size it is normally freed to operate as an independent business within the Virgin Group, and the intrapreneur retains an equity stake. Some, though, are sold and cease to be part of Virgin. Branson has always been willing to 'take punts' – and some do go wrong. Simply, on balance, he expects (and needs) to succeed more than he fails. 'Opportunities are like London buses. If you look at why you missed the last one, you will miss the next one as well.'

Virgin 'overseas'

Branson has been willing to take Virgin overseas, with varying degrees of success. He started a low cost airline in Australia – Virgin Blue – which has performed well and forced a serious reaction from Qantas, the national carrier. Qantas was forced to lower its own prices and also establish a specialist low-cost subsidiary, Jet Star. Branson's deal-making didn't work out quite as he wanted in this case, though, and he lost control of the business.

Inevitably his fame and reputation will encourage people to approach him – as Nelson Mandela did in 2001. Mandela asked whether he would take over the bankrupt Health and Racquet Club chain of health clubs in South Africa and thus save 6000 jobs. He agreed and has since transformed the business into a successful chain of health and fitness clubs across the country. He has since invested further in South Africa through Virgin Money (a low-cost credit card) and Virgin Mobile (with a competitively priced network). Virgin Atlantic has been flying into the country for several years.

He has also declared his commitment to 'giving something back' and with a focus on where in the world he believes he can do most good.

Branson owns an island in the Caribbean, in the British Virgin Islands, where he has a retreat and holiday home and where his global think tanks are likely to meet. The Caribbean and South Africa have become two important targets for his Virgin Unite non-profit Foundation. He has established Branson Centres of Entrepreneurship in both Johannesburg and Jamaica. Here people are encouraged to start businesses and provided with appropriate support – work space, business training, individual mentoring, networking opportunities and introductions to financiers. These centres are basically business incubators and each has a focus on businesses that are relevant for the locale – the one in Montego Bay targets tourism, but the one in South Africa has a strong technology focus.

Questions

1 What are Richard Branson's strengths and limitations as a strategic leader?
2 How have they been manifested as Virgin has developed?
3 Can this diverse business outlive its founder?
4 Or would Virgin be split into its many constituent businesses without Branson to lead it?
5 What other activities might Branson consider if he wants to help new businesses develop around the world?

Gladwell (2000) refers to unpredicted events that open up unexpected opportunities as 'tipping points', but, of course, organizations must be in a position to take advantage. One such event happened to Hush Puppies in the mid-1990s. This once very popular brand of casual shoe had declined markedly in popularity and its owners were barely supporting it. However, a number of young people in New York started wearing them as something of a fashion statement, and mainly because nobody else was wearing them. This trend started when they bought them from charity shops! What they were doing was spotted and copied and suddenly there was a resurgence in the popularity of the brand. It had nothing to do with any marketing by the manufacturers. The owners then had a huge challenge restoring the **supply chain** to meet demand.

The critical point that emerges from the Hush Puppies example is that, in contrast to the view that strategies are planned, successful strategies can emerge without prior planning.

Other classic business school examples of emergent or unintended strategies are Xerox, who set out to sell photocopiers when customers only really wanted the copies and not the machines, and Gillette, actively promoting shavers when the real desire of the customer is for a shave. The razor blade is what is wanted by the consumer. Arguably, it is better to give the razor away if this ensures you sell the blades.

In more recent times, we have seen the demise of many products relating to the delivery of music – including music cassette tapes, DAT and of course vinyl. When the compact disk was introduced, it was seen as being the 'nail in the coffin' of the old vinyl format. Yet vinyl has not died quite as anticipated. Vinyl is still sold in most music outlets as new types of music become popular, including dub step, reggae and techno, that are sold in the 12 inch vinyl size – previously the format for what was known as LPs. Driving this forward has been the fact that vinyl has also been used for the hand mixing of tracks by DJs in clubs all over the UK and beyond. Other innovations include MP3s, Spotify and SoundCloud. See also Case 4.2.

Will the same happen with Kodak? The company filed for bankruptcy protection in the US in January 2012 due to rapidly declining sales of photographic film in the face of competition from digital photo technology mainly in smart phones.

Case 1.4 above on Richard Branson and Virgin looked at the strategic impact of a truly entrepreneurial strategic leader. We included in this case an example of how one successful 'Western' entrepreneur has helped businesses to start and grow in developing countries. In doing this Branson is not unique.

We can now argue that there are two distinct elements to emergent strategic change.

Incremental strategic change

In dynamic and turbulent competitive environments, detailed formal planning is seen to be problematic. The plans are only as good as any forecasts, which must be uncertain. It can make sense, therefore, not to rely on detailed plans, but instead to plan broad strategies within a clearly defined mission and purpose.

Having provided this direction, the strategic leader will allow strategies to emerge in a decentralized organization structure. Managers will meet regularly, both formally and informally, to discuss progress and changing trends; they will plan new courses of action and then try them out: a form of 'real-time planning'.

Adaptive strategic change

Some organizations will be characterized by extensive decentralization, empowerment and accountability. Here, managers throughout the organization are being encouraged to look for opportunities and threats and to innovate. The underlying argument is that managers 'at the coal face' are closest to the key changes in the organization's environment and should, therefore, be in a position where they can, on the one hand, react quickly and, on the other hand, be proactive or intrapreneurial in attempting to change or manage the external environment. Managers will be encouraged and empowered to make changes in their areas of responsibility and, ideally, rewarded for their initiatives. The implication is that functional changes will impact upon competitive strategies in a positive way as the organization adapts to its changing environment. Conceptually this is similar to incremental change.

Proponents of chaos theory such as Stacey (1993) argue that intentional strategies are, *per se*, 'too inflexible for unknown futures'. Relying on this approach is a 'recipe for stagnation and failure because of the extent of the complexity'. Companies must seek to 'achieve a state of creative tension on the edge of instability'. These theorists accept that organizational hierarchies and planning are needed to control day-to-day operations but, in the long-term, strategies must be allowed to emerge from the 'self-organizing activities of loose, informal, destabilizing networks'.

Team working and learning are at the heart of the adaptive and incremental modes. Managers must learn about new opportunities and threats; they should also learn from the successes and mistakes of other managers. Managers must be willing to take measured risks; for this to happen, understandable mistakes and errors of judgement should not be penalised harshly.

Change is gradual and comes from experimentation; new strategies involve an element of trial and error. Success is very dependent upon communications. Managers must know of the opportunities and threats facing them; the organization must be able to synthesize all changes into a meaningful pattern, and spread learning and best practice.

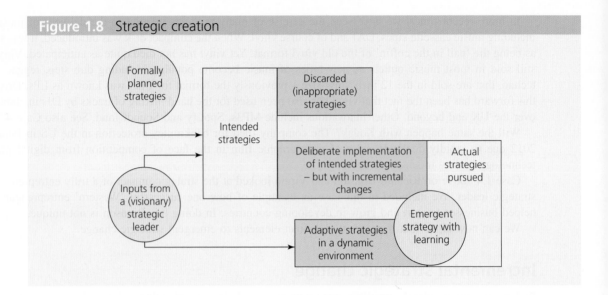

Figure 1.8   Strategic creation

Mintzberg (1989) argues that organizations should be structured and managed to ensure that formulators of strategies (managers whose decisions lead to strategic changes) have information, and that the implementers of strategies and changes have the appropriate degree of **power** to ensure that the desired changes are brought about.

Figure 1.8 pulls these ideas together and highlights that it is quite normal to find all of these modes in evidence simultaneously in an organization, although there is likely to be one dominant mode. Moreover different managers in the same organization will not necessarily agree on the relative significance of each mode; their perceptions of what is actually happening will vary.

The message for managers is that they need to recognize this process of emergence and to intervene where appropriate, killing off bad emergent strategies but nurturing potentially good ones. To make such decisions, however, managers must be able to judge the worth of emergent strategies. They must be able to think strategically. This viewpoint is probably the best argument for the continued use of the rationalist approach.

Strategy is necessarily incremental and adaptive, but that does not in any way imply that its evolution cannot be, or should not be, analyzed, managed and controlled.

PASCALE, 1984

Strategy at work

We conclude this section with Figure 1.9, which has its origins in Mintzberg's work cited earlier. Here we can see it proposed that strategy comprises:

- **Learning** from the past
- **Understanding** (making sense of) the present
- **Imagining** the future and
- **Competing** and innovating to stay ahead of rivals and seize new opportunities.

Some authors would describe such different but linked perspectives as 'lenses'. Individually, but especially collectively, they can help us make sense of strategy. Simply, they are all legitimate ways of looking at strategy.

Individually, we are all different and if we think about ourselves we would be able to explain which of these perspectives we find most natural and which we struggle with the most. Indeed, some people are naturally analytical; others are naturally creative. Some of us see opportunities before others do because we

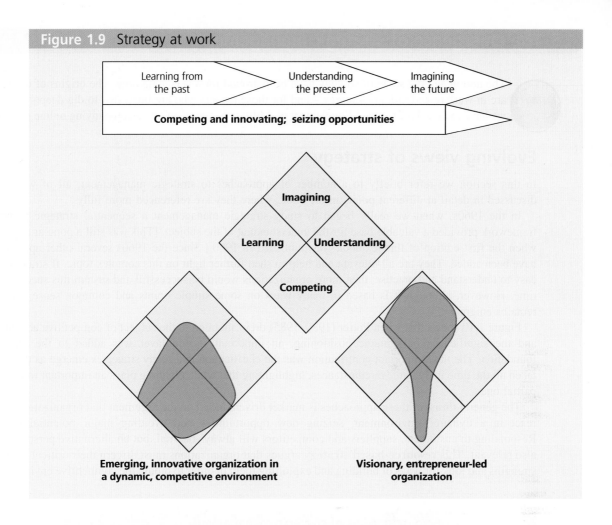

Figure 1.9 Strategy at work

Learning from the past → Understanding the present → Imagining the future

Competing and innovating; seizing opportunities

Imagining

Learning   Understanding

Competing

Emerging, innovative organization in a dynamic, competitive environment

Visionary, entrepreneur-led organization

form different mental patterns from what we see and observe. And, finally, some of us are very tactical and enjoy the buzz of competition; we are flexible in the face of adversity.

Metaphorically, organizations are the same as individuals. And their behaviour will reflect the type of organization they are strategically. Moreover, the circumstances they face will influence the type of organization they ideally need to be or become, if they are to be strong and effective.

An emerging and innovative (entrepreneurial) business in a dynamic, competitive environment might be expected to be strong in the bottom diamond (competing) and less strong in the other three. One led by a visionary entrepreneur might be less strong in the other three. That said, to some degree, it is important to have some strength in every segment.

Before we explore the business model – in Chapter 2 – it is useful to consider just how the subject of strategic management has emerged in recent years and views have changed on what is and what isn't significant. In 'the early days' strategy was taught from a strongly analytical viewpoint but as time has gone on the more subjective elements have become increasingly significant. At the end of the chapter through Strategy in Action, we reflect on two examples of historic change and through an Appendix we discuss strategic management in a number of different contexts. Additionally, we also make use of a web supplement on military strategy. From all of this you will see that whilst there are many common elements there are significant areas of difference – such that people dealing with strategy in one context will find certain issues more or less critical. We strongly recommend that you read this Appendix material so that when you discuss strategy with people whose background and perspective differ from yours you will appreciate why.

1.5 The emergence of strategic management

 The notion and the study of strategy have been around for a very long time. The origins of our study are in warfare and military strategy – and for those readers who are interested to dig deeper into this we have included a Chapter 1 Supplement on Military Strategy on our accompanying online platform.

Evolving views of strategy

In this section we refer briefly to a number of approaches to strategic management, all of which are discussed in detail at different points in the book, where they are referenced more fully.

In the 1960s, when we really began to study strategic management a sequential strategic planning framework provided a valuable base for the understanding of the subject. [This was still a popular approach when the first edition of this textbook was published in 1990.] Since the 1960s several other approaches have been added. They are all relevant and help to shed further light on this complex topic. If strategy was easy to understand and practise, then more organizations would be successful and sustain this success over time. However, although it is based in many ways on some simple points and common sense, strategy remains enigmatic.

Figure 1.10 shows that when Porter (1980, 1985) drew attention to the subject of competitive advantage, and the significance of strategic positioning, an important second layer was added to the planning foundation. The next important contribution was the clarification that many strategies emerge as decisions taken all the time in dynamic circumstances, highlighting that while planning plays an important role, it is a partial one.

The general thrust of these approaches is market driven, based on the argument that organizations must react in a dynamic environment, seizing new opportunities and avoiding major potential threats. Responding to customers, suppliers and competitors will always be vital, but an alternative perspective is also relevant. This **resource-based strategy** argues that organizations must discern their critical strategic strengths and look for ways of building and exploiting them in order to mould the competitive environment.

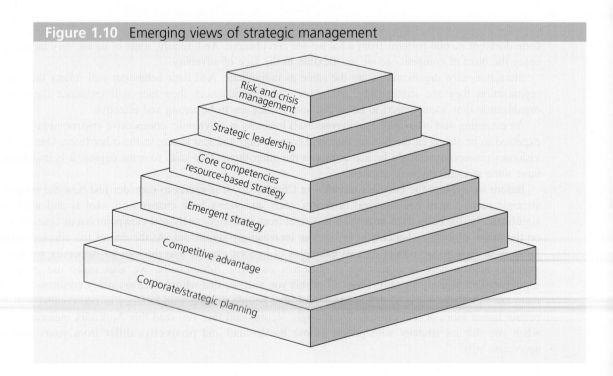

Figure 1.10   Emerging views of strategic management

In the supplement to this chapter we look at the relevant issues of core competency and **strategic capability**. Successful organizations will blend both the market and resource perspectives so that they do not overlook potentially good opportunities.

In recent years the subject of strategic leadership has received greater prominence, stimulated in part by the media. Business success stories have been popular items for newspapers and magazines, especially where there is a high-profile figure who can be identified with the organization and the story. In addition, the 'falls from grace' of some very high-profile business people have proved newsworthy. The accompanying autobiographies of some of these people have added to this understanding.

Critical Reflection 1.1 provides an alternative perspective on these important approaches.

Critical Reflection 1.1   Directions of Strategic Thought

The Classical Approach – *planning*

Driven by the 'rational man' paradigm and based on the economists' profit-maximizing model.

Planning is the vehicle for rational strategy creation.

There are elements of creation and implementation, the classical strategy-structure framework.

Strategic positioning is at its heart. Appropriateness is, therefore, a key test.

Strong central leadership is required to drive the process.

The Evolutionary Approach – *opportunity-driven emergent strategy*

Driven by competition – and, in this respect, the work of Michael Porter – it is based around responding to identified opportunities and threats.

The idea is that only the best performers survive in a dynamic world, accepting there is always an element of luck and chance.

The approach questions whether organizations can create differences by a largely rational approach.

'Strategizing' – or thinking long-term – can be dangerous if it reduces organizational flexibility.

Rather, strategy is about tactical moves (changes) in response to external events.

The appropriate resources are essential to put the organization in a position to 'engage the enemy'.

Appropriateness and feasibility are the key tests.

The Processual Approach – *resource-based emergent planning*

This is driven by internal stakeholders and assumes that adaptation to the outside world is through internal political bargaining, compromise and accommodation.

Along the lines of Mintzberg, strategies are crafted by trial, error and learning.

The organization needs to develop key strengths (core competencies and strategic capabilities) which become the foundation for resource-based strategies.

Feasibility and desirability for key internal stakeholders are important tests.

The Systemic Approach – *visionary strategy driven by key players*

Strategies emerge from the culture and values of key players, typically the strategic leader.

Very much affected by the 'wider picture' perspective, although this could embrace the needs of a local community as much as concerns for the global environment.

In some economies the systemic approach can correspond to the profit-seeking paradigm behind the classical approach.

Developed from

Whittington, R (1993) *What Is Strategy – And Does It Matter?* Thomson / Cengage Learning

Commentary

Whittington sees the Classical and Processual approaches as internally driven, on the grounds that the classical approach is driven by an internal desire to maximize profits. Evolutionary and Systemic are then external.

However, we might argue that the Classical approach (like the Evolutionary) is external as they are both based on a search for economic opportunities in a competitive environment.

The Systemic (like the Processual) is internal because it is based on the values of powerful strategic leaders.

Most recently, **risk management** and **crisis management** have joined the debate. Organizations have recognized that scenario building can help their understanding of uncertainty, where the future may depend in part on the past but will not replicate it. For some industries, such as pharmaceuticals (where huge investments in new drugs are required but carry no guarantee of success) and electronic commerce (which is changing by the day) serious risk assessment is vital. The environment is busy with information and triggers, never more so than now, thanks to the Internet, but discerning the real commercial opportunities is probably harder rather than easier than it was in the past. Organizational fortunes can, therefore, change rapidly, and crises can arise suddenly to catch out the unwary organization. The study of learning, and the involvement of people in an empowered and intrapreneurial culture, is a key element both of this topic and of emergent strategy.

The following discussion on strategic disturbances supports the significance of this sixth layer in Figure 1.10.

Strategic disturbance

Stacey (1993) advocates that strategy is about handling disturbance, and this is related to changing both competitive advantage and competitive capability. We can see how disturbances constitute risk and, if mishandled, crises.

To Stacey, strategy is not about a comprehensive and integrated set of actions or routes to objectives; instead it is about a comprehensive and integrated total control system, which will enable the strategic leader to deal with unforeseeable disturbances, changes in competitive advantage and capability as they occur. Handling disturbance effectively is, therefore, a question of control in its widest sense.

The starting point is not the mission, and certainly not detailed long-term objectives, but the appropriate style of control.

Disturbances can arise from anywhere and everywhere. The basic business flows, of orders/ requisitions, inputs/outputs and money, all give rise to disturbances; machine breakdowns, material shortages, unpaid debts, rising stock levels, changes in the pattern of orders also give rise to disturbances. The environment impacts on the flows, feeding disturbances into the organization – through, for example, the loss of a major customer, changing customer tastes and the appearance of a new competitor. The environment also feeds disturbances directly to the instruments of control – public opinion, changes in work culture, pressures to install training, reward pressures and so on. The environment could also directly contribute to disturbance – changes in taxation, changes in health and safety requirements, trade union law, environmental legislation imposing uniform standards throughout the EU and so on. The instruments of control can directly contribute to disturbance – new staff and managers may join the company with different cultural values. Roles can directly contribute to disturbance through individual dissatisfaction with roles or a poor fit of people to their roles.

Disturbances are continuously bombarding the business from all directions and wherever they come from they have to be handled at the core of the control system by managers and workers who apply processes to control elements. The outcome is some form of action. This action is based on structured thinking, but not some analytical straitjacket.

A serious drawback to the formal planning approach, then, is the problem of trying to foresee strategic disturbance over a period which extends much into the future. We all know that the early decades of this century will see a rapid growth in the age group over 60s in most industrialized countries. We know that this group will be healthier and wealthier than ever before in history. But just what does this mean for business? What will these rich, healthy pensioners be looking for – Club 65+ instead of Club 18–30? Moreover, when does it make sense for anyone to do anything about it? This major demographic change is a strategic disturbance, but should an entrepreneur start building holiday villas for the elderly now?

In Chapter 2 we develop further ideas introduced in this introductory chapter. We look at the constituent elements in the business model and argue that for any organization to be able to show that it is strategic it must have – and been seen to have – a credible business model.

One feature of most chapters is the 'Research Snapshot', which reviews some of the most cutting-edge contemporary research on that sub-theme of strategic management. While we review relevant research on strategy as practice below, we will keep you waiting until Chapter 17, after you have digested this contents of this book, for a thorough discussion and some concluding thoughts on this theme.

Research Snapshot 1.1

Strategy as practice, extensively reviewed recently (e.g. Miettinen et al., 2009; Jarzabkowski and Spee, 2009; Vaara and Whittington, 2012) relates to: 'detailed aspects of strategizing; how strategists think, talk, reflect, interact, embellish and politicize, what tools and techniques they use and the implications of different forms of strategizing for strategy as an organizational activity' (Jarzabkowski, 2005: p.3), and has been contrasted with the process-based and other views of strategy. Or which Chia and MacKay (2007) refer to as being 'post-processual', with a focus upon both 'agency' and 'structure', and clear differentiation from other viewpoints of strategy (itself assumed by them to be 'discernible patterns of actions arising from habituated tendencies and internalized dispositions rather than from deliberate, purposeful goal-setting initiatives' (ibid: p.635)).

The early work by Paula Jarzabkowski (2004, 2005) made a significant contribution to the field. For example, she examined recursive and adaptive practice in strategic management and highlighted a 'tension' between such practices and in terms of implementing strategy (Jarzabkowski, 2004). Indeed, Whittington (2006: p.613) contends for a need for further research, given the focus 'either on strategy activity at the intra-organizational level or on the aggregate effects of this activity at the extra-organizational level'; and thus he, along with others, argues for an approach or 'overarching conceptual framework' linking three elements of strategy: 'praxis', 'practices' and 'practitioners' (Whittington, 2004; Jarzabkowski et al., 2007). The literature on strategy as practice (SAP) has been comprehensively reviewed and profiled in terms of concepts of practitioners, praxis and practices, and finally its outcomes (Jarzabkowski and Spee, 2009), demonstrating its status as a developed field and yet one that has much scope for future research studies.

Other authors link strategy as practice with e.g. dynamic capabilities, particularly in terms of 'organizational assets' (Regnér, 2008), sense-making by middle managers and the link between 'intended

strategies' and 'unintended outcomes' (Balogun and Johnson, 2005), framing in uncertain conditions (Kaplan, 2008), strategy teams (Paroutis and Pettigrew, 2007), the concept of 'social practice' (Rasche and Chia, 2009) and a Heideggerian view on the role of 'practical coping' (Chia and Holt, 2006). The latter is a particularly interesting and relevant paper in that they identify two strategizing 'modes' – 'building' ('purposeful' and planned) and 'dwelling' ('non-deliberately through everyday practical coping' and without 'strategic intent' or 'goal-orientation') – and they conclude that: 'actions may be consistent and organizationally effective without (and even in spite of) the existence of purposeful strategic plans' (ibid: p.635). In some respects, Chia and Holt's (2006) paper mirrors the two alternative cognitive approaches of predictive-and-planning-oriented causation (akin to building) and the much more entrepreneurial, controlled, future-changing effectuation (à la dwelling) theorized by Sarasvathy (2001) and extended by Venkataraman and Sarasvathy (2002) in terms of strategic management.*

Jarzabkowski and Whittington (2008a, b) argued for greater alignment between SAP and learning and teaching at universities given the clearer and more real-world insight that practice can give students and future managers/strategists. Corradi et al. (2010), perhaps, more critically, consider SAP to be something of a 'bandwagon', suggesting that 'the collective appropriation of the label has not been achieved, and therefore, the bandwagon is heading for a partition'. Finally, as a counterweight to this more critical or negative viewpoint, Vaara and Whittington (2012: p.285) find that SAP's: 'power ... lies in its ability to explain how strategy-making is enabled and constrained by prevailing organizational and societal practices ... SAP research has helped to advance social theories in strategic management, offered alternatives to performance-dominated analyses, broadened the scope in terms of organizations studied and promoted new methodologies. In particular, it has provided important insights into the tools and methods of strategy-making (practices), how strategy work takes place (praxis) and the role and identity of the actors involved (practitioners).'

Students will find these articles particularly useful in developing a comprehensive understanding of strategy as practice.

*Sarasvathy, S. D. (2001) 'Causation and effectuation: Towards a theoretical shift from economic inevitability to entrepreneurial contingency', *Academy of Management Review*, Vol. 26, No. 2, pp. 243–263.

Venkataraman, S. and Sarasvathy, S. (2002) 'Strategy and entrepreneurship: Outlines of an untold story', in Hitt, M., Freeman, E. and Harrison, J. (Eds), *Handbook of Strategic Management*, Wiley, London, pp. 650–668.

Further Reading

Balogun, J. and Johnson, G. (2005) 'From Intended Strategies to Unintended Outcomes: The Impact of Change Recipient Sense-making', *Organization Studies*, Vol. 26, No. 11, pp. 1573–1601.

Chia, R. and Holt, R. (2006) 'Strategy as Practical Coping: A Heideggerian Perspective', *Organization Studies*, Vol. 27, No. 5, pp. 635–655.

Chia, R. and MacKay, B. (2007) 'Post-processual challenges for the emerging strategy-as-practice perspective: Discovering strategy in the logic of practice', *Human Relations*, Fol. 60, No. 1, pp. 217–242.

Corradi, G., Gherardi, S. and Verzelloni, L. (2010) 'Through the practice lens: Where is the bandwagon of practice-based studies heading?', *Management Learning*, Vol. 41, No. 3, pp. 265–283.

Fenton, C. and Langley, A. (2011) 'Strategy as Practice and the Narrative Turn', *Organization Studies*, Vol. 32, No. 9, pp. 1171–1196.

Jarzabkowski, P. (2004) 'Strategy as Practice: Recursiveness, Adaptation, and Practices-in-Use', *Organization Studies*, Vol. 25, No. 4, pp. 529–560.

Jarzabkowski, P. (2005) *Strategy as Practice: An Activity Based Approach*, Sage: London.

Jarzabkowski, P. and Spee, A.P. (2009) 'Strategy-as-practice: A review and future directions for the field', *International Journal of Management Reviews*, Vol. 11, No. 1, pp. 69–95.

Jarzabkowski, P. and Whittington, W. (2008a) 'Directions for a Troubled Discipline: Strategy Research, Teaching, and Practice—Introduction to the Dialog', *Journal of Management Inquiry*, Vol. 17, No. 4, pp. 266–268.

Jarzabkowski, P. and Whittington, R. (2008b) 'A Strategy-as-Practice Approach to Strategy Research and Education', *Journal of Management Inquiry*, Vol. 17, No. 4, pp. 282–286.

Jarzabkowski, P., Balogun, J. and Seidl, D. (2007) 'Strategizing: The challenges of a practice perspective', *Human Relations*, Vol. 60, No. 1, pp. 5–27.

Kaplan, S. (2008) 'Framing Contests: Strategy Making Under Uncertainty', *Organization Science*, Vol. 19, No. 5, pp. 729–752.

Miettinen, R., Samra-Fredericks, D. and Yanow, D. (2009) 'Re-Turn to Practice: An Introductory Essay', *Organization Studies*, Vol. 30, No. 12, pp. 1309–1327.

Paroutis, S. and Pettigrew, A. (2007) 'Strategizing in the multi-business firm: Strategy teams at multiple levels and over time', *Human Relations*, Vol. 60, No. 1, pp. 99–135.

Rasche, A. and Chia, R. (2009) 'Researching Strategy Practices: A Genealogical Social Theory Perspective', Organization Studies, Vol. 30, No. 7, pp. 713–734.

Regnér, P. (2008) 'Strategy-as-practice and dynamic capabilities: Steps towards a dynamic view of strategy', *Human Relations*, Vol. 61, No. 4, pp. 565–588.

Vaara, E. and Whittington, R. (2012) 'Strategy-as-Practice: Taking Social Practices Seriously', *The Academy of Management Annals*, Vol. 6, No. 1, pp. 285–336.

Whittington, R. (2004) 'Strategy after modernism: recovering practice', *European Management Review*, Vol. 1, pp. 62–68.

Whittington, R. (2006) 'Completing the Practice Turn in Strategy Research', *Organization Studies*, Vol. 27, No. 5, pp. 613–634.

Summary

Strategies are means to ends – they are the means through which organizations seek to achieve objectives and fulfil their mission or purpose.

All managers can be strategy makers because of their influence in both strategy creation and **strategy implementation**.

Strategic management is a process which embraces the strategies together with the themes of excellence in their implementation, creativity and innovation when they are changed and the effective and timely management of these changes.

There is evidence that strategic thinking, and hence strategic management, could be improved in many companies by:

- *segmenting* and *targeting* markets more crisply and definitively
- appreciating clearly what the *key success factors* are in the targeted markets and segments
- creating real *competitive advantage*
- out-thinking rivals.

There are three levels of strategy:

- *corporate* – the overall portfolio of businesses within an organization
- *competitive* – the search for, and maintenance of, competitive advantage in each and every business, product and/or service
- *functional* – the activities that deliver the competitive advantage.

These activities, products, services and businesses should not be analyzed exclusively at an individual 'ring-fenced' level, but also in terms of the whole organization. Links should be forged wherever possible to generate *synergies*.

Strategies should not be thought of as having one single definition or perspective. Five have been discussed: visionary strategies, planned strategies and tactics, all of which address the future; present strategic positions, and patterns that have emerged with past decisions and strategies.

Strategy, then, comprises elements of learning, understanding, imagining and competing.

E–V–R (Environment–Values–Resources) is a simple but very useful framework for examining the effectiveness of the current strategies and strategic position of an organization.

There are three ways in which strategies are created: with visionary leadership, from a planning process, and adaptively and incrementally as new decisions are taken in real-time.

Additional themes complement, but do not replace, strategic planning in the understanding of the realities of strategic management and strategic change, namely competitive advantage, emergent strategy creation, strategic competency, strategic leadership and risk and crisis management.

Strategy and strategic management in different sectors, such as small and global businesses, the public sector and not-for-profit organizations, have many similarities, but there are clear differences, especially of emphasis.

Online cases for this chapter

Online Case 1.1: P&O

References

Ansoff, H.I. (1968) Corporate Strategy Penguin Coliginally publishd by, McGraw Hill

Bettis, R. and Prahalad, C.K. (1995) The dominant logic: retrospective and extension, *Strategic Management Journal*, Volume 16, January.

Campbell, A. and Alexander, M. (1997) What's wrong with strategy? *Harvard Business Review*, November–December.

Courtney, H., Kirkland, J. and Viguerie, P. (1997) Strategy under uncertainty, *Harvard Business Review*, November–December.

Drucker, P.F. (1994) The theory of business, *Harvard Business Review*, September–October.

Gladwell, M. (2000) *The Tipping Point - How Little Things Can Make a Big Difference*, Little Brown.

Mathur, S.S. and Kenyon, A. (1998) *Creating Value: Shaping Tomorrow's Business*, Butterworth-Heinemann.

Mintzberg, H., Ahlstrand, B. and Lampel, J. (1998) *Strategy Safari*, Prentice Hall.

Mintzberg, H. (1989) *Mintzberg on Management*, Free Press, Prentice-Hall.

Morrison, R. and Lee, J. (1979) From planning to clearer strategic thinking, *Financial Times*, 27 July.

Pascale, R.T. (1984) Perspectives on strategy - the real story behind Honda's success, *California Management Review*, 26, 47–72.

Porter, M.E. (1980) *Competitive Strategy*, Free Press.

Porter, M.E. (1985) *Competitive Advantage*, Free Press.

Porter, M.E. (1996) What is strategy? *Harvard Business Review*, November–December.

Pümpin, C. (1987) *The Essence of Corporate Strategy*, Gower.

Quinn, J.B. (1980) *Strategies for Change: Logical Incrementalism*, Irwin.

Stacey, R.D. (1993) *Strategic Management and Organizational Dynamics*, Pitman.

Web supplement related to this chapter

Military Strategy I
In additional to the web supplement, there are some additional questions for this chapter on the online platform.

Appendix

Strategic management in specific contexts

Strategic ideas are relevant for all types of organization, and many of the key issues are the same, although they may differ in their relative significance. At the same time there are some important differences, which are introduced in this section. Throughout the book an attempt is made to use examples and cases that reflect a range of different types and size of organization but, inevitably, large manufacturing and service businesses feature prominently, largely because they are the organizations and brand names that most readers will recognize and relate to easily.

Small businesses

Typically, small businesses will focus on a single product or service, or at least a restricted range of related products and services, targeted at a defined market niche. Competitive and functional strategies are important, but many of the corporate strategy issues discussed herein will not be relevant until the organization grows larger, assuming that it does so. In addition, their customers may be concentrated in a single geographical area, but this will certainly not always be the case especially with the Internet available to drive sales. In some large organizations,

the structure is designed to encourage the individual businesses to behave as a typical small business in some of its operations.

There is generally a great reliance on the owner–manager for all major strategic decisions. The advantage can be speed, as decisions need not become lost or slowed down in discussion or committee; the corresponding disadvantage can be an overreliance on one person who may become overstretched as the business develops. Hence, there is an emphasis on visionary strategy creation and on emergence, as new ideas are tried out. Sophisticated analysis and planning is less likely, and sometimes a lack of attention to detail can constitute another weakness.

The real challenge for small businesses is to develop and strengthen their resources once they start growing: if they fail they will lose their competitiveness. Some never possess any real competitive advantage in the first place and, while they may survive if they are run efficiently, they are unlikely to grow to any significant size.

Where a small business fails to grow it will always be dependent on the actions of others. Both its suppliers and customers could be larger and consequently more powerful. In this case it could be paying cash for its supplies and giving extended credit to its customers, resulting in cash-flow problems. It is also likely to be very reactive to competitor initiatives until it can become more prominent and proactive. The helpful publicity and visibility given to larger organizations may be withheld, even at a local level. High-quality managers and employees, who could fuel the growth, may not find a small, and perceptually inconsequential company, attractive to work for. Nevertheless, all companies start small: they are, after all, the seedbed for those successful entrepreneurs who create growth businesses.

The success, or lack of it, then, will be hugely dependent on the strategic leader, and his or her culture and style. The future will be dictated by their skill and also by their ability to acquire resources, particularly in terms of finance. A lack of capital can often be a real restraint to growth. Banks often demand security and collateral and venture capitalists often only become interested once the business has reached a certain size and proved itself. The web supplement on Military Strategy illustrates how guerrilla warfare provides a useful metaphor for the strategic use of tactics by small businesses.

Some of the traditional logic concerning small businesses, however, has to some degree been turned on its head in the case of many new Internet or 'dot.com' companies who have been able to raise millions of dollars and pounds on the strength of a barely proven idea that appeared to offer a golden opportunity. Financiers have taken risks that they would previously have shunned because of the speed and growth of this sector and its inherent uncertainty. Some of the new organizations have grown rapidly and become huge in a very short space of time; equally many have failed.

Global companies

Here the emphasis is very much on corporate strategy: diversity, geographical scope and co-ordinating the countries where products are made with the countries where they are sold. Using low-cost labour factories in Eastern Europe and the Far East can prove controversial while still being an economic necessity. In addition, these are often very powerful companies whose annual turnover exceeds the gross national product (GNP) of many of the world's smaller countries. Nevertheless, issues of competitiveness and competitive advantage are as relevant as they are for a small business. One key complication can be currency fluctuations when component supplies and finished goods are moved around the world.

The major dilemma for many global companies concerns their need to achieve global scale economies from concentrating production in large plants whilst not sacrificing their local identity and relevance in the various markets. To accomplish this they must stay close to their customers and markets, whose specific tastes and preferences may differ markedly, even though they are buying essentially the same product.

The organizational structure can be, and often is, just as important as the strategy. This, in turn, raises a number of important people issues. People may be switched from business to business and from country to country as part of their personal progression. This movement also helps the whole organization to transfer skills and knowledge and to learn good practices from different parts of the business.

Global corporations also need to develop expertise in financial management. Attractive development grants and packages will be available in certain countries and influence strategic developments. Interest rates are not the same around the world and consequently loans can be more attractive in certain countries and not in others. Moreover, tax rates vary and it can be very beneficial to be seen to be earning profits in low-tax countries instead of high-tax ones.

Not-for-profit organizations

Organizations such as churches and charities clearly fit into this sector very well, but certain other profit-generating businesses, such as museums, zoos and local theatres, are relatively closely aligned. In the case of the latter examples, the profit objective is often designed to create a 'war chest' for future investment rather than to reward an owner or a group of investors. For this reason there are many common characteristics. Many *Social Enterprises* demonstrate issues described above in the section on small businesses and in the comments here.

Money and surpluses may be perceived differently in not-for-profit organizations than in profit-seeking businesses, but there is still a need to create a positive cash flow. A charity, for example, can only spend on good causes if it can generate funds. For this reason, churches and charities can legitimately appear very commercial in their outlook, and this must be accepted alongside the cause that they are targeting.

These not-for-profit organizations need social entrepreneurs or strategic leaders who, in many ways, will be similar to those found in the profit-seeking sector. They will possess similar entrepreneurial and leadership qualities, but they will be driven by a cause, which attracts them to the particular organization and sector. This, in turn, guides the mission, purpose and culture. In addition, there is likely to be a greater reliance on voluntary helpers and possibly managers and others who readily accept salaries and wages below those that they might earn in the profit sector.

There are likely to be variations on the modes of strategy creation discussed herein. There is likely to be some committee structure, involving both salaried employees and unpaid volunteers, the latter often in senior roles. Decision-making can be slow and political in nature, although clearly it does not have to be this way. However, strong and dominant leaders (either paid or unpaid) quite often emerge and are at the heart of strategy making. Because there is a need for accountability for the funds raised, planning systems are likely to be prominent.

Public-sector organizations

In countries all round the world governments – national, regional and/or local – will be concerned with business in their countries and communities. Sometimes they will run certain critical services directly; on other occasions they will allow these services to be in the hands of private business owners but ensure they are regulated in some way. Political ideology is often a feature and complexity is added because governments often think short-term, always with an eye on winning the next election. Many businesses caught up in this sector require long-term investment.

In many countries around the world the composition of this sector has changed over recent years. Typically in the developed world, essential service industries, such as telecommunications, gas, electricity, water, and air, bus and rail transport, have been privatized if they were previously in public ownership – to encourage both operating efficiencies and a competitive spirit. This has often led to the creation of a number of complementary or even competing businesses. The outcome in each industry has been one or more private companies, some of which have since merged or been acquired, sometimes by overseas parents. In the case of the UK this privatization programme has also included individual companies such as British Airports Authority (BAA), which manages several airports but is largely a retail organization. Outside direct government control, BAA has expanded overseas and now manages a number of other airports around the world. Since privatization it has been sold to a Spanish parent and also required by the UK competition authorities to reduce the number of airports it **controls**, especially in London.

The trend towards privatization has gathered momentum for many reasons, one factor in Europe being the stronger stance on government subsidies to individual industries by the European Commission. The key appears to lie in the effectiveness of the regulation, which must attempt to balance the needs of all key stakeholders: customers, employees and investors.

As a result, we now tend to think of local authorities and public health and emergency services as the archetypal **public sector organizations**. Clearly these are service businesses, and ones which will always have to choose and prioritize between different needs and stakeholders. In general, they will always be able to achieve more outcomes if they can acquire more resources. However, they remain largely dependent on central government for their resources and are, therefore, influenced by the political agenda of the day.

Chapter 2

The business model and the revenue model

**PART 1
Understanding strategy**

1   What is strategy and who is involved?
   • Appendix
2   The business model and the revenue model
3   Strategic purpose
   • Supplement: Using frameworks to analyze strategy cases

**PART 5
Strategy implementation**

14   Strategy implementation and structure
15   Leading change
16   Managing strategy in the organization
17   Final thoughts and reflections: the practice of strategy

STRATEGIC MANAGEMENT: AWARENESS AND CHANGE

**PART 2
Analysis and positioning**

4   The business environment and strategy
5   Resource-led strategy
6   The dynamics of competition
7   Introducing culture and values

**PART 4
Strategic growth issues**

11   Strategic control and measuring success
12   Issues in strategic and international growth
13   Failure, consolidation and recovery strategies

**PART 3
Strategy development**

8   Creating and formulating strategy: alternatives, evaluation and choice
9   Strategic planning
10   Strategic leadership and intrapreneurship: towards visionary leadership?

Learning objectives

Having read to the end of this chapter, you should be able to:

● appreciate how organizations utilize business models to make strategic decisions and identify ways of creating a winning business model (**Section 2.1**)

● understand how **revenue models** help organizations to maximize their performance (**Section 2.2**)

● through examples, realize different types and contexts of business model (**Section 2.3**).

This chapter is short and largely descriptive but very important.

Introduction

In Chapter 1 we saw how 'strategy' is effectively a process or a set of questions where we need to examine **who** decides **what** an organization should do, **why** (the context of the overriding purpose), **how** and **when**. The outcome is a series of decisions and actions that determine how distinctive an organization is and how strong a competitor it is – and, in turn, how strong a performer it is in the short term – and, with change, how sustainable it is. The decisions and actions are manifest in the business model; whilst the revenue model illustrates the level of performance.

The business model explains **what** the organization does, **for whom** it does it (its target customers), **why** they are (ideally loyal and sustained) customers – their compelling reason to choose this organization's products – **how** the strategy is executed and **when** it needs to change. The revenue model deals with the financial implications of the business model; it examines revenue and costs and thus reflects both viability and performance.

It explains both the business and revenue models and provides several examples to illustrate the points. We deliberately provide more illustrations than we do in other chapters – we want to show that good business models can be found in every industry, with some organizations standing out as strong competitors. But what works in one sector might not be appropriate for another industry. Customers and markets are different; therefore, there is no single best way of satisfying them.

The need for a clear and persuasive business model is a key plank in strategy. In essence, the business model involves a clear understanding of:

● What product or service is on offer?
● Who will buy it?
● Why will they buy it?

At a conceptual level, the business model can appear simple and straightforward – and it probably is for those companies who succeed in getting it right – but many don't succeed in this challenge. Their business models are flawed in some way. In addition, what appears to be a sound model 'on paper' may not deliver to its potential if the organization fails to manage the implementation of its ideas and intentions. There are several examples of good business models that demonstrate the robustness of this process and the importance of getting it correct and in this chapter we will describe and evaluate a number of successful models.

Yet we are left with questions to answer regarding companies with apparently sound businesses and business models who got into difficulty for one reason or another. In recent years, we can look at a number of less successful business stories that are relevant to this debate and reinforce the argument of the importance of a continued sound business model.

- Northern Rock got into severe difficulty because the underlying business model was wrong – they had lost sight of the key success factor that you should only lend where you can borrow for lower cost. Simply, the building society was making too many loans, some of them to people who had inadequate security; as a consequence their own borrowing costs escalated. At the same time certain other banks were making similar high-risk mortgage loans and then bundling these loans into packages that they were selling on to raise money for further high-risk lending. Once defaults kicked in, the fragility of this business model was all too apparent.

- eBay acquired Skype – which it owned for a period – but it is questionable whether there was ever any synergy. The business model for the combined operation didn't stack up. The product on offer did not suit the needs and wants of the customer. eBay had apparently assumed that the people who were buying and selling goods through its website would find it useful and beneficial to be able to talk to each other easily and cheaply through their computers – but maybe this was addressing a need that did not really exist.

- Starbucks has grown rapidly over the years and its popularity has been retained in the face of competition from Costa, Caffè Nero and others – as well as adverse publicity from time to time. Some rivals never quite made it; Coffee Republic, although successful to a point, might be considered as an example here. These businesses all have the same business model by-and-large – the menu looks the same; the prices are not significantly different; they are often located close to each other – but they don't all execute the business model in the same way. Implementation and service matter. As they say, 'the devil is in the detail'. The realities of competition in this sector are at least as much about levels of customer service and outlet ambience as they are about the actual cup of coffee.

  Moreover, Starbucks had a 2-3-year period when its profits fell. Observers would suggest it opened too many new branches too quickly and, in part to help finance this, increased its prices a tad too far. Customers resisted and Starbucks had to take a step back in order to restore its profit growth trajectory.

- Ryanair continues to outperform its rivals in the low-cost no-frills end of the market. Again there are few fundamental differences in the underlying business model – although there are differences in routes and destinations and sometimes prices. But Ryanair again scores with implementation and its never-ending search for ways to reduce costs and stay more efficient with greater scale economies than its rivals. Significantly customers will privately have a moan about certain features and examples of service trimming, but they appreciate the low prices and believe they are getting value for money.

One of the more recent examples of the need to rethink the business model is the change that has come about in the news and magazine market. Charging money for the news linked to advertising revenues was the basis of the industry in the US and the UK. In 2008 the news industry reached a tipping point when the number of people getting news online for free outstripped those paying for the news. The most vocal response to this issue was that of Rupert Murdoch who has led the attempt to get consumers to pay for news online. Will it change anything in terms of what is happening to news revenue? It can be argued that business models need to innovate by looking forward not looking back. Trying to still charge for news can be argued as a way of looking back and not forward and, therefore, it will not work.

2.1 The business model

When we argue that an organization needs a sound, or a winning, business model we mean that there is a need for a very clear picture concerning what the organization is – and what it isn't – and who will buy its products and services, and why. The business model thus embraces three key themes: the product (or service); the market; and the 'compelling reason to buy'.

It is important to remember here that strategy always involves choices. Organizations have to make decisions about what they intend to do – at the same time ruling out things it is less appropriate or desirable for them to do. Maybe it is because competition is too intense. Or perhaps they do not possess the required competencies and capabilities. This picture then needs to be communicated and understood throughout the organization. Moreover, the model – and the strategies that underpin it – needs to be reviewed constantly. The picture should embrace the business as it is now, and how it will be in the future – where and how it will change and grow.

The business model provides an explanation of an organization's 'recipe for success', and it contains those factors that essentially define the business. Case 2.1 provides a comparison of two business models by analyzing the two 'no-frills' business models of Aldi and Lidl.

Case 2.1   No-Frills Retailing – the Aldi and Lidl business models   Ger

Aldi and Lidl – two German-owned no-frills grocery retail chains – both have a business model that challenges that of the leading supermarket groups in the UK in a similar way to how Ryanair has challenged the business operating model of the airline industry over the last 25 years. The low-cost airlines in the UK, dominated by Ryanair and easyJet, have seized market leadership for short-haul European flights from flag carriers such as British Airways. The story in grocery retailing is not the same. Aldi and Lidl are both successful and profitable businesses but their combined market share is estimated to be around 6 per cent. This is less than half of the share of the smallest of the four dominant retailers, who comprise market leader Tesco, Asda (owned by Wal-Mart), Sainsbury's and Morrisons. There are other no-frills retailers competing for the same customers as Aldi and Lidl, such as Iceland. The Danish Netto was another direct competitor but it was acquired by Asda in 2011 and will inevitably now increase the proportion of main brand products it sells and thus set it further apart from Aldi and Lidl. Historically, with around one-third of its products leading brand items, Netto was already different from Aldi and Lidl, which both shun leading brands. Premium retailers such as Waitrose and Marks and Spencer choose to offer a very different shopping experience.

Ryanair's success is based on keeping costs to a minimum and adopting a simple, effective service offering; this is energized by an open and candid culture orientated towards cutting out waste but without compromising on the essential safety and quality aspects of the commercial airline business. Ryanair, then, has succeeded by looking for every opportunity to reduce costs whilst not sacrificing value that would cause serious customer resistance. Some of the tactics (such as charging for hold baggage) may not be popular, but customers seem willing to accept them if the reward is still a fare lower than that of rival airlines. Aldi and Lidl offer a limited frills product and service package and very competitive prices. It works well but it is a niche and not a market-dominating approach. Clearly there are benefits and limitations to the strategy. Opening new branches in new areas will always help, but to grow their market share further then arguably Aldi and Lidl will have to look at issues of differentiation and how they and their market position are perceived by customers. So what are the real growth and development opportunities for Aldi and Lidl? The UK supermarket industry is one of the most established and competitive in the world. The dynamics are relentless and changeable – and those businesses that opt for broad competitive positions also have to work hard to appeal to very different customer segments.

Aldi

Aldi (**Al**brecht **Di**scount) is a family based, discount supermarket chain based in Germany. The company started in 1913 with the opening of a small food store in the German town of Essen. This little 'service store' quickly became a popular place to shop. It was during the 1940s that an expansion programme was created and more Aldi stores opened. By the 1960s there were 300 stores in Germany. The chain is now international and made up of two separate groups, Aldi Nord (North) headquartered in Essen – and covering North Germany, France, Denmark, Holland and Belgium – and Aldi Süd (South) – covering Southern European countries but including the UK, US and Australia – headquartered in Mulheim an der Ruhr. These organizations operate independently from each other within specific market boundaries. The individual groups were originally owned and managed by brothers Karl and Theo Albrecht. Karl has since retired and is now Germany's richest man. Theo was Germany's second richest man until his death in July 2010. A senior manager at Aldi has commented that although the stores look and feel different (Nord and Sud) the business results and performance are very similar. The core values and principles upon which the brothers founded the business continue to be central to the strategic direction and decision-making principles today. These are:

- consistency – for reliability – along the lines of McDonald's
- simplicity – for efficiency
- responsibility – to all the company's stakeholders.

As a business Aldi prefers to stay relatively low profile and – unlike Ryanair which enjoys considerable low-cost publicity from being controversial – does not court publicity. But like Ryanair, Aldi claims to have 'cost control built into the DNA and culture of the business'; it has lower levels of staffing and a payroll cost that is significantly lower than its competitors. It rewards people with rates of pay that are higher than the industry average and demands they work hard and smart. Allied to this, Aldi has invested in sophisticated till systems (products have the bar code in more than one place for rapid scanning) and place a lot of emphasis on staff training. Not everyone, however, is supportive of Aldi's people management practices and critics point to the fact, that similar to rival German discounter Lidl, there is an anti-union stance.

In contrast to many of its UK rivals, all Aldi stores operate limited opening hours. Aldi only recently extended trading to 12 hours a day (8.00 am to 8.00 pm) when many competitors are moving towards 24/7 and 365 days opening. There is a clear strategic intention not to keep shoppers at the store longer than necessary. Aldi have declined to follow the pack regarding introducing add-on facilities such as cafe's, lottery terminals, children's rides, photo booths, toilets, dry cleaning services, currency exchanges, newsagent/ tobacco counters and sweet counters on entry and exit and so forth. The argument is that these facilities have to be paid for in some shape or form and therefore will add to the end cost. They are not seen as essential.

Anyone who shops at Aldi will notice other subtle aspects of cost saving. Car parks tend to be relatively small. Aldi only take debit cards and cash, not credit cards, thereby eliminating the accompanying charges. Customers are expected to collect and return trolleys themselves from a single collection and drop point,

saving on staffing costs. There are no baskets because people might buy more if they have a trolley. Merchandising and shelf presentation is fairly basic with some products stacked on pallets and left in packing boxes. The aisles are relatively narrow to yield more selling space. All small actions on the surface but ones which, when aggregated, contribute to significant cost savings across the business.

In June 2011 there were 440 stores in the UK and this number was forecast to expand by 20–30 new stores per year. Store size is relatively low in comparison to its competitors at an average floor space of between $650m^2$ to $1000m^2$. Only recently have larger stores been trialled (at $1125m^2$) and the new international optimum standard for new build stores has recently been agreed and set at $990m^2$. Aldi requires that store size be conducive to the scope of one manager and a small team, who are expected to run the whole operation efficiently and profitably.

A small regional team – there are 70 around the world in the Aldi structure – supports the stores and the centralized logistics operations. Each region has ultimate responsibility for purchasing for its stores and negotiates its own arrangements (and prices) with a list of approved suppliers from around the world.

In terms of sales philosophy, Aldi adopts a very simple approach – get the product and price right and it will sell. Branded products carry much less operating profit so Aldi – though not wholly averse to stocking these brands – tends to steer away from the most popular iconic brands and instead focuses on 'brand equivalent' products – lesser known brand names but ones that Aldi buyers think replicate the product quality which consumers have come to expect. These products state who the manufacturer is and explain they are produced exclusively for Aldi. There is, though, no generic Aldi brand. In contrast to around 700 product lines in Aldi, a large Tesco or Sainsbury's store will typically stock up to 50 000 lines, of which 50 per cent will be clearly identified own label items. These much larger supermarkets also offer a wide range of non-food items which the no-frills grocers tend to avoid. Both Tesco and Sainsbury's have smaller 'Metro' and local stores which sell a smaller range, but still with the same mix of leading brands and own label.

A key part of Aldi's strategy is for their buyers to work closely with suppliers, especially on food and drink products. The aim is to refine as many products as possible to match the taste and consumer experience of more well-known branded names that are on their competitors' shelves. Aldi focuses on decent quality products in modest packaging at low prices. There are always 'special offers' of low price bargain items which will only be available whilst stocks last – and these could be almost anything.

Rather than prefer to do all the 'weekly shop' in one store, the average customer that currently shops at Aldi and Lidl does so for basic items; they are likely to then go elsewhere to top up with any branded products they want as well as luxury items and treats. If in the future Aldi attempts to attract and retain a 'full shop' customer it will need to expand its range, as M&S has done.

Lidl

Lidl is also German-owned and in many ways is very similar to Aldi in its operating strategy. Lidl has stores in 23 countries and it has more than Aldi in the UK. These stores tend to be slightly larger than the ones Aldi has opted for historically – but Lidl still has a slightly smaller market share than its rival. Lidl strives for 'top quality at low prices' and again focuses on own label brands rather than leading brands. It has a wider range than Aldi, with a typical store offering between 800 and 1400 products, all of which must be fast-in, fast-out. In-store decorations are sparse and many products are sold direct from cartons and pallets. Prices are always kept low and competitive; there are few discount offers at any time but there are, as with Aldi, special promotion items for sale for a limited period. Purchasing decisions are made at the country level but within a clear international supply chain system.

Published accounts do not make it easy to compare the relative profitability of these two rival operators in any one country. Lidl could be more profitable in terms of margins whilst posting lower overall revenues than Aldi.

Some commentators would point out that the changes required to grow market share in any serious way could present a paradox for these two rivals and perhaps for Aldi in particular. From this company's inception the ethos that has brought them success has been one of 'sticking to the knitting' – that is resisting the temptation to change and instead to maintain a steadfast adherence to principles. Dieter Brandes, a former executive, has commented: 'What is visible – store decorations, product ranges and prices – have been easily copied by competitors. It is the invisible that has determined Aldi's success. To understand the company, you must understand the essential defining characteristics that lie beneath the surface. Standards, values, the unwritten cultural rules. That is what the company sees as "good or bad", "permitted or forbidden" what it "rewards and what it punishes"'. It is argued, by the advocates of Aldi, that this 'secret culture' is a key source of competitive advantage for Aldi.

Quotations from: Bare Essentials: The Aldi Way of Retailing, Dieter Brandes.

Question

Compare and contrast the two business models described here. Is there an argument that one is stronger than the other or are they simply 'different'? *Be prepared to defend your position if challenged …*

In many respects, the business model is the vehicle for delivering the purpose or mission. It encapsulates both 'big picture' and 'little picture' elements and it can be applied to both the present and the future. Over time the model, and the strategies it encapsulates, are likely to change, even if the basic purpose remains constant. Put simply, the business model should clearly show how the business is going to make money. Many dot.com businesses essentially failed because they did not address the issue of how they were going to make money. They offered technology to deliver a product that customers simply were not prepared to pay for. They failed to blend business and technology innovation. In Case 2.2, it was the reluctance of the consumer to pay the very high price of designer eyewear that led to the creation of Glasses Direct by Jamie Murray Wells.

Case 2.2   Glasses Direct   UK

Glasses Direct is a story of entrepreneurship in action. It illustrates how someone with entrepreneurial potential, a keen motivation and a simple but winning idea can quickly become established with a widely recognized brand. It is also the story of a business and an entrepreneur that have won multiple awards.

Jamie Murray Wells comes from something of a business background – his father is an investment analyst and his maternal grandfather was involved when both Chrysler and Ford established plants in the UK – but he chose to read English at University in Bristol. He confesses he had been searching for business ideas when, and whilst studying for his final exams, he was told he needed glasses. He was surprised at the prices of around £150 that opticians were charging for glasses and thought there must be a lower cost alternative. When he checked he discovered professional labs can make glasses with quality prescription lenses at relatively low cost. He had his idea – glasses supplied through online ordering – which he then researched thoroughly before taking the metaphorical plunge. Customers with a prescription from an optician could log on, choose a frame (or frames) and provide details of the lenses they needed. A trial pair (or pairs) would be sent out – which the customer would return and which would then be sent to another prospective customer. New glasses would be produced and posted out with little delay. The prices they would pay for good quality products have always been substantially lower than the traditional high street. With up-front payments from their customers and trade credit for their laboratory suppliers the business had a sound cash flow. The business model also passes the test advocated by the founders of Innocent Smoothies – one's granny could understand it in no time at all. That said, some grannies might still need help from their grandchildren with ordering online!

Jamie used his own funds to pay a fellow student to produce the website and his early marketing involved him distributing flyers to rail commuters and passengers in the West Country. His simple viral marketing approach worked. Reflecting current trends, Glasses Direct now makes extensive use of online social networks but Jamie Murray Wells has always looked for valuable publicity opportunities and relevant stories for the press. Although there are aspects of creative irreverence such as fun cleaning sprays, Murray Wells acknowledges that glasses are a serious purchase for most people and is careful to preserve the right image for the business.

The first base for Glasses Direct (in 2004) was his parents' home in Wiltshire but as others started to join the business it became necessary to decamp to a nearby converted barn. As the business grew he expanded in the same area but now the head office and marketing are based in London with manufacturing – Glasses Direct originally relied on laboratories but switched to producing their own – and distribution in Swindon. Qualified opticians were recruited to the business to support the business experts. As time has gone on varifocal lenses have been added to the range – supported by opticians who will travel to people's homes – as have designer frames and a wide range of prescription and non-prescription sunglasses. Innovation is taken seriously, but Glasses Direct has so far chosen not to supply non-prescription reading and distance glasses with 'standard' lenses. Venture Capital funding (from Index Ventures and Highland Capital Partners) supplemented business angel funding which itself had helped the business move on from a personal and family funding dependency. Straightforward prescription glasses can be bought for £39 but there are more expensive alternatives. The leading designer frames are, not unexpectedly, the most expensive with typical prices of £159 (glasses) and £220 (sunglasses).

With annual sales revenue now in the millions of pounds, Glasses Direct has become the leading online supplier in the industry sector it created. He reckons he has saved customers in the UK over £50 million in 6 years. Again not unexpectedly Murray Wells' success provoked a reaction from high street opticians, most noticeably the high-advertising Specsavers – but threatened legal actions have led to nothing of consequence. Invoking reminders of how the then small Ben & Jerry's saw off competition from the owners of Häagen-Dazs (Pillsbury Corporation) in the USA, Murray Wells published letters from Specsavers' lawyers on the Glasses Direct website.

A more recent diversification (2010) is Hearing Direct, a separate company based in Andover. Murray Wells supplies, again online, digital hearing aids with prices ranging from £99 to £299, depending on looks and specification. Prospective customers can take a simple hearing test online and again be supplied with a trial hearing aid (which they return) before they make a final choice. Industry experts have been recruited to ensure the products are reliable and appropriate.

Going forward, Murray Wells appreciates that businesses have to develop and move on if they are to preserve their existing markets and open new opportunities. He knows he must explore the potential of the 'higher end' of the market for glasses where margins will be higher but not threaten his volume sales of lower price glasses by doing this. He also appreciates there are strategic opportunities overseas.

The main lessons

Jamie Murray Wells believes he has learnt a number of simple but important lessons:

First, all staff in the business should engage with customers on a regular basis.

Second, it can pay off to stir things up occasionally if it brings valuable publicity. Michael O'Leary and Ryanair would undoubtedly agree with this, as would James Watt of Brewdog (Case 10.3).

Third, it is important to build the right team and to exploit people's talents.

Fourth, in the end the product is going to be more important than the marketing, but marketing, especially social marketing, does matter – as does customer service.

Fifth, a business evolves and revolves around its culture. A set of understood and practiced guiding principles can really help.

Questions

1 Why do you think this is a successful business?
2 How different and distinctive is it?
3 Is Hearing Direct a logical extension? Why? Why not?

glasses direct

Every organization is practising a model, even though it may not have thought it through in any depth. Where this is the case, any success could well be short-lived as it implies there is a reliance on good fortune rather than analytical insight. One might argue that if the model can't be articulated or written down, then the organization's managers don't know what the model is.

It is, of course, important to recognize that good ideas and a plausible outline model are relatively easy to imagine and define … the secret lies in delivering the model and implementing the strategies. In military terms, tactics can be trickier than the grand strategy – even though we clearly need both.

The business model is outlined in Figure 2.1 and the elements of this diagram are discussed below.

The three fundamental elements of the model itself are shown at the top, metaphorically mounted on an important base.

Products and services constitute *what* the organization produces or markets. The range can be broad or narrow, focused or diversified. The choice, like the selection of target customers and competitive strategies, implies a decision concerning what to do and what not to do. There needs to be a clear strategic logic for what is in the range. Everyone should be able to make a contribution to the business; none of them should be in a position where they bring harm to any of the others because, perhaps, they are under-performing and demanding cash subsidies.

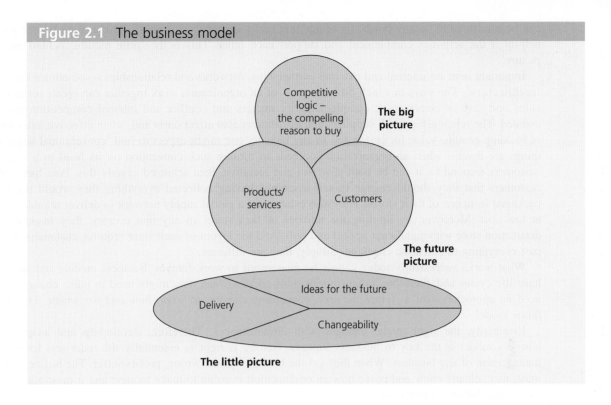

Figure 2.1   The business model

Customers make up markets – they are the *who* in the model. Again the coverage can be narrow or broad. The scope of the business can be localized, national or international. And these can vary between the various products.

The link between products and customers represents the organization's strategic or competitive position. If it is a strong, or a winning, position, then there is a good reason for this.

When we add the third element, **competitive logic**, we have our *why*, our compelling reason to buy. These three together constitute the organizational 'big picture'. The competitive logic can be based on price; equally it can be based on difference.

We shall see later in the book that there are four basic approaches to the positioning element of the model:

- A narrow product (or service) range for a broad range of customers – the basics of the business model for Starbucks and the low-cost airlines.

- A broad product range for a defined segment of the market – Harrods provides a vast choice of items for those people who are willing to pay premium prices and who enjoy being seen out with a Harrods bag.

- A narrow range for a targeted niche – handmade Morgan cars appeal to a limited number of people who want a sports car with an essentially pre-war style and who are willing to join a waiting list of some 4-years duration.

- A broad range for a wide market – Amazon.com has added a diverse range of products to its original books and it sells to anyone who is interested in buying online.

The *delivery* section of the base is an essential adjunct, even though it may not strictly be part of the outline model. Without a clear strategy for implementing and delivering the model, the organization will be compromising on **efficiency** and **effectiveness**. This aspect is the how element, and it includes the structure of the organization and the operations and activities carried out by people within the structure. Cost management and synergy are key themes. Unnecessary costs should be avoided; equally it can be a mistake to 'penny-pinch' on things that really matter to customers. At the same time it can be helpful if the activities complement and support each other. This is the 'little picture' behind the 'big picture'.

Important here are internal and external partnerships, networks and relationships – sometimes known as '**architecture**'. The ways in which different parts of an organization work together can create (or destroy) value and save or create costs; complementarity matters and conflict and internal competition must be avoided. The relationships with suppliers and distributors also affect costs and, when effective, are capable of building genuine value for customers. In any industry one might expect to find 'conventional ways' that things are done – when an organization succeeds in turning such convention on its head in a way that customers respond to, it can be both powerful and lucrative. Ikea achieved exactly this. Ikea 'persuaded' customers that they should engage in self-assembly, having collected everything they would need pre-packaged from one of their stores. They also established a global supply network to deliver reliable quality at low cost. Moreover, by limiting the number of Ikea stores in any one country, they made them a destination store with significant appeal and pull. And the layout of each store requires customers to walk past everything to reach the checkout. Simply, they are different.

What works successfully today cannot be guaranteed to work forever. Business models and strategies have life cycles and, therefore, organizations must address *when* they might need to make changes. They need an appreciation of a 'future picture', concerning changes to *what, how and for whom*. This is the *future model*.

Essentially, the right model changes with circumstances. Therefore, developing and adapting the business model is the key to business success. Getting it right is essentially the main test for the top management of any business. When they get the business model wrong, profits suffer. The business model must, then, clearly show and prove how an organization is going to make money; and it must address and answer the following questions:

- What is different about our value proposition?
- Who are our customers?
- What do customers value today?
- What will customers value tomorrow?

The questions asked of customers should also be addressed to investors. The capital markets need to be convinced that a business understands the needs of investors. If not, they will not buy into the business model.

Ensuring the future model can also be delivered when it is needed means that the organization needs *changeability*, which in turn will be very dependent upon its strategic leadership.

Hamel (2000) argues that new business models are emerging all the time as fresh opportunities are found. Amongst the examples he cites are:

1 Consolidation in the SME sector as large organizations grow bigger by systematically absorbing a series of small (and sometimes local) businesses. Examples include funeral services in the UK; this industry now comprises national organizations which own several 'subsidiaries' which trade as local businesses and small independents which have often evolved as family businesses. We see the same with opticians' practices.

2 Throwaway varieties of such products as watches and cameras.

3 Individual customizing. Collector's editions of the ubiquitous Barbie doll appeal to certain enthusiasts and command a premium price. Apple's iPod allows people to download music of their own choosing to compile a CD of their favourites.

The case illustration of Enterprise Cars (Case 2.3) shows a very successful business model and the following examples of some very different organizations provide further insight into the reality that there is any number of possible models – some of which imply clear choices and compromises. The Dell story (also part of Case 2.3) illustrates that their relative value may diminish over time.

Case 2.3   The business models for Dell Computers and
Enterprise Cars   US

Dell

It has been said that Michael Dell, founder and CEO of Dell Computers, became the Henry Ford of the information age – as a mass producer of standardized products. Dell assembles and sells PCs and laptops and, more recently, servers and storage hardware. The company began when Dell was a university student in the 1980s. In the early days Dell sold only to the business market, and, although this remains important, home consumers have been a vital growth area. The business model was simple and powerful – and unusual for the industry.

Dell buys in standardized components in order to minimize the need for any expensive research and development. The company has relied extensively on Intel chips. Sales are direct to customers, typically over the Internet or telephone. Together with a telephone helpline, this alleviates the need for middlemen and the consequential distributor margins. Dell builds to order and carries very little inventory of finished products. This cannot happen effectively without strict attention to detail and constant process re-engineering. The assembly time for a PC was reduced to 4 minutes, with a further 30 seconds allowed to fix the holograms and logos for Microsoft and Intel.

Dell, now the second largest computer maker in the world, never set out to be a high-technology company, but instead relied on sales and logistics, driven by low costs. Dell then adopted a very aggressive pricing policy in order to seize market share from any competitor who had 'taken its eye off the ball' and let its costs increase. The assumption was that this business model could be used for other consumer electrical products such as digital music players and flat screen televisions. Some critics always argued that the model has to be limited as a substantial proportion of consumers would be unwilling to buy without being able to inspect a model in a store. But the logic of this argument becomes thinner as more and more of us know people who have bought a Dell – we can inspect theirs.

However by 2005 it was apparent that the sales growth was slowing down. New products – servers and printers, which amounted to two-thirds of sales – were not as successful as PCs, where Dell was selling one in every three bought in the USA.

It was less successful with notebooks, which were being supplied direct from manufacturers in Taiwan. Competitors, especially Hewlett Packard and Acer, had narrowed the price advantage. Between 2000 and 2005 Dell's cost advantage reduced from 20 per cent to 10 per cent and its price advantage more dramatically from 25 per cent to just 5 per cent. In addition it was developing a reputation for inadequate service when something was wrong with a product.

In 2006 the CEO resigned. Kevin Rollins had worked as an external management consultant for Dell prior to joining the business full-time in 1996. He was Number Two to Michael Dell and replaced him as CEO in 2004. He had been responsible for much of the manufacturing efficiency and cost saving. But Dell was accused of 'tunnel vision with its sales model' and Michael Dell felt it necessary to take over again.

Alongside job cuts, the company soon announced a renewed emphasis on product design, confirmed it would increase sales through third-party vendors, including systems installers, and seek to acquire other businesses which had more of a customer services focus. In 2009 Dell bought into IT services (essentially consulting) believing this would help revenues in unpredictable economic cycles.

Enterprise cars

Enterprise Cars was founded in St. Louis, Missouri, in 1957 as a car leasing business. Rentals began in 1963. Today, with a turnover of multi-billion US dollars, it is the largest car rental business in the USA and growing in Europe. It is still a private business controlled by the founding family. The company has over 500 000 vehicles, making it the largest buyer of cars in America. The real growth has occurred in and since the 1990s when the market began to realize the value of the Enterprise business model – which is different from the other majors like Alamo, Avis and Hertz.

The Product and the demand

Whereas most car rental businesses specialize in the travelling public, Enterprise focuses on those car owners

SOURCE: THIS CASE STUDY WAS PREPARED USING PRIMARILY PUBLICLY AVAILABLE SOURCES OF INFORMATION FOR THE PURPOSES OF CLASSROOM DISCUSSION; IT DOES NOT INTEND TO ILLUSTRATE EITHER EFFECTIVE OR INEFFECTIVE HANDLING OF A MANAGERIAL SITUATION.

who have been parted from their own vehicles. This segment has generally been avoided by the other leading competitors. Enterprise customers' cars might be in a garage for service; more likely they have been subject to accident or breakdown. Enterprise staff collect customers from whichever garage they leave their car and drive them to their own compound. That said, Enterprise does also rent cars to people who just want to hire a vehicle.

The customers

Some customers can plan and book in advance, but most are making an inevitable late booking. Consequently they are often people experiencing some sort of distress and agitation because of the uncertainty. In addition, the actual customer might be an insurance company rather than the car owner themself.

Operational aspects

Enterprise is decentralized into over 5000 individual offices with an average of ten employees each. They are all profit centres. There is extensive monitoring and tracking of cash and profit and customer satisfaction. The stated intention is to make every office feel like a local family business with staff who are 'passionate about service'. There is an extensive graduate recruitment programme to find able young people to work alongside mature, experienced front-line staff. Coffee and doughnuts are provided whilst customers fill in their paperwork.

Questions

1 How would you assess these two business models?
2 Is Dell becoming more robust again?
3 Does Enterprise have a defensible and sustainable model?

The attempt to get consumers to pay for online newspapers (discussed earlier) is one example of a business trying to compete by tweaking the established business model. We would argue that sometimes what is needed is a more radical approach to business model development. The theme of **Blue Ocean Strategy**, a concept developed by Kim and Mauborgne (2005) (and discussed in detail in a later chapter) is relevant for Case 2.4, Cirque du Soleil. Blue Ocean includes the four action themes of eliminate, reduce, raise and create in the search for a new value proposition and a distinctive competitive edge; and we can see these in evidence in Cirque du Soleil as follows:

ELIMINATE: Star performers; animal shows

REDUCE: Fun and humour; thrills and danger

RAISE: Unique venues

CREATE: Themes; refined environment

'This revamped Value Proposition allowed Cirque du Soleil to broaden its appeal to theatregoers and other adults seeking sophisticated entertainment, rather than the traditional circus audiences of families. As a consequence it was able to substantially raise ticket prices.' Osterwalder and Pigneur (2010)

Case 2.4   Cirque du Soleil   Ca

The big top travelling circuses of the type pioneered by showmen such as the legendary PT Barnum – and which featured animals, typically lions, tigers and elephants, alongside acrobats and the ubiquitous clowns – still exist, but they cannot command the audiences they once did. And there are fewer of them. The main ones include the Ringling Brothers and the Russian and Chinese State circuses. Competition for the 'entertainment spend' has increased.

Spectacular specialist acts featuring animals became popular in Las Vegas many years ago, although when a

white tiger mauled one of the partners in the Siegfried and Roy Show in 2003, serious questions were raised about them. There were, of course, already many animal lovers who were critics of shows such as this. Meanwhile the circus industry had been reinvented without needing animals.

Dubbed 'the New American Circus', Cirque du Soleil was started in Montreal, Quebec, Canada, in 1984, the invention of a small group of street performers led by partners Guy LaLiberte and Daniel Gauthier. By the end of the century they had entertained some 30 million people with a range of innovative and daring production shows. The shows combine circus acts with performing arts and they typically feature jugglers, trampolinists, trapeze artists and clowns – who work together rather than have individual feature spots. The shows are operatic as well as acrobatic, they are choreographed, they stretch the talents of the performers, they are visually impressive and they all have a clear theme or story.

The shows are different and innovative – and relatively high price – and so Cirque du Soleil enthusiasts are likely to attend regularly, if they can get to where the shows are. Originally the focus was on a traditional moveable 'big top' but quite soon Cirque du Soleil moved into dedicated resident theatres and also introduced some shows that worked in existing venues such as the Royal Albert Hall in London, which they visit regularly.

Las Vegas was an obvious early target, with the first venue being the Treasure Island hotel and casino. The specialist show 'O', which needs a tank filled with 1.5 million gallons of water, was put on in a dedicated 1800 seat theatre at the Bellagio. Walt Disney World Resort is another home. When this case was written there were eight long running shows on offer in different Las Vegas hotels, including some built around music, namely 'Live' (The Beatles) and Viva Elvis. Perhaps not unexpectedly one show, 'Zumanity' has strong 'sensual themes'. Vegas is Vegas, after all. New residences are being prepared in Moscow and Dubai.

Fundamentally Cirque du Soleil has eliminated animals and markedly cut down on the sales of food and other merchandise whilst the show itself is live – something quite different from the traditional circus and most American sporting events. There is less emphasis on thrills and danger – something circuses used to try to create competitive advantage – and a more creative use of different venues. What really sets it apart from the original circus model is the 'seamless' element of the

show where music, opera, dance and acrobatics are combined into a holistic show.

Over 30 different shows have been created and the majority are still operational; some have been retired. Cirque du Soleil will typically trial a new travelling show for approximately a year in Montreal before sending it out to America for some 3 years. Europe and then Asia follow. There are few price concessions for children and so it is clear the target audience is not the families for whom the traditional circus was appealing.

It has been reported that Cirque du Soleil has received several takeover offers, but so far it remains independent. Guy LaLiberte is still the controlling shareholder. In summer 2008 a proportion of the equity was sold for US$2 billion to one fund controlled by the government of Dubai.

Questions

1 Do you agree that Cirque du Soleil 'reinvented the circus industry'?
2 Given that prices for Cirque shows are relatively expensive how might they sustain their position? How much is it about the content of the shows and how much about the overall service?

We conclude, then, that the business model matters – but so too does the way the business is run. The 'devil is in the detail' of implementation and execution and it is here that really we switch from the business to the revenue model. They are both critical. They both need to be 'right'.

2.2 The revenue model and business value

The revenue model focuses on activities and what the business does to (a) conserve resources, using only what it needs to use, (b) manage its resources efficiently and (c) prioritize those resources that create and build value for customers.

In the context of our framework for the book, we are here asking:

- Why are our profits at the level they are – what is the trend – are we doing better or worse than our leading rivals?
- Where are they going with current strategies – up or down?
- How do we improve the numbers – what do we have to do?

Businesses use cash and knowledge to invest in resources and instigate and execute activities that help them with what they need to do. They are implementing their strategies within the confines of their business model. In turn, they should be generating more cash and also new knowledge and insights as they learn how to do things better and also explore what they might do differently. **Income should exceed spending**. We deliberately use the word 'should' rather than 'must' because of timescales. Amazon provides a wonderful example of a business which spent more than it earned for several years – accumulating trading losses – until it had **critical mass** in terms of size and product ranges. There was always logic to Jeff Bezos' business model but it required significant investment to build the infrastructure and the business. FedEx (Federal Express delivery service) was not dissimilar at the outset. In recent years, and in no small way thanks to the Kindle, Amazon has repaid the investment and become a very profitable and powerful organization.

In this context, though, we should never overlook the reality that 'cash is king'. Unless the business can generate surplus cash to invest (from its trading activities), it will need to borrow money to fund its growth – as long as it is in a position to do this. This will need to be repaid at some point or, simply, the business is insolvent.

The strategic logic and longer-term value of certain courses of action will always be an important issue – but so too are short-term returns and financial considerations – however valuable the desired action might appear to be, it has to be financially possible.

The key issue with any decision concerning what to do next is whether it will lead to an increase or deterioration in the value of the business for its owners (shareholders). This again can be looked at over the longer term rather than the immediate future as long as those involved are fully aware and supportive. In other words, the net present value of the return on any investment we make must be positive – and, essentially, more positive than other alternatives. There might be alternative options/investments to evaluate. It might sometimes be more beneficial to the organization to sell a part, say one business unit (unless it has a hidden strategic worth and significant opportunity cost), and spend the money on perhaps developing a new product or buying an alternative business.

Businesses make money when they sell things at a profit. In order to have things to sell they incur costs. They need to spend on:

- direct costs to acquire resources and pay people
- indirect costs on marketing and promotion
- investment to make sure the business can stay resourced in the future and that there is a flow of new ideas, products, services.

These (eventually) all have to be recovered from sales revenues.

Revenues and costs, the cash implications and the margin (profit) from revenues exceeding total costs are the basic components of the revenue model.

In other words, the execution of the business model must be profitable. And ideally more profitable than other alternatives – as otherwise these alternatives would imply more value for the business and its owners.

The revenue model is, therefore, about the financial implications of a series of tactical decisions. These tactical decisions are taken in the context of the overall strategy and the business model. Revenues, of course, can be increased with additional marketing and selling activities – but, naturally, these incur fresh costs. There are often opportunities to cut costs – and really organizations should always be looking to manage their cost drivers to generate savings. At the same time, it is important to remember that some costs (and some activities) should not be sacrificed as they make significant contributions. They are valued by key stakeholders.

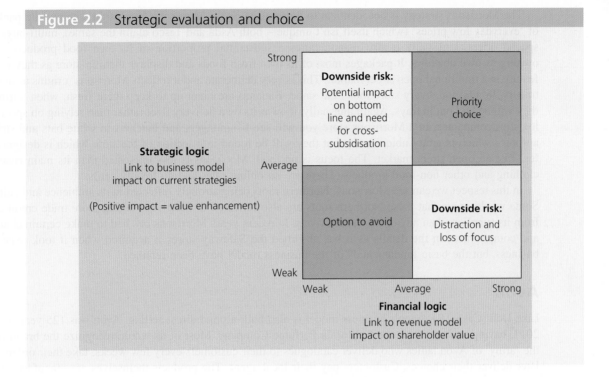

Figure 2.2 Strategic evaluation and choice

The basic argument, therefore, is that there needs to be both a strategic logic and a financial logic to the strategic decisions and actions that organizations take. New activities should help to improve both – there will always be a downside risk if they have a positive impact on just one of the two, but that may not mean they are automatically the wrong thing to do. Such potential actions require very careful thought and evaluation. Sometimes financial needs and priorities dictate the choice; an alternative might make more sense strategically but not add sufficient financial value to the organization. On other occasions the strategic importance of certain actions is such that something that would be more lucrative financially should not be preferred. If any proposals under consideration have a negative impact upon both the strategic logic and the finances they should be avoided. These points are illustrated in Figure 2.2 – but we do not develop the arguments in depth here but instead return to them when we examine Strategic Choice in Chapter 8.

2.3 More examples of business models

William Morrison

The WM Morrison supermarket group, strongest in the North of England and still a family company in many respects, competes directly and successfully with Tesco, Sainsbury's and Asda. Aldi and Lidl (Case 2.1) are also competitors but with a different business model. Fundamentally, the large supermarket chains offer broadly the same product ranges, although there will be some clear differences. Across a wide range of goods, there are the leading brands and own-label alternatives, which normally are cheaper.

Morrisons' customers are not going to be markedly different from those who pick Tesco or Asda. They all emphasize competitive prices. Location, of course, and convenience will influence customer choice. Sainsbury's is somewhat different as their prices overall have traditionally been slightly higher. Waitrose (owned by John Lewis) and Marks and Spencer, with a greater focus on premium products and higher prices, have a different market appeal. So where is the Morrisons 'compelling reason to buy'?

The Morrisons strategy is not identical to those of its rivals. Morrisons focuses on a composite package of 'everyday low prices' (which itself isn't unique – both Asda and Tesco claim the same), multi-buys and special offers. Unusually it also manufactures a substantial proportion of its own food products, even owning its own abattoirs. It packages most of its own fresh foods and displays them in-store as they would feature in a traditional open street market. This is very deliberate and it reflects Morrisons' origins as market traders. In addition, every store looks the same. Bananas are hung up to keep them fresh, when normally they will be laid out in trays. Again unusually, it owns its own delivery fleet rather than relying on specialist logistics companies. In a Morrisons store you will see fishmongers and butchers in white hats and striped aprons – which is pretty ubiquitous – but they will be found in a section of the store which is designed to feel like an open street market. The focus is on food; Morrisons is less interested than its main rivals in clothing and other non-food products. There are no online sales and no loyalty cards.

In this respect we can see Morrisons' Northern roots being strongly reflected in its ambience and culture. Some would argue that these Northern roots are also reflected in Morrisons taking more trade credit days from its suppliers than any of its leading rivals. In recent years Morrisons has had to make certain changes and compromises in the details as it has absorbed the Safeway stores it acquired when it took over that business, but the basic fundamentals of the business model have been retained.

Avon

Like Dell (Case 2.3), Avon's business model is also built around direct selling. Avon was 125 years old in 2011, having started life as the California Perfume Company. Most of us would recognize the brand from the 'army' of Avon ladies who deliver catalogues to their customers every few weeks, take their orders and later deliver their choices. Customers pay their local agent. The products themselves are manufactured in various countries around the world.

Although the direct selling remains constant, other elements of the model are constantly changing. Existing product ranges are likely to change at any time; and new products are added, often replacing poor-selling items. Packaging often changes to freshen the appearance of products. No two catalogues are identical, although some products do appear regularly; and there are always special offers. More recently 'well-ness' products for health- and fitness-conscious customers have been included. These range from vitamin supplements to yoga mats. Avon 'Cosmeceuticals', brands endorsed by dermatologists, fit somewhere between medications and cosmetics.

Avon has also diversified to widen its overall customer appeal. It became prominent as a convenient supplier to 'middle-class mothers' who were short of time for personal shopping, but this is no longer adequate. Although the average age of Avon's customers is around 39, this average is falling slowly. In part this is affected by the wider product choices; it is also enhanced by the choice of younger role models to promote the products. Actress Reese Witherspoon, model Yasmin le Bon, singer Alesha Dixon and, in the past, tennis stars, Serena and Venus Williams, are included here. In addition, in the USA, Avon has developed its new Mark range for 16–24-year-old customers.

Like Ikea, Avon has seen the benefit of moving into China and Russia, two huge consumer markets. When, direct selling was illegal in China (from 2001–08), Avon traded through specialist boutiques.

Andrea Jung became CEO in 1999 and spawned 6 years of relatively high growth and renewed success. Annual revenues exceeded US$10 billion from 100 countries. But arguably she failed to make sure the surpluses were invested in developing the business model. Non-cosmetics had grown to one-third of sales, but with lower margins. There were logistical problems in certain countries and inventory management was poor. Between 2005 and 2011 her second 6 years were less successful than her first 6 and at the end of 2011 she took on the role of Chairperson to allow a new face to become CEO and hopefully refresh the brand and the business model.

Poundland and Poundstretcher

These two examples of 'value retailers' represent a retail sector that has grown dramatically in recent years. We saw earlier how M&S began as a market stall where everything was priced at a penny – the intention here is to charge a pound for everything, with 'everything' focusing on various household and bathroom products, although not exclusively. Anything might appear because the business model is based on sourcing 'anything anywhere' which can be sold profitably for a pound. Surplus stock from other retailers who are in trouble, plus imported goods, are all likely to appear. The range changes in line with availability and the uncertainty concerning what might suddenly appear is attractive to some customers. The certainty is the price – which puts great pressure on sourcing and the supply chain. The margins on goods sourced overseas, for example, are affected by currency movements. There might be an expectation that such stores would have a down-market profile but the careful choice of high street locations helps alleviate this. That said, these discount stores are more likely to appear at the 'poorer end' of the high street where rents are lower.

London Zoo

In the case of London Zoo (in the next chapter) we can see evidence of difficult decisions concerning 'products' and customers. Without at least some retailing activities London Zoo would be out of business. A part of the Zoological Society of London, the zoo has a key scientific purpose related to conservation and the preservation of endangered species. However, those animals that are particularly attractive to most paying visitors are often not the most endangered. Moreover, there is a duty to educate as a large proportion of the visitors are children. Many national animal collections around the world are much more heavily subsidized, but in recent years London Zoo has not been allowed to become grant-dependent. It has had to establish a revenue-generating business model without losing sight of its origins and fundamental purpose – within the constraint of its location in a Royal Park which seriously affects any possibility of expansion. London Zoo has, therefore, had to build a model which balances conservation, education and entertainment.

The Opera

Globally, opera can only survive if it is subsidized, so again the business model must embrace this. The subsidy can be from government – in the UK the Arts Council, which, for example, accounts for 30 per cent of the budget at The Royal Opera House – or corporate and private donors.

Customers are willing to pay very high prices for the best seats as long as the quality of the performance merits it. And many opera-goers are discerning. In part, opera is expensive because it demands a large number of singers and musicians. In the UK, prices for The Royal Opera House Covent Garden rise to over £160.00 – although the cheapest restricted view seats can sometimes be bought for £3.00. The Metropolitan in New York has top prices of around US$300.00. But opera houses have to be maintained throughout the year and orchestras retained. They are not going to be full of customers every night of the year. The market is too limited for that.

Opera has long enjoyed an elitist image; opera-goers are so-called aficionados. And yet the reality has changed in recent years. The opera 'product' now extends well beyond the world's leading opera houses. The change began when *Nessun Dorma* was used as the theme music for the 1990 football World Cup and, on the back of this, the concert by 'The Three Tenors' was broadcast to the world on television and the accompanying CD became the best-selling classical album of all-time. Tickets for today's leading tenors, such as Roberto Alagna, Andrea Bocelli and Rolando Villazon, will quickly sell out. Recently, more populist singers like Lesley Garrett, Russell Watson, Alfie Boe and Katherine Jenkins have brought operatic arias to an ever-wider audience.

In other words, the opera 'product' now encapsulates CD and popular television as well as actual performances for a growing and changing market. The leading singers have been very carefully 'packaged' and marketed to give them a wider appeal.

Manchester United

Manchester United – like Barcelona and certain other leading European clubs – is far more than a successful football club. It is a collection of diversified but related activities that can be associated with a distinctive brand – a brand which signifies success, such that association with it automatically implies being part of something that is successful. Manchester United may not be unique in what it does but it still attracts fans and loyalty around the world. Manchester United reflects high quality both on and off the pitch – and consequently customers expect to have to pay premium prices to buy this association. The 'core market' might be the 70 000 plus fans who turn up at Old Trafford for Premier League matches, but there are many more people all round the world who are interested in having some part of this success story. Some fans travel long distances to attend the home matches; support in parts of the Far East is fanatical. In Porter terminology, Manchester United is very clearly differentiated – and very profitable.

Divine Chocolate

The main chocolate brands in the UK and elsewhere might be Cadbury's and Nestlé, but there are clear niche opportunities as well. Divine Chocolate is marketed as 'heavenly chocolate with a heart'. It is, though, a Fairtrade social enterprise, one of a number in this industry. The business was set up in 1997 by a Farmer's Co-operative in Ghana, and the farmers retain a 45 per cent share. The lead owner is a Dutch Fairtrade enterprise, but the business is based in the UK where there are 16 employees. Manufacture is close to where the cocoa beans are grown. The European turnover is some £10 million per year, but the UK chocolate market alone is some £4.6 billion a year. But Divine is available in leading supermarkets, including Tesco, Waitrose and Asda, and it provides own-label products to Starbucks. The cocoa bean growers are guaranteed a fair price for their beans and they receive annual dividends; as a consequence, customers will generally be asked to pay a premium price. Divine Chocolate is examined in more detail as a short case in Chapter 14 (Case 14.1).

The chapter concludes with Case 2.5, the Chinese business Daphne Shoes, which is a good example of a large business having to cope with the twin pressures of brand development and high quality against the backdrop of trying to control and reduce costs. For Daphne Shoes the new innovative business model going forward will be all important if it is to survive and develop its share of the market.

Case 2.5   Daphne Shoes   Ch

This short case tells the story of the rapid growth and success of a Chinese manufacturing company and the challenge it now faces if it is to become a more international business.

The company was first established as the Prime Success International Group in Taiwan in the 1970s – manufacturing shoes for established shoe companies in the USA and Europe. During the 1980s production was relocated to mainland China; it was when the company was left with a stockpile of surplus leather in 1990 that it decided to make shoes that it would sell under its own brand name. These 'Daphne' winter boots sold out within 3 weeks and the company decided this was a route it should now follow. Success was rapid and the company was listed on the Hong Kong Stock Exchange in 1995. It has since become one of China's leading shoe companies and China's leading brand for ladies' shoes.

Two ranges of Daphne-branded shoes were created – one for young ladies between the ages of 15 and 30 and the other for slightly older women aged 20 to 45. The company also struck new deals with both Nike and Adidas to produce and distribute their shoes. Daphne shoes were relatively low price – but by no means the cheapest available – and so the business was very dependent on a limited section and the middle market. Consequently there was a need for some range diversification. A second major brand was developed – Shoebox – with lower price points, different age targets and a range of men's as well as women's shoes. The Sofft (casual comfortable shoes) and Born (high quality but not the most fashionable) ranges were created; and Arezzo shoes were marketed as an internationally fashionable and more expensive brand. The biggest threat had come from Bella Shoes, the market leader for ladies' shoes and a business that had a wider distribution network – and whose shoes sold at prices some 50 per cent higher than Daphne's. In 2003 Bella established its own American business.

Bella were available in the main department stores whilst Daphne was not. Daphne focused distribution on more specialist outlets or 'street stores'. By the early 2000s there were over 5000 sales points (dedicated shops or counters or displays in other stores) around the world, some 3000 of these in mainland China and Taiwan. The company's sales reached 50 million pairs a year – with Daphne accounting for 66 per cent of revenue, Shoebox 20 per cent, and all the other brands together 14 per cent. One in eight ladies' shoes sold in China was labelled Daphne.

Daphne had reacted well to competitive threats but other challenges waited in the wings. In 2007 one of the family founders was arrested in Macao and charged with insider trading. As the global recession hit, Daphne realized that it would need to reduce its production costs and set about renegotiating its deals with its suppliers. It needed high quality but at low prices if it was to protect its margins. Increasingly the supply chain became focused on China – Daphne was in a strong position as there was over-supply in the market.

By around 2010 the company was still trading satisfactorily but the perceived quality of its shoes – as well as price points – was inferior to those of many international brand names and it did not have a truly recognizable global brand. It believed it needed to strengthen its reputation first in China and then around the world – such repositioning is a formidable challenge for a Chinese manufacturer in this industry. As a first step in 2010 Daphne agreed a joint venture with Taiwanese shoemaker Pou Chen to develop shoes for the global high end women's shoe market. Pou Chen was a younger company (just 5 years old) and with less market reach for ladies shoes, although its Aee brand was well placed with a high-quality product and a good reputation.

Pou Chen is actually the world's largest shoe manufacturer but its presence in fashionable ladies shoes was limited to Aee. Pou Chen mainly manufactures sports shoes for all the leading brands – Adidas, Asics, New Balance, Nike, Puma and Reebok – but it also produces for Merrell and Timberland. The intention of the joint venture was to explore and develop markets outside China for ladies' fashion shoes. Daphne in effect purchased 60 per cent of the Aee brand.

Questions

1   Does Daphne Shoes have a strong and distinctive business model?

2   Would you change it? Why? Why not? And if yes, how?

SOURCE: THIS CASE STUDY WAS PREPARED USING PRIMARILY PUBLICLY AVAILABLE SOURCES OF INFORMATION FOR THE PURPOSES OF CLASSROOM DISCUSSION; IT DOES NOT INTEND TO ILLUSTRATE EITHER EFFECTIVE OR INEFFECTIVE HANDLING OF A MANAGERIAL SITUATION.

Research Snapshot 2.1

The literature on the *business model* concept, and exemplar business models, reveals a lack of conceptual clarity and a limited range of research. However, over the last 10 years, significant advances have been made in our understanding of this concept, the rationale for the business model, and good practice in terms of design/implementation (typologies and exemplars). There is growing interest in business models as a concept and various definitions exist (Amit and Zott, 2001; Teece, 2010). An important component of any business model ought to be ethics and morals, rather than just 'reductionist' thinking and the application of models, such as the 'MBA wholly trinity' (sic) of vision, mission and strategy, argue Lissack and Richardson (2003). Clearly, while business models can make a key contribution to a firm's success, it is also distinct from other concepts and constructs, such as innovation and marketing, and ought to have a strong ethical element.

Business models are very clearly linked with the innovation literature, as well as that on strategic management (SM). A number of prominent scholars from both fields, for example Teece (2010) and Chesbrough (2007), have crossed the intersection between SM and innovation with their studies on business models. Teece (2010) notes the lack of a conceptual foundation for business models, particularly in the economics or management literature, then reviews examples of business models (e.g. traditional industries, e-business models), and then considers their linkage with strategy and sustainable competitive advantage, barriers to imitation, technological innovation.

A number of key pointers that are identified in developing open business models including clear definition of 'co-development' partnership objectives, classification of research and development capabilities ('core, critical and contextual') and, therefore, aligning the partners' business models (Chesbrough and Schwartz, 2007). Chesbrough (2007) explores various exemplar business models in terms of the six functions: value proposition (GE aircraft engines), target market (Ryanair), value chain (Wal-Mart), revenue mechanisms (Xerox), value network/ecosystem (Ryanair) and competitive strategy (Southwest Airlines), and then presents an indicative typology of business models:

i **undifferentiated**
ii **some differentiation**
iii **segmented**
iv **externally aware**
v **'integrates its innovation process with its business model'**
vi **adaptive platform**, which involves 'experimentation', through corporate ventures, spin-offs, joint ventures, etc. e.g. Intel, Microsoft and Wal-Mart where 'key suppliers and customers become business partners, entering into relationships in which both technical and business risk may be shared' and in which its business models are integrated with both suppliers and top customers (Chesbrough, 2007, pp 13-15).

The role of discovery and experimentation is also important (McGrath, 2010). Exemplars of business models can be replicated by other businesses, and may be considered as taxonomies or typologies (Baden-Fuller and Morgan, 2010). There is particular interest in business models from the e-venture and electronic business field; indeed, early work on business models hailed from this arena (Amit and Zott, 2001). Business models have also been identified to be highly relevant to the entrepreneurial context, i.e. in the design and execution of new ventures, (e.g. Morris *et al.*, 2005; Rajala and Westerlund, 2007, the latter focusing on assets and capabilities). Furthermore, other novel business models include social ventures, for example, which have social objectives, including poverty reduction, and a distinct business model (Seelos and Mair, 2007).

One particularly pertinent example is Grameen Bank, whose business model exposes three key lessons, *viz* 'challenging conventional wisdom', 'finding complementary partners', 'undertaking continuous experimentation', 'favouring social profit-oriented shareholders' and 'specifying social profit objectives clearly' (Yunus *et al.*, 2010). Consequently, Yunus *et al.* (2010) have developed a social business model framework which has four elements: (i) social and environmental profit equation, (ii) value proposition (stakeholders and product/service), (iii) internal and external value constellation and (iv) economic profit equation.

It is beyond the scope of this commentary to review these particular exemplars in any further detail, suffice to say that there are many case study examples in a number of industries that provide additional insight and illumination into the diversity of business models that exist.

This brief review has uncovered a developing and emergent literature on business models in the past 10 years, with a number of varied definitions and a clear rationale for a business model in terms of improved performance. Furthermore, there are a number of studies indicating the key elements of the design of business models – or in terms of business model innovation – as well as typologies and exemplars, particularly in specific industries. As a still immature concept within the strategic management and innovation fields, there are opportunities for research into the business model, not just in terms of clarifying the concept and building theory, but also empirical research into what makes a good business model and how it contributes to performance and firm strategy (particularly in terms of social enterprises, and not just the commercial sector). Students will find these articles particularly useful in developing a comprehensive understanding of the concept and its practical application, and in critically challenging the conventional wisdom around business models.

Further Reading

Amit, R. and Zott, C. (2001) 'Value Creation in E-Business', *Strategic Management Journal*, Vol. 22, No. 6, pp. 493–520.

Baden-Fuller, C. and Morgan, M.C. (2010) 'Business models as models', *Long Range Planning*, Vol. 43, No 2–3, pp. 156–171.

Chesbrough, H. (2007) 'Business model innovation: it's not just about technology anymore', *Strategy & Leadership*, Vol. 35, No. 6, pp. 12–17.

Chesbrough, H. and Schwartz, K. (2007) 'Innovating business models with co-development partnerships',

Research Technology Management, Vol. 50, No. 1, pp. 55–59.

Lissack, M.R. and Richardson, K.A. (2003) 'Models without Morals: Toward the Ethical Use of Business Models', *Emergence: A Journal of Complexity Issues in Organizations and Management*, Vol. 5, No. 2, pp. 72–102.

McGrath, R.G. (2010) 'Business Models: A Discovery Driven Approach', *Long Range Planning*, Vol. 43, No 2–3, pp. 247–261.

Morris, M., Schindehutte, M. and Allen, J. (2005) 'The entrepreneur's business model: toward a unified perspective', *Journal of Business Research*, Vol. 58, pp. 726–735.

Rajala, R. and Westerlund, M. (2007) 'Business models – a new perspective on firms' assets and capabilities', *Entrepreneurship and Innovation*, Vol. 8, No. 2, pp. 115–127.

Seelos, C. and Mair, J. (2007) 'Profitable Business Models and Market Creation in the Context of Deep Poverty: A Strategic View', *Academy of Management*, Vol. 21, No. 4, pp. 49–63.

Teece, D.J. (2010) 'Business Models, Business Strategy and Innovation', *Long Range Planning*, Vol. 43, No 2–3, pp. 172–194.

Yunus, M., Moingeon, B. and Lehmann-Ortega, L. (2010) 'Building Social Business Models: Lessons

Summary

Drawing upon this introduction to the business model we can restate strategy as a set of four visions or articulated pictures for:

- The businesses and industries the organization should be in – its corporate strategy.
- How it will compete in each one in its search for advantage – which takes in its targeted customers.
- How every activity which supports these strategies can be linked effectively to create synergy and avoid fragmentation.
- How and when to change strategies.

It will be appreciated that all of these support the essential purpose of the organization.

At this point it would be useful to revisit the section in Chapter 1 on functional, competitive and corporate strategies.

The revenue model examines revenue and costs and thus evaluates business performance. It deals with financial implications and the implementation of the business model.

Finally, the following conclusions from Collins (2001) can be used to draw together a number of our early themes. Collins had been examining what characterized companies that had achieved and sustained high performance. The three main conclusions can be seen as essential tests of a sound business model and they can also be related directly to the E–V–R framework we introduced in 1. They are:

They sought to be seen as 'the best in the world' at what they did, which gave them a serious competitive advantage they could exploit – *environment*.

They exercised control over the 'economic engine'. In other words they managed their resources efficiently and had a robust revenue model – *resources*.

They are passionate about what they do – *values*.

References

Collins, J. (2001) *Good to Great*, Random House Business Books.

Hamel, G. (2000) *Leading the Revolution*, Harvard Business School Press.

Osterwalder and Pigneur. (2010) *Business Model Generation*, John Wiley & Sons.

Kim, W.C. and Mauborgne, R. (2005) *Blue Ocean Strategy*, Harvard Business School Press.

Chapter 3

Strategic purpose

PART 1
Understanding strategy

1 What is strategy and who is involved?
 - Appendix

2 The business model and the revenue model

3 Strategic purpose
 - Supplement: Using frameworks to analyze strategy cases

PART 5
Strategy implementation

14 Strategy implementation and structure

15 Leading change

16 Managing strategy in the organization

17 Final thoughts and reflections: the practice of strategy

STRATEGIC MANAGEMENT: AWARENESS AND CHANGE

PART 2
Analysis and positioning

4 The business environment and strategy

5 Resource-led strategy

6 The dynamics of competition

7 Introducing culture and values

PART 4
Strategic growth issues

11 Strategic control and measuring success

12 Issues in strategic and international growth

13 Failure, consolidation and recovery strategies

PART 3
Strategy development

8 Creating and formulating strategy: alternatives, evaluation and choice

9 Strategic planning

10 Strategic leadership and intrapreneurship: towards visionary leadership?

Learning objectives

Having read to the end of this chapter, you should be able to:

- explain the terms vision, mission, and objectives **(Section 3.1)**

- identify and summarize how stakeholder theory and economic theories of the firm impact upon objectives and decisions **(Section 3.2)**

- discuss the significance of profits in for-profit and not-for-profit organizations **(Section 3.4)**

- differentiate between **policies**, and official and operative objectives, and assess the impact of personal objectives **(Section 3.4)**

- identify the key issues involved in **social responsibility** and **business ethics** **(Section 3.5)**.

Introduction

Strategies are means to ends, and organizations have a purpose, which ideally will be understood, shared and supported by everyone in the organization: leading to a clear, if broad, direction for its activities and strategies. Strategic leaders must establish the organization's purpose and direction, as well as the more detailed objectives and performance targets for individual managers and employees. Whilst there can often be internal conflicts over these, what individual people actually do and achieve affects organizational performance. Hence, this chapter looks at the idea of purposeful activity by considering the organizational mission and objectives, which, as we saw in Chapter 2, need a clear business model.

A number of economic and behavioural theories influence strategic purpose, such as the potentially conflicting expectations of different stakeholders, the role of institutional shareholders, and whether the profit motive should be the key driving force, including within certain not-for-profit organizations.

If you don't know where you are going, any road will take you there.

RAYMOND G VIAULT, WHEN CHIEF EXECUTIVE OFFICER, JACOBS SUCHARD, SWITZERLAND

A voyage of a thousand miles begins with a single step. It is important that that step is in the right direction.

OLD CHINESE SAYING, UPDATED

Life can only be understood backward, but it must be lived forward.

S KIERKEGAARD

3.1 Vision, mission and objectives

This chapter is about strategic direction and objectives. Figure 3.1 defines the terms vision, mission and objectives, provides a range of examples from the private and public sectors and shows the relationships between these terms. It shows how the overall vision ultimately drives measurable key **performance indicators** which relate to specific objectives that have been derived from the high-order vision. Strategy in Action 3.1 illustrates the relevant points, not because of comparative superiority or inferiority. Kaplan and Norton (2000) have emphasized the significance of enabling factors, resources and support that ensure that targets are attainable.

Figure 3.1   Vision, mission and objectives: a hierarchy of terminology

VISION
to become

|

MISSION
to be in order to become
how the organization will make a difference

|

VALUES
behaviours to support the vision and mission

|

BROAD AIMS & OBJECTIVES
to deliver the mission and vision

|

ENABLING FACTORS
things that need to be in place to support this process and achievement

|

KEY PERFORMANCE INDICATORS (KPIs)
specific targets and milestones for a defined time period linked to each and every aim,
objective and enabler

BASED IN PART ON THEMES FROM KAPLAN, R AND NORTON, D (2000), THE STRATEGY FOCUSED ORGANISATION, HARVARD BUSINESS SCHOOL PRESS

Strategy in Action 3.1   Examples of Vision, Mission and Objectives Statements

1. Vision Statements

A vision statement describes what the company is to become in the (long-term) future.

The Sony Spirit

'Sony doesn't serve markets; Sony makes markets. Sony is a trail blazer, always a seeker of the unknown. Sony will never follow old trails. Through this progress Sony wants to serve mankind.'

SONY **http://www.sony.com**

British Airways

'The world's favourite airline.'

This vision, first adopted in the 1990s, focuses on employees and customers; and the related mission emphasized BA's desire to be the world's first truly global airline. In turn, the corporate strategy focused on carefully selected alliances, which required BA staff to believe in the vision and act accordingly. In recent years staff trust and morale has declined as costs have been cut dramatically. The strapline has effectively been abandoned.

BRITISH AIRWAYS **http://www.britishairways.com**

The Girl Guides Association

'To help a girl reach her highest potential.'

These eight words cut straight to the heart of the movement and its clear and direct statement of purpose.

GIRL GUIDES ASSOCIATION
http://www.wagggsworld.org

2. Mission Statements

The mission statement *reflects* the essential purpose of the organization, and ideally captures why it is in existence, the nature of its business(es), the customers it seeks to serve and satisfy and how it will do so.

Google

Google set out to 'organize the world's information and make it universally available'.

Pithy and to the point – and allowing considerable flexibility in the way strategies would emerge and evolve.

Financial Times Conferences

'The mission of the FTC is to organize conferences on subjects of interest to the international business

community, using the highest calibre speakers and providing attending delegates with the finest service, thereby providing a low-cost and time-efficient means of both obtaining impartial quality information and making senior-level industry contacts.'

Here we can see a clear definition of the business, a formulation of objectives, delivery strategies, means of differentiating the service and stakeholder relevance.

FINANCIAL TIMES

3. Long-Term Objectives

Objectives are desired (and measurable) states or results linked to particular timescales and concerning the size or type of organization, the nature and variety of the areas of interest and levels of success. Measurement can be straightforward – for example, 'a minimum return of 20 per cent of net capital employed in the business' – or it might be less specific, e.g. 'continued customer satisfaction, a competitive return on capital employed and real growth in earnings per share next year', requiring a comparison of competitor returns and the monitoring of customer satisfaction through, say, the number of complaints received. We can distinguish between clearly and typically finance based measurable objectives ('closed') and those that are less specific and essentially continuing ('open') (Richards, 1978).

British Airports Authority (BAA): Open Objectives

'BAA aims to enhance the value of the shareholders' investments by achieving steady and remunerative long-term growth. Its strategy for developing and operating world-class international airports that are safe, secure, efficient and profitable is based on a commitment to continuously enhancing the quality of service to passengers and business partners alike. This process of constant improvement includes cost-effective investment in new airport facilities closely matched to customer demand.'

These were in the context of a declared mission to 'make BAA the most successful airport company in the world' and before the new Spanish owners of BAA were required to sell a number of airports.

BRITISH AIRPORTS AUTHORITY **http://www.baa.co.uk**

4. The Coca-Cola Roadmap

This 'roadmap' has been summarized from the company's website and it shows how the mission and vision can be used to drive further layers of detail.

Mission

- to refresh the world
- to inspire moments of optimism and happiness
- to create value and make a difference.

Leading to

A Vision for each of the following:

profit
people
products
partners (especially bottlers and distributors)
the Planet
productivity.

This then leads on to (for each one of these six)

Goals

Priorities for strategies and tactics

Measurement metrics

All of this is rooted in the Coca-Cola culture spelled out as:

- live our values
- focus on the market
- work smart
- act like owners – in other words be responsible and accountable
- be the brand.

Whilst a mission statement captures how an organization will create and add value for its customers, '**values**' (see below) are important as they relate to the corporate values that should be held by employees, be visible to the outside world and support the organization in pursuing its mission.

The term *aims* is sometimes used interchangeably with mission, and goals with objectives. While it has been argued that objectives overall define the specific kinds of performance and results that the organization seeks to produce through its activities, the *long-term objectives* relate to the desired performance and results on an ongoing basis; *short-term objectives* are concerned with the near-term performance targets that the organization desires to reach in progressing towards its long-term objectives (Thompson and Strickland,

1980). Accordingly, these performance targets can be agreed with individual managers, who are responsible and held accountable for their attainment. Similarly, Gerber (2008) theorizes an entrepreneur creating a new business with growth potential having four differently ordered themes or elements descending from higher- to lower-order: (i) the *dream*, a mental conceptualization of the ultimate outcome for the customers being targeted, (ii) the vision, a statement of what the business seeks to achieve, (iii) the purpose, a clarification of why they are doing the planning activity and (iv) the mission, an explanation of what they (and the business) are going to create.

Values: corporate social responsibility (CSR) and business ethics

We do not propose reviewing CSR and business ethics substantially here because it is too wide a field that is developing separately from strategic management and other disciplines and functional areas of business, and there are a number of textbooks focusing on this area (for example, Griseri and Seppala, 2010). How responsible a firm might choose to be, and why – simply, firms can be socially responsible (proactive) or socially responsive (reactive to pressure) – can embrace, for example, product safety, working conditions, honesty, environment, discrimination, community relations, etc. Social responsibility and **profitability** can be improved simultaneously (The Performance Group, 1999). Many companies mistakenly see environmental legislation as a threat, but should perhaps see regulation as an indication the company is not using its resources efficiently (Porter, 1995). Case 3.1. on Selco demonstrates what is possible when true entrepreneurs get to work. We expand on these points in an extended section later in the chapter.

Case 3.1 Selco Ind

Selco is short for the Solar Energy Light Company, which is a declared 'for profit social enterprise' based in Bangalore, India. Its activities are concentrated in the poor rural areas away from, but relatively close by, the wealth-creating software businesses in that part of India.

Selco was established to help improve the living conditions of poor rural households, many of whom are local farmers growing a few crops or producing milk they can sell to yield some income. Annual incomes of around US$1000 would be typical. The company provides solar 'interventions' for lighting and heating water and also low-smoke cooking stoves. When solar panels appear on houses in the developed world they are normally placed flat to the tiled roof to attract the sun's rays. But these rural farmers are more likely to have thatched roof houses and so the panels are raised above the roof and mounted on a post which protrudes through the roof itself. They look rather like television aerials. They are not a replacement for electricity – which is available in some places but from a system that is likely to crash at any time, especially if there is peak demand. Instead kerosene burners are more popular.

Dr Harish Hande was a PhD student in America – an engineer – when he imagined what Selco could become. The conceptual model was part of his thesis. In 1994 he returned to India and persuaded Tata-BP Solar to let him have a single solar panel on credit to sell and install to a wealthy small farmer. Once he had a customer and a sale and was paid for the installation he carried on in the same vein to prove the concept. The problem was that his target market would not be able to pay in full for the solar installations.

Hande got to know Neville Williams, founder of a non-profit solar energy business in the USA and he agreed to co-found Selco with a modest personal investment. This got the business off the ground in 1995 and in 1997 they received a loan of US$130 000 from USAID. Later some US$1.5 million equity capital was provided by five social investors.

Hande's business revenue model was based on the premise that a customer would be expected to pay between 15 and 25 per cent of the installation cost, ideally at the higher end of this range. A basic installation would cost US$450 and so for many this amounted to a month's income. The intention would be that the rest be paid in monthly instalments at an agreed affordable level. It has been said that the prevailing borrowing philosophy amongst local farmers was that '300 rupees a month is expensive; ten rupees a day is affordable'. Loans and repayments was not something they were necessarily used to – in large part because nobody was willing to lend them money.

Hande set out on a charm-offensive with local banks and suggested they see loans to fund the down payments as a form of well-intended micro financing – even though it was really directed at improving lives rather than supporting a business. But he did succeed and millions have been lent. The default percentage is under ten per cent. The banks were not being commercially negligent – the local people would actually be able to save on their energy costs with solar power and so be in a position to pay the interest on the loans as well as pay Selco. Over 125 000 systems have been installed at a cost of over US$50 million. The investment in Selco and the local bank finance has circulated well.

It was 2000 before Selco broke even – but the ambitious Hande was drawn to establish a franchised dealer network in the state. This did not turn out to be a sound strategic move and it proved expensive for Selco, which lost money. The problem was the global cost of solar panels was increasing and the opportunity for franchisees was less than forecast. Selco managed to get emergency funding from the International Finance Corporation, part of the World Bank, and this kept the business going. The loan is still being serviced.

Selco now employs some 170 people who work through 25 service centres, each with a dedicated rural area.

Questions

1 How would you summarize the Business Model for Selco?
2 How important was it, for the success of this venture, to build a network of committed stakeholders?
3 Can you think of any similar 'win-win' opportunities?

Meanwhile, dissenting voices include Milton Friedman (1979), the economist, arguing that 'the business of business is business … the organization's only social responsibility is to increase its profit', and Drucker (1974) advocating that businesses' role is, 'to supply goods and services to customers and an economic surplus to society … rather than to supply jobs to workers and managers, or even dividends to shareholders'.

Disasters such as the explosion at the chemical plant in Bhopal, India, in 1984 have long raised the question of how far companies should go in pursuit of profits. More recent cases, such as Tyco and Enron, have raised different but related issues of ethical behaviour. Houlden (1988) suggests that business ethics encompasses the views of people throughout society concerning the morality of business, and not just the views of the particular business and the people who work in it. Issues such as golden handshakes, pensions, insider dealing and very substantial salary increases for company chairpeople and chief executives are topical and controversial. But is it ethical for large companies to pursue high-risk strategies which might leave several small suppliers financially exposed? Another ethical concern is individual managers or employees who adopt practices which senior managers or the strategic leader would consider unethical; for example, phone hacking in the UK newspaper industry has led to the humiliation and, in some cases, prosecution of their strategic leaders. Badaracco and Webb (1995) also highlight how internal decisions can be influenced by unethical practices, quoting instances of invented market-research findings, and altered investment returns which imply, erroneously, that the organization is meeting its published targets.

Because ethical standards and beliefs are aspects of the corporate culture, they are influenced markedly by the lead set by the strategic leader and their awareness of behaviour throughout the organization. If a proper lead is not provided, managers will be left to 'second guess' what would be seen as appropriate behaviour. Power, then, can be used ethically or unethically by individual managers. Section 3.5 is an extended version of the above text.

Vision statements

Despite the increasing popularity of organizational mission statements, vision statements are less prevalent – which does not necessarily indicate a lack of vision – but, when present, they reflect the company's vision of some idealized and achievable future state. Terminology and themes such as a 'world-class manufacturer', a 'quality organization', a 'provider of legendary service' and a 'stimulating, rewarding place to work' might well appear. The essential elements focus on: those values to which the organization is committed, appropriate standards of behaviour for all employees, along with possible improvement paths, employee development programmes and measures or indicators of progress for each element of the vision.

> *Strategy development is like driving around a roundabout. The signposts are only useful if you know where you want to go. Some exits lead uphill, some downhill – most are one-way streets and some have very heavy traffic indeed. The trick is in picking the journey's end before you set out – otherwise you go around in circles or pick the wrong road.*
>
> GERRY M MURPHY, WHEN CHIEF EXECUTIVE OFFICER, GREENCORE PLC, IRELAND

Mission statements

Whilst often seen as the organization's overriding *raison d'être*, many corporate mission statements, according to Ackoff (1986), still resonant today, prove 'worthless' consisting of loose – and essentially indeterminable – expressions, such as 'maximize growth potential' or 'provide products of the highest quality'. Primarily, the mission statement 'should not address what an organization must do in order to survive, but what it has chosen to do in order to thrive' (ibid). He suggests that a good mission statement has five characteristics: (i) a formulation of objectives enabling progress towards them to be measured; (ii) differentiating the company from its competitors; (iii) defining the business(es) that the company wants to be in; (iv) is relevant to all stakeholders in the firm, not just shareholders and managers; and (v) is exciting and inspiring.

Campbell (1989) argues that effective mission statements must reflect corporate values and thus be pursued visibly by the strategic leader and the organization as a whole, and identifies four key issues involved in developing a useful mission. These are to: (i) clarify the purpose of the organization, i.e. why it exists; (ii) describe the business and its activities, and the market position it seeks to achieve; (iii) state its values, e.g. how it will treat its employees, customers and suppliers; and (iv) ensure that the organization behaves as promised, thus inspiring trust within employees and other stakeholders.

In successful companies, middle and junior managers know where the strategic leaders are taking the company and why, whilst confusion may abound in less successful organizations.

Mission statements, like vision statements, can easily 'state the obvious', thus having little real value, whereas they should clarify what makes a company different and a more effective competitor. A generic mission (or vision) statement is, simply, of no great value. Companies that succeed long-term create competitive advantages and sustain their strong positions with flexibility and improvement, as supported by the vision and mission.

While such statements facilitate external and internal communication, organizations benefit from the forced thinking in order to establish sound statements. And yet, many are still worded poorly. Mission (or vision) must be more than a plaque in a foyer – given that employees must translate the words into actions to achieve the desired outcomes, and so must feel and *trust* that the organization actually means what it is saying.

The mission clearly corresponds to the basic philosophy underlying the business and, if it is sound, will derive strategies that generate success.

The points we have covered so far are illustrated in Case 3.2 on The Republic of Tea.

Case 3.2   The Republic of Tea   US

The Republic of Tea is a relatively new business derived from the old regime of tea drinking, given tea has allegedly been drunk in China since 2737BC. It was founded in California in 1992 to market organic and exotic teas from all round the world. There were three founders: Mel and Patricia Ziegler, who had earlier started the Banana Republic fashion store chain which they had sold to Gap, and Bill Rosenzweig, an academic at the Haas Business School, University of California Berkeley. They wrote a book on how the business started after an exchange of letters discussing their perception of a need and a possible business model. It is clear that, in their own words, the founders 'delight in drinking tea'.

The business was sold after just 2 years to an entrepreneur, Ron Rubin, who has grown it from essentially a 'fun idea' into a sizeable and profitable venture – but retained many of the founders' idiosyncrasies. The emergence and growth of the company has happened roughly parallel to the very rapid growth of the modern coffee bar, led by Starbucks. The persuasive argument would be that both tea and coffee benefit from using the best quality raw materials and preparing the drinks carefully and properly. In the UK the number of cups of tea drunk every day continues to exceed the number of cups of coffee, although the gap has been closed in the last 20 years.

The Zieglers and Rosenzweig had set out to 'create a tea revolution' and their early letters to each other postulated a mythical country – hence the business name. Employees are still described as ministers; customers are citizens; and retail outlets are embassies. There is, however, a strong focus on mail-order sales and tea can be couriered to anywhere in the US in 2 working days and anywhere in the world in 10–14 days.

The Republic of Tea sells only full leaf tea, not the ground tea leaves that most of us buy as loose tea or tea bags. The argument is that full leaf tea provides a better taste and aroma as well as being healthier. The company works closely with its growers and uses only young leaves. Its supply chain provides red, black, green and white varieties, as well as certain specialty teas, such as Moroccan Mint. Most branded tea consumed is black tea. Some varieties are very scarce and limited edition; and there is also a wide range of herbal infusions. Generally different tea leaves are not blended.

Company documentation proclaims the following:

The *purpose* is 'to enrich people's lives through the experience of fine tea' – there is a key balance between health and well-being.

The *mission* is to become 'the leading purveyor of fine teas and herbs in the world' and 'to be respected for unsurpassed quality'.

These will be achieved by providing 'outstanding products delivered in innovative ways'.

Questions

1 Do you believe these statements of purpose and mission capture the spirit of the business effectively?
2 Do you believe this is a sustainable business model?

3.2 Objectives – the influence of economic theories and stakeholder theory

A full consideration of objectives incorporates three aspects:

- an appreciation of the objectives that the organization is actually pursuing and achieving – where it is going and why

- the objectives that it might pursue, and the freedom and opportunity it has to make changes
- specific objectives for the future.

This section considers the issues that affect and determine the first two of these, while decisions about specific future objectives feature later in the book. We begin, though, by looking briefly at a number of theories of business organizations and considering the role and importance of stakeholders.

Market models and other economic theories

Basic micro-economic theory states that firms should seek to maximize profits, which is achieved where marginal revenue is equal to marginal cost; and is underpinned by assumptions such as firms' clear understanding of the nature of the demand for their products, and why people buy, and that they are willing and able to control production and sales as the model demands. In reality, decision-makers do not have perfect knowledge, and production and sales are affected by suppliers and distributors.

However, four market models have been derived from such theory (Table 3.1), the characteristics of these in respect of barriers to entry into the industry and the marketing opportunities (**differentiation** potential; price and non-price competition) determining the opportunity to achieve significant profits.

In markets which approach pure competition (pure competition as such is hypothetical), firms will only make 'normal' profits, the amount required for them to stay in the industry. Products are 'commodities', not differentiated, and so premium prices for certain brands are not possible. There are no major barriers to entry into the industry and so new suppliers are attracted if there are profits to be made. Competition results, and if supply exceeds demand the ruling market price is forced down and only the efficient firms survive.

In monopolistic competition there are again several suppliers, some large, many small, but products are differentiated. However, as there are once more no major barriers to entry, the above situation concerning profits applies. Newcomers increase supply and, although those firms with distinctive products can charge some premium, they will still have to move in line with market prices generally, having a dampening effect on profits.

Only in **oligopoly** and monopoly markets, where a small number of large firms is dominant, is there real opportunity for 'supernormal' profits, in excess of what is required to stay in business. However, in oligopoly the small number of large firms tend to be wary of each other and prices are held back to some extent for fear of losing market share. Suppliers are interdependent and fear that a price decrease will be matched by competitors (thus reducing profits) and price increases will not (hence market share will be threatened). There are two types of oligopoly, depending on whether opportunities exist for significant differentiation. In all of these models competition is a major determinant of profit potential and, therefore, objectives must be set with competitors in mind. In a monopoly (again somewhat theoretical in a pure sense), excess profits could be made if government did not act as a restraint. In the UK, although such **public sector organizations** as British Gas and British Telecom have been privatized, their actions in terms of supply and pricing are monitored and regulated.

A number of other authors have offered theories in an attempt to explain the behaviour of organizations and the objectives they seek. Baumol (1959) argues that firms seek to maximize sales rather than profits, but within the constraint of a minimum acceptable profit level. Williamson (1964) theorized that managers can set their own objectives, which are different from those of shareholders, and that managerial satisfaction, which is crucial, increases if a manager manages a large staff, if there are lavish perks and if profits exceed the level required for the essential development of the business and the necessary replacement of equipment. Marris (1964) postulates growth as a key concern, as managers derive utility from growth in the form of enhanced salaries, power and status – but, if, as a result of growth strategies pursued by the firm, the firm's profits are constrained, its share value may fall and it may become increasingly vulnerable to takeover. Penrose (1959) argues that firms seek to achieve the full potential from all their resources, and they grow if there are unused resources, diversifying when they can no longer grow with existing products, services and markets or other limits (e.g. production facilities, the capacity of managers to plan and implement growth strategies). Finally, large corporations, with large investments and long-term commitments, attempt to control their environment, influencing both government and consumer, and being controlled by 'technocrats', teams of powerful experts and specialists (Galbraith, 1969).

Table 3.1   Structural characteristics of four market models

Market	Number of firms	Type of product	Control over price by supplier	Entry conditions	Non-price competition*	Examples[†]
Pure competition	Large	Standardized Identical or almost identical	None	Free	None	Agricultural products; some chemicals; printing; laundry services
Monopolistic competition	Large	Differentiated	Some	Relatively easy	Yes	Clothing; furniture; soft drinks; plumbers; restaurants
Oligopoly**	Few or a few dominant	Standardized or differentiated	Limited by mutual interdependence Considerable if collusion takes place	Difficult	Yes	Standardized: cement; sugar; fertilizers Differentiated: margarine; soaps; detergents
Pure monopoly	One	Unique	Considerable	Blocked	Yes	Water companies in their regions (at the moment); local bus companies in certain towns

* Non-price competition occurs in many ways, e.g. by attempts to increase the extent of product differentiation and buyer preference through advertising, brand names, trade marks, promotions, distribution outlets; by new product launches and innovation, etc.

** There are many oligopoly models of a collusive and non-collusive type. They make varying behavioural and structural assumptions.

[†] Useful further reading: Doyle, P and Gidengil, ZB (1977) An empirical study of market structures. *Journal of Management Studies*, 14(3), October, 316–328. Some of the examples are taken from this.

Stakeholder theory

Profit-maximizing theory by early theorists, identifying owners and managers as synonymous, assumed that the first priority in decision-making is held by shareholders. Later thinking on strategic management rejects this assumption, however, and demonstrates the important role played by competitors and by government as a restraining force: as well as considering the concerns and impact of external market forces, such as suppliers and distributors, and internal forces, e.g. employees and managers (Newbould and Luffman, 1979). For example, managers' decisions create incremental changes that are influenced by the objectives and values they believe to be important, while as employees they also regard growth and their own security as important. In Cyert and March's (1963) behavioural theory of the firm, organizational goals are compromises between members of an internal coalition (production, inventory, sales, market and profit), linked to relative power and inevitable conflicts of interest, with the perceived importance of the short-, as opposed to long-, term because these issues are more tangible and decisions have to be taken as situations change. In Simon's (1964) theory of satisficing, managers seek courses of action (although not necessarily optimal courses), which are acceptable in the light of known objectives, because of internal and external constraints such as time pressure, a lack of information and the vested interests of certain powerful groups or individuals. He also argued that some of the ends that strategies are designed to achieve are not freely set objectives, but constraints imposed on the organization by powerful stakeholders or agencies. For example, many of the world's leading drug companies have been forced, due to Government reluctance to fund expensive drugs and treatments, to close plants, relocate in lower cost regions and to focus research on treatments that are most likely to receive funding, arguably at the expense of potential breakthroughs.

These are all *stakeholders*, defined by Freeman (1984) as 'any group or individual who can affect, or is affected by, the performance of the organization'. Hence its objectives will consider stakeholder's needs, virtually representing an informal coalition, with their relative power being a key variable. Therefore, the organization occasionally 'trades off' one against the other, effectively prioritizing them into a hierarchy, whilst Table 3.2 illustrates the importance of different aspects to different stakeholders.

Stakeholder interests may be consistent or conflicting, such as investment in new technology improving product quality and thus profitability, benefiting customers and shareholders respectively, but employees, possibly managers and their trade unions, may be dissatisfied by job losses and, consequently, if any related redundancies result in militant resistance, the government may become involved.

Stakeholders are not affected in the same way by every strategic decision. Therefore, their relative influence will vary from decision to decision. In 1995 Shell, supported by the UK government which was convinced by the scientific case for the decision, planned to sink its redundant Brent Spar oil platform in deep seas some 150 miles west of Scotland. The environmental pressure group Greenpeace objected and protesters boarded the platform, claiming that it still contained 5000 tonnes of oil which would eventually be released to pollute the sea. Following a professional campaign which fuelled public opinion, and which made Shell appear socially irresponsible, the company agreed to investigate other possibilities for disposal, whilst the UK government was angry and disappointed by this decision. Independent inspectors later proved that the residual oil was much less than 5000 tonnes. The press concluded:

> 'Shell went wrong in spending too much time convincing government of the case for sea-bed dumping, but not attaching enough importance to consulting other stakeholder groups.'

Waterman (1994) contends that successful companies, by prioritizing employees and customers (and not shareholders), perform more effectively than their rivals, leading to superior profits and wealth creation for their shareholders. Whilst many organizations fail because they do not incorporate the important motivational concerns of key stakeholders (Simon, 1964), small businesses in particular may neglect their larger suppliers, and if they do not pay their accounts on time they will find their deliveries stopped. Similarly, if new products or services fail to provide consumers with what they are looking for, however well produced or low priced they might be, they will not sell.

Figure 3.2 shows that organizations must satisfy shareholders, employees and customers, but if they fail with any group long-term they will place the organization in jeopardy through a spiral of decline.

Table 3.2   Examples of stakeholder interests

Shareholders	Annual dividends; increasing the value of their investment in the company as the share price increases. Both are affected by growth and profits
	Institutional shareholders may balance high-risk investments and their anticipated high returns with more stable investments in their portfolio
Managers	Salaries and bonuses; perks; status from working for a well-known and successful organization; responsibility; challenge; security
Employees	Wages; holidays; conditions and job satisfaction; security – influenced by trade union involvement
Consumers	Desirable and quality products; competitive prices – very much in relation to competition; new products at appropriate times
Distributors	On time and reliable deliveries
Suppliers	Consistent orders; payment on time
Financiers	Interest payments and loan repayments; like payment for supplies, affected by cash flow
Government	Payment of taxes and provision of employment; contribution to the nation's exports
Society in general	Socially responsible actions – sometimes reflected in pressure groups

Figure 3.2   Satisfying stakeholders

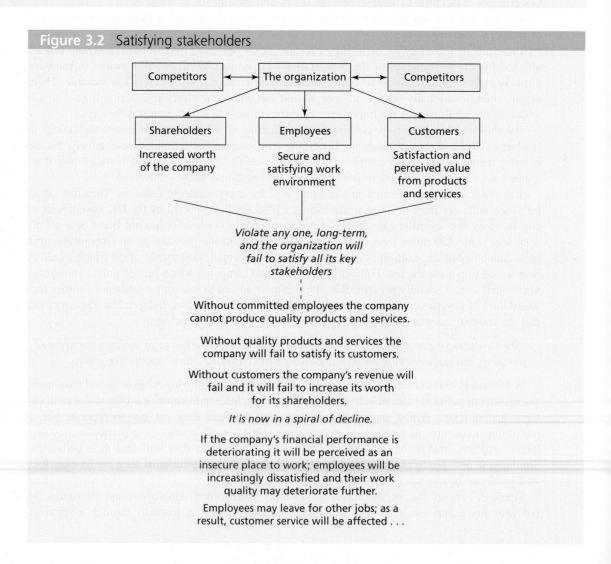

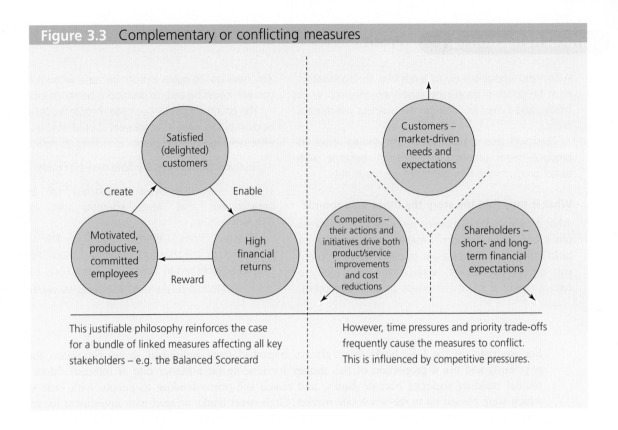

Figure 3.3 Complementary or conflicting measures

Figure 3.3, alternatively, presents a virtuous circle of growth and prosperity with satisfied, perhaps delighted, customers (on the left) enabling high financial returns, used in part to reward employees (with a perception of fairness motivating employees to keep customers satisfied) and (on the right) showing how customer needs can sometimes conflict with the demands of some shareholders, especially those who are willing to trade off long-term achievement for short-term financial returns. Competitors are always trying to persuade customers to switch allegiance and thus impact on an organization's success.

3.3 Profit as an objective: for-profit versus not-for-profit

Critical Reflection 3.1 discusses whether profit is the ultimate objective of profit-seeking business organizations or whether it is merely a means to other ends, which themselves constitute the real objectives. Ackoff (1986) argues that profit is necessary for the survival of a business enterprise, but is neither the reason for which the business is formed nor the reason why it stays in existence. Instead, Ackoff contends,

Those who manage organizations do so primarily to provide themselves with the quality of work life and standard of living they desire … their behaviour can be better understood by assuming this than by assuming that their objective is to maximize profit or growth.

Although one must also consider the quality of life of investors (shareholders), customers, suppliers and distributors, it is non-decision-making employees who are the major stakeholders, because if the firm fails they incur the greatest losses. Ultimately, it is irrelevant whether profit is an objective or a means of providing service and satisfaction to stakeholders, as long as both are considered and not seen as mutually exclusive. However, the 'feel' and culture of an organization will be affected. In simple terms, an organization will succeed if it survives and meets the expectations of its stakeholders (Table 3.3). But how it prioritizes its objectives can have a marked effect. Company B is following a more growth-oriented approach.

Critical Reflection 3.1   Profit

A business school is likely to teach that an organization must be good to people because then they will work harder; and if they work harder the business will make a profit.

They will also teach that a firm should strive to produce better products and services, because with better products the firm will make greater profits.

What if they told the story the other way round?

What if they taught managers: you have got to make a profit, because if you do not make a profit you cannot build offices that are pleasant to be in. Without profit you cannot pay decent wages. Without profit you cannot satisfy a lot of the needs of your employees.

You have got to make a profit because without a profit you will never be able to develop a better product.

The profit would still be made. People would still get decent wages. Most employers would still make an effort to improve their products as they do now.

'But you would have a whole new ball game.'

It is clear that these approaches will lead to organizations that 'feel' different, that manifest different cultures.

Adapted from Cohen, P (1974) *The Gospel According to the Harvard Business School*, Penguin. Originally published by Doubleday, New York, 1973.

HARVARD BUSINESS SCHOOL **http://www.hbs.edu**

For example, in the UK, banks have always borrowed from individual savers (in return for interest payments) and use a proportion of this money for lending (at a higher rate of interest). More recently, mutual building societies became banks, and risked sub-prime lending to people with little collateral, which were passed on to the wholesale market. High street banks merged with investment banks, and the savings of the 'general public' were now at risk of being gambled by professional bankers whose life is spent taking short-term risks on fluctuating future commodity and stocks prices, in return for very generous performance bonuses. Banks now seem reluctant to lend very much, even after the government supported them with taxpayers' money.

> *The purpose of industry is to serve the public by creating services to meet their needs. It is not to make profits for shareholders, nor to create salaries and wages for the industrial community. These are necessary conditions for success, but not its purpose.*

> DR GEORGE CAREY, RETIRED ARCHBISHOP OF CANTERBURY

> *The responsibility of business is not to create profits but to create live, vibrant, honourable organizations with a real commitment to the community.*

> ANITA RODDICK, FOUNDER, THE BODY SHOP

While some commentators argue that too many companies are still encouraged to seek short-term profits in order to please their major institutional shareholders (Constable, 1980) and that it is only by considering the long-term and the interests of all stakeholders that companies will become more effective competitors in world markets, institutions such as pension funds effectively control the UK's largest companies through the sizeable blocks of shares that they own. These managers have a remit to earn the best returns that they can obtain for their members. Since the mid-1990s, there has been a drive to increase the transparency of these large shareholder blocks, and companies have been required to publish more information.

Table 3.4 shows how organizational strategic leaders and institutional investors do not share completely the same perspective on stakeholder priorities, although there are clear similarities with the most important stakeholders. Interestingly, suppliers, key partners in the **supply chain**, receive a higher priority from strategic leaders, while the institutions rate politicians more highly than do organizational leaders. It is both significant and realistic that small, individual shareholders are not particularly powerful, because they are generally too disparate to become organized.

Table 3.3 Contrasting company objectives

Company A	Company B
1 Return on net assets, 1–3 year time horizon	1 Maintenance and growth of market share
2 Cash flow	2 Maintenance and growth of employment
3 Maintenance and growth of market share	3 Cash flow
4 Maintenance and growth of employment	4 Return on net assets

Objectives, strategies, tactics and the strategic leader

We can think in simple terms of 'objectives' relating to desired ends and so a 'why'? theme. Strategies then concern 'what' to do (the means) to achieve the desired end. Tactics break strategies down further and address 'how', given that activities are what organizations do. Different people in the same organization will be able to relate to activities that are happening, activities that sometimes they are responsible and accountable for. A particular activity, though, can be one person's objective but a strategy carried out by someone else. Take the following list of activities:

1 achieve a higher value (and hence price) for my property

2 improve the appearance of my house

3 paint my house

4 do the painting myself

5 buy some paint.

These are deliberately listed as a hierarchy. Our question to you is: which of these is an objective, a strategy, a tactic? Number 1 easily makes sense as an objective, making 2 a strategy and 3, 4 and 5 are, therefore, tactics. But 2 could be seen as an objective – and maybe so too could 3 – at a lower order. If the key influencer (perhaps one of our wives!) decides Number 1 is important she might delegate the required tasks to one of us. That is her strategy for making sure something happens; it is now our objective! These arguments are extended in Strategy in Practice Box 3.1.

Table 3.4 Perceptions of stakeholder importance

Stakeholder	Prioritization by industry strategic leaders	Prioritization by analysts with institutional investors
Existing customers	1	1
Existing employees	2	3
Potential customers	3	2
Institutional investors	4	4
Suppliers	5	7
Potential employees	6	6
City analysts	7	5
Private (individual) shareholders	8	10
Business media	9	9
General media	10	11
Local communities	11	12
Members of Parliament/Local authorities	12	8

SOURCE: BASED ON RESEARCH BY MORI (2000). MORI http://www.mori.com

Strategy in Practice 3.1

The list of do-it-yourself activities linked to house painting pre-supposes strategic intent. The implication is that a higher order objective (or purpose) has led to a broad strategy and subsequently tactical actions. But why does this necessarily have to have been the reality?

Conceptualize a quite different scenario.

A neighbour and close friend has recently been treating his garden fence and it looks fantastic. Because he wasn't really sure what he was doing, he bought far too much wood treatment and rather than just store it in the back of his garage he offers it to you to treat your fence. You take him up on his kind offer.

When your fence looks really good it becomes obvious you should also paint your garage door – which also looks weather-beaten. Naturally as soon as the garage is painted, the house exterior looks drab in comparison and in need of freshening. Soon the house is looking far more attractive. The outcome – were it to be offered for sale the value of the house would have increased. It is conceivable that improving the house and its value opportunistically could even persuade someone actually to move property.

In this scenario, strategy creation is emergent rather than intended. Activity builds on activity in an incremental way – but through opportunity and circumstance rather than clear intent with a specific outcome in mind. It is for this reason that we argue all

managers are potential strategy makers and that when people try out something – linked to either an opportunity or a competitor tactic – it can lead on to subsequent actions and 'change one's plans'.

In Chapter 1 we explained that strategies are means to ends; and with the intentional approach to strategy, actions are created and executed with specific ends in mind. Here the argument is that people are more like explorers – they draw the map as they go along but remain always mindful of the impact of their actions. What they do and what they achieve is evaluated for its value. If things are seen as positive and progressive they will be continued; if the evaluation is more negative they are likely to be abandoned in favour of an alternative. *These issues will be explored further in Chapter 8 when we examine strategy creation and strategy selection.*

The strategic leader, and their values, establish the main objectives and the direction in which they take the organization. Personal ambitions to build a large conglomerate or a **multinational company** may fuel growth; a determination to be socially responsible may restrain certain activities that other organizations would undertake; a commitment to high quality will influence the design, cost and marketing approach for products. These points are illustrated in Case 3.3, Trade Plus Aid.

Case 3.3   Trade Plus Aid   Int

Trade Plus Aid began more by chance than design in 1992. Charlotte di Vita, then aged 25, was in Ghana when drought ruined thousands of farms – something she realized when she was waiting to see a doctor for treatment for the severe dysentery she had contracted and witnessed the death of a baby in its mother's arms. Wanting to help in some way, she had an idea when the local elders refused her offer of money to buy seed. She suggested to local tribal chiefs that she would spend her £800 savings on seed for them if they would make her 800 pendant-size carvings. The deal was struck. Back in London, and calling on her friends to help her out, she began selling the pendants at Camden and Portobello Markets, plucking a price of £3.99 each out of thin air. Somewhat to her surprise,

the carvings sold quickly and easily. The risk she took had paid off, and she was encouraged to want to do more. She envisioned a seed bank from which local farmers could borrow seed without any payment until they harvest their crops. To progress her idea, she negotiated an alliance with an established mail-order business in Japan – and pendant sales were strong once the infrastructure and supply chain was in place. Her seed bank was started in 1995. The venture grew rapidly with a comprehensive Japanese mail-order catalogue, which included jewellery, clothing and toiletries from various countries in Africa and South America. Unfortunately the 1995 earthquake at Kobe, in Japan, destroyed the warehouse that di Vita's partner owned; the mail-order company was in trouble and the

Japanese market disappeared overnight. Exhibiting courage in the face of setbacks, she managed to survive and rescue the business by spending hours and days searching out new mail-order buyers in America and Germany – but they would only buy her supplies at cost.

Many of the Third World village supply groups she helped establish are now trading independently; they no longer need her help. 'A good year is seeing my groups become self-sufficient, not increasing my turnover.' The ever creative Trade Plus Aid, however, continued to experiment with new initiatives. Charlotte di Vita was able to raise money from business people around the world – who believe in what she does – to establish a 140-employee factory in China for producing hand-enamelled teapots. She started selling these at the Victoria and Albert Museum and various up market department stores. Underestimating demand forced her to resort to airfreighting. A similar venture was started to produce wind chimes in South Africa. Altogether some 500 employees were employed in her factories in China and South Africa. In the UK, Trade Plus Aid relies more on volunteer helpers than it does on paid employees and di Vita herself took only a limited salary from the operation. In 2003 Charlotte di Vita agreed a world-wide licensing deal for her Collection (as it is now called) of gifts with leading giftware company Goebel – this guaranteed a minimum revenue of US$1.3 million over 4 years.

In 13 years di Vita's efforts had enabled over $5 million to be returned to producer communities around the world – Africa, South America and the Far East – in payment for their handicrafts. Her charitable trust (founded in 1997) has also funded special projects in various countries.

Charlotte di Vita's more recent new project was developed with the encouragement of Nelson Mandela. Entitled 'Twenty-First Century Leaders' her project invited famous people – leaders, sports stars, musicians and actors – to provide a simple design that reflects their message of hope for the world, together with a stick diagram self-portrait. These are then used as designs for plates, mugs, t-shirts and any other relevant product where she can secure a licence agreement with a suitable manufacturer. In the case of the plates, the illustrated message is on the front, the stick diagram on the back and they are being sold as limited edition collectibles. In the case of wristbands and other smaller items, the production runs are unlimited. The surpluses from all sales of every item will be 'handed back' to their designers, who will choose which charity will receive them. The intention is to raise money to help tackle key global issues: poverty, child abuse and environmental conservation. This charity has grown in prominence and is now based in Doha.

Questions

1 How would you apply the Gerber themes of dream, vision, mission and purpose (Section 3.1 Introduction of this chapter) to this case?
2 To what extent is this organization dependent upon Charlotte Di Vita?
3 Is a high level of dependency on a leader driven by a personal cause good or bad?

SOURCE: THIS CASE STUDY WAS PREPARED USING PRIMARILY PUBLICLY AVAILABLE SOURCES OF INFORMATION FOR THE PURPOSES OF CLASSROOM DISCUSSION; IT DOES NOT INTEND TO ILLUSTRATE EITHER EFFECTIVE OR INEFFECTIVE HANDLING OF A MANAGERIAL SITUATION.

While it is possible for small firms to enjoy competitive advantage by providing products or services with value added to appeal to local customers in a limited geographical area, many are not distinctive in any marked way. Where this is the case, and where competition is strong, small firms will be price takers, and their profits and growth will be influenced substantially by external forces. Some small firm owners will be entrepreneurial, willing to take risks and determined to build a bigger business, whereas others will be content to stay small. Some small businesses are started by people who essentially want to work for themselves rather than for a larger corporation, and their objectives could well be concerned with survival and the establishment of a sound business which can be passed on to the next generation of their family.

Objectives of public sector and not-for-profit organizations

For not-for-profit organizations, stakeholders are important, particularly providers of financial support. Not-for-profits have a number of potentially conflicting objectives, some of which are financial (i.e. quantitative and easily measurable) but are not the most essential in terms of the mission, likely to be qualitative and less measurable. Therefore, the efficient use of resources becomes an important objective. These points will now be examined in greater depth.

Although governments have attempted to construct acceptable and effective measures of performance (e.g. **break-even** and return on capital employed), for large public sector and non-profit *nationalized industries* with essentially monopoly markets there has always been an inbuilt objectives conflict between social needs (many of them provided essential services) and a requirement that the very substantial resources involved were managed commercially in order to avoid waste. The Conservative government of the 1980s followed a policy of privatizing certain nationalized industries partly on the grounds that in some cases more competition will be stimulating and create greater efficiency.

The UK's National Health Service's (NHS) purpose relates to the health and well-being of the nation, and attention can be focused on both prevention and cure. Resources improve treatments and open up new opportunities for prevention; and these in turn stimulate demand, particularly where they concern illnesses or diseases which historically have not been easily treated. However, these developments are often very expensive, and decisions have then to be made about where funds should be allocated, and these relate to priorities and, therefore, some employees in the NHS feel as if they are working for an organization whose purpose is to ration scarce resources given by the State.

Customers are concerned with such things as the waiting time for admission to hospital and for operations, the quality of care as affected by staff attitudes and numbers, and arguably privacy in small wards, cleanliness and food. Doctors generally are concerned with the quantity of resources and their ability to cope with demand; some consultants are anxious to work at the leading edge of their specialism; while administrators must ensure that resources are used efficiently.

The government, as the major funder of the NHS, is a key influencer and is very concerned with the political fallout from perceived weaknesses in the service, which inevitably affect its priorities. Pfeffer (1981) has argued that the relative power of influencers is related to the funds that they provide. The less funding that is provided by customers, the weaker is their influence over decisions. Hence, a not-for-profit organization such as the NHS may be less customer orientated than a private competitive firm. Some would argue that the private medical sector is more marketing conscious. Without question, and in simple terms, the NHS is about patient care within imposed budgetary constraints, but patients may perceive that it feels like a service driven by a culture of care or by a culture of resource-management efficiency.

Whilst organizations may focus on the aspects that are most easily measured (e.g. the number of hospital admissions, the utilization of beds and theatres, the cost of laundry and food, etc.), these measures of the *efficient use of resources* may be perceived as the most important objectives, whereas who is being treated relative to the real needs of the community, i.e. the *effectiveness of the organization*, should be paramount. Profit may not be an important consideration, but costs are, and there may be a resultant conflict between medical and administrative staff, leading to disagreement and confusion over what are the key objectives. Hence, objectives that are perceived to be important and are pursued at any time are dependent on the relative power of the *influencers* and their ability to exercise power, for example where not-for-profit organizations have advisory bodies, or boards of trustees.

Tourist attractions such as London Zoo (Case 3.4) and leading museums have a potential conflict of objectives concerning their inevitable educational and scientific orientations and the requirement that they address commercial issues. Museums can earn money from shops and cafeterias and they receive some private funding, but to a great extent they are reliant on government grants. A controversial issue in the UK in the 1980s was the introduction of museum admission charges (following a reduction in government subsidies), leading to reduced admissions but these began to increase again in subsequent years as people became more accustomed to charging. Although admission to the main halls of national museums is now generally free once again, visitors pay for the special exhibitions, which is what attracts many of them in the

Case 3.4   London Zoo

UK

London Zoo, in Regent's Park, is one of two zoological gardens which are controlled and administered by the Zoological Society of London (ZSL). The other is Whipsnade Park, in Bedfordshire, and this covers 600 acres compared with just 36 acres in London. London Zoo, opened in 1828, is the world's oldest scientific zoo; Whipsnade opened in 1931.

The Society's original charter laid down its primary purpose as 'the advancement of zoology and animal physiology, and the introduction of new and curious subjects of the animal kingdom', but this has been modified in the current mission. ZSL now exists to 'promote and achieve the worldwide conservation of animals and their habitats'. Its vision is 'a world where animals are valued and their conservation assured'. These are pursued by:

- keeping and presenting animals at the two zoos
- prioritizing threatened species
- helping people become more aware of animal welfare and conservation issues
- maintaining an education programme
- undertaking both conservation work and serious zoological research
- publishing activities.

However, ZSL has to generate an income from visitors to supplement its other sources of revenue. Therefore from the mission must stem a fundamental dilemma: how much is a zoo a place of entertainment and relaxation, with customers paramount, and how much is it an organization with primarily educational and scientific purposes? One commercial constraint for London Zoo is the fact that Regent's Park is a Royal Park, and that bylaws restrict certain activities such as on-site advertising.

There are basically five main activities: London Zoo, Whipsnade Park, The Institute of Zoology (conferencing and publishing), conservation programmes and the world-renowned library.

At times in the past the zoo has received a series of annual grants from the Department of the Environment, and in 1988, for example, it was given £10 million as a designated one-off payment 'to put it on a firm financial footing'. It remains 'the only national collection in the world not publically funded on a regular basis'.

Income is essentially from visitors, the majority of whom live within comfortable travelling distance of London, through membership and admission fees and merchandising, but there are some research grants.

Many of the visitors are on organized school trips, and weather conditions are very important in attracting or deterring people.

Many visitors are attracted by big animals, as evidenced by the commercial success of safari parks, but these are costly and dangerous, and well researched and relatively safe as far as endangered species go. Quite often the most endangered species are relatively unattractive to visitors. Whipsnade is regarded as more ideal for big animals. London Zoo for many years has had no hippos (since the 1960s – although there are pygmy hippos in the collection) – and no bears (since 1986), but more recently some large animals have been brought back to counter visitor criticism. There are, for example, giraffes, lions, tigers and leopards. However, in 2001, and following an incident with a visitor, London Zoo's elephants were moved to Whipsnade. Visitors can drive around Whipsnade, parking in various places en route, but it is not a safari park. There are some 750 species at London Zoo, of which over 100 can be classified as 'threatened'. There are breeding programmes for 130 species.

Critics have sometimes argued that London Zoo's management has failed to fully exploit the zoo's conservation work by featuring it in informative displays and that much of the zoo's important and scientifically renowned research is not recognized by the general public. This may be correct, but the fact remains that much of the important conservation work involves species which are relatively uninteresting for many public visitors, for example the rare Rodriguez fruit bat.

The Department of the Environment paid for a report by independent consultants (1987–8) and concluded that 'management at London Zoo did not reflect the commercial emphasis which was essential for survival and prosperity without a permanent subsidy'. They recommended the establishment of a new company to manage London and Whipsnade Zoos, separate from the scientific research of the Zoological Society. This company was established in October 1988, with the aim of reversing the falling trend in admissions and returning the zoo to profit in 3 years.

The numbers of visitors did increase in 1989 and 1990, but below the level required to break even. In April 1991 newspapers first reported that London Zoo might have to close, with some animals destroyed and others moved to Whipsnade. The government refused further financial assistance, not wholly convinced of the need for urban zoos. Cost reduction *per se* was ruled out as this was likely to provoke a new fall in admissions. Instead, rescue plans concentrated on a smaller zoo with a new concept: natural habitats such as an African rainforest complete with gorillas, and a Chinese mountain featuring the pandas. There would be less emphasis on caged animals. These developments have taken place but there have still been criticisms from some groups that the space for gorillas is inadequate when compared with the facilities they enjoy in some other zoos. The reality is, of course, that only so much can be done in 36 acres whilst still retaining a collection that is attractive to visitors.

Although changes were made, attendances continued to fall. The zoo's closure was announced formally in June 1992. New external funding provided a reprieve.

Since 1992 the zoo has secured its survival by emphasizing its role as a conservation centre, breeding endangered species and returning them to the wild. During the 1990s ZSL managed to break even by using publicity more effectively to attract some one million visitors a year.

More recently the zoo has stopped providing pony rides for children, declaring that this is not an appropriate form of entertainment. The Mappin Café was renovated in 2002. There is an ongoing renovation project in London to replace cages with enclosures which recreate the animals' natural environments, thus providing a better lifestyle for the animals and a more realistic visitor experience. In 2005 two walkthroughs for African birds and monkeys were opened, followed by a new Gorilla Kingdom and Rainforest Lookout in 2007. In 2008 the Bird House was reopened as a tropical rainforest. 2009 brought the 'Giants of the Galapagos' exhibit to house giant tortoises. The new 'Penguin Beach' that opened in 2011 is the largest penguin pool in England and it is used to inform visitors about ZSL's conservation work in Antarctica. When the Tiger SOS appeal was launched in February 2011 to help protect and conserve Sumatran tigers it was the zoo's largest ever fundraising campaign.

Whilst some changes in the last 20 years have been forced on the zoo by external pressures, others have been voluntary. In the end London Zoo has to find a business model that attracts sufficient visitors and revenue in the face of competition from a wide range of other tourist attractions. New rhino and cheetah exhibits were opened at Whipsnade in 2008.

In 2002–3 ZSL had incoming resources of £34 million – of this £13.1 million came from members' subscriptions and admission charges; £4.2 million from merchandising and catering and £3.7 million from grants. These grants did not amount to public subsidies; half of the total was HEFCE (Higher Education Funding Council) research funding chanelled through the University of Cambridge. Most of the other half came from individual grants related to specific projects. Profit after tax was £1.4 million. In this year there were 815 000 paying visitors at London Zoo, with a further 445 000 at Whipsnade.

Five years later, in 2007 the corresponding figures were as follows. London Zoo attracted 1.1 million visitors and Whipsnade 475 000. The increase in numbers during the year was the highest for 15 years. ZSL had incoming resources of £40.1 million and it spent 36.6 million, yielding a surplus of £3.5 million. There had been some grants for specific projects and a capital spend of nearly £8 million.

By 2011–12 the incoming resources had grown to £45.8 million. Subscriptions and admissions contributed £21.7 million; merchandising and catering £10.0 million; and grants £5.8 million. The after-tax surplus was £4.2 million. Visitor numbers in London were much the same as 2007, but those at Whipsnade had grown further to 503 000. The finances had been helped by a 'healthy increase' in voluntary income and donations. Over the years the more visible collection has helped with both visitor numbers and donations.

Questions

1 What should the objectives of London Zoo be?
2 Who are the major stakeholders, and how important are they?
3 If you were in charge (and remembering the constraints) what strategies would you recommend?

London Zoo **http://www.londonzoo.co.uk**

SOURCE: THIS CASE STUDY WAS PREPARED USING PRIMARILY PUBLICLY AVAILABLE SOURCES OF INFORMATION FOR THE PURPOSES OF CLASSROOM DISCUSSION; IT DOES NOT INTEND TO ILLUSTRATE EITHER EFFECTIVE OR INEFFECTIVE HANDLING OF A MANAGERIAL SITUATION.

first place! Whilst with either admission charges or larger grants, the museums could employ more curators and provide more frequent exhibits, a balance has to be found between the level of service and the number of visitors.

Cathedrals face a similar dilemma with the costs of repairs and maintenance forcing some to charge visitors fixed amounts rather than to rely on voluntary donations and, although their mission is concerned with religion (if not the gospel) and charity, they are not immune from commercial realities.

Charities frequently have sets of interdependent commercial and non-commercial objectives. Oxfam's mission concerns the provision of relief and the provision of aid where it is most needed throughout the world, as well as additionally teaching people to be self-sufficient through irrigation, better farming techniques, etc. and publicizing the plight of the needy. Their ability to pursue these objectives is constrained by resource availability and they have fund-raising objectives, and strategies (including retailing through Oxfam shops) to achieve them, and it is not clear which is most prioritized given their interdependence.

While the coverage of not-for-profit organizations in this section has been partial, as many other organizations such as schools and universities are fundamentally non-profits, the points are representative of the sector.

Quantitative performance indicators are relatively easily carried out and measurable, with the efficient use of resources replacing profit as the commercial objective which, though perhaps not an essential aspect of the mission, will be seen as important by certain stakeholders. Attention has shifted from evaluating outputs and outcomes (the real objectives) to measuring inputs (resources) because it is easier to do, and major sponsors, such as government, will insist upon cost-effectiveness. Many non-profits are managed by people trained and naturally orientated towards arts or science, leading to feelings of conflict with regard to objectives. Hence, the organization will pursue certain objectives for a period of time, satisfying the most influential stakeholders in the coalition, and then change as the preferences of stakeholders, or their relative power and influence, change.

While profit-seeking and not-for-profit organizations have essentially different missions, the issue of profit-making is complex, with some relying on subsidies enabling low prices. Customer service has been seen to be important in nationalized industries, with prices controlled or at least influenced by the government, and an independent regulator appointed when nationalized businesses have been privatized. However, unless the providers of grants and subsidies are willing to bear commercial trading losses and at the same time finance any necessary investment, there is a necessity for the organizations to generate revenue at least equal to the costs incurred. Where investment finance also needs to be generated, a surplus of income over expenditure is important. This basically is profit. While profit may not, therefore, be an essential part of the mission, it is still required.

> *The objectives pursued by organizations frequently differ from those proclaimed. Some years ago I assumed that the principal objective of universities was the education of students. Armed with this assumption I could make no sense of their behaviour. I learned that education, like profit, is a requirement not an objective and that the principal objective is to provide their faculties with the quality of work life and the standard of living they desire. That's why professors do so little teaching, give the same courses over and over again, arrange classes at their convenience, not that of their students, teach subjects they want to teach rather than students want to learn and skip classes to give lectures [elsewhere] for a fee.*
>
> RUSSELL ACKOFF, 1986

Hopefully, Ackoff would not be able to make quite the same arguments today!

3.4 The impact of personal objectives

Organizations, due to their size and complexity, set or change several objectives – due to (i) decisions by the strategic leader, (ii) influence from managers and/or (iii) influence or constraints from external stakeholders – with varying degrees of relative importance. With *emergent strategy* the decisions made by managers determine the actual strategies pursued, and revised, implicit, objectives come to replace those that were previously declared as intended objectives. The culture of the organization, the relative power bases of managers, communication systems, and the rigidity of policies and procedures (or more informal management processes allowing managers considerable freedom) are key determinants. While Key Terms 3.1, defines policies and discusses their role in strategy implementation, this topic is exemplified by a multiple store that sells DVDs as one of its products and a nearby smaller independent competitor appealing to different customers. If the small store closed down, there could be new opportunities for the manager of the multiple store if they changed their competitive strategy for DVDs by changing their displays, improved their stock levels and supported these moves with window displays promoting the changes. Head office merchandizing policies concerning stocks and displays may or may not allow them this freedom.

In the case of *intended strategy*, the strategic leader – influenced by his or her style and values and the culture of the organization – determines and states the objectives, strategies and proposed changes for the organization; may be influenced to some extent by external stakeholders and internal managers consulted; and to ensure their implementation (and achievement of objectives) will design and build an organization structure, either restricting or empowering managers; and will determine policies which may be mandatory or advisory.

Key Terms 3.1   Policies

You must provide a framework in which people can act. For example, we have said that our first priority is safety, second is punctuality and third is other services. So if you risk flight safety by leaving on time, you have acted outside the framework of your authority. The same is true if you don't leave on time because you are missing two catering boxes of meat. That's what I mean by a framework. You give people a framework, and within the framework you let people act.

JAN CARLZON, WHEN PRESIDENT AND CHIEF EXECUTIVE OFFICER, SAS (SCANDINAVIAN AIRLINES SYSTEM)

- *Policies* are guidelines relating to decisions and approaches which support organizational efforts to achieve stated and intended objectives.
- They are basically *guides to thoughts* (about how things might or should be done) and *actions*.
- They are, therefore, *guides to decision-making*. For example, a policy which states that for supplies of a particular item three quotations should be sought and the cheapest selected, or a policy not to advertise in certain newspapers, or a policy not to trade with particular countries all influence decisions. Policies are particularly useful for routine repetitive decisions.
- Policies can be at corporate, divisional (or strategic business unit [SBU]) or functional level, and they are normally stated in terms of management (of people),

marketing, production, finance and research and development.

- If stated objectives are to be achieved, and the strategies designed to accomplish this implemented, the appropriate policies must be there in support. In other words, the behaviour of managers and the decisions that they make should be supportive of what the organization is seeking to achieve. Policies guide and constrain their actions.
- Policies can be mandatory (rules which allow little freedom for original thought or action) or advisory. The more rigid they are, the less freedom managers have to change things with delegated authority, and this can be good or bad depending on change pressures from the environment.
- *It is vital to balance consistency and coordination* (between the various divisions, SBUs and departments in the organization) *with flexibility.*
- Policies need not be written down. They can be passed on verbally as part of the culture.
- Policies *must* be widely understood if they are to be useful.

Footnote

For governments, *policies* has a slightly different meaning. Government policy relates to what government 'intends to do' regarding specific issues and priorities.

Although the types of policy and the authority and freedom delegated to managers guide, influence and constrain decision-making, the motives, values and relative power of individual managers, the relative importance of particular functions, divisions or strategic business units in the organization and the system of communications are also influential. The stated or *official objectives* may or may not be achieved; there may be appropriate incremental decisions which reflect changes in the environment; or managers may be pursuing personal objectives, which Perrow (1961) has termed *operative goals* when the behaviour taking place cannot be accounted for by official company objectives and policies. The aggregation of these various decisions determines the emergent strategic changes, the actual objectives followed and the results achieved.

Operative goals may complement or conflict with official goals; for example, *complement* them if a stated objective in terms of a target return on capital employed was achieved through operative goals of managers and decisions taken by them regarding delivery times, quality and so on; or *conflict* if a sales manager was favouring particular customers with discounts or priority deliveries on low-profit orders, or a production manager was setting unnecessarily high quality standards (as far as customers are concerned) which resulted in substantial rejections and high operating costs, profits would be threatened. In such cases, operative goals would conflict with official goals.

3.5 Social responsibility and business ethics

Having looked at some of the theories which are relevant for a study of objectives, and examine typical objectives that organizations pursue and why, it is appropriate to conclude this chapter with a consideration of wider societal aspects. Realistically, this topic is a book in itself (e.g. Griseri and Seppala, 2010) but we feel a relatively short section is important to stress its significance.

Objectives that relate to **social responsibility** may be affected by stakeholders; in some cases they result from legislation, but often they are voluntary actions. The issue is one of how responsible a firm might choose to be, and why – simply, firms can be socially responsible (proactive) or socially responsive (reactive to pressure). Again, the particular values of the strategic leader will be very influential. There is, though, often an interesting 'Catch-22' at work. Starbucks promotes itself as a socially responsible business, citing its dealings with coffee growers and pickers in developing countries. That it makes a serious effort is not in doubt. And yet Starbucks gets singled out by environmental and other campaigners – because they believe that a company which promotes itself as responsible is a softer target and more easily influenced than one that is either hostile or ambivalent. In addition, one might question the social message being conveyed when a company seeks to minimize (some would say avoid) the tax it pays in certain countries, as has been the case in the UK, though it has agreed to make 'symbolic' tax payments due to political and media bullying.

There are numerous ways in which a firm can behave responsibly in the interests of society, and examples are given below. It should not be thought, however, that social responsibility is a one-way process; organizations can benefit considerably from it. Social responsibility and profitability can be improved simultaneously (The Performance Group, 1999).

- Product safety: this can be the result of design or production and includes aspects of supply and supplier selection to obtain safe materials or components. Product safety will be influenced to an extent by legislation, but an organization can build in more safety features than the law requires. Some cars are an example of this, such as Volvo which is promoted and perceived as a relatively safe car. Product safety will have cost implications. Sometimes the safety is reflected in perceived higher quality, which adds value that the customer is willing to pay a premium for, but at other times it will be the result of the organization choice to sacrifice some potential profit.

- Working conditions: linked to the previous point, these can include safety at work, which again is affected by legislation which sets minimum standards. Aspects of job design to improve working conditions and training to improve employees' prospects are further examples.

- Honesty, including not offering or accepting bribes.
- Avoiding pollution.
- Avoiding discrimination.

The above points are all subject to some legislation.

- Community action: this is a very broad category with numerous opportunities, ranging from charitable activities to concerted action to promote industry and jobs in areas which have suffered from economic recession. Many large organizations release executives on a temporary basis to help with specific community projects.

- Industry location: organizations may locate new plants in areas of high unemployment for a variety of reasons. While aspects of social responsibility may be involved, the decision may well be more economic. Grants and rate concessions may be important.

- Other environmental concerns: these include recycling, waste disposal, protecting the ozone layer and energy efficiency. Porter (1995) contends that many companies mistakenly see environmental legislation as a threat, something to be resisted. Instead, he argues, they should see regulation as an indication the company is not using its resources efficiently. Toxic materials and discarded packaging are waste. The costs incurred in eliminating a number of environmental problems can be more than offset by other savings and improvements in product quality. Companies should be innovative and not reluctantly just complying with their legal requirements. However, the European chemical industry has argued that bulk chemical manufacture has been largely driven out of EU countries by the costs of complying with environmental regulation. Standards in many Far Eastern countries are less restrictive.

- Attitude of food retailers: for example, accurate labelling (country of origin), free-range eggs, organic vegetables, biodegradable packaging, CFC-free aerosols and products containing certain dubious E-number additives. It is a moot point whether retailers or consumers should decide on these issues.

Objectives of this nature become part of the organization culture. Social responsibility is at the heart of activities and objectives because it is felt that the organization has an obligation both to the community and to society in general. However, it must not be assumed that the approach receives universal support. Milton Friedman (1979), the economist, argues that, 'the business of business is business ... the organization's only social responsibility is to increase its profit'. Friedman also comments that donations to charity and sponsorship of the arts are 'fundamentally subversive' and not in the best interests of the shareholders. Social responsibility would then be the result of legislation. Drucker (1974) argues businesses have a role in society which is 'to supply goods and services to customers and an economic surplus to society ... rather than to supply jobs to workers and managers, or even dividends to shareholders'. The latter, he argues, are means not ends. Drucker contends that it is mismanagement to forget that a hospital exists for its patients and a university for its students.

The topic is complex, and although the outcome of certain decisions can be seen to be bringing benefit to the community or employees the decision may have been influenced by legislation or perceived organizational benefit (enlightened self-interest) rather than a social conscience. One could argue that the organization will benefit if it looks after its employees; equally, one could argue that it will suffer if it fails to consider employee welfare. The two approaches are philosophically different, but they may generate similar results. Some organizations feature their community role extensively in corporate advertising campaigns designed to bring them recognition and develop a caring, responsible image.

Business ethics

Disasters such as the explosion at the chemical plant in Bhopal, India, in 1984 have long raised the question of how far companies should go in pursuit of profits. More recent cases, such as Tyco and Enron, have raised different but related issues of ethical behaviour. The CEO of Tyco has been prosecuted for using corporate funds to provide a lavish personal lifestyle – at the same time as sponsoring a number of creative accounting practices to hide the company's true financial performance. Enron lost huge sums of shareholder money as it developed future trading for energy including trying to hold the state of California to ransom for power supplied through Enron.

Ethics is defined as 'the discipline dealing with what is good and bad and right and wrong or with moral duty and obligation' (*Webster's Third New International Dictionary*). Houlden (1988) suggests that **business ethics** encompasses the views of people throughout society concerning the morality of business, and not just the views of the particular business and the people who work in it.

Issues such as golden handshakes, pensions, insider dealing and very substantial salary increases for company chairpeople and chief executives are topical and controversial. But is it ethical for large companies to pursue high-risk strategies which might leave several small company suppliers financially exposed? Again, when some large (and smaller) companies come to grief (often through ill-advised or ill-judged strategic choices) many employees may find their pension funds have disappeared. Is this also an ethical issue?

The high-profile (at the time) case of British Airways and Virgin Atlantic, where BA was accused of using privileged information to evaluate Virgin's route profitability and to persuade Virgin customers to switch airlines, suggested that BA acted unethically. Much more recently, BA and Virgin colluded (illegally) to fix fuel surcharges when oil prices rose. Virgin decided after the event to confess to its role and was thus exempted from prosecution when the issue was investigated. BA was fined and a number of senior executives individually charged for a criminal act. If they had ended up in prison, would Virgin's role have been seen as ethical or unethical? In contrast, Hewlett-Packard, the US electronics multinational, which has often been cited as being highly ethical, has not always been. In September 2006 Newsweek published a story revealing that the chairwoman of HP, Patricia Dunn, had hired a team of independent electronic-security experts who had spied on HP board members and several journalists to determine the source of a leak of confidential details regarding HP's long-term strategy that had been published as part of a CNET article in January 2006. HP operates an internal ban on the use of improper means for obtaining competitor information. The company also insists that any statements about its competitors must be fair, factual and complete.

Public attention is drawn to these issues, and people's perceptions of businesses generally and individually are affected. However, their responses differ markedly. Some people feel disgruntled but do nothing, whereas others take more positive actions. Managers, however, should not ignore the potential for resistance or opposition by their customers, who may refuse to buy their products or use their services.

Another ethical concern is individual managers or employees who adopt practices which senior managers or the strategic leader would consider unethical. These need to be identified and stopped. If they remain unchecked they are likely to spread, with the argument that 'everyone does it'. Sales staff using questionable methods of persuasion, even lying, would be an example. However, it does not follow that such practices would always be seen as unethical by senior managers – in some organizations they will be at least condoned, and possibly even encouraged.

In the UK the Co-operative Bank is one organization that decided to use an ethical stance to create a competitive advantage – and it thus provides an interesting contrast to some of the other comments we have made on UK banks and their role in the **credit crunch**.

Ethical dilemmas

One classic ethical dilemma concerns the employee who works for a competitor, is interviewed for a job and who promises to bring confidential information if he is offered the post. Should the proposition be accepted or not? The issue, featured at the beginning of this section, is how far companies should go in pursuit of profits. In such a case as this, long-term considerations are important as well as potential short-term benefits. If the competitor who loses the confidential information realizes what has happened, it may seek to retaliate in some way. Arguably, the best interests of the industry as a whole should be considered.

Another example is the company with a plant that is surplus to requirements and which it would like to sell. The company knows the land beneath the plant contains radioactive waste. Legally, it need not disclose this fact to prospective buyers, but is it ethical to keep quiet? Research commissioned by the Joseph Rowntree Foundation (see Taylor, 1997) concluded that house-builders and estate agents generally do not warn buyers when new homes are built on previously contaminated industrial land. The three further examples below are developed from Badaracco (1997).

A well-established European pharmaceutical company (X), in a country with a moderate but not large Catholic community, has developed and patented a new contraceptive drug, which has demonstrable health-care benefits. For a variety of reasons, largely economic (health-care savings, benefit reductions and corporation tax revenues), its government is encouraging it to launch the drug in the home country and around the world at the earliest opportunity. Profits to the company would be good, but they would not have a dramatic impact on the company's overall profits. They would, however, ensure the future viability of a small production plant in an area of high unemployment. However, a sizeable block of the company's shares (but not a controlling interest) has recently been acquired by a foreign mini-conglomerate whose chief executive is a Catholic and opposed to the drug on religious grounds. As X's managing director, you also know from your personal experience that if you launch the drug in America, one of your key export markets, you can expect protests from demonstrators. What should you do?

A business manager for a well-known high street bank is told by her manager that her function is shortly to be moved to a new regional centre some 25 miles away and that her own position is secure. She is personally delighted as her travel-to-work commute will be reduced, but she knows that there will be redundancies. Under instruction that for the moment the news is embargoed from other staff, she is concerned when her personal assistant approaches her a few days later. She has heard unsubstantiated rumours on the bank's grapevine and she would, for family reasons, be unable to move. She wants to know what she should do as she is about to pay a deposit on a new house. What should the business manager do? What is 'right by her employer' and what is 'right by her subordinate'?

A young consultant with a relatively new and small but fast-growing management consultancy is invited out of the blue to be joint presenter (with the senior partner) of a bid to a potentially very large client. He is surprised; he has had no involvement in preparing the bid. Moreover, it is not in his area of expertise. Flattered with the wonderful opportunity, but at the same time concerned, he discusses the request with his mentor in the consultancy. He is informed that the contact person in the client organization is, like him, from an ethnic minority background. The senior partner felt that the client would like to see that the consultancy's only non-white consultant was a key member of the team. How should he react?

Badaracco and Webb (1995) also highlight how internal decisions can be influenced by unethical practices. They quote instances of invented market-research findings, and altered investment returns which imply, erroneously, that the organization is meeting its published targets. They distinguish between 'expedient actions' and 'right actions'.

In contrast, a serious dilemma faces individuals in an organization who feel that their managers are pursuing unethical practices. There are several examples of individuals who have acted and suffered as a result of their actions. An accountant with an insurance company exposed a case of tax evasion by his bosses and jeopardized his career. Stanley Adams, an employee of Hoffman la Roche, the Swiss drug company, believed that his firm was making excessive profits and divulged commercially sensitive information to the European Commission. He also lost his career and suffered financially. There are similar examples of engineers who felt that design compromises were threatening consumer safety, complained, and lost their jobs. When the UK government started to probe in greater detail the banking crisis, it emerged that one ex-employee of HBOS, Paul Moore, a senior Risk Manager, was claiming to have warned the bank's CEO, Sir James Crosby, that the level of exposure was dangerous. He was sacked, he claims, for this intervention. Crosby himself left but became a government adviser and later Deputy Director of the FSA (Financial Services Authority). Protesting that he had done nothing wrong, but wished to clear his name, Crosby then resigned from the FSA in February 2009. He later relinquished his knighthood.

Many of the ethical issues that affect strategic decisions are regulated directly by legislation. Equally, many companies do not operate in sensitive environments where serious ethical issues require thought and attention. However, some companies and their strategic leaders do need a clear policy regarding business ethics. Often they have to decide whether to increase costs in the short run, say to improve safety factors, on the assumption that this will bring longer-term benefits. Short-term profitability, important to shareholders, could be affected. Increased safety beyond minimum legal requirements, for example, would increase the construction costs of a new chemical plant. If safety were compromised to save money, nothing might actually go wrong and profits would be higher. However, an explosion or other disaster results in loss of life, personal injury, compensation and legal costs, lost production, adverse publicity and tension between the business and local community. The long-term losses can be substantial. Reidenbach and Robin (1995) have produced a spectrum of five ethical/unethical responses.

- *Amoral companies* seek to 'win at all costs'; anything is seen as acceptable. The secret lies in not being found out.

- *Legalistic companies* obey the law and no more. There is no code of ethics; companies act only when it is essential.

- *Responsive companies* accept that being ethical can pay off.

- *Ethically engaged companies* actively want to 'do the right thing' and to be seen to be doing so. Ethical codes will exist, but ethical behaviour will not necessarily be a planned activity and fully integrated into the culture.

- *Ethical companies* such as Body Shop have ethics as a core value, supported by appropriate strategies and actions which permeate the whole organization.

Because ethical standards and beliefs are aspects of the corporate culture, they are influenced markedly by the lead set by the strategic leader and his or her awareness of behaviour throughout the organization. If a proper lead is not provided, managers will be left to 'second guess' what would be seen as appropriate behaviour. Power, then, can be used ethically or unethically by individual managers.

Frederick (1988) contends that the corporate culture is the main source of any ethical problems. He argues that managers are encouraged to focus their professional energies on productivity, efficiency and leadership, and that their corporate values lead them to act in ways which place the company interests ahead of those of consumers or society.

Business ethics is arguably important and worthy of serious attention. However, a consideration of ethical issues in strategic decisions typically requires that a long-term perspective is adopted. Objectives and strategies should be realistic and achievable rather than overambitious and very difficult to attain. In the latter case, individual managers may be set high targets which encourage them to behave unethically, possibly making them feel uneasy. Results may be massaged, for instance, or deliberately presented with inaccuracies. Such practices spread quickly and dishonesty becomes acceptable. The longer-term perspective can reduce the need for immediate results and targets which managers feel have to be met at all costs. However, pressure from certain stakeholders, particularly institutional shareholders, may focus attention on the short term and on results which surpass those of the previous year. The longer-term perspective additionally allows for concern with processes and behaviour, and with how the results are obtained. The drive for results is not allowed to override ethical and behavioural concerns.

Houlden (1988) concludes that strategic leaders should be objective about how society views their company and its products, and wherever possible should avoid actions that can damage its image. If an action or decision that certain stakeholders might view as unethical is unavoidable, such as the closure of a plant, it is important to use public relations to explain fully why the decision has been taken. The need for a good corporate image should not be underestimated.

Other chapters (particularly Chapter 6) include discussions on how organizations might achieve competitive advantage. Ethical considerations can make a significant contribution to this. A commitment to keeping promises about quality standards and delivery times, or not making promises which cannot be met, would be one example. If employees are honest and committed, and rewarded appropriately for this, then costs are likely to be contained and the overall level of customer service high, thereby improving profits.

Research Snapshot 3.1

There has been a large body of recent literature relating to strategic purpose, building on the earlier studies. In particular, vision and mission have been widely researched. Quite a lot of literature has also been published building upon Freeman's (1984) seminal stakeholder theory and these are also related to objectives and the other elements of strategic purpose. Furthermore, recent research has also examined what is a growing area of interest: ethics, corporate responsibility and values. Inevitably, these three elements, *strategic purpose* (objectives, vision and mission), **values** (ethics and social responsibility) and **stakeholders** are inextricably intertwined and, indeed, a number of articles have made linkages between them, including in *SMEs* and social enterprises.

Examples of vision include IKEA and its 'revolutionary' vision and use of 'experimentation and adaptation to market circumstances rather than through preplanned strategy formulation', or so-called logical incrementalism which involves refinement, ongoing experimentation with potential errors, conversion of 'problems into opportunities' and also learning from 'other people's ideas' (Barthelemy, 2006). Reflection and models can be used to construct vision (Mumford and Strange, 2002). The relationship between vision and goals, on the one hand, and firm performance on the other has been examined, in relation to behaviour (e.g. Kantabutra, 2009), as well as upon the level of innovation within an organization (Bart, 2004). A number of papers include those which prescribe how a vision can be written and communicated, for example, as a 'corporate story', and executed (Marzec, 2007).

While organizational vision and particularly its link with firm performance has been widely researched recently, there would seem to be considerably less literature on mission statements: even the extensive research in the last two decades has only established a tenuous link, and it is difficult to establish whether mission statements directly influence performance, i.e. causality is not clear (Desmidt *et al.*, 2001). Building on Freeman's (1984) stakeholder theory, literature has focused upon definitions, firm/stakeholder behaviour, performance and theory (Laplume *et al.*, 2008), the link with corporate social responsibility (Munilla and Miles, 2005) and more recently defended, and clarified, by its originator (e.g. Freeman, 2011). In summary, there is continuing interest in strategic purpose, values and stakeholders.

The articles below provide deeper understanding of strategic purpose, stakeholder theory and their relationship with values, ethics and corporate responsibility (though see Chapter 7 for further references on culture and values). The further reading from this literature will help students to develop their perception and critical awareness of the utility and value of mission and vision, and also to highlight the developing thinking in relation to stakeholder theory and wider ethical considerations.

Further Reading

Bart, C. (2004) 'Innovation, mission statements and learning', *International Journal of Technology Management*, Vol. 27, No. 6-7, pp. 544–561.

Barthelemy, J. (2006) 'The Experimental Roots of Revolutionary Vision', *MIT Sloan Management Review*, Vol. 48, No. 1, pp. 81–84.

Desmidt, S., Prinzie, S. and Decramer, A. (2011) 'Looking for the value of mission statements: a meta-analysis of 20 years of research', *Management Decision*, Vol. 49, No. 3, pp. 468–483.

Freeman, R.E. (2011) 'Some thoughts on the development of stakeholder theory' In R. Phillips Ed, *Stakeholder Theory: Impact and Prospects*, Edward Elgar: Cheltenham, pp. 212–234.

Kantabutra, S. (2009) 'Toward a behavioral theory of vision in organizational settings', *Leadership & Organization Development Journal*, Vol. 30, No. 4, pp. 319–337.

Laplume, A.O., Sonpar, K. and Litz, R.A. (2008) 'Stakeholder Theory: Reviewing a Theory That Moves Us', *Journal of Management*, Vol. 34, No. 6, pp. 1152–1189.

Marzec, M. (2007) 'Telling the corporate story: vision into action', *Journal of Business Strategy*, Vol. 28, No. 1, pp. 26–33.

Mumford, M. D. and Strange, J. M. (2002). Vision and mental models: The case of charismatic and ideological leadership. In B. J. Avolio and F. J. Yammarino (Eds.), *Transformational and charismatic leadership: The road ahead* (pp. 109–142). Oxford, England: Elsevier.

Munilla, L.S. and Miles, M.P. (2005) 'The Corporate Social Responsibility Continuum as a Component of Stakeholder Theory', *Business and Society Review*, Vol. 110, pp. 371–387.

Summary

The corporate *mission* represents the overriding purpose for the business, and ideally it should explain why the organization is different and set it apart from its main rivals. It should not be a statement that other organizations can readily adopt. Its main purpose is communication.

It is useful to separate the mission statement from a statement of corporate vision which concerns 'what the organization is to become'. Both can provide a valuable starting point for more specific *objectives* and strategies. Shorter-term objectives will normally have timescales or end-dates attached to them and ideally they will be 'owned' by individual managers.

It is, therefore, feasible to argue that organizations (as a whole) have a purpose and individual managers have objectives. Mission, vision and objectives all relate to the *direction* that the organization is taking – the ends from which strategies are derived.

It is not, however, feasible to assume that the organization will always be free to set these objectives for its managers: there may be constraints from key stakeholders. A number of theories and models, mainly from a study of economics, can help us to understand why organizations do the things they do. In addition, individuals will have *personal*

objectives that they wish (and intend) to pursue, which should not be allowed to work against the best interests of the organization.

External *stakeholders* also have expectations for the organization. These will not always be in accord with each other, and important trade-offs and priorities must be established. There is always the potential for conflicts of interest. As a result, the organization will be seen to have a multitude of objectives, but all contributory to a single purpose.

Profit is necessary for profit-seeking businesses; a positive cash flow is essential for not-for-profit organizations. Profit (or cash) can, however, be seen as either a means or an end, and this will impact upon the 'feel' or culture of the organization.

Regardless, there is a virtuous circle of financial returns, motivated employees and satisfied customers.

Issues of *social responsibility* and *business ethics* are important for all organizations. They will be seen by some organizations as a threat or constraint and encourage a strategy of compliance. Other organizations will perceive them as an opportunity to create a difference and in turn a positive image. They are becoming increasingly visible, issues which organizations should take seriously and not ignore.

Online cases for this chapter

Online Case 3.1: New York's Yellow Cabs
Online Case 3.2: National Theatre
Online Case 3.3: Nike

Online Case 3.4: The Co-operative Bank
Online Case 3.5: BAE Systems

Questions and research assignments

1 Using a case from this chapter, clarify what you think the business model is. How would you define that company's vision and mission?

2 Think of any organization with which you have personal experience. Do you believe that profit (or cash in the case of a non-profit organization)

is seen as a means or an end by the key decision-makers? Do they all agree on this?

3 What key issues do you believe should be incorporated if a company opts to publish a statement on ethics?

Internet and library projects

1 From the Fast Track website, pick a rapidly growing business of your choice from within the top ten businesses listed. In 400 words or less can you identify the business objectives of that business? **http://www.fasttrack.co.uk**

2 When Tottenham Hotspur became the first English Football League club with a stock exchange listing (in 1983), the issue prospectus said: 'The Directors intend to ensure that the Club remains one of the leading football clubs in the country. They will seek to increase the Group's income by improving the return from existing assets and by establishing new sources of revenue in the leisure field.'

   a Research the strategies followed by Tottenham Hotspur plc since 1983. Do you believe that the interests of a plc and a professional football club are compatible or inevitably conflicting?

   b Which other clubs have followed Tottenham? Have they chosen similar or different strategies? How have they performed as businesses?

3 Have the objectives (in particular, the order of priorities) of the Natural History Museum changed since the introduction (and later abandonment) of compulsory admission charges in April 1987?

4 In March 2009 it was announced that Cadbury was 'to become the first mass-market chocolate brand to adopt the Fairtrade certification mark'. How significant was this? Do you see this as reactive to changing consumer views or a very smart proactive move – or both? What has been the impact?

5 In January 2009 an investigation by the BBC found that clothes sold in Primark stores were being made in factories in the UK where workers were being paid less than the official minimum wage – and also working very long hours in poor conditions. How did the company deal with this revelation?

Strategy activity

Ben and Jerry's Ice-Cream

This idiosyncratic business was founded and developed by two partners, both entrepreneurs but, at face value, unlikely businessmen. Ben Cohen was a college dropout who had become a potter. His friend from his schooldays was Jerry Greenfield, a laboratory assistant who had failed to make it into medical school. They had become 'seventies hippies with few real job prospects'. They decided they wanted to do something themselves and 'looked for something they might succeed at'. They 'liked food, so food it was'! They could not afford the machinery for making bagels, their first choice, but ice-cream was affordable. In 1977 they opened an ice-cream parlour in Burlington, Vermont, where there were 'lots of students and no real competition'. They fostered a relaxed, hippy atmosphere and employed a blues pianist. Their ice-cream was different, with large and unusual chunks.

They were instantly successful in their first summer, but sales fell off in the fall and winter when the snow arrived. They realized they would have to find outlets outside Vermont if they were to survive. Ben went on the road. Always dressed casually, he would arrive somewhere around 4.00 am and then sleep in his car until a potential distributor opened. He was able to 'charm the distributors' and the business began to grow. Ben and Jerry's success provoked a response from the dominant market leader, Häagen-Dazs, owned by Pillsbury. Their market share was 70 per cent of the luxury ice-cream market. Häagen-Dazs threatened to withdraw their product from any distributors who also handled Ben and Jerry's. The two partners employed a lawyer and threatened legal action, but their real weapon was a publicity campaign targeted at Pillsbury itself, and its famous 'dough boy' logo. 'What's the Dough Boy afraid of'? they asked. Their gimmicks generated massive publicity and they received an out-of-court settlement. More significantly, the publicity created new demand for luxury ice-cream, and the company began to grow more rapidly than had ever been envisaged. A threat had been turned into a massive opportunity. Soon Ben and Jerry's had a segment market share of 39 per cent, just 4 per cent behind Häagen-Dazs. The company has expanded internationally with mixed success. They have enjoyed only limited success in the UK 'because there was only limited marketing support'.

Perhaps not unexpectedly, given their background, Ben and Jerry have created a values-driven business; some of their ice creams have been linked to causes and interests they support and promote. Rainforest Crunch ice-cream features nuts from Brazil; the key ingredients for Chocolate Fudge Brownie are produced by an inner-city bakery in Yonkers, New York; and they favour Vermont's dairy-farming industry. When the business needed equity capital to support its growth, local Vermont residents were given priority treatment. Ben and Jerry argue they are committed to their employees who 'bring their hearts and souls as well as their bodies and minds to work' but acknowledge that their internal opinion surveys show a degree of dissatisfaction with the amount of profits (7.5 per cent) given away every year to good causes.

The two realists with an unusual but definite ego drive later dropped out of day-to-day management '… the company needed a greater breadth of management than

we had …' and were content to be 'two casual, portly, middle-aged hippies'.

In early Spring 2000 the business was acquired by Unilever, the multinational foods, detergents and cosmetics business. Unilever already owned the UK market leader, Wall's ice-cream. Unilever and Wall's had recently been investigated by the UK competition authorities because of their strategy of insisting that retailers only stock Wall's ice-cream if Unilever provide them with a freezer cabinet on loan.

Questions

1 Do you think the objectives of Ben and Jerry's will have had to change after this acquisition?
2 Do you think it will now feel like 'a different place to work', with different priorities?

Ben and Jerry's **http://www.benjerry.com**

References

Ackoff, R.L. (1986) *Management in Small Doses*, John Wiley.

Badaracco, J.L. (1997) *Defining Moments – When Managers Must Choose Between Right and Wrong*, Harvard Business School Press.

Badaracco, J.L. and Webb, A. (1995) Business ethics: a view from the trenches, *California Management Review*, 37 (2), Winter.

Baumol, W.J. (1959) *Business Behaviour, Value and Growth*, Macmillan.

Campbell, A. (1989) Research findings discussed in Skapinker, M. (1989) Mission accomplished or ignored? *Financial Times*, 11 January.

Constable, J. (1980) The nature of company objectives. Unpublished paper, Cranfield School of Management.

Cyert, R.M. and March, J.G. (1963) *A Behavioural Theory of the Firm*, Prentice-Hall.

Drucker, P.F. (1974) *Management: Tasks, Responsibilities, Practices*, Harper & Row.

Frederick, W.C. (1988) An ethics roundtable: the *culprit is culture*, *Management Review*, August.

Freeman, R.E. (1984) *Strategic Management: A Stakeholder Approach*, Pitman.

Friedman, M. (1979) The social responsibility of business is to increase its profits. *In Business Policy and Strategy* (eds D.J. McCarthy, R.J. Minichiello and J. R. Curran), Irwin.

Galbraith, J.K. (1969) The New *Industrial State*, Penguin.

Gerber, M. (2008) *Awakening the Entrepreneur Within*, Collins.

Griseri, P. and Seppala, N. (2010) *Business Ethics and Corporate Social Responsibility*, first edition, Cengage.

Houlden, B. (1988) The corporate conscience, *Management Today*, August.

Kaplan, R. and Norton, D. (2000) *The Strategy Focused Organization*, Harvard Business School Press.

Marris, R. (1964) *The Economic Theory of Managerial Capitalism*, Macmillan.

Martinson, J. (1998) Ethical equities perform well, *Financial Times*, 21 July.

Newbould, G.D. and Luffman, G.A. (1979) *Successful Business Policies*, Gower.

Penrose, E. (1959) *The Theory of the Growth of the Firm*, Blackwell.

Performance Group, The (1999) *Sustainable Strategies for Value Creation*, Oslo, Norway.

Perrow, C. (1961) The analysis of goals in complex organizations, *American Sociological Review*, 26, December.

Pfeffer, J. (1981) *Power in Organizations*, Pitman.

Porter, M.E. (1995) Interviewed for the Green Management letter, *Euromanagement*, June.

Reidenbach, E. and Robin, D. (1995) Quoted in Drummond, J: Saints and Sinners, *Financial Times*, 23 March.

Richards, M.D. (1978) *Organizational Goal Structures*, West.

Simon, H.A. (1964) On the concept of organizational goal, *Administrative Science Quarterly*, 9 (1).

Taylor, A. (1997) Home buyers unaware of contamination, *Financial Times*, 24 October.

Thompson, A.A. and Strickland, A.J. (1980) *Strategy Formulation and Implementation*, Irwin.

Waterman, R. (1994) *The Frontiers of Excellence: Learning from Companies that Put People First*, Nicholas Brealey Publishing.

Williamson, O.E. (1964) *Economics of Discretionary Behaviour: Managerial Objectives in a Theory of the Firm*, Kershaw.

Part 1

Supplement

A summary of strategy frameworks

This supplement has a different format from the rest of the book. We use it to list and cross-reference a number of frameworks that can all be adopted for carrying out a strategic analysis of an organization. Most of those not already mentioned in Chapters 1 and 2 are to be found in Chapters 4–9. Part 2 (Chapters 4–7) and Part 3 (Chapters 8 and 9) examine *strategic analysis* and *strategic decision-making* respectively.

We feel it is appropriate to present this checklist here, rather than later, to provide an overview before we discuss the various frameworks. It has been written as a reference chapter to help you analyze strategy case studies – specifically longer cases than the ones we include within this text and the sorts of case you are likely to use in class discussion and particularly in examinations. You will soon be in a position to start doing this. Obviously the frameworks will also help you to carry out a strategic audit of any organization for which you are in a position to gather data.

Different people will have personal preferences and favourite techniques and consequently may opt not to use all of the frameworks – especially as there is some clear overlap in a number of instances.

The analysis frameworks from Chapters 1–7 all help us to understand where the organization – or a selected, relevant part of it – is at the moment. The others, those that blend analysis and decision-making, address where it might seek to develop in the future, given the circumstances it faces.

However, the key decisions that an organization faces concern 'what' changes to make and 'how' to implement the chosen strategic decisions. Whilst analytical frameworks can provide valuable insight into these issues, by themselves they cannot provide the answers. Consequently the final section of this chapter outlines three key tests for evaluating the effectiveness of current and proposed strategies – and we look at these in more detail in Chapter 8.

Strategic purpose

1. MOST Analysis (Chapter 3)

Mission – Objectives – Strategies – Tactics
The key 'check' issues are:

- Are M and O explicit, widely appreciated and shared?
- Are M, O and S externally consistent and do they fit environmental and stakeholder needs?
- Are O and S – the important ends and means – internally consistent? Do they make the most effective use of resources and capabilities?
- Do the potential benefits from S and T justify the inherent risks and uncertainties?

Strategy or strategies

2. The Business Model (Chapter 2)

The key questions being addressed in a Business Model are:

- What are the products and services we are concerned with?
- Who are the target customers?

- What is their compelling reason to buy our product?
- How to we deliver it efficiently and effectively?

We might also add:

- When do we need to make changes?

External analysis frameworks

3. PEST or PESTLE Analysis (Chapter 4)

Political – Economic – Social – Technological – Legal – Environmental issues

This framework enables the evaluation of key environmental variables or forces in an attempt to judge their potential future impact upon the organization. Sometimes 'Ethical' is added as a seventh factor.

It also informs the Opportunities and Threats elements of a SWOT Analysis.

4. Five Forces Industry Analysis (Porter, 1980) (Chapter 4)

- The threat of new entrants.
- The threat of substitute products and services.
- The bargaining power of suppliers.
- The bargaining power of buyers.
- Rivalry amongst existing firms in the industry.

Provides an assessment of how attractive – potentially profitable – an industry is.

5. Key Success Factors (Chapter 4)

The things an organization must be able to perform both efficiently and effectively if it is to compete in an industry. The strengths, competencies and capabilities it has to have.

6. Generic Strategies (Porter, 1985) (Chapter 6)

Introduces Cost Leadership and Differentiation as key drivers of competitive advantage. This framework enables an organization to check the logic of its current competitive strategy or begin a search for new competitive opportunities.

7. Stakeholder Analysis (Chapter 3)

Assessing and prioritizing the needs and expectations of both external and internal stakeholders to ensure nothing of consequence is overlooked.

These external frameworks all inform the Opportunities and Threats element of a SWOT Analysis – Framework 13 below.

Internal analysis frameworks

8. Resource Audits (Chapter 5)

A straightforward analysis of the relative strengths and weaknesses of the organization. Typically based on a framework of functions and key activities – marketing, operations, human resources, etc.

9. Distinctive Competencies (Kay, 1993) (Chapters 4 and 5)

A framework for exploring those distinctive competencies that separate strong and successful organizations from their weaker competitors.

- Architecture – internal and external links and processes.
- Strategic assets – factors (such as industry structure) which enable organizations us to enjoy competitive advantage through, say, cost leadership or differentiation.

- Reputation – the value of a distinctive image and brand.
- Innovation – harnessing the change agenda.

10. The Value Chain (Porter, 1985) (Chapter 5)

Provides a framework for evaluating the relative significance of various activities undertaken by an organization – from the perspectives of cost and value added.

11. Activity Mapping (Porter, 1996) (Chapter 5)

A diagrammatic approach to the inter relationships of the organization's activities.

These resource-based frameworks all inform the Strengths and Weaknesses element of a SWOT Analysis.

Frameworks combining internal and external themes

12. Scenarios (Chapter 4)

Conceptual possibilities of possible future events and circumstances, used to add creativity to the opportunities and threats elements of a SWOT. Has the added advantage of helping managers think through how they might react if events unfold in unexpected ways.

13. SWOT Analysis (Chapter 4)

Strengths – Weaknesses – Opportunities – Threats

14. The Culture Grid (Chapter 7)

Analyzes the culture of the organization in a framework of three clusters of criteria: manifestations; people; and power.

Informs the values element of E–V–R Congruence to supplement the SWOT.

15. E–V–R Congruence (Chapter 1)

Adds 'values' to a traditional SWOT Analysis to capture the theme that effective strategic positions have to be both managed and changed.

16. Strategic Value Drivers (Chapters 4, 5 and 6)

Links to Key Success Factors, and examines those factors that characterize a particular industry and highlight the implications of being a competitor in that industry. Examples might include:

- Growth rates and investment needs.
- Planning horizons for investment and linked capital requirements.
- Operating profit margins and sales volume requirements.
- Credit given and taken, and cash requirements.
- Perceived risk and the **cost of capital**.

The following framework is one that we haven't discussed in this book but is sometimes used in connection with a resource audit.

17. The McKinsey 7–S Framework (Peters and Waterman, 1982)

An alternative (or additional) framework for analyzing resources, based on seven inter related internal elements:

- Strategy – in particular functional strategies such as operations, marketing, innovation, research and development, human resources.
- Structure – internal structures and processes.
- Systems – external linkages and processes.

- Style – of leadership and management.
- Staff – 'people'.
- Skills – competencies and capabilities.
- Shared values – relating to the culture of the organization.

18. Financial Analysis (Web Appendices)

- The ability to raise capital and use it to generate higher returns.
- Performance and profitability.
- Solvency and liquidity.

These are critical issues for every organization and many cases include sufficient data for you to calculate and analyze key financial ratios.

Strategic decision-making

19. Portfolio Analyses (Chapter 8)

Grids which allow a range of businesses, products or services to be plotted against certain criteria – providing an indication of appropriate strategies.

Some plot the attractiveness of an industry on one axis and the relative competitive strength of an organization on the other, thus utilizing Frameworks 4 and 6 above.

20. The Ansoff Grid (Chapter 9)

A simple grid attributed to H. Igor Ansoff (1987) which provides a valuable framework to explore possible directions for strategic growth.

Based on existing and new markets and existing and new products/services it provides basic strategies for **market penetration, market development, product development** and diversification.

Strategy evaluation (Chapter 8)

If we review these 20 frameworks, we can see three questions emerge and these are fundamental for the success of any strategic choice:

- Is there a market opportunity?
- Does the organization have the necessary competencies and capabilities?
- Does the organization have the requisite financial resources?

But the 'personal preference' element should not be overlooked. The strategic leader – possibly the owner of the business, perhaps the strategic leader and his or her senior team – must be fully committed. Moreover, the strategy must fit the culture and values of the organization unless there is a drive to change these. There are, then, three fundamental issues to consider in strategy evaluation – and where there are choices to be made, it is rare that one alternative comes out on top on all three. The 20 frameworks above can all inform the following criteria:

- **Appropriateness** – in the context of environmental and competitive forces.
- **Feasibility** – relative to resources, competencies and capabilities.
- **Desirability** –the preferences of key decision-makers and the fit with the existing culture.

It will be realized that these three themes are closely linked to E–V–R congruence, which, as a framework, has the advantage of spanning the analysis and choice elements of strategic management.

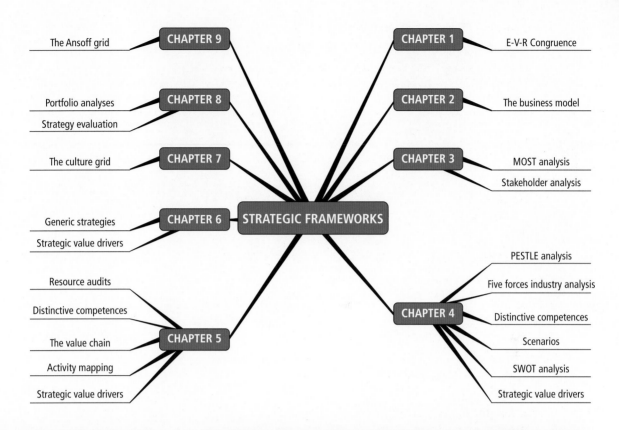

References for appendix

Ansoff, H.I. (1987) *Corporate Strategy*, revised edition, Penguin.

Kay, J.A. (1993) *Foundations of Corporate Success: How Business Strategies Add Value*, Oxford University Press.

Peters, T.J. and Waterman, R.H. Jr. (1982) *In Search of Excellence: Lessons from America's Best Run Companies*, Harper and Row.

Porter, M.E. (1980) *Competitive Strategy: Techniques for Analysing Industries and Competitors*, Free Press.

Porter, M.E. (1985) *Competitive Advantage: Creating and Sustaining Superior Performance*, Free Press.

Porter, M.E. (1996) What Is Strategy? *Harvard Business Review*, November/December.

Part 2 Analysis and positioning

In Part 2 we see how the concept of environmental fit and a PEST (political, economic, social and technical) analysis illustrate the presence, absence or loss of strategic positioning, competitiveness and strategic effectiveness. We believe that culture and values hold the key to the existence and sustenance of positioning, competitiveness and effectiveness. This part looks in detail at positioning and competitiveness, and useful techniques for carrying out the appropriate analyses are explained.

There are three distinct approaches to strategy and strategy creation. They should not be seen as opposing approaches, however, but as complementary approaches to opportunity finding. The entrepreneurial organization will certainly take account of all three, placing an appropriate emphasis on each one. They are:

- Market-driven. The market-based approach implies an active search for new products and marketing opportunities in the external environment. These might be found in industries in which the organization already competes or in new ones.

- Resource-based. Here the organization clarifies its distinctive core competencies and strategic capabilities – perhaps technologies and processes – which set it apart from its competitors in ways that customers value. It then seeks to build on these competencies and capabilities to build new values for both existing and new customers. This approach has the advantage of encouraging the organization to focus on what it can do well – as long as there is a market for it.

- **Competitor-influenced Strategy**. This is a more tactical approach which implies short-term vigilance. Whilst seeking to build the future, an organization must never lose sight of the present day. Its existing positions must be protected against active competition. This means an ability to react to competitor moves and proactive initiatives designed to surprise competitors. Of course, it is important not to become over-reliant on this tactical approach as this is likely to make the organization more reactive rather than proactive.

Organizations should be looking for ways of being different from their competitors. This is unlikely to come from imitation, from monitoring and copying what rivals do – although this approach can be seen in many organizations. In the end, such mimicry will make all competing organizations look remarkably similar, making it difficult for customers to distinguish between them and placing too much emphasis on price competition. Instead organizations should be looking to innovate to achieve two purposes – one intention is to always be ahead of rivals with new ideas; the second intention is to draw apart from competitors with radical differences that they find hard to imitate in the short term. There are two important provisos. First, the differences should mean something positive to customers; it is not simply a question of being different for the sake of being different. Second, it should never be assumed that any gap or advantage is anything but temporary; all ideas can be copied eventually, and all good ones will be!

We look at these approaches in Part 2 before developing our understanding of culture and values in Chapter 7 to complete our study of the E–V–R Congruence themes.

Chapter 4

The business environment and strategy

PART 1
Understanding strategy

1 What is strategy and who is involved?
- Appendix

2 The business model and the revenue model

3 Strategic purpose
- Supplement: Using frameworks to analyze strategy cases

STRATEGIC MANAGEMENT: AWARENESS AND CHANGE

PART 2
Analysis and positioning

4 The business environment and strategy

5 Resource-led strategy

6 The dynamics of competition

7 Introducing culture and values

PART 3
Strategy development

8 Creating and formulating strategy: alternatives, evaluation and choice

9 Strategic planning

10 Strategic leadership and intrapreneurship: towards visionary leadership?

PART 4
Strategic growth issues

11 Strategic control and measuring success

12 Issues in strategic and international growth

13 Failure, consolidation and recovery strategies

PART 5
Strategy implementation

14 Strategy implementation and structure

15 Leading change

16 Managing strategy in the organization

17 Final thoughts and reflections: the practice of strategy

Learning objectives

Having read to the end of this chapter, you should be able to:

- assess the impact of a number of environmental forces and analyze the attractiveness of an industry (**Section 4.1**)

- summarize the important role of government policy and regulation upon competition (**Section 4.2**)

- appreciate the significance of key success factors, effective strategic positioning, adding value and SWOT analysis (**Section 4.3**)

- identify how changes might be forecast (**Section 4.4**).

Introduction

Matching, exploiting and changing the linkages between resource competency and environmental opportunity is an expression of organizational competitiveness, and the presence (or absence) of competitive advantage. Chapter 6 later illustrates how it is essential for organizations to seek competitive advantage for every product, service and business in their portfolios.

Figure 4.1 illustrates the organization in the context of its external environment, showing how its suppliers and customers, upon whom it depends, and its competitors – both existing and new-in-the-future – have an immediate impact. Wider environmental forces, shown in the outer circle as political, economic, social and technological (*PEST*) forces, affect all the 'players' in the industry. The forces and influences have been deliberately shown in concentric circles. Often an organization is conceived as a group of activities (and/or functions) with everything and everyone else, including suppliers and customers, in a

Figure 4.1   The business environment

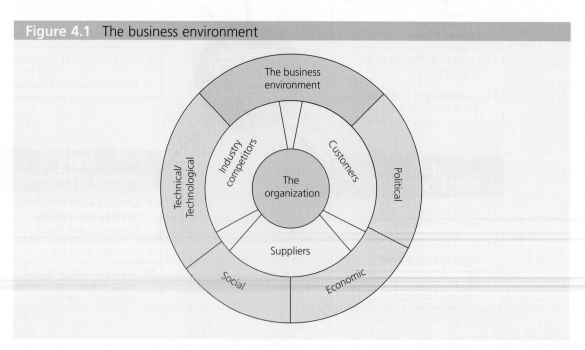

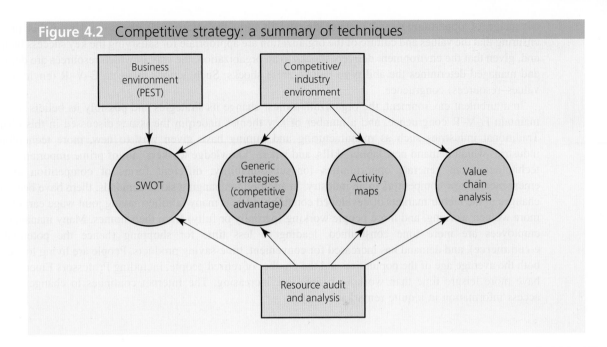

Figure 4.2   Competitive strategy: a summary of techniques

so-called external **business environment**. Increasingly, it makes considerable sense for the organization to see itself working in partnership with its suppliers, distributors and customers. When this perspective is adopted, then only competitors from the middle ring would be placed in the external environment, together with the general forces which impact upon the whole industry.

Figure 4.2 illustrates the various concepts and techniques discussed in this part of the book.

4.1   Analyzing the business environment

To explain the fit between an organization and its external environment, strategic positions are related to the organization's ability to create and add value, which can be examined in relation to a SWOT (strengths, weaknesses, opportunities and threats) analysis. This chapter continues by examining the nature of the business environment, followed by a consideration of the impact of competition regulations on industry and company strategies. Positions have to be changed, which may be a continuous and incremental process, or alternatively more dramatic or discontinuous.

One thing is clear. Even if you're on the right track, you'll get run over if you just sit there!

SIR ALLEN SHEPPARD, WHEN CHAIRMAN, GRAND METROPOLITAN PLC
(NOW DIAGEO)

Managing in an increasingly turbulent world

We will now examine in detail the environment in which the organization operates and consider how the forces present in the environment pose both opportunities and threats. Several of the environmental forces which affect the organization clearly have a stake in the business and are, therefore, stakeholders (as discussed in Chapter 3) who have power and must be satisfied, especially if they are also interested in the activities of the organization (Freeman, 1984). Competitors inevitably constitute a major influence on corporate, competitive and functional strategies and they are the subject of Chapter 6, thus allowing us to better understand the strategic situation and also to build relevant **scenarios**.

A firm must control the forces that influence its growth and, therefore, needs to be aware of environmental forces and environmental change, thus managing the organization's resources to take advantage of opportunities and counter threats. In turn, the strategic leader should lead this process, ensuring that the values and culture of the organization are appropriate for satisfying the key success factors – and, given that the environment delivers shocks to an organization, the way in which resources are deployed and managed determines the ability to handle these shocks. Such actions relate to E–V–R (environment–values–resources) congruence.

In a turbulent environment, the organization must change its strategies and possibly its beliefs if it is to maintain E–V–R congruence, and a number of key themes underpin the issues discussed in this chapter. Traditional industries such as manufacturing and mining have given way to new, more technological industries which demand new labour skills, and where 'knowledge workers' are of prime importance. New technologies can generate opportunities for substitutability: different forms of competition and the emergence of new competitors in an industry. In addition to changing skills demands, there have been other changes in the labour markets of developed countries, such as many families having joint wage earners with more women working, and more people working (partially or fully) from their homes. Many managers and employees are more time constrained, leading to less time for shopping (hence the potential for e-commerce), and demand has increased for convenient, time-saving products. People are living longer and both the average age of the population and the number of retired people, including Professors Emeritus who have more leisure time than working people, are increasing. The Internet continues to change how we access information in a quite remarkable way.

Case 4.1   BHP Billiton   Int, Africa

BHP Billiton is the 'world's largest diversified natural resources company'; its main rivals are Rio Tinto and Anglo American.

The world needs natural resources to be discovered, extracted and utilized for energy and manufacturing – as well as providing a supply chain of precious commodities such as gold and diamonds. Some of these resources are to be found in well developed countries but many are mined in the developing world. Trade and transport are important. This, then, is an industry where poor countries can benefit in all sorts of ways as long as everything is managed responsibly.

Mining and extraction affects landscapes. Whilst reinstatement might be possible in the long term there are also potentially massive short-term impacts. This might be seen as less significant if the work is in under-populated regions – for example much of the modern coal mining is in inland barren parts of Australia. But there are clearly cases where places of true natural beauty are affected. In addition the health and safety of the people involved is a critical issue. Whenever there is a disaster underground there is controversy. There was an argument that when some 30 miners were trapped underground in Chile for 69 days, their mine was still operational because commodity prices made it economical, but really it was in need of investment and improvement. Rescue teams drilled a shaft and brought up the miners one-by-one in a capsule.

BHP

'Broken Hill Proprietary' began mining silver, lead and zinc in New South Wales, Australia, in 1885. BHP added iron ore extraction in South Australia in 1890, steel production in 1915, again in New South Wales; and in 1931 it bought a gold mine. By 1965 it was capturing natural gas from the Bass Strait between Australia and Tasmania. Some years later, and linked to a serious expansion programme, it invested heavily outside Australia – with coal mining in Indonesia, copper mining in Chile and gold in Mali.

Billiton

This was an older company, Dutch owned and established in 1851 to mine tin in 'Billiton' island in Indonesia. In 1928 tin and lead smelting was started in Holland; and around the time of the Second World War the company began bauxite mining in Indonesia and then South America. Some time later, Thailand. In 1970 Billiton became a subsidiary of Royal Dutch Shell. Whilst there was some deliberate contraction there was also investment in South Africa.

BHP and Billiton merged in 2001 and an aggressive expansion programme began. Acquisitions and local investments were both important elements. Oil and natural gas were prioritized, with investment in Western Australia, Algeria and the Gulf of Mexico. Soon after the merger the annual corporate turnover exceeded US$25 billion.

There were also strategic deals. For example, in 2004 BHP Billiton secured a 10 year supply agreement for iron ore with Chinese steel mills – and in return these mills bought a 40 per cent stake in a BHP ore mine in Western Australia.

The company was spread across Australia, Africa, South America, Canada and the Far East – and it divided its activities as follows:

- aluminium
- base metals – copper, zinc, gold and silver
- diamonds and titanium
- iron ore, manganese and coking coal
- coal
- petroleum
- stainless steel materials – chrome, nickel and cobalt.

The 'modern BHP Billiton' has declared itself to be concerned with sustainable development. Economic development must be accompanied by environmental, social and ethical development. The environmental issues would involve the future impact on landscapes and communities, water pollution and the carbon footprint. Social concerns include working conditions, physical dangers, heat, noise, gas emissions and general health. In some cases the company would be focusing on positive outcomes and supporting communities; in other cases it would be seeking to behave responsibly and limit any negative impacts.

Is it, though, ever possible to satisfy all critics and stakeholders?

Aluminium smelting in Africa

Mozambique borders South Africa on the east coast of southern Africa. It is a relatively poor country. When a feasibility study into a new aluminium smelting plant was begun in 1995 the country was around 1 year on from a 17 year civil war. The infrastructure was fragile; there had been no major development project such as this for 30 years. Disease – including HIV/AIDS – was rampant; skills were low; roads were poorly maintained; the housing stock was inadequate. From BHP Billiton's perspective one might not have thought this an obvious choice of location. From the perspective of the Mozambique government things might seem different! The potential could be massive – as long as the country could cope with the upheaval. The development, which was christened Mozal, would have to be supported by, and the responsibility shared with, a number of community stakeholders.

In the event the development was given a green light. Mitsubishi (Japan) became involved; and the International Finance Corporation (IFC), which is linked to the World Bank and has a remit of reducing global poverty, provided a loan of US$120 million to mitigate some of the financial risk. In return a number of community safeguards had to be specified.

The project had a total budget of US$1.8 billion, split roughly 50:50 over two phases. Phase 1 began in 1998 and came in 6 months early and $120 million under budget. Aluminium production and export began in 2000. Phase 2, which started a year later and which doubled capacity, came in 7 months early and $195 million under budget in 2003.

A sustainability audit by the IFC showed that Mozal had:

- created local jobs – in both construction and smelting – altogether 15 000
- had a major economic impact as people earned and spent money – there had been a serious positive impact on Mozambique's GDP and foreign exchange earnings
- brought investment in community health, especially malaria, HIV/AIDS and maternity clinics
- done 'minimal environmental harm' with the construction
- been sympathetic when families affected by the construction had to be moved and rehoused

- helped affected farmers to grow new crops
- built schools
- trained the local workforce
- resulted in new roads, bridges and water supply
- supported local SMEs which supplied Mozal.

In 2010 a pressure group drew attention to the release of tars and toxic gases into the atmosphere and suggested this was down to poor operating conditions and poor maintenance and that this had begun in 2003. BHP Billiton responded that they were operating within World Health Organization limits for emissions.

Questions

1 Do you agree that with developments of this nature it is possible to satisfy all critics and stakeholders?
2 Do you feel the report on the release of tars and gases was probably a serious issue demanding a critical response or more likely activists at work?
3 Might one expect BHP Billiton's reaction and response to be the same as it would be if such an issue was raised in Australia?

Multinational businesses have grown in strength and significance and they have become the norm for mining and manufacturing industries. Case 4.1 on BHP Billiton highlights the value of taking a responsible attitude when developing businesses abroad. Manufacturers from the UK, USA, Germany, Japan and other nations with a longstanding tradition in manufacturing have relocated factories in developing countries with lower wage costs. Technology, which allows increasing levels of output from the same size factory has facilitated these changes, e.g. Hornby switched its production to China, leading to visibly higher quality for the same market price. Consequently, the competitive arena has been changing with, until recently, the highest economic growth being enjoyed by the USA, although during the early and mid-1990s it was the Pacific Rim countries. During the early years of this century, China, India and Brazil have all experienced relatively strong economic growth. In many industries, global supply potential exceeds demand, placing downward pressures on real prices.

Product and service markets, supply chains, capital markets and communication systems have become global in nature. The speed of change in most industries and markets has increased and product life cycles have shortened. For some companies, success can be very transient: a classic example being the computer games industry for both hardware and software.

Governments have masterminded increasing degrees of deregulation. Other countries have followed the UK's lead and privatized public-sector utilities; air travel and telecommunications markets have been opened up to more competition. Consumers are more aware and more knowledgeable; and environmental groups have begun to wield increasing influence. Changes in politics and regimes in different parts of the world, such as Eastern Europe and the Far East, have introduced an element of chaos and greater unpredictability, whilst opportunities open up but carry a significant downside risk.

Simply, environments are more turbulent; managing them and managing in them both demand more flexibility and more discontinuity than in the past.

There is no doubt that the world is becoming one marketplace. Capital markets, products and services, management and manufacturing techniques have all become global in nature. As a result, companies increasingly find that they must compete all over the world – in the global marketplace.

MAURICE SAATCHI, WHEN CHAIRMAN, SAATCHI AND SAATCHI COMPANY PLC

In my experience, corporate life-threatening problems in large manufacturing companies have developed over a long period. These problems should never have been permitted to grow so large, but they were allowed to do so by top management who were lethargic and self-satisfied, who engaged in self-delusion and congratulated themselves on their exalted status. In short, the managements were the problem.

EUGENE ANDERSON, EX-CHAIRMAN AND CHIEF EXECUTIVE, FERRANTI INTERNATIONAL PLC

How can we expect to succeed when we are playing cricket and the rest of the world is practising karate?

SIR EDWIN NIXON, WHEN CHAIRMAN, AMERSHAM INTERNATIONAL

Figure 4.3   World-class strategic performance

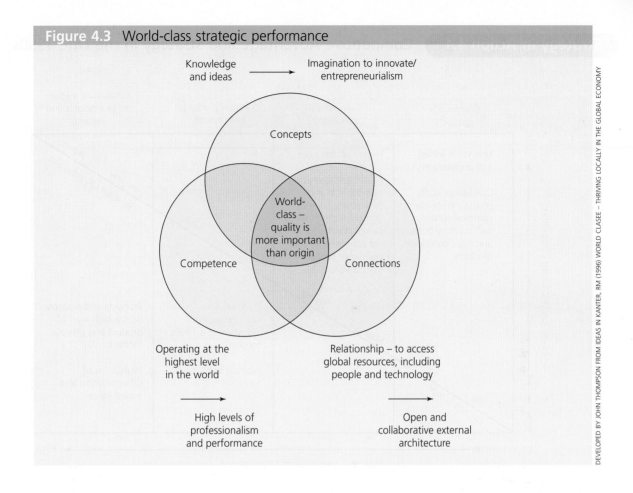

Figure 4.3 emphasizes that, as industries and markets become increasingly global, quality is more important than origin. To achieve world-class quality and **reputation**, companies must use knowledge and ideas to be innovative, operate at the level of the best in the world and form international networks and partnerships to access the best resources from around the world.

In this dynamic environment, the USA became the most competitive nation by taking a lead in technically advanced industries, transforming itself into a service economy, generating the private-sector finances required for investment in new and relatively high-risk sectors and ensuring that regulations do not inhibit labour force flexibility. The USA also has a compelling cultural will to win, the importance of which should never be underestimated. Europe is generally more restrictive, although practices do vary between countries, even within the European Union (EU).

The competitive future for any developed country does not lie in reducing wages to compete with the Far East and Eastern Europe: rather, it lies in finding new ways of innovating, adding value, differentiating and *leading* consumers. These points are explored further in Strategy in Action 4.1.

There are several frameworks for studying the environment of an organization. In addition to considering the company's *stakeholders* in terms of their relative power, influence, needs and expectations, a **PEST analysis**, an objective and straightforward consideration of changing political, economic, social and technological influences, can prove useful (discussed in detail later in this chapter).

The nature of the stakeholders and the environmental forces is a useful indicator of the most appropriate strategic approach for the organization to take – with it being (i) vigilant and speedily reactive where the environment is complex, turbulent and uncertain, (ii) carefully planning in stable and predictable circumstances and (iii) a positive and proactive approach where the environment can be changed or influenced.

Strategy in Action 4.1   Competitive Advantage and Strategy in the Late 1990s

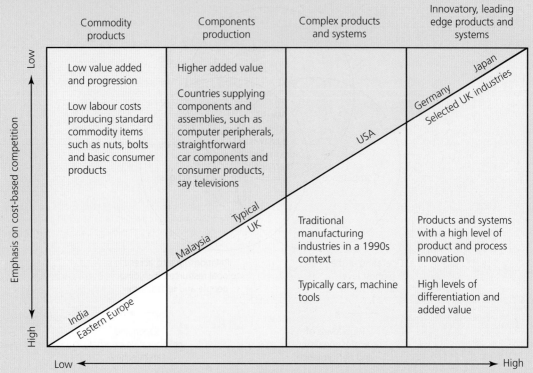

- Countries progress up and down the diagonal over time.
- Within each country, different industries will be in different sectors. The position shown here on the diagonal is that with which the country is typically associated.
- The UK has drifted down to 'components' by offering incentives and relatively low labour costs to attract inward investments. However, for example, aerospace and pharmaceuticals the UK is clearly in the innovatory sector.
- Arguably, the UK should focus more intently on innovation to reverse the trend – otherwise the UK

will increasingly become a mere supplier to the industry leaders and drivers. However, innovation requires managerial and workforce strengths and skills which the UK may not have.
- Innovation relates to products and services (radical improvements in value, reconceiving form and function) and market boundaries (attracting new customers, and providing new values by satisfying individual needs more effectively).

Based on ideas in Kruse, G and Berry, C (1997) A nation of shopkeepers, *Management Today*, April.

Uncertainty, complexity and dynamism

The environment is more uncertain the more complex or the more dynamic it is (Duncan, 1972), e.g. historically a small rural village post office faced a generally stable, non-dynamic and hence fairly certain environment, but their position has become more uncertain and many have closed. Meanwhile, their 'parent company', the UK Post Office (which has branches in every town and city that possess both spare capacity and a secure environment for handling cash) attempted to offer a new range of banking services, spotting a window of opportunity as high-street banks consolidate and shut small branches, but requiring support and co-operation from these banks, only some of whom have co-operated, seeing them as competitors.

Dynamism can be increased by a number of factors, such as rapid technological change involving either products, processes or uses, meaning that organizations must stay aware of the activities of their suppliers and potential suppliers, customers and competitors. Where competition is on a global scale, the pace of change may vary in different markets, and competition may be harder to monitor, and the future is likely to be uncertain. Risk-taking and creative entrepreneurial leadership may well be required because previous strategies, or modifications of them, may no longer be appropriate.

An environment is complex where the forces and the changes involving them are difficult to understand, and complexity and dynamism may occur together, for example technology- and Internet-based businesses. The structure of the organization, the degree of decentralization and the responsibility and authority delegated to managers throughout the organization, and information systems can render complexity more manageable. Managers will need to be open and responsive to the need for change and flexible in their approach if they are to handle complexity successfully.

Managerial awareness and the approach to the management of change are key issues in uncertain environments and thus managers can perceive the complex and dynamic conditions as manageable, while less aware managers may find the conditions so uncertain that they are always responding to pressures placed on the organization rather than appearing to be in control and managing the environment. Hence a crucial aspect of strategic management is understanding and negotiating with the environment in order to influence and ideally to control events.

Case 4.2 looks at issues of dynamism and complexity in the music industry.

Case 4.2 The Recorded Music Industry   UK

The recorded music industry has enjoyed a period of growth since the emergent popularity of Elvis Presley and The Beatles. From the mid-1980s to the mid-1990s the growth and prosperity was boosted by people's willingness to rebuild their collections by replacing their vinyl LPs and cassettes with compact discs. Since 1997, however, the popularity of singles has declined whilst sales of compilation albums and classical music has increased. Global revenues reached almost $40 billion dollars in 1999 but by 2003 these had declined by almost 20 per cent to $32 billion.

There are many forces at work driven by the public perception that they were paying too much for the product:

- People were downloading music from the Internet, sometimes legally, sometimes illegally. Eventually legal action would be taken to restrain the activities of Napster, a leading provider of online free downloads. The impact of Apple's iPod and associated iTunes software on music downloads was dramatic. The Internet also provided the opportunity to purchase CDs at significant discounts on high street prices.
- Pirate copies of CDs were increasingly available – some on the black market, some inadvertently through legitimate channels.

- The CD replacement market has matured as people have rebuilt their collections.
- More recently people have been able to make good home copies of their friends' CDs by purchasing a CD burner for the personal computer. To complete the task, CD labels can be downloaded from the Internet!
- The ways and means that people listen to music have changed to iPod and other MP3 players. Computer game playing and satellite television have competed for the same leisure time. In the past people would play CDs time and time again; now many people only play them infrequently. New cars invariably provide a CD player, many have bluetooth connections for MP3 players and there are, as well, more radio stations to tune in to.
- In 2007, and for the first time, songwriters and publishers earned more from downloads than from the copyright payments resulting from the sales of their CDs.
- Young people – teenagers and others not in full-time employment – have often switched their discretionary purchasing away from music to their mobile phones.
- Retail competition has increased, stimulated in part by supermarkets increasing their sales of best sellers. As a result prices and margins have declined.

SOURCE: THIS CASE STUDY WAS PREPARED USING PRIMARILY PUBLICLY AVAILABLE SOURCES OF INFORMATION FOR THE PURPOSES OF CLASSROOM DISCUSSION; IT DOES NOT INTEND TO ILLUSTRATE EITHER EFFECTIVE OR INEFFECTIVE HANDLING OF A MANAGERIAL SITUATION.

- Some analysts believe there is less creative talent being discovered than was the case in the past. Assuming this is true, there are potential causes. The industry is dominated by global conglomerates; the significance of small and entrepreneurial independent record labels has declined, although they are still around. The growth in popularity of television programmes designed to find new artistes and to form new boy and girl bands has also, for some, been a negative force. The real test is often whether sales of second and third albums exceed or fall below those of debut albums. In the past the successful groups and artistes saw sales grow; now it is less likely to happen.

By 2002 five companies controlled some 75 per cent of the global market, with the following market shares:

Universal (MCA and Polygram)	25.9 per cent
Sony Music	14.1 per cent
EMI (incl. Virgin)	12.0 per cent
Warner Music	11.9 per cent
Bertelsmann (BMG)	11.1 per cent

EMI was seriously interested in acquiring Warner Music from Time Warner Corporation, but the European competition regulators ruled against this in 2000. A year later a proposed merger between EMI and Bertelsmann received the same treatment. Meanwhile Bertelsmann and Sony started planning a joint alliance which subsequently became a merger – and which the European regulators approved in 2004. Ironically the European Court later concluded this was a poor decision. Together they were roughly the same size as Universal.

EMI was eventually bought by Guy Hands' private equity vehicle, Terra Firma, in 2007. Hands declared there would need to be annual savings of some £200 million and that between 1500 and 2000 jobs would need to be lost. Sir Paul McCartney and Sir Mick Jagger opted to leave EMI and Robbie Williams refused to deliver his latest album to them as a protest. Things did not go to plan and Hands was unable to justify his

investment. He sold to Citibank who shortly afterwards (in 2011) sold EMI Music to Universal and EMI Publishing to Sony. The industry was now even more concentrated than it had been. Fortunately the independent record labels are strong and thus able to drive innovation and creativity.

Interestingly, and also in 2007, Madonna parted company with Warner Music, with whom she had recorded for 25 years. In the future she would work with Live Nation, a concert promotion business, which would sell her albums as well as stage and promote her concerts. In 2009 a merger was proposed between Live Nation and leading distributor of tickets for shows, concerts and sporting events, Ticketmaster.

The most recent trends are being set by artists like Lady Gaga, who uses social media (particularly Facebook and Twitter) to stay in daily touch with her millions of fans/followers and to make sure they are fully up-to-speed on her latest songs and recordings.

Questions

1 What future changes do you foresee – and will these have a predominantly positive or negative impact on (a) consumers and (b) the record companies?
2 How have your own musical tastes and listening habits been changing in recent years?
3 What have been the implications of the proposed merger between Live Nation and Ticketmaster?

Adams (1995) tries to explain why different organizations and managers adopt different approaches to the way they deal with the external environment, reflecting underlying beliefs and values held by the organization and the apparent nature of the environment. He uses the metaphor of a round ball.

When nature (the environment) is benign, the ball comes to rest in the bottom of a bowl and, if the bowl is moved, the ball returns to its position. The environment appears predictable, stable and forgiving, and managers tend to be relaxed and non-interventionist, given limited opportunities to grow, with change being unnecessarily disruptive. When the environment is ephemeral, it is a ball balanced precariously on an upturned arch, i.e. fragile, precarious and unforgiving. Therefore, if managers make the wrong decisions they cause serious damage, e.g. combinations of human and technical error in train, airplane and space shuttle disasters, where safety is compromised by the quest for speed and cost reduction. The appropriate style is one of caution and careful risk management, if not risk aversion.

If the environment is perverse or tolerant, the ball is in a valley and can roll around, so it behaves predictably but within limits, and modest shocks can be tolerated. The organization knows the other inhabitants in the valley (its customers and competitors), but the next valley might be more attractive, perhaps more fertile (potentially more profitable) or quieter (fewer competitors), but the complete picture is not fully visible and to climb out and change valley requires courage and faith. There is, though, generally a way back which reduces the risk and allows management of the downside, and is the measured way of some entrepreneurs and entrepreneurial managers. A capricious environment is represented by a ball able to roll freely on a flat surface, and it is very difficult to predict where the ball might come to rest again. Any change of position or direction involves a degree of risk, but staying put is also high risk since, if other balls are moving freely, the organization can get hit and moved out of position by competitors. Vigilance is essential but care must be taken with any change of direction.

Environmental influences

Typically an organization is one of a number of competitors in an industry, with all being affected by the decisions, competitive strategies and innovation of the others. Given how crucial these interdependencies are, strategic decisions should always involve (i) some assessment of their impact on other companies, and their likely reaction, and (ii) being fully aware of what competitors are doing at any time.

Furthermore, this industry will be linked to, and dependent on, other industries from which it buys supplies, or to which it markets products and services, relating to Porter's model of the forces that determine industry profitability (the subject of the next section in this chapter).

The relationships between a firm and its buyers and suppliers are crucial because they might be performing badly, and future supplies might be threatened; equally, they might be working on innovations that will impact on organizations to which they supply. Buyers might be under pressure from competitors to switch suppliers. Firms must be strategically aware, and to seek to exert influence over organizations where there are (inter)dependencies.

These industries and the firms that comprise them are additionally part of a wider environment that is composed of forces that mutually influence each other, some of which are more or less important for individual organizations and in certain circumstances. Managers need to appreciate the existence of these forces, how they might influence the organization, and how they might be influenced.

Mintzberg (1987) has used the term 'crafting strategy', analogous to a potter moulding clay and creating a finished object, to explain how managers learn by experience and by doing and adapting strategies to environmental needs. If an organization embarks upon a determined change of strategy, certain aspects of implementation will be changed as it becomes increasingly clear with experience how best to manage the environmental forces. Equally, managers adapt existing competitive and functional strategies as they see opportunities and threats and gradually change things. In each case, the aim is to ensure that the organization's resources and values are matched to the changing environment.

External forces: a PEST analysis

A PEST analysis is merely a framework that categorizes environmental influences as political, economic, social and technological forces, and sometimes environmental and legal are added to make a PESTEL analysis.

Politics and government policy influence economic conditions and vice versa. Either exported or imported goods can seem expensive or inexpensive, dependent upon currency exchange rates. Capital markets can be subject to government **controls**, or by government spending which can increase the money supply and make capital markets more buoyant, thus affecting shareholders' expectations with regard to company performance and their willingness to provide more equity funding or sell their shares. The rate of interest charged for loans, though affected by inflation and by international economics, may be fixed by a central bank. The labour market is affected by training, which is influenced by government and its agencies. Labour costs will be influenced by inflation and by general trends in other industries, and by the role and power of trade unions.

Economic conditions affect how easy or how difficult it is to be successful and profitable at any time because they affect both capital availability and cost, and demand. If demand is buoyant, for example, and the **cost of capital** is low, it will be attractive for firms to invest and grow with expectations of being profitable. In opposite circumstances, firms might find that profitability throughout the industry is low. The timing and relative success of particular strategies can be influenced by economic conditions; for example, a growing economy creates demand for a product or service, or the opportunity to exploit a particular strategy successfully, which would not be in demand in more depressed circumstances.

S The *sociocultural environment* encapsulates demand and tastes, varying with fashion and disposable income, providing both opportunities and threats for particular firms. Over time, most products change from being a novelty to a situation of market saturation, and as this happens pricing and promotion strategies have to change. Similarly, some products and services will sell around the world with little variation, but these are relatively unusual. Figure 4.4 shows how washing-machine designs are different for different European countries to reflect consumer preferences. Organizations should be aware of demographic changes as the structure of the population by ages, affluence, regions, numbers working and so on can have an important bearing on demand as a whole and for particular products and services. Threats to existing products might be increasing; opportunities for differentiation and **market segmentation** might be emerging.

T *Technology* is used for the creation of competitive advantage, and technology external to the industry can also be captured and used, and can be influenced by government support and encouragement. Technological breakthroughs can create new industries which might prove a threat to existing organizations whose products or services might be rendered redundant, and those firms which might be affected in this way should be alert to the possibility. Equally, new technology could provide a useful input, perhaps in both manufacturing and service industries, but in turn its purchase will require funding and possibly employee training before it can be used.

Table 4.1 provides a list of environmental influences and forces, which managers the need to appreciate how they affect their organization. Strategy in Action 4.2 provides a short and very selective PEST analysis of environmental forces affecting the credit-card industry and picks out a number of key influences. It will be realized how such an analysis can be useful for helping to identify emerging opportunities and threats.

Figure 4.4   European preferences for washing machines

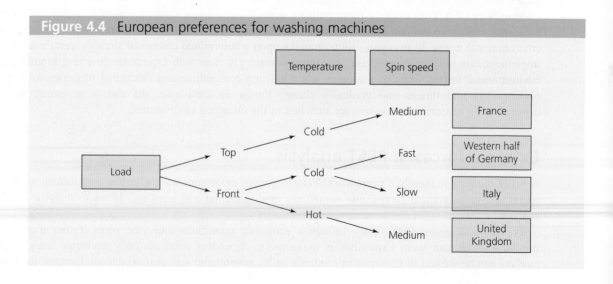

Table 4.1   Environmental influences

Influence	Examples of threats and opportunities
The economy	The strength of the economy influences the availability of credit and the willingness of people to borrow. This affects the level of demand. Interest rates and currency fluctuations affect both the cost and demand of imports and exports
Capital markets	This includes shareholders and their satisfaction with company success. Are they willing to buy more shares if offered them to increase equity funding? Would they willingly sell if someone bid for the organization? Also included are the banking system and the cost and availability of loan capital
Labour market	Changes in structure with an ageing population and more women seeking work Availability of skills, possibly in particular regions Influence of trade unions Contribution of government training schemes
Technology	Robotics in manufacturing in industries such as car assembly Computers for design and manufacturing Information technology such as electronic point of sale in retailing
Sociocultural environment	Pressure groups affecting demand or industry location Changing population – by age groups Changing tastes and values Regional movements
Government	Regional aid policies Special industry initiatives, e.g. where high technology is involved The legal environment is part of this, including the regulation of competition Restraints on car exhaust emissions (pollution control) and labelling requirements would be other examples
Suppliers	Availability and cost of supplies, possibly involving vertical integration and decisions concerning whether to make or buy-in essential components
Customers	Changes in preferences and purchasing power Changes in the distribution system
Competitors	Changes in competitive strategies Innovation
The media	Effects of good and bad publicity, drawing attention to companies, products and services

Strategy in Action 4.2   A PEST Analysis of the Credit-Card Industry

Political	Legislation allowing young people to own credit cards. The threat of restrictions on Internet trading.
Economic	The future presence – or not – of the UK, Denmark and Sweden in the eurozone and the European single currency, and the impact of the single currency on interest rates generally. Future economic trends which will affect demand for consumption and credit. Freedom for, or restrictions on, new entrants to the industry.
Social	The willingness or reluctance to buy on credit – while credit is readily available for many people, there can be a rebellion against high interest charges. The increasing acceptance of Internet shopping, which depends on credit-card transactions – possibly affected by the age profile of the population.
Technical	Internet and e-business possibilities – and security.

For any organization, certain environmental influences – e.g. customers for some manufacturing and service businesses, while for others it is competition or, for small businesses, suppliers who influence their cash flow by paying on time will constitute powerful forces which affect decision-making significantly.

Ansoff's model

Ansoff (1987) contends that, 'to survive and succeed in an industry, the firm must match the aggressiveness of its operating and strategic behaviours to the changeability of demands and opportunities in the marketplace.' The extent to which the environment is changeable or turbulent depends on six factors:

- changeability of the market environment
- speed of change
- intensity of competition
- fertility of technology
- discrimination by customers
- pressures from governments and influence groups.

Ansoff suggests that firms need to pursue more aggressive competitive strategies, entrepreneurialism or change orientation to succeed in more turbulent environments. A small number of firms in an industry will be insufficiently aggressive for the requirements of the industry, being unprofitable or going out of business; whilst another small number will be above average in terms of success because they are best able to match the demands of the environment. Many will achieve results above average; and some others may also fail because they are too aggressive and try to change things too quickly through lack of awareness.

Where an organization is multi-product or multinational, the various parts of the business are likely to experience some common environmental influences and some which are distinctive, which reinforces the need for managers who are closest to the market and to competitors to be able to change things.

Ansoff suggests that the environment should be analyzed in terms of competition and entrepreneurship or change. The degree of competitive and entrepreneurial turbulence can be calculated by attributing scores to various factors. The competitive environment is affected by market structure and profitability, the intensity of competitive rivalry and the degree of differentiation, market growth, the stage in the life of the products or services in question and the frequency of new product launches, capital intensity and **economies of scale**. Certain of these factors, namely market growth, the stage in the life of the product and profitability, also help to determine the extent to which the environment is entrepreneurial. Changes in structure and technology, social pressures and innovation are also influential.

The culture of the organization and managerial competencies should then be examined to see whether they match and be changed as appropriate if they do not. Again, scores are attributed to various factors. Culture encompasses factors such as values, reaction and response to change and risk orientation. Problem-solving approaches, information systems, environmental forecasting and surveillance, and management systems are included in the competencies. Ansoff is arguing that the resources of the organization and the values must be congruent with the needs of the environment.

Analyzing an industry

Porter (1980) argues that five forces determine the profitability of an industry. At the centre of his 'Five Forces industry analysis' framework are the competitive rivals and their strategies linked to, say, pricing or advertising. He contends that it is important to look beyond one's immediate competitors as there are four other forces or determinants of profitability which impact on the central core of rivalry. He includes competition from substitute products or services, which may be perceived as substitutes by buyers even though they are part of a different industry. In the case of plastic bottles, cans and glass bottles for packaging soft drinks, there may be a potential threat of new entrants, although some competitors will see this as an opportunity to strengthen their position in the market by ensuring, as far as they can, customer loyalty. This is then a third force. Companies purchase from suppliers and sell to buyers who, if they are powerful, are in a position to bargain profits away through reduced margins, by forcing either cost increases or price decreases (relating to the strategic option of **vertical integration**, where a company acquires, or merges with, a supplier or customer thereby gaining greater control over the chain of activities which leads from basic materials through to final consumption, which is considered later in the book). The relative power of suppliers and buyers are the fourth and fifth forces. You can easily download Porter's 5 forces diagram if you search online.

To achieve its objectives and to establish appropriate strategies, a firm must seek to understand the nature of its competitive environment and to be in a stronger position to defend itself against threats and to influence the forces with its strategy: it must fully understand the nature of the five forces, and particularly appreciate which one is the most important. As the situation is in flux, with the nature and relative power of the forces changing, the need to monitor and stay aware is continuous.

The threat of new entrants: barriers to entry

Where barriers to entry are high, new entrants are likely to be deterred: if they do attempt entry, they are likely to provoke a quick reaction from existing competitors. Low barriers generally mean that responses will be slower, offering more opportunities. A number of factors can create barriers:

- **Economies of scale:** some of the possible ways of achieving economies of scale have been considered earlier. In addition, the **experience curve (or learning curve)** can be important. If there is a need for substantial investment to allow a new entrant to achieve cost parity with existing firms, this may well be a deterrent. In such a case, if a newcomer enters the market with only limited investment and is not able to achieve comparable economies of scale, they will be at a cost disadvantage from the start, in which case substantial differentiation will be required, introducing another issue. (See the associated web supplement on the experience curve for this chapter.)

- **Product differentiation:** if consumers perceive rival products or services to be clearly differentiated then newcomers must also seek to establish a distinct identity. Newcomers will, therefore, have to invest in advertising and promotion to establish their new brand, and this may be expensive. The major brewers and chocolate manufacturers, for example, spend millions of pounds each year promoting specific products and brands.

- **Capital requirements:** any requirement for substantial investment capital in order to enter a market is a barrier to entry. The investment may be on capital equipment, research and development, or advertising to establish a market presence, and it may deter many aspiring competitors. However, large multi-product companies that wish to break into a market may finance the necessary investment with profits from other areas of the business. Pharmaceutical companies require huge investments to develop and test possible new products over several years. Whilst patent protection allows the costs to be recouped through prices, the investment is all 'up front'.

- **Switching costs:** these are not costs incurred by the company wishing to enter the market but by the existing customers. If a buyer were to change his or her supplier from an established manufacturer to a newcomer, costs may be incurred in a number of ways. New handling equipment and employee training are examples. Buyers may not be willing to change their suppliers because of these costs, thereby making it very difficult for any newcomer to poach existing business.

- **Access to distribution channels:** existing relationships and agreements between manufacturers and the key distributors in a market may also create barriers to entry. Some manufacturers may be vertically integrated and own or control their distributors. Other distributors may have established and successful working relationships with particular manufacturers and have little incentive to change. Companies aspiring to enter a market may look for unique distribution opportunities to provide both access and immediate differentiation.

- **Cost advantages independent of scale:** this represents factors which are valuable to existing companies in an industry and which newcomers may not be able to replicate. Essential technology may be protected by patent; the supply of necessary raw materials may be controlled; or favourable locations near to supplies or markets may not be accessible. Government restrictions on competition may apply in certain circumstances.

Case 4.3 illustrates the absence of significant barriers to entry in the DVD industry. The outcome is that an innovative business model can be copied by powerful rivals.

Potential entrants, attracted by high margins in an industry and not discouraged by any of the above barriers, must try to gauge any likely retaliation by existing manufacturers; and Porter argues that this can be assessed by examining:

- past behaviour when newcomers have entered or tried to enter the market
- the resource capabilities of existing companies which will affect their ability to retaliate
- the investment and commitment of existing companies which may make retaliation inevitable if they are to protect their investment and position
- the rate of growth of the industry – the faster it is the more possibilities for a newcomer to be absorbed.

Existing firms may be prepared to reduce prices to deter entry and protect their market shares, especially if supply already exceeds demand. As a result, even in an oligopoly, profitability can be contained.

Case 4.3   Barriers to Entry: Netflix and DVD Rentals   US

Netflix Inc is an American provider of on-demand Internet streaming media in the USA, Canada, Latin America, the Caribbean, the UK and Ireland, and DVD-by-mail in the USA.

Netflix is an online DVD rental site begun by entrepreneur Reed Hastings in America in 1998. There was a monthly subscription which started out at $19.95 (£12.50) but which was soon reduced as customer numbers increased, and for this customers could borrow DVDs and keep them for as long as they like. It is a simple model. Once people joined and subscribed they picked out a large number of titles they would like to borrow. Three are sent out with return envelopes, and when these are returned three more are dispatched from their list, based on prioritization and availability. Originally there were about 12000 titles to choose from, but after 3 years this had grown to 50000. Typically customers have to wait between 2 and 5 days after emailing their order, but turnaround is speeded up by Netflix having distribution points across the USA. Operatives basically unpack and repack – the systems are driven by IT at relatively low cost. By 2002, when 30 per cent of USA households had a DVD player, Netflix had enrolled some 750000 subscribers, and this number was growing at the rate of 100000 every quarter. However, in 2002, a new and very powerful rival opted to enter the market and there was little Netflix could do to stop it happening. Wal-Mart, which already sold DVDs, set up a rival service, undercutting Netflix's price by 10 per cent. Amazon, partnering with other organizations for which it provided a marketing vehicle, also entered the market with an almost identical business model to that of Netflix.

But by 2009 Netflix was offering a collection of 100000 titles on DVD and had surpassed ten million subscribers. In February 2007, Netflix had announced the billionth DVD delivery. By 2011, the total digital revenue for Netflix reached $1.5 billion from its customers around the world. Netflix of course has diversified and now streams products via televisions, computers and games consoles direct into people's homes. The original target for 2012 was always 20 million subscribers but this number was achieved years ahead. One can soon realize this implies substantial revenues every year from a very simple business idea.

The leading competitor, although not offering the same service, was Blockbuster video, which rents videos to over 50 million customers through its ubiquitous retail outlets. Blockbuster will rent and even post out DVDs, but there is an individual item charge. It is a different business model. Netflix believes it has a competitive advantage because it can post summaries and reviews of all its DVDs on its website that all its customers have to use.

Project

Check out the performance of Netflix and evaluate how this entrepreneurial business dealt with the threat from Wal-Mart and Amazon. Examine the progress made by LoveFilm in the UK.

The bargaining power of suppliers

The behaviour of suppliers, and their relative power, can squeeze industry profits. Equally, the ability of a firm to control its supplies by vertical integration (acquiring its suppliers) or long-term supply arrangements can be very beneficial. The relative power is affected by five major factors:

- Concentration amongst suppliers *vis-à-vis* the industry they sell to: if the supply industry is very concentrated then buyers have little opportunity for bargaining on prices and deliveries as suppliers recognize that their opportunities for switching suppliers are limited.
- The degree of substitutability between the products of various suppliers and the amount of product differentiation: a buyer could be tied to a particular supplier if his or her requirements cannot be met by other suppliers.
- The amount of, and potential for, vertical integration which might be initiated by either the supplier or the buyer: again government regulation on competition may prevent this.
- The extent to which the buyer is important to the supplier: if a buyer is regarded as a key customer he or she may well receive preferential treatment.
- Any switching costs that might be incurred by buyers will strengthen the position of suppliers.

The bargaining power of buyers

Any competitive action by buyers will act to depress industry profits, but specific arrangements with distributors or customers can be mutually beneficial. Vertical integration is again a possibility. The major supermarket grocery stores with their multiple outlets nationwide are in a very strong bargaining position with most of their suppliers.

This power has been strengthened by the success of private label brands, whose prices for 'basic ranges' can be up to 60 per cent below those of the recognized major brands. Private labels have grown to well over one-third of UK retail food sales. They have proved most successful with chilled meals, frozen vegetables, fruit juices and cheese; and least successful with pet foods, sugar, coffee and, for a long time, breakfast cereals. Barriers against private label products are provided by innovation and aggressive marketing and promotion.

The bargaining power of buyers is determined by:

- the concentration and size of buyer
- the importance to the buyer of the purchase in terms of both cost and quality (the more important it is, the more he or she must ensure good relations with the supplier)
- the degree of product standardization, which affects substitutability
- the costs, practicability and opportunity for buyers to switch supplier
- the possibility of vertical integration, initiated by either the supplier or the buyer.

The threat of product substitutes

The existence or non-existence of close substitutes helps to determine the elasticity of demand for a product or service. In simple terms, this is price sensitivity. If there are close substitutes, demand for a particular brand will increase or decrease as its price moves downwards or upwards relative to competitors. Price changes can be initiated by any firm, but other competitors will be affected and forced to react. If products are not seen as close substitutes then they will be less price sensitive to competitor price changes.

For this reason, firms will seek to establish clear product or service differentiation in order to create customer preference and loyalty and thereby make their product or service less price sensitive. Where this is accomplished industry profits are likely to rise, which of course may be attractive to prospective newcomers who will seek to create further differentiation in order to encourage customers to switch to them and enable them to establish a presence in the market.

Products and services can be substituted for something completely different, reflecting the ever-present possibility that new competitors can change the 'rules of competition' in a market or industry.

Rivalry amongst existing competitors

Porter terms rivalry amongst existing competitors 'jockeying for position'. Competition may take the form of price competition, advertising and promotion, innovation or service during and after sale. Where competitive firms are mutually interdependent, retaliation is a key issue. Before deciding upon aggressive competitive actions firms, must attempt to predict how their competitors will react; when other firms are proactive, an organization must at least be defensive in order to protect market share and profitability. The intensity of competition is affected by the market structure and depends on the following:

- the number of competitors and the degree of concentration
- the rate of growth of the industry – slow growth increases the pressure upon competitors to fight for market share
- the degree of differentiation – the less there is, the more likely is price competition
- cost structures – where fixed costs are high relative to variable costs, companies are very sensitive around the **break-even** point. Profits are very dependent upon volume.

An example of dedicated assets which have no obvious alternative use is multiplex cinema complexes. As the number of these has grown, cinema audiences have also grown, and an industry in decline has been given a new lease of life. In addition, it is quite normal for several fast food and retail outlets to open alongside the cinemas, helping to boost their traffic. But what would happen to the cinema buildings if audiences declined again? Additionally, it could be argued that cinema going is now becoming more expensive – but not when compared to prices for live theatre. The early alternative product offering in the market was easyCinema.com. This failed to make any real dent in the market against the power of the major cinema chains. History would suggest that sooner or later new competitive pressures will hit this industry. This may come from film downloads once the speed of broadband connections improves significantly and people have invested in home cinema systems.

Manufacturers of consumer electronics products have to invest continually to maintain the technology required for the necessary product improvements. To generate revenues to fund further investment, they need volume sales; to create these they price with low, competitive margins. Profits are very slim, but the sunk costs are such that the cycle continues; it is too costly to come out of the industry. The cycle is reinforced by consumer purchasing behaviour. Consumers know which brands they are happy to consider, their shortlist depending upon the quality and differentiation they are seeking. They then buy on price, seeing certain brands as interchangeable. Inevitably, the retailers also earn only low margins.

Table 4.2 provides a summary checklist of factors for industry analysis, and Strategy in Action 4.3 analyzes the supermarket industry against Porter's model of five forces.

Table 4.2 A checklist for industry analysis

- How many firms are in the industry, and what size are they?
- How concentrated is the industry?
- To what degree are products substitutes?
- Is the industry growing or contracting?
- What are the relative powers of suppliers? Buyers? Competitors?
- What are the prevailing competitive strategies?
- What entry barriers exist?
- What economies of scale are present?
- What experience/learning curve effects are important?
- What exit barriers exist (if any)?
- What important external factors affect competition?

Strategy in Action 4.3   Industry Analysis – Supermarkets

Threat of New Entrants

Barriers to entry are very high, because of the necessary supply network and distribution infrastructure. The continual investment in EPOS (electronic point-of-sale) and EDI (electronic data interchange) systems creates further barriers. In addition, it is very difficult and very expensive to acquire new sites in prime positions. It is possible, given financial reserves, to build a position in selected market niches.

Of course, powerful companies, able to command huge financial resources, can break in with an acquisition, as we saw when Wal-Mart bought ASDA.

Relative Strength of Suppliers

Supply agreements with major retail chains, using EDI, make the leading suppliers and supermarkets more and more interdependent. Ownership of a leading brand yields power, but secondary and tertiary brands must be more vulnerable. Further interdependency with own-label supply agreements.

Relative Strength of Buyers

Invariably, buyers will have more than one supermarket that they can access, especially if they are car owners. The power of the Internet to promote home deliveries also opens up choice. There will be some loyalty, but only if prices and service are competitive.

Threat of Substitutes

Small independent stores have a niche and a role, but the supermarkets are dominant. However, they are vulnerable on price for those products/brands offered by smaller, discount stores, especially where customers are willing to multi-shop. Home shopping via IT continues to be a sector of the market the supermarkets must develop rather than relinquish.

Existing Rivalries

The industry is very competitive, with four or five chains competing for the family shopping budget. Tesco, ASDA, Sainsbury's and Morrisons (after their takeover of Safeway) have different competitive strategies (product ranges, pricing strategies, etc.) and have differing appeals, but they remain largely interchangeable. These companies must all invest to try to create differences as well as pricing competitively. The relatively speedy demise of the Co-op to a predominantly niche role illustrates how intense the rivalry is. The recent growth of the new price-led supermarkets Lidl and Aldi show where things are now going as consumers cut their spending.

Summary

Barriers to entry	high
Power of suppliers	medium
Power of buyers	medium/high
Threat of substitutes	medium
Existing rivalries	intense

The rivalry factors discussed above, and the rivalry strategies, are both affected by any slowing down in the rate of industry growth, by acquisitions, and by changes in the marketing strategy of any one competitor resulting from the perception of new opportunities for differentiation or segmentation.

To be an effective competitor, a company must:

- appreciate which of the five forces is the most significant (it can be different for different industries) and concentrate strategic attention in this area
- position itself for the best possible defence against any threats from rivals
- influence the forces detailed above through its own corporate and competitive strategies
- anticipate changes or shifts in the forces – the factors that are generating success in the short term may not succeed long-term.

Much will depend upon the strategic leader, the quality of management in the organization and the prevailing culture.

The role of government

Rather than incorporation as a separate sixth factor, Porter maintains that the importance of government lies in an ability to affect the other five forces through changes in policy and new legislation. For example, the introduction of competition and an internal market in the National Health Service, a Conservative policy abandoned by the Labour government under Tony Blair and Gordon Brown.

Many industries in the UK, such as the main utilities of gas, electricity and water, were privatized – in order to prevent these (new) businesses becoming national or local monopolies in private ownership, with enormous potential to exploit their customers, industry regulators have been appointed in a number of cases. The regulators and the newly privatized businesses have at times disagreed over important **strategic issues**. Individual regulators are given freedom to establish specific guidelines within clear broad principles, and some would argue that this makes conflict between them and the regulated businesses inevitable. One of the reasons for the diversification strategies by privatized companies is that they create business activities which are outside the direct control of the regulator. Given a general trend away from diversification to a concentration on core businesses and competencies, this has sometimes proved to be risky. Perhaps the impact of the regulators also needs regulating.

High and low profit industries

Porter (2008) revisited his earlier work on industry analysis. He identified soft drinks, pre-packaged software, pharmaceuticals and spirits as attractive, relatively high **profit** potential, industries and air travel, wines and hotels as more naturally unattractive – and, therefore, very competitive. Scattered through this book you will find cases on most of these industries. Porter based his conclusions on return on investment data.

He emphasized that high growth does not guarantee high profits – and neither does the presence of innovation and the latest technology.

In terms of using Porter's ideas to evaluate any 'industry', one must be clear on what the word 'industry' means, as there might be a very broad definition – such as public transport – or a very narrow one. An interpretation that is too wide will obscure the identification of opportunities to be genuinely different; or if too narrow, it is possible to undervalue the potential to create synergy by linking different products and market niches.

4.2 Competition and the structure and regulation of industry

Readers who are familiar with the four economic models of pure or perfect competition, monopolistic competition, oligopoly and monopoly, will appreciate the links to Porter's industry analysis model. The opportunity for substantial profits is most likely to be found in oligopoly and **monopoly structures**. Competition in the other models, resulting mainly from lower barriers to entry, has the effect of reducing profit margins. We consider which models are dominant in the UK, and most other developed nations, as this influences the ways in which firms compete. Specifically, it affects the opportunities for differentiation and for the achievement of cost advantages which, as we discuss in Chapter 6, are major determinants of competitive advantage.

Monopoly power

As far as the regulatory authorities are concerned, a 25 per cent market share offers opportunities for a company to exploit monopoly power. Hence, although the model of pure monopoly assumes only one producer with absolute power in the marketplace, a large producer with a substantial share will be regarded as having **monopoly power**. Such power is not necessarily used against the consumer, but large companies with market shares in excess of their rivals may be able to produce at lower cost (and sell at lower prices) because of their ability to invest in high output, low unit cost technology, to buy supplies in bulk and receive discounts, or to achieve distribution savings, or due to the opportunity to improve productivity as more and more units are produced (*economies of scale*).

Many industries have a limited number (perhaps three, four or five) of large mass market competitors with a broad product range and a number of much smaller niche producers, with the largest companies possibly controlling their costs well, and a consequent reduction in margin as market shares decline (or competitors whose products are very specialist and with very limited market appeal to clearly defined niches or segments will enjoy higher margins than other niche producers whose products are less specialized, with margins declining as market share increases).

A cost advantage, then, can be a major source of competitive advantage, and this point will be developed in greater detail later. The producer who is able to produce at a lower cost than his or her rivals may choose to price very competitively with a view to driving competitors out of the market and thereby increasing market share. Equally, they may not; and by charging a higher price can make a greater profit per unit and thereby seek profit in preference to market share. In the first case, the consumer benefits from lower prices and, therefore, monopoly power is not being used against the consumer. However, once a firm has built up a truly dominant market share, it might seek to change its strategy and exploit its power more, and governments will intervene in some way, for example both the EU and the US government's attempts to curb the power of Microsoft.

Concentration

Concentration is the measure of control exercised by organizations. There are two types.

Aggregate concentration, which will be mentioned only briefly, considers the power of the largest privately owned manufacturing firms in the economy as a whole.

Sectoral or market concentration traditionally considers the percentage of net output or employment (asets, sales or profits can also be measured) controlled by the largest firms in a particular industry, be it manufacturing or service. High **concentration ratio** figures tend to encourage monopoly or oligopoly behaviour, most probably the latter, which implies substantial emphasis on differentiation and non-price competition, with rivals seeing themselves as interdependent.

Many industries worldwide are essentially oligopolistic in structure, with a limited number of major competitors and barriers to entry in individual countries. In general, competition will be non-price rather than price, but price competition will be seen in situations where supply exceeds demand and there is aggressive competition for market share.

There may well be marketing and distribution advantages for companies which belong to conglomerates and this could increase their relative market power. Similarly, products which dominate particular market segments will yield advantages. Consequently, there is still opportunity for smaller companies to compete successfully in certain oligopoly markets, especially if they can differentiate their product so that it has appeal for particular segments of the market.

In the UK chocolate industry, Thornton's has been successful with a limited range of high-quality chocolate products distributed through the company's own specialist and franchised outlets. It is only recently, in 2009, with changing purchase habits of consumers that sales of high quality and, therefore, high price boxed chocolates seemed under pressure. At the same time, sales of high quality chocolate bars seemed to be on the increase. This trend is not confined to the chocolate industry, but is widespread. One must assume that once the recession is over and discretionary purchasing power grows back that this situation will also change back.

The regulation of monopoly power

Governments monitor the forces of competition to minimize any waste of resources due to economic inefficiency, to guard against any exploitation of relatively weak buyers or suppliers and to ensure that powerful companies do not seek to eliminate their competitors purely to gain monopoly power.

Regulations are passed and implemented to police these issues (illustrated in this section by reference to the UK) but the principles and general approach apply elsewhere. A new UK Competition Bill, passed in 1997 and operational in 1999, put the following structure in place.

In ultimate charge was the Department (or Minister) of Trade and Industry (DTI) now renamed as the Department for Business, Innovation and Skills (BIS). The Office of Fair Trading (OFT), headed by a Director-General, has powers to carry out preliminary investigations of all proposed **mergers** or takeovers involving market shares of 25 per cent or more, or combined assets in excess of £75 million. If the OFT believes that major competition concerns are present, then it can refer the proposal to a second body, the Competition Commission, for further investigation. The Competition Commission is the delegated arbiter of referrals.

Each case is considered on merit, and the presumption is not automatically that monopoly power is against the public interest. High profitability is considered acceptable if it reflects efficiency, but not if it is sustained by artificial barriers to entry. The OFT also investigates cartels.

The delay involved in an investigation can be important strategically. The process is likely to take at least 6 months and in that time a company which opposes the takeover bid against it will work hard to improve its performance and prospects. If this results in a substantial increase in the share price, the acquisitive company may withdraw on the grounds that the cost has become too high. Companies may seek to prevent a reference by undertaking to sell off part of the businesses involved in an acquisition if competition concerns are raised. Recently, the UK government has mused about legislation to make company executives personally liable for competitive misdemeanours, but it has not been passed.

Since September 1990, the European Commission has also been able to influence the growing number of corporate mergers and acquisitions in the EU. Mergers are exempted, though, if each company has more than two-thirds of its EU-wide turnover in any one EU country. The intervention of the European authorities has been controversial and some judgements have been criticized. There is a voice of opinion in the USA that the European Commission is hostile to American mergers where the companies enjoy substantial sales in Europe. The EU in effect prevented General Electric acquiring another American business, Honeywell.

Examples of intervention

In February 2000, the Competition Commission in the UK ruled that Unilever should be banned from distributing its own Wall's ice-cream direct to retailers. Wall's ice-cream products hold the largest market share in the UK, in excess of 50 per cent. The argument was that a newly formed subsidiary, Wall's Direct, was undermining independent wholesalers and, as a consequence, competitors such as Nestlé and Mars were being squeezed out of the supply chain. The DTI chose to water down the ban and recommended a capping of the scope and extent of the distribution operation. Unilever, however, concluded that a cap was not feasible and it began to wind down its distribution.

In parallel with this investigation, the Competition Commission had also examined Unilever's practice of providing retailers with free freezer cabinets but insisting that they were used only for Wall's products. Small retailers, with room for just one freezer cabinet, were effectively prevented from stocking other brands. The Commission recommended that retailers should be allowed to fill up to half of the cabinet with rival products.

In July 2003 Manchester United, JJB (the UK's leading sportswear retailer) and Umbro (sportswear manufacturer) were all fined for colluding to fix the retail prices of replica football kits. Those concerned all denied the allegations. In a case brought in 2003 and ruled on in 2004, Ryanair fell foul of the Commission for accepting unfair landing subsidies from municipal airports in Europe.

Highlighting the global nature of competition regulation, Microsoft, dominant in personal computer operating systems, has been judged by an American court to be exploiting its monopoly power. In early 2000, it was ruled that the basic operating systems (based on Windows) and the applications (Microsoft Office and Internet Explorer) should be separated into two separate businesses, and that Microsoft should also be required to give away to its competitors some of its operating systems code. The contention was that Microsoft had driven Netscape out of the Internet browser market by tying its own browser, Explorer, to Windows. Inevitably, the company appealed against the ruling, and after a Democratic President was replaced by a more sympathetic to business Republican President in George W. Bush, this requirement was relaxed. Microsoft could stay intact. However, the European competition authority has also taken a very firm line, convinced that Microsoft has exploited its monopoly power. The *Financial Times* commented at one stage: 'Surely, most seriously of all, is that at a time Microsoft should be focusing all its talent on keeping up with technological innovation, it is hamstrung by this case.'

4.3 Key success factors, strategic positioning, adding value and SWOT

Key success factors

Firms must produce to high and consistent quality levels and meet delivery promises to customers, with delivery times reducing gradually in very competitive industries. Suppliers and subcontractors expect regular orders and accurate forecasting when very quick deliveries are demanded from them or **just-in-time (JIT)** production systems, which rely on regular and reliable deliveries from suppliers in order to maintain constant production without the need for high parts inventories, are impractical.

Firms will try to minimize their stockholding to improve both cash flow and costs. Conglomerate subsidiaries will have to generate a positive cash flow in order to meet the financial expectations of the parent company who, in effect, act as its bankers. Costs have to be controlled so that companies remain price competitive, although low prices are not always a marketing weapon.

These stakeholder requirements represent *key success factors*, those things that an organization must do well if it is to be an effective competitor and thrive. In addition, many companies have to be innovative and improve both their product range and their customer service if they are to remain a leading competitor in a changing industry.

Some key success factors will be industry and sector specific, e.g. charities need skills in fundraising and public relations, given intense competition for donations, as they can only spend what they can raise, and must use their money appropriately, are seen to be doing so and are recognized for their efforts, such that the differing demands of fundraising and aid provision lead to complex cultures and organizations.

Resources must be managed with stakeholder needs in mind, with everyone in the organization recognizing and being committed to meeting key success factors, and being responsive to change pressures in a dynamic and competitive environment, without which firms will be unable to sustain a match with the changing environment.

Figure 4.5 illustrates that if organizations are to satisfy their stakeholders, especially their customers, while outperforming their rivals, their competitive offering should comprise:

- the ability to meet the recognized key success factors for the relevant industry or market
- distinctive competencies and capabilities which yield some form of competitive advantage, and
- the ability and willingness to deploy these competencies and capabilities to satisfy the special requirements of individual customers, for which a premium price can often be charged; or 'customerizing' rather than marketing, reflecting the importance of customers as individuals rather than as a generic group who constitute a market (Hall, 1992).

Strategic positioning

A Strengths, Weaknesses, Opportunities and Threats (SWOT) analysis implies that an organization's resources (its strengths and weaknesses) should match the demands and pressures from its external environment (opportunities and threats) as effectively as possible and, with change, stay matched in dynamic and turbulent times. The overlap of products and services (the outcome of the use of the organization's resources) with market needs is shown as a strategic fit in Figure 4.6.

Here we can see illustrated two different, but complementary, approaches to strategy creation and strategic change.

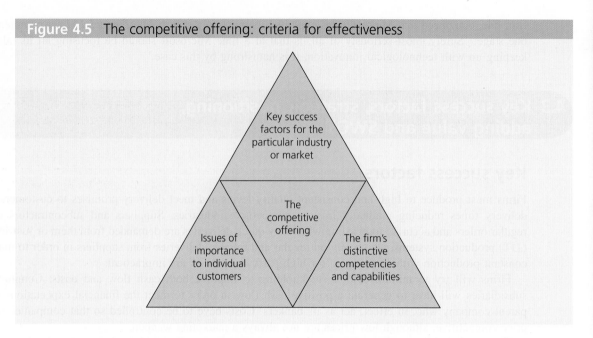

Figure 4.5 The competitive offering: criteria for effectiveness

Market-driven strategy (or **opportunity-driven strategy**) reflects the adoption of the marketing concept, and implies that strategies are designed – and resources developed and deployed – with customer and consumer needs in mind. Carefully and creatively defining the industry or industries in which an organization competes can influence its perspective on the products and services it supplies. Marketing students will always remember that railway companies are in the transportation business! The approach is market-pull, and the value of a distinct competitive advantage is clearly synonymous with this approach. It should, however, never be forgotten that different sectors of the same industry require different competencies, and that the demands of creating new competencies may be readily underestimated.

It is convenient but too simplistic just to see resources as organizational strengths and weaknesses (which they very clearly are) and the environment as the source of opportunities and threats. Resources can also constitute both opportunities and strengths – as we can see in Case 4.4 on Flying Brands. This case also highlights how strengths can become weaknesses and hoped-for synergies may often not materialize.

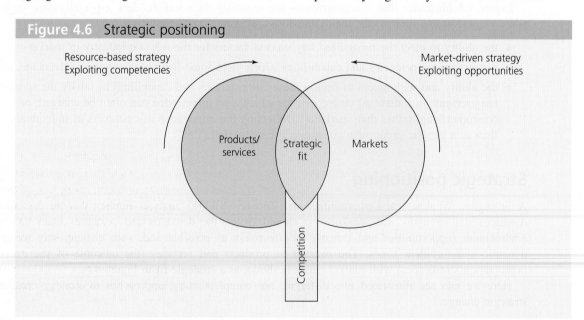

Figure 4.6 Strategic positioning

Case 4.4   Flying Brands   UK

Flying Brands began life as Flying Flowers, which, as the name suggests, sold flowers by post. The company was set up in Jersey in the Channel Islands in the early 1980s to save a struggling glasshouse business – a loss-making nursery needed and created a new opportunity. By 1996 turnover had grown to £35 million, with pre-tax profits of £4 million.

There are four key elements to the strategy and the success. First, the company held only low stocks of the actual flowers, many of which it bought in cheaply from countries such as Colombia: flowers *from* Jersey does not have to mean flowers grown in Jersey!

Demand fluctuates markedly, peaking twice, at Christmas and Mother's Day, when the company typically receives 15 000 postal and 5000 telephone orders per day for a short period. Christmas sales amounted to five million carnations in 330 000 boxed deliveries. Coping with this surge in demand is critical for success. The second key element therefore is staffing and staff management. As tourism is a leading source of employment in Jersey, and is strongest during the summer months, Flying Flowers was able to use casual hotel and restaurant staff. They are relatively plentiful on an island of scarce labour resources, and critically they are often laid off temporarily over Christmas and Mother's Day when tourism falls off.

Third, the company used a disused glasshouse to house a noisy, steam-breathing machine which produces polystyrene boxes every working day of the year. These are then piled high to ensure that any demand peak can be catered for.

Fourth, and very critically, Flying Flowers invested in IT to support both control and marketing. It soon built up a database of one million people and carefully targeted its direct mail, analyzing all responses and orders in detail. It opened a telephone call centre in Essex.

Flying Flowers as a concept adds value for customers – high-quality, fresh flowers delivered directly to the door. Its operating costs are relatively low for the reasons described above and, of course, there are no returns to deal with.

The skills and competencies the company developed were exploited further with the acquisition of other businesses – hence the change of name to Flying Brands. The company bought Gardening Direct (mail-order bedding plants), Listen2Books and Stanley Gibbons (publisher and stamp supplier) and another supplier of first-day stamp covers. It operated as three divisions, which clearly could share resources and competencies.

In 2006 Scottish entrepreneur and venture capitalist, Sir Tom Hunter, bought a 29.9 per cent stake in the business. He was already a part owner of Wyevale Garden Centres and almost certainly expected synergy opportunities.

Flying Brands then became a multi-brand home shopping centre using catalogues, press advertising and the Internet to promote its many product ranges. For example, garden bird foods had been added to work alongside the bedding plants. As more and more products were considered and added the challenge was to find the right mix and balance.

SOURCE: THIS CASE STUDY WAS PREPARED USING PRIMARILY PUBLICLY AVAILABLE SOURCES OF INFORMATION FOR THE PURPOSES OF CLASSROOM DISCUSSION; IT DOES NOT INTEND TO ILLUSTRATE EITHER EFFECTIVE OR INEFFECTIVE HANDLING OF A MANAGERIAL SITUATION.

Theeconomic recession hit Flying Brands and sales suffered. To consolidate the business, a decision was made to sell certain businesses within the portfolio; unfortunately this seemed to have an adverse impact and the bad publicity (about falling sales and profits) affected the products that remained. Everything was for sale at an appropriate price. When the original Flying Flowers business was sold (in February 2012) to Interflora, Flying Brands was all but finished.

Questions

1 How did Flying Brands add value?
2 What was the nature of its strategic position?
3 At the time, did the acquisitions make sense in relation to its competencies and capabilities?

Resource-based strategy (covered in more detail in Chapter 5) implies that the organization clarifies its core strategic competencies and capabilities and seeks to exploit these by finding new market opportunities where they can be used to create new value and competitive advantage – such that the organization can mould and develop its market with innovatory new ideas, sometimes changing the rules of competition in an industry and possibly creating new customer preferences and perspectives in the process.

All the time, competitors (Chapter 6) will be attempting to accomplish the same ends so that, while a company is trying to create a stronger fit between itself and its customers, its competitors will be attempting to force them apart by offering something superior which draws customers away and destroys fit. Hence, a third and more tactical approach to strategy is **competitor influenced** which implies short-term vigilance to deal with any threatening competitor initiatives. Whilst significant, it is important that an organization does not become over-reliant upon this tactical approach. We can also see this reflected in the Online Case 4.1 on Sainsbury's.

Moreover, emerging opportunities can attract competitors with different backgrounds and motives, for example how developments in computer software and hardware (high-quality monitors, scanners and printers) have opened up an opportunity for digital cameras, with Kodak, Canon and Hewlett-Packard all being interested but the challenge for each rival was quite different.

Figure 4.7 emphasizes that effective strategic positions ensure that corporate strategic resources meet and satisfy **key (or critical) success factors** for customers and markets. Strategically valuable resources translate into core competencies and strategic capabilities (which are explained in more detail in Chapter 5), which are then manifest in a whole range of activities that the organization undertakes. Competencies and capabilities can be separated by thinking of core competencies being built around technologies and technological skills, and strategic capabilities referring to processes and ways of doing things.

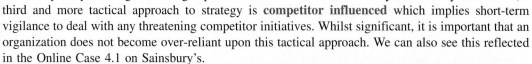

Figure 4.7   Strategic positioning revisited

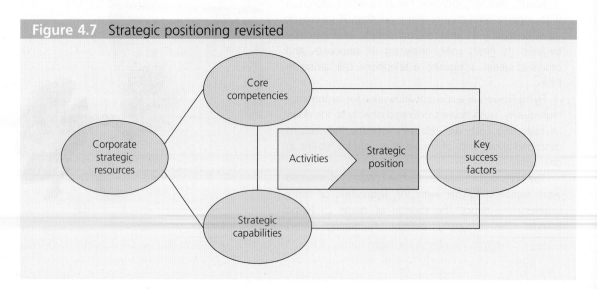

Capabilities thus exploit the competencies; technology must, however, be developed to a particular level for a company to be influential in an industry or market. Hence, while the real competitive strength of an organization can be built around either competencies or capabilities, both must be present for relative success, and both competency and capability must be improved with innovation over time. In Chapter 10 it is shown that people, learning and information are critical elements of this innovation. In addition, companies can benefit markedly from exploiting the linkages and relationships that they have with their suppliers and distributors.

Strategic positioning, *per se*, is not a source of competitive advantage because any relative advantage enjoyed by the organization comes from the resources and activities which establish and support the position, whether tangible or intangible in nature, i.e. these are the ways through which it creates and adds value.

Added value

To be successful, a business must add value (value added being defined as the difference between the value of the outputs from an organization and the cost of the inputs or resources used), particularly as supply potential has grown to exceed global demand in the majority of industries.

The traditional paradigm, based on the accountancy measure, is that prices reflect costs plus a profit margin. The lack of differentiation, for which a higher price can be charged, implies enormous downward pressures on costs. Performance measurement is then based upon economy of scale (low input costs) and efficiency (minimizing the actual and attributed costs of the resources used for adding further value).

While all resources must be used efficiently and properly, firms must ensure that the potential value of the outputs is maximized by ensuring that they fully meet the needs of the customers for whom they are intended – by seeing its customers' objectives as its own objectives and enabling them to easily add more value or, in the case of final consumers, feel that they are gaining true value for money.

In the new paradigm, the key is value for the customer so that, if resources are used to provide real value for them, they will pay a price reflecting its worth to them.

Kay (1993) researched the most successful European companies during the 1980s, measured by their average costs per unit of net output, finding that each company had developed an individual strategy for adding value and creating competitive success. Glaxo (number one in the ten at that time) successfully exploited the international potential for its patented anti-ulcer drug Zantac. LVMH (Louis Vuitton, Moet Hennessy), sixth in the list, generated synergy from the global distribution of a diverse range of high-quality, premium-brand products. Benetton, second, enjoyed beneficially close links with its suppliers and distributors, again worldwide. Marks and Spencer (tenth, and Case 1.2 in the opening chapter) was also expert at supply-chain management and further benefited from its value-for-money image and reputation. In contrast, low-price food retailer Kwik Save, fifth in the list, was selling its products with a low margin but enjoying a relatively very high turnover to capital employed. BTR (number nine) had expertise in the management of a diversified conglomerate. The relative fortunes of some of these organizations have declined, such as BTR and Kwik Save, which no longer exist, since what constitutes value for customers at some point in time will not always constitute value. As needs and requirements change, companies must find new ways of creating high added value.

The important elements in adding value are:

- understanding and being close to customers, in particular understanding their perception of value
- a commitment to quality
- a high level of all-round service
- speedy reaction to competitive opportunities and threats
- innovation.

Organizations can seek to add value by, first, adding positive features, such as air conditioning, comfortable bucket seats and CD players in cars and, secondly, by removing any features perceived as negatives or drawbacks. Antilock braking systems and four-wheel drive gearboxes reduce the concerns that some people have about driving in bad weather, while extended warranty schemes remove the fear of unknown future repair costs. Each of these additions has a value for which some customers, not all, will pay a premium. Case 4.5, PlayPumps, illustrates a creative way of adding value for communities.

It is quite conceivable that organizations are pursuing strategies or **policies** which make life harder for their customers. Minimum order quantities and, possibly, volume discounts, may force or encourage customers to buy more than they need or can afford to stock, but obsolescence can then become an issue. Organizations could evaluate the merit of discounts based on annual sales rather than only on individual orders, and should be looking to ensure that they follow the top loop of Figure 4.8 and not the bottom one.

Organizations that truly understand their customers can create competitive advantage and thereby benefit from higher prices and loyalty, so that high-capacity utilization can then help to reduce costs.

Opportunities for adding value which attracts customers must be sought and exploited. Numerous possible opportunities exist at corporate, competitive and functional strategy levels, so that resources must be deployed to exploit these possibilities. Pümpin (1991) argues that multiplication, i.e. strategic

---

Case 4.5   PlayPumps   Africa

PlayPumps is a South African social enterprise with a different perspective on children playing and having fun. It is based on the belief their energy can be captured and used to create community value.

In rural areas in developing countries there is no piped water routinely available. The main source of fresh water is boreholes where springs, streams and rivers are missing or unsuitable. Water is raised using hand pumps and many women and children invest hours of time fetching and carrying water for their family's needs. Individually we each need a minimum of 5 litres a day. If petrol or diesel is available and can be afforded, motorized pumps can be used – as long as they can be maintained for a lengthy period of time – otherwise communities have to rely on hand pumps. Typically a hand pump will deliver 150 litres per hour to ground level, and that water will need to be used relatively quickly as there is unlikely to be anywhere to store it hygienically. Installing a hand pump costs in the region of 10 000 South African Rand, something over £1000. For between three and five times that amount a PlayPump could be installed.

The idea of the inventor was to build a special playground roundabout to be the main power source and encourage children to have fun spinning it round and round – which is something young children have always enjoyed doing! Clean borehole water is pumped up and collected in large aboveground storage tanks. Because there is no engine, maintenance is straightforward and relatively inexpensive. The equipment used is standard windmill equipment which is readily available and does not require special sourcing. Below the ground is a positive displacement cylinder using rising rods and pipes – which very simply converts the rotational movement of the roundabout into a vertical movement.

Each rotation of the roundabout can pump up to 4 litres of fresh water, allowing for some 1400 litres per hour to be raised into the storage tank if the depth does not exceed 40 metres. The system can support raising water 100 metres but obviously the capacity is substantially reduced. Storage tanks will typically hold up to 5000 litres on a 6-metre-high stand. Water is drawn by a simple tap arrangement. The outer skin of the storage tank can also be used for advertising, and the revenue from this will certainly pay for all the maintenance and may, over time, repay the cost of the installation. The advertising works as women will generally be the ones to come and collect the water.

Women do not have to labour as they do with hand pumps. Children have fun. Communities get fresh water. And the project is self-sustaining.

The South African government has funded a project in KwaZulu Natal to install PlayPumps in school playgrounds wherever this is appropriate and water can be harnessed and drawn. Clearly this is an invention that has relevance for other countries in Africa and Asia.

Question

PlayPumps – as an organization – adds considerable value to African communities – but they are unlikely to be able to pay for the installation. The community benefits socially more than it does economically. Whose responsibility is it to fund such initiatives?

Project

Research the One Foundation – specifically the branded product, One Water – and its role in helping fund PlayPumps.

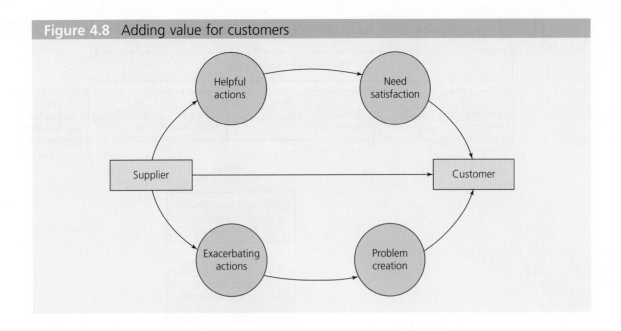

Figure 4.8 Adding value for customers

consistency and performance improvement by concentrating on certain important strategies and learning how to implement them more effectively, promotes growth. The matching process is led and championed by the strategic leader, who is responsible for establishing the key values. While striving to improve performance with existing strategies, the organization must constantly search for new windows of opportunity. McDonald's (Case 1.3) provides an excellent example. Ray Kroc spotted an opportunity in the growing fast-food market and exploited it by concentrating on new product ideas and franchised outlets, supported by a culture that promoted 'quality, service, cleanliness and value'.

Figure 4.9 shows that organizations must add value, and continue to find new ways of adding fresh value for their customers by developing, changing and exploiting core resource-based technological competencies, involving organizational processes and capabilities, together with strong linkages with other companies in the supply chain (**strategic architecture**), in order to create differentiation and effective cost control and, thus, establish a superior competitive position. The situation is always fluid, though; organizations cannot assume that currently successful products, services and competitive strategies will be equally successful in the future, and they must be changed at appropriate times. In turn, this requires competency in awareness, thinking and learning, such that realizing which competencies are most important for long-term success, concentrating attention on them, developing them and measuring the desired improvements is critically important for the strategic leader.

All the time, companies should carry out efficiently those activities which are essential for creating a distinctive or differentiated competitive position, and avoid incurring unnecessary costs by providing non-essential value – implying that they clearly understand their markets, their customers and the key success factors that they must meet (their defined competitive strategy), and should constantly seek improvement by driving their operating efficiencies.

Firms use their various resources, both tangible and intangible, to create value so that customers who recognize and appreciate that value and are happy with the price being asked are likely to buy, influencing profit. Figure 4.10 delineates two value-adding cycles, both of which can establish superior profits and allow for ongoing investment and innovation. They are not mutually exclusive because, whatever the competitive strategy, strong cost management is essential.

To be successful, products and services must fit into markets. Marketing and operations strategies are critical elements of competitive strategy, which could be global or local markets, mass or niche markets, with products that are commodities or substantially customized, or the market (or the relevant niche) could

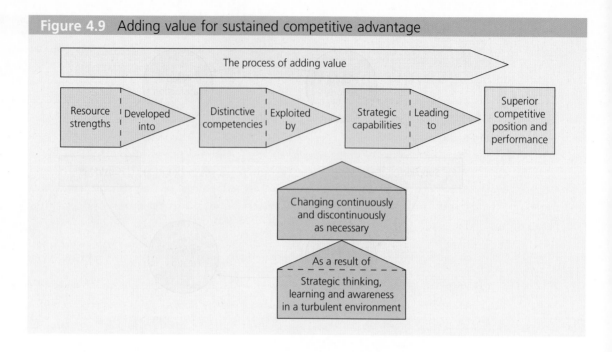

Figure 4.9 Adding value for sustained competitive advantage

be growing, static or declining. Each one can be profitable, but in different ways, with different strategies. Companies which target new markets, segments or niches may find that they are hard to penetrate, unless they have developed something radically new and different which is seen as a valuable alternative by customers. Most successful companies have realized that it is more expensive to win new business than it is to retain existing customers and, as a result, look after their customers. While patents can provide a barrier to new entrants and new rivals, so too can loyal customers!

However, some markets may equally be difficult to defend, such as where the wider business environment is dynamic and turbulent, where the organization enjoys only a relatively weak strategic fit and where the service being provided is below the level expected. Hence, positioning and fit can be improved with customer care, product and service innovation and improvement, and by developing new products.

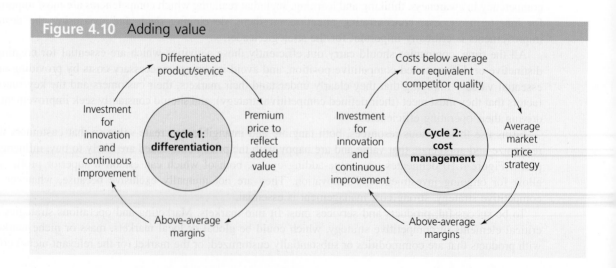

Figure 4.10 Adding value

All of this requires that companies take their competitors seriously, defend against any initiatives that they start and, on occasion, attack them, implying any or all of:

- finding and opening new windows of opportunity
- product and service development, improvement and enhancement
- direct attacks, such as price wars, either 'all-out' and sustained or short-term and guerrilla. Special discount promotions would be an example of the latter
- attempting to change the 'rules of engagement or competition' either openly (with genuinely new ideas) or more deviously (lobbying government for new regulations or buying out a key supplier or competitor)
- a 'war of words', seeking publicity for your activities and carefully disparaging your competitors. Sir Richard Branson was able to strengthen the image and position of Virgin Atlantic when he drew attention to British Airways' so-called 'dirty tricks' campaign to win over Virgin customers
- networking and collaboration with key partners in the supply chain.

To summarize this section, Markides (1999) provides a list of six factors for competitive and strategic success. These are:

1   Choose a potentially winning position. This requires understanding *who* your customers are, *what* they require and expect and *how* they can be reached. This corresponds with Porter's (1996) view that it is essential to focus on certain activities and ignore others, not attempting to be 'all things to all people'.

2   Make this choice by a proper exploration of options.

3   An active search for opportunities to be different in a meaningful way, not just adopting a strategy because it seems to work.

4   Ensure all the support activities work together effectively and synergistically.

5   Create a real strategic fit and position which links the organization with its customers.

6   Ensure there is flexibility in both the activities and the fit so that innovation and change can sustain competitiveness.

Appropriability

Kay (1993) stresses '**appropriability**', that organizations must seek to ensure that they see the benefits of the value which they create and add, since few things cannot be copied and some positions of advantage will be transient without improvement.

Value can be provided for customers in a whole variety of ways, but unless they are willing to pay a premium price which at least offsets the cost of adding the value, then it is the customer and not the organization that benefits. Even if a premium price can be charged, if this is then used to reward suppliers and employees, additional profits may not accrue. Sometimes higher profits are used primarily to reward shareholders, or owner–managers in the case of small organizations. All of these possibilities imply that the organization is not creating and sustaining a position where it makes superior profits and uses these (at least in part) to reinvest and help to build new values through improvement and innovation. Quite simply, the ideal scenario is a virtuous one, where every stakeholder benefits.

SWOT (strengths, weaknesses, opportunities and threats) analysis

Environmental opportunities are only potential opportunities unless the organization can utilize resources to take advantage of them and until the strategic leader decides that it is appropriate to pursue the opportunity – by evaluating environmental opportunities in relation to the strengths and weaknesses of the organization's resources, and in relation to the organizational culture. Real opportunities exist when there is a close fit between environment, values and resources. Similarly, the resources and culture will determine the extent to which any potential threat becomes a real threat, or E–V–R congruence, which was explained in Chapter 1.

All of the resources at the disposal of the organization can be deployed strategically, including strategic leadership, and firms must evaluate the resources in terms of strengths and weaknesses to provide an indication of their strategic value – not a list of absolute strengths and weaknesses seen from an internal perspective, but only in relation to the needs of the environment and in relation to competition. The views of external stakeholders may differ from those of internal managers (who, in turn, may disagree among themselves) when evaluating the relative strength of a particular product, resource or skill. Resources should be evaluated for their relative strengths and weaknesses in the light of key success factors.

Even though an organization may be strong or weak in a particular function, the corresponding position of its major competitors must also be taken into account. For example, it might have sophisticated computer-controlled machine tools in its factory, but if its competitors have the same or even better equipment, the plant should not be seen as a relative strength – distinctive competencies, relative strengths which can be used to create competitive advantage. As any resource can be deployed strategically, competitive advantage can be gained from any area of the total business.

An evaluation of an organization's strengths and weaknesses in relation to environmental opportunities and threats is generally referred to as a SWOT analysis.

Figure 4.11 illustrates a popular and useful framework for a SWOT analysis applied to ASDA earlier in the 1990s, before the introduction of new strategies focusing on the product ranges, in-store layouts and a clear distinction between large ASDA superstores and smaller units with a limited range and discounted prices and then its acquisition by Wal-Mart before it later acquired (and rebranded) the Netto stores.

Figure 4.11   ASDA – SWOT analysis, early 1990s

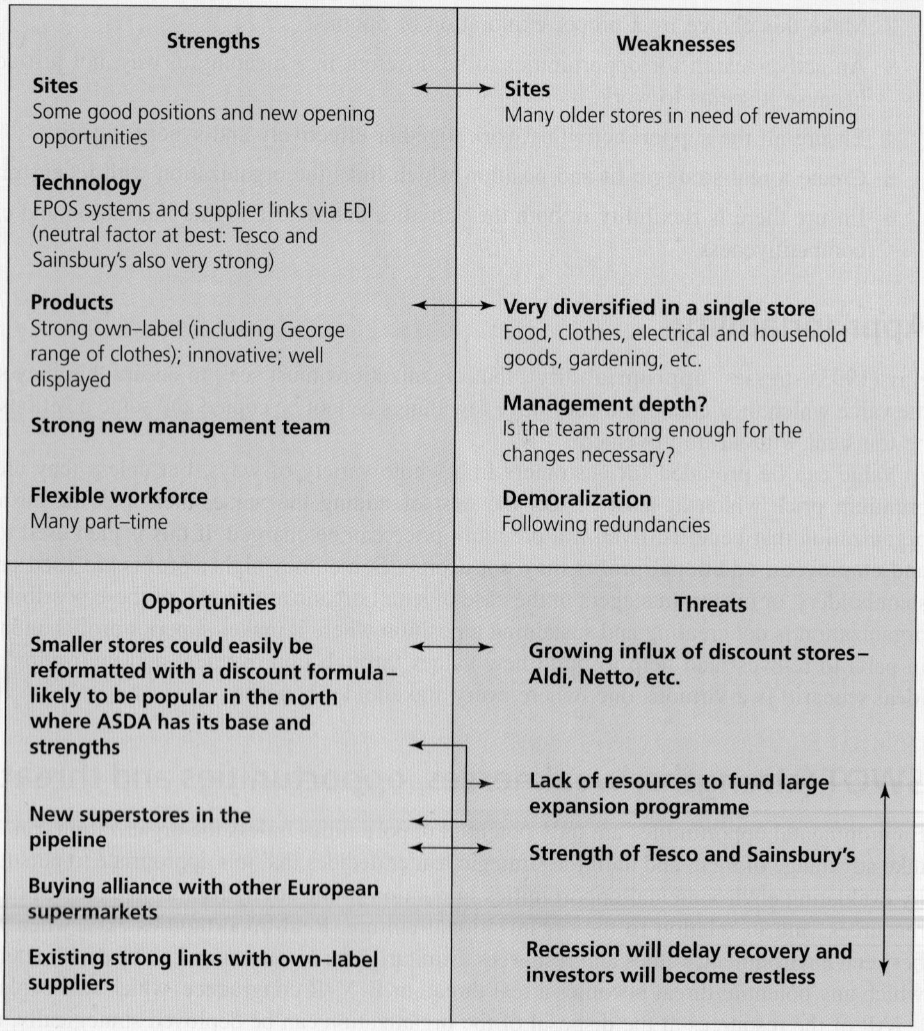

Strengths	Weaknesses
Sites Some good positions and new opening opportunities	**Sites** Many older stores in need of revamping
Technology EPOS systems and supplier links via EDI (neutral factor at best: Tesco and Sainsbury's also very strong)	
Products Strong own–label (including George range of clothes); innovative; well displayed	**Very diversified in a single store** Food, clothes, electrical and household goods, gardening, etc.
Strong new management team	**Management depth?** Is the team strong enough for the changes necessary?
Flexible workforce Many part–time	**Demoralization** Following redundancies

Opportunities	Threats
Smaller stores could easily be reformatted with a discount formula – **likely to be popular in the north where ASDA has its base and strengths**	**Growing influx of discount stores – Aldi, Netto, etc.**
	Lack of resources to fund large expansion programme
New superstores in the pipeline	**Strength of Tesco and Sainsbury's**
Buying alliance with other European supermarkets	
Existing strong links with own–label suppliers	**Recession will delay recovery and investors will become restless**

The chart highlights how certain issues can be considered as either a strength or a weakness, an opportunity or a threat, depending on how they are managed in the future.

Once all of the important *strategic issues* have been teased out from a long list of strengths, weaknesses, opportunities and threats, the following questions should be asked:

- How can we either neutralize critical weaknesses or convert them into strengths?
- Similarly, can we neutralize critical threats or even build them into new opportunities?
- How can we best exploit our strengths in relation to our opportunities?
- What new markets and market segments might be suitable for our existing strengths and capabilities?
- Given the (changing) demands of our existing markets, what changes do we need to make to our products, processes and services?

Finally, alongside a general SWOT analysis, it is essential to evaluate the relative strengths and weaknesses of the company's leading competitors.

4.4   Forecasting the environment

External events and competitor activities can trigger a chain reaction of responses and new **scenarios**; but Handy (1989) contends that 'those who know why changes come waste less effort in protecting themselves or in fighting the inevitable.' However, despite the difficulty of forecasting environmental change, organizations must (i) attempt to stay strategically aware, (ii) reflect upon their experiences and seek emerging patterns or trends in the industry and business environment, (iii) be vigilant in tracking technological and other developments which may affect, possibly radically, their industries and markets and (iv) look for, and maybe even borrow appropriate ideas.

> *Don't try to eliminate uncertainty … embrace it. Despite overwhelming evidence to the contrary many of us still view the future as an extension of the past.*
>
> CLEM SUNTER, ANGLO AMERICAN CORPORATION OF SOUTH AFRICA (THE WORLD'S LARGEST MINING GROUP)

> *The world's changing. People in the US and Europe aren't going to live the way they do 100 years from now unless they do a lot of things differently. Who says that because we have 240 million people on this big piece of land [USA] we should have two cars and second homes, while 800 million people in India and one billion in China should live the way they live? We've only been wealthy in this country for 70 years. Who said we ought to have all this? Is it ordained?*
>
> JOHN F. WELCH, CHAIRMAN AND FORMER CEO, GENERAL ELECTRIC

Scenario planning

Scenario planning was first properly used in a business context by Shell over 40 years ago; however, it still remains a fringe activity for many organizations.

Scenarios are often used in strategic management to explore future possibilities, which are considered by looking at potential outcomes from particular causes and seeking to explain why things might occur. The value is in increased awareness by exploring possibilities and asking and attempting to answer 'what if' questions. Although scenario planning can be predictive and can be used to plan strategic changes, it can also help decision-making by providing managers with insight so that they can react better when things happen or change, and can be helpful for conceptualizing possible new competitive paradigms.

Environments for many organizations have become – and continue to become – increasingly dynamic, turbulent and uncertain, featuring an element of competitive chaos, where companies continually thrust and parry with new ploys and stratagems in an attempt to, at the very least, 'stay in the game' and, ideally, get ahead of their rivals. Scenarios and scenario planning concern the medium- or long-term future and they embrace the possibility of real and dramatic change. Anticipation and creativity can be invaluable in dealing with the turbulence and uncertainty. By considering and evaluating future possibilities, organizations can put themselves in positions where they might be better placed to deal with the unpredictable challenges of the future. Put another way: simply engaging in the process of acknowledging and anticipating change enables managers to be less shocked by whatever change does occur.

Three central themes underpin effective scenario planning:

- Clarifying just what a business can and cannot change. Small farmers, for example, cannot enjoy the scale economies of large farms, nor can they affect the climate, but they can, within reason, improve their soil and they can change their crops.

- What seems trivial or a pipe dream today could be crucial in the future. In 1874, Western Union in America turned down Alexander Graham Bell's prototype telephone!

- Multiple scenarios need to be explored and then *held* as real possibilities. Shell, which pioneered scenario planning, is arguably ready to respond quickly to shocks which affect supply or prevailing prices.

The scenarios considered may involve modified versions of current competitive paradigms (the future is not the past, but at least the two are related) or radically new paradigms (everything changes in the end). The implications of the scenarios will tend towards one of two themes: first, there will be environmental changes but organizations can learn to cope with, and influence or manage events, and thereby enjoy some degree of relative stability; second, the environmental turbulence will be so great that the competitive situation will become ever more chaotic in nature.

Readers might like to consider a number of emerging issues in the UK, evaluate their significance and implications and, where appropriate, consider how they might apply in their own countries.

- In recent years UK residents have increasingly become home owners. This trend has been in part caused by the long-term growth in property values, but in turn it has helped to fuel rises and falls in house prices. Negative equity (owning a mortgage that is greater than the price of the property) and repossessions have become a problem for some people at certain times. At the same time, more and more people have been tempted to become owners of buy-to-let properties, many of them apartments. The availability of these properties and the inability of first-time buyers to afford the deposits required to secure a mortgage have worked together. There is an argument that one outcome is a housing stock that is inappropriate for the future. The credit crunch of 2008 brought many of these issues to a head with record numbers of repossessions and significant increases in negative equity. The amount of deposit required to secure a new mortgage has increased.

- People are living longer; there is an ageing population. But will the more recent trend of people retiring earlier, many on good pensions, continue? As people are healthier, is it not logical for them to work longer, as long as employers do not discriminate on age grounds? Of course, for some jobs, skills can become outdated and people do become less useful. There is also the key dilemma of pensions. If people retire relatively early and live longer, there are two implications: one is that they will have to accept lower pensions; the other is that those people still in employment will have to pay far higher contributions to build up and sustain the pension funds. Many employers have had to reassess the pensions they provide – as they cannot afford them.

- In part thanks to television programmes such as *Dragons' Den* on BBC, an increasing number of people seem attracted to the idea of self-employment and starting their own businesses. It is debatable whether our education and business support networks are truly effective in terms of providing the support they need.

- According to most published statistics, unemployment had been consistently coming down, yet, at the same time, there are growing skills shortages in trades such as plumbing. Developing one point above, raising the retirement age could help here, but only for some jobs. In a knowledge-based society, does the need for skill retraining and updating become more critical through a person's working life?

- There are some who argue that there is 'grade deterioration' with school-leaving qualifications and many young people are inadequately prepared. At the same time as this, and at the same time as there is a shortage of people in skilled trades, the numbers attending universities has been increasing. Adding to this point, the increase in university tuition fees may well make students more discriminating.

- The NHS is stretched and private medicine is expensive. This could become more problematical as people live longer and especially if pensions are reduced. Hence, economically, people might need to work longer.

- However, if the relative balance between salaried and 'permanent' career posts and self-employed people who contract themselves to various organizations continues to change, this issue of the length of working lives could be exacerbated.

- In addition, it is becoming increasingly difficult for many families to prepare for retirement because of the increasing costs of educating their children. In turn, this increases the number of two-income families and creates a larger number of childcare positions.

- The UK is a member of the enlarged European Union. This allows workers from other European countries to come to the UK and seek work without a visa. Although there are tighter rules for would-be immigrants from non-EU countries this has created some tensions in the recent economic recession.

In a wider context it might also be valuable to look at the implications of global climate change, the ever-increasing power of computing technology and the growth of new economies, such as China.

Developing useful scenarios

Organizations should really be looking to develop a number of scenarios that can be used to provoke debate among managers and possibly generate new creative ideas in the process – ideas that can be used as a basis for new strategies and action plans. As Schwartz (2003) points out, most future predictions will prove to be wrong – the real test of scenario planning is whether or not it changes how people manage their businesses, not whether the predictions are right.

The first step is to clarify the *key strategic issues*, mainly external, which will impact on the future that the company will face. Internally, many managers will already have formed views, which may not always accord, and which may be partial rather than comprehensive, but these preliminary views will have caused the development of current working assumptions about future trends. It is invariably invaluable also to consult outside experts.

There are three types of issue to consider:

- *predetermined elements* – for example, *social* and demographic changes to the size and structure of the population, lifestyles and values

- *key uncertainties* – *political* changes and the inevitable *economic* changes which accompany it; the entry of new competitors; possible changes of corporate ownership

- *driving forces* – developments in *technology* and education.

The link to a PEST analysis will be clearly seen.

The next step is to examine a number of *plausible outcomes* from the various key issues, and debate issues of positive and negative synergy, specifically the impact of interconnectedness, with discussions generating some consensus, or possibly, and more realistically, accommodation on priorities, in the form of *viable scenarios* to test further. These will often be presented as *stories*, illustrated creatively to generate interest and enthusiasm.

The *tests* against which they will be ultimately evaluated are:

- What has been left out? – in effect, the extent of the comprehensiveness and the absence of key omissions – and

- Do they lead to clearer understanding which informs future decisions and actions, while winning the commitment of everyone involved?

Yet in our rapidly changing world can even well-meaning scenario planning work?

Jensen (1999) contends that we shall soon be living in a 'dream society' where the stories attributed to products and services – their image and reputation – will be an increasingly significant aspect of competitive advantage. Examples might relate to free-range eggs, organic vegetables and celebrity-endorsed training shoes. Simply, the story adds value. Jensen provides a number of themes for those organizations interested in creating 'dreams':

- *Adventure*. Involvement in the 'great outdoors' or leisure activities. Manchester United branded clothing appears to combine both.

- *Networks*. BT (British Telecom) capitalized on this with its 'family and friends' name for its discounted call scheme as well as the television advertisements which feature a family of two children, a mother who has a new man in her life and various changes in their situation all based on telephone and Internet connections.

- *Self-discovery* linked to products which allow people to say something about themselves. This theme has been exploited by VW (Volkswagen) with advertisements for the Golf which claim the only statement it needs to make is 'gone shopping'.

- *Peace of mind*. Security, often linked to the perceived safety of the known past. Perhaps this explains why VW has been able to relaunch the Beetle model and BMW a new Mini (a model that it acquired when it owned Rover).

- *Caring* businesses that can exploit their community links and programmes.

- *Convictions*. Ethical and environmental concerns are prominent. The Body Shop built a successful business around this, as shown in online Case 7.1.

Critical Reflection 4.1   Scenario Planning

Task One

Outlined below are the skeletons for four quite different scenarios relevant for 2020. Expand each of these skeletons into a 150 word scenario and either individually or in groups assess or debate the implications of each one for you as an individual. Although there might be relevant elements in each one, which one of the four do you see as being the most realistic?

Scenario 1

Green thinking and climate warming concerns are dominant forces in consumer purchasing and consumption.

Sustainability is a 'mandatory' consideration for any new product.

Healthy living and an outdoor lifestyle are prominent in most people's lives.

Scenario 2

We live in a high-tech society.

There is far more home working and online shopping than we have at the moment.

Living rooms are entertainment systems with all needs met through one central processor.

Our cars have technology that controls our speed and route.

Scenario 3

Society has become much more violent with high levels of education drop-out and unemployment.

There are more prisons and prisoners.

People live in more segregated areas. Those who can afford gated and secure communities live in this way.

More extreme political parties perform well at election time.

Scenario 4

There has been a rebellion against all these three trends and people have become more spiritual and creative.

People enjoy more leisure time and work less. They travel more and generally they are less materialistic as far as consumer goods are concerned.

A demand for better transport has forced improvements.

Task Two

Taking as your themes 'international politics', 'religious differences', 'the continued emergence of the East' and 'global terrorism', create four scenarios of your own and consider the implications.

We conclude this chapter with the exercise on scenario planning (Critical Reflection 4.1) above and a case on eBay – Case 4.6. eBay developed resources to seize a new opportunity that was being offered by the Internet and, typical of most of the truly successful Internet businesses to date, eBay provides a service rather than selling a specific product.

Case 4.6   eBay   US, Int

eBay is fundamentally an online auction house, dealing in almost anything – although many small businesses use it for online sales transactions. In fact, 70% of its business now involves new stock as eBay has courted retailers and small businesses. The most popular products include cars and motor cycles, computers, books, music and electronic goods – but eBay once sold a Gulfstream jet aircraft for $4.9 million. Altogether there are thousands of categories and it is not unusual for several million items a day to be featured.

Described as an online flea market in the late 1990s, eBay had actually started life in 1995 when its founder, French-born computer programmer Pierre Omidyar, set up a site so that his wife, who collected Pez sweet distributors, could make contact with other collectors around the world. It was not the first online auction house – and, unlike a number of its rivals, it has always charged a commission rather than provided a free service. Omidyar was a Silicon Valley resident and he went in search of venture capital to expand the business in 1997. He raised $6.7 million for a third of his business. The company was and always has been profitable. In just over 5 years of trading it was able to boast 40 million customers and deals amounting to almost $10 billion a year.

Head-hunters found Meg Whitman for Omidyar and she joined as CEO in 1998. Whitman had a corporate background – she had been working for Hasbro, the toy company, where she was running the Mr Potato Head franchise and masterminding the import into America of the Teletubbies. She recalls that she found a black and white website with a single typeface – courier. Despite the fact the company was successful and growing, she believed the website was 'confused'. She set about changing all this. She built up a fresh, strong management team and prepared the business for an IPO. When this happened late in 1998 it was the fifth most successful ever in US corporate history. Whitman made the company international. Where sales have been disappointing – the case in Japan – she simply closed the country site down. eBay arrived in the UK in December 1999.

Online auctions have an interesting business model. There are no supply costs and there is no inventory. Goods are never handled – they simply move from seller to buyer and a percentage margin taken. Once established there is little need to advertise. Overall very little capital expenditure is required. Regular customers spend an average of 90 minutes when they are surfing the site – but they will make other quick visits to check progress when they are bidding for an item. To put this approach in perspective, eBay expects global transactions on mobile phones alone to exceed £12 billion, which is now between one third and one half of transactions. Countless small businesses have increasingly found eBay a useful opportunity for selling their products. In 2007 eBay trade by UK based businesses exceeded £2 billion. Success has to depend on satisfied customers and eBay invests in customer feedback, which is collected for every transaction and made available as data for other customers to access. Whitman is strong on performance orientation. eBay maintains that it has always listened to its customers and responded whenever appropriate.

Interestingly there was little evidence of dishonest customer activity for quite a long time. Very few cheques ever seemed to bounce, for example. Moreover, customers have been very quick to respond if they notice any apparently rogue products being offered for sale – alleviating the need for eBay to invest heavily in security monitoring. However, in 2008 eBay were faced with a bill for huge damages when it was shown they had inadvertently allowed fake designer goods, mainly Louis Vuitton brands, to be passed off as originals. There were also concerns that people were trading Marks and Spencer credit notes which some were convinced had been obtained by returning stolen goods to stores. Perhaps it was inevitable that certain 'rogue traders' would find opportunities to beat eBay's security. In 2013 eBay was accused of (legal) corporation tax avoidance in the UK.

An ever-increasing proportion of the transactions are now handled online and eBay has had to develop the necessary competency. In July 2002 eBay bought PayPal, the world's largest online payment system. It is clearly possible to expand the scope of the business by offering the facility for customers to offer their products at a fixed price through the site – but this is different from the concept of an auction.

A further acquisition, in 2005, was Skype, the Internet voice company that allows free conversation between people who are able to link their computers online. Although one can see how discussions between buyers and sellers could lift eBay to a new dimension the strategic value of this was always questionable. Skype was sold to Microsoft for just over £5 billion in 2011.

Towards the end of 2008, as the economic recession bit in the UK, an interesting scenario evolved. It was reported that many people were no longer taking 'everything they no longer wanted' to charity shops but instead were looking to sell their 'best waste' through eBay. But at the same time, charity shops were taking trade away from the main high street retailers as customers looked to save money. It was around this time that Whitman left. In 2010 she stood for Governor of California but was not successful; she is now CEO of Hewlett-Packard.

Projects

1 Use the eBay website to track the bidding for a product that interests you. *You could, if you wish, sell something on eBay as an alternative.*
2 Use eBay as a topic for scenario planning – either individually or as part of a small group.

Now answer the following questions

Questions

1 Why do you think this simple business concept has been so successful?
2 Why does it make sense for small businesses to use eBay as a retail channel?

3 What might affect the prospects for eBay in the future?

Note

This chapter does not include a Research Snapshot due to the general and introductory nature of its content.

Summary

The external environment is perceptibly 'layered', with suppliers, customers and competitors comprising the inner layer; and the PEST (political, economic, social and technological) factors are the outer layer as they affect the industry.

Organizations operate with external environments that spring surprises on them from time to time, with many industries and markets characterized by a form of 'competitive chaos' which arises from the natural dynamism, turbulence and uncertainty of both the industry and the environment.

A firm can visualize its boundary with the environment as relatively fluid, such that, while suppliers, distributors and customers can be seen as outside the organizational boundary, they can also be identified as partners in a collaborative network which, more holistically, bounds with a number of external influences and forces.

Organizations must be able to react to the change pressures imposed by their environment (potential threats) and, at the same time, take advantage of opportunities which seem worthwhile. And yet, leading organizations will create and sustain positions of strength by seeking to influence – and maybe even manage – their external environment.

A PEST (political, economic, social and technological forces) analysis provides a valuable framework for analyzing relevant environmental forces.

All organizations should seek to understand the industries in which they compete since industry attractiveness affects profitability and it can be assessed by considering five forces: barriers to entry; the relative power of suppliers; the relative power of buyers; the potential for substitutability; and inter-firm rivalry, with governments affecting all five.

Over time, strong competitors create and seek to hold positions of power in markets and industries, while governments everywhere will seek to exercise some degree of control. Regulation is rarely clear-cut or black and white and sometimes the outcomes are not quite the ones desired.

To manage and manage in its environment, an organization will need strong strategic positions, implying finding and exploiting opportunities for adding value in ways that consumers value and for which they will reward the organization with prices that imply superior margins – finding an effective blend between the opportunity-driven approach to strategy creation and the resource-based approach.

As organizations seek to exploit their *core competencies* and *strategic capabilities* to add value in this way, the value must be appropriable such that the benefits should not all go to shareholders (through high dividends), consumers (in, say, the form of relatively low prices) or employees (generous remuneration) so the organization has inadequate resources for investment to build new ways of adding value for the future.

A SWOT (strengths, weaknesses, opportunities and threats) analysis is a second valuable framework for evaluating the position of an organization in relation to its environment, but should be used to create ideas and is not just seen as a static statement of position.

Organizations should attempt to forecast their environment, however difficult this may prove, with *scenario planning* making a very valuable contribution here if well done!

Online cases for this chapter

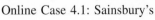

Web supplement related to this chapter

Finance in Action: the experience curve

Questions and research assignments

1 Draw a diagram incorporating the environmental influences and stakeholders for any pub, discotheque or nightclub with which you are familiar. From this evaluation, develop a SWOT analysis and consider the strategic implications.

2 One of the growth sectors in the UK economy has been in the area of call centres. Many thousands of people are employed in UK call centres. Many of these jobs have been threatened with removal to India and other cheaper wage areas. How should the managers and workers of UK call centres respond?

3 Possibly in a group discussion, build a scenario relevant for the motor vehicle industry in 10 years' time. How will people be using their cars? What will they expect in terms of size, performance and external and interior design? Will electric cars have made a significant impact?

Internet and library projects

1 How have changes in competition from around the world affected the UK footwear industry? What are the strategies of the leading, remaining manufacturers? You may wish to use a leading manufacturer such as C&J Clark as a key reference point. You should also look at a specialist such as Jimmy Choo, Grenson or Church's. You might also investigate the source of your personal wardrobe of shoes, boots and trainers.

C&J Clark **http://www.clarks.com**

Church's **http://www.churchsshoes.com**

Grenson **http://www.grensonshoes.co.uk**

2 From your own experience, and from newspaper and other articles you have read or seen, list examples of where monopoly power and restrictive practices have been investigated, and where proposed mergers have been considered by the Competition Commission (or its predecessor the Monopolies and Mergers Commission). Evaluate the recommendations and outcomes. If you wish to follow up any of these investigations, all of the reports are published by HMSO.

3 Take an industry of your choice, perhaps the one you work for, and assess it in terms of:

a concentration

b Porter's model of five forces.

From this, analyze one or more of the major competitors in terms of their chosen competitive strategies.

As well as the Internet, the following library sources might prove useful sources of information:

- Business Monitors (PA and PQ series)
- Annual Report of the Director General of Fair Trading (as a source of ideas)
- Monopolies and Mergers Commission reports, and Competition Commission reports, which usually feature a comprehensive industry analysis
- McCarthy's (or similar) Index (press cutting service for firms and industries).

4 How could Porter's five forces model be applied to Camelot, the monopoly supplier of the UK's lottery? On the one hand, Camelot operates under licence for a fixed period of years without any direct competition; on the other hand, it provides only one gambling opportunity amongst many. Why has Camelot needed to introduce several new games during the period of its licence?

Strategy activity

Cream O' Galloway

The ice-cream business that is Cream o' Galloway was started by David and Wilma Finlay in 1992 with the realization that if the family business Rainton Farm started in 1927 by the Finlay family was to survive it had to change. Although they had a relatively comfortable existence running the dairy farm, David and Wilma realized that if they wanted a sustainable business they had to move away from their dependence on small scale dairy farming. They investigated cheese, yoghurt and ice-cream and decided to major in ice-cream based on: the farm being located in a popular tourism area for families being based in the Dumfries and Galloway area of the South-West of Scotland; the luxury end of the ice-cream market was growing; and the ice-cream business did not seem an expensive business to enter.

The Finlays identified the following key success factors that needed to be in place to start their new business. They needed: milk, land, office space, employees, product knowledge, equipment and market knowledge. In-depth product and market knowledge was missing alongside some equipment. The farming side of the business was kept going as they spent the next 2 years on research and development. In 1994 they felt that they were ready to launch their new business and they did so at the Royal Highland Show in Edinburgh in 1994 with ten flavours of ice-cream. Customer feedback was so good they took the decision to move from small scale dairy farming to making ice-cream to sell in the UK market. As a couple, their skills were complementary. David provided the farming expertise, whilst Wilma provided the friendly and driven personality and was the face of the business.

To support the development of their business, they decided to take advantage of the family friendly image of ice-cream and turn their farm into a tourist attraction creating an ice-cream visitor centre out of their home. Initially, the centre was little more than a shed where you could buy ice-cream with a few tables and a couple of swings for children. Over time the visitor centre has grown to accommodate a total of 70 000 visitors each year. The Finlays have created an adventure playground on the farmland with amongst other things a 50 foot viewing tower, Scotland's only 3D maze, nature trails and much more.

Since that time the business has developed and grown into one producing 30 different flavours of organic ice-cream, smoothies and frozen yoghurts using only natural ingredients and organic milk. Their new 'Made Fair' product range is Fair Trade certified. They soon produced 200 000 litres of ice-cream a year with a turnover in 2007 of just over £1 million.

Their continued philosophy centres around being a sustainable business making a contribution to the local economy at the same time minimizing the impact on the environment:

'Bets are currently being taken on what is having the biggest negative environmental impact from our business whether it is the tourists travelling to our visitor centre; the distribution of our ice-cream; the energy needed to make the ice-cream; or the milk production.' (Wendy Finlay)

www.creamogalloway.co.uk

Question

1   What is the 'common' business model that Cream O'Galloway seems to fit?

References

Adams, J. (1995) *Risk*, UCL Press.

Benoit, B. (1999) Nearing 50, hale and hearty on home ground – a corporate profile of SAGA, *Financial Times*, 23 November.

Duncan, R. (1972) Characteristics of organizational environments and perceived environmental uncertainty, *Administrative Science Quarterly*, 313–27.

Freeman, R.E. (1984) *Strategic Management: A Stakeholder Approach*, Pitman.

Hall, D. (1992) *The Hallmarks for Successful Business*, Mercury Books.

Handy, C. (1989) *The Age Of Unreason*, Hutchinson.

Jensen, R. (1999) *The Dream Society*, McGraw Hill.

Kay, J.A. (1993) *Foundations of Corporate Success*, Oxford University Press.

Markides, C. (1999) Six principles of breakthrough strategy, *Business Strategy Review*, 10(2).

Mintzberg, H. (1987) Crafting strategy, *Harvard Business Review*, July–August.

Porter, M.E. (1980) Competitive Strategy: *Techniques for Analyzing Industries and Competitors*, Free Press.

Porter, M.E. (1996) What is strategy?, *Harvard Business Review*, November–December.

Porter, M.E. (2008) The Five Competitive Forces That Shape Strategy, *Harvard Business Review*, January.

Pümpin, C. (1991) *Corporate Dynamism*, Gower.

Schwartz, P. (2003) *Inevitable Surprises: Thinking Ahead in Times of Turbulence*, Gotham Books.

Chapter 5

Resource-led strategy

PART 1
Understanding strategy

1	What is strategy and who is involved?
	• Appendix
2	The business model and the revenue model
3	Strategic purpose
	• Supplement: Using frameworks to analyze strategy cases

PART 5
Strategy implementation

14	Strategy implementation and structure
15	Leading change
16	Managing strategy in the organization
17	Final thoughts and reflections: the practice of strategy

PART 2
Analysis and positioning

4	The business environment and strategy
5	Resource-led strategy
6	The dynamics of competition
7	Introducing culture and values

STRATEGIC MANAGEMENT: AWARENESS AND CHANGE

PART 4
Strategic growth issues

11	Strategic control and measuring success
12	Issues in strategic and international growth
13	Failure, consolidation and recovery strategies

PART 3
Strategy development

8	Creating and formulating strategy: alternatives, evaluation and choice
9	Strategic planning
10	Strategic leadership and intrapreneurship: towards visionary leadership?

Learning objectives

Having read to the end of this chapter, you should be able to:

- explain the resource-based view of strategy (**introduction and Section 5.1**)

- discuss the critical strategic contribution of people, including employee empowerment, and the **learning organization** (**Section 5.2**)

- appreciate the importance of information in strategic decision-making, the contribution of information technology and the Internet (**Section 5.3**)

- describe and produce an organizational **value chain** and explain how it might be used for evaluating competitive advantage (**Section 5.4**)

- discuss the significance of branding and corporate reputation as an intangible organizational asset (**Section 5.5**).

Introduction

The resource-based view of strategy gradually emerged during the 1980s and 1990s with a series of important contributions helping to explain why some *individual* organizations (not all competitors) succeed in creating competitive advantage and earning superior profits, while others do not – through an understanding of industries and markets leading to market opportunities being identified and satisfied individually and distinctively. Its supporters argue that, as long as there are opportunities which can be identified to sustain any competitive advantage, it will normally be easier and less risky for organizations to exploit their existing resources in new ways, by innovating, than to seek to acquire and learn new skills and competencies. Just having a resource is not enough and, therefore, it is helpful to have particular strengths that are *inimitable*, i.e. not easily learned and imitated by rivals and linked to core competency and strategic capability. The opening case, Case 5.1, on Dyson shows how innovation and new ways of creating and adding value through design can markedly change an industry by allowing a newcomer to establish a position of market dominance and force a reaction from established manufacturers.

This chapter looks first at the idea of a resource audit before considering resource linkages and synergy through **architecture** and the notion of the value chain. The chapter includes a section on human resource strategies.

People feel the best about their work when they do a high-quality job! Getting a job done quickly is satisfying. Getting a job done at low cost is rewarding. But getting a job done quickly, at low cost and with high quality is exciting!

ROBERT C STEMPEL, WHEN CHAIRMAN, GENERAL MOTORS CORPORATION

5.1 Strategic resources, core competency, capabilities and adding value

Environments spring surprises, sometimes either opportunities or threats, on organizations. The most vigilant and aware are better placed to respond by predicting opportunities and responding in some individual way, ideally genuinely different, appreciated by customers and inimitable – due to individuals, specific to the organization's competencies and capabilities, emanating from the organization's *resources*.

Case 5.1   James Dyson   UK

James Dyson is an entrepreneur who challenged the industry giants, in his case with a revolutionary vacuum cleaner. His dual cyclone cleaner built a UK market share in excess of 50 per cent and international sales are blooming. A Hoover spokesman has said on the *BBC Money Programme*: 'I regret Hoover as a company did not take the product technology of Dyson ... it would have been lain on a shelf and not been used.' Dyson has been compared by Professor Christopher Frayling, Rector of the Royal College of Art, with 'the great Victorian ironmasters ... a one-man attempt to revive British manufacturing industry through design'. Dyson is creative, innovative, totally focused on customers and driven by a desire to improve everyday products. His dedication and drive is reflected in the following comment: 'the only way to make a genuine breakthrough is to pursue a vision with a single-minded determination in the face of criticism ...' and this is exactly what he has done. Clearly a risk taker, he invested all of his resources in his venture. In the end his rise to fame and fortune came quickly, but the preceding years had been painful and protracted, and characterized by courage and persistence. They reflect the adage that 'instant success takes time'.

James Dyson's schoolmaster father died when he was just 9 years old. The public school to which he was then sent 'made him a fighter'. At school he excelled in running, practising by running cross-countries on his own; and it was on these runs that he began to appreciate the magnificence of the railway bridges constructed by Brunel in the nineteenth century, an experience which helped to form his personal vision. An early leap in the dark came when he volunteered to play bassoon in the school orchestra, without ever having seen a bassoon! Naturally artistic, he won a painting competition sponsored by the *Eagle* comic when he was 10 years old. Art became a passion and he later went on to complete a degree in interior design. Dyson may be an inventor, but he has no formal engineering background.

Dyson's first successful product and business was a flat-bottomed boat, the Sea Truck. At this time he learnt how a spherical plastic ball could be moulded, an idea that he turned to good use in the wild garden of his new home. His wheelbarrow was inadequate as the wheels sunk into the ground, so he substituted the wheel with a light plastic ball and thus invented the Ballbarrow. Backed by his brother-in-law on a 50:50 basis, Dyson invested in his new idea. Made of colourful, light plastic the barrow was offered to garden centres and the building trade, both of whom were less than enthusiastic. With a switch to direct mail via newspaper advertisements, the business took off. A new sales manager was appointed but his renewed attempt to sell the barrow through more traditional retail channels was again a failure. The financial penalty was the need for external investors, who later persuaded Dyson's brother-in-law to sell the business. A second painful experience came when the sales manager took the idea and design to the USA, where Dyson later failed with a legal action against him.

Dyson's idea for a dual cyclone household cleaner came in 1979, when he was 31 years old. Again, it was a case of a need creating an opportunity. He was converting his old house and becoming frustrated that his vacuum cleaner would not clear all of the dust that he was creating. Particles were clogging the pores of the dust bags and reducing the suction capability of the cleaner. He needed something to collect paint particles For his plastic spraying operation for the ballbarrows, Dyson had developed a smaller version of the large industrial cyclone machines, which separate particles. For air by using centrifugal forces in spinning cylinders. He believed that this technology could be adapted for home vacuum cleaners, removing the need for bags, but his partners in the Ballbarrow business failed to share his enthusiasm. Out of work when the business was sold, his previous employer, Jeremy Fry (for whom he had developed the Sea Truck), loaned him £25 000. Dyson matched this by selling his vegetable garden for £18 000 and taking out an additional £7000 overdraft on his house. Working from home, risking everything and drawing just £10 000 a year to keep himself, his wife and three children, he pursued his idea. Over the years he produced 5000 different prototypes.

When he ultimately approached the established manufacturers his idea was, perhaps predictably, rejected. Replacement dust bags are an important source of additional revenue. A series of discussions with potential partners who might license his idea brought mixed results. Fresh legal actions in the USA for patent infringement – 'with hindsight I didn't patent enough features' – were only partially offset by a deal with Apex of Japan. Dyson designed the G-Force upright cleaner which Apex manufactured and sold to a niche in the Japanese market for the equivalent of £1200 per machine, from which Dyson received just £20. At least there was now an income stream, but this had taken 7 years to achieve. Finally, in 1991 Lloyds Bank provided finance for the design and manufacture of a machine in the UK. Several venture capitalists and the Welsh Development Agency had turned him down. Dyson was determined to give his latest version the looks of NASA technology, but further setbacks were still to occur. Dyson was let down by the plastic moulder and assembler with whom he contracted, and was eventually forced to set up his own plant. Early sales through mail-order catalogues were followed by deals with John Lewis and eventually (in 1995) with Comet and Curry's. In this year a cylinder version joined the upright. Dyson continues to improve the designs to extend his patent protection. By 1999 his personal wealth was estimated to be £500 million.

Dyson has always seen himself as more of an inventor than a businessman. He established two separate businesses, both in Malmesbury, Wiltshire, and he kept Dyson Manufacturing and Dyson Research (design and patenting) apart. The dress code for employees is perpetually informal and communications are predominantly face-to-face. Memos are banned and even emails discouraged. Every employee is encouraged to be creative and contribute ideas. Most new employees are young – 'not contaminated by other employers' – and they all begin by assembling their own vacuum cleaner, which they can then buy for £20. Designers work on improvements to the dual cyclone cleaners as well as new product ideas.

In early 2000 Dyson launched a robot version of the dual cyclone cleaner, which is battery-powered, self-propelled and able to manoeuvre itself around furniture. It retailed at some £2500, which limited it to a select segment of the market and it was slow to take off. He has since launched 'The Ball', a version which has a large ball instead of wheels to make the cleaner more versatile. Later in 2000 Dyson launched a revolutionary super-fast washing machine with short wash cycles and an ability to spin clothes almost dry, presenting a challenge to the manufacturers of both washing machines and tumble dryers. This time, however, Dyson had his own resources to launch the product. He has also succeeded in penetrating the US and Japanese markets with his dual cyclone cleaners; he had to design a small version with a digital motor for Japan.

Another Dyson product is his own design of wall-mounted hand dryer – users don't hold their hands under a hot air outlet but place them between two flat plates. The machines are extremely powerful. More recently he has launched what he calls the 'Air Multiplier' which is effectively a blade-free fan which blows cold hair; a variant of this is his (warm air) room heater. Both look like rings – the secret lies in the way the air is circulated. Dyson controls 100 per cent of the shares in his business. He has learnt some painful lessons but is now enjoying the rewards of his dogged

determination. In recent years Dyson has transferred the majority of his manufacturing to lower cost plants in Malaysia and Singapore. Perhaps inevitably this was opposed by the UK workforce and it has brought him adverse publicity. Before the transfer there were 1800 employees in the UK. This reduced to 1000, but has since been increased to between 1400 and 1500 none of them actually making any products. Several hundred people work in research and development and design.

Dyson himself has become a passionate spokesman for engineering and design and has funded the Dyson School of Design Innovation in Bath. He believes the UK must focus on what it can do well and accept that the actual manufacture should take place in lower-labour-cost countries overseas.

Questions

1 Thinking about the issues of core competency and strategic capability, what is the 'secret' of James Dyson's competitive advantage?
2 Has he been able to appropriate the rewards of the value he has added?

DYSON: **http://www.dyson.com**

SOURCE: THIS CASE STUDY WAS PREPARED USING PRIMARILY PUBLICLY AVAILABLE SOURCES OF INFORMATION FOR THE PURPOSES OF CLASSROOM DISCUSSION; IT DOES NOT INTEND TO ILLUSTRATE EITHER EFFECTIVE OR INEFFECTIVE HANDLING OF A MANAGERIAL SITUATION.

In this chapter this argument is explored in greater depth and frameworks are provided which can help us to audit and evaluate strategic resources.

There are many ways of studying strategic resources. We can, for example, look at key resource drivers – such as labour, the need for investment in technology, supplies (i.e. their cost as a proportion of total costs, their role in creating and adding value for customers, and their scarcity), and knowledge – and tangible (e.g. capital equipment, physical supplies and technology) and **intangible resources** (often the hardest to copy or replicate, e.g. organizational processes, networks, alliances, corporate reputation and strategic thinking).

Auditing strategic resources

Not every organizational resource is strategically significant, but can be evaluated by:

- *Competitive superiority*, the relative value when compared to rivals, since a resource is not a competitive strength if possessed by every competitor.

- *Barriers to replication*, which can stop rivals from imitating or replicating any valuable resources.

- *Durability*, a time advantage relating to 1 and 2.

- *Substitutability*, whether competitors neutralize the value of a resource by substituting an alternative.

- *Appropriability*, whether the organization, rather than a supplier or distributor, genuinely benefits from the resource it possesses (Kay, 1993).

Figure 5.1 shows: (i) selected products, services and markets (which are environment-driven), (ii) the competitive environment, stakeholders, resources and values as key strategic elements – which can be changed, but often not readily and not quickly, and consequently they are reasonably fixed – and which determine whether or not the corporate objectives are achieved and (iii) six operating elements (or *functional areas*) – marketing, manufacturing, finance, research and development, human resources and the organizational structure – which are affected to varying degrees and in quite different ways by different stakeholders, with their impact upon the whole organization influenced by the organizational structure and relative power and influence within the firm, thus highlighting the strategic value of functional managers taking a more holistic view of the organization and their role and contribution (Kelly and Kelly, 1987).

Figure 5.1   Matching the organization and the environment

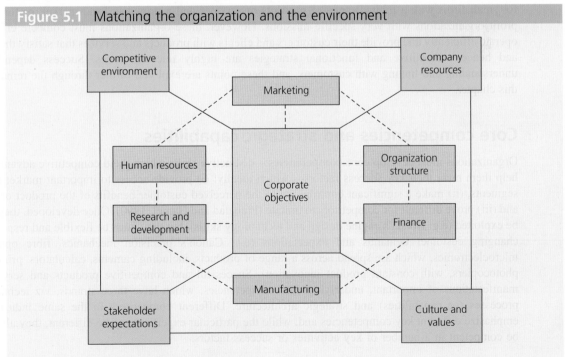

ADAPTED FROM KELLY, FJ AND KELLY, HM (1987) *WHAT THEY REALLY TEACH YOU AT THE HARVARD BUSINESS SCHOOL* PIATKUS

To audit and evaluate these operating elements or strategic resources, an internal analysis should be a three-stage process:

1 an evaluation of the profile of the principal skills and resources of an organization
2 a comparison of this resource base with the requirements for competitive success in the industry
3 a comparison with competitors to determine the relative strengths and weaknesses and any significant comparative advantage.

It is inevitable that internal managers, when carrying out this analysis, will have some subjective judgement, influenced by their position in the organization. For example, a SWOT (strengths, weaknesses, opportunities and threats) analysis of resources must consider them in relative and not absolute terms, i.e. whether they are managed, controlled and used effectively as well as efficiently (influenced by control systems, such as production and **financial control**), not purely whether they exist. In addition, the functional areas of the business, i.e. where the human, financial and physical resources are deployed, are considered. And yet, although a successful marketing manager might seem to represent a strength, if there is no adequate cover for him/her and he/she leaves or falls ill, it is arguable that the firm has a marketing weakness.

Table 5.1 provides a sample, but not a comprehensive list, of key resource considerations; e.g. efficiency measures of the salesforce might include sales per person or sales per region, but sales force effectiveness relates to their ability to sell the most profitable products or those products or services that the organization is keen to promote at a particular time, perhaps to reduce a high level of inventory. Other relative strengths and weaknesses relate to competition, marketing, production/operations management (i.e. innovation and quality), human resources management and financial management. In terms of the latter, organizations must control costs so that profit is achieved and value is added to products and services primarily in areas that matter to consumers. While lower costs and differentiation are important themes in competitive strategy, they relate to both an awareness of consumer needs and the management of resources to satisfy these needs *effectively* and, where relevant, profitably.

Functional and competitive strategies are important for an understanding of strategic management in all types of organization, and they are especially important for a large proportion of small businesses and many not-for-profit organizations. Corporate strategic changes such as major diversification and acquisition, divestment of business units which are under-performing or international expansion may not be relevant for small firms with a limited range of products or services and a primarily local market, or for not-for-profit organizations with very specific missions. However, these organizations must compete effectively, operate efficiently and provide their customers and clients with products and services that satisfy their needs and hence competitive and functional strategies are highly relevant issues. Success depends upon understanding and linking with customers, and these points are explored further through the remainder of this chapter.

Core competencies and strategic capabilities

Organizations must develop **core competencies** – distinctive skills which yield competitive advantage and help them meet their key success factors – which ideally: (i) provide access to important market areas or segments, (ii) make a significant contribution to the perceived customer benefits of the product or service and (iii) prove difficult for competitors to imitate (Prahalad and Hamel, 1990). Once developed, they should be exploited (e.g. Honda's engine design and technology skills), but they must be flexible and responsive to changing customer demands and expectations (e.g. Canon's precision mechanics, fibre optics and microelectronics, which are spread across a range of products, including cameras, calculators, printers and photocopiers, with constant product innovation). Successful and competitive products and services are manifestations of important, underlying core competencies, which have three strands, viz technologies, processes (or capabilities) and strategic architecture. Different competitors in the same industry may emphasize different key competencies and, while the particular expertise may be different, they all need to be competent in a number of key activities or success factors.

Table 5.1   Aspects of the resource audit

Resource/function	Key considerations
Marketing	Products and services: range, brand names and stage in life cycle
	Patents
	Strength of salesforce
	Distribution channels
	Market information
Operations	Location and plant
	Capital equipment
	Capacity
	Processes
	Planning and manufacturing systems
	Quality control
	Supplies
Research and development	Annual budget
	Technology support
	Quality of researchers
	Record of success and reputation
	Spending in relation to industry norm
Information	Organizational knowledge and extent of sharing
	Information systems
	Problem-solving capabilities and procedures
Finance	Capital structure
	Working capital
	Cash flow
	Costing systems and variances
	Nature of shareholders
	Relations with bankers
Human resources	Numbers and qualifications
	Skills and experience
	Age profile
	Labour turnover and absenteeism
	Flexibility
	Development and training record and policies
	Motivation and culture
	Managerial competencies and capacity

Strategic success is, arguably, based on **strategic capabilities** – processes that enable the company to be an effective competitor – such as distribution networks that achieve both high service levels (effectiveness) and low costs (efficiency), and which cut across whole organizations, rather than being product specific, relying heavily on information systems and technology (Stalk *et al.*, 1992). In many respects Stalk's capabilities are the processes embedded in Hamel and Prahalad's core competencies, but a valuable distinction can be made between competencies that are largely rooted in technologies and process-based capabilities which, although delivering similar outcomes, are very different conceptually.

Retailers such as Boots in the UK (which has encompassed high-street department stores, specialist pharmacies, optical retailing, Halfords car products and service bays, Fads, Homestyle and Do-It-All DIY at various times) operate a number of different retail formats, capitalizing on their expertise in supply-chain, information and service management.

Understanding processes should generate intelligence that can be used to create added or greater value from resources, in order to strengthen or enhance competitiveness, or **stretching resources** (Hamel and Prahalad, 1993), while both core competencies and strategic capabilities must be capable of exploitation and be *appropriable* by the firm rather than rivals, suppliers or customers (Kay, 1993). Indeed, he proposed a three-strand framework for evaluating or auditing strategic resources: (i) *strategic architecture*, internal and external relationships and links, (ii) reputation, including branding and (iii) innovation by continually improving, the organization's products, services and processes, partially in response to competition and partially to drive competitiveness in the industry. For example, Marks and Spencer (M&S)'s functional competencies and brand technology create both an image and a capability which enable it to trade in clothes, foods, cosmetics, household furnishings and credit. These competencies also bestow on the company the power to demand and obtain from its suppliers worldwide both a strict adherence to M&S' technological specifications and very keen prices. The important themes in architecture are *internal*, including 'systemic thinking' leading to synergy from the fostering of interdependencies between people, functions and divisions in organizations, and *external*, i.e. the establishment of linkages or even alliances between organizations at different stages of the added **value chain** (Kay, 1993). Successful internal architecture requires that managers think 'organizationally' rather than put themselves first or promote their particular part of the organization to the detriment of other parts, and also depends on the ability of the divisions or businesses in a conglomerate to support each other, transferring skills, competencies and capabilities, and sometimes sharing common resources. This, in turn, is partially dependent on the ability of the organization to learn, and share learning; and is affected by the actual portfolio of businesses managed by a corporation, with Goold *et al.* (1994) using the term '**heartland**' to describe that range of businesses to which a corporate head office can add value, rather than see value destroyed through too much complexity and diversity.

Case 5.2 on Piano Manufacturing in China illustrates these points.

Case 5.2   Piano Manufacturing in China   Int, US, Ch

Pearl River Piano

Pearl River Piano is a piano company that started in 1956 in Guangzhou, China and now lays claim to have the largest piano factory in the world with 3 million square feet of manufacturing in a single location. Pearl River pianos have become the fastest sellers in the USA and Canada, with over 300 dealers selling the products. This success and the recent development of a new state-of-the-art woodworking facility has given Pearl River Piano the ability to produce over 100 000 pianos per year and they export to over 80 countries. This outcome is part of a strategy of heavy investment in both technology and people development by Pearl River Piano.

Pearl River pianos feature hardwood rims, sand-cast plates and lower tension scales, features found in the world's best pianos, such as those produced by Steinway and Bosendorfer. Pearl River Piano has been awarded the ISO 9001 certificate for its complete line of grand and vertical pianos; indeed Pearl River Piano was the first piano company in China to receive this award along with the award of ISO 14001 for the environmental standards practice by the company. Pearl River Piano was the first Chinese piano manufacturer to both market pianos under its own name and to distribute them directly to dealers through opening (in 2000) its own distribution business. The company not only manufactures pianos, Pearl River Piano is one of the world's largest guitar and violin manufacturers as well as selling drums, brass and woodwind instruments around the world.

One of the crucial elements of the success of Pearl River Piano is its strategic alliances with Yamaha and Steinway. In 1995 Yamaha formed a joint venture with Pearl River Piano to establish a factory to build Yamaha-branded pianos for the Chinese market. This factory is located east of Guangzhou in an 'economic development zone' some 35 miles from the Pearl River Piano factory. In turn, Pearl River Piano produce a line of pianos which Yamaha distributes, and benefit from the exchange of expertise between the two manufacturers. Pearl River Piano also manufactures three designs of pianos for the German company, Steinway, a true 'heavyweight' in this industry. This is testimony to its quality. Pianos branded Pearl River are not, and do not pretend to be, the best available, but they are both good quality and good value for money.

Gibson Guitar and Dongbei Piano

In December 2006, Gibson Guitar Corporation of the USA announced that it had acquired 100 per cent ownership of Dongbei Piano Co Ltd, another of the largest piano producers in China. This acquisition of Dongbei Piano was an important and significant strategic move for Gibson after it had acquired the US piano maker Baldwin a few years earlier. Inward investment of this nature might be seen as unusual. Dongbei Piano Co is based in Yingkou, a city in Northeast China's Liaoning Province. Dave Berryman, President of Gibson Guitar Corp., said 'As a major producer in the Chinese mainland, Dongbei Piano boasts a great reputation the world over. Gibson will fully bolster Dongbei Piano's development by introducing advanced manufacturing and marketing concepts to upgrade its competitiveness in global markets.' Dongbei Piano was now on track to become the second-largest piano manufacturing facility in China and a major manufacturing base for Gibson, according to Henry Juszkiewicz, Chairman and CEO of Gibson. The new company was named Baldwin Dongbei Piano Instrument Co. Ltd.

Dongbei Piano had been founded in 1952 and prior to the acquisition it employed more than 2000 workers and produced 30 000 upright pianos and 10 000 grand pianos every year, making it the third-largest piano producer in China. Dongbei Piano sells its products to more than 20 countries. 'There is no doubt that joining

Gibson is the right choice for Dongbei Piano. Cooperation with an industry leader like Gibson greatly enhances our strengths, and we are expecting Dongbei Piano's continued and further success in both the domestic and overseas markets' – Zhang Daming, General Manager of Dongbei Piano. Gibson was a much older company – it started out making mandolins in 1902 but it became a leading and world-renowned manufacturer of guitars and other musical equipment.

Questions

1 Identify the main classic elements of the strategy of Pearl River Piano. What should now be the tactics of Pearl River Piano?
2 What is the competitive strategy of Gibson?
3 How is Gibson trying to achieve competitive advantage?

The value and constituency of these networks and partnerships may be hard to quantify or even explain, since they owe much to people and to their history, and they are relationships which emerge and strengthen over many years and are dependent upon personal relations and interactions, and as they are difficult to replicate they are even more powerful. Consequently, architecture can be a vital element of competitive advantage. Some organizations have chosen to **outsource** their manufacturing, for example Dyson's (Case 5.1) switch to Malaysia to reduce costs and Hornby Hobbies' (Case 5.3) to China to devote two labour hours for every one used in the UK and thus produce models with much higher quality and detail at the same total cost without changing its prices, while being highly innovatory with new products (e.g. Eurostar, the Hogwarts Express from the Harry Potter stories); with Royal Doulton (china and tablewear) now focusing on design and marketing and outsourcing production from Indonesia, and Dr Martens boots and shoes being made in China.

Buckingham and Coffman (1999) draw attention to the importance of architecture in their delineation of four levels of customer service: Levels 1 (accuracy) and 2 (availability), which are relatively easy and generally taken for granted, but required to win repeat business, with Levels 3 (working partnerships) and 4 (provision of advice and support) relating to strategic architecture. Before looking in-depth at Porter's value chain framework, which helps us to identify valuable differences and manage cost drivers, we next consider two critically important strategic resources – *people* and *information* – that are the key drivers of change and are crucially important in the implementation of chosen strategies.

Case 5.3   Hornby Hobbies   UK, Ch

Hornby is a rare survivor in the UK toy industry, which has a past characterized by (in their day) leading brands but which has been subject to intense competition from manufacturers in the Far East and by the growth and popularity of electronic and computer toys and games which has hit demand for more traditional toys.

Hornby began over 100 years ago in Liverpool; its founder, Frank Hornby, invented Meccano, a construction set based on the principle of 'mechanical engineering made easy'. Trevor Baylis, inventor of the clockwork radio, has always said he 'cut his teeth' with Meccano during and after World War II. The company would follow this with model electric railway sets and Dinky Toys, scale model vehicles. The first Hornby trains were O gauge, but these were replaced by the Double O gauge that is most popular today. OO gauge is half the size of O gauge.

Meccano reached its heyday in the period between the 1930s and 1950s, but it is still available today. The company that manufactures it is joint French and Japanese, and sets are manufactured in both France and China. Modern Meccano is different, but the principle is the same. Pieces are bolted together to produce a whole variety of finished models. Like Lego bricks, which for many people were a substitute product, small engines can be added to provide power.

Dinky Toys competed with Corgi Toys – which were roughly the same size – and Matchbox Toys, which were much smaller. These were all die-cast and produced absolutely to scale and finished to look just like the original in respect of design and colour. Dinky eventually became part of Matchbox (started by Lesney) but are now most likely to be found as collector's items on eBay.

The Hornby company would eventually be merged with Triang, which, amongst other toys, also produced model railways, which it had started to do with encouragement from Marks and Spencer. Scalextric slotcar racing was later merged into the business. The combined business was first owned by Lines Brothers, but after this company went into liquidation, by Dunbee Combex Marx, from which there would be a management buy-out. During the 1990s, and with new owners, Hornby diversified quite widely – one new product was Cassy dolls, which competed head-on with the more popular Barbie and Sindy dolls, although at 7 inches tall they were a good 5 inches shorter than their rivals. These changes were not a success; and after a few years of very mixed results a new Chief Executive took over in 2001. Frank Martin would succeed in rejuvenating the business with a number of important strategic changes.

- The company was located at Margate in Kent, where it manufactured everything. This was changed.

Production was moved to China where there are now 3000 employees. The 130 staff in Kent control design and marketing and look after distribution. Although some organizations opt to manufacture in China to save as many costs as possible, Martin saw it as an opportunity to invest over twice the number of people hours into every product and thus increase its quality, whilst maintaining the existing market price and improving profitability. Quality improved markedly through this strategy and improved the 'model feel' (as distinct from a toy) with the railway equipment. In turn this opened up a new market opportunity for adult enthusiasts, who are now a main purchaser.

- New models of both railways and Scalextric have reflected licensing opportunities. One railway is based on the Hogwarts Express (from Harry Potter) and cars have been linked to cars from the James Bond movies. There are also deals with racing drivers such as Fernando Alonso, Lewis Hamilton and the McLaren Team.
- There has been product innovation, with engines that emit real steam and digital controls for Scalextric.
- Hornby has actively encouraged and supported Collectors' Societies.
- Distribution has been extended, with sets specifically for Marks and Spencer, for example. In addition sales across Europe have been targeted.
- To support this strategy Hornby has acquired rival (model railway) companies in Spain, Italy, France and Germany.
- In 2006 the company also bought another 'brand from the past' – Airfix, manufacturer of construction kits, mainly aircraft and warships. This business had started in Hull but, like Meccano, moved to French ownership. After this purchase, one TV production company went into a school in South London to test whether the young teenagers (both boys and girls) could be persuaded to work on construction kits at the expense of playing computer games, and found that they could!
- In 2008 Corgi was added to the business portfolio. In recent years Corgi has focused on customized vehicles for the corporate gift market, a very lucrative niche.

Company profits – and its share price – have reflected a resurgent company and Hornby has been seen as a 'star performer'. There have been periodic falls in monthly and quarterly sales during the recent economic recession but Hornby has been innovative with new models, by becoming the official toymaker for the 2012 Olympics, and by direct association with the movie Toy Story 3.

Questions

1 How would you define Hornby's business activities – is it, for example, a toy company or a model maker?
2 How will this affect its key success factors and the competencies and capabilities it needs?
3 Do you agree that the move to China probably saved the business?

SOURCE: THIS CASE STUDY WAS PREPARED USING PRIMARILY PUBLICLY AVAILABLE SOURCES OF INFORMATION FOR THE PURPOSES OF CLASSROOM DISCUSSION; IT DOES NOT INTEND TO ILLUSTRATE EITHER EFFECTIVE OR INEFFECTIVE HANDLING OF A MANAGERIAL SITUATION.

5.2 People as a strategic resource

Human resource strategies: The 'people contribution'

To meet the needs and expectations of their customers more effectively than their competitors and to generate acceptable financial returns, successful organizations need to attract, motivate, develop, reward and (in lean periods) retain skilled and competent managers and other employees, who are critically important strategic resources, and who can create and implement strategic changes in a supportive culture in which they share the values of the organization. Although technology and IT can make a major strategic impact, it is people who exploit their potential, and managers and employees are needed to implement strategies, and must be committed to the organization and must work together well. At the same time, where an organization is decentralized and operating in a turbulent environment, the strategic leader will rely on people to spot opportunities and threats, to adapt and create new strategies and, consequently, it is people who ultimately determine whether or not competitive advantage is created and sustained. Adding new value with innovation, they can be an opportunity and a source of competitive advantage; equally, unenthusiastic, uncommitted, untrained employees can act as a constraint. People's capabilities are infinite and resourceful in the appropriate organizational climate, and the basic test of their value concerns how much they – and their contribution – would be missed if they left or, possibly worse, left and joined a competitor, and could take customers with them and not be easily replaced. Achieving the highest level of outcomes that people are capable of producing will, therefore, depend upon the human resource practices adopted by the organization. One issue here is whether the business is being driven by a small number of identifiable, key decision-makers or by the employees collectively. Case 5.4 (Semco) illustrates an unusual approach to people management in a Brazilian family business.

| Case 5.4 | Ricardo Semler and Semco | Br |

Ricardo Semler was just 21 years old when he took over as chief executive of his family's business, Semco. This Brazilian company manufactured pumps, food mixers, meat-slicing equipment and dishwashers. Brazil is a country characterized by high inflation and a massive relative wealth gap between the rich and the poor. His father believed that if he handed over the reins when Ricardo was still young, 'he could make his mistakes while he was still around to fix them'! His father had run the business along traditional and autocratic lines; Ricardo was to change everything, and the company has thrived and prospered.

Although he has an MBA from Harvard, Ricardo Semler's stated business philosophy is: 'follow your intuition'. He inherited a company where 'people did not want to come to work and managers watched everything and everybody constantly, trusting nobody', and transformed it into one which is 'ultimately democratic' and based on 'freedom, respect, trust and commitment'. Things did not happen instantaneously; many new approaches and experimental methods were tried and abandoned. However, in a 10-year period from the mid-1980s Semco achieved 900 per cent growth.

There is no reception area, no secretaries and no offices. Managers walk around constantly to provide help and assistance when it is requested; the workers organize their own flexible working time arrangements. Employees work in small clusters, and they can also rearrange their working space and environment as they wish. Semco has come to believe that clusters of no more than ten are required if this approach is to work effectively. Twelve layers of a management and supervisory hierarchy have been reduced to three. The appointment of any manager has to be approved by the workforce, and managers are subjected to regular assessment by their subordinates and shopfloor employees. People talk openly and 'when someone says they'll do something, they do it'. Consequently, managers also feel that they can spend time away from the plant, with customers and suppliers.

Profit sharing is by consultation and negotiation – 23 per cent of after-tax profits is available for the workforce – and all employees are trained to ensure that they can read the company accounts. There is no longer a formal chief executive post for Ricardo, who is now President. Instead, there is an informal board of six associates (the most senior managers) who elect a nominal chief executive for a 6-month period. Ricardo sometimes attends their meetings as an adviser.

Ricardo has recently taken his ideas further, encouraging employees to consider starting up satellite supply companies and subcontracting for Semco. Those who have opted for this entrepreneurial route have been allowed to take Semco machines with them, leasing them on favourable terms. One advantage for Semco is the fact that it is no longer responsible for the maintenance and safety of the equipment. In addition, there is an opportunity for the machinery to be used more effectively as the satellite companies are free to work for other organizations; their efficiency gains can be passed through in the form of lower prices. If the venture fails, Semco takes back the equipment and the people. It is a relatively low and managed risk for all concerned.

Semco continues to thrive – although Semler himself remains at a relative distance from strategic decisions – and it comprises four main divisions:

- Semco Capital Goods – refrigeration and other white goods and the like
- Pitney Bowes Semco – a joint venture for intelligent systems for processing and automating documents
- Brenco – producing ethanol from sugar cane
- Tarpon Investments – asset management and investments.

Ricardo Semler has not been a man who has hidden his achievements! He has written the story of his role at Semco with the title *Maverick*. He helps other companies as a consultant and he has become a recognized member of the management guru circuit around the world. He has also campaigned against corruption in Brazil, and he has exposed government officials who have been demanding bribes for domestic planning permission. As a result, he has generated hostility from certain prominent people in his country.

'Successful companies will be the ones that put quality of life first. Do this and the rest – quality of product, productivity of workers, profits for all – will follow.'

Questions

1 Is Ricardo Semler really a 'maverick'?
2 Have these changes been sustainable?
3 Has Semco become even more 'maverick' or has it mellowed?

Sources

Semler, R (1993) *Maverick*, Century
Semler, R (2003) *The Seven Day Weekend*, Century

To bring out the best in people, they have to be managed well, which requires leadership, e.g. in an orchestra every member (manager/employee) is a specialist, with some making a unique contribution which, on occasions, can take the form of a solo performance, but all the contributions must be synthesized to create harmony (synergy), which is the role of the conductor (strategic leader). A single musician (weak link) can destroy a performance, since a chain is only as strong as its weakest link.

A successful organization, therefore, needs people with appropriate skills and competencies who can work together effectively, and who must be committed, competent, cost-effective, and in sympathy with the aims of the organization.

Where people grow, profits grow.

DR ALEX KRAUER, WHEN CHAIRMAN AND MANAGING DIRECTOR, CIBA-GEIGY

There are two recognized approaches to human resource management: the 'hard' approach (centralization for control) and the 'soft' approach (decentralization for greater empowerment), which imply contrasting styles, but they can both be appropriate in certain circumstances. Indeed, companies can be hard on certain aspects and soft on others, and when times are difficult and a company must rationalize and downsize, a hard approach may prove to be appropriate for driving through the changes quickly, whereas a softer, more empowered style may be required to rejuvenate the company and bring new sources of competitive advantage.

Soft human resource management argues that people are different from other resources (and often more costly) but they can create added value and **sustainable competitive advantage** from the other resources

Figure 5.2   Manager's discretionary layer

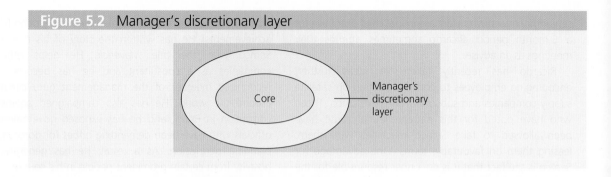

and, therefore, this approach places greater emphasis on control through review and evaluation of outcomes, such that employees are led rather than managed. Empowerment means freeing employees from instructions and controls and allowing them to take decisions themselves. As empowerment is increased, employees must be adequately informed and knowledgeable, must be motivated to exercise power, and must be rewarded for successful outcomes. In flatter organization structures, there are fewer opportunities for promotion. For many organizations, empowerment implies that the core organization strategies are decided centrally, with individual managers delegated a discretionary layer around the core (as shown in Figure 5.2). It is crucial first to find the right balance between the core and discretionary elements, and second to ensure that managers support and own the core strategy. With extensive empowerment can come the notion of an inverted pyramid structure with leaders focusing on a nurturing, supporting, mentoring style (Figure 5.3).

The deciding factors are competitive strategies and the relative importance of close linkages with customers in order to differentiate and provide high levels of service; putting the 'right' people in place and ensuring that they are able to do their job, which they understand and own, and making them feel important; the extent to which the environment is turbulent and decisions are varied rather than routine; the expectations and preferences of managers and employees, and their ability and willingness to accept responsibility, with a coaching style of management, and linking-in monitoring systems together with rewards and sanctions. Finally, resources must be made available to support those who will embrace empowerment.

Some companies seek to develop their employees and managers, invariably promoting from within, and a strong culture and vision should foster both commitment and continuous, emergent change – with necessary new competencies being *learned* – and teamworking and networking likely to be prominent. The challenge for companies growing from within is that they need to become and stay very aware strategically if they are to remain ahead of their rivals; they will actively benchmark and look for new ideas that might be helpful. Other organizations prefer to search for the best people who might be available and willingly recruit outsiders by *buying in* the new competencies that they require, but people may feel less committed to such organizations in the long-term, hence the inevitable greater reliance on individualism and individual contributions.

Figure 5.3   Inverted pyramid structure

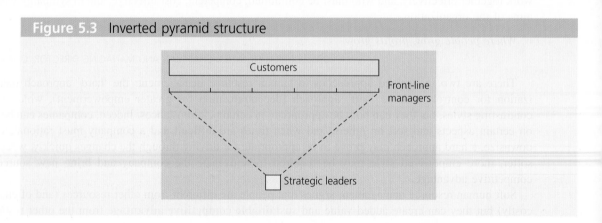

Indeed, if the competencies are available, and can be bought by any competitor, how can they ensure that they find the best ideas and people, and how can they generate some unique competency and competitive advantage?

Some companies will look to do both to find an appropriate balance, for example a leading football club which buys expensive, talented players in the transfer market, while simultaneously nurturing young players: and experienced players may not fit in at a new club and, when several arrive at once, it can be very disruptive until they are moulded into an effective team.

Companies may either compete by moving quickly, perhaps by necessity, responding speedily to new opportunities, typically finding it more appropriate to recruit from outside, or developing a more sustainable advantage in a long-standing market, strong internal and external architecture and new competencies internally, but making them too slow to gain early advantage from new opportunities (Capelli and Crocker-Hefter, 1995). In general, industries and markets are becoming more dynamic and turbulent, demanding that companies develop new product and market niche opportunities, thus implying an increasing reliance on recruiting strong, competent people from outside. In turn, this means that internal relationships and the culture may be under constant pressure to change. Companies are recruiting and rewarding individual experts; at the same time, synergistic opportunities demand strong internal architecture and co-operation; and those that succeed in establishing a strong, cohesive and motivating culture while developing new competencies flexibly and quickly are likely to be the future high performers. Reinforcing points from other chapters, this demands effective strategic leadership and a shared, understood vision for the organization. The extent to which an organization can become a 'learning organization', discussed later in this chapter, is of great significance.

Figure 5.4 repackages the notion of manager competency in the form of five distinct mindsets, all of which managers, to different degrees, will and must possess – with some managers being extremely competent in certain areas, but their profile, approach and style may not be appropriate for the demands placed on them, and they may find it difficult to find time to think, reflect and challenge. Short-termism and 'more-of-the-same' can all too readily be the result.

Because these questions are complex, some organizations will adopt and build human resource practices that help to create and sustain a competitive advantage that is peculiar to that organization's environmental

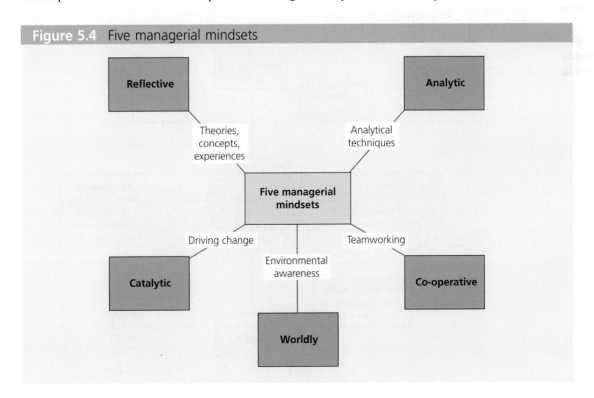

Figure 5.4 Five managerial mindsets

matching challenge. Such organizations enjoy strong E–V–R (environment–values–resources) congruence, and the competitive value of their competencies lies in the general approach being transferable, but the specifics are not.

Organizations need the appropriate people with the required and desired competencies, and/or the potential for growth and development, if they are to foster effective emergent strategy. Such people require clear objectives to give them both direction and performance yardsticks, backed by training and development opportunities, with outcomes which should be measured, performance reviewed and rewarded as appropriate, leading to action against underperformance or failure. Organizational success and performance are affected by the congruence between the objectives of managers and those of their subordinates, such that the organization can only accomplish its objectives if those of managers and subordinates are supportive of each other and of the organization (Hersey and Blanchard, 1982). Moreover, people need objectives to direct their efforts, or they will create their own (McGregor, 1960), whilst managers are orientated towards economic goals and see profit as being important (Schein, 1983), with personal objectives likely to be allowed more freedom if managers are not given clear objectives, and objectives pursued by managers being dependent on personal motives, their understanding and perception of what the strategic leader and their colleagues expect them to contribute, and organizational culture (Porter *et al.*, 1975), such that in recent years bankers and investment traders took high levels of risk to generate profit and personal rewards. Figure 5.5 summarizes an array of different ways of rewarding people.

A number of organizations, including BP, WH Smith and Federal Express, have at times experimented with formalized upward feedback, as well as manager/subordinate appraisal. Although difficult to implement successfully, as these companies have all found, such systems can be very useful for increasing managers' awareness concerning their style and effectiveness. Any performance evaluation systems which influence or determine rewards should be open and fair, and perceived as such.

Rewards depend upon the success of the organization as a whole, as well as individual contributions to that success. Employees at the so-called grassroots level are likely to know the details of the business and what really happens better than their superiors and managers. If they are involved and encouraged to

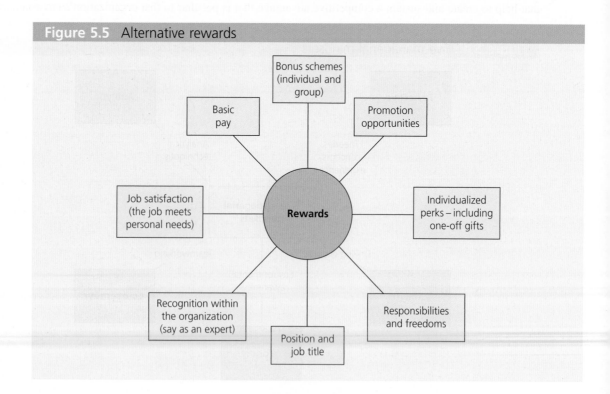

Figure 5.5   Alternative rewards

contribute their ideas for improvements, the result can be innovation or quality improvement. Moreover, if managers and other employees are to make effective strategic contributions, it is important that they feel motivated, such as achievement, recognition, promotion, interesting work and responsibility (Hertzberg, 1968), and the need for achievement, power, close or friendly working relationships manifested, say, by not working in isolation (McClelland and Winter, 1971). When organizations are **downsizing**, and people are being made redundant, it is both essential and difficult to maintain the commitment of those remaining, since they are the people upon whom new competitive advantages will depend, without which the company cannot successfully rejuvenate. Indeed, research by Roffey Park Management Centre (1995) established that while there is considerable enthusiasm among authors, consultants and senior managers for teamworking, empowerment and flexibility, many employees remain 'cynical, overworked, insecure and despondent' about the impact of flatter organization structures and the consequent reduction in promotion prospects. Employees frequently perceive **delayering** to be a cost-cutting exercise which actually reduces morale. When such rationalization is essential, and often it is, the real challenge comes afterwards, in encouraging the remaining managers to look for innovative new ways of adding value and to take risks, albeit limited and measured risks, reinforcing the importance of the most appropriate reward systems, and involving, managing and leading people to achieve superior levels of performance.

Furthermore, succession problems can concern both strategic leadership and managerial positions throughout the organization, for example small firms, whose growth and success have been dependent upon the founder, often experience problems when he or she retires, especially where there has been a failure to develop a readymade successor. Similarly, some very large organizations also experience problems when particularly charismatic and influential strategic leaders resign or retire, and subsequently there may be unsuccessful changes to the strategy and/or culture. Succession problems are evident with key people in any specialism and at any level of the organization.

Both formal and informal teams exist within organizations, with formal teams comprising sections or departments of people who work directly together on a continuous basis and in pursuit of particular specified objectives, and teams of senior managers who meet on a regular basis with an agreed agenda; and informal teams of managers from different departments, or even divisions, who agree informally to meet to discuss and deal with a particular issue, or who are charged with forming a temporary group to handle an organization-wide problem. In both cases, relationships determine effectiveness, where all members contribute and support each other, with synergy resulting from their interactions, as opposed to simply putting a group of people together in a meeting.

A successful team needs shared and agreed objectives, a working language or effective communications, and the ability to manage both the tasks and the relationships. Individual contributions to the overall team effort are determined by personal growth needs (for achievement and personal development) and social needs, i.e. perceived benefits from working with others to complete tasks, rather than working alone (Cummings, 1981). A good team of people will have complementary strengths and weaknesses – relating to the provision of ideas, leadership, the resolution of conflict, the gathering and analyzing of data and information, carrying out certain detailed work, organizing people to make their most useful contributions and developing relationships within the group – so that they will be able to perform a series of necessary and related tasks (Belbin, 1981), with the strategic leader and his or her team of senior or departmental managers considering these, dealing with missing areas and seeking to develop them into an effective and cohesive team.

The 'learning organization'

Building strong, cohesive and integrated teams suggests small groups of employees, and yet the same themes can be scaled up to the whole organization, such that where the parts can be integrated effectively, share with each other and learn from each other strategically and synergistically in a 'learning organization',

Figure 5.6   The learning organization – leadership and vision (based on the ideas of Charles Handy)

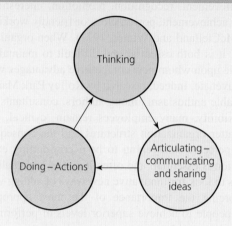

a self-reinforcing process develops in which managers objectively review their progress (Senge, 1991), as shown in Figure 5.6. The basic arguments concerning **learning organizations** are as follows:

- When quality, technology and product/service variety are all becoming widely available at relatively low cost, speed of change is essential for sustained competitive advantage.

- If an organization, therefore, fails to keep up with, or ahead of, the rate of change in its environment, it will either be destroyed by stronger competitors, or lapse into sudden death or slow decline. The ideal is to be marginally ahead of competitors – opening up too wide a gap might unsettle customers.

- An organization can only adapt if it is first able to learn, and this learning must be cross-functional as well as specialist.

Hence a learning organization encourages continuous learning and knowledge generation at all levels, has processes which can move knowledge around the organization easily to where it is needed, and can translate that knowledge quickly into changes in the way the organization acts, both internally and externally.

SENGE, 1991

Strategically important information, together with lessons and best practice, will thus be circulated, and ideally protected from competitors.

The essential requirements are:

- Systemic thinking, such that decision-makers will be able to use the perspective of the whole organization; and there will be significant environmental awareness and internal co-operation. For many organizations, the systemic perspective will be widened to incorporate collaboration and **strategic alliances** with other organizations in the added value chain.

- Management development and personal growth – to enable effective empowerment and leadership throughout the organization, and in turn allow managers to respond to perceived environmental changes and opportunities.

- A shared vision and clarity about both core competencies and key success factors. Changes should be consistent through strategic and operational levels.

- Appropriate values and corporate culture – to exploit core competencies fully and satisfy key success factors.

- A commitment to customer service, quality and continuous improvement.

- The appropriate culture is one which is capable of constant adaptation as the needs of customers, shareholders and employees change (Kotter and Heskett, 1992).

- Team learning within the organization through problem sharing and discussion.

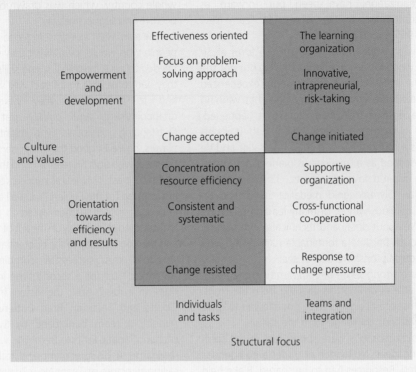

Figure 5.7 Learning organizations

These points have been used to develop the above matrix (Figure 5.7), which draws together a number of issues discussed in this chapter and relates them to key issues of change management.

Case 5.5 then looks at the attributes of a learning organization in the context of Team New Zealand, the relatively small team of sailors who took the America's Cup from the US, whereas creating a learning organization in a large company is no easy task, but if achieved to some creditable degree there are likely to be substantial benefits.

Case 5.5 Team New Zealand   NZ

The America's Cup series of yacht races, between the current holder and a preselected challenger, lasts over several weeks and requires considerable preparation and dedication. When New Zealand won in 1995 it was only the second time a team from outside America had won in 144 years, the first being Australia in 1985. Moreover in the final races, New Zealand won 41 races and lost just one, an incredible margin of victory. The team had 'continually expanded its ability to create its destiny'. There had been a driving vision throughout the preparation and the race series: 'to build, modify and sail the fastest boat on any given day'. This vision had brought together the (technical) designers with the users, the sailors and created synergy where often there is conflict. Their respective perspectives are, quite simply, different.

Team New Zealand was successful in defending the trophy in 2000, but then events would take an unexpected turn.

There are 17 sailors on board an America's Cup boat. The skipper has overall responsibility and is the leader whilst the team are at sea. He relies on his tactician (who keeps the boat on course) and navigator (who looks after the sophisticated electronic tracking instrumentation). A helmsman drives the boat and a strategist monitors the slightest changes of wind speed and direction. Decisions to alter course or rigging are often made very quickly and they need implementing instantaneously. There are then 11 sailors with specific roles mainly related to the deployment of the huge sails. The seventeenth man is really something of a spectator and is often a team sponsor.

Several factors, all characteristic of a successful learning organization, have been put forward as important contributors to the success of Team New Zealand in 1995 and 2000:

There was an *inspirational leader* in the form of Sir Peter Blake, who was an experienced sailor, but not the skipper of the actual crew. Nor was he an experienced boat designer. Blake convinced everyone that winning was possible, and he then made sure that happened. The skipper was Russell Coutts. Blake had built his reputation as a round-the-world challenge sailor and he has been described as a 'meticulous planner and gifted leader who inspired loyalty'. Coutts, 33 years old in 1995, was an Olympic gold medallist for sailing (in 1984) and a previous winner of many leading races. He was 'obsessive about detail and technically very skilled'. Blake and Coutts became a formidable partnership who provided leadership onshore and at sea.

There was a *strong sense of community* in the team. Blake was visible in driving this, leading from the front. He ensured that the designers were not allowed to drive the agenda without challenge from the sailors.

Open communications were sponsored, in the form of free-flowing ideas. No hidden or undeclared agendas were permitted. Resources had to be shared. Blake held meetings between the designers and sailors at regular intervals during the build-up period and ran them without ceremony or hierarchy. He encouraged people to be creative in their search for different and unusual answers to problems and issues. It was noted that the secretary at one meeting felt comfortable contributing an idea that turned out to be really valuable.

There was a *sustained record of improvement* in product design and racing skills right through to the end of the race series. Team New Zealand did not stop searching for improvements even when they were winning every race! They built on their successes to reinforce their advantage. There was a willingness by the sailors to accept design modifications if they made the boat go faster, even where it made their task of sailing it more difficult or uncomfortable. During the pre-race trials Team New Zealand sailed two identical boats, rather than two different designs in competition. Their choice of design had been made by simulation. Because the two boats began as identical, any successful modifications to the design of one could be copied by the team sailing the other. As a result, considerable emphasis was placed on improving sailing skills as well.

There was clear evidence of a very *strong commitment* by the individual team members, who were convinced that winning the America's Cup mattered immensely to the whole country, which was drawn behind the team in a positive and supportive way.

The *team* was *carefully selected* to ensure that they were people who would 'own' what they were taking on. They needed to have individual sailing skills and experience, but they had to be able to interact well with others. They also had to demonstrate they were able to handle disappointment and quickly put it behind them. Outstanding individuals who might be reluctant team players, however good they were personally, were rejected by Blake, who built his team around the tasks. (Interestingly, and in contrast, it sometimes appears that certain footballers are selected for the England football team because of their individual skills, and then asked to play out of position. Right-footed players play on the left of the field, for example, and then do not play to their potential.)

Could this successful combination defend the America's Cup for a second time in 2003 and make it three in a row? After the victory in 2000 both Russell Coutts and Tactician Brad Butterworth 'defected' to Alinghi, a team bankrolled by Swiss billionaire and yachting fanatic Ernesto Bertarelli, who would sail as the navigator. A disagreement and fall-out with the non-sailing directors of Team New Zealand was given as the reason by Coutts. The final Alinghi team for 2003 would include seven New Zealanders and just two Swiss sailors. Its successful challenge was devastating for New Zealanders as really it was the core of the previous winning teams that won the America's Cup for a third time in a row – but this time not for New Zealand. Blake, unfortunately, was unable to contribute to either team. In December 2001 he was shot on board his boat by people described as pirates whilst sailing up the Brazilian Amazon.

Alinghi would go on to defend the Cup successfully in Europe. Coutts left Alinghi in 2004, and he was replaced by Brad Butterworth. In 2007 Alinghi again defeated Team New Zealand (but only by the narrowest of margins in the final deciding race). Coutts was later recruited by Oracle-founder, entrepreneur and racing enthusiast Larry Ellison to lead his Oracle team in a serious American bid for the 2010 America's Cup – and they were successful.

Questions

1 Do you agree that Team New Zealand was a learning organization?

2 How important do you think individuals are in building such a team?

3 How significant is it that their behaviour is transferable?

4 In the end how reliant is a team on its leader and why is it that strong, effective leaders can often move and build new winning teams?

Source of basic material: Maani, K. and Benton, C. (1999) Rapid team learning – lessons from Team New Zealand's America's Cup campaign, *Organizational Dynamics*, Spring. Team New Zealand
http://www.teamnz.org

5.3 Information and information technology (IT)

The strategic value of information

People make decisions, with information being the fuel they use in decision-making, and an important source of competitive advantage in certain circumstances. It must be stressed that IT, *per se*, is rarely a source of advantage, but information management can be. In this section we define 'information' and how it might be exploited.

Information has been defined as 'some tangible or intangible entity that reduces uncertainty about a state or event' (Lucas, 1976), such that information increases knowledge in a particular situation and, when received, some degree of order can be imposed on a previously less well-ordered situation. The more information managers and other employees have about what is happening in the organization, and in its environment, the more strategically aware they are likely to be – with information about other functional areas and business units being particularly helpful.

Ackoff (1967), however, suggested that management information systems can easily be based on three erroneous assumptions:

- Managers are short of information and may have too much irrelevant information.

- Managers know the information they require for a decision but they play safe and ask for all information which might be relevant, thereby contributing to the overabundance of irrelevant information.

- If a manager is provided with the information required for a decision, he or she will have no further problem in using it effectively. How information is used depends on perceptions of the issues involved. If any additional quantitative analysis or interpretation is required, many managers are weak in these skills.

While the right information available at the right time can be extremely useful, the real value of information relates to how it is used by decision-makers, particularly for generating and evaluating alternative possible courses of action. In designing and introducing IT and management information systems into organizations, the likely reaction of people and the potential benefits that can accrue from having more up-to-date and accurate information available are important. Information gathering should never become an end in itself, for the expertise and experience in people's heads can be more useful than facts on paper.

Moreover, it is important to evaluate who actually needs the information, rather than who might find it useful for increasing awareness, and to ensure that those people receive it. Although information technology and information systems can be expensive to introduce, those organizations that receive information, analyze and distribute it to the appropriate decision-makers more quickly than their competitors can achieve a competitive edge, particularly in a turbulent environment. Hence, the structure and culture of the organization should ensure that managers who need information receive it, and at the right time. However, it can also reduce decision-making effectiveness if potentially useful information is withheld, negligently or deliberately, by political managers pursuing personal objectives.

Information is used through a filter of experience and judgement in decision-making, and its relative value varies between one decision-maker and another, being accurate, reliable and up-to-date to some, but to others it may already be biased due to being someone's subjective interpretation of a situation. Some managers, perhaps those who are less experienced, will rely more heavily on specific information than others, for whom experience, general awareness and insight into the situation are more important.

To complicate matters further, Day (1996) argues that organizations do not know what they know, being awash with data that do not get translated into valuable information and hence real organizational knowledge, and they also fail to realize the value of some of the information that some people in the organization possess. Consequently, they also do not know what they do not know, and thus remain unaware of certain opportunities that others will seize and that they would have found valuable if they knew of their existence, or perhaps about certain threats.

The strategic information challenge

Being close to customers, and in touch with new developments in a dynamic and possibly chaotic marketplace, requires information, intelligence and learning. Successful organizations monitor the activities of their customers, suppliers and competitors, asking questions, testing out new ideas and expressing a willingness to learn and to change both their perspective on competition – their mindset concerning which factors determine competitive success – and the things they actually do. Sophisticated analyses and models of past and current results and behaviour patterns make an important contribution but, as Day (1996) argues, it is also necessary to think through how a market might respond to actions designed to retain existing customers and win new business, while outflanking and outperforming competitors. One of the reasons for Canon's continued success has been its ability to spot new market opportunities for its advanced technologies and exploit them early, and hence the company has managed to remain a force in digital cameras and accessories.

In order to become and remain strategically successful, organizations must create and sustain competitive advantage by continuing to enjoy E–V–R congruence, frequently in a dynamic and turbulent environment, by gathering and sharing information, but it is not merely a question of designing a new information system.

The important elements for strategic success are:

- tracking events in the market and the environment, choosing responses (both proactively and reactively) and monitoring the outcomes of the actions which follow. Competitor initiatives must be dealt with; benchmarking best practices and general awareness can suggest new ideas

- making sure that important information from the questioning and learning from these emergent changes is disseminated effectively

- reflecting upon outcomes in the context of E–V–R congruence to ensure that the organization can sustain an effective match with its environment

- where appropriate, adapting policies and procedures to better guide future decisions.

Therefore, they need a constant willingness to be flexible and to change as necessary, and to work from the twin perspectives of opportunity and threat. Strategically successful organizations **leverage** their innovative competitive ideas with speed and act quickly by obtaining market feedback continuously and rapidly, adapting to the feedback ahead of their rivals, and exploiting the potential of strategic as well as competitive and operating information systems (Gilbert, 1995).

There are three levels of information systems:

- *Operating information systems* – Cost accounting systems, sales analyses and production schedules are essential for efficiency and control. Used creatively as, for example, is the case with airline reservation systems, they can create competitive advantage, but they are not designed to drive strategic change.

- *Competitive information systems* – Important elements of the various operating systems need to be integrated and synthesized to ensure that the organization is using its resources efficiently, effectively, and meeting the needs and expectations of important external stakeholders. Competitive information systems, therefore, relate to competitive advantage and E–V–R congruence, requiring managers to think and work across functional boundaries and consider the total service package provided to customers, encapsulating all the ways in which an organization can add value in a co-ordinated way. However, Gilbert (1995) argues that managers will not always be aware of or understand the information they have used to make a competitively successful formula, thus that success may be fragile.

● *Strategic information systems* – While competitive information systems will typically focus on existing competition, organizations must also be able to learn about the business environment in order that they can anticipate change and design future strategies. Marchand (1995a) stresses that strategic information management should not be confined to the level of the strategic leader, but rather it should be dispersed throughout the whole organization, implying an innovative culture and an organization structure which facilitates the sharing of information – one essential element of a learning organization.

Hence, as one moves up these three levels of decision-making, the contribution of IT and information systems to decision-making changes. Once operating systems are established, they can be used to make a number of decisions and drive the operations. By measuring performance, the systems can again make a valuable contribution and highlight when things are going wrong. For strategic decisions, however, IT is primarily an aid to decision-making. Systems cannot realistically make the decisions, and consequently interpretation and meaning systems are particularly important. For such decisions, the systems should be designed to provide information in a form that is useful to decision-makers. Expanding this point, Marchand (1995b) distinguishes four important and distinct uses for information at these three decision-making levels:

● *Command and control* – The formal gathering of information to allow centralized control and decentralized accountability, including budgeting and resource allocation. Command and control is valuable for managing resources efficiently but, used in isolation, it does not drive rapid change.

● *Improvement* – Here the emphasis is on integrating the functions to improve both efficiency and effectiveness through better all-round service.

● *Opportunities for organizational synergy* – If complex multi-business organizations can find new opportunities for internal synergy, sharing and interdependency, they can clearly benefit.

● *Environmental opportunities* – Market intelligence, competitor monitoring and benchmarking best practice can generate new ideas and opportunities, as we have seen.

Figure 5.8 illustrates that an organization must be able to manage all four information needs simultaneously and harmoniously if it is to benefit from improved efficiencies and manage change both continuously and

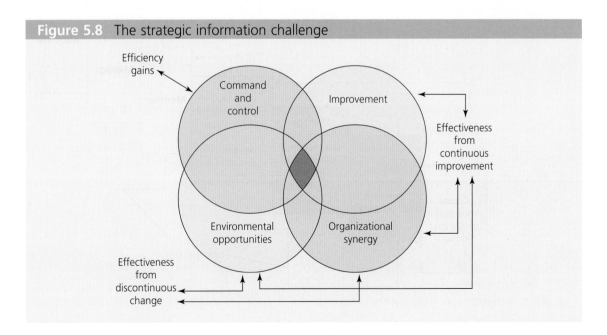

Figure 5.8   The strategic information challenge

discontinuously. Herein lies the real strategic information challenge, where the deployment of organizational resources, the corresponding style of management and the cultural implications vary between the four information needs and the decision-making processes that they support.

Figure 5.9 illustrates how organizations need, first to develop a perspective on how they can add value and create competitive advantage since, through monitoring, measurement, continuous improvement and innovation, they should seek to become increasingly efficient and effective, which represents **single-loop learning**, essential if competitive advantage is to be sustained in a dynamic environment. However, organizations must always be looking for new competitive paradigms, new ways of adding different values, ahead of existing competitors and potential new entrants, looking for an opportunity to break into the market, and effective strategic information systems, relying on informality, networking and learning, are required for this **double-loop learning**.

Organizations that invest in strategic planning, research and development and new product/service programmes are locked into the process, but the real benefits cannot be gained if these activities and the requisite learning are confined to head office departments and specialist functions, since they must permeate the whole organization and become embedded in the culture. This reflects a key organizational tension and dilemma: the paradox of stability (running existing businesses efficiently and effectively, exploiting strategic abilities and continually looking to create higher returns from the committed resources) and instability (the search for the new competitive high ground ahead of one's rivals).

Information, however, as well as being a vital element in decision-making, can also be a source of competitive advantage, as shown in the next section.

The online British Airways case offers an example of this section's theory in practice.

Information, information technology and competitive advantage

Although IT offers many potential strategic opportunities, harnessing these opportunities involves changes in attitude and culture among managers. McFarlane (1984) claims that IT strategies should relate to how dependent the organization is on IT systems which are constantly reliable, and whether IT is crucial if the organization is to meet its key success factors.

Figure 5.9 Single- and double-loop learning and strategic change

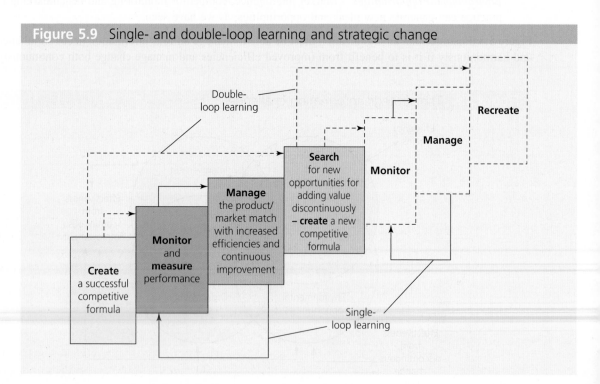

Rayport and Sviokla (1995) argue that competition is now based on two dimensions: the physical world of resources and a virtual world of information, which clearly supports and enhances every activity in an organization, but it can itself be a source of added value and consequently competitive advantage as long as organizations are able to extract that value. Porter (1985) had earlier suggested that technological change, and in particular IT, is among the most prominent forces that can alter the rules of competition because most activities in an organization create and use information. Porter and Millar (1985) contend that IT could affect competition in three ways:

- *IT can change the structure of an industry, and in so doing alter the rules of competition.* IT could influence the nature of Porter's (1980) five forces, thereby changing the attractiveness and profitability of an industry, particularly where the industry has a high information content, e.g. airlines and financial and distribution services. Firms that were either slow or reluctant to introduce IT might be driven out of the industry, because they would be unable to offer a competitive service. Where the cost of the necessary IT, both hardware and software systems, is high it can increase the barriers to entry for potential new firms.

- *IT can be used to create sustainable competitive advantage by providing companies with new competitive weapons.* If costs are reduced to a level below competitors' costs and this advantage is maintained, above-average profits and an increased market share can result, and they suggest that while the impact of IT on lower costs has historically been confined to activities where repetitive information processing has been important, such restraints no longer apply. IT can lead to lower labour costs by reducing the need for certain production and clerical staff, so there should be both lower direct production costs and reduced overheads. Differentiation can be created in a number of ways, including quality, design features, availability and special services that offer added value to the end consumer.

- *As a result of IT, new businesses can be developed from within a company's existing activities.* Telecommunications led to the development of facsimile services; micro-electronics made personal computing possible; and IT created demand for high-speed data communications networks that were previously unavailable. In addition, organizations have diversified into software provision stemming from the development of packages for their own use, whilst the Internet spawned a number of new and very entrepreneurial businesses – every organization must now develop a strategy for harnessing its potential.

In summary, implementing IT for competitive advantage requires:

- an awareness of customer and consumer needs, changing needs, and how IT can improve the product's performance or create new services
- an awareness of operational opportunities to reduce costs and improve quality through IT
- an appreciation of how the organization could be more effective with improved information provision, and how any changes might be implemented. The impact upon people is very significant.

The argument is that competitive advantage can stem from any area of the organization.

5.4 The value chain

Developing his earlier work which highlighted the significance of the relative power of buyers and suppliers (Porter, 1980), Porter (1985) argues that in the search for competitive advantage a firm must be considered as part of a wider system:

suppliers > firm > distributors > consumers.

Thus, a firm should assess the opportunities and potential benefits from improving its links with other organizations – for example, the marketing and selling activities of its suppliers; and the purchasing and materials handling activities of its distributors or customers. Prahalad and Krishnan (2008), instead of conceptualizing 'chains', emphasize the critical links between suppliers, manufacturers and customers, arguing that managers should seek to build 'constellations' of suppliers that can be reconfigured in different patterns to meet different needs, which can only work if people are flexible and IT is harnessed. Similarly, and reinforcing points from earlier in the chapter, Davenport and Harris (2007) argue that organizations, for example Wal-Mart (and also UPS, FedEx and Amazon), have more information than ever before about their environment and their competitors, thanks to IT – but they must use it to become more effective strategic thinkers, understand what makes them different, and exploit what they term 'analytics'. The supply chain is a process, and managing it is a key strategic capability, to achieve cost savings and service differentiation.

Organizations can create synergy, and enjoy the appropriate benefits, if they can successfully link their value chain with those of their suppliers and distributors. Just-in-time (JIT) deliveries integrate a supplier's outbound logistics with the organization's inbound logistics. Stock and costs can be reduced for the manufacturer, whose delivery lead time and reliability should also be improved. An effective JIT system can enable suppliers to plan their work more effectively and reduce their uncertainty. This approach requires an open exchange of reliable, up-to-date information and medium- to long-term supply arrangements. When Nissan was developing the supply chain for its UK manufacturing plant in Sunderland, it deliberately forged links with its suppliers' suppliers in its search to control costs without sacrificing quality and service. A retail bookseller, taking orders for non-stock items, needs to be sure of the delivery lead time from its publishers or wholesaler before quoting a date to the customer. This again demands accurate information, supported by reliable supply.

Carphone Warehouse, a leading retailer of mobile phones, has retailed telephones at prices ranging from 50p to over £300. Where the phone is sold as part of a package which involves a monthly line rental, the phone will typically have been provided free to Carphone Warehouse by one of the major networks, such as O2, Orange or Vodafone, who in turn will have a supply arrangement with a manufacturer, perhaps Nokia or Motorola. The retailer will later receive a share of the future call revenues, normally between 3 per cent and 5 per cent. The ultimate value to Carphone Warehouse of the sale might average £300, regardless of the apparent selling price. In the case of phones used for prepaid calls without any monthly line rental, a typical sale could yield £200.

The incentive of the giving of laptop computers for customers signing up to a specific mobile Internet rental agreement offers companies the opportunity for new business streams. Organizations launching a new product must ensure that their supply and distribution networks are in place so that retailers can be convinced of a new product's viability and potential before stocking it, normally taking something else off their shelves, while manufacturers must be sure that stocks are available where customers expect to find them before they proceed with launch advertising.

The key lies in an integrated network, where all members of the supply chain see themselves as mutual beneficiaries from an effective total system. Preece *et al.* (1995) use the value chain to explain how Levi Strauss has created value and used its value-creating activities carefully to establish a distinctive corporate reputation, which is a form of competitive advantage, due to established links with global suppliers, team manufacturing, global advertising and branding, alliances with retailers who exclusively stock Levi's jeans, and a programme of 'marketing revitalization' designed to reduce lead times and improve the availability of the products.

Strengthening the processes involved in managing the supply chain relates to the level of service that companies are able to offer their customers and to total quality management. Some years back, managers in ICI's explosives manufacturing division also developed expertise in detonating explosions. Since quarry managers (who buy the explosive products) really want stones and rocks on a quarry floor, ICI offered to produce a three-dimensional map of a quarry for their customers, indicating where the charges need to be placed, and then, when suitable holes have been drilled in the quarry face (by the quarry owners), carry out controlled explosions, thus adding value for their customers and linking the two value chains.

The organization's value chain

While strategic success depends upon the way in which the organization as a whole behaves, and the ways in which managers and functions are integrated, competitive advantage stems from the individual and discrete activities that a firm performs. A cost advantage can arise from low-cost distribution, efficient production or an excellent salesforce that succeeds in winning the most appropriate orders. Differentiation can be the result of having an excellent design team or being able to source high-quality materials or high-quality production.

Value-chain analysis is a systematic way of studying the direct and support activities undertaken by a firm, thus providing greater awareness concerning costs and the potential for lower costs and for differentiation. Competitive advantage is created and sustained when a firm performs the most critical functions either more cheaply or better than its competitors (Porter, 1985).

Porter (1985) developed his value chain framework which is now used extensively; the same basic outline can be shown in a number of different formats, which can be seen by carrying out a simple online search for it. There are five primary activities in the value chain, namely inbound logistics, operations, outbound logistics, marketing and sales, and service – illustrated as a chain moving from left to right – and they represent the activities of physically creating the product or service and transferring it to the buyer, together with any necessary after-sales service. They are linked to four support activities – procurement, technology development, human resource management and the firm's infrastructure – which are drawn laterally as they can affect any one or more of the primary activities, although the firm's infrastructure generally supports the whole value chain. Every one of the primary and support activities incurs costs and should add value to the product or service in excess of these costs. It is important always to look for ways of reducing costs sensibly; cost reductions should not be at the expense of lost quality in areas that matter to customers and consumers. Equally, costs can be added justifiably if they add qualities that the customer values and is willing to pay for. The difference between the total costs and the selling price is the margin. The margin is increased by widening the gap between costs and price. The activities are described in greater depth below.

Primary Activities

- *Inbound logistics* are activities relating to receiving, storing and distributing internally the inputs to the product or service and include warehousing, stock control and internal transportation systems.

- *Operations* are activities relating to the transformation of inputs into finished products and services; e.g. machining, assembly and packaging.

- *Outbound logistics* are activities relating to the distribution of finished goods and services to customers.

- *Marketing and sales* includes such activities as advertising and promotion, pricing and salesforce activity.

- *Service* relates to the provision of any necessary service with a product, such as installation, repair, extended warranty or training in how to use the product.

Each of these might be crucial for competitive advantage, with the nature of the industry determining which factors are the most significant.

Support Activities

- *Procurement* refers to the function or process of purchasing any inputs used in the value chain, as distinct from issues of their application. Procurement may take place within defined policies or procedures, and it might be evidenced within a number of functional areas. Production managers and engineers, for example, are very important in many purchasing decisions to ensure that the specification and quality are appropriate.

- *Technology development:* technology is defined here in its broadest sense to include know-how, research and development, product design and process improvement and information technology.

- *Human resource management* involves all activities relating to recruiting, training, developing and rewarding people throughout the organization.

- *The firm's infrastructure* includes the structure of the organization, planning, financial controls and quality management designed to support the whole of the value chain.

Again, each of these support activities can be very important in creating and sustaining competitive advantage.

Porter argues that it can often be valuable to subdivide the primary and support activities into their component parts when analyzing costs and opportunities for differentiation. For example, it is less meaningful to argue that an organization provides good service than to explain it in terms of installation, repair or training, since the competitive advantage is likely to result from a specific sub-activity. Similarly, the marketing mix comprises a set of linked activities which should be managed to complement each other. However, competitive advantage can arise from just one activity in the mix, possibly the product design, its price or advertising, technical support literature, or from the skills and activities of the sales force.

Although competitive advantage arises from one or more sub-activity within the primary and support activities comprising the value chain, the chain is a *system of interdependent activities*, and is not merely a set of independent activities. Linkages in the value chain, which are relationships between the activities, are very important. Behaviour in one part of the organization can affect the costs and performance of other business units and functions, and this quite frequently involves trade-off decisions. For example, more expensive materials and more stringent inspection will increase costs in the inbound logistics and operations activities, but the savings in service costs resulting from these strategies may be greater. The choice of functional strategies and where to concentrate efforts will relate to the organization's competitive and corporate strategies concerning competitive advantage.

Similarly, several activities and sub-activities depend on each other. The extent to which operations, outbound logistics and installation are co-ordinated can be a source of competitive advantage through lower costs (reduced stockholding) or differentiation (high-quality, customer-orientated service). This last example uses linkages between primary activities, but there are also clear linkages between primary and support activities. Product design affects manufacturing costs, purchasing policies affect operations and production costs and so on.

Having introduced and discussed the concept of the value chain, it is now important to consider how it might be applied in the evaluation of costs and differentiation opportunities.

The value chain and competitive advantage

Cost leadership and differentiation strategies. While in Chapter 6 we introduce Porter's **generic strategies** built around **cost leadership** and differentiation (Porter, 1985), we examine how these themes relate to the value chain framework.

Cost leadership

Porter (1985) argued that the lowest cost producer in either a broad or narrow competitive scope (the broad market or specialist segments):

- delivers acceptable quality but produces the product or service with lower costs than competitors
- sustains this cost gap
- achieves above-average profits from industry-average prices.

This cost advantage will be achieved by the effective management of the key determinants of costs.

The differentiation strategy

Similarly, Porter argues that the successful application of a differentiation strategy involves:

- the selection of one or more key characteristics which are widely valued by buyers (there are any number of opportunities relating to different needs and market segments)
- adding costs selectively in the areas perceived to be important to buyers, and charging a premium price in excess of the added costs.

Firms aim to find strategic opportunities for differentiation which cannot be matched easily by competitors, and being clear about the costs involved and the price potential. For example, costs in areas not perceived to be significant to buyers must be controlled, and in line with competitor costs, for otherwise above-average profits will not be achieved.

The successful implementation of both of these strategies, therefore, requires an understanding of where costs are incurred throughout the organization, and the search for appropriate cost reductions, which involves an appreciation of how costs should be attributed to the various discrete activities which comprise the value chain. Table 5.2 compares a possible cost breakdown for a manufacturing firm with that for a firm of professional accountants. For an analysis of the value chain to be meaningful, the costs must be genuinely attributed to the activities that generate them, and not simply apportioned in some convenient way, however difficult this might prove in practice. The figures in Table 5.2 (which are only indicative, and should not be seen as targets for any particular firm) suggest that the manufacturing firm may not be spending enough on human resources management and marketing, while the accountancy practice may be spending too much.

Cost drivers

The following cost drivers, some of which may be more significant, can all influence the value chain:

- economies of scale and potential experience and learning curve benefits
- capacity utilization, linked to production control and the existence of bottlenecks
- time spent liaising with other departments can incur costs, but at the same time create savings and differentiation through interrelationships and shared activities

Table 5.2   Indicative cost breakdown of a manufacturing and a service business

	Manufacturing firm (% of total)	Professional firm of accountants (% of total)
Primary activities Inbound logistics	4	8 (data collection for audits)
Operations	64	26 (actual auditing)
Outbound logistics	1	5 (report writing and presentations)
Marketing and sales	7	21 (getting new business)
Service	1	3 (general client liaison)
	77	63
Support activities Procurement	1	1
Technology development	10	8 (IT development)
Human resources management	2	16
Firm's infrastructure	10	12
	100	100

- Interrelationships and shared activities, possibly a shared salesforce, shared advertising or shared plant can generate savings by increasing quality and ensuring that the needs of customers are matched more effectively.

- The extent to which the organization is vertically integrated (e.g. manufacturing its own component parts instead of assembling bought-in components, or designing and manufacturing its own machinery) can influence costs and differentiation. Strategy in Action 5.1 (YKK) illustrates this.

Strategy in Action 5.1   YKK – the World's Leading Manufacturer of Zips

The Japanese zip manufacturer YKK, the world market leader, grew to enjoy a superior competitive position, and the company's strategy is analyzed against the value chain in this box. The underlying philosophy of YKK, the 'Cycle of Goodness', is a cultural issue described in Chapter 7.

YKK succeeded in creating both cost leadership and substantial differentiation with its corporate, competitive and functional strategies, and these have resulted in effective barriers to entry into the industry and close relationships with customers. The conceptual idea is illustrated in Figure 5.10.

The essential components of the strategy, summarized in outline here, are illustrated in Figure 5.11, which places them in the context of the value chain and highlights the linkages.

YKK was structured as a multi-plant multinational company with both wholly owned subsidiary companies and joint ventures throughout the world. The latter organizations were primarily the result of local politics, particularly in low-labour-cost countries in the Far East. While the subsidiaries were decentralized and enjoyed some local autonomy, they were often managed at the top by Japanese executives on a period of secondment. Consequently, there was substantial influence from the Japanese parent.

YKK invested a significant percentage of after-tax profits back in the business, and as a result became heavily automated and able to enjoy the benefits of the experience/learning curve. Moreover, YKK priced its finished products very competitively both to generate customer satisfaction and to create barriers to entry. The company was vertically integrated, designing and manufacturing its own production machinery, and this gave it a unique competitive edge. It was also particularly innovative as far as both machinery and finished products were concerned.

Coils of semi-finished zips were produced in the Far East, particularly Japan, and exported to such countries as the UK, where they were cut to size and finished in response to customer orders. This resulted in both cost advantages and speedy deliveries from semi-finished stocks. A wide range of colours and sizes was kept ready for finishing. In the UK the key garment manufacturers and the retail outlets that they serve were targeted by YKK and given special service.

The 'Cycle of Goodness' philosophy was not exported in its complete form, but employee relations were an important aspect of the human resources strategy. Participation and involvement were essential features, and total quality management was a key feature.

Figure 5.10   YKK's competitive advantage

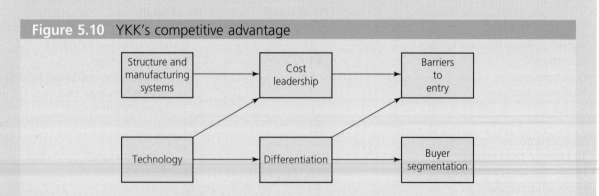

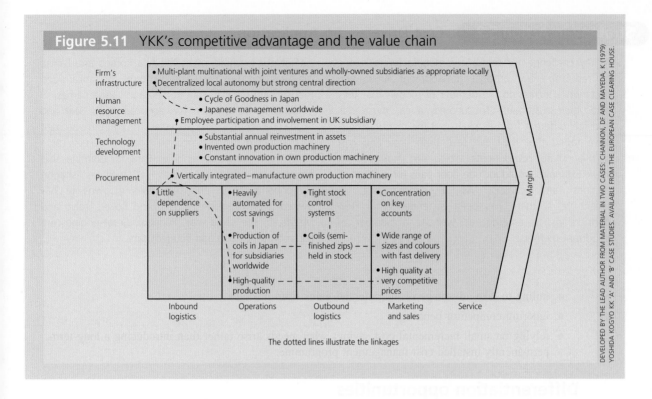

Figure 5.11 YKK's competitive advantage and the value chain

DEVELOPED BY THE LEAD AUTHOR FROM MATERIAL IN TWO CASES: CHANNON, DF AND MAYEDA, K (1979) YOSHIDA KOGYO KK 'A' AND 'B' CASE STUDIES. AVAILABLE FROM THE EUROPEAN CASE CLEARING HOUSE.

- Buying and selling at the appropriate time, for example investing in stocks to ensure deliveries when customers want them, but also stockholding costs must be monitored and controlled.
- Policy standards for procurement or production may be wrong and, if set too low, quality may be lost and prove detrimental, whereas, if too high in relation to the actual needs of the market, costs are incurred unnecessarily.
- Location issues include wage costs, which can vary between different regions, and the costs of supporting a particular organization structure.
- Institutional factors comprising specific regulations concerning materials content or usage, for example.

Porter argues that sustained competitive advantage requires effective control of the cost drivers, and that scale economies, learning, linkages, interrelationships and timing provide the key opportunities for creating advantage. The cost advantage in a cost leadership strategy is relative to the costs of competitors, and over time these could change if competitors concentrate on their cost drivers. Consequently, it is useful to attempt to monitor and predict how competitor costs might change in the future linked to any changes in their competitive and functional strategies.

Strategy in Action 5.2 provides details of some cost drivers in the car industry.

Common problems in cost control through the value chain

Whilst it can prove difficult to assign costs to activities properly, Porter contends that there are several common pitfalls in managing costs for competitive advantage:

- misunderstanding of actual costs and misperceptions of the key cost drivers
- concentrating on manufacturing when cost savings are required. Often it is not the area to cut if quality is to be maintained, especially once a certain level of manufacturing efficiency has been achieved

Strategy in Action 5.2   Cost Drivers – an Application

A key challenge for motor car manufacturers is one of reducing new product development times and costs while increasing the number of models that they offer their customers. To succeed, a car must look and feel different from its rivals, but the manufacturers have found that they can save both time and cost if they share components *which are hidden from view*. Examples would include floor pans (or platforms), engines and chassis. As a consequence, in recent years, there has been a tendency for new partnerships to emerge, as well as a number of important mergers.

Fiat, for example, owns the Alfa Romeo and Lancia marques and uses the same platforms for similar-sized models with the Fiat, Alfa Romeo and Lancia names.

Similarly, Volkswagen has acquired Audi, Seat and Skoda and adopts similar strategies. The platforms account for one-third of the costs incurred in designing a new car.

Manufacturers trade engines. Ford, for example, sells engines to other companies, as well as sharing components across the businesses it owns or has owned, which include Jaguar, Land Rover, Volvo and Mazda. In the same way, Peugeot diesel engines are common to Citroën and Peugeot cars.

- failing to take advantage of the potential gains from linkages
- ignoring competitor behaviour
- relying on small incremental cost savings when needs arise rather than introducing a long-term, permanently installed cost-management programme.

Differentiation opportunities

Competitive advantage through differentiation can arise from any and every area of the business, for example:

Primary Activities

- *Inbound logistics* – careful and thoughtful handling to ensure that incoming materials are not damaged and are easily accessed when necessary, and the linking of purchases to production requirements, especially important in the case of JIT manufacturing systems.
- *Operations* – high quality; high-output levels and few rejections; delivery on time.
- *Outbound logistics* – rapid delivery when and where customers need the product or service.
- *Marketing and sales* – advertising closely tied to defined market segments; a well-trained, knowledgeable and motivated salesforce; and good technical literature, especially for industrial products.
- *Service* – rapid installation; speedy after-sales service and repair; and immediate availability of spare parts.

Support Activities

- *Procurement* – purchasing high-quality materials (to assist operations); regional warehousing of finished products (to enable speedy delivery to customers).
- *Technology development* – the development of unique features, and new products and services; the use of IT to manage inbound and outbound logistics most effectively; and sophisticated market analyses to enable segmentation, targeting and positioning for differentiation.
- *Human resources management* – high-quality training and development; recruitment of the right people; and appropriate reward systems which help to motivate people.

● *Firm's infrastructure* – support from senior executives in customer relations; investment in suitable physical facilities to improve working conditions; and investment in carefully designed IT systems.

In searching for the most appropriate means of differentiating for competitive advantage, one must look at which activities are the most essential to consumers, and to isolate the key success factors. It is a search for opportunities to be different from competitors in ways which matter, and through this the creation of a superior competitive position. The Japanese zip manufacturer YKK, the world market leader, grew to enjoy a superior competitive position, and the company's strategy was analyzed against the value chain in Strategy in Action 5.1 seen earlier.

The value chain can provide an extremely useful framework for considering the activities involved in producing products and services and considering their significance for customers.

Activity mapping and strategy mapping

Porter (1996) later developed activity maps as an adjunct to the value chain, in order to produce a framework of the critically important activities, together with those that support them, and show how they all link together.

Activity mapping, described here in outline only, provides a useful framework to explain how all the selected activities and resources fit together, add value, and complement the corporate and competitive strategies in order to yield uniqueness and synergy. Porter (1996) uses the metaphor of a comparison of two people who may have functionally similar eyes, hands and feet, but where the real difference is in the way all the parts combine into a whole, and where individual differences in parts – such as colour blindness or arthritis in a hand – do not in themselves explain different behaviours and outcomes. Thus we need to understand more about the workings of the brain and, if we are to understand organizations and organizational differences, we must understand how different organizations acquire and use knowledge – which is frequently related to the synergy created by the interactions of the functions and activities.

Figure 5.12 is an example of Porter's activity mapping idea based on Lilliput Lane, a manufacturer of plaster cottages and other collectable items which, along with nearby business, Border Fine Arts (best known for resin models of wildlife), is owned by the American collectables business, Enesco, which derives synergy from distributing different collectable products from suppliers around the world through common retail channels. Using innovative moulding technology, much of it invented by founder, David Tate, Lilliput Lane casts intricate figures and models out of plaster, a cheap and readily obtainable commodity. Individual painters then transform a relatively bland model into a unique finished article.

The five larger circles in Figure 5.12 represent the key activities in terms of difference and competitive strength, while the smaller circles are important support activities, with the key activities all linked and complementary and the other activities support often more than one key activity. As time progresses, activities will be abandoned, added or changed to affect the competitive position. How activities are carried out by people is important and so the culture and style of management in the organization is a major determinant of the organization's ability to change and find new opportunities for creating different values for customers.

Strategy mapping, developed by Kaplan and Norton (2000) from their earlier work on the Balanced Scorecard, which is explained in Chapter 11 (Kaplan and Norton, 1992), has usefully applied to the public sector (Irwin, 2002).

Since financial *performance measures* alone are inadequate to evaluate performance, the Balanced Scorecard includes measures relating to customers, internal processes and improvement that give an all-round view on the extent to which the organization is progressing towards its vision and long-term purpose. Strategy mapping works oppositely, demanding that managers question what is going to be required (in terms of activities) to progress systematically and synergistically towards the vision and then to set targets for performance against these activities. In other words, one starts with the vision and then questions what needs to be done, how and when. Whilst the Balanced Scorecard measures activities and reviews outcomes, strategy mapping starts with desired outcomes and then seeks to make sure the necessary activities are in place – with performance targets attached – and it embraces how activities can be used to create competitive advantage.

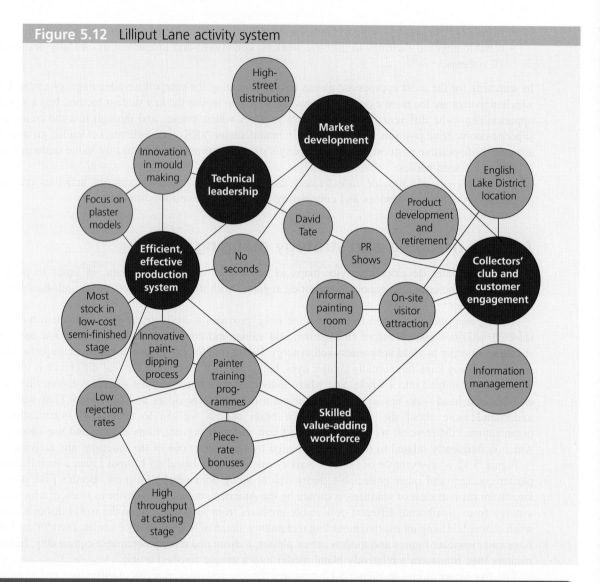

Figure 5.12 Lilliput Lane activity system

5.5 Reputation and branding

Reputation and branding are clearly linked but are not synonymous, since a brand is a label that is attached to an organization's reputation. Kay (1993) sees reputation as a key element of differentiation, and that both reputation and branding are key intangible resources in determining how customers perceive the difference and its meaning and are, therefore, qualitative indicators of quality – where quantitative measurement may be difficult – enabling decision-making and choice.

The reputation of particular brands can allow certain organizations to diversify into a wide range of activities, with customer confidence in the brand providing reassurance and even allowing them entry into areas where they have little previous experience or expertise. However, they must never disappoint customers in ways which tarnish a reputation, and thus there can be a huge downside risk for companies with the strongest reputations if they make strategic errors of judgement.

In a similar vein, a strong reputation provides a safe choice for customers who are new entrants to a market, helping to sustain and build a strong position in a market, and can even sometimes be used to justify a premium price. Famous-name endorsements provide an ideal opportunity for enhancing a company's reputation, as they make a statement about a person who is held in very high regard by the public – whether or not they actually use the products and services that they endorse!

Branding

Brand is only important when two products are identical. It is not important if one of the products has better technology or a better design than the other.

JAMES DYSON

Many differentiated products and services are identified by brand names which, possibly along with the identity of the companies that own them, convey an image to customers by reflecting reputations. Advertising is often used to create and reinforce this image and reputation. As competition intensifies, more products are perceived as commodities, sold essentially on price and so differentiation and branding become increasingly significant. The product needs a clear brand identity; a supportive corporate image, a company brand, is also valuable. Brands add value, possibly the promise of some particular satisfaction or experience, a 'guarantee' of a specific level of quality, or reliability and a brand can be seen as an actual product or service augmented by some additional added value. The drive to establish and maintain a recognized brand image can bring about differentiation and innovation, e.g. Nescafé instant coffee has had several variants and improvements over the years. However, the value added must be real, as informed customers today will quickly see through any marketing hype; and the distinctiveness will not be achieved without investment, in both research and development and advertising, as discussed later.

Ideally, successful branding will generate customer loyalty and repeat purchases, enable higher prices and margins, and provide a springboard for additional products and services. Customers expect to find the leading brand names widely available in distribution outlets but supermarkets will typically only offer the number one and number two grocery brands alongside their own-label brand, since strong branding has been essential for enabling the leading manufacturers to contain the growing power of the leading supermarket chains, but it has not exempted them from tight pricing strategies. Edwin Artzt, until the mid-1990s a powerful and renowned Chief Executive of Procter & Gamble, has stated that 'winning companies offer lower prices, better quality, continuous improvement and/or high profits to retailers'.

The quality of own-label products has increased, and consequently the magnitude of the premium that customers will pay for the leading manufacturer brand has declined in recent years. Procter & Gamble, which is not alone in this strategy, has adopted perpetual 'everyday low prices' for all of its products. In the competitive food sector, product innovation, quality, specific features and, to a lesser extent, packaging are seen as the most effective means of distinguishing brands from own-label alternatives.

Examples of leading brands

- *Persil* and *Pampers:* brand names not used in conjunction with the manufacturer's name – they are produced by Unilever and Procter & Gamble, respectively.

- *Coca-Cola:* manufacturer's name attributed to a product. *Levi's* is derived from Levi Strauss. An online case on Levi's looks at how a company with a significant brand and image has changed tactics in a dynamic and competitive environment.

- *Cadbury's Dairy Milk* and *Barclaycard Visa:* the first is a combination of a company and a product name, the second a combination of an organization (Barclays) and a service provided by a separate business.

- *St Michael:* the personalized brand name used historically on all products sold by Marks and Spencer to signify UK manufactured. Now no longer a viable cost concept and replaced with clothing related band names such as Per Una.

- Apple through new **product development** has created the iPod, iPhone, iTunes, MacBook and the ultra thin MacBook Air which have all regenerated a struggling business to be a major player in the multimedia arena.

Several large organizations have, through strategic acquisitions and investments in brands, established themselves as global corporations. Examples include:

- *Unilever:* now owns a variety of food (Birds Eye, Batchelors, Wall's, John West, Boursin, Blue Band, Flora), household goods (Shield soap, Persil, Lux and Surf detergents) and cosmetics (Brut, Fabergé and Calvin Klein) brands.

- *Nestlé:* including Chambourcy (France), Rowntree (UK) and Buitoni (Italy).

These companies can afford substantial investments in research and development to innovate and strengthen the brand by extending the range of products carrying the name, develop new opportunities (e.g. Mars Bars ice-cream with its price premium over normal ice-cream bars), and transform competition in the market (e.g. Pampers disposable nappies' segmented products in the USA and Europe). Strong brand names are clearly an asset for an organization and the value of the brand – the so-called brand equity – relates to the totality of all the stored beliefs, likes/dislikes and behaviours associated with it. Customer and distributor attitudes are critical.

A brand commanding a certain amount of shelf space in all leading stores carries a value. However, creating and maintaining the image is expensive, and manufacturers spend on average 7 per cent of sales revenue to support the top ten leading brands, covering all product groups, increasing as the brand recognition factor decreases. Because of this, manufacturers need to control the number of brands that they market at any time; Procter & Gamble withdrew over 25 per cent of their brands in the 1990s. Similarly, new product launches need to be managed effectively.

However, not all brand names are strong and effective. Prudential, best known as an insurance business, launched its Internet bank in 1999, calling it 'Egg' partly to provide a distinctive and unusual launch platform. The business developed successfully and in 2004 Egg had between three and four million customers. Recognizing that Egg needed investment at a level that would stretch its own resources, Prudential attempted to find a buyer for the business, but none was forthcoming at the right price, providing wonderful ammunition for some to criticize the name 'Egg', with phrases such as 'egg on its face', 'half-baked' and 'gone off the boil' all appearing in the press. Changing brand names is not always for the better, such as the UK's Post Office changing its corporate identity to Consignia, with some design team creating a clever play on the word 'consignment' but the public reaction was hardly supportive and the name was changed back!

Branding helps to establish, build and cement relationships among manufacturers, their customers and their distributors. The term 'relationship marketing' is used to reinforce the argument that marketing should be perceived as the management of a network of relationships between the brand and its various customers. Marketing, therefore, aims to enhance brand equity and thus ensure continued satisfaction for customers and increased profits for the brand owner. Implicit in this is the realization that new customers are harder, and more expensive, to find than existing ones are to retain. This potent mix of brand identity and customer care is clearly related to the whole service package offered by manufacturers to their customers, and to total quality management.

Research Snapshot 5.1

In this snapshot we review articles on resource-led strategy which is linked to a firm's competitive advantage and performance (Clulow *et al.*, 2007), focusing on two key areas: (i) the resource-based view and (ii) strategic resources, including in terms of HR. Other key elements, such as core competencies, strategic architecture, networks and IT, are also covered briefly in the more recent literature but to a more limited extent. Overall, the resource-based view still holds, although it has been rather eclipsed by Teece's dynamic capabilities perspective, whilst one paper argues the case for a hybrid dynamic resources view (Helfat and Peteraf, 2003). For students, these papers provide a deeper insight into modern thinking and development in the resource-based view, building, of course, upon the Penrosian origins of the theory and the other classical (e.g. 1980s and 1990s) literature – (Prahalad and Hamel, 1990; Hershey and Blanchard, 1982 etc) covered in this textbook. This perspective builds upon Penrose's theory of the growth of the firm (see also Acedo *et al.* (2006), Armstrong and Shimizu (2007), Lockett *et al.* (2009) and Kraaijenbrink *et al.* (2010) for reviews), and has since been extended to include strategy. Other key studies include Helfat and Peteraf's (2003) capability life cycle concept. The link between the RBV and performance and competitive advantage has been examined, e.g. in manufacturing (Schroeder et al., 2002; Größler, 2007), service firms (Ray et al., 2004) and the impact of information technology (Rivard et al., 2006). Key reviews include a meta-analysis of strategic resources and performance (Crook et al., 2008).

These papers provide a key understanding of the link between strategic resources, capabilities, strategy, competitive advantage and performance, focusing on more recent thinking on the theory and its link to practice. There is not so much that has been published on strategic architecture, but the dynamic capabilities view has gained quite a lot of traction and yet does not have to be contradictory of RBV.

Further Reading

Acedo, F.J., Barroso, C. and Galan, J.L. (2006) 'The resource-based theory: dissemination and main trends', Strategic Management Journal, Vol. 27, pp. 621–636.

Armstrong, C.E. and Shimizu, K. (2007) 'A review of approaches to empirical research on the resource-based view of the firm', Journal of Management, Vol. 33, No. 6, pp. 959–986.

Clulow, V., Barry, C. and Gerstman, J. (2007) 'The resource-based view and value: the customer-based view of the firm', Journal of European Industrial Training, Vol. 31, No. 1, pp. 19–35.

Crook, T.R., Ketchen, D.J., Combs, J.G. and Todd, S.Y. (2008), 'Strategic resources and performance: a meta-analysis', Strategic Management Journal, Vol. 29, pp. 1141–1154.

Größler, A. (2007) 'A dynamic view on strategic resources and capabilities applied to an example from the manufacturing strategy literature', Journal of Manufacturing Technology Management, Vol. 18, No. 3, pp. 250–266.

Helfat, C.E. and Peteraf, M.A. (2003) 'The dynamic resource-based view: capability lifecycles', Strategic Management Journal, Vol. 24, pp. 997–1010.

Kraaijenbrink, J., Spendr, J.-C. and Groen, A.J. (2010) 'The Resource-Based View: A Review and Assessment of Its Critiques', Journal of Management, Vol. 36, No. 1, pp. 349–372.

Lockett, A., Thompson, S. and Morgenstern, U. (2009) 'The development of the resource-based view of the firm: A critical appraisal', International Journal of Management Reviews, Vol. 11, pp. 9–28.

Ray, G., Barney, J.B. and Muhanna, W.A. (2004) 'Capabilities, business processes, and competitive advantage: choosing the dependent variable in empirical tests of the resource-based view', Strategic Management Journal, Vol. 25, pp. 23–37.

Rivard, S., Raymond, L. and Verreault, D. (2006) 'Resource-based view and competitive strategy: An integrated model of the contribution of information technology to firm performance', The Journal of Strategic Information Systems, Vol. 15, No. 1, pp. 29–50.

Schroeder, R.G., Bates, K.A. and Junttila, M.A. (2002) 'A resource-based view of manufacturing strategy and the relationship to manufacturing performance', Strategic Management Journal, Vol. 23, pp. 105–117.

Summary

The resource-based view of strategy looks at how organizations acquire, deploy and exploit resources in an individual and effective way, and at how their core competencies and strategic capabilities determine their competitive advantage.

A simple *resource audit* is an attempt to assess the strengths and weaknesses of an organization and can be carried out in conjunction with an assessment of opportunities and threats, but it should be relative, and be in the context of, first, the key success factors for the markets and industries in question and, second, the comparable strengths and weaknesses of competitors for the same customers.

Strategic architecture refers to the linkages inside the organization (between different divisions, departments and managers) and the relationships, possibly partnerships, that an organization has with other members of the relevant value chain, such as suppliers and distributors. Synergy, mutual dependency and trust are key issues in the relationships.

People in organizations must be in a position where they feel stretched and rewarded. For some organizations, *empowerment* is a wonderful idea but they find it difficult to create the appropriate climate and culture; their employees may not wish to be empowered to some considerable degree. Emergent strategy possibilities are enhanced where people work well together and collectively. There is a team spirit, sharing and learning. *Synergy* is the outcome. Extended to the level of the organization, this constitutes a learning organization. Like empowerment, this can seem attractive as a theoretical idea and ideal but be difficult to implement effectively.

The information that feeds the whole process of decision-making comes from a variety of internal and external sources, both formal and informal. Formal information systems and *information technology* can both make a valuable input, but information is more than information technology. However much information they have, managers are still not 'seeing reality', rather they are put in positions where their perception of events can be more informed and hopefully more insightful. As well as informing decision-making, information and information technology can be a source of competitive advantage in its own right. The emergence of the *Internet* has spawned a host of new businesses and requires every company to formulate a strategy.

Michael Porter has provided a useful value-chain framework for helping to understand where differences are created, where costs are incurred and how synergy might be generated through linkages (see table below). His value chain comprises:

Five primary activities	inbound logistics
	operations
	outbound logistics
	marketing
	sales service, and
Four support activities	procurement
	technology development
	human resource management, and
	the firm's infrastructure.

Organizations must understand and manage their cost drivers. They should not attempt to cut corners with things that really matter for customers; at the same time, they should not incur unnecessary costs with things that do not add value for customers.

The value of a strong reputation must not be underestimated. A sound corporate reputation reassures customers. It generates sales and, very significantly, repeat sales, can enable price premiums, is an important intangible resource, and is frequently manifested in a strong, visible and readily identified brand name.

Online cases for this chapter

Online Case 5.1: British Airways
Online Case 5.2: Benetton
Online Case 5.3: Britt Allcroft
Online Case 5.4: The UK Holiday Travel Industry

Online Case 5.5: Tesco (IT case)
Online Case 5.6: Befair
Online Case 5.7: Burberry
Online Case 5.8: Levi's

Questions and research assignments

1 What are the opportunity-driven and resource-based views of strategy? Where and why are they different? Why is it important for organizations to embrace both views simultaneously?

2 Think about your own buying habits and choices. Where do you specifically choose high-profile branded items, and where are you less concerned? Why? What do you think this behaviour is saying about you?

3 Consider how strategic changes in one retail sector, from an emphasis on hardware stores that specialize in personal service and expert advice to customers from all employees, to a predominance of do-it-yourself supermarkets and warehouses, might have affected issues of staff motivation, personal development needs and appropriate reward systems.

4 Albeit by rule of thumb, take a team of people with whom you associate closely and evaluate their behaviour characteristics Where is the team strong? Where is the team weak? Do you believe it is balanced? If not, what might be done to change things?

5 Consider how the increasing utilization of information technology in retailing has affected you as a customer. Do you feel that the major retail organizations who have introduced and benefited from the greater utilization of IT have attempted to ensure that the customer has also benefited and not suffered?

6 Consider why it is argued that the increasing utilization of IT by organizations is a cultural issue. How might managers be encouraged to make greater use of the technology which is available?

7 How do you personally use the Internet? Do you feel you are exploiting its potential?

Internet and library projects

1 Use the Internet to look at the current status of Dyson and the other main manufacturers of vacuum cleaners. To what extent has James Dyson transformed an industry? How has he now extended the product range of the business?

Dyson **http://www.dyson.com**

2 Selecting an organization of your choice, and ideally one with which you are familiar, carry out a resource audit. Make sure that you take account of industry key success factors and competitors' relative strengths in your evaluation.

3 Using the same organization, apply Porter's value chain. As far as you are able, and accepting that there may be elements of subjectivity, allocate the costs and consider whether your breakdown matches your initial expectations. Where are the all-important linkages?

4 For an organization of your choice ascertain the range of products and services offered and answer the following questions:

- What are essential information needs from outside the organization (the environment) for managing these products and services both now and in the future?
- Where are the limitations in availability?
- What role might IT play in improving availability?

5 By visiting and talking to staff at an appropriate level and with several years' work experience in that environment, in both a travel agency and a retail store which makes extensive use of an EPOS (electronic point of sale) system, ascertain the effect that IT has had on their decision-making. Do the staff feel they are more aware strategically? If so, has this proved valuable?

Strategy activity

Lagardere

Lagardere is France's largest media company, but not a 'world leader' in the industry. Its magazines include Elle, Paris Match and Psychologies, all of which are published in different language editions. It owns the Europe 1 radio station and two television stations in France. It also publishes *Le Journal de Dimanche*, one of two national Sunday newspapers. It promotes live concerts and has developed into Internet advertising. Since 2006 it has been divesting unprofitable regional newspapers.

In 2008 Lagardere was seeing a downturn in the advertising spend upon which it depends for most of its activities. As a consequence, it sought to build on its existing competencies and seek out growth opportunities in China and Russia, as well as increasing its Internet presence. Perhaps these could even be combined?

These ideas presented some interesting challenges. China is well established as a provider of both typesetting and printing – but this is different from penetrating the 'reading industry' in China. Lagardere was also thinking about possible scale economies and synergies across its range of activities. Did shared content offer an opportunity? Could advertising packages be constructed?

Question

1 Does this resource-based approach make strategic sense? Are the possible synergies realistic or very ambitious?

References

Ackoff, R.L. (1967) Management misinformation systems, *Management Science* 14, December.

Belbin, R.M (1981) *Management Terms: Why They Succeed or Fail*. Heinemann.

Buckingham, M. and Coffman, C (1999) *First, Break all the Rules*, Simon and Schuster.

Capelli, P. and Crocker-Hefter, A. (1995) HRM: The key to competitive advantage, *Financial Times Mastering Management Series*, No. 6, 1 December.

Cummings, T.G. (1981) Designing effective work groups. In *Handbook of Organizational Design* (eds PC Nystrom and WH Starbuck), Oxford University Press.

Davenport, T. and Harris, J. (2007) Competing on Analytics – The New Science of Winning, *Harvard Business School Press*.

Day, G. (1996) How to learn about markets, *Financial Times Mastering Management Series*, No. 12, 26 January.

Gilbert, X. (1995) It's strategy that counts, *Financial Times Mastering Management Series*, No. 7, 8 December.

Goold, M., Campbell, A. and Alexander, M. (1994) *Corporate Level Strategy*, John Wiley.

Hamel, G. and Prahalad, C.K. (1993) Strategy as stretch and leverage, *Harvard Business Review*, March–April.

Hersey, P. and Blanchard, K. (1982) *The Management of Organisational Behaviour*, 4th edn, Prentice-Hall.

Hertzberg, F. (1968) One more time how do you motivate employees? *Harvard Business Review*, January–February.

Irwin, D. (2002) *Strategy Mapping in the Public Sector*, Long Range Planning, Vol 35, Pp 637–647.

Kaplan, R. and Norton, D. (1992) The Balanced Scorecard – Measures that Drive Performance, *Harvard Business Review*, January-February.

Kaplan, R. and Norton, D. (2000) *The Strategy Focused Organization*, Harvard Business School Press.

Kay, J.A. (1993) *Foundations of Corporate Success*, Oxford University Press.

Kelly, F.J. and Kelly, H.M. (1987) *What they Really Teach you at the Harvard Business School*, Piatkus.

Kotter, J.P. and Heskett, J.L. (1992) *Corporate Culture and Performance*, Free Press.

Lucas, H. (1976) *The Analysis, Design and Implementation of Information Systems*, McGraw-Hill.

Marchand, D.A. (1995a) Managing strategic intelligence, *Financial Times Mastering Management Series*, No. 4, 17 November.

Marchand, D.A. (1995b) What is your company's information culture? *Financial Times Mastering Management Series*, No. 7, 8 December.

McClelland, D. and Winter, D. (1971) *Motivating Economic Achievement*, Free Press.

McFarlane, F.W. (1984) Information technology changes the way you compete, *Harvard Business Review*, May–June.

McGregor, D.M. (1960) The Human Side of Enterprise, McGraw-Hill.

Porter, L.W., Lawler, E.E. and Hackman, J.R. (1975) *Behaviour in Organisations.*, McGraw-Hill.

Porter, M.E. (1980) *Competitive Strategy: Techniques for Analysing Industries and Competition*, Free Press.

Porter, M.E. (1985) *Competitive Advantage: Creating and Sustaining Superior Performance*, Free Press.

Porter, M.E. (1996) What is strategy? *Harvard Business Review*, November–December.

Porter, M.E. and Millar, V.E. (1985) How information gives you a competitive advantage, *Harvard Business Review*, July–August.

Prahalad, C.K. and Hamel, G. (1990) The core competency of the corporation, *Harvard Business Review*, May–June.

Prahalad, C.K. and Krishnan, M.S. (2008) *The New Age of Innovation – Driving Co-created Value through Networks*, McGraw Hill.

Preece, S., Fleisher, C. and Toccacelli, J. (1995) Building a reputation along the value chain at Levi Strauss, *Long Range Planning*, 28, 6.

Rayport, J.F. and Sviokla, J.J. (1995) Exploiting the virtual value chain, *Harvard Business Review*, November– December.

Roffey Park Management Centre (1995) *Career Development in Flatter Structures*. Research report.

Schein, E.H. (1983) The role of the founder in creating organizational culture, *Organisational Dynamics*, Summer.

Senge, P. (1991) *The Fifth Discipline – The Art and Practice of the Learning Organization*, Doubleday. Skandia (1994, 1995) Annual Reports and Accounts.

Stalk, G., Evans, P. and Shulman, L.E. (1992) Competing on capabilities: the new rules of corporate strategy, *Harvard Business Review*, March–April.

Roffey Park Management
... agement in Europe, Roffey Park
Saban, E.H. (1997) The role of ...
competency of the corporation, Harvard Business
Review, May–June.

Prahalad, C.K. and Krishnan, M.S. (2008) The New Age
of Innovation — Driving Co-created Value through ...
Networks, McGraw Hill.

Treece, S., Vissenrer, C. and Beninello, ...
Building a reputation along the value chain at ...
Siemens, Long Range Planning, 28.5.

Rayport, J.F. and Sviokla, J.J. (1995) Exploiting the
virtual value chain, Harvard Business Review,
November–December.

Porter, M.E. and Millar, V.E. (1985) How information
gives you a competitive advantage, Harvard Business
Review, July–August.

Chapter 6

The dynamics of competition

PART 1
Understanding strategy

1 What is strategy and who is involved?
- Appendix

2 The business model and the revenue model

3 Strategic purpose
- Supplement: Using frameworks to analyze strategy cases

PART 5
Strategy implementation

14 Strategy implementation and structure

15 Leading change

16 Managing strategy in the organization

17 Final thoughts and reflections: the practice of strategy

PART 2
Analysis and positioning

4 The business environment and strategy

5 Resource-led strategy

6 The dynamics of competition

7 Introducing culture and values

STRATEGIC MANAGEMENT: AWARENESS AND CHANGE

PART 4
Strategic growth issues

11 Strategic control and measuring success

12 Issues in strategic and international growth

13 Failure, consolidation and recovery strategies

PART 3
Strategy development

8 Creating and formulating strategy: alternatives, evaluation and choice

9 Strategic planning

10 Strategic leadership and intrapreneurship: towards visionary leadership?

Learning objectives

Having read to the end of this chapter, you should be able to:

● explain the notion of dynamic, tactical change in a competitive environment **(Section 6.1)**

● define product (service) differentiation and cost leadership and explain their role in the creation and maintenance of (sustainable) competitive advantage through Porter's generic strategies **(Section 6.2)**

● show how an organization can evaluate its competitive strategies against those of its competitors, e.g. 'blue ocean' strategy **(Section 6.3)**.

They say: 'Do you sleep well at night with all the competition?' I say: 'I sleep like a baby.' They say: 'That's wonderful.' I say: 'No, no. I wake up every 2 hours and cry!' Because it's true, you know. You have to feel that restlessness.

ROBERTO GOIZUETA, LATE CHIEF EXECUTIVE, COCA-COLA CORPORATION

Introduction

Few companies enjoy the luxury of having no serious competitors or little likelihood of any need to change their competitive strategy. Companies must seek opportunities to create – and sustain – a competitive edge over their rivals and build customer loyalty that provides something of a comfort zone, which logically should lead to superior profits.

Yet some organizations easily misunderstand competitive advantage, as a term, and clearly believe, and thus delude themselves, that a clear competitive strategy constitutes advantage – whereas advantage comes from being better or different in some meaningful way.

Even the strongest companies cannot afford to stand still: Nintendo (Online Case 6.1) has been successful because (a) it understands its industry, (b) it found a winning opportunity and (c) it surprised both Sony and Microsoft. A cynic, of course, would argue that a company must change more rapidly than its rivals can steal its ideas!

This chapter begins by examining the nature of competition in general, before discussing models and frameworks that help us to understand competitive strategy, competitive advantage and competitive dynamics.

The online case 'Nintendo's Rise From The Ashes' provides an extended example of this section's theory in practice.

6.1 Competition and competitive advantage

Causes generate effects, actions lead to outcomes, such that companies introducing an innovation affect the relative success of rivals, possibly provoking several reactions, depending on the extent of the impact and the general nature of competition. Each reaction, in turn, further affects the other rival competitors in the industry, and new responses will again follow. What we have in many markets and industries, as illustrated by Figure 6.1, is a form of *competitive chaos*, i.e. a competitive business environment which is permanently fluid and unpredictable. British Telecom (BT), for example, continues to face competition from cheap

Figure 6.1 Dynamic competition

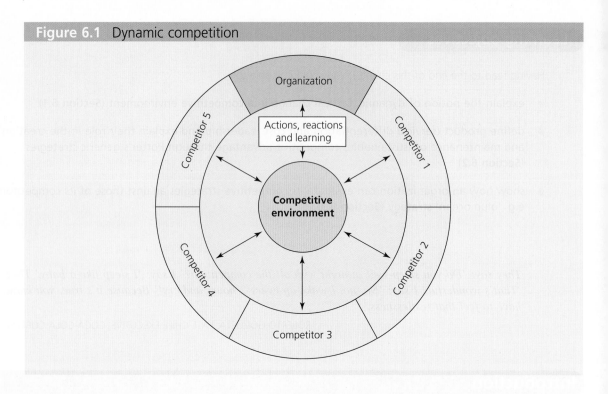

telephone call and Internet service providers, as well as demands that it provides free and open access to its network, leading to falling telephony revenues (approximately £500 million per year) as business drifts to both fixed line rivals and mobile companies. With its broadband services, BT must adapt and respond to defend its place in the market, or eventually the government might force further regulatory change on them resulting in a weakened business. Case 6.1 shows how one competitor, Mattel, reacted to a serious competitive threat.

There are two sets of similar, but nevertheless different, competitive decisions. First, some actions are innovatory where one competitor acts upon a perceived opportunity ahead of its rivals and opens up a gap; other actions constitute reactions to these competitive initiatives. Second, some decisions imply incremental strategic change to existing, **intended strategies**; on different occasions, companies are adapting their strategies (**adaptive strategic change**) as they see new opportunities which they can seize early, or possible future threats which they are seeking to avoid. The process is about *learning and flexibility*. Often, as we see later in Chapter 10, they involve an *intrapreneur*, an internal (or 'intra-corporate') entrepreneur. Organizations, therefore, need to be able to discern patterns in this dynamic environment and competitive chaos, and spot opportunities ahead of their rivals; anticipate competitor actions and reactions; and use this intelligence and insight to lead customer opinion and outperform competitors.

Ocean Spray was identified by Kanter (1990) as a US company which spotted a potentially lucrative competitive opportunity, in this case 'paper bottles' for soft drinks that were being used in Europe – an opportunity which its leading US rivals did not spot; nor were they enthusiastic about it. Ocean Spray, which manufactures a range of products, including drinks, from cranberries (sometimes mixed with other fruits) had empowered a middle manager from their engineering department to look for new ideas for the company – an aspect of their planned strategy – and he saw the potential, resulting in an 18-month exclusive rights agreement, and a packaging concept that proved attractive, substantially increasing the popularity of cranberry juice drinks. Simply, children liked the package and came to love the drink. Thus competition can come from unexpected sources, so any organization is playing dangerously if it assumes that future competitive threats will only come from rivals, products and services that they already know and understand. In reality, the unrecognized, unexpected newcomers may pose the real threat because, in an

Case 6.1 Barbie and Mattel   US, Int

Barbie dolls were launched in 1959 and they have enjoyed constant popularity with young girls. People can buy multiple outfits for the same doll but there are also special collector's editions with distinctive outfits. They are manufactured by leading toy maker, Mattel, which is based in California. The dolls are 11.5 inches tall and the idea came to designer Ruth Handler when she saw her daughter imagining paper dolls in grown-up roles.

In 2001 MGA Entertainment, also based in Los Angeles, launched a rival product, Bratz. The 10-inch-tall Bratz doll features racier outfits – it is more 'urban fashion' than Barbie – and facially she is different. She has accentuated lips and, with a relatively large head, has more of a cartoon appearance. The inspiration came from 'children walking home from school and the cover of a Dixie Chicks album'. But MGA sold 150 million dolls in 6 years and was becoming a real threat to Barbie's market leadership.

Mattel then sued MGA and claimed the designer, Carter Bryant, had come up with the designs whilst he was employed by Mattel, who were entitled to his designs through the terms of his contract. MGA countered that Bryant had come up with the idea in the time between two contracts with Mattel. One might speculate Mattel would not be interested in launching a new doll that might threaten sales of Barbie and so any real interest in developing the designs was always likely to be with a competitor. Mattel had in fact launched a new doll to try to affect the popularity of Bratz, but the doll had by this time established herself; this reaction had maybe come too late.

Mattel won the case and was awarded multimillion dollar damages. Mattel had asked for $2 billion but MGA was told to pay just over $20 million. However, and much more significantly, MGA was told to hand over its designs to Mattel and to withdraw the dolls from sale. It appealed – and this latter requirement was suspended. When the Appeals Court ruled everything changed. This time Mattel was told to pay MGA $310 million in damages. Almost inevitably Mattel appealed against this new judgement. More recently, in 2012, MGA sued Lady Gaga! She had agreed to help with a doll in her image, which was to be launched in time for Christmas 2012 sales; she was alleged to be slowing down the process and deadlines were being missed.

Questions

1 Do you believe MGA took a calculated risk that might not have worked out or were they naïve or were they intuitively entrepreneurial?

2 Did Mattel get its defence right? With hindsight might it have been better to compete with a 'better product' than rely on the courts – accepting they had tried once to do this?

3 What do you feel about legal interventions being used to establish the rules of competition?

attempt to break into an established market, they may introduce some new way of adding value and 'rewrite the rules of competition'.

Bill Gates' view of the future, based on personal computers on every desk, was radically different from long-time industry leader IBM's, enabling Microsoft to enter and dominate the computer industry. Direct Line, with its telephone insurance services at very competitive prices, provoked a response from competitors, and price comparison websites emerged, forcing Direct Line to change its pricing offer – both have changed and improved the nature of their service dramatically for customers.

Figure 6.2 shows how organizational resources need to be used to drive the competitive cycle as constant, or ideally growing, sales and market share can lead to economies of scale and learning and, in turn, cost reductions and improved profits. The profits could, in a particularly competitive situation, be passed back to

Figure 6.2   The competitive cycle

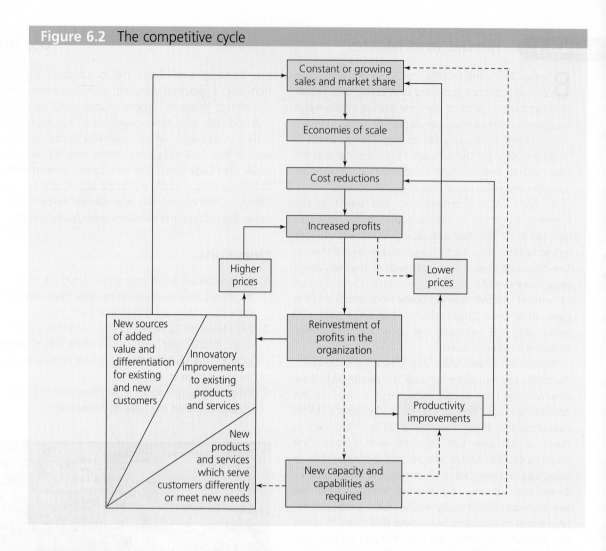

customers in the form of lower prices, but more normally they will be reinvested in the organization, improving productivity, adding new capacity, lower prices and/or further cost reductions.

The investment can also bring about new sources of added value and differentiation, possibly allowing higher prices and further profit growth. The improved competitiveness should also increase sales and market share and drive the cycle round again. These changes might take the form of gradual, continuous improvements or radical changes to establish new rules of competition.

In this regard, the market for DVD players has grown dramatically and had massive price reductions. When first introduced, a DVD player was a premium item, but they are now being sold in supermarkets for a fraction of the initial entry price.

With future uncertainty, changes in popularity, and different competitors tomorrow than today's, Sull (2006) argued that all organizations competing in an industry, as well as those thinking of entering the industry, have the opportunity to look for trends and signals and search for competitive opportunities. He contends that the winners are 'actively waiting', and (a) *anticipate*, perhaps using scenarios, (b) *prepare* for opportunities and threats that they can neither fully predict nor control, remaining vigilant and prepared and (c) *screen and evaluate* the significance of potential opportunities and threats (*ibid*).

Competitive advantage is achieved not from simply being different, but if and when real value is added for customers, often requiring companies to stretch their resources to achieve higher returns (Hamel and Prahalad, 1993), successfully harnessing and exploiting their **core competencies** and *capabilities*, perhaps leading to improved productivity, employees generating innovations (new and better ways of doing things for customers), followed by lower costs, differentiation or a faster response to opportunities and threats. Such employees must be empowered in a decentralized organization, allowing them to make their own decisions, making them able and willing to look for improvements, possibly changing the rules of competition. Organizations, therefore, should seek to encourage 'ordinary people to achieve extraordinary results' by rewarding and recognizing achievement. Whilst people are naturally reticent about taking risks, 3M (which developed Post-it Notes), Sony, Hewlett-Packard and Motorola are highly creative and innovative, and all actively encourage their employees to look for, and try out, new ideas. In such businesses, the majority of products in the corporate portfolio will have only existed for a few years, whilst effective empowerment can bring continual growth to successful companies and also provide ideas for turning around companies in decline.

Competitive advantage is also facilitated by good internal and external communications, achieving one of the potential benefits of linkages, and enabling businesses to share and learn best practice. Information is a fundamental aspect of organizational control, such that they can learn from suppliers, distributors, customers, other members of a large organization and competitors. Companies should never overlook opportunities for communicating their achievements, strengths and successes, given that image and reputation are vital intangible resources, which also help to retain business.

Competitive themes and frameworks

Porter (1980) and Ohmae (1982) are two authors who contend that business strategy is all about competitive advantage, because its sole purpose is to enable the company to gain, as effectively as possible, a sustainable and strong edge over its competitors in the most efficient and cost-effective way; for example, by undertaking actions improving its health (value engineering or improved cash flow which improve profitability), thus widening its range of alternative strategies *vis-à-vis* its competitors.

There are basically four ways, according to Ohmae (1982):

- Identify the key success factors in an industry and concentrate resources in a particular area with potentially the most significant competitive advantage.

- Exploit any area where a company enjoys relative superiority, e.g. using technology or the sales network developed elsewhere in the organization for other products or services.

- Aggressively attempt to change the key success factors by challenging the accepted assumptions concerning the ways in which business is conducted in the industry or market.

- Innovate: open up new markets or develop new products.

Therefore, by avoiding doing the same thing, on the same battleground, as the competition, the company's competitive situation will enable it to: (i) gain a relative advantage through measures that its competitors will find hard to follow and (ii) extend that advantage further. Accordingly, he offers a framework for studying competitive advantage focusing on three Cs:

- *Customers* ultimately determine a company's success by buying or not buying the product or service, but they cannot be treated *en masse* and specific preferences should be sought and targeted, with products differentiated to appeal to defined market segments.

- *Competitors* similarly differentiate their products, goods and services, incurring costs, with competition based e.g. on price, image, reputation, proven quality, particular performance characteristics, distribution or after-sales service.

- *Corporations* are organized around particular functions (production, marketing, etc.) and their structure and how they are managed determines the cost of the product or service.

Competitive advantage can be created by differentiating in several areas of business – such as product design, packaging, delivery, service and customizing – but they can increase costs, which must be related to the price that customers are willing to pay based upon the perceived qualities of a product, again in relation to competitors. A clear understanding of market needs and of specific segments and targeting customers more effectively and profitably than competitors leads to strategic success.

Prahalad and Ramaswamy (2004) argue that the best way to create new value is by proper co-operation with customers, rather than assuming it is best created from within the organization. It implies a level of engagement that extends beyond either consultation or test marketing; it involves real listening and collaboration. The focus is 'meeting requirements' rather than 'delivering a great experience'. They cite allowing customers to put fuel in their own cars at service stations (providing them with greater freedom of choice and lower prices) and ATM machines, 'holes in the wall' outside banks and in other convenient locations, as examples where requirements have been met. Asking customers to do more for themselves is, though, not always going to be universally popular and successful – as was the case with asking people to weigh their own fruit and vegetables in supermarkets.

According to Michael Porter (1980), effective strategic management is the positioning of an organization, relative to its competitors, in such a way that it outperforms them. Marketing, operations and personnel and all other aspects of the business, are capable of providing a competitive advantage, leading to superior performance and profits.

Two aspects of the current position of an organization are important:

1 *The nature and structure of the industry* in terms of the number of firms, their sizes and relative power, the ways they compete and the rate of growth. A company may or may not be attracted to a particular industry, depending on that industry's prospects in terms of both profit and growth potential and growth, and the contribution to achieving the firm's objectives (which are, in turn, influenced by the nature of the industries in which it does compete). The flow chart illustrated in Figure 6.3 reinforces the basic principles.

2 *The position of the firm within the industry*, involving its size and market share, how it competes, whether it enjoys specific and recognized competitive advantage and whether it has particular appeal to selected segments of the market. The extent of any differentiation is crucial here.

Figure 6.3   Industry growth prospects

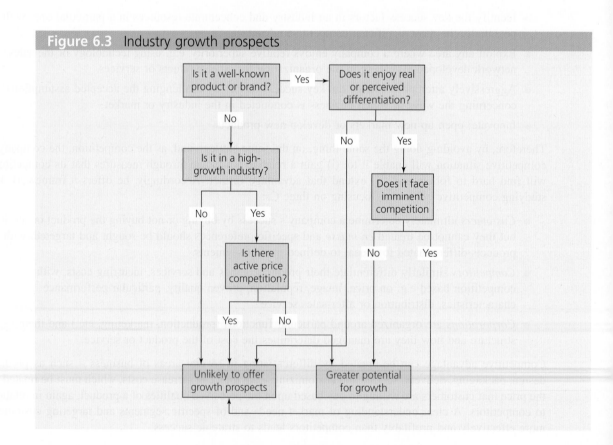

The most successful competitors will create value, create competitive advantage in delivering that value and operate the business effectively and efficiently. For above-average performance, all three are required. A business could be run well, i.e. efficiently, but never create competitive advantage. An effective and superior organization will be in the right industry and in the right position within that industry. Size can matter – as we see in Figure 6.4 – such that the largest of the mainstream competitors, as long as it is run effectively and efficiently, will be able to enjoy superior margins in comparison to its nearest rivals because it can generate scale economies. And yet, the small competitor with a very carefully defended niche can also enjoy superior margins.

A good new product may offer the consumer something new, something different and thus add value; but if it is easily imitated by competitors there is no sustainable competitive advantage. For example, Freddie Laker pioneered cheap transatlantic air travel but went out of business in the face of competition and management weaknesses.

Sustaining competitive advantage, rather than creating it initially, presents the real challenge. The imperative is, therefore, for constant innovation – changes in products, services and strategies which take account of market demand, market saturation and competitor activity – given that people's tastes change, the size of markets is limited, not infinite and competitors will seek to imitate successful products, services and strategies. Case 6.3 later considers how Coca-Cola retains global leadership of the soft drinks market.

Heller (1998) has suggested that organizations which sustain competitive advantage over time will be addressing seven questions effectively:

1 Are we supplying the 'right' things?

2 Are we doing it in the most effective way?

3 And at the lowest possible economic cost?

4 Are we as good as – and ideally better than – our strongest competitor?

5 Are we targeting and serving the widest possible market?

6 Do we have a unique selling proposition – something which will persuade customers to buy from us rather than anyone else?

7 Are we innovating to make sure the answer to all these questions will remain 'yes'?

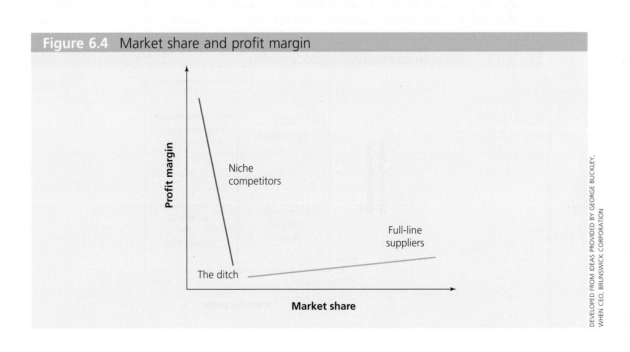

Figure 6.4 Market share and profit margin

DEVELOPED FROM IDEAS PROVIDED BY GEORGE BUCKLEY, WHEN CEO, BRUNSWICK CORPORATION

6.2 Competitive strategy

For customers, the link between price and perceived quality must make sense, i.e. products and services should be neither overpriced (resulting in a loss of goodwill and often lost business) nor underpriced (leading to lost profits and lost orders due to lower perception of the relative quality).

As an activity, we suggest you run a quick online search to discover Porter's generic strategy framework and view his simple matrix. His original framework is the basis for both Figures 6.5 and 6.6.

Porter (1985), building on earlier work on industry analysis, identified how a firm might create sustainable competitive advantage through generic strategies of **lower costs** or **differentiation**, as illustrated in Figure 6.6. Competitive strategy and competitive advantage, although clearly linked, are not synonymous, with the former concerning the way in which organizations choose to compete and position themselves, while the latter may or may not be an outcome of this. To achieve true advantage, an organization must find opportunities to be different in ways which are meaningful for customers, and thus the activities which create the position are the key to advantage.

Porter argues that the organization must be *the* cost leader, and be unchallenged in this position, and if there is competition for market leadership based on this strategy there will be price competition. Cost leadership does not imply that the company will market the lowest price product or service in the industry, because these are often perceived as inferior, appealing to only a proportion of the market – so low price related to lower quality is a differentiation strategy. Low-cost companies can have up market rather than down-market appeal. Equally, low cost does not imply lower rewards for employees or other stakeholders, as successful cost leaders can be very profitable, aiming to secure a cost advantage over their rivals, price competitively and relative to how their product is perceived by customers and achieve a high profit margin. Where this applies across a broad range of segments, turnover and market share should also be high for the industry. They are seeking above-average profits with industry-average prices.

Cost focus strategies can be based on finding a distinct group of customers whose needs are slightly below average, and saving costs by meeting their needs specifically and avoiding unnecessary additional costs.

Figure 6.6 illustrates the above points and relates the generic strategies to efficiency and effectiveness. The advantage lies not in being only one of a number of low-cost producers, but by superior management, concentrating on cost-saving opportunities, minimizing waste, in any and every area of the business.

Porter argues that in the motor vehicle industry Toyota became the overall cost leader, and the company remains successful in a number of segments with a full range of cars, and its mission is to be a low-cost producer.

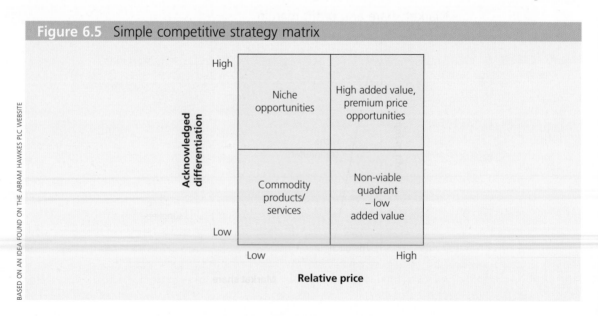

Figure 6.5   Simple competitive strategy matrix

Figure 6.6   Competitive strategies

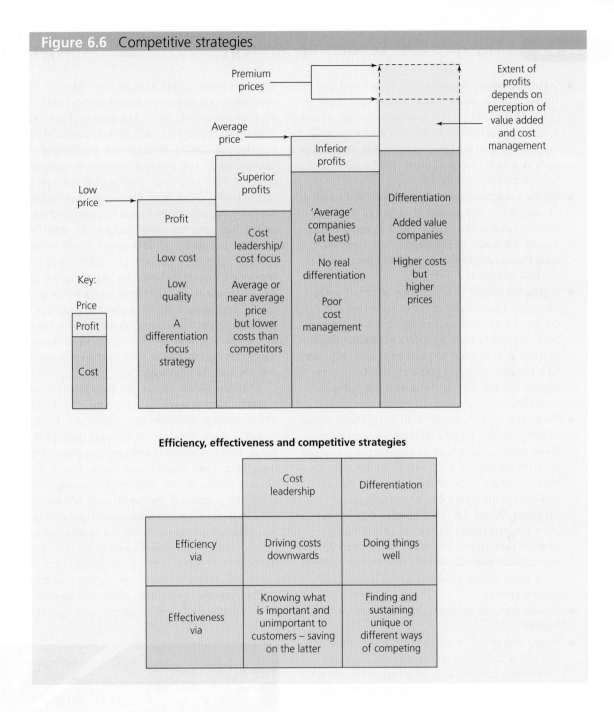

Case 6.2 outlines Toyota's competitive strategy. In contrast, in the USA, General Motors (GM) competes in most segments of the market, seeking to differentiate each of its products with superior styling and features and by offering a wider choice of models for each car in its range – but its cost of production is not in line with its overseas rivals. Hyundai became successful around the world with a restricted range of small- and medium-size cars which it produced at relatively low cost and priced competitively. Neither Toyota nor Hyundai markets the *cheapest* cars available.

Differentiation adds costs in order to add value for which customers are willing to pay premium prices, and the market must be capable of clear segmentation.

SOURCE: THIS CASE STUDY WAS PREPARED USING PRIMARILY PUBLICLY AVAILABLE SOURCES OF INFORMATION FOR THE PURPOSES OF CLASSROOM DISCUSSION; IT DOES NOT INTEND TO ILLUSTRATE EITHER EFFECTIVE OR INEFFECTIVE HANDLING OF A MANAGERIAL SITUATION.

Case 6.2 Toyota's Cost Leadership Strategy   Jpn, Int

- Toyota historically has enjoyed a 40 per cent plus market share in Japan, supplemented by a growing percentage of the US and European markets (where it also manufactures) – Toyota followed Nissan in manufacturing in the UK. This strategy is clearly long-term as it took Toyota 17 years (1989 – 2006) to become profitable in the UK.

- Toyota has focused on organic growth and avoided the acquisition and alliance strategies of its major rivals. It has invested in local plants in key countries around the world. Its European plants, however, have traditionally been less profitable than those in the USA and Japan.

- Toyota has sought to sell a range of cars at prices marginally below those of comparable Ford and General Motors cars. Historically Ford and GM have both sold more cars than Toyota worldwide. Toyota overtook Ford in 2006 and was 'neck-and-neck' with GM. However, Toyota's operating profits have ex-ceeded those of its rivals because it has ruthlessly controlled its costs.

- Production systems, based on JIT (just-in-time supply of components), are very efficient. Toyota claims fewer defects than any other manufacturer, resulting from the vigilance of each worker on the assembly lines. The Lexus range of top-quality cars requires one-sixth of the labour hours used to build a Mercedes. During the mid-1990s the best Toyota plant was assembling a car in 13 person-hours, whereas Ford, Honda and Nissan all required 20. Its sophisticated assembly techniques eliminate waste at every stage and are driven by strong just-in-time delivery systems.

- 'Toyota does not indulge in expensive executive facilities.'

- Toyota also spends 5 per cent of sales revenue on research and development (as high as any major competitor), concentrating on a search for contin-uous improvements 'to inch apart from competitors', rather than major breakthroughs.

- Continuous improvement is a 'way-of-life' as Toyota strives to ensure its costs are always below the prices customers are willing to pay.

- There is a policy of fast new model development. In the 1990s Toyota models had an average age of 2 years; Ford and GM cars averaged 5 years. Many cars tend to be a refinement of previous models rather than revolutionary designs. Some would argue this implies many Toyota cars lack passion, of course.

Revenues began to fall back in 1995. Sales of Toyota's new, revamped version of its best-selling Corolla saloon were disappointing. 'In its hot pursuit of cost savings, Toyota had produced a car that lacks character.' Overall cost leaders, slicing through the competitive middle market, must still produce distinctive, differentiated products to justify their near-market-average pricing policy. In the UK at least the Corolla was replaced by the Auris. More recently Toyota has launched the Yaris, which has received wide acclaim. In addition, the growing popularity of four-wheel drive recreational vehicles affected saloon car sales, but Toyota responded with its own models, especially the popular Rav 4. Toyota is an established world leader in hybrid cars – beginning with its successful Prius car it has extended this option to other models; and it has started to manufacture and sell pick-up trucks in America. Its Tundra brand has begun to take market share in this critically important segment.

Chairman Hiroshi Okuda described Toyota as a 'clever engineer that is quick to spot consumer trends and which captures customers with high-quality products'.

But is there a danger in growing quickly? In 2007 some commentators questioned whether this was happening when Toyota was involved in a series of product recalls. It was experiencing quality problems; whilst the number of incidences was not excessive in industry terms it was still unusual for Toyota. At the time the Japanese plants remained the quality leaders but Honda and Subaru were beating Toyota in quality surveys. Three years later, in 2010, there were more significant recalls. Drivers of certain models had complained the accelerator pedal was getting stuck when depressed and braking was problematic.

Particularly because of the inherent danger the media coverage was very critical at times. Toyota's President expressed a view that inadequate staff training might be the root cause of the problem. 'Sales expanded faster than we could train people.'

Questions

1 What do you believe the competitive position of Toyota to be now? (To answer this it would be useful to look at the margin and profitability figures for the leading manufacturers.)

2 Can you find any evidence that Toyota has suffered because of these recent developments?

3 How difficult is it to manage cost drivers, especially whilst growing rapidly, and not lose something which is critically important?

TOYOTA **http://www.toyota.com**

Firms, therefore, serve customer needs differently, ideally uniquely, so the more sustainable is any advantage which accrues. Differentiation inevitably adds costs, but only in areas that customers perceive as important *in any area of the business*, for example quality of materials used (related to purchasing), superior performance (design), high quality (production; inspection), superior packaging (distribution), delivery (sales; production), prompt answer of queries (customer relations; sales) and efficient paperwork (administration).

Furthermore, it is insufficient merely to add value; customers must recognize and appreciate the difference.

The differentiation strategy can be easily misjudged, however, for a number of reasons, including:

- choosing something that buyers fail to recognize, appreciate or value
- over-fulfilling needs, thus failing to achieve cost-effectiveness
- selecting something that competitors can either improve on or undercut
- attempting to overcharge for the differentiation
- thinking too narrowly, missing opportunities and being outflanked by competitors.

Case 6.3 illustrates four distinct differentiation strategies.

Case 6.3 ▶ Four Differentiation Strategies   Int

BMW, Miele, Bang & Olufsen and James Purdey

BMW

BMW follows a number of strategies designed to protect its market niche, especially from Japanese competition. Notably, these cover both the cars and the overall service package provided by BMW for its customers.

- Cars can be tailored and customized substantially. Customers can choose any colour they want, a benefit normally restricted to Rolls Royce and Aston Martin; and there is a wide range of interior options and 'performance extras'.
- Safety, environment, economy and comfort are featured and stressed in every model.

- National BMW sales companies are wholly owned, together with strategically located parts warehouses. The independent distributors place their orders directly into BMW's central computer.
- There are fleets of specially-equipped cars to assist BMW motorists who break down.
- In 1994 BMW became the first European car manufacturer to produce in the USA.
- Historically, BMW chose to ignore sports cars and hatchbacks, which it saw as downmarket from luxury saloon cars. However, market trends and preferences brought a change of heart. The 1994 BMW Compact was launched as a hatchback version of the successful 3-series; a BMW sports model was used for the James Bond film *Goldeneye*.

The acquisition of Rover gave BMW a range of successful, smaller hatchbacks, along with Land Rover recreational

SOURCE: THIS CASE STUDY WAS PREPARED USING PRIMARILY PUBLICLY AVAILABLE SOURCES OF INFORMATION FOR THE PURPOSES OF CLASSROOM DISCUSSION; IT DOES NOT INTEND TO ILLUSTRATE EITHER EFFECTIVE OR INEFFECTIVE HANDLING OF A MANAGERIAL SITUATION.

and multipurpose vehicles. But the two companies, with their very different histories and cultures, were not easily integrated. In 2000 Rover was bought back by a financial consortium and Land Rover was sold to Ford.

When BMW divested Rover it retained the rights to the Mini, which it has redesigned and successfully relaunched. It is quite normal for demand to exceed supply, such that there is a waiting list for new models. It is significant that, although they may be adjacent on the same site, mainstream BMW and Mini models are typically sold from separate showrooms.

BMW **http://www.bmw.com**

Miele

The German company Miele is a global leader in high quality domestic appliances – washing machines, vacuum cleaners and dishwashers. The business was formed in 1900 and it is still run by two great-grandsons of the founding partners. Around 90 per cent of the sales are in Europe, where the company has a 6 per cent market share. The other 10 per cent come from America. It does not look to compete on price – indeed the prices of a Miele can be up to 70 per cent higher than some rival branded products. The brand stands for quality. The typical life of a Miele machine is 20 years, and the company enjoys a tradition of loyal customers and repeat purchases.

Most of the products are manufactured in Germany, regarded as a relatively high-wage country. Miele even manufactures its own motors at a plant near Cologne. However, as a result of the German recession at the end of the 1990s/early 2000s, Miele has established a small production plant in the Czech Republic – where wages are one-quarter of those it is paying in Germany. It already had one plant in Austria and a joint venture in China. Some 12 per cent of revenues are re-invested in product development, a figure much higher than the industry average. The company has around 700 different patents to protect its designs. There is a strategy of rigorous and lengthy product testing.

Innovation is simply seen as routine and significant. The drums in large front-loading washing machines, for example, have some 4000 holes for letting the water in and out. Miele reduced this to 700 without reducing performance, thus making the drums both stronger and easier to manufacture at the same time. Interesting Miele has not copied the principle of the Dyson vacuum cleaner – it continues to believe bags are superior.

Bang & Olufsen

Now over 80 years old, Bang & Olufsen is a Danish manufacturer of hi-fi equipment and televisions, which enjoys an elite reputation and status worldwide for the quality of its products. Its customers tend to be very loyal.

The company has adopted sleek, tasteful designs, clever technologies and high standards of manufacture for many years. During the 1980s its performance deteriorated because it was seen as too much of a niche competitor. As a response, ranges of slightly less expensive – but still exceptionally high-quality – products were launched. From this a new philosophy has emerged – that the products are about lifestyle and technical excellence is more of a 'given'.

Company advertising uses the slogan 'a life less ordinary' to suggest that 'distinctiveness is a value in itself'.

Bang & Olufsen never asks its customers about future designs and products. Instead, its 'freethinking designers plant their ideas in the marketplace'. The company sees itself as a fashion leader. In addition, the company is very concerned to maintain control over who retails its products and how they are displayed in stores.

The company's niche must be potentially under threat if its rivals are able to improve the quality and reliability of their designs and exploit the manufacturing competencies of lower-cost labour countries. However, it is probably the case that only poor decision-making by Bang & Olufsen can threaten their niche.

BANG AND OLUFSEN
http://www.bang-olufsen.com

James Purdey

Purdey firearms would be classified as a super-luxury product; they retail at 'prices more normally associated with small houses'. The company manufactures something in the order of 60 guns per year, over 85 per cent of which are sold abroad. America and, in recent years, Russia are the main markets. Purdey is an iconic upmarket British brand but the company is now Swiss-owned.

There is close attention to detail, and quality control is incredibly tight. Every order is perceived as a special; nothing is seen as standard. The Turkish walnut stocks are polished several times in linseed oil and beeswax rather than varnished in what is a lengthy, labour-intensive process; and buyers can choose almost any special, idiosyncratic feature as long as they are happy to pay the appropriate premium. It takes some 650 hours to make a basic side-by-side 12 bore rifle and 750 hours to make the more complicated 'up and under' where the barrels are one above the other. The basic prices of these hover below and above £50 000 respectively for each rifle. Once refinements and customizing are factored in the bill for a pair (they are always sold in pairs) will be in the region of £250 000. Typically, orders are placed 2 years in advance of delivery.

Because they appeal to a very limited market segment, and because they literally last a lifetime (and frequently longer!), growth potential for James Purdey, without diversification, is clearly limited. Despite the special market position it holds, Purdey struggles to make a profit from rifles and in recent years has divested into related outdoor clothing and accessories.

JAMES PURDEY **http://www.purdey.com**

Question

1 To what extent are these companies successfully defending their differentiation focus strategies?

BMW and Mercedes have both succeeded historically by producing a narrow line of more exclusive cars for the price-insensitive, quality-conscious customer. Both companies have widened their ranges in recent years without fundamentally changing their basic strategy. There are several cars available from both companies but they are clearly targeted at people who are willing to pay premium prices for perceived higher quality.

Critical perspectives on Porter's generic strategies, and recent developments

Porter argues that successful organizations select and concentrate their efforts on effectively implementing one of his generic strategies, and will avoid being 'stuck in the middle'. However, while cost leadership and differentiation may be seen as mutually exclusive, successful strategies can be based on a mix of the two.

Hendry (1990) has suggested that, as there can be only one cost leader, cost leadership is not so much a strategy as a position that one company – which is almost certainly differentiated – enjoys. Toyota may be overall cost leader, but it still differentiates all of its cars, with different models for different market segments, as well as the associated Lexus range. Because it is a position, and because competitors are always likely to be following cost reduction strategies, it can be a very risky position if other opportunities for adding value are ignored. Although cost leadership is based on efficiencies and sound cost management, being different still matters.

Similarly, differentiation may be concerned with adding value and, therefore, costs but these must still be managed. We must understand the cost drivers of any business, and incur and add costs only where they can be recouped in the form of premium prices. Yet, where a company is particularly concerned with issues of size and market share, it may deliberately choose to charge relatively low prices and not attempt to recover the extra costs it has added in its search to be different. It sacrifices superior profits, at least in the short term, while it builds a power base.

Hendry (1990) also questions the value of broad and narrow focus, arguing that internal industry boundaries are always changing, enhanced by the speed of technological change. New niches are emerging all the time, such that what appears to be a solid niche can quickly become a tomb. The ideas of Michael Porter can be questioned and debated, but they nevertheless provide a useful framework for analyzing industries and competitive strategy. One must not assume that the idea of generic strategies is the key which unlocks the secret of competitive advantage.

While competitive strategies are *built around* differentiation and cost leadership, competitive advantage is *reflected in* and accrues from perceived differences and real cost advantages, both of which are relative to competitors. Hence, competitive advantage is *dependent upon* strategic positioning (not the same thing), and normally, at least in the long-term, results in superior margins. Table 6.1 shows that any individual functional area, or a combination of several functions, can be the actual source of the advantage.

Porter (1996) later reinforced these points, and attempted to answer some of the criticisms of his generic strategy approach, when he restated that competitive success is based on one of two alternatives. First, an organization can aim to be better than its rivals and focus on operating efficiencies to achieve this. Second, it can seek either to do different things, or to do things differently. He identified three broad approaches to positioning in which a firm can:

- Focus on a particular product or service – or an identifiable and limited range – and sell it to every customer who is interested, which is the approach favoured by BMW and easyJet.

- Target a segmented group and provide a wider range of products which can serve a variety of their needs, which is the IKEA approach.

- Identify and focus on a carefully defined niche with a single product or service, e.g. James Purdey (Case 6.3).

Porter pointed out that it is activities – what the organization actually does both directly and indirectly for its customers, its functional strategies – that create and build value and, in turn, advantage. Together, these activities determine the strategic position that an organization enjoys, and competitive advantage comes from the strength of the position. While being able to do something better or differently is essential, the way in which the activities are combined to generate synergy is also critical. Most individual activities can be copied, but it is much more difficult to replicate what might be a unique combination of activities, and so Porter (1996) developed activity maps, which we explained briefly in Chapter 5.

Consequently, organizations must choose what to do and what not to do, which activities to undertake and which to ignore, and how they might be fused into a powerful mix. Activities that affect the value

Table 6.1   Functional strategies and competitive advantage

Functional strategy	Competitive strategy	
	Low Cost	Differentiation
Marketing	Large companies can obtain media discounts	Image – reinforced by well-known strategic leader
Operations	Efficient plant management and utilization (productivity); re-engineered processes which reduce costs	Low defect rate and high quality; and re-engineered processes which add extra value
Human resources	Training to achieve low rejections and high-quality; policies which keep turnover low	Incentives to encourage innovation
Research and development	Reformulated processes which reduce costs	New, patented breakthroughs
Finance	Low-cost loans (improves profit after interest and before tax)	Ability to finance corporate strategic change, investments and acquisitions
Information technology	Faster decision-making in flatter organization structure	Creative use of information to understand customer needs, meet them and outperform competitors
Distribution logistics	Lower stock-holding costs	Alliances with suppliers and/or distributors which are long-term and mutually supportive

This list of examples is indicative only, and not an exhaustive set of possibilities.

proposition must not be neglected, but those that have little impact should not consume resources. Critical trade-offs must be made in an attempt to find a unique position. It can be expensive, even self-destructive, to try to do too much and not focus on what does make a difference.

IKEA has chosen to trade off in a number of ways, for example; it sacrifices being able to offer a wide range of bought-in products by designing and manufacturing its own. By choosing to hold stock in all of its stores and warehouses, IKEA sacrifices the low inventory costs some of its competitors enjoy by only delivering against orders. It sacrifices the use of the highest quality materials in favour of function and affordable prices. IKEA also sacrifices sales assistance in favour of self-service; and it opts for only out-of-town locations.

We conclude this section with a short case on Galanz, Case 6.4. This Chinese manufacturer declares it pursues cost leadership – but it also differentiates its products. In the case of its new microwave, one might reflect upon whether this would demonstrate the theme of co-creation with customers that we discussed earlier.

Many companies spend a lot of time and money researching customers' views, but most spend nothing like enough on observing competitors. The main reason for change is to keep ahead of competitors or to catch up on the complacent market leaders. Companies must invest in development – it's a case of 'duck or no dinner'.

SIR SIMON HORNBY, EX-CHAIRMAN, WH SMITH PLC

Case 6.4 Galanz   Int

Galanz is now one of the world's biggest home appliance manufacturers with over 40 000 employees spread over three global manufacturing bases: microwaves, air conditioning and home appliances. For example, in 2006 global sales of microwaves were a total of 20 million units. Many of the products are produced for someone else and badged. For example Galanz supplies the French supermarket giant Carrefour with microwaves that have the Carrefour trademark on them.

Galanz has come a long way from when it was established in 1978 as a producer of feather products in a small town within Guangdong Province. Indeed it was only in 1993 that Galanz actually moved to become a producer of microwaves. To engineer such a dramatic change and successfully penetrate the market, Galanz adopted the strategy of cost leadership in all areas of its business.

An example of this attitude to cost leadership is given in the following commentary:

'Transformers are an important part of the micro-wave. One Japanese transformer costs more than 20 dollars. In Europe and in the US the transformer is more than 30 dollars each. We moved an advanced production line from the US to China by agreeing to

supply the US company at a unit price of eight dollars. Once their needs were met the line was ours. We adopted three shift working. Of the six-and-a-half working days we only spent one day on the needs of the US company. With our superior technology and lower labour costs, one-tenth that of the US and Japan, we could supply the transformer at five dollars. Eventually the Japanese transformer production line was moved to China and Galanz supplied them at five dollars.'

(Zhang Jinsong, European Sales Manager)

Galanz follows an internationalization strategy based on being the lowest cost producer and able to sell at the lowest price, coupled with advanced technology to ensure quality. Over time this has developed through attention to branding, product and after-sales service – all connected to economies of scale. In 2000 microwave production was 12 million units. By 2006 it was 20 million units with 18 million units going for export. This was around eight times the level of sales of the nearest local producer. The same tactic of aggressive pricing, allied to advanced technology (Galanz has an research and development facility in the USA to develop proprietary technologies) and economies of scale are other tactics used by Galanz in its air conditioning and domestic appliance sales both in China and in export markets.

In recent years Galanz has proudly launched a combined microwave and multimedia player. The robust microwave (with a stainless steel casing) can also play music and it has a small television screen. It believes this will help with its ambition to become one of the world's leading white goods manufacturers. One might question whether this development was carried through 'because they could' or because there was an expressed wish by customers for such an innovation.

Questions

1 How do you think Galanz should be categorized in the context of the frameworks discussed in this chapter?
2 Is an aggressive cost-driven strategy of this nature appropriate for Chinese manufacturers with global ambitions?
3 Do you believe a combined microwave-multimedia player reflects co-creation with customers?

Sustaining competitive advantage

Few positions are defensible long-term against rivals – who will copy good ideas and perhaps even improve on them. Having created a competitive advantage, companies should strive to stay ahead by innovating and looking for improvements on a continuous basis and, at the same time, looking for discontinuous opportunities to effect change on industries and markets (e.g. Coca-Cola, Case 6.5).

Figure 6.7 combines a number of the points made here, emphasizing that successful companies create advantage and success by being committed to their customers through careful positioning and managed change. The differences and cost advantages which create a position must be supported by high levels of service in strategy implementation and ideally by a strong reputation and brand, as discussed in Chapter 5.

Figure 6.7 Competitive advantage through customer commitment

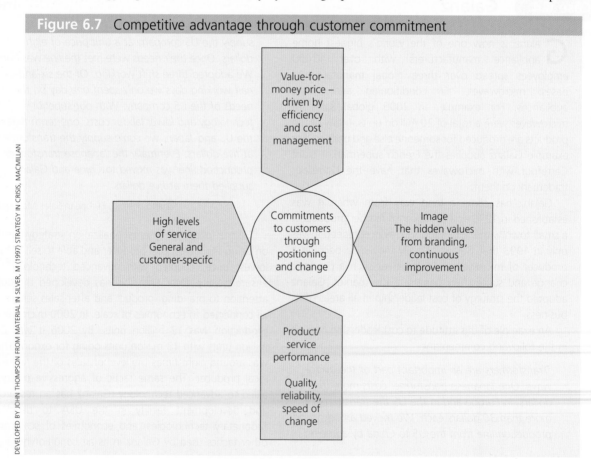

DEVELOPED BY JOHN THOMPSON FROM MATERIAL IN SILVER, M (1997) STRATEGY IN CRISIS, MACMILLAN

Coca-Cola   Int

Although it is typically priced higher than many competing products, Coca-Cola (Coke) remains the world's best-selling soft drink and it is amongst the world's best-known (and most valuable) brand names. Coca-Cola is reputed to see its only serious competitor as water! Ideally an adult requires a daily liquid intake of 64 ounces, and overall Coke provides just two of these. The soft drinks industry has been categorized in the following way:

- refreshment – typical carbonated drinks, such as Coke
- rejuvenation – ready-to-drink teas and coffees, for example
- health and nutrition – juices, vitamin-enhanced and milk drinks
- replenishment – bottled water and sports drinks.

The Coca-Cola company was 125 years old in 2011, and today it remains largely focused; Columbia Pictures was acquired some years ago, but later sold to Sony. Seventy per cent of Coke's sales and 80 per cent of its operating profits are now earned outside the USA. The company has enjoyed a 50 per cent share of the world market for carbonated drinks, including 44 per cent of the US market. It is now around 42 per cent of the US market, some 12 per cent ahead of its nearest rival, Pepsi. A typical American adult who drinks Coke will consume 400 eight-ounce servings in a year, just over one a day. Because Americans own very large refrigerators which can store the largest bottles available, this can work out relatively inexpensive. By contrast, a regular British Coke drinker consumes 120 eight-ounce servings in a year, often from smaller and more expensive bottles and cans. The UK is still perceived to be a developing market for the product. Other 'established' territories, which include Switzerland, Chile and Mexico, have a consumption of 300 eight-ounce servings per year. Most recently sales have been growing well in the fastest growing economies, including China and India. The company recently claimed that there are 1.8 billion servings every day around the world of Coca-Cola products. As a consequence the company is responsible for 700 000 jobs when its partners (bottlers and distributors) are included in the total.

Over the years critics have predicted that something would happen to stem the continual and successful growth of the business, possibly changing tastes, stronger competition or market saturation. This really has not happened; Coca-Cola has continued to increase worldwide sales through clever marketing and occasional new products. In 1996 Coca-Cola was America's most admired company in the Fortune rankings but it has not sustained this position in the late-1990s and early 2000s, although it continues to enjoy high global admiration. In terms of increases in shareholder wealth, Coca-Cola was unrivalled in the USA throughout the leadership of its charismatic chief executive, Roberto Goizueta. Goizueta was the strategic leader from 1981 until his death in post in 1997. Coca-Cola made a number of strategic misjudgements during his time in charge, but overall he was perceived to be a hero in the company's folklore. He kept Coca-Cola strongly focused on Coke when, with hindsight, he should have introduced other drinks – as his competitors were doing.

Competitive strategies

Coke had successfully established Fanta (the fizzy orange drink launched in 1960) and Tab (sugar-free Coca-Cola, 1963) when Goizueta took over. In 1982 Diet Coke was launched. Diet products are particularly important for the American market, but generally less significant elsewhere.

However, in 1985, New Coke was launched to replace the original blending, but subsequently withdrawn after a consumer outcry. It was sweeter and some critics suggested it had been developed because of the increasing popularity of the sweeter Pepsi Cola. One lady Coke fan who lived on the East coast went round all the local stores in her district buying up all their remaining stock of the original blend. Two middle-aged men on the West coast started a society pledged to restore the original taste. Members from across the nation paid to join and the group organized demonstrations. Inevitably there was huge publicity. The company eventually backed down and re-launched the original blend as Coca-Cola Classic. Some time later New Coke was withdrawn. Whilst one might have imagined the company would be damaged, it actually benefited from the enormous publicity it generated. The debacle cost money, but sales increased.

The Fresca range had also been launched. Sprite is another famous Coca-Cola brand, as are Minute Maid fruit juices. Under Goizueta's successor, in 1998, an agreement to buy the Schweppes soft drinks businesses outside the USA from Cadbury's was thwarted by the European regulatory authorities. Coca-Cola has also been affected by economic crises and recessions in countries where it is particularly popular, especially Russia and Asia. In 1999 it was forced to withdraw the product in Belgium after a health scare resulting from minor contamination. Arguably, the company's public relations could have been better. Five years later it had to deal with an even more significant self-imposed crisis. Dasani Water in Europe was exposed as treated tap water and not natural spring water. The company never claimed anything else, but consumer expectations were that it was. It was withdrawn. In the USA the product is different; simply the same brand name is used.

In 2001 Coca-Cola formed a joint venture with Procter & Gamble to link its soft drinks with P&G's snacks, such as Pringles. This was really following a strategy developed by PepsiCo. Also in 2001 Coca-Cola allied with Disney to allow it to use Disney characters for promotional purposes. The company has also extended its product ranges into Fruitopia, a 'new age' fruit drink, bottled water (the Dasani brand mentioned) and Lemon and Vanilla Coke.

Coke had really become popular overseas when it was shipped out to GIs during World War II, and systematically it has been introduced to more and more countries. For many years its stated goal was to 'always have Coca-Cola within an arm's reach of desire' and preferably in chilled storage, whether this was on retail shelves or through vending machines. It has benefited from being associated with the image and persona of America. When GIs drank it during World War II – and subsequent wars in Korea and Vietnam – it was seen as a reminder of exactly what they were fighting for. Early in 1999 Coca-Cola's name was linked to a line of fashion and sports clothing, the first significant extension of the brand.

Coca-Cola controls production of the concentrated syrup from Atlanta; mixing, bottling/canning and distribution is franchised to independent businesses worldwide. In truth, the issue of the 'secret formula' is more mystique than necessity, but it provides another valuable story to reinforce the brand and its image. Goizueta inherited a distribution network which was underperforming and he set about strengthening it with proper joint venture agreements and tight controls. Effective supply management is absolutely vital for the business.

Goizueta chose to acquire its smaller, underperforming bottlers, invested in them and, when they were turned around, sold them to stronger anchor bottlers – specifically those with the financial resources to invest in developing the business. 'Coca-Cola's distribution machine is [now] the most powerful and pervasive on the planet.'

Coca-Cola has always advertised heavily and prominently; and Goizueta has also negotiated a number of important promotional agreements. Coca-Cola has special aisles in Wal-Mart stores; Coke's Hi-C orange juice is supplied to McDonald's, for example. In recent years there has been increased emphasis on branding and packaging at the expense of pure advertising. 'We had really lost focus on who our customer was. We felt our customer was the bottler, as opposed to the McDonald's and the Wal-Marts (Goizueta).

Faced with increased competition from retail own-label brands sold mainly through supermarket chains, Coca-Cola has carefully defended and strengthened its other distribution outlets such as convenience stores, fast-food restaurants and vending machines.

Competitors

Coca-Cola's main rival is Pepsi Cola, which has a 30 per cent share of the US market and 20 per cent of the world market. Its share has been growing since the 1993 introduction of Pepsi Max, a sugar-free product with the taste of the original Pepsi. Pepsi diversified into snack foods (Frito-Lay in the USA, Walkers and Smiths crisps in the UK) and restaurants (Pizza Hut, Taco Bell and Kentucky Fried Chicken in the USA); just one-third of global profits came from soft drinks in the mid-1990s. Pepsi also owns much of its bottling network. In 1996 the Pepsi brand was relaunched with a massive international promotional campaign. The new Pepsi colours, predominantly blue, were chosen to appeal to the younger buyer. In 1997 PepsiCo divested its restaurants into a separate business, and followed this up with the acquisition of the French company, Orangina – after the European competition regulators had prevented Coca-Cola from buying the business. A year later Pepsi acquired Tropicana, the world's largest marketer of branded juices, which it bought from the Canadian company Seagram. With this purchase, Pepsi controlled 40 per cent of the US chilled orange juice market, twice the share of Coca-Cola.

Another significant competitor is Cott of Canada, which produces discounted colas with acceptable alternative tastes. Cott produces concentrate for Wal-Mart in the USA and for Sainsbury in the UK.

Renewal

In 2004 Douglas Daft, the second CEO since Goizueta, announced he would retire at the end of the year. He would be 61 and have completed 5 years in charge. The company had a succession problem all over again and moreover it was not performing particularly well. It was rumoured Coca-Cola might seek to split the Chairman and CEO posts but that did not happen. Instead retired executive Neville Isdell (an Irishman) was persuaded to return and he would stay firmly in charge until 2008, by which time Coca-Cola was much stronger.

Isdell immediately declared there would be investment in marketing, brand building and brand protection. Where there were gaps in the product line they would be filled. In 2005 Vault was launched to compete with Pepsi's citrus flavoured Mountain Dew. Rockstar was acquired to add to Full Throttle – both would compete with Red Bull. Powerade, launched to compete with Pepsi's Gatorade was doing well but it had a lot of ground to catch up. Coca-Cola Zero was launched in 2005 to complement Diet Coke. Coca-Cola also bought a minority share in Honest Tea (organic teas and juices) in 2007 and also acquired the French company, Glaceau, which produces and markets a range of different enhanced water drinks. They all have added vitamins and distinct fruit flavours. In three stages Coca-Cola has bought Innocent Drinks (fruit smoothies) in the UK – although this company operates with a degree of independence.

When Isdell stepped down, Coca-Cola was already showing healthy sales in four key emerging markets: China, India, Russia and Brazil. Isdell was replaced by an internal candidate, Mushtar Kent.

Questions

1 Why is Coca-Cola 'number one' in its industry?
2 Where is its competitive advantage?
3 If it avoids serious mistakes, does it need to do anything radically different to retain its position?
4 Can you think of anything its leading rivals might do to 'upset the applecart'?

COCA COLA **http://www.coca-cola.com**

Figure 6.8 shows that competitive advantage can be rooted in technology, organization and people, but people and people-driven processes are the real source of *sustained* advantage, because these are the most difficult for rivals to copy. People must be convinced that they are important, and that their contribution is valued – logically through an appropriate reward system – as otherwise they may not deliver and improve the all-important service. This will always prove difficult in a culture where cost management and resource savings have become dominant.

There are many examples where once-powerful and prominent companies have lost their edge and failed to sustain their competitive advantage.

With the clothing retailer Next, George Davies opened a niche for stylish clothing for slightly older age groups. However, once such a niche has been opened, it is relatively easy for rivals to copy the broad strategy, and they did. When Next failed to defend its position by improvements, and instead committed resources to the acquisition of other retail brands and formats, its early advantage was lost. Davies was a corporate casualty. However, as a designer, George Davies has proved much more resilient than many retailers with successful retail clothing developments within both ASDA and Marks and Spencer. His Per Una range of fashionable clothing designed exclusively for M&S provided one of the few welcome highlights for the embattled retailer in 2003. In October 2004 M&S bought Per Una from George Davies for £125m.

Figure 6.8   Sustainable competitive advantage – the need to grow the business

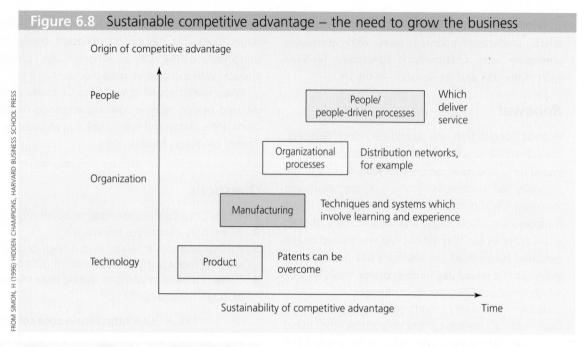

However, in 2005 Davies walked out after a row with Sir Stuart Rose, the then Chief Executive: only to return. From this, Per Una surged ahead and in 2007 Per Una accounted for 25 per cent of M&S womenswear sales of £500m. In December 2008, Davies stepped down as Chairman of Per Una at a time when M&S had suffered a 34 per cent decline in pre-tax profits. Per Una is seen by some business analysts as having lost its edge, especially in failing to cater for the younger element amongst M&S customers.

Toys R Us is the American toy superstore chain which grew at the expense of independent retailers, and which suffered at the hands of Wal-Mart which used its purchasing power to compete on price and gain a significant market share. Wal-Mart simply focuses on the best-selling toys which it offers at rock-bottom prices. Toys R Us has a wider choice but that clearly is not what every customer wants. According to Tomkins (1998), 'the company's big mistake was complacency ... they stopped renewing and refreshing their stores', and thus provided a way in for Wal-Mart. Toys R Us became 'stuck in the middle'. The remaining high-street independents are often more convenient and the discounters are cheaper. Their demise was exacerbated by a reputation for relatively poor in-store service.

Competitive platforms

Building on issues incorporated in Figure 6.8, George Buckley (2003), when Chairman and Chief Executive of the Brunswick Corporation – he moved on to become CEO of 3M – contended that costs, technology and people provide the three key **competitive platforms** for strong competitors to build on, but suggests that six platforms should always be considered:

- The best (not the lowest) cost manufacturing when set alongside direct competitors. Cost, after all, is the ultimate competitive weapon as it becomes increasingly significant in the toughest trading conditions.

- Technology, innovation and styling. Good design and style does not have to cost a great deal but it can be an ideal differentiator.

- Customer service.

- Brands, marketing and reputation.

- Distribution. The best products in a design sense will be wasted opportunities if their manufacturers cannot put them in front of potential customers where and when they expect them.

- People. Competitors can acquire equivalent technology and tooling and copy processes, but it is much harder to replicate the contribution made by people.

6.3 Competitor benchmarking

All companies should continually search for innovative differentiation opportunities and for ways of improving their cost efficiencies. As seen in earlier chapters, leveraging resources and setting stretching targets for employees can help to bring about innovation and savings. Benchmarking against good practice in other organizations (a process of measurement and comparison) can provide new ideas and suggestions for reducing costs and improving efficiency. Organizations from different sectors and industries can be a useful source of ideas if they have developed a high level of expertise. This process is a search for ideas that can be customized for a different organization, rather than being a copying exercise. Managers should be open-minded and inquisitive and look *everywhere* for ideas.

At the same time, it is vital for an organization to understand clearly its position relative to its competitors. Table 6.2 provides a general framework for considering competitive strategies and Figure 6.9 shows how we might benchmark competitors in comparison with an organization and with customer preferences, with the key success factors listed down the left-hand side and ranked (top-down) in order of their importance to customers; their relative significance plotted against the horizontal axis; and the ability

Table 6.2	A framework for evaluating competitive strategies
Scope	Global; industry-wide; niche
	Single or multi-product/service
	Focused or diversified
	Vertical linkages with suppliers/distributors
Objectives	Ambitious for market or segment leadership
	Market presence just to support other (more important) activities
Success	Market share
	Image and reputation
	Profitability
Commitment	Aggressive – willing to acquire to grow
	Passive survivor
	Willing to divest if opportunity arises
Approach	Offensive – attacking other competitors
	Defending a strong position. Note that the same strategy (new products, price cuts) can be used both offensively and defensively
	Risk-taking or risk averse
	Teasing out new segments or niches
Strategy	High quality – perhaps with technological support
	High service
	Low price
Position	Cost advantage or even cost leadership enjoyed
	Clearly differentiated
Competitive resources	High-technology base; modern plant
	Location relative to markets
	Quality of people (ability to add value)
	Reputation

The examples provided for each of the eight criteria are not offered as an exhaustive list.

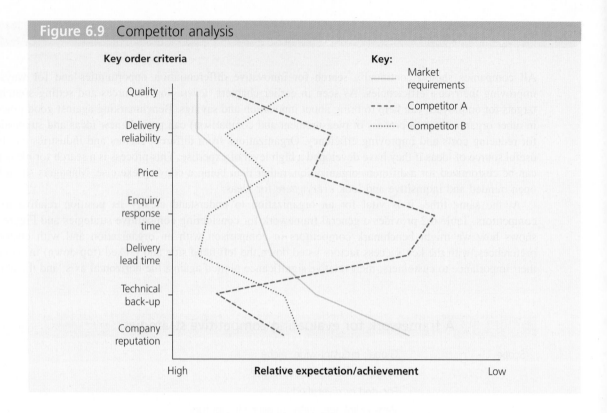

Figure 6.9   Competitor analysis

of different competitors to meet these key success factors illustrated by the dotted lines. Competitor A is clearly relying on its quality and technical backup, for which it has a good reputation, but is it truly satisfying customer needs? Competitor B seems to offer an all-round better service, and in some areas is providing a service beyond that demanded, which may be good as it will indicate a reliable supplier.

How would our customers rank our products/services in relation to those of our competitors?

- *Not as good as. We must improve!*
- *No worse than. This implies a general dissatisfaction, so there must be real opportunities to benefit from improvement and differentiation.*
- *As good as the others, no better, no worse. Again opportunity to benefit if new values can be added and real differentiation perceived.*
- *Better than. We must still work hard to retain our lead.*

I subscribe absolutely to the concept of stealing shamelessly! Wherever you come across a good idea, if it's likely to work, pinch it. There's nothing wrong with that. There is a quite respectable word – benchmarking – which is the same thing if you think about it.

BILL COCKBURN, WHEN GROUP CHIEF EXECUTIVE, WH SMITH PLC

Changing competitive positions

A successful competitive position implies a match between customers' perceptions of the relative quality or value of a product or service and its price, both in relation to the prices of competing products or services. **Competitor gap analysis** can be conducted in the segment or segments in which an organization chooses to compete; and, in addition, the total price should be used for comparison purposes. Customers, for example, may willingly pay a premium purchase price initially for a particular brand of, say, an electrical good or car if they believe that over its life it will incur lower maintenance and service costs than competing brands. Products offered at initially lower prices may be perceived to be more expensive overall.

Figure 6.10 (which develops Figure 6.5) features a competitive positioning grid. Three basic positions are shown by sectors 1, 2 and 3. Sector 6, high perceived prices but only average (at best) quality, is an untenable position in the long run. Sector 4 illustrates a company competing on price, which can be a successful strategy, but it can provoke competitive responses; in which case, it may only serve in driving down all prices and making all competitors less profitable. Do-it-yourself chains, such as B&Q, have come to believe that the key to survival in a crowded market is to offer permanently competitive prices as well as developing a unique identity. Sporadic high discounts are being replaced by 'everyday low prices' and success is more dependent on volume sales than the actual margins on individual products.

Effective differentiators, commanding premium prices and earning superior profits with high margins, are shown as Sector 5. Their success is partially dependent upon sound cost management.

Figure 6.11 illustrates a number of optional/improvemental competitive strategy changes for companies in selected positions in the matrix. Change to 'something better' is hardly optional for companies towards the bottom right of the diagram.

Blue Ocean Strategy

The basic presumption of Kim and Mauborgne (2005) is that some dynamic and leading organizations are successful because they discover radical new opportunities for competitive advantage. They do not set out to

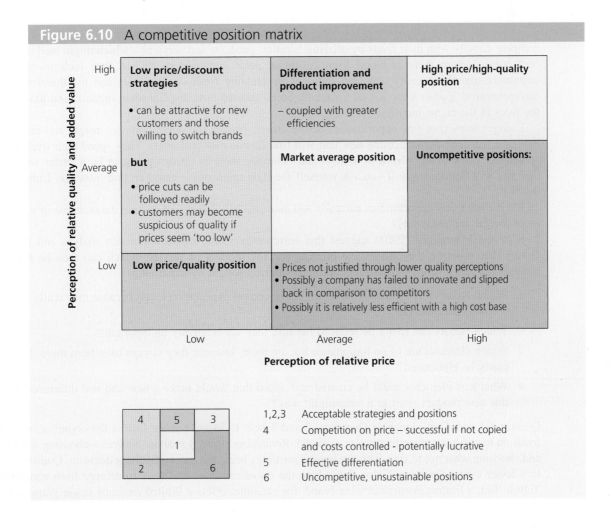

Figure 6.10 A competitive position matrix

Figure 6.11 Possible competitive strategy changes

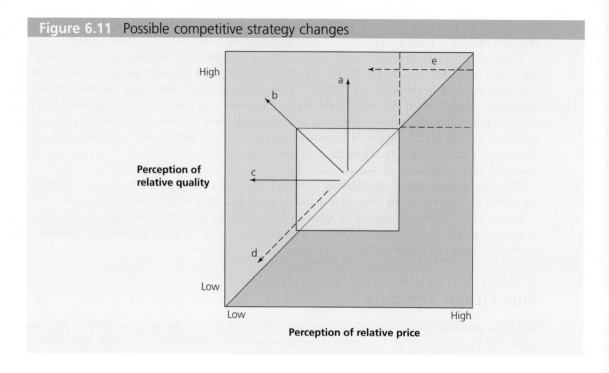

compete directly with their rivals by offering 'similar' products and services – which might well result in a 'red ocean' where there is blood from cut-throat price competition. Rather, they look to offer their customers something really new and different by creating fresh opportunities and by, therefore, being entrepreneurial. Earlier Case 2.4 on Cirque du Soleil showed how this Canadian organization has changed the rules in the circus industry.

Entrepreneurs spot new opportunities before others, finding the opportunity by insight and inspiration, having a 'gut-feel' for something new that will find favour with customers. They spend their lives looking at what is, questioning why it is as it is and believing there is always going to be a better way – and that you will find that way if you ask yourself the right questions – based around 'how can I improve on this?'

But are such new opportunities naturally and automatically subjective and not the outcome of something more logical and analytical?

Kim and Mauborgne (2005) suggest that entrepreneurs and organizations can analyze and list those factors that make up the competitive offering for any product or service, which can then be examined individually and a new business model/product offering sought by examining:

1 Which factors might usefully be raised above current expectation levels because they really matter to (certain) customers?

2 Which factors can easily be reduced because they are relatively unimportant?

3 Which elements are of no importance but are there 'because they always have been there' but could easily be eliminated?

4 What new elements could be created and added that would make a new and real difference and set this new product apart in a meaningful way?

Questions 1 and 4 set alongside Questions 2 and 3 help to identify those factors the organization should focus on to create a compelling business model. Remember strategy is about choices – choosing what to do and choosing what not to do – with the latter sometimes being the more important decision. Question 4 and to a lesser extent Question 1 also flag where the organization should seek to diverge from competitors. Yellow Tail, a leading Australian wine brand, for example, offers a limited range of single grape branded wines and has capitalized on the surging demand for wine in recent years. Against the above four criteria, the following answers were generated:

1 There is no requirement to be the cheapest wine available as this affects perceptions of quality. So the price should be affordable and the wine readily available through the leading supermarkets and other relevant outlets. Company staff must be enthusiastic and champion the product.

2 Customers do not expect a huge range of different grapes and so a limited range of 'favourites' will suffice. Similarly, many customers are not really interested in the prestige of the vineyard (but they are interested in the taste).

3 Wine aficionado technology is important to only a minority of people and not the mainstream buyer, and relatively few concern themselves with ageing properties. Availability and word-of-mouth are more important than above-the-line advertising.

4 Easy drinking, easy selection and a sense of fun and adventure can be utilized to marked effect to promote a new brand.

It is relatively straightforward to apply the same criteria to the no-frills airlines (Case 1.1), which also created a whole new market opportunity.

Kim and Mauborgne (2005) also suggest organizations can make use of what they call a 'buyer utility map' – see Table 6.3 – drawn up to try to identify just which messages are most compelling for their customers: again based on focus and divergence: and the grid for the map illustrated in Table 6.3 would be relevant for a new model of a car.

Kim and Mauborgne (2005) argued that the Model T Ford focused on two things that set it apart from rival models at the time (marked in the grid with an x): the car was small, strong and rugged and could be used on the roads and lanes available at the time with little risk to the driver or the vehicle, and the engineering was simple and straightforward and the maintenance would be easy. The car was also readily available (because of the new production line manufacturing systems) and, in part because of this, relatively affordable.

In this context, it is interesting to evaluate the new Tata Nano car, launched in 2008 for the Indian subcontinent at a very affordable price. Huge numbers of people who could not previously afford a car now can – but this will add to the world's carbon emission problems in a big way! The story is outlined in Case 6.6.

Strategic groups

The argument about strategic groups (see, e.g., Hunt (1972) and Leask and Parker (2007)) is that organizations must be able to identify and stay fully aware of developments with those competitors who are in the same 'group'. These are the companies closest to you, competing with similar products and services for the same customers.

Table 6.3 Buyer utility map applied to the Model T Ford

	Showroom experience	Availability and delivery	Model capability	Extras available	Service costs	Residual value or scrapping issues
Perceived price relative to quality		(X)				
Ease of handling						
Size and convenience				X		
Image						
Safety issues and risks					X	
Environmental issues						

Case 6.6   The Tata Nano – a Low-Cost, No-Frills Car   Ind, UK

SOURCE: THIS CASE STUDY WAS PREPARED USING PRIMARILY PUBLICLY AVAILABLE SOURCES OF INFORMATION FOR THE PURPOSES OF CLASSROOM DISCUSSION. IT DOES NOT INTEND TO ILLUSTRATE EITHER EFFECTIVE OR INEFFECTIVE HANDLING OF A MANAGERIAL SITUATION.

We typically associate 'low cost and no frills' with the airline industry but it clearly has a relevance as a competitive strategy elsewhere. Historically, certain cars have been seen as relatively low-quality and low-price – Eastern European brands such as Lada, Trabant and Skoda before its acquisition by Volkswagen – might be included.

But low price and lower quality is not necessarily quite the same as low cost, no frills. Passengers on airlines such as easyJet and Ryanair sacrifice certain services in order to get low prices, but the seats are comfortable enough, the safety records stand scrutiny and the planes generally fly on time. This is different from low quality leading to unreliability.

In this context two recent strategies by two quite different competitors are worthy of evaluation.

Renault is a long-established French car manufacturer with a defendable reputation. In 2007 it chose to enter the 'global emerging markets' sector with a new car, the four-door Renault Logan saloon. The car was launched in India, where it was manufactured in a joint venture with Mumbai based car manufacturer, Malindra & Malindra.

Priced at around £5000, the car was certainly not ultra-cheap, but it was certainly competitive. It was not described as 'stylish' and it dispensed with frills. Costs were contained by certain design features: almost flat windscreens which are cheaper to make; identical right- and left-wing mirrors, for example. It uses interior parts designed for other Renault cars and it has the Clio engine. Development costs were shaved by relying on computer modelling rather than actual mock-ups.

The Tata Nano is different. The diversified Indian conglomerate Tata is perhaps best known as the world's leading tea company, but it has bought Jaguar and Land Rover from Ford in the recent past.

The Nano is marketed as the world's cheapest car. It is again manufactured in India and at its launch priced at just £1275. The Nano is a five door four-seat car with a rear mounted 624cc engine. It offers 50 miles to a gallon of fuel. Air conditioning, electric windows and power steering are all features that simply are not available. It is designed to be affordable to less affluent buyers and thus make cars more widely available. It is basically 'safe, affordable and all-weather transport'. In this respect it is the Model T Ford story all over again, which, on the face of it, seems a positive development.

However, whilst it does meet minimum standards, its emissions are higher than other small cars. One question, therefore, is whether increasing the number of cars on the planet that add to the carbon footprint in a relatively inefficient way is genuine progress or a mixed blessing. Sales have not met all of Tata's expectations – perhaps, after all, car buyers don't flock to the cheapest car that is available. Nevertheless the car has won awards for its design.

Questions

1. Is the Tata Nano 'Blue Ocean' or has Tata more realistically discovered a new niche which could, in time, be potentially very valuable?

2. Is being described as the 'world's cheapest car' potentially more of a detriment than an advantage? Or could the niche grow into something very substantial?

Some may be located close by in a so-called cluster; some may sell through the same retail outlets. They may not all be the same size and they may not overlap fully in terms of price, quality and niche appeal – but they are still very close rivals. When competition 'heats up', some organizations will seek to reposition themselves in a different group, whilst more entrepreneurial ones might even try to start a new group.

The rivals in strategic groups might well find themselves converging as they compete – some mimic and copy, but logically without any formal collusion which might be illegal. Prices and/or packaging become similar. This is perhaps based on a fear that rivals cannot be allowed to do something too individual which might set them apart. The logic: if it matters to customers and it works we too must do it. Of course, this is the opposite of differentiation.

Such tendencies and behaviour will drive the industry leaders to innovate further, in part because there is reinforcement that what they are doing already is powerful. Rivals can become increasingly reactive rather than proactive. At the same time leaders, will seek to find ways to protect what they are introducing from being copied.

The core issue for any organization, then, is appreciating just what you cannot afford not to do if you are to be an effective competitor. Once sorted, and from that base, you can seek to build defensible differentiation.

6.4   Concluding comments

This chapter has concentrated on how an organization can gain a deeper understanding of its competitive environment with a view to becoming a stronger, more effective competitor through creating and sustaining competitive advantage. The closer a business is to its customers, the more it will understand the market and the industry. Competitive strategy, essential for every product and service that the organization makes and markets, involves a vision about how best to compete. There are a number of ways to generate competitive advantage, and the process is both logical and creative. The choice will also be influenced by the strategic leader and by the organization's culture. However, every employee contributes in some way to both lower costs and uniqueness and, therefore, it is important that the competitive strategy is communicated and understood throughout the organization.

In the end, the most successful companies will be those with:

- differentiated products and services which are recognized for their ability to add value, and are:
- produced efficiently
- upgraded over time through innovation and improvement, and which
- prove relevant for international markets.

Porter contends that competitors can be viewed as good or bad. Good ones differentiate, innovate and help to develop an industry; bad ones just cut prices in an attempt to drive others out of business.

New windows of competitive opportunity are always opening as identified by Peter Drucker (1985):

- Products and services can be improved to open up new markets and segments, as was the case with PDA organizers which compete for the market pioneered by Filofax.
- New technologies change behaviour and demand, e.g. mobile phones, personal computers and MP3 players such as the iPod.
- Changes in attitude – concern for the environment created the opportunity for unleaded petrol – and in the recent acceptance of organic food.

Research Snapshot 6.1

Competitive strategy has been prevalent in the strategic management field since the seminal work of Porter, on generic strategies and the five competitive forces, in the 1970s and 1980s. Recently for example, he defined strategy in distinctly competitive terms, i.e. 'what makes one unique, gives one a distinct competitive advantage, provides direction, builds brand reputation, sets the right goals, adds superior performance, defines a market position and creates a unique value proposition' (Porter, 2005: p. 14). Indeed, regarding the vital link between competitive strategy and firm performance (Parnell, 2002; Parnell et al., 2006), there is a debate about whether firms should mix and match generic strategies or not, and it has been found that 'strategic purity', i.e. choosing one and only one strategy, leads to enhanced performance (Thornhill and White, 2007).

Weerawardena (2003a) suggests that innovative firms need to have particular marketing capabilities, hence contributing to the firms' competitive strategies and thus sustainable competitive advantage; and further that they need a market learning capacity (Weerawardena, 2003b). Knowledge, as a resource, can also assist competitive strategy through effective knowledge management (Halawi *et al.*, 2006). Furthermore, networks and alliances can support competitive strategies, particularly in terms of the structure of these networks and the influence of geography (Tracey and Clark, 2003); networks being confirmed as important to competitive strategy by other authors (Ehrhardt, 2004; Rajasekar and Fouts, 2009).

Brown and Blackmon (2005) also suggest that, due to 'strategic dissonance' – which occurs because of tensions between strategies that are either resource- or market-based, – therefore, the new concept of strategic resonance is required, where resources (or manufacturing strategy and operations) and markets (or competitive strategy) are aligned. The use of strategic tools, such as SWOT, PEST, etc., in the contemporary development of competitive strategy has been critiqued, but Jarratt and Stiles (2010: p. 28) found that, 'methods and tools are adapted as they are contextualized in alternative practices'.

The articles below provide a deeper understanding of competitive strategy and particularly its link with firm performance and the role of networks. The further reading from this literature will help students to develop their perception and critical awareness of the role of different competitive strategies, in relation to the dynamics of competition that is covered in this chapter, and that there is no 'one size fits all' or automatic response strategy, hence highlighting the complexity of competitive strategy and strategic choice.

Further Reading

Brown, S. and Blackmon, K. (2005) 'Aligning manufacturing strategy and business-level competitive strategy in new competitive environments: The case for strategic resonance', *Journal of Management Studies*, Vol. 42, pp. 793–815.

Ehrhardt, M. (2004) 'Network effects, standardisation and competitive strategy: how companies influence the emergence of dominant designs', *Journal International Journal of Technology Management*, Vol. 27, No. 2-3, pp. 272–296.

Halawi, L.A., McCarthy, R.V. and Aronson, J.E. (2006) 'Knowledge management and the competitive strategy of the firm', *Learning Organization*, Vol. 13, No. 4, pp.384–397.

Jarratt, D. and Stiles, D. (2010) 'How are methodologies and tools framing managers' strategizing practice in competitive strategy development?', *British Journal of Management*, Vol. 21, pp. 28–43.

Parnell, J.A. (2002) 'Competitive strategy research: Current challenges and new directions', *Journal of Management Research*, Vol. 2, No. 1, pp. 1–12.

Parnell, J.A., O'Regan, N. and Ghobadian, A. (2006) 'Measuring performance in competitive strategy research', *International Journal of Management and Decision Making*, Vol. 7, No. 4, pp. 408–417.

Porter, M. (2005) 'Michael Porter on strategy', *Leadership Excellence*, Vol. 22, No. 6, pp.

Rajasekar, J. and Fouts, P. (2009) 'Strategic alliances as a competitive strategy: How domestic airlines use alliances for improving performance', *International Journal of Commerce and Management*, Vol. 19, No. 2, pp. 93–116.

Thornhill, S. and White, R.E. (2007) 'Strategic purity: A multi-industry evaluation of pure vs. hybrid business strategies', *Strategic Management Journal*, Vol. 28, pp. 553–561.

Tracey, P. and Clark, G.L. (2003) 'Alliances, networks and competitive strategy: Rethinking clusters of innovation', *Growth and Change*, Vol. 34, pp. 1–16.

Weerawardena, J. (2003a) 'The role of marketing capability in innovation-based competitive strategy', *Journal of Strategic Marketing*, Vol. 11, No. 1, pp. 15–35.

Weerawardena, J. (2003b) 'Exploring the role of market learning capability in competitive strategy', *European Journal of Marketing*, Vol. 37, No. 3/4, pp. 407–429.

Summary

Many industries and markets are characterized by competitive 'chaos' – they are dynamic and uncertain. All the time, rivals may be trying out new initiatives which cannot be ignored. To succeed in the long term, organizations must be able to manage both continuous and discontinuous change pressures, achieved with a mix of incremental and more dramatic changes to competitive and corporate strategies.

In an endeavour to manage their competitive environment, organizations must understand the nature and attractiveness of their industry, and their relative position in it.

Positioning can be examined against a framework of generic strategies, which are based on differentiation and cost leadership. The issue of a broad or narrow market focus is another important consideration.

Michael Porter has provided two useful frameworks to help with these assessments.

However, competitive positions, *per se*, do not yield competitive advantage. Advantage is a reflection of a strong position, but it is the result of the activities which create the position and, in particular, the synergistic links between them. Successful organizations achieve a unique mix which is hard to replicate, although the individual activities, at a basic level, can be copied.

While competitive advantage comes from technologies, organization and people, it is the people-driven processes that enable advantage to be sustained and extended.

All the time, the pace of change and competition is speeding up in many markets and industries. To deal with this, it is essential for organizations to benchmark both their competitors and other high-performing organizations in a search for good ideas and best practice. Specifically, they are looking for new opportunities to add or build value in ways that are meaningful for customers.

Kim and Mauborgne have introduced the term 'Blue Ocean Strategy' to explain those entrepreneurial organizations that innovate in a distinctive way and impact upon the rules of competition in an industry.

Understanding rival behaviour in strategic groups can help organizations to identify just what it is they cannot afford not to do.

Online cases for this chapter

Online Case 6.1: Nintendo's Rise from the Ashes

Online Case 6.2: Schick versus Gillette

Questions and research assignments

1. What is the difference between competitive strategy, competitive advantage and strategic positioning?

2. Study Porter's Generic Strategy framework and consider where you would place British Airways and other major carriers such as Air France as opposed to easyJet and Ryanair.

3. Apply Figures 6.10 and 6.11 to this industry.

Internet and library projects

1. Take an industry of your choice and analyze one or more of the major competitors in terms of their chosen competitive strategies. As well as the Internet, the following library sources might prove useful sources of information:

   - *Business Monitors* (PA and PQ series)

   - *Annual Report of The Office of Fair Trading* (as a source of ideas)
   - Monopolies and Mergers Commission reports, and Competition Commission reports, which usually feature a comprehensive industry analysis
   - McCarthy's (or similar) Index (press-cutting service for firms and industries).

2 How successful has Porsche been since the introduction of its new models? Do you believe that the size of its niche is viable, or might the company have to extend its range? Porsche **http://www.porsche.com**

Strategy activity

The Fiat 500 (Cinquecento)

The Fiat Cinquecento is similar to two other iconic cars – the BMW Mini and the Vokswagen Beetle. It is a relatively old brand, but one with enduring qualities. Although it would be categorized as a supermini, it also competes in the same sector of the market as the Mini and the Beetle.

The Italian family-dominated Fiat organization (owner of the Alfa Romeo brand and allied to Ferrari) lost some of its shine and popularity, but with a series of new models, including the Panda and the Punto, it was able to restore some of its past glory. In 2007 the Fiat 500, the Cinquecento, was proclaimed European Car of the Year. Made in Poland, demand exceeded supply.

The original Cinquecento was launched in 1957 (exactly 50 years earlier) and it was soon popular, especially in certain Hollywood movies. It predated the original Mini by a few years. It lasted almost 20 years before it was seen as unfashionable and withdrawn.

With a completely fresh design and improved technology this car carries a premium price, and in this respect the strategy is the same as BMW has for the Mini. The car can be customized in various ways and Fiat claim that 500 000 permutations are possible. It has a high crash rating and is a relatively safe car; it offers high fuel consumption and is energy efficient. In a world of high fuel prices and carbon emission concerns, one can see logic in Fiat's strategy.

Fiat set out to develop a sports version for the American market, which it would promote alongside Alfa Romeo models when these were relaunched in 2009.

Questions

1 Do you see this as effective differentiation by Fiat?
2 Do you think the 2008 link between Fiat and Chrysler would have improved the prospects for the American market?

References

Buckley, G. (2003) Presentation at the University of Huddersfield, November.

Drucker, P.F. (1985) *Innovation and Entrepreneurship: Practice and Principles*, HarperCollins.

Hamel, G. and Prahalad, C.K. (1993) Strategy as stretch and leverage, *Harvard Business Review*, March–April.

Heller, R. (1998) *Goldfinger – How Entrepreneurs Grow Rich by Starting Small*, HarperCollins.

Hendry, J. (1990) The problem with Porter's generic strategies, *European Management Journal*, December.

Hunt, M.S. (1972) *Competition in the Major Home Appliance Industry 1960–70*, Harvard university Press.

Kanter, R.M. (1990) Strategic alliances and new ventures, Harvard Business School Video Series.

Kim, W.C. and Mauborgne, R. (2005) *Blue Ocean Strategy*, Harvard Business School Press.

Leask, G. and Parker, D. (2007) Strategic groups and performance in the UK pharmaceutical industry: improving our understanding of the competitive process, *Strategic Management Journal*, Vol 28, Pp. 727–745.

Ohmae, K. (1982) *The Mind of the Strategist*, McGraw-Hill.

Porter, M.E. (1980) *Competitive Strategy: Techniques for Analysing Industries and Competitors*, Free Press.

Porter, M.E. (1985) *Competitive Advantage: Creating and Sustaining Superior Performance*, Free Press.

Porter, M.E. (1996) What is strategy? *Harvard Business Review*, November–December.

Prahalad, C.K. and Ramaswamy, V. (2004) *The Future of Competition: Co-creating value with customers*, Harvard Business School Press.

Sull, D. (2006) Good things come to those who actively wait, *Financial Times*, 6 February.

Tomkins, R. (1998) Trouble in toyland pushes Toys R Us on the defensive, *Financial Times*, 29 May.

Chapter 7

Introducing culture and values

STRATEGIC MANAGEMENT: AWARENESS AND CHANGE

**PART 1
Understanding strategy**

1   What is strategy and who is involved?
   • Appendix
2   The business model and the revenue model
3   Strategic purpose
   • Supplement: Using frameworks to analyze strategy cases

**PART 2
Analysis and positioning**

4   The business environment and strategy
5   Resource-led strategy
6   The dynamics of competition
7   Introducing culture and values

**PART 3
Strategy development**

8   Creating and formulating strategy: alternatives, evaluation and choice
9   Strategic planning
10 Strategic leadership and intrapreneurship: towards visionary leadership?

**PART 4
Strategic growth issues**

11 Strategic control and measuring success
12 Issues in strategic and international growth
13 Failure, consolidation and recovery strategies

**PART 5
Strategy implementation**

14 Strategy implementation and structure
15 Leading change
16 Managing strategy in the organization
17 Final thoughts and reflections: the practice of strategy

Learning objectives

Having read to the end of this chapter, you should be able to:

- explain the manifestations and determinants of organizational culture and its impact upon the organization, its managers and other employees (**Section 7.1**)

- distinguish how different organizational structures, philosophies and styles are influenced by, and in turn influence, organizational culture (**Section 7.2**)

- list and define different sources of power (**Section 7.3**)

- show how cultures differ throughout the world (**Section 7.4**).

The online case 'The Body Shop' provides an introductory example of this section's theory in practice.

Introduction

This chapter examines the manifestations, impact and determinants of culture (and cultural differences), which influences strategic positioning, strategic choices and the feasibility of change and, in turn, helps to determine success. Whilst culture varies between organizations, some elements will be common and transferable, with the relative competitiveness of industries and organizations in different countries being influenced by cultural variations. Whilst we discuss an organization's culture in the singular, it is important to realize that especially in the case of those that are large and diverse, they invariably exhibit different cultures across different parts of the organization.

7.1 The manifestations and impact of culture

When any group lives and works together for any length of time, certain beliefs about what is right and proper (so-called *norms*) are formed and shared, along with behaviour patterns based on their beliefs, and actions that are matters of habit which are followed routinely – these are their **culture**.

In organizational settings, culture is reflected in the way in which people perform tasks, set objectives and administer resources to achieve them. Culture affects the way that they make decisions, think, feel and act in response to opportunities and threats. Culture also influences the selection of people for particular jobs which, in turn, affects the way in which tasks are carried out and decisions are made. Culture is so fundamental that it affects behaviour unconsciously. Managers do things in particular ways because it is implicitly expected behaviour.

The culture of an organization is, therefore, related to the people, their behaviour and the operation of the structure, and it is encapsulated in beliefs, customs and values, and manifested in a number of symbolic ways. **In a nutshell, attitudes and assumptions form the core of the organization's culture. Values represent implicit aspects of the culture; and behaviour is the explicit element**.

The formation of, and any changes to, the culture of an organization is dependent on the leadership of, and example set by, particular individuals – and their ability to control or influence situations, which is dependent on a person's ability to obtain and use power.

Online Case 7.1, The Body Shop, shows how the values of the founder, Anita Roddick, inspired employees and attracted customers. The distinctive culture enabled The Body Shop to grow and prosper, but it was not totally appropriate for the large, international business that The Body Shop became. Eventually, in 2006, The Body Shop was sold to L'Oreal as a way of making sure that the business could survive and prosper as part of a large multinational. Anita Roddick died in September 2007, leaving a legacy of a lifetime of philanthropy and of campaigning for ethical issues.

Culture and power, then, affect the choice, incidence and application of the modes of strategy creation, which will also reflect the values and preferences of the strategic leader. The preferred mode must, however, be appropriate for the organization's strategic needs, which are affected by competition. Moreover, culture and power are such strong forces that, if the prevailing culture is overlooked, implementation may not happen. Strong cultures can obstruct strategic change, particularly if companies are in decline and people feel vulnerable.

Quite simply, culture is at the heart of all strategy creation and implementation. Organizations are seeking to respond to perceived strategic issues. Resources must be deployed and committed, but successful change also requires the 'right' attitude, approach and commitment from people. This mindset – which might, for example, reflect a strong customer and service focus – could imply further empowerment and, consequently, cultural change.

Berry (1983) claimed prematurely that the focus of strategic management had switched from analytical models (the marketplace!) to softer aspect of culture (how managers can resolve internal problems): by using culture, companies could become more strategically effective. The perspective of this book is, though, that both hard and soft aspects of strategy have important roles to play in strategic management.

Strong cultures can be an important strategic asset, with internalized beliefs motivating people to achieve exceptional levels of performance. An effective strategic leader will understand and mould the culture to pursue a vision and implement intended strategies. Although the most successful companies develop strong cultures, the major doubt concerns an organization's ability to change its culture.

Moreover, large organizations formed by a series of acquisitions, especially internationally, will frequently exhibit different cultures in the various divisions or businesses. Therefore, the challenge for corporate headquarters is to ensure that certain critically important values are reflected in all branches of the corporation and cultural differences do not inhibit internal architecture and synergy. The acquisition of Compaq by Hewlett-Packard in 2002 (Case 7.1) provided exactly this challenge – and it would ultimately lead to the downfall of the strategic leader behind it.

Case 7.1 Hewlett-Packard US

Hewlett-Packard (HP) began life in a garage in Palo Alto, California, in 1939. It happened because Stanford Professor Fred Terman brought together two of his PhD students, Bill Hewlett and Dave Packard, and encouraged them to start a business based on their research. Not long after the business started Bill Hewlett was called up for military service and in his absence Dave Packard held everything together. When Hewlett returned after the war he was able to introduce fresh ideas. The two partners were different in character but they complemented each other well. HP not only became a leading computer company, it was also the foundation upon which Silicon Valley was built. Some 60 years later HP was probably best known for its computer printers – it had some 40 per cent of the world market and also earned substantial revenues from sales of replacement ink and toner cartridges. But HP was a diversified business and also supplied PCs, laptops, servers, scanners and digital cameras as well as providing IT consultancy services. In 1999 Carly Fiorina became the new CEO and she was determined to strengthen HP's position in the market and make it the number two company behind IBM. Fiorina had been CEO of the newer and 'fashionable' Lucent Technologies. Today HP is the world's largest maker of personal computers.

Fiorina soon launched an agreed $19 billion bid for Compaq. The opposition to this strategy was led by Walter Hewlett, the son of Bill Hewlett, who believed that instead of moving further into computers, HP should become more focused on printers and associated digital businesses. Fiorina's logic was that sales of computers, scanners and digital cameras drive printer sales. HP had a special range of photo printers.

In contrast Compaq was a much younger company which had been founded in 1982 by three senior managers from Texas Instruments. They set out to make affordable and portable PCs to run the software being developed for the IBM PC. These were commonly known as IBM clones, and the design for the first model was sketched out on a restaurant placemat.

The emphasis was on volume production and managed costs to fuel competitive prices.

The company became one of America's fastest growth businesses. Over 50 000 were sold in the first year of operations. By 1994 Compaq was the world's leading PC supplier. However, in 1998 Compaq acquired Digital Equipment for $9.6 billion in cash. Digital provided high-end servers, operating systems and chip technology. It might have been complementary, but it was certainly not a direct competitor. At the same time Compaq was experiencing more intense competition from the aggressive and fast-expanding Dell, started in Texas by the entrepreneurial Michael Dell, whose business model relies on sourced-in components and direct sales (see Case 2.3). There were post-acquisition problems and soon Compaq was carrying expensive excess inventory. The product lines and distribution had to be rationalized. Jobs, including senior executives, were lost. Fast, aggressive and competitive, for some analysts the company had lost its way strategically. Under a new CEO, however, the decline was staunched and the situation was stabilized with a stronger focus on services – but not sufficiently to withstand a market slump in 2001, when more jobs were lost.

Compaq Computer lived the Hank Williams life – it ran hard, got famous and died before its time.

CNET News.com

HP's values, known widely as 'The HP Way' were based on trust, respect, passion for customers, speed and agility of service. HP believed in involving managers in decision-making. These had all evolved over 60 years. The company saw itself as process-intensive and very much technology-based. One strap line used by the company is 'HP Invent' and this really tells its own story.

At HP we believe ideas thrive on teamwork. Everyone at every level in every function is encouraged to have original ideas and to share them. We believe anything can be achieved if you really believe in it and will invest in your ideas to change lives and working practices. That's because we work across borders and without limits. Global virtual teams share resources and pool their brainpower to solve business issues and meet personal goals. You will be valued for your unique skills, experiences and perspective. You will add value with every idea you have.

Statement to employees

One analyst, John Madden (Summit Strategies, Boston) mused that it was unclear whether a combined HP-Compaq would have a cohesive strategy but acknowledged that 'culture issues aside, services for both companies are at the heart of the bulls-eye'.

One interesting and maybe significant development in 2004 was HP's decision to launch a range of notebook computers with the Linux open-source operating system installed. Started by the entrepreneur, Linus Torvalds, a Swedish-speaking Finn, Linux has been made available either free of charge or for a small licence fee from certain organizations who will provide technical support. It is a growing competitor to the ubiquitous Microsoft Windows, but, as yet, had only had a limited impact on the market. Leading rival, Dell, sells 'naked' machines – with no operating system installed – but it has yet to offer Linux pre-installed, possibly concerned about its long-term relationship with Microsoft. HP was the first to do so. The price saving was not huge – some $60 in a $1000 plus notebook; the real issue is one of consumer choice.

In 2005 Carly Fiorina resigned over 'differences of opinion over strategy' with the Hewlett-Packard Board. The company had been missing earnings targets. Given the opposition to her acquisition of Compaq by some members of the Board, it was always going to be necessary to deliver on earnings promises. HP shares had lost two-thirds of their value since she had been appointed.

Some new strategies were being developed in-house.

In March 2006 HP entered retail photo printing in competition with Kodak and Fuji, another strategy some questioned. The company had developed a number of machines that it would sell to stores and others which were integral in a stand-alone kiosk. Wal-Mart became an early customer for the kiosks. Store machines were available which would digitally print posters and promotional material to a very high quality. HP was 'moving from being a printer company to being a printing company'. But did this make sense?

Later in 2006 HP launched new high-end video conferencing equipment.

Also later in the same year HP acquired Mercury Interactive for $4.5 billion. This was a business software company, and the latest in a line of recent software acquisitions. HP wanted to be able to help its customers with a range of packages and systems that would help with their more complex needs, and thus provide a 'complete package' of products and services.

In January 2007 the Chairman, Patricia Dunn, resigned. She had apparently employed private detectives to tap directors' telephone calls in an attempt to plug an information leak. There were clearly still problems at Hewlett-Packard – and they would continue.

In 2010 HP acquired 3PAR, a storage technology company which provided proper access to cloud computing. HP had beaten off competition from Dell. A year later HP bought the UK software business Autonomy.

Also in 2011, and after other senior management changes, Meg Whitman moved from eBay to become the new CEO. Could she reinvigorate a company that had yet to deal with the growing competition from tablet computers? HP had been unsuccessful in its first attempt to launch a tablet that could compete with the rivals, especially the iPad. In 2012 Whitman announced that the workforce would be reduced by 27 000 over 2 years (some 8 per cent) and the savings invested into the organization, into innovation and research and development.

However, late in 2012 HP announced it was taking action against the previous owners of Autonomy, the UK software business acquired in 2011. 'Hidden issues and financial improprieties' were cited, although these were immediately denied by those accused. HP believed the company's value had been overstated and too high a price paid for the acquisition.

Questions

1   How different do you imagine the HP and Compaq cultures were when Compaq was thriving as a manufacturer of PCs and laptops? How difficult might it be to reconcile the differences and create a cohesive culture? In a company like Hewlett-Packard, would it have been inevitable that the CEO would have to go if results did not follow a controversial strategic decision?

2   What do you think the decision to launch a notebook with Linux installed is saying about the HP culture?

3   Is there a defensible strategic logic in the moves into imaging and printing (favoured by Walter Hewlett) and software?

4   How might a company like HP become more naturally innovative – which it needs to be in the face of competition?

5   Do some of the strategic decisions and actions cause one to question HP's competency with acquisitions?

SOURCE: THIS CASE STUDY WAS PREPARED USING PRIMARILY PUBLICLY AVAILABLE SOURCES OF INFORMATION FOR THE PURPOSES OF CLASSROOM DISCUSSION; IT DOES NOT INTEND TO ILLUSTRATE EITHER EFFECTIVE OR INEFFECTIVE HANDLING OF A MANAGERIAL SITUATION.

After the problems of the merger of Chrysler and Daimler in 1998 and the break-up of the group in 2007 with the sale of Daimler's equity stake in Chrysler to Cerebus Capital Group, its chairman Dieter Zetsche commented on leading across cultures. 'Some stereotypes seem based in individual cultures such as the notion that American businesses have a relaxed style and German managers hold long meetings. At the end of the day, my experience is that those differences are minor. For me, the same issues are important everywhere. People want to see that you mean what you say. If they feel you are not straightforward, you are lost. This is important whether you work in Asia or Africa or whatever.'

Figure 7.1 summarizes manifestations of culture, power and other aspects discussed below.

Figure 7.1 Aspects of culture – the culture grid

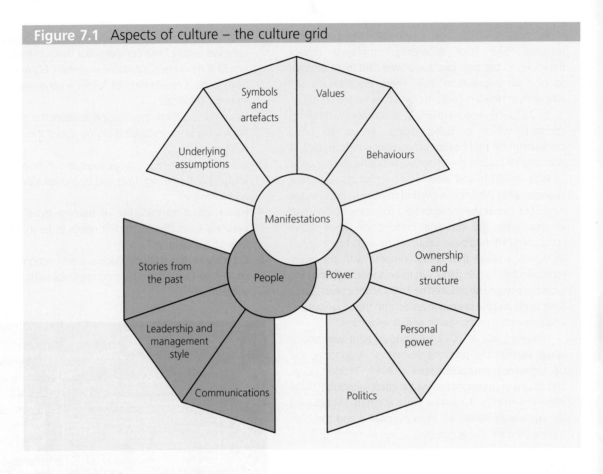

Manifestations of culture

Schein (1985) contends that culture has a number of levels (numbered below), some of which are essentially manifestations of underlying beliefs:

1 *Artefacts* include the physical and social environment and the outputs of the organization, including written communications, advertisements and the reception received by visitors.

2 *Values* represent a sense of 'what ought to be' based on convictions held by certain key people, e.g. if an organization has a problem such as low sales or a high level of rejections in production, decisions (based on the values of the decision-maker or strategic leader, though debatable or perhaps questionable) might be made to advertise more aggressively or to use high-quality but more expensive raw materials.

3 *Underlying assumptions* are the taken-for-granted ways of doing things or solving problems – i.e. if the alternative is successful, it may be tried consecutively until it becomes common practice, such that the value becomes a belief and ultimately an assumption about organizational behaviour.

One belief accepted by employees within a bank might be that all lending must be secure, whereas a football team could be committed to always playing attractive, open football. A university might be expected to have clear beliefs about the relative importance of research and teaching, but this is likely to be an issue where employees 'agree to disagree', leading to a fragmented culture. Examples of *behaviour* include speedy new product development, long working hours, formal management meetings and regular informal meetings or contacts with colleagues, suppliers and customers. Certain organizations may state that they have particular values, but in reality these will be little more than verbal or written statements or aspirations for the future.

Schein argues that cultural paradigms are formed which determine how 'organization members perceive, think about, feel about and judge situations and relationships' and these are based on a number of underlying assumptions.

People and culture

For Schwartz and Davis (1981), culture is: 'a pattern of beliefs and expectations shared by the organization's members, and which produce norms that powerfully shape the behaviour of individuals and groups in the organization.' Such beliefs are key elements of corporate policy, being developed from interactions with, and in turn forming policy towards, the marketplace. As a result, rules or norms for internal and external behaviour are developed and eventually both performance and reward systems will be affected: aspects of the culture which are often transmitted through stories of past events, glories and heroes.

Success is measured by, and culture therefore becomes based on, past activities. Current decisions by managers reflect the values, beliefs and norms that have proved beneficial in the past and in the development and growth of the organization, and reinforcing the organization's corporate culture and expected behaviour.

Culture affects the all-important suppliers and customers who will feed back impressions about the organization. Successful organizations will ensure that there is congruence between these environmental influences and the organization culture, such that key success factors can be achieved if resources are administered, controlled and developed appropriately.

Organizations need a cohesive blend of the philosophies introduced earlier. A cohesive culture would exhibit strong *leadership*, whereby the strategic leader is sensitive to the degrees of decentralization and informality necessary for satisfying customer needs efficiently, and managing change pressures, in order to keep the business strong and profitable. At the same time, a centralized information network will ensure that communications are effective and that managers are both kept aware and rewarded properly for their contributions. A fragmented culture, in contrast, would suggest that the needs of certain stakeholders were perhaps not being satisfied adequately, or that strategies and changes were not being co-ordinated, or that managers or business units were in conflict and working against each other, or that the most deserving people were not being rewarded.

Linked to this is *communication*, an essential aspect of culture, as the organization might be seen as open or closed, formal or informal. Ideally, employees from different parts of the business, and at different levels in the hierarchy, will feel willing and able to talk openly with each other, sharing problems, ideas and learning. 'Doors should be left open.' Employees should also be trusted and empowered to the appropriate degree. Good communications can stop nasty surprises. If employees know how well competitors are performing, where they are particularly strong, they can commit themselves to high levels of achievement in order to outperform their rivals.

Communication is clearly essential for creating effective internal and external architecture. Indeed, Hampden-Turner (1990) argues that culture is based on communication and learning. The strategic leader's vision for the organization must be communicated and understood; events and changes affecting the organization also need to be communicated widely. Managers should be encouraged to seek out new opportunities by learning about new technology and customer expectations, and to innovate; and the organization should help them to share their experiences and their learning.

Power and culture

Power is reflected in the *ownership* of the business, which may be a family company with strong, concentrated power, or a small group of institutional shareholders could control the business – in which case it is conceivable that short-term financial targets will dictate strategies. *Structural issues* include the extent to which the organization is centralized or decentralized, the role and contribution of corporate headquarters and control and reward systems. Personal power is discussed later in this chapter (Section 7.3); politics refers to the ways in which managers use power and influence to affect decisions and actions.

Case 7.2 analyzes IKEA, a low-cost competitor with its complex supply-chain network, with its ability to be flexible in response to local opportunities, which could easily add costs as well as value. The company is product- and production-driven, but is able to capture and use ideas from customers and employees.

Case 7.2   IKEA   Eur

IKEA was started in Sweden by Ingvar Kamprad, who pioneered the idea of self-assembly furniture in handy packs. Now well into his 80s he is still involved but not running the company himself; that is left to Michael Ohlsson. Kamprad's vision of 'a better, more beautiful, everyday life for the many' led to 'a wide range of home furnishings, of good function and style, at low prices, for mass consumer markets'. Kamprad began with a mail-order business in 1943; the first IKEA store was opened in 1958. Every year IKEA prints over 110 million catalogues – this is by far the single largest print run of any comparable item anywhere in the world.

Growth has been carefully regulated. IKEA waited for 7 years before opening a second branch; the first branch outside Sweden was in the early 1970s; the first US store opened in 1985, with typically one new store being added every year. This approach allows IKEA to establish local supply networks and ensures that it does not become stretched financially. The expansion programme has always been funded from cash generated by the retail activities. IKEA does not have a large market share in any single country; instead, it has a global brand and an intriguing reputation which draws customers from substantial distances away.

By 2011, IKEA had some 332 shops in 38 countries. There are 18 stores in the UK and one in Ireland. IKEA's strategy has always involved high-quality merchandise at prices which undercut the competition. In the mid-1990s IKEA's annual turnover passed the $5 billion mark; after-tax profits were estimated to be 8 per cent of revenue. Sales have risen in every year of its existence, and by 2001 revenues had doubled to $10 billion. They were growing at 15 per cent per year and reached 23.5 billion Euros in 2011. A private company, IKEA has always been reticent about the financial data it releases. Moreover, as IKEA has only recently started to target Russia and China, growth prospects appear to remain healthy. In 2006 IKEA returned to Japan, a country it had abandoned in 1994 after being there for 20 years.

IKEA stores focus on sales of self-assembly packs which customers take away themselves. IKEA will, however, deliver fully assembled pieces for a premium price. The stores have a wide range of facilities, typically including restaurants and games and video rooms for children; these are normally on the top floor, which is where customers come in. People are then routed carefully through a series of display areas to the downstairs purchase points which resemble a typical discount warehouse.

The furniture packs are commissioned from over 2300 suppliers in some 70 countries, many of them low-labour-cost countries in the Far East and Eastern Europe. IKEA has an equity stake in several of its suppliers and insists on tight stock control programmes to reduce costs through the whole supply chain. IKEA designs all its own products and aims to lead customer taste. There is just one range of products for the global market, but not every country and store stocks the full range. IKEA chooses not to have mini-ranges for specific countries and prides itself on an ability to respond to local fashion and opportunities by quickly adjusting the range in any one store. Sales per square foot invariably exceed industry averages.

Manifestations of IKEA's distinctive culture

The *artefacts* clearly include the stores, the products and the prices. There are no brands other than IKEA's own. There are no annual or seasonal sales; prices stay valid for a whole year. There is a plethora of in-store information and communications, but no commissioned sales people.

Values – IKEA's mission statement emphasizes 'functionality, good design, low price and good quality'. The company uses the word 'prosumers' to imply that value is added by both IKEA and their customers in partnership. Employees are empowered to be innovative and helpful and challenged to 'dare to be different'. IKEA recognizes that always offering prices substantially below those of its competitors places considerable pressure on its staff. IKEA also expect, and get, some complaints about busy stores and slow checkout service – a price they claim that has to be paid for low prices. Even though IKEA prices could easily have been increased, Kamprad has stuck with his original approach and mission.

Underlying assumptions can be summarized in the following quotes:

We do not need to do things in traditional ways (window manufacturers have been approached to make table frames; shirt manufacturers for seat cushions).

Break your chains and you are free; cut your roots and you die. IKEA should look for constant renewal.

Experiments matter; mistakes (within reason) will be tolerated.

IKEA also emphasizes the shared experience – *if we contribute 50 per cent and you [the customer] contributes 50 per cent, we both save.*

Behaviours – Every IKEA manager flies economy class and uses taxis only if there is no suitable alternative. In the Netherlands, managers have been encouraged to stay with typical IKEA customer families to learn more about their needs. Kamprad himself, despite his enormous wealth (estimated at £15 billion), drives a 15-year-old Volvo car and uses budget airlines, especially easyJet. In this respect he can be likened to the late Sam Walton of Wal-Mart who opted for a pick-up truck.

People

A variety of **stories** permeates the IKEA culture. Initially customers in the US stores were simply not buying any beds – there had been no market research into US tastes; it was IKEA's global product. Eventually, it was realized that Americans sleep in bigger beds than Swedes. Similarly, kitchen units had to be adjusted to handle extra-large pizza plates.

Kamprad denies that there is any truth in the story that his parsimony stretches to him buying cans of Coca-Cola from local supermarkets to replenish hotel room mini-bars because he is reluctant to pay hotel prices for soft drinks.

One less desirable but well-publicized story concerns a stabbing during crowd trouble at the midnight opening of a new store in North London in 2007. IKEA openings are always popular!

Leadership and management style – Kamprad rarely shows his face to the public. At one stage there was some adverse publicity concerning alleged wartime allegiances, but no lasting damage. The lack of published financial information reinforces this hidden aspect of IKEA.

Communications – Both customers and employees are encouraged to provide ideas and suggestions, which may be translated into new products. Information enters the system from several points. When Kamprad visits stores he encourages staff to use his Christian name and he spends time with them and IKEA customers receiving feedback.

Power

Ownership and structural issues – IKEA remains a private company which owns all of its sites. It pays for new sites in cash. 'We don't like to be in the hands of the banks.' There are no plans to become a limited company either; Kamprad has criticized the short-term interests of many investors.

The company operates as three distinct activities. The core retailing business is now a Dutch-registered charitable foundation. The profits of the operations are subjected to a top-slice of 3 per cent to fund a separate business which has responsibility for managing the brand and IKEA's franchisees. The third arm is a banking and finance business; IKEA, for example, owns a majority shareholding in Habitat in the UK.

Power – The organization is structured as an inverted pyramid and based on managers and co-workers. 'Employees are there to serve customers.' Kamprad was always concerned that IKEA should not become inflexible as it grew in size. There are no directors, no formal titles and no dining rooms or reserved parking spaces for executives. Managers are quite likely to switch between functions and countries. The organization is fundamentally informal with 'few instructions'. Every year there is an 'anti-bureaucracy' week when everyone dresses casually.

Questions

1 IKEA believes that fashionable and modern furniture and furnishings can be affordable for most families. It need not be prohibitively expensive. How does it achieve this?

2 Do you believe IKEA enjoys E–V–R congruence? If so, what are the key congruency themes? If not, in what way is it incongruent?

IKEA **http://www.ikea.com**

Determinants of culture

Deal and Kennedy (1982) argue that employees must be rewarded for complying with the essential cultural aspects if these values are to be developed and retained over time, concluding that people who build, develop and run successful companies invariably work hard to create strong cultures within their organizations.

Deal and Kennedy isolated five key elements or determinants of culture:

- The *environment* and key success factors which the organization must do well to be an effective competitor, e.g. innovation and fast delivery.
- The *values* that the strategic leader considers important and wishes to see adopted and followed in the organization, and which should relate to the key success factors, and to employee reward systems.
- *Heroes* are the visionaries who create the culture, and can come from any background and could be, for example, product or service innovators, engineers who build the appropriate quality into the product, or creative marketing people who provide the slogans which make the product or brand name a household word.
- *Rites and rituals* are the behaviour patterns in which the culture is manifest, for example employees helping each other out when there are difficulties, the way in which sales people deal with customers and the care and attention that go into production.
- *The cultural network* is the communications system around which the culture revolves and which determines just how aware employees are about the essential issues.

When the culture is strong, people know what is expected of them, they understand how to act and decide in particular circumstances, and they appreciate the issues that are important. When it is weak, time can be wasted in trying to decide what should be done and how. Moreover, employees may feel better about their companies if they are recognized, known about and regarded as successful, aspects reflected in the culture.

The various separate strands to the culture in any organization should complement each other, e.g. relating to the strategic leader, the environment and the employees. There could be a strong power culture related to an influential strategic leader who is firmly in charge of the organization and whose values are widely understood and followed – and which could be linked to a culture of market orientation, which ensures that customer needs are considered and satisfied, and to a work culture if employees feel committed to the organization and wish to help in achieving success.

Implications and impacts of culture

Pümpin (1987) suggests that seven aspects comprise the culture of an organization, and that the relative significance of each of these will vary from industry to industry. The seven are:

1 The extent to which the organization is marketing orientated, giving customers high priority.
2 The relationships between management and staff, manifested through communication and participation systems, for example.
3 The extent to which people are target orientated and committed to achieving agreed levels of performance.
4 Attitudes towards innovation, with the risks associated with failure being perceived as acceptable by all levels of management.
5 Attitudes towards costs and cost reduction.
6 The commitment and loyalty to the organization felt, and shown, by staff.
7 The impact of, and reaction to, technology and technological change and development; for example, whether or not the opportunities offered by information technology are being harnessed by the firm.

Many of these aspects are developed further in later chapters of the book.

Hampden-Turner (1990) believes that the culture is a manifestation of how the organization has chosen to deal with specific dilemmas and conflicts. Each of these can be viewed as a continuum, and the organization needs a clear position on each one. As shown earlier, one dilemma might be the conflict between, on the one hand, the need to develop new products and services quickly and ahead of competitors and, on the other hand, the need for thorough development and planning to ensure adequate quality and safety. Another dilemma is the need for managers to be adaptive and responsive in a changing environment, but not at the expense of organization-wide communication and awareness. Such change orientation may also conflict with a desire for continuity and consistency of strategy and policy.

Tables 7.1 and 7.2 take this idea further, Table 7.1 highlighting how every apparent virtue also has a 'flip side', and consequently something which is positive at one point may suddenly prove disadvantageous; and Table 7.2 examining the advantages and drawbacks of three business paradigms (market-orientation, resource efficiency or growth-driven). Taken together, these confirm that there can never be one best or ideal culture since the culture needs to be flexible and adaptive as circumstances change. The cultural factors that bring initial success may need to be changed if success is to be sustained. Similarly, it is not enough simply to analyze what other successful organizations are doing and copy them. Benchmarking and teasing out good practices is both important and beneficial, but these practices again need customizing and adapting to the unique circumstances facing an individual organization.

Table 7.1   Every coin, every virtue, has a flip side!

Team players	May be indecisive and avoid risks
Customer focus	Can lead to reactivity and lack of innovation
Action orientation	Can become reckless and dictatorial
Analytical thinking	Can result in paralysis
Innovation	Which is impractical, unrealistic, ill thought-through, wastes time and money
A global vision	May mean valuable local opportunities are missed
Being a good 'people manager'	May allow someone to become soft and walk away from tough decisions

(DEVELOPED FROM IDEAS IN McCALL, MW (1998) HIGH FLYERS, HARVARD BUSINESS SCHOOL PRESS.)

Table 7.2   The imperfect world of organizations

A market-driven business is likely to be:	An efficient operations-driven business is likely to be:	A growth-orientated business is likely to be:
Resourceful	Efficient	Competitive
Entrepreneurial	Strong on team working	Strong on targets and achieving results
Risk oriented	Good at executing plans	Full of hard-working people
Pragmatic in terms of getting things done	Sophisticated with its systems and procedures	Flexible
		Changing quickly
But it may not be:	*But it may not be:*	*But it may not be:*
Consistent	Responsive to customers	Taking a long-term perspective
Disciplined in what it does	Good at managing change	Offering a balanced lifestyle for its employees
Adhering to systems and procedures	Able to see 'the big picture'	Sensitive to people's needs
Strong on teamworking		

(DEVELOPED FROM IDEAS IN McCALL, MW (1998) HIGH FLYERS, HARVARD BUSINESS SCHOOL PRESS.)

Culture, strategy creation and its impact and outcomes

We have already seen that the essential cultural characteristics will dictate the preferred mode of strategy creation in an organization; all the modes are likely to be present to some degree.

The culture will influence the ability of a strategic visionary to 'sell' his or her ideas to other members of the organization and gain their support and commitment to change. The planning mode is ideal for a conservative, risk-averse, slow-to-change organization or is most suitable in a reasonably stable and predictable environment – but in a more unstable situation it can lead to missed opportunities. Where environmental opportunities and threats arise continuously in a situation of competitive chaos, an organization must be able to deal with them in order to survive. It is the culture, with its amalgam of attitudes, values, perceptions and experiences, which determines the outcomes and relative success. The structure must facilitate awareness, sharing and learning, and people must be willing and able to act. People 'learn by doing' and they must be able to learn from mistakes and, indeed, Peters (1988) states that 'managers have to learn how to make mistakes faster'. The reward system is critical, such that managers and employees should be praised and rewarded for exercising initiative and taking risks which prove successful; failures should not be sanctioned too harshly, as long as they are not repeated!

Berry (1983) argues that if a strategic leader really understands the company culture they must, by definition, be better equipped to make wise decisions. They might conclude that 'cultural change will be so difficult we had better be sure to select a business or strategy that our kind of company can handle well', which is just as valid as, and perhaps more useful than, believing that one can accomplish cultural change in order to shift the firm towards a new strategy.

If business strategies and culture are intertwined, the ability both to analyze and construct strategies and to manage and inspire people are also intertwined. Hence, a good strategy acknowledges, 'where we are, what we have got, and what, therefore, managerially helps us to get where we want to be', which is substantially different from selecting business options exclusively on their product/market dynamics. In other words, developing and implementing strategy is a human and political process that starts as much with the visions, hopes and aspirations of a company's leaders as it does with market or business analysis. Ideas drive organizations.

With ever-shortening product life cycles, intense global competition and unstable economies and currencies, the future is going to require organizations that are ready to commit themselves to change. Strategy will be about intertwining analysis and adaptation, with the challenge being to develop more effective organizations.

Miles and Snow (1978), whose research has been used to develop Table 7.3, have suggested a typology of organizations in relation to culture and strategy formation. The typology distinguishes organizations in terms of their values and objectives, and different types will typically prefer particular approaches to strategy creation. Defenders, prospectors and analyzers are all regarded by Miles and Snow as positive organizations; reactors must ultimately adopt one of the other three approaches or suffer long-term decline. Suggested examples of each type are as follows. GEC, despite being in high-technology industries, was for most of its life relatively conservative and a defender. It built up cash reserves that protected it during cyclical downturns – but was accused of not taking risks! The risk-oriented, innovative Amstrad has always been a prospector. Sometimes Amstrad struggled to implement its innovative ideas. The respective strategic leaders of these organizations, the late Lord Weinstock (until his retirement in 1996) and entrepreneur (Lord) Alan Sugar adopted different styles of management and leadership and exhibited different corporate values. Weinstock's successor, Lord Simpson, changed to a far higher risk 'prospector' strategy, divesting defence businesses and acquiring telecommunications companies. The outcomes were disappointing and led to the collapse of the company, which was subsequently renamed Marconi. Arguably, as we shall see, cultural change can be disturbing.

Historically, many public-sector bureaucracies have been stable analyzers, while Marks and Spencer has long been a changing analyzer. Prior to its decline and acquisition by BTR, Dunlop, in the 1970s, exhibited many of the characteristics of a reactor organization, and failed to change sufficiently in line with environmental changes. BTR turned the company around and it was then sold on; the Dunlop and Slazenger branded sporting goods are still popular today. Acquisition saved the business.

Table 7.3   Organizational values and strategies

Type	Characteristics	Strategy formation
Defenders	Conservative beliefs	Emphasis on planning
	Low-risk strategies	
	Secure markets	
	Concentration on narrow segments	
	Considerable expertise in narrow areas of specialism	
	Preference for well-tried resolutions to problems	
	Little search for anything really 'new'	
	Attention given to improving efficiency of present operations	
Prospectors	Innovative	Visionary mode
	Looking to break new ground	
	High-risk strategies	
	Search for new opportunities	
	Can create change and uncertainty, forcing a response from competitors	
	More attention given to market changes than to improving internal efficiency	
Analyzers	*Two aspects: stable and changing*	
	Stable: formal structures and search for efficiencies	Planning mode
	Changing: competitors monitored and strategies amended as promising ideas seen (followers)	Adaptive/Incremental mode
Reactors	Characterized by an inability to respond effectively to change pressures	Adaptive mode
	Adjustments are therefore forced on the firm in order to avert crises	

Miles and Snow argue that, as well as being a classification, their typology can be used to predict behaviour. For example, a defender organization, in a search for greater operating efficiency, might consider investing in the latest technology, but reject the strategy if it has high risk attached.

The power of 'corporate culture' should not be underestimated, both for a company's success and, if it is inappropriate, in frustrating change. Values, strategies, systems, organization and accountabilities – the components of culture – are a very strong mix which can either make a company successful or, alternatively, lead to its decline. The task of corporate leadership is to apply energy and judgement to the corporate culture to ensure its relevance.

SIR ALLEN SHEPPARD, WHEN CHAIRMAN, GRAND METROPOLITAN PLC

7.2 Culture, structure and styles of management

Handy (1976), building on earlier work by Harrison (1972), has developed an alternative classification of organizations based on cultural differences, as illustrated in Figure 7.2.

Figure 7.2 Handy's four cultures

ADAPTED FROM HANDY, CB (1976) UNDERSTANDING ORGANIZATIONS, PENGUIN

Culture	Diagrammatic representation	Structure
Power or club		Web
Role		Greek temple
Task	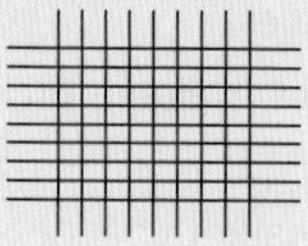	Net
Person or existential	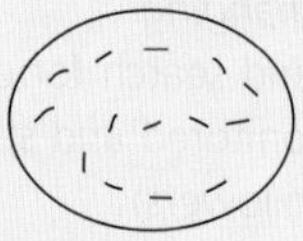	Cluster

The club culture or power culture

Work is divided by function or product and a diagram of the organization structure would be quite traditional. There would be departments for sales, production, finance and so on, and possibly product-based divisions or strategic business units if the organization was larger. However, this structure is mostly found in smaller firms.

These functions or departments are represented in Handy's figure by the lines radiating out from the centre, but notably there are also concentric lines representing communications and power – the further away from the centre, the weaker is the power and influence. This structure is dominated by the centre and, therefore, is typical for small entrepreneurial organizations. Decisions can be taken quickly, but their quality is dependent on the abilities of managers in the inner circle.

In its heyday, Hanson, a large and diverse UK/US conglomerate, was described by a former director as a 'solar system, with everyone circling around the sun in the middle, Lord Hanson' (see Leadbeater and Rudd, 1991). This analogy suggests both movement and dependency.

Decisions depend a great deal on empathy, affinity and trust, both within the organization and with suppliers, customers and other key influences.

People learn to do instinctively what their boss and the organization expect and require. Consequently, they will prove reliable even if they are allowed to exercise a degree of initiative. Foreign-exchange dealers provide an illustration of this point.

For this reason, the culture can be designated either 'club' or 'power'. Employees are rewarded for effort, success and compliance with essential values; and change is very much led from the centre in an entrepreneurial style. A culture such as this may prevent individual managers from speaking their minds, but decisions are unlikely to get lost in committees.

The role culture

Here the culture is built around defined jobs, rules and procedures and not personalities. People fit into jobs, and are recruited for this purpose. Hence, rationality and logic are at the heart of the culture, which is designed to be stable and predictable. The design is the Greek temple because the strengths of the organization are deemed to lie in the pillars, which are joined managerially at the top. One essential role of top management is to co-ordinate activity, and consequently it will be seen that both planning systems and incremental changes can be a feature of this culture. Although the strength of the organization is in the pillars, power lies at the top. As well as being designed for stability, the structure allows continuity and changes of personnel, and for this reason dramatic changes are less likely than more gradual ones.

High efficiency is possible in stable environments, but the structure can be slow to change and is, therefore, less suitable for dynamic situations.

Aspects of this culture can prove beneficial for transport businesses such as railways and airlines, where reliability and timekeeping are essential. Unfortunately, it is not by nature a flexible, service-orientated culture. **Intrapreneurship** or elements of the task culture are also required for effectiveness.

The task culture

Management in the task culture is concerned with the continuous and successful solution of problems, and performance is judged by the success of the outcomes – and the challenge is more important than the routine. The culture is shown as a net, because for particular problem situations people and other resources can be drawn from various parts of the organization on a temporary basis. Once the problem is dealt with, people will move on to other tasks, thus discontinuity is a key element of this culture. Expertise is the major source of individual power and it will determine a person's relative power in a given situation. Power basically lies in the interstices of the net, because of the reliance on task forces.

The culture is ideal for consultancies, advertising agencies and research and development departments, and within the role culture for tackling particularly difficult or unusual problem situations.

A major challenge for large organizations operating in dynamic environments is the design of a structure and systems which allow for proper management and integration without losing the spirit and excitement typical of small, entrepreneurial businesses. Elements of the task culture superimposed over formal roles can help by widening communications and engendering greater commitment within the organization. However, this culture is expensive as there is a reliance on talking and discussion, experimentation and learning by trial. Although Handy uses the expression 'problem solving', there can be problem resolutions or moves towards a solution along more incremental lines, as well as decisions concerning major changes. If successful changes are implemented, the expense can often be justified.

The person culture or existential culture

The person culture is completely different from the other three, for here the organization exists to help the individual rather than the other way round, e.g. groups of professional people: doctors, architects, dentists and solicitors. The organization, with secretarial help, printing and telephone facilities, provides a service for individual specialists and reduces the need for costly duplication. If a member of the circle leaves or retires, they are replaced by another who may have to 'buy in' to the partnership.

Some professional groups exhibit interdependencies and collaboration, allocating work among the members, although management of such an organization is difficult because of individual expertise and because the rewards and sanctions are different from those found in most other situations.

However, in an environment where government is attempting to increase competition between professional organizations (in some cases to reduce barriers to entering the profession), it is arguable that effective management, particularly at the strategic level, will become increasingly necessary. Efforts will need to be co-ordinated and harnessed if organizations are to become strong competitors.

Management philosophies

Press (1990) suggests that the culture of an organization is based upon one or more philosophies (Figure 7.3), which relate to the various stakeholders in the business, and are determined by two intersecting axes. One relates to whether the business is focused more internally or externally, and the other is based on performance measures. Do they concentrate more on resource management and efficiency, or outcomes and effectiveness? This creates four discrete philosophies:

● the resource focus, which concentrates on internal efficiencies and cost management

● the shareholder focus, which sees the business as a portfolio of activities which should be managed to maximize the value of the business for its shareholders

● the people focus, which emphasizes the skills and contribution of employees, and their needs and expectations

● the market focus, which stresses the importance of satisfying customers by adding value and differentiating products and services.

All of these are important and none can be ignored. The culture can be analyzed in terms of how these four philosophies are perceived and prioritized. As pointed out earlier, the philosophy may have to change if success is to be sustained.

A company which relies heavily upon formal strategic planning, for example, is likely to appear to concentrate more upon shareholders and resources. General Electric (GE) of the USA, on the other hand, is a diversified conglomerate, which is perceived to focus on people empowerment and decentralization, and its style and culture has proved more enduring. That said, this did not prevent GE being accused of being bottom-line oriented. Japanese companies, discussed later in this chapter, exhibit a particular and distinctive blend of people, markets and resources.

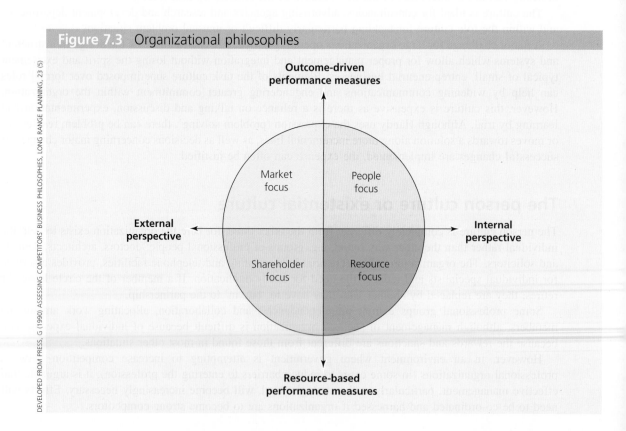

Figure 7.3 Organizational philosophies

DEVELOPED FROM PRESS, G (1990) ASSESSING COMPETITORS' BUSINESS PHILOSOPHIES, LONG RANGE PLANNING, 23 (5)

Styles of management

The style adopted by the strategic leader – whether autocratic or democratic, visionary or champions of the past, orientated towards markets more than towards financial controls – can have a strong influence on the culture of the organization, and is also related to power, as discussed in Section 7.3 below.

Styles which differ from the 'normal and traditional' can prove to be very effective in particular circumstances. The John Lewis Partnership, Britain's third largest department store chain after Debenhams and House of Fraser, is employee-owned and has also diversified into supermarkets with its Waitrose chain. The company has a chairman, a board of directors and a management structure, as do most companies, but parallel to this commercial structure stands a second structure which represents the interests of the ordinary worker who is also a partner in John Lewis. In terms of power, while a partner working in a department in a store cannot directly influence management decisions, he or she is nonetheless in ultimate control of the company for which he or she works – and this collective power is supplemented by a profit-sharing scheme. Decision-making and communications within the organization must be affected by high levels of participation. John Lewis's motto of 'never knowingly undersold' is based on value for money which is helped by employee involvement.

> *Everyone in the business feels (and is) involved. Everyone also feels (and is) accountable, especially those at the top. Top management are given lots of freedom to determine and change strategy, but they can be questioned on anything by the rank-and-file partners ... this ... makes people think ahead and consider the consequences of their actions.*
>
> STUART HAMPSON, CHAIRMAN, JOHN LEWIS PARTNERSHIP SPEAKING IN 1993. HAMPSON WAS ONLY THE FOURTH CHAIRMAN SINCE THE PARTNERSHIP WAS FORMED IN 1929

7.3 Culture and power

In Charles Handy's classification of organizations in terms of their culture, power is an important element which needs further consideration. While an introduction to the topic is included here, the subject of power is explored more fully in Chapter 15, when its impact on strategy implementation and strategic change is considered.

Power is related to the potential or ability to do something. Consequently, strategic change will be strongly influenced by the bases of power within an organization and by the power of the organization in relation to its environment.

Internal power

Change is brought about if the necessary resources can be harnessed and if people can be persuaded to behave in a particular way. Both of these require power, which results in part from the structure of the organization, and it needs exercising in different ways in different cultures in order to be used effectively. At the same time, power can be a feature of an individual manager's personality, and managers who are personally powerful will be in a position to influence change.

The ways in which managers apply power are known as 'power levers'. The theorized classifications of power bases differ only slightly. Critical Reflection 7.1, identifying seven major sources of power, has been developed from a classification by Kakabadse (1982), who has built on the earlier work of French and Raven (1959).

To understand organizational change and how it is managed, one must consider where power lies and which managers are powerful, and identify their sources of power. While a visible, powerful and influential strategic leader is often a feature of an entrepreneurial organization, the nature and direction of incremental change will be influenced by which managers are powerful and how they exercise their power.

A power culture has strong central leadership as a key feature and power lies with the individual or small group at the centre who controls most of the activity in the organization. In contrast, role cultures are based

Critical Reflection 7.1   Power Levers

1 Reward power is the ability to influence the rewards given to others. These can be tangible (money) or intangible (status). Owner managers enjoy considerable reward power, managers in larger public sector organizations very little. For reward power to be useful, the rewards being offered must be important to the potential recipients.

2 Coercive power is power based on the threat of punishment for non-compliance, and the ability to impose the punishment. The source can be the person's role or position in the organization, or physical attributes and personality.

3 Legitimate power is synonymous with authority, and relates to an individual manager's position within the structure of the organization. It is an entitlement from the role a person occupies. The effective use of legitimate power is dependent on three things: access to relevant information; access to other people and communication networks inside the organization; and approaches to setting priorities – this determines what is asked of others.

4 Personal power depends on individual characteristics (personality) and physical characteristics. Charm, charisma and flair are terms used to describe people with personality-based power. Physical attributes such as height, size, weight and strength also affect personal power.

5 Expert power is held by a person with specialist knowledge or skills in a particular field. It is particularly useful for tackling complex problem areas. It is possible for people to be attributed expert power through reputation rather than proven ability.

6 Information power is the ability to access and use information to defend a stance or viewpoint – or to question an alternative view held by someone else – and is important as it can affect strategic choices.

7 Connection power results from personal and professional access to key people inside and outside the organization, who themselves can influence what happens. This relates particularly to information power.

on the legitimacy of rules and procedures and individual managers are expected to work within these. Task cultures are dependent on the expertise of individuals, and their success, in some part, depends on the ability of the individuals to share their power and work as a team. Managers are expected to apply power levers in ways that are acceptable to the predominant culture of the organization, and at the same time the manner in which power levers are actually used affects what happens in the organization. Power is required for change, which itself results from the application of power. Hence the implementation of desired changes to strategies requires the effective use of power bases, whilst other strategic changes will result from the exercise of power by individual managers. It is important for the organization to monitor such activity and ensure that such emergent changes and strategies are desirable or acceptable.

The relative power of the organization

The ability of an organization to effect change within its environment will similarly depend on the exercise of power. A strong competitor with, say, a very distinctive product or service, or with substantial market share, may be more powerful than its rivals. A manufacturer who is able to influence distributors or suppliers will be similarly powerful. The issue is the relative power in relation to those other individuals, organizations and institutions – its stakeholders – on whom it relies, with whom it trades, or which influence it in some way.

Culture and competitive advantage

Barney (1986) has examined the relationship between culture and 'superior financial performance', using micro-economics for his definition of superior financial performance, arguing that firms record either below-normal returns (insufficient for long-term survival in the industry), normal returns (enough for survival, but no more) or superior results, which are more than those required for long-term survival.

Superior results, which result from some form of competitive advantage, attract competitors who seek to copy whatever is thought to be the source of competitive advantage and generating the success – which, in turn, affects supply and margins and can reduce profitability to only normal returns and, in some cases, below normal. Therefore, sustained superior financial performance requires sustained competitive advantage. Barney concluded that culture can, and does, generate sustained competitive advantage, and hence long-term superior financial performance, when three conditions are met:

- The culture is valuable. The culture must enable things to happen which themselves result in high sales, low costs or high margins.
- The culture is rare.
- The culture is imperfectly imitable, i.e. it cannot be copied easily by competitors.

Peters and Waterman (1982), in a study that was in part discredited because some apparently successful companies experienced declining fortunes, identified a number of factors which appeared to explain the success of a number of large American businesses by focusing on corporate culture and its impact on corporate performance. At the time, the question raised was: if the cultural factors identified by Peters and Waterman were in fact transferable easily to other organizations, could they be the source of superior financial performance? Barney contends that valuable and rare cultures may be difficult, if not impossible, to imitate. Indeed, it is difficult to define culture clearly, particularly in respect of how it adds value to the product or service; whilst culture is often tied to historical aspects of company development and to the beliefs, personality and charisma of a particular strategic leader.

Online Cases 7.1 (The Body Shop) and 7.2 (Club Méditerranée) both provide examples of companies which have gained success and renown with a culture-based competitive advantage. While maintaining the underlying principles and values, both companies have had to rethink their strategies to remain competitive. Club Méditerranée highlights how difficult it can be to sustain competitive success when values are core but the competitive environment changes, also demonstrating the use of power by external shareholders to change the strategic leader when the strategy is proving unsuccessful.

The limits to excellence

Although some firms do appear to obtain superior financial performance from their cultures, it does not follow that firms who succeed in copying these cultural attributes will necessarily also achieve superior financial results. Organizations which pursue the excellence factors must surely improve their chances of success, but clearly there can be no guarantees. Ignoring these issues may increase the chances of failure.

The need to maintain E–V–R congruence in a dynamic, competitive environment must never be forgotten. During the early 1980s, Jan Carlzon turned around the struggling SAS (Scandinavian Airlines System) by focusing on improvements in service and communications. Profits were restored with improved revenues, but costs later increased as well. As a driving philosophy, the service culture had to give way to a focus on strategy and rationalization.

Changing culture

The culture of an organization may appear to be in need of change for any one of a number of reasons: e.g. the culture does not fit well with the needs of the environment or with the organization's resources, or that the company is not performing well and needs major strategic changes or even that the company is growing rapidly in a changing environment and needs to adapt.

Ideally, the culture and strategies being pursued will complement each other and, again ideally, the organization will be flexible and adaptable to change when it is appropriate. But these ideals will not always be achieved.

The culture of an organization can be changed, but it may not be easy. Strong leadership and vision is always required to champion the change process. If an organization is in real difficulty, and the threat to its survival is clearly recognized, behaviour can be changed through fear and necessity. However, people may not feel comfortable and committed to the changes they accept or are coerced into accepting. Behaviour may change, but not attitudes and beliefs. When an organization is basically successful the process of change again needs careful management – changing attitudes and beliefs does not itself guarantee a change in behaviour. It is not unusual for a team of senior managers to spend time, frequently at a location away from the organization itself, discussing these issues and becoming excited about a set of new values that they proclaim are the way forward. After the workshop, any commitment to the new values and to change can be easily lost once managers return to the daily grind and they become caught up again in immediate problems and difficulties. Their behaviour does not change and so the culture remains largely untouched.

The potential for changing the culture is affected by:

- the strength and history of the existing culture
- how well the culture is understood
- the personality and beliefs of the strategic leader, and
- the extent of the strategic need.

Lewin (1947) contends that there are three important stages in the process of change: unfreezing existing behaviour, changing attitudes and behaviour and refreezing the new behaviour as accepted common practice.

The first steps in changing culture are recognizing and diagnosing the existing culture, highlighting any weaknesses and stressing the magnitude of the need to change.

One way of changing behaviour would be the establishment of internal groups to study and benchmark competitors and set new performance standards, which would lead to wider discussion throughout the organization, supported by skills training – possibly including communication, motivation and financial awareness skills. People must become committed to the changes, which requires persistence by those who are championing the change and an emphasis on the significance and the desired outcomes.

Unless the changes become established and part of the culture, there will be a steady drift back to the previous pattern. While critical aspects of the culture should remain strategically consistent, it must not mean that the organization becomes resistant to change without some major upheaval. Competitive pressures require organizations to be vigilant, aware and constantly change-orientated, not change-resistant.

Resistance to change should always be expected. People may simply be afraid because they do not understand the reasons behind the proposed changes; they may mistrust colleagues or management because of previous experiences; communications may be poor; motivation and commitment may be missing; internal architecture may be weak, causing internal conflict and hostility; and the organization may simply not be good at sharing best practice and learning.

7.4 Culture – an international dimension

(In my mind) the England (football) team plays with passion; Germany is about determination; the French have subtlety and Spain demonstrate[s] pride.

ARSENE WENGER, MANAGER, ARSENAL FC

Cultural differences between nations and ethnic groups mean that what constitutes acceptable behaviour in one country (for example, communal nakedness in gender-segregated saunas in Finland) would be totally unacceptable in others. Ways of conducting discussions and deals vary, for example Indians always like and expect to negotiate. Some countries, such as France, have a high respect for tradition and the past, while others, such as the US, are more interested in future prospects. National (and ethnic) cultures influence the extent to which both individuals and organizations are judged on their track record and on their promise, and such differences are important because business is conducted across frontiers and because many organizations have bases in several countries. Organizations, therefore, have to adjust their style for different customers and markets and accept that there will be cultural differences between the various parts of the organization, and this affects the ability of the strategic leader to synthesize the various parts of the organization and achieve the potential synergies.

Related to these issues, research by Kanter (1991) drew out different perspectives on competitive success between the leading nations, where she argued that these stemmed from national cultures and cultural differences, indicating the following priorities:

- Japan   Product development
                 Management
                 Product quality
- USA   Customer service
                 Product quality
                 Technology
- Germany   Workforce skills
                 Problem-solving
                 Management

These conclusions may be summarized by arguing that Japan is driven by a commitment to innovation, America to customers and Germany to engineering.

Interestingly, the report highlighted how UK competitiveness had been enhanced by its drive to privatize public services and other state-owned organizations, the opening up of its capital markets and its encouragement of inward investment. At the same time, it is arguably inhibited by an education system which discourages rather than encourages creativity, individualism and entrepreneurship, by a general lack of language skills (including English amongst many of the 'indigenous' Caucasians) and, for many, a preference for leisure (referred to as 'the dole') over work.

Differences in international cultures have been examined by various authors (including Hofstede, 1991; Kluckhohn and Strodtbeck, 1961; Trompenaars and Hampden-Turner, 1997). The following points have been distilled from their findings and, although general conclusions may be drawn about cultural differences between nations, certain organizations in the same country do not automatically fit the national picture in every respect. In some respects, for example, Sony is typically Japanese whilst, in other respects, it behaves more like an American company, such that research has confirmed that many US citizens think that Sony is American!

Some cultures have…

1 Preferences for a watertight contractual approach, while others are more comfortable with trust and a handshake, such that the appropriate way of conducting business, therefore, varies accordingly.

2 Managers who operate with individual freedom and responsibility and with negotiations on a one-to-one basis, whilst in others there will invariably be a team of people involved. Where there are multiple decision-makers, there will sometimes be a clear hierarchy and recognition of the relative power of various individuals, whereas at other times such demarcations will be less obvious or visible.

3 Individual managers who can be relatively selfish in their outlook, or far more corporate, which can have a particular bearing on where managers' natural competitive energy is channelled. Is it directed at outside competitors, as realistically it should be, or at perceived internal rivals? Simply, would a culture of internal rivalry inside an organization be typical or rare?

4 Women managers, and some do not have any: either at all, or at least in positions of real authority.

5 Different attitudes to leisure activities, e.g. the image of the British bank manager who enjoys long lunches and regular golf matches with clients has been largely confined to history, but negotiations and networking away from the place of business (e.g. corporate hospitality at major sporting events) can still be important.

6 Varied senses of humour, which affects advertising and promotion, such that the same campaigns cannot necessarily be used on a global scale.

7 Similar or different perspectives on uncertainty, with some being relatively risk orientated (viewing environmental turbulence as a source of opportunity), looking to be proactive; while others seek to be more reactive and adaptive, attempting to find positions of stability amongst the perceived chaos.

Case 7.3, Kungkas Can Cook, discusses an Aborigine business in Australia's Northern Territory which has a strong cultural underpinning.

Case 7.3   Kungka's Can Cook   Aus

Kungka's Can Cook is the trading name of an indigenous outback catering business based in Alice Springs in the centre of Australia. 'Kungka' is an aboriginal word for women – and indeed the business was started in 2000 by two aboriginal mothers who between them had seven children. It has become a successful business – but there is far more to the story.

One of the co-founders, Rayleen Brown, has been the sole owner since her friend Gina Smith relocated to Tennant Creek, some 315 miles due north of Alice Springs on the main road to Darwin, in 2006 – too far to commute to work. She moved to help look after family, something quite normal amongst the Aboriginal people.

Rayleen and Gina both worked – Rayleen already ran a cafe that served both healthy and less healthy (too much fat, sugar and salt) dishes – but they envisioned a business that focused on natural bush foods which would (a) enable local people to eat more healthily given diet is a key part of a lifestyle and (b) introduce non-Aboriginals to tasty Aboriginal delicacies. Rayleen herself had spent a nomadic childhood 'living in nearly every town in the Northern Territory'. Her family sheltered in a bus when the notorious cyclone devastated Darwin in 1974. She learnt to be independent; one of six children, she had to. She was steeped in the culture of her people and determined to preserve key aspects of it. Both she and Gina were disappointed with the number of unhealthy options they saw on offer at catered functions they attended and believed passionately that food from natural sources could be tasty, nutritious and healthy all at the same time. Whilst they have succeeded with both objectives it wasn't an easy road.

The two women spent a year discussing the concept and drawing up a business plan that would allow them to apply for a relevant loan. They believed they needed a clear story, a clear direction and full compliance within the strictly regulated catering industry. Using a popular Aboriginal term they spent time 'dreaming'. They also wanted to be ready for the hurdles and barriers they knew they would have to face; they were seeking to understand the inherent risks in the business. In 2001,

and whilst waiting for the loan decision, Rayleen and Gina decided to tender for the contract to provide catering for 1400 people at a Dreaming Festival in Alice Springs, to which Aboriginals from across Australia would be coming. This was really a huge risk for them but they took it. They were awarded the contract but 'had nothing to use'. They had to 'gather, beg and borrow' and even persuaded someone in Sydney to send them a large warmer. At the end of a successful but very fraught venture they declared 'Now we could do bloody anything!'

The publicity they received and the subsequent loan was all they needed to get the business off the ground properly and they started catering for more and more events, with both Indigenous and non-Indigenous customers becoming keen fans of their cooking. They used the money to establish a fully equipped commercial kitchen in dedicated premises. The business remains largely focused around Alice Springs and the surrounding communities.

Their dishes would include slow-cooked (in a fire pit) kangaroo tails and honey extracted from honey ants; but even though the infamous witchetty grubs might be a delicacy and a treat for Aboriginal people they are not ubiquitously popular! They rely extensively on natural products from trees and bushes but always offer a mix of bush tucker and Western food. People can 'try the real thing' when they feel ready to do so; when they do they most quickly become a fan.

Today there are six full-time employees and others brought in as and when necessary. Family members are often involved and Rayleen has said (maybe quite seriously) that it is 'easier to fire members of your family if they don't perform'.

Suppliers from the Aboriginal community are preferred; young women are trained and mentored and offered opportunities many would not otherwise have. Rayleen has become an accomplished networker and is often heard on the radio and seen in schools 'telling her story'. Recipes are willingly shared. As a consequence Kungka's Can Cook plays a valuable community role, adhering to the Aboriginal culture, helping to preserve this culture and showing that entrepreneurial people are to be found amongst the Indigenous people. This is not a widely held view. Some in the Aboriginal community were openly critical – some would say this is an example of the Australasian '*Tall Poppy Syndrome*' where successful people are vilified for standing tall and independent. Not all non-Aboriginals would see Indigenous people as naturally entrepreneurial. Rayleen now wants Alice Springs to become the centre for bush tucker food in Australia – what she calls the 'first foods of the first Australians'. She is an entrepreneur and an enabler.

And what about the future? Maybe for her own ambitions Rayleen has done enough but there must be growth opportunities, albeit with greater risks. Perhaps she could look to widen the territorial reach, but given the distances in that part of Australia it would be hard to do this direct from Alice Springs. She might look to gather, process, package and distribute some of the foods she uses – in much the same way that some successful Asian restaurants in the UK have done with limited ranges of their own meals and sauces. But she would need a route to market, and the local market is very dispersed with a very thinly spread population.

Questions

1 How have aspects of Aborigine culture and values driven the strategy for this business?
2 Kungka's Can Cook appears to have developed E–V–R congruence – at least for a limited market in the Northern Territory. How transferable might this be?

Would it be fair to assume that there actually are market opportunities but resource constraints?

Japan rose in the second half of the twentieth century to become a major global economic force, with some Japanese companies extremely prominent in certain industries. The Japanese style of management is different from that found in most Western countries and, while it cannot simply be copied – largely because of cultural differences – it offers a number of important and valuable lessons. Consequently, this chapter continues with a section on Japanese culture and management style, and afterwards a brief and contrasting summary of China. In recent years, China's economy has grown rapidly as China has emerged as a leading global manufacturer. One key difference is that the Chinese (despite large numbers of PhD graduates of Chinese origin from Western universities) have not – as yet – provided the technological inspiration that has come from Japan. We also include a short discussion on the Indian way of doing business. India is another fast-growing economy in the developing world.

The Japanese culture and style of management

Without question, Japanese companies have become formidable competitors in several industries. In recent years Toyota and Sony have been the only two non-American businesses to appear in the world's top ten most respected companies. For many years they have been the principal challengers of Western firms serious about world markets. More recently domestic recession, a high yen and intensifying competition from other Pacific Rim countries (many with lower wages) have restrained Japan's global expansion. Woodford (2012) demonstrated that top-level corruption has been found and covered up in one leading Japanese business, Olympus. However, a study of the philosophies, strategies and tactics adopted by Japanese companies will yield a number of valuable insights into competitive strategy, even though it is impractical to suggest that Western businesses could simply learn to copy their Japanese rivals. This section looks at some of the reasons for Japan's economic rise and success; it has to be acknowledged that since the 1990s some of the practices have changed but the differences with the American and European approaches provide real food for thought.

Deal and Kennedy (1982) have argued that 'Japan Inc.' is a culture, with considerable co-operation between industry, the banking systems and government. For this reason, certain aspects of the Japanese culture are difficult to imitate (although the UK government has done its best inadvertently to move towards a Japanese model in some respects – although banks in the UK have historically been public companies with their own shareholders, many are now at least partially nationalized following the banking crisis of 2009 onwards).

Another key structural feature historically has been the *keiretsu*, or corporate families, whereby a unique mix of ownerships and alliances makes hostile takeovers very unlikely. At its height, for example, the powerful Mitsubishi *keiretsu* represented 216 000 employees in 29 organizations as diverse as banking, brewing, shipping, shipbuilding, property, oil, aerospace and textiles. The companies held, on average, 38 per cent of each other's shares; directors were exchanged; and the fact that 15 of the companies were located together in one district of Tokyo facilitated linkages of various forms, including intertrading wherever this was practical. The *keiretsu* influence is fading as Japanese companies are locating more and more production overseas in their search for lower manufacturing costs. Mitsubishi's shipping company, for instance, has begun to buy vessels manufactured in Korean yards; Japanese shipbuilders are no longer an automatic low-price competitor.

Culture plays a significant role at the heart of the Japanese strategy process.

In Japan the historic focus has been on human resources (Pucik and Hatvany, 1983) which became the basis for three key strategic thrusts which are expressed as a number of management techniques, and which have acted as key determinants of the actual strategies pursued (Figure 7.4). The three strategic thrusts are the notion of an internal labour market within the organization, a unique company philosophy and intensive socialization throughout the working life.

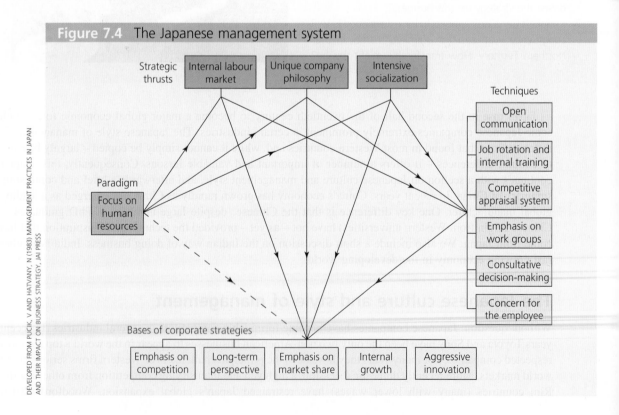

Figure 7.4   The Japanese management system

DEVELOPED FROM PUCIK, V AND HATVANY, N (1983) MANAGEMENT PRACTICES IN JAPAN AND THEIR IMPACT ON BUSINESS STRATEGY, JAI PRESS

The internal labour market is based on the tradition of lifetime employment whereby young men (not women) who joined large companies after school or university were expected to remain with them for life and in return were offered job security. Commitment and loyalty to the employer result. With recession in recent years and the growing use of sub-contractors, this practice has been less widespread.

The articulated and enacted unique philosophy is again designed to generate commitment and loyalty with the argument that familiarity with the goals of a company helps to establish values and provides direction for effort and behaviour. YKK's 'Cycle of Goodness' (Strategy in Action 7.1) is an excellent example; we analyzed YKK in Chapter 5.

The potential benefits of a company philosophy will only be gained if the philosophy is communicated to employees and demonstrated by managers. Hence this is a key aspect of company socialization in Japan, which starts with initial training and continues with further training throughout the working life.

These three strategic thrusts are closely linked to six management techniques used extensively in Japanese firms.

Open communication and sharing information across departmental boundaries aims to develop a climate of trust and a team spirit within the organization, which is enhanced by close integration between managers and employees. Job rotation and the internal training programmes supplement this communication system because through them employees become more aware of what happens throughout the organization. Because of relatively low labour turnover, promotion opportunities are very limited and advancement is slow and often based on seniority. However, performance is essential, and employees are carefully and regularly appraised in their abilities to get things done and to co-operate with others – particularly important, since Japanese companies revolve around groups rather than individuals, with work being assigned to teams of employees. Together with the use of quality circles (whereby groups of employees are encouraged to discuss issues and problems and suggest improvements), this approach is seen as a key motivator. There is considerable emphasis on consultative decision-making, involving these working groups, and a desire for consensus decisions.

Strategy in Action 7.1 The Cycle of Goodness

The Cycle of Goodness was created by Tadeo Yoshida, President, YKK.

YKK is the world's leading manufacturer of zip fasteners. YKK produces and markets zips throughout the world, and is vertically integrated, designing and manufacturing much of its own machinery.

I firmly believe in the spirit of social service.

Wages alone are not sufficient to assure our employees of a stable life and a rising standard of living. For this reason we return to them a large share of the fruits of their labour, so that they may also participate in capital accumulation and share in the profits of the firm. Each employee, depending on his means, deposits with the company at least ten per cent of his wages and monthly allowances, and 50 per cent of his bonus; the company, in turn, pays interest on these savings. Moreover, as this increases capital, the employees benefit further as stockholders of the firm. It is said that the accumulation of savings distinguishes man from animals. Yet, if the receipts of a day are spent within that day, there can be no such cycle of saving.

The savings of all YKK employees are used to improve production facilities, and contribute directly to the prosperity of the firm. Superior production facilities improve the quality of the goods produced. Lower prices increase demand. And both factors contribute to the prosperity of other industries that use our products.

As society prospers, the need for raw materials and machinery of all sorts increases, and the benefits of this cycle spread out not just to this firm, but to all related industries. Thus the savings of our employees, by enhancing the prosperity of the firm, are returned to them as dividends that enrich their lives. This results in increased savings which further advance the firm. Higher incomes mean higher tax payments, and higher tax payments enrich the lives of every citizen. In this manner, business income directly affects the prosperity of society; for businesses are not mere seekers after profit, but vital instruments for the improvement of society.

This cycle enriches our free society and contributes to the happiness of those who work within it. The perpetual working of this cycle produces perpetual prosperity for all. This is the cycle of goodness.

YKK **http://www.ykk.com**

This generates greater loyalty to the decisions and to implementation. Finally, managers are encouraged to spend time with employees discussing both performance and personal problems. Companies have also frequently provided housing and various other services for employees.

Several Japanese companies have invested in manufacturing plants in the USA and Europe in recent years. In a number of cases, they have selected industries where the country had already ceased to manufacture products because of an inability to compete (e.g. television sets and video recorders) or where the competitive edge had declined, for example motor vehicles. The British car industry fell behind the Japanese and German producers in terms of quality and productivity and has struggled to catch up. The first Japanese car plant in the UK was built by Nissan near Sunderland and, using a Japanese approach – rather than adopting all the techniques described in this section – it has become the most productive car plant in the UK, and one of Nissan's most efficient anywhere in the world. Yet again, Nissan's most productive plant has had to reduce output in 2009 as its market had declined.

Hill (1990) explains that the key human resources aspects of the Nissan UK strategy are as follows:

- There is a single union agreement, with the Automotive Employees' Union (AEU).
- All employees (including managers) have the same conditions of employment, and wear similar blue overalls at work.
- There are no (inflexible) written job descriptions.
- There is no clocking on and no privileged parking.
- Absenteeism has remained very low.
- There are daily communications meetings – searching for continuous improvement.
- Employees often go to Japan for training – skilled workers learn both operational and maintenance skills.
- The training budget, equivalent to 14 per cent of sales revenue, is exceptionally high for a British company. A typical employee will receive 9 days on-the-job and 12 days off-the-job training each year.
- Supervisors are empowered managers. They recruit and select their own staff (individually they are responsible for about 20 employees), and they control the layout and operation of their own part of the production line.

The core of management is the art of mobilizing every ounce of intelligence in the organization and pulling together the intellectual resources of all employees in the service of the firm. We know that the intelligence of a handful of technocrats, however brilliant and smart they may be, is no longer enough. Only by drawing on the combined brain power of all its employees can a firm face up to the turbulence and constraints of today's environment.

MR. KONOSUKE MATSUSHITA, MATSUSHITA ELECTRICAL INDUSTRIAL COMPANY LTD

Quality and competition

Prahalad and Hamel (1985) have suggested that the Japanese, 'rewrite the rules of the game to take their competitors by surprise'. Through technology, design, production costs, distribution and selling arrangements, pricing and service they seek to build 'layers of competitive advantage' rather than concentrate on just one aspect. Many competitors in the West think more narrowly. They suggest that Japanese companies are successful in part because they have a clear mission and statement of strategic intent, and a culture which provides both opportunity and encouragement to change things incrementally (Prahalad and Hamel, 1985). Getting things right first time and every time – total quality management – is endemic in the culture.

Internationally, Japanese companies may not be consistent with their strategies; instead they will seek the best competitive opportunities in different places and they will change continually as new opportunities arise and are created.

Japanese companies benchmark against the best in the world and willingly customize their products to meet local market demand.

Long-term perspective

While many Western companies concentrate on short-term strategies, influenced often by financial pressures, the Japanese take a long-term perspective.

Emphasis on market share

Japanese companies are competitive, growth orientated and anxious to build and sustain high market shares in world markets, enabling them to provide the job security that is a fundamental aspect of the culture. They often use their experience (and the concept of the experience curve) to develop strategies aimed at market dominance with a long-term view of costs and prices.

Internal growth

Mergers, acquisitions and divestitures are relatively uncommon in Japan – the Japanese favour the internal production system and innovation.

In a book on Japanese manufacturing techniques, Schonberger (1984) argued that a major reason for Japan's success has been its ability to use its resources well, better than many Western competitors. In many factories, he contends, the equipment is no better than that used elsewhere in the world but, wherever they can, Japanese companies invest in the best equipment available. Managerial skills are used in improvement drives, a search for simple solutions and, in particular, a meticulous attention to detail. Simplicity is important since the management and shop floor can relate better to each other; and flexible techniques and workforces result in low stock production systems, efficiency and lower costs. We can see this reflected in Case 6.2, where we discussed Toyota's cost leadership strategy.

The ability to trust and establish close links with other companies in the supply chain allows focused specialization and just-in-time manufacturing with low inventories. However, this type of dependency can act as a hindrance to global expansion until comparative supplier links can be established.

Innovation

Research and development is deemed important and funded appropriately. As a result, much of Japan's technology has advanced quickly, and firms who fail to innovate go out of business. Ohmae (1985) has described Japan as a 'very unforgiving economy', with thousands of corporations destroyed every year through bankruptcy. He points out that Japan is selective about the industries in which research and development will be concentrated. Japan has, for example, spent a relatively high proportion of its research and development money in ceramics and steel and, as a result, has become a world leader in fibre optics, ceramics and mass-produced large-scale integrated circuits. For similar reasons, the USA is a world leader in biotechnology and specialized semiconductors, and Europe in chemicals and pharmaceuticals.

Product innovation in Japan is fast and competitive. For example, Sony launched the first miniaturized camcorder (hand held video camera and recorder) in June 1989. Weighing less than 700g (1.5lb), it was one-quarter of the size of existing camcorders. Within 6 months, Matsushita and JVC had introduced lighter models. Within a further 6 months, there was additional competition from Canon, Sanyo, Ricoh and Hitachi. Sony introduced two new models in summer 1990. One was the lightest then available; the other had superior technical features. More recent models feature larger viewfinders and allow the user to hold the camcorder at arm's length instead of up to the eye. In recent years, we have seen exactly the same trend with laptop computers.

This faster model replacement is linked to an ability to break even financially with fewer sales of each model. Japan has achieved this with efficient and flexible manufacturing systems and a greater willingness to use common, rather than model-specific, components.

Individual Western companies have proved that it is possible, with determination and distinctive products, to penetrate Japanese markets successfully, but contenders can expect fierce resistance and defensive competition.

The approach in China

Although they are relatively close neighbours in the Far East, China and Japan are very different in their approach and culture.

Research evidence suggests – and obviously there are some generalizations here – that Chinese workers will strive very hard to solve crises and they take direction well. They are hungry to learn and very committed to the organization. Chinese businesses are more risk oriented than is the case with Japan. Whilst Japanese companies are very innovative, they are not as intuitively entrepreneurial.

On the other hand, the Chinese are not as natural at teamworking as their counterparts in Japan – where a team culture is endemic – and their punctuality can sometimes be questioned. They do not readily share their knowledge and insights – and they are unlikely to challenge and question strategic direction, but rather obey instruction. There is some evidence of resistance to change.

Our final case, Case 7.4 on Aiptek, a Taiwanese business, allows you to consider the cultural features of both Japan and China in a particular context.

Case 7.4   Aiptek   Taiwan

Aiptek was founded in 1997 by Peter Chen in Taiwan and was located in the HsinChu Industrial Park. This location is commonly known as Taiwan's 'Silicon Valley'. The company set out to develop a range of innovative products based on electronic handwriting, digital video, wireless communication and opto-electronic technologies. In 2000 the company launched its first generation PenCam and the product soon became available in retail stores in Japan and in the USA. In 2001 its PenCam II was a big success in the CeBit Computer Exhibition in Germany. From this point Aiptek sales and profits increased rapidly.

The company continued to launch new innovative products. In 2003 it launched the world's first MP3 digital video player called Pocket DV. Peter Chen the founder of Aiptek hoped to take advantage of the surging demand for hi-tech products brought about in part by the rapid decrease in the cost of crucial hi-tech components brought about by standardization in the manufacturing processes involved. In Taiwan the government sought to assist companies such as Aiptek with tax incentives for investing in technology based research and development.

The initial success of Aiptek was based on the adoption of a simple management structure with all employees directly involved in projects with the company actively promoting its share plan for all employees. As Aiptek became an international business it became involved in product diversification, joint ventures and alliances. Issues began to arise with poor product quality and rushed new product development whereas initially the success of the business had been based on the swift development and launch of new products. The resources of Aiptek became stretched between conflicting demands for capital to fund research as opposed to marketing. The company found itself unable to quickly expand production capacity as it took too long to install manufacturing equipment and recruit and train new skilled employees. Because of these conflicting pressures Aiptek formed a strategic alliance with an OEM called YHi Company who could provide the high volume manufacturing capacity Aiptek needed to meet the demand for its products.

To raise further funds Aiptek had successfully offered an IPO in Taiwan in May 2001. However major concerns over increasing competition led Aiptek to both relocate and expand its production capacity by moving its production facility to China. This meant that Aiptek could consolidate back in Taiwan its research and product development, marketing and brand development functions away from its manufacturing division. On the opposite side the termination of the OEM alliance with YHi due to poor quality issues meant that Aiptek had to shoulder all the risks relating to product quality. At this time Aiptek formed another strategic alliance with AVAC Co. Ltd to co-ordinate the development of crucial components inside digital cameras thus sharing research and development risks.

By 2003 Aiptek had become an international based company with a manufacturing subsidiary in China employing 1000 people, three marketing subsidiaries in the USA, Europe and China respectively with its headquarters in HsinChu in Taiwan. However Aiptek had problems. As indicated, its move to China had presented quality problems. The previous alliance with YHi saw losses due to bad quality at 3 per cent of inventory value. By 2007 losses from bad quality had surged to 30 per cent of inventory value. The initial strategy of having production in China but research and development and marketing in Taiwan had not worked as well as the company intended. Research groups had to support product manufacturing in China to such an extent that the research crews were complaining of exhaustion. The pressures on them led to delays in new product development. In addition, marketing subsidiaries were feeling the pressures on them from bad product quality. As a result the company was facing a worsening cash-flow problem.

The solution that they arrived at in 2007 was to sell the manufacturing subsidiary in China to Gemtek Co. Ltd and to sign a long-term deal with Gemtek as the OEM supplier to Aiptek.

Questions

1 What are the main lessons of the Aiptek change of strategy in 2007? Is being a manufacturer incompatible with a major research and development function in such a fast-moving industry as digital cameras and camcorders?

2 Can you see evidence of the Chinese culture in this case? Is Aiptek more Japanese than Chinese in its culture?

3 Aiptek continues as a robust business – has it needed to make further strategic changes?

AIPTEK **www.aiptek.com.tw**

The India way

India is another developing country that has been enjoying above average (in global terms) economic growth. Software development is one example where India has been able to develop and sustain a strong competitive position. The ability to work naturally in the English language and to electronically transfer data files instantly have been valuable – as we see later (in Chapter 12) in the case of Infosys. At the same time, there is still considerable poverty in India, and the gap between the wealthiest and the poorest remains immense.

Capelli *et al.* (2010) show that behind this success is an innovative and exportable (replicable) way of doing business. As with Japan, there are serious lessons to be learned. India has the advantage of low-labour costs but many educated people understand and speak English. Traditional values of respect (for, say, government and family) have been retained – some aspects are a legacy from the years of Colonial control – and yet Indian employees can be intuitive in their search for competitive advantage. There are some very large and powerful conglomerates, such as Tata, which, as we saw earlier, is a large steelmaker and now owner of Jaguar and Land Rover. Case 6.6 earlier described the development of the Tata Nano car. In conceiving this car, Tata took a different perspective on competitiveness and asked 'how much can we realistically leave out'? They designed a small and very basic car which could be produced at low cost and thus marketed as the cheapest car in the world. When thinking about production, they worked on a 'kit' approach such that semi-assembled car sections could be moved around India for final assembly close to local markets in this huge country.

Capelli *et al.* (2010) argue that the India Way is about focusing on the long-term and not short-term shareholder expectations; and that the combined prosperity of company, employees and community matters. It helps develop valuable trust amongst the workforce. They emphasize four themes:

- A holistic engagement with employees – where people are seen as assets which should be developed and not 'costs to be reduced'. Their knowledge and innovativeness must be harnessed. We can again see evidence of this in another later case, the one of the Dabbawallas of Mumbai in Chapter 9.

- Improvisation and adaptiveness – in a sense instinctive entrepreneurship, but reacting to opportunities rather than creating opportunities.

- Constantly sharing information and knowledge to create new value for customers – always embracing the reality that many Indian customers will have only relatively modest spending power.

- Shared corporate values that embrace a social and community purpose.

Note

We do not offer a Research Snapshot in this section because culture is a generic theme, but please see the bibliography at the back of the book.

Summary

Culture is the way in which an organization performs its tasks, the way its people think, feel and act in response to opportunities and threats, the ways in which objectives and strategies are set and decisions made: reflecting emotional issues and it is not easily analyzed, quantified or changed. Nevertheless, it is a key influence on strategic choice, strategy implementation and strategic change – until we understand the culture of an organization we cannot understand strategic management in that organization.

A large organization is unlikely to be just one single, definable culture as it is more likely to be a loose or tight amalgam of different cultures.

It is quite normal for culture to be influenced by a strong strategic leader and his or her beliefs and values.

In a very broad sense, we can think of culture as a mixture of behaviour (the manifestations of culture) and underlying attitudes and values, such that it is easier to change one of these rather than both simultaneously.

There is no 'ideal culture' as such, because key elements typically have a flip side and, therefore, a style and approach that is appropriate at a particular time can quickly become out of date and in need of change.

A useful grid for analyzing the culture of any organization would comprise:

- manifestations – artefacts; values; underlying assumptions; behaviour
- people – stories; leadership; communications

- power – ownership and structure; personal power; organizational politics.

Handy proposes four cultural types which help to explain the culture, style and approach of different organizations. These are the power culture (typical of small, entrepreneurial organizations), the role culture (larger and more formal organizations), the task culture (the complex organization seeking to achieve internal synergies through effective linkages) and the person culture (built around the individual managers' needs).

In an alternative and equally significant contribution, Miles and Snow differentiate *defenders* (conservative and low-risk organizations), *prospectors* (innovative and entrepreneurial), *analyzers* (limited change with measured steps) and *reactors* (followers), which can be readily linked to styles of strategy creation.

We can only understand culture when we understand power inside an organization. Who has power, how do they acquire it and how do they use it?

A number of books on the general theme of 'organizational excellence' have highlighted how it is culture that is at the heart of success. Although general themes and lessons can be teased out, an organization cannot simply replicate the culture of another successful organization and become successful itself.

There are important cultural differences between nations. This has implications for businesses which operate or trade globally.

Online cases for this chapter

Online Case 7.1: The Body Shop

Online Case 7.2: Club Méditerranée

Questions and research assignments

1 Use the text in Case 7.2 (IKEA) to complete a culture grid (Figure 7.1) for IKEA.

2 Take an organization with which you are familiar and evaluate it in terms of Handy's and Miles and Snow's typologies.

3 List other organizations that you know which would fit into the categories not covered in your answer to Question 2.

For both Questions 2 and 3, you should comment on whether or not you feel your categorization is appropriate.

4 Considering the organization that you used for Question 2, assess the power levers of the strategic leader and other identifiable managers.

5 Thinking of the identified cultural priorities for Japan, Germany and the USA, listed in the text, what do you think the cultural priorities of your own national businesses are?

Internet and library projects

1 The National Health Service

British Prime Minister John Major announced a new Citizen's Charter in July 1991. This implied a change of attitude for the NHS: patients should be seen as customers with rights, rather than people who should be grateful for treatment, however long the wait. From April 1992, hospitals would have to set standards for maximum waiting times.

This followed on from the 1989 NHS White Paper, Working for Patients, which was designed to achieve:

- increased performance of all hospitals and general practitioners (GPs) to the level of the best (significant differences existed in measured performances)
- patients receiving better health care and a greater choice of services through improved efficiencies and effectiveness in the use of NHS resources
- greater satisfaction and rewards for NHS staff.

In subsequent years, how did this impact on NHS strategies?

2 In 1997 a Labour government was elected and it set about changing the Conservative philosophy, dismantling and replacing a number of strategies.

What was the Labour approach? Has it changed the culture in any way? Indeed, did the culture need changing? The new Coalition government (elected in 2010) decided it did and introduced new legislation in 2012, where in essence GPs became more influential and competition from the private sector more evident. What impact might this have on the NHS culture and employees?

3 Can the relative success of the NHS ever be evaluated effectively without imputing political and cultural concerns?

4 Research how profitable John Lewis and Waitrose have been in comparison with their major competitors in the last 5 years. What conclusions can you draw?

John Lewis Partnership **http://www.johnlewis .co.uk Waitrose http://www.waitrose.com**

5 Find out where your nearest John Lewis or Waitrose store is and if possible visit it. Can you detect any differences in attitude between the John Lewis staff and those who work in similar mainstream department stores?

John Lewis Partnership **http://www.johnlewis .co.uk Waitrose http://www.waitrose.com**

Strategy activity

BP and Shell: cultural roots

British Petroleum (BP) and Anglo-Dutch Shell are two of the leading oil companies in the world. American Exxon-Mobil and the amalgamation of Total and Elf (both French) and Petrofina (Belgian) are the others. They are all involved in exploration, drilling, refining and transporting oil and its derived products.

The industry has been characterized by mergers and consolidation in a search for scale and critical mass. The oil companies are pressurized by the countries where oil is located (who, not unexpectedly, want to control both access and prices) and governments in consumer countries who are worried about escalating oil prices. The powerful OPEC (Organization of Petroleum Exporting Countries) acts as a cartel to regulate commodity prices.

In recent years both BP and Shell have had to deal with crises, some of them self-created. Shell was found to have misreported its assets by overestimating reserves. BP had to deal with the fallout when its highly acclaimed Chairman, Lord Browne, resigned following published details about his personal life. The company was also in trouble: first, after a fatal explosion at one of its refineries in Texas and, second, after it was deemed culpable when oil was spilled into the Gulf of Mexico. BP's commitment to safety was in question.

In the context of the supply chain, BP is seen as primarily a downstream business. Started over 100 years ago in what is now Iran, BP began in exploration. Year-on-year, it replaces in reserves at least as much as it takes out. It is currently developing fields in Azerbaijan, Egypt, Angola, Libya and Oman. But in recent years, its upstream refineries have not been operating at full capacity.

In contrast, Shell is more upstream having started as a shipping company. Shell pioneered bulk oil tankers. Having been caught out for overestimating its reserves, it is seen to be weaker than BP in terms of future supply potential. But its refineries deliver three times the profits of those owned by BP. Shell is investing heavily in different sources of energy, such as liquefied natural gas.

Before the Gulf crisis, one analyst commented that BP looked strong in the short term but Shell might be a better long-term prospect.

Question

1 How much do you think cultural roots will affect strategy and culture?

References

Barney, J.B. (1986) Organization culture: can it be a source of sustained competitive advantage? *Academy of Management Review*, 11 (3).

Berry, D. (1983) The perils of trying to change corporate culture, *Financial Times*, 14 December.

Capelli, P., Singh, H., Singh, J. and Useem, M. (2010) *The India Way*, Harvard Business Press.

Deal, T. and Kennedy, A. (1982) *Corporate Cultures. The Rites and Rituals of Corporate Life*, Addison-Wesley.

French, J.R.P. and Raven, B. (1959) The bases of social power. *In Studies in Social Power* (ed. D. Cartwright), University of Michigan Press.

Hampden-Turner, C. (1990) Corporate culture – from vicious to virtuous circles, *The Economist*.

Handy, C.B. (1976) *Understanding Organizations*, Penguin. The ideas are elaborated in Handy, CB (1978) Gods of Management, Souvenir Press.

Harrison, R. (1972) Understanding your organization's character, *Harvard Business Review*, May–June.

Hill, R. (1990) Nissan and the art of people management, *Director*, March.

Hofstede, G. (1991) *Cultures and Organization: Software of the Mind*, McGraw Hill.

Kakabadse, A. (1982) *Culture of the Social Services*, Gower.

Kanter, R.M. (1991) Transcending business boundaries: 12000 world managers view change, *Harvard Business Review*, May–June.

Kluckhohn, C. and Strodtbeck, F. (1961) *Variations in Value Orientations*, Peterson.

Leadbetter, C. and Rudd, R. (1991) What drives the lords of the deal? *Financial Times*, 20 July.

Lewin, K. (1947) Frontiers in group dynamics: concept, method and reality in social science, *Human Relations*, 1.

Miles, R.E. and Snow, C.C. (1978) *Organization Strategy, Structure and Process*, McGraw-Hill.

Ohmae, K. (1985) *Triad Power*, Free Press.

Peters, T.J. (1988) *Thriving on Chaos*, Knopf.

Peters, T.J. and Waterman, R.H. Jr (1982) *In Search of Excellence: Lessons from America's Best Run Companies*, Harper and Row. Original article: Peters, TJ (1980) Putting excellence into management, Business *Week*, 21 July.

Pramalhad, C.K. and Hamel, G. (1985) Address to the Annual Conference of the Strategic Management Society, Barcelona, October.

Press, G. (1990) Assessing competitors' business philosophies, *Long Range Planning*, 23 (5).

Pucik, V. and Hatvany, N. (1983) Management practices in Japan and their impact on business strategy, *Advances in Strategic Management*, vol. 1, JAI Press.

Pümpin, C. (1987) *The Essence of Corporate Strategy*, Gower.

Schein, E.H. (1985) *Organizational Culture and Leadership*, Jossey Bass.

Schonberger, R.J. (1984) *Japanese Manufacturing Techniques*, Free Press.

Schwartz, H. and Davis, S.M. (1981) Matching corporate culture and business strategy, *Organizational Dynamics*, Summer.

Trompenaars, F. and Hampden-Turner, C. (1997) *Riding the Waves of Culture: Understanding Cultural Diversity in Business*, Nicholas Brealey Publishing.

Woodford, M. (2012) *Exposure: Inside the Olympus Scandal*, Portfolio Penguin.

Part 3 Strategy development

In Part 2 we examined the techniques for conducting an analysis based on positioning and competitiveness. We examined the following approaches; market-driven, resource-based and competitor-influenced. Part 3 looks at how organizations might, and in reality do, generate new ideas for future strategies. The following chapters will cover:

- Alternatives and choice – Chapter 8. Organizations will change their directions and strategies and they do not always pursue the same strategy in the same way. We cannot finally judge the worthiness of a particular choice until we take account of the organization's ability to implement the strategy that it has chosen. This chapter outlines the various strategic alternatives that might be available to an organization in thinking and deciding where it wants to go, and for helping to close the planning gap.

- Planning in strategy – Chapter 9. Strategic planning using techniques and formalized procedures is just one of the ways in which strategies are created. Strategies can also be provided by the strategic leader and be decided by managers in real time. Intended strategies, say those selected by the leader or through a formal planning system, have to be implemented, and during this implementation they may well be changed incrementally. In addition, flexible organizations will adapt all the time by responding to new opportunities and threats. Our contemporary approach to strategic planning is based on a mixture of planning techniques, intellectual input and action plans for implementing strategies; and central to the whole process are current strategic issues.

- Leadership – Chapter 10. As well as leading from the front, it is also important for a leader to create a climate that facilitates emergent change – appropriate employees should be empowered, encouraged and energized. Intrapreneurs then lead the emergent change initiatives. Leadership is both a job and a process – a process concerned with influence and change. It requires both personal characteristics and leadership skills. The skills can be learned, but effective leaders need to possess certain characteristics in the first place. Successful leaders also tend to build effective teams to support them. In exploring these issues, this chapter also looks at how some leaders are perceived to fail, and at the vital issue of leadership succession.

Chapter 8

Creating and formulating strategy: alternatives, evaluation and choice

PART 1
Understanding strategy

1 What is strategy and who is involved?
- Appendix

2 The business model and the revenue model

3 Strategic purpose
- Supplement: Using frameworks to analyze strategy cases

PART 5
Strategy implementation

14 Strategy implementation and structure

15 Leading change

16 Managing strategy in the organization

17 Final thoughts and reflections: the practice of strategy

STRATEGIC MANAGEMENT: AWARENESS AND CHANGE

PART 2
Analysis and positioning

4 The business environment and strategy

5 Resource-led strategy

6 The dynamics of competition

7 Introducing culture and values

PART 4
Strategic growth issues

11 Strategic control and measuring success

12 Issues in strategic and international growth

13 Failure, consolidation and recovery strategies

PART 3
Strategy development

8 Creating and formulating strategy: alternatives, evaluation and choice

9 Strategic planning

10 Strategic leadership and intrapreneurship: towards visionary leadership?

Learning objectives

Having read to the end of this chapter, you should be able to:

- describe the planning, visionary and emergent approaches to strategy and how emergent strategy includes adapting to new opportunities and changing intended strategies incrementally as they are implemented **(Section 8.1)**

- identify and describe a number of possible strategic alternatives, separated into limited growth, substantive growth and **retrenchment** clusters, with additional focus on innovation and temporal differences **(Section 8.2)**

- define the key criteria for evaluating the appropriateness, feasibility and desirability of a particular strategic alternative, and discuss why there might be a trade-off between these factors **(Section 8.3)**

- summarize a number of alternative theories of decision-making and explain why subjectivity can sometimes result in poor decisions, hence the importance of judgement **(Section 8.4)**.

Introduction

The following chapters show why it is the case that every manager can be a strategy maker, although it should be said that not every manager can be either a leader or an entrepreneur. This chapter outlines the various strategic alternatives that might be available to an organization in thinking and deciding where it wants to go, and for helping to close the planning gap. The appropriate strategy always matches the environment, values and resources congruently.

> *If you're in the penalty area and aren't quite sure what to do with the ball, just stick it in the net and we'll discuss your options afterwards.*

BILL SHANKLY (1914–1981), MANAGER, LIVERPOOL FOOTBALL CLUB

Football or any professional sport provides a useful metaphor for understanding strategy creation. Planning, vision, emergence, competition, team and individual contributions, setbacks and unexpected events are all relevant. The extent of significance of each will vary with the sport and the level at which it is played. Teams or, in the case of sports such as tennis, individuals will begin all important matches with a game plan. They will have studied their opponents, assessed their relative strengths and weaknesses, thought about their natural game and about how they might approach this particular match and worked out how they might be beaten. In a football game, coaches will have helped the players with the analysis and the tactics. Normally, the objective will be about winning. In some instances it can be about not losing (a subtle difference) or winning might be qualified by adding a 'means' objective related to approach and style. These game plans will undoubtedly *inform* the players, but it may be impossible to carry them out to the letter, ensured by unexpected tactics from their opponents.

Once the game is underway, the intended plans and strategies will be adjusted through incremental changes. Broadly, however, they will be implemented, certainly as long as the game is being won and not lost. At the same time, new and unexpected opportunities will be presented during the game, and good teams will be able to adapt.

Of course, and keeping with the literary flavour of this introduction, 'the best laid plans o' mice and men gang aft a gley' (Robert Burns). The opponents may prove stronger and more disciplined than predicted and may take the lead in the first minute and seize control of the game. In this case, there will be a need to adapt to the threats and change the tactics and thus the ability to remain cohesive and disciplined as a team is essential. In football pundit terminology, this scenario is usually described as 'keeping your shape'. In other words, don't panic.

At any time, there is an opportunity for individuals to show initiative and to shine. A strong, experienced and maybe visionary team manager (the strategic leader in this example) can act as a master tactician and an inspiration both beforehand and from the sidelines during the game. Talented players – with individual goals, spectacular saves or important tackles at key moments – will often make important contributions and, by doing so, encourage their colleagues also to make the extra effort that tips the balance. As commentators always say, a game is not lost until the final whistle: teams often do go one or two goals down before recovering to win.

8.1 Strategy creation

Chapter 1 explained how strategy creation involves three strands:

- *planning*, both systematic and formal strategic planning systems and informal cerebral planning
- *vision* and visionary leadership, and
- *emergent strategies*, incremental, adaptive changes to predetermined intended strategies involving learning and responsiveness to opportunities and threats.

Strategy and strategic management embrace the corporate portfolio of businesses and the search for competitive advantage, which arises from the functional activities that an organization undertakes (Figure 8.1). Visionary ideas *pull* the organization forward and, where these result in significant changes, they will often be associated with the strategic leader. Planning *pushes* everything forward. Emergent intrapreneurial changes initiated and implemented by individual managers throughout the organization *support* and complete the process.

If all strategies were planned formally, then organizations could look back and review the decisions that they had made over a period of time since they would have had a clear recorded statement of intent which matched these events closely. In reality, stated plans and actual events are unlikely to match closely because, in addition to strategies that have emerged and been introduced entrepreneurially, there are likely to have been expectations and planned possible strategies that have not proved to be viable. However, broad directions can be established and planned and then detailed strategies emerge as part of an ongoing internal learning experience.

Figure 8.1   Strategy creation

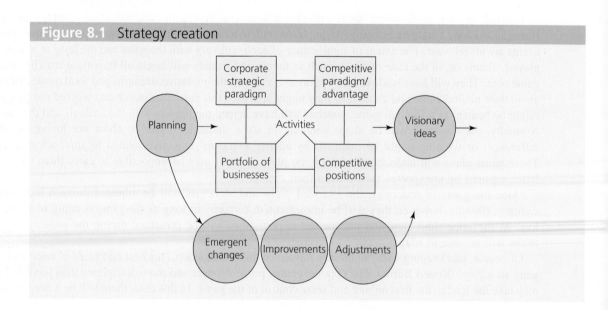

Idenburg (1993) distinguishes between formal planning systems, learning or real-time planning (a 'formal' approach to adaptive strategy creation), incremental change and logical incrementalism (with flexibility for managers to experiment) and emergent strategies (where the organizations do not create objectives, but are very flexible). Mintzberg and Waters (1985) and Bailey and Johnson (1992) have also shown how the simple three-mode categorization might be extended, but the underlying implications remain unchanged. A number of points should be noted:

- Although it is not made explicit, some strategies, especially those formulated by a visionary entrepreneur, attempt to shape and change the environment, rather than react to changing circumstances.

- The organization structure and the actual planning process will affect the nature of planned objectives and strategies. Wherever a group of managers is involved in planning, their personal values and relative power will be reflected. See Cyert and March's behavioural theory in Chapter 3.

- Adaptive changes also reflect the values, power and influence of managers.

The three modes described above are not mutually exclusive, and one mode frequently leads on from another. The implementation of visionary ideas and strategies typically requires careful planning, for example, which will invariably bring about incremental changes. In Chapter 1 it was confirmed that all three modes will be found in an organization simultaneously, but the mix and prioritization will be particular to an individual company. This key point is illustrated in Figure 8.2. It was also emphasized that individual managers, depending largely on their position within the organization, will not necessarily agree on the relative significance of each mode but they must understand and support the processes.

The mixed approach is both sensible and justifiable. In some manufacturing industries the time taken from starting to plan a substantive innovation to peak profit performance can be 10 years – and needs planning, although the concept may be visionary. Throughout the implementation, there has to be adaptive and incremental learning and change. Where strategies are being changed in a dynamic environment, it is also useful on occasions to evaluate the current situation and assess the implications, which could be part of an annual planning cycle.

Chris Gorman operates very much within the strategic entrepreneurial leader role. Immediately prior to his involvement with the Gadget Shop (unfortunately an unsuccessful acquisition for him), Gorman had the very interesting title of 'Chief Entrepreneur' within Great Universal Stores (GUS), which had bought the Reality Group from Gorman, and after the acquisition Gorman had this new role. However, Gorman did not stay long within GUS because: 'it was not my skill set … I am not someone who is comfortable as a manager working through the layers that make up a large PLC.'

Case 8.1 (Sole Rebels) illustrates a mix of roles.

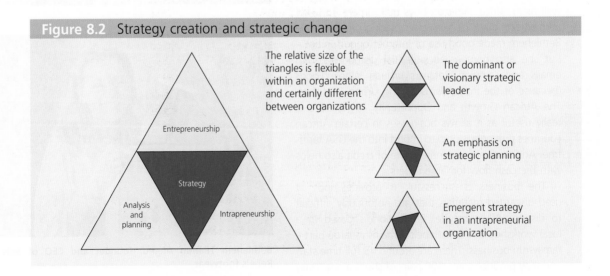

Figure 8.2   Strategy creation and strategic change

Case 8.1   Sole Rebels   Africa

Sole Rebels is a story about innovation and how an innovative young African company has found opportunities to reach international markets.

The company is based in Addis Ababa, Ethiopia. Ethiopia is heavily dependent on foreign aid; and whilst micro businesses such as this are not at all unusual, successfully accessing foreign markets is.

Sole Rebels was founded in 2005 by a local entrepreneur, a young lady accountant, Bethlehem Alemu, who was in her mid 20s when she saw an opportunity to create jobs for local people. She saw a *business* opportunity in something people, particularly soldiers, had been doing for some while. She started making shoes largely, or even entirely, from recycled materials. She cut up old truck tyres to make the soles and initially used old camouflage jackets and trousers for the tops. Because she wanted something more fashionable, she found some people who would use traditional spinning methods to produce hard-wearing cloth (in attractive designs) for the uppers. It so happened these suppliers lived in a leprosy area, and so again there was a strong social element underlying the decision. Local strips of leather are also used.

Many of her shoes are causal – sandals, boat shoes, loafers and flip-flops. For one design she reinforces the toecaps (on the outside) with inner tube rubber. She is constantly trawling the Internet to find ideas for new designs and improving her range – which boasts names such as Night Rider, Pure Love, New Deal, Class Act, Gruuv Thong and Urban Runner.

The shoes can be bought online from Amazon, as well as direct from the business itself, and through physical outlets in the USA, Canada and Australia as well as in Africa. Amazon buys bulk orders from her and expects quick delivery after placing orders. Again Bethlehem made good use of Internet opportunities – but she also bombarded potential distributors with emails and samples. Retailers include Whole Foods (because of the materials used) and Urban Outfitters. The African Growth and Opportunity Act (AGOA) is really useful as it allows businesses in certain African countries (Ethiopia is one) to import into the USA tariff-free. An Ethiopian government line of credit also helps with the cash flow for large orders.

The business is successful; it provides jobs; it used discarded materials that are notoriously difficult to dispose of or recycle. Production is based in a local workshop but Sole Rebels remains in large part a family-run business. There are around 45 full-time staff and they produce some 500 pairs of shoes a day. Daily wages range from £1.50 for a trainee to £7.00 for a skilled worker. In a global context this is competitively low; in Ethiopian terms it is relatively generous. Customers can scan in the outline of their sole and have shoes hand cut to size. Retail prices range from £21.00 to £40.00. Bethlehem sees her shoes as the 'Timberland or Skechers of Africa' and always seeks to offer uniquely designed products that have international appeal at affordable prices. She does not want Sole Rebels to look too African. She wants people to buy because they are good shoes that they will enjoy wearing and not because by buying from her they are helping Ethiopia's poor people.

Questions

1 Evaluate Sole Rebels against the framework in Figure 8.2.
2 Can you thinks of additional ways in which Sole Rebels might seek to innovate?

Bethlehem Tilahun Alemu, founder and CEO of Sole Rebels footwear

Table 8.1   Levels of strategy and modes of creation

Modes of strategy creation	Levels of strategy	
	Corporate strategy	Competitive and functional strategies
Planning	Formal planning systems	Planning the detail for implementing corporate strategies
Visionary	Seizing opportunities – limited planning only	Innovation throughout the organization
Adaptive/incremental	Reacting to environmental opportunities and threats, e.g. businesses for sale: divestment opportunity	Reacting to competitor threats and new environmental opportunities. Learning and adjustment as planned and visionary strategies are implemented

Table 8.1 further relates these themes to the three levels of strategy: corporate, competitive and functional. In large organizations, much of the responsibility for corporate strategic change will be centralized at the head office, although the businesses and divisions can be involved or consulted. Competitive and functional change decisions are more likely to be decentralized, but again not exclusively. Corporate policies can require or constrain changes at these levels.

For a more detailed analysis of strategic planning, see Chapter 9.

The adaptive and incremental modes

Strategies are formed as managers throughout the organization learn from their experiences, adapt to changing circumstances and also respond to pressures and new strategic issues. They perceive how tasks might be performed, and products and services managed, more effectively, and they make changes. There will again be elements of semi-consciousness and informality in the process. Some changes will be gradual, others spontaneous, and they will act collectively to alter and improve competitive positions. As individual decisions will often involve only limited change, little risk and possibly the opportunity to change back, it is essentially the **'squirrel approach'**. Managers learn whether their choice is successful or unsuccessful through implementation.

Hence this mode implies limited analysis preceding choice and implementation, which are intertwined and difficult to separate. A proper analysis follows in the form of an evaluation of the relative success:

$$\text{Analysis (limited)} \rightarrow \text{Choice and implementation} \rightarrow \text{Analysis}$$

Adaptive strategic change requires decentralization and clear support from the strategic leader, who also aims to stay aware of progress and link the changes into an integrated pattern. It may be based on setting challenges for managers – to hit targets, improve competitiveness and stretch or exploit internal systems and policies to obtain the best possible returns – and the greater the challenge, the more care needs to go into establishing a suitable reward system. When the structure enables effective adaptive change, then **intrapreneurship** can be fostered throughout the organization and individual managers can be allowed the necessary freedom. However, if adaptive changes are taking place in a highly centralized organization, despite rigid policies, there is a problem which should be investigated. The major potential drawbacks concern the ability of the organization and the strategic leader to synthesize all the changes into a coherent pattern, and the willingness and ability of individual managers to take an organization-wide perspective. This latter point is examined later in Chapter 12.

Figure 8.3 provides a short summary of the processes with planning shown at the top as a 'closed funnel' activity. The entrepreneurial, visionary style is about diverging and opening things up, widening the scope

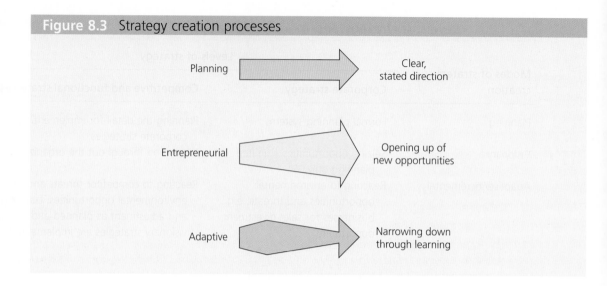

Figure 8.3 Strategy creation processes

Planning → Clear, stated direction

Entrepreneurial → Opening up of new opportunities

Adaptive → Narrowing down through learning

of the ideas considered. Adaptive strategy (responding to new opportunities) is, conversely, illustrated as a convergent process where learning and synthesis are required to form cohesive patterns which bind the emerging strategies. In the entrepreneurial mode, planning is required during implementation; and in the adaptive mode, individual managers are doing their own planning, sometimes informally, sometimes more formally.

Figure 8.4 considers the alternative ways in which strategies are created in the context of approaches to strategy that were introduced in Chapter 1.

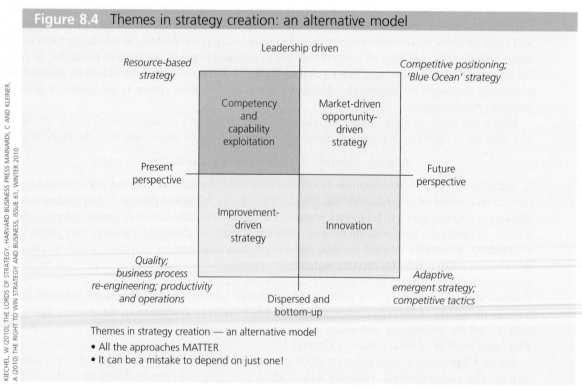

Figure 8.4 Themes in strategy creation: an alternative model

Leadership driven

Resource-based strategy

Competitive positioning; 'Blue Ocean' strategy

Competency and capability exploitation

Market-driven opportunity-driven strategy

Present perspective

Future perspective

Improvement-driven strategy

Innovation

Quality; business process re-engineering; productivity and operations

Dispersed and bottom-up

Adaptive, emergent strategy; competitive tactics

Themes in strategy creation — an alternative model
• All the approaches MATTER
• It can be a mistake to depend on just one!

KIECHEL, W (2010), THE LORDS OF STRATEGY, HARVARD BUSINESS PRESS. MAINARDI, C AND KLEINER, A (2010) THE RIGHT TO WIN STRATEGY AND BUSINESS, ISSUE 61, WINTER 2010

Changing strategies

Two important strategic pressures can leave the unprepared organization weakened: competitive and other environmental pressures, and focusing too much on controls at the expense of flexibility.

Hurst (1995) found that management and control becomes increasingly necessary as organizations grow and become more complex, but that this development contains the seeds of potential failure. Figure 8.5 shows that organizations often start life with an *entrepreneurial vision* but that the significance of this vision soon gives way to learning and emergence as the entrepreneur and the organization learns to cope with the pressures of a dynamic and competitive environment. This flexibility means that the momentum is maintained and the organization grows and prospers. To ensure that the organization is managed efficiently, planning and control systems run by specialist professional managers become increasingly prominent, but this often reduces the flexibility which has proved so valuable. If the flexibility is lost, if the organization fails to address what it is doing wrong while it is still succeeding, the momentum for innovation subsequently slows. Unless the entrepreneur and the organization foresee the impending problem and find a major new initiative, a crisis is likely to happen. For the organization to survive the crisis, it needs a substantial new opportunity, together with a renewed reliance on innovation and learning. **This scenario is the key determinant of long-term survival in business**.

Businesses hit these crisis points when they run short of money, usually because they have failed to remain competitive and to attract sufficient resource contributions from customers and other important resource suppliers. **Turnaround** may be possible, with a change of strategic leader to input the new vision and inspiration but, on other occasions, the intervention is too late and so the organization either collapses or is taken over as a means of providing the necessary new leadership and resourcing.

Businesses in trouble, then, may be realistically irrecoverable, recoverable but only to a level of survival, or capable of genuine renewal. The immediate need is to stop any financial haemorrhaging before new opportunities are sought and pursued. The first step, being largely based on technique backed by a

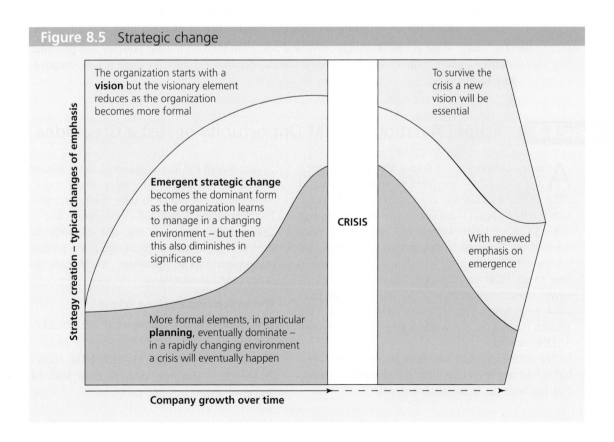

Figure 8.5 Strategic change

The organization starts with a **vision** but the visionary element reduces as the organization becomes more formal

To survive the crisis a new vision will be essential

Emergent strategic change becomes the dominant form as the organization learns to manage in a changing environment – but then this also diminishes in significance

CRISIS

With renewed emphasis on emergence

More formal elements, in particular **planning**, eventually dominate – in a rapidly changing environment a crisis will eventually happen

Strategy creation – typical changes of emphasis

Company growth over time

willingness to take tough decisions, does not need someone with entrepreneurial talent and temperament – but the second stage does.

Hurst further argues that on occasions it can be valuable to engineer an internal crisis and upset in order to drive through major changes in an organization that has lost its dynamism and become too resistant to change. A controlled crisis is better than one resulting from external events as it can be used for positive change rather than constitute a more desperate reaction.

Stasis is less likely to happen if the company employs and encourages creative people who drive innovation and intrapreneurship. But if momentum is lost, the company may need more than creative people: it may need a 'maverick', perhaps someone who is normally ill-at-ease in a typical organization or a new strategic leader who will come in for just a short period. The maverick manager is unorthodox, individualistic and outspoken, and will challenge mediocrity and existing ways of doing things and someone who is not afraid to upset others in the drive for change.

Another way of presenting these arguments is the following four-stage model of organizational progression and development:

- The first step is a *creative* one, when new ideas are put forward.

- *Reflection and nurturing* involve ideas being crafted into winning opportunities, but the idea generator may not exploit it in the most opportune way.

Case 8.2, Eclipse Aviation, examines the difference between a great idea and a true market opportunity. A similar idea is the Terrafugia Transition, a road car that becomes a plane in 15 seconds. The airplane that becomes a car – and *vice versa* – was designed by ex NASA technicians, runs on a petrol engine and fits into a normal car garage. Its main test flight was in March 2009 and it sells for $195 000. Would you invest in this vehicle? It might be the future and it might not. It is also a great idea but what kind of an opportunity is it?

- The third stage is an *action* stage as the organization grows by developing a business from the opportunity. As the business takes off, and more and more products are sold, some element of order becomes vital if the organization is to control events, manage its cash flow and deliver on time.

- The fourth stage is one of *management* and administration with clear policies and procedures which deliver smooth running and efficiencies, but can become a dangerous stage if new, creative ideas are not forthcoming.

Case 8.2   Eclipse Aviation – Great Opportunity or Just a Great Idea? US

A new jet aeroplane, the Eclipse 500, made its first – and successful – test flight in America in August 2002. Eclipse Aviation was attempting an 'aviation first' with this new aircraft – the first commercial jet priced at under $1 million (approximately £650 000). At this price it would be 75 per cent cheaper than a near rival, the Cessna Citation. To achieve this price, Eclipse would have to sell 1000 aircraft a year. The intention was full airworthiness certification in 2003 with deliveries from 2004. Four separate certifications were required – the aircraft, the engine, the welding technique being used and the avionics.

The first Eclipse 500 may have tested successfully – but it had not been built with the production tooling that has been put in place subsequently.

Any one of the four areas could fail certification and thus delay the project. Any delay would require even more investment capital to bring the project to market. The first plane (after full certification) was actually delivered for service at the end of 2006. Industry experts were always sceptical about the proposal, but non-experts were generally in favour of the entrepreneurial venture.

The entrepreneur behind Eclipse

Vern Raburn had a background in technology, not aviation. He was, in fact, the eighteenth person to join Microsoft in its early days. He believed he could use his experience in improving value to drive new sales and also drive down costs and prices.

The specification

The aircraft has six passenger seats but no toilet. Its flying speed is 400 miles an hour and its range is 1300 miles. It is powered by a new single Williams engine (which, like the plane, had to be certified) with double the thrust-to-weight ratio of rival engines. Eclipse had found a suitable supplier for its avionics, which it believed it could purchase for $50 000, whilst Cessna pay $700 000. Manufacturing processes are based on high-volume techniques, and a new type of welding was being adopted. Sceptics believe the overall extent of technological change is too ambitious.

The aims of the business model

Eclipse hopes to expand jet travel beyond 'executive elites' and to open up a new market opportunity for 'taxis in the sky'.

The idea for a taxi service would require an independent operator to create a service which links hundreds of small airports. As a concept it is unproven. Fractional, part-ownership share schemes have been tried out, but they have been largely unprofitable, as much as anything because of the complex logistics. Forecasting demand and dealing with planes flying return or collection journeys without passengers are a big issue.

Funding

By 2003 some $240 million had been invested in the development. Investors included Bill Gates and an ex-Ford CEO. There had been $25 million in customer deposits which was used for working capital. Through the development phase the business was burning at least $5 million every month and needed more funding to see it through certification.

In 2008 control of the business fell to the Etirc Fund controlled by entrepreneur, businessman and financier Roel Pieper – who was something of a veteran of the computing and IT industries. The fund is based in Luxembourg and Pieper had links with Russia. His intent was to move production there, to a new custom-built factory. Etirc already owned the distribution rights to Russia, Asia and Eastern Europe.

The market

2001 was a record year for business jet manufacture. 738 were built. *Forecast International* suggested a market of 1900 between 2002 and 2011, with Eclipse perhaps achieving 400 of these.

Eclipse aimed for sales of 140 in 2004, 500 in 2005, 900 in 2006 and then 1500 by 2007 from the replacement of existing jets as well as new sales and air taxis. It claimed it already had 1350 firm orders. By the end of 2007 just 104 had been produced, and this caused the financial strains which led to the takeover by Etirc. But mysteries always abounded.

A Russian entrepreneur, who had built a substantial perfume chain, said he had a company called Nimbus which had access to $1.2 billion for an air taxi service with 1000 aircraft. Nimbus turned out to be an online auction business. Another Swiss entrepreneur announced that Aviace would acquire 112 planes to start a business in Europe. Aviace paid a deposit but the rest of its funding was never put in place.

Early in 2008 there were still 1950 'firm orders' – apparently.

The underlying risk

Since 1960 only one new entrant to the market – Embraer of Brazil – has managed to deliver more than one new business jet per month.

Questions

1 Eclipse has been described as 'the last great dream in aviation' … but does this imply a 'half full' or a 'half empty' perspective?
2 Is it a good dream or a bad dream?

Task

Use the Internet to determine what has happened with the venture and with the Terrafugia Transition.

SOURCE: THIS CASE STUDY WAS PREPARED USING PRIMARILY PUBLICLY AVAILABLE SOURCES OF INFORMATION FOR THE PURPOSES OF CLASSROOM DISCUSSION; IT DOES NOT INTEND TO ILLUSTRATE EITHER EFFECTIVE OR INEFFECTIVE HANDLING OF A MANAGERIAL SITUATION.

Clearly, each stage has a downside. A constant stream of new ideas may not constitute entrepreneurial opportunities, too much deliberation may inhibit action and an overemphasis on 'doing' and competitiveness may mean that inadequate attention is given to structural necessities. Finally, too much bureaucracy can mean missed opportunities. The organization begins to need a fresh input of creative ideas. Individually, we are all different and our affinity and fit with each of these stages varies; some of us are not able to switch styles. While the most successful and habitual entrepreneurs will ensure that there is a constant flow of activity between these stages and the potential downsides do not materialize, other strategic leaders will need to recognize their relative strengths and weaknesses and recruit other people carefully to ensure that there is a balance of skills and constant progression. Moreover, the positive organization implied here will be in a better position to exploit and retain its most talented intrapreneurial managers.

Changing strategies and strategy drivers

So far we have seen how opportunities, resources and competition are key drivers of strategy – and we have also seen that the organization's culture can be either a facilitator or an inhibitor of change. These are drawn together in Figure 8.6. In reality, we might think of resources and competition as 'push' forces and opportunities and aspiration as 'pull' factors.

Figure 8.7 presents these themes in an alternative form. It again uses the market and resource-based views of strategy, this time with the analytical (planning in a competitive environment) and aspirational (visionary and emergent) approaches to strategy creation that we also introduced and explained in Chapter 1. The market-based approach can be manifest in either an analytical insight into the competitive environment or an endeavour to envision new opportunities for building value through an instinctive understanding of customers and their needs. The resource-based approach can build analytically on core competencies and capabilities. At the same time, real breakthroughs in processes or technologies can help to rewrite the rules of competition in an industry.

In their consideration of strategic alternatives, some organizations will be entrepreneurial and actively search for opportunities for change. Others will only consider change if circumstances dictate a need.

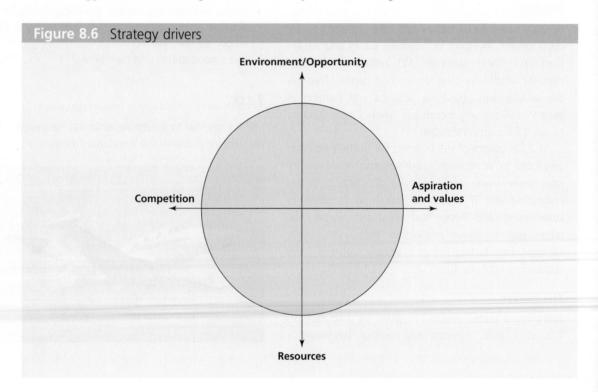

Figure 8.6   Strategy drivers

Figure 8.7   Changing strategies

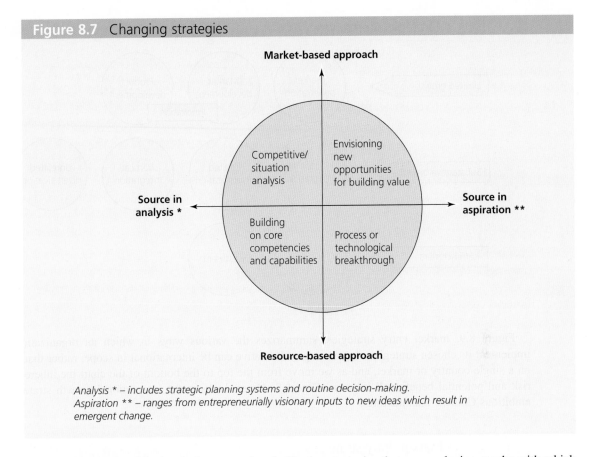

Analysis * – includes strategic planning systems and routine decision-making.
Aspiration ** – ranges from entrepreneurially visionary inputs to new ideas which result in emergent change.

Some organizations will already have sound and effective strategies that are producing results with which they are satisfied. Others may ignore the need to change. The essential criteria for strategy evaluation and selection are appropriateness, feasibility and desirability. These involve a mixture of objective and subjective factors. Not every strategic decision will be objective and consequently we need to understand how managers (and in turn organizations) make decisions and the impact of uncertainty and judgement on these decisions.

8.2 Strategic alternatives

Figure 8.8 provides a summary of the main strategic alternatives, which are separated into three clusters: *limited growth*, *substantive growth* and *retrenchment*. In addition, an organization can opt to do nothing; and on occasions the whole business will be sold or liquidated.

From origins in a single business concept, **market penetration** and product and **market development** are shown as limited growth strategies as they mainly affect competitive strategies rather than imply major corporate change, but invariably they involve innovation. The substantive growth strategies imply more ambitious and higher risk expansion which is likely to change the corporate perspective or strategy. These options, explained below, may involve either a strategic alliance or an acquisition, and these *strategic means* are discussed later in the chapter. It was established in Chapter 1 that it is important for organizations to seek competitive advantage for each business in the portfolio. Consequently, once an organization has diversified, it should then look for new competitive opportunities, or limited growth strategies, for the various individual businesses.

The bottom section of Figure 8.8 shows the main strategies for corporate reduction, namely turnaround and divestment, which are discussed in detail in Chapter 13.

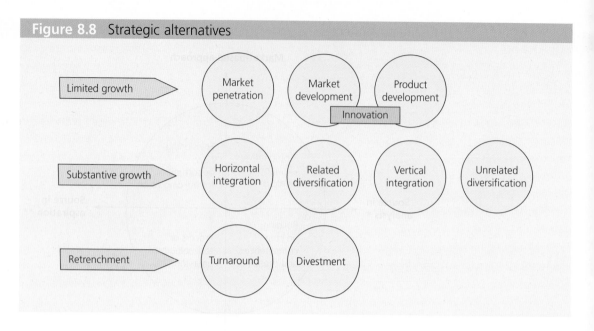

Figure 8.8   Strategic alternatives

Figure 8.9, market entry strategies, summarizes the various ways in which an organization might implement its chosen strategies. Any strategic alternative can be international in scope, rather than focused on a single country or market, and as we move from the top to the bottom of the chart the inherent scope, risk and potential benefits all increase. Case 8.3 (Haier) looks at the international growth strategy of an ambitious Chinese manufacturer.

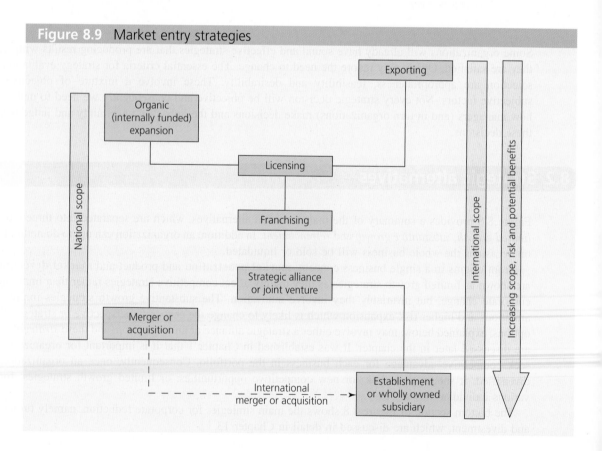

Figure 8.9   Market entry strategies

Case 8.3   Haier

Ch, Int

Haier is the fourth largest white household appliance manufacturer in the world. In terms of employment its global workforce reached 50 000 some 5 years ago, and now exceeds 70 000. It owns more than 200 subsidiary companies and has established design centres, manufacturing bases and trading companies in more than 30 countries. 2011 turnover was around US$23 billion. A crucial role in the development of Haier has been played by one man – Zhang Ruimin, the Chairman and CEO of the Haier Group. Born in 1949 he graduated from the Chinese University of Science and Technology and obtained an MBA in 1995. In 1984 Zhang Ruimin was appointed as a director of Haier's Qingdao Refrigerator Factory; at that time the company's products were perceived to be relatively shoddy and the workers poorly paid. The business had started in the 1920s and become State-owned around 1950. Zhang Ruimin was the fourth new director of the factory appointed that year; none of the others had been able to make serious improvements. It appeared to some observers that nobody in authority really cared about the quality of the product and this was giving rise to a large number of defects. Customers did not trust Haier; and in 1984 losses of 1.47 million RMB were incurred. This almost led to bankruptcy. When a number of defective refrigerators were discovered Zhang Ruimin ordered the workers to destroy the defective products in public using sledgehammers. From then on he stated there would be 'no more defects'. As the company became more and more successful under Zhang, Haier was encouraged to take over more and more Chinese manufacturing businesses and change their cultures. It now manufactures domestic electrical products (TVs, microwaves) as well as white goods.

From that event major changes in attitude and product development have taken place. In 2006 the Haier Group developed a dual power washing machine which washed clothes without the need to use soap powder. The 'natural cleansing' dual power washing machine has 32 technological patents, and it exceeds international standards in saving water and electricity.

Under Zhang Ruimin, Haier Group has successfully implemented a brand strategy, a diversification strategy and an internationalization strategy before moving on to what it described as the fourth stage of development, that of a globalization strategy. In 2008 Haier was one of the major sponsors of the Beijing Olympic Games.

The competitive strategy of Haier is now based largely on product quality – every employee is educated into the Haier culture of product quality. Sub-standard products are simply not acceptable. The second competitive strategy is one of constant product development. Haier has also developed what it calls its '24 hours strategy' where service support for Haier products is available 24 hours a day.

In seeking to enter the European market, Haier first chose to enter the German market because it believed it was the most difficult to penetrate. It set itself a challenge. Initially it began with a strategic alliance with Liebherr, and then it went on its own once the products were seen to meet the German VDE Quality Certificate.

Because the strategy is based on their reputation for quality and after-sales support, Haier have avoided participating in price wars. It is the perceived view that Haier customers are willing to pay a higher price for a higher technology, premium product with built-in quality and reliability. Haier regards R&D as very important and between 1997 and 2007 the amount invested in research and development doubled from 4 per cent to just over 8 per cent of sales revenues. In a typical year Haier will apply for 800 patents of which half will be classed as inventions.

Additionally Haier has opted to spend heavily on marketing. Overseas Haier directly uses foreign partners with existing distribution market and service networks. Haier has also grown through what it terms its 'stunned fish' strategy, looking to acquire white goods companies who have good products, facilities and distribution channels but poor senior management. Companies it can turn around.

Question

How does Haier illustrate the key themes of this chapter?

SOURCE: THIS CASE STUDY WAS PREPARED USING PRIMARILY PUBLICLY AVAILABLE SOURCES OF INFORMATION FOR THE PURPOSES OF CLASSROOM DISCUSSION; IT DOES NOT INTEND TO ILLUSTRATE EITHER EFFECTIVE OR INEFFECTIVE HANDLING OF A MANAGERIAL SITUATION.

The choice must take into account the risk that the strategic leader considers acceptable given any particular circumstances, and the ability of the organization to deal with the risk elements. Some organizations will not select the most challenging and exciting opportunities because they are too risky.

The options should not be thought of as being mutually exclusive – two or more may be combined into a composite strategy, and at any time a multi-product organization is likely to be pursuing several different competitive strategies.

Table 8.2 combines the themes of this chapter by providing examples, many of which are discussed in greater detail throughout the book, of seven growth directions related to three alternative means of pursuing each of these strategic alternatives.

Limited growth strategies

The do-nothing alternative A continuation of the existing corporate and competitive strategies, which might be highly appropriate, considered and justified, but it can result from managers lacking awareness, being lazy or complacent or deluding themselves into believing that things are going well when in fact the company is in difficulties. Doing nothing when change is required is a dangerous strategy.

A company might appear to an outsider to be doing nothing when in reality it is holding back its innovation while a competitor introduces its version into the market, thus allowing the initial reaction of consumers to be monitored and evaluated, and competitive and functional strategies reviewed before eventual launch. Timing is the key to success with this strategy, so that the company can be sure that its approach is likely to prove successful, whilst reacting sufficiently quickly so that it is not perceived to be copying a competitor. In general, the rather more theoretical than realistic do-nothing alternative could conceivably be viable in the short term but is unlikely to prove beneficial or plausible in the long-term as environmental factors change.

Market penetration This *organic growth* strategy can either seek assertively to increase market share or more defensively to retain existing customers by concentrating (perhaps by investing in brands and brand identity), specializing and consolidating, which implies what Peters and Waterman (1982) designated 'sticking to the knitting'. Growth is an objective and there is an implicit search for ways of doing things more effectively and, because market environments are dynamic, it overlaps with the ideas of market and product development described below. This strategic alternative is particularly applicable to small businesses which concentrate their efforts on specific market niches.

Resources are directed towards the continued and profitable growth of a 'single' product in a 'single' market, using a 'single' technology, accomplished by attracting new users or consumers, increasing the consumption rate of existing users and, wherever possible, stealing consumers and market share from competitors. The word *single* needs careful interpretation, in the context of the limited growth strategies, as companies such as Kellogg's (breakfast cereals) and Sony (music) would be classified as organizations which have succeeded with specialization strategies based around a core brand identity. An extensive product line of differentiated brands designed to appeal to specific market segments would periodically have new additions and withdrawals. Productivity and more effective cost management can make significant contributions, perhaps by investing in new technology at the expense of labour.

The two main advantages are, first, that the strategy is based on known skills and capabilities and is generally low risk. Second, because the organization's production and marketing skills are concentrated on specialized products and related consumers, and not diversified, these skills can be developed and improved to create competitive advantage. The company has the opportunity to be sensitive to consumer needs by being close to them, and may build a reputation for doing so. Market penetration strategies are likely to succeed, more so than most other alternatives, but have limitations such that they may be inadequate for closing an identified planning gap.

Whilst market penetration is a growth strategy, the long-term growth is likely to be gradual, which on the positive side can be more straightforward managerially. Any firm pursuing this strategy is susceptible to: (i) changes in the growth rate or attractiveness of the industry in which it competes and, therefore, the strategy can become high risk if the industry goes into recession and (ii) competitors' innovations which

Table 8.2 Examples of strategic growth and change

Means of growth	Direction of growth						
	Inventing a new way of doing business	Market penetration/ divestment	Globalization	Vertical integration/ divestment	Related diversification	Unrelated diversification	Focus by divestment
Organic/ internal	Southwest Air Amazon.com Hotmail	Toyota (with Lexus)	McDonald's Canon	Exxon (with refineries) Disney (with stores)	Sony Disney (with cruise ships)	Tata* (India) Virgin Atlantic Airways	Hanson Burton/ Debenhams
Strategic alliance	Benetton and IKEA (with their supply chains)	General Motors and Saab	Star Alliance† Coca-Cola and its bottlers	MBNA/Co-op Bank credit cards	Nokia and 3 Com (Internet mobile phones)	Siam Cement‡ (Thailand)	Yorkshire Water's onion outsourcing strategy
Merger, acquisition takeover	Royal Bank/ Direct Line	Ford with Jaguar, Land Rover, Volvo, Daewoo	Astra/Zeneca	Merck with Medco, a distributor	Disney/ABC Television; Wal-Mart and ASDA	General Electric (GE) and NBC Television	ICI's sale of non-core businesses after splitting from Zeneca

* Tata: steel, construction machinery, engineering, locomotives; tea (where it has global leadership)
† Airline code sharing alliance: includes United Airlines, Air Canada, Air New Zealand, Singapore Airlines, Lufthansa, SAS
‡ Siam Cement: also pulp and paper, construction materials, machinery and electrical products, marketing and trading

may become a major threat, so that competitors must be constantly monitored. Consumer behaviour has been affected by new supply opportunities that have provided market penetration opportunities, e.g. buying products online, watching television programmes 'on demand' using innovative devices and the Internet. Although the traditional product life cycle suggests that sales of new products take off slowly and then grow rapidly before flattening out and then declining, innovation means that the life cycle can be extended and extended again and the ultimate decline delayed for possibly many years. Some fashion and fashionable products thus have a very short lifespan, whilst others can continue for decades (for example, see the 'retro' clothing that many academics, particularly professors, wear), albeit with changes and improvements at various intervals (the products, not the academics, that is). Whilst the theory would imply a 'tipping point' of the type outlined by Gladwell (2000) that once a product is experiencing a decline in popularity it should be scrapped (given the expense of production, storage and distribution) and that products sell if they are available where and when people expect to find them (at appropriate prices), Anderson (2006) contends that for some products these principles no longer apply, as much as anything because of changes in distribution and channel preference. In this context, Anderson quotes one Amazon employee as saying, 'we sold more books today that didn't sell at all yesterday than we sold today of all the books that did sell yesterday.' A breakdown of sales would perhaps reinforce the Pareto principle, even not strictly 80:20 – i.e. a limited number of current bestsellers would amount to X per cent of total sales, but very small individual sales of a very **long tail** of almost-forgotten-about but previously popular items would constitute Y per cent – and Y would be greater than X. Although persuasive, new products which do have a chance of high sales over a short period of time are still needed, but opportunities now exist to continue to sell them and buy them, and some new books and music that would previously have been as a 'miss' rather than a 'hit' can make money over their life, albeit an extended life. Hence, it allows producers more freedom to release products they are less convinced about and give them a chance to see if they find favour.

Market development Together with product development, this organic growth strategy is closely related to a strategy of specialization by building on existing strengths, skills, competencies and capabilities. It is a relatively low-risk strategy of marketing present products, with possible modifications and range increases, to customers in related market areas, perhaps by a product range to increase its attractiveness to different customers in different market segments or niches. Clearly, therefore, this strategy is about modifications to strategic positioning typically supported by changes in distribution and advertising.

In summary, the key themes are:

- modifications to increase attractiveness to new segments or niches
- new uses for a product or service
- appropriateness for different countries with particular tastes or requirements.

One example of a market development strategy, therefore, would be a firm which decided to modify its product in some minor way to make it attractive to selected export markets where tastes and preferences are different, supported by advertising and new channels of distribution.

In the last 20–25 years China, since the implementation of its 'One Child Policy', has become an increasingly attractive market for specialized children's products, including nutritional supplements and certain upmarket toys. Two parents and four grandparents for each child amounts to significant purchasing power, given that 20 million babies are born in China every year.

Product development This organic growth strategy implies substantial modifications or additions to present products in order to increase their market penetration within existing customer groups, perhaps by attempting to extend or prolong the product life cycle; for example, the second (or seventh!) and revised edition of a successful textbook, or the relaunch of a range of cosmetics with built-in improvements which add value. As product life cycles contract and time becomes an increasingly important competitive issue, this strategy becomes more significant.

Case 8.4 shows how BUPA has developed a new business in care homes, whilst the company was divesting hospitals.

Case 8.4 BUPA

UK

Many people in the UK would say 'private health care' if asked to explain what BUPA provides. BUPA has in fact been a lead player in this industry for many years. It established its position by both providing the care – in its own hospitals – and also providing health care insurance. Typically private hospitals are ideal for non-critical procedures; they do not have accident and emergency rooms and they would not normally have intensive care facilities. The operations are generally, but not exclusively, carried out by consultants who also have contracts with the NHS (the National Health Service). It has long been recognized that this implies a dual culture. Insurance is driven by numbers – income from premiums must exceed payments to claimants – and it is very competitive. Customers can be corporate clients (insuring their workforce) or private individuals. Hospitals might be expected to exhibit a caring culture, even though they have to be financially viable.

In the UK some 7.5 million people are covered, around 12 per cent of the population. This may, of course, be partial cover rather than the complete package.

Over the years BUPA had acquired a national network of care homes – both residential care and the more specialized nursing care. This is again a competitive industry and one that is very tightly regulated. Homes are individual but there are clearly scale economies in a group. Like hospitals one might expect a manifest caring culture but in a context of financial viability.

In 2008 the current CEO stepped down. Val Gooding had been in post for 10 years and had executed a number of major changes. In her 10 years she had doubled BUPA's revenues but increased profits by a factor of nine. From a zero base, overseas income now accounted for a third of the total. She had invested in insurance businesses in Australia and the Middle East and nursing homes in Australia and New Zealand.

In 2007 Gooding decided BUPA did not need to own its 26 UK hospitals and sold them to Cinven for almost £1.5 billion. The insurance part of BUPA could direct clients to any UK provider. That said, Gooding bought the Cromwell Hospital in London in early 2008 – but claimed this was not a strategy reversal. It was a one-off investment.

BUPA's hospitals were rebranded 'Spire' and they benefited from being able to actively promote their services to NHS patients as the UK government has been willing to allow the NHS to pay money over to the private sector if they can help reduce the waiting lists and thus meet government targets.

Questions

1 Do you see these changes as positive moves by BUPA?
2 Do you believe they will have left the organization stronger?

Innovation Linked to the three strategies described above, innovation often involves more significant changes to the product or service (see Critical Reflection 8.1). As a strategy, innovation can imply the replacement of existing products with ones which are really new, as opposed to modified, and which imply a new product life cycle.

The line which differentiates a really new product from a modification is difficult to quantify. In the case of cars such as the Ford Focus or Ford Fiesta, for example, which have appeared in new forms every few years, the changes for each new model were typically marked differences rather than essentially cosmetic. Each new model was very different from the existing model, simply the name was the same.

Similarly, one should consider which product life cycle is being addressed. The Sony Walkman and similar personal cassette players enjoyed their own successful life cycle and they extended the product life cycle of cassette players in general far beyond their technical life. As shown in Table 8.2, innovation can be behind the invention of a new way of doing business. Case 8.5 shows how Lego has largely (but not exclusively) stayed focused on building bricks but innovated constantly.

It can be risky not to innovate in certain industries as a barrier against competition. Innovative companies can stay ahead by introducing new products ahead of their rivals and concentrating on production and marketing to establish and consolidate a strong market position. All the time, they will search for new opportunities to innovate and gain further advantage by limiting the market potential for retailer own -brands.

Critical Reflection 8.1   Innovation

Innovation takes place when an organization makes a technical change, e.g. produces a product or service that is new to it, or uses a method or input that is new and original. If a direct competitor has already introduced the product or method then it is imitation, not innovation. However, introducing a practice from a different country or industry rather than a direct competitor would constitute innovation.

Innovation implies change and the introduction of something new. Creating the idea, or inventing something, is not innovation but a part of the total process. While at one level it can relate to new or novel products, it may also be related to production processes, approaches to marketing a product or service, or the way in which jobs are carried out within the organization. The aim is to add value for the consumer or customer by reducing costs or differentiating the product or total service in some sustainable way. In other words, innovation relates to the creation of competitive advantage; and, to summarize, there are four main forms of innovation:

- new products, which are either radically new or which extend the product life cycle
- process innovation leading to reduced production costs, and affected partially by the learning and experience effect
- innovations within the umbrella of marketing, which increase differentiation
- organizational changes, which reduce costs or improve total quality.

Where the innovation reflects continuous improvement, product or service *enhancement*, and only minor changes in established patterns of consumer behaviour, the likelihood of success is greater than for those changes that demand new patterns of usage and consumption. Examples of the latter include personal computers and compact disc players. Discontinuous innovations such as these are more risky for manufacturers, but if they are successful the financial payoffs can be huge. By contrast, continuous improvements – which, realistically, are essential in a dynamic, competitive environment – have much lower revenue potential.

Innovation can come about in a variety of ways:

- Ideas can come out of research and development departments, where people are employed to come up with new ideas or inventions. Some would argue that there is a risk that departments such as this are not in direct touch with customers; however, while customers may sense that a product or service has drawbacks, they may have no idea how it might be improved. This requires a technical expert.
- People from various parts of an organization working on special projects.
- Employees being given freedom and encouragement to work on ideas of their own, e.g. the 3M approach.
- Everyday events as people interact and discuss problems and issues.

There is a mix of routine, structured events and unstructured activities.

Changes in the service provided to customers and the development of new products and services imply changes in operating systems and in the work of employees, and some of the proposed changes may well be the result of ideas generated internally. However, many of the ideas for innovations come from outside the organization, from changes in the environment. This emphasizes the crucial importance of linking together marketing and operations and harnessing the contribution of people. For example, Ford in the USA realized some years ago that a number of its engineers had a tendency to 'over-engineer' solutions to relatively simple problems. As a result, its costs were higher than those of its rivals, particularly Japanese and Korean companies, and its new product development times were considerably longer. Instead, the company needed 'creative engineers' with a fresh perspective and greater realization of customer expectations.

Combination strategies A firm with a number of products or business units will typically pursue a number of different competitive strategies at any time, such as product development, market development and innovation. The organic growth strategies discussed in this section are primarily concerned with improving competitive strategies for existing businesses, but may not prove adequate for closing the planning gap (which we discuss in the next chapter) and, consequently, higher risk growth strategies may also be considered, which may involve a new strategic perspective.

Case 8.5 Lego

In a volatile and competitive environment we have concentrated and used our strength to go deeper into what we know about.

KJELD KIRK KRISTIANSEN, DEPUTY CHAIRMAN
AND GRANDSON OF THE FOUNDER

Lego, the brightly coloured plastic building bricks, was launched in 1949, and has always proved popular in an industry renowned for changing tastes and preferences and for innovation. The name was derived from Leg Godt, which is Danish for 'play well'. Ironically Lego in Latin means 'I put together'. On the strength of this one product Lego has become Europe's largest and the world's fourth largest toy maker. Lego is Danish, family owned and based on strong principles. For example, no toys will be developed that have a military theme. Lego has five stated values: creativity, innovation, learning, fun and quality. Historically it has been relatively secretive, hiding its actual sales and profit figures. In 2011 turnover was reported to be 9.13 billion Kroner (£972 million) and net profit 2.02 billion Kroner (£215 million).

The basic strategy is one of product development, with Lego developing an enormous number of variations on its basic product theme. Wheels and electric motors were added in the 1960s. By the mid-1990s some 300 different kits (at a wide range of prices) were available worldwide. There were 1700 different parts, including bricks, shapes and miniature people, and children could use them to make almost anything from small cars to large, complex, working space stations with battery-operated space trains. Brick colours were selected to appeal to both boys and girls; and the more complex Lego Technic sets were branded and promoted specially to make them attractive to the young teenage market. Well over 200 billion plastic bricks and pieces had been produced since Lego was introduced.

In a typical year Lego has replaced one-third of its product range, with many items having only a short lifespan. New ideas are developed over a two- to three-year period and backed by international consumer research and test marketing. Lego concentrates on global tastes and buying habits. The Pacific Rim was perceived to offer the highest growth potential during the 1990s. 'If you differentiate too much you start to make difficulties for yourself, especially in manufacturing.' Competition has forced Lego to act internationally and aggressively. One US company, Tyco, markets products that are almost indistinguishable from Lego. Lego has attempted unsuccessfully to sue for patent infringement and now views this competition as undesirable but stimulating. More recently new competition has come from another rival construction product, K'Nex, again American.

In the mid-1990s sales were being affected adversely by changing tastes and by the growing popularity of computer games. In 1997 Lego opted for a new range extension. Using technology as an enabler, Lego began to market construction kits with microchips and instructions on CD-ROMs. In 1998 the company introduced a new Mindstorms range, built around a brick powered by AA batteries, which could be incorporated into a variety of different models that could then be instructed to move with the aid of an infra-red transmitter and a typical personal computer. Lego had had the technology for some while but had been waiting until it could reduce costs to a realistic level. More recently, Lego has ventured into the computer games market with CD-based products enabling users to 'build' train sets, vehicles, etc., on screen. 'Design by Me' allows children to design their own finished Lego model and then have the required parts shipped to them. It has also agreed licensing deals for kits based on Bob the Builder, Star Wars and Harry Potter.

When Lego launched Serious Play in 2002, a corporate training package, it was capitalizing on Lego-based activities developed by independent trainers over many years. Vision Lab is a new research centre built in 2002 to develop scenarios on future families and play.

Lego has manufactured in Switzerland, the Czech Republic, South Korea and the USA as well as Denmark, making its own tools for the plastic injection moulding machines. Bricks were only moulded in Denmark and Switzerland but there were finishing factories in other countries. Tool-making could easily be concentrated in one plant, but took place in three to engender competition and to emphasize quality. Lego deliberately maintained strong links with its machinery suppliers. In this and other respects Lego sees itself as being closer culturally to a Japanese company than a US one. Investments in production and improvements are thought to have been in the region of at least £100 million per year. In 2006 production was outsourced to

Flextronics, a Singapore-based company – manufacture would take place in Mexico and eastern Europe.

Some years ago, in 1968, Lego diversified with a theme park, featuring rides and displays built with Lego bricks, in Denmark. This has been followed with a similar development on the site of the old Windsor Safari Park in the UK and followed by a third in San Diego, USA, and a fourth in Gunzburg, Germany. In the late 1990s the UK park was attracting 1.5 million visitors every year. Recently Lego has opted to outsource the management of the Theme Parks.

Lego recorded record trading losses in 2000 and set about restructuring. Jobs and plants were lost. There was a new logo – with a new strapline, 'Play On' – and new packaging. Diversification trials for clothing, bags and accessories were abandoned. In 2001 the company was profitable again. Unfortunately this would only last 2 years, before Lego plunged into loss again. Many believed it had been over-ambitious with its licensing agreements as many of these were only short-term windows of opportunity. There has been further restructuring 'in a drive to remain independent'.

Kjeld Kirk Kristiansen, grandson of the founder, stepped down as CEO, but remained as Deputy Chairman. Sales revenues had fallen some 20 per cent from their 2002 high point of 10 billion Kroner.

In recent years Lego has enjoyed genuine success from a new range of products designed for girls. Jorgen Vig Knudstorp became CEO in 2004; his background was consultancy with McKinsey after graduating in America. He was convinced a large proportion of children were missing out on Lego because it was too boy focused. The 'Friends' series comprises around 30 miniature dolls which are sold with storybooks and kits to make 'sets' where the dolls can be deployed and played with. Extensive use is made of pink Lego bricks. Knudstorp has also streamlined the number of different parts that Lego will use and supply.

In 2006 Lego employed 1500 people in Denmark (it had once been as high as 5000) and 3000 worldwide (down from 8300). But there was no corporate debt. Another shining light was the range of robot toys, including Spike, AlphaRex, TriBot and RoboArm, all part of the Mindstorms range. With packs selling for as much as US$250 the appeal was to older children and even some adults.

Some believe Lego brought problems on itself by taking some focus away from traditional bricks and experimenting with other products and activities. Yet in

2009 Lego was reported to be planning the launch of a mobile phone with a casing that looks like Lego bricks. Parts can be removed and replaced to allow for colour changes to suit different moods. The target market would be children in the USA and Asia. There are also reported plans for a Lego MP3 Player and digital camera.

Lego is not a lifestyle brand.

JORGEN VIG KNUDSTORP, THE NEW CEO

Questions

1 Can Lego realistically anticipate further growth and prosperity if it relies on its focused strategy or will it become increasingly vulnerable to competitive threats?
2 What would you recommend?
3 Should Lego consolidate or continue to seek to grow?

LEGO **http://www.lego.com**

Substantive growth strategies

While this section provides an overview of four substantive growth strategies – **horizontal integration**, **vertical integration**, *related and unrelated diversification* – many of the key issues are discussed in more detail in Chapter 12. Substantive growth strategies are frequently implemented through acquisition, merger, **joint venture** or franchising rather than organic growth.

Non-organic growth can involve the purchase of, or an arrangement with, firms that are behind or ahead of a business in the added value chain, spanning raw material to ultimate consumption. Similarly, it can involve firms or activities that are indirectly related businesses or industries, those which are tangentially related through either technology or markets, and unrelated businesses. The key objectives are additional market share and the search for opportunities that can generate synergy. The outcome from this will be larger size and increased power, and ideally improved profitability from the synergy. In reality, as will be explored in greater depth in Chapter 12, the outcome is more likely to be increased size and power than improved profitability.

Horizontal integration When a firm acquires or merges with a major competitor, or another firm operating at the same stage in the added value chain, possibly appealing to different market segments rather than compete directly, market share will increase, and pooled skills and capabilities should generate synergy. Horizontal integration is, therefore, concerned with issues of **critical mass**, which are discussed later in this chapter.

Brewing, motor cars, banking and insurance are all industries where there has been extensive horizontal integration, where it has been allowed by competition authorities. As we saw earlier, the competition rules were 'relaxed' to allow the 2009 creation of the Lloyds Group from the old Lloyds TSB and HBOS. In the oil industry in recent years there have been mergers between Exxon and Mobil, Fina and Elf, BP and Amoco and between Texaco and Chevron.

The online case on Electrolux is an example of international horizontal integration and it shows how difficult it can be to pull everything together and achieve synergy, despite broadly similar competencies and products. Adidas, Nike and Umbro, another online case, also looks at horizontal integration but incorporates the role of a 'spoiler' determined to stop others merging.

Vertical integration This strategy involves the acquisition of a company which supplies a firm with inputs of raw materials or components, or serves as a customer for the firm's products or services (a distributor or assembler). If a shirt manufacturer acquired a cotton textile supplier, this acquisition would be known as **backward vertical integration**; if the supplier bought the shirt manufacturer, its customer, this would constitute **forward vertical integration**.

At times, firms will reduce the extent to which they are vertically integrated if they are failing to obtain the appropriate benefits and synergy from the fusion of two sets of skills and capabilities. In 1988 the UK clothing retailer Burton Group, which once had been one of the leading clothing manufacturers in Europe (before made-to-measure suits were substantially replaced in popularity by ready-made suits), sold the last of its suit-making factories in order to concentrate on retailing.

Backward vertical integration aims to secure supplies at a lower cost than competitors, but after the merger or acquisition it becomes crucial to keep pace with technological developments and innovation on the supply side, or competitive advantage may be lost. In 1987 Rover divested its parts distribution business, Unipart – an example of vertical disintegration – and 8 years later, after its acquisition by BMW, Rover sought unsuccessfully to buy Unipart back, arguing that it needed to control its parts distribution to support its increasingly international role.

Forward vertical integration secures customers or outlets and guarantees product preference, and can give a firm much greater control over its total marketing effort. At the consumer end of the chain, retailers generally are free to decide at what final price they sell particular products or services, and their views may not always accord with those of the manufacturer. However, greater control over distribution might mean complacency and a loss of competitive edge through less effective marketing overall. In addition, manufacturing and retailing, if these are the two activities involved, require separate and different skills, and for this reason synergy may prove elusive.

Many benefits of vertical integration can be achieved without merger or acquisition. Joint ventures, discussed later, are one option. In addition, there may simply be agreements between companies who appreciate that there can be substantial gains from proper co-operation. Marks and Spencer (M&S) provides an excellent example historically: M&S has benefited from long-term agreements with its suppliers with whom it has worked closely, whilst many suppliers of a wide variety of products sold by M&S rely very heavily upon them as their major customer. At the same time, M&S set exacting standards for cost, quality and delivery, and guarantee to buy only when these standards are met continuously; hence suppliers are aware that they will always have competitors who would like them as a customer.

The effect of vertical integration can be created organically, without merger or acquisition, which is likely to be more risky because, for example, new skills have to be developed from scratch (such as a manufacturer deciding to make components rather than buying them from specialist suppliers, or starting to distribute independently rather than relying on external distributors).

Related (or concentric) diversification Any form of diversification involves a departure from existing products/services and markets, which may be related through either technology or marketing, and is known as **concentric** (rather than conglomerate) diversification, e.g. a specialist manufacturer of ski clothing who diversified into summer leisure wear to offset seasonal sales. Potential consumers may or may not be the same, distribution may or may not change, and the existing production expertise should prove beneficial. Similarly, when retailers such as WH Smith add different new lines and products, they are seeking to exploit their resources and their retailing skills and expertise (core competencies) more effectively.

It is often assumed that synergy can be created from the two businesses or activities, such that ideally the new, diversified, company enjoys strengths and opportunities which decrease its weaknesses and exposure to risks.

Any organization seeking concentric diversification will look for companies or opportunities where there are clearly related products, markets, distribution channels, technologies or resource requirements with related benefits that are clear and genuinely capable of generating synergy. However, diversification might be adopted as a means of covering up weaknesses or previous poor decisions. Benefits will not be expected immediately, and the change involved may divert interest and attention away from existing problems or difficulties.

Unrelated (or conglomerate) diversification In this strategy, there is no discernible relationship between existing and new products, services and markets, since the diversification is justified as a promising investment opportunity. Financial benefits and profits should be available from the new investment, and any costs incurred will be more than offset. Financial synergy might be obtained in the form of greater borrowing capacity or acquired tax credits.

The strategy is regarded as high risk because the new technologies, new skills and new markets involved constitute unknowns and uncertainties. Moreover, because the change is uncertain and challenging, it can be tempting to switch resources and efforts away from existing businesses and areas of strength, and this compounds the element of risk involved.

Conglomerate diversification is often linked to **portfolio analysis**, and sometimes the search for businesses which might remedy any perceived strategic weaknesses. A company with reserves of cash to invest, because it has a number of cash cow businesses, might seek to buy businesses with growth potential in new industries. Some acquisitive and financially orientated companies adopt this strategy to rationalize businesses that they buy, retaining parts which add value and divesting other parts. In such cases, the critical issue is the opportunity cost of the money involved, i.e. the long-term return on capital employed should exceed alternative uses for the money, including simply keeping it banked! While some companies hoard substantial capital reserves to survive future recessions, others will use the cash to buy back equity. Shareholders wish to see a company enjoying sound financial health, but may prefer a 'cash mountain' to be used to pick up 'bargains' in a recession. Hence, it can be a difficult balance. Referring to points made earlier, where a company is anxious to grow, it might initially look for closely related acquisitions but find such routes blocked by competition authorities who are convinced that customers might be disadvantaged. When such companies opt for unrelated acquisitions, they are likely to argue that there is more relatedness than there is in reality!

Unrelated diversification became less popular in the 1990s, especially under the onslaught of management guru thinking that favoured focus strategies. We develop this later in this chapter as well as in Chapter 16. The real issue concerns whether the strategic leadership can deliver value for all key stakeholders from the diversification. At this point, it would be useful to read the online case on Granada.

Some companies diversify to build a bigger business, reducing the likelihood of being acquired, but if they do not achieve synergy, they may look attractive to an outside bidder who sees value in buying them to split them up.

Diversification or 'focus' as growth strategies

As Figure 8.10 demonstrates, the growth challenge is to find opportunities for developing and deploying technologies, processes and competencies in ways that generate a more effective and beneficial match between the organization's products and services and its customers and markets. Some of the key themes include potential synergy from internal and external linkages and alliances; the diversification/focus dilemma; opportunities for, and abilities in, transferring skills and competencies; and opportunities emerging from the exploitation of a successful corporate brand name.

Table 8.3 provides a brief summary of the advantages and drawbacks of *organic growth* (from within, utilizing the organization's own resources and developing new competencies as required), **acquisitions** (including the friendly purchase of one company by another, an unfriendly purchase (a *takeover*) and a straightforward merger of the assets of two or more organizations), **strategic alliances** (an agreement between two or more companies), or **joint ventures** (alliances, plus the exchange of minority shareholdings between the companies involved or the establishment of an independent company, jointly owned by the organizations who start it).

Although not all acquisitions aim to do so, the majority appears to represent either related or unrelated diversification. Furthermore, when a business is acquired by another, be it in a friendly or hostile manner, the assets of the acquired business are revalued before they are absorbed into the balance sheet of the acquirer. Any difference between the new valuation and the price paid to buy the business would be reflected in the value of goodwill such that, wherever they can, businesses will seek to treat any form of acquisition as a merger for the balance sheet.

Channon's (1983) analysis of diversification in the UK's largest firms over the previous 30 years included *single-product companies* (over 95 per cent of sales from 'one basic (or core) business'), *dominant-product companies* (70–95 per cent), *related-product companies* (related but 'no single business accounts for 70 per cent of sales', e.g. vertically or horizontally integrated or concentrically diversified), and *conglomerate/unrelated-product companies* (unrelated but 'no single business accounts for 70 per cent of sales'). He found that, in many cases, a company started its life as a single-product enterprise, then went through the dominant-product stage to become a related business and then a conglomerate – but this model is not intended to be generalizable or to apply to all companies. Whilst this trend continued through the 1980s, since then there has been an increasing tendency for organizations to stay more focused.

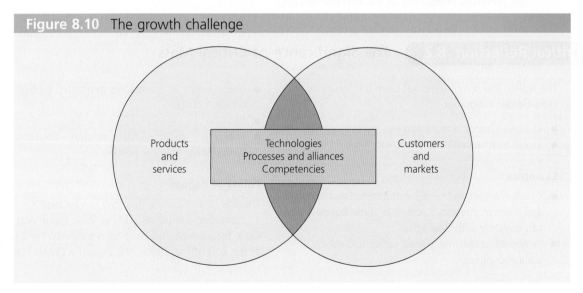

Figure 8.10   The growth challenge

Products and services

Technologies
Processes and alliances
Competencies

Customers and markets

Table 8.3 Alternative growth strategies

	Advantages	Possible drawbacks
Organic growth	Lower risk Allows for ongoing learning More control	Slow Lack of early knowledge – may be misjudgements
Acquisition	Fast Buys presence, market share and expertise	Premium price may have to be paid High risk if any misjudgement Preferred organization may not be available May be difficult to sell unwanted assets
Strategic alliance	Cheaper than takeover Access to market knowledge Useful if acquisition impractical	Possible lack of control Potential managerial differences and problems
Joint venture	As for strategic alliance plus: ● Greater incentive and closer contact ● Can lock out other competitors more effectively	As for strategic alliance

As markets and industries become increasingly global, a certain minimum size and market share – known as **critical mass** – is often thought to be necessary for competitive viability, and explains the growing incidence of mergers and alliances between related and competing organizations. Critical mass, discussed in detail in Critical Reflection 8.2, ensures: sufficient investment in research and development to keep pace with the market leader; that the important cost benefits of the experience curve can be realized; and that marketing activities achieve visibility and a competitive presence.

Because of both competitive requirements and regulatory and cultural issues, which can inhibit 'full' merger and acquisition activity, many links between businesses are between existing competitors, and often take the form of joint ventures and strategic alliances as an alternative to mergers or acquisitions. On occasions, there will have been clear strategic arguments in favour of linking two organizations – but pressure from shareholders, managers or governments may mean that the acquisition is not feasible. However, joint ventures and alliances should not be regarded as 'second best' choices; indeed, they can be the preferred alternative as we will discuss later.

Critical Reflection 8.2   The Significance of Critical Mass

The reality: The recent trend has been for horizontal and cross-border integrations:

● to establish critical mass and
● as industry rationalization to create global players.

Examples:

● Airbus (combining the relevant British, French, Italian and German interests to create a single business that can compete with Boeing)
● oil companies (as mentioned earlier and driven by scale economies)

● pharmaceuticals companies (prompted by high research costs)
● banking
● telecoms – Vodafone/Mannesmann – for European/ world power and economies.

Points of debate

There is clear evidence that 'big can be best'?

Dominant companies such as Shell, Exxon and Coca-Cola, for example, are long-term survivors. For example at the end of the 1990s, the powerful Lloyds TSB bank *was* the best performing British bank. But do they always stay the best? Are they more vulnerable to the external rule changer? After all, size is no protection against lost competitive advantage. The share price of the new Lloyds Group since early 2009 tells an interesting story.

Glaxo grew from semi-obscurity to become the top pharmaceuticals company in the world on the back of a single new drug, Zantac, but arguably the rules in this industry have changed since then. Governments are cutting back their spending; generic drugs are becoming more popular all the time; and smaller, entrepreneurial biotechnology companies are having an impact on the industry giants.

On the other hand, privatization and the splitting up of the utilities has improved efficiencies – although these improvements may sometimes have resulted in higher profits rather than lower prices.

At the same time, many dominant industry leaders do falter and fail. United Steel was once the world's largest company and is now 'nowhere in sight'.

Sometimes an industry declines, but sometimes large organizations become sluggish with power. Others diversify and get it wrong strategically, and then get taken over and possibly split up.

What, then, goes wrong?

- loss of control
- lack of co-ordination and communication
- lost momentum/motivation/hunger.

The key issue

Big must think and behave small! Because:

- speed is critical as product life cycles are getting shorter
- information can be dispersed quickly and electronically.

The final question

Do alliances make more sense than mergers?

Although their popularity has waned in the 1990s, *research evidence* confirms that successful diversified conglomerates have been very profitable at certain times and in certain circumstances. Generally, these conglomerates succeeded because they carefully targeted their acquisitions, avoided paying too much (normally), adopted an appropriately decentralized structure and control systems; and corporately added value. Much akin to the concept of core competency discussed in Chapter 4, and in keeping with the theme of a **focus strategy** as an alternative to diversification, Goold *et al.* (1994) use the term *heartland* to describe a range of business activities to which a corporation can add value rather than destroy value by trying to manage a conglomerate which is too diverse, including:

- common key success factors – often market driven
- related core competencies and strategic capabilities
- related technologies.

Whilst we discuss some of these strategic alternatives in Chapter 16, it should not be forgotten that a strategy of focus is not immune from the risk of over-dependency.

> *As soon as things go wrong, companies start talking about focus. Focus is the crutch of mediocre management … If you are trained in the techniques of management … you should be able to apply them across a range of companies. Diversified companies possess both defensive qualities in recession and a springboard for new ventures in more expansive times.*

A COMMENT IN DEFENCE OF CONGLOMERATE DIVERSIFICATION BY SIR OWEN GREEN, PREVIOUSLY A SUCCESSFUL CHAIRMAN OF BTR. SOURCE *MANAGEMENT TODAY*, JUNE 1994

Constable (1986) argued that the UK had the highest rate of diversification among the leading industrial nations (even Japan) between 1950 and 1985 largely through acquisitions and mergers and, as a result, developed the most concentrated economic structure alongside a weak small firm sector. He contends that Japan, the USA and Germany have concentrated more on product and market development and on adding value to current areas of activity, hence have enjoyed greater economic prosperity. Hilton (1987) suggested that Germany and Japan have placed a greater emphasis on the respective banking systems, rather than shareholders, providing funding – thus influencing both the number of takeover bids and expectations of performance.

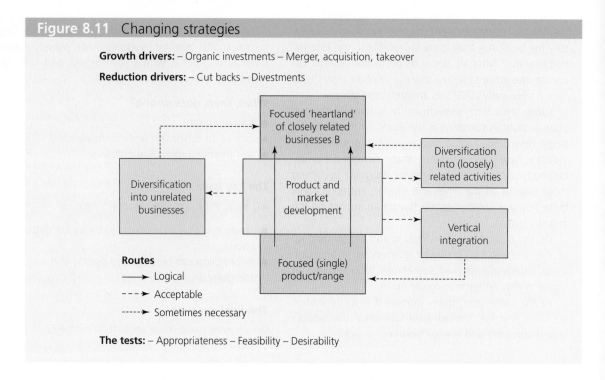

Figure 8.11 Changing strategies

Diversification and acquisition strategies, and tests to establish whether or not a proposed diversification seems worthwhile, will be considered further in Chapter 12, while an online case explains how Kodak has had to shift its focus as the demand for 'traditional' film has dropped significantly.

Figure 8.11 tracks alternatives, with the most logical strategic choices built around relatedness and the consequent synergy, and product and market development being used to extend a single product range while retaining a clear focus. Acceptable diversification strategies may be followed, but are later reversed as the organization returns to a more focused alternative. The three evaluative tests – appropriateness, feasibility and desirability – at the bottom of the chart are considered next.

8.3 Introducing strategy evaluation

No single evaluation technique or framework will provide a definite answer to which strategy or strategies a company should select or follow at any given time, but particular techniques will prove helpful in particular circumstances.

A sound choice will always address four issues:

1 competitiveness and competitive advantage
2 strategic logic and synergy
3 the financial returns, which should normally exceed the cost of capital
4 the ability to implement.

Figure 8.12 (which is a reproduction of Figure 2.2) links this argument back to the key topics of the business and revenue models which we discussed in Chapter 2. An ideal choice will make a positive impact on both the business and revenue models; and where a choice needs to be made between an option that would benefit either the business or the revenue model but not the other, there is an identifiable downside risk to factor in to the decision. When you read the next section, you will appreciate that in such cases desirability on the part of the decision-makers will be an important force.

Figure 8.12 Strategic evaluation and choice

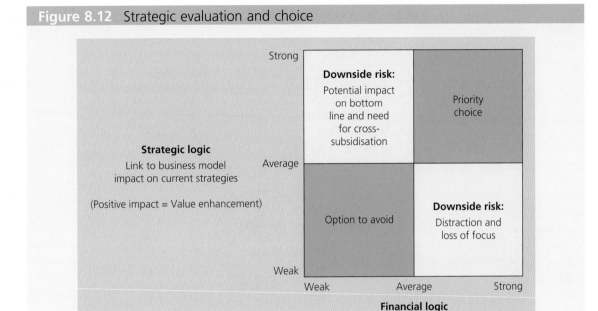

Several frameworks and techniques which are often classified as means of analyzing strategy have been discussed in earlier chapters and are listed in Box 8.1, together with a number of additional financial considerations. **These are explained and discussed in the Finance in Action supplement which is provided on the online platform**.

Certain essential criteria, however, should be considered in assessing the merits and viability of existing strategies and alternatives for future change. This section considers how one might assess whether or not a corporate, competitive or functional strategy is effective or likely to be effective in terms of *appropriateness, feasibility* and *desirability*. Some of the considerations are likely to conflict with each other, and consequently an element of judgement is required in making a choice. The most appropriate or feasible option for the firm may not be the one that its managers regard as most desirable, for example.

In many respects, the key aspects of any proposed changes concern the *strategic logic*, basically the subject of this book so far, and the *ability to implement*. Implementation and change are the subject of the final chapters.

Strategic logic relates to four elements, first the relationship and fit between the strategies and the mission or purpose of the organization; and the current appropriateness of the mission, objectives and the

Box 8.1 The Main Strategy Evaluation Techniques

SWOT analysis
E–V–R congruence
Planning gap analysis
Porter's industry analysis and competitive advantage
    frameworks
Portfolio analyses
Scenario modelling
Break-even analysis

Investment appraisal techniques using **discounted cash flows**
Net present value
Internal rate of return
Payback
Cash-flow implications
(The public sector often also uses cost–benefit analysis.)

Figure 8.13 E–V–R congruence restated

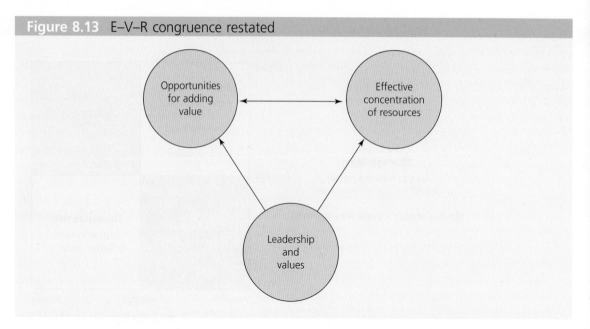

strategies being pursued (in which synergy is an important concept). Second, the ability of the organization to match and influence changes in the environment, third, its competitive advantage and distinctiveness and finally, the availability of the necessary resources. Figure 8.13, which recrafts the earlier model of E–V–R (environment–values–resources) congruence, shows that organizations must seek and exploit opportunities for adding value in ways that are attractive to customers at both the corporate strategy (to establish a heartland of related businesses and activities) and competitive strategy (to create and sustain competitive advantage) levels. Indeed, resources must be deployed to exploit the new opportunities, and this is driven or, in some cases, frustrated by strategic leadership and the culture of the organization.

When evaluating any corporate, competitive or functional strategy it is worth considering ten strategic principles, which are listed in Box 8.2 and all of which are discussed in detail elsewhere in the book. Where these principles are evident, and particularly where they are strong and powerful forces, the likelihood of strategic success and effectiveness is enhanced. In addition, the financial returns should always exceed the costs involved, unless there is a defensible strategic reason for cross-subsidization.

Corporate strategy evaluation

Rumelt (1980) argues that corporate strategy evaluation at the widest level involves seeking answers to three questions:

- Are the current objectives of the organization appropriate?
- Are the strategies created previously, and which are currently being implemented to achieve these objectives, still appropriate?
- Do current results confirm or refute previous assumptions about the feasibility of achieving the objectives and the ability of the chosen strategies to achieve the desired results?

It is, therefore, important to evaluate, retrospectively, the outcomes and relative success of previous decisions, and also to look ahead at future opportunities and threats. In both cases, strategies should be evaluated in relation to the objectives that they are designed to achieve, which can be facilitated by a quantitative chart along the lines of Table 8.4. In this illustration, and in order to evaluate current and possible future strategies and help to select alternatives for the future, the objectives are listed at the top of a series of columns, with some clear and objective measurement criteria, while others are more subjective. The alternatives, listed down the left-hand side, could be ranked in order of first to last preference in each column, or given a numerical score. In making a final decision based on the rankings or aggregate

Box 8.2   Ten Principles of Strategy

1 Market orientation and customer relevance
2 Innovation
3 Distinctiveness – relating to differentiation and competitive advantage
4 Timeliness (appropriate for the current situation) and
5 Flexibility (capable of change)
6 Efficiency – relating to cost control and cost efficiency, particularly in production and operations
7 Building on strengths and competencies
8 Concentration and co-ordination of resources (rather than spreading them too widely) to achieve synergy
9 Harmonization of strategy creation and implementation
10 Understanding – remembering that if a strategy is to be supported by employees who are motivated and enthusiastic it must be communicated and understood

marks, it may well prove appropriate to weight the objectives in the light of their relative importance. This table could simply be used as a framework for discussion without any scoring or ranking, if this approach is preferred. In terms of assessing the suitability of strategic alternatives in particular circumstances, Thompson and Strickland (1980) suggest market growth and competitive position as key elements.

Table 8.5 summarizes their argument. Concentration, for example, is seen as an appropriate strategy where market growth is high and the existing competitive position is strong. By contrast, where market growth is slow and the competitive position is weak, retrenchment may be the most suitable strategy for the organization.

Table 8.4   Evaluating strategies in terms of objectives

	Objectives*					
Strategic alternative	Ability to achieve specific revenue or growth targets	Ability to return specific profitability targets	Ability to create and – sustain relationship competitive with other advantage activities	Synergy potential - relationship with other activities	Ability to utilize existing (spare) resources & skills	and so on
Existing competitive strategies for products, services, business units	Score out of say 10					
And Possible changes to corporate and competitive strategies	*Or* Rank in order of preference					

* For evaluation purposes, each objective could be given a relative weighting

Table 8.5   Strategic alternatives: their appropriateness in terms of market growth and competitive position

Strategy	Market growth	Competitive position
Concentration	High	Strong
Horizontal integration	High	Weak
Vertical integration	High	Strong
Concentric diversification	Not material	Not material
Conglomerate diversification	Low	Not material
Joint ventures into new areas	Low	Not material
Retrenchment	Low	Weak
Turnaround	High	Weak
Divestment	Not material	Weak
Liquidation	Not material	Weak

Source: Developed from ideas in Thompson, AA and Strickland, AJ (1980) *Strategy Formulation and Implementation*, Irwin.

Where 'not material' is listed in a column, the contention is that the strategy is appropriate for either high or low growth or strong or weak competitive positions.

Criteria for effective strategies

When assessing current strategies, and evaluating possible changes, there is no such thing as a right or wrong strategy or choice in absolute terms. However, certain factors will influence the effectiveness of strategies and the wisdom of following certain courses of action. A number of authors, including Tilles (1963) and Hofer and Schendel (1978), have discussed the factors that determine the current and future possible effectiveness of particular strategies.

The factors that they suggest, and others, are summarized in Figure 8.14 and considered in three criteria or categories – *appropriateness*, *feasibility* and *desirability* – which have been selected, and factors linked to each of the them, for convenience. Although there is some overlap between the sections and some of the factors clearly impact upon more than one criterion, they are simply linked to the criteria to which they have the strongest link. The term 'the strategy' refers to each particular current strategy or future proposed strategic alternatives being considered.

Appropriateness

In reviewing 'the strategy', one must gauge that strategies are consistent with the needs of the environment, the resources, values and mission of the organization. In addition, is it acceptable to the strategic leader and other influential stakeholders?

Does the strategy proposed have the potential for improving the strategic perspective and general competitive position of the organization? In other words, will the individual business not only have a strong competitive position (possibly drawing upon strengths and competencies from elsewhere in the organization) but also be able to make a positive and synergistic contribution to the whole organization?

The company, therefore, must be responsive to changes in the environment and it may wish to be proactive and influence its market and industry. All the time it should seek to become and remain an effective competitor.

Is the strategy appropriate for the current economic and competitive environment? Is the strategy able to capitalize and build on current strengths, competencies and opportunities, and avoid weaknesses and potential threats? To what extent is the strategy able to take advantage of emerging trends in the environment, the market and the industry?

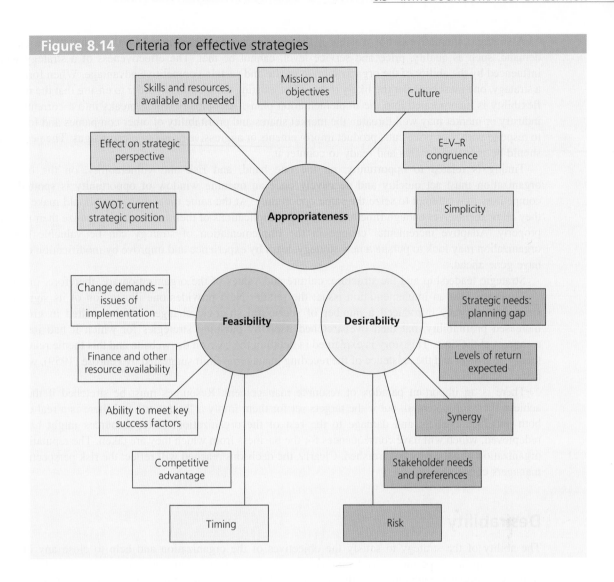

Figure 8.14 Criteria for effective strategies

Are the strategies being pursued and considered sufficiently consistent that skills, competencies and resources are not spread or stretched in any disadvantageous way? Does any new proposal exploit key organizational competencies? For current businesses and strategies: can the organization effectively add value, or would a divestment strategy be more appropriate? It will be appreciated that this consideration embraces both the opportunity-driven and resource-based perspectives on strategy.

Does the strategy fit the culture and values of the organization? If not, what are the implications of going ahead?

Is the strategy simple and understandable? Is the strategy one which could be communicated easily, and about which people are likely to be enthusiastic? These factors are also aspects of desirability.

Feasibility

Is the strategy feasible in resource terms? Can it be implemented effectively? Is it capable of achieving the objectives that it addresses? Can the organization cope with the extent and challenge of the change implied by the option? A lack of any key resource can place a constraint on certain possible developments. The cost of capital is explained in the Finance in Action web supplement accompanying this chapter.

A strategic alternative is not feasible if the key success factors dictated by the industry and customer demand, such as quality, price and service level, cannot be met. The effectiveness of a strategy will be influenced by the ability of the organization to create and sustain competitive advantage. When formulating a strategy, one must consider the likely response of existing competitors in order to ensure that the necessary flexibility is incorporated into the implementation plans. A company which breaks into a currently stable industry or market may well threaten the market shares and profitability of other companies and force them to respond with, say, price cuts, product improvements or aggressive promotion campaigns. The new entrant should be prepared for this and ready to counter it.

Timing is related to opportunity, on the one hand, and risk and vulnerability, on the other. An organization must act quickly and decisively once an opening window of opportunity is spotted, since competitors may attempt to seize the same opportunity. At the same time, managers should make sure that they allow themselves enough time to consider the implications of their actions and organize their resources properly. Adaptive incremental change in the implementation of strategy can be valuable here. An organization may look to pursue a new strategy, learn by experience and improve by modification once they have gone ahead.

Strategic leadership and the structure, culture and values of the organization are, therefore, important.

Timing is also an implementation issue; the retailer Next provides one illustration of its significance, since the company introduced a number of successful strategic changes which resulted in growth and increased profitability, but then overstretched itself by pursuing strategies for which it had insufficient resources at the time. This story is explained in detail in the case on the website and this theme relates to the theory of growth and the existence of the receding managerial limit suggested by Penrose (1959), which was discussed earlier.

There is an important paradox of resource management. Resources must be stretched if they are to achieve their full potential, but if the targets set for them imply a 'bridge too far' there is a real danger of both underachievement and damage to the rest of the organization. Here, resources might have to be redeployed, which will have consequences for the business from which they are taken. The reputation of the organization might easily be tarnished. Clearly, the decisions reached will reflect the risk perspective of the managers concerned.

Desirability

The ability of the strategy to satisfy the objectives of the organization and help to close any identified planning gap are important considerations. Timing may again be an important issue. The ability of the strategy to produce results in either the short or the longer term should be assessed in the light of the needs and priorities of the firm.

Decisions concerning where a company's financial resources should be allocated are known as investment or capital budgeting decisions. The decision might concern the purchase of new technology or new plant, the acquisition of another company or financing the development and launch of a new product. Competitive advantage and corporate strategic change are both relevant issues. The ability to raise money, and the cost involved are key influences, and should be considered alongside two other strategic issues:

- Does the proposed investment make sense strategically, given present objectives and strategies?
- Will the investment provide an adequate financial return?

The latter question is partly answered by the company's cost of capital and the topic of investment decisions is explored in the Finance in Action web supplement. Strategic fit is a broad issue and is addressed in the main part of the chapter.

Effective synergy should lead ideally to a superior concentration of resources in relation to competitors. The prospects for synergy should be evaluated alongside the implications for the firm's strategic perspective and culture, which were included in the section on Appropriateness. These factors in combination affect the strategic fit of the proposal and its ability to complement existing strategies and bring an all-round improvement to the organization. Diversification into products and markets with which the organization has no experience, and which may require different skills, may fit poorly alongside existing strategies and fail to provide synergy.

It has already been pointed out that risk, vulnerability, opportunity and timing are linked. Where organizations, having spotted an opportunity, act quickly, there is always a danger that some important consideration will be overlooked. The risk lies in these other factors, many of which are discussed elsewhere, which need careful attention in strategy formulation:

- the likely effect on competition
- the technology and production risks, linked to skills and key success factors. Can the organization cope with the production demands and meet market requirements profitably? Innovation often implies higher risks in this area, but offers higher rewards for success
- the product/market diversification risk – the risk involved in overstretching resources through diversification has been considered earlier in this chapter
- the financial risk – the cash flow and the firm's borrowing requirements are sensitive to the ability of the firm to forecast demand accurately and predict competitor responses
- managerial ability and competence – the risk here involves issues of whether skills can be transferred from one business to another when a firm diversifies, and whether key people stay or go after a takeover
- environmental risks – it is also important to ensure that possible adverse effects or hostile public opinion are evaluated.

Many of these issues are qualitative rather than financial, and judgement will be required. The ability of the organization to harness and evaluate the appropriate information is crucial, but there is a trade-off. The longer that the organization spends in considering the implications and assessing the risks, the greater the chance it has of reducing and controlling the risks. However, if managers take too long, the opportunity or the initiative may be lost to a competitor who is more willing to accept the risk. The subject of risk is revisited in Chapter 16.

> *In my experience those who manage change most successfully are those who welcome it in their own lives and see it as an opportunity for stimulation and learning new things. Implicit is the willingness to take risks, including making intelligent mistakes.*
>
> *I am much more interested in important failures that prepare the way for future success than I am in cautious competence and maintaining the status quo.*
>
> ROBERT FITZPATRICK, WHEN PRESIDENT DIRECTEUR GÉNÉRAL, EURO DISNEYLAND SA

Another consideration is the expectations and hopes of key stakeholders, the ability of the organization to implement the strategy and achieve the desired results, and the willingness of stakeholders to accept the inherent risks in a particular strategy.

Strategic changes may affect existing resources and the strategies to which they are committed, gearing, liquidity and organization structures, including management roles, functions and systems. Shareholders, bankers, managers, employees and customers can all be affected; and their relative power and influence will prove significant. The willingness of each party to accept particular risks may vary, such that trade-offs may be required. The power and influence of the strategic leader will be very important in the choice of major strategic changes, and their ability to convince other stakeholders will be crucial.

8.4 Decision-making, subjectivity and judgement

Although strategies can form or emerge as well as be formulated or prescribed, strategic change results from decisions taken and implemented in response to perceived opportunities or threats. The management of change, therefore, requires strategic awareness and strategic learning, which implies the ability to recognize and interpret signals from the environment. Signals from the environment are recognized by the organization all the time and in numerous ways, and they must be monitored and filtered in such a way that the important messages reach decision-makers. If strategic change is to some degree dependent on a planning system, that planning system must gather the appropriate data. Equally, if there is greater reliance on strategic change emerging from decisions taken within the organization by managers who are close to the market, their suppliers and so on, these managers must feel that they have the authority to make decisions that change things. In both cases, appropriate strategic leadership is required to direct activity.

This section looks at decision-making in practice, at how decisions are taken and might be taken, and at why some bad decisions are made. Strategy in Practice 8.1 focuses on strategic decision-making.

Strategy in Practice 8.1

Strategy concerns decisions and activities – both those intended to help meet desired ends and others which are circumstantially responsive. Typically, one decision starts off a chain reaction. The basic idea is that resources are used (at a cost) to produce products and services which are distributed, sold and consumed. The outcome should be that revenues exceed costs and that customers are sufficiently satisfied that they return.

Assume an organization wants to increase its profits. It can look to increase revenue or reduce costs – or, of course, both. Revenue can be improved by selling more products and by increasing prices (but only as long as demand doesn't suffer unduly). To which end a price rise should be accompanied by adding value in some way. Costs can be reduced by increasing throughput to gain scale economies (but that might require a price reduction to stimulate demand!) or by improving productivity at no extra cost. One might argue that strong organizations will be looking at all of these options all of the time. Sometimes the requirements for something to work in the desired way might not be met – and the side-effects can be counter-productive.

Let us apply this theme to a specific business issue, one fraught with issues. Airports really have no option but to take security seriously; they must screen passengers and their luggage. But they know they will come in for criticism when they keep people queuing for any serious length of time – especially if they have already been delayed at check-in. So how might an airport – and the various airlines – look to improve passenger satisfaction during check-in and security without increasing costs? The airport executive know that if the airlines get waiting times down people will be less grumpy and maybe even more willing to spend money in the various shops and outlets. If airlines can reduce waiting times with lower staff, then that is even more beneficial to their bottom line.

One tactic that is used now is to allow people to check in before they even arrive at the airport and print off their boarding card. They only need to queue at the airport if they have hold bags to check in. Printing boarding cards is often easier to achieve 'at home' and more difficult 'away from home' where access to a printer might be restricted. But it is difficult, perhaps impractical, to allow check-in too many days ahead. It also assumes people are willing to do this. One alternative is electronic check-in at the airport – but if several people arrive at once and they are unfamiliar with the systems, this can cause even longer delays. If the equipment breaks down or if the queue builds up too much it rather demands that check-in staff are flexible and willing to intervene. But they may themselves have only limited slack they can utilize. So the risk and trade-off: either don't make too many changes but make sure there are plenty of people checking passengers in – this can be costly and work its way through to fares. Or implement these types of changes in order to both speed up passenger lines and save costs (with fewer staff) – accepting that if things do go wrong passengers might be aggrieved and complain and eventually seek an alternative airline that either does it differently or has a better reputation for doing so.

One can see a similar 'whinge or walk' risk with some other decisions certain airlines take. The decision to charge passengers to check in hold bags is designed to speed up things at the airport by persuading people not to have much luggage. It also means those with luggage pay whilst those without luggage save. But whilst queuing is reduced at check-in it, can take longer to board a plane if most passengers have the maximum possible carry-on baggage. Delaying a plane on the ground can be costly in a number of ways, especially if one delay leads to further delays in a busy system. Everything involves some element of trade-off.

Of course, and returning to our earlier argument about real-time decisions that people take when something unexpected or undesirable is happening … individuals (who are allowed the freedom to do so) will intervene to try to make a system work better. If what they do actually works, it can eventually become practice and the system is changed. So, on the one hand, decisions and actions have a strong top-down element, with a clear outcome driving them, but at the same time bottom up practices might be the ones that come up with the real answers to the dilemma.

When things are working well in practice

- Activities deliver desired or desirable outcomes – in terms of profits and customer satisfaction.
- Costs are managed and controlled.

- Decision-makers are making sense of what's happening.
- There are no serious unintended consequences.

When things are not working well in practice

- What someone thought would work in a particular way doesn't in practice – *the idea was flawed*.
- What was intended has 'got lost in translation' and something else happens – and this can be both deliberate or accidental – *the execution of the idea was flawed*.
- Deadlines (and targets) are missed.
- Problems are not spotted quickly enough to take remedial action, or they are ignored.

Decision-making and problem-solving

Decision-making is a process related to the existence of a problem, and it is often talked about in terms of problem-solving. A problem, in simple terms, exists when an undesirable situation has arisen which requires action to change it. In other words, a problem exists for someone if the situation that they perceive exists is unsatisfactory for them and they wish to see something different or better happening and achieving different results.

However, in many instances, the problem situation is very complex and can only be partially understood or controlled and, therefore, decisions are not so much designed to find ideal or perfect answers but to improve the problem situation. In other instances, managers may find themselves with so many problems at any time that they can at best reduce the intensity of the problem rather than systematically search for a so-called right answer.

Ackoff (1978) distinguishes between solving, resolving, dissolving and absolving problems. A *solution* is the optimum answer, the best choice or alternative, and rational decision-making (developed below) is an attempt to find it. A *resolution* is a satisfactory answer or choice, not necessarily the best available, but one that is contingent upon circumstances, such as time limitations or lack of real significance of the problem, again developed below. A *dissolution* occurs when objectives are changed in such a way that the problem no longer seems to be a problem. Feelings about what *should* be happening are changed to bring them in line with what is happening; current realities are accepted. Typically managers accept new, weaker objectives which allow them to feel that there is no longer a problem. For example, achieving a target revenue growth of 5 per cent in a static market might be proving difficult; a revised (downwards) figure of 2 per cent would be much more achievable! *Absolution* happens when problems are simply ignored in the hope that they will rectify themselves; indeed, some people tend to treat minor illnesses in this way.

While there will always be an objective element in a strategic decision, other more subjective influences will also play a part. Figure 8.15 shows that the ultimate decision will have been affected by three elements. First, the results of whatever analyses have been used to evaluate the data available. Second, the intuition and perspective of the person or people involved. Past experiences and their willingness to trust the reliability and validity of the information that they have will both be influential issues. Some managers and strategic leaders, particularly those whom we would describe as entrepreneurial, often have an uncanny and barely explicable understanding of a market or industry and of which strategy would work. They do not appear to carry out any formal analysis or use any of the techniques described here. But such managers are a minority and others are well advised to use formal analysis! And, third, the political realities of the various

Figure 8.15 Decision-making

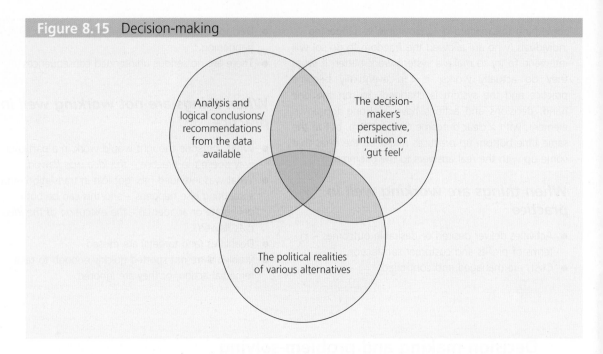

alternatives, in the sense that the contingent decision is the one that people believe can be implemented and not necessarily the alternative that on paper promises the highest rewards. To be effective, all managers must be able to handle political issues, as discussed in Chapter 15.

Figure 8.16 slightly differently illustrates the four key issues in any decision:

1 The nature of the actual intervention – the person or people involved will be involved for a reason, perhaps it is their direct responsibility, or they have been asked to advise and help, or they have been brought in because those responsible for the problem are simply not coping. What the problem 'means' to them, how they interpret and perceive the situation becomes a critical issue. Simply, they bring their own perspective, interpretation and objectives to the situation, which will naturally have an important bearing on:

2 The relevant power issues and political realities.

3 The quality and reliability of the information available.

4 Cultural issues, in particular norms, values and key roles because the decision taken should never ignore the likelihood of it being implemented successfully. If people oppose the changes or strategy proposed, for whatever reason (again discussed in Chapter 15), they may try to block its implementation. Where the change complements existing values and practices, it should be more acceptable than if it implies a change of culture and behaviour. Radical change is sometimes essential, and should not be avoided because it is likely to attract opposition. However, it must be realized that it will take longer to implement.

'Good' and 'bad' decisions

Decision-making, then, involves both information and people. While the strategic leader must develop an appropriate information system, they must also ensure that a good team of people has been gathered and manage them well.

The conductor is only as good as his orchestra.

ANDRÉ PREVIN

Figure 8.16 Key issues in decision-making

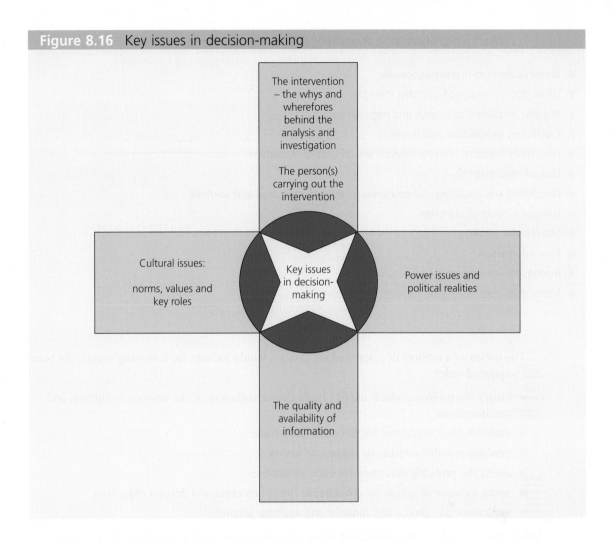

Considerable research has been conducted on group behaviour, and it is beyond the scope of this book to review it. Yet, no leadership style is universally better than others, and much depends on the personality, power and charisma of the leader.

Just as we would like to see evidence of more objectivity in some decisions, we would also like to see organizations being proactive as well as reactive in their decision-making – and yet they risk missing new windows of opportunity because they are perpetually 'crisis fighting'. Table 8.6 lists the characteristics of a fragmented organization with a likelihood of both inadequate decision-making for internal cohesion and synergy, and to be engaging in considerable crisis fighting. Organizations should usefully evaluate the extent to which any, or all, of these factors are present in the decisions that their managers are making. Improvements could then foster increased co-operation and sharing and allow managers who do seem to be perpetually crisis fighting to be more proactive in seizing new opportunities.

Because of the nature of the issues, it is not being suggested that there are obvious and quantitative measures available for assessing them. Rather, managers should be encouraged to confront and discuss the ways in which they behave, make decisions, carry out the decisions they make and, in the process, help or hinder their colleagues and other stakeholders. Hopefully, this approach will persuade people to reflect on the inherent style weaknesses without the process being either hostile or confrontational. While a personal self-audit is possible, the process is enhanced with groups of managers and frank exchanges. How often, when managers gather for a meeting, is the purpose task-orientated, with the process element being either ignored or taken for granted? Increased attention to process can strengthen the decision-making and, although not novel, the fact that it is frequently missing requires that it is restated.

Table 8.6   Manifestations of a fragmented organization

- Irrational decision-making (processes)
- Weak decision-making/leadership (people)
- Rigidity, reluctance to change and negative politics
- Conflicting perspectives and interests
- Over-hasty decisions (decisive!) which are difficult to implement
- Lack of clear purpose
- Dissolution and absolution (of problems) instead of resolution and solution
- Unhelpful personal objectives
- Stakeholder conflicts
- Poor information
- Inadequate measurement and control
- Managerial inability to take a holistic perspective.

The notion of a rational decision-making process would include the following stages, not necessarily in this sequential order:

- clarify the problem, which implies more than a statement of the obvious symptoms and manifestations
- establish clear objectives for the desired outcome
- generate possible alternative courses of action
- assess the probable outcomes for each alternative
- select a course of action by considering likely outcomes and desired objectives
- implement this choice and monitor and evaluate progress.

Whilst most decisions and managerial actions do not follow such a sequence, or incorporate all of these stages, short-cuts are often taken because of a lack of time or a lack of information, and sometimes through laziness. Simon (1976) identifies how the idea of 'satisficing' explains the acceptance of a satisfactory course of action (not necessarily the best solution), which at least deals with the problem. Lindblom (1959), and later Quinn (1980), offer alternative theories based around the concept of trial and error in incremental, learning stages as distinct from a more hands-off decision. Etzioni (1967) argues that managers make a judgement on the relative importance and priority of an issue or problem, and then base the time and attention that they give to the issue on this judgement. All of these are logical and defensible. The issue concerns the extent to which managers are avoiding – consciously or unconsciously – the elements of the rational approach, especially in the case of major, serious problems and, in the end, making poor decisions which fail to deal adequately with the problem.

Weak decision-making involves managers realizing and discussing the extent of:

- their tunnel vision, leading to a lack of internal synergy
- information flows and communications which prevent the right information reaching the people who need it when they can make best use of it
- personal objectives and agendas which lead to subjectivity, selfishness and internal tensions
- willingness to ignore the potential downside impact of their actions on other managers and other parts of the organization
- unwillingness to compromise to 'accommodate' other managers.

Many of these issues are ever-present, or are possibly being ignored – causing frustration and maybe even despair – if not being dealt with. There might be accommodation among managers, as distinct from consensus, given the existence of multiple objectives and perspectives.

Heirs and Farrell (1987) identify three 'destructive minds', the impact of which organizations must minimize if they are to manage change effectively:

- the rigid mind which stifles originality and creativity and ignores the need to change
- the ego mind which fosters subjectivity and makes collaboration very difficult
- the 'Machiavellian mind' which uses political activity to achieve personal objectives at the expense of others.

All effective managers will be political; they will use their power and influence to bring about decisions and actions which serve the needs and interests of the organization. Negative politics occurs when this power and influence is used against the best interests of the organization. How many of these minds are evident in a crisis fighting organization that is largely reactive to events?

Crisis fighters are typically pragmatic and decisive, but sometimes decisions taken in haste prove difficult to implement, as valuable time is spent trying to justify the decision. Taking time initially to search for support and agreement, involving a range of people and opinions in the process, can be hard to justify when time pressures are tight. However, if decisions enjoy people's support because they have been consulted and understand the background, implementation can be smoother, actually saving time in the end. We can learn a great deal from the Japanese here – but in how many organizations are managers listening and learning?

All the preferences of every internal and external stakeholder are unlikely to be met in full and so accommodation is necessary, hence managers ought to appreciate and accept that different people have different perspectives on problems and issues. There is a saying: 'the way we see the problem is the problem'. Too narrow a perspective leads to a poor decision with adverse impacts on others, whereas taking account of different perspectives demands dialogue and sharing.

Finkelstein *et al.* (2009) argue that bad decisions come in two stages. In the first instance, an individual or group exercises poor judgement; but then, and second, there is a failure to correct the mistake. They cite four key causes: misleading experiences; misleading prejudgements; inappropriate self-interest; and inappropriate attachments. Sometimes emotional attachments get in the way of logic. They see the Sinclair C5 (electric car) and the acquisition of ABN Amro by Royal Bank of Scotland as 'bad mistakes'. They comment that, due to what is known as post-hoc rationalization, managers will retrospectively argue that 'it seemed like a good idea at the time', which it perhaps did because of the causal factors involved. Often the managers involved are not stupid and they are not setting out to destroy their organizations, but they simply make mistakes and the risks they take do not work out for them.

Implementing decisions

A decision can only be effective if it is implemented successfully and yields desirable or acceptable results. Although spending time involving and gaining commitment from the people who must implement a decision is likely to lead to smoother implementation, the 'speedy decisive approach' may prove to be less effective because, if not supported, the alternative chosen may result in controversy and reluctance on the part of others to implement it. Vroom and Yetton (1973) have developed a model of five alternative ways of decision-making:

1 The leader solves the problem or makes the decision himself or herself using information available at the time.

2 The leader obtains necessary information from subordinates and then decides on the solution to the problem. Subordinates are not involved in generating or evaluating alternative solutions.

3 The leader shares the problem with relevant subordinates individually, obtaining their ideas and suggestions without bringing them together as a group. Then the leader makes the decision, which may or may not reflect the influence of subordinates.

4   The leader shares the problem with the subordinates as a group, collectively obtaining their ideas and suggestions. Then they make the decision, which again may or may not reflect their influence.

5   The leader shares the problem with the subordinates as a group, and together the leader and subordinates generate and evaluate alternatives and attempt to reach an agreement on a solution.

Vroom and Yetton (1973), as well as using the subjective expression 'solve' throughout, contend that the choice of style should relate to the particular problem faced, and their model includes a series of questions which can be used diagnostically to select the most appropriate style. While the model is useful for highlighting the different styles and emphasizing that a single style will not always prove to be the most appropriate, it is essentially a normative theory – 'this is what you should do' – and, therefore, should be treated with caution.

I make every decision, but get lots of advice. I don't delegate. It's 'What do you think?' 'What do you think?' 'What do you think?' Then boom, I decide.

JEFF INMELT, CEO, GENERAL ELECTRIC

Judgement

Judgement, per se, cannot be taught or learned; instead it comes from experience. Experience is gained by making mistakes, which, of course, are the result of poor judgement! Managers exercise poor judgement because it cannot be taught or learned.

Strategic changes can be selected by an individual manager, often the strategic leader, or a team of managers, and Vickers (1965) stresses that three contextual aspects have a critical impact on the decision:

● the decision-makers' skills and values together with aspects of their personality (*personal factors*)

● their authority and accountability within the organization (*structural factors*)

● their understanding and awareness (*environmental factors*).

Related to these, the decisions taken by managers are affected by their personal judgemental abilities, and understanding judgement can, therefore, help us to explain why some managers appear to 'get things right' while others 'get things wrong'. Vickers (1965) suggests that there are three types of judgement:

1   Reality judgements – Strategic awareness of the organization and its environment and which is based upon interpretation and meaning systems.

2   Action judgements – What to do about perceived strategic issues.

3   Value judgements – Concerning expected and desired results and outcomes from the decision.

Figure 8.17 shows how these are interconnected, given that decision-makers need to understand 'what is' (*reality*), 'what matters' (*values*) and 'what to do about it' (*action*). Their choice will be based upon a conceptualization of what might or what should be a better alternative to the current situation and, ideally, will incorporate a holistic perspective, implying either an understanding or a personal interpretation of the organization's purpose or mission, and an appreciation that what matters is a function of urgency and time horizons. A company with cash difficulties, for example, might need a strategy based upon immediate rationalization or consolidation; a liquid company evaluating growth options has greater flexibility. The choice will be influenced by managers' relative power and influence, their perception of the risks involved and their willingness to pursue certain courses of action.

Tichy and Bennis (2007) suggest that managers and leaders must exercise good judgement in three critical areas: the selection of key people, the choice of strategy to follow and how to handle crises when something unexpected happens. Effective leaders, they argue, are better briefed and better prepared and they 'make good calls'. It is, they say, all too easy for a leader to be: 'dazzled by an exciting strategy without thinking hard enough about how achievable it is, given the resources available' and quote a corporate strategic leader: 'things seem very different now it's my ultimate responsibility than they did when I was a McKinsey consultant in the past.'

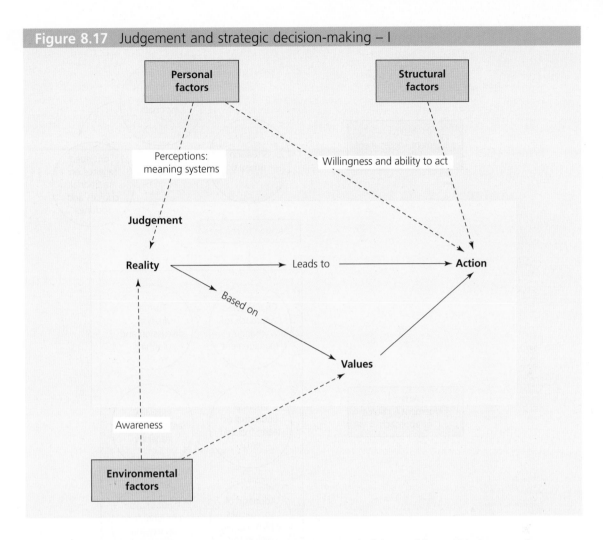

Figure 8.17 Judgement and strategic decision-making – I

Figure 8.18 draws together key points from the sections on decision-making and judgement, its top part explaining that managers have to assess any problematical situation and determine the extent to which it is normal or unusual: their reality judgement of the situation. Where they perceive that there is a real degree of normality to the events, they will likely continue to rely on traditional routines and approaches. However, where the situation is seen as more unusual, a decision has to be made about how to deal with it. This choice reflects action judgement, and there are six (and possibly more) alternatives to choose from:

1 Continue to rely on approaches which have worked well in the past.

2 From a position of leadership, take decisive action – reflecting an entrepreneurial style.

3 Involve others in formal analysis, discussion and planning.

4 Possibly involving others, adopt a trial-and-error approach to craft a new strategy adaptively or incrementally.

5 Seek input from an expert, maybe an external consultant.

6 Establish that there is a change project under way and follow a 'textbook' approach – along the lines of the one explained in Chapter 15.

The outcomes will be dependent upon the people who become engaged and involved, their relative positions, power and competency and the time and resources allocated to the decision-taking and implementation. This final part is the relevant value judgement.

Figure 8.18 Judgement and strategic decision-making – II

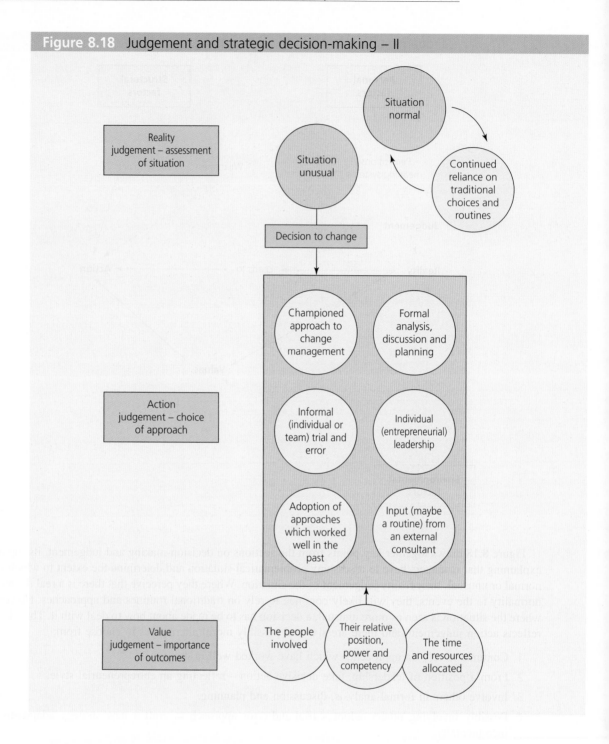

Finally, Case 8.6 looks at the respective decisions by Airbus and Boeing when they were considering where to focus their energy and investment. Their views and judgement on which new planes were most worthy differed. Maybe in their own way they were both right, as they targeted different markets … maybe they both wanted to avoid head-on competition.

Case 8.6   Airbus and Boeing   Eur, US

Airbus and Boeing are the two leading suppliers of commercial airplanes to airlines around the world; they are also both suppliers of military planes. Historically Boeing of the USA (which absorbed rival McDonnell Douglas) has been the leading supplier, but Airbus, a European consortium involving France, Germany, Italy and the UK, has made serious progress. In recent years they have been following quite different strategies – and both have struggled to implement their strategies. Boeing provided the world with the 747 'Jumbo' and the 737, the favourite plane of the low-frills carriers. Airbus pioneered fly-by-wire technology.

New airliners require huge investments in time and money to develop and test. Airlines will, however, sometimes order well ahead and pay deposits to help fund such investment – but only if they are convinced by the promise of the new plane. Consequently delivering on time is critically important.

Airbus chose to focus on a new 'Superjumbo' with passengers on two levels. A typical first-business-economy configuration would imply 555 passengers – but all economy it could easily seat 840. This A380 is four-engined. Singapore Airlines was the first to take delivery of a plane but early deliveries fell behind schedule. One complication was that this plane is so big only certain runways and terminals can handle it. Boeing has provided a stretch version of the 747 but has opted not to compete with a genuinely new plane in this sector of the market.

Instead Boeing has been developing its 787 Dreamliner plane – which was also delivered behind schedule. First deliveries – promised 2008 – were made in 2009. There had been problems with the supply chain. Boeing opted for global sourcing and what was meant to be a virtue appears to have turned into

something of a nightmare. Before the economic recession started to bite Boeing had a strong order book, with the first deliveries going to All Nippon of Japan.

The first Dreamliner (the 787-8) could seat between 210 and 250 passengers, depending on configuration. It has two engines and a 15 000 km range. It is smaller than Boeing's 747, 767 and 777 planes but bigger than the 737 and similar to the 757. It is fuel efficient (offering savings of around 20 per cent) and boasts a relatively low CO_2 emission figure. Carbon fibre is used extensively in the construction. It also offers greater humidity in the cabins and, for this reason, is seen as less likely to cause jet lag.

By 2012 there were scheduled to be two further models. The 787-3, seating between 290 and 330 passengers and with a flying range of some 6000 km; the 787-9, seating 250-290 and with a range of 8500 km. But at this time there were new problems with batteries and planes were grounded.

Airbus, which has grown on the back of the A320 and A340 models has also been working on an A350 long range medium size plane, but it is some years behind Boeing's Dreamliner. But in the end will it matter?

Question

Airbus and Boeing both developed their strategies when economies were healthy around the world. When demand started falling in 2008, and passengers were being asked to pay fuel surcharges, which of the two strategies would have looked to be the more appropriate?

Use the Internet to determine whether your instinctive answer to this question is in fact correct.

SOURCE: THIS CASE STUDY WAS PREPARED USING PRIMARILY PUBLICLY AVAILABLE SOURCES OF INFORMATION FOR THE PURPOSES OF CLASSROOM DISCUSSION; IT DOES NOT INTEND TO ILLUSTRATE EITHER EFFECTIVE OR INEFFECTIVE HANDLING OF A MANAGERIAL SITUATION.

Research Snapshot 8.1

Strategic choice and decision-making, while it was first conceptualized by John Child (1972), is an important element of strategic management that has been widely researched in recent years. More recently, he and a colleague have developed and tested (in Egypt) an 'integrated model of strategic decision-making

rationality', which incorporates variables related to the decision itself, the environment and the firm, and which resulted in the findings that these aspects influence strategic decision-making to differing extents but that the national cultural context also must be taken into account (Elbanna and Child, 2007a). Indeed, Elbanna and Child (2007b) modelled influences upon the 'effectiveness' of strategic decisions (measured by 'rationality, intuition and political behaviour'), plus seven other variables (again: decision, environment and firm), testing the model in Egypt, and they found that: '(i) both rational and political processes appear to have more influence on strategic decision effectiveness than does intuition, (ii) strategic decision effectiveness is both process- and context-specific and (iii) certain results support the "culture-free" argument, while others support the "culture-specific" argument' (*ibid*: p.431).

Key top management (so-called 'upper echelons' of organizations) factors influencing strategic choice and performance (the latter indicated by *, whereas other factors which are not directly shown to thereby influence performance are shown as §) include, for example: (i) their diversity*, including both their age and 'functional heterogeneity', in terms of strategic choices including innovation and acquisitions (Olson *et al.*, 2006), (ii) how they utilize social capital*, 'a vital operative mechanism through which links between executive characteristics, strategic choice, and performance occur' (Shipilov and Danis, 2006), or with regard to external social capital in 'late movers' (Yoo *et al.*, 2009), (iii) their other characteristics§, including of their CEOs, and it was noted that one major factor, 'TMT's "aggressiveness" (commitment to beating the competition, attitude to innovation, willingness to take risks)' (Papadakis and Barwise, 2002), suggesting more entrepreneurial strategic choices, (iv) the top manager's 'core self-evaluation' (CSE)§, including 'self-esteem, self-efficacy, locus of control and emotional stability', or even more so 'hyper-CSE', who exhibit hubris i.e. 'self-confidence, self-potency and conviction that they will prevail' (Hiller and Hambrick, 2005), again which are characteristics also of more entrepreneurial individuals, (v) their 'cognitive diversity, task conflict and competence-based trust'§ (Olson *et al.*, 2007) and (vi) the use of advisers§ by CEOs and top management teams (Arendt *et al.*, 2005). If managers completely comprehend their 'competitive environment' and 'competitive dynamics' of their firm, they can then make effective strategic decisions that enhance performance (proxied, in this case, by profitability), specifically in terms of: '(1) Whether to enter a new market? (2) How to respond to a competitive attack? (3) If and how to pursue growth in existing markets? (4) Whether to compete or co-operate?' (Ketchen *et al.*, 2004).

Amason and Mooney (2008: p.407), in theorizing the 'The Icarus paradox revisited', found that: 'organizations

that perform well sometimes squander their success subsequently through poor decision-making' due to 'a defensive mindset that may lead to dysfunctional outcomes', Vos (2005) highlighted how managers lack the 'skills … to reflect on themselves strategically', particularly with regard to innovation, and suggests a 'Quick Scan' that can 'support managers of SMEs in developing strategic self-descriptions that highlight the need for innovation', thus they 'initiate strategic sense-making in the context of SMEs'. Leavy (2003) suggested that, rather than just adopting *either* a Porterian market position oriented *or* the Prahalad and Hamel core competence method of strategic choice, managers should adopt both of these strategic choice methodologies. Mazzarol and Reboud (2006) noted that, in terms of social capital, smaller innovative firms were less reliant upon advisers from outside the firm, relying upon customers to influence the strategic decision to commercialize their innovation. Furthermore, in service SMEs, Jansen *et al.* (2011) uncovered how: 'Evaluative judgements (risk acceptance and confidence) explain the negative effects of social capital on [strategic] decision effectiveness. Service delivery and dependency on tacit know-how account for differences between SMEs in different service sectors and serve as explanations for different effects of social capital as a decision aid.' Finally, a recent model helps non-profits evaluate whether they are 'doing the right things', financially, and in terms of quality and thus assist their strategic decision-making (Krug and Weinberg, 2004).

The role of prior experience in strategy formulation has been investigated, with the concept of 'analogical reasoning', where strategists 'transfer useful wisdom from similar settings they have experienced in the past', and thus, 'Faced with a novel industry, they seek a familiar industry which matches the novel one along that subset of characteristics. They transfer from the matching industry high-level policies that guide search in the novel industry' (Gavetti *et al.*, 2005). Other antecedent factors include their personalities and traits, in this case in SMEs with the 'pragmatist' and the 'charismatic entrepreneur', the latter adopting 'a more rational, planned approach', due to their 'review[ing] their propensity to take risk, share power and involve more people' in making decisions (McCarthy, 2003).

Performance measurement, also addressed in Chapter 11, can also be linked to strategy formulation and, indeed, there are an extensive number of performance measurement 'systems' or 'initiatives' that could be utilized (Pun and White, 2005). Andrews *et al.*

(2009), furthermore, attempted to establish the influence of both strategy formulation and content upon performance, finding that performance is exacerbated by 'logical incrementalism' and 'strategy absence', whereas the strategy content variables of 'prospecting' and 'defending' improve performance. Noy and Ellis (2003) observed that, within strategy formulation, risk is a 'neglected component', with relatively little use of 'risk-assessment models', with the notion of risk being a key element supported elsewhere (Parnell and Lester, 2003). Moizer and Tracey (2010) use a 'causal-loop' to illustrate the trade-off between the allocation of resources to both their commercial and social activities.

The articles below provide a deeper understanding of strategic choice, strategy formulation, strategic alternatives and strategic decision-making. The further reading from this literature will help students to develop their perception and critical awareness of the choice of strategies from a set of alternatives, and also to highlight the developing thinking in relation to what is a long-established (over 40 years) theory of strategic choice, in particular how it is applied practically in varied organizational, economic and geographical contexts.

Further Reading

Child, J. (1972) 'Organization structure, environment and performance: The role of strategic choice', *The Journal of the British Sociological Association*, 6, pp. 1–22.

Amason, A.C. and Mooney, A.C. (2008) 'The Icarus paradox revisited: how strong performance sows the seeds of dysfunction in future strategic decision-making', *Strategic Organization*, Vol. 6, No. 4, pp. 407–434.

Andrews, R., Boyne, G.A., Law, J. and Walker, R.M. (2009) 'Strategy formulation, strategy content and performance: An empirical analysis', *Public Management Review*, Vol. 11, No. 1, pp. 1–22.

Arendt, L.A., Priem, R.L. and Ndofor, H.A. (2005) 'A CEO-adviser model of strategic decision making', *Journal of Management*, Vol. 31, No. 5, pp. 680–699.

Elbanna, S. and Child, J. (2007a) 'Influences on strategic decision effectiveness: Development and test of an integrative model', *Strategic Management. Journal*, Vol. 28, pp. 431–453.

Elbanna, S. and Child, J. (2007b) 'The influence of decision, environmental and firm characteristics on the rationality of strategic decision-making', *Journal of Management Studies*, Vol. 44, pp. 561–591.

Gavetti, G., Levinthal, D.A. and Rivkin, J.W. (2005) 'Strategy making in novel and complex worlds: the power of analogy', *Strategic Management Journal*, Vol. 26, pp. 691–712.

Hiller, N.J. and Hambrick, D.C. (2005) 'Conceptualizing executive hubris: the role of (hyper-) core self-evaluations in strategic decision-making', *Strategic Management Journal*, Vol. 26, No. 297–319.

Jansen, R.J.G., Curseu, P.L., Vermeulen, P.A.M., Geurts, J.L.A. and Gibcus, P. (2011) 'Social capital as a decision aid in strategic decision-making in service organizations', *Management Decision*, Vol. 49, No. 5, pp. 734–747.

Ketchen, D.J. Jr., Snow, C. and Street, V.L. (2004) 'Improving firm performance by matching strategic decision-making processes to competitive dynamics', *The Academy of Management Executive*, Vol. 18, No. 4, pp. 29–43

Krug, K. and Weinberg, C.B. (2004) 'Mission, money and merit: Strategic decision making by nonprofit managers', *Nonprofit Management and Leadership*, Vol. 14, pp. 325–342.

Leavy, B. (2003) 'Assessing your strategic alternatives from both a market position and core competence perspective', *Strategy & Leadership*, Vol. 31, No. 6, pp. 29–35.

Mazzarol, T. and Reboud, S. (2006) 'The strategic decision making of entrepreneurs within small high innovator firms', *International Entrepreneurship and Management Journal*, Vol. 2, No. 2, pp. 261–280.

McCarthy, B. (2003) 'The impact of the entrepreneur's personality on the strategy-formation and planning process in SMEs', *Irish Journal of Management*, Vol. 24, No. 1, pp. 154–172.

Moizer, J. and Tracey, P. (2010) 'Strategy making in social enterprise: The role of resource allocation and its effects on organizational sustainability', *Systems Research*, Vol. 27, pp. 252–266.

Noy, E. and Ellis, S. (2003) 'Risk: a neglected component of strategy formulation', *Journal of Managerial Psychology*, Vol. 18, No. 7, pp. 691–707.

Olson, B.J., Parayitam, S. and Bao, Y. (2007) 'Strategic decision making: The effects of cognitive diversity, conflict, and trust on decision outcomes', *Journal of Management*, Vol. 33, No. 2, pp. 196–222.

Olson, B.J., Parayitam, S. and Twigg, N.W. (2006) 'Mediating role of strategic choice between top management team diversity and firm performance: Upper echelons theory revisited', *Journal of Business and Management*, Vol. 12, No. 2, pp. 111–127.

Papadakis, V. M. and Barwise, P. (2002) 'How much do CEOs and top managers matter in strategic decision-making?', *British Journal of Management*, Vol. 13, pp. 83–95.

Parnell, J. A. and Lester, D. L. (2003) 'Towards a philosophy of strategy: reassessing five critical dilemmas in strategy formulation and change', *Strategic Change*, Vol. 12, pp. 291–303.

Pun, K. F. and White, A. S. (2005) 'A performance measurement paradigm for integrating strategy formulation: A review of systems and frameworks', *International Journal of Management Reviews*, Vol. 7, pp. 49–71.

Shipilov, A. and Danis, W. (2006) 'TMG social capital, strategic choice and firm', *European Management Journal*, Vol. 24, No. 1, pp. 16–27.

Vos, J-P. (2005) 'Developing strategic self-descriptions of SMEs', *Technovation*, Vol. 25, No. 9, pp. 989–999.

Yoo, J. W., Reed, R., Shin, S. J. and Lemak, D. J. (2009) 'Strategic choice and performance in late movers: Influence of the top management team's external ties', *Journal of Management Studies*, Vol. 46, pp. 308–335.

Summary

Some strategies are intended, while others are emergent in real time. Intended strategies can emanate from planning and also from ideas input by key decision-makers or influencers, typically an owner-manager or a visionary strategic leader. Emergent strategies happen when intended strategies are changed incrementally as they are implemented or when organizations respond to environmental opportunities and threats. We would expect to find at least some evidence of all of these modes in every organization – simply the relative significance of each one will vary.

There is a range of strategic alternatives and strategic means that organizations might review and possibly choose at any time. Organizations will change their directions and strategies and they do not always pursue the same strategy in the same way. Normally, they will aim to be proactive and purposeful about this. Sometimes, however, they are constrained: an option that they would like to pursue is unrealistic.

Over time, the corporate portfolio migrates. It should be built around a defensible heartland of related businesses, accepting that at times there will be diversification into related and unrelated activities. We cannot finally judge the worthiness of a particular choice until we take account of the organization's ability to implement the strategy that it has chosen.

The key strategic alternatives are *limited growth* (market penetration, market development and product development), *substantive growth* (horizontal integration, vertical integration, related diversification or unrelated diversification) and retrenchment. *Innovation* is an important aspect of market and product development – organizations should be constantly on the lookout for opportunities to improve and thus stay ahead as a competitor. The key strategic means are *organic growth*, internal investment to develop new competencies, *acquisition* (friendly purchase), *merger* (two companies simply joining together), *takeover* (hostile purchase), *strategic alliances* (partnerships, whatever the form) and *joint ventures* (alliances which involve a major financial investment by the parties concerned).

When evaluating and selecting strategies, it is important for organizations to address the following questions: What constitutes a good strategic choice? What can the organization do and what can it not do? What should the organization seek to do and what should it not seek to do?

An effective strategy is one that meets the needs and preferences of the organization, its key decision-makers and influencers – ideally better than any alternatives – and can be implemented successfully. The techniques introduced in earlier parts of the book can all make a contribution, but there are likely to be subjective elements as well. There are three broad criteria for evaluating strategies:

Appropriateness: Its fit, and ability to strengthen, the existing portfolio of activities; compatibility with the organizational mission; impact on opportunities and weaknesses, on E–V–R congruence; and whether it can stretch the organization's resources and exploit its core competencies further, or requires diversification.

Feasibility: Its ability to be implemented successfully (without any detrimental impact upon present activities); the organization's possession of, or ability to acquire, the skills and competencies required; whether the implied costs can be met; and whether there is an opportunity to build and sustain a strong competitive position.

Desirability: Whether: the option truly helps to close the planning gap; the organization is comfortable with the risks implied; it is a justifiable (and, in certain cases, the most profitable) use of organizational effort and resources; and potential synergy is acquired and stakeholder needs will be met and satisfied.

When reviewing options, it is unlikely that one will turn out to be the most appropriate, the most feasible and the most desirable. Trade-offs will have to be made.

The decision-making processes used will inevitably have elements of subjectivity. Judgement will have to be applied alongside any technique-driven strategic analyses. Decision-making, therefore, must embrace issues of intuition and political reality alongside the available information and analyses. There are a number of explanations – all easily appreciated – for 'poor' decision-making.

Online cases for this chapter

Online Case 8.1: Adidas, Nike and Umbro
Online Case 8.2: Granada/ITV: Granada's Acquisition of Forte
Online Case 8.3: Kodak
Online Case 8.4: Next
Online Case 8.5: Easy Group – *which is also relevant for* Chapter 9

Online Case 8.6: Diageo
Online Case 8.7: Electrolux
Online Case 8.8: Airtours
Online Case 8.9: Mars
Online Case 8.10: Nokia

Web supplement related to this chapter

Finance in Action: Financial management

Questions and research assignments

1 What is the difference between planned strategy, visionary strategy and emergent strategy? Distinguish between adaptive and incremental change.

2 Thinking about any project or sporting event you have been involved with, how relevant are the introductory comments on professional football? What have you learned about strategy creation from your own experiences in either a business or other context?

3 For each of the following strategic alternatives, list why you think an organization might select this particular strategy, what they would expect to gain, and where the problems and limitations are. If you can, think of an example of each one from your own experience:

 • do nothing; no change
 • market penetration
 • market development
 • product development

 • innovation
 • horizontal integration
 • vertical integration
 • concentric diversification
 • conglomerate diversification.

4 What are the relative advantages and disadvantages of organic growth as opposed to external growth strategies?

5 Which of the evaluation techniques listed in the chapter (Box 8.1) do you feel are most useful? Why? How would you use them? What are their limitations?

6 From your experience and reading, which evaluation criteria do you think are most significant in determining the effectiveness of strategies? List examples of cases where the absence of these factors, or the wrong assessment of their importance, has led to problems.

Internet and library projects

1 For an organization of your choice, trace the changes of strategy and strategic direction over a period of time. Relate these changes to any changes in strategic leadership, structure and, wherever possible, culture.

2 Walt Disney Corporation became hugely successful and influential on the back of cartoon films, beginning with Mickey Mouse. In more recent years, theme parks and 'mainstream' movies have also been vitally significant. In addition, a

number of proposals have bitten the dust. As a consequence, in 2004, the CEO Michael Eisner was under considerable pressure from some shareholders to resign. Research and evaluate the various strategic options pursued by Disney. Where should it seek to develop next?

3 Mumtaz started life as an Indian restaurant in Bradford, West Yorkshire, in the UK. It was started by a son and his mother in 1979. A second brother – who was a medical doctor – later opted

to join the business. Mumtaz boasts Sir Alex Ferguson, various high-profile footballers and other celebrities as its customers. Her Majesty the Queen has eaten their food. There is now a second restaurant in Leeds and the business has diversified into Halal baby food (with 50 per cent of the sales going to white customers) and a range of supermarket meals – starters, mains desserts and breads.

Why has Mumtaz been as successful as it has with its strategic choices when there are numerous Indian restaurants in the UK?

4   In 1983 Tottenham Hotspur became the first English football club to be listed on the Stock Exchange. Subsequently, the club diversified, acquiring a number of related leisure companies. The intention was to subsidize the football club with profits from the new businesses. Initially this happened, but in the recession of the late 1980s football had to prop up the other activities. Businesses were closed or divested, and the

ownership of Tottenham Hotspur changed hands in 1991. During the 1990s entrepreneur Alan Sugar acquired the club, only to relinquish control when he proved unpopular with many Spurs fans. Sugar claimed the Club forced him to take his eye off the ball with his business. Since then, despite several changes, including a new owner and several new managers (the most recent being Redknapp and Villas-Boas) and spending heavily on new players, Tottenham Hotspur has struggled to win trophies as frequently as in the past. Research the various changes and evaluate the strategies. Was it appropriate and desirable for Tottenham to become a public limited company at the time it did? How different was the approach taken some years later by Manchester United? What strategies have made Manchester United the richest football club in the world?

Tottenham Hotspur plc **http://www.spurs.co.uk**
Manchester United FC **http://www.manutd.com**

Strategy activity

Reuters

Started in 1850 by a German living at the time in Belgium, Reuters is prominent and well-known as a news agency; it has employed journalists to report conflicts and events across the world.

But 'news' has never been Reuter's main revenue earner! The provision of financial data has always been the principal business, and for this it is the current world leader. In the early days pigeons were used to fly data from one stock exchange to another across Europe and further afield.

In 2001, and some 150 years old, Reuters was thought to be near to collapse because of the growing prominence of US rival, Bloomberg, which runs its own satellite TV channel and also owns Thomson Financial.

Reuters' main customers are banks, brokerages and fund managers. It opted to rationalize its product range

and to target these customers more effectively. It would look to provide data and analysis packages suited to specific needs in a more differentiated way. This implied higher added value products and in some cases premium prices. There was a downside risk that some customers would 'trade down' for a cheaper, more generic, package. There would also be fewer global centres. This would save on overheads; but, thanks to IT, customers were unlikely to be affected. In 2008 Thomson and Reuters merged.

Question

Do you think this more focused approach and the merger were perhaps risky in the economic recession and credit crunch of 2008 and 2009?

References

Ackoff, R. (1978) *The Art of Problem Solving*, John Wiley.

Anderson, C. (2006) *The Long Tail*, Hyperion

Bailey, A. and Johnson, G. (1992) How strategies develop in organizations. In *The Challenge of Strategic Management* (eds G Johnson and D Faulkner), Kogan Page.

Channon, D.F. (1983) *Strategy and Structure in British Industry*, Macmillan.

Constable, CJ. (1986) Diversification as a factor in UK industrial strategy, *Long Range Planning*, 19 (1).

Etzioni, A. (1967) Mixed scanning: a third approach to decision making, *Public Administration Review*, 27, December.

Finkelstein, S., Whitehead, J. and Campbell, A. (2009) *Why Good Leaders Make Bad Decisions and How to Keep it From Happening to You*, Harvard Business School Press.

Gladwell, M. (2000) *The Tipping Point – How Little Things Can Make a Big Difference*, Little Brown.

Goold, M., Campbell, A. and Alexander, M. (1994) *Corporate Level Strategy*, John Wiley.

Heirs, B. and Farrell, P. (1987) *The Professional Decision Thinker*, Sidgwick and Jackson.

Hilton, A. (1987) Presented at 'Growing Through Acquisition', Conference organized by Arthur Young, London, 31 March.

Hofer, C.W. and Schendel, D. (1978) *Strategy Evaluation: Analytical Concepts*, West.

Hurst, D.K. (1995) *Crisis and Renewal – Meeting the Challenge of Organizational Change*, Harvard Business School Press.

Idenburg, P.J. (1993) Four styles of strategy development, *Long Range Planning*, 26 (6).

Lindblom, C.E. (1959) The Science of *Muddling Through*, reprinted in *Organization Theory*, Pugh, D.S. (ed.) 2nd edn (1987) Penguin.

Mintzberg, H. and Waters, J.A. (1985) Of strategy deliberate and emergent, *Strategic Management Journal*, 6 (3).

Penrose, E. (1959) *The Theory of the Growth of the Firm*, Blackwell.

Peters, T.J. and Waterman, RH Jr (1982) *In Search of Excellence: Lessons from America's Best Run Companies*, Harper and Row.

Quinn, J.B. (1980) *Strategies for Change: Logical Incrementalism*, Richard D Irwin.

Rumelt, R. (1980) The evaluation of business strategy. In *Business Policy and Strategic Management* (ed. WF Glueck), McGraw-Hill.

Simon, H.A. (1976) *Administrative Behavior: A Study of Decision Making Processes in Administrative Organizations*, 3rd edn, Free Press.

Thompson, A.A. and Strickland, A.J. (1980) *Strategy Formulation and Implementation*, Richard D Irwin.

Tichy, N. and Bennis, W.G. (2007) *Judgment – How Winning Leaders Make Great* Calls, Portfolio.

Tilles, S. (1963) How to evaluate corporate strategy, *Harvard Business Review*, July–August.

Vickers, G. (1965) *The Art of Judgment: A Study of Policy Making*, Chapman & Hall.

Vroom, V. and Yetton, P. (1973) *Leadership and Decision Making*, University of Pittsburgh Press.

Chapter 9

Strategic planning

Learning objectives

Having read to the end of this chapter, you should be able to:

- distinguish between planning as a cerebral activity carried out by all managers and systematic strategic (or corporate) planning (**Section 9.1**)

- describe a number of corporate planning approaches and, in relation to these, discuss who should be involved in planning (**Section 9.2**)

- explain the concept of the planning gap (**Section 9.3**)

- discuss what is involved in a contemporary approach to planning, and assess the contribution of a number of planning techniques (**Section 9.4**).

Introduction

Mintzberg (1989) contends that the strategic leader should be the chief architect, in conjunction with planners, of corporate plans, that the process should be explicit, conscious and controlled, and that issues of implementation should be incorporated. Analysis leads to choice, which leads on to implementation. The process is sequential:

$$\text{Analysis} \rightarrow \text{Choice} \rightarrow \text{Implementation}$$

Certain organizations might claim that detailed long-term planning is essential for them, such as an airline which must plan capacity several years ahead because of the long delivery lead times for new aeroplanes and the related need to manage cash flow and funding. In addition, resources must be co-ordinated on an international scale. While planes are utilized on most days and fly as many hours in the day as possible, crews work only limited hours, and typically finish a flight or series of flights in a location which is different from their starting point.

However, Mintzberg argues that such planning of the implications and consequences of the strategic perspective is not necessarily the perspective itself, so detailed planning of this type should not inhibit creativity concerning the perspective. Planning of some form will always be required in large organizations because it forces thinking and enables and supports resource allocation and budgeting. And yet, the extent and nature of the overall planning contribution will relate to the industry and the environment and be affected by both leadership and culture.

Planning the future – thinking about the most appropriate strategies, and changes in strategic direction – is essential for organizations, particularly those experiencing turbulent environments. Rigid systematic planning, based on techniques and formalized procedures is no longer as fashionable as it was, nor is it the only way in which strategic change decisions are made. Organizations that become reliant upon professional planners and where the only outcome of planning is a plan may not allow for effective strategic thinking, and may not result in a clear direction for the future.

There are dangers, then, in thinking that all strategic changes can be planned systematically and procedurally. Whether it is the result of formal and systematic planning, or much more informal and *ad hoc* leadership and management – which, paradoxically, still implies an element of planning – an organization will have strategies and processes whereby these strategies are changed. The processes need to be understood, and in many cases improved – for example, where and how should it change and develop in the light of market opportunities and competitive threats? Lessons can be learnt about their appropriateness to certain strategic opportunities. Managers should know clearly where the organization is, and where it might sensibly go, and start making appropriate changes and they should then monitor progress and be aware of changes in the environment, in order to be flexible and responsive since they are, after all, strategy makers.

In this context, this chapter now considers what is meant by the term planning, and what is involved in the systematic planning cycle approach to the management of strategic change. The contribution of a number of planning techniques is evaluated, and possible pitfalls and human issues in planning are pinpointed.

Readers may notice that a number of the references in this chapter are rather dated because, whilst at one time strategic planning and strategic management were almost synonymous, that is no longer the case and relatively little is being written on strategic planning that improves on earlier material (though see the Research Snapshot at the end of the chapter). The earlier writings on the topic, however, remain important and valid since the points they make have not changed, although we must place strategic planning within the wider context of strategy creation.

Planning is one of the most complex and difficult intellectual activities in which man can engage. Not to do it well is not a sin; but to settle for doing it less than well is.

RUSSELL ACKOFF, 1970

9.1 Strategic thinking and strategic planning

Case 9.1 (FedEx) shows two key elements of strategy creation in action and working together – **planning** focusing on project management and the implementation of a visionary idea. Without sound planning, the venture could not possibly have worked. When we talk about 'strategic planning', it is not exactly what we mean: planning can also be used to identify future strategies, although it is only one way of identifying future opportunities. This section looks at planning's contribution to strategy making.

Case 9.1   Federal Express   US

Federal Express provides an excellent example of an organization (and an entrepreneur) that opened up an unrealized market opportunity and began a new industry. 'The greatest business opportunities arise when you spot things your customer didn't have a clue they needed until you offered it to them.'

The idea behind FedEx is simple. It is to provide a speedy and reliable national and international 'overnight' courier service for letters and parcels based upon air cargo. FedEx rightly claim to have invented the concept of overnight delivery, creating a whole new market where previously there was none. The company had a peripheral but significant role in the film *Castaway*, which featured Tom Hanks as a FedEx manager who survived the crash of a FedEx airplane only to spend several years marooned on a desert island. He held on to one of the packages from the plane and finally succeeded in delivering it.

FedEx is, however, unusual in a number of ways. Before it could even begin, FedEx needed a nationwide

(North American) distribution system with a fleet of planes and trucks – a huge investment in planning and resources.

The business was the idea of Fred Smith, whose father was also an entrepreneur who had founded and built a successful bus company. When Fred was a student at Yale in the 1960s he wrote a paper outlining his idea for a freight-only airline which delivered and collected parcels to and from a series of hubs. Traditionally parcels were shipped on scheduled passenger airlines as normal mail, whilst Smith proposed flying at night when the skies were relatively quiet. His paper was graded as a C. After graduating, Smith served as a pilot in Vietnam before he bought a controlling interest in Arkansas Aviation Sales, a company which carried out modifications and overhauls. Determined to implement his idea for a courier service he invested a $10 million family inheritance and raised a further $72 million from various sources based on a number of independent but positive feasibility studies.

FedEx took to the skies in 1973, offering a service in and out of 25 East coast cities with 14 jet aircraft. The demand was there, as he had forecast. Unfortunately the rise in the OPEC oil price made FedEx uneconomical almost as soon as it started. Two years of losses and family squabbles – Smith was accused of 'squandering the family fortune' – were followed by profits and Smith's belief, courage and persistence were rewarded.

FedEx opened a hub in Paris in 1999 and opted for a standard price across the eurozone; and in 2006 it acquired UK-based competitor ANC – which it rebranded FedEx UK. In 2004 FedEx acquired Kinko's, an American high street franchise that provides a range of office services. This allows customers to more readily access FedEx services.

FedEx is successful because it delivers on time and speedily, and because it has a sophisticated tracking system – SuperTracker which it introduced in 1986 – for when something does go astray. It uses as a slogan 'The World on Time'. There are now nearly 700 FedEx aircraft flying over 1 million miles every 2 days. The central hub remains in Memphis in the USA but the flights are international. Six million packages from 220 countries are handled every night. FedEx's courier vans cover another 2 million miles every day collecting and delivering these parcels. To ensure FedEx can maintain its service it flies empty aircraft every night, which track close to the pick-up airports and which are brought into service if they are needed.

Its success has, of course, spawned competition. But with learning and emergence FedEx has stayed at the forefront of the industry it invented.

Questions

1 What role did planning play in the beginning of the FedEx story and how do you think it is utilized now?
2 Is it more or less significant than visionary ideas and emergent strategy?

Task

Use the Internet to compare and contrast FedEx with UPS.

Robinson (1986) argues that the role of the planner should not be to plan but to enable good managers to plan, as the planner's task is not to state the objectives, but he or she should elicit and clarify them. Planning should concentrate on understanding the future, which is uncertain and unpredictable, and helping managers to make decisions about strategic changes. Thus, the aim of planning should be to force people to think and examine, not to produce a rigid plan. Hence the real value of planning is not the plan which emerges, and which might be produced as a summary document which is worth little more than the paper it is printed on, but rather the value lies in the **strategic thinking** that the act and process of planning forces people to do.

Undoubtedly, planning techniques, used carefully, can help to provide a valuable description and analysis of where the organization is 'now'. But for managing the future and its inherent uncertainties, vision and flexibility will also be essential, alongside a clear direction and purpose. New thinking is essential for reaching the new competitive high ground first.

Strategic planning systems, popular and dominant in the 1960s and 1970s, became less fashionable in the 1980s and 1990s since they were perceived to be too time-consuming and mechanistic, unable to keep up with the changes going on in business. In most companies planning had not contributed to strategic thinking and, because strategic thinking is essential, a new role has had to be found for strategic planning – which became fashionable, and is arguably still needed, since it enabled allocation of resources and management of budgets in new complex multi-product organizations and helped to pull together organizations' disparate activities and businesses.

The outcome for many organizations was the downside – formal planning systems, heavily reliant on financial data, and supported by thick planning manuals and too many staff at the centre.

On the upside, planning can encourage managers to think about the need and opportunities for change, and to communicate strategy to those who must implement it, particularly important in the 1960s and early 1970s when there was an abundance of investment opportunities and a dearth of capital and key priorities needed to be established. In complex multi-activity organizations, decisions have to be made concerning where to concentrate investment capital in relation to future earnings potential, thus generating a number of portfolio analysis techniques, some of which are studied later in this chapter. Rather than use these techniques for gaining greater awareness and insight, for which they are well suited, managers sought to use them prescriptively to determine future plans.

Formal strategic planning had become unfashionable by the 1980s because:

- Planning was often carried out by planners, rather than the managers who would be affected by the resultant plans.
- As a result, the outcome of planning was often a plan which in reality had little impact on actual management decisions and, therefore, was not implemented.
- The planning techniques used were criticized primarily because of the way in which they were used.
- The important elements of culture and total quality management were ignored.

And yet, many industries continue to experience turbulent environments caused by such factors as slower economic growth, globalization and technological change and so strategic thinking is extremely important, leading to the following questions:

- What is the future direction of competition?
- What are the future needs of customers?
- How are competitors likely to behave?
- How might competitive advantage be gained and sustained?

Organizations must ensure that these questions are constantly addressed rather than addressed occasionally as part of an annual cycle. Line managers who implement plans must be involved throughout the process, and every executive needs to understand how to think strategically. Rigorous frameworks and planning manuals are not necessary as long as the proper thinking takes place.

There should be a strategic plan for each business unit in a complex organization, i.e. clear competitive strategies built around an understanding of the nature of the industry in which the business competes, and sources of competitive advantage. Chosen strategies must have action plans for implementing them, including an assessment of the needs for finance and for staff training and development, which is generally less difficult than formulating a corporate strategy for a whole organization.

All managers plan how they might achieve objectives. However, a clear distinction needs to be made between the cerebral activity of informal planning and formalized planning systems.

A visionary strategic leader aware of strategic opportunities and convinced that they can be capitalized upon may decide independently where the organization should go and how the strategies are to be implemented. Very little needs to be recorded formally, since conversations between managers may result in plans which again exist only in individual managers' heads or in the form of scribbled notes. Equally, time, money and other resources may be invested by the organization in the production of elaborate and formally documented plans.

In all cases, planning is part of an ongoing continuous activity which addresses where the organization as a whole, or individual parts of it, should be going. At one level, a plan may simply describe the activities and tasks that must be carried out in the next day or week in order to meet specific targets. At a much higher level, the plan may seek to define the mission and objectives, and establish guidelines, strategies and policies that will enable the organization to adapt to, and to shape and exploit, its environment over a period of years. In both cases, if events turn out to be different from those which were forecast, the plans will need to be changed.

Like Case 9.1 (FedEx), Case 9.2 on the Dabbawallas of Mumbai also shows the link between vision and planning. It is interesting to consider how much information is stored in people's heads and how flexible their behaviour might have to be on any particular day if the trains do not run on time.

Case 9.2   The Dabbawallas of Mumbai   Ind

The Mumbai Dabbawallas is a 100-years-old lunchbox delivery system whereby tins of hot curry, rice and chapattis are delivered to people in their places of work. The tins are of a standard size and shape – they form a stackable cylinder – and up to 250 000 of them are delivered (and returned) every day by some 5000 wallas. Dabba means lunchbox; a walla (sometimes written as wala, sometimes as wallah) is a person carrying out basic work.

The origins of the business go back to 1885 when a banker hired a man to collect a dabba from his home and bring it to him at work, wait until he had eaten the meal and then return the empty tin to his home. Other colleagues caught on to the idea and did the same thing. One employee, Mahadev Haji Bache, saw the opportunity to build a business. He was really the founding entrepreneur who saw potential in an idea someone else had had. In 1890 Bache created his delivery business, employing 35 wallas from his home village. They made use of the commuter railway network that was growing in and around Mumbai. This original business has grown into today's network – known formally as the Nutan Mumbai Tiffin Box Suppliers Charity Trust – which appears to mix organization and systems with entrepreneurship in a flat structure.

The food has traditionally been cooked by wives, sisters and maids – but as more and more women are now working, other women have seen a business opportunity and established small catering businesses to produce food to order. The food is cooked and put into the sealed tins for a particular time each day. The dabba is then collected by a walla, either on foot and with a hand cart or more likely on a bicycle, from either the home or the micro business where it is prepared to someone's place of work and later taken back in readiness for the next day. Each tin is uniquely identifiable (with a set of numbers and letters painted on the lid or handle) and provided by the organization. The system is popular because it ensures people get a home-cooked meal each day – the trains they use for work are so crowded it would be very difficult for them all to be carrying lunch pails.

After collection any time after 7.00 am by a particular walla, and always the same walla, the tins are taken to the nearest railway station, sorted by their destination, and put onto a train at around 10.00 am. They may travel on more than one train, depending on the complexity of the route they must take, and they eventually end up in the hands of the walla who will deliver them. The system operates in reverse later in the day. All empty dabbas are returned by 6.00 pm. Teamwork is vital as there is a chain of people who all depend on the reliability and punctuality of everyone else. The chain cannot have weak links. Those involved appear to take great pride in the work they do and they are relatively well paid. They carry no paperwork; there are no scannable bar codes; in fact, there is no computer information system behind the operation although online ordering has recently been made possible. Social ingenuity rules and the reliability is such that no more than around ten dabbas go astray in a year – in the order of 1 in 6 million. One might wish to reflect on how this compares with many airline baggage systems.

The system is favoured by people who work in offices, schools, hospitals and government buildings. They are invariably 'white collar' workers. Because of religious and other preferences many have personal food tastes that are better satisfied from home than by local restaurants. Unless internal security systems require delivery to a nearby collection point then every dabba is delivered to the consumer's desk – and always by 12.30 am. If someone has forgotten something, perhaps their glasses or mobile phone, this can be delivered along with their lunch.

The wallas normally have only a modest school education and they come from one of a series of 30 villages around Mumbai. Many do not read or write very well. They all wear jackets and white caps to identify who they are and also to offer some protection from the wind and rain. There are just four women dabbawallas. Each dabbawalla provides his own uniform as well as two bicycles and a wooden crate for carrying a stack of dabbas.

A typical operation at a specified railway station within the network might see four independent groups of between 20 and 30 wallas who each collect from 35–40 customers near to that station. Each full dabba weighs around 2 kilos. In other words, easily between 3000–4000 dabbas are brought to the station every morning for the same time and for sorting. Four thousand full dabbas would weigh some 8 tonnes! The individual wallas have their own agreed route which they seem to memorize. They negotiate the price with each house – based on weight, distance and number of collections in the week – and they typically collect the meals at the same time every day. They also collect the money at some point in the week, normally on the evening return. Each of the four groups will be supervised by around four Mukadams, who are typically experienced dabbawallas themselves. They can cover for absent colleagues – so they must know the procedures and the routes. They also maintain records of every daily transaction and movement.

The tins might arrive at the station at around 9.00 am and at around 10.00 am they will be loaded onto a train. In between they will have been sorted and re-crated by the dabbawalls for their route and destination, using the details painted on the tin. The 'code' identifies originating and destination stations, the delivery dabbawalla and the relevant building, floor and room for the delivery. When the dabbas complete the final train journey on their route they will end up with the walla who will deliver them. Every collecting walla rides a train and delivers dabbas, in the main ones they did not collect themself. The system has to be very slick indeed. Whilst space has been booked in the luggage compartments of the trains, they are normal commuter trains and they only stop for the time it takes for passengers to get off and on. More dabbas and wallas are loaded at every subsequent station and the sorting continues on the train.

The revenues collected for the service are pooled and split equally amongst the group of dabbawallas and mukadams. They are effectively self-employed and easily replaceable (there is always a demand to be accepted into the pool) but they operate as a co-operative and share equally. A small top slice pays the costs of the Trust.

Questions

1 What role do you think planning plays in this organization? Is this 'strategic planning' or planning the implementation of a visionary concept?
2 How significant might it be that so much information is kept in people's heads?
3 Can some of the issues the wallas might have to face on a daily basis be dealt with via planning or do they require *ad hoc* flexibility?

The value of strategic planning

When managers and organizations plan strategies, they are seeking to be clearer about the business(es) that the organization is in, and should be in; increase awareness about strengths and weaknesses; be able to recognize and capitalize on opportunities, and to defend against threats; and be more effective in the allocation and use of resources.

Irrespective of the quality or format of the actual plans, engaging in the planning process can valuably help individual managers to establish priorities and address problems; and it can bring managers together so that they can share their problems and perspectives. Ideally, the result will be improved communication, co-ordination and commitment, hence there can be real benefit from planning or thinking about the future. What form should the thinking and planning take? Should it be part of a formalized system making use of strategic planning techniques?

Corporate and strategic plans concern the number and variety of product markets and service markets in which the organization will compete, together with the development of the necessary resources (people, capacity, finance, research and so on) required to support the competitive strategies. Strategic plans, therefore, relate to the whole organization, cover several years and are generally not highly detailed. They are concerned with future needs and how to obtain and develop the desired businesses, products, services and resources. The actual timescale involved will be affected by the nature of the industry and the number of years ahead that investments must be planned if growth and change are to be brought about.

Functional plans are derived from corporate strategy and strategic plans, and they relate to the implementation of functional strategies. They cover specific areas of the business; there can be plans relating to product development, production control and cash budgeting, for example. Functional plans will usually have shorter time horizons than is the case for strategic plans, and invariably they will incorporate greater detail. However, they will be reviewed and updated, and they may become ongoing rolling plans. While strategic plans are used to direct the whole organization, functional plans are used for the short-term management of parts of the organization, for example as applied to Federal Express.

Competitive strategies and functional strategies and plans are essential if products and services are to be managed effectively, but they should be flexible and capable of being changed if managers responsible for their implementation feel it necessary. Ohmae (1982) emphasizes that individual products must be seen as part of wider systems or product groups/business units and that, although short-term plans must be drawn up for the effective management of individual products, one must ensure that thinking about the future is done at the appropriate level. As an example, a particular brand or type of shampoo targeted at a specific market segment would constitute a product market. The company's range of shampoos should be produced and marketed in a co-ordinated way, and consequently they might constitute a strategic planning unit. The relevant strategic business unit might incorporate all of the company's cosmetics products and there should be a competitive strategy to ensure that the various products are co-ordinated and support each other. In terms of strategic thinking, Ohmae (1982) suggests that it is more important to consider listening devices as a whole than radios specifically, and that this type of thinking resulted in the Sony Walkman and similar products. In the same way, the Japanese realized a new opportunity for black and white television receivers in the form of small portable sets, when other manufacturers had switched all of their attention to the development of colour sets. If the level of thinking is appropriate, resources are likely to be allocated more effectively.

9.2 Alternative approaches to planning

Taylor and Hussey (1982) feature seven different approaches to planning:

- *Informal planning* takes place in someone's head, and the decisions reached may not be written down in any extensive form. While often practised by managers with real entrepreneurial flair, and often highly successful, it is less likely to be effective if used by managers who lack flair and creativity.

- *Extended budgeting*, primarily financial planning based on the extrapolation of past trends, is rarely used as it is only feasible if the environment is stable and predictable.

- *Top-down planning* relates to decisions taken at the top of the organization and passed down to other managers, who will have had little or no input into the planning process, for implementation. Major change decisions reached informally may be incorporated here, and then a great deal depends upon the strength and personality of the strategic leader in persuading other managers to accept the changes. At the other extreme, top-down plans may emanate from professional planners using planning techniques extensively and reporting directly to the strategic leader, and are the type of plans that may not be implemented.

- *Strategic analysis/policy options*, using planning techniques, involves creating and evaluating alternative options. Where future possible scenarios are explored for their implications, and possible courses of action are tested for sensitivity, this form of planning can be valuable for strategic thinking, being an appropriate use of planning techniques, yet one must consider its potential impact on people.

- *Bottom-up planning* involves managers throughout the organization and, therefore, ensures that people who will be involved in implementing plans are consulted. Specifically, functional and business unit managers are charged with evaluating the future potential for their areas of responsibility and are invited to make a case for future resources. All of the detail is analyzed and the future allocation of resources is decided. In an extreme form, thick planning manuals will be involved and the process may be slow and rigid. Necessary changes may be inhibited if managerial freedom to act outside the plan is constrained, and a formal system of this nature is likely to involve an annual planning cycle.

- *Behavioural approaches* can take several forms, but essentially require that managers spend time discussing the future opportunities and threats and areas in which the organization might develop. The idea is that if managers are encouraged to discuss their problems and objectives for the business freely, and if they are able to reach agreement concerning future priorities and developments, then they will be committed to implementing the changes. However, not all of the conflicts concerning resource allocation and priorities may be resolved, so scenario planning can be useful here.

- The term *strategic review* was coined to take the best features of the other six approaches and blend them together into a systematic and comprehensive planning system. All of these approaches have individual advantages and disadvantages, and they are not mutually exclusive. The approach adopted will depend on the style and preferences of the strategic leader, who must: (i) clarify the mission and corporate objectives and establish the extent and nature of changes to the corporate perspective; (ii) approve competitive and functional strategies and plans for each part of the business, however they might be created; and (iii) establish appropriate control mechanisms, which may or may not involve substantial decentralization.

Planning thus may be either informal (which cannot be taught) or formal (which can).

9.3 The planning gap

A number of authors have developed a number of essentially similar models of systematic planning, which all use the concept of gap analysis (e.g. Argenti, 1980; Hussey, 1976; Cohen and Cyert, 1973; Glueck and Jauch, 1984). The concept of the **planning gap** can be summarized as 'project the known – develop the new' (see Garvin and Levesque, 2006). It addresses two questions: Where do we want to go? Where can we go realistically?

When deciding future organizational strategies, one must consider both the *desired objectives* (where the strategic leader and other decision-makers would like to take the organization if possible) and *realistic objectives* (the influence and expectations of the various stakeholders, the existence of suitable opportunities, and availability of the necessary resources). Indeed, evaluating the risk involved in the alternative courses of action is crucial, such as diversification with its high failure rates (as discussed in Chapter 13), and so may be the only *feasible* strategy to achieve future, or maintain present, high growth rates – such that the strategic leader, under pressure from City investors, shareholders and analysts expecting growth rates to be at least maintained, may be forced to pursue high-risk strategies.

Table 9.1 illustrates how two well-known organizations, specifically Virgin and Sony, pursued several different strategies over a period of years.

While undue risk should be avoided wherever possible, nonetheless a certain level of risk must be accepted and stretching targets set for managers and businesses.

The planning gap should be seen as an idea which can be adapted to suit particular circumstances, although gap analysis could be regarded as a planning technique.

An example of the planning gap is illustrated in Figure 9.1 in which the horizontal axis represents the planning time horizon, stretching forward from the present day; either sales volume or revenue, or profits, could be used on the vertical axis as a measure of anticipated performance. The lowest solid line on the graph indicates expected sales or profits if the organization continues with present corporate, competitive and functional strategies; *it does not have to slope downwards*. The top dashed line represents ideal objectives, which imply growth and which may or may not ultimately be realized. The difference between these two lines is the gap: the difference between the results that the organization can expect to achieve from ongoing present strategies and the results that the strategic leader would like to attain.

Table 9.1   Applications of the simple growth vector

	Virgin	Sony
Market penetration	Publicity, self-publicity and exploitation of Virgin name, e.g. Branson's balloon challenges	Sony as a brand
Market development	Before divesting the businesses: opening Virgin Megastores around the world and a music business in the USA	The Sony Walkman and associated derivatives: existing products repackaged
Product development	Music retailing led to music production and publishing and later music videos	Tape recorders to videos; televisions; compact discs (some limited diversification involved)
Related diversification	Films, computer games	Computers, Sony Playstation (related technologies, e.g. PDAs)
Unrelated diversification	Virgin Atlantic Airways, Virgin Holidays, Virgin Cola, Virgin Financial Services	CBS Records, Columbia Pictures (vertical integration that some would argue was related diversification for Sony. The fact it happened facilitated the development of PlayStation.

The example illustrated in Figure 9.1 shows the gap filled in by a series of alternative courses of strategic action ordered in an ascending hierarchy of risk, which is constituted by the extent to which future products and markets are related to existing ones, as developed further in Figures 9.2 and 9.3. The lowest risk alternative is to pursue **market penetration** in the simple growth vector developed by Ansoff (1987) and illustrated in Figure 9.2, and which can be extended to strategies of *market and product development* (as discussed in relation to Figure 8.8 in Chapter 8).

Figure 9.1   An example of the planning gap

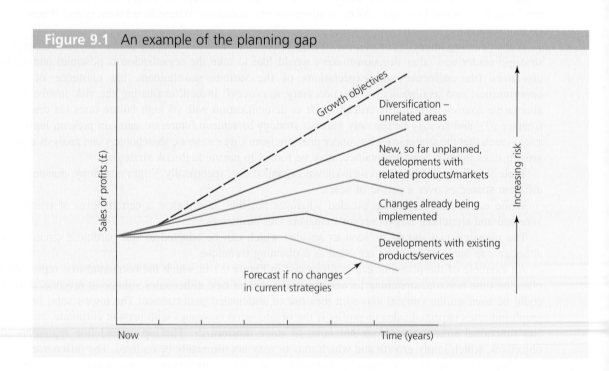

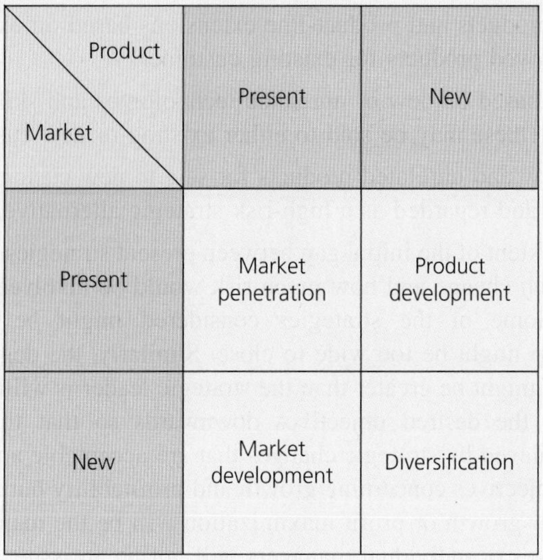

ANSOFF, HI (1987) CORPORATE STRATEGY, REVISED EDN, EDN, PENGUIN

Figure 9.2 Ansoff's growth vector

	Product	
Market	Present	New
Present	Market penetration	Product development
New	Market development	Diversification

Figure 9.3 An extended growth vector

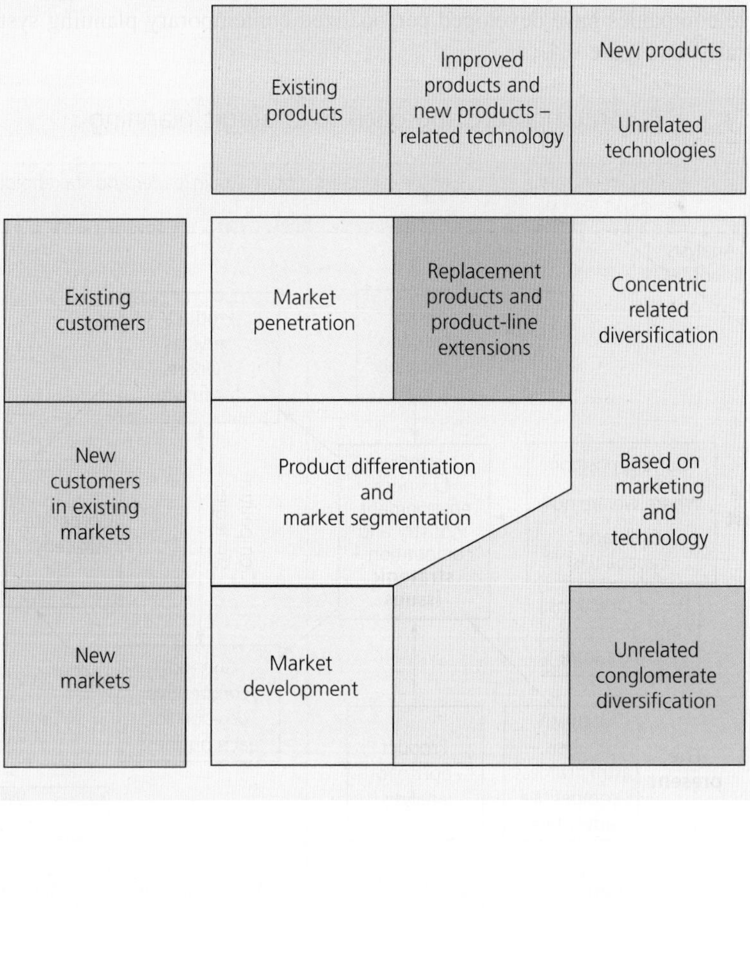

	Existing products	Improved products and new products – related technology	New products / Unrelated technologies
Existing customers	Market penetration	Replacement products and product-line extensions	Concentric related diversification
New customers in existing markets	Product differentiation and market segmentation		Based on marketing and technology
New markets	Market development		Unrelated conglomerate diversification

The highest risk alternative is diversification because this involves both new products and new markets. Figure 9.3 develops these simple themes further and distinguishes between the following:

- Replacement products and product-line extensions based on existing technologies and skills, which represent improved products for existing customers.

- New products based on new or unrelated technologies and skills, which constitute concentric diversification (these may be sold to either existing or new customers).

- Completely new and unrelated products for sale to new customers, known as conglomerate diversification and regarded as a high-risk strategic alternative.

Thinking about the extent of the initial gap between present strategies and ideal objectives enables managers to consider how much change and how much risk would be involved in closing the gap and achieving the target objectives. Some of the strategies considered might be neither feasible nor desirable, and consequently the gap might be too wide to close. Similarly, the degree of risk, especially if a number of changes is involved, might be greater than the strategic leader is willing to accept. In these cases, it will be necessary to revise the desired objectives downwards so that they finally represent realistic targets which should be achieved by strategic changes that are acceptable and achievable. This type of thinking is related to specific objectives concerning growth and profitability but it does not follow, as was discussed in Chapter 3, that either growth or profit maximization will be the major priority of the organization, or that the personal objectives of individual managers will not be an issue.

9.4 A contemporary approach to strategic planning

To avoid planning becoming an end in itself, and to ensure that planners facilitate management thinking, many large companies have developed personalized contemporary planning systems along the lines of the one illustrated in Figure 9.4.

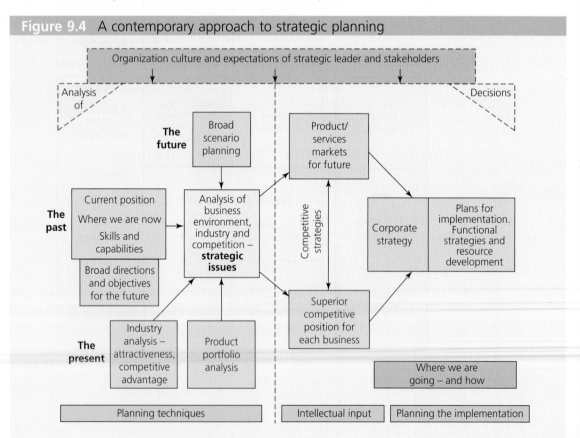

Figure 9.4 A contemporary approach to strategic planning

The organization's culture and the expectations of the strategic leader and the key stakeholders influence the whole process of analysis and decision-making – starting with an assessment of the current position of the organization, its skills and resources, and an evaluation of whether there is a clear understanding of the mission, the broad objectives and directions for the future.

Then the business environment is analyzed thoroughly, concentrating on the industries in which the organization currently competes and those in which it might apply its skills and resources. Feeding into this analysis are three other analyses:

- Broad scenario planning – conceptualizing a range of different futures with which the organization might have to deal, to ensure that the less likely possibilities, threats and opportunities are not overlooked, and to encourage a high level of flair and creativity in strategic thinking (see Chapter 4).

- Product portfolio analyses, which are discussed in greater detail in the next section; and contingency and possible crisis planning considerations can be incorporated in this.

- Industry analyses, following Porter's criteria for judging attractiveness and opportunities for competitive advantage (see Chapters 4 and 6).

This environmental analysis should focus on any *strategic issues* – current or forthcoming developments, inside or outside the organization, which will impact upon the ability of the organization to pursue its mission and achieve its objectives. Ideally, these would be opportunities related to organizational strengths. Wherever possible, any unwelcome but significant potential threats should be turned into competitive opportunities. The band across the bottom of Figure 9.5 shows how this contemporary approach blends planning techniques with an intellectual input and later action plans for implementing strategic choices.

Identifying strategic issues is the transition point from analysis to decisions regarding future strategy, where techniques give way to more intuition and intellectual inputs before implementation issues are explored.

From these analyses, competitive strategy decisions must be reached concerning:

- The reinforcement or establishment of a superior competitive position, or competitive advantage, for each business within the existing portfolio of products and services.

- Product markets and service markets for future development, and the appropriate functional strategies for establishing a superior competitive position.

When amalgamated, these functional and competitive strategies constitute the corporate strategy for the future which, in turn, needs to be broken down into resource development plans and any decisions relating to changes in the structure of the organization: i.e. those reflecting where the organization is going and how the inherent changes are to be managed.

Simply, planning techniques and analyses are used to clarify the key strategic issues. Discerning the issues and deciding what should be done to address them requires creativity (the search for something different) and hence a more intellectual input. Once broad strategic directions are clarified, detailed implementation planning will follow. Like the strategies, these detailed implementation plans are not inflexible.

New strategic issues ought to be spotted and dealt with continuously, enabled by the organization structure, either by decentralization and empowerment or by effective communication.

Case 9.3 examines the experiences of the international mining conglomerate Rio Tinto in 2008/09 given that the organization, which relies on huge investments and projects which take years from conception to fruition, must plan and yet must stay flexible and be ready to deal with issues that can threaten to jeopardize its plans.

A systematic approach to corporate planning may well succeed in the essential task of co-ordinating the plans for all the divisions and businesses in a large organization, enabling the strategic leader to exercise control over a conglomerate – and this is good. However, the system should not prohibit vision and learning within the corporation, since these are the two modes of strategy creation most likely to take the organization forward in a competitive and uncertain environment. Unfortunately, the vision and learning may be concentrated within individual divisions when in an ideal scenario it should permeate the whole organization.

Case 9.3   Rio Tinto

Aus

This case illustrates the speed at which the strategic issues that companies must deal with can change.

Rio Tinto is one of the world's leading mining groups and the second largest producer of iron ore. It is also involved in coal mining as well as uranium, copper and gold. It owns Alcan, the Canadian aluminium producer, which it bought in 2007. Its main base is in Australia, but it has other operations as far afield as Indonesia and Chile. A Chinese metals (mainly aluminium) group, the Chinese state-owned Chinalco, has for a while owned a 9 per cent stake.

In early 2008 Rio Tinto was looking for partnerships with Chinese steel and construction businesses to help with the development with a new iron ore mine in Guinea, Africa. With anticipated production of around 170 million tonnes every year this could become the third largest iron ore mine in the world. The problem is that it is in a remote location some 750 km from the sea. There is no infrastructure of consequence and a new railway will have to be constructed. This implies an alliance between a mining company and its customers further down the supply chain.

The issue is a complex one. Guinea is not Australia, but the challenge of mining development is similar. BHP Billiton (Case 4.1), a rival Australian mining corporation with interests in iron ore and aluminium, built and operates a private railway line in Western Australia to move material from its mines to the coast. A smaller rival, Fortesque Metals, wanted access to move its ore – which BHP refused – but, in 2008, Fortesque's claim was supported by the courts. BHP had argued that the track was an integral part of its production system and never meant to be a freely available resource for others to access, and that it was running 'close to capacity'. But this argument was not accepted.

At roughly the same time in early 2008 two global businesses were considering bidding to buy Rio Tinto. One represented vertical integration, the other horizontal integration. Whilst the price – at around $70 billion – would be an issue in any decision by Rio Tinto's shareholders, which would make the better strategic sense? BHP was one bidder; the other was Lakshmi Mittal, an Indian steelmaker with interests in Europe and thus an iron ore customer. The steel industry generally was concerned with the implications of a possible merger between BHP and Rio Tinto. This may just have been a defensive spoiler bid. But demand for steel fell in 2008 as car production and other key industries declined. Later in the year, when everyone's share prices fell, interest in the acquisition disappeared. Rio Tinto had determinedly opposed both bids.

By October 2008 the demand for iron ore and other natural resources had changed. China was not exempt from the economic slowdown and demand for steel and hence iron ore was falling. Once this downward trend in demand took hold, commodity prices also started to fall from a record high level in the summer of 2008 – simply compounding the problem for the mining businesses. Rio Tinto found it necessary to revise all its capital investment and expansion plans. That said, Rio Tinto was still trading profitably – but for how long? Rio Tinto's problem was relatively high debt of nearly $40 billion; it needs a strong cash flow to fund the interest payments. As demand fell it was able to save money by laying people off – in December the loss of 14 000 jobs was announced; and quite quickly it was clear that offers for asset sales would be considered. BHP, of course, could well be a bidder for selected interests.

Companies can always look to try and raise money through rights issues of new equity. Rio Tinto is dual listed in London and Sydney. Was this a real possibility in the credit crunch and recession – on the promise of guaranteed future growth once demand for minerals takes off again and commodity prices increase, as they inevitably will? In February 2009, Chinalco announced plans to double its stake from 9 per cent to 18 per cent by investing $19.5 billion. This happened just 3 days after one senior non-executive director resigned over disagreements about how to deal with the debt burden.

However many investors were opposed to Chinalco taking a larger stake and actively campaigned against it. The Australian government also expressed concern. By June the deal looked unlikely to happen. Without this Rio Tinto would probably need a rights issue – in a depressed market. And in the meantime Rio Tinto and BHP Billiton had been discussing the possibilities for a joint venture of their iron ore interests in Western Australia. Also in 2009 Rio Tinto and its Chinese customers had been struggling to reach an agreement over future iron ore prices.

Questions

1 What does this case teach us about long-term strategic intent and the need to respond to shorter-term opportunities and threats?
2 Is it possible to run a business such as Rio Tinto without long-term investment planning?
3 Would you expect planning to be the dominant mode of strategy creation?

Typically, strategic planning systems grew to be very formal such that all ideas from the individual businesses had to be supported by comprehensive, documented analyses. Now it is frequently accepted that many proposals cannot be fully justified quantitatively and instead the assumptions and justifications will be probed and challenged by divisional boards. Care must also be taken to ensure that the evaluation and resource allocation processes do not create too high a level of internal competition. Divisions and businesses should have to justify their intentions and proposals, and it is inevitable they will be competing for scarce resources. Nevertheless, the real enemy is external competitors, not other parts of the organization, which must not be forgotten.

In addition, some organizations still tend to use performance targets as the primary means of control, which sometimes results in short-term thinking. Once a business drops below its target, it becomes pressurized to reduce costs, which may restrict its ability to be creative and innovative. Many strategic planning systems could be improved if the head office corporate planners, who sometimes tend to be remote and detached, had more contact and involvement with the businesses.

In summary, formalized planning systems may be imperfect, but a system of some form remains essential for control and co-ordination. Alone it cannot enable the company to deal with competitive uncertainties and pressures – vision and learning are essential, but planning must not be abandoned.

This section has considered the important role and contribution of strategic planning in large, and possibly diverse, organizations. Strategy in Action 9.1 examines a number of relevant planning issues in local government, whilst the next section considers strategic planning in small businesses.

Strategy in Action 9.1   Strategy and Local Government

A typical UK local authority is likely to perceive the aim of the activities it carries out as the provision of more, and ideally better, services for the local community. These services fall into three broad categories: front line (housing, education and leisure), regulatory (environmental health, planning and building control) and promotional (economic development and tourism).

How does local government 'work' strategically? Strategic decisions at the top policy level demand an input from two groups of people: the elected councillors who exert a controlling influence, and the salaried managers. The councillors may be politically very experienced and, working on behalf of their constituents, they should be in a position to reflect local needs. The specialist expertise is more likely to come from the salaried staff, although there are some very well qualified and expert councillors. There are, therefore, two strategic leaders – the Leader of the Council and the Chief Executive – who ideally will be able to work together harmoniously and synergistically. On occasions, there will be clear evidence of visionary leadership. Some leaders, either individually or in partnership, will transform the character and infrastructure of a town or city. At the other extreme, other leaders really do little more than manage budgets and carry through central government initiatives.

There is an obvious role for strategic planning as local authorities have to work within guidelines and budget restraints set by central government. They have to decide upon how, at least, to maintain local services, improve efficiencies and implement any central government requirements.

Councillors will form policy-making groups, with the head of each group holding a place in the Cabinet – which is akin to the Cabinet in central government. The salaried employees will operate with some degree of delegated authority in discrete service areas. Each service will have policy guidelines, output targets and a budget. Normally they will be free to develop and adapt strategies and programmes as long as they operate within their budget and achieve their outputs.

Many councils will want to increase spending wherever possible, as more or better services are popular with the electorate. In simple terms, spending minus income (including grants from central government) equals the sum to be raised from householders and businesses, and generally more spending is likely to lead to higher local taxes. The freedom to increase these is constrained by central government. Borrowing is used primarily to fund new capital programmes and for managing the cash flow on a temporary basis. It is, for example, still being suggested that in the future many more local councils will borrow money to build new roads, or improve existing ones, and repay the money with congestion charges on motorists, at least in part following the lead of London. Since the residents of Manchester were allowed a vote on this possibility in early 2009 – and rejected it even though it would open the door to external public investment – the future remains uncertain. Some councils establish partnerships with specific developers. An independent company might, for example, develop a new shopping centre in partnership with a local authority. Together they will put up or raise substantial sums of development capital which will be repaid later through rents and business rates.

It is very difficult to measure quantitatively the benefits that accrue from certain services, such as parks and gardens for public recreation. Information from the Audit Commission enables one authority to compare its costs and spending in total, and per head of the population, for individual services with those incurred by similar authorities in the UK. Where this is utilized, it is basically a measure of efficiency, rather than an assessment of the overall effectiveness of the service provision, as shown in Chapter 11.

Until the 1980s, it was usual for a local authority to carry out most of its activities in-house. External contractors were used for some building and engineering work, and in other instances where very specialized skills were required. However, the first Thatcher government required that councils put out to tender all major new build projects, together with significant projects in housing and highways maintenance. Later in the 1980s school catering, refuse collection, street cleaning and most white-collar services were also subject to compulsory competitive tendering (CCT). Where services were put out for tender, an authority continued to determine the specific level of service to be provided, and then sought quotations for this provision. Tendering organizations neither suggested nor influenced the actual level of service. This power remained firmly with the local authority. As more and more services were compulsorily put out to tender, local authorities essentially became purchasers of services on behalf of the local community.

The Blair-led Labour government, elected in 1997, was determined to abolish CCT and replace it with 'Best Value'. CCT was abandoned in 2000. Best Value requires a local authority to review each of its services over 5-year periods, assessing whether it should be provided in-house, via social enterprises and the voluntary sector or by private-sector contractors. There are four key themes:

- challenge
- consult (stakeholders)
- compare (by benchmarking external and other local authority providers)
- compete (with the best providers that can be identified).

In recent years, the contribution of social enterprises and the voluntary sector in providing services that local (and national) government cannot or will not provide has grown – and without this contribution many individuals and communities would be far worse off.

Some councils have spun-out services they once ran into private ownership in the form of management buyouts. Building maintenance for council houses would be a typical example. The new business must tender for the work periodically, but it is free to seek other work and contracts as well. The assumption is a blend of public service and entrepreneurship.

Local councils are constrained by both central government financial rules and by legislative requirements. After the Blair Labour government came to power in 1997, it tightened up on the rules that govern residential care homes for the elderly. Room sizes and facilities had to meet certain minimum standards. As a result many closed, although some have been rebuilt, making homes with fewer but better rooms. In some communities, it is significant that it is the public sector homes, rather than those run by the private sector, that have closed down.

Strategic planning and small businesses

Many small businesses stay focused and do not diversify or acquire another business. Their corporate perspective stays the same, but they still need to create some form of competitive advantage and develop and integrate functional plans. In this respect, small business planning is similar to that for an individual business inside a conglomerate. Unfortunately, many small owner–managers misguidedly believe that strategic planning is too expensive and only belongs in large organizations, that formalized processes requiring expert planners are essential, and that the benefits are too long-term and there are no immediate pay-offs.

As a result, they adopt a more reactive approach and both vision and flexibility are important features of most successful small businesses, but these can be built on to provide greater strength and stability. Reinforcing the points made earlier in the chapter, small businesses can benefit in the same way as large ones from discerning the important strategic issues and from involving managers from the various functions in deciding how they might best be tackled.

Small businesses should involve all relevant managers in discussions about priorities, opportunities, problems and preferences and should look ahead and not just consider immediate problems and crises. Objective information and analyses (albeit limited in scope) are required to underpin the process, which must be actively and visibly supported by the owner–manager or strategic leader, who, in turn, must be willing to accept ideas from other managers. Adequate time must also be found, and sound financial systems should be in place to support the implementation of new strategies and plans. If they needed to raise finance from the banking system or elsewhere, they would have had to draw up a business plan to support their request. All too often these plans are then put in a drawer and largely forgotten, rather than being used as a framework for budgeting and monitoring performance, such that some small firm owner-managers never really develop a discipline of planning.

Strategic planning issues

Corporate planning authors who have been cited earlier in this chapter share a consensus that strategic planning should not be undertaken by the chief executive alone, planning specialists divorced from operating managers, marketing executives or finance departments. An individual or specialist department may be biased and fail to produce a balanced plan. Instead, in some way, all managers who will be affected by the plan, and who will be charged with implementing it, should be involved. However, all of these managers together cannot constitute an effective working team, and, therefore, a small team representing the whole organization should be constituted, and other managers consulted, which will require a schedule for the planning activities and a formalized system for carrying out the tasks. As discussed above, it is important that planning systems do not inhibit ongoing strategic thinking by managers throughout the organization, because threats must still be spotted early and potential opportunities must not be lost.

Planning traps   Ringbakk (1971) and Steiner (1972) have documented several reasons why formal planning might fail and have discussed the potential traps to avoid, concluding the following:

- Planning should not be left exclusively to planners who might see their job as being the production of a plan and who might also concentrate on procedures and detail at the expense of wide strategic thinking.

- Planning should be seen as a support activity in strategic decision-making and not a once-a-year ritual.

- There must be a commitment and an allocation of time from the strategic leader. Without this undertaking, managers lower down the organizational hierarchy might not feel that planning matters within the firm.

- Planning is not likely to prove effective unless the broad directional objectives for the firm are agreed and communicated widely.

- Implementers must be involved, both in drawing up the plan (or essential information might be missed) and afterwards. The plan should be communicated throughout the organization, and efforts should be made to ensure that managers appreciate what is expected of them.

- Targets, once established, should be used as a measure of performance and variances should be analyzed properly. However, there can be a danger in over-concentrating on targets and financial data at the expense of more creative strategic thinking.

- The organizational climate must be appropriate for the planning system adopted, and consequently structural and cultural issues have an important role to play.

- Inflexibility in drawing up and using the plan can be a trap. Inflexibility in drawing up the plan might be reflected in tunnel vision, a lack of flair and creativity, and in assuming that past trends can be extrapolated forwards.

- If planning is seen as an exercise rather than a support to strategy creation, it is quite possible that the plan will be ignored and not implemented.

The impact of planning on managers

Unless the above traps are avoided and the human aspects of planning are considered, the planning activity is unlikely to prove effective. Abell and Hammond (1979) and Mills (1985) highlight the following important people considerations:

- Ensure the support of senior executives.

- Ensure that every manager who is involved understands what is expected of them and that any required training in planning techniques is provided.

- Use specialist planners carefully.

- Keep planning simple, and ensure that techniques never become a doctrine.

- Particularly where doing detailed planning and forecasting, ensure that the time horizon is appropriate, since it is harder to do so further into the future.

- Never plan for the sake of planning.

- Link managerial rewards and sanctions to any targets for achievement which are established.

- Allow managers of business units and functions some freedom to develop their own planning systems rather than impose rigid ones, especially if they produce the desired results.

In summary, planning activities can take a number of forms, and organizations should seek to develop systems that provide the results they want. Ideally, these should encapsulate both strategic thinking and the establishment of realistic objectives and expectations and the strategies to achieve them. Planning techniques can be used supportively, and their potential contribution is evaluated in the next section. Systematic corporate planning, though, should not be seen as the only way in which strategic changes are formulated.

The role of planning and planners

In the light of the comments above on strategy formulation (and also in Chapter 8), this section concludes by considering further the role of planning and planners. Planning and strategy creation are different in the sense that planners may or may not be strategists but strategists might be found anywhere in the organization. Mintzberg (1989) suggests that planning activities are likely to involve a series of different and very useful analyses, but it does not follow that these must be synthesized into a systematic planning system. Planners can make a valuable contribution to the organization and to strategic thinking by:

- Programming strategies into finite detail to enable effective implementation (this will involve budgeting and ensuring that strategies are communicated properly, plus the establishment of monitoring and control processes).

- Formalizing ongoing strategic awareness by carrying out SWOT analyses and establishing what strategic changes are emerging at any time.

- Using scenarios and planning techniques to stimulate and encourage thinking.

- Searching for new competitive opportunities and strategic alternatives, and scrutinizing and evaluating them.

In other words, all of the activities incorporated in the planning systems discussed earlier in the chapter are seen to be making an important contribution, but they need not be component parts of a systematic model. Rather, they are contributors towards strategic thinking, awareness and insight.

Johnson (1992) further points out that occasionally plans are documented in detail only because particular stakeholders, say institutional shareholders or bankers, expect to see them as justification for proposals. There is never any real intention that they should be implemented in full.

Figure 9.5 draws together a number of these themes and illustrates the various contributions that planning and planners can make. In conjunction with this, the next section considers the relative value and contribution of selected planning techniques.

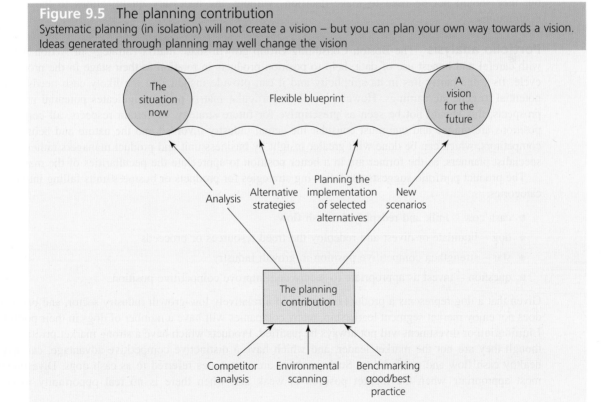

Figure 9.5 The planning contribution
Systematic planning (in isolation) will not create a vision – but you can plan your own way towards a vision. Ideas generated through planning may well change the vision

The key macro and micro variables of our business are so dynamic that poker becomes more predictable than planning and reactivity more profitable than rumination.

DR JOHN WHITE, EX-MANAGING DIRECTOR, BBA, WHOSE CUSTOMERS WERE INVOLVED IN THE
MOTOR VEHICLE INDUSTRY

I have a saying: 'Every plan is an opportunity lost' ... because I feel that if you try to plan the way your business will go, down to the last detail, you are no longer able to seize any opportunity that may arise unexpectedly.

DEBBIE MOORE, FOUNDER CHAIRMAN, PINEAPPLE DANCE STUDIOS LTD

Strategic planning techniques

While different strategists and authors of strategy texts adopt different stances on the significance of vision, culture and strategic planning techniques in effective strategic planning, our collective view is that the role of the strategic leader, styles of corporate decision-making and organization culture are key driving forces in strategy creation and implementation. However, strategic planning techniques, which rely heavily on the collection and analysis of quantitative data, do have an important contribution to make. They help to increase awareness, thereby reducing the risk involved in certain decisions, and can indicate the incidence of potential threats and limitations which might reduce the future value and contribution of individual products and services. They can help in establishing priorities in large complex multi-product multinational organizations, and can provide appropriate frameworks for evaluating the relative importance of very different businesses in a portfolio.

However, their value is dependent on the validity and reliability of the information fed into them such that, where comparisons with competitors are involved, the data for other companies may well involve 'guesstimation'. Judgement is required for assessing the significance of events and competitor strategies; vision is essential in discontinuous change management.

We would argue that strategic planning techniques should be used to help and facilitate decision-makers, but they should not be used to make decisions without any necessary qualifications to the data and assumptions.

Portfolio analysis   The Boston Consulting Group growth-share matrix (Strategy in Action 9.2) can, with careful and honest use of data, help to position products in relation to their stage in the product life cycle. Its value partly lies in its simplicity and it can provide insight into the likely cash needs and the potential to generate earnings. However, while a particular matrix position indicates potential needs and prospects, this should not be seen as prescriptive for future strategy. In certain respects, all competitive positions are unique and one must consider the actual industry involved and the nature and behaviour of competitors, which can be done with greater insight by business unit and product managers rather than by specialist planners, as the former are in a better position to appreciate the peculiarities of the market.

The product portfolio suggests the following strategies for products or business units falling into certain categories:

● cash cow – milk and redeploy the cash flow

● dog – liquidate or divest and redeploy the freed resources or proceeds

● star – strengthen competitive position in growth industry

● question – invest as appropriate to secure and improve competitive position.

Given that a dog represents a product or service in a relatively low-growth industry sector, and one which does not enjoy market segment leadership, many companies will have a number of dogs in their portfolios. **Liquidation** or divestment will not always be justified. Products which have a strong market position, even though they are not the market leader, and which have a distinctive competitive advantage, can have a healthy cash flow and profitability. Such products are sometimes referred to as cash dogs. Divestment is most appropriate when the market position is weak and when there is no real opportunity to create

Strategy in Action 9.2   The Boston Consulting Group (BCG) Growth-Share Matrix

Basic premises

Bruce Henderson (1970) of BCG has suggested first that the margins earned by a product, and the cash generated by it, are a function of market share. The higher the market share, relative to competitors, the greater the earnings potential; high margins and market share are correlated. A second premise is that sales and revenue growth requires investment. Sales of a product will only increase if there is appropriate expenditure on advertising, distribution and development; and the rate of market growth determines the required investment. Third, high market share must be earned or bought, which requires additional investment. Finally, no business can grow indefinitely. As a result, products will at times not be profitable because the amount of money being spent to develop them exceeds their earnings potential; at other times, and particularly where the company has a high relative market share, earnings exceed expenditure and products are profitable.

Profitability is, therefore, affected by market growth, market share and the stage in the product life cycle. A company with a number of products might expect to have some that are profitable and some that are not. In general, mature products, where growth has slowed down and the required investment has decreased, are the most profitable, and the profits they earn should not be reinvested in them but used instead to finance growth products that offer future earnings potential.

The matrix

The matrix is illustrated in Figure 9.6. Chart (a) shows the composition of the axes and the names given to products or business units which fall in each of the four quadrants; chart (b) features 15 products or business units in a hypothetical company portfolio. The sterling-volume size of each product or business is proportional to the areas of the circles, and the positioning of each one is determined by its market growth rate and relative market share.

The market growth rate on the vertical axis is the annual growth rate of the market in which the company competes, and really any range starting with zero could be used. The problem is where to draw the horizontal dividing line which separates high-growth from low-growth markets.

The relative market share on the horizontal axis indicates market share in relation to the largest competitor in the market. A relative market share of 0.25 would indicate a market share one-quarter of that of the market leader; a figure of 2.5 would represent a market leader with a market share that is 2.5 times as big as that of the nearest rival. The vertical dividing line is normally 1.0, so that market leadership is found to the left-hand side of the divider. It is important to consider market segmentation when deciding upon the market share figure to use, rather than using the share of the total market.

Figure 9.6   The Boston Consulting Group growth-share matrix

(a)

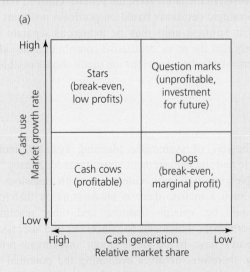

(b)

An example of a balanced portfolio

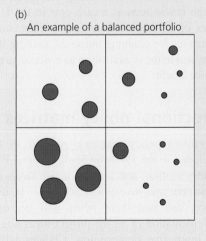

The growth-share matrix is thus divided into four cells or quadrants, each representing a particular type of business.

- Question marks are products or businesses which compete in high-growth markets but where market share is relatively low. A new product launched into a high-growth market and with an existing market leader would normally constitute a question mark. High expenditure is required to develop and launch the product, and consequently it is unlikely to be profitable and may instead require subsidy from more profitable products. Once the product is established, further investment will be required if the company attempts to claim market leadership.
- Successful question marks become stars, market leaders in growth markets. However, investment is still required to maintain the rate of growth and to defend the leadership position. Stars are marginally profitable only, but as they reach a more mature market position as growth slows down they will become increasingly profitable.
- Cash cows are, therefore, mature products which are well-established market leaders. As market growth slows down, there is less need for high investment, and hence they are the most profitable products in the portfolio. This is boosted by any economies of scale resulting from the position of market leadership. Cash cows are used to fund the businesses in the other three quadrants.
- Dogs describe businesses that have low market shares in slower growth markets. They may well be previous cash cows, which still enjoy some loyal market support although they have been replaced as market leader by a newer rival. They should be marginally profitable, and should be withdrawn when they become loss makers, if not before. The opportunity cost of the resources that they tie up is an important issue in this decision.

BOSTON CONSULTING GROUP **http://www.bcg.com**

sustainable competitive advantage, as long as a buyer can be found. Turnaround strategies for products which are performing very poorly are examined further in Chapter 13.

According to Hamermesch (1986), many businesses that are classified as cash cows should be managed for innovation and growth, especially if the industry is dynamic or volatile, or can be made so. In other words, strategies that succeed in extending the product life cycle can move it from a state of maturity into further growth, for example coffee which experienced renewed growth when the success of automatic coffee makers increased demand for new varieties of fresh ground coffee.

When 'milking' products, care also has to be taken not to reduce capacity if there is a chance that demand and growth opportunities might return as a result of scarcities or changes in taste. When restrictions on the import of Scotch whisky into Japan were eased in the late 1980s, the product enjoyed star status, even though it was seen as a cash cow in the UK. Strategic decisions based on portfolio positions may ignore issues of interdependence and synergy, such that business units may be treated as separate independent businesses for planning purposes, making it likely that the more qualitative contributions to other business units, and to the organization as a whole, are overlooked when decisions are made about possible liquidation or divestment.

Directional policy matrices

Directional policy matrices, popular in the heyday of systematic planning systems, included those developed in the 1970s by Shell, General Electric and the management consultants McKinsey. They are all broadly similar and aim to assist large complex multi-activity enterprises with decisions concerning investment and divestment priorities. In using such a matrix, there is an assumption that resources are scarce, and that there never will be, or should be, enough financial and other resources for the implementation of all the project ideas and opportunities which can be conceived in a successful, creative and innovative organization. Choices will always have to be made about investment priorities. The development of an effective corporate strategy, therefore, involves evaluating the potential for existing businesses together with new possibilities in order to determine the priorities.

Typically, the matrix would be constructed within two axes: the horizontal axis representing industry attractiveness, or the prospects for profitable operation in the sector concerned; the vertical axis indicating the company's existing competitive position in relation to other companies in the industry, linked closely to Porter's models and frameworks (Chapters 4 and 6). Existing and potential new products can both be evaluated initially along the vertical axis by considering their likely prospects for establishing competitive advantage. The **directional policy matrix**, like other matrices, is a technique which assists in determining the industry and product sectors that are most worthy of additional investment capital. Issues of synergy and overall strategic fit require further managerial judgement before final decisions are reached.

Rowe *et al.* (1989) have developed a model based on four important variables:

- the relative stability/turbulence of the environment
- industry attractiveness
- the extent of any competitive advantage
- the company's financial strengths: profitability, liquidity and current risk exposure.

Scores are awarded for each factor, and then put into a diagram (see Box 9.1), which features a financially strong company (or division or product) enjoying competitive advantage in an attractive industry with a relatively stable environment. The appropriate strategy is an aggressive one. The table (Table 9.2) shows the appropriate strategies for four clearly delineated positions, and judgement has to be applied when the situation is less clear-cut.

This technique usefully incorporates finance, which will affect the feasibility of particular strategic alternatives and the ability of a company to implement them. It has similar limitations to directional policy matrices. Box 9.1 can be applied very effectively to the banking industry in the UK and also, we believe, to Scottish and Newcastle.

Scottish and Newcastle was a large UK brewing business which in 2003 sold its 1450 pubs in the UK to Spirit for £2.5 billion, and then followed a strategy of concentrating on brewing, rather than follow a diversified strategy by owning the outlets for its products. It also rationalized the location of its brewing

---

Box 9.1   SPACE (strategic position and action evaluation)

Figure 9.7   SPACE

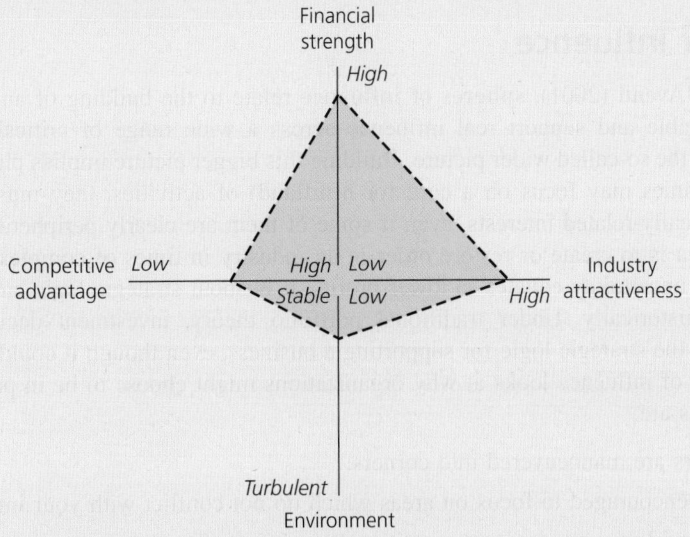

Table 9.2   SPACE

Strategic thrust	Aggressive	Competitive	Conservative	Defensive
Features:				
Environment	Stable	Unstable	Stable	Unstable
Industry	Attractive	Attractive	Unattractive	Unattractive
Competitiveness	Strong	Strong	Weak	Weak
Financial strength	High	Weak	High	Weak
Appropriate strategies	Growth, possibly by acquisition	Cost reduction, productivity improvement, raising more capital to follow opportunities and strengthen competitiveness	Cost reduction and product/service rationalization	Rationalization
	Capitalize on opportunities		Invest in search for new products, services and competitive opportunities	Divestment as appropriate
	Innovate to sustain competitive advantage	Possibly merge with a less competitive but cash-rich company		

activities and entered into partnerships with smaller scale real ale brewers such as the Caledonian Brewing company in Edinburgh, who brew the award-winning Deuchar's IPA. At the same time S&N (Tony Frogatt) pursued a strategy of 'turning its back on acquisition activity and focusing on operational efficiencies, increased marketing investment and improved utilization of capital'. (Source: Ian Shackleton, Credit Suisse First Boston.) It could be argued that S&N was pursuing all four of the strategic thrusts identified above. S&N was sold to Heineken and Carlsberg in 2007.

Spheres of influence

According to D'Aventi (2001), **spheres of influence** relate to the building of an arsenal of products and services that enable and support real influence across a wide range of critical interests – they imply consideration of the so-called wider picture. Building this bigger picture implies planning linked to a vision. Although companies may focus on a core (or heartland) of activities, they must not neglect to build a portfolio of logically-related interests, even if some of them are clearly peripheral.

The basic idea is to create or restore order in an industry in times of complexity and chaos. After all, more chaos and uncertainty equates to lower profits. It is about strategic logic and it mimics how nations have behaved historically. Under traditional portfolio theory, investment decisions do not require a consideration of the strategic logic for supporting a business, even though it could be relatively low profit, whereas spheres of influence looks at why organizations might choose to be in particular businesses. The desired outcomes are:

- Competitors are manoeuvered into corners.
- Rivals are encouraged to focus on areas which do not conflict with your interests directly.
- There is less destructive price competition lowering profits.
- There are fewer opportunities for new, rule-changing competitors to enter an industry.

There are five key planning elements:

1 *Core geographic and product markets*. The centre of the sphere of influence and where a company is seeking domination.

2 *Vital interests*. Geographic or product zones which are critical for protecting the core, including complementary products, key supplies and providers of valuable resources such as know-how or employee skills. Sometimes, but not always, they exploit competencies and capabilities associated with the core.

3 *Pivotal zones*. Markets that could, in the long-term, tip the balance of power or control away from a company in favour of a rival, if freely dominated by a competitor. A position is needed more for defensive purposes than dominance.

4 *Buffer zones*. Positions in expendable, non-committed, markets simply to constrain competitor activities, an important bargaining weapon – forward positions

5 *Forward positions*. Front-line products located close to the core activities of key rivals, which can be used for purposes of attack, but they are mostly defensive, and cause competitors to think carefully about attacking any company which has them in place – there is a fear of a possible response.

We can apply these five elements to the development of Microsoft as follows:

- *Core* – desktop operating systems; graphical user interfaces; Internet browsers.
- *Vital interests* – where it seeks to be a winner – operating systems for networks and for portable devices.
- *Pivotal zones* – e-portals and e-commerce businesses.
- *Buffer zones* – computer games and the X-Box, because rivals might use their dominance of this sector to develop operating systems.
- *Forward positions* – initially bundling Explorer with Windows was a forward position, partly synergistic, partly competitive, to deter Netscape – but it became core.

Much of Microsoft's history – and phenomenal success – is characterized by 'catch-up' strategies where it has been quick to capitalize on rival initiatives, but then overtake them with alternative products and services. The Windows computer operating system lagged behind – but grew to dominate – the Apple Mac, which at one time was market leader. Whilst it remains the system of choice for some, especially designers, the Mac still has only a fraction of the market share of Windows. Word similarly grew to dominate and displace WordPerfect. Its commercial database SQL was developed to take on Oracle; Windows (Internet) Explorer eventually sidelined Netscape's Navigator although some believe there was an element of 'foul play' in the way Explorer was bundled with other Microsoft products. The Pocket PC was launched as a rival to the Palm hand-held organizer, and its Internet portal MSN was a follower of AOL. X-Box, of course, was designed to rival the Sony PlayStation, but realistically Microsoft has never truly managed to seize market leadership. Microsoft has bought a minority stake in Facebook and attempted (unsuccessfully) to acquire Yahoo. In large part, these decisions are affected by the strong position of Google and that company's ability to attract billions of dollars in online advertising revenue. In addition, Microsoft and Nokia entered into a strategic alliance that resulted in Nokia mobile phones carrying the Windows Phone 7 (and eventually Windows Phone 8) operating system, in addition to its existing alliance with camera lense manufacturer Carl Zeiss.

Other examples   Wal-Mart focuses on establishing and sustaining dominance of key product markets and territories around the world by, in part, establishing and nurturing relationships with key suppliers, and exploiting these through its huge buying power to force its rivals into either unoccupied niches or those in which Wal-Mart is not particularly interested which, of course, is a very typical retail strategy.

Disney retains a presence in children's book publishing and in branded retail stores to give it countervailing bargaining power against potential rivals should it ever need to use it.

Johnson & Johnson (J&J) is describable as 'The Baby Company' and Procter & Gamble (P&G) 'The Soaps and Shampoo Business'. These two businesses have activities and interests which overlap, but they avoid destructive rivalry. J&J opts not to compete directly with P&G's diaper business and its powerful Pampers brand, a massive baby product (not massive in the sense of obesity); and, similarly, P&G focuses on adult soaps and shampoos and does not address the children's market. Why? Because J&J owns the Neutrogena brand of mild adult soaps and shampoos, tightly niched and not mainstream, but this provides the company with competencies and capabilities which it could use to expand if it wished. Equally, P&G has the competencies and capabilities to produce children's soaps and shampoos. Competition from powerful rivals in core areas could destroy position and power, so no-one would win and victory would be pyrrhic. Simply, potential threats are keeping rivals at bay.

Research Snapshot 9.1

The rationale behind strategic planning includes evidence that the process can, in fact, create sustainable competitive advantage by allowing senior managers to have 'prepared minds' and, therefore, leading to effective decision-making (Kaplan and Beinhocker, 2003). Clearly, as bureaucracy, formalism and also limited integration and implementation were and have been problematic and raised ethical concerns, it is important not only to ensure effective conduct of strategy as well as an ethical approach (Bonn and Fisher, 2005). Formal strategic planning, apart from 'internal financial analysis', in smaller and medium-sized firms appears to be relatively rare (Stonehouse and Pemberton, 2002) and, yet, that would be too simplistic given evidence that, 'entrepreneurial firms tend to adopt more formal strategic planning approaches, while conservative firms adopt more incremental approaches' (Gibbons and O'Connor, 2005: p.170). In other words, 'small' does not always equal 'entrepreneurial', nor does 'large' necessarily equal 'strategic'. Strategic planning and performance is 'mediated' by different approaches to flexibility (Rudd et al., 2008). Strategic planning is critical for less innovative family firms in enhancing their performance (Eddleston et al., 2008). Further, Andersen (2004) notes that performance is enhanced in manufacturing plants by a, 'simultaneous emphasis on decentralized strategy making and strategic planning processes', in other words it is not an 'either … or' approach to flexibility or rigorous strategy, which somewhat gives the lie to the notion, e.g. that firms must be either entrepreneurial or strategic. Indeed, performance needs to be added into the mix when considering these issues. O'Regan and Ghobadian (2002) found that SMEs that adopt formal strategic planning were less constrained in implementing their strategies – as well as high- and low-technology differences (O'Regan and Ghobadian, 2006).

Examples of strategic planning include: multinationals (Brock and Barry, 2003); General Electric with its changing processes over the years (Ocasio and Joseph, 2008); and the oil and gas sector where the actual process changes in conditions of uncertainty, which involved adaptation and 'responsiveness' but 'showed limited innovation and analytical sophistication' (Grant, 2003: p.491). Indeed, performance measurement is used in strategic planning by both the larger and more uncertainty-facing firms (Tapinos et al., 2005), the latter confirmed elsewhere (Brews and Purohit, 2007). Whatever the evidence on the role of strategic planning in enhancing performance and sustainable competitive advantage more generally, there might well be a spectrum of the extent of planning, though it can also be categorized, for example, as 'non-planners, informal planners, formal planners and sophisticated planners' (French et al., 2004), they found that informal planning positively influences net profit. Significant further research is still clearly needed not only to establish whether strategic planning impacts upon performance, but also how and why particular approaches make a firm operate more effectively vis-a-vis its competitors. The balance between entrepreneurial, dynamic, and flexible versus strategic planning needs to be achieved. Whilst knowledge is limited on how strategic planning is 'initiated' (Harris and Ogbonna, 2006), there are new techniques that assist strategic planning. Whilst defining strategic planning, 'as a process of actively developing and managing portfolios of corporate real options in the context of competitive interactions', such options can conceivably be valued, as can the related resources and capabilities, to assist decision-making (Smit et al., 2006). Visualization (utilizing 'real-time, interactive visual representations') of strategy can also contribute to the process of strategic planning (Eppler and Platts, 2009).

The articles below provide deeper understanding of strategic planning. The further reading from this literature will help students to develop their perception and critical awareness of this concept and practice, and also to highlight the developing thinking in relation to how they can enhance performance.

Further Reading

Andersen, T.J. (2004) 'Integrating decentralized strategy making and strategic planning processes in dynamic environments', *Journal of Management Studies*, Vol. 41, pp. 1271–1299.

Bonn, I. and Fisher, J. (2005) 'Corporate governance and business ethics: insights from the strategic planning experience', *Corporate Governance: An International Review*, Vol. 13, pp. 730–7310.

Brews, P. and Purohit, D. (2007) 'Strategic planning in unstable environments', *Long Range Planning*, Vol. 40, No. 1, pp. 64–83.

Brock, D. and Barry, D. (2003) 'What if planning were really strategic? Exploring the strategy-planning relationship in multinationals', *International Business Review*, Vol. 12, No. 5, pp. 543–561.

Eddleston, K.A., Kellermanns, F.W. and Sarathy, R. (2008) 'Resource configuration in family firms: Linking resources, strategic planning and technological opportunities to performance', *Journal of Management Studies*, Vol. 45, pp. 26–50.

Eppler, M.J. and Platts, K.W. (2009) 'Visual strategizing: the systematic use of visualization in the strategic-planning process', *Long Range Planning*, Vol. 42, No. 1, pp. 42–74.

French, S.J., Kelly, S.J. and Harrison, J.L. (2004) 'The role of strategic planning in the performance of small, professional service firms: A research note', *Journal of Management Development*, Vol. 23, No. 8, pp. 765–776.

Gibbons, P.T. and O'Connor, T. (2005) 'Influences on strategic planning processes among Irish SMEs', *Journal of Small Business Management*, Vol. 43, pp. 170–186.

Grant, R. M. (2003) 'Strategic planning in a turbulent environment: evidence from the oil majors', *Strategic Management. Journal*, Vol. 24, pp. 491–517.

Harris, L.C. and Ogbonna, E. (2006) 'Initiating strategic planning', *Journal of Business Research*, Vol. 59, No. 1, pp. 100–111.

Kaplan, S. and Beinhocker, E.D. (2003) 'The real value of strategic planning', *MIT Sloan Management Review*, Vol. 44, No. 2, pp. 71–76.

O'Regan, N. and Ghobadian, A. (2002) 'Effective strategic planning in small and medium sized firms', *Management Decision*, Vol. 40, No. 7, pp. 663–671.

O'Regan, N. and Ghobadian, A. (2006) 'Strategic planning—a comparison of high and low technology manufacturing small firms', *Technovation*, Vol. 25, No. 10, pp. 1107–1117.

Ocasio, W. and Joseph, J. (2008) 'Rise and fall - or transformation?: The evolution of strategic planning at the General Electric Company, 1940–2006', *Long Range Planning*, Vol. 41, No. 3, pp. 248–272.

Rudd, J.M., Greenley, G.E., Beatson, A.T. and Lings, I.N. (2008) 'Strategic planning and performance: Extending the debate', *Journal of Business Research*, Vol. 61, No. 2, pp. 99–1010.

Smit, H. T. J. and Trigeorgis, L. (2006) 'Strategic planning: valuing and managing portfolios of real options', *R&D Management*, Vol. 36, pp. 403–419.

Stonehouse, G. and Pemberton, J. (2002) 'Strategic planning in SMEs – some empirical findings', *Management Decision*, Vol. 40, No. 9, pp. 853–861.

Tapinos, E., Dyson, R.G. and Meadows, M. (2005) 'The impact of performance measurement in strategic planning', *International Journal of Productivity and Performance Management*, Vol. 54, No. 5/6, pp. 370–384.

Summary

As organizations grow and become more complex, we find an increasing reliance on planning at the expense of the other modes of strategy as there is an increasing need for effective control mechanisms. However, the risk is that bureaucracy and stasis accompanies the reliance on planning, which must not be allowed to happen.

Planning techniques can be extremely useful, particularly as they force managers and organizations to ask themselves many relevant and searching questions and compile and analyze important information. But the techniques do not, and cannot, provide answers: they merely generate the questions.

The danger is that some managers may perceive the output of a technique such as matrix analysis as an answer to strategic issues.

Strategic planning – using techniques and formalized procedures – is just one of the ways in which strategies are created. Strategies can also be provided by the strategic leader and be decided by managers in real time. Intended strategies, say those selected by the leader or a formal planning system, have to be implemented, during which they may well be changed incrementally. After all, intended strategies imply forecasting, and, to some extent, all forecasts are wrong. In addition, flexible organizations will adapt all the time by responding to new opportunities and threats.

In the 1960s and 1970s, the predominant view of academics and organizations was that formalized strategic planning was at the heart of strategy creation, and should be used to manage future direction. It became clear, however, that a planning approach that relies on quantitative data, forecasts and manuals, can restrict creativity, thinking, flexibility and, critically, the support and engagement of the managers who must implement strategy. Many organizations fell into the trap of believing the key outcome of planning is the plan!

Nevertheless, it is important to realize that all managers plan all the time. Evaluating the current situation, and discussing possible changes and improvements with colleagues, implies planning. Simply, this is informal planning rather than the formalized systems implied by the term strategic planning.

There are at least seven approaches to planning, which should not necessarily be seen as mutually exclusive. Formal planning is separate from informal planning. The process can be largely top-down or bottom-up, and can involve extended budgeting and be numbers driven, or be more behavioural in approach, possibly using scenarios.

The '*planning gap*' is a very flexible concept and technique which can be used in a variety of ways, and is used to clarify the extent of the revenue or profits gap that might emerge if current strategies are left largely unchanged. The more ambitious the objectives set by the company, the greater the risk that is likely to be involved in the strategies required to close the gap.

Our contemporary approach to strategic planning is based on a mixture of planning techniques, intellectual input and action plans for implementing strategies; and central to the whole process are current strategic issues.

With any form of strategic planning, one must decide who should be involved and what they should contribute. Professional or specialist planners have an important role to play, but others must be involved as well. Where there is an over-reliance on planners, or where there is inadequate flexibility with the plan itself, the organization is likely to fall into one of the obvious planning traps.

Planning has a number of important contributions to make and individual organizations will not all adopt the same approach.

There is a number of useful planning techniques, specifically:

- The Boston Consulting Group (BCG) 2 × 2 matrix
- Directional policy matrices
- SPACE.

In various ways, all of these techniques can be valuable but they will always be dangerous if they are used too rigidly and allowed to drive decisions without reference to, or qualification by, managerial judgement. The thinking behind spheres of influence concerns the big picture, contending that companies should look to develop a portfolio of products that strengthen its all-round ability to compete by opening up competitive fronts both proactively and reactively.

Online cases for this chapter

Online Case 9.1: Starbucks

Online Case 9.2: Unilever

Online Case 9.3: Strategic Issues and High Street Banking

Web supplement related to this chapter

Military Strategy II

Questions and research assignments

1 Mintzberg has distinguished between 'grass-roots' strategies (which can take root anywhere in the organization but eventually proliferate once they become more widely adopted) and 'hothouse' strategies which are deliberately grown and cultured. What do you think he means?

2 A manufacturer of industrial products is structured around five separate strategic business units (SBUs). Use the data below to construct a Boston matrix and assess how balanced the portfolio seems. Where are the strengths? Where are the weaknesses?

SBU	Sales (£ million)	Number of competitors	Sales of top three companies (£ million)	Market growth rate (%)
A	0.4	6	0.8, 0.7, 0.4	16
B	1.8	20	1.8, 1.8, 1.2	18
C	1.7	16	1.7, 1.3, 0.9	8
D	3.5	3	3.5, 1.0, 0.8	5
E	0.6	8	2.8, 2.0, 1.5	2

3 In the context of the Boston matrix, is the Big Mac a cash cow? What do you feel McDonald's competitive strategy for the Big Mac should be?

4 For an organization of your choice, ideally one with which you are familiar:

a Ascertain how the planning, entrepreneurial and emergent modes might apply currently to strategic change in the organization. Which mode is predominant? Why do you think it is the preferred mode? How successful is it?

b What would be the opportunities and concerns from greater utilization of the other modes?

Internet and library projects

1 Use the Internet to look at all the businesses started by easyJet founder Stelios Haji-Ioannou – other than easyJet – and consider where he might have made a visionary impact. What do you think are the main contributions planning might make to the business? How much have the strategies changed as Stelios has striven to make these various businesses profitable?

2 Follow up the web case on UK high street banks. Take any one of the leading banks and examine its portfolio of activities – including the investment banking, international and other financial services businesses. In the current climate, do you believe the structure makes sense?

Strategy activity

The Channel Tunnel

The Channel Tunnel between England and France was named the greatest construction achievement of the twentieth century. Passenger and freight shuttles began operating in 1994; Eurostar passenger services began a short while later, but growth was constrained until the fast access route between London and Folkestone began opening (in stages) in 2003. Freight trains also use the tunnel. The tunnel operator, Eurotunnel, has made operating profits since 1997 but other charges have meant net losses. In 2003 Eurotunnel identified the following strategic issues:

- the expensive infrastructure was under-utilized
- operator access charges were too high
- there were conflicts between the various stakeholders, many of them caused by the financial losses.

Eurotunnel decided to reduce access charges to stimulate demand. There was a belief that demand was sufficiently price-elastic for this to improve profitability. Debts would have to be restructured – and not for the first time. There would be fresh investment in the Folkestone freight terminal to allow it to handle Continental gauge trains for the first time. And the terminal areas of Kent and the region around Calais would be promoted to stimulate tourism.

There have been two serious fire incidents. Both resulted in major disruptions which Eurotunnel had to deal with at immediate notice. The company has been restructured financially yet again, the shares are worth very little, and the business is controlled from France.

Questions

1 Overall, has the Channel Tunnel been a success or a failure?
2 Can you identify additional strategic issues to those listed here?
3 What alternative strategies might be considered to improve the fortunes of Eurotunnel?

EUROTUNNEL **http://www.eurotunnel.com**

References

Abell, D.F. and Hammond, J.S. (1979) *Strategic Market Planning*, Prentice-Hall.

Ackoff, R.L. (1970) *A Concept of Corporate Planning*, John Wiley.

Ansoff, H.I. (1987) *Corporate Strategy*, revised edn, Penguin.

Argenti, J. (1980) *Practical Corporate Planning*, George Allen & Unwin.

Cohen, K.J. and Cyert, R.M. (1973) Strategy formulation, implementation and monitoring, *Journal of Business*, 46 (3), 349–67.

D'Aventi R.A. (2001) *Strategic Supremacy – How industry leaders create growth, wealth and power through spheres of influence*, The Free Press.

Garvin, D.A. and Levesque, L.C. (2006) Project the known – deliver the new, *Harvard Business Review*, October.

Glueck, W.F. and Jauch, L.R. (1984) *Business Policy and Strategic Management*, 4th edn, McGraw-Hill.

Hamermesch, R. (1986) Making planning strategic, *Harvard Business Review*, July–August.

Henderson, B. (1970) *The Product Portfolio*, Boston Consulting Group.

Hussey, D. (1976) *Corporate Planning – Theory and Practice*, Pergamon.

Johnson, G. (1992) Strategic direction and strategic decisions, presented at 'Managing Strategically: Gateways and Barriers', Strategic Planning Society Conference, 12 February.

Mills, D.Q. (1985) Planning with people in mind, *Harvard Business Review*, July–August.

Mintzberg, H. (1989) Presentation to the Strategic Planning Society, London, 2 February. Further details can be found in Mintzberg, H (1973).

Ohmae, K. (1982) *The Mind of the Strategist*, McGraw-Hill.

Ringbakk, K.A. (1971) Why planning fails, *European Business*, Spring.

Robinson, J. (1986) Paradoxes in planning, *Long Range Planning*, 19 (6).

Rowe, A.J., Mason, R.O., Dickel, K.E. and Snyder, N.H. (1989) Strategic Management: *A Methodological Approach*, 3rd edn, Addison-Wesley.

Steiner, G. (1972) *Pitfalls in Long Range Planning*, Planning Executives Institute.

Taylor, B. and Hussey, D.E. (1982) *The Realities of Planning*, Pergamon.

Strategic leadership and intrapreneurship: towards visionary leadership?

Learning objectives

Having read to the end of this chapter, you should be able to:

- define, and contrast the role of, strategic leaders(hip) and entrepreneurs(hip), identifying factors contributing towards their (or its) effectiveness (**Section 10.1**)

- describe the conditions for making an organization intrapreneurial (**Section 10.2**)

- analyze the function of visionary leadership (**Section 10.3**)

- discuss a number of critical leadership issues such as finite shelf-lives and succession (**Section 10.4**).

Introduction

Strategic leaders have to be able to think, make things happen, engage the support of other people and, on occasions, be the public face of the organization, but few strategic leaders will be good at all four of these tasks. The strategic leader has an overall responsibility for clarifying direction, for deciding upon strategies by dictating or influencing others around them and for ensuring that strategies are implemented through the decisions that they make on structure, style and systems. Perhaps the basic nature of the strategic leader will have an impact on the style and culture of an organization over time: dull leaders, belligerent bullying leaders, adventurous leaders and risk averse leaders spawn companies with similar characteristics. Some leaders are entrepreneurial and visionary and may be very effective in that role but ineffective as managers, hence balancing visionary leadership and managerial competence affects the success or failure of any business.

Our opening case (Case 10.1) on Innocent Smoothies features the growth and success of an entrepreneurial business started and run by a team of three friends who share the strategic leadership role and responsibilities.

As well as leading from the front, a leader should create a climate that facilitates emergent change – appropriate intrapreneurial employees should be empowered, encouraged and energized (see Chapter 5) and can lead these emergent change initiatives. Leadership is both a job and a process – a process concerned with influence and change – which requires both personal characteristics (which effective leaders need to possess) and leadership skills (which can be learned). Successful leaders also tend to build effective teams to support them.

This chapter also looks at how some leaders are perceived to fail, and at the vital issue of leadership succession.

Case 10.1   Innocent Smoothies   UK

Innocent Smoothies was started in 1998 by three friends who had met when they were students at St John's College in Cambridge. They had graduated in the early 1990s. On a snowboarding holiday – which they still enjoy – they decided to start a business, but didn't immediately plan to 'give up the day job'. They had run social events together at University and stayed close friends.

Adam Balon was the son of an ENT surgeon. Brought up in Surrey he read Economics at Cambridge and afterwards worked for Virgin Cola. Richard Reed's father was a manager with the Yorkshire Rider bus company. Reed read Geography and then worked in advertising. Jon Wright was a Londoner, son of an IT Manager and he read Engineering before becoming a management consultant.

After discarding a number of ideas the trio decided to invest £500, buy some fresh fruit, have it crushed and bottled and sell it from a stall at a music festival. They had decided that none of them really lived a healthy lifestyle and truly fresh fruit drinks would be one answer. They placed two large baskets on their stall and erected a large sign – *Should we start this business?* It was the philosophy that 'if there's something I want and can't readily get, and other people are saying the same thing, then there must be an opportunity'. The 'yes' bucket was soon full! They resigned from their jobs and embarked on the entrepreneur's journey. They were about to start one of the UK's fastest growing food and drink businesses which would be turning over £10 million after 5 years. Turnover in 2007 (just under 10 years) exceeded £100 million; Innocent had 70 per cent of the UK market for smoothies. When it started there was little competition – but the market and competition would grow, partly as a consequence of what they did.

Money to establish a 'proper' business was hard to come by until they decided to email all their contacts with a simple question – *Do you know anyone who is rich?* One did, and after some discussions the three were offered £235 000 for 18 per cent of the equity in the business. Their investor was a veteran American serial entrepreneur who had spent some time on the staff at London Business School and become a private venture capitalist. The three partners would retain 70 per cent, with the remaining 12 per cent split amongst their colleagues in the business, a number of whom also knew them at Cambridge. Because of the need to comply with legislation and restrictions over manufacture and distribution, things did not go smoothly at first. There were a number of 'false starts' but the trio persisted.

The three always had separate roles in the business based on their skills and preferences. Initially they split the key roles into production (Wright), trade sales (Balon) and consumer marketing (Reed) but there was no designated leader or Chief Executive. They recognized each other's strengths and worked as a team. The same principle continued but more responsibilities were added – and Reed became the public face of Innocent.

Although there are now more bottle sizes and blends than in the early days, with some flavours now targeted specifically at children, the business remains focused on crushed fruit juices, fruit-flavoured water, yoghurt-based fruit smoothies and the more recent 'veg pots'. They only use natural fresh products – with no additives or concentrated juices. The ingredients are sourced carefully from around the world – 'only the best' approach linked to ethical and environmental concerns. They are not, however, organic. They continue to charge premium prices although there are invariably supermarket offers to be found.

The products can be bought widely – in Tesco, Sainsbury's and Waitrose, for example. Their markets soon extended to Dublin, Paris and Hong Kong. Their early success pioneering bottled fruit smoothies provoked competition. Established 'giants' such as Del Monte and Ocean Spray (part of Gerber, itself recently acquired by Nestlé) have been unable to dislodge them from their market position. The most serious competition has come from the Tropicana brand, owned by Pepsi.

The company has always maintained a fun image and the trio dress casually. Their offices in South London are called 'Fruit Towers'. They are very creative and their logo is distinctive. It comprises an apple shape face with two eyes and a halo above. They want to be seen as fun and funky. They proclaim that their staff, with an average age of 27, are empowered and constantly on the lookout for new ideas. Their website has been likened to a student blog and they regularly email their online subscribers. They push the health message and feature mentions of daily fruit and vegetable intakes on their packages. In 2007 they launched new packaging made from polyactic acid which is fully degradable. Ten per cent of Innocent's annual profits have been given over to aid projects in countries such as Bangalore, Africa and Brazil; and they maintain a 'Sustainability Squad' to monitor environmental issues. Innocent are on record as saying that they try to 'leave things better than they find them'. Richard Reed was once asked whom he most admired. Instead of a business leader he chose 'a guy named Paulo who is running a Greenpeace campaign to save the Amazon rainforest'.

After nearly 10 years of growth and success Innocent 'took its eye off the ball'. In 2008 the founders sold a further stake to raise £35 million to help fund the development of new food products. Sales fell back in the second half of the year and there appeared to be some concern that smoothies, very much a discretionary consumer purchase, might suffer in the anticipated economic recession. Competition and increases in fruit prices were also issues. A profitable company was about to become a loss maker for a short period. At this time Innocent were keen to expand in selected overseas markets – especially in Europe – and in April 2009 Coca-Cola bought a 20 per cent stake for £30 million. Press reports stated the founders would continue to run the business and they remained confident the socially and environmentally-aware stance of Innocent was not under threat. The logic of the investment was that Coca-Cola can help secure new distribution opportunities. Coca-Cola's stake has since been expanded and they now own the company – but they seem to prefer a hand's-off role and the three founders are still involved – Innocent has been restored to growth and profitability and the founders had secured their exit strategy.

Asked to explain just why Innocent has been as successful as it has, and what they have learned, Richard Reed focused on five themes:

● Be clear about your purpose – Innocent's was about making healthy food both fun and popular.
● Start with a 'clear big picture' but then focus on getting the details right. Implementation is critical and opportunities for innovation and improvement start with activities.
● Business is ultimately about people – consistent values matter.
● So does an ethical approach – which gives substance to what happens.
● Listening comes free – and doing it can be a real source of added value.

Questions

1 What are the key determinants of the success of Innocent Smoothies?

2 Visit one local supermarket and check out the presence of Innocent drinks and the competition. Can you see any visible threats to the business?
3 Do you see any longer-term risks to the idiosyncratic nature of this business from the investment and then acquisition by Coca-Cola?

The most important quality of a CEO (Chief Executive Officer) is communicating a clear vision of the company's strategy – and the reputation of the CEO directly contributes to the company's ability to attract investment, recruit talent and survive crises.

BURSON-MARSTELLER, US PUBLIC RELATIONS BUSINESS

The task of leadership, as well as providing the framework, values and motivation of people, and allocation of financial and other resources, is to set the overall direction which enables choices to be made so that the efforts of the company can be focused.

In this quotation, Sir John Harvey-Jones emphasizes the need for a clear direction for the organization. The chief executive is responsible for clarifying the mission and objectives of the organization, for defining the corporate strategy which is intended to achieve these and for establishing and managing the organization's structure. Personal ideas, vision and planning systems are all involved in defining the strategy.

The corporate strategy will be implemented within the structure, and the ways in which people behave – and are allowed to behave – within the organization structure will impact upon changes in competitive and functional strategies. The chief executive will also be a major influence on the organization's culture and values, which are key determinants of the ways in which strategies are created and implemented.

However, managers who are in charge of divisions or strategic business units (often referred to as 'general managers') are also responsible for strategic changes concerning their own products, services or geographical territories – as are functional managers, the chief executive, the chairman of the board (whether the same person as the chief executive or a part-time, non-executive chairman) or chief operating officer. Throughout this book, the term *strategic leader* is used to describe the managers who head the organization and who are primarily responsible for creating and implementing strategic change, particularly corporate strategic change.

While the strategic leader has overall responsibility for managing strategy in the organization, all employees can, and should be encouraged to, make a contribution since they are then more likely to accept changes and the organization can become a strong competitor. Leaders should not – and realistically cannot – do everything themselves, but they remain the catalyst for what does happen.

The strategic leader gathers and receives information about all aspects of the business, and should monitor the environment and the organization and watch for important opportunities and threats that could affect the whole business, hence they need both analytical skills and insight (or awareness) to provide an intuitive grasp of the situation that faces the organization.

Strategic leaders are put in a position of **power**, but have discretion over how they use it; some are very motivated by power, others use it to impose their own ideas, others seek to share power and responsibility with others to empower them.

Strategic leaders also draw upon their experiences and expertise, as well as their background, which affects their relative preference for analysis and planning or for working through people and allowing them individual freedom in strategy creation.

These are the key themes of this chapter.

The strategic leader is responsible directly to the Board of Directors of the organization, and through the Board, to the stakeholders in the business. The responsibilities of the Board and, in effect, the strategic leader, could be summarized as follows:

1 Manage the business on behalf of all the stakeholders (or interested parties).

2 Provide direction in the form of a mission or purpose.

3 Formulate and implement changes to corporate strategies.

4 Monitor and control operations with special reference to financial results, productivity, quality, customer service, innovation, new products and services and staff development.

5 Provide policies and guidelines for other managers to facilitate both the management of operations and changes in competitive and functional strategies.

Responsibility 5 is achieved through the organization structure; 2 and 4 are dependent on an effective communications network.

Figure 10.1 summarizes these points by explaining that, essentially, the strategic leader has a meta-level responsibility for deciding how strategies are to be created and implemented to pursue the mission and direction. They may impose strategies and at the same time decide upon the nature, scope and significance of strategic planning systems. The choices of structure and management style will affect emergent strategy making, as will be seen in Chapters 14 and 16.

Hooper and Trompenaars (2009) suggest that strategic leaders' results are partly driven by personal motives and ambitions, which affect personal values and the specific concerns these bring to the organization. In terms of their style, are they by nature more analytical (like corporate leaders) or more intuitive (like entrepreneurs)? And how effective is the leader at communicating – are they trusted, and, do they trust those that work for them?

10.1 Strategic leaders(hip) and entrepreneurs(hip): same or different?

Kets de Vries (1996) found that the most successful strategic leaders perform two key roles, a *charismatic* role and an *architectural* one, effectively (see Figure 10.2), such that their strategies are owned, customers are satisfied, employees enjoy work and things can, and do, happen and change quickly. The charismatic role involves establishing and gaining support for a (winning) vision and direction, empowering employees and energizing them, gaining their enthusiastic support for what has to be done. The architectural role concerns building an appropriate organization structure, together with systems for controlling and rewarding people. Hence, these roles embrace visionary leaders, entrepreneurs and intrapreneurs.

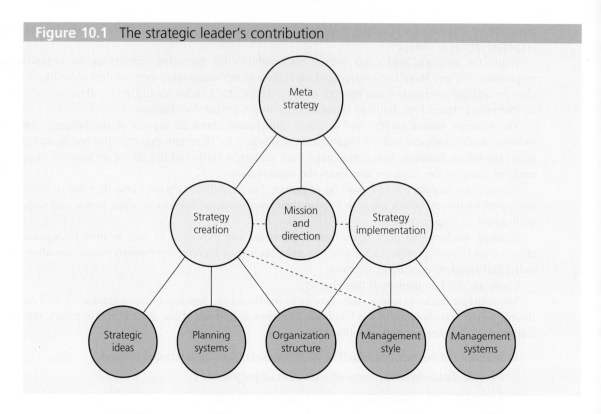

Figure 10.1   The strategic leader's contribution

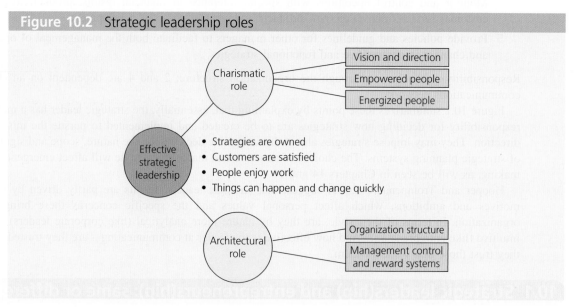

Figure 10.2   Strategic leadership roles

Hamel (1999) distinguishes between the often inadequate *stewardship* – the continued exploitation of *past* opportunities with costs managed for efficiencies and some incremental changes and improvements to reinforce the strategic position in a competitive environment – and the more dynamic *entrepreneurship* – combining new ideas, talented and entrepreneurial managers, and resources to exploit *new* opportunities entrepreneurially and driven by aspiration rather than analysis.

Table 10.1 features ten quite different strategic leaders, including the late Anita Roddick, Tim Waterstone, Archie Norman and others.

Table 10.1   Ten strategic leaders, each of whom has or had a vision, and is linked irrevocably with their company's strategy, structure and performance

Anita Roddick	The Body Shop	Built up and 'stuck with it'
Richard Branson	Virgin	Built up and sold parts
Alan Sugar	Amstrad	Built up and split up
Tim Waterstone	Waterstone's	Built up, sold off and started again
Archie Norman	ASDA	Turned around and rejuvenated
Jack Welch	General Electric	Transformed
James Dyson	Dyson	Built up and remains in control
Gerald Ratner	Ratner's	Inherited, grew and lost
Freddie Laker	Laker Airways (Skytrain)	Built up, lost and retired eventually
Stelios Haji-Ioannou	EasyGroup	Built up; stepped down from original business

Strategic awareness and change involves: becoming aware – listening, being on the shop floor more than in the office whilst, most important of all, staying humble – and taking action – sharing with others.

MICHEL BON, ex-PDG, CARREFOUR SA

The role of the strategic leader

The strategic leader must *direct* the organization and ensure that feasible and achievable long-term **objectives** and **intended strategies** (which are more likely to be supported) have been determined and that they are understood and supported by managers who implement them through the *organization structure* adopted by the strategic leader. Some will not be feasible due to wrong assumptions or changing circumstances. Decisions taken by general and functional managers within a decentralized structure will lead to new, incremental and adaptive changes in competitive and functional strategies. A third major responsibility of the strategic leader is a system of *communications* which both enables managers to be strategically aware, and ensures that the strategic leader stays informed of changes taking place.

Strategic leaders need to articulate a clear mission for the organization that is understood and supported by committed employees and which provides guidance and direction when managers make decisions and implement strategies determined by others. Similarly, the actual strategies – corporate and competitive – for achieving long-term objectives may be created personally by a strong or visionary strategic leader, or they may be ideas from anywhere inside the organization. Strategic leaders need not be personally visionary, as discussed later, but they must ensure that the organization has a clear direction and resources are committed to its achievement.

Figure 10.3 develops the E–V–R (environment–values–resources) congruence framework introduced in Part 1 with effective strategic positioning being central and reflecting competitive advantage. Positions have to be changed, perhaps due to innovation and incremental changes, or more dramatic and discontinuous changes reflecting a change in the vision.

Strategic leaders must make things happen and bring positive results such that the organization's resources are managed efficiently and effectively. Some strategic leaders will be *doers*, active in carrying strategies through, and others will be delegators who rely instead on their skills for motivating and inspiring, and they will need control systems for monitoring results and strategic effectiveness. Pragmatic but non-visionary leaders can be highly effective but they must still ensure that the organization has a clear and appropriate purpose and direction. However, short-term success results from a combination of efficient management and friendly market forces, which can change quickly, or when previously successful strategies are in need of renewal, a non-visionary may fail to provide the appropriate leadership and champion the necessary changes. Vision is crucial and some believe that the most effective leaders are those with ideas (Bennis, 1988), perhaps because their vision and track record helps obtain and maintain the confidence and support of influential stakeholders, such as institutional shareholders.

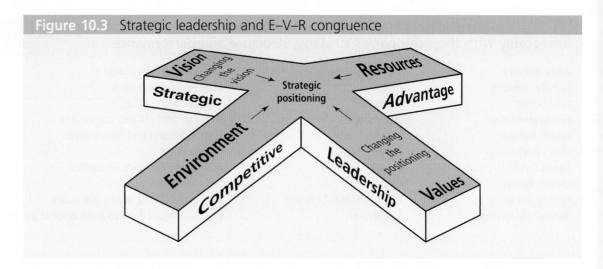

Figure 10.3   Strategic leadership and E–V–R congruence

As well as vision and pragmatism, the leader should build a structure and culture that captures the abilities and contributions of other managers and employees, through which existing strategies are implemented where there is proper momentum for change. See Chapter 15.

The organization's culture and values (Chapter 7) is very often influenced, or imposed, by the strategic leader, for example the attitudes and behaviour of people and their willingness to accept responsibility and take measured risks. Although over time a strategic leader is likely to become more of a generalist than a specialist, a leader with a financial background may focus on financial targets and analysis; a marketing background on consumers and competition; or an engineering background on product design and quality.

Figure 10.4 delineates six key leader styles, as every leader may have a dominant style, but must make sure that the others are not neglected because all of the contributions are required. The balance between the

Figure 10.4   Strategic leadership style

Table 10.2 E–V–V–R and leadership styles

E–V–V–R	Leadership styles
Vision	Aspirational
Values	Human resources
Environment	Public relations; analytical
Resources	Financial engineering; operational/Tactical; analytical

six, which ones are strong relative to the others, will affect the culture and management style of the whole organization. Arguably, use of this framework can help us to understand why things happen as they do in any organization being analyzed and will help to explain the relative balance between visionary, planned and emergent strategy creation. Table 10.2 now links Figures 10.3 and 10.4.

Effective formal and informal communication systems help to share the strategic vision and inform people of priorities and strategies and to ensure that strategies and tasks are carried out expeditiously. In a decentralized organization, an effective communications network feeds information *upwards and laterally* inside the organization to avoid control being lost. In quite different ways, both 'managing by wandering around' and budgetary control systems can help to achieve this co-ordination. Good lateral communications also help managers to learn from other parts of the business, which can lead to good practice being shared. The strategic leader must champion relationships with important stakeholders, particularly its financiers, suppliers and major customers, and government agencies and the media.

Corporate governance, although beyond the scope of this book, means that the leader should ensure that there is a strong, competent and balanced executive team at the head of the organization whether or not the roles of chairman (often a part-time post) and chief executive are split or not, or in terms of the role and contribution of part-time non-executive directors. Topics of **governance** controversy frequently involve senior management remuneration packages.

The importance attached to formal planning processes and emergent strategy creation in an organization will depend upon the personal preferences and the style of management adopted by the strategic leader. The organization must be able to respond to the change pressures of a competitive environment, and curiosity, creativity and innovation should become part of the corporate culture. Although learning and incremental change are crucially important, discontinuous change and strategic regeneration will be necessary for organizations at certain stages in their life cycles. When this is the case, and strategies, structures and styles of management need re-inventing simultaneously, an effective, visionary leader will be essential.

An organization needs an *effective* strategic leader, but they cannot and should not attempt to do everything and should be able to understand personal strengths and limitations and to appreciate the most appropriate ways of contributing. There is no single, recommended behaviour for effective strategic leadership: some are autocratic, others democratic, some rely on planning and analysis, others are more intuitive and visionary, some accept risk or uncertainty, others are averse to these elements, some pursue growth through efficiency and cost savings, others by adding new values in an innovatory climate, some set ambitious growth objectives and others are more modest. All of these styles can prove effective but the challenge lies in creating and maintaining E–V–R congruence.

The strategic leader's position and situation should be evaluated, given that they may have founded the organization and still be in control; maybe in a later family, generation; may have 'risen through the ranks' to take control; or may have been brought in specially, possibly to turn around a company in difficulty; and may be relatively new or have been in the post for some time. The style of leadership adopted depends upon the leader's preferred style, background and current circumstances.

Critical Reflection 10.1 provides a summary of the qualities and skills required for effective leadership, together with a list of the factors that typically characterize ineffective leadership. Figure 10.5 features

Critical Reflection 10.1 Effective and Ineffective Leadership

Qualities and skills for effective leadership

- A vision – articulated through the culture and value systems.
- The ability to build and control an effective team of managers.
- Belief in success and in corporate strengths and competencies that can be exploited.
- The ability to recognize and synthesize important developments, both inside and outside the organization. This requires strategic awareness, the ability to judge the significance of an observed event and conceptualization skills.
- Effective decentralization, delegation and motivation (the appropriate extent will vary).
- Credibility and competence. Knowing what you are doing and having this recognized. This requires the ability to exercise power and influence and to create change.
- Implementation skills; getting things done, which requires drive, decisiveness and dynamism.
- Perseverance and persistence in pursuing the mission or vision, plus mental and physical stamina.
- Flexibility; recognizing the need (on occasions) to change strategies, structures and style. Some leaders are single style and inflexible.

Characteristics of ineffective leadership

After a period in office, some leaders appear to coast, enjoying their power and status, but no longer adding any real value to the organization. Specifically:

- There are few new initiatives; instead there is a reliance on tinkering with existing strategies to try to update past successes.
- Good new products and services are not developed.
- The leader surrounds him- or herself with loyal supporters, rather than enjoying the stimulus of newcomers with fresh mindsets.
- Moreover, discordant views are either ignored or not tolerated.
- Cash reserves, beyond those needed to sustain a period of depressed sales, are allowed to accrue.
- The leader becomes out of touch with the views of customers and the activities of competitors.
- Too much time is spent by the leader on external activities, without ensuring that other managers are dealing with important organizational issues.

Figure 10.5 Leadership requirements

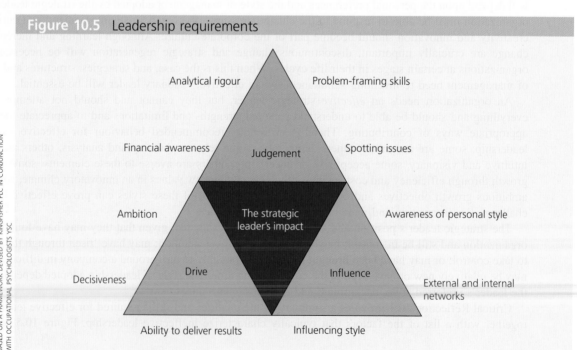

BASED ON A FRAMEWORK DEVISED BY KINGFISHER PLC IN CONJUNCTION WITH OCCUPATIONAL PSYCHOLOGISTS YSC

requirements that determine the extent of the impact made by a strategic leader and presents the issues in three clusters:

- Drive – concerns motivation and ambition and a person's ability to accept demanding targets and achieve results.
- Judgement – related to decision-making style and abilities. The softer or more conceptual issues of opportunity-spotting and problem-framing (awareness and insight into a situation) blend with harder analytical abilities.
- Influence – a person's appreciation of how others might be influenced and their way of doing it. Networks and contacts are an important element of this.

A number of these themes are also illustrated in Case 10.2 on Sir Tom Farmer, founder of Kwik-Fit, who imported his vision from the USA and whose success has involved opportunism and innovation backed up by sound business sense. Sir Tom Farmer could legitimately be described as an entrepreneur as discussed later in this section when we examine the link between entrepreneurs and strategy before examining visionary strategic leadership.

Case 10.2   Sir Tom Farmer and Kwik-Fit   UK

Tom Farmer was born into a working-class family in Edinburgh, Scotland, in 1940; he was the seventh child. Brought up a Roman Catholic in a largely Protestant city, he left school at the age of 15 and began working in a tyre company. In 1964 he set up his own business, retailing tyres at discount prices. New legislation on minimum tyre depths opened a window of opportunity and he quickly expanded from one to four outlets. After 4 years he sold the whole business for £450 000 to Albany Tyres, 'retired' and went to live in California. Within 3 years he and his wife were bored. He returned to Scotland but, because of his agreement with Albany, he could not start a new tyre-retailing business until a number of years had elapsed.

Instead, he brought over an idea he had seen in the USA: a fast-change exhaust shop. Again, he quickly expanded from one to four outlets, so that he could re-employ a number of his old friends! Tyres were added later. As for the Kwik-Fit name, he just dreamed it up. The distinctive blue and yellow colours, pervasive to this day, were chosen because these were the colours of some paint that someone gave him free of charge!

Farmer is a workaholic and was always very committed to his business and his employees. He is also very religious. All of Tom Farmer's employees were put on profit-share schemes; about half became individual shareholders in the business. Private garages and repair shops are often thought to involve dubious commercial practices; one of Tom Farmer's major achievements has been to bring a high level of

perceived (and real) integrity into the industry. He places a strong emphasis on good customer service and friendliness, attributes which are featured in distinctive Kwik-Fit advertisements.

By the early 1980s there were 200 depots; arguably the business grew too quickly. Inadequate management control left the company vulnerable to takeover for a while, but it managed to retain its independence. For 29 years the company grew organically and stayed focused. There was some geographical expansion, successfully in Belgium and the Netherlands, but Kwik-Fit entered and then withdrew from France. 'There are cultural differences. The French want to close for lunch. French managers are reluctant to bond with their employees. These are key Kwik-Fit values.'

In 1994 Kwik-Fit acquired 95 Superdrive Motoring Centres from Shell, a related business. In 1995 Kwik-Fit Insurance was launched, exploiting Kwik-Fit's large customer database. Farmer argues that it is based on the same principles: high service using someone else's products. In 1999 Kwik-Fit was sold to Ford for £1 billion. By this time there were 1900 outlets, 9000 employees and eight million customers a year. Tom Farmer, by this time Sir Tom, stayed active in the business for some time after the sale to Ford, before effectively retiring for a second time. In August 2002, Ford sold Kwik-Fit to the private equity group CVC Partners for £330m. In 2001/2 Ford had global losses of $5billion and needed to raise cash by selling off non-core activities. Kwik-Fit continues to thrive with

SOURCE: THIS CASE STUDY WAS PREPARED USING PRIMARILY PUBLICLY AVAILABLE SOURCES OF INFORMATION FOR THE PURPOSES OF CLASSROOM DISCUSSION; IT DOES NOT INTEND TO ILLUSTRATE EITHER EFFECTIVE OR INEFFECTIVE HANDLING OF A MANAGERIAL SITUATION.

over 2500 service centres and 11 000 employees. This time there was no going back to Kwik-Fit for Sir Tom. But he remains active, encouraging other young entrepreneurs.

Yet Farmer has always been seen as a demanding man to work for, and many employees have been 'rather frightened of him'.

In an interview with *Management Today* (August 1995) Tom Farmer made the following comments.

If the customer is king, the staff are emperors.

We don't have a head office; we have a support office. We don't have senior management; we have support management.

All sound businesses are built on good Christian ethics: don't steal, don't exploit your customers or your people, always use your profits for the benefit of your people and the community.

We are in business to make a profit and we should not be ashamed of that, provided we stick to sound principles, and, at the end of the day, do proper things with that profit.

Questions

1 Why was Kwik-Fit so successful?
2 Is Tom Farmer a visionary leader, an entrepreneur or both?
3 Does the fact that he lives in a large house and owns both a corporate jet and a helicopter contradict any of his stated beliefs?

KWIK-FIT **http://www.kwik-fit.com**

Charan (2006) argues that effective strategic leaders should demonstrate necessary qualities and know-how, which, he argues, are:

- The ability to position the business in order to make money – which implies an ability to satisfy customers and respond to environmental changes.
- Connecting external events to the internal workings of the business – in order to drive the change agenda.
- 'Managing the social system' of the organization so that there are effective networks and communications.
- Judging, selecting and developing both other and future leaders.
- Moulding an effective leadership team.
- Deciding upon and pursuing realistic but stretching goals, linked to direction.
- Clarifying priority issues – which will affect the likelihood of achieving the desired outcomes.
- Finally, dealing with the inevitable, ubiquitous and unexpected challenges. The world is uncertain.

He does argue that it is unlikely any one person will be outstanding in all of these!

Entrepreneurs and entrepreneurship

Bolton and Thompson (2013) define an entrepreneur as a person who: 'habitually creates and innovates to build something of recognized value around perceived opportunities'. Entrepreneurs start organizations, run organizations and work in organizations as employees (as **intrapreneurs**, shorthand for *intra-corporate entrepreneurs* (Pinchot and Pinchot, 1978). Here we examine strategic leaders as entrepreneurs; and then whether the strategic leader has built an organization which fosters intrapreneurship (Section 10.2).

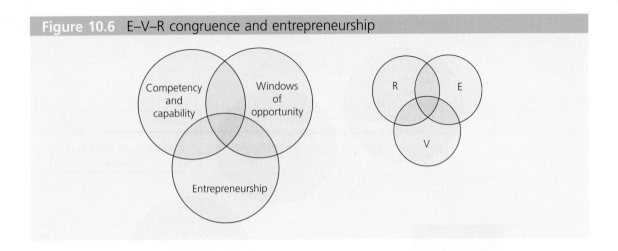

Figure 10.6   E–V–R congruence and entrepreneurship

Strategic management is concerned with environmental fit in terms of achieving congruence between environment, values and resources for both existing and potential future products and services (Figure 10.6 implies E–V–R action rather than an expression of a state, in terms of the environment as windows of opportunity and resources as organizational competencies and capabilities). Thus entrepreneurship in the organization, both at the level of the leader and throughout the whole organization, is required to ensure that resources are developed and changed and used to exploit the windows of opportunity ahead of rival organizations.

Existing business leaders should ensure that attention is focused on costs and prices, which determine profits, and on ways of reducing costs by improving productivity perhaps by technology changes and new operating systems, which may equally improve product quality, for which premium prices might be charged. Future developments might concern new products (or services) or new markets or both, and might involve diversification. For different alternatives, the magnitude of the change implied and the risk involved will vary, and the changes can be gradual or incremental, or can be more dynamic or individually significant. Real innovation can be costly in terms of the investment required and is (often necessarily) risky.

Figure 10.7 shows alternative development paths for a business given that, although entrepreneurs are normally conceptualized as people who develop new ideas and new businesses, alternative conceptualizations theorize entrepreneurs as individuals who introduce innovative ideas into a situation of some stability and create disequilibrium (Schumpeter, 1934) or, conversely, create equilibrium (in the form of E–V–R congruence) by matching demand and supply in a creative way (see Kirzner, 1973). However, it is the path of future progress that really matters.

The business could initially be successful but then fail, without further innovation and renewal (Path I), as the original window of opportunity closes and the business fails to find or capitalize on a new one.

Many archetypal small 'lifestyle' businesses – not run by 'real' entrepreneurs as they fail the 'habitual' requirement included in the definition, but by lifestyle entrepreneurs – never improve and grow (Path II), sometimes by deliberate choice, sometimes through lack of insight and awareness; but survive by satisfying a particular niche or localized market and find a new window of opportunity if that one closes, and are reactive rather than proactive. They may *expand*, as distinct from true growth based on improvement and excellence.

Paths III and IV feature more proactive entrepreneurial businesses which *grow* via productivity improvements and/or by leveraging their resources to develop new products and service opportunities and sometimes, but certainly not always, they will be decentralized, empowered and *intrapreneurial*.

Path V implies discontinuous change and requires visionary leadership, either from the original founding entrepreneur or a new strategic leader: involving opportunity-based strategy-making, growth orientation, decentralized power and significant strategic change achieved despite conditions of uncertainty (Mintzberg, 1973). Implicit is an attempt to be proactive and manage the environment. Paths III, IV and V are clearly not mutually exclusive and can exist simultaneously.

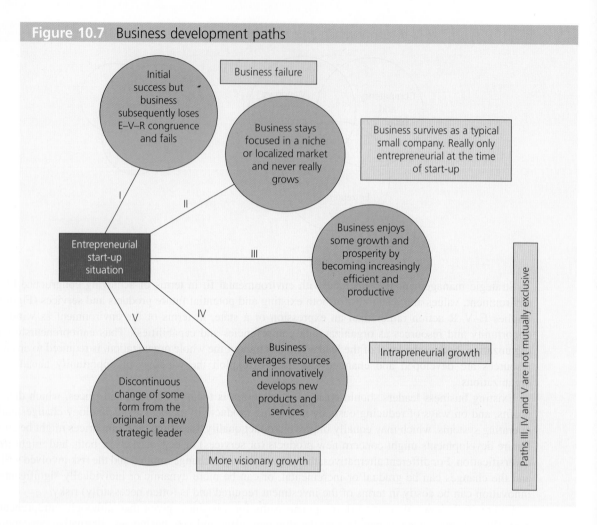

Figure 10.7   Business development paths

While Paths I and II are not genuine 'entrepreneurial' businesses, nor is an acquisitive-growth organization which fails to add new value and improve along either Paths III or IV, although at times its revenue might grow dramatically. When any company merges or gets taken over, there is likely to be a change of strategy, culture and possibly leadership and hence the acquired business may, therefore, experience a Path V change.

The role of the entrepreneur

The word 'entrepreneur' continues to suggest the sharp trader, so-called dodgy dealer or less-than-honest used car salesmen. Entrepreneurs are often linked exclusively to the business world; and yet entrepreneurial people are to be found in most walks of life, for example social entrepreneurs have a commitment to deliver social and environmental as well as financial outcomes. In this section we explore how our understanding of the term has developed in the last 250 years.

Cantillon (1755) cites the entrepreneur as any individual who operates under conditions where expenditures are known and certain, but incomes (sales revenues) are unknown and uncertain. Cantillon's entrepreneur possesses foresight and the confidence to operate under conditions of uncertainty, and his or her main qualities are the creation of entrepreneurial income through decision-making and risk-taking rather than orthodox effort. Cantillon was a natural trader and dealer with a relatively shrewd approach to opportunistic profit, and he was reportedly a successful speculator because he could perceive and predict the actions and reactions of other speculators better than they could predict his own – revealing a character combining intelligence and perceptiveness with a willingness to take risks. The word 'entrepreneur' first referred to Frenchmen – appointed by noblemen acting on the King's orders – who were granted the right to supervise the construction of a road or bridge and to collect the tolls, in return for a suitable donation to the royal treasury or some other favour. The entrepreneur took the risk and guaranteed the nobleman a fixed annual payment and kept the profit, while noblemen generally wished to earn a steady income without getting their hands dirty. Since entrepreneurs tended to be smart and closely involved with the project, and the noblemen who nominally owned the projects were usually neither, profits were often substantial – because they managed the risk carefully.

In the German–Austrian tradition, the entrepreneur is characterized as someone who manages the inputs into a process with higher level outputs, i.e. trying to manage demand and supply and who, by coping with uncertainty, is a risk-bearer.

Schumpeter (1934) saw the role of the entrepreneur as driving through innovation, which leads to the creation of new firms, to the demise of old firms, and thus the creation of wealth. Schumpeter believed that only large firms would have the resources to both innovate and prevent the competition from new entrepreneurs threatening them. However, small firms continue to be the engine of innovation in any economy and these firms are led by people we call entrepreneurs.

The Chicago tradition, outlined in the work of Knight (1921), indicates that the fundamental characteristic of the entrepreneur is risk-taking and being able to deal with the uncertainty that exists within any economy.

Schultz (1962) suggested that the entrepreneur should not have a limited role as a business person, but should be the agent of economic change driving the economy forward. The Modern–Austrian Tradition portrays the entrepreneur as demonstrating 'great ingenuity' and thus reaches the higher level of promoting economic change, meaning that they can contribute more to the economy and are more than just an effective manager: the entrepreneur must be alert to opportunity.

For Kirzner (1973), the entrepreneur is not interested in routine managerial tasks but is concerned to demonstrate qualities of creativity and perception, and is alert to changes in the economy and takes advantage of this. This view could return the perception of the role of the entrepreneur as a wheeler dealer who creates nothing except for spotting and taking profitable opportunity. To some extent, it will depend on what form opportunity takes: asset stripping or the opportunity to innovate and, as both might create wealth, but for whom and how will the wealth be used?

Liebenstein (1966) moved towards confirming the more complex profile of the effective entrepreneur, with the theory of x-inefficiency and x-efficiency highlighting the basic concept that only through innovation will firms progress. He identifies two types of entrepreneurs: a routine or managerial figure allocating inputs to the production process in a traditional manner; or the Schumpetarian entrepreneur who can produce a new product or process through innovation.

At this point, we can link in the work of the Classicists and particularly of Say (1815) who perceived the entrepreneur as someone who can effectively manage all of the factors of production (such as materials, labour, finance, land and equipment), e.g. someone who has mastered the art of administration and superintendence. This type of entrepreneur is a real team player and capable of managing the growth of a larger organization. Few entrepreneurs show these capabilities and many have no desire to manage, co-ordinate and combine all of the factors of production, but if this was not the case, the organization would ultimately fail and, therefore, the qualities of the entrepreneur are crucial, giving added importance to the concept of the entrepreneurial team who can provide the wide range of skills needed.

As well as sustained entrepreneurial behaviour, new entrepreneurs are required to start new businesses to replace the jobs which are lost when other companies collapse and certain industries decline, as have coal mining, steel making and shipbuilding, for example. Typically, a different type of business, with dissimilar labour requirements, will emerge. In general, the issue is not so much stimulating business start-ups, but in encouraging them to grow; and yet growth demands changes in structure and style and requires the owner-manager to relinquish some power and control. Case 10.3 features two interesting examples of visionary entrepreneurs, James Watt and William Chase, and the businesses they have helped to create. Case 10.4 allows you to reflect upon how these views of entrepreneurs and entrepreneurship might be applied to the story of a successful Chinese businessman.

Case 10.3 James Watt and BrewDog and William Chase and Tyrrell Chips   UK

James Watt grew up in the North East of Scotland in a small fishing village called Gradenstown near Fraserburgh. James would help his father run and maintain his fishing boat. This exposure to hard labour is something that James Watt felt was a good beginning to his business career. After leaving school, Watt moved to Edinburgh to study law and economics at Edinburgh University. Following his graduation, Watt obtained a job in an Edinburgh law office. Pretty soon after joining the law firm, James realized he hated the job and discovered he actually had little real interest in his law career. At this point Watt moved back to his home village and to temporary work on his father's boat.

During this period his friend Martin Dickie (who James had met at Peterhead Academy) had completed a degree in brewing at Heriot Watt University. After graduation, Dickie had obtained employment as head brewer at Thornbridge Brewery in Derbyshire. However, the two friends had kept in touch and shared a passion for beer especially what Watt describes as 'real, honest natural beer not all that mass-produced beer that is full of junk and additives with marketing onslaughts designed to change your life'.

BrewDog was founded in 2006 by James Watt and Martin Dickie. The two friends started the business with £120 000 obtained from many sources including their savings and loans from a variety of sources including the Prince's Scottish Youth Business Trust (PSYBT). No external equity was given away, thus leaving the two partners firmly in control.

The brewery at the Kessock Industrial Estate in Fraserburgh produced its first brew in April 2007 and would go on within 1 year to become Scotland's largest independently owned brewery producing about 120 000 bottles per month for export all over the world. This soon grew to over 200 000 bottles per month with 80 per cent for export to the USA and Scandinavia supported by sales in Tesco and Sainsbury's in the UK. The BrewDog promise states that they will:

- only use the finest natural ingredients
- not include preservatives or additives within their beer
- always make great tasting beers and promote them in a way which makes people smile.

What is clear about the business is the fervour and style that the two friends brought to the start-up. Watt was very much the driving force behind the marketing of the beers with Dickie happy to brew beer rather than sell beer. Watt recognized that there was a gap in the market between traditional real ale drinkers who were mainly male and over 50, compared with the new beer drinker who is aged 18 to 30 and either male or female. In realizing there was a profit to be made from changing consumer tastes Watt demonstrates the typical entrepreneurial trait of taking advantage of change for profit.

The nature of the different approach to brewing bottled beer that BrewDog has is very well demonstrated in the names given to their beers, which include:

- Hop Rocker (Lager)
- Punk IPA (India Pale Ale)
- The Physics (Amber Ale)
- Rip Tide (Stout)
- Hardcore IPA (India Pale Ale)
- Paradox Imperial Stout, matured in various malt whisky casks.

The quirky nature of how BrewDog is run and their attitude to business, customers, beer creation and development can be examined through the company website: **www.brewdog.com**

In 2008 Paradox won the Gold Medal from the Brewers Association of the USA in the strong beer category, beating 53 other entries. This award is generally regarded as the most prestigious one that can be won worldwide for the brewing of beer. In 2008 BrewDog and James Watt won a number of other accolades, including Entrepreneur of the Year in the National Business Awards for Scotland; BrewDog was runner-up for the HSBC 2008 Start-Up Stars Award.

It was not however all 'plain sailing' for BrewDog. Their Fraserburgh location, to which they were fiercely attached, made it difficult to recruit the staff they would need for expansion and it inevitably added to their distribution costs.

In 2008 BrewDog was challenged by UK drinks industry watchdog, the Portman Group. Portman claimed BrewDog was in breach of their Code of Practice on the Naming, Packaging and Promotion of Alcoholic Drink. BrewDog refuted these allegations and countered that Portman was impeding the development of smaller brewing companies.

After an 8-month-long dispute and a preliminary adjudication which had ruled against the company, BrewDog was cleared of all breaches of the Code of Practice in December 2008, and was permitted to continue marketing their brands without making any changes to the packaging.

In February 2009, BrewDog announced plans to sell their beer in pubs and clubs up and down the UK stating that 'world domination is very much on the agenda'.

Questions

1 In terms of the theory and practice of entrepreneurship, what theories best explain the actions of James Watt in the creation of BrewDog?
2 What type of entrepreneur is James Watt?
3 Have they been able to continue with their ambitious programme of expansion?

FOR FURTHER DETAIL ON JAMES WATT

**http://www.bbc.co.uk/lastmillionaire/
entrepreneur/jamesw.shtml**

William Chase

At the ripe old age of 20, William Chase purchased the Tyrrell Court Farm from his father in 1984. Poor sales and a recession saw his investment turn sour with Chase being made bankrupt. However, not to be put off, William Chase fought back. He leased his farm back from the lenders and eventually bought the farm back and moved on to become a successful potato farmer in his own right.

However, Chase believed that the only people making any money out of farming were the supermarkets who were forever forcing down the prices they gave to the farmer. On this basis Chase felt that his business of supplying potatoes would not be profitable for much longer. As with many examples of business change the new direction for William Chase came about through circumstance. A batch of his potatoes scheduled to be turned into oven ready chips by McCain were rejected. Chase quickly found an alternative customer for the potatoes and sold them to a crisp maker. Upon tasting the final product Chase thought he could do better. In 2002 he decided to do market research by going to America to taste as many handmade potato chips as he could. Upon returning he set about making his own handmade potato chips. He knew that success of his chips had to be based upon selling them as a new innovative product. He invested a great deal of money in marketing and packaging to put across the quality hand made image Chase felt was crucial to the success of his chips.

Over the next few years Chase built up his hand made potato chip business by selling firstly to independent retail stores, farm shops and to delicatessens rather than to the big supermarkets, who he would not let dictate to him. In September 2006, Chase won a legal battle against Tesco preventing them from stocking his products without his permission. He does however sell to other supermarkets whom he is happy to deal with and they include, Waitrose, Sainsbury's and the Co-op. By 2007 the turnover of the business had reached £8.5 million selling not only the original potato chip but also flavoured potato chips such as Strawberry Sweet Chili and White Wine potato chips. His next great product idea was to launch in 2008 the first British pure potato vodka.

Chase personified the business. Whilst very ambitious, he was very keen on keeping the business based around the Tyrrell Farm and he is a firm believer in the happy personalized team approach to doing business. Would this approach be appropriate into the future?

Questions

1 To what extent is business development of this type very much a rare example of how to succeed in business?
2 Profile William Chase. Is he part of a new breed of businessman? How successful is his business today?

www.tyrrellspotatochips.co.uk

SOURCE: THIS CASE STUDY WAS PREPARED USING PRIMARILY PUBLICLY AVAILABLE SOURCES OF INFORMATION FOR THE PURPOSES OF CLASSROOM DISCUSSION; IT DOES NOT INTEND TO ILLUSTRATE EITHER EFFECTIVE OR INEFFECTIVE HANDLING OF A MANAGERIAL SITUATION.

Case 10.4   Jack Ma and Alibaba.com   Ch

Jack Ma is now the Chairman and CEO of the Alibaba Group of companies with a personal wealth estimated in 2011 to be over $1.5 billion dollars. In the world of business Jack Ma is the epitome of the successful Chinese businessman who has, from nothing, created a major Chinese company. What lies behind his success and what, if anything, can be learned from and applied to other businesses, especially those based in Asia?

Ma was born in Hangzhou, Zhejiang Province, China. He graduated in 1988 with a Bachelor's degree in English having initially failed the entrance exam for the Hangzhou Teachers College on two occasions. From his graduation he followed what could be anticipated as the expected or traditional route and became a lecturer in English and International Trade at the Hangzhou Dianzi University. In 1995 Jack Ma visited the USA for the first time. He was able to go on this trip, on behalf of a public body in his province, through his superior skills in English – and it was then that he saw the Internet in operation.

Following on from his trip to the USA Ma, in 1995, was behind an Internet b2b start-up that had to be effectively shut down through the lack of businesses wishing to trade online. The main product of this web business set up by Ma was Haibao.net, which had, as its b2b platform, a product called China Page. This was one of the earliest Internet companies in China – and Jack Ma had invested 20 000 Yuan of his own money in it. At this time Ma experienced very heavy competition for the local b2b market from Hangzhou Telecom and he was eventually forced to co-operate with this local Telecom company and in order to survive he sold different equity stakes in China Page. Subsequently Ma became the minority shareholder in his own business and as a result he decided to withdraw dividing his 21 per cent of shares in China Page amongst the staff who had helped him to start up China Page.

Closely following this Ma was given the opportunity, in 1997, to join the Ministry of Foreign Trade and Economic Cooperation, where he was given responsibility to develop the Ministry's official site for the online trading of Chinese products. Ma was however not willing to settle for the Ministry position and resigned his post in 1999. What the post had given him, though, was further experience in the needs of Chinese businesses wanting to sell their products on the Internet. Ma became convinced that the answer to his need for revenue development was based on helping small-to-medium Chinese businesses get online and trading both with each other and with other businesses outside China.

With a start-up fund of 500 000 Yuan Ma bought the domain name of Alibaba.com and other related domain names e.g. Alibaby.com. To get the site up and running the staff recruited by Ma all worked 16 hours a day sleeping on the floor of Jack Ma's house. The site was in operation by March 1999 and almost immediately started to attract venture capital offers. The key to success for Ma was that he believed that China must have its own mode of Internet and that if Alibaba stuck to providing services for small and medium enterprises then the business would grow as these enterprises grew.

'Those who need our help are not nationally owned business firms – while international corporates don't need us either. We should always help those who need our help,' said Jack Ma in 2001. He realized he must 'put the customer first'.

This focus on the needs of the Chinese business or consumer has seen the Alibaba group of companies grow rapidly since 2001. Alibaba China is now the world's largest online business-to-business marketplace with over 500 000 people visiting the site everyday. Alternatively eBay, Google and Amazon have struggled in the Chinese market through not being able to adjust their US business practices to the needs of a Chinese SME wanting to sell in the world market whether that be in New York or not.

In 2003, Jack Ma, through Alibaba.com, started an auction website, Taobao.com, which made use of an escrow payment system called Alipay which was needed at the time to work with the cash based payment system that was the norm for transactions in China. In 2011 Taobao was ranked the 21st most popular global website in terms of traffic by Alexa.com, a subsidiary of Amazon.com, that measures global Internet traffic. Taobao now has a 67 per cent share of the Chinese auction online market and the value of the transactions on the site has reached $1billion.

In recent years Alibaba.com has opened a European office and in Spring 2009 it opened its UK office. Ma has not stopped at this and has in 2011 added Alibaba Cloud to the stable of businesses within the Alibaba group.

In a shareholders meeting in May 2009 Ma urged those attending to take matters into their own hands. He reminded everyone there that the great fortunes of the world were made by people who saw opportunities that others missed and that the present global recession provided the opportunity for people to take matters into their own hands in the form of starting businesses to cope with the economic downturn rather than waiting for government or businesses to help them.

Questions

1 Do you agree that Jack Ma is a typical entrepreneur?
2 What actions has he done that represent the blend of entrepreneurial characteristics found in the literature profiling entrepreneurs?
3 What is the basic business model of Alibaba.com?

It is, therefore, important for us to understand the motivation of entrepreneurs and how they see and activate opportunities. McClelland and Winter (1971) argue that all managers, in fact all workers, are influenced and motivated by three desires – the desire to achieve, the desire for power and the desire for affiliation at work – whose relative strength varies between individuals. Management thus needs to understand what motivates people, rather than to believe that all people can be motivated in the same way. Entrepreneurial behaviour is characterized by high achievement motivation, a power motive and affiliation. Achievement motivation concerns doing a job well, or better than others, and accomplishing something unusual or important, and with advancement. Such managers thrive where they are responsible for finding answers to problems, and tend to set moderate achievable goals and take calculated risks – but, if the targets are too modest, they are not challenged or satisfied and, if too high, consider them too risky. Actually achieving the goal is important and they also prefer constant feedback concerning progress. Achievement motivation is closely linked to the desire to create something, and entrepreneurial behaviour also features a desire for power, influence and independence. Entrepreneurs need both creativity and confidence if they are to seek out and exploit new ideas; and they must be willing to take risks. While McClelland and Winter describe achievement-motivated people as those who take very measured risks, there are some entrepreneurs who thrive on uncertainty and are successful because they take chances and opportunities that others would and do reject, but they will not always succeed.

Therefore, one might expect to see people who aspire to be leaders to be driven more by a desire for power, although McClelland and Winter believe achievement motivation is also strong in the most effective leaders.

10.2 Intrapreneurship

Entrepreneurial activity, innovation and growth are affected greatly by the ambition and style of the strategic leader, their values and the culture that they create, but arguably these should be spread throughout the organization. Intrapreneurship or intra-corporate entrepreneurship (Pinchot and Pinchot, 1978; Pinchot, 1985) is the establishment and fostering of entrepreneurial activity within large organizations. Many new ideas for innovation, for product or service developments, can come from managers within organizations if the structure and climate encourage and allow them to contribute – such as through special task forces, development groups or allowing individual managers the opportunity, freedom and, if necessary, the capital to try new ideas. Success requires that change is perceived more as an opportunity than a threat, that the company is aware of market opportunities and is customer orientated, and that the financial implications are thought through.

Although effective leaders possess a number of characteristics, set direction and inspire others, their strong leadership should not stifle flexibility and learning by a resistance to trusting other managers and involving them in key decisions or by trying to do everything themselves. Instead, they should build a team to whom they can delegate important decisions and contributions. While some of these people will, by necessity, be specialists, professionals and technocrats, Horovitz (1997) stresses the importance of also recruiting or developing entrepreneurial managers to ensure the flow of innovation and change and prevent entropy, arguing that one of the reasons for Club Méditerranée losing momentum in the 1990s was the result of a failure to accomplish this back-filling effectively (see the online case on Club Med). Quinn (1980) also emphasizes the importance of innovation and ongoing learning by this team because not all of the issues and difficulties that will have to be faced can be foreseen.

The aim in a global business is to get the best ideas from everywhere. [In General Electric] each team puts up its best ideas and processes – constantly. That raises the bar. Our culture is designed around making a hero out of those who translate ideas from one place to another, who get help from somebody else. They get an award, they get praised and promoted.

JACK WELCH, ex-CHIEF EXECUTIVE, GENERAL ELECTRIC

Horovitz (1997) contends that organizations should look for the problems before they even arise, by questioning what the (possibly very successful) organization is doing wrong. At times, products, services and strategies which have served the organization well in the past, as they are not the future, should be abandoned. De Geus (1997) contends that businesses need to become 'living organizations' if they are to enjoy long and sustained success requiring that the company:

- knows 'what it is about'
- understands where 'it fits in the world'
- values new ideas, new people and fresh views and opinions
- manages its resources (especially financial resources) in a way which places it in a position to govern its own future; in other words, it is prudent and does not spend beyond a level it can earn.

These requirements are manifest in:

- clear direction and purpose (awareness of its identity)
- strategic positioning (its sensitivity to its environment)
- the management of change (its tolerance of new ideas) and
- the efficient use of its capital investment.

People, then, must be seen as key assets and managed accordingly; controls must have some element of looseness and flexibility; and constant learning must be possible.

Kanter (1989) clearly supports this view when she argues that the whole organization holds the key to competitive advantage and that five criteria are found in successful intrepreneurial organizations:

- *focused* on essential core competencies and long-term values
- *flexible* – searching for new opportunities and new internal and external synergies with the belief that ever-increasing returns and results can be obtained from the same resources if they are developed properly and innovative
- *friendly* – recognizing the power of alliances in the search for new competencies
- *fast* and able to act at the right time to get ahead and stay ahead of competitors
- *fun* – creative and with a culture which features some irreverence in the search for ways to be different; people feel free to express themselves.

In her earlier work, Kanter (1983) warned about how innovation can be stifled by:

- blocking ideas from lower down the organization, on the grounds that only senior or very experienced managers are in a position to spot new opportunities. On the contrary, she argues, younger people with fresh minds are in an excellent position to question and challenge the status quo
- building too many levels in the hierarchy so that decision-making is slowed almost to a point of non-existence
- withholding praise from people who do offer good, innovative ideas, and instilling a culture of insecurity so that people feel too terrified even to question authority, policies or procedures
- being unwilling to innovate until someone else has tried out the idea – a fear of leading change.

Critical Reflection 10.2   Innovation and Marketing

In 'The Purple Cow', Seth Godin argues that the traditional model of marketing/advertising where high spending drives long-life brands can still work for some but it is not the way forward for most companies and certainly not small businesses.

The traditional model of innovators (Rogers, 1995), namely early adopters, early and late majority and laggards is again still relevant but for many organizations the emphasis should be on reaching the innovators and early adopters rather than thinking of big spends on the majority. After all, many people are now becoming very adept at ignoring brand advertising.

The implication is that we try to find people who are 'sneezers' and spread the word. One seeks to seed an 'idea virus' and ride the bandwagon of social media and viral marketing. The secret to success lies in the product itself and not the power of advertising.

The ideal is a remarkable product, remarkable because it is innovative. But, of course, we also need a good route to market – we have to be able to access customers.

This should be the approach from the beginning – a search for 'something worth talking about'.

How might we achieve this? By clearly targeting improvement and looking to break the existing rules of competition. Witness the success of Classic FM and also composers who now see film scores as the new classical music; Ryanair; Starbucks; the Calendar Girls calendar.

In looking around, we can look at existing products and dissect them by the marketing P's. Product, price, promotion, positioning, packaging. All of these can offer opportunities to improve.

In all the above cases, those involved stuck to products people already wanted and consumed. They *simply* provided a new business model that worked.

In this context, it is always worth remembering that rule breakers usually get criticized. That said, playing safe will remain a risky strategy. The world changes.

The marketing spend that accompanies these new ideas doesn't necessarily have to be huge as long as it gets talked about. Again think about the cheap-and-cheerful Ryanair adverts emphasizing low-low prices.

Ryanair also confirms that a modest beginning can still result in a very large and successful business with wide appeal – if the product is distinctive in a meaningful way.

The advertising should target the customer who is likely to be interested from the outset. But as time goes on, it is important to stay vigilant and remember there is a difference between someone who, say, uses online banking every day and someone who uses it once a month. They might all be online bankers, but they are very different in their usage.

Critically, you can never predict success. This is the world of the unpredictable.

In the end, a passion for the product is always going to help. You live and breathe it. And the initial ideas can be found with consumers who are passionate about the product and can see better ways of doing something.

Later on in the life of a product there is nothing wrong with 'milking a cash cow'. There never has been. The issue comes when this becomes the values and paradigm of the business.

Reference

Rogers, E.M. (1995) *Diffusion of Innovation*, 4th edition, Free Press.

Source

This Critical Reflection is summarized from: Godin, S. (2002) *Purple Cow*, Penguin.

Critical Reflection 10.2 provides another perspective on innovation. Case 10.5 illustrates how Richer Sounds has benefited substantially from involving employees widely in new strategy creation.

While robust questioning and assumption-testing of new ideas is crucial, many people fear change, partly because of uncertainty about its impact on them personally and thus will seek to resist valuable change initiatives, and may even attempt to mount an active and orchestrated opposition. Managing change effectively, therefore, requires continuous effort and sometimes patience, reinforcing the significant contribution made by the project champion.

The process of intrapreneurship

Bridge *et al.* (2009) highlight the importance of recruiting, spotting and using people with entrepreneurial talent who are motivated to use their abilities and initiative and do something on their own, but who may not

Case 10.5 Richer Sounds   UK

Electrical goods retailers are not new. The dominant name in the UK is Curry's, but Richer Sounds is different, and very successful. Richer is more focused than its main rival, specializing in hi-fi, especially separate units. According to the *Guinness Book of Records*, Richer achieved the highest sales per square foot of any retailer in the world. Sales per employee are also high. Stock is piled high to the ceilings in relatively small stores in typically low-rent locations. All the main brands can be found; the latest models feature alongside discontinued ones, these at very competitive prices. 'We just aren't that ambitious [to justify diversifying] ... we feel that by staying with what we know best we can concentrate our effort and resources in one field and hopefully do it well.'

Julian Richer was born in 1959; his parents both worked for Marks and Spencer. He was just 19 when he opened his first shop at London Bridge: 'seventy thousand commuters passed the shop every day'. He now owns some 50 stores in the UK and Eire and two more in the Netherlands. Apart from Christmas, Richer will not open on Sundays. His employees are known as colleagues and they are empowered to work 'The Richer Way'. He claims that his suggestion scheme has generated the highest number of suggestions per employee of any scheme anywhere in the world, and the best ideas are rewarded with trips on the Orient Express. The most successful employees (in terms of sales) can win free use of a holiday home; the most successful shops earn the free use of a Bentley or Jaguar for a month. Every employee is allowed £5 per month 'to go to the pub and brainstorm'. Julian Richer has advised ASDA on suggestion schemes, and ex-ASDA Chairman, Archie Norman, has said: 'Julian has gone to great lengths to create a system that works without him, but, to a great extent, his business is his personality.'

Richer has established a parallel consulting arm, with eight consultants who offer 'The Richer Way as a philosophy for delighting customers'. Consultancy is provided free to charities and good causes. Richer has also established a foundation to help selected good causes, and he owns a number of other small businesses. These include a retail recruitment agency, a property portfolio and an award-winning tapas bar in Fulham. He has, however, 'one business and a number of hobbies'. He has, he says, stayed focused because of the perpetual threat from Internet sales.

Questions

1 Is 'The Richer Way' a key to sustained competitive advantage?
2 Why do you think it has been successful?

RICHER SOUNDS **http://www.richer-sounds.co.uk**

want to start their own business. Intrapreneurship results in incremental improvements to existing products and services and occasionally to brand-new products, and Strategy in Action 10.1 is an idealized version of this situation, an example of one large company's approach.

Figure 10.8 shows that both entrepreneurship (creating outcomes which imply a real difference) and intrapreneurship (less ambitious changes which are more likely to be based around improvements than major changes of direction) are broadly similar. They both begin when someone has a personal vision from which an idea and a related opportunity emerge, which must then be engaged and resources acquired as prerequisites to action and implementation. Intrapreneurship happens as individual managers promote and sell their ideas inside the organization and build a team of supporters, driving change (e.g. 3M and Post-it Notes). And yet, innovation is more likely to be a minor but significant improvement to a product, service or process.

Intrapreneurs, typically, are strategically aware, ideas-driven, creative, flexible, innovative, good networkers, individualistic but also able to work well in a team, persistent and courageous. If frustrated by a lack of freedom, they will underachieve or possibly leave. But they are volunteers; intrapreneurship is not right for everyone.

According to Pinchot (1985), the key lies in engaging people's efforts and energy for championing, capturing and exploiting new ideas and strategic changes, which must stretch beyond the most senior managers in the organization, who do not have a monopoly on good ideas. On the contrary, the potentially most valuable and lucrative ideas are likely to come from those people who are closest to the latest

Strategy in Action 10.1   Jack's Dream

I'm Jack Dupont. I work for Sunlite PLC, one of the world's largest fruit juice manufacturers. I am an assistant manager in the staff canteen. I was having a shower after a hard game of squash when it suddenly hit me. If you can put shampoo in a sachet, why not fruit juice? When the sun is beating down, as it nearly always does in most countries of the world, what better than a quick squirt of juice to lubricate the tonsils? No cumbersome bottles or glasses, it can be carried in a shirt's top pocket or in a handbag.

I became excited. We could put, say, 100 millilitres of juice in each sachet. Ten to a litre. Each sachet could be sold for 20p – £2 per litre of juice compared to 50p for a full litre pack. I rushed to see Jim McIlroy, my boss. Mary Dignum, his secretary, gave me her usual friendly smile. 'Want to see Jim? He is very busy but I will see what I can do.' She came back with a twinkle in her eye. 'He can fit you in between appointments at eleven.'

I explained my idea. 'Hum' beamed Jim. 'Let's get it off the ground at once. We need a proper business plan of course, to convince the board we have done things properly. Ring James Petrie at Price Water-house (Mary has the number) and ask him to do a market assessment for us. Harry in Packaging will know who to contact for the machinery to sachet the juice. You'll need money. We were about to launch a campaign to expand our market in Singapore, but I am sure they would not miss a few grand to help start your new venture. While you develop this idea, I will instruct Catering to buy in a substitute for you for 1 year. There are some spare rooms in 'D' division where you can pilot some juice sachets.
If the piloting is successful, come back to help me arrange further finance. That's all for now, except to say, well done. There will be a rise for you in this.'

I felt inspired as I launched into the project with all the energy I could muster. There were, of course, many problems to overcome, but I had so many experts to help me. I had the full support of Jim and the board, with all the resources of Sunlite behind them. The first sachet rolled off the production line within a year, and is now being sold worldwide under the brand name 'KOOOL'. I never did go back to the catering department. I am currently working on a new project putting gin into small plastic sachets.

Interim question: Have you ever had an idea and a dream like Jack's? If so, how did you feel? What were you minded to do about it? Read the following story of Shell's Game Changer project and consider the parallels.

Royal Dutch Shell, with revenues of around £85 billion and over 100 000 employees worldwide, is an industrial giant in an established industry: petroleum. Historically, access to capital has been carefully controlled and radical ideas from internal entrepreneurs have been rare. Managers switch between divisions and countries for experience and promotion, but they are generally disciplined and loyal to corporate policies and procedures. In 1996, Tim Warren, Director of Research and Technical Services in Exploration and Production (Shell's largest division), was determined to change this, and to free up ideas, talent and resources. He was concerned that competition was intense in the dynamic and turbulent oil industry and Shell was 'not inventing radically new businesses'. Moreover, he firmly believed that Shell possessed the talent to drive a different behaviour.

In November 1996 he secured the resources to launch *Game Changer* and £12.5 million was set aside to fund radically new ideas submitted by employees. A group of key people would evaluate the ideas put forward by their peers. Consultants were brought in to run a series of creativity laboratories for volunteers; 72 turned up to the first one.

The focus was on:

- identifying and challenging industry conventions
- identifying emerging discontinuities
- leveraging and exploiting existing competencies to create new competitive opportunities.

The ideas began to flow from the laboratories and their interactive sessions. Some of the money set aside was used to ensure that the ideas which passed the first selection and screening were put into action. The creativity laboratory was supplemented by further work on project management.

As the programme developed, Shell's intranet was used increasingly to move ideas around the organization. Initial funding averaged some £60 000 per project selected, but it has been as high as £350 000. Employees were encouraged to stay involved. Once the concept was proven, further funding could be arranged. A number of important new Shell initiatives have emerged from *Game Changer*.

Follow-on questions

Why do you think many large organizations ignore the potential of initiatives such as this?

What are the dangers in their approach?

Developed from:
Hamel, G. (1999) Bringing Silicon Valley inside, *Harvard Business Review*, September–October.

developments in technology or to customers, perhaps through suggestion schemes. The ideas need to be taken forward, and they can only be developed if the potential intrapreneurs are able to obtain the necessary internal resources and, moreover, they are willing to do something which, in turn, requires encouragement and appropriate rewards for success. People must feel involved in the process and comfortable that they are being supported. Morris and Kuratko (2002) added that intrapreneurs should manage expectations and never over-promise.

Intrapreneurship cannot work where people feel frozen out or metaphorically 'dumped on'. Churchill (1997) summarizes the philosophy as skills following opportunities, with people in entrepreneurial businesses seeing the opportunities and setting about acquiring the necessary resources. The whole process of change then becomes gradual and evolutionary, while the momentum for change and improvement is never lost and the organization is less likely to be exposed and weakened by its competitors, resulting in it having to cross a 'bridge too far'. Maitland (1999) described how Bass developed new pub brands replacing its traditional customers (older working-class people) with young people through the involvement of an intrapreneur.

To summarize these points, Hurst (1995) likens entrepreneurial strategic leaders to gardeners, as they prune, clear out and plant (by recruiting other entrepreneurial managers), they feed (by encouraging and rewarding managers for being creative and innovative) and nurture and manage the organization as they would a garden. Paradoxically, many good ideas begin in the same way that weeds emerge in a garden, i.e. randomly, and they need spotting and looking after, and transferred to a hothouse.

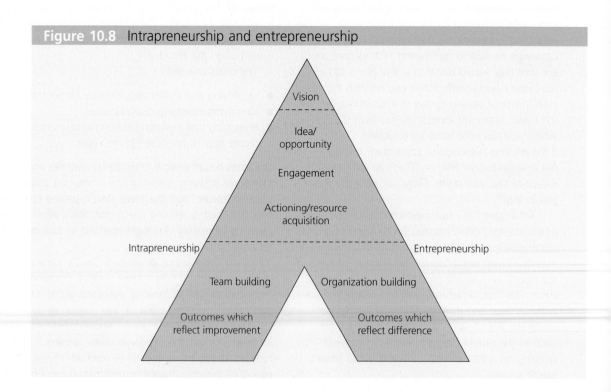

Figure 10.8 Intrapreneurship and entrepreneurship

The intrapreneurial organization

Fradette and Michaud (1998) describe four main elements in an organization which succeeds with intrapreneurship. First, the strategic and structural environment is 'right' in the sense that it has a realistic, widely understood and shared vision, and that formal systems and controls do not stifle innovation and people are free to make limited changes. Second, an appropriate workforce has been built including enterprising people trained in key skills with an appropriate reward system, with the organization's main heroes being the entrepreneurial ones. Third, the workforce is backed by the necessary support systems with a natural triumvirate of teamworking, collaboration and networking, and information shared and learning fostered. Fourth, successes are visibly rewarded and mistakes are not punished so harshly that people are dissuaded from further initiatives.

An intrapreneurial organization will often feature a relatively flat structure with few layers in the hierarchy to speed up decision-making, and a culture and atmosphere of collaboration and trust. The style of management will be more coaching than instructional, and mentoring will be evident, and ideally it will be an exciting place to work since the entrepreneur's enthusiasm will have spread to others.

Terazano (1999) also observes that effective intrapreneurship is not that easily achieved, and that many organizations fail to reap the anticipated rewards. Balancing control (to ensure that current activities and strategies are implemented efficiently) with flexibility (to foster and embrace changes to the same strategies) can imply different cultures, which are difficult to achieve without tension and conflict. Another difficulty lies with finding the appropriate reward and remuneration systems to ensure fairness. Managers in established companies often find it difficult to handle setbacks and disappointments when initiatives fail. But there always has to be the risk of failure, albeit temporary, when experimenting with new and unproven ideas. While intrapreneurs often have the security of large company employment, such that the penalty for failure is to some extent reduced, the rewards for real success are unlikely to equal those of the true entrepreneur. Nevertheless, 'increased competition in global markets and the pressure for innovation is forcing Britain's large companies to look for methods to stimulate ideas for new products' (Terazano, 1999).

10.3 Visionary leadership

Visionary leadership is often associated with organizations and leaders that might be described as entrepreneurial but this is not always the case, nor is it necessary that an effective strategic leader has to be personally visionary. Mintzberg *et al.* (1998) contend that visionary strategic leaders perceive strategy as a mental representation of the successful position or competitive paradigm, which is either thought through quite carefully or largely intuitive, and then serves as an inspirational driving force for the organization. The vision or idea alone is inadequate since the leader must ensure that it is seen, shared and supported by customers, partners, employees and suppliers – and that it is flexible with detail emerging through experience and learning.

Mintzberg *et al.*'s (1998) visionary entrepreneurs often, but not always, conceptualize the winning strategic position as a result of immersion in the industry, either simply though a genuine interest or because they may have worked in the industry for some time. Their secret is an ability to learn and understand, making sense of experiences and visible signals of which others cannot make sense.

Given the two opposing views of entrepreneurs – Schumpeter's (1934) *market equilibrium* (stability) *disturbing innovators* and the Kirznerian *equilibrium creating* opportunity-spotters, Blanchard and Waghorn (1997) claim that Ted Turner (with CNN 24 hour network news) and Steve Jobs, like entrepreneurs in the mobile phones business, have been instrumental in changing the world we know.

Successful visionary, aspirational leaders and entrepreneurs are clearly not all from the same mould and it has been argued that there is a well of talent and as individuals we possess the potential most suitable for us to become either a leader, an entrepreneur, an intrapreneurial manager, an inventor, a follower or whatever (Bolton and Thompson, 2013). They argue that individuals remain in the well until released, or

Figure 10.9 Four dimensions of entrepreneurship

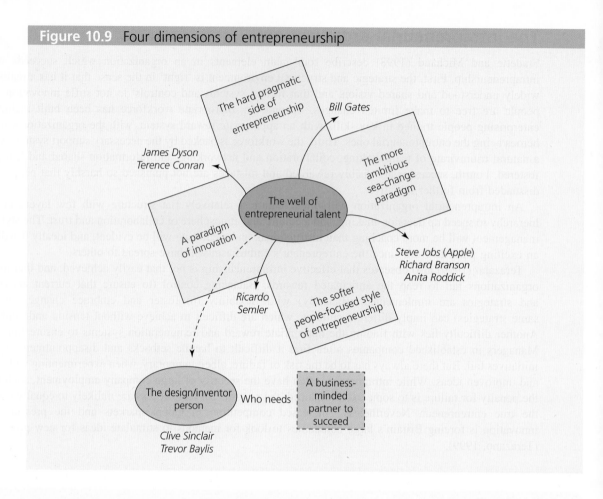

propel themselves out with sheer determination, or are spotted, nurtured and encouraged. When people with entrepreneurial talent emerge from the so-called well, they follow different paths. Figure 10.9 represents hard entrepreneurship as the paradigm of the independent, pragmatic, opportunistic and competitive entrepreneur, who are achievement-orientated people and typical managed risk-takers and natural networkers in search of a deal. Not every entrepreneur fits this pattern, since some present a softer image and operate in a more informal manner, being strong on communication and sell their vision to engage and motivate others. The hard and soft approaches lead to quite different cultures.

Some visionary, adventurous entrepreneurs set out to change the world as they are people with a real ability to galvanize others, and they work hard, play hard and operate at the leading edge, having a need to have enormous energy and generally they would be described as 'having a presence'. Again, this approach is not, and need not, be ubiquitous. The fourth arm, innovation, still requires imagination, creativity, passion and a commitment to bring about change (see Lessem, 1986, 1998).

> *Entrepreneurs are risk-takers, willing to roll the dice with their money or reputation on the line in support of an idea or enterprise. They willingly assume responsibility for the success or failure of a venture and are answerable for all its facets.*

VICTOR KIAM (REMINGTON RAZOR)

Bill Gates (Case 10.6) is perhaps a typical hard adventurer given that Microsoft has literally changed the world of computing, while James Dyson (Chapter 5 Case) is a hard innovator, and Ricardo Semler (also a Chapter 5 Case) is a visionary as far as management style is concerned, but Semco's engineering products, including pumps and industrial dishwashers, are hardly revolutionary so he appears to typify the soft innovator.

Case 10.6 Bill Gates US

Bill Gates had a vision for transforming the lives of ordinary people, 'foreseeing a single operating system for every personal computer around the world' to complement Steve Jobs' (Apple) vision of 'a personal computer on every desk in every home and office around the world'. Dedicated pursuit of this focused vision through Microsoft has made him the world's richest person. At the beginning of 2000 Microsoft was valued at $600 billion; Gates' personal wealth exceeded $85 billion. Gates was born to wealthy parents; he was energetic and inspired to work 'ridiculously long hours', and he has inspired criticism and, inevitably, jealousy.

There are several reasons behind Gates' phenomenal success. Among them are his ability to absorb information quickly and his technical expertise – he can actually write computer code. He understands consumers and is uncannily aware of market needs. He has an eye for the main chance coupled with an ability and will to make things happen. Moreover, he is an aggressive defender of his corner, which in the end may have worked against him with the American anti-trust authorities.

Born in 1955 in Seattle, Gates quickly became interested in science fiction and unusually went to a school which had a computer that students could use. A 'nerd' from an early age, it has been said Gates 'preferred playing with computers to playing with other children'. He nevertheless teamed up with his friend, Paul Allen, and together they 'begged, borrowed and bootlegged' time on the school computer, undertaking small software commissions. Gates and Allen went to Harvard together, where Gates proved to be an unpopular student because of his high self-opinion. Surreptitiously using Harvard's computer laboratories they began a small business on the campus. Gates later left Harvard to start Microsoft, never completing this formal part of his education. Allen was his formal partner in the venture, but Gates always held a majority control. Bill Gates' visionary contribution was the realization that operating systems and software (rather than the computer hardware) held the key to growth and industry domination.

Gates took risks in the early days but, assisted by some good luck, his gambles largely paid off. When the first commercial microcomputer (the Altair) needed a customized version of the BASIC programming language, Gates accepted the challenge. His package was later licensed to Apple, Commodore and IBM, the companies which developed the personal computer market. When IBM decided to attack seriously the personal computer market Gates was commissioned to develop the operating system. Innovatively improving an existing off-the-shelf package and renaming it MS-DOS (Microsoft Disk Operating System) Gates was now on his way. Since then Windows has become the ubiquitous first-choice operating system for most PC manufacturers.

By and large, his success has depended on his ability to create standard products, the benchmark against which others are judged.

Gates hired the 'best and brightest' people and he made many of them millionaires. He preferred a college-style working environment with a culture dedicated to learning, sharing and overcoming hurdles. Gates personally thrives on combat and confrontation. His colleagues have to be able to stand up to him, but it does generate creative energy. However, he is also seen as enormously charismatic, and employees desperately 'wanted to please him'. In his younger days he was branded a risk-taker; stories are told of his love of fast cars and his tendency to leave late for meetings in order to provide him with an excuse for driving quickly. After a 2-year investigation by the American anti-trust authorities it was ruled (in 2000) that Microsoft should be split into two businesses – one for operating systems and one for applications, including the Internet – and should also be required to give away some of its coding. Gates and Microsoft had been found guilty of exercising monopoly power to the detriment of their competitors. Gates was incensed and appealed against the verdict, which was largely overturned in a higher court. In 2004 the European Competition Commission also ruled against Microsoft, arguing that it had created an effective monopoly by bundling its own Media Player with Windows. Microsoft said that again it would appeal the verdict.

Since the US ruling Gates has announced two key things. First, in the future Microsoft would focus its resources and energies on developing software that would be delivered as services via the Internet rather than loaded into individual PCs. Second, he was standing down as chief executive. He would continue as chairman and adopt a new role as the company's top software architect. He was returning to his roots.

I'm returning to what I love most – focusing on technology. These are dramatic times in our industry. We recognize that we must refocus and reallocate our resources and talents.

In July 2008, Gates left Microsoft in terms of day-to-day involvement but remained Chairman. Between 2006 and 2008 what is described as a top management transition took place at Microsoft. The new role for Gates allows him to spend more time on his health and education work through the Bill and Melinda Gates Foundation.

The CEO is Steve Ballmer, who had joined Gates during the Harvard days, where he was a fellow student. Having been a successful vice president for sales, support and marketing he had later been appointed president. Ballmer is recognized as an aggressive hardliner who will have the tricky job of trying to keep the growth of Microsoft going.

Questions

1 What are the strategic issues that confront Microsoft today?
2 What exactly did the European Competition authorities decide and what has developed since the announcement in March 2004?

In considering these questions you might review the commentary on Microsoft in the Spheres of Influence section in the previous chapter.

MICROSOFT **http://www.microsoft.com**

There is, however, one final category: the designer–inventor who lacks the necessary business acumen or interest to build the business on their own, but who can, with help, be part of a successful and entrepreneurial business. Sir Clive Sinclair, a designer–inventor who came up with a number of truly innovative ideas and products, never found the right partner to build a winning business. Trevor Baylis also fits here, as he found the right partner and his BayGen radio has been a successful business.

Visionary leadership and strategy creation

Visionary leadership thus implies a strategic leader with a personal vision for the future of the organization and at least a broad idea of the strategies for pursuing the vision. Such leadership often appears to be based on intuition and possibly experience rather than detailed analysis, but truly visionary leaders possess strategic awareness and insight, and do not require extensive analyses to understand key success factors and how the organization can use its abilities and competencies to satisfy needs and expectations. There is a 'feel' for which strategies will be appropriate and feasible and for the potential of the opportunity.

When a visionary leader pursues new opportunities and introduces changes, the detailed plans for implementing the new strategies are unlikely to be in place but they will rely on incremental learning, flexibility and adaptation. For the approach to succeed, the leader must be able to inspire others and persuade them of the logic and merits of the new strategies and, although true for all important strategic changes, when new proposals have emerged from a more formal strategic planning system, there will be substantive detail and analysis to justify the case instead of a strong reliance on vision and intuition.

Where major changes to the corporate strategy are being considered, it may be necessary for the strategic leader to convince other members of the Board of Directors and, if new funding is needed, the institutional shareholders and bankers.

The strategy cannot be successful until it has been implemented and has brought the desired results and rewards. Such outcomes require the support and commitment of other managers and, consequently, effective visionaries are often articulate, communicative and persuasive leaders.

Therefore, visionary strategic leadership implies three steps:

1   the vision

2   selling it to other stakeholders and managers

3   making sure it happens – aspects of vision, communication and pragmatism.

Richardson (1994) suggests that visionary leaders typically adopt 'covert', cerebral planning rather than formal planning, are passionate, develop a specific culture, convince others about their strategy and are charismatic and powerful.

A visionary leader is not a synonym for an entrepreneur such that we view a visionary leader, typically, as someone who is a persuasive and charismatic agent of change, either starting a new, differentiated business which takes off, or changing the direction and corporate strategy of a business in order to maintain or improve its rate of growth – implying major, discontinuous change, and growth fuelled by astute acquisition. Entrepreneurial growth is not necessarily visionary, nor must entrepreneurs be charismatic figures, whereas visionary strategic leadership involves a visionary impact on strategy creation.

Yet a strategic leader who succeeds in turning around a company in crisis and *restores growth* – a process sometimes called corporate entrepreneurship – can be a visionary. But visionary leadership is not necessary for either new ventures or successful turnaround situations. When a company is in trouble, a good, analytical 'company doctor' who can restructure, rationalize and refocus the business can be very effective – for example, the management buy-in to Clyde Blowers plc orchestrated by Jim McColl OBE, provided as Case 10.7.

Case 10.7   Jim McColl   UK

Jim McColl had spent 17 years (1968–1985) working as an engineer in various UK companies. He followed this with a period of 3 years as a senior consultant with Coopers and Lybrand working mainly in corporate care work. From 1987–1992 he worked as an independent company doctor. In his own words, 'all the time looking for an opportunity to buy into an engineering business'. In 1992 he was offered that opportunity when he bought a 29 per cent stake in Clyde Blowers a public listed engineering company whose principal business activity was sootblowing from coal-fired boilers. Established in 1924 as a family firm, Clyde Blowers was still controlled and run by the original family in 1992. Instead of being an engineering business, Clyde Blowers had become a property company which also earned some revenues from sootblowing. McColl set about 'realizing the value in the engineering business' by selling off the property interests and investing the cash in the engineering business which had been starved of investment. Additionally, he set about building up the business through a series of acquisitions. During the period 1992–1997, seven companies were acquired worldwide which took the market share enjoyed by Clyde Blowers to over 25 per cent of the world market for sootblowing. In 1992,

the turnover of Clyde Blowers was £3.3m and 100 per cent within the UK. By the year 2000, the geographical spread of sales was: 56 per cent USA, 34 per cent Europe, 7 per cent UK and 3 per cent China on a total turnover of £70m. McColl describes his strategy for Clyde Blowers as a classic example of textbook consolidation involving: rationalizing of activities; simplified product lines; 43 per cent reduction in manpower; elimination of the competition; and internationalizing the business.

Described thus it all looks very simple. However, it was McColl who spotted the opportunity and had the vision and drive to see the strategy through to completion including delisting Clyde Blowers from the London Stock Exchange and taking the company private when the share price of the business was marked down by analysts.

Question

1   What has happened to Jim McColl and Clyde Blowers in recent years?

http://www.clydeblowers.co.uk/

Maccoby (2000) notes that strategic leaders, especially those described as visionary, are typically more visible today due to being self-publicists and the media being more interested in business stories, especially about new industries. Consequently, Maccoby (2000) concludes that an increasing number of strategic leaders are narcissists, inspirational personalities who have a major impact upon culture and style, who enjoy the visibility and notoriety, and who often believe that they are 'something special'.

A lot of people want to be led – yet there are very few leaders in life. When people have a good leader who instils team spirit, and they work in an environment that demands excellence, energy and the keeping of momentum in order to achieve a goal, then they want to stay … or, if they leave, they want to come back!

LINDA J WACHNER, WHEN CEO, WARNACO (US)

To be effective, leadership has to be seen, and it is best seen in action. Leadership must be communicated in words, but even more importantly in deeds. Leaders must be seen to be up-front, up to their jobs and up early in the morning.

LORD SIEFF OF BRIMPTON, CHAIRMAN, MARKS AND SPENCER, 1972–1984

Big-picture visionaries are associated with risks, appear to be charming personalities, are typically entrepreneurial and competitive – and yet they can be unrealistic dreamers with delusions of grandeur, a poor listener, a relatively isolated loner, and uncomfortable with challenge or criticism.

10.4 Critical issues in strategic leadership: towards visionary leadership?

Chief executives of large UK businesses stay in post for an average of just 4 years, while their equivalents in the USA last, on average, a year longer. These short 'shelf lives' are because of the visibility mentioned above which leads to perceived poor performers being dismissed more readily than in the past. A price has to be paid for perceived failure and, although as it would appear with the collapse of banks, the price is not necessarily financial but more in terms of their reputation amongst the general public.

Charan and Colvin (1999) suggest that these people are normally bright and experienced executives who can articulate a vision and strategy for their organization, but their shortcomings lie in an inability to implement strategy which in an age of visibility, visions and broad strategies soon become public property. Rivals can attempt to copy them if they wish and hence, as was shown earlier, sustained competitive advantage lies not in ideas and strategic positions, but in the way strategies are executed. Charan and Colvin (1999) specify a number of typical strategic leader misjudgements:

- underestimating the importance of people – a topic we discussed in Chapter 5
- failing to put people in the right jobs – people's individual strengths and natural behaviours can be used to judge where they are most likely to make their best contribution (Buckingham and Coffman, 1999)
- failing to deal with underperforming managers, especially if they are people they have appointed and who remain loyal
- not stretching people to the highest levels of performance that they can reach
- failing to put in effective decision-making processes such that important decisions are either not made or not carried through, relating to empowerment, another topic discussed in Chapter 5
- misjudging the balance between strategy and operations, and between the external and internal focus of their efforts, linked to poor corporate governance, with the outcome that a good vision and broad strategy may neither be implemented effectively nor updated in changing circumstances.

All leaders, including the most successful, have finite shelf lives, periods of time when they can contribute effectively to an organization. Some know when to step down and either retire or move on, before they cease to be effective, but others stay too long and risk being remembered for their later shortcomings rather than their earlier successes. In recent times, the departure of Tony Blair as Labour Prime Minister may prove to have been an example of someone staying too long and thus tarnishing his reputation, while Case 10.8 (Volvo) looks at another longstanding strategic leader who eventually lost the confidence of his board.

Case 10.8   Volvo   Eur

Volvo was led from 1971 to 1993 by Pehr Gyllenhammar, a lawyer who was married to the daughter of the previous chief executive. Gyllenhammar has been credited as a visionary leader who failed to implement many critical strategic proposals.

In the early 1970s he concluded Volvo was reliant on a limited product range (essentially large cars, trucks and buses) and constrained by Sweden not being a member of the European Union. He acquired Daf from the Dutch government; a prolonged period of learning was required before Volvo's subsequent range of small cars proved successful. He began to build the first foreign-owned car assembly plant in the USA, but production never started. He opened the revolutionary Kalmar assembly plant in Sweden in 1974, based on autonomous work groups rather than the traditional assembly line; the idea was successful, but not outstandingly so, and Kalmar was closed in 1993. In 1977 a proposed merger with Saab-Scania was abandoned when Saab had second thoughts. In 1978 Gyllenhammar agreed to sell 40 per cent of Volvo to the Norwegian government in exchange for oil rights, but Volvo's shareholders revolted.

In the 1980s Volvo acquired the US White truck business and diversified into the food and drug industries in Sweden, but not without some friction with the Swedish government. Throughout this period Volvo's car subsidiary enjoyed continuing success, albeit with its relatively staid image and reputation.

In 1989 Volvo and Renault cemented a strategic alliance with the exchange of minority shareholdings, and in 1993 a full merger was proposed. Fearing the future role of the French government (Renault was nationalized but due for privatization), Volvo's shareholders again refused to back Gyllenhammar. After this defeat he resigned but has since been active in other business and civil engineering ventures. Despite all the setbacks, Volvo proved to be robust and, under Gyllenhammar, grew into one of Sweden's leading businesses.

The diversification strategies had been focused on less cyclical industries to offset the uneven cash flow characteristics of car manufacturing, but a new corporate strategy was announced in April 1994. Non-vehicle interests would be divested systematically. Vehicle joint ventures with a series of companies worldwide would be sought.

Gyllenhammar's immediate successor as chief executive, Sören Gyll, appeared to be adopting a different style. He was more of a team player. The new strategy for cars became the responsibility of a new divisional head. In 1995 Volvo changed the marketing strategy for its cars, attempting to shift away from an image built wholly on safety, reliability and (more recently) environmental friendliness, to one of 'safe but sexy'. Advertisements claimed that (when accelerating in top gear) a Volvo 850 could outpace a Ferrari. The aim was to attract younger 'pre-family' and older 'post-family' buyers without losing the core family customers, and increase output by one-third.

In 1999 Volvo's car division was sold to Ford, which was concerned that 'Volvo had failed to attract younger buyers' and this needed addressing urgently. There would be further changes of management. The sale was possibly inevitable – the group was no longer generating an adequate cash flow for sustainability.

In 2000 Volvo – which by now was largely trucks – bought Renault's truck businesses (which included the American Mack business) and became Europe's largest heavy truck maker. Some time earlier Volvo had been prevented by the European competition authorities from acquiring Swedish rival Scania. In recent years the business has suffered from declining demand in key American and European markets.

Perhaps ironically Volvo cars – under Ford ownership – has prospered and become a very profitable brand. Quality, design and profits have all improved. Some analysts insist this is the result of its managers being allowed to focus exclusively on cars.

As for Gyllenhammar, he withdrew from Swedish public life and did not take on any major business executive commitments thereafter.

Questions

1 Do you think that those who criticize Gyllenhammar for being an overambitious and individualistic strategic leader are being altogether fair?

2 What do you think his strengths and his failings might have been?

VOLVO **http://www.volvo.com**

Kets de Vries (1994) argues that chief executives who fail to make a timely exit go through a three-phase life cycle:

1 the entry of a new strategic leader into the organization, followed by experimentation with new strategies – downsizing, acquisitions, re-engineering and a drive for improved service and quality – and results improve, certainly in the short term

2 consolidation, when the changes are likely cemented in a new culture such that, if an organization was in crisis, the risks are now perceived to have fallen back, and herein can lie the seeds of a new crisis

3 decline and a new crisis.

Visionary leadership is frequently associated with entrepreneurial strategies for companies enjoying prosperity in growth markets. As the organization continues to grow, a more formal structure, together with robust control systems, will be required. The leader must, therefore, be flexible, capable of adapting and willing to relinquish some personal control and ideally other managers will be empowered and encouraged to be entrepreneurial and visionary – however, some visionary leaders tend to be inflexible and a change of leader would benefit the organization. Similarly, a leader who is skilled at managing detail and resources to generate productivity is required by companies in trouble, facing a strategic crisis or which need rationalizing.

Unless proper plans are made, succession be can be hampered by many visionary leaders, who may be driven by personal ambition and a personal vision and can be difficult to work with, hence failing to build a pipeline, which may raise several 'possible problem' scenarios. Owner-managed businesses may need to be sold but, once an entrepreneurial leader has left, what is the true value of the remaining assets? On a visionary's retirement, a complete outsider may be needed, implying major change; or the leader could have an accident (by falling under the proverbial bus) or illness, leaving a gap which cannot be filled in time to prevent a crisis.

The former leader of the successful diversified American conglomerate, General Electric (GE), Jack Welch, had an alleged conversation with a New York yellow cab driver, who claimed he sold his GE shares every August and bought them back in September: 'Jack goes on holiday in August and who knows what might happen when he's away.' When Welch gave GE advance notice that he would retire in April 2001, succession planning got underway and three internal divisional heads were identified as possible successors. They were all interviewed by GE's main board members, as were the key staff who reported to them, to assess their style and suitability. Furthermore, to ensure that one of them could be moved up without leaving a gap at the top of their division, a new chief operating officer was appointed in each case to provide for a second-stage orderly succession. 'Few large companies approach their succession planning with such care, but, of course, they do not always have as much notice!'

Welch's successor has proved to be effective – but in a different way – and the two disappointed executives both left to take up CEO roles at other companies, both in retailing, Albertson's and Home Depot, and both businesses were in trouble and have been turned around successfully by their new strategic leaders.

In contrast, an Online Case 10.1 looks at how succession issues have contributed to the declining fortunes at Boots.

Bower (2007) argues strategic leaders must engage three challenges: judging where the world is going, identifying managerial and leadership talent and engaging that talent. Planning for succession is integral to the talent challenge and should not be an occasional decision but an ongoing issue. Bower suggests that succession should come from within, as external appointments can be too disruptive, and he would argue in favour of the GE approach to succession of appointing business heads and making sure they are put to the test as strategic leaders.

When a new strategic leader is appointed, things may not be the same, strategically, culturally and stylistically. If real changes are required because the company has lost momentum or is in difficulty, then logically a new leader with a different style is being brought in to make changes. Where a company is successful, then 'change for the sake of change' may be a mistake but it is not unusual for a new leader to want to be seen to be his or her own person and to make an early mark. Returning to Figure 10.4, new leaders normally have a different preferred style.

Businesses 'fail' when they fail to meet the needs and expectations of their key stakeholders, or when decisions that they take lead to outcomes which are unacceptable to the stakeholders, which may generate crises with which the business is able to deal, usually at a cost, or they may also lead to its ultimate collapse. The outcomes can take a variety of different forms, but authors such as Slatter (1984) have clearly identified three main, direct causes of corporate failure and collapse:

- weak or inappropriate strategic leadership
- marketing and competitive failings
- poor financial management and control.

These failings imply *incongruency*, or lack of fit, between environment, values and resources, resulting from a lack of strategic awareness, with leadership issues also underpinning the marketing and financial weaknesses.

Richardson *et al.* (1994) have identified a number of discrete failure crisis situations, against which we can consider strategic leadership:

- A *niche becomes a tomb* when a small company, locked into a successful product or service, lives in the past and fails to change – an invariable sign of poor leadership, and perhaps succession problems.

- When *markets are not understood* small companies will fail to establish a position in their target market and not take off and grow, due perhaps to attention being concentrated on production, where the would-be entrepreneur may have expertise, but may not satisfy customer needs and expectations, or may achieve an insufficient volume of sales.

- *Strategic drift* with larger organizations is the result of introversion and inertia in a changing environment due to complacency from past success, or a concentration on day-to-day reactive or crisis management, leading to potential failure. The Online Case 10.1 Boots is an example of a previously successful large business's problems adapting to a changing environment.

- *Overambition* occurs in the guise of the failed entrepreneur (who enjoys early success and rapid growth due to a good product or service, but in desiring to maintain high growth diversifies into less profitable areas), or a conglomerate kingmaker (who wants to build a large and powerful corporation and is tempted to acquire businesses that cannot be justified financially, paying a price which either overvalues the assets or which cannot be recouped from earnings, or overestimate the potential for synergy with the existing businesses, e.g. the Royal Bank of Scotland).

Failures of this nature are frequently characterized by strong, powerful strategic leaders, inadequate attention to critical financial measures and controls, and inadequate governance by not looking after the stakeholder interests. In October 2008, the Baugur Investment Group was facing meltdown having built up a mountain of debt buying top retail assets in the UK, such as House of Fraser, Hamleys, Mappin & Webb and Oasis. With the credit crunch and the collapse of the Icelandic banks, Baugur owed at least £2bn to these banks. What seemed like an integrated strategy of buying related assets including department stores, fashion stores, speciality businesses and food retailers such as Iceland (the company not the country), all unraveled. Similarly, a number of so-called corporate scandals have been widely publicized and generated considerable cynicism and distrust about the world of business and especially about high-profile, celebrity leaders of Enron, Tyco, etc.

Sonnenfeld and Ward (2007) believe that the most effective strategic leaders are those who can deal with adversity, crises and setbacks to avoid failure. Failure is viewed differently in the USA such that many American entrepreneurs consider failure as an invitation to get up and do something else. Success, although an issue of temperament, also involves being able to learn from events and mistakes.

Research Snapshot 10.1

We do not consider the more recent literature on entrepreneurship, which is much too big to attempt even to scan the surface; however, see an entrepreneurship textbook (such as Bolton and Thompson, 2013; or Storey and Greene, 2010) for further insight. Relatively few articles have been written in recent years specifically on strategic leadership, though a large body of research has focused on leadership more generally, including at the strategy level, and there has been much interest in top management teams. We review briefly some recent research on strategic leadership, but also direct the reader's attention to the literature on leadership, which is vast and will provide some insights into strategic leadership, which clearly remains an area ripe for future research. Indeed, Storey (2005: p. 89) notes that: 'Despite the massive growth in activity directed towards leadership development, little of this has been directed at the top level; instead most activity has been focused on junior and middle levels of organizational leadership. Three key interrelated themes are identified: structural/relational issues; functional issues; and legitimacy issues.' Grandy and Mills (2004: p. 1153) define strategic management as 'the third order of simulacra … a model of simulation whereby reality has been replaced by hyperreality'.

Hitt and Ireland (2002) promote an 'effectuation' approach to strategic leadership, where competitive advantage is achieved by, 'building company resources and capabilities with an emphasis on intangible human capital and social capital'. Jansen et al. (2009) have found that – in linking innovation (i.e. exploration and exploitation), organizational learning and strategic leadership – 'transformational' leadership inculcates 'adopting generative thinking and pursuing exploratory innovation', whilst 'transactional' leadership 'facilitate improving and extending existing knowledge and are associated with exploitative innovation'. There are also cases where 'religion' has an influence upon how strategic leadership is conducted (Worden, 2005). Marion and Uhl-Bien (2010) note that strategic leadership tends to have a 'leader-centric (upper-echelon) approach to strategy' but, in order to ensure competitive advantage, openness and social capital connections need to be exploited, e.g. co-operation, alliances and partnerships.

Intrapreneurship as a 'niche' of the larger discipline of entrepreneurship has received increasing, though limited, interest in the academic literature, and we use the terms *intrapreneurship* synonymously and interchangeably with (intra)*corporate entrepreneurship*. Following research on external and internal factors, as shaped by managers, that influence intrapreneurship in South African firms can be measured (Goosen et al., 2002), it was observed that the importance of employees has been overly downplayed in research into CE, which overstate the middle manager's role (Heinonen and Toivonen, 2008).

Evidence from at least one study indicates that there is a direct link between employee satisfaction, on the one hand, and intrapreneurship and thus the organization's performance (proxied by its growth), on the others (Antoncic and Antoncic, 2011). Furthermore, Antoncic and Hisrich (2003) highlighted that our understanding or definition of intrapreneurship is clarified by: 'emergent behavioural intentions and behaviours that are related to departures from the customary ways of doing business in existing organizations.'

Indeed, Parker (2011: p. 19), in considering entrepreneur–intrapreneur differentials and the role of social and human capital, found that, 'Nascent entrepreneurs tend to leverage their general human capital and social ties to organize ventures which sell directly to customers, whereas intrapreneurs disproportionately commercialize unique new opportunities which sell to other businesses. Implications of the findings are discussed.' Bosma et al. (2011) also compare intrapreneurship and entrepreneurship, finding (i) double the incidence of intrapreneurship in countries with higher than lower income and (ii) while education impacts upon the likelihood to start an intra- or entreprise, 'intrapreneurs are much more likely to have the intention to start a new independent business than other employees'. Indeed, in terms of intrapreneurial strategy, Ireland et al.'s (2009) model theorizes its 'antecedents', 'elements' (including 'vision, organizational architectures' and the generic forms of entrepreneurial process that are reflected in 'entrepreneurial behaviour') and 'outcomes', such as competitiveness and 'strategic repositioning'.

Further Reading

Antoncic, B. and Hisrich, R.D. (2003) 'Clarifying the intrapreneurship concept', *Journal of Small Business and Enterprise Development*, Vol. 10, No. 1, pp. 7–24.

Antoncic, J.A. and Antoncic, B. (2011) 'Employee satisfaction, intrapreneurship and firm growth: a model', *Industrial Management & Data Systems*, Vol. 111, No. 4, pp. 589–607.

Bolton, W.K. and Thompson, J.L. (2013) 'Entrepreneurs: Talent, Temperament, Opportunity, 3rd edn., Routledge.

Bosma, N.S., Stam, E. and Wennekers, S. (2011) 'Intrapreneurship versus independent entrepreneurship: A cross-national analysis of individual entrepreneurial behavior', Discussion Paper Series, Tjalling C. Koopmans Research Institute, Vol. 11, No. 4, pp. 1–32.

Goosen, C.J., De Coning, T.J. and Smit, E. V d M. (2002) 'The development of a factor based instrument to measure corporate entrepreneurship : a South African perspective', *South African Journal of Business Management*, Vol. 33, No. 3, pp. 39–51.

Grandy, G. and Mills, A. J. (2004) 'Strategy as simulacra? A radical reflexive look at the discipline and practice of strategy', *Journal of Management Studies*, Vol. 41, pp. 1153–1170.

Heinonen, J. and Toivonen, J. (2008) 'Corporate entrepreneurs or silent followers?', *Leadership & Organization Development Journal*, Vol. 29, No. 7, pp. 583–5911.

Hitt, M.A. and Ireland, R.D. (2002) 'The essence of strategic leadership: Managing human and social capital', *Journal of Leadership & Organizational Studies*, Vol. 9, No. 1, pp. 3–14.

Ireland, R. D., Covin, J. G. and Kuratko, D. F. (2009) 'Conceptualizing corporate entrepreneurship strategy', *Entrepreneurship Theory and Practice*, Vol. 33, pp. 19–46.

Jansen, J.P., Vera, D. and Crossan, M. (2009) 'Strategic leadership for exploration and exploitation: The moderating role of environmental dynamism', *The Leadership Quarterly*, Vol. 20, No. 1, pp. 5–18.

Marion, R. and Uhl-Bien, M. (2010) 'Complexity and strategic leadership', in R. Hooijberg, J.G. Hunt, J. Antonakis, K.B. Boal and Nancy Lane (Eds) *Being There Even When You Are Not*, Monographs in Leadership and Management, Vol. 4, Emerald Group Publishing Limited, pp. 273–287.

Parker, S.C. (2011) 'Intrapreneurship or entrepreneurship?', *Journal of Business Venturing*, Vol. 26, No. 1, pp. 19–34.

Storey, D.J. and Greene, F.J. (2010) *Small Business and Entrepreneurship*, Harlow: Pearson.

Storey, J. (2005) 'What next for strategic-level leadership research?', *Leadership*, Vol. 1, No. 1, pp. 89–104.

Worden, S. (2005) 'Religion in strategic leadership: a positivistic, normative/theological, and strategic analysis', *Journal of Business Ethics*, Vol. 57, No. 3, pp. 221–2311.

Summary

The *strategic leader* of an organization affects both strategy creation and strategy implementation and is responsible for establishing the basic direction of the organization, the communications system and the structure – which influence the nature and style of decision-making within the firm. In addition, decision-making and change is affected by the personal ambitions of the strategic leader, his or her personal qualities such as entrepreneurialism and willingness to take risks, the style of management adopted and the management systems used. Power, however obtained and used, will also affect the style and approach of the strategic leader.

Strategic leaders may be personally visionary, but this is not a prerequisite for effective leadership, and leaders must ensure that the organization has a vision and clear direction and that resources are committed towards its achievement. They must ensure, perhaps by delegating to others, that: (i) the organization thinks strategically, (ii) people are engaged and committed, (iii) there is positive action and (iv) the organization has an appropriate public face and visibility.

The leader can contribute by starting a new business or venture, by turning around a company in trouble, by transforming an already successful company or even by splitting up a company to exploit the true value of its subsidiary parts. Six different *leadership* styles (analytical, aspirational, public relations, financial engineering, operational and people-based) were identified, often related to past experiences. The leader's natural or preferred style has a major impact on organizational culture. Visionary leaders typically provide a strategic vision, rely less on formal planning systems, are persuasive, charismatic and operate through the culture.

Entrepreneurs are similar in many respects, but are also different as they build value around opportunities with intra-corporate entrepreneurs (intrapreneurs) being provided with opportunity and encouragement in some organizations where they will drive emergent strategic change.

Clearly, some strong leaders are instrumental in the success and prosperity of organizations, but on other occasions they are perceived to fail. In reality, the shelf-life of many large company chief executives is relatively short. Where they are seen to fail is often the result of poor implementation, which implies that leaders are more likely to know what they would like to achieve than how to do it, suggesting that it is easy to think that success lies in a good idea, in a strategic position – but ideas and positions can be copied, sustained competitive advantage lies in the ways in which things are done. Processes and behaviours are harder to replicate.

Succession is a crucial issue, particularly for someone who has been especially successful or charismatic, and a newcomer may want to make changes, possibly to establish his or her personality and preferences in the organization.

Online cases for this chapter

Online Case 10.1: Boots
Online Case 10.2: Philip Green
Online Case 10.3: David Bruce
Online Case 10.4: Michelle Mone and MJM International

Online Case 10.5: Pilgrim Jewellery
Online Case 10.6: Wynn Las Vegas
Online Case 10.7: JK Rowling

Questions and research assignments

1   Using the Volvo case (Case 10.8) as background, discuss why effective leadership involves both strategy creation and strategy implementation. From your experience and reading, which other well-known strategic leaders do you believe are strong on:

a   creation
b   implementation
c   both?

2 Research the real ale sector. What might the further development of BrewDog entail?

3 Where do the entrepreneur and the visionary leader overlap and where are they different?

4 Apply Figure 10.4 (alternative styles of leadership) to any strategic leader whom you are in a position to evaluate.

Internet and library projects

1 What has happened recently with respect to the ambitions of Sir Philip Green, the owner of BHS and Arcadia? Will he ever get his hands on M&S?

2 Re-examine Figure 10.4 Can you attach a particular entrepreneur to each one of the six key leader styles?

3 How effectively has the General Electric succession issue been resolved?

Strategy activity

Friends Reunited   UK

In 1999 Julie Pankhurst was pregnant and walking near where she lived in Barnet, North London. She had an idea that it would be interesting to get back in touch with people she had known at school to check which ones were now parents. She shared her thoughts with her husband, Steve, a computer programmer. They came up with the idea for a website and enlisted the additional expertise of Jason Porter, an IT developer.

The site was launched in 2000; the business was being run from the Pankhursts' home. They gained publicity and people soon started clicking on the site and became subscribers. After 6 months, Friends Reunited was talked about on Radio One and this had an immediate impact. Daily subscriptions doubled overnight. Eventually 'half the online population signed up'.

The Pankhursts held 30 per cent of the shares and Porter another 30 per cent. The remaining shares were distributed amongst the managers who joined the growing business. When it was sold to ITV in 2005, the founders became multimillionaires. ITV paid £175 million – but interest in Friends Reunited then started to fade and by early 2009 the business was valued at £40 million *maximum*, possibly quite a bit less. ITV sold it to DC Thomson for just £25 million in August 2011.

The idea is incredibly simple. It is in effect an *alumni* society for schools, colleges and universities which goes way back and supplements anything the schools and universities might organize themselves. In fact, many universities use Friends Reunited to track their *alumni!*

There are obvious benefits and outcomes – such as getting to rekindle friendships from way back and organizing reunions – but there have been negative impacts. There are cases of people being libelled on the site. In the end, the competition from Facebook and others was too strong.

Questions

1 Why would Friends Reunited be attractive to a business like ITV?

2 Revenue comes mainly from subscriptions, but is this business so much more than that?

3 Were the founders right to sell out whilst they could get a deal?

4 Is Friends Reunited a genuinely entrepreneurial business or what we might call a 'one trick pony'?

References

Bennis, W., Interview recorded in Crainer, S. (1988) Doing the right thing, *The Director*, October.

Blanchard, K. and Waghorn, T. (1997) *Mission Possible*, McGraw Hill.

Bolton, W.K. and Thompson, J.L. (2013) *Entrepreneurs: Talent, Temperament, Opportunity*, 3rd edn., Routledge

Bower, J.L. (2007) The CEO *Within: Why Inside Outsiders are the Key to Succession Planning*, Harvard Business School Press.

Bridge, S., O'Neill, K. and Martin, F. (2009) *Understanding Enterprise, Entrepreneurship and Small Business*, Third Edition, Palgrave.

Buckingham, M. and Coffman, C. (1999) *First, Break all the Rules*, Simon and Schuster.

Cantillon, R. (1755) Essai sur la Nature du Commerce en General, London and Paris.

Charan, R. and Colvin, G. (1999) Why CEOs fail, *Fortune*, 21 June.

Charan, R. (2006) *Know-How: The eight skills that separate people who perform from those who don't*, Random House.

Churchill, N.C. (1997) Breaking down the wall, scaling the ladder. *In Mastering Enterprise* (eds S. Birley and D. Muzyka), Financial Times/Pitman.

De Geus, A. (1997) The living company, *Harvard Business Review*, March–April.

Fradette, M. and Michaud, S. (1998) *The Power of Corporate Kinetics – Create the Self-adapting, Self-renewing, Instant Action Enterprise*, Simon and Schuster.

Hamel, G. (1999) Bringing Silicon Valley inside, *Harvard Business Review*, September–October.

Hooper, L. and Trompenaars, F. (2009) *The Enlightened Leader*, Jossey Bass.

Horovitz, J. (1997) Growth without losing the entrepreneurial spirit. In *Mastering Enterprise* (eds S. Birley and D. Muzyka), Financial Times/Pitman.

Hurst, D.K. (1995) Crisis and Renewal – *Meeting the Challenge of Organizational Change*, Harvard Business School Press.

Kanter, R.M. (1983) *The Change Masters – Innovation and Entrepreneurship in the American Corporation*, Simon and Schuster.

Kanter, R.M. (1989) *When Giants Learn to Dance*, Simon and Schuster.

Kets de Vries, M.F.R. (1996) CEOs also have the blues, *European Journal of Management*, September.

Kets de Vries, M. (1994) Leaders who make a difference, *European Management Journal*, 14 (5).

Kirzner, I.M. (1973) *Competition and Entrepreneurship*, Cambridge University Press.

Knight, F. (1921) Risk, Uncertainty and Profit, Chicago, University of Chicago Press.

Lessem, R. (1986) *Enterprising Development*, Gower.

Lessem, R. (1998) *Managing Development Through Cultural Diversity*, Routledge.

Liebenstein, H. (1966) Allocative efficiency vs. "x-efficiency", *American Economic Review*, June.

Maccoby, M. (2000) Narcissistic leaders, *Harvard Business Review*, January–February.

Maitland, A. (1999) Strategy for creativity, *Financial Times*, 11 November.

McClelland, D. and Winter, D. (1971) *Motivating Economic Achievement*, Free Press.

Morris, H.M. and Kuratko, D.F. (2002) Corporate Entrepreneurship, Fort Worth: Harcourt College Publishers.

Mintzberg, H. (1973) Strategy making in three modes, *California Management Review*, 16 (2).

Mintzberg, H., Ahlstrand, B. and Lampel, J. (1998) *Strategy Safari*, Prentice-Hall.

Pinchot, G. and Pinchot, E. (1978) Intra-corporate Entrepreneurship. Avaialble online: http://www.intrapreneur.com/MainPages/History/IntraCorp.html. Accessed 23/04/12

Pinchot, G. (1985) *Intrapreneuring*, Harper and Row.

Pinchot, G. III (1994) *Intrapreneuring*, Harper and Row.

Quinn, J.B. (1980) *Strategies for Change: Logical Incrementalism*, Irwin.

Richardson, B. (1994) Towards a profile of the visionary leader, *Small Business Enterprise and Development*, 1 (1).

Richardson, B., Nwanko, S. and Richardson, S. (1994) Understanding the causes of business failure crises, *Management Decision*, 32 (4).

Say, J.B. (1815) Catechisme d'Economie Politique, translated (19210 by John Richter, Catechism of Political Economy.

Schultz, T.W. (1962) Investment in human beings, Chicago, University of Chicago Press.

Schumpeter, J. (1934) *The Theory of Economic Development*, Harvard University Press; original German edition, 1911.

Slatter, S. (1984) *Corporate Recovery: Successful Turnaround Strategies and their Implementation, Penguin*.

Sonnenfeld, J. and Ward, A. (2007) *Firing Back: How Great Leaders Rebound After Career Disasters*, Harvard Business School Press.

Terazano, E. (1999) Fresh impetus from the need to innovate, *Financial Times*, 25 June.

Part 4 Strategic growth issues

This part of the book first considers what constitutes strategic success and how a number of choices are driven by the related ambitions – Chapter 11. At the most basic level of argument, an organization is successful if it is meeting the needs and expectations of its stakeholders, such that their support and commitment are maintained. We will explore the logic of constantly seeking to grow, which sometimes implies serious risk.

Chapter 12 concentrates on managing growth by discussing diversification, acquisition strategies and strategic alliances. Chapter 12 also covers the broader topic of international strategy. It is broader in the sense that all of the growth strategies discussed in Chapter 8 can have an international dimension. Therefore, internationalization needs to be examined as a strategic action in its own right.

Chapter 13 looks at business failure, consolidation and recovery strategies. If anything in human life is certain then it is death. This applies to many businesses. At some point in the life of any business, elements of Chapter 13 will be relevant. Corporate level failure is a fact of life; no business of any size is immune to this possibility and, just as failure can happen, so can it be avoided or recovered from by the correct strategic actions.

Chapter 11

Strategic control and measuring success

Learning objectives

Having read to the end of this chapter, you should be able to:

- distinguish between efficiency and effectiveness, and how success might be measured and assessed in financial terms (**Section 11.1**)

- appreciate how strategic competency and admiration are important themes in a holistic approach to evaluation (**Sections 11.2 and 11.4**)

- identify the difficulties involved in measuring the effective performance of many not-for-profit organizations (**Section 11.3**).

Introduction

The performance of a company – in terms of the outcomes of its realized (as distinct from intended) strategies – is typically evaluated by financial ratios and other quantitative measures. We argue in this chapter that, while these are an essential element of the evaluation process, they are inadequate alone such that we need to take a more holistic perspective which embraces both subjective performance indicators and recognizes the underlying causes of relative success and failure.

We show how different measures and assessments can provide conflicting conclusions and provide a comprehensive model based on E–V–R (environment–values–resources) congruence.

Since financial ratio analysis remains an important aspect of management case-study analysis, a section explaining the main ratios is included as a Web Supplement – which was first highlighted in the appendix to Part 1. You might wish to revisit this.

11.1 Defining and measuring success

An organization is successful if it meets the needs and expectations of its stakeholders, implying a mixture of common sense and competency, as it must understand the 'why' and 'how' behind the 'how well'.

We may think we know instinctively whether an organization is doing relatively well or relatively poorly, but more precision is needed – since we could be deluding ourselves, misjudging a situation, feeling complacent and/or ignoring environmental changes. Success, assuming it is real and not imagined, can be transient.

Figure 11.1 implies that organizations and their managers must know where, how and why a company is doing relatively well or relatively poorly and that they use this information to sustain success by improvement and change or actively remedy weaknesses. Otherwise, if they take relative success for granted or fail to understand relative failure, they will experience slow or rapid decline.

Explanations are sought, and attention is focused, when results or outcomes are disappointing or below target but is not always so with success. Managers may proverbially pat themselves on the back and assume that the success is a result of their personal abilities and brilliance – whereas the success may, in reality, lie more in good fortune and an absence of any strong, threatening competitors. Such advantages can prove very short-lived since success, when taken too much for granted, can quickly turn to failure, a manifestation of the prevailing culture.

Organizations must face up to the real issues and not attempt to 'spin' the figures to provide an attractive, but not entirely honest, explanation. Companies like to present and discuss their results in terms of absolute

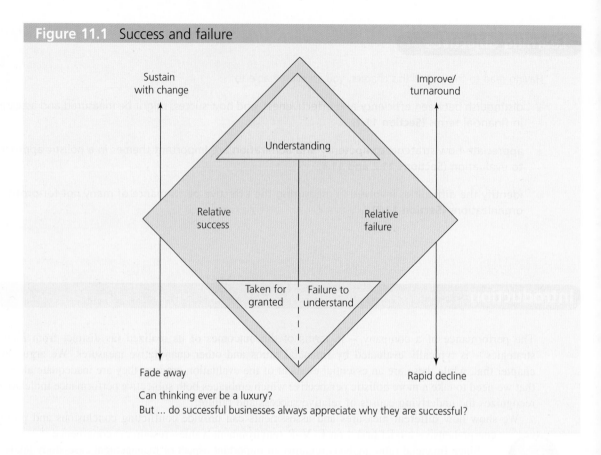

Figure 11.1 Success and failure

Can thinking ever be a luxury?
But ... do successful businesses always appreciate why they are successful?

figures for revenue and profits, and the media seem happy to report these figures, frequently headlining any growth. Absolute growth in this form can – and can be used to – hide deterioration in true performance. Profitability, for instance, is more important than profit *per se* for understanding how well a company is doing since growth alone can be a very dubious and misleading measure of success, since *sales revenue is vanity; cash flow is clarity; profits are sanity.*

Companies may, not unusually, concentrate measurement on factors that can be measured most easily or readily, such as inputs, resources and efficiencies, because outcomes and effectiveness are more difficult to measure. Yet, as we have already seen, satisfying the needs and expectations of key stakeholders is critical for long-term prosperity. Critical Reflection 11.1 on efficiency and effectiveness reinforces the point and it incorporates a summary of relevant measures for British Airways. Thompson and Richardson (1996) have shown how generic strategic competencies can be categorized into three broad groups which influence the organization's efficiency and effectiveness and have relevance for all of its stakeholders. *Content* competencies reflect the ways through which organizations add value, differentiate and manage their costs, including functional and competitive strategies. *Process* competencies deal with the ways by which these content competencies are changed and improved in a dynamic and competitive environment, such as strategy implementation and quality and customer care. Meanwhile *awareness and learning* competencies inform the change management process, e.g. the ability to satisfy stakeholders, ethical and social issues and the ability to avoid and manage crises.

Possible performance measures for British Airways – an application

Whilst we have specified British Airways, this list would be relevant for any similar airline.

An airline is a people-dependent service business. Unquestionably its revenue, profits, profitability, liquidity and market share (explained and discussed in the web supplement to this chapter) are all important. But alone they are inadequate for assessing the overall performance.

Critical Reflection 11.1   Efficiency or Effectiveness?

There are three important measures of performance:

- Economy, which means 'doing things cost effectively'. Resources should be managed at the lowest possible cost consistent with achieving quantity and quality targets.
- Efficiency, which implies 'doing things right'. Resources should be deployed and utilized to maximize the returns from them.

Economy and efficiency measures are essentially quantitative and objective.

- Effectiveness, or 'doing the right things'. Resources should be allocated to those activities which satisfy the needs, expectations and priorities of the various stakeholders in the business.

In essence, there is no point being the world's best producer of something, e.g. large CRT computer monitors when everyone wants a flat screen!

Effectiveness relates to outcomes and need satisfaction, and consequently the measures are often qualitative and subjective.

Although it is rarely used, there is a relevant fourth 'e' – efficacy. Is the organization doing 'what it says on the tin'? In effect, is it practising and demonstrating its declared mission or purpose and values?

Where economy, efficiency and effectiveness can be measured accurately and unambiguously, it is appropriate to use the expression 'performance measures'. However, if, as is frequently the case with effectiveness, precise measures are not possible, it can be more useful to use the term 'performance indicators'.

As the following table indicates, only efficient and effective organizations will grow and prosper. Effective but inefficient businesses will survive but underachieve because they are not using minimum resources; efficient but ineffective companies will decline as they cease to meet the expectations of their stakeholders – simply, the things they are doing are wrong, however well they might be doing them.

	Ineffective	Effective
Inefficient	Corporate collapse	Survival
Efficient	Gradual decline	Growth and prosperity

The following list contains examples of appropriate measures that might also be used.

Economy measures

- Costs, e.g. the cost of fuel
- The cost of leasing aircraft
- Staff levels and costs – slimming these is acceptable as long as the appropriate quality of service is maintained. This could be measured as an overhead cost per passenger.

Efficiency measures

- Timekeeping/punctuality
- Revenue passenger kilometres (RPK), the number of passengers carried multiplied by the distances flown
- Available seat kilometres (ASK), the number of seats available for sale multiplied by the distances flown
- The overall load factor = RPK/ASK. (Similar measures for freight are also relevant.)

Solid performance with these measures is essential if the airline is to run at all profitably, but increasing them requires the airline to be more effective in persuading more customers to fly, utilizing marketing and consistently good service.

A related measure is:

- Passenger revenue per RPK. Improving this implies increasing the return from each flight, given that on any aircraft there are likely to be several pricing schemes in operation. BA has changed its strategy to address this issue (Online Case 12.1).

- Income (from all sources) related to the numbers of employees

- Reliability of the aircraft, i.e. continuous flying without breakdown (as a result of efficient maintenance, see below)

- The average age of the aircraft in the fleet.

Effectiveness

- Ability to meet all legislative requirements

- Image – which is based on several of the factors listed in this section

- Staff attitudes and contributions – both on the ground and on board the aircraft: care, courtesy, enthusiasm, friendliness, respect and efficiency

- The aeroplane – does it look and feel new and properly looked after?

- Other aspects of the on-board service, such as the cleanliness of the seating and toilet areas, food and entertainment

- Innovation – new standards of passenger comfort

- Safety record

- The number of routes offered, the timing of flights and the general availability of seats (this requires good links with travel agents)

- Recognition of, and rewards for, regular and loyal customers, reflected in the accumulation of Air Miles by passengers and the numbers of passengers who become 'gold-card' holders in regular flyer schemes

- Having seats available for all people with tickets who check in. While airlines, like hotels, often overbook deliberately, they must ensure that they are not 'bumping' people onto the next available flight at a level which is causing ill-will and a poor reputation

- The compensation package when people are delayed

- Time taken at check-in

- Reliability of baggage service, particularly making sure that bags go on the right flight. This also involves the issue of bags being switched from one flight to another for transit passengers

- The time taken for baggage to be unloaded (this is partially in the hands of the airport management)

- The absence of any damage to luggage. *Issues of lost and delayed bags plagued the opening of BA's new Terminal 5 at London Heathrow in 2008.*

- The systems for allocating particular seats in advance of the flight and at check-in

- The number of complaints; the number in relation to the number of passengers

- The way in which complaints are handled

- The ability to balance the cost of maintenance with the costs incurred if things go wrong. If there is inadequate maintenance, there are likely to be incidents or accidents which are costly in lost revenue and goodwill. At the same time, airlines could over-maintain to a level where they are no longer able to compete because of too-high costs.

The additional factors below are not wholly the responsibility of airlines as they also involve the airport owners:

- Terminal provisions and comfort – seating, escalators, restaurants, duty-free shopping and toilets

- Security – evidence of security and the perception that it is being taken seriously
- Availability of trolleys and wheelchairs for disabled passengers.

Endnotes

It is also important to consider how all these factors might be measured and evaluated. Observation, passenger surveys, complaints and comparisons with other airlines are all possibilities.

The distinction between indicators – aspects of service which are actually difficult to measure – measures and performance targets – standards to measure against – needs to be recognized.

The following points are also worth noting:

- it is sensible not to be overambitious with both measures and targets
- if something cannot be measured, it is perhaps better to leave it out
- the chosen measures must be relevant and easily understood; hopefully, the very act of measurement will foster improvements.

Improving competency

Where organizations need to become more successful and less crisis prone, they must improve and/or reprioritize their competencies. Thompson and Richardson (1996) argue that it is necessary, first, to evaluate which competencies are critical for strategic and competitive success and, second, to ensure that the organization possesses these competencies at an appropriate level. To facilitate these needs, and to ensure that there is improvement and change, they need to measure their competencies. Figures 11.2 and 11.3 expand the strategic implications of these points.

The four-quadrant box on the left of Figure 11.2 has been adapted from May and Kruger (1988), whose ideas on personal competency have been extrapolated to an organizational context and it can be linked to E-V-R congruence. An *unconsciously incompetent* organization does not appreciate just which factors are

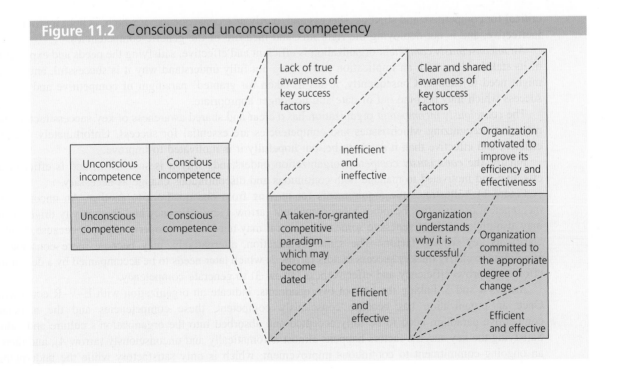

Figure 11.2 Conscious and unconscious competency

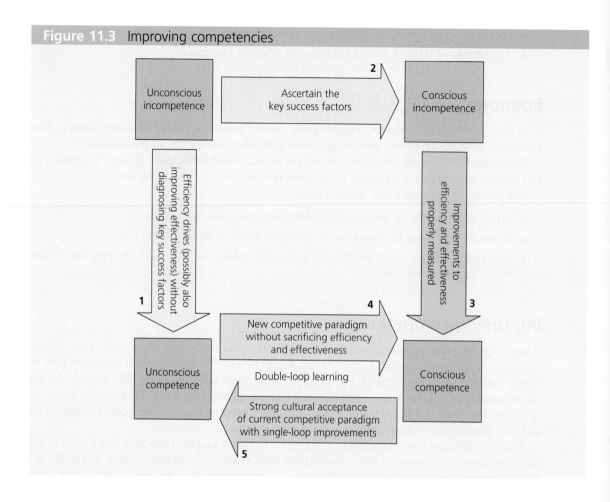

Figure 11.3 Improving competencies

critical for competitive and strategic success and, partly as a consequence of which, is both inefficient and ineffective, and is not deploying the right mix and measure of the generic competencies.

An *unconsciously competent* organization is efficient and effective, satisfying the needs and expectations of its stakeholders, with an implication that it does not fully understand why it is successful, and when it might need to change. Consequently, it has a 'taken for granted' paradigm of competitive and strategic success which may become out of date and no longer appropriate.

The *consciously incompetent* organization has a clear and shared awareness of key success factors, with managers recognizing which issues and competencies are essential for success. Unfortunately, it is less efficient and effective than it needs to be, but hopefully it is motivated to improve.

Finally, the *consciously competent* organization understands why it is successful; and is efficient and effective and motivated to manage both continuous and discontinuous change as necessary.

Figure 11.3 illustrates the requirements for moving from one quadrant to another. An unconsciously incompetent organization becomes more competent (arrow 1) by efficiency and productivity drives, which may also improve effectiveness to some extent, but it may not become properly effective because it fails to clarify its key success factors. The same organization, alternatively, may become more conscious by attempting to clarify the key success factors (arrow 2) which later needs to be accompanied by a determined effort to improve efficiency and effectiveness (arrow 3) to generate competency.

Arrows 4 and 5, linking the bottom two quadrants, indicate an organization with E–V–R congruence. Once an organization has become consciously competent, these competencies and the associated competitive paradigm need to be fully accepted and absorbed into the organization's culture and values. Satisfying the key success factors happens almost automatically and unconsciously (arrow 4), and there is an ongoing commitment to continuous improvement, which is only satisfactory while the underpinning competitive paradigm remains appropriate. Competitive pressures will at some stage require most organizations to search for a new perspective of effective competition, and ideally reach the new competitive high ground ahead of their rivals so that the competency package – and key success factors – should be evaluated constantly to ensure that they remain appropriate. When the competitive strategy is changed, efficiency and effectiveness must not be sacrificed (arrow 5).

11.2   What should we measure? A holistic model

If you can measure it you can manage it.

PETER DRUCKER

Not everything that can be counted counts; and not everything that counts can be counted.

ATTRIBUTED TO ALBERT EINSTEIN

The three most important things you need to measure in business are customer satisfaction, employee satisfaction and cash flow.

JACK WELCH, EX-CHIEF EXECUTIVE OFFICER, GENERAL ELECTRIC (US)

The ultimate measure of success for any organization will invariably have a quantitative element: revenue growth, profits and profitability for profit-seeking firms, and an ability to raise sufficient funding to fulfil its purpose and objectives effectively for nonprofit-seeking concerns. However, simply focusing on financial measures, important as they are, is woefully inadequate as they pay insufficient regard to issues of cause and outcome.

The basic principles are explained in Figure 11.4, which links to the business and revenue models. The quality of the opportunity and its execution (strategy and implementation) indicate strategic effectiveness. It is the opportunity and its execution that generate revenue; the efficiency of the execution determines costs. The gap between costs and revenue is profit.

Accepting these reservations, we should look at performance measures within a comprehensive cause and outcome framework. Kets de Vries (1996) argues that strategic leaders play two key roles: a charismatic

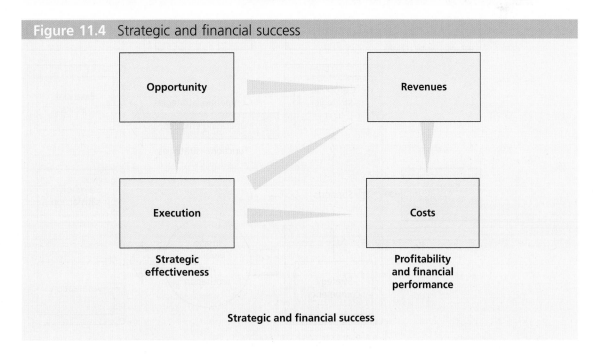

Figure 11.4   Strategic and financial success

one, through which they ensure that the organization has an understood vision and direction, people are empowered and as a consequence they energize, stimulate and galvanize change; and an architectural role of establishing an appropriate structure and style for both control and reward. Effective leaders succeed when strategies are owned by those who must implement them, customers are satisfied, people enjoy their work and things happen in the organization – specifically, the necessary changes are quick and timely. This was explored more fully in Chapter 10.

Figure 11.5 reinforces the importance of strategic leadership for establishing (and changing) both competency and the corporate strategic logic of the organization. With the latter, we are considering whether or not the organization's corporate portfolio and its competitive strategy or strategies make sense and can be justified, or appear to be a recipe for poor or disappointing performance.

A strong and well-managed portfolio will be reflected in successful and effective competitive and functional strategies and in operating efficiency, as well as its image, visibility and reputation, its strategic leader and its products and services – which can be managed and can have a bearing on many things, but which are difficult to evaluate and measure, particularly by the organization itself. Largely, they are the subjective opinion of external experts and stakeholders.

There are three distinctive broad approaches to measuring outcomes. These are:

● *financial results* and other market-driven quantitative measures such as market share
● *stakeholder satisfaction*, reflected in the Balanced Scorecard and similar packages
● *admiration*, for example the annual reviews carried out by *Fortune* in the US and *Management Today* in the UK.

We now examine briefly corporate logic, admiration, image and reputation, financial measurement and stakeholder measures to explain the linkages in Figure 11.5.

Corporate strategic logic

Caulkin (1995) stresses that the average life expectancy of successful UK companies is some 40–50 years, such that only nine of the 30 companies in the first *Financial Times* share index in 1935 still existed in their

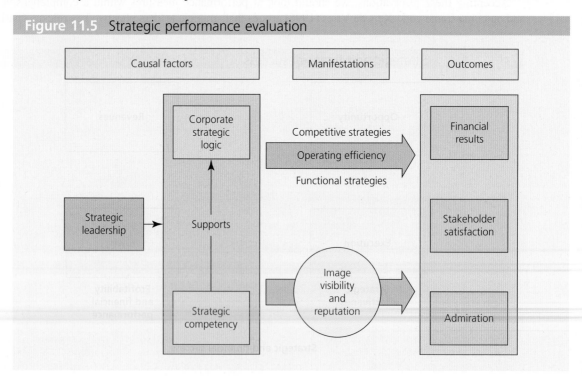

Figure 11.5 Strategic performance evaluation

own right 60 years later, whilst several others were under new ownership, some had been liquidated, and many had been acquired and absorbed by their new corporate parents. Inevitably, every one of the companies will have seen major strategic and/or structural changes of some kind.

Sadtler *et al.* (1997) support a clear focus built around a defensible core of related activities, and in this they reflect current practice, as debated in Chapters 12 and 16.

Admired companies

Sound profits and a strong balance sheet are very important, but alone they will not necessarily lead to a company being 'admired'. In the 1980s, and based on research in the USA by *Fortune*, *The Economist* began to investigate which companies are most admired by other business people, particularly those with whom they compete directly. More recently, *Management Today* has taken over the project in the UK and the *Financial Times* in association with Price Waterhouse later initiated a parallel European and then a global study. Business people are asked to allocate marks against certain criteria for their main rivals, which in the UK survey are: quality of management; financial soundness; value as a long-term investment; quality of products and services; the ability to attract, develop and retain top talent; capacity to innovate; quality of marketing; and community and environmental responsibility. These reflect multiple perspectives and stakeholder interests and, consequently, *The Economist* (1991) argues that admiration encourages customers to buy more and to stay loyal, employees to work harder, suppliers to be more supportive and shareholders also to remain loyal.

The 2011 UK *Management Today* top ten is listed below, with some selected relevant 2010 positions shown to the right:

1	Berkeley Group (House building and property)	6th
2	Diageo (spirits)	22nd
3	Rotork (valves)	
4	Aggreko (power, heating and cooling systems for gigs and festivals)	
5	Derwent London (commercial property)	
6	Paddy Power (betting shops)	
7	Royal Dutch Shell (oil)	3rd
8	Unilever (foods and detergents)	1st
9	Rolls-Royce (aircraft engines)	7th
10	Shaftesbury (property investment).	

The most significant point to make is the strong showing of property companies, which has not been as evident in previous years. It is interesting to reflect upon which sectors and industries have been most affected by the economic recession – and which ones might be expected to lead the economy out of recession.

The list below shows comparative data for 2008 (with 2007 places to the right) and it will be readily observed how significantly things have changed in 3 years.

1	Diageo (spirits)	9th
2	Johnson Mathey (chemicals and metals)	5th
3	Unilever (foods and detergents)	
4	BskyB (media)	3rd
5	Tesco (grocery retailing)	2nd
6	Stagecoach (bus and rail travel)	
7	Rolls-Royce (aircraft engines)	10th
8	Man Group (investment products)	
9	Kingspan (building products)	
10	3i (private equity funding).	

In 2007 the other five winners in the top ten (not there a year later) were: Marks and Spencer (first), Serco (support services), ICAP (finance), Sainsbury's and Capita (support services again).

Sir Terry Leahy of Tesco was the most admired strategic leader in both 2007 and 2008. Interestingly, by 2010 Tesco had dropped a little to eighth position – but by 2011 it was forty-first. Had the retirement of Sir Terry been instrumental in this fall in confidence? Also interestingly, given the ranking for the business, Sir Stuart Rose of Marks and Spencer was runner up in both 2007 and 2008. In 2007 third place went to the now disgraced banker, Sir Fred Goodwin, CEO of Royal Bank of Scotland, RBS. In 2007 RBS and HBOS (another bank that collapsed in 2008) were ranked first and fourth in the banking section.

The most admired strategic leader in 2011 was Terry Pidgley of the Berkeley Group. Pidgley was a true entrepreneur rather than a career executive who had risen to be CEO of a blue chip corporation – and the first entrepreneur to win the 'most admired leader' accolade. He had founded the business in 1976 and stayed with it as it grew and prospered. Given he had a deprived background, and was, in fact an orphan, a 'Barnado boy', one can appreciate he started by building a single house as a sole trader. This has been a remarkable achievement.

Listed below are the 20 most admired American companies in 2012 on the Fortune website:

1 Apple
2 Google
3 Amazon.com
4 Coca-Cola
5 IBM
6 FedEx
7 Berkshire Hathaway
8 Starbucks
9 Procter & Gamble
10 Southwest Airlines
11 McDonald's
12 Johnson & Johnson
13 Walt Disney
14 BMW
15 General Electric
16 American Express
17 Microsoft
18 3M
19 Caterpillar-(earth-moving equipment)
20 Costco Wholesale.

A number of observations can be made about the American poll:

- In an era of strategic focus, an extensively diversified company, GE, was the most admired – and globally the most respected – for a number of years up to 2007. GE was only deposed when its highly regarded chief executive, Jack Welch, retired. The important contribution made by Jack Welch, in ensuring that there is a cohesive and synergistic link between strategy, structure and style will emerge throughout this book.

- By 2000 the chart of winners was dominated by computing, networks and semiconductor companies, of which there were five in the top ten. Cisco, Intel and Lucent have since disappeared. Later Apple and Google came into the top ranks – but there is still no top ten place for Microsoft. Amazon.com also made the breakthrough to real admiration when it became profitable after a number of years of investment and reinvestment; this change was helped enormously by the success of the Kindle e-reader.

- The extremely successful and remarkable Berkshire Hathaway is included. Run by entrepreneur Warren Buffett, Berkshire Hathaway is neither a manufacturing nor a service business; instead it is an investment vehicle for its shareholders' funds. Minority shareholdings in a range of companies, including Coca-Cola, are typically held for the long-term. Notably, high-technology companies are avoided because of their perceived inherent uncertainty.

Financial success alone certainly does not guarantee admiration from competitors and popularity with all the stakeholders; at the same time, as evidenced by the Body Shop over a period of years, deteriorating financial returns will bother shareholders far more than customers!

Image and reputation

Could reputation, inevitably a subjective judgement, actually help to cover up a relatively poor financial performance, itself a more objective measurement? Fombrum (1996) contends that reputations create economic value with image, embodying the company's uniqueness, being a key competitive tool, thus favouring benchmarking those companies perceived to be the leading performers to avoid critical gaps.

Brands can give a company visibility, sometimes internationally; and, when a prominent brand becomes associated with trust and quality, its corporate owner should be in a position to command premium prices, although some may be needed to cover the extra promotional costs required to sustain the brand's visibility. Companies are increasingly including their brands as balance-sheet assets and attempting to place a value on them. Usefully for consumers, sensible companies will invest in their brands in order to improve them and sustain their competitive leadership.

Financial measures

A plethora of financial performance measures has long been used to help evaluate the relative success and progress of a business, including ratios such as return on capital employed and return on shareholders' funds, earnings per share, the share price itself and the price to earnings ratio. Typically, a company's share price performance will be evaluated against the relevant industry average and against one of the *Financial Times* indices. While these are objective within the constraints of accounting practice and convention, there are two points to note. First, although analysts always seem to stress profitability, relating pre- or after-tax profits to either sales, capital employed or shareholders' funds, press headlines are more likely to focus on the specific growth or decline in revenues and actual profits made. Second, share prices are also affected by future expectation, and a plausible and convincing strategic leader can be persuasive about 'better times being on the way'.

An analysis of financial ratios is useful for a number of reasons. It enables a study of trends and progress over a number of years to be made, and comparisons with competitors and with general industry trends are possible. It can point the way towards possible or necessary improvements – necessary if the organization is performing less and less well than competitors, useful if new opportunities are spotted. It can reveal lost profit and growth potential, and can emphasize possible dangers – for example, if stock turnover is decreasing or ratios affecting cash flow are moving adversely. Financial analysis concentrates on efficiency rather than effectiveness unless the objectives are essentially financial or economic ones. The real measures of success, as far as the strategic leader and the various stakeholders are concerned, is whether or not the objectives perceived as important are being achieved.

Outside analysts, such as students and interested readers, can gain insight into the apparent objectives of an organization by reading annual reports, articles, press releases and so on, but only the people involved in decision-making know the real objectives and whether they are being achieved. Financial analysis from the published (and easily obtained) results can be very informative and lead to conclusions about how well a company is performing, but certain aspects remain hidden. Decision-makers inside an organization use financial analysis as part of the wider picture, but outsiders are more restricted. Financial analysis is a very useful form of analysis, which should be used, but its wider aspects should not be overlooked. *Economic value added* (EVA) has been adopted as another measure, which compares a company's after-tax operating profits with its cost of capital (see Lynn, 1995).

A more detailed treatment of financial measures is included as the Finance in Action Web Supplement.

Stakeholder measures

The *Tomorrow's Company* report (RSA, 1995), written in an attempt to improve the competitiveness of UK industry in global markets, concluded that there was:

- complacency and ignorance about world-class standards
- an over-reliance on financial measures which often focus attention on the short rather than the long-term
- a national adversarial culture which fails to integrate stakeholders into a cohesive network of interdependent organizations.

We might ask: has much changed since this research was published?

We believe that the preferred solution lies in a more holistic approach which incorporates the interests of multiple stakeholders, with a clear realization that both measurement and organizational learning must encompass internal and external (environmental) aspects, according to the ideas behind the '*Balanced Scorecard*' approach of Kaplan and Norton (1992, 1996).

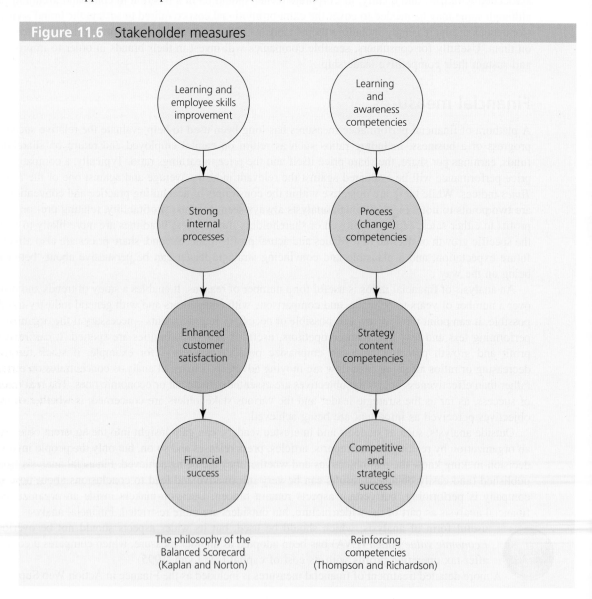

Figure 11.6 Stakeholder measures

Kaplan and Norton suggest that organizations should focus their efforts on a limited number of specific, critical performance measures which reflect stakeholders' key success factors, so that managers can readily concentrate on those issues which are essential for corporate and competitive success.

Kaplan and Norton use the term 'Balanced Scorecard' to describe a framework of four groups of measures, and argue that organizations should select critical measures for each one of these areas:

- financial – return on capital employed; cash flow
- customers – perceived value for money; competitive prices
- internal processes – enquiry response time; enquiry to order conversion rate
- growth and improvement – number of new products/services; extent of employee empowerment.

These measures encapsulate both efficiency and effectiveness. Figure 11.6 illustrates the synergistic dependencies and linkages between the four groups of measures, which have a close relationship with the competency linkages mentioned at the start of this chapter, and featured on the right-hand side of the figure.

Measuring effectiveness requires recognition that quality does not mean the same for every customer. Organizations must determine what will generate repeat business and seek to provide it: supermarkets, for example, can offer service in the form of a wide range of products, brand choice for each product in the range, low prices, fast checkout and ample car parking, perhaps by focusing aggressively on one or more of these or seek a balanced profile, such that the major chains will have a basic competitive posture and then tailor each store to meet local conditions.

Case 11.1 – Classic FM – describes how a radio station has introduced classical music to millions of new listeners, causing an increase in classical CD sales, whilst not meeting its own financial expectations and being criticized by 'musical purists'. Case 11.2 invites you to consider the reasons behind the success of fast food business, Ajisen Rahmen and how changes in China might impact upon its future. In addition you might like to read the online case on Lastminute.com and reflect upon how we evaluate success in modern-age dot.com businesses.

Case 11.1   Classic FM   UK

Owned by radio group, Global Radio, Classic FM was launched in 1992. It is now a 24-hour commercial radio station which plays classical music in typically 4-minute extracts. As GWR also owns a jazz radio station Classic FM sometimes plays jazz during the early hours of the morning – otherwise it is exclusively classical. As its audience ratings have continued to grow – they now exceed 7 million – and making extensive use of its website, Classic FM has increasingly involved its listeners in choosing the playlist. This began with an annual popularity poll for people's favourite classical music; now people vote for their favourites from a predetermined list every day of the week. As with popular music, there is also a Classical Top 20 (best-selling CDs) which is featured every week.

In the beginning some 'purists' were incensed. This was different from the approach of the 70-year-old BBC Radio 3 which had always targeted 'high-brow' listeners. Opera and theatre director, Jonathan Miller commented that he saw it as part of a 'global decline where all thought is reduced to soundbites'.

The Times feared it would 'relegate serious music from high art to low entertainment'.

Diarist and playwright Alan Bennett described Classic FM listeners as 'Saga-louts'.

But there have been some notable achievements:

- Classical music has acquired a mainstream audience
- Classic FM is one of the best-known brands in the UK
- The company has found opportunities to diversify – into a magazine, retail organization, record label, credit card and dating agency
- Compilation albums of favourite classical music have been spawned and sold in large numbers by both Classic FM and mainstream labels
- Record stores feature classical music more extensively, especially the chart albums
- Classic FM has helped launch the careers of such popular artists as Russell Watson, Andrea Bocelli, Bond and The Opera Babes

SOURCE: THIS CASE STUDY WAS PREPARED USING PRIMARILY PUBLICLY AVAILABLE SOURCES OF INFORMATION FOR THE PURPOSES OF CLASSROOM DISCUSSION; IT DOES NOT INTEND TO ILLUSTRATE EITHER EFFECTIVE OR INEFFECTIVE HANDLING OF A MANAGERIAL SITUATION.

- It has also popularized the soundtracks of films such as *Titanic*, *Lord of the Rings* and *Harry Potter* – all of which have sold in huge quantities.

Although turnover exceeded £30 million by the early 2000s, with the company profitable from 1997, advertising revenues have fallen short of early targets. Part of the issue lies with the age profile of the listeners it attracts. The median age is 52; half are over 45, half under. There is a strong student audience, but students are not big spenders! Indeed much of this book has been written with the station playing quietly in the background. Simply, the biggest spending advertisers want to see evidence of the key 35–44 age group.

have for increasing its popularity with the key 35–44 age group.

Question

Visit the Classic FM website and tune into the station (101.1 FM) and consider what options Classic FM might

Case 11.2   Ajisen Ramen (China)   Ch

Ajisen Ramen (China) Holdings Limited is based in Hong Kong and is one of the biggest fast food noodle restaurant chains in China, selling Japanese ramen noodle soup dishes. The 420 plus chain of outlets is mainly to be found in the Far East but also as far away as Australia and Canada and, in the USA, in California and New York. Originating from Kumamoto in western Japan, Ajisen was a moderately successful family owned Ramen chain best known for its white broth, which is made by simmering different kinds of bones including fish bones for many hours. Ajisen (China) Holdings is the Hong Kong-based holder of the Japanese brand's Chinese franchise. In Japan the ramen industry as a whole has been facing declining demand, mainly due to the falling birth rate in Japan. For the business the growth market now is China.

Rapid Growth

The first bowl of Ajisen Ramen noodle was sold in Shenzhen, China in 1997. The Chinese diet at this time very much favoured a fast food noodle business, as opposed to what might be considered as Western fast food. The Japanese Ramen noodle is served in a wooden bowl and is much more refined than the Chinese 'la mian' equivalent and is considered by the Chinese customer to

be a better quality, more fashionable and desirable taste – despite being more expensive. This made the Ramen noodle more attractive to younger white-collar workers in China. The rapid growth enjoyed by Ajisen was based on the perception that the Ramen noodles were a healthier casual food, as opposed to a Western style fast food. Ajisen (which means 'a thousand tastes' in Japanese) design their outlets with their own distinctive lantern style ambience based on the original Japanese restaurant look; this includes the 'byobu' screen which is illustrated with pictures and a good evening in Japanese from the Chinese waitresses as you enter the restaurant.

The business model behind the success of Ajisen Ramen was this casual food positioning allied to the creation of a chain of noodle outlets that were set up based on unified purchase of raw materials and unified methods of production which has the aim of keeping the noodle taste consistent across the chain. In contrast the Chinese 'la mian' is varied in its taste, depending on what area the outlet is based and the type of noodle that is being used. The standardization of the products of the Ajisen Ramen noodle bar enabled each outlet to serve its customers very quickly. The standardization also gave Ajisen Ramen large cost advantages.

In March 2007 Ajisen (China) had a successful listing on the Hong Kong stock exchange that raised $210 million and saw the stock valued at $1.4 billion. Ajisen has now successfully built a brand in China on the back of being seen as representatives of high quality Japanese Ramen and Japanese fast food. Turnover exceeds Hong Kong $2 billion (some US$2.6 billion).

Ajisen Ramen (Holdings) Limited is now committed to rapid growth on the back of a major expansion in factory capacity in China, where a new $13.7 million noodle factory in Shanghai, will be big enough to supply noodles for 500 restaurants. Ajisen also manufactures and sells packaged noodles, with 7500 points of sale around the world.

Questions

1 What are the key features of the success of Ajisen Ramen in China?

2 Do you believe the urbanization and wealth development amongst the Chinese population will actually detract or encourage the growth of the noodle restaurant chain?

www.ajisen.com.hk

11.3 The measurement of success in not-for-profit organizations

In Chapters 1 and 3 we suggested that the objectives of not-for-profit organizations are often stated in terms of resource efficiency because of the difficulty of quantifying their real purpose, and thus measures of their success that are used in practice may not be closely related to their real mission and purpose. Where this happens, financial and other quantitative measures are being used as the measures of performance, and efficiency, not effectiveness, is being evaluated. In other words, performance and success is being measured, but despite the usefulness of, and need for, the measures being used, they may not be assessing strategic performance directly in relation to the mission.

Drucker (1989) observed that many not-for-profit organizations are more money conscious than business enterprises, because their required funding is hard to raise, and they could invariably use more money than they have available. Money, however, is less likely to be the key element of their mission and strategic thinking than are the provision of services and the satisfaction of client needs. Given this premise, the successful performance of a not-for-profit organization should be measured in terms of outcomes and need satisfaction, with money being a major constraint upon what can be accomplished and the appropriate level of expectations. The outcomes, in turn, must be analyzed against the expectations of the important stakeholders, involving for many not-for-profits both beneficiaries of their service and volunteer helpers, as well as financial supporters and paid employees. Typically, their personal objectives and expectations will differ. But what is the case in reality?

The performance and effectiveness of the education system relates to the impact on pupils after they leave the system, their parents, the taxpayers who fund education and future employers. Their perspectives will differ, and their individual aspirations and expectations will be difficult to quantify and measure, such that it is easier to measure efficiency in the way that resources are utilized, for example by class sizes, staff/student or staff/pupil ratios, building occupancy and examination performance.

A charity seeking to save money by minimizing its administration and promotion expenditures (perhaps then spending only 20 per cent of its income on these functions) is focusing on short-term efficiency, but one that increases its long-term effectiveness (raising more money) by investing in marketing and administration (perhaps spending 60 per cent on administration and marketing) – such that the latter could be more effective over the long-term than the former. Charities aim to establish the most appropriate structure, administration network and promotional expenditure to achieve the purpose, and then run it efficiently. The not-for-profit sector is increasingly attempting to measure effectiveness in terms of impacts and outcomes rather than efficiency alone, a task that is not straightforward.

Value for money looks at the relationship between the perceived value of the output (by the stakeholders involved) and the cost of inputs, and is used as a comparative measure. There are too many uncertainties for there to be any true agreement on the magnitude of 'very best value' and, consequently, the provision of good value (in comparison to 'competitors') is being sought.

Both inputs and outcomes enable a consideration of the efficiency and effectiveness of the organization's transformation processes, and its ability to add value. Jackson and Palmer (1989) emphasize that if performance is to be measured more effectively in the public sector, then the implicit cultural and change issues must also be addressed. The climate must be right, with managers committed to thinking clearly about what activities should be measured and what the objectives of these activities are, perhaps involving different reward systems linked to revised expectations. This approach, they suggest, leads managers, for example, to move on from measuring the numbers of passengers on the railway network to analyzing how many had seats and how punctual the trains were. Jackson and Palmer also emphasize the importance of asking users about how effective they perceive organizations to be.

Case 11.3 (Masdar) describes a remarkable project in the Middle East and again invites you to reflect upon how its success will be evaluated as time goes on.

Case 11.3　Masdar　UAE

Masdar is a radical 'project' in Abu Dhabi in the United Arab Emirates that raises interesting questions about how one might evaluate success.

The UAE relies heavily on oil – Abu Dhabi has some 8 per cent of the known supplies in the world – which should last it for another 100 years. But it is a desert region with a hot and humid climate. Summer temperatures can easily exceed 50 degrees centigrade and sandstorms are normal. Air conditioning is ubiquitous. Research by the World Wildlife Fund and others (working together) has concluded that per capita it has the 'world's worst environmental footprint'.

Masdar is a planned city designed by UK architects Foster & Partners. It is being built by the Future Energy Company with seed capital from the government. Located next to the international airport, the new city will be entirely dependent on solar and other renewable energy and there will be a zero carbon and a zero waste ecology. In the first instance a solar energy plant is being constructed to (amongst other things) provide the energy for wind farms on the peripheries of the city, a hydrogen power plant and geothermal facilities. The intention is to attract 'cleantech' companies that both carry out research and design and manufacture environmentally friendly products.

The city project was started in 2006 with an intended timescale of 8 years to completion and with a first phase completion in 2009. But this was before the global financial crisis. Phase one is now scheduled to be finished in 2015 and with everything else some 5 to 10 years down the line. At the same time the budget has been reduced by between 10 and 15 per cent. The Masdar Institute of Science and Technology (with links to the Massachusetts Institute of Technology, MIT, in the USA) is already open and operating within the developing city. Large companies such as General Electric are 'signed up', and it seems as if a solid cluster of related businesses will co-locate there.

When complete, Masdar will be a large block of around 6 square kilometres. There will be a perimeter wall to block out the hot desert winds but to also channel air movement in order to create an air flow down the carefully designed streets and reduce the need for extensive air conditioning. Between 45 000 and 50 000 people will live in the city and up to 60 000 will commute in to work. There will be no cars and instead a new rapid transit system. With around 100 stations and 3000 pods people will be able to access transport within 150 metres of where they are anywhere inside the city boundary. This system will connect to the public transport outside the city. Water will come from a solar powered desalination plant and will be recycled as much as possible. Crops will be watered with grey water. Biological waste will be treated to make fertiliser. Plastics and metals will be recycled locally. Palmwood (taken from trees that no longer bear fruit) is being used extensively.

So how much is Masdar an exciting model for the future and how much is it an indulgence for the wealthy elite of Abu Dhabi?

The city is meant to be commercially viable. Revenues will be earned from its commercial and trading activities. There will be an income from selling and licensing its new technologies. Ideally there will be synergy from learning from doing and exploiting the new knowledge. There is the potential to learn lessons that are valuable for improving living conditions in desert countries everywhere.

A long-term sustainability perspective is being taken – given Abu Dhabi's oil reserves are thought to be finite. Throughout the world there is increasing interest in renewable energy sources not dependent on oil and other fossil fuels. There is perhaps an assumption that over time Abu Dhabi can become a knowledge economy and therefore more sustainable – at the same time, helping the rest of the world.

But there is perhaps one irony. The future energy company is a subsidiary of Mubadala – an organization that is also committed to revenue generating from its

attractions including the Formula 1 racetrack and a Ferrari-themed Amusement Park. Neither of these will be carbon neutral. Hence there is the potential for a cynical view that Masdar is largely a 'balancing act'. We must all decide for ourselves.

Question

Over time how do you think the relative success of Masdar will be evaluated? Are you in favour of the 'measures' you believe will be used? Are they sufficiently holistic?

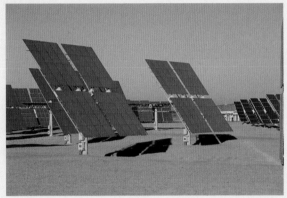

11.4 A holistic framework of measures – revisited

Figure 11.7 offers an outline framework for reflecting on the measurement demands facing an organization, based on the premise that a competitive and strategically successful organization will achieve and – with changes – sustain a congruency among its environment (key success factors), resources (competencies and capabilities) and values (the ability to manage appropriate and timely continuous and discontinuous change). A small reminder of this E–V–R congruence model is provided in the top right corner.

While corporate strategic success is concerned with the mission and purpose of the organization, it will frequently be assessed by financial measures of some form, as highlighted earlier. Long-term strategic success requires that the interests of stakeholders are met, and are seen to be met, is accomplished efficiently with capable resources, and that there is a commitment to the mission reflected in organizational values. The implication is that, in addition to resource efficiency and stakeholder satisfaction, organizations should attempt to measure values to ensure that the culture is appropriate. However, the true complexity of this task is realized when we question whether we really know what the culture of an organization in an era of continuous change – and incorporating periodic restructurings and downsizings – should be like.

In a very turbulent, rapidly changing time what we need to give people is something they can depend on, something lasting. Every company needs to rethink what are the values and what are the operating principles that will be unchanging in time so that we can truly establish a new contract with all employees.

GEORGE FISHER, CHAIRMAN, EASTMAN KODAK

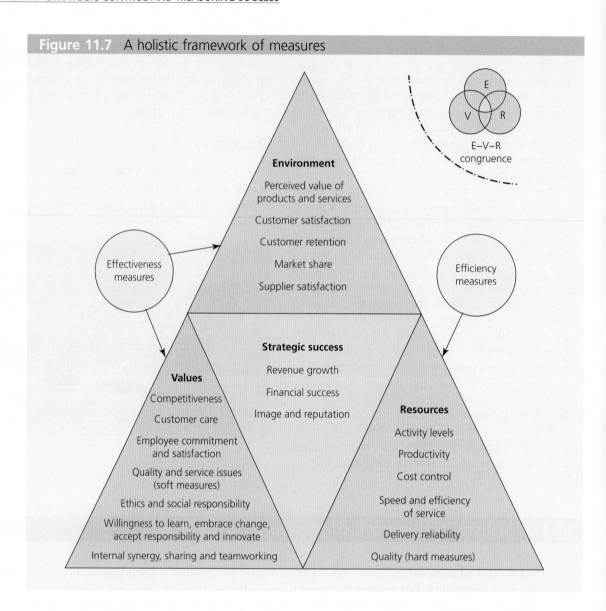

Figure 11.7   A holistic framework of measures

Research can capture a snapshot of currently held values and the extent to which particular behaviour is being manifested, e.g. some organizations will prefer to use volunteers from among the workforce rather than select a sample. The findings should be evaluated against a set of expectancies, and follow-up research can track both positive and negative developments. The organization must then decide what action to take if there is any deterioration or the initial absence of a critical value or behaviour pattern. The Figure 11.7 framework implies a series of both 'hard' and soft' measures and indicators, and some will be straightforward, others far more difficult and subjective. Arguably, the real key to success lies in those issues that are most difficult to assess – not an excuse for not attempting a robust assessment of some form.

Note

Given the rather descriptive and technical nature of this chapter, it does not include a Research Snapshot, whilst issues of performance have been explored in other chapters' Snapshots in specific reference to those particular themes.

Summary

An organization is successful if it is meeting the needs and expectations of its stakeholders, such that their support and commitment are maintained.

Strategically, this definition will imply a clear direction, from which are derived corporate, competitive and functional strategies, the implementation of which brings about the desired results, and needs both common sense and strategic competency.

Measurement matters such that apparent success cannot, and must not, be taken for granted, nor must weaknesses be overlooked, and those issues which really matter must be measured. The act of measurement focuses attention and endeavour on that which is being measured: being brilliant at things that do not really matter to stakeholders will not add and build value.

Some key elements will, through their very nature, be difficult to measure since they are essentially subjective and qualitative issues rather than objective and quantifiable – no excuse to avoid tackling them – and instead we have to rely on indicators rather than measures of performance.

In some cases, attention is focused on efficiency measures, which largely concern the utilization of resources, such as whether or not we are 'doing things right', while measures and indicators of effectiveness look more at outcomes (for stakeholders) and provide a check on whether we are 'doing the right things'.

Most organizations use a raft of quantitative measures, embracing sales and production. Analysts external to the organization, such as students – and lecturers, come to that – will not normally have access to this information to draw conclusions from. However, financial data have to be published and can be used to calculate a number of valuable ratios which provide some insight into organizational performance. In the web supplement to this chapter, investment, performance, solvency and liquidity ratios are explained.

The balanced scorecard provides a comprehensive set of measures which cover stakeholders: finance; customers; internal processes; and growth and improvement.

Issues of admiration, image and reputation can be examined, evaluations that are normally by people inside the relevant industries and, therefore, provide an insight into how organizations are rated by their competitors and peers – but with a short-term focus. Companies that are highly regarded will not necessarily be those with the strongest financial results.

In isolation, therefore, any single (type of) measure must be treated cautiously.

Online cases for this chapter

Online Case 11.1: Lastminute.com
Online Case 11.2: National Health Service (I)

Online Case 11.3: Arsenal Football Club
Online Case 11.4: BTA – British Tourist Authority

Web supplement related to this chapter

Finance in Action: Financial statements

Questions and research assignments

1 The purpose of the Metropolitan Police Service is to: 'uphold the law fairly and firmly; to prevent crime; to pursue and bring to justice those who break the law; to keep the Queen's peace; to protect, help and reassure people in London; and to be seen to do all this with integrity, common sense and sound judgement.'

How might they measure their success?

2 The Royal Charter for the Royal National Institute for the Blind (RNIB), granted originally in 1949, states that the RNIB exists in order to:

- 'promote the better education, training, employment and welfare of the blind;
- protect the interests of the blind; and
- prevent blindness'.

How might they assess how well they are doing?

Internet and library projects

1 In early 2000 Microsoft was judged by the American courts to have been operating as a monopoly and stifling competition. How have its reputation, respect and admiration been affected by this judgement and also by subsequent moves by both the company and the competition authorities in both America and Europe?

Microsoft **http://www.microsoft.com**

2 Select a number of organizations from the 'Admired Company' section of this chapter, picking out ones that interest you personally. Obtain their financial results for at least 2 years which correspond with the admiration rankings. To what extent are financial performance and admiration linked? By also checking the movements in the company's share prices over the same period, does the company's market valuation more closely reflect financial performance or a wider perception of its relative performance?

3 The National Health Service

British Prime Minister John Major announced a new Citizen's Charter in July 1991. This implied a change of attitude for the NHS: patients should be seen as customers with rights, rather than people who should be grateful for treatment, however long the wait. From April 1992 hospitals would have to set standards for maximum waiting times.

This followed on from the 1989 NHS White Paper, Working for Patients, which was designed to achieve:

- raising the performance of all hospitals and general practitioners (GPs) to the level of the best (significant differences existed in measured performances)
- patients receiving better health care and a greater choice of services through improved

efficiencies and effectiveness in the use of NHS resources
- greater satisfaction and rewards for NHS staff.

In subsequent years, how did this impact on NHS strategies?

In 1997 a Labour government was elected and it set about changing the Conservative philosophy, dismantling and replacing a number of strategies.

What was the Labour approach? How have these changes impacted upon performance measurement? How have things changed again with the (new, 2013) policies of the Coalition Government? Can the relative success of the NHS ever be evaluated effectively without imputing political concerns?

4 Research how profitable John Lewis and Waitrose have been in comparison with their major competitors in the last 10 years. What conclusions can you draw?

John Lewis Partnership
http://www.johnlewis.co.uk

Waitrose **http://www.waitrose.com**

5 Find out where your nearest John Lewis or Waitrose store is and if possible visit it. Can you detect any differences in attitude between the John Lewis staff and those who work in similar stores?

John Lewis Partnership
http://www.johnlewis.co.uk

Waitrose **http://www.waitrose.com**

6 In conjunction with the financial analysis exercise at the end of the Web Supplement to which we have referred, determine just how successful in a relative and competitive sense you believe Shepherd Neame to be.

References

Caulkin, S. (1995) The pursuit of immortality, *Management Today*, May.

Drucker, P.F. (1989) What businesses can learn from nonprofits, *Harvard Business Review*, July–August.

Fombrum, C.J. (1996) *Reputation – Realizing the Value from the Corporate Image*, Harvard Business School Press.

Jackson, P. and Palmer, R. (1989) *First Steps in Measuring Performance in the Public Sector*, Public Finance Foundation, London.

Kaplan, R.S. and Norton, D.P. (1992) The balanced score-card – measures that drive performance, *Harvard Business Review*, January–February.

Kaplan, R.S. and Norton, D.P. (1996) *The Balanced Scorecard*, Harvard Business School Press.

Kets de Vries, M. (1996) Leaders who make a difference, *European Management Journal*, 14 (5).

Leadbeater, C. and Rudd, R. (1991) What drives the lords of the deal? *Financial Times*, 20 July.

Lynn, M. (1995) Creating wealth: the best and the worst, *Sunday Times*, 10 December.

May, G.D. and Kruger, M.J. (1988) The manager within, *Personnel Journal*, 67 (2).

RSA (1995) *Tomorrow's Company: The Role of Business in a Changing World*, Royal Society of Arts.

Sadtler, D., Campbell, A. and Koch, R. (1997) *Break-up. When Large Companies are Worth More Dead Than Alive*, Capstone.

Thompson, J.L. and Richardson, B. (1996) Strategic and competitive success – towards a model of the comprehensively competent organization, *Management Decision*, 34 (2).

Chapter 12

Issues in strategic and international growth

PART 1
Understanding strategy

1 What is strategy and who is involved?
- Appendix

2 The business model and the revenue model

3 Strategic purpose
- Supplement: Using frameworks to analyze strategy cases

PART 5
Strategy implementation

14 Strategy implementation and structure

15 Leading change

16 Managing strategy in the organization

17 Final thoughts and reflections: the practice of strategy

STRATEGIC MANAGEMENT: AWARENESS AND CHANGE

PART 2
Analysis and positioning

4 The business environment and strategy

5 Resource-led strategy

6 The dynamics of competition

7 Introducing culture and values

PART 4
Strategic growth issues

11 Strategic control and measuring success

12 Issues in strategic and international growth

13 Failure, consolidation and recovery strategies

PART 3
Strategy development

8 Creating and formulating strategy: alternatives, evaluation and choice

9 Strategic planning

10 Strategic leadership and intrapreneurship: towards visionary leadership?

Learning objectives

Having read to the end of this chapter, you should be able to:

- compare and contrast diversification and acquisition as growth strategies, in terms of alternative forms, geography, motives for and risks of these strategies, as well as effective implementation (**Section 12.1**)

- explain why strategic alliances and joint ventures might be preferable strategic means of growth, again exploring forms, and implementation, plus some additional modes, i.e. franchising and licensing (**Section 12.2**)

- explain what is meant by a global strategy and its importance, different stage models, and issues of effective implementation (**Section 12.3**)

- evaluate the value and relevance of different market entry strategies in an international context (**Section 12.4**)

- discuss a number of constraints and outline a selection of possible future influences on international growth (**Section 12.5**).

Introduction

This chapter explores different forms of growth strategies, both domestic and international, and considers how to manage and implement these strategies effectively. Whilst they are popular alternatives for many companies, particularly larger ones, research suggests that growth strategies often fail to meet expectations: they need careful, thorough and objective analysis before they are pursued, and care and attention in implementation. We explore acquisition, diversification, joint ventures and alliances, as well as – in the international context – alternatives ranging from 'simply' exporting to a fully fledged global strategy and structure. The attractiveness of these alternatives will be influenced by the company's objectives. Some companies will be proactive, others reactive; but not all need to, or should, take advantage of every potential international opportunity. The appropriate strategy will always match the environment, values and resources congruently.

A number of the studies cited in this chapter are rather dated and summarize research from several years back, and are used deliberately, as this foundation research in this topic has been reinforced rather than questioned by later work.

12.1 Diversification and acquisition

As we discussed in Chapter 8, companies can grow organically by investing their own resources to develop new competencies and capabilities and open up new market opportunities; and/or select strategies involving acquisitions, joint ventures (JVs) or strategic alliances (SAs). The latter strategies either involve integration with another company (acquisition) or establishing linkages (JVs/SAs) with a proven supplier with the appropriate competencies and the necessary customers, and which will also typically be faster but often higher risk because the partnerships have to be implemented successfully. Diversification (a route) and acquisition (a means) often go hand-in-hand, and both imply some uncertainty and risks. In addition,

Constable (1986) argues that the high level of strategic energy devoted to these consolidation strategies have created an illusion of real growth, with an emphasis on the shorter-term financial aspects of strategic expertise as opposed to the operational and market-based aspects which are of great significance in the long-term.

If a growth-oriented company faces limited existing markets, as well as barriers to entering international markets, diversification may be an attractive option – but there may already be intense competition in domestic markets which the company considers entering, especially in attractive and profitable industries. Direct entry may thus seem less appropriate than acquiring an existing competitor.

Although as we explored earlier, government policy on competition may restrain particular lines of development for certain companies, such that large firms may diversify into unrelated businesses where there is little apparent threat to the interests of consumers. An ambitious company which has grown large, successful and profitable in a particular industry is perhaps likely to seek diversification while it is strong and has the resources to move into new business areas effectively by acquiring an existing organization rather than growing organically.

In choosing whether to diversify or not, Markides (1997) recommends that organizations should address five key questions:

1   What can we do better than our competitors, around which we should focus and build?

2   What strategic resources are required in the possible new sector(s) or segment(s)? What are the implications of this requirement?

3   Can we beat the competition and become a strong player?

4   Is there a downside risk? In particular, might existing businesses be affected in any detrimental way?

5   What learning potential is there? Can the new business enhance synergy and improve our existing businesses and the organization as a whole? Assuming, of course, that the organization is able to exploit the learning potential.

Endless (high) growth may be a delusion and low growth the norm, such that managing growth wisely is a key managerial skill for organizations and that new business areas should be entered cautiously (Harding and Rovit, 2004; Campbell and Park, 2005). Diversification and acquisition strategies often proving less successful than expected is less likely to be due to the choice of diversification as a strategy but rather because of a poor choice of acquisition target, and implementation problems.

Diversification may be chosen because the existing business is perceived to be vulnerable, perhaps because of its limited growth potential; further investment in internal growth not being justified; threats from new technology; undervaluation by the stock market, leading to them being a takeover target if they do not diversify. Or because a company has developed a particular strength or expertise – whether financial (high cash reserves or borrowing capacity), marketing, technical or managerial – and feels that it could benefit from transferring this asset into other possibly unrelated businesses. If genuine synergy potential exists, both the existing and newly acquired businesses can benefit from a merger or acquisition. A company which has become stale or sleepy, or which has succession problems at the strategic leader level, may see an acquisition as a way of obtaining fresh ideas and new management, apparently more important than how related the businesses are. Sometimes it concerns risk and establishing or restoring an acceptable balance of yesterday's, today's and tomorrow's products in a complex portfolio – especially attractive where a company is relying currently on yesterday's products. Another reason is connected to the ambitions of the strategic leader, who may feel that they can run any type of business successfully regardless of the degree of unrelatedness. Some may be very keen to grow quickly, possibly to avoid takeover, and acquisitions may happen because a company is available for purchase rather than as the outcome of a careful and detailed analysis.

As the major beneficiaries of an acquisition are often the existing shareholders of the company being acquired, some people argue that the self-interest of the City and large institutional shareholders might motivate certain mergers and acquisitions.

Figure 12.1 summarizes related and unrelated diversification opportunities, with its upper section suggesting that the degree of unrelatedness increases when the **tangible resources** involved (both plant and

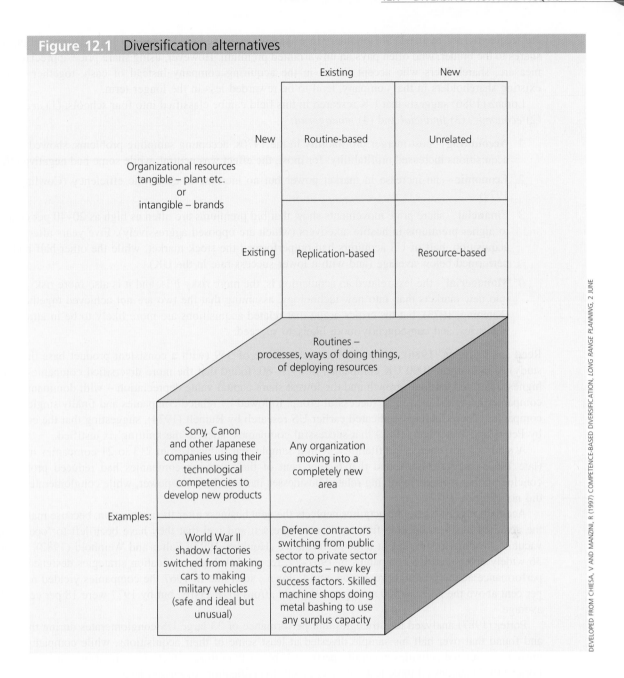

Figure 12.1 Diversification alternatives

equipment and intangible brands) are different rather than similar, and the processes – the ways in which these resources are deployed and utilized – also change. Its lower section provides examples of each situation, and with strategic risk rising, along with the extent of newness and learning.

The relative success of diversification and acquisition

A number of UK and US research studies have investigated the relative success of diversification and acquisition strategies and, despite problems with researching this topic due to the availability of longitudinal data as well as comparing the performance of businesses over time, most of the findings are consistent.

General conclusions from the research suggest that no more than 50 per cent of 'diversification through acquisition' strategies are successful because the synergies that were considered to exist prior to acquisition are frequently not realized. Shareholders in a taken-over or acquired company benefit from selling their shares to the bidder, who often pays an unwarranted premium. However, using share price appreciation as a measure, shareholders who accept shares in the acquiring company instead of cash, together with the existing shareholders in that company, tend to be rewarded less in the longer term.

Lorenz (1986) suggests that UK research in this field can be classified into four schools, (1) *accounting*, (2) *economic*, (3) *financial* and (4) *managerial*:

1 **Accounting** – post-merger profitability in the 1970s, accepting sampling problems, showed that few acquisitions increased profitability: for most, the effect was neutral, while some had negative effects.

2 **Economic** – an increase in market power but no increase in economic efficiency (Cowling *et al.*, 1979).

3 **Financial** – share price movements show that bid premiums are often as high as 20–40 per cent, due to higher premiums in hostile takeovers (which are opposed aggressively). Five years after acquisition, half of US acquirers had outperformed the stock market, while the other half had performed below average (and with a lower success rate in the UK).

4 **Managerial** – the less related an acquisition is, the more risky it is, and it is also more risky to move into new markets than into new technology, assuming that the two are not achieved together (Kitching, 1973), but his critics argue that related acquisitions are more likely to be in attractive industries, and consequently more likely to succeed.

Reed and Luffman (1986), analyzing the performance of 349 (with a consistent product base during the study) of the largest 1000 UK companies in 1970–80, found that the more diversified companies had the highest sales and earnings growth and the lowest share capital value depreciation – with dominant-product companies being the next most successful group, followed by related companies and finally single-product companies. These findings replicated earlier US research by Rumelt (1974), suggesting that the contention by Peters and Waterman (1982) that successful companies 'stick to the knitting' is justified.

A study of post-merger profitability, with a sample that reduced from 213 to 21 companies in 7 years (late 1960s-early 1970s), found that 62 per cent of the surviving companies had reduced profitability, concluding that mergers involving related businesses increased market power, while conglomerate mergers did not (Meeks, 1977).

Acquisitions fail where the acquirer neglects the new business after the acquisition, because managers in the acquired business become frustrated and depressed and feel that they have been left to 'operate in a vacuum', leading to subsequent underperformance (Houlder, 1997). Salter and Weinhold (1982), studying 36 widely diversified US companies in 1967–77, reported that 'diversification strategies designed to raise performance actually brought return on equity down', such that in 1967 the companies yielded returns 20 per cent above the *Fortune* 500 average, and could afford to diversify, but by 1977 were 18 per cent below average.

Porter (1987) analyzed the strategies and performance of 33 large US conglomerates during the 1970s, and found that over half his sample divested at least some of their acquisitions, while companies which moved into related activities generally performed better than those which diversified into unrelated areas. Porter (1987) suggested three tests for successful diversification, discussed later.

McKinsey (1988), documenting the performance of 116 large UK and US companies since 1972, found that 60 per cent failed to earn back the cost of capital on the funds invested in acquisitions, rising to 86 per cent for large unrelated acquisitions. Nesbitt and King (1989) examined the progress of 1800 US companies between 1978–1988, concluding that corporate performance is dependent on strategy implementation rather than the strategy itself: the degree of diversification as opposed to specialization, taken in isolation, has little impact.

Burgman (1985), studying 600 US acquisitions between 1974–1978, found that:

● the higher the premium paid to acquire a company, the less likely it was to be successful

● prospects for success were greater where the acquirer had a functional appreciation of the business being acquired

- success depended upon the ability to retain key managers in the acquired company
- larger acquisitions were often more successful, possibly because the sheer size and financial commitment necessitated a thorough appraisal beforehand.

The studies above and papers by Biggadike (1979) and Kitching (1967) suggest a number of reasons why acquisitions fail, and these are considered below.

A key reason why acquisitions fail is that they do not generate the synergy that was anticipated or at least hoped for, particularly true for conglomerate rather than concentric diversification. In general, companies can more easily gain synergy from production and operations than from marketing, due to difficulties gaining real additional benefit from selling more than one product or service into one market.

In many cases, the real weaknesses of the acquired company are hidden until after the acquisition, and consequently are underestimated, as are the cultural and managerial problems of merging two companies and then running them as one. Insufficient managerial resources may be devoted to the process of merging, such that the hoped-for synergy remains elusive, or the acquirer concludes that skills they planned to transfer in order to generate synergy are unavailable. Key managers responsible for the past growth and success of the acquired company may choose to leave the new conglomerate and thus past successes may not be repeatable.

The amount paid for the acquisition, and the extent of the premium, can have an impact; for example, in a contested takeover where the bidding company has become overenthusiastic and optimistic about the prospects of the acquisition, overstretched itself financially and then cannot afford the necessary investment to generate benefits and growth in the new company.

In order to recoup quickly a premium that has been paid, the acquirer may set high targets initially for the new company and, when these unrealistic targets are missed, enthusiasm may be lost and feelings of hostility may develop. Arguably, if synergy really is available, price is less significant as an issue, and a premium may well be justifiable – but, if an acquisition is fundamentally misconceived, a low or a cheap price will not achieve successful implementation.

Finally, the reaction of competitors may be misjudged, such as the long-established and family-owned Cadbury's that was persuaded by management consultants to believe that 'successful managers can manage anything' and diversified into Schweppes soft drinks (related distribution channels) and the unrelated Jeyes (disinfectants). Jeyes was quickly divested when it became clear that the core chocolate business was suffering as managers became preoccupied with the new activities. Interestingly, the same consultants also persuaded Cadbury's to abandon its paternalistic style of management, manifested in the Bournville village and community which the Quaker family had built for its workforce. When it was still independent, General Accident acquired a related insurance business in New Zealand in 1988 and, as part of the purchase, inherited the NZI Bank whose loan book deteriorated in the worldwide recession and, lacking the necessary turnaround skills, General Accident decided to close the bank.

In reality, acquisition is an uncertain strategy and, no matter how sound the economic justification may appear, implementation or managerial issues ultimately determine success or failure, which are the subject of the next section.

Managing and implementing diversification and acquisition

Where two companies choose to merge, they have an opportunity for a reasonably comprehensive assessment of relative strengths and weaknesses, although one of them may conceal certain significant weaknesses. Even less information will be available in the case of a contested takeover. It is never easy to determine from outside an organization what its style of management is, or its managers' attitude to risks, or how decisions are made, and whether managers are largely self-reliant. In the final analysis, the success of an acquisition or merger will be influenced markedly by the way the companies fit (or do not fit) together, as well as by the logic used to justify the strategy (see Figure 12.2). As a result, financial analysis may be used to justify the acquisition, but it will not answer questions relating to implementation. Table 12.1 highlights significant information that is normally unavailable until after the acquisition.

Figure 12.2   Strategy creation and implementation

Vision

		Good	Poor
Implementation	Good	Effective strategic management	Opportunist and likely to underperform
	Poor	Wasted opportunity	Ill-conceived mistake

BASED ON A MATRIX DEVISED BY BOOZ, ALLEN AND HAMILTON

Key considerations to be addressed by a company before acquiring another are:

- how the acquiring company should restructure itself in order to absorb the new purchase, and thus implications for existing businesses and people
- what the acceptable minimum and maximum sizes are for proposed diversifications in relation to present activities
- what degree of risk it is appropriate for the company to take
- how to value a proposed acquisition and how much to pay
- how to maintain good relationships with key managers during negotiations to try to ensure that they stay afterwards
- how to maintain momentum and interest in both companies after a successful offer
- how quickly to move in merging organizational parts and sorting out problems
- reporting relationships and the degree of independence allowed to the acquired company, particularly where the business is unrelated
- whether and how to send in a new management team.

Table 12.1   Information available before and after an acquisition

Before	After
Organization charts	Inner philosophy and culture
Data on salaries of top management	Real quality of staff in decision roles
Reasonably detailed information on board members and key executives – but only brief details on middle management	Salary and reward structures and systems
	Decision processes
	Interrelationships, power bases, hidden conflicts and organizational politics
Products	Individual objectives being pursued
Plants	
Corporate identity, image and reputation	
Past record, especially financial	

Some of these issues are considered below, where effective acquisition strategies are discussed, but many of them are taken up in later chapters which consider the implementation aspects of strategic change. Figure 12.2 illustrates that an effective strategy is one that is based upon good vision (in relation to its strengths and market opportunities) and sound implementation prospects (i.e. how the two organizations will be merged together and the changes required to structures, cultures and systems in order to achieve their potential synergy). If the logic behind an acquisition is poor, the merged company is likely to underperform, however well the two companies might be managed as one corporate whole. If the vision is good but implementation is weak, under-performance is again likely because synergy will not be created.

If companies develop by a series of acquisitions, typically several banks will become involved, which may be spread worldwide – and, therefore, their cultures and lending philosophies may differ, their levels of exposure will vary, the assets securing the loans will not be the same and certain banks may see themselves as lenders to just one part of, rather than the whole, acquired company. Problems arise if a bank gets into financial difficulties or if the company seeks to extend a loan or adjust the terms.

Effective acquisition strategies

A number of authors have suggested ways of improving the effectiveness of acquisition strategies. Drucker (1982), for example, argues that there are five rules for successful acquisitions:

1 It is essential for the acquiring company to determine exactly what contribution it can make to the acquired company: it must be more than money.

2 It is important to search for a company with a 'common core of unity', say in technology, markets or production processes.

3 The acquiring company should value the products, services and customers of the company that it is taking over.

4 Top management cover for the acquired company should be available in case key managers choose to leave after the acquisition.

5 Within a year, managers should have been promoted across company boundaries.

Business International (1988) offers the following guidelines:

- *Plan first* – As a company, know exactly what you are going to do. Ascertain where the company being acquired has been, and maybe still is, successful, and ensure that it can be maintained – taking special account of any dependence on key people. Appreciate also where it is weak, as it may have good products but overheads which are too high.

- *Implement quickly* – People in the acquired company expect decisive action, and delay prolongs speculation. At the same time, do not act without thinking things through first.

- *Communicate frankly* – Explain the acquisition or merger, the expected benefits and the changes which will be required. In addition, ensure that there is an understanding of the values and expectations of the acquiring company.

- *Act correctly*, particularly as far as redundancy is concerned.

Ramsay (1987) argues that effective acquisition strategies have four stages, which are illustrated in Figure 12.3, and are discussed and unpacked below:

1. *The formulation of a clear strategy* needs to consider how much to concentrate and how much to diversify; build on existing strengths and develop synergy around them, thereby transferring skills and competencies and achieving economies of scale; spot an opportunity and act quickly and decisively to capitalize on it; and match resources (strengths) and opportunities relating to the way the company is managed and to its culture and values.

2. The *search for, and review of, possible acquisitions* needs an active and positive search process, must be realistic and must assess just how resources will be shared, where and how skills will be transferred, and where and how economies of scale will be obtained. Porter (1987) contends that a portfolio of unrelated

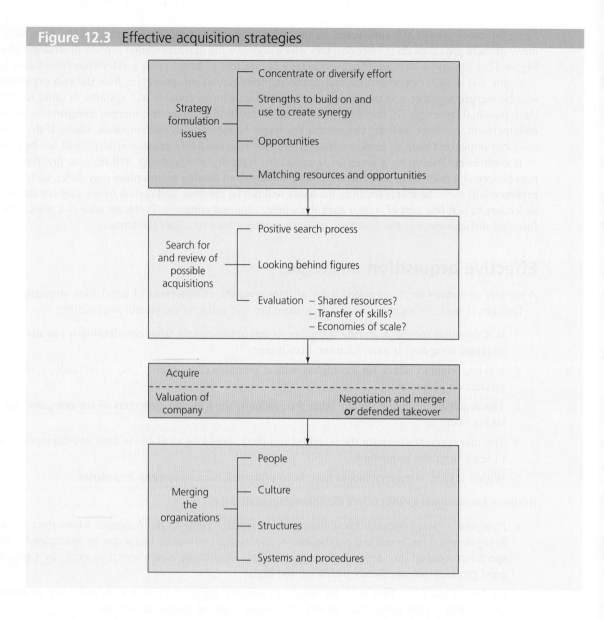

Figure 12.3   Effective acquisition strategies

companies is only a logical corporate strategy if the aim is restructuring (i.e. the strategy pursued by conglomerates), requiring the identification of companies which are underperforming and which can be transformed with new management skills; and argues that three tests should be passed:

(i) The industry involved should be, or could be, made structurally attractive

(ii) The entry cost should not be so high that future profit streams are compromised

(iii) One of the companies should be able to gain competitive advantage, and the newly acquired business should be better off in the new corporation than elsewhere. The interrelationships, based on shared activities and transferred skills, must give added value which outweighs the costs incurred.

Although there was a switch during the 1990s from conglomeration to mergers with a more defensible strategic logic, there has also been a concurrent increase in hostile takeovers because higher premiums are being paid (van de Vliet, 1997). Figure 12.4 pulls these points together diagrammatically. In the context of these arguments, did the acquisition of Jaguar-Land Rover by Tata (Case 12.1) make strategic sense?

Figure 12.4   The effective acquisition

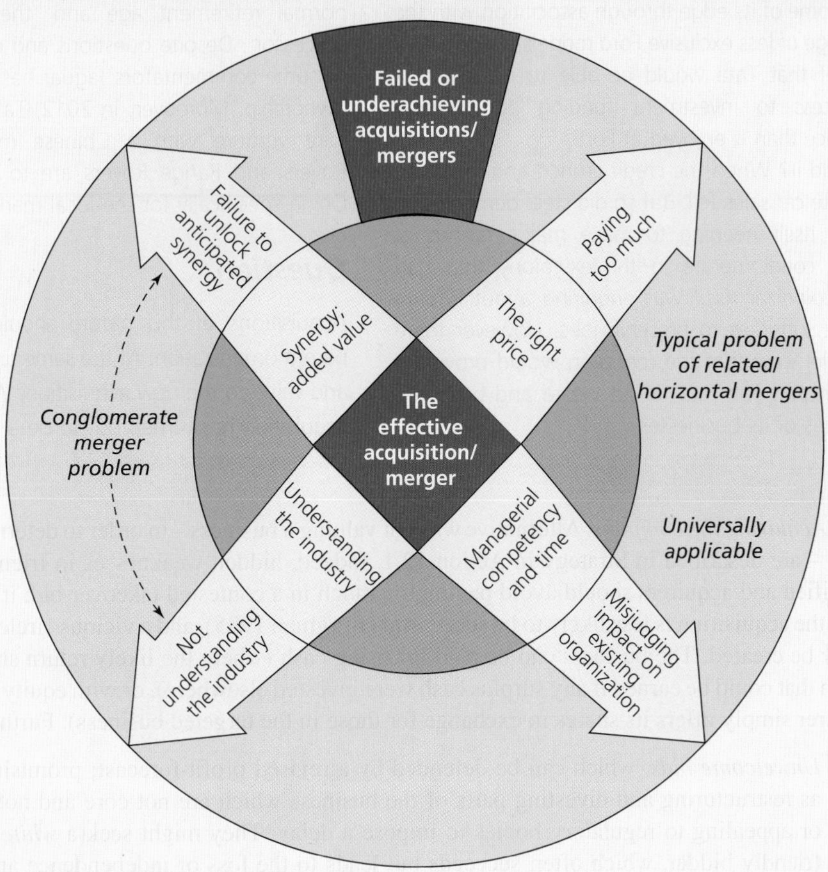

Case 12.1   Tata and the Acquisition of Jaguar   Int

Tata is India's largest conglomerate, with interests spanning tea, motors, steel and software consultancy. It is over 140 years old. It is controlled by three family-run trusts and the CEO is Ranan Tata, who took over from an uncle in 1991. He set about 'modernizing' the conglomerate to 'make it ready for international expansion'. Ranan Tata initially made the group more centralized to bring cohesion to the 90 operating companies around the world. There have since been selective investments – but also disposals – with a general drive to become more international. IT has been developed and used to drive control systems which allow for increasingly decentralized authority.

The international strategy began to really gather pace in 2000.

Tetley tea, bought in 2001, is part of Tata, as are Daewoo Trucks, NatSteel of Singapore (2004) and Teleglobe, the Bermuda-based wholesale telecoms group it bought in 2005. In 2007 Tata paid US$13 billion to acquire the UK's largest steelmaker, Corus. Linked to Corus Tata was keen to develop iron ore mining in South Africa and Canada in order to extend its control of the supply chain. Steel, of course, is a key material for car manufacture.

In 2007 Tata bought Jaguar and Land Rover from Ford of America. This was an interesting move, given Tata's parallel strategy of developing the so-called People's Car, the Tata Nano, the truly low price car discussed in a separate case. Tata really had no previous experience of luxury brands. There were commentators who expressed the view that they could not understand this move. After all, Tata was more used to building rudimentary trucks for relatively poor roads across India.

SOURCE: THIS CASE STUDY WAS PREPARED USING PRIMARILY PUBLICLY AVAILABLE SOURCES OF INFORMATION FOR THE PURPOSES OF CLASSROOM DISCUSSION; IT DOES NOT INTEND TO ILLUSTRATE EITHER EFFECTIVE OR INEFFECTIVE HANDLING OF A MANAGERIAL SITUATION.

Jaguar was thought to be in need of repositioning – it had lost some of its edge through association with the broader range of less exclusive Ford models. There was a stated belief that Tata would be able to offer Jaguar greater access to investment funding and greater independence than it enjoyed at Ford.

But would it? When the credit crunch and recession began to bite car sales fell. But so did steel demand and Tata found itself needing to make major savings at Corus. The conglomerate in the ex-colony that had become a colonizer itself was enquiring about foreign government subsidies to preserve jobs. However there was a parallel view that the recession would provide a good opportunity for Tata to cut waste and build the core strengths of its businesses.

Another problem was that Ranan Tata was past normal retirement age and 'there was no obvious successor'. Despite questions and concerns on the part of some commentators Jaguar has thrived under Tata's ownership. Moreover, in 2012, Tata announced a new joint venture with a Chinese manufacturer – Land Rovers and Range Rovers are to be manufactured in China specifically for the local market.

Question

Acquisitions of this nature should add value to the parent organization. At the same time the parent should add value to the new acquisition. Why do you think this acquisition has turned out to be a 'win-win'?

3. *Acquiring the company.* Alternative ways of valuing a business – in order to determine an appropriate bid price – are described in Strategy in Action 12.1. Indeed, hidden weaknesses in friendly mergers should be identified and acquirers should avoid paying too much in a contested takeover bid: if too high a premium is paid, the acquisition is less likely to be successful (Burgman 1985), and a vicious circle of disillusionment can easily be created. The business can be paid for using cash (where the likely return should exceed either the return that could be earned if any surplus cash were invested elsewhere), or with equity (whereby a predator or acquirer simply offers its shares in exchange for those in the targeted business). Further, there might be:

- *Unwelcome bids*, which can be defended by a revised profit forecast; promising improvements such as restructuring and divesting parts of the business which are not core and not contributing synergy; or appealing to regulatory bodies to impose a delay. They might seek a *white knight*, a preferred friendly bidder, which often succeeds but leads to the loss of independence and, in the absence of a white knight, cash bids are more difficult to defend against than equity bids (Jenkinson and Mayer, 1994). A targeted company may seek the support of its employees or trade unions, on the grounds that their jobs could be affected detrimentally; or may acquire fresh assets to make the acquisition less attractive to the predator but, of course, might have to pay a strategic price later if the bid collapses. These issues are explored further in Strategy in Action 12.2.

Strategy in Action 12.1   Valuing a Company

Acquisition of another company constitutes an investment, although one major strategic objective might be to avoid being taken over by another firm. Whatever the strategic reason, the current value of an organization is important. Assuming that we are not talking about a merger (of assets), a company will normally be acquired when another company buys an appropriate percentage of its shares. While the bid price will always be influenced substantially by their current market price in trading, the likely purchase price in both a hostile and a bidding situation (where more than one prospective buyer is in evidence) will reflect a premium. However, the market price at any time may or may not reflect the value of the organization.

Alternative valuation methods

Rule of thumb

A typical rule of thumb valuation of a company would be to multiply the most recent annual profits (or an average of the last few years) times an x factor. Relatively small x's will be selected for small companies (which have fewer customers and fewer key people) and service businesses, where it is easier for key people to be lost during or after the acquisition. The x factor might vary from three up to 13 for large, established manufacturing businesses.

The balance sheet valuation

The balance sheet value of a company is normally taken from the value of the net assets. Divided by the number of ordinary shares issued, this yields the asset value behind every ordinary share and it can, therefore, be useful in assessing what an appropriate bid price for the ordinary shares might be. However, caution is needed because the balance sheet traditionally records historical costs rather than present values, which can be misleading in the case of property. In addition, although some companies do account for this, the value of such intangible assets as brand names is rarely reflected in the balance sheet.

The market valuation

The market valuation of a company is the number of ordinary shares issued multiplied by their present price plus the inherited debt. This will reflect the likely lowest cost to a buyer, as any bid for shares at a price below their existing price is unlikely to succeed. In reality, the price of shares is likely to increase during the period between when current shareholders realize that a bid is likely, or when one is announced, and when control is finally achieved by the bidder.

The current share price and the asset value of shares should be looked at together.

Earnings potential

Many contend that it is future earnings potential that determines how valuable a company is, not historical results – see, for example, Allen (1988). An analysis of past and current performance is, therefore, limited in its usefulness. In isolation, a high return on capital employed, for example, can hide the reality of an asset base which is declining in real terms. Therefore, one should estimate the future cash flows that the company is capable of generating and discount these by the cost of capital. The current value of the company is determined by this net present value calculation.

The decision to acquire a company, however, will not be based solely on the discounted future earnings, nor the purchase price, but both of these are very important. Future earnings potential for both the acquiring and the acquired companies could be improved with a merger if valuable synergy of some form is derived, and for this potential a premium price might be justified. To a large extent, the price will often be determined by what improvements to the bottom line the acquiring management believe they can achieve.

A multifactor approach

Consequently, Copeland et al. (1990) recommend a five-level valuation approach:

- The first level is the current market value, described above.
- The second level is the earnings potential, the value of the projected cash flow, discounted.
- The third level projects a value once internal improvements have been undertaken. New business processes, for example, could improve the cash flow.
- The fourth level is the value after restructuring, when non-core or poorly performing activities have been sold or divested.
- The fifth level combines level three and four benefits. Significantly, the improvements implied in these three levels may require a fresh management team and style.

References

Allen, D. (1988) *Long Term Financial Health – A Structure for Strategic Financial Management*, Chartered Institute of Management Accountants (CIMA).

Copeland, T., Kotter, T. and Murrin, J. (1990) *Valuation: Measuring and Managing the Value of Companies*, John Wiley.

Strategy in Action 12.2   Hostile Takeovers

In a research sample year (1989) in the UK, there were 161 bids for publicly listed companies; 35 of these were hostile takeover attempts as distinct from agreed or friendly acquisition bids. In one sense, the year was seen as typical: some 70 per cent of the largest acquisitions/takeovers were hostile. Of these, about half will normally succeed; in the other cases, the target company will be able to mount an effective defence strategy.

By contrast, Germany had experienced just three hostile takeover bids since 1945. They are equally rare in France and almost unheard of in Japan. They remain popular in the USA, where a larger number of defence mechanisms are available than is the case in the UK.

Alternative Defence Strategies

(Listed in order of popularity in the UK.)

1   *Financial responses* Companies will hope to be able to announce forthcoming profit improvements – they have been targeted because, although fundamentally competitive and sound, recent profits have been disappointing. They may also seek to revalue their assets to make the bid appear to be undervaluing the true worth of the business.

2   *Legal and political tactics* Political lobbying and attempts to get a bid referred to the competition authorities: the latter, at the very least, to buy time and allow a company to mount a stronger defence.

3   *Attempted white knight bids* An alternative, preferred, outside bidder is sought.

4   *Corporate restructuring* Typically, disposals are announced. Bidders will claim that attempts to rationalize and downsize, while appropriate and desirable, have been provoked by the bid and are indicative of reactive senior management. Sometimes the strategic leadership will attempt to mount a management buy-out as an alternative to the outside bid.

5   *Poison pills* This strategy, most popular in the USA, describes shareholder rights plans which effectively increase the price to the bidder. An example would be preferentially priced stock being available to existing shareholders, giving them a later right to new ordinary shares. Similarly, the term *golden parachutes* describes special departure terms for directors in the event of an unwelcome acquisition.

In 1999, for example, American Airlines (linked to Canadian Airlines and allied with British Airways in the Oneworld alliance) was interested in bidding for Air Canada, which was experiencing financial difficulties. However, Air Canada was part of the Star Alliance, dominated by American's main rival, United Airlines. A poison pill was in evidence – whoever might own Air Canada, it would remain a member of the Star Alliance for 10 years or United and its partners would be entitled to huge damages. The presence of this arrangement was sufficient to deter American Airlines.

Outcomes

In general, a well-formulated and strategically logical bid for a poor performer should succeed; a strong performer will clearly be in a stronger position to defend itself and its record. However, in isolation, a strong financial performance is not everything – simply, there may appear to be more strategic logic in the business being parented by the bidder instead of staying as it is.

Cash bids have the greatest likelihood of success. In 1989, 21 per cent of the 161 bids were equity based and just 11 per cent of these succeeded; 43 per cent were cash only with a 56 per cent success rate; the remaining 36 per cent were mixed cash/equity bids and 53 per cent of these succeeded. Normally, the value of a hostile bid will be increased once the nature and robustness of the defence is revealed.

Cash bids are most likely to fail if an alternative white knight bidder is found. The likelihood of the success of equity and mixed bids appears to depend upon the quality of the financial defence.

Source

Jenkinson, T. and Mayer, C. (1994) *Hostile Takeovers: Defence, Attack and Corporate Governance,* McGraw-Hill.

- *Abandoned discussions* where merger talks fail for a number of different reasons due to problems involved in creating a partnership, strategic leadership differences, being blocked by shareholders who feel left out of the process, or a collapse of trust (Walton and McBride, 1998).

4. *Post-acquisition activities.* The nature of the post-acquisition challenge depends upon the type of acquisition and the objectives behind it, which include, as identified by Ernst and Young (1995):

  (i) *financial acquisitions* brought into a **holding company**, sometimes for the purpose of restructuring, and implementation issues concern timing and decisiveness

  (ii) *geographical acquisitions*, expanding the acquirer's core business across new frontiers, with problems merging different country cultures and job losses in the acquired business being the key challenges

  (iii) *symbiotic acquisitions*, where newly acquired products and competencies are absorbed into the parent's business but the acquired company retains some independence, where the establishment of an appropriate new structure, culture and communications system are the implementation issues

(iv) *absorption acquisitions*, where the two businesses are fully integrated, with one effectively losing its identity, being challenging to implement as everything changes.

For any acquiring company to gain financially, sales must be increased and costs reduced to a level which compensates for any price premium paid, which researchers suggest is rarely less than 20 per cent. Merging two organizations involves decisions about the integration of strategic capabilities, in particular operating resources (sales forces, production facilities), functional skills (product development, research and development) and general management skills (strategy development, financial control, human resource strategies). There needs to be a strategy for the implementation, ideally developed after the merger or acquisition when fuller details are available, in particular concerning (i) people, (ii) culture and (iii) structure and systems.

(i) Many chief executives and other senior managers leave acquired companies either immediately or within 1 to 2 years after the acquisition, especially after hostile takeovers.

(ii) Different cultures must be reconciled.

(iii) As also addressed in Chapter 14, when companies become larger and more complex, they must be broken down into business units, and managers must be given some degree of independence – to motivate them and to ensure that functional and competitive strategies can be adapted in response to environmental changes. However, if activities are to be shared, or skills transferred, independence must not inhibit, or even prohibit, the implementation of the necessary interdependencies.

In summary, first, the price paid for an acquisition should reflect its acquirer's ability to add value, share resources and transfer skills. Second, its strategy should be soundly based, and the potential synergy real rather than imagined. Third, post-acquisition management should recognize that, while changes must be made to add value, two cultures must be integrated if the strategy is to be implemented effectively.

Finally, five factors for implementing acquisitions and mergers successfully are:

1 Tread warily and carry out sufficient analysis – especially where there is a hostile reaction from the target.

2 Evaluate any prospective partner fully, carrying out a culture and style assessment as well as a financial evaluation.

3 Take on board the best practices from both (all) businesses to increase the prospects for synergy. It is highly unlikely that one partner will have a monopoly on good ideas.

4 Communicate with those people affected to the maximum extent that is expedient.

5 Ensure that key people are identified and stay.

12.2 Strategic alliances and joint ventures

Partnership can be one of the quickest and cheapest, but also toughest and riskiest, ways to grow or develop a new (and perhaps global) strategy. Many alliances fail, since the needs of both partners must be met and, consequently, the *why*, the *who* and the *how* must be answered satisfactorily:

1 *Why* use an alliance?

2 *Who* to select as a partner?

3 *How* to implement the agreement?

Many European companies have conceived alliances from a defensive perspective rather than as a proactive growth opportunity (Garrette and Dussauge, 1999), or they may be a fall back when the competition authorities stand in the way of a merger or acquisition. It is important to note that several successful American and Japanese companies have taken a different view and favoured alliances.

An online case shows how British Airways (BA) has used both mergers and alliances, together with both proactive and reactive strategies for its alliances, in an ongoing attempt to create the world's first truly global airline.

Although strategy authors are still arguing over the meaning and definition of the terms 'joint venture' and 'strategic alliance', we consider a **strategic alliance** to be all forms of agreement between partners, and a **joint venture** to be those agreements which involve either the establishment of a new, independent company owned jointly by the partners, or the minority ownership of the other party by one or both partners.

The term *consortium* is also used in this context, e.g. where companies in an industry generally collaborate or share, perhaps through a trade association. The Japanese *keiretsu* (or family of businesses) is another, quite different example where companies, often in a geographical cluster, own stakes in each other and share and collaborate wherever possible, perhaps by intertrading or by seconding staff to help with a particular problem or difficulty.

An alliance (or joint venture) could involve:

1 direct competitors, possibly sharing common skills, and with the objective of increased market share

2 less direct competitors with complementary skills, where the intention is more likely to be benchmarking and learning for mutual benefit, and possibly developing new ideas

3 related companies sharing different skills and competencies and, although they might be within the same added-value chain (e.g. a manufacturer and either a supplier or a distributor), the alliance should generate synergy through co-operation, innovation and lower costs, while allowing each partner to concentrate on its core competencies.

Thus companies can increase competitive advantage without either merger or acquisition and, moving from an alliance to a joint venture and from 1 to 3 in the above hierarchy, the significance increases for the partners involved. Some companies will be involved in several alliances with different companies at the same time. For instance, Toshiba has created a global network of allies for different products and technologies (including Alstom, Siemens, Ericsson, General Electric, Motorola, Time Warner and Apple), seeing this 'circle of friends' as an opportunity to share ideas to obtain the latest technology and to gain competitive advantage through learning.

Case 12.2 describes how Yorkshire Water adopted an onion strategy to allow it to concentrate more on its core service competencies, and the necessary learning curve it faced, since the company needed to form a network of partnerships and develop capabilities in managing such a network.

Case 12.2 Yorkshire Water's Onion Strategy   UK

Since being privatized in 1989 most of the ten water companies in the UK have pursued diversification strategies. The core business activities are water supply and the management of waste water (i.e. sewage treatment). Prices and quality standards are closely regulated, and consequently the diversification is aimed at offsetting the perceived risks and constraints inherent in regulated businesses. The most popular activity has been waste management, the collection and disposal of industrial and domestic waste. For example, Severn Trent Water acquired Biffa, and Wessex formed a joint venture with Waste Management of the USA, one of the world's largest companies in the industry. South Staffordshire diversified into Homeserve, which organizes plumbing services for clients who take out insurance policies with them. Yorkshire Water developed a similar business but sold it to South Staffs. Homeserve has been split off from its original parent and is thriving.

After privatization Yorkshire Water (YW) basically created two separate, but linked, businesses: Yorkshire Water Services to control the core businesses, and Yorkshire Water Enterprises, later renamed Yorkshire Environmental Solutions, for other commercial ventures. Eventually these would become a £1 billion business. In recent years Yorkshire Water has been renamed Kelda and acquired by a private equity company. The holding company has three subsidiaries: Yorkshire Water itself (turning over some £700 million); Kelda Water Services (what was Yorkshire Water Enterprises and turning over some £100m); and Keyland Development (property, £20 million). A fourth company, Aquarion, has been divested – as explained below.

Kelda continues to be focused on water and waste management, with Yorkshire Water providing core services in the Yorkshire Region and Kelda Water Services operating water and waste management contracts and private finance initiatives primarily for other water companies throughout the UK.

Yorkshire Water Enterprises (now Kelda Water Services)

This business became active in the following areas:

- *Waste management* – Industrial effluents and clinical waste. This was sold in 1998 to Waste Recycling, but Yorkshire Water (YW) retained a 49 per cent shareholding in the enlarged Waste Recycling business – until it was sold off completely.
- *Engineering consultancy and support* – A joint venture with Babcock International. Since 1989 YW have been investing in treatment plants (mainly) and water-distribution networks, the latter to free up engineering resources which the joint venture would seek to deploy and exploit. This was sold to Earthtec.
- *'Pipeline Products'* – The sale of existing stores items to external customers – now a ceased activity.
- *'Waterlink'* – A network of approved subcontractor plumbers. YW provided an arrangement service before selling the business to South Staffordshire Water. This business is now part of Spice Holdings which also embraces a number of other related activities.
- *Laboratory services* – Providing analytical services and environmental testing to a range of businesses and agencies – before being sold.
- *Loop* – A separate subsidiary to provide customer service management, billing, payment and debt collection. Services are sold to external customers; control lies with Yorkshire Water.
- *Management training* – Primarily exploiting existing markets and competencies. This has also been stopped.
- Keyland Developments – Property development and representing 'real' diversification. This continues and is focused on maximizing the value of Kelda and Yorkshire Water assets.

The Director General of OFWAT, the industry regulator, always emphasized that he was not going to ignore these strategic developments. 'Customers of core services must not be affected adversely.' For example, the water companies were prevented from selling services from the associated businesses to the core at contrived prices which benefited shareholders at the expense of captive water customers. In addition, 'the required investment funds for the water supply services must not be put at risk'.

Yorkshire Water Services

YW stated quite early that it did not intend to build and then manage a diversified corporation. Once the appropriate business had been constructed, with YW's resources deployed effectively, the layers would be peeled away systematically – an onion focus strategy – until only the core business remained. The defined core activity was *water delivery*, which incorporated the removal of sewage and water treatment. The pursuit of this strategy entailed divesting certain non-core or support activities into either wholly owned subsidiaries or independent contractors (in properly negotiated alliances), and possibly more joint ventures, but only where there were providers able to deliver the range and quality of services.

Four alternative implementation approaches for this strategy are illustrated below.

The services divested by YW are also highlighted. Where there were agreements with multiple outside contractors (Approaches 2 and 3), separate geographical regions were typically the predominant logic. For example, the pipework to sewage treatment works was initially divested to individual local authorities.

This corporate onion strategy aims to improve a company's competitiveness with the premise that non-core services can invariably be acquired more effectively from an experienced outside provider, selected because it already has competitive advantage. It is essential to define the core carefully and to establish the appropriate ongoing relationships in order to minimize risk. The order and timing of each divestment is also an important issue. The company benefits because it can concentrate on its core activities; it has access to a wider skill and resource base, which should promote best practice, enable greater service flexibility and lead to overall quality improvements. Resources should match needs more effectively. In addition, clearer accountability should foster cost reductions, and the introduction of controlled competition should enhance the quality of in-house service provision and act as a catalyst for change throughout the organization. YW, for example, set up contracts to buy all the pipes that would be needed by its contractors. The contractors were then able to take advantage of the favourable prices negotiated, but they bought the pipes and held the inventory. To implement this strategy successfully the central organization must develop competency in network management. Effective partnership sourcing such as this requires unambiguous long-term agreements, clear performance measures and shared risk. It is most appropriate where the service is a core activity for the contracted supplier. The partners should engage in ongoing dialogue and maybe even exchange personnel periodically.

However, in the mid-1990s a summer drought caused Yorkshire Water considerable embarrassment. Public relations were clumsy; the managing director suggested people could easily wash with just a basin of water as opposed to having a bath, for example. The company ended up hiring road transporters to move water from different parts of Yorkshire to its own reservoirs, but supplies were never cut off. In the end the chairman and managing director both retired and, with a new strategic leader, the parent company was then renamed Kelda. The company bought Aquarion, an American water company, in 2000. Since then this New England business was active acquiring related businesses in other New England states. However the potential returns were always limited by US regulations and the business was consequently sold on.

When YW started with this onion strategy the supplier market was relatively immature and considerable learning took place. YW came to realize that it was difficult to drive innovation when it relied extensively on independent suppliers, and so it needed to rethink aspects of the strategy to make sure this could happen. It also became apparent that if efficiency improvements were to be driven then it needed YW to find ways of rewarding 'high performers' at the expense of poorer performers. YW also realized that it needed to be able to exercise some control over work planning and scheduling of critical activities, even if they were provided by external organizations and this also had to be tackled as an issue. In recent years most other water companies have followed a similar route and the market has become more mature. There have been new entrants and consolidation. Basically the trend over the time this onion strategy has evolved has been to reduce the number of contractors, to enable stronger, and more strategic, alliances to be developed.

Four alternative onion-focus strategies applied in Yorkshire Water Services

Strategy 1

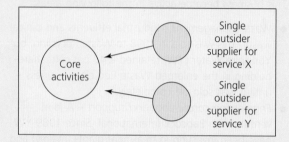

Examples: Fleet services and laboratory services.

Strategy 2

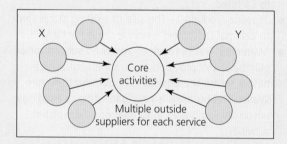

Examples: Electrical and mechanical maintenance; repair and maintenance.

Key success factor: Partnership sourcing, establishing firm alliances with each supplier.

The suppliers were generally based in specific geographic locations and looked after a 'territory'. The most efficient were rewarded in two ways. First any financial benefits from beating agreed targets were shared with Yorkshire Water. Second their territory was increased in size at the expense of poorer performers.

Strategy 2 became the dominant and preferred model of the four alternatives.

Strategy 3

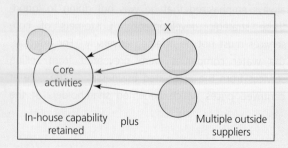

Objective: Develop the in-house capability into a centre of excellence.

Example: Waste detection.

This model was only applied sparingly. Sewage management – the pipework to the sewage treatment works – was given over to local authority control, but it has since been taken back in-house.

Strategy 4

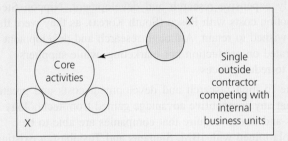

Objective: Form an alliance with an outside expert and benchmark to drive internal improvement.

In the end this model was abandoned quite quickly and absorbed into Strategy 2.

In 2000 Kelda announced a radical proposal. It indicated intent to sell all of its physical assets (pipes, sewage works and reservoirs) to a new mutual company, which would be owned by Kelda's customers and financed with debt capital. Kelda would simply lease back the assets and employ contractors. Other activities would also be sold to leave a water *services* company. Environmental groups, customers and the water regulator all opposed the plan, which was subsequently abandoned.

Water meter reading is one key activity that was contracted out but has been brought back in-house – as much as anything to drive improvement and innovation. Yorkshire Water has also used its experience to form relevant alliances outside the water industry. For example it has looked to expertise developed for the oil industry to drive innovations in water leak detection.

Questions

Can alliance-based networks such as the one developed (and proposed) by Yorkshire Water deliver the equivalent or even greater value to customers than a company which owns and manages all of its activities?

Footnote

Michael Smith, retired Director of Human Resources, has provided invaluable support in clarifying the specific details described in this case.

Reasons for joint ventures and strategic alliances include the cost of acquisition being too high, or legislation preventing acquisition (in cases where the larger size is required for critical mass), or political or cultural differences meaning that an alliance is the most likely approach that would facilitate integration. The increasing significance of a total customer service package suggests linkages through the added value chain – to secure supplies, customize distribution and control costs – while at the same time individual companies may prefer to specialize in those areas where they are most competent. Furthermore, the threat from Japanese competition has driven many competitors, who do not wish to merge, into closer collaboration; such as American and European car manufacturers who have taken stakes in Japanese businesses where outright acquisition is unlikely. Covert protectionism in certain markets necessitates a joint venture with a local company, particularly in China, one of the world's fastest growing economies.

The likely outcomes of joint ventures and strategic alliances include increased competency, synergy, a stronger global presence, greater innovation from the pooling and sharing of ideas and competencies, lower costs (through a virtuous circle of learning where each partner learns new skills and competencies from one another) and access to new markets and technologies. In short, an alliance is a means to an end, since it is not necessarily a permanent arrangement, and can be changed as time goes on. Indeed, Connell (1988) contends that companies collaborate strategically for three primary reasons:

1 To gain access to new markets and technologies as markets become increasingly international. In 1989 Pilkington, the UK float glass manufacturer, sold 20 per cent of its US vehicle glass subsidiary (which supplied the Toyota plant in the USA) to Nippon Sheet Glass (Japan). Pilkington had 17 per cent of the world market for vehicle glass at the time, Asahi (Japan) 19 per cent and Nippon already had 9 per cent. Nippon and Pilkington gained respective access to the US and Japanese markets.

2 To share the costs and risks of increasingly expensive research and development. Nippon Steel developed an alliance designed to cut production costs with Posco (South Korea), as they were the world's largest steelmakers, a position they wished to retain. Although research and development resources were pooled, they neither collaborated on production nor marketing, while suppliers suggested that they might use their alliance to reduce prices.

3 To manage innovation more effectively, due to high research and development costs and greater globalization, which together often ensure that any competitive advantage gained from technology is relatively short-lived. Both the opportunities and threats require that companies are able to be flexible and change quickly. In 1995 Motorola joined with IBM, Siemens and Toshiba (an existing alliance) to develop the next generation of advanced memory chips, which have always been highly complex and extremely costly to develop and make.

Two more recent alliances in 2008 appear to address all three reasons: Peugeot and Mitsubishi started working together on the development of motors for electric cars, and Bosch and Samsung formed a 50:50 joint venture to develop, manufacture and sell automotive lithium-ion batteries.

A fourth reason is, arguably, to attempt to regain lost competitiveness in a marketplace – believed to have spawned a series of agreements among European electronics manufacturers, and links between them and Japanese and US competitors.

While there are a number of reasons and justifications for such strategic alliances, they can be difficult strategies to implement effectively, as shown later in the chapter.

Forms and examples of strategic alliances and joint ventures

Strategic alliances and joint ventures can take a number of forms, six being illustrated below, which are not mutually exclusive, as some joint ventures cover more than one:

1 Component parts of two or more businesses might be merged. Case 10.7 illustrated the opportunity that Jim McColl grasped to conduct a management buy-in to Clyde Blowers which, funded by its bank, acquired six of its worldwide competitors for a total of £33.2m, thus achieving a new market share of over 50 per cent when the market share had previously been 8 per cent. Clyde Blowers also acquired a number of materials handling businesses, leading to the creation of a new division, Clyde Bergemann Power, with a total spend of £25.7m. Clyde Blowers rationalized its activities, simplified product lines and reduced manpower by 43 per cent, what McColl described as 'a classic MBA textbook strategy'.

2 Companies might agree to join forces to develop a new project. Philips and Nintendo jointly developed a new generation of video games on compact discs (CDs) compatible with Philips' CD-i (compact disc-interactive) players, which linked up to high-definition televisions. Nintendo went on to develop the Wii with its wireless controller and the Wii remote which can be used as a handheld pointing device to detect movement in three dimensions. Psion, the UK manufacturer of palm-size computers and electronic organizers, joined forces with the world's largest mobile telecommunications companies, Nokia, Motorola and Ericsson, to develop Internet-linked mobile phones and other products which use WAP (wireless application protocol) technology – an alliance that was perceived

to be a means of counteracting the power of Microsoft in one of the fastest growing areas of the computing industry. More recently, Nokia and Microsoft's strategic alliance has led to the development of the Nokia Lumia series of mobile phones, with Nokia changing from its Symbian operating system to Windows Phone 7 and later 8, with always the possibility of a 'blockbuster' future product emerging from this alliance.

3   Companies might agree to develop a new business jointly. Cereal Partners Worldwide is a joint venture designed to strengthen market access for the two companies involved – General Mills, an American rival to Kellogg's, which had developed a number of popular products (particularly Cheerios) but was not geared up to distribute them outside America, and Nestlé which owned a formidable distribution network and could provide access to most of Europe but had earlier tried to break into this industry without any marked success.

4   There might be specific agreements between manufacturers and their suppliers. American Express (AMEX), like many other large corporations, had a travel department which organized the global travel arrangements for its managers, a competency which it now provides as a service to other corporations who prefer to outsource this task; and AMEX has since moved into consumer travel as well.

5   A company might make a strategic investment in another firm. British Telecom (BT) has used minority stakes and joint ventures as its path to a global presence, for example becoming the second largest competitor in Sweden, France, Germany, the Netherlands, Spain, Portugal and Italy. BT, which has the most extensive portfolio of assets in the European telecommunications industry, claims that acquisitions were 'never on the cards' but does not rule out increasing its stake in the partner organizations.

6   Companies might form international trading partnerships. Disney Corporation, McDonald's and Coca-Cola, owners of three of the most powerful brands in the world, have a loose partnership which varies from country to country depending upon how local managers wish to exploit its potential:

● McDonald's is Coca-Cola's largest customer and buys its soft drinks exclusively from Coca-Cola
● McDonald's sponsors activities and exhibits at Disney attractions, as well as running restaurants on site
● Disney collaborates with McDonald's on special worldwide promotions which feature Disney characters, especially when new movies are released
● Coca-Cola is also the sole supplier of soft drinks to Disney's theme parks.

Key issues in joint ventures and strategic alliances

Various authors have examined the relative success of alliances and joint ventures. Kanter (1990) suggests that key success factors include the strategic importance for both partners of the alliance/joint venture, combining complementary (not the same) competencies, open information sharing, 'genuine' integration despite cultural differences which requires trust, and which should have some sort of formal institutional framework, management of which would be a strategic capability. Ohmae's (1989) aspects of effective implementation include: (i) mutual commitment of resources and time to the collaborative arrangement, with the brightest and the best management being moved into the alliance or 'seconded', (ii) mutual benefits which may cause some 'sacrifices' to each partner, rather than any sort of unbalanced partnership, (iii) flexibility to deal with emergent changes throughout the alliance's existence and (iv) aligning, or resolving, any variations in organizational or national cultures. Alliances enable learning, and a distinction can be made between 'migratory knowledge', for example capabilities that can be transmitted in a straightforward manner, and more deeply 'embedded knowledge' (such as trade secrets and expertise), which helps partners to understand new markets (Badaracco, 1991).

Like acquisitions, joint ventures and strategic alliances should be evaluated in terms of their ability to generate synergy. The strategic wisdom behind the decision to form an alliance in the first place, the choice of partner, and the management of the alliance once it has been agreed are other critical success factors

(Devlin and Bleackley, 1988). Both partners should improve their position as a result of their alliance and, if synergy truly exists, joint ventures can effectively enable the implementation of strategic change. However, although some of the inherent difficulties of acquisition are avoided by this type of agreement, implementation issues exist which, if not tackled properly, will make the joint venture expensive and tie up resources which might otherwise be deployed more effectively.

Alliances can fail and/or be dismantled for various reasons and thus the extent to which any organization is dependent upon its alliances should be carefully monitored.

Franchising and licensing

Two other means of growing the organization avoid the risks and pitfalls of acquisitions and joint ventures, but still require relationship building and trust:

1. **Franchising** takes many forms, providing established businesses with an opportunity for rapid growth and franchisees with a relatively low risk means of starting a small business with an already established brand and an extant market if they have sufficient investment capital. A number of small independent businesses can, therefore, operate as part of a chain and can compete against larger organizations. Service businesses are more common than manufacturing in franchising, e.g. Tie Rack, a retail organization which has concentrated on specific market segments and grown rapidly with franchising, as have Thornton's chocolate shops, Prontaprint printing and copying shops and the British School of Motoring, plus Subway (Case 12.3), Kentucky Fried Chicken, Burger King and Spud-U-Like. A company which chooses franchising as a means of strategic growth enters into contractual arrangements with a number of small businesses, usually one in each selected geographical area. In return for a lump sum initial investment and ongoing royalties, the typical franchiser provides exclusive rights to supply a product or service under the franchiser's name in a designated area, know-how, equipment, materials, training, advice and national support advertising – thus allowing the business to grow rapidly in a number of locations without the investment capital which would be required to fund organic growth of the same magnitude. Another advantage for the franchiser is alleviation of the need to develop managers, such that efforts can be concentrated on expanding market share. Effective monitoring and control systems must be established to ensure that franchisees are providing the necessary level of quality and service. Franchising would appear to offer valuable opportunities to Ajisen Ramen (Case 11.2), which you might like to review in this context.

Case 12.3   Fred DeLuca and Subway   US

Many entrepreneurial businesses and fortunes have been built with franchising – McDonald's is an excellent example. However, by 2003, McDonald's had been overtaken by Subway in terms of the largest number of fast-food outlets in America. The company has also grown overseas – and all of it through franchising.

The company, which sells freshly made sandwiches and salads to order – its trademark is the long 'submarine' roll – was started in 1965 by the 17 year old Fred DeLuca, in partnership with a family friend – and nuclear physicist – who invested $1000. The first sandwich shop struggled, but it survived and was joined by a second and then a third. By 1968 DeLuca owned five outlets. In 1974 he switched to franchising. Rapid growth followed such that 200 outlets in 1981 became 5000 in 1990 and 11000 in 1995. In 1983 Subway outlets began baking all their own bread.

Subway is successful for a number of reasons:

- It is simple – an easy model to replicate
- It is innovative. Menus are changed constantly with new breads as well as fillings
- There is distinct advantage in the healthy option sandwiches and salads
- It has a very clear focus and business model. Franchisees are not creators of new ideas; rather they are there to deliver products and service. Their overheads are low because the franchisor supplies most of the

equipment they need. Franchisees organize their own local food purchases – which is quite different from the way many franchised fast-food outlets are supplied with centrally sourced materials.

Questions

1 Was franchising the most logical growth route for Subway? Why? Why not?
2 What do you think are the key competencies and capabilities for managing international growth of this magnitude using franchising?

2. **Licensing** is an arrangement whereby a company is allowed to manufacture a patent-protected product or service which has been designed by someone else, possibly in a different country. Pilkington, for example, patented float glass and then licensed its production throughout the world and earned money from the arrangements and established world leadership, whereas they could not have afforded to establish production plants around the world. In contrast, Mary Quant, designer of cosmetics, tights, footwear, beds and bed linen, never manufactured the products she designed, as they were all licensed and some were marketed under the Quant name and some under the manufacturer's name (e.g. Myers beds and Dorma bed linen). Licensing also provides an ideal opportunity for the owners of valuable **intellectual capital** to earn revenues from their knowledge-based resource without having to invest in manufacturing. One argument in favour of licensing has been that production and labour relations problems are avoided, enabling the business to focus on its expertise and competitive advantage.

The role of private equity funds

Private equity funds appear to be the new conglomerates, as they seek to acquire struggling businesses (usually as a whole) or buy selected parts of existing businesses that the current owners are happy to divest, put in a new management team (often described as a management buy-in), turn them around and prepare them for flotation. Their logic is to borrow money at competitive rates and seek to earn a handsome return from the flotation in a relatively short period of time. A number of success stories bear out the logic of this approach, with the Debenhams Strategy activity (at the end of this chapter) providing an example.

However, private equity funders have been criticized and accused of 'job cutting and asset stripping'. Although many of the businesses they target are under-performing, analysis of the largest businesses currently owned by private equity funds at the end of 2007, tracking back to when they had been acquired, suggested that they had created jobs and increased the investment in fixed assets, and had increased productivity and value added, well ahead of the UK average (see Arnold, 2009). Although such a study may appear credible, it is nonetheless only one study, and perhaps the jury is still out on the socio economic contribution of private equity.

12.3 Global strategy

In future we will have local [retail] companies and global companies and not much in-between. Globalization pressures will lead to those who are not in the first division and those who are purely national to make alliances.

DAVID BERNARD, CHAIRMAN, CARREFOUR HYPERMARKETS

Growth strategies may involve a complex international dimension, since countries differ economically (e.g. variable growth rates), culturally (behaviours, tastes and preferences) and politico-legislatively (markets that cannot be penetrated effectively without joint ventures with local companies). International organic growth strategies include exporting to new markets overseas, or developing special varieties of a product or service in order to target it to the specific needs and requirements of overseas customers. Alternatively, they could establish distribution or assembly bases, joint ventures and licensing agreements with foreign companies, or a comprehensive global organization through acquisition or strategic alliances. Kay (1990) recommends that they should determine the smallest area within which they can be a viable competitor; e.g. while a retail newsagent can succeed by concentrating on a local catchment area, many other industries and service businesses see their relevant market as a global one. The term *multinational* is generally applied to any company which produces and distributes in two or more countries, while a *transnational* global corporation is one with a large proportion of its sales, assets and employees outside its home base. Using these criteria, Nestlé is the most global business in the world.

Porter (1990) believes that **global strategies** essentially supplement the competitive advantage created in the home market. Wickham (2001) indicates that there are six main types of competitive advantage:

- a lower price than competitors
- features or performance that differentiates the product offering
- better service
- branding
- brand imagery
- better distribution and easier access to the product.

Firms can achieve sustainable competitive advantage and achieve a higher profit by being the *low cost* producer in the industry (Lynch, 2000), or by a *differentiation* strategy with more reliable products and better levels of service, or *focus* where the business seeks to achieve a competitive advantage in specific target segments. As well as these three generic strategies, Porter (1990) contended that firms must retain their national strengths when they cross national borders, whilst Ohmae (1990) argued that global firms should shake off their origins with managers adopting an international perspective, avoiding the near-sightedness which often characterizes companies with centralized and powerful global headquarters. He suggests that markets are driven by the needs and desires of customers around the world, and managers must act as if they are equidistant from all these customers, wherever they might be located (ibid), perhaps a futuristic vision of how things may become as global forces strengthen.

Chandler (1990) stresses the continuing importance of *economies of scale* (which are cost advantages with large-scale production) and *economies of scope* (involving the use of common materials and processes to make a variety of different products profitably), since they imply carefully targeted investment in large-scale operations and a search for international marketing opportunities.

The competitive, growth and internationalization strategies of Galanz and Haier were discussed in earlier cases and again you might like to revisit them.

Definitions of internationalization

As with many other academic concepts, definitions of *internationalization* are contested, incoherent, inconsistent and varied. However, the concept could, for example, be defined as: 'an approach to management which allows an organization to integrate domestic and international opportunities with internal resources' (Yanacek, 1988). Alternatively, international business can be said to consist of transactions that are devised and carried across national borders to satisfy the objectives of individuals, companies and organizations, with primary types of international business being export-import trade and direct foreign investment (Czinkota *et al.*, 2005).

Internationalization research originates from studies in the 1960s on the nature of export behaviour, when the promotion of an 'international outlook' or 'internationalization' among managers was identified as a more successful route to increasing exports than any appeal to nationalistic motives. Models of export behaviour were developed by Swedish researchers, including Johanson and Wiedersheim-Paul (1975) who viewed the interaction of attitudes and actual behaviour to characterize the internationalization process, echoed by Joynt and Welch (1985) who suggested that the 'internationalization of people and their attitudes' is crucial.

Although some people might suggest that selling across borders could be achieved through management contracts or licensing agreements (rather than the firm having a physical presence in another country), the proprietary information possessed by the firm and its people is a vital source of competitive advantage, which can only be accessed by a physical presence. Another theme in some definitions is that internationalization is a gradual process during which firms acquire, integrate and utilize their knowledge about foreign markets and over time the firms gradually increase their commitment to international markets. Research has suggested that internationalization develops through firms gradually increasing their commitment and exposure to risk, which is reflected in their market entry mode which may progress through: (i) exporting, (ii) agency representation, (iii) overseas licensing, (iv) overseas sales subsidiary and finally (v) the establishment of an overseas production subsidiary.

Motives for internationalization

Daniels *et al.* (2007) explain that internalization is about control through the self-handling of operations internal to the organization, a concept that has been derived from transaction cost theory, which holds that companies should seek the lower cost of handling something internally and contracting another party to handle it for them. In reality, it might actually be better to let another company handle things for you if they have a significant technology or cost advantage.

Generally, the decision to go international is based on an actual opportunity, rather than a decision to search for global investment opportunities (Ghauri, 2000). At this stage, the company has limited knowledge but will benefit from its early experiences and its subsequent investment decisions, and hence needs a strong push and/or commitment to go abroad. Ghauri (2000) identified three organizational and three environmental factors that influence the internationalization decision:

Organizational	The ambitions of the management team
	The objectives and motives of the organization
	The company's success record in its home market
Environmental	Unsolicited proposals
	The bandwagon effect
	Strong overseas competition in the home market

An unsolicited proposal can come from a foreign government, distributor or customer. The bandwagon effect can be created by competitors going international or a general belief that a presence in a certain market is somehow essential, e.g. investment in the former communist states of Eastern Europe post-1989 and the current focus on China.

In this context, significant amounts of time should be invested in relationship building and on being sensitive to the cultural differences in both business and personal relationships.

Firms enter the international arena, therefore, for a variety of reasons, and no classification is inclusive of all possible reasons but they act as a shorthand guide. Likewise, all firms operate within a framework of constraints, such that not all opportunities can be responded to positively, and they need to be evaluated within the overall context of the businesses aims. Motives are also directly related to the mode of market entry adopted by a company.

Although a range of generally recognized export motives exist, classifications vary and are in some cases unclear, but the literature regards export motives as push (internal) and pull (external) factors. The main *push factors* are having: excess capacity, a unique product, a company-specific advantage, a marketing advantage or being driven by the ambitions of the strategic leader. And the main *pull factors* are receiving an unsolicited order, having a saturated domestic market, experiencing competitive pressures and identifying an attractive export development or incentive programme. Inevitably, this classification is

Table 12.2   A classification of international involvement motives

	Internal	External
Proactive	• Driven by owner–manager/key decision-makers • Desire to increase profits • To increase market share/market power • Having a unique product/service/brand • Extend life cycle or seasonality • New product/service development • Having a company-specific advantage, e.g. in marketing, technology • To serve customers better by being closer to where they are	• Perceived international market opportunities, e.g. removal of trade barriers • Export development activity by governments, trade associations, banks • Improvements in IT, physical infrastructure, e.g. transport links
Reactive	• Excess production capacity • Spreading costs and risk	• Unsolicited order • Small domestic market • Declining domestic market • Saturated domestic market • Peer competitive pressure • Service existing customers who have gone international

contested, since the difference between a pull factor and a push factor can be difficult to judge (e.g. a saturated home market could be both a pull factor and a push factor), but greater clarity emerges from the terms **proactive** and **reactive**, as identified in Table 12.2.

Proactive internationalization is in line with the ambitions of the strategic leader (the owner–manager in a small organization) and thus strong market development in the domestic market that provides finance for international activities. Alternatively, the company may internationalize rapidly because of a strong product concept, brand or service. Internationalization in this context is deliberate and planned, reflecting the owner's commitment to the process and the associated risks. Quite often, proactive internationalization can be the result of a conscious policy of recruiting people, often younger graduates, who have a positive attitude to international business.

Reactive internationalization tends to be based, at least initially, on an extension of domestic marketing practice with very little adaptation to local customer needs. The whole internationalization process tends to be more gradual and it emerges in an *ad hoc* and incremental way, which is often based on a chance order from abroad which the company follows up without any grand design. Market spreading tends to be more common than concentration as opportunities are followed without, at least initially, any strategic plan in mind.

Case 12.4 explores the drive and motivation behind Bata Shoes' global expansion.

12.4 Market entry strategies

The most likely options for going global are developing new markets for existing products and diversification, the latter being the riskiest since it takes the company away from its core expertise in production and domestic distribution. Going global may seem ambitious, but is a viable strategy if well managed by the leadership team.

Bata Shoes   Eur

Although not a familiar name in the UK, Bata is one of the world's leading footwear retailers. The company remains family owned and with headquarters in Lausanne, Switzerland. It manufactures and retails all round the world – there is production in 25 different countries and retailing in 50. Approximately 1 million customers buy Bata shoes every day, and in its life the company has sold 14 billion pairs. The company seeks to stay ahead by innovation in both products and processes. Its shoes are designed for comfort as well as fashion and design. This market position has been brought about because Bata has been able to deal with a variety of environmental shocks.

The company was founded in 1894 in Zlin, which today is in the Czech Republic but then was classified as the Austro-Hungarian Empire. Thomas Bata was a descendant of a family of cobblers who had been shoemakers for centuries. Real growth started during World War I when the company received orders for military boots, which allowed it to move from a small family concern to mass production. Bata has been described as the 'Henry Ford' of Eastern Europe. He was always concerned about his employees and built houses and recreation facilities for them. When Thomas died in a plane crash in 1932 there were 16 500 employees.

His half-brother, Jan, took over the business and he set about expanding throughout Europe – previously the company had been concentrated in the East – and adding new products such as toys and tyres. After 10 years of Jan's leadership there would be over 100 000 employees and various overseas subsidiaries.

But Germany occupied Czechoslovakia in 1939 and Jan Bata was forced to leave the country. He was a recognized supporter of the Czech in exile. The Czech factories were handed over to a distant family member and Thomas' grandson, another Thomas, was left controlling all the overseas subsidiaries from a new base in Toronto, Canada. It is reported that during World War II Jan Bata helped many Czech and Slovak Jews to escape the Nazi occupation, finding them work in the various factories.

When the war was finished there were ownership disputes over the Czech factories and eventually they were nationalized in 1945. Jan Bata was put on trial (in absentia) by the new Communist government and convicted; it was clear he would be unable to return. His conviction would eventually be quashed in 2007.

Quite soon the family name disappeared from the business in Czechoslovakia, which was renamed Svit.

But the business, known worldwide as Bata Shoe Company, has continued to expand. Private label ranges were added to the basic name in the 1970s: Bubblegummers, Power, North Star and Marie Claire. In the 1980s the retail formats were changed to reflect current trends; there were now city stores, large format stores and speciality sports stores. As was happening with many shoe manufacturers, production in developed countries largely ceased during the 1990s. After the fall of the communists in Czechoslovakia in 1989, named the so-called 'Velvet Revolutions', Thomas Bata, the new CEO, was invited to invest in the ailing Svit business, but it could not be returned to its original ownership. Instead he bought a number of stores and also established partnership agreements with businesses in Russia, Poland, Croatia and Slovenia. The original Czech company was simply unable to compete in a new, free market and it went bankrupt in 2000. There is, however, a shoe museum in Zlin and the Bata family still have a small shoe trading business. The actual business may have gone full circle but the company name is revered in the Czech Republic for what it has achieved.

Questions

1 How well do you think Bata dealt with the challenges and threats it faced?
2 Do you think the enforced trigger caused the development of an international strategy that otherwise might not have happened?

SOURCE: THIS CASE STUDY WAS PREPARED USING PRIMARILY PUBLICLY AVAILABLE SOURCES OF INFORMATION FOR THE PURPOSES OF CLASSROOM DISCUSSION; IT DOES NOT INTEND TO ILLUSTRATE EITHER EFFECTIVE OR INEFFECTIVE HANDLING OF A MANAGERIAL SITUATION.

This approach involves simultaneous entry into numerous different geographical markets, and is most viable for companies (or entrepreneurs) that have internationally transferable technology- or knowledge-based products. It is based on assumptions that the world is becoming more homogeneous and that distinctions between national markets are fading and will eventually disappear for some products, and only the brands will survive in any scale. Coca-Cola and Levi Strauss have based their global marketing effort over the past decades on the premise that universal appeal exists, such as Coke's 'one sight, one sound, one sell'. Global marketing strategies must change as the world does. Yet a single advertising approach exploits the similarities to stimulate sales everywhere, while being lower cost than many national campaigns.

Organizations developing their corporate strategy internationally must consider:

1 marketing strategies

2 financial strategies

3 the structure of the organization – including location issues

4 cultural and people issues.

Before discussing these factors individually, Figure 12.5 endeavours to link them and implicitly reinforce the notion of E–V–R (environment–values–resources) congruence. The situational factors have to be right for an international strategy to make sense, i.e. the returns must exceed the investment, as shown in Figure 12.6.

Gupta and Govindarajan (1998) argue that the potential pay-off can be assessed by addressing a number of obvious questions:

● Which product lines are (most) suitable for internationalization?

● Which markets should be targeted – and in what order of priority?

● What are the most appropriate ways of entering these target markets?

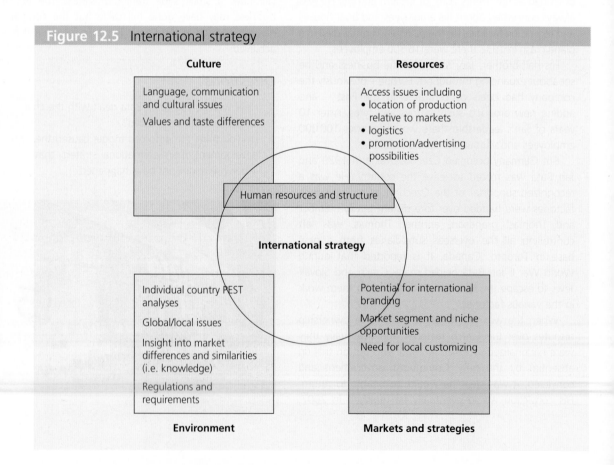

Figure 12.5 International strategy

Figure 12.6   The attractiveness of the international opportunity

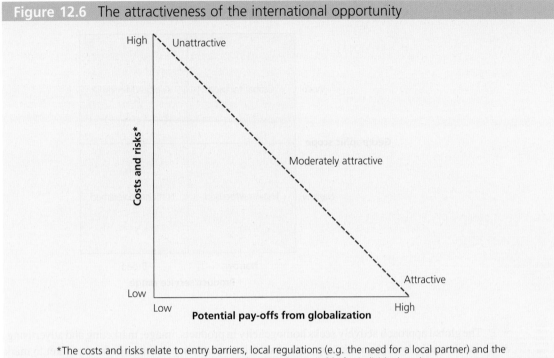

*The costs and risks relate to entry barriers, local regulations (e.g. the need for a local partner) and the extent of investment required to make products/services suitable for individual markets

- How rapidly does it make sense to expand? Does a fast-track approach (such as Glaxo licensing Zantac for production in various countries simultaneously) make more sense than a slower approach (IKEA deliberately restricting the number of new branch openings every year to retain tight control)?

Marketing

Both how global products and services can be made and the extent to which they have to be tailored to appeal to different markets are critical. Markets vary from those termed *multi-domestic* (where the competitive dynamics of each separate country market are distinctive and idiosyncratic) to **global** (where competitive strategies are transferable across frontiers). Coca-Cola, Levi jeans and the expensive perfumes and leather goods marketed by Louis Vuitton Moët Hennessy (LVMH) attract a global consumer with identical tastes, but they are more exceptional than normal. Clearly, different competitors in the same industry adopt a variety of competitive strategies. A follow-up issue concerns the appropriate range of products or services, illustrated by the framework, a 2 × 2 four-quadrant matrix, in Figure 12.7, which is a useful starting point for analyzing both opportunities and competitor strategies:

Product/service range	*Geographic scope*
1 Narrow	National
2 Broad	National
3 Narrow	Global
4 Broad	Global

Organizations that need to be located close to customers to provide delivery and other services can establish strategic stockholding, rather than manufacturing.

Going global differs from a multi-level domestic approach in three basic ways:

1   The global approach looks for similarities between markets, while the multi-level domestic approach ignores similarities.

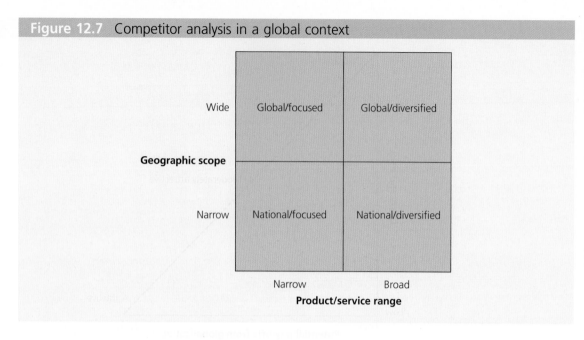

Figure 12.7 Competitor analysis in a global context

2 The global approach actively seeks homogeneity in products, image, marketing and advertising message; and the multi-level domestic approach results in unnecessary differences from market to market.

3 The global approach asks, '*is this product or process suitable for world consumption?*', but the multi-level domestic approach, relying solely on local autonomy, never asks the question.

Marketing in a multi-level domestic strategy is the most localized of the business functions, but differences exist in marketing mix elements and between firms. Elements that are strategic such as positioning are more easily globalized, while tactical elements such as sales promotions are typically determined locally. Adaptation is present even at Coca-Cola, which is acknowledged to be one of the world's most global marketers. The key is the worldwide use of ideas and methods rather than absolute standardization.

The global approach involves centralizing decision-making, which is invariably beyond the resource or management capability of a small fast-growth company. Adaptability – or localization – invariably takes place, influenced by three factors:

- the markets targeted and their level of sophistication
- the product and its ability to transfer across boundaries, to include issues of conformity and supply-chain management
- company culture including factors such as resources and experience in overseas markets.

Thus a company can be global if it has the vision and means to adapt products or services to suit local circumstances, which means that the process of being a global company involves an infinite number of alterations to the marketing mix.

The characteristics of a global business are summarized in Table 12.3.

Finance

The management of currency transfers and exchange rates adds complexity, since floating exchange rates imply uncertainty, although companies can, and do, reduce their risk by buying ahead. The European Exchange Rate Mechanism (superseded by the single European currency, the Euro) was originally designed to minimize currency fluctuations, but economic pressures still cause periodic devaluations. For example, the Euro can still fluctuate widely against pound sterling to such a degree as to make many transactions in Euros very expensive and *vice versa*. Predictable or fixed rates may benefit a car manufacturer which

Table 12.3	Characteristics of a global business
Criteria	Measurement
Mission	Clear mission statement signalling that the company has significant international ambitions
Objectives	Quantifiable objectives showing ambition to operate or market on two or more continents
Size	>£5m turnover Minimum 30 per cent turnover from overseas
International markets	Sales: minimum two continents
Overseas operations	On a minimum of two continents: employment or assembly or manufacture or distribution channels
HQ	CEO based in and board meetings held in founding country. Overall operational control there
Strategic independence	Strategic decision-making in 'home' country
Growth	Five year turnover growth
Influence on markets	Global market share. Global brands
Integration of operations	Operational control or Brand management on at least two continents
International recruitment	Significant numbers of non-home nationals at senior managerial level
International sourcing	Company seeks inputs worldwide

produces engines and transmission systems in one country, transfers them to assembly plants in a second and third country, each specializing in different cars, and then finally sells them throughout Europe. Costs and estimated profits must be based on predicted currency movements, and any incorrect forecasting could result in either extra or lost profits.

Where such an organization structure is created, transfer pricing arrangements are required. If managers of the various divisions or business units are motivated or measured by their profitability figures, there will be some disagreement about the **transfer price** which affects their value-added figures. Equally, the organization may be seeking to manage transfer arrangements for tax purposes, seeking to show most profit where taxes are lowest.

Companies with a main base in a country whose currency is strong and appreciating may find their international competitiveness weakened since exported products will become relatively expensive, and competing imports cheaper – and such companies may be tempted to invest and relocate elsewhere.

Structure

The two key structural questions are:

1 Where to make the various products and services to obtain the necessary people and other resources required in order to be as close as appropriate to each defined geographic market and to manage costs efficiently, and

2 How best to structure the organization in order to control it effectively but simultaneously ensuring sufficient responsiveness to changing environments. The speed and nature of change pressures may be uneven, while IT increasingly offers opportunities for more effective control of globally dispersed businesses.

One obvious way for a firm to expand is by offering its existing products in foreign markets, perhaps by exporting from its domestic production base, and employing the services of agents and distributors to handle its products in export markets. Alternatively, and implying greater commitment, the firm may decide to relocate production itself by establishing manufacturing plants in selected overseas markets.

The company may decide to become vertically integrated on a global basis, sourcing some of its raw material requirements and intermediate products from overseas subsidiaries or suppliers, and establishing overseas sales subsidiaries in order to put its international marketing operations on a more dedicated footing. Likewise, the company may diversify its business by acquiring suitable foreign companies. These multichannel strategies are consistent with becoming a global entity.

The structural alternatives available are:

- A globally centralized organization, remote from markets and relying on exporting, which is likely to prove cost-efficient but possibly out of touch.

- Manufacturing plants located close to markets in order to satisfy local needs and preferences. This structure, known as both international and multi-domestic, could still be controlled centrally, or substantially decentralized into fully autonomous units, in which case the plants may be independent or co-operate in some way. This structure is more expensive, but one which can offer higher levels of service. Unilever, which relies on localized manufacturing and marketing, is an example. Whilst cement is an international commodity product, companies are structured in this way because there is no benefit to be gained from transporting cement across frontiers.

- Centralized manufacture of key components, possibly in a low-wage country, with final assembly or finishing nearer to markets, e.g. Caterpillar Tractors.

- An integrated global structure with production locations chosen on resource or cost grounds, in which finished goods will be transported to markets. In this structure, the organization will have an international presence but e.g. in Country X its sales could consist mainly of products imported from other locations, whilst most of Country X's production is exported. Marketing, production control, purchasing and research and development will all be co-ordinated globally if they are not centralized.

- Centres of excellence may be established where cultural values and behaviour are most appropriate. Philips chose to concentrate technology development in the Far East, where a long-term perspective is natural; IBM has established research and development facilities in Italy, which it regards as suitably intuitive and innovative. When Lenovo (China) bought the PC business from IBM, the company moved the HQ of the new business to New York. However, if national preferences and requirements are markedly different, dedicated research and development facilities could arguably be established in several countries. ICI opened a technical centre in Japan for developing special chemicals and materials in collaboration with the major car and electronics manufacturers, in order to sell its products to Japanese plants throughout the world. Japanese companies appear to prefer to collaborate with chemicals suppliers which have scientists and engineers in Japan, and a factory to produce material locally.

- A global network via strategic alliances. This alternative has many strategic advantages but can be complex to control and costly in overheads. For example, Coca-Cola based in Atlanta commands some 50 per cent of the world's soft drinks market and over 40 per cent of the US domestic market. The key success factor is obtaining distribution and access to markets, and because Coca-Cola is mostly water this aspect of the business is decentralized, while branding and marketing is global and centralized. The strategy is to sell concentrate or syrup to local bottlers, whether independent businesses or joint venture partners. Pricing is based on what can be afforded locally, and a variety of support mechanisms are offered. Coke is frequently promoted with local endorsements, but marketing and advertising feature sponsorship of international sporting events.

International location

The international location decision is affected by a number of factors, including the existence of any national resources which influence competitive advantage in any significant way. Nike and Reebok have built factories in China, Thailand and the Philippines for labour cost savings. Even small businesses are using overseas factories to produce goods at a low price whilst retaining home-based research and development and sales and marketing. A number of leading computer and semiconductor businesses are located in California's Silicon Valley because of the pool of skilled labour and acquired expertise to support research and development. Consumer electronics and pharmaceuticals are industries where the headquarters of the leading companies are concentrated in one or a few countries. Case 12.5 shows how Infosys chose to locate where specialist people resources were available and affordable.

Case 12.5) Infosys   Ind

Infosys is a software business based in India, but which targets markets around the globe. It was set up with this strategy in mind.

Infosys was started in 1981 with 10 000 (Indian) rupees, equivalent to some US$1200; it is now one of India's most dynamic wealth generators. The company was floated in 1993; within 6 years, and after growing by some 50 per cent per year, the share value had increased 85 times. Infosys became the fifteenth largest company quoted on the New York NASDAQ and the first Indian business to be listed there.

Founder Narayana Murthy, who was around 35 at the time, left an American computing business, together with six Indian colleagues, and they started Infosys in Murthy's home in Poona, near Mumbai. Infosys would write software for established businesses in the G7 countries, and also provide systems integration and consultancy services. Murthy was the son of a teacher, and, although he had been working abroad extensively, particularly in Paris, he was to be the only one of the seven to stay based in India. The others would work in America, close to their key clients. The business would be global from 'day one'; there was no local market of any consequence for what they were doing. Their first major client was Reebok.

'The market for the idea did not exist in India...we had to embrace globalization. I believe globalization is about sourcing capital from where it is cheapest, producing where it is most cost-effective and selling where it is most profitable, all without being constrained by national boundaries' (Murthy).

India was able to offer well-educated, English-speaking staff who were proficient in IT. They had a strong work ethic and the prevailing salaries were well below those of their client countries. America has generally provided two-thirds of the company's revenues. Infosys was able to offer very competitive prices for high-quality work. But things were not altogether smooth. 'It took 1 year for a specialist telephone connection, 2 years to get a licence to import a computer and 2 weeks every time we needed foreign currency to travel abroad.'

In 1987 Infosys began a joint venture with a management consultancy based in Atlanta. The US staff would seek out business; Infosys would provide the skilled personnel to deliver the product. This gave Infosys market credibility and opened up a host of fresh opportunities. New clients included Nestlé, General Electric and Holiday Inn.

The joint venture was abandoned in 1995 when Infosys felt it was sufficiently established and well-known to open its own offices in the US. In 1991, back in India, Infosys had moved from Poona to a new 55-acre complex in Bangalore, home of India's burgeoning software industry. There was now to be a focus on a broader product range with an extended set of staff skills and competencies; this would involve selective acquisitions. The company was restructured around strategic business units. The emphasis would be on service and customer focus. Additional business from existing clients was sought energetically – it amounted to 80 per cent of revenues – as well as the active search for new clients.

There are a number of reasons why Infosys has been as successful as it has:

- World-class operations and high-quality products and service.
- A recognition that in software human resources are the core resources and they must be nurtured. Systems and conditions were created which would attract and retain the best. Good young talent was sought and, unusual for India, Western-style stock options offered.
- Expertise in project management.
- A clear structure (in Bangalore) that was dedicated to servicing overseas clients. However, as relative salaries in India have risen (albeit still well below those of the USA and UK!) Infosys has started to set up overseas supply operations. It now employs software writers at its operation in Shanghai, China, for example.

- Ensuring that whilst large clients are sought, Infosys avoids dependency on any single client. At one time GE provided 25 per cent of revenues; this has been reduced to 10 per cent over time as the company has grown.

Infosys has not been without its critics in India. Its 'social perspective' on working conditions and rewards has not endeared it to everyone. Murthy has proclaimed that 'all profitable exporters should give 20 per cent of their earnings before interest and tax to help fund higher education in India', which has detractors as well as supporters.

As for Murthy himself, he has stepped down from the Chief Executive position he held for over 20 years but he remains as Chairman. In 2003 he became the company's 'Chief Mentor' responsible for helping to 'create future leaders' within Infosys.

Questions

1 What factors might threaten the type of global strategy practised by Infosys?
2 What do you think are the most realistic growth options available to Infosys?

Footnotes

In 2008 the global credit crunch and recession hit India's outsourcing industry quite markedly. Infosys slashed its earnings targets by 30 per cent. The main problem: the demise of the US financial sector. Also in 2008 Infosys looked at acquiring Axon, a UK-based specialist in business software. It backed away, saying it was 'no longer prudent' at the existing valuation.

By 2011, the company's thirtieth birthday, there were 125 000 employees. Competition from Tata Consultants (mentioned in Case 12.1) and others was robust and at this time Tata was growing at a faster annual rate. Critics argued that Infosys' decision-making was too slow, in part because 'some of the best managers had left', and that margins were being protected rather than prices shaved to secure business. Infosys was perceived to be reluctant to sacrifice its margins. In addition, it was said, its marketing and customer service could both be improved. It was also very significant that in the global recession, and problems in banks and financial services, some of Infosys' leading customers were spending less on IT and software. On a more positive note Infosys were becoming increasingly committed to cloud computing for those customers who would accept it.

Whatever the structural form, a truly international business must develop a global mission and core values (such as consistent quality worldwide), and achieve integration through effective communications. The corporate strategy must be centralized even if the company has a number of independent subsidiaries and operates in several multi-domestic markets. However, the organization must be able to embrace the different national cultural traits and behaviours, which presents an important managerial challenge. Decisions have to be made concerning the balance of local managers and mobile 'international' managers who are easily transferable between divisions and countries.

Bartlett and Ghoshal (1989) summarized the above points as three potentially conflicting issues which must be reconciled, which are the need:

- for efficiency through global centralization
- to respond locally through decentralization
- to innovate and transfer learning internationally.

Bartlett and Ghoshal (1992) have also concluded that the concept of a 'universal international manager' is misconceived, since global firms require those who are specialized in particular functions and also managers based locally. Further, they suggest that combining worldwide operations ought to be focused upon the firm's upper hierarchy such that 'international managers' are not needed.

Culture

Two perspectives of culture, a national perspective as well as a policy perspective, often lead to the creation of strategies that allow entrepreneurial companies to think globally and yet still deliver products and services that are locally suited. Differences – especially cultural differences – are revealed through values, rituals, heroes and symbols (Hofstede, 1991). Following on the discussion of his thinking in Chapter 7, Hofstede developed five dimensions to describe the cultural variations between 58 countries, which include: masculinity, e.g. money focus, ambition and aggression (UK/Germany) versus femininity, i.e. kindness and good relationships (Nordic countries); individualism versus collectivism; uncertainty avoidance; distance from power or hierarchy; and long-term versus short-term orientation (Hofstede, 1991).

Similarly, he found that more prosperous nations were more individualistic and the poorer ones more collectively orientated, with uncertainty avoidance being more evident in the Latin European and Mediterranean nations, with Latin countries having higher power distance while most countries studied had a short-term orientation (ibid).

Wherever this type of analysis is used, cultural differences must influence the market entry strategies of firms. McAuley (2001) notes that:

> The European retailers prefer to enter geographically close countries first and often, but not always, these were culturally close. It was also found that standardized retail formats are first exported to culturally close countries (Ikea). In addition those countries (France, Germany and Belgium) with a high degree of uncertainty avoidance apply entry modes giving them a high degree of control. The same was true for power distance in the case of the examples from France and Germany.

However, a dilemma can be created for firms that seek rapid internationalization, in terms of whether they should opt for an efficient distribution network and tackle countries that are closer or better to account for cultural similarities. Geographic proximity and logistics can be overridden by cultural empathy, i.e. having an understanding of a particular market or a feeling of national closeness.

Stage models

Frameworks based on various stages such as the one featured in Figure 12.8 build upon the premise that internationalization is a process which develops over time and consists of a number of phases. Two concepts strongly associated with the models are *psychic distance*, the tendency for those people involved in first

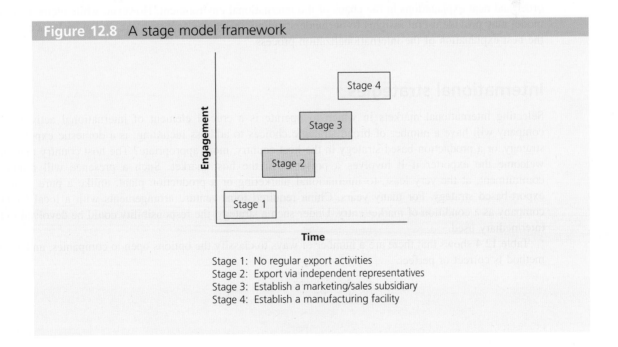

Figure 12.8 A stage model framework

Stage 1: No regular export activities
Stage 2: Export via independent representatives
Stage 3: Establish a marketing/sales subsidiary
Stage 4: Establish a manufacturing facility

time exporting to trade with countries with which they feel comfortable culturally, and **geographic proximity**, where initial exporting will take place to countries nearby.

The models draw on organizational behaviour and learning theory to capture both firm behaviour and managerial learning over time, as the following story illustrates:

A company was founded in 1981 in Newcastle, England, UK – its setup was, in itself, an interesting process. It was started by a Swedish entrepreneur and, because of patent protection in the UK, was immediately forced to export – a truly international firm from the outset. Whilst not directly reflecting the classic stages model, its history does help to illustrate stages of gradual market expansion and product development. The first main products which the company marketed were surf boards and surf skis. These were sold into identified markets in France, Australia and the USA. Five years after it was founded, the company acquired a clothing manufacturer in order to develop a range of leisure wear, which it again sold to the same markets where it had successfully marketed its surf boards. This time, of course, it had benefited from the market knowledge and experience gained from the first round of international involvement. Further new product development produced a kayak which again was to be sold into the company's already established key markets.

Johanson and Wiedersheim-Paul's (1975) model suggested that internationalization activities occur incrementally, influenced by increased market knowledge and commitment. Hence the perceptions and beliefs of managers influence, and are shaped by, incremental involvement in foreign markets – and they shift from having little or no interest in international markets, to trial initiatives in, and evaluation of, psychically close markets, then active expansion into more challenging and unknown markets, becoming increasingly committed to international growth.

Since the late 1980s, research has shown that many companies are engaging in rapid and more direct forms of internationalization and, therefore, the stage models are ill-equipped to deal with this dynamic process as many early models were based on very small samples of large firms, whose wider relevance must be questioned. Further, the implied sequential process is not inevitable and there is evidence of companies moving backward and forwards or even jumping stages within the model. Evidence of rapid internationalization by high-technology products, whose window of opportunity on the world market can be quite limited, has further added to the criticism.

An online case on Volkswagen illustrates this theory in practice. This theory has survived for as long as it has because nothing better has come along, and the model remains intuitively appealing to our search for order and neat explanations in the chaos of the international environment. However, while elements of the model may provide useful insights to our understanding, the stages approach can no longer be accepted as the best explanation of the internationalization process.

International strategies

Selecting international markets in which to operate is a crucial element of international activity. Any company will have a number of broad strategic choices to address including: is a domestic export-based strategy, or a production-based strategy in the host country, more appropriate? The host country may only welcome the exporter if it involves a presence in the host market. Such a presence will require a commitment, at the very least, to international marketing or a production plant, unlike a pure domestic export-based strategy. For many years, China required joint venture arrangements with a local Chinese company as a condition of market entry. Under such a strategy, the responsibility could be devolved to the intermediary used.

Table 12.4 shows that there are a number of ways to classify the options open to companies, and no one method is correct or perfect.

Table 12.4   Classification of modes of market entry

Indirect market entry	Strategies without foreign investment

• Unsolicited orders
• Domestic-based intermediaries
 	
  Courier/express services
  Export management companies
  Export houses
  Trading companies
  Piggybacking
  Brokers
  Jobbers
	• Licensing
	• Franchising
	• Management contracts

Direct market entry	**Strategies with foreign investment**

Domestic-based intermediaries
 	
• Freight forwarders
• Consortium exporting
• Export department
 	
Foreign-based intermediaries
 	
• Agents
• Distributors
	• Marketing subsidiary
	• Manufacturing subsidiary
	• Joint ventures
	
	  Joint equity venture
	  Contractual joint venture

Ensuring successful market entry

Nothing, not even a monopoly situation (as many state-owned businesses have found), can guarantee success, as the environment does not stand still, and market awareness and knowledge is important, as the following story illustrates:

> For one company that attempted to exploit the Dutch market from a base in the UK, failure was based on poor market research. A showroom was opened in Holland to sell female clothing. The company attempted to simply transfer the product to the new market, and in so doing made the mistake in marketing of giving the market the wrong product. Colours and styles which had gone down well in England were found to be unacceptable in the Dutch market. The company also encountered problems with regard to the size of its garments. It did not take into account the difference in stature between customers in the two markets. The company found, too late, that the Dutch customer was taller and larger than ones in the UK. Formal market research would have revealed the special characteristics of the new market, and allowed the company to adapt its products to the fashion tastes of the Dutch buyers.

However, the very best information-gathering exercise is only as good as the interpretation of the individuals concerned. There is perhaps a rather understated view, which says that marketing cannot guarantee success, but that an enterprise will fail less badly because of it. Not everything goes smoothly all the time for market entry and the literature is full of famous errors. Failure can occur for all sorts of reasons, e.g. poor intermediaries, poor communication or not getting paid.

Export readiness

Few companies have the management resources, experience or financial resources to launch products globally and, therefore, the choice of market entry options is more restricted for smaller and newer companies. Nor can one be prescriptive about the method of entry chosen: different international markets require different solutions!

In understanding market entry decisions, there is trade-off between having a high level of control set against the cost of achieving this status. Most writers on this subject make the distinction between indirect and direct modes of entry, which have different levels of foreign (or direct) investment available for overseas expansion. For example, a new firm or a firm new to exporting, may, for financial reasons, choose to use domestic intermediaries to respond to unsolicited orders. As these types of orders grow in numbers and regularity, the company may then choose to appoint a representative in-country who will be given the task of actively seeking new orders.

Case 12.6, Li Ning, looks at export readiness.

Case 12.6   Li Ning Company   Ch

SOURCE: THIS CASE STUDY WAS PREPARED USING PRIMARILY PUBLICLY AVAILABLE SOURCES OF INFORMATION FOR THE PURPOSES OF CLASSROOM DISCUSSION; IT DOES NOT INTEND TO ILLUSTRATE EITHER EFFECTIVE OR INEFFECTIVE HANDLING OF A MANAGERIAL SITUATION.

The Li Ning Sports Wear company was first established in 1989 by Li Ning, one of the outstanding Chinese athletes of the twentieth century – at the 23rd Los Angeles Olympic Games Li Ning won three gold medals, two silver medals and one bronze medal. As a gymnast he won over 106 medals in various competitions over a career in sport that lasted 17 years. Li Ning retired in 1989 and by 1990 he had founded the Li Ning Sportswear business. In August 1990, Li Ning Sportswear was selected to provide the designated clothing for the Chinese delegation at the 11th Asian Games and in 1992 for the 25th Barcelona Olympic Games.

Encouraged by this success Li Ning was cross-listed in the Hong Kong Stock Exchange in 2004 and was the first Chinese sports good business to do this. Throughout this period Li Ning had been trying to succeed in international markets. He set up within Li Ning Sportswear an international trade department and signed agreements with European distributors; he also hired designers of sportswear and equipment in Italy and France. The company was represented at European Trade Fairs in major cities such as Munich. All of this activity failed to help the business reach its overall target of sales of one billion RMB. The brand simply had not taken off outside China. It appeared that European markets were not ready for a Chinese sportswear business competing head on with Adidas and Nike and other multinational brands.

During this period, when the focus of the company was on developing its international trade, the domestic market had become extremely competitive. The Li Ning Company then decided to concentrate on the domestic market in order to achieve the original sales objective set by the founder, that of sales of one billion RMB. 'To some extent China is the world', Li Ning commented. At this point international sales were less than 2 per cent of total sales.

However Li Ning did not give up on his quest to create an international business. In part this was driven by the corresponding success of Adidas and Nike in the Chinese market, where from 2004 they took advantage of the booming Chinese sports goods market to open two stores a day in the major cities. The Chinese brands such as Li Ning, and Anta faced the real possibility of being relegated to second tier businesses. To combat this Li Ning decided to combine the Chinese oriental elements of design into the sportswear, in order to differentiate the business, and also to invest heavily in technology based research and development for its sportswear and equipment. At the same time he adopted the 'best of overseas management practices' in terms of IT, stock control and marketing. European companies were hired to install and implement the management systems needed.

Li Ning had started to sponsor foreign sports groups in 2001. Between 2001 and 2006 this was stepped up, and in 2006 Li Ning successfully sponsored the French gymnastics team and became the designated supplier for the Spanish male and female gymnastics and basketball teams. At the same time Li Ning was investing in the home market with major new stores in Beijing and Shanghai.

Li Ning was now perceived to be a real success story both inside and outside China. This was highlighted in 2008, when, at the Beijing Olympic Games, Li Ning himself flew across the stadium to light the Olympic torch. This fitted in with the company's slogan of 'Anything is Possible'.

Following on from this Li Ning, in March 2009, signed a major sponsorship agreement worth $7.5 million over 5 years with Elena Isinbayeva, the double Olympic gymnastic champion at the Beijing games. Elena was to become the international face of Li Ning as it sought to combine what they believe is the unique combination of oriental style with advanced technological developments in sportswear and equipment. The aim now was to make Li Ning into one of the top five world sports brands at some point between 2013 and 2018. There was still a long way to go for this to be achieved. Revenue reached 9479 million RMB in 2010 (95 per cent of the target) – but this fell to below 9000 million in 2011, when earnings also halved. Slower industry growth, increased competition and increased costs were all cited as contributing causes.

Clearly, for a business solely based in China, becoming a truly international brand is a major challenge.

Questions

1 Research the Li Ning business. What can you learn from this in terms of how the business has developed?

2 What steps are needed for Li Ning to be a truly international business?

http://www.lining.com

Indirect exporting

Indirect exporting According to McAuley (2001), 'the indirect method of exporting is often referred to as passive exporting or as being a result of an 'export pull' effect, since people outside the company stimulate the activity', suggesting that the strategies that came under this category are 'responding to unsolicited or chance orders'. For some companies, such unsolicited orders are their first introduction to international markets, which may stimulate them to explore the feasibility of exporting more seriously as the stage models would suggest. It does have that advantage of being new, unexpected business which illustrates that there are potential, as yet unreached, customers in the world, and it involves no product adaptation costs or promotion costs. The downside of this approach is that the company: 'is not geared up for exporting, and therefore there are relatively high costs involved because of the learning curve which has to be gone through. For example, a one-off distribution channel will be relatively expensive as no economies of scale are available. The potential benefits of this initial involvement depend on the company's medium-term response to the unsolicited order' (*ibid*).

Direct entry

The direct entry approach involves finding and appointing in-country representatives, usually in the form of agents or distributors, an active form of exporting which relies on in-country intermediaries. Inevitably, the commitment and investment required are greater than for direct exporting, but the rewards are potentially greater.

The options involved are as shown in Table 12.5.

Whilst agents and distributors are the most common form of entry by newer growth firms, this form of representation requires management and control which is sometimes learnt the hard way!

A limitation of working through an intermediary is that a firm will not own its distribution network or its customers within a foreign market, and the exporter can be starved of information on market trends and competitor activities, which an intermediary may control. In fast-moving markets or with products at the early stages of growth, access to information can be crucial to gaining entry – hence licensing and joint ventures are more common methods of entry for technology-based businesses.

Agents and distributors will usually seek exclusivity for a territory. The difference between an agent and a distributor is that the distributor will, like a foreign customer, be placing orders, holding stock and accepting responsibility for the sale of goods. Despite best intentions, a growth business with a limited track record and product innovation is less likely to attract a distributor who is willing to hold stock. Agency agreements are, initially, the more common form of entry, especially where more than one market is being addressed.

Table 12.5 Options for direct entry

Agents	Generate customers for products on a commission basis	Exporter's control is high but the method involves close management if market coverage is to be achieved
Distributors	Take title of goods and earn a profit from the mark-up Handle local distribution and marketing	Low level of initial control but offers rapid coverage
Direct selling	Supply to direct customers who order through catalogues, online or through trade fairs	Potentially high level of control but lack of country presence may limit penetration
Sales office	Exporter's own personnel actively target customers Office handles all sales functions	Country presence helps develop sales but coverage may not be sufficient for larger markets such as the US
Subsidiary	Dedicated sales and operations may range from assemblage to locally sourced manufacturing	High potential control but coverage can be limited

In this case, most agreements are set out between sole agents rather than the larger multichannel agency that is more likely to deal with public limited companies.

An agent for whom the company's business is significant should be found, such that they will provide adequate support and prioritize the products amongst the range they represent and promote. At the same time, no agent will willingly expose him- or herself to the risk of being supplanted by a branch of the company's own sales organization. Exclusivity is usually central to negotiations for the agency agreement, but many unsuspecting firms give away too much territory to a single agency.

In market situations where there is slow growth for the company's product in an otherwise high-growth market, the agent concerned may either be overstretched or may be the wrong agent, someone for whom the products and the business are insignificant or have a low priority. On the other hand, high-market growth can create pressures within the company to take over the territory or replace the agent, which may often require compensating the agent handsomely, especially where local legislation exists to protect his or her position. Elsewhere, the company may wish to expand its product line or else diversify into a quite different product – but if the local agent is unable to meet this new expansion, but still holds a company agreement to exclusivity of sales territory, then contracts will need renegotiating or terminating.

These factors may explain why finding an agent is comparatively easy when entering a new market, but finding one that is right for the company is extremely difficult. An agent is normally paid commission only on sales, so loyalty rests purely on the company currently providing them with the greatest earnings, which may be problematic since agents may represent a number of separate companies and product lines. Meanwhile, the company holds responsibility for whatever unsold inventory is held by the agent.

Other direct entry choices tend to rely on strategic alliances or partnering relationships, which can take many forms, such as:

1 **Licensing** involves agreements providing unilateral technology access (frequently through patents) to a licensee in return for a fee. Cross-licensing is a bilateral form of licensing where companies usually swap packages of patents to avoid patent infringements or to exchange existing, codified technological knowledge.

2 **Second-sourcing agreements** regulate the transfer of technology through technical product specifications in order to produce exact copies of products. In the case of mutual second sourcing, this transfer takes place between two or more companies that transfer technical specifications of different products.

3 **Customer–supplier relationships** are co-production contracts and co-makership relations that basically regulate long-term contracts between vertically related, but independent, companies that

collaborate in production and supply. A specific case of customer–supplier relationships are research and development contracts where one company is subcontracted by another company to perform particular research and development projects.

4 **Joint research and development pacts and joint development agreements** are contractual relationships through which companies perform jointly funded research and development projects or, in the case of joint development agreements, jointly work on the development of new products or processes.

5 **Joint ventures** are the combinations of the economic interests of at least two separate companies in a distinct organizational entity, where profits and losses are usually shared in accordance with the equity investments by the parent companies. Joint ventures act as separate organizations that have regular company objectives such as production, marketing and sales, but if relevant also research and development, as a specific objective of the partnership.

Distinguishing between these alternatives is not always possible, and experienced companies often mix and match the methods according to their market and resources. The characteristic that all the methods share is that they promote collaboration through two or more firms, and the factor which increasingly encourages and enables this form of business activity is information and communications technology (ICT).

Arguably, the world has become too large and the competition too strong for even the largest multinational corporations to do everything independently! Technologies are converging and markets are becoming integrated, making the costs and risks of both product and market development ever greater. Partly as a reaction to and partly in order to exploit these developments, entrepreneurial management has become more pragmatic about what type of alliance it takes to be successful in global markets.

The emerging business model, especially amongst technology-centred companies, favours the formation of strategic alliances with suppliers, customers, competitors and companies in other industries, which can take many forms, ranging from informal co-operation to joint ownership of plants and operations.

Dunning's (1980) *Eclectic Paradigm* – sometimes called the OLI Framework – merged a number of existing theories to explain why firms would logically opt for a strategy of licensing, exporting or foreign direct investment (FDI) based on three discrete categories of advantage. The three advantages are:

- Ownership – it owns something valuable, such as a trademark or patent, or specific knowledge and/or skills that others do not possess. If this is the only advantage it possesses then licensing is the most logical.

- Internalization – implying that internal transaction costs (the cost of doing something oneself) are lower than the costs if an external party is involved. In this case, producing and then direct exporting now make more sense than licensing – and there may well be a case to invest in a subsidiary exporting business.

- Location – if, and only if, there are further specific potential advantages available, such as direct access to raw materials, low wage opportunities or favourable tax or tariff advantages, then establishing an overseas production facility comes to the fore and this implies foreign direct investment. Of course, where strong location advantages exist, there will sometimes be internal pressure from the government and local businesses to be able to share in the benefits. China, for example, has favoured joint venture arrangements for this reason. There is a recognition that foreign investors have something to offer and something to gain – as has the country.

Franchising (discussed in Section 12.2) has also enabled a number of prominent companies to open up access to a global market without the financial and other resource implications of acquisition, and a number of models are dependent on franchise relationships:

1 *Manufacturer-Retailer* – Where the retailer, as franchisee, sells the franchiser's product directly to the public; for example, new motor vehicle dealerships.

2 *Manufacturer-Wholesaler* – Where the franchisee, under licence, manufactures and distributes the franchiser's product; for example, soft drink bottling arrangements.

3 *Wholesaler-Retailer* – Where the retailer, as franchisee, purchases products for retail sale from a franchiser wholesaler, typically a wholesale co-operative set up by the franchisee retailers, who are contractually obliged to purchase from it; for example, hardware and automotive product stores.

4 *Retailer-Retailer* – Where the franchiser markets a service or a product under a common name and standardized system through a network of franchisees.

Companies can expand in a number of ways, and full ownership of new outlets is perhaps the most obvious way forward. However, having fully assessed the costs and risks of expansion, some organizations decide to follow the franchising route because of the following three key reasons:

1 *Resource scarcity* means that a company needs access to management talent or other knowledge not available to them and, at the same time, may not have a large amount of money to invest in the expansion.

2 *Agency theory* is about the way in which those people who manage the outlet are motivated and monitored. Because franchisees have considerable financial investments at stake, and because they receive profits from the outlet, they are more motivated than managers of company-owned units to work hard to make the franchise profitable.

3 *Risk spreading*, compensating for the decisions surrounding any expansion, is accomplished through franchising. The investment risk is lowered through franchising compared with joint ventures, which can involve large capital investments and legal complications. Franchising creates sales and brand recognition at a much lower cost. In international expansion, the political risk and the overall risk of failure are primarily borne by the franchisee.

The timescale required by franchising is seen as faster than self-owned expansion, which will often require more monitoring. The process of establishing a chain of franchises increases the knowledge of the franchiser, and the time required for each new outlet is reduced as expertise increases. With experience, the franchiser develops sensitivity to site selection, store layout, procurement and operating policies appropriate to particular environmental settings.

Case 12.7 (Sanyo) looks at a very particular, but very successful, alliance approach.

Case 12.7   Sanyo   Jpn, Int

Sanyo is an innovative and pioneering Japanese electronics company, and a global leader for certain consumer electronics goods. Once best known for its low prices, Sanyo has been described as unusual amongst Japanese businesses – it drops products and businesses that under-perform rather than persisting with them. Sanyo became the world's leading manufacturer of digital still cameras, a very high growth business – it captured a 30 per cent share. This fact would not be realized by looking at the camera displays in stores around the world – the vast majority of the cameras Sanyo makes are marketed with other leading brand names attached. This approach helps overcome the relative weakness of its own brand, when compared with other leading Japanese electronics companies – and also provides a revenue stream to fund research and investment. It also became a leader with optical pick-ups, a key component of CD and DVD players. Many of its various semiconductor products enjoy niche dominance; and it produces the rechargeable batteries for a large proportion of the world's mobile phones.

Sanyo is successful because it focuses its resources on carefully identified opportunities:

● It concentrates on where it can be 'Number One' globally.

'Unless you choose what to focus on, you will not survive' (Yukinori Kuwano, CEO).

● It rates all its businesses by their growth potential and achievable margins – basically following the portfolio approach.

● It constantly searches for new opportunities, especially acquisitions that would strengthen critical mass and market (segment) dominance.

● Sanyo has also developed a joint venture in China with Haier, China's largest consumer electronics group, to provide access to this important and growing market.

Question

What do you think are the relative merits and disadvantages of Sanyo's strategy of producing digital still cameras for some of the leading brand names?

12.5 Internationalization constraints and influences on future global growth

Not all companies are in a position to take advantage of all the international opportunities which may present themselves and, indeed, not all opportunities will even be recognized by the decision-makers in the company. Morgan and Katsikeas (1997) identified four barriers explaining why business owners are discouraged from participating in international business:

1   An insufficient pool of resources can create strategic obstacles.

2   A firm's cost base and margins can lead to operational (and logistical) obstacles.

3   A lack of fit between a firm's strategy and its environment may result in limited knowledge of market opportunities, creating informational obstacles.

4   A firm may be unable to maintain necessary interactions with key parties because of limited resources leading to process-based obstacles.

Little, quoted in Yanacek (1988), identified ten constraints faced by companies marketing products or services internationally, which are:

1   building distribution networks

2   designing market entry strategies

3   identifying market opportunities

4   dealing with political and commercial risks

5   obtaining information on alternatives to direct exporting

6   securing working capital and export financing

7   collecting foreign receivables

8   providing after-sales customer service

9   dealing with tariff barriers and quotas

10   dealing with export laws, regulations and procedures.

Further, not all companies wish to become internationally active for a variety of reasons, which can be associated with the personal characteristics of the strategic leader or founding entrepreneur, particularly in smaller companies, who may find it difficult to delegate responsibility or who have reached the 'comfort level' and do not wish to expand the business. While outsiders may wish to see growth in a frustratingly underachieving company, one must not force change upon such a company. As well as what might be termed these 'softer' constraints, the more traditional ones relate to worries about resources (mainly finance and people), time available, market uncertainties, marketing costs, payment terms, exchange rates, the cost of insurance, information shortages, political uncertainties and cultural differences.

Any firm faces many decisions in its attempt to internationalize its activities, and must decide what volume of trade is desirable, how many countries to market in and which countries to select. The degree of market attractiveness will be influenced by a number of factors related to geographic, demographic, economic, technological and sociocultural characteristics. Once it has evaluated the relative attractiveness of the potential markets in relation to the company's product/service, a company should be better placed to select those markets where the 'fit' is apparently best. For each business, the selection of entry mode will then be linked to their international strategy, which in turn is influenced by motives and constraints. For example, the use of export or international production strategies, the use of intermediaries or how much control over marketing activities the business wishes to retain. There will also be issues regarding expected payback on the investment, the degree of flexibility required and how the strategy fits with broader business objectives. All of these issues prepare the way for one of the dominant decisions of the internationalization process, namely, the mode of market entry decision. Clearly, the constraints on internationalization can act as barriers to the initiation of international activity as well as affecting the process of international business by influencing the choice of market entry.

The future potential internationalization opportunities are influenced by the interaction of external and internal forces, for example when pressure built for a return to the Doha Development Round which is the trade negotiation forum for the World Trade Organization (WTO), aiming to lower global trade barriers. Discussions started in November 2001 in Qatar but stalled in 2008. Global trends include the creation of enterprises based on the knowledge-based economy, such that firms must be must be aware of opportunities and be prepared to take advantage of windows of opportunity as they open – just as relevant for **small and medium-sized enterprises** as for the multinational. Decades of constant progress in ICT have triggered a complex pattern of change in international business relationships, providing the process of globalization with new tools and infrastructures with which entrepreneurial companies capture global opportunities. Unlike previous transformations, the international economy now encompasses global consumers who have local tastes, preferences and servicing requirements.

Drucker (1988) defined the term knowledge management as being the criterion that would define companies in the next 20 years, as the knowledge economy differed from the traditional economy in several key respects including that knowledge is measured by its abundance rather than its scarcity, and is sharable unlike other strategic resources. Thus business alliances across international frontiers have been encouraged, while the effect of location has been diminished. Using appropriate technology and methods, virtual marketplaces and virtual organizations have been created that offer speed and agility, round the clock operation and global reach. These characteristics require new thinking and approaches by entrepreneurial companies, policy-makers, senior executives and knowledge workers alike. To do so, though, requires leadership and risk taking, against the prevailing and slow changing attitudes and practices of many existing institutions and business practice. Like most assets, knowledge is only valuable if it can be transmuted into goods and services that people will pay for. Chapter 5 earlier explored knowledge as a strategic resource.

Knowledge management, combined with the enabling technology associated with e-business, is changing nearly all that companies do, from the procurement of supplies to the delivery of finished products and services. New types of competitors, value-added services and new delivery channels are shifting the boundaries between customers, suppliers, partners and competitors, and profoundly altering industry value chains. Web-based organizations exist because market conditions are changing, as customers demand more specialized products, and thus companies have to develop a wider range. At the same time, they expect a high degree of customization as well as localization to suit conditions that prevail in any particular market. Virtual companies are able to command resources beyond those immediately available to them through collaboration and alliances – a strategy ideally suited to those organizations who wish to cross geographic frontiers.

Specialization and individualization of products leads to shorter production cycles which in turn increase the investment and costs of research and development, production, and sales. As a counter-balance to this trend, ICT has dramatically improved the speed, quantity and quality of communication and especially the co-ordination of economic actions and transactions. In this respect, ICT can be viewed as an enabler and at the same time as a driving force towards the virtual organization. A key objective of a virtual company is to improve its flexibility, which is needed to meet the fast changing market conditions. In order to decrease complexity and increase flexibility, companies seek to create, nurture and exploit relevant core competencies. This strategy means that companies concentrate on what they can do best – specializing in certain areas, developing and constantly improving their core competencies.

However, as we pointed out in Chapter 3, a core competence on its own does not create any value; therefore, companies have to search internationally for value chains where they can integrate their core competencies. Those core competencies are then flexibly configured in different value chains whereby those value chains are made of many different core competencies provided by different economic actors, which leads theoretically to an optimum value creation process.

The emergence and development of virtual organizations is being forced by changing market conditions: in particular, the increased requirement to offer specialized products, to reduce the time to market process, the increased international competition (globalization) and the need to satisfy individual customer needs to which organizations have to respond. Some commentators expect multinationals to be losers in this world order. Others anticipate that the large global companies will form strategic alliances with the small technology innovators and between them they will have the capability to squeeze out the existing market leaders. This process of change offers an increasing number of opportunities for entrepreneurial firms that are knowledge-based and willing to play on the global stage.

Finally, firms involved in internationalization must be concerned with the quest for 'global' sustainability, defined as 'the ability to meet the needs of the present without compromising the ability of future generations to meet their needs' (Peng, 2009), for example through Fair Trade and other ethical practices.

Research Snapshot 12.1

Some authors have argued the case for organic – 'by enhancing current customer relationships and building new relationships' – rather than acquisitive growth (Dalton and Dalton, 2006). Meer (2005) suggested that firms should appoint 'Chief Growth Officers' to give them: 'a more disciplined approach to growth, better organizational capabilities for driving growth and a more supportive culture'. High-growth entrepreneurial businesses have various 'patterns' of growth, being influenced by age, size and sector (Delmar et al., 2003), high-growth 'Gazelles' creating jobs (Davidsson and Henrekson, 2002; Henrekson and Johansson, 2010) and, with the wry observation that, 'The development of firm growth research has been notably slow,' McKelvie and Wiklund (2010) observed that too much attention has been given to the growth rate rather than the growth mode.

As well as a literature review of diversification focusing upon 'antecedents, environmental factors, performance and process outcomes, moderators and the characteristics' (Hitt et al., 2006), studies on diversification have researched matters such as its link with performance (e.g. Miller, 2004), itself impacted by factors including higher levels of competition from abroad (Bowen and Wiersema, 2005), and also corporate coherence, 'the ability of the firm to generate and explore synergies of various types', or a 'dynamic interconnectedness between the company's technological competencies and its downstream activities' (Piscitello, 2004). Related and unrelated diversification have been studied, showing: 'inter-temporal economies of scope that firms achieve by redeploying resources and capabilities between related businesses over time, as firms exit some markets while entering others' (Helfat and Eisenhardt, 2004).

Inter-firm collaboration as a growth strategy has been investigated, e.g. Kumar and Malegeant (2006) on 'closed-loop' supply chains between manufacturers, e.g. Nike, allying with 'eco-non-profit community organizations', i.e. Throwplace.com. How strategic partners are chosen has also been studied (Nielsen, 2003) and why, along with performance (Pansiri, 2005), and how the legitimacy conferred upon firms by strategic alliances – in relation to how they are governed and how they have chosen partners – can, therefore, contribute to their performance (Dacin et al., 2007). The advantages of strategic alliances have been investigated, i.e. 'accessing rather than acquiring knowledge', where they can 'contribute to the efficiency in the application of knowledge', and 'by improving the efficiency with which knowledge is integrated into the production of complex goods and services, and second, by increasing the efficiency with which knowledge is utilized' (Grant and Baden-Fuller, 2004). Performance in the Chinese context is influenced by, 'the parent companies' experience of international business and joint ventures, and the quality of resources they provide to the joint ventures in respect of capital investment, new facilities and operational inputs' (Child and Yan, 2003).

As for SMEs, performance is impacted upon by 'host country knowledge' and 'size-based resources' in the sense that: 'SMEs' IJVs with local partner(s) may be associated with decreases in longevity, especially when SMEs acquire host country knowledge', whilst, 'the size of Japanese partner(s) increases the longevity of IJVs but may have negative effects on IJV profitability when large Japanese partners have low equity ownership in IJVs' (Lu and Beamish, 2004).

The further reading from this literature will help students to develop their perception and critical awareness of strategic growth and its modes and also to highlight developing thinking.

Further Reading

Bowen, H.P. and Wiersema, M.F. (2005) 'Foreign-based competition and corporate diversification strategy', *Strategic Management Journal*, Vol. 26, pp. 1153–1171.

Child, J. and Yan, Y. (2003) 'Predicting the performance of international joint ventures: an Investigation in China', *Journal of Management Studies*, Vol. 40, pp. 283–320.

Dacin, M.T., Oliver, C. and Roy, J.-P. (2007) 'The legitimacy of strategic alliances: an institutional perspective', *Strategic Management Journal*, Vol. 28, pp. 169–187.

Dalton, D.R. and Dalton, C.M. (2006) 'Corporate growth: Our advice for directors is to buy "organic"', *Journal of Business Strategy*, Vol. 27, No. 2, pp. 5–7.

Davidsson, P. and Henrekson, M. (2002) 'Determinants of the prevalance of start-ups and high-growth Firms', *Small Business Economics*, Vol. 19, No. 2, pp. 81–104.

Delmar, F., Davidsson, P. and Gartner, W.B. (2003) 'Arriving at the high-growth firm', *Journal of Business Venturing*, Vol. 18, No. 2, pp. 189–216.

Grant, R.M. and Baden-Fuller, C. (2004) 'A knowledge accessing theory of strategic alliances', *Journal of Management Studies*, Vol. 41, pp. 61–84.

Helfat, C.E. and Eisenhardt, K.M. (2004) 'Inter-temporal economies of scope, organizational modularity, and the dynamics of diversification', *Strategic Management Journal*, Vol. 25, pp. 1217–1232.

Henrekson, M. and Johansson, D. (2010) 'Gazelles as job creators: a survey and interpretation of the evidence', *Small Business Economics*, Vol. 35, No. 2, pp. 227–244.

Hitt, M.A., Laszlo Tihanyi, L., Miller, T. and Connelly. B. (2006) 'International diversification: antecedents, outcomes, and moderators', *Journal of Management*, Vol. 32, No. 6, pp. 831–867.

Kumar, S. and Malegeant, P. (2006) 'Strategic alliance in a closed-loop supply chain, a case of manufacturer and eco-non-profit organization', *Technovation*, Vol. 26, No. 10, pp. 1127–1135.

Lu, J.W. and Beamish, P.W. (2004) 'International diversification and firm performance: the S-curve hypothesis', *The Academy of Management Journal*, Vol. 47, No. 4, pp. 598–609.

McKelvie, A. and Wiklund, J. (2010) 'Advancing firm growth research: a focus on growth mode instead of growth rate', *Entrepreneurship Theory and Practice*, Vol. 34, pp. 261–288.

Meer, D. (2005) 'Enter the "chief growth officer": searching for organic growth', *Journal of Business Strategy*, Vol. 26, No. 1, pp. 13–17.

Miller, D.J. (2004), 'Firms' technological resources and the performance effects of diversification: a longitudinal study', *Strategic Management Journal*, Vol. 25, pp. 1097–1119.

Nielsen, B.B. (2003) 'An empirical investigation of the drivers of international strategic alliance formation', *European Management Journal*, Vol. 21, No. 3, pp. 301–322.

Pansiri, J. (2005) 'The influence of managers' characteristics and perceptions in strategic alliance practice', *Management Decision*, Vol. 43, No. 9, pp. 1097–1113.

Piscitello, L. (2004) 'Corporate diversification, coherence and economic performance', *Industrial and Corporate Change*, Vol. 13, No. 5, pp. 757–787.

Summary

Periodically, organizations must make decisions about how focused and how diversified they wish to be. Horizontal integration, such as acquiring or merging with a competitor, will engender critical mass but may be restrained by the relevant competition authorities. Diversification can be into related or unrelated businesses, or vertically forwards or backwards in the supply chain.

Where a company does choose to diversify, it is more likely to implement this strategy through acquisition (friendly purchase), merger (bringing together the assets of two businesses) or takeover (hostile purchase) than through organic growth.

Unrelated diversification is invariably high risk, but it may be justified or chosen because of the weakness of the present businesses, existing businesses having strengths and competencies that could be exploited in other industries, or the ambitions of the strategic leader.

Research in both the UK and USA consistently indicates that diversification through acquisition has only a 50 per cent likelihood of success, specifically delivering the hoped-for benefits. The typical reasons for failure are that the synergy potential is overestimated, managerial problems and issues are underestimated, key managers leave after the acquisition, hidden weaknesses are not spotted until it is too late, or too much money is paid and the premium cannot be recovered.

The companies that succeed with this strategy follow a number of simple rules: they carefully target their acquisitions; learn from previous experiences and become 'professional acquirers'; avoid paying too high a premium; adopt an appropriate post-acquisition structure and style and ensure that the businesses are integrated effectively; and corporately they add value.

Strategic alliances and joint ventures (a stronger type of alliance where shares are exchanged or an independent company is set up) provide an alternative to an acquisition or merger. While they are designed to deliver synergy, cost savings and access to either technology or markets, they will have implementation challenges.

The Japanese, in particular, have developed real capabilities in alliance management whilst many Western companies have looked upon them from a more defensive perspective. For example, they are an alternative when an acquisition is not feasible for whatever reason, with the three main reasons lying behind this strategy being to gain access to new markets and technologies, to share expensive research and development costs, and to manage innovation more effectively.

There are six particular, and overlapping, forms of alliance and joint venture:

1 the merging of component parts of two or more businesses

2 companies joining forces to develop a new project

3 companies joining forces to develop a new business together

4 agreements between partners in the same supply chain

5 where companies purchase a stake in another business for strategic, rather than purely financial, reasons

6 international trading partnerships.

For alliances and joint ventures to work successfully, commitment from all parties is required. Everyone must appreciate that they can benefit and commit accordingly. Trust, sharing and collaboration become essential, even though different cultures and languages might be involved.

Franchising and licensing can sometimes provide valuable means of growing. The risks are different but the capital required is considerably less.

Private equity funding, described as the 'new conglomerate' can result in *strategic renewal* in the case of under-performing companies. New ways are often found to add value and engineer growth.

All strategic options can have an international dimension – ranging from exporting to a global corporation where products are manufactured in various places around the world and then marketed globally as appropriate. Some companies will 'go global' with existing products and services they market overseas – others will tailor complete strategies for local markets – and the motivation to do so can be organization-driven or driven by environmental opportunities. The deciding factors can thus be push or pull and involve either a proactive or reactive stance.

The key issues in developing an international strategy concern products, markets, entry considerations and timing. The main considerations are marketing (the global and multi-domestic approaches), finance, structure, location (where to produce in relation to market opportunities) and culture (which differs between countries).

There are useful stage models which provide some insight into a typical (if not universally adopted) path to internationalization. Similarly, there are a number of market entry opportunities, although sometimes there will be a given element which acts as a constraint.

Entry into a market can be either direct or indirect and it may or may not require foreign investment. Good overseas agents (a crucial element of the direct approach) are worth their weight in gold, but it is all too easy to appoint the wrong agent.

Strategic alliances can also be very significant in developing internationally. Franchising is an approach used by many companies to develop internationally, which can allow for controlled investment and more limited resource implications. However, not all options are always going to be available or suitable.

Constraints thus limit opportunities – here resources, costs and knowledge may be relevant – and the ability to gain market access will always be critical.

Some companies will deliberately avoid the risks and uncertainty associated with internationalization. Finally, we outlined how e-commerce and the knowledge economy are changing the nature of global strategy by opening up new, exciting opportunities.

Online cases for this chapter

Issues in strategic growth

Online Case 12.1: British Airways
Online Case 12.2: Asda–MFI.

This case was originally written to illustrate the three tests described in the section entitled 'The search for, and review of, possible acquisitions'. The anticipated synergy was not achieved. Asda, of course, is now owned by Wal-Mart. MFI went into administration in December 2008 and all of its branches closed.

Online Case 12.3: Daimler-Chrysler
Online Case 12.4: Delta-Northwest
Online Case 12.5: Ford-General Motors

Issues in international growth

Online Case 12.6: Volkswagen
Online Case 12.7: Matsushita and Canon
Online Case 12.8: Tesco
Online Case 12.9: Constellation Wines

Questions and research assignments

1   From the various points and issues discussed in this chapter, list the possible advantages and disadvantages of diversification and acquisition strategies, and from your experience list one successful and one unsuccessful example of this strategy. Why have you selected these particular cases?

2   What are the key arguments for and against strategies of unrelated diversification and focus? Again, from your own experience, list examples of each.

3   What exactly is the difference between a strategic alliance and a joint venture? Can you provide examples of each – in addition to those included in the text?

4   Do you agree with the view that, if they are established and managed carefully, strong alliances can provide all the benefits of an acquisition or merger without most of the drawbacks?

5   Revisiting Chapter 8, for each of the following strategic alternatives, list why you think an organization might select this particular strategy as a means of international growth. What would they expect to gain, and where are the problems and limitations? If you can, think of an example of each one from your own experience:

● market development
● product development
● innovation
● horizontal integration
● vertical integration

- concentric diversification
- conglomerate diversification.

6 What are the relative advantages and disadvantages of direct market entry as opposed to indirect entry strategies?

7 What are the essential differences between an export, an international and a global organization?

Internet and library projects

1 Obtain statistics on either a selection of large companies which interest you, or the 20 largest companies in the UK, and:

a ascertain the extent to which they are diversified and classify them as either single, dominant, related or conglomerate product companies

b determine their relative size in relation to their competitors in the USA, Japan and Europe.

2 In 2003 Cadbury Schweppes became more diversified – albeit relatedly – when it acquired Adams Confectionery, a leading manufacturer of chewing gum. We can see in online case 8.9 that Mars had considered buying Adams – and that it eventually bought Wrigley instead. Was this a justifiable move by Cadbury Schweppes? Why? Why not? Has it turned out to be a successful strategy? Did it force the hand of Mars?

3 Take any well-known Japanese manufacturer, such as Toshiba or Sony, and determine how many alliances and joint ventures they have and what they are designed to contribute strategically.

4 Using actual examples as your base point, could the high-technology things we currently take for granted (such as mobile phones, personal computers and the Internet) have been developed to the stage they have if companies had worked in isolation? Has the co-operation approach been more sensible and realistic than a series of cross-border mergers?

5 Take any leading investment by private equity funders and explore the impact of the intervention. You might, for example, choose from Fitness First, Madame Tussauds, National Car Parks or Travelodge – depending on your personal interests.

6 Consider the most appropriate strategy for a UK-based company with international ambitions in the following industries (assume that your choice could be implemented):

- men's fashion
- real ale
- baby clothes
- ladies' handbags.

7 For an organization of your choice, trace the changes of international strategy and strategic direction over a period of time. Relate these changes to any changes in strategic leadership, structure and, wherever possible, culture.

8 Abrakebabra became the Republic of Ireland's premier fast food chain. It grew rapidly in Ireland through franchising. Can you ascertain why? Before the company got into difficulties, it opted not to develop internationally (apart from in the UK), but instead developed other franchises. Was this strategy sensible?

Abrakebabra **http://www.abrakebabra.com**

9 Find two businesses that have grown internationally through franchising, one a product business and the other a service business. Compare and contrast their development. To what extent are they similar and to what extent different?

Strategy activity

Debenhams

The hostile acquisition of Debenham's department stores by Burtons – which later changed its own name to Arcadia – took place in 1985. Debenhams was then owned by Burton for 12 years until 1997 before it was demerged as an independent company with a separate listing on the Stock Exchange. It was generally acknowledged that it had not been able to prosper as part of the larger group. At this time sales exceeded £1 billion from the 92 stores. The managing director in post at the time, Terry Green, stayed on until 2000, when he left to run BHS (British Home Stores).

Belinda Earl was then promoted to the top job. 38 years old, she had extensive experience in 'trading' but was less experienced in the property and financial aspects. Her strategy was focused on improving customer service and introducing a wider, more differentiated product range. The ranges would not be the same in every store; she wanted the individual units to be as flexible as possible and able to respond to regional taste variations. She also wanted to increase the number of stores to 150 – but gradually over a period of time. She also opted to join Barclaycard, BP and Sainsbury's in the Nectar loyalty card scheme.

Prices were reduced in 2001 and 2002 to boost sales; and by 2002 turnover had risen to £1.7 billion. Pre-tax profits were £150 million. Many analysts believed Debenhams was being set up for sale.

In 2003 two prospective external buyers came on the scheme. Both were venture capitalists, anxious to buy a successful business. First to bid was Permira, once called Schroder Ventures. It offered 425 pence per share, valuing the business at £1.54 billion. Permira were experienced in these deals, having bought Homebase from Sainsbury's before strengthening it for sale on to Great Universal Stores (GUS). In 2 years Permira had generated a cash return of six times its original investment. Belinda Earl and her Finance Director were given permission by the Debenham's Board to co-operate fully; and it was assumed that if Permira were successful, Earl would stay on as Managing Director and as a substantial shareholder.

The alternative bidder was CVC Capital Partners in association with Texas Pacific Group. They bid 455 pence per share, valuing the business at £1.65 billion. Some independent non-executive directors on the Debenhams Board backed them, but it was clear CVC would not be retaining Belinda Earl if they succeeded. CVC were successful and they installed a new management team. In charge was Rob Templeman, who was currently the Chairman of Halfords, which CVC had bought from Boots. He had also been in charge of Permira's turnaround of Homebase after its purchase from Sainsbury's.

The business changed hands in December 2003. The CVC buy-in team had four main planks to its strategy: improve cash management; cut costs; increase top-line sales – the new target audience was to be young females interested in fashion – and better supply-chain management. Templeman commented that Debenhams 'is a good business with a good brand – but we think

we can do it better'. Head office staffing levels were soon reduced and supply chain costs saved through inventory reductions of £50 million, coupled with an increased stock turn. The number of suppliers was reduced. Stores were remortgaged and bonds issued to replace expensive debt capital. Prices for some slow-moving items were slashed to clear stocks. By mid 2004 sales were running some 5.5 per cent ahead of 2003 levels; profits were up by round 14 per cent. Five new outlets were planned for 2005. New overseas suppliers were being targeted. It seemed only a matter of time before Debenhams followed Halfords and Homebase as a sale or flotation business in a relatively short space of time.

The IPO took place in 2006. When this was complete the business had generated well over £1 billion for the new investors. The company was being valued around £3 billion. Templeman stayed on as CEO after the flotation. CVC and Texas Pacific still held (smaller) stakes.

Some of the new Debenhams early success had coincided with problems at Marks and Spencer, but, and like John Lewis, this business started to improve its performance. Moreover key staff left Debenhams for other retailers. 2007 saw the share price fall and there was a series of profit warnings. Capital expenditure for new stores and refurbishments would have to be curtailed which would hit performance further. The question was – *could Templeman be as effective at building new value as he was at cost cutting and retrenchment?*

Christmas trading at the end of 2007 was also disappointing – although Debenhams was not alone in this – and in 2008 the share price continued to fall. At the beginning of the year Angela Spindler joined the business from Asda, where she had been in charge of the George clothing range. She had the title Managing Director and was being talked about as a future CEO. But she left before completing 12 months. Under Templeman the trading position of Debenhams continues to fluctuate.

When Principles, the fashion chain that was owned by collapsed Icelandic investor Baugur, went into administration in 2009 Debenhams took on the in-store concessions it already had. High street Principles stores closed. Debenhams was able to acquire the name and any stock it wanted. Debenhams has also announced plans to open more stores. However, the shares slumped due to worries over the debt pile.

In June 2009 CVC Capital Partners made its exit. Texas Pacific remained involved, reiterating its confidence in the business and its management team. That said, Debenhams' debt burden still stood at £925 million.

Question

1 Clearly when strategic leaders fail, their replacement by someone capable of turning around the business can be justified. But Belinda Earl was successful. In whose interests is a management buy-in along the lines described here?

Project

1 By either visiting a Debenham's store or using the Internet (or both) try to ascertain what benefits have subsequently accrued from this change of ownership and management. Can you see ways in which they might have created new value for customers?

References

Arnold, M. (2009) Brickbats and bouquets for private equity, *Financial Times*, 15 January.

Badaracco, J.L. (1991) *The Knowledge Link: How Firms Compete Through Strategic Alliances*, Harvard Business School Press.

Bartlett, C. and Ghoshal, S. (1989) *Managing Across Borders: The Transnational Solution*, Harvard Business School Press.

Bartlett, C. and Ghoshal, S. (1992) What is a global manager? *Harvard Business Review*, September–October.

Biggadike, R. (1979) The risky business of diversification, *Harvard Business Review*, May–June.

Burgman, R. (1985) Research findings quoted in McLean, RJ, How to make acquisitions work, *Chief Executive*, April.

Business International (1988) *Making Acquisitions Work: Lessons from Companies' Successes and Mistakes*, Report published by Business International, Geneva.

Campbell, A. and Park, R. (2005) *The Growth Gamble*, Nicholas Brealey.

Chandler, A.D. (1990) The enduring logic of industrial success, *Harvard Business Review*, March–April.

Chiesa, V. and Manzini, R. (1997) Competence-based diversification, *Long Range Planning*, 2 June.

Connell, D.C. (1988) Strategic partnering and competitive advantage, Presented at the 8th Annual Strategic Management Society Conference, Amsterdam, October.

Constable, C.J. (1986) Diversification as a factor in UK industrial strategy, *Long Range Planning*, 19 (1).

Cowling, K., Stoneman, P. and Cubbin, J. (eds) (1979) *Mergers and Economic Performance*, Cambridge University Press.

Czinkota, M., Ronkainen, I.A., and Moffet, M. (2005) *International Business*, Seventh Edition, Thomson, South-Western.

Daniels, J., Radebaugh, L. and Sullivan, D. (2007) *International Business*, Seventh Edition, Pearson Prentice Hall, Upper Saddle River, New Jersey.

Devlin, G. and Bleackley, M. (1988) Strategic alliances – guidelines for success, *Long Range Planning*, 21 (5).

Drucker, P.F. (1982) Quoted in Drucker: The dangers of spoonfeeding, *Financial Times*, 15 October.

Drucker, P.F. (1988) The coming of the new organization, *Harvard Business Review*, January–February.

Dunning, J.H. (1980) *International Production and the Multinational Enterprise*, Allen and Unwin.

Ernst and Young (1995) Key success factors in acquisition management, Research project with Warwick Business School, Ernst and Young, London.

Garrette, B. and Dussauge, P. (1999) Strategic alliances – why Europe needs to catch up, *Financial Times Mastering Global Business*, No. 5.

Ghauri, P. (2000) Internationalization of the firm, in Tayeb, M. (ed.) *International Business – Theories, Policies and Practices*, FT-Prentice Hall.

Gupta, A. and Govindarajan, V. (1998) How to build a global presence, *Financial Times Mastering Global Business*, No 1.

Harding, D. and Rovit, S. (2004) Building Deals on Bedrock, *Harvard Business Review*, September.

Hofstede, G. (1991) *Cultures and Organization: Software of the Mind*, McGraw Hill.

Houlder, V. (1997) Neglect of the new addition, *Financial Times*, 5 February.

Jenkinson, T. and Mayer, C. (1994) *Hostile Take-overs: Defence, Attack and Corporate Governance*, McGraw-Hill.

Johanson, J. and Wiedersheim-Paul, F. (1975) The internationalization of the firm – four Swedish cases, *Journal of Management Studies*, 12 (3).

Joynt, P. and Welch, L. (1985) A strategy for small business internationalization, *International Marketing Review*, 2 (3).

Kanter, R.M. (1990) *Synergies, Alliances and New Ventures*, Harvard Business School video package.

Kay, J.A. (1990) Identifying the strategic market, *Business Strategy Review*, Spring.

Kitching, J. (1967) Why do mergers miscarry? *Harvard Business Review*, November–December.

Kitching, J. (1973) *Acquisitions in Europe: Causes of Corporate Successes and Failures*, Report published by Business International, Geneva.

Lorenz, C. (1986) Take-overs. At best an each way bet, *Financial Times*, 6 January.

Lynch, R. (2000) *Corporate Strategy*, Second Edition, Prentice Hall.

Markides, C. (1997) To diversify or not to diversify, *Harvard Business Review*, November– December.

McAuley, A. (2001) *International Marketing – Consuming Globally*, Thinking *Locally*, John Wiley.

Meeks, J. (1977) *Disappointing Marriage: A Study of the Gains from Merger*, Cambridge University Press.

Morgan, R.E. and Katsikeas, C.S. (1997) Obstacles to export initiation and expansion, *International Journal of Management* Science, 25.

Nesbitt, S.L. and King, R.R. (1989) Business diversification – has it taken a bad rap? *Mergers and Acquisitions*, November–December.

Ohmae, K. (1989) The global logic of strategic alliances, *Harvard Business Review*, March–April.

Ohmae, K. (1990) *The Borderless World*, Harper.

Peng, M.W. (2009) *Global Business*, South-Western, Cengage Learning.

Peters, T.J. and Waterman, R.H. Jr (1982) *In Search of Excellence: Lessons from America's Best Run Companies*, Harper & Row.

Porter, M.E. (1987) From competitive advantage to corporate strategy, *Harvard Business Review*, May–June.

Porter, M.E. (1990) *The Competitive Advantage of Nations*, Free Press.

Ramsay, J. (1987) The strategic focus: deciding your acquisition strategy, Paper presented at 'Growing Through Acquisition', Conference organized by Arthur Young, London, 31 March.

Reed, R. and Luffman, G. (1986) Diversification: the growing confusion, *Strategic Management Journal*, 7 (1).

Rumelt, R.P. (1974) *Strategy, Structure and Economic Performance*, Division of Research, Harvard Business School.

Salter, M.S. and Weinhold, W.A. (1982) *Merger Trends and Prospects for the* 1980s, Division of Research, Harvard Business School; quoted in Thackray, J. (1982) The American takeover war, *Management Today*, September.

van de Vliet, A. (1997) When mergers misfire, *Management Today*, June.

Walton, C. and McBride, J. (1998) Broken engagements, *Financial Times*, 26 February.

Wickham, P.A. (2001) *Strategic Entrepreneurship*, Second Edition, Prentice Hall.

Yanacek, F. (1988) The Road to Exports, *Transportation and Distribution*, 29 (2).

Failure, consolidation and recovery strategies

Learning objectives

Having read to the end of this chapter, you should be able to:

● identify the four possible outcomes of strategic change when companies are in difficulties (**Section 13.1**)

● define corporate decline and failure and identify their main symptoms and causes (**Section 13.2**)

● describe and discuss strategies related to retrenchment, turnaround, divestment, management buy-outs and buy-ins, and implementation issues involved (**Section 13.3**)

● summarize the possible strategies for individual competitors in declining industries (**Section 13.4**).

13.1 Outcomes of strategic change for companies in difficulty

Ultimate business failure implying closure or liquidation – where the organization has failed to satisfy certain key stakeholders, has ceased to be financially viable, and is beyond turning around by new management – happens with many small businesses and also with much larger and established organizations. However, at least some part of a larger organization can potentially be rescued. A business that is in crisis, where radical strategic changes are required, also represents a failure of strategic management, even if (with sound retrenchment and turnaround strategies) the business can be rescued: mistakes have been made, either poor judgement or relative inactivity in the face of a need to change. If a business, or a part of a business, is sold because it is unprofitable, it may represent failure by the current management team. Although commonly assumed that the business has a stronger future in different hands, all divestments of this nature do not imply failure but rather may be because of poor strategic fit and perhaps a past misjudgement. Hence our study of failure concerns why the performance of a business can sink to a crisis level which demands either drastic remedial action, sale or closure – or, arguably, under-performance and under-achievement (against potential) may be a form of failure.

Poor strategic leadership, insufficient control of the essential aspects of financial management and the failure to be competitive are key causes of corporate decline and failure; for example, in Case 13.1 Jinan Sanzhu failed because, *inter alia*, it grew very quickly and executives 'took their eye off the ball'.

Case 13.1   Jinan Sanzhu Group   Ch

The Jinan Sanzhu Group was founded in 1993 by Bingxin Wu. He started the business with the equivalent of £20 000 or RMB 300 000 (RMB conversion of 15 to £1). By 1996 the turnover of the Sanzhu Group had reached RMB 8 billion. The basic product of the business was a health food drink which was claimed to both prolong life and cure a range of diseases. The founder of the business, Mr Wu, was a self-made man who, after the death of his parents and six brothers, had been forced to feed and clothe himself from an early age. He had successfully built up his first

business when he was struck down with a serious illness. Fortunately he recovered and it was this brush with cancer that led him to set up his latest venture selling the health food drink. Mr Wu is very typical of the kind of self-made Chinese entrepreneur who, after starting a business from humble beginnings, is able to create a large business by sheer force of their personality and power within the business.

The company grew rapidly, setting up 2000 offices throughout China and with a salesforce of 150 000 people recruited mainly as agents. The advertisements for the product implied that it could cure a range of diseases; and within 3 years the company was selling 0.4 billion bottles of the product per annum. During its period of success the Sanzhu Group diversified very rapidly – entering a range of business sectors including medicine, bioengineering, chemical and cosmetics industries. However, in 1996, a man called Boshun Chen died suddenly at the age of 60 in Hunan province. His family suspected that the health product of Sanzhu had caused the death of Mr Chen. The event received widespread media publicity within China and within a few months the turnover of the company rapidly declined. A lawsuit was also lost in 1998 and the army of sales agents built up by the group quickly dropped

away. Most of the existing health products of the business were now worthless and two modern factories set up to manufacture the product were closed. Unlike many sophisticated multinational businesses, the Sanzhu Group was unable to make effective use of the media to defend the product so as to retain the loyalty of their customers. Within 5 years of start-up the Jinan Sanzhu Group had failed.

Question

1 What are the classic management problems that a careful reading of the Jinan Sanzhu Group situation can identify?

SOURCE: THIS CASE STUDY WAS PREPARED USING PRIMARILY PUBLICLY AVAILABLE SOURCES OF INFORMATION FOR THE PURPOSES OF CLASSROOM DISCUSSION; IT DOES NOT INTEND TO ILLUSTRATE EITHER EFFECTIVE OR INEFFECTIVE HANDLING OF A MANAGERIAL SITUATION.

At any given time, certain industries will provide attractive growth prospects for those companies who already compete in them, and for potential newcomers. Concomitantly, other industries will be in terminal decline either slowly (where profitable opportunities may still exist for those companies that can relate best to changing market needs) or rapidly (where prospects are likely to be very limited); or undergoing significant change where adaptable companies can survive and grow. Shipbuilding is a good example. There has been a migration to yards in the Far East, whilst some (but certainly not all) European yards have thrived by switching to building modern cruise ships by adapting to, and exploiting, changes in lifestyle holiday patterns and demographics (the population's age profile).

Any recovery is influenced by improved marketing effectiveness, competitiveness and revenue; and also managing the organization more efficiently in order to reduce costs. Where these changes prove inadequate, more drastic strategic change is necessary: **retrenchment**, i.e. changes in functional strategies that increase revenue and reduce costs by concentrating and consolidating, or **turnaround**, i.e. changes in competitive strategies frequently featuring repositioning for competitive advantage. Retrenchment and turnaround strategies are often collectively called *recovery strategies*, while **divestment** occurs when part of an organization, which is diverting resources which could be used more effectively, is sold. Sometimes this happens just to raise money. These all result in changes to the company's corporate strategy.

Businesses succeed when a number of things are in place, in particular a sound business and revenue model where there is real demand and an opportunity to earn revenues in excess of costs; a solid cash flow; good relationships with customers; and strong relationships with employees. These themes are particularly relevant when times are tough – such as in a recession – and point the way to understanding what business should look to achieve and protect all the time.

Arguably, a company is failing when it does not meet objectives set by its stakeholders, or if it produces outputs that are considered undesirable by those associated with it. The outcome may not be ultimate failure, closure or liquidation, but – when the failure or the decline reaches a certain level or continues for some time – it may act as a trigger for remedial action. Such action might be spurned, of course, or prove inadequate, such that the business deteriorates and is finally liquidated.

A company which polluted or harmed the natural environment in some way would be classified as unsuccessful – and maybe even perceived as a failure – by certain stakeholders, but would not necessarily fail financially and go out of business. Companies sometimes develop and launch new products that fail because very few people buy them – the Ford Edsel car and Strand cigarettes are well-quoted examples from business history and over the years Sony has launched recording products (e.g. DAT tapes and the mini disk) that were market failures. Such companies have particularly unsuccessful competitive strategies with some products, but do not thus experience corporate failure.

Corporate failure, liquidation and lack of success should not then be seen as synonymous terms. A private-sector, profit-seeking organization would certainly be classified as a failure if it ended up in liquidation and was closed down with its assets sold off piecemeal, whereas a similar company might be unsuccessful and in decline but able to avoid liquidation. Appropriate strategic action that addresses the causes of the decline may generate recovery; e.g. major shareholders might insist upon the appointment of a new strategic leader, or the financial or competitive weaknesses might be acted upon. Such a company might also be acquired by another, possibly because its shareholders are happy to sell their shares, or the company has been placed in *receivership* (unable to pay its creditors: its suppliers or bank loan interest) and the *receiver* (normally a professional accountant charged with saving the business if possible) has arranged the sale of the business as a going concern. An alternative is the process of 'members voluntary liquidation', where the owners are still in control of the business having chosen to close it by selling off the assets themselves rather than a forced sale of assets by the receiver.

Similarly, major financial stakeholders or trustees could orchestrate the closure or replacement of strategic leader(s) of a non-profit-seeking organization.

Figure 13.1 tracks the potential outcomes once difficulties and potential failure are realized and acted upon. The timing of the intervention is critical here, such that sometimes businesses can be turned around, and sometimes it may be too late to undo the effects of weaknesses and poor decisions in the past.

A company might be relatively unsuccessful compared with its competitors for a prolonged period if its key stakeholders allow it, but is never perceived to be failing.

For example, a small private company whose shares are not quoted on the stock exchange might be making only very limited profits and growing at a rate slower than its industry, but its owners may be happy for it to stay in existence while it is solvent: perhaps because the owners are drawing substantial earnings and not reinvesting to build a future, as the business exists to provide them with a lavish lifestyle. Major English football clubs have perhaps exhibited such symptoms; however, a lack of success consistently will weaken the company, cause it to exhibit symptoms of decline (discussed below) and may ultimately lead to failure. Case 13.2 looks in detail at the rapid collapse of Leeds United.

The next sections examine factors typically leading to corporate decline and failure and at how managers might realize that their company is heading for failure unless remedial action is taken.

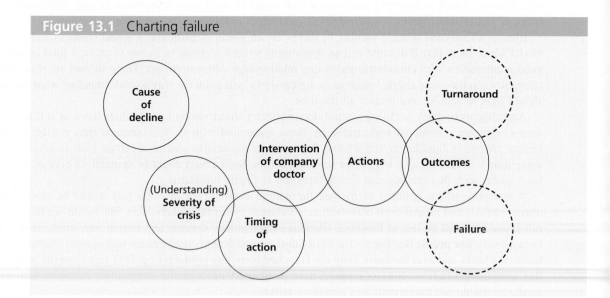

Figure 13.1   Charting failure

Case 13.2 Leeds United Football Club   UK

Under manager Don Revie, Leeds United enjoyed their so-called 'Glory Days' in the 1960s and early 1970s, when they were successful in both England and Europe. In 1974 Revie left to become England manager. Six years later – after five changes of manager including Brian Clough's short stay – the club was relegated from the first to the second division. In 1982, with Eddie Gray (a star player from the Revie era) now installed as manager, crowd trouble and continuing poor performance made this a 'low period' in the club's history. Another ex-star player, Billy Bremner, who lasted until 1987, replaced Gray. Gray retained a support role and in 2004 was again caretaker manager as Leeds struggled to avoid relegation from the (now) Premier League, having just been sold in a last ditch attempt to avoid possible liquidation.

With Howard Wilkinson as the manager, Leeds gained promotion and became League Champions in 1991/2, the season before Division One became the Premier League. Fortunes continued to be cyclical and George Graham, who left in 1996 to manage Tottenham Hotspur, replaced Wilkinson. David O'Leary, who was deputy manager, took over in 1998. By this time Leeds United had been acquired by external investors and was, in reality, a PLC, Leeds Sporting. The new Chairman was Peter Ridsdale, a lifelong supporter of the club who had been managing director of the Burton retail chain, which was a major club sponsor. Some commentators were astonished that Ridsdale reportedly offered George Graham a salary package of £1 million a year in an attempt to persuade him to stay. O'Leary's contract was, however, also worth £6 million over 5 years. Leeds was successful, in part due to a number of young players who had been recruited as youths in the Graham years. However, by 1999, leading players were asking for £50 000 per week salaries. The wage bill was spiralling upwards and the club also began to spend millions of pounds to bring in new players. Both Ridsdale and O'Leary were gambling on success, which, really, they were attempting to buy. In one respect, it made sense – if it was achievable. The winning Premier League clubs attract the most television income and success opens up a variety of commercial and sponsorship opportunities. The fact that this strategy failed to work for Leeds United did not make them in any way unique. At the very least, to remain financially viable, Leeds United had to qualify for a place in the very lucrative European Champions League and

this meant either winning the FA Cup or finishing in the top three of the Premier League. In 2001 Leeds United were beaten semi-finalists in the European Champions League. In one sense getting as far as they did was a real achievement. In another sense, defeat was a setback – but less of a setback than failing to qualify for the competition in the following season.

Leeds Sporting was profitable until 2000, but the financial situation began to deteriorate in 2001, which coincided with yet another decline in the club's playing success. During this period Manchester United was the dominant club in England, although Arsenal enjoyed some more limited success. Manchester United, of course, is a hugely successful global brand which opens up a myriad of income-generating opportunities. The situation had been made worse for Leeds United in 2000 when two players, Lee Bowyer and Jonathan Woodgate, were charged with assault outside a nightclub in Leeds City Centre.

In 2001 Ridsdale began to receive hate mail from fans who opposed his proposal to move Leeds United out of their Elland Road ground to a new purpose-built stadium – something which has never happened. He was now England's highest-paid football club Chairman. Bowyer and Woodgate were acquitted, but Ridsdale disciplined Bowyer, which again angered certain fans. The club was beginning a spiralling cycle of decline.

Results on the field were poor, despite some European success. O'Leary was sacked (with a multi-million pound payoff). Terry Venables and Peter Reid preceded Eddie Gray's second chance as manager. The tendency to replace the manager when results are poor was continuing. Recent signing, Rio Ferdinand was sold to Manchester United for £30 million, yielding a £12 million profit. But he was just one of several players 'divested' to help offset the now unprofitable club's debts, which were growing rapidly as Leeds United was unable to generate an adequate cash flow without European football.

Ridsdale himself resigned in March 2003. To many outsiders he had enjoyed too much power and his willingness to spend money on players and wages had been largely unchecked. Within 12 months, and with debts approaching £100 million, Leeds United's leading creditors accepted a deal and new owners bought the football club from Leeds Sporting, whose shareholders lost everything they had invested. It was now crucial the club avoided relegation at the end of the 2003/4

SOURCE: THIS CASE STUDY WAS PREPARED USING PRIMARILY PUBLICLY AVAILABLE SOURCES OF INFORMATION FOR THE PURPOSES OF CLASSROOM DISCUSSION; IT DOES NOT INTEND TO ILLUSTRATE EITHER EFFECTIVE OR INEFFECTIVE HANDLING OF A MANAGERIAL SITUATION.

season. But this was not to happen. Rumours that the club was to be sold again (literally within months) came to nothing when one interested businessman could not secure the necessary funding. Gray was sacked as manager and it was obvious that a number of players would be sold to raise money and reduce the wage bill. What was going to be required now to secure promotion back to the Premier League, let alone to restore the 'Glory Days'?

Ken Bates, who had sold his share in Chelsea FC to the Russian billionaire, Roman Abramavich, bought Leeds United in January 2005 and took over as Chairman. Bates was acting on behalf of anonymous investors whose identity has been protected. This again led to some disquiet. Leeds competed for 2 more years in the Championship (one league below the Premier League) but failed to secure promotion in an end-of-year play off final in May 2006. A year later they were relegated. To make this situation worse the club went into administration with debts of £35 million they could not meet – some of this to the Inland Revenue. Controversially Bates was then able to buy the club back from the Administrator, but the debts were not paid in full. Leeds United was required to start the 2007/8 season in a lower division and with a 15 points penalty. They had a remarkably good season and managed to win a place in the play-offs – but they lost again in the final. They would then be ousted from the FA Cup before Christmas 2008 by a non-league team. Managers have continued to 'come and go'. There has also been considerable player movement as the club has tried to keep its debts to a minimum. The next appointment generated controversy, yet again. After sacking Gary McAllister, following a run of five defeats, Leeds appointed Simon Grayson, manager at Blackpool, in December 2008. Blackpool accused Leeds of making an illegal approach. Grayson was sacked in 2012 although by then Leeds were competing in the Championship again. His replacement: Neil Warnock, who had a reputation for being strong-willed and willing to offer an opinion, and who also left in 2013.

David O'Leary, seen by many as one of the culprits for spending money to build a winning side that failed to deliver results, became manager at Aston Villa for a time – under his leadership Villa almost qualified for a place in the European Champions League in 2004. He is no longer in club management. Peter Ridsdale became Chairman of Barnsley FC, another club that had experienced financial difficulties in recent years, but left for Cardiff City. When Ridsdale left Barnsley the club was in debt. Most Leeds fans always believed Ridsdale had more questions to answer than O'Leary. Before he left the club Ridsdale had had to employ security staff because of threats to the safety of his family.

In 2007 Ridsdale published a book – *United We Fall* – where he maintained the bulk of the blame should lie with O'Leary; he blamed other managers as well. Ken Bates has commented that many of the club's ongoing problems are largely the result of Ridsdale's debt legacy.

Many have opinions, some driven by insight, others by emotion, but will we ever know the truth about exactly what happened? Maybe Peter Ridsdale was right when he commented that 'nobody at Leeds United ever seems to have been honest with one another'.

Questions

1 What exactly had gone wrong?
2 Is it ever possible to apportion blame in circumstances like these?
3 And should we seek to do this anyway?
4 Are there any lessons in this case that might allow other clubs to avoid the same problems, given that ambition demands investment? You might have a look at Newcastle United.

How different is the situation at Chelsea and Manchester City – two Premiership clubs which have also gambled on success by investing huge amounts on players from around the world? Although in each case there is a wealthy benefactor, he could change his mind if the club doesn't win trophies consistently.

13.2 Symptoms and causes of decline

Symptoms of decline

These symptoms do not cause failure but are indicators that a company might be heading for failure, and appear when a company is performing unsuccessfully relative to what might be expected by an objective outsider or analyst. Slatter (1984), building on the earlier work of Argenti (1976), analyzed 40 declining UK companies which were either turned around or have failed, concluding that the ten major symptoms are:

1 falling profitability
2 reduced dividends, because the firm is reinvesting a greater percentage of profits
3 falling sales, measured by volume or revenue after accounting for inflation
4 increasing debt
5 decreasing liquidity
6 delays in publishing financial results, a typical indicator that something is wrong
7 declining market share
8 high turnover of managers
9 top management fear, such that essential tasks and pressing problems are ignored
10 lack of planning or strategic thinking, reflecting a lack of clear direction.

Causes of decline

Slatter's work remains definitive, affirmed by recent research, including the Society of Practitioners of Insolvency (1995) which found that the greatest single cause of business failure was the loss of market (29 per cent of insolvencies), inadequate cash flow (25 per cent), and leadership failings (16 per cent). Once such symptoms are evident, the underlying causes – categorized below as leadership, finance and competitiveness – should be identified before attempting remedial action:

1. Inadequate or weak strategic leadership Derived largely from Heller (1998) and Oates (1990), warning signals (mainly in smaller firms) include:

- *The existence of (too many) 'would-be's'* where something critical is missing, e.g. a good new idea, some key competence, true commitment.

- *The single-dimension paradox*: Start-up progressed well, but there was a lack of ability or opportunity to grow the business beyond the initial stages.

- *The business is a half-way house*, i.e. a franchise or co-operative (or something similar) that is critically dependent upon the continued support and engagement of others who may be outside the business.

- *The business is impoverished* and fails to achieve (or loses) a winning strategic position; funding may be difficult or mismanaged and is under-capitalized; insufficient attention is paid to the right quality for customers; under-developed management team; key people leaving (key skills are missing); or cannot cope when succession is an issue.

- *The business is blinkered* with too much self-belief (perhaps driven by production, not customer, orientation): the 'we know best' syndrome where the strategic leader is unwilling to accept outside views/advice.

- *The business is technology shy*, a tension where the business needs capital and technology, which costs money, so its key question is: Just when do you invest and how much do you spend?

- *The business has become smothered* and too bureaucratic, perhaps due to legislation, or its large size has caused a loss of its creative spark.

- *The business is (now) run by a crisis manager* who relies too much on an ability to deal (or not deal!) with setbacks and crises as they arise, implying the wrong trade-off between reactive and proactive strategies.

- *The business has started making (too many) mistakes*, possibly having become too ambitious, perhaps with misjudged diversification or acquisition, or may have ignored warning signs such as a cash shortage, or may be simply too greedy.

Inadequate strategic leadership can be manifested in a number of ways, which in turn cause key strategic issues to be neglected or ignored (Chapter 10), and a company could be controlled or dominated by one person whose pursuit of particular personal objectives or style of leadership might create problems or lead to inadequate performance. The organization might fail to develop new corporate or competitive strategies such that previous levels of performance and success are not maintained when particular products, services or strategies go into decline. This issue can be compounded or alleviated by weak or strong managers and by the quality of non-executive directors on the board. Specialists (e.g. accountants or engineers) might ignore aspects outside their expertise. Other examples include: (i) companies undergoing diversification concentrating their resources on areas of new development and neglecting core businesses; (ii) acquisitions failing to match expectations (Chapter 12), due to a poor choice by the strategic leader; (iii) mismanagement of big projects, including developing new and different products and entering new markets (possibly abroad), where over-optimistic revenue forecasts prove to be wrong, or the company stretches its financial and managerial resources, causing healthier parts of the business to suffer. Another possibility is dishonesty, whereby some strategic leaders and businesses take chances and risks which rely on not being found out, but ultimately the business may find survival difficult.

2. Poor financial management Poor financial control includes a failure to manage cash flow, temporary illiquidity due to overtrading, or inadequate costing systems (a lack of awareness of the costs of their products/services) moving them from profit to loss if the product mix changes. A firm investing in expensive equipment for potentially lower costs or product differentiation automatically increases its fixed costs or overheads and its break-even point, making the company more volume sensitive. Finally, some companies in decline situations (e.g. Case 13.2 on Leeds United) appear not to budget properly and, therefore, experience unexpected financial difficulties.

Companies without scale economies (or who are not vertically integrated) can be at a cost disadvantage relative to larger competitors and face low profits or a failure to win orders. Large multi-product companies can subsidize the cost of certain products and again put pressure on their rivals; or, conversely, may have higher costs than their smaller competitors because of the overhead costs of the organization structure, such as an expensive head office. Further, poor operating management can mean low productivity and higher costs, thereby causing decline. These cost problems all affect competitiveness and they are, therefore, linked to the additional competition factors discussed below. Finally: the debt ratio should be controlled to avoid not being able to pay interest charges because of low profits; companies relying on loan capital may find that in years of low profits they cannot invest sufficiently, leading to decline; or, conversely, may decline because of underinvestment due to conservatism rather than financial inability, a weakness of strategic leadership.

3. Competitive forces While all the relevant Porterian forces (Chapter 4) can be managed to create competitive advantage, each of them could cause a weak competitor to be in a decline situation. If companies' products or services cease to be competitive (perhaps due to a loss of clear differentiation and, in turn, a failure to maintain competitive advantage) or if costs increase (perhaps due to increased labour costs which competitors manage to avoid), pressure will be put on prices or profit margins and it may no longer be worthwhile manufacturing the product or service. As well as increased labour costs, a company may experience cost problems as a result of currency fluctuations if it has failed to buy forward appropriately to offset any risk, and with property rents if leases expire and need renegotiating during a period of inflation. Companies whose competitive strategies rely on differentiation must ensure that customers recognize and value the source of the differentiation – requiring creative and effective advertising and promotion targeted to the appropriate segments, potentially expensive, especially if the industry is characterized by high advertising budgets. Companies failing to market their products/services effectively may decline because they are failing to achieve adequate sales.

Case 13.3 looks at a company where rapid growth and success put strains on the business and led to a perception of underlying difficulties.

Case 13.3 Nine Dragons Paper Limited   Ch

Nine Dragons Paper Holdings Limited (ND Paper) was established in 1995 to meet the needs of the growing Chinese business economy for paperboard packaging. Its operations serve as a one stop shop for a broad range of high-quality paperboard products. The growth of ND Paper has been extraordinary – as witnessed by the group sales for 2010/11 of RMB 14.2 billion representing an increase of 36 per cent when compared with the previous year. At the same time gross profit amounted to RMB 2.2 billion, an increase of 8 per cent over the previous year.

The intention of the Group was stated as continuing steady growth in 2012 and beyond, with six new paper machines coming on stream for 2012 and 2013, which would bring the Group's total production capacity to over 14 million tonnes per annum – an increase in production capacity of 21 per cent when compared to the current capacity.

Behind all of this growth and success is the figure of Chair and founder of ND paper Cheung Yan (her Cantonese name), otherwise known as Zhang Yin, who, with the continuing success of ND Paper, became the richest woman in greater China.

How did she achieve this position and become the Chair of such a business enterprise?

Zhang Yin was born in 1957 in Shaoguan, Guangdong. She is the daughter of a lieutenant in the Red Army who subsequently became the general manager of a metallurgy company in Guangdong. When Yin finished school she started working as an accountant in a textile factory in Guangdong. From the textile company Yin moved to Shenzhen to work in a paper trading business. This happened at the time when the whole area around Shenzen was starting to boom because of its economic zone status. In 1985, when she was 27 years old, Yin gave up working in Shenzhen and rejected the opportunity to work in a joint venture company. Instead she was entrusted by a papermaking factory to purchase waste paper in Hong Kong. Due to the relative scarcity of forest resources in China most high grade paper raw material requires the import of waste paper and pulp. Yin saw the opportunity this represented. She moved to Hong Kong in 1985 with her savings of US$3800 and became engaged in the business of purchasing waste paper for recycling.

After working for less than 2 years in Hong Kong Yin had accumulated enough experience to establish her own paper-making factory – Dongguan Zhongnan Paper – in Dongguan City to produce paper for daily use. However the supply of waste paper in Hong Kong and in China continued to be limited by volume. In order to seek greater sales and business development opportunities she moved to the USA and founded, in collaboration with her (new) second husband, the paper exporting company America Chung Nam. Not only was the USA rich in waste paper resources it also had a mature recycling industry.

The ambitious Yin set herself the goal of building the largest business in the world for the supply of raw material for paper making. Yin also saw an advantage in being located in the USA – by shipping her waste paper to China in containers that otherwise would be returning empty to China from the USA. At this time it was the case that for every ten full containers that left China for the USA, nine empty ones went back to Hong Kong. Yin was thus able to secure a low price for shipping her waste paper back to China and the shipping company made an unexpected profit. This gave her a core element of price competitiveness in the Chinese market-place. This was coupled with the business model adopted by Yin of being a Chinese company buying cheap scrap paper from the USA, importing it into China to be recycled into cardboard boxes to export Chinese goods mainly back to the USA.

Yin's ambition led her take a different strategic course from other Chinese paper-making factories – who typically limited their production capacity to around 50 000 tons per annum due to the size of the local domestic market. Yin planned to become the leading packaging manufacturer in the world; and her first paper-making machine had a production capacity of 200 000 tons. At this time she bought paper-making factories in both Dongguan City and Taicang City, giving her additional production capacity. Yin supplemented this by purchasing capacity and paper from overseas paper-making machinery that, although more expensive, was much more productive at high volumes.

In 1995 Yin returned to Hong Kong and co-founded Nine Dragons Paper (NDP) with her husband and her younger brother. Yin demonstrated the nature of her single-minded determination to stay focused on one activity when she said: 'Nine Dragons Paper will not enter the field of newsprint.' A total of US$110 million was invested in Nine Dragons Paper at this time with the headquarters of NDP remaining in Dongguan. For the next 10 years Yin and the management team at Nine Dragons set about meeting their declared target of becoming the world's largest supplier of paper for the packaging industry. In March 2006 Nine Dragons Paper floated on the Hong Kong Stock Exchange and the IPO raised almost US$500 million. By the end of 2006 investors were enjoying a 300 per cent increase in the value of their stock. Through the success of this flotation, a further doubling of production capacity took place – and this continued each year so that by 2009, NDP was indeed the world's largest manufacturer of packaging paper, with an ever-increasing focus in high margin paper products such as coated duplex board and food grade and pharmaceutical grade white board. In 2010/11 high grade paper products accounted for 24 per cent of the tonnage produced – up from 11 per cent in the previous year.

The Group's paper machines in China are currently located in four areas, including Dongguan, Guangdong Province, the Pearl River Delta and Taicang, Jiangsu Province in the Yangtze River Delta Region; and is actively involved in both further organic growth and growth by acquisition having in 2011 entered into an agreement for the controlling interest in Habel Yongxin Paper Co Ltd.

With the strategy of measured steady long-term growth in production capacity, a focus on core paper products and the twin targets of economies of scale and environmental protection called for in the PRC (People's Republic of China) Government's 'Twelfth 5-year programme', then Nine Dragons Paper appeared to be set for continued sales and profit growth.

Yet in June 2011 Standard and Poor's Rating Services, quoted in Reuters, announced that it had withdrawn its 'BB' long-term corporate credit rating on Nine Dragons Paper (Holdings) Ltd and also the 'BB' issue rating on the company's outstanding senior unsecured notes. Standard and Poor's is quoted as saying; 'In our view, Nine Dragons has an aggressive debt-funded growth appetite. We withdrew the ratings because we have insufficient access to the management and therefore cannot fully understand the company's strategy or assess its further credit risks.'

At the end of December 2011, Nine Dragons had about HK$19.97 billion (US$2.6 billion) in bank borrowings and a net borrowings total equity ratio of almost 88 per cent. Zhang Yin defended the performance of Nine Dragons saying 'These six new production lines will allow the company to produce new products and not just increase production of what we already have. This year will be a peak for debt levels. Once we are through this year we will see debt levels falling next year and the year after next.'

**http://www.ndpaper.com/eng/aboutnd
/chairman.htm**

Questions

1 Is a sustained existence 'inevitable' for Nine Dragons Paper or could a business with such a growth record actually fail?

2 Has Nine Dragons been guilty of repeating mistakes made in the past by companies with ambitious business growth targets?

3 Alternatively, is this a typical stock market scare mongering to act as a check on an aggressive and dynamically led focused business?

13.3 The feasibility of recovery

When a company's sales or profits are falling because of non-competitiveness or because its industry is in decline, recovery may or may not be possible. A single-product firm, or one heavily reliant on the industry in question, may be in real difficulties and in danger of liquidation unless it can diversify successfully, though this may be difficult to fund with lower profits. Where the situation applies to one business unit in an already diversified company, the company as a whole may be less threatened. However, a change of strategy will be required, depending whether or not a successful recovery can be brought about and sustained.

The likelihood of a possible recovery improves where the causes of the problems can be overcome, depending upon how serious and deep-rooted they are; and the industry as a whole, or particular segments of the industry which might be targeted, remains attractive; and where there is potential for creating/enhancing competitive advantage. Slatter and Lovett (1999) identified four steps to turnaround management:

1 take control and manage the immediate crisis

2 rebuild stakeholder support

3 fix the business

4 resolve future funding

Recovery situations

Four types of recovery situation are illustrated in Figure 13.2(a) (derived from Slatter, 1984). Changing the strategy is essential when the profits of the firm or business unit have declined to a crisis stage, but the industry and competitive factors might be such that recovery simply is not feasible. Insolvency is inevitable, whatever alternative strategies might be tried, or successful retrenchment strategies might be implemented and profits returned to a non-crisis level. Unless the industry remains in some way attractive and potentially profitable, or the firm retains its competitive advantage, the retrenchment might subsequently fail. A third alternative is a successful turnaround but no real growth and sustained recovery. Insufficient funds may be generated in a low-profit industry to finance investment for further growth and diversification. A sustained recovery implies real growth, and possibly further changes in functional, competitive and corporate strategies.

Weitzel and Johnson (1989) drew attention to the issue of timing and highlighted that the later an organization delays attempting recovery from a downward trend, the more difficult the task. Figure 13.2(b) shows that sustained survival/recovery is a much steeper challenge (with less likelihood of success) when remedial action is delayed, given the point in time – a 'crisis zone' – when recovery is unrealistic.

Non-recoverable situations involve little chance of survival and the likelihood that both retrenchment and turnaround strategies will fail, characterized by (Slatter, 1984):

- The company is not competitive and its potential for improvement is low, perhaps the result of a cost disadvantage that cannot be remedied. Certain businesses and industries that have declined in the face of foreign competition, especially from countries with low wage costs, are testament to this scenario.

- The company is not diversified and lacks both the resources and access to resources to remedy this weakness.

- Demand for the basic product or service involved is in terminal decline.

Temporary recovery occurs where a retrenchment strategy is implemented successfully and may or may not be sustained (Slatter, 1984). New forms of competitive advantage may be found and sustained, or the product or service may be effectively repositioned, averting subsequent insolvency. However, if costs are reduced or additional revenues are generated in an essentially unattractive and declining industry, the effect will be limited. In such cases, the company should invest the cash generated from the retrenchment to diversify, if that is possible.

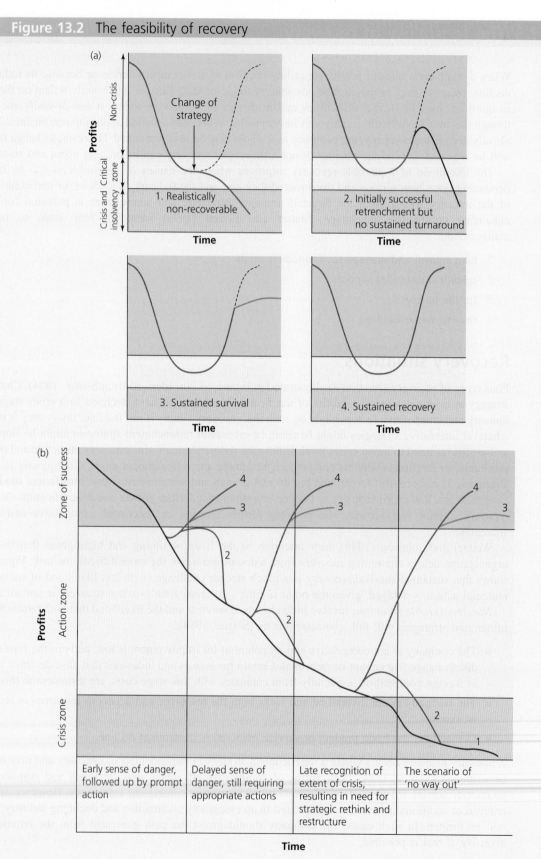

Figure 13.2 The feasibility of recovery

(a)

1. Realistically non-recoverable

Change of strategy

2. Initially successful retrenchment but no sustained turnaround

3. Sustained survival

4. Sustained recovery

(b)

Early sense of danger, followed up by prompt action

Delayed sense of danger, still requiring appropriate actions

Late recognition of extent of crisis, resulting in need for strategic rethink and restructure

The scenario of 'no way out'

(A) DEVELOPED BY AUTHORS BASED ON IDEAS FROM SLATTER, S (1984) CORPORATE RECOVERY, PENGUIN

(B) ADAPTED FROM WEITZEL, W AND JOHNSON, E (1989) DECLINE IN ORGANIZATIONS – A LITERATURE INTEGRATION AND EXTENSION. ADMINISTRATIVE SCIENCE QUARTERLY, 34 (1)

If an organization has captive customers who are in some way dependent and face high short-term exit costs, possibly because of agreed specifications, they can exploit them for a period by charging high prices – although profit will improve temporarily, the customers will be lost in the medium to long-term – so the company needs to use the extra revenue and the time that they buy to develop new strategic opportunities.

Sustained survival implies that a turnaround is achieved but there is little further growth (Slatter, 1984). The industry may be in slow decline, or generally competitive and unprofitable; and, while survival potential and limited profit opportunities continue to exist, there is little more. Sustained survival would also apply where a company failed to use its increased earnings effectively and did not diversify into new, more profitable opportunities which could provide growth prospects.

Sustained recovery is likely to involve a genuine and successful turnaround, possibly new product development or market repositioning, perhaps followed by a growth strategy such as acquisition and diversification.

The recovery is helped if the industry is strong and attractive and the company's decline has been caused by poor management rather than because of industry decline.

Both a sustained survival and a sustained recovery may involve divestment of assets or part of the business to enable the company to concentrate on selected market segments or products.

Slatter (1984) studied a number of successful and unsuccessful attempts at turnaround, and concluded that there are three main features of a sustained recovery:

1 Asset reduction is invariably required in order to generate cash, which is quite frequently achieved by divestment of part of the business.

2 A new strategic leader is usually necessary, who will typically be associated with a restructuring of the organization, the introduction of new strategies and a redefinition of roles and policies.

3 Better financial control systems are also a normal feature.

While retrenchment and initial survival can be achieved by concentrating on improving efficiencies, sustained survival and recovery invariably require more effective competitive and corporate strategies. Case 13.4 provides an example of a more sustained recovery at Pringle where the strategic leader involved, Kim Winser, then left to try to do the same for Aquascutum.

Case 13.4   Kim Winser, Pringle and Aquascutum   UK, Int

This case describes the impact Kim Winser has had in reviving the fortunes of two long-established brands. Winser herself has been described as having that 'unnerving mix of friendliness and control that powerful women have'.

Pringle is a long-established clothing and knitwear manufacturer based in the Scottish borders. Formed in 1815 Pringle is believed to be the UK's oldest clothing brand. The company became known for the 'twinset' matching jumper and cardigan for ladies – which was worn and popularized by movie stars such as Audrey Hepburn, Vivienne Leigh and Margaret Lockwood in the 1950s – the shruggie 'ballet cardigan' and the Argyle check sweater worn by golfers.

In 2002 the current owner, Dawson International, a Scottish yarn and clothing manufacturer, was keen to refocus its business around cashmere products, and opted to sell Pringle for £10 million to Fang Brothers Knitting of Hong Kong. At the time Pringle was in decline. A number of reasons were cited. Sales had fallen in key Asian markets; the value of sterling was high; the clothes were staid and unfashionable; the brand had failed to keep up with changing tastes. Dawson had closed the Pringle factory in Berwick and reduced the headcount elsewhere – but the overall health of the business had not improved markedly. New owner Kenneth Fang decided he needed a fresh chief executive if the brand was to be rejuvenated.

He recruited Kim Winser, at the time a marketing director with Marks and Spencer, where she had worked since she was 18. Feisty, she had once criticized M&S chief, Lord Sieff, in a meeting, arguing against his plan to appoint a female board director. The argument is that she herself wanted to be the first woman on the M&S Board! She had been promoted through the ranks and was credited with turning around the womenswear business in the 1990s. She came with a reputation for being driven, career-minded and organized. Fang was willing to give her considerable autonomy.

She concluded the brand needed reconceptualizing and repositioning in a short period of time – her target was just 3 months. She set out to simultaneously lower costs and develop new products and market opportunities. More jobs, including senior management posts, were lost. The long-standing retail concession with Edinburgh Woollen Mills was abandoned in favour of high end/high fashion outlets such as Selfridges and Harvey Nichols. A celebrity endorsement deal with golfer Nick Faldo was terminated.

A new collection was quickly designed – with a more modern look – although the product range overall was being reduced. Aspects of the past – the Argyll check, the twinset and the cashmere yarns – were retained, but new colours, new styles and new ways of displaying the famous Pringle motifs were sought. The range was promoted in glossy fashion and lifestyle magazines; model Sophie Dahl was recruited for the campaign. The effect was instantaneous and sales jumped 30 per cent. A confident Pringle joined the London catwalk for the first time in its history. When Madonna, David Beckham and Robbie Williams were all seen in public wearing Pringle clothes (a hugely valuable free endorsement) the brand was 'hot'. It was now 'nightclub' rather than 'golfclub'.

Winser decided to enter retailing, another first for Pringle. She began with a shop at Heathrow Airport, but with plans for Central London, New York, Tokyo and other European cities. The range has also been extended beyond knitwear into complementary skirts, trousers, dresses, coats, swimwear and accessories. Baby wear and homewear were on the future agenda. It helped that any spare capacity in the Pringle factories could be used to manufacture other products for the Fang Brothers.

In 2006 Kim Winser joined Aquascutum, which she described as a 'sleeping giant of a business'. Aquascutum had also been described as 'Britain's noblest fading brand'. Could she repeat her turnaround achievements?

Aquascutum became a popular choice for consumers willing to pay premium prices for good quality, stylish clothing; it is perhaps best known for its trenchcoat – a distinctive, classic, light tan coloured, belted, double-breasted raincoat with sleeve straps and epaulettes. The company is 150 years old – younger than Pringle! – and now owned by a Japanese business, Renown.

The flagship London store has photographs of Hollywood celebrities wearing the products – the fact that most of these are 'older' rather than 'youthful' stars is indicative of the typical buyer. Annual turnover exceeds £200 million, mainly in the UK and Japan, but the business had been losing money. One question

concerned whether it would lend itself to a more youthful appeal with endorsement by models such as Kate Moss or Sophie Dahl.

Winser believed she needed to 'have fun with the style' but not sacrifice the brand's heritage – an interesting challenge. She wanted to attract new customers without losing the existing ones. More accessories were on the cards, especially bags.

In 2009, and after 3 years of losses, Winser sought to acquire the business as a management buyout, but her bid failed 'at the eleventh hour'. She resigned and left immediately. Renown continued with its attempt to sell the business and started discussions with a Hong Kong trader who already acted as a wholesaler in the Far East for Aquascutum trenchcoats – but again no deal was concluded. 'The chances of the brand surviving as a British business were fading fast.' It began to appear that Renown might move everything, including design and manufacture, to the Far East.

Meanwhile Kim Winser's name had been linked to a senior post at Versace and also as a possible successor to Sir Stuart Rose as CEO of Marks and Spencer. Neither happened and she now acts as an adviser to other fashion retail groups.

Questions

1 How do you perceive the similarities and differences of the two turnaround challenges faced by Kim Winser?

2 Given that in the world of high fashion little stays still for long, what would you recommend Pringle should be doing to make sure Pringle does not once again switch from growth into decline?

3 Had Kim Winser succeeded in buying Aquascutum what changes do you think she might have made/needed to make?

4 Given her record would she appear to have been a likely candidate for the leadership role at M&S?

SOURCE: THIS CASE STUDY WAS PREPARED USING PRIMARILY PUBLICLY AVAILABLE SOURCES OF INFORMATION FOR THE PURPOSES OF CLASSROOM DISCUSSION; IT DOES NOT INTEND TO ILLUSTRATE EITHER EFFECTIVE OR INEFFECTIVE HANDLING OF A MANAGERIAL SITUATION.

Rescue, to provide a platform for recovery, could well take 12–18 months and involves making the business cash rich by selling assets, obtaining a new injection of funding and restructuring debt; and tightening operations by strengthening margins, better cost control, better working capital management and better information.

True renewal and recovery could then require a further 3–5 years.

The skills required for the rescue and recovery stages are different, and a change of strategic leader – as happened at Pringle – may be logical. A vision for recovery is of little use until the business has been rescued and consolidated; equally, consolidation without a future vision is likely to show only limited and short-term benefits.

van de Vliet (1998) identified useful questions to assess recovery potential:

1 Is there some part of the business worth rescuing?

2 What are its key core activities?

3 Does it have the people it needs, who truly understand it operationally?

4 Do these managers have the freedom to manage?

5 Are there ways in which the product(s) and/or service(s) could be improved?

6 Can the necessary resources (other than people) that are required be secured?

Having considered the background feasibility of recovery, the actual recovery strategies are now examined in greater detail.

Retrenchment strategies

Essentially functional, rather than competitive or corporate, retrenchment aims to make firms more productive and profitable while retaining essentially the same products and services, although there might be some rationalization. By concentrating on financial issues, it often addresses major causes of the company's decline.

Organizational changes While (as discussed above) a change in strategic leadership is frequently involved in recovery strategies, firms might also need to strengthen their management team in other areas. Personnel changes are unimportant, but the subsequent changes to strategies, structure and policies, and the effect on the existing staff and their motivation, do matter. Reorganizations take place, with new definitions of roles, responsibilities, policies and management and control systems to give managers new opportunities to achieve, and convince them that recovery is possible.

Financial changes Poor financial control systems, e.g. badly managed cash flow, are often a feature of companies in difficulties; while overheads may have become too high in relation to direct production costs, such that the company may not know the actual costs of producing particular products and services or be unable to explain all expenditures. The establishment of an effective costing system, and greater control over the cash flow, can improve profitability and generate revenue. Another retrenchment strategy is restructuring debt to reduce the financial burden of the company. Possibly repayment dates can be extended, or loan capital converted into preference shares or equity, thereby allowing the company more freedom through less pressure to pay interest.

Cost-reduction strategies Traditionally, highly acquisitive companies such as Hanson sought businesses with high gross margins and relatively low after-tax profitability: indications of overgrown overheads, which provide opportunities for improving profits by reducing organizational slack and waste. Companies can address their overheads, without being acquired, if they recognize the extent of the problem and are determined to reduce costs to improve their competitiveness and profitability – which happened increasingly in the late 1980s and 1990s, reducing the number of attractively priced acquisition targets. Companies that could not reduce their costs were often liquidated as the economy tightened. A starting point for cost-cutting is labour costs, thus improving productivity, but reductions that are too harsh threaten the quality of both the product and the overall service offered to customers. One opportunity is to examine working patterns and attempt to manage overtime, part-time arrangements and extra shifts both to meet demand and to contain costs. Companies can slip easily into situations where overtime and weekend working are creating costs which cannot be recovered in competitive prices.

Redundancies may be required to reduce costs and bring capacity more into line with demand, but can be implemented well or poorly. In most cases, the issue is not losing particular numbers of people and thereby saving on wages, but losing non-essential staff or those who fail to make an effective contribution – and in a voluntary redundancy programme good people may choose to leave or take early retirement. Costs can be reduced anywhere and everywhere in the value chain. Better supply arrangements and terms can reduce costs; products can be redesigned to cost less without any loss in areas significant to customers; and certain activities, such as public relations, training, advertising and research and development, might be cut. The rationale is often that these activities are non-essential, which might be perfectly plausible in the short term, but may not be the case for the longer term and, therefore, they would need to be reinstated when extra revenues had been generated.

Asset-reduction strategies *Divestment* of a business unit, or part of the business, is considered in greater detail later and, while being more of a corporate than a functional strategy, the decision should not be made on financial grounds alone. While the sale of a business can raise money, it may be more than offset if there is existing synergy with other parts of the company which suffer from the divestment. *Internal divestment or rationalization* can take a number of forms – for example, plants might be closed and production concentrated in fewer places, or production might be rescheduled to generate increased economies of scale – to reduce both overheads and direct costs. *Assets might be sold and leased back* and, as far as the balance sheet is concerned, assets have been reduced and in turn cash has been generated; the scope and capacity of the business may be unaffected, since the changes are exclusively financial.

Revenue-generating strategies Revenue can be generated by improving certain management control systems: freeing cash by reducing stocks by better stock management or a review of the whole production system and a move towards just-in-time; or improving cash flow by persuading debtors to settle accounts more speedily.

We weren't making money at SAS [Scandinavian Airlines System] when I came here. We were in a desperate situation, and that's the worst time to focus on preventing mistakes and controlling costs. First, we had to increase revenues. We had to decide what business we were going to do – before you can start managing effectively you must know who is your customer and what is your product – and go to work on the revenue side. Then we could think about cutting costs, because only then would we know which costs could be cut without losing competitiveness.

JAN CARLZON, WHEN PRESIDENT AND CHIEF EXECUTIVE OFFICER,
SCANDINAVIAN AIRLINES SYSTEM

Case 13.5 examines the revenue-increasing approaches of Gap, Gucci and Maserati.

Case 13.5   Gap, Gucci and Maserati   US, Eur, Int

Gap

Gap is a US clothing retailer which also owns the Old Navy and Banana Republic brands. The business was founded by Don Fisher and throughout the 1990s he continued to work closely with his hands-on CEO, who designed clothes and specified inventory quantities. When Paul Pressler was recruited from Disney in 2002, and appointed CEO, the business was in some difficulty. Sales were falling and Gap appeared to have 'lost touch with its customers'. Could Pressler restore its previous performance levels?

Gap's original target customers were the so-called baby boomers, those born between 1946 and 1964. As they matured, married and had children the brand was extended – with Gap Kids (1986) and Baby Gap (1990). The business did very well with smart casual clothes when 'dress-down Fridays' were introduced. But competition from 'more sassy brands' such as Abercrombie & Fitch and American Eagle hit Gap. The company reaction was to target the younger market, but critics felt the focus was more on teenagers than people in their twenties and this was a mistake. Gap had failed to get the range quite right. Profits were affected because costs were relatively high through inadequate investment in retail systems.

Pressler was more detached in his style and he was determined to 'replace intuition with science'. He respositioned the brands – with Banana Republic the most upmarket, followed by Gap and then Old Navy. Products were segmented for discrete groups such as mums, mums shopping for families, fashionable young people and more conservative young people. Considerable work was done on sizing – with sales data used to determine which sizes would feature in different stores. Where sales were inadequate, stores were closed. But 3 years after his appointment, Gap was still struggling.

Gucci

Gucci began life in Florence in 1923 as a manufacturer of superior quality leather goods – but since 2001 it has been owned by the French business Pinault Printemps Redoute (PPR); it is now based in London. During the 1990s the company had enjoyed something of a revival in its fortunes.

Gucci is perhaps best known for its shoes and handbags – which are sold in boutiques and specialist department stores around the world. Many of its customers are wealthy Asians. The company has systematically diversified and the Gucci group also includes Yves Saint Laurent (clothing, perfumes and other luxury items), the Alexander McQueen, Stella McCartney and Balenciaga fashion labels and the French Boucheron jewellery business. Yves Saint Laurent had been acquired in 1999. Group sales were in the region of 2.5 billion Euros when PPR acquired the business.

PPR appointed a new CEO, Robert Polet, from Unilever. Although he had been responsible for revenues some three times Gucci's turnover, his main experience was with ice-cream.

He targeted a number of things:

- Sales of Gucci-branded products needed to double (from 1.5 billion Euros) by 2010 – by exploiting opportunities in Asia and India.
- The group overall should adopt the 'lighter style' of YSL.
- Shoes and jewellery sales should be increased.
- The specialist fashion labels needed to be lifted to at least break-even performance.

- Marketing and customer awareness was not strong enough.
- The supply chain should be strengthened to 'best in class' performance levels.

Maserati

Maserati started making cars in 1914; and its success as a sports car manufacturer peaked in the 1950s. There have been six owners of the business, the most recent being Ferrari, itself owned by Fiat. Ferrari bought 50 per cent of the business in 1997 and the remaining half in 1999.

In the early years of the twenty-first century Maserati was losing money. It was not alone. The two luxury brands owned by Volkswagen – the Italian Lamborghini and the French Bugatti – were also struggling. Ferrari inherited a 'ramshackle factory' making 700 cars a year. It 'wasn't really a business any more' but Ferrari was determined to remedy this. Money was invested and capacity increased to 5000 cars a year. This was 300 cars more than Ferrari itself, which was being kept at that level. The realistic target for Maserati was thought to be 10 000. To put these figures in perspective, the UK's specialist sports car builder, Morgan – albeit a different offering – makes around 700 cars a year. A new CEO, Martin Leach, from Ford, was appointed in 2004.

There was a stated desire to introduce new models, but this takes time. Maserati uses Ferrari engines, as one might expect. The focus of investment would be on the engine, gearbox and electronics – the car must be distinguishable on performance. The most popular model is the sporty Quattro Porte saloon, which competes against the top of the range BMW and Mercedes models. 'The Maserati brand has an intrinsic value that can justify a high price – 10 per cent to 20 per cent above BMW and Mercedes – if the product is right.'

Questions

1 How difficult is it to revive a flagging brand and target new customers in a very competitive market?
2 What has happened to Gap and Gucci since 2009, a period when many retailers have been struggling?
3 Was the timing of the attempt to rejuvenate Maserati 'right' or 'wrong'?

SOURCE: THIS CASE STUDY WAS PREPARED USING PRIMARILY PUBLICLY AVAILABLE SOURCES OF INFORMATION FOR THE PURPOSES OF CLASSROOM DISCUSSION; IT DOES NOT INTEND TO ILLUSTRATE EITHER EFFECTIVE OR INEFFECTIVE HANDLING OF A MANAGERIAL SITUATION.

Turnaround strategies

Whilst retrenchment strategies usually have short time horizons, do not affect customers directly and will be designed to yield immediate results, turnaround strategies are likely to address those areas which must be developed if there is to be a sustained recovery – involving changes in the overall marketing effort, including the repositioning or refocusing of existing products and services, together with the development of new ones. They are designed to bring quick results and at the same time contribute towards longer-term growth. They overlap with the internal limited growth strategies outlined in Chapter 10, and they may also be a stepping stone to growth through diversification. The turnaround strategies below are designed to improve the effectiveness of the company's marketing and, consequently, address customers and consumers directly thus changes should be implemented cautiously.

Changing prices Prices can be changed at very short notice, with price increases or decreases resulting in increased revenue. Price rises can increase revenue as long as the elasticity of demand ensures that sales do not thus decline unacceptably. Price decreases can improve demand and hence revenue, again depending on the elasticity of demand. Hence, an insight into the demand elasticity for individual products and services is required – although forecasting the effect of price changes is somewhat uncertain. In general, the opportunity to increase prices is related to the extent of existing differentiation, and the opportunity to differentiate further and create new competitive advantage.

Unless particular products and services are regarded as under-priced by customers in relation to their competition, a price rise should be accompanied by advertising support and possibly minor changes and improvements in the product or packaging, and the price change must be justified. The likely reaction of competitors, in turn influenced by the structure of the industry and the degree and type of competitive rivalry, should be gauged. Markets with an oligopoly structure, an essential feature of UK industry, tend to follow price decreases but not price rises. Discount structures might be altered to favour certain groups of customers at the expense of others, thus both raising revenue and improving attractiveness to certain market segments. Any negative effect on other customer groups should be monitored carefully.

However, some firms increase prices immediately after being acquired, assuming that existing customers are for now committed and locked in, and can be 'exploited'. The new parent is willing to lose them in the medium term as it has other plans for the business, which might involve rationalization and selling on to someone else.

Refocusing By concentrating its efforts on specific customers and specific products, relating the two closely together, refocusing requires careful thought and attention in relation to why people buy and to identify the opportunities for differentiation, segmentation and competitive advantage. The selection of particular product/market and service/market niches for concentrating effort will depend upon revenue and growth potential, gross margins, the extent and type of competition for the segment or niche and the potential to create a response to marketing activity, such as advertising. In the short term, products or services that sell quickly and generate cash quickly may be attractive opportunities even if their gross margin is small; and there may be a group of customers for whom an appropriate package can be created.

New product development The replacement of existing products with new ones may be required to effect a turnaround if a company has been losing competitiveness in an attractive industry by falling behind competitors in terms of innovation and product improvement. Equally, product improvements, designed to prolong the product life cycle, can be useful in low-growth or declining industries, by helping a company to concentrate on particular segments of the market that remain relatively strong.

Rationalizing the product line Variety reduction can enable efforts to be concentrated on stronger market segments and opportunities, particularly where the industry overall is losing attractiveness. This strategy needs a proper understanding of costs, and which individual products and services are most and least profitable. In a multi-product organization, with interdependencies between the business units, transfer price arrangements can distort profitability. As mentioned earlier, certain products and services can be vital contributors to overall synergy, but individually not very profitable, and care needs to be taken with these.

Emphasis on selling and advertising Selected additional expenditure (e.g. advertising, below-the-line promotions and the salesforce to promote products and services in order to generate sales revenue) can generate greater revenue, or there might be an examination of all current marketing expenditure to try to ascertain the best potential returns from the spending. However, all of these activities are investments, and their potential returns should be considered. The increased revenue expected from any increased spending should certainly exceed the additional costs incurred, and perhaps the opportunity cost of the investment funds should also be assessed. While five alternative approaches to improving marketing effectiveness have been considered in this section, a number of them may be used in conjunction at any time. Moreover, these turnaround strategies may also be combined with the retrenchment strategies discussed earlier, both to reduce costs and to improve revenue at the same time. As discussed above, the divestment of products or business units can reduce assets in retrenchment strategies and also to rationalize the product line.

Rejuvenating mature businesses Baden-Fuller and Stopford (1992) define a mature business as 'one whose managers believe themselves to be imprisoned by their environment and unable to succeed' and, as a consequence, they are invariably giving poor service to their customers and achieving barely adequate financial returns. Often, with a more creative, entrepreneurial, innovative approach, they can be rejuvenated by simply becoming a stronger competitor. This transformation is likely to require a number of developmental steps over an extended period, rather than being achieved with a one-off major project; it implies a change of culture and style. Success will not be instantaneous and will need building. Baden-Fuller and Stopford (1992) have developed a four-stage model for rejuvenation, which is summarized in Figure 13.3.

1 *Galvanization* is when there is a clear recognition of the true state of the business and the establishment of an able management team which is committed to dealing with the problem, which may only need a change of strategic leader; on other occasions, the changes will be more extensive. Managers who are responsible for bringing about the crisis, through poor decisions and judgement, or negligently allowing the situation to deteriorate, will need to change their approach if they do stay.

   Progress requires resources. Independent businesses are likely to require fresh capital and possibly new owners, while subsidiaries of larger organizations will have to justify new, corporate investment.

2 *Simplification* follows, implying a clearer focus and the concentration of scarce resources on a smaller agenda to build a strong and sustainable core. Strategies, structures and styles may all have to change, which is sometimes termed strategic regeneration (Chapter 15). The business must next:

3 *Build* new competencies and competitive advantages which, because of resource pressures, is again likely to take time and prove highly challenging. Finally, true rejuvenation requires it to:

4 *Exert leverage* to extend its new competencies and capabilities into new products, services, markets and opportunities.

These points are illustrated in Case 13.6, where a turnaround specialist intervenes at two businesses, New Covent Garden Foods and Green and Black's Chocolate.

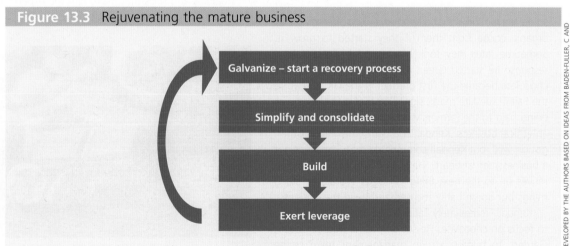

Figure 13.3 Rejuvenating the mature business

Galvanize – start a recovery process

Simplify and consolidate

Build

Exert leverage

DEVELOPED BY THE AUTHORS BASED ON IDEAS FROM BADEN-FULLER, C AND STOPFORD, J (1992) *REJUVENATING THE MATURE BUSINESS*, ROUTLEDGE

Case 13.6 William Kendall – Turnaround Specialist   UK

William Kendall has demonstrated expertise in turning around companies. He will join a company and allow its founder to make an exit; he will then build the business in terms of both scale and profitability before selling it on as a viable concern.

Kendall is the son of a Bedfordshire farming family and he grew up passionate about both food and business. After school he spent a year in the army before reading law at Cambridge. He trained and practised as a barrister before becoming an investment banker. After the crash of 1987 he opted to study for an MBA at Insead.

In 1989 he joined the New Covent Garden Food Company, best known in the UK for its fresh soup in cartons, a product the supermarkets have come to copy with their own branded ranges. The company was not making money when Kendall arrived, and this continued for 5 years. But with innovation, new products, diversification into fresh gravies, fresh baked beans and fresh sweet sauces, and with more robust management systems, its fortunes were changed around. In 1998 it was sold for £24 million to existing food business, S. Daniels, a related business that had moved from canned to fresh and chilled fruit and drinks products.

His next challenge was Green and Black's chocolate, where he and a business partner bought an 85 per cent stake. He was able to do this at a favourable price because the company was 'losing money thanks to a mish-mash of a product range'. The business had been set up by Craig Sams, an American who had come to the UK from California. Sams had been an early campaigner for organic living and he set up Whole Earth Foods in 1967 to make peanut butter, jams, baked beans and cereals. Whilst on a holiday in Belize he met some Mayan Indians and spontaneously offered to buy organic cocoa from them if they started to grow it. Sometime later they took him up on his offer! As a response he started Green and Black's in 1991 and its chocolate became the first product in the UK to feature the Fair Trade kite mark, signalling that a fair price was being paid to the farmers who supplied it. It symbolizes an ethical business. Kendall and Sams knew each other, got on well, but Kendall commented that Sams was not a businessman at heart. 'He has brilliant ideas, but soon moves on to the next thing.' In other words, he starts things but doesn't stay focused and build the business.

Kendall immediately rationalized the product range to focus on chocolate. He set out, as he had at Covent Garden, to build a strong management team so he could step back from operational commitments. To generate funding he negotiated a sale of 5 per cent of the equity to Cadbury Schweppes. The product was clearly a luxury product, not an essential foodstuff, and it was priced higher than the main branded chocolate bars. But it was high quality and customers 'get their chocolate hit from eating less than they would of the main brands'. Kendall recognized the importance of supermarkets and targeted them. Supermarket sales of £2 million in the 1990s increased sevenfold in the first 4 years Kendall was in control, and the annual growth was around 40 per cent through this channel. Margins might be tight but it was a very significant route to market for a confectionery product. Improved marketing, new products and ever-increasing quality standards went hand-in-hand with the supermarket strategy. In 2006 the whole business was sold to Cadbury Schweppes for some £20 million. Inevitably there were sceptics who did not believe the new owner would preserve the strong ethical values of the business. Kendall dismissed this argument and said they had been able to work with Cadbury Schweppes successfully for 3 years and 'big business is not automatically evil'. Cadbury has since extended its committee to Fair Trade.

William Kendall is now the Chairman of Nemadi Advisers, investors in early stage consumer goods businesses with an environmental element.

Questions

1 Would you think any strategic leader who 'under-stands the theory' could be a turnaround specialist like William Kendall, or do you think he has certain qualities and skills that make him the expert he is?
2 What is the 'secret of his success'?

The whole enterprise must become more customer-focused, committed to efficiency and improvement, and responsive to environmental demands.

Returning to the theme of Figure 5.10 earlier in the book, through double-loop learning an uncompetitive firm has found new opportunities for adding value and creating advantages, and has then used single-loop learning initially to leverage this new advantage.

Divestment strategies Divestment can be *internal*, the closure of a plant as part of a rationalization programme, or *external*, the sale of part of the business. The justification will be similar for each, with resources that have been saved or generated being reallocated. Pharmaceutical companies have been divesting non-core assets such as medical devices and manufacturing plants to cut costs and focus on core strategies, primarily drug development. However, while some Pharma companies are narrowing their focus, targeting specific disease areas for future growth, others are taking a broader approach in an effort to spread risk and return on investment.

Davis (1974) argues that divestments are often sudden decisions rather than decisions reached as part of a continual evaluation process which reviews all of the products and services in the firm's portfolio periodically. Companies that utilize portfolio analysis as part of their planning will be in a position to identify which parts of the business are the poorest performers and possible candidates for divestment. However, Devlin (1989) contends that effective divestment is a skill that few strategic leaders actually possess – which itself is a critical strategic issue, given that many acquisitions fail to achieve their expected returns. While divestment may suggest an admission of failure, it can be used positively. There will be reluctance to sell a business unit to another company, especially a competitor, who might succeed and transform the business into an effective performer – particularly important if such success could pose a future threat to business units that have been retained. For these reasons, divestments are often associated with a change of strategic leader, as an outsider is less likely to feel any loyalty to past decisions.

In selecting a divestment candidate, both financial and strategic aspects are important: the current position in the product life cycle, and the likely future potential for further growth and profitability; the current market position, and opportunities for competitive advantage; the future potential for cash generation and future investment requirements in order to remain competitive (linked to this is the opportunity cost of the resources being utilized); identified alternative uses for the resources which could be freed up, and in certain cases the extent of the need to free up resources for relocation; and the ability to find a suitable buyer willing to pay an acceptable price.

Once the decision to divest has been taken, there are further considerations. First, how active and how secretive the search for a buyer should be. Arguably, there should be an active search for an acceptable buyer who is willing to pay an appropriate premium, on the grounds that it is all too easy to sell a business cheaply. A low price might be expected where the sale is hurried, perhaps because there is a pressing need to raise money or where a first offer is accepted without an exploration of other options. Another argument is in favour of secrecy and speed, as opposed to prolonged and publicized negotiations. Employees may leave if they feel that their company is no longer wanted by its existing parent, and relationships with important suppliers and customers may also be affected. In addition, simply offering a business for sale may not be productive. Sales must be negotiated and potential buyers must be vetted. The terms of the sale should be financially acceptable, and the buyer should not be an organization that can use the newly acquired business to create a competitive threat to retained activities. Devlin (1989) suggests that, in general, speed is of the essence. Long delays are likely to mean lost confidence. However, some businesses may be difficult to sell. Second, buyers can be categorized into different types, and the potential of the business for them needs careful consideration during negotiations:

- *Sphere-of-influence buyers* might expect immediate synergy from the acquisition. These would include competitors for whom it would be horizontal integration, and buyers and suppliers for whom it would imply vertical integration. These are the buyers who are most likely to pose future threats unless the divestment removes any involvement in the industry in question.

- *Related industry companies* – these might not be current competitors but companies for whom it might be possible to share activities and transfer skills.

- *Management buy-outs* involve the purchase of a business from its existing owners by the current managers in conjunction with one or more financial institutions. Some buy-outs occur because family owners have no organized succession and a sale to the existing managers is more desirable than sale to an unknown outsider. Financiers are attracted to management buy-outs, which offer the potential to earn higher returns than investing in large companies and lower failure rates than traditional start-up businesses, but will typically look to earn back their investment – normally through a public share offering – in around 4 years. Banks will normally agree to a higher percentage of debt in relation to equity (gearing) or in relation to total capital employed (the debt ratio) than is conventional, and will look for a cash flow that can both pay the interest and repay the debt after an agreed number of years. Managers must be able to make the business more competitive and overcome the constraints imposed by the high debt burden, and to generate a positive cash flow. The Strategy Activity in Chapter 12 shows how private equity was invested in Debenhams and how a handsome return was earned quite quickly.

- *Management buy-ins* occur when a group of outside managers is brought in to run a company which is sold to them and their backers rather than to existing managers. The disadvantage is the loss of continuity and the lack of insight and experience in the particular company; a possible advantage in certain circumstances is the influx of fresh ideas.

Third, some argue that the cash raised from the sale should be deployed effectively and without undue delay. If a company is decreasing in size, building up reserves of cash and can find no suitable investment opportunities, it might become vulnerable to acquisition. Ideally, a use for the cash will be determined before the sale, but implementation of a combined sale and investment may prove difficult. Devlin argues that where these changes can be managed effectively, divestment can provide a source of new competitive advantage.

Having explored retrenchment, turnaround and divestment strategies, these strategies are discussed specifically in the context of an economic recession, and this chapter concludes by considering alternative strategies for declining industries and how the most appropriate strategy might be selected.

13.4 Managing in a recession and a declining industry

Managing in a recession

The early 1990s was characterized by an economic recession, not unusually as economies experience cycles. Typically, the latter years of the decade provided clear evidence of an economic recovery in the UK, but this time the real beneficiaries were service businesses rather than the manufacturing sector, which was affected by the high value of the pound sterling. This early 1990s recession was global and it affected most countries, industries and businesses, regardless of size or sector. Since then, other world economies have performed worse than the UK, which has benefited from low inflation and low interest rates and from investment in the public sector.

While it was always likely that another recession would occur at some stage, when it happened it was a deep recession affecting America, Europe and Asia, which then impacted upon the developing countries such as China and India that supply them with manufactured goods, and the rest of the world as the fallout from the banking crisis spread worldwide. The recession that began in 2008/9 has seen the traditional economic downturn – accompanied by limited and expensive credit, the so-called credit crunch brought about by the banks becoming defensive as they try to recover from the imprudent lending that had characterized the previous few years, fuelled by policing and regulation of financial services. The government put pressure on the banks to lend but things were slow to happen. In Ireland, the government would only lend money to the (needy) banks if they promised to lend rather than shore up their capital reserves, which was only likely to happen if the government offered 'guarantees' against loan defaults. The latest recession was also particularly volatile and uncertain, and was manifest by the suddenness and steepness of the downturn in orders, and the uncertainty caused by the lack of clarity and agreement on its length. Running a business became more uncertain – a threat to some and an opportunity to others, such as eBay making much money helping companies clear surplus stocks.

For those companies that could survive the recession with their capacity and employees largely intact, the turnaround in the economy would be a genuine opportunity. In 2009 some companies – for example, all the leading car manufacturers – were giving their workers extended holidays on part pay, while others were reducing hours and some reduced pay. Large companies – where they were able – took extended credit, something that is always easier if the suppliers are small companies with only limited power and influence. For any that could grant extended credit, there was a chance to pick up fresh orders.

Figure 13.4 illustrates possible competitive outcomes from a recessionary period, with the two key variables being sales and market share. During the recession, sales overall in an industry will go down. A neutral effect for all (or any single competitor) would be reduced sales but retained market share. A 'perfect' result would be increased sales and market share, if some competitors are forced to close. A good result would be constant sales which would imply an improved market share. Reducing both sales and market share would be a disaster and reflect a weak competitor.

Retrenchment strategies are frequently required in a recession as demand falls and costs need containing; at the same time, there is a need, wherever practical, to invest and prepare the organization to benefit from the recovery when it comes. Recession alone will not necessarily put a company into a crisis or turnaround situation; rather, it highlights existing weaknesses either created, or hidden, in boom conditions. The organizations that are best prepared to cope with a recession are those with relatively low borrowings. Highly geared companies may be forced to divest assets in order to raise cash to cover their interest and repayment needs.

Clifford (1977) has suggested that companies that survive a recession most successfully are characterized by superior management which emphasizes the protection of margins, the efficient use of capital – and a concentration on markets or segments where distinctive competitive advantage is possible.

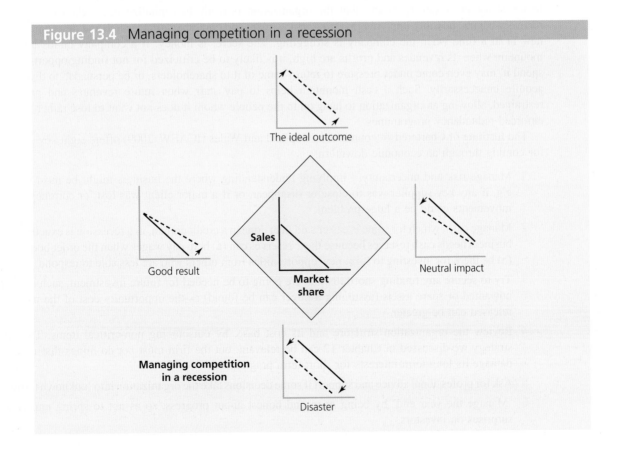

Figure 13.4 Managing competition in a recession

Such competitive advantage will result from more effective cost control, innovative differentiation, a focus on service and quality and speedy reaction and change in a dynamic environment. An economic recession will typically force organizations to be creative in their search for cost reductions, especially if productivity drives (perhaps IT related) have already eliminated a number of operational inefficiencies. Cost savings must then be controlled to ensure that they do not creep up again, and the focus of the cost cutting is critical. Training and research and development, for example, should not be sacrificed unnecessarily because new ideas and service quality are increasingly important for adding value, helping customers to find new competitive opportunities themselves and persuading consumers to buy when their spending power is limited. Research and development, then, should be managed better rather than cut, and directed more towards short-term improvements. However, the long-term needs should not be wholly ignored, in particular the development time for new products and services should be speeded up.

Dividend payments and investment funding may have to be traded off against each other. Some organizations will reduce dividends when profits fall to conserve their resources; others will maintain them to appease shareholders. Moreover, increasing global competition has forced companies to target markets and niches more effectively and, in many cases, increase their marketing rather than cut expenditure. The emphasis has typically focused on efficiencies and savings rather than luxury – consumers with less discretionary purchasing power have been more selective.

Whittingham (1991) reinforces points made earlier in the book and contends that innovation and product and service improvement is a more effective use of scarce resources in a recession than is diversification, and that cutting back too much leaves companies exposed and under capacity for the recovery. Ideally, organizations will consult and involve employees, seeking negotiated pay freezes and reduced hours rather than making staff redundant – providing greater flexibility to grow. And yet many firms will not have sufficient resources to pursue their preferred option.

When companies emerge from a recession and attempt to satisfy increasing demand, they need to control events, monitor the cash flow and guard against overtrading. Paradoxically, a recession can be an ideal time to invest for the future to ensure that the organization is ready to capitalize fully when the economic recovery begins, possibly implying investing in new plant and equipment, in research and development or in new IT at a time when the company is struggling. The secret is money: if a company builds up a cash mountain when its revenues and profits are high, it is likely to be criticized for not finding opportunities to spend it, may even come under pressure to return some of it to shareholders, or be persuaded to diversify or acquire unnecessarily. Such a cash mountain helps to pay staff when future revenues and profits are restrained, allowing an organization to hang on to the people whom it does not want to lose rather than face enforced redundancy programmes.

The Institute of Chartered Accountants in England and Wales (ICAEW, 2009) offers eight key strategies for coming through an economic downturn:

1 Manage risk and uncertainty – implying understanding where the business might be most exposed, e.g. if any key supplier was to close or disappear, or if a major client was lost, or currency movements could be a huge problem.

2 Manage cash, which for some is easier said than done in a credit crunch, as a recession is exactly when a business needs cash reserves because these reserves can (a) help pay wages when the order book is thin, (b) be there for investing to seize new opportunities from others who are less able to respond.

3 Try to secure any funding shortfalls that are going to be needed for future investment, such as selling unwanted or spare assets (assuming a buyer can be found) as the opportunity cost of the money released can be greater.

4 Review the organization structure and its cost base, by outsourcing non-critical items. The onion strategy we discussed in Chapter 12 can be relevant, but the firm must not do things that might damage its long-term interests for short-term pragmatism.

5 Ask for professional advice and support if some decisions take the organization into 'unknown territory'.

6 'Manage the year end' by being open and honest about progress, so as not to spring unnecessary surprises on investors.

7 Engage and involve employees, who know where savings can be made, and if painful decisions have to be made then there are 'good' and 'bad' ways of dealing with the problem.

8 Finally, look ahead, plan ahead. The recession will end; new opportunities will arise. Is the company's business model appropriate for the future?

Table 13.1 provides a useful bullet-point summary of these and other points.

Accenture (2003) suggested the following companies as examples of strategic successes during the 1990s recession:

- Nokia divested a range of businesses and invested in mobile telephones, becoming the world's leading manufacturer of handsets.
- Southwest Airlines continued to expand, opening up new routes and cities, never deviating from its winning competitive formula and was consistently profitable when other airlines were losing money.
- Wal-Mart also grew (opening up more and more new stores) and remained focused on its existing strategies, whilst many other rivals changed their strategy in an attempt to boost sales.
- In contrast, Samsung decentralized to give managers more autonomy.

In every case, we can see evidence of investment in a clear business model, indicating that successful companies do not spend excessively in boom times; instead they generate cash, reduce debt and build up their resource base, providing flexibility. But other businesses will perish in a recession.

At this point you might like to think of businesses you know that have done well in the recession since 2008 and consider the reasons why.

Table 13.1 Managing in a recession

In a recession, companies should:

- Determine and clarify strategic priorities
- Be willing to act rather than procrastinate with some tough decisions
- Stay fully informed about trends and changes in relevant industries, making use of IT for this and other potential benefits
- Monitor gross profits and cash flow very carefully
- Identify where there is any overcapacity
- Spend carefully
- Seek to extend payment times to creditors
- Look for possibilities to reduce overheads or fixed costs
- Cut back on borrowings if at all possible
- Monitor currency fluctuations if the company trades in foreign currencies, buying forward where appropriate
- Recognize that high prices may be unsustainable and act sooner rather than later
- Keep staff informed of the situation, taking as positive a stance as is realistic
- Tighten staffing levels where appropriate, but not by losing key people
- Make any necessary redundancies all at once
- Invest in training for those who remain and look to retain morale
- Stay in close contact with customers and look for opportunities where both parties can help each other
- Seek out relevant marketing opportunities at home and abroad – recessions are uneven in their impact
- Accept that flexibility and innovation are crucial.

Strategies for declining industries

Rarely is an industry unattractive for every company competing within and, indeed, mature and declining industries can be made attractive for individual competitors if they can find appropriate and feasible opportunities for adding value and creating competitive advantage. Although tea is a more popular drink than coffee in the UK, consumption has been declining for a number of years. Tetley became the market leader in the 1990s and it has adopted a number of strategies to retain its leadership, such as promoting more specialist teas such as Earl Grey, Red Bush and Lapsang, and it introduced draw-bag tea bags, and the increasingly popular fruit flavoured infusions. After being bought out by its managers (from Allied Domecq) in 1995, Tetley formed a joint venture with Indian tea grower, Tata, now its new owner. Some firms experiencing decline in a mature industry will cause their own demise through dated, inappropriate competitive strategies. US company Republic of Tea (see the case in Chapter 3) has succeeded in the same industry with a very different niche approach.

In some cases, an innovative new strategy by one competitor can rejuvenate the whole industry. When an industry has reached maturity or begun to decline, while demand overall is declining, the pattern can vary markedly – some sectors or segments may be static or expanding. Consumers will be knowledgeable because the product or service has been around for a while, and many will become increasingly price conscious and prices will tend to fall in real terms. The 'commodity' perception of products will increase, and distribution is likely to become more concentrated.

Companies will again attempt to find new ways of adding value and differentiating, but as time goes on the opportunities become increasingly limited. Paradoxically, they will often find it harder to justify both research and development spending (to develop new variations) and marketing expenditure to inform and persuade customers of the differentiation. However, as the decline continues and overcapacity emerges, the weakest or least profitable producers will tend to withdraw from the industry, relieving some of the pressure on those who remain.

Harrigan (1980) considers whether retrenchment, turnaround or divestment is the most appropriate strategy for an individual competitor in a declining industry. Strategies of leadership and **niche marketing** (turnaround), exploiting or harvesting (retrenchment) and divestment are considered in the light of the overall attractiveness of the industry while it is declining and the opportunities for an individual competitor to create and sustain competitive advantage, as illustrated and defined in Figure 13.5.

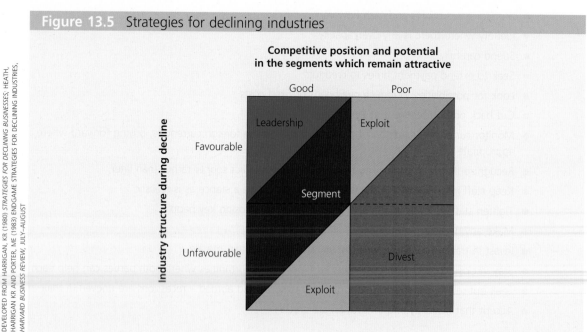

Figure 13.5 Strategies for declining industries

DEVELOPED FROM HARRIGAN, KR (1980) *STRATEGIES FOR DECLINING BUSINESSES*; HEATH, HARRIGAN KR AND PORTER, ME (1983) ENDGAME STRATEGIES FOR DECLINING INDUSTRIES, *HARVARD BUSINESS REVIEW*, JULY–AUGUST

Leadership	Selective investment: turnaround
	Invest as appropriate to give real competitive advantage
	Idea: become one of the strongest competitors in the declining industry with either the lowest costs or clear differentiation
Segment or niche	Selective investment: turnaround
	Identify one or more attractive segments, those with greatest potential for longer-term survival or short-term returns, and seek a strong position whilst divesting from other segments
Exploit or harvest	Phased withdrawal; retrenchment
	Controlled disinvestment, reducing product alternatives, advertising and so on in order to cut costs
	Problem: losing the confidence of suppliers and buyers as they witness the obvious reduction of commitment
	Must lead eventually to divestment or liquidation
Quick divestment	Immediate sale or liquidation

Harrigan contends that the most appropriate strategy depends on four factors:

1 The nature of the decline, and the causes – the speed at which decline is taking place, and whether specific segments are still surviving and offering differentiation and niche marketing opportunities for companies who can create and sustain competitive advantage – which affect the industry attractiveness.

2 The ability of a company to target these market segments effectively and create consumer preference, which is affected by company strengths and weaknesses.

3 The exit costs for all competitors, which influence the degree of urgency that companies feel towards finding a way of remaining competitive rather than simply withdrawing and relate to:

– the inability to find a buyer for the business, and the cost of closure
– the strategic significance for the company as a whole, particularly if vertical integration strategies are affected
– the possible effect upon key stakeholders, such as shareholders, managers and the strategic leader, especially if they have had a long-term commitment to the product service or business unit.

4 Linked to all these, the opportunities or threats which exist as a result of competitor activities, what they choose to do and why. If the product is strategically significant to them, certain competitors may choose not to withdraw, accepting very low profits or even no profits, and thereby making it more difficult for others.

Figure 13.5 encapsulates the first two points but the decision also involves the last two. Competitive advantage is likely to be attained by companies who are aware early of the decline, and the opportunities present during the decline, and who seek to create the most advantageous positions ahead of competitors. Companies reacting when things have already started to go wrong are less likely to create an effective strategy.

In Chapter 12 we stressed that organizational issues and difficulties often result in the failure of the diversification and acquisition strategies to yield the desired results. Organizational issues will again be important in the case of recovery strategies. Time is likely to be limited and proposed changes will have to be implemented quickly. The support and co-operation of managers and other employees will be essential, particularly where redundancies, changes in organization structures or changes in working practices are required. Quite possibly, changes in attitudes – an issue of organizational culture – will be involved. Although the gravity of the situation may be visible, and the dangers of failing to change clearly understood, the changes will need managing properly if they are to prove effective. The issues involved in managing change are discussed in Chapter 15.

Research Snapshot 13.1

Business failure – along with turnaround and recovery – has been emergent within the academic literature, particularly where these phenomena are most pertinent, in the entrepreneurship and small business field, rather than just large corporates. However, given the niche nature of this topic, this section is necessarily shorter given the need to focus upon a small(er) number of studies.

Entrepreneurial learning after business failure can be impeded by the process of 'grief recovery' – with grief being defined as 'a negative emotional response interfering with the ability to learn from the events surrounding that loss' – although there are tactics by which this process can actually enhance such learning (Shepherd, 2003), later noting that delayed failure hampers recovery, suggesting 'anticipatory grief as a mechanism for reducing the level of grief triggered by the failure event, which reduces the emotional costs of business failure' (Shepherd *et al.*, 2009). Concomitantly, 'recovery and re-emergence from failure is a function of distinctive learning processes that foster a range of higher-level learning outcomes', particularly that, 'entrepreneurs learn much not only about themselves and the demise of their ventures but also about the nature of networks and relationships and the "pressure points" of venture management", and that, "these powerful learning outcomes are future-oriented, increasing the entrepreneur's level of entrepreneurial preparedness for further enterprising activities" (Cope, 2011). A more realistic or even pessimistic perspective on 'subsequent ventures' may be taken by entrepreneurs with prior failure experiences, more particularly noting that 'portfolio' entrepreneurs were less optimistic than 'serial' entrepreneurs (Ucbasaran *et al.*, 2010).

Some authors challenge the notion that closure = failure, notably that even relatively well financed, bigger businesses may have closed for various reasons, including simply because of owner-managers having an 'exit strategy, closed a business without excess debt, sold a viable business or retired from the work force' (Headd, 2003). Stokes and Blackburn (2002), also critiquing the erroneous closure-failure link, found that (serial) entrepreneurs learn: 'the closure process can represent a positive, learning experience. Even owners who have had unsuccessful ventures are motivated and more able to make it work next time because of lessons learned', and a distinction between 'compulsory' and 'voluntary' exits, hence 'the longer one can survive and prevent involuntary exit, the more successful one is' (van Praag, 2003) is needed. Furthermore, Cope *et al.* (2004) found that venture capitalists (VCs) considered prior failed entrepreneurs sympathetically given that they (VCs), 'recognize the complex, contextual nature of failure and do not necessarily perceive the entrepreneur to be the primary cause of the venture's demise', hence they take 'a tolerant, flexible and open-minded attitude to failure and are keen to understand the circumstances in which it occurred', and might still invest in an excellent idea whether or not the entrepreneur had prior failure(s). Indeed, research into failure has identified a 'self-serving attribution bias among entrepreneurs when they enumerate the factors that contribute to or impede their business success' (Rogoff *et al.*, 2004).

Research into turnaround and recovery, on the other hand, while being not so well developed, provides some interesting and relevant pointers to strategies for firms experiencing financial problems and the risk of failure. Morrow Jr. *et al.* (2004) note that such strategies vary by whether the sector is 'growing' or 'declining', such that for 'growth industries', asset retrenchment enhanced performance, while in 'declining industries', cost retrenchment did the same, whereas 'asset retrenchment' exacerbated performance. Distinguishing the public and private sector, turnaround is essential, with 'failure' in the public sector being conceptualized quite differently from private sector firms running out of money, for example schools or hospitals not meeting their objectives to the necessary quality required, and hence exploring endeavours to achieve a 'turnaround in their performance' (Walshe *et al.* 2004). Accordingly, private and public sector turnaround have been compared and contrasted, with key distinct features in the public arena rather than a one-size-fits-all application of the generic corporate turnaround model (Paton and Mordaunt, 2004).

The articles below provide a deeper understanding of business failure and turnaround with the further reading helping students to develop their perception and critical awareness of this topic, and also to highlight the developing thinking in relation to why and how smaller, entrepreneurial firms especially fail and what can be done in response to such scenarios.

Further Reading

Cope, J. (2011) 'Entrepreneurial learning from failure: An interpretative phenomenological analysis', *Journal of Business Venturing*, Vol. 26, No. 6, pp. 604–623.

Cope, J., Cave, F. and Eccles, S. (2004) 'Attitudes of venture capital investors towards entrepreneurs with previous business failure', *Venture Capital: An International Journal of Entrepreneurial Finance*, Vol. 6, Nos 2-3, pp. 147–172.

Headd, B. (2003) 'Redefining business success: Distinguishing between closure and failure', *Small Business Economics*, Vol. 21, No. 1, pp. 51–61.

Morrow Jr., J.L., Johnson, R.A. and Busenitz, L.W. (2004) 'The effects of cost and asset retrenchment on firm performance: The overlooked role of a firm's competitive environment', *Journal of Management*, Vol. 30, No. 2, pp. 189–208.

Paton, R. and Mordaunt, J. (2004) 'What's different about public and non-profit 'turnaround'?', *Public Money & Management*, Vol. 24, No. 4, pp. 209–216.

Rogoff, E. G., Lee, M.-S. and Suh, D.-C. (2004) '"Who Done It?" Attributions by entrepreneurs and experts of the factors that cause and impede small business success', *Journal of Small Business Management*, Vol. 42, pp. 364–376.

Shepherd, D.A. (2003) 'Learning from Business Failure: Propositions of Grief Recovery for the Self-Employed', *The Academy of Management Review*, Vol. 28, No. 2, pp. 318–328.

Shepherd, D.A., Wiklund, J. and Haynie, J.M. (2009) 'Moving forward: Balancing the financial and emotional costs of business failure', *Journal of Business Venturing*, Vol. 24, No. 2, pp. 134–148.

Stokes, D. and Blackburn, R. (2002) 'Learning the hard way: the lessons of owner-managers who have closed their businesses', *Journal of Small Business and Enterprise Development*, Vol. 9, No. 1, pp. 17–27.

Ucbasaran, D., Westhead, P., Wright, M. and Flores, M. (2010) 'The nature of entrepreneurial experience, business failure and comparative optimism', *Journal of Business Venturing*, Vol. 25, No. 6, pp. 541–555.

van Praag, C.M. (2003) 'Business survival and success of young small business owners', *Small Business Economics*, Vol. 21, No. 1, pp. 1–17.

Walshe, K., Harvey, G., Hyde, P. and Pandit, N. (2004) 'Organizational failure and turnaround: Lessons for public services from the for-profit sector', *Public Money & Management*, Vol. 24, No. 4, pp. 201–208.

Summary

Ultimate business failure happens when a business is liquidated or sold because its managers have made strategic errors or misjudgements and may have simply avoided the need to change in a dynamic environment. However, a business can similarly fail to meet the needs and expectations of key stakeholders, experience financial difficulties but survive, where one or more factors might be involved. A new strategic leader might be appointed who succeeds in turning the company around. Part, or all, of the business might be sold.

Companies fail for a variety of reasons, and normally more than one factor is in evidence, the main ones being: poor management; competition; a decline in profits; a decline in demand for the product or service; misjudged acquisitions or other changes in corporate strategy.

At any time, certain industries will be declining and others will be relatively unattractive as far as particular companies are concerned, generally because of intense competition. Individual companies might be performing poorly and in need of either a recovery strategy or an appropriate divestment, and the feasibility of recovery varies from situation to situation, and four possible outcomes of a change in strategy are a failure to recover, temporary recovery, sustained survival and sustained recovery.

The likely outcome is inevitably affected by the timing of the intervention such that, if a company realizes the gravity of a pending situation at an early stage, it will be better placed to deal with it. Recovery will be more difficult to achieve if the organization waits until it is facing a real crisis. *Retrenchment* – to create a platform for possible expansion later – concerns stronger cash management and tighter operations. Renewal brings in marketing and the search for new opportunities for adding value and differentiating, and is about building new forms of competitive advantage. *Divestment* can be an important theme in retrenchment and consolidation. Management buy-outs can be used as a convenient means of divesting a business which has the potential to grow but which is no longer core to its existing parent. A four-stage model of the process can be summarized as:

1 galvanization – engaging the problem
2 simplifying the situation so it can be dealt with
3 building new competencies
4 exerting leverage to develop and sustain new competitive advantages.

Economies move from boom conditions into recessions, the depth and length of which vary markedly, when company revenues and profits will fall and a number of the issues and strategies discussed in relation to retrenchment and consolidation become relevant and is, paradoxically, often an ideal time for a company to invest if it has the appropriate resources. If it can afford to hold on to its staff, they will have time to deal with the changes; and new plant, equipment and technology could be in place in time for when the economy turns around, strengthening its position. Several possible strategies exist for individual competitors in mature and declining industries, e.g. withdrawal from the industry or finding attractive niches, and an industry being in decline does not automatically make it unattractive for everyone.

Online cases for this chapter

Questions and research assignments

1 Do the causes discussed in this chapter provide an adequate explanation for any corporate failure with which you are familiar?

2 Why might a company wish to remain a competitor in an industry despite low or declining profitability? Classify your reasons as objective or subjective. Can the subjective reasons be justified?

3 What factors do you feel would be most significant to all parties involved in a proposed buy-out during the negotiations? Where are the major areas of potential conflict?

Internet and library projects

1 Chariot was described as a 'small but brazen' lottery provider. In 2006 it attempted to launch an alternative to Camelot and the National Lottery in the UK. It claimed the existing lottery 'gave money to unworthy causes', the opposite of its mission. The business lasted less than 6 months. What happened to cause it to fail?

2 Coffee Republic was one of the forerunners with coffee bars providing freshly made and relatively expensive coffees in the UK. Its founders, Sahar and Bobby Hashemi, wrote a book for would-be entrepreneurs – *Anyone Can Do It*. But competitors like Starbucks, Caffe Nero and Costa Coffee were far more successful. Again, what went wrong? What are the lessons in this particular case?

Strategy activity

Northern Foods

Northern Foods in the UK is best known for certain brands: Fox's Biscuits, Goodfella's Pizza and Dalepak burgers. It had also produced own-label foods for Marks and Spencer and the leading supermarkets. Changes to the M&S supply chain and price demands from the supermarkets had hit its margins. A number of reasons were offered as to why Northern Foods got into difficulties:

- It had been more concerned with sales than cash.
- It operated from too many (dispersed) sites.
- It was too ready to say 'yes' to its leading customers without examining the implications of the choices this approach implied.
- There had been inadequate innovation – say, with healthy option foods.

- Across the business there was inadequate learning and sharing.

As a result, it faced some difficult decisions in 2009. One concerned the future of Fox's Biscuits. The factories were in need of improvement. There were two key sites, one in Batley (West Yorkshire) and one in Uttoxeter. Neither was adequate. One new factory was needed – but where should it be sited? Wherever was chosen, redundancies were implied.

Questions

1 Once Northern Foods was through these difficulties what do you think it should have done differently to deal with future challenges?

2 What has happened with Fox's Biscuits?

References

Accenture (2003) *Investing for the Upturn*. Summarized from the Accenture website at the time: **www.Accenture.com/upturn**

Argenti, J. (1976) *Corporate Collapse*, McGraw-Hill.

Baden-Fuller, C. and Stopford, J. (1992) Rejuvenating the Mature Business: The Competitive Challenge, Routledge.

Clifford, D.K. (1977) Thriving in a recession, *Harvard Business Review*, July–August.

Davis, J.V. (1974) The strategic divestment decision, *Long Range Planning*, February.

Devlin, G. (1989) Selling off not out, *Management Today*, April.

Harrigan, K.R. (1980) *Strategies for Declining Businesses*, Heath.

Heller, R. (1998) *Goldfinger – How Entrepreneurs Get Rich by Starting Small*, Harper Collins.

ICAEW (2009) *Surviving the Downturn*, Institute of Chartered Accountants in England and Wales, Publication No. 5760.

Oates, D. (1990) *The Complete Entrepreneur*, Mercury.

Slatter, S. (1984) *Corporate Recovery: Successful Turnaround Strategies and Their Implementation*, Penguin.

Slatter, S. and Lovett, D. (1999) Corporate Turnaround, Penguin

Society of Practitioners in Insolvency (1995) *Personal Insolvency in the UK*, SPI, London.

van de Vliet, A. (1998) Back from the brink, *Management Today*, January.

Weitzel, W. and Johnson, E. (1989) Decline in organizations – a literature extension and integration, *Administration Science Quarterly*, 34 (1).

Whittingham, R. (1991) Recession strategies and top management change, *Journal of General Management* 16 (3).

Part 5 Strategy implementation and strategic management

Parts 1 and 3 – Understanding strategy and strategic management, and Strategy development – have addressed a number of important 'how' (and some 'who') questions, in particular how strategies are created; while Parts 2 and 4 (Analysis and positioning, and Strategic growth issues) have been more focused on 'what', 'where' and 'why' issues. This final part of the book addresses a number of additional 'how' questions regarding the management of strategy.

In particular, the following issues are addressed:

- How intended strategies might be implemented (Chapter 14)
- How emergent strategy actually happens (Chapter 14)
- How the organization should (might) be structured and designed to ensure that both happen (Chapter 14)
- How the strategic leader can manage both the organization structure and resources to achieve corporate-level synergy, ideally making sure the various functions, activities and businesses are co-ordinated and
- Contributing towards clearly understood objectives (Chapter 14)
- How the organization should seek to deal with the pressures and demands of change, appreciating that cultural and behavioural changes may be required (Chapter 15)
- How resources should (might) be deployed and managed (Chapter 16)
- How the organization might seek to manage risk and avoid managing crises (Chapter 16).

We conclude the book with Chapter 17 which reviews:

- What strategy is and what the practice of strategy involves
- What the purpose of strategy is.

Chapter 14

Strategy implementation and structure

PART 1
Understanding strategy

1 What is strategy and who is involved?
   - Appendix

2 The business model and the revenue model

3 Strategic purpose
   - Supplement:
     Using frameworks to analyze strategy cases

PART 5
Strategy implementation

14 Strategy implementation and structure

15 Leading change

16 Managing strategy in the organization

17 Final thoughts and reflections: the practice of strategy

STRATEGIC MANAGEMENT: AWARENESS AND CHANGE

PART 2
Analysis and positioning

4 The business environment and strategy

5 Resource-led strategy

6 The dynamics of competition

7 Introducing culture and values

PART 4
Strategic growth issues

11 Strategic control and measuring success

12 Issues in strategic and international growth

13 Failure, consolidation and recovery strategies

PART 3
Strategy development

8 Creating and formulating strategy: alternatives, evaluation and choice

9 Strategic planning

10 Strategic leadership and intrapreneurship: towards visionary leadership?

Learning objectives

Having read to the end of this chapter, you should be able to:

● explain how strategy and structure are linked in a circular process (**Section 14.1**)

● discuss the processes and problems involved in the effective implementation of both intended and emergent strategies (**Section 14.2**)

● discuss the advantages and disadvantages of centralization and decentralization (**Section 14.3**)

● identify and describe five basic structural forms which an organization might adopt (**Section 14.4**).

Introduction

In Chapter 8 we considered how an effective (appropriate, feasible and desirable) chosen intended strategy must be implemented – i.e. translating ideas into actions and generating positive outcomes, sometimes swiftly, itself a source of competitive advantage – successfully and competently. New strategies may be selected because they offer opportunities and potential benefits but their implementation, involving change, implies risk (Reed and Buckley, 1988). Strategy implementation should, therefore, seek to maximize benefits and minimize risks. Accordingly, this chapter examines the linkages between strategy and structure, in terms of a number of alternative structural forms and the centralization/decentralization dichotomy, and the forces that influence and determine structure.

14.1 Strategy → structure or structure → strategy?

The structure of an organization is designed to break down the work to be carried out – the tasks – into discrete components, which might comprise individual businesses, divisions and functional departments. People work within these divisions and functions, and their actions take place within a defined framework of objectives, plans and policies which are designed to direct and control their efforts. In designing the structure and making it operational, key aspects include empowerment, employee motivation and reward, as well as information and communication systems to ensure that efforts are co-ordinated to the appropriate and desired extent and that the strategic leader and other senior managers are aware of progress and results.

As mentioned earlier, one essential contribution of the strategic leader in a competitively chaotic environment is providing and sharing a clear vision, direction and purpose for the organization (see Figure 14.1). From this, and taking into account whether the strategy is visionary, planned and/or emergent, actions and action plans (the middle column in the figure) need to be formalized. Strategies and proposals for change are inextricably linked to the implementation implications (the right-hand column in Figure 14.1). Four questions must then be asked:

● Is the structure capable of implementing the ideas?

● Are resources deployed effectively?

● Are managers suitably empowered?

● Do organizational policies support the strategies?

Figure 14.1 Strategy implementation

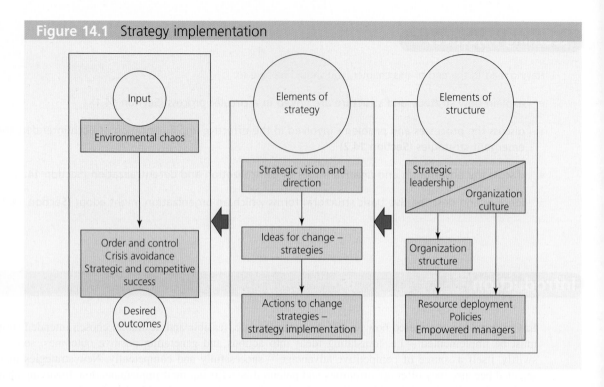

If any answers are negative, then either the strategic ideas themselves, the structure, organizational policies or aspects of resource management will need to be reviewed and rethought. The final decisions will either be determined or strongly influenced by the strategic leader, and affected by the culture of the organization.

If appropriate, feasible and desirable strategies that *are* capable of effective implementation are selected and pursued, the organization should be able to establish some order and control within the chaotic environment, hence avoiding major crises (the left-hand column), which still requires that strategies, products and services are managed efficiently and effectively at the operational level. Responsibility for operations will normally be delegated, and consequently, to ensure that performance and outcomes are satisfactory, sound monitoring and control systems are essential.

While structures are designed initially – and probably changed later at various times – to ensure that *intended* strategies can be implemented, the day-to-day decisions, actions and behaviours of people within the structure lead to important emergent strategies. There is, therefore, a continual circular process in operation:

Although this chapter is a later one in this book, structure and implementation are not the end point in the strategy process and, indeed, they may be the source of strategic change.

Figure 14.2 illustrates that, when implementing intended strategies, the strategic leader must ensure that there are appropriate targets and milestones, must establish a suitable organization structure and must secure and allocate the relevant strategic resources, such as people and money. People then use the other strategic resources, working within the structure, to carry out the tasks that they have been allocated and their actions should be monitored and evaluated to check that the targets and objectives are being achieved.

Figure 14.3 summarizes that, in the (less prescriptive) emergent strategy process, the strategic leader provides a broad strategic direction such that empowered managers – whilst constrained by any relevant rules, policies and procedures – work within a decentralized structure. The strategies that emerge are

Figure 14.2 Intended strategy implementation

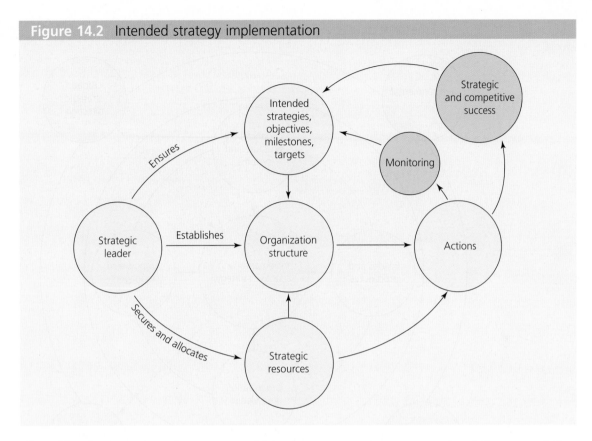

affected by the constraints, the extent to which managers accept empowerment and the accumulation, sharing and exploitation of organizational knowledge. The outcome of the strategies is related to the extent to which they deal with the competitive and environmental pressures with which the organization must deal.

The outcome, in terms of strategic management and performance, depends on: the direction provided by the strategic leader; the culture of the organization; managers understanding, supporting and owning the mission and corporate strategy, and appreciating the significance of their individual contribution; empowered managers' willingness and ability to be innovative, add value and take measured risks; and the effectiveness of the information sharing, monitoring and control systems. See Case 14.1.

> *Business is a game, a game to win. My job is to set the strategy and have a team that can deliver it, to review their performance, handle the regulatory issues and set targets and objectives to grow the business.*
>
> CHARLES ALLEN, WHEN CHAIRMAN, ITV

14.2 Implementation and change

Some of the aspects of implementation can be changed directly; and some that can only be changed indirectly are more difficult for a strategic leader to control and change. Their success in managing these aspects influences the effectiveness of both: (i) the implementation of strategies and strategic changes which are determined through the planning and visionary modes of strategy creation and (ii) the ability of the organization, and its managers, to respond to changes in the environment and adapt in line with perceived opportunities and threats.

Aspects of implementation that can be changed directly include, *inter alia*, the organization structure (the actual, defined structure, not necessarily the way in which people behave within the structure), management systems, policies and procedures, action plans and short-term budgets and management information systems.

Figure 14.3 Emergent strategy

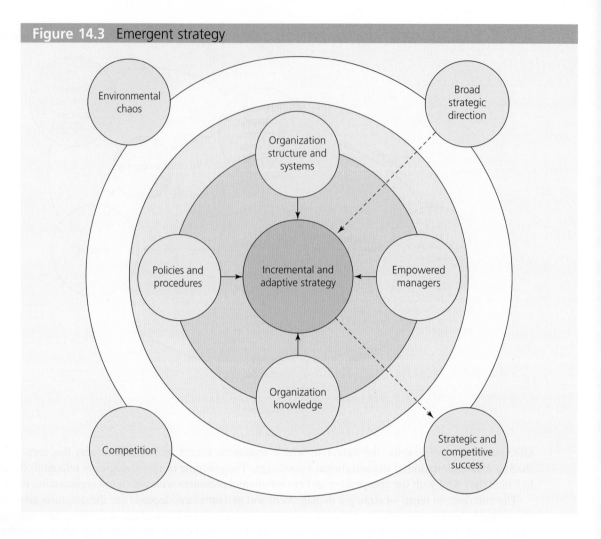

Cocoa was first farmed in Ghana when plants were taken over from Equatorial Guinea. Ghana turned out to have ideal soil (the beans take their taste from the soil) and a suitable climate; high-quality coffee beans with a good taste are grown in the humid, shady conditions of the rainforest. Coffee beans are now an important export product and Cadbury's a major buyer. Most of the coffee is grown on small family farms; the land does not lend itself to large plantations. The trees are vulnerable to disease and so yields vary, meaning demand and supply are sometimes out of alignment. Bean prices fluctuate and life can be very uncertain for small farmers.

In 1993 a group of local farmers formed their own co-operative, Kuapa Kokoo, with help from Twin Trading in London. Twin was a charity set up to promote and sponsor Fairtrade; behind it was a group of individuals with an interest in regeneration, economic development and public policy. They were also keen to act and (in collaboration with Oxfam) they had already been instrumental in the establishment of Café Direct, which distributes Fairtrade coffee.

Every village in one particular area of Ghana has representation in the co-operative, which acts on behalf of some 67 000 small farmers. Many of the farms are run by 'the women in the family' as it is claimed they have the stronger work ethic. The 'chief weigher' is a farmer and villager and everyone is entitled to check he or she is being fair.

Again with direction and support from Twin Trading, Divine Chocolate was set up in 1998. Divine was established to manufacture and distribute chocolate products and the Kuapa Kokoo Co-operative is the largest shareholder. This system makes sure the farmers can get their product to market and obtain a realistic price. When Divine was established, the UK Government helped with overseas aid and The Body Shop was an investor. Later, when Body Shop was acquired by L'Oreal in 2006, its 12 per cent shareholding was gifted to the Kuapa Kokoo Co-operative, thus increasing its shareholding from 33 to 45 per cent. A Dutch financial and development group, Oikocredit, and Twin Trading also hold shares; Comic Relief and Christian Aid both have a direct interest. Now the co-operative's beans are handpicked, fermented and carefully dried in the sun on large tables. Whilst the beans are used in chocolate, the oil is used for soap manufacture and the husks for animal feed. The co-operative is willing to sell its high-quality beans to other customers than Divine, but typically at higher prices. Divine's dried beans are then shipped to Europe (Germany) for manufacturing into chocolate bars. The range has 85 per cent and 70 per cent cocoa solid black chocolate, milk and white chocolate, and bars flavoured with orange, ginger, raspberries, mint and hazelnut. It is a premium price product and available in UK supermarkets. Divine also produces own label chocolate for the Co-op Retail supermarkets in the UK and for Starbucks. The bars are now sold in Ireland, Scandinavia, the Netherlands and, since 2007, the USA.

Divine has its head office in London and there are some 16 employees. The Managing Director is Sophi Tranchell, who started with the company shortly after it was set up. Previously she had run Tartan Films but she came from a family who had campaigned on social issues. She had also sold Fairtrade products at University. The idea is that Ghanaian farmers always receive US$1600 per tonne (minimum) for their beans plus a further $150 which is ploughed directly into community projects such as new schools. In addition, 2 per cent of Divine's turnover is paid as a shareholder dividend to them. Divine's turnover of between £8 and £9 million is a tiny proportion of the global £3 billion market for chocolate.

In Divine we can see entrepreneurship in action at a number of levels – the story also provides insight into how a vision can become a reality with a sound business and revenue model if various interested parties can find ways to work together.

Question

How would you design a structure that could embrace the ethos and values of Divine Chocolate and ensure strategy implementation such that the objectives of all key stakeholders might be met?

SOURCE: THIS CASE STUDY WAS PREPARED USING PRIMARILY PUBLICLY AVAILABLE SOURCES OF INFORMATION FOR THE PURPOSES OF CLASSROOM DISCUSSION; IT DOES NOT INTEND TO ILLUSTRATE EITHER EFFECTIVE OR INEFFECTIVE HANDLING OF A MANAGERIAL SITUATION.

Aspects of implementation that are changed indirectly, for example, are communication systems, managing and developing quality and excellence, manifested values and the organization culture and the fostering of innovation.

While the management information system can affect formal information flows, the network of informal communications truly determines awareness. Such communications are affected by, and influence, the degree and spirit of co-operation between managers, functions and divisions.

Attention to detail, production on time and to the appropriate quality and the personal development of managers and other employees are all factors in managing and developing quality and excellence. As well as developing managers' skills and capabilities generally, the quality of management in particular areas and the cover for managers who leave or who are absent should be considered – and the organization structure should provide opportunities for managers to grow and be promoted.

Manifested values and the organization culture involves the way in which things are done, including standards and attitudes which are held and practised.

The fostering of innovation is about the willingness of people to search for improvements and better ways of doing things, with their encouragement and reward being very much influenced by the strategic leader, with leadership by example often proving significant.

Those aspects that can be changed directly generally imply physical changes in the way in which resources are allocated. Behavioural aspects, which imply changes in beliefs and attitudes, can only be modified indirectly. Both are considered in the forthcoming chapters.

Owen (1982) identified problems faced in successful strategy implementation:

1   Strategy and structure need to be matched and supportive of each other, with products and services being managed independently (or in linked groups or business units) in order to be matched closely and effectively with their environments. Alternatively, the strategic leader might prefer a centralized structure without delegated responsibilities, or the organization might possess certain key skills and enjoy a reputation for strength in a particular area. Indeed, certain skills might be absent which need to be compensated for, or managers might be unwilling or reluctant to change jobs or location within the structure – given that structures depend upon the people involved and their individual skills. Related products may be produced in various plants nationally or internationally, leading to a geography-orientated structure keeping the plants separate. The structure cannot feasibly be changed every time there is a change in corporate strategy, so acceptable modifications to the existing structure are preferred to more significant changes.

2   The information and communications systems are inadequate for reporting back and evaluating the adaptive changes that are taking place, and hence the strategic leader is not fully aware of what is happening, leading to the performance of the existing structure not being monitored properly and thus ineffective control mechanisms.

3   Implementing strategy involves change, which in turn involves uncertainty and risk, and the development of new skills; and managers may be reluctant to implement changes. Their motivation might need to be addressed.

4   Management systems within the structural framework, developed to meet the needs of past strategies, may not be ideal for the changes that are taking place currently and modifying them continually is difficult.

In addition, managers and leaders often do not anticipate challenges and the length of time that implementation entails, or they may be too focused – in terms of time and resources – on other tasks to concentrate on implementation of a new strategy, or predictions were predicated on circumstances or assumptions that no longer hold, or were downright incorrect, and the organization is not dynamic enough to deal with the changes required (Alexander, 1985). All of these problems presuppose that the formulated strategic change is sound and logical, but a poorly thought-out strategy will create its own implementation problems.

To counter these problems, without changing the structural framework but reconfiguring how people operate within it, Owen (1982) suggests the following:

● Clear responsibility for the successful outcome of planned strategic change should be allocated.

● The number of strategies and changes being pursued at any time should be limited, and the ability of the necessary resources to cope with the changes should be seen as a key determinant of strategy and should not be overlooked.

● Necessary actions to implement strategies should be identified and planned, and again responsibility should be allocated.

● Milestones, or progress measurement points, should be established.

● Measures of performance should be established, as well as appropriate monitoring and control mechanisms.

Moreover, Alexander (1985) contends that people who will be affected by the strategic changes should be involved and their commitment gained, and that the implications should be communicated widely and awareness created, underpinned by incentives and reward systems. While no 'best way' of implementing strategic change and 'no right answers' exist, there are various lessons, considerations and arguments.

Three final points must be made to conclude this section.

First, although there are no right answers to either strategy formulation or strategy implementation, the two must be consistent if the organization is to be effective. Arguably, how the organization does things, and manages both strategy and change, is more important than the actual strategy or change proposed.

Second, the style of strategic leadership will be very influential. We also argue that the preference of the strategic leader affects the desirability of particular strategic alternatives. The structure of the organization, the delegation of responsibilities, the freedom of managers to act, their willingness to exercise initiative, and the incentive and reward systems will all be determined and influenced by the strategic leader. These, in turn, determine the effectiveness of implementation. The strategic leader's choices and freedom to act, however, may be constrained by any resource limitations and certain environmental forces.

Third, the timing of when to act and make changes will also be important. In this context, for example, Mitchell (1988) points out that timing is particularly crucial in the implementation decisions and actions that follow acquisitions. Employees anticipate changes in the organization, especially at senior management level, and inaction, perhaps beyond 3 months, causes uncertainty and fear. As a result, there is greater hostility to change when it does occur. The dangers of hasty action, such as destroying strengths before appreciating that they are strengths, are offset. Mitchell (1988) concludes that it is more important to be decisive than to be right, and then learn and adapt incrementally.

14.3 Structural alternatives

While the organization structure provides the framework through which intended strategies are or are not implemented, the structure also provides a foundation for emergent strategy creation and allocates tasks to people in certain roles with certain expectations. The accompanying systems, which in part are designed to co-ordinate all of these tasks into a meaningful whole and thus create synergy, help to determine the freedom that individual managers have to change things. The style of management, influenced by the strategic leader, which determines how co-ordinated the efforts are; how co-operative managers, functions and businesses are with each other; and how willing managers are to accept empowerment and make changes. We now examine strategy-structure linkages in terms of various alternative structural forms, in particular centralization and decentralization, as well as the forces that influence and determine structure.

Lawrence and Lorsch (1967) have argued that organizations should be structured so they can respond to environmental pressures for change, thus pursuing any appropriate opportunities. As strategies relate the organization's resources and values to its environment, strategy and structure are inextricably linked and, indeed, structure enables the organization to achieve its strategic objectives and implement strategies and strategic changes. While strategy formulation requires the abilities to conceptualize, analyze and judge, implementation involves working with and through other people and instituting change, such that implementation poses the tougher management challenge (Thompson and Strickland, 1980).

The essential criteria underpinning the design of the organization structure are, first, the extent to which decision-making is *decentralized* as opposed to centralized, and, second, the extent to which policies and procedures are *formalized*.

Critical Reflection 14.1   Centralization and Decentralization

Centralization and decentralization relate to the degree to which the authority, power and responsibility for decision-making are devolved through the organization. There are several options, including the following:

- All major strategic decisions are taken centrally, at head office, by the strategic leader or a group of senior strategists. The size of any team will depend upon the preference of the overall strategic leader together with the size, complexity and diversity of the organization. Strictly enforced policies and procedures will constrain the freedom of other managers responsible for business units,

products, services and functional areas to change competitive and functional strategies. This is centralization.
- Changes in the strategic perspective are decided centrally, but then the organization is structured to enable managers to change competitive and functional strategies in line with perceived opportunities and threats.
- The organization is truly decentralized such that independent business units have general managers who are free to change their respective strategic perspectives. In effect, they run a series of

independent businesses with some co-ordination from the parent headquarters.

The extent to which true decentralization exists may be visible from the organization's charted structure. It is always useful to examine the membership of the group and divisional/business unit boards, regardless of the number and delineation of divisions. The organization is likely to tend towards decentralization where there is a main board and a series of subsidiary boards, each chaired by a member of the main board. The chief executive/strategic leader, who is responsible for the performance of each subsidiary, will not necessarily have a seat on the main board. The organization will tend towards greater centralization where the main board comprises the chairperson/chief executives of certain subsidiaries, generally the largest ones, together with staff specialists. Hence decentralization and divisionalization are not synonymous terms.

The ten main determinants

- The size of the organization.
- Geographical locations, together with the
  - homogeneity/heterogeneity of the products and services
  - technology of the tasks involved
  - interdependencies.
- The relative importance and stability of the external environment, and the possible need to react quickly.
- Generally, how quickly decisions need to be made.
- The workload of decision-makers.
- Issues of motivation via delegation, together with the abilities and willingness of managers to make decisions and accept responsibility.
- The location of competence and expertise in the organization. Are the managerial strengths in the divisions or at headquarters?
- The costs involved in making any changes.
- The significance and impact of competitive and functional decisions and changes.
- The status of the firm's planning, control and information systems.

Advantages and disadvantages

There are no right or wrong answers concerning the appropriate amount of centralization/decentralization. It is a question of balancing the potential advantages and disadvantages of each as they affect particular firms.

It has been suggested that companies which achieve and maintain high growth tend to be more decentralized, and those which are more concerned with profits than growth are more centralized. The highest performers in terms of both growth and profits tend to retain high degrees of central control as far as the overall strategic perspective is concerned. Child (1977) contends that the most essential issue is the degree of internal consistency.

Advantages of centralization

- Consistency of strategy.
- Easier to co-ordinate activities (and handle the interdependencies) and control changes.
- Changes in the strategic perspective are more easily facilitated.

Disadvantages of centralization

- May be slow to respond to changes which affect subsidiaries individually rather than the organization as a whole, depending upon the remoteness of head office.
- Easy to create an expensive head office that relies on management information systems and becomes detached from customers, and for which there are too many diverse interests and complexities.
- General managers with real strategic ability are not developed within the organization. Instead the organization is dependent on specialists and, as a result, the various functions may not be properly co-ordinated. Does this achieve a fit between the organization and its environment?

Advantages of decentralization

- Ability to change competitive and functional strategies more quickly.
- Improved motivation.
- Can develop better overall strategic awareness in a very complex organization which is too diverse for a head office to control effectively.

Disadvantages of decentralization

- May be problems in clarifying the role of head-office central services which aim to co-ordinate the various divisions and business units and achieve certain economies through, and the centralization of, selected activities.
- Problems of linking the power that general managers need and the responsibility that goes with the power. General managers must have the freedom to make decisions without referrals back.

Decentralization is required to some degree if incremental and adaptive strategic change is to take place (see Critical Reflection 14.1) with formality relating to the degree of specialization of tasks and jobs, and how defined and 'rigid' jobs are (i.e. how long they have remained roughly the same) – such that the longer the 'rigidity', the greater will be the resistance to changing them. Clearly, communications and formality are linked with a formal organization relying on vertical communications, with instructions passing downwards and information on results passing upwards, and often good news tending to flow upwards quickly and readily and bad news being covered up. More informal organizations have stronger and more effective horizontal communications as people across the organization are encouraged to talk and share.

A key organizational challenge, therefore, is to find the appropriate degrees of decentralization and informality to enable them to maintain control while innovating and managing change in a dynamic and turbulent environment, in turn requiring that managers are empowered. As suggested by various small business growth models (e.g. Greiner, 1972), organizations are often centralized and informal at start-up but, as limited power and responsibility is devolved to identifiable managers, the structure becomes more formalized – while the central power of the strategic leader remains strong – and with a later switch to a decentralized structure with formal controls through policies, procedures and reporting relationships.

Case 14.2 Oxfam – A Structure for Emergent Strategy UK

Oxfam is a well-known international charity engaged in:

- 'doing good' around the world, both through routine operations (such as improving fresh-water availability in developing countries) and responding to emergencies such as the Indian Ocean tsunami a few years ago with both physical goods and people
- campaigning and lobbying
- fundraising and promotion
- running a chain of charity shops and warehouses.

These activities might be (and clearly are) related, but they are different in respect of key success factors, competencies and culture. The challenge is compounded by the fact that Oxfam operates globally – but it is not one single operation. The charity was started in the UK, in Oxford, in 1942; and whilst the UK operation remains substantially the largest, there are now 12 Oxfams around the world. There are national operations in Spain, Germany, Holland, Hong Kong, Australia and the USA, for example – all 'working together' and co-ordinated from Oxford.

Each national operation has something of a distinctive and preferred *modus operandi*. For example, the Dutch Oxfam prefers to ally with local partners whilst the UK is big enough to deploy its own field workers.

When some new disaster or emergency arises and Oxfam's help is needed, there are a number of things to co-ordinate. The delivery of actual aid to various points of need must be overseen. Staff need to be deployed to those areas where they can be of most help – some quite senior staff have to be available on a flexible basis to travel at short notice. Oxfam's efforts overall must link with parallel work by the United Nations and other aid agencies.

Decision-making must be speedy and to a genuine degree devolved. Moreover it is important that Oxfam is genuinely responsive – its efforts should be targeted at the needs its clients have, rather than in the pursuit of a provider's agenda.

It was clear not very long ago that sometimes the different national operations were working 'side-by-side' at least as much as they were behaving as a single operation with joined-up thinking and effort. As a consequence Oxford took on a stronger centralized co-ordination role – helped by (subsidized) investment in new IT systems.

Question

1 Given the nature of the needs and challenges outlined, to what extent do you think Oxfam should be centralized and to what extent decentralized?

SOURCE: THIS CASE STUDY WAS PREPARED USING PRIMARILY PUBLICLY AVAILABLE SOURCES OF INFORMATION FOR THE PURPOSES OF CLASSROOM DISCUSSION; IT DOES NOT INTEND TO ILLUSTRATE EITHER EFFECTIVE OR INEFFECTIVE HANDLING OF A MANAGERIAL SITUATION.

Two contrasting cases explore how the international charity Oxfam (Case 14.2) and the entrepreneurial US-based Nantucket Nectars (Case 14.3) have dealt with the centralization-decentralization challenge. Oxfam needed centralization to achieve co-ordinated effort, while the need for a formal structure developed and became urgent as Nantucket Nectars grew in size.

Case 14.3 Nantucket Nectars   US

SOURCE: THIS CASE STUDY WAS PREPARED USING PRIMARILY PUBLICLY AVAILABLE SOURCES OF INFORMATION FOR THE PURPOSES OF CLASSROOM DISCUSSION; IT DOES NOT INTEND TO ILLUSTRATE EITHER EFFECTIVE OR INEFFECTIVE HANDLING OF A MANAGERIAL SITUATION.

Nantucket Nectars is an unusual but very successful business which was started by two friends. When Tom First and Tom Scott graduated from Brown University in Rhode Island they decided they wanted to live on Nantucket Island, off the New England coast, and find some way of earning a living. In the summer of 1989 they started a small business for servicing the yachts belonging to visitors to the island. This was always going to be seasonal. They travelled around the harbour in a distinctive red boat, delivering newspapers, muffins, coffee, laundry and any other supplies for which there was a demand. They also washed boats, emptied sewage and shampooed dogs. This seemed to lead naturally to them later opening the Nantucket Allserve general store, which still exists. They used the following promotional slogan in the early days: 'Ain't nothing those boys won't do'.

Once the summer was over, demand for their services fell as the yachts disappeared. They decided to experiment with fruit juices, mixed in a household blender. They first sought to replicate a peach-based nectar that they had sampled in Spain. During the following summer they sold their bottled juices from their red boat. They always produced distinctive flavours from the best quality ingredients. By investing their joint savings they were able to hire a bottler to produce 1400 cases. Overall, though, the business merely struggled on for a couple of years, until one wealthy yacht owner offered them a $500 000 loan to develop the business. They seized the opportunity. Nantucket Nectars then expanded quickly to cover a number of states on the American east coast. Initially they did their own bottling, but they switched to subcontracting. As the business has grown they have also switched to independent distribution.

If I were on the outside looking in, I'd say Nantucket Nectars was an overnight success. Being on the inside, it's been a long, long time. We almost went out of business a thousand times.

TOM SCOTT

By the late 1990s Nantucket Nectars employed over 100 people and sold in over 30 US states and a number of selected export markets. Values were always a key element. The partners remained determined to 'create the best quality product in the juice market', and yet the company remained enigmatic. The bottle labels stated: 'We're juice guys. We don't wear ties to work'; folksy radio commercials were utilized extensively in America; but a new head office was established in an old Men's Club near Harvard University. It was furnished with antiques, and managers had private offices instead of the open-plan arrangement which is increasingly popular in many informal organizations. First and Scott typically took their dogs into work. Each week every head-office manager focused on talking personally with one of their salespeople in the field, staff who would otherwise have little contact with head office.

The founders claim that the company was always run on gut instinct and trial and error. Few people had any formal business qualifications. In 1997 Nantucket Nectars was awarded a contract to provide juice for Starbucks, and later that year Ocean Spray – leading manufacturer of cranberry juices and other products – acquired a 50 per cent stake. The companies believed that they could make extensive savings on supplies if they joined forces. First and Scott continued to run the business that they founded.

One other related diversification is the Juice Guys Juice Bar which sells freshly prepared smoothies made from fruit, yogurt and Nantucket Nectars fruit juices, as well as sandwiches and memorabilia.

Nantucket Nectars was acquired by Cadbury Schweppes in 2002 but today it is part of Plano, the Texas-based owner of Dr Pepper, Snapple and a number of other refreshment beverages. The founders are not involved in day-to-day operations but they do still contribute to the marketing effort and provide the voice-over for the radio advertisements.

Questions

1 How easy would it have been for First and Scott to maintain their informal style and culture as Nantucket Nectars grew?
2 Would more formality really be required?
3 How are strategy and structure linked?
4 What is the balance between intended and emergent strategy?

You might usefully apply Figures 14.1–14.3 to this case.

Whilst these structural types will be evidenced in the organization frameworks and structural designs which are next explored in detail, structure involves more than the organization chart or framework used for illustrative purposes and to explain where businesses, products, services and people fit in relation to each other – since structures are dynamic and involve behaviour patterns.

In my experience, the key to growth is to pick good managers, involve them at the outset of discussions on strategy and objectives and then devolve as much responsibility as they will accept. That's the only way you know if they are any good.

SIR MICHAEL GRADE, WHEN CHIEF EXECUTIVE, CHANNEL FOUR TELEVISION

14.4 Structural forms

Individual firms grow from being a small business with a simple **entrepreneurial** structure, developing a more formal **functional structure** to cope with the increasing complexity and the demands of decision-making, later becoming diversified with a **divisionalization** structure, and eventually a *matrix* within a multi-product, multinational organization with interdependencies accommodated to achieve synergy (Chandler, 1962; Salter, 1970). A number of discrete structural forms can be adapted and personalized by an organization when attempts are made to design an appropriate structure to satisfy its particular needs. The structural forms described in this section are only a framework, and the behavioural processes within the structure, the way in which resources are managed and co-ordinated, really determines effectiveness. In turn, these aspects are related to the way in which authority, power and responsibility are devolved throughout the organization, and whether generally the firm is centralized or decentralized. These forms are illustrated, but not exhaustively, below:

1. The entrepreneurial structure (Figure 14.4)

Typically utilized by early-stage small firms, totally centralized, with key decisions being made by the strategic leader to whom employees refer everything significant back. A new business founder (who has contacts and expertise in the firm's line of business, and whose investment is at risk) can control its growth and development. Although perhaps not really a formal structure (as all responsibility, power and authority lie with one person), some small firms give selected specialized employees job titles and some limited responsibility for production, sales or accounting (in which the founder may have potential skills gaps) and, as such, is more like the functional structure below. Its limitations relate to both skills gaps (discussed above) and growth, since the demands of both day-to-day problems and longer-term planning mean decision-making will become too complex for one person, leading to pressure to establish a more formal functional organization. When faced with relinquishing some responsibility for short-term decisions in order to have greater opportunity to concentrate on the more strategic aspects of the business, some owner-managers – who started their own business because they wanted total control over something, or because they were frustrated with the greater formality of larger companies – will be faced with a major dilemma.

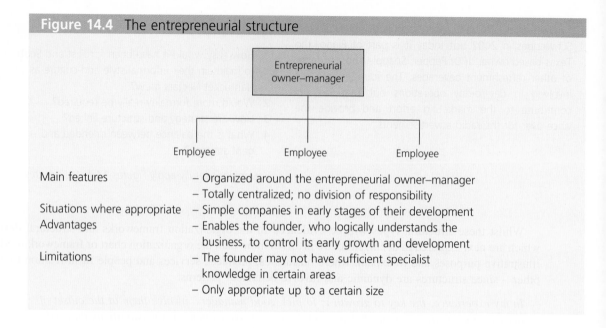

Figure 14.4 The entrepreneurial structure

Main features	– Organized around the entrepreneurial owner–manager
	– Totally centralized; no division of responsibility
Situations where appropriate	– Simple companies in early stages of their development
Advantages	– Enables the founder, who logically understands the business, to control its early growth and development
Limitations	– The founder may not have sufficient specialist knowledge in certain areas
	– Only appropriate up to a certain size

2. The functional structure (Figure 14.5)

Small firms that have outgrown the entrepreneurial structure, larger firms that produce only a limited range of related products and services and the internal divisions and business units that comprise larger diversified organizations all may adopt this structural form which, being centralized with corporate and competitive strategies controlled by the strategic leader, is more suited to a stable rather than turbulent environment. Structured around specialist functional tasks, the managers – who may possess delegated authority to change functional strategies – run departments responsible for these functions. Their effectiveness depends on teamwork by specialist managers and the co-ordination of the strategic leader. This structure is highly efficient with low overheads, and allows functional managers to develop specialist expertise that can help create competitive advantage, and communication between these specialists and the strategic leader facilitates a high degree of strategic awareness at the top of the organization. Limitations, however, include managers with greater specialist expertise rather than a more corporate perspective found in general managers, leading to the likely succession of a functional-specialist chief executive. Although possibly having a dynamic entrepreneurial strategic leader, functional organizations tend to be less entrepreneurial than more decentralized forms. Functional managers (not being responsible for strategy or profit) may concentrate on short-term issues rather than longer-term strategic needs, or on building mini-empires around their specialism, leading to *intra-firm* rivalry (for resources and status) and making co-ordination and team-building difficult. Further, as the firm grows from a limited range of related products to unrelated ones, co-ordination becomes difficult, necessitating some form of divisionalization and a revised role for the strategic leader. Their choice of future corporate growth strategy will have a major bearing upon the structural developments, with Figure 14.6 showing the structures discussed linked (indicatively not prescriptively) to relevant growth strategies.

Case 14.4 allows us to consider how such a structure would have been developed in Boda Porcelain as the operational challenges for the strategic leader grew with the success of the business.

3. The divisional structure (Figure 14.7)

An organization can be divisionalized using product groups (as illustrated by the figure); geographical regions; or manufacturing, assembly and distribution activities in vertically integrated organizations. They have decentralized divisions or business units (led by a general manager responsible for strategy implementation and, to some extent, formulation), themselves likely to contain a functional structure, and which are profit centres. Such structures are found when complexity and diversity increase, where turbulent environmental conditions make it appropriate to decentralize some responsibility, or where there are major

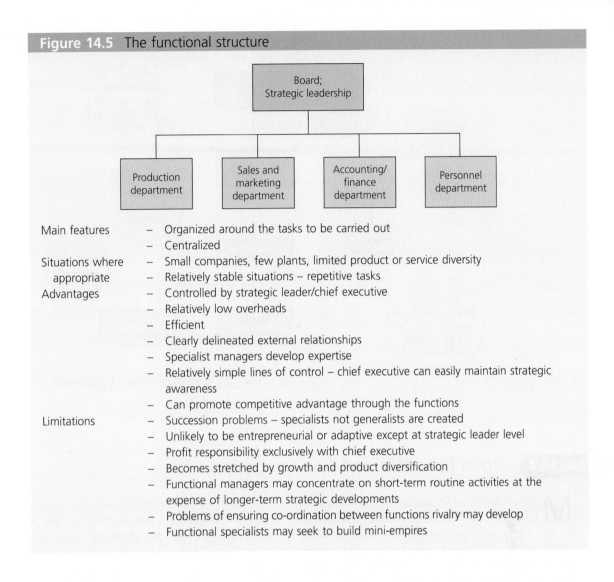

Figure 14.5   The functional structure

Main features	– Organized around the tasks to be carried out
	– Centralized
Situations where appropriate	– Small companies, few plants, limited product or service diversity
	– Relatively stable situations – repetitive tasks
Advantages	– Controlled by strategic leader/chief executive
	– Relatively low overheads
	– Efficient
	– Clearly delineated external relationships
	– Specialist managers develop expertise
	– Relatively simple lines of control – chief executive can easily maintain strategic awareness
	– Can promote competitive advantage through the functions
Limitations	– Succession problems – specialists not generalists are created
	– Unlikely to be entrepreneurial or adaptive except at strategic leader level
	– Profit responsibility exclusively with chief executive
	– Becomes stretched by growth and product diversification
	– Functional managers may concentrate on short-term routine activities at the expense of longer-term strategic developments
	– Problems of ensuring co-ordination between functions rivalry may develop
	– Functional specialists may seek to build mini-empires

differences in needs and tastes in the company's global markets. The organization can thus manage the strategies of a number of disparate products and markets effectively; and can spread profit responsibilities between the divisions or business units, thus motivating managers and enabling each activity's contribution to the organization as a whole to be evaluated. By delegating functional strategies, the strategic leader can concentrate on corporate strategy and avoid involvement in routine decisions. Acquisitions and divestments can be handled so that only parts of the firm are affected directly. Innovation and intrapreneurship throughout the corporation, if encouraged by the strategic leader, is facilitated. Difficulties and challenges include designing the most appropriate structure (which involves changing the power structure, the relative amount of decentralization and managers' jobs, thus proving disruptive) and also implementation since it may be difficult to establish (perceived) equitable profit targets – used as a basis for assessing performance and effectiveness – given that divisions may (a) be of uneven sizes, (b) be operating in markets which differ in their attractiveness, (c) have strong or weak relative market shares, (d) be interdependent upon each other or (e) have to compete with each other for scarce corporate resources. Further, conflict may arise if certain divisions are favoured in transfer prices at the expense of others. Profit orientation means that buying divisions may seek internal discounts, or selling divisions may expect other parts of the company to pay the going market price, or divisions may be oriented towards short-term financial measures rather than strategic issues. Organizations with various different products, all depending on core skills and technologies, must

Figure 14.6 Growth strategies and related structural formats

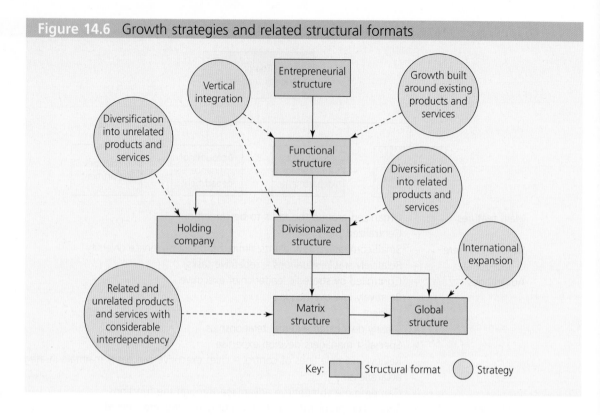

Key: ▢ Structural format   ◯ Strategy

Case 14.4   Boda Porcelain and Gao Songming   Ch

Most of the porcelain produced in China comes from one City – Jingdezhen –which is renowned for the quality of its porcelain. For this reason it would seem natural for anyone wishing to build a new porcelain business to locate in that city. Jingdezhen Boda Art Ceramics Limited was no exception to this tradition when it started up.

In order to assist the development of businesses within China, especially new start-ups and growing small businesses, the PRC (People's Republic of China government) has encouraged the development of Technology Industrial Parks. Boda Porcelain chose to locate in such a Park when it started up; and today Boda now has over 600 staff working in all areas of development within the business, including research and development, coloured drawing and manufacture.

Boda was founded by Gao Songming, and his personal success story is noteworthy for the nature of the difficulties he has had to overcome to build Boda Porcelain into the business it presently is.

Gao Songming was born in 1976; and, when he was 20 years old in 1996, he moved away from home with little money to obtain employment in the porcelain industry in Jingdezhen. Prior to this, Gao had been a factory worker near to where he lived. For Gao, Jingdezhen offered a new and better opportunity in a different industry. In what we might describe as 'typical lone entrepreneur style' Gao worked hard in the porcelain factory and saved his money. Later, and assisted by borrowings, he would be able to start his own small-scale porcelain factory – also in Jingdezhen.

When he did set up on his own, and not unusually, Gao did everything. He undertook every task that needed doing. As well as being a talented porcelain artist, he was in charge of production; and he packaged and posted the finished products. The danger will always be that people who start that way will continue as such a 'technician', in effect employing themselves but never finding a genuine expansion opportunity.

In an area famous for its porcelain Gao knew that competition would be severe from factories similar to his. He needed to be, and he wanted to be, different. Gao decided on a strategy of producing the very best products through large-scale development and artistic design of delicate porcelain. His time and money was spent on assembling a high-quality art and design team so as to make his products stand out from his rivals. To help his staff understand the strategy of the business Gao developed a slogan which loosely translates to: 'Art up the daily porcelain ware and industrialize the delicate porcelain'. This slogan has been followed throughout the development of the business – and he has succeeded in reaching a competitive higher ground in porcelain ware than his rivals.

The strategy followed by Gao is based on three principles:

1 employing people with strong talent
2 technical advantage
3 large scale production.

To achieve this Gao has invested a great deal of money and resources in the development of high standard delicate porcelain. The concept is that if delicate, well drawn porcelain can be produced in large quantities and sold at a good price point, it can be used in the home much more extensively than before. He has always sought creative ideas from his employees, with 10 per cent of business revenues being allocated as rewards for staff who come up with viable new design and product ideas. This drive for quality and artistic design has been very successful for Gao and Boda Porcelain. In 2008 his products passed the certification ISO9001–2000 and in 2009 Boda Porcelain was given the honour of the title 'China Famous Brand'. This emphasis on quality has continued

with the award of a gold medal at the 2010 Shanghai World Expo. This was added to by the continued certification stamp of ISO9001–2008 Quality Series.

The importance of Gao Songming to the success of Boda Art Ceramics is personified by the Chinese saying; 'It is the engine that contributes to the fast-running train'.

Questions

Do you believe Gao Songming has succeeded in moving on from being the 'founding technician' and put both himself and Boda Porcelain in a position where it is no longer dependent on him? Has he, in fact, done enough to secure the future of the business that he started?

harness and improve these skills (i.e. corporate resources) while ensuring competitiveness and operating efficiency for each product range. Each division is likely both to contain a functional structure and to have functional support from headquarters. The overall company may be able to negotiate better borrowing terms than an individual division could. They also need to minimize the potential waste from duplicate resources, especially where there are layers of divisions and, as organizations develop globally, the structural issues are compounded. Case 14.5 (later) discusses ABB, a company which deliberately followed a strategy of devolution when growing and diversifying.

4. The holding company structure (Figure 14.8)

Ideal for diversified conglomerates where there are few interdependencies between the businesses, as the small head office acts largely as an investment company, acquiring and selling businesses and investing money as appropriate. The subsidiaries, which may or may not be wholly owned, are independent, and their general managers are likely to have full responsibility for corporate strategy within any financial constraints or targets set by headquarters. Subsidiaries commonly trade under individual names rather than the name of the parent organization, especially where they are acquisitions which may at any time be sold again. The holding company structure is particularly appropriate for companies pursuing restructuring strategies, buying, rationalizing and then selling businesses when they can no longer add further value. Advantageously, this structural form has low central overheads and considerable decentralization, while

Figure 14.7 The divisional structure. A product divisional structure is illustrated. Geographical divisions, or a mixture of the two, are also used

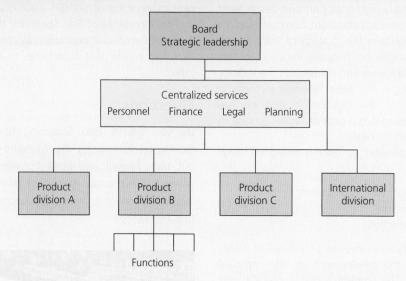

Main features	–	Divisions are likely to be profit centres and may be seen as strategic business units for planning and control purposes
	–	Divisions/business units are headed by general managers who enjoy responsibility for their own resources
	–	Decentralized
Situations where appropriate	–	Growing size and complexity
	–	Appropriate divisional/business unit splits exist
	–	Organizations growing through merger and acquisition
	–	Turbulent environments
	–	Product/market divisions/business units most appropriate where there is a diverse range of products
	–	Geographic divisions are common where there are cultural distinctions between the company's markets – especially if distances are great
	–	Divisionalization may also be a mix of products and geography or based on different production processes
Advantages	–	Spreads profit responsibility
	–	Enables evaluation of contribution of various activities
	–	Motivates managers and facilitates the development of both specialist and general managers
	–	Enables adaptive change
	–	Chief executive can stay away from routine decisions and concentrate on corporate strategy
	–	Growth through acquisition more readily implemented
	–	Can be entrepreneurial throughout the organization
	–	Divestment can also be handled relatively easily
Limitations	–	Conflict between divisions, say for resources
	–	Possible confusion over focus of responsibility (head office and divisions) and duplication of efforts and resources
	–	Divisions may tend to think short term and concentrate on profits
	–	Divisions may be of different sizes and some may grow very large – evaluation of relative performance may be difficult
	–	Co-ordinating interdependent divisions and establishing transfer prices between them

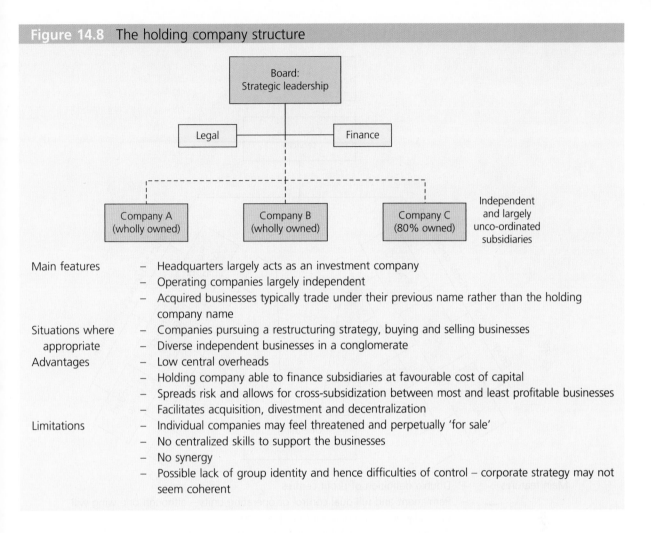

Figure 14.8 The holding company structure

Main features	– Headquarters largely acts as an investment company
	– Operating companies largely independent
	– Acquired businesses typically trade under their previous name rather than the holding company name
Situations where appropriate	– Companies pursuing a restructuring strategy, buying and selling businesses
	– Diverse independent businesses in a conglomerate
Advantages	– Low central overheads
	– Holding company able to finance subsidiaries at favourable cost of capital
	– Spreads risk and allows for cross-subsidization between most and least profitable businesses
	– Facilitates acquisition, divestment and decentralization
Limitations	– Individual companies may feel threatened and perpetually 'for sale'
	– No centralized skills to support the businesses
	– No synergy
	– Possible lack of group identity and hence difficulties of control – corporate strategy may not seem coherent

enabling the head office to finance the subsidiaries at a favourable cost of capital, helping to provide competitive advantage. In addition, risks are spread across a wide portfolio, and cross-subsidization is possible between the most and least profitable businesses, but a fair reward structure is needed for the general managers. The key benefit to headquarters lies in their ability to earn revenue and profits from the businesses, ideally in excess of pre-acquisition earnings, and being able to sell for a real capital gain. Limitations include the vulnerability that general managers may feel if they suspect that their business may always be for sale at the right price; the existence of fewer centralized skills and resources supporting the businesses, little co-ordination and, therefore, few opportunities for synergy; and no group identity among the business units and a lack of coherence in the corporate strategy. Several control issues which face head offices of divisionalized and holding company structures have been mentioned in the above sections, and these will be explored in greater detail in Chapter 16.

5. The matrix structure (Figure 14.9)

These attempt to combine the benefits of *decentralization* (motivation of identifiable management teams, closeness to the market, speedy decision-making and implementation) with those of *co-ordination* (achieving economies and synergy across all the business units, territories and products). They require dual reporting by managers, for example, to a mix of functional and business unit heads or geographical territory and business unit general managers, and are found typically in large multi-product, multinational organizations where there are significant inter-relationships and inter-dependencies, as

Figure 14.9 The matrix structure

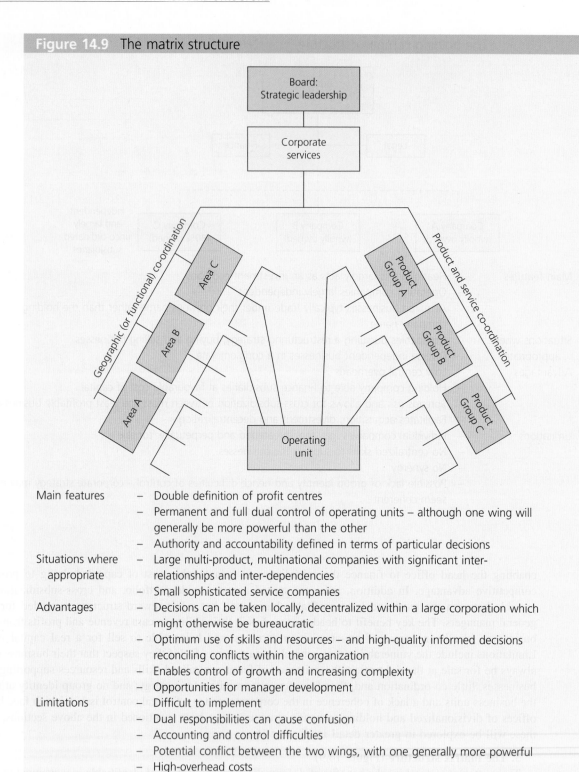

Main features	–	Double definition of profit centres
	–	Permanent and full dual control of operating units – although one wing will generally be more powerful than the other
	–	Authority and accountability defined in terms of particular decisions
Situations where appropriate	–	Large multi-product, multinational companies with significant inter-relationships and inter-dependencies
	–	Small sophisticated service companies
Advantages	–	Decisions can be taken locally, decentralized within a large corporation which might otherwise be bureaucratic
	–	Optimum use of skills and resources – and high-quality informed decisions reconciling conflicts within the organization
	–	Enables control of growth and increasing complexity
	–	Opportunities for manager development
Limitations	–	Difficult to implement
	–	Dual responsibilities can cause confusion
	–	Accounting and control difficulties
	–	Potential conflict between the two wings, with one generally more powerful
	–	High-overhead costs
	–	Decision-making can be slow

illustrated in Case 14.5, and in small sophisticated service businesses such as a business school. The matrix structure in Figure 14.9 illustrates an organization split into a series of divisions with co-ordination responsibilities *viz*: (i) product groups: production and marketing of their particular products in a series of plants which might be based anywhere in the world and (ii) geographical divisions: sales, marketing and distribution of all of the corporation's products, regardless of where they are manufactured, within their territorial area. The operating units are the production plants, members of one or more product groups, depending upon the range of products manufactured in the plant, and whose products are marketed in more than one territory or geographical region. Consequently, the general manager in charge of each operating unit is responsible in some way to a series of product and territory chiefs (four in the illustration), all of whom have profit responsibility. The matrix is designed to co-ordinate resources and effort throughout the organization. Ideally, resources and efforts should be concentrated on *both*, not just one of, the product groups and the geographical territories.

Case 14.5 ABB (Asea Brown Boveri)   Eur

Barnevik's Matrix Structure

ABB was formed in 1988 when the Swedish company ASEA merged with Brown Boveri of Switzerland to create a global electrical engineering giant. At the time this was the largest cross-border merger in modern history. ABB would later acquire over 100 additional, but smaller, businesses in Europe and America, all of which have needed integrating effectively. The chief executive who masterminded the merger and consequent restructuring was Percy Barnevik (of ASEA), who realized that he had a major challenge if he was to maintain both drive and dynamism during the integration. He became committed to an individualized matrix structure and his aim was to make ABB the global low-cost competitor. His creation has been declared 'the ultimate global organization' – a decentralized structure with centralized control over information and knowledge development. Simply, ABB became a 'multinational without a national identity'.

Barnevik was Swedish and he has been described as soft spoken, intense and philosophical. He was noticeably strong on information technology (IT) and he was very committed to the economic development of Eastern Europe and to the fostering of 'clean' energy and transportation. During his 8 year reign as Chief Executive revenues doubled and net profits trebled. The share price rose by 20 per cent every year.

Under Barnevik ABB was divided up into 1300 identifiable companies and 5000 profit centres. These were aggregated into eight business segments and 59 business areas. There were over 200 000 employees worldwide.

The eight segments were:

- power plants, further subdivided into

  - gas turbine plants
  - utility steam plants
  - industrial steam plants
  - hydro power plants
  - nuclear power plants
  - power plant controls

- power transmission
- power distribution
- electrical equipment
- transportation (such as high-speed trains)
- environmental controls
- financial services
- other activities.

The segments were responsible for organizing manufacture around the world and for product development. Horizontally, ABB was divided up into a mix of countries and regions. Figure 14.10 summarizes the basics of the matrix. There was a 12 member executive board representing products, regions and corporate operations, and a slim head office (under 200 employees) in Zurich. It was not seen as essential that the divisional headquarters for the eight business segments were located in Zurich. Some years earlier ASEA had had a head office staff complement of 2000; Brown Boveri employed 4000 in its head office.

Zurich essentially retained control over acquisitions; shifting production to Asia and Eastern Europe; and raising and managing corporate finance.

Financial reporting and evaluation was on a monthly basis.

Figure 14.10   Component businesses in the ABB matrix

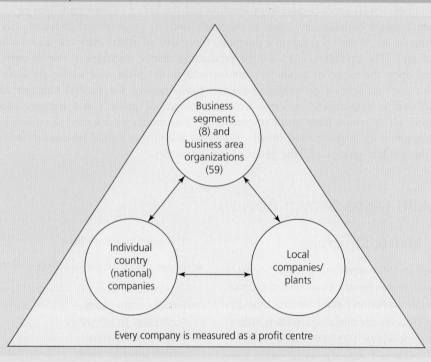

Business segments (8) and business area organizations (59)

Individual country (national) companies

Local companies/ plants

Every company is measured as a profit centre

The basic structure, therefore, was based on small units (of 50 people each on average) supported by good communications and IT. Although ABB comprised distinct businesses, both technology and products were exchanged. Under Barnevik, every employee had a country manager and a business sector manager. Dual responsibilities such as this have often been key issues in matrix structures which failed. However, Barnevik insisted that ABB's version was 'loose and decentralized' and that it was easily recognized that the two bosses are rarely of equal status.

Barnevik was obsessed with the idea of creating a small company and entrepreneurial climate within his large corporation. Extra costs and some fragmentation in the structure were seen as 'a small price to pay for speed and flexibility, with employees staying close to customers and understanding the importance of their own individual efforts for the success of their profit centre'. He also believed that if a large company is to manage internal communications effectively it must develop a 'horizontal integration process'.

The front-line managers, the heads of the 1300 businesses, were no longer implementers of decisions from the strategic leader; instead they were initiators of entrepreneurial action, creating and chasing new opportunities. The role of middle managers – in this flatter structure – concerned coaching and technology and skill transfer. Strategic leadership was about creating purpose, challenging the status quo and setting stretching, demanding targets for front-line managers; it was not simply, as historically it was, to allocate corporate resources and resolve internal conflicts.

Barnevik also commented that the biggest problem was 'motivating middle and lower level managers and entrenching corporate values – particularly a customer and quality focus'. He believed that his executives should see the business as their number one priority and assumed that high-fliers would spend up to 30 hours a week (in addition to their regular tasks) travelling, attending conferences and evening seminars and lectures.

It is the responsibility of every manager to network within the family of companies, developing informal relationships and looking for synergistic opportunities.

BARNEVIK

Life – and structure – after Barnevik

In 1997 Barnevik gave up the chief executive role and became non-executive Chairman of ABB. His successor was Göran Lindahl, perceived as more of a detail and less a concept person. Under Lindahl the process of transferring manufacturing to Asia and Eastern Europe from America and Western Europe accelerated. He initially reduced the importance of those executives with geographical responsibilities to focus more emphasis on manufacturing and to iron out some of the complex, dual-reporting issues. But he waited 18 months before dismantling the matrix structure of his predecessor. He was, however, anxious to retain the learning style and the concentration on small units.

Lindahl decided to take ABB out of capital-intensive and low-margin activities, here targeting transportation and power generation. He wanted to focus more on automation businesses. In 3 years the number of employees would fall from 215 000 to 160 000. Lindahl resigned in 2000 after initiating these changes of strategic direction. When he left the share price was half the value when he took over. At this time there were four industrial divisions – power transmission; power distribution; building technologies; and automation.

In fairness to Lindahl, some of ABB's markets had been declining and many agreed the company had diversified too quickly and too far. Adverse interest rate movements affected pre-tax profits and an ill-judged acquisition in America left ABB saddled with asbestos liabilities.

His successor, Jörgen Centerman opted to restructure ABB again, this time around four consumer segments – utilities; process industries; manufacturing and consumer industries; oil, gas and petrochemicals – and two product segments – power technology and automation technology. The product divisions both provided technology support to all the consumer divisions. It took him just 1 month to instigate this change. In recent years, sales growth had fallen back and Centerman believed ABB had to focus more on its customers. However he also created a stronger central executive team. The general assumption was that he would focus even more on automation and exit power transmission and distribution.

In November 2001 Barnevik resigned as Chairman, 'accepting responsibility for the collapse of the business'. The share price was now back to the 1988

merger value. Barnevik was replaced by Jurgen Doorman, who was recruited from Avensis (created through the merger of German and French chemical/pharmaceutical companies Hoechst and Rhône Poulenc). He was a 'hard-headed numbers man'.

You may have a brilliant vision … but if your bottom line is bad, your vision will be called into question very quickly … you have to implement your ideas.

DOORMAN

When Centerman also left in September 2002, Doorman took over his role as well.

Almost immediately, ABB's financial services business was sold to General Electric and oil and petrochemicals were put up for sale. An initial deal for part of the business was concluded in 2003. ABB was to be structured around two core activities: automation technologies and power technologies. There would be 12 business areas. Current staff levels of 150 000 would shrink further. ABB was now a 'mid-size engineering group with a lot of debt and a list of disposable assets'.

ABB had once been renowned for its growth and imaginative structure, for which it had sought publicity and notoriety. But 'arrogance and complacency are contagious … successful organizations have a tendency to become bureaucratic. The company went from the very entrepreneurial spirit under Percy [Barnevik] in his early days to then having become too successful. People felt there was too much power out there and wanted to centralize management control. This went far beyond what should have happened. It's operational excellence that's required now … and improving operating margins … some might say that's [more] boring [than in the past].' (Doorman)

ABB began its recovery in 2003, but it was a dramatically different company from when Asea and Brown Boveri were merged. Fred Kindle (from Sulzer) was appointed in 2004 to succeed Doorman as CEO from 1 January 2005. Doorman would progressively reduce his commitment to the business. There were 115 000 employees and the 2003/4 financial year showed a profit after three consecutive trading losses.

In 2004 ABB announced it was to build the world's largest underwater HVSC power cable link, joining Norway and Holland. The asbestos liabilities were finally settled in 2006. At this time a HVSC link between Finland and Estonia was completed. When the final oil and gas interests were sold in 2008, ABB was 'free to focus on power and automation'.

The current interests are:

- power products – which distribute electricity
- power systems – such as substations
- automation products – drives, motors and generators
- process automation – plant control systems
- robotics – for industry.

Profits exceeded $1 billion in 2007 – although the global economic downturn would follow, ABB appeared to be once more a robust – if different – organization. But in February 2008 Fred Kindle announced he was leaving – because of 'irreconcilable differences about how to lead the company'. It was announced that these differences did not relate to strategy or to acquisitions, and they did not imply 'problems lurking in the bushes'.

Questions

1 While the idea of a matrix structure is very attractive, it is inherently complex. Why do you think Barnevik's structure was at one time described as the 'ultimate global organization'?

2 Is the swing between decentralization and centralization flagged in the Doorman quote towards the end of the case an inevitability?

3 What is the situation today? Have further strategic changes required more structural changes?

4 How do you think it would feel to work within a structure such as this?

6. Post-matrix alternatives

Matrices have been too complicated to be effective, due to organizations' inability to deal with the issue of dual responsibility. And yet Fayol (1916) established the basic management principle 'unity of command', the need to be responsible only to one manager which, originally challenged by the matrix, has now been established to be uncannily accurate. Decisions have been stifled by confusion, complexity and delay because managers have not been sufficiently sophisticated to operate effectively within this theoretically ideal structure. The need for a structural form which offers the potential advantages of the matrix to large complex multi-product, multinational organizations, and which can be implemented, remains. An organization that is unable to design and operate a structure that enables the effective linking of a diverse range of related interests to achieve synergy – and at the same time permits the various business units to be responsive to environmental change – may need to be split up. Philips, Ciba-Geigy and Texas Instruments are examples of multinationals that introduced and then retreated from the pure matrix structure (Hunsicker, 1982), while ABB (Case 14.5) changed its matrix to adjust the balance of power, then largely abandoned it. Hunsicker (1982) argues that matrices were designed to co-ordinate activities, but the real strategic need is the development of new initiatives, hence a greater emphasis on temporary project teams, and the development and encouragement of managers within the organization so that they are more innovative and intrapreneurial, implying changes in behaviour rather than structure. Pitts and Daniels (1984) list the following opportunities for obtaining the benefits of a matrix-type structure within more unitary forms:

- Strengthen corporate staff to look after corporate strategic developments, e.g. seeking new opportunities that existing business units could exploit.

- Rotate managers between functions, business units and locations, increasing their awareness and providing input of fresh ideas.
- Locate executives responsible for product co-ordination in territories closer to those managers responsible for production of the key products.
- Create liaison groups meeting periodically to co-ordinate related issues, groups which might attempt to co-ordinate the global strategies of a number of related products in a search for synergy and mutual benefits.
- Build the notion of agreed contributions between business units into both the performance management systems and the compensation schemes.
- Periodically review and amend the constitution of the divisions without restructuring the whole organization.

Drucker (1988) suggested that the organization of the future would have fewer managers and fewer hierarchical layers, that IT would give individual managers more autonomy and more informed decision-making when specialists have decentralized responsibility for key activities within the organization, but that strategy co-ordination would still constitute a major challenge. We are now in a position to judge his prediction. Virtually every manager has access to a personal computer, an organizational intranet and the Internet. For many, letters, memos and telephone calls have been replaced by emails. In reality, what has changed? Emails and electronic file transfers have led not to better decision-making through more autonomy, but to rushed decision-making due to having less time to consider the next move.

At this point in the book you might like to reflect on whether certain strategic decisions can lead to serious implementation and structural challenges and consider why the notion of 'sticking to the knitting' might seem very plausible and persuasive. One irony is that **some** strategic leaders manage complex strategic situations very effectively. We might wonder why this does not prove possible for many other strategic leaders. See Research Snapshot 14.1.

Research Snapshot 14.1

There has been a moderate level of interest in strategy implementation, but it is dwarfed by the literature on strategy formulation and strategic management more generally, suggesting a field of research with significant gaps and opportunities for future studies. That said, the implementation of strategy is covered by other related papers but not necessarily explicitly. Here we explore issues of its link with performance, and barriers to effective strategy implementation and ways to overcome these.

Considering the link between firm performance and the implementation of strategy, some studies have identified particular barriers to strategy implementation (Heide *et al.*, 2002; Atkinson, 2006; Hrebiniak, 2006). In particular, achieving 'effective' implementation, with strategy failure being due to a lack of investment, no 'buy-in' by implementers, being unfocused, poorly designed, and 'unanticipated market changes' or powerful competitors' responses (Sterling, 2003), with responses to these being modelling, achieving 'buy-in', making priorities clear, designing better strategies and

using competitive intelligence (*ibid*). Another barrier can be 'communication problem[s] which may be influenced to some extent by the organizational structure, constitute the key barriers to the implementation of planned strategic activities' (Heide *et al.*, 2002). Resistance to change and leadership tactics by 'saboteurs, groupies, double agents and mavericks' suggest that 'mavericks need to be supported and rewarded for their contributions, groupies must be driven and encouraged, double agents have to be persuaded and convinced and saboteurs must be handled carefully and effectively and must not be allowed to become the focal point of leadership efforts' (Speculand, 2006). Dobni and Luffman (2003) investigated a major driver of performance, market orientation, 'the collective of employee behaviours that affects strategy implementation, how an organization interacts with its environment and adjusts to changes within that context'. Meehan and Baschera (2002) noted the role of contact with customers and employees in effective implementation of strategy.

Chimhanzi and Morgan (2005) found that marketing strategy can be effectively implemented in non-profits, taking into account 'relationship effectiveness' and 'interfunctional conflict', whilst 'psychosocial outcomes do have important effects on marketing strategy implementation effectiveness, a paradox is observed in the effects of process-based dimensions upon psychosocial outcomes'. Crittenden and Crittenden (2008) noted that, 'implementation is a critical cornerstone or ally in the building of a capable organization, and the use of the appropriate levers of implementation is the pivotal hinge in the development of the organization. Ultimately, strategy implementation helps create the future, not inhibit it.' Other studies include how, rather than parachuting managers from their home countries, multinationals operating in China can improve the implementation of their strategy by recruiting local managers (Fryxell et al., 2004).

It has also been studied how, over time, strategy implementation consistency (SIC), 'the alignment between firms' resource allocation decisions and their articulated corporate concept', shows no particular trends, in fact such 'firms tend to "zig-zag" over time – swaying off and pulling back to their strategic course independent of the timing of the announcement of a corporate concept' (Brauer and Schmidt, 2006). The consistency of the implementation of strategy may, in addition, differ drastically across different organizations of the same type, for example in local government where the four-fold factors of 'ideological vision, leading to change, institutional politics and implementation capacity', underpinned by an overarching concept of 'receptivity for organizational change', in the practices of particular strategies in such organizations, such as in those cases that are outsourcing (Butler, 2003), whilst achieving effective strategy implementation within subsidiaries has a major impact on performance (Lin and Hsieh, 2010).

The articles below provide a deeper understanding of strategy implementation and, accordingly, the further reading from this literature will help students to develop their perception and critical awareness of the barrier to, and drivers of, effective implementation of strategy, its link with firm performance, and also to highlight the developing thinking in relation to this topic.

Further Reading

Atkinson, H. (2006) 'Strategy implementation: a role for the balanced scorecard?', *Management Decision*, Vol. 44, No. 10, pp. 1441–1460.

Brauer, M. and Schmidt, S.L. (2006) 'Exploring strategy implementation consistency over time: the moderating effects of industry velocity and firm performance', *Journal of Management and Governance*, Vol. 10, No. 2, pp. 205–226.

Butler, M.J.R. (2003) 'Managing from the inside out: Drawing on 'receptivity' to explain variation in strategy implementation', *British Journal of Management*, Vol. 14, pp. S47–S60.

Chimhanzi, J. and Morgan, R.E. (2005) 'Explanations from the marketing/human resources dyad for marketing strategy implementation effectiveness in service firms', *Journal of Business Research*, Vol. 58, No. 6, pp. 787–796.

Crittenden, V.L. and Crittenden, W.F. (2008) 'Building a capable organization: The eight levers of strategy implementation', *Business Horizons*, Vol. 51, No. 4, pp. 301–309.

Dobni, C. B. and Luffman, G. (2003) 'Determining the scope and impact of market orientation profiles on strategy implementation and performance', *Strategic Management Journal*, Vol. 24, pp. 577–585.

Fryxell, G.E., Butler, J. and Choi, A. (2004) 'Successful localization programs in China: an important element in strategy implementation', *Journal of World Business*, Vol. 39, No. 3, pp. 268–282.

Heide, M., Grønhaug, K. and Johannessen, S. (2002) 'Exploring barriers to the successful implementation of a formulated strategy', *Scandinavian Journal of Management*, Vol. 18, No. 2, pp. 217–231.

Hrebiniak, L. (2006) 'Obstacles to effective strategy implementation', *Organizational Dynamics*, Vol. 35, No. 1, pp. 12–31.

Lin, S.L. and Hsieh, A-T. (2010) 'International strategy implementation: Roles of subsidiaries, operational capabilities, and procedural justice', *Journal of Business Research*, Vol. 63, No. 1, pp. 52–59.

Meehan, S. and Baschera, P. (2002) 'Lessons from Hilti: How customer and employee contact improves strategy implementation', *Business Strategy Review*, Vol. 13, pp. 31–39.

Speculand, R. (2006) 'Strategy implementation: we got the people factor wrong!: How to lead your saboteurs, groupies, double agents and mavericks', *Human Resource Management International Digest*, Vol. 14, No. 6, pp. 34–37.

Sterling, J. (2003) 'Translating strategy into effective implementation: dispelling the myths and highlighting what works', *Strategy & Leadership*, Vol. 31, No. 3, pp. 27–34.

Summary

To be successful, an intended strategy must be implemented, which requires that the organization's strategic resources are developed, deployed and controlled appropriately – accomplished through the design of the organization (the structure) and the processes encapsulated within the structure.

The structure can be described as the means by which an organization seeks to achieve its strategic objectives. However, the structural processes are a reflection of culture, power and political activity, and where people are empowered in a decentralized organization, these processes determine the actual (adaptive and/or incremental) strategies pursued.

Consequently, the structure must be capable of both creating and implementing strategy. The key issues which impact upon strategy creation and implementation are the extent of any decentralization, the need for co-ordination and the relative degree of formality–informality.

Organization structures are designed to ensure that intended strategies can be implemented effectively, and the processes within the structure also affect and facilitate emergent strategy. Particularly significant for ensuring that both happen is the location of power, responsibility and authority in the organization, and the extent to which these are centralized and decentralized. In large organizations, the relationship between the head office and the various subsidiaries (businesses or divisions) relates to this issue.

Centralization yields consistency and control, but it can result in an organization being slow to respond to the pressures for change in its external environment. In addition, entrepreneurial managers may feel constrained. Decentralization enables flexibility, but control is more difficult because it is dependent upon an effective information system which can gather together the various changes that are taking place as empowered managers make and take decisions.

Centralization/decentralization and formality/informality (the nature of control mechanisms and communications) determine the broad structural type. There are five + one main structural forms:

1 The *entrepreneurial structure* is found in the typical small business where everything is centred around a key person, often the owner–manager.

2 The *functional structure* emerges as departments and managers are created to deal with the increasing number of tasks.

3 The *divisionalized structure* is a popular structure for organizations with several products or services which may or may not be related.

4 The *holding company* is adopted by a diversified business with largely unrelated activities or businesses which can advantageously be kept separate for control purposes.

5 The *matrix structure* – or some variant of it – is most frequently used where there is a need to co-ordinate both products and countries in a business which manufactures and markets worldwide. Because of its inherent complexities, alternative forms of integration might be sought.

6 What we might call the *post-matrix* structure that may attempt to combine the matrix's benefits yet overcome its limitations.

Organizations change their structures as they grow; they may also be changed in line with alterations to the corporate portfolio to try to keep the two in balance. The main determinants of structure are: size, tasks to be carried out, environment and ideology. The basic structure divides up the tasks but, of course, the structure is merely a framework for allocating tasks and roles and positioning people. The real follow-up challenge is one of integration.

Online cases for this chapter

Questions and research assignments

1 It was stated in the text that decentralization and divisionalization are not synonymous. What factors determine the degree of decentralization in a divisionalized organization?

2 For an organization with which you are familiar, obtain or draft the organization structure chart. How does it accord with the structural forms described in the text? Given your knowledge of the company's strategies and people, is the structure appropriate? Why? Why not? If not, in what way would you change it?

3 How uncertain and traumatic might it be to work in a middle or senior management position in a large organization which changes its structure relatively frequently? Despite this, is change inevitable?

Internet and library projects

1 Evaluate the divisionalized or holding company structure of a large, diverse, multi-product, multi-national, considering the main board status of the key general managers. Does this suggest centralization or decentralization? If you are familiar with the company, do your findings accord with your knowledge of management styles within the organization? To what extent is performance determined by structure?

Strategy activity

WH Smith

In the last 20 years WH Smith has worked hard to clarify its strategic position in the retail industry. There is serious competition for all its products. As a consequence, its performance has both improved and deteriorated. There have been changes of leadership and occasional rumours of a possible takeover or sale to private equity. The data below provides a summary of the organization structure in 1995, 1999, 2003 and 2008. Research the company's progress over this period and (if you wish) update the data provided below. Has the structure merely changed to reflect changes of strategy? Or might the structural changes have been a serious attempt to drive the business both competitively and in fresh directions? What new formats are WH Smith experimenting with in 2013?

WH Smith: Group Structure, 1995

Retailing: UK and Europe

WH Smith Retail	High street stores – books, sounds, stationery
	Airports and stations
	Specialist Playhouse video stores
Virgin Our Price (75 per cent holding)	Virgin Megastores – *sold 1998*
Waterstone's	Specialist booksellers – large towns and cities – *sold 1998*

Retailing: USA

WH Smith Inc.	Gift shops, typically in hotels and airports
The Wall Inc.	Specialist bookselling in major cities and airports – *sold 1998*

Distribution: UK and Europe

WH Smith News and Books	Newspaper and magazine wholesaling and distribution
	Book distribution to retailers, schools and libraries
WH Smith Business Supplies	Five acquired suppliers of commercial stationery and office products amalgamated under the Nice Day brand – *sold in 1996 to Guilbert of France*

| **Do It All** | DIY retailers, at this time a 50:50 joint venture with Boots – *sold to Boots in 1996* |

WH Smith: Group Structure, 1999

WH Smith High Street	545 stores – books, sounds, stationery in the main
WH Smith Europe Travel Retail	183 station and airport stores
WH Smith USA Travel Retail	412 gift shops mainly in hotels and airports
WH Smith Asia Travel Retail	Hong Kong, Singapore and Sydney airports
WH Smith Direct	Internet retailing, with terminal access in selected stores
Hodder Headline	Consumer books publisher – with an 8.5 per cent share of the relevant market segment
WH Smith News Distribution	51 depots, making WHS the UK's leading wholesaler of newspapers and magazines. (The High Street and Europe Travel Retail included the rebranded John Menzies stores acquired by WH Smith in 1998.)

WH Smith: Group Structure, 2003

UK Retailing	The high street, airport and station stores plus WH Smith Direct (online sales)
WH Smith Asia Pacific	Stores in Australia (Angus & Robertson) and New Zealand (Whitcoulls) had been acquired. *The US Travel Retail Business had been sold in 2003*
WH Smith News Distribution **Publishing**	Publishers John Murray and Robert Gibson had been acquired to strengthen Hodder Headline.

Publishing was floated off as an independent business in 2004.
Also in 2004 the Asia Pacific business was sold to private equity.
In 2006 the business was split into two and existing shareholders given shares in both.
WH Smith Retail and Smiths News

WH Smith Retail: Group Structure, 2008

WH Smith High Street	557 stores, selling newspapers, magazines, stationery, books and entertainment. There were Post Offices in 82 of these and Bureau de Change facilities in 50 branches.
WH Smith Travel	449 outlets at airports, railway stations, hospitals and motorway services – selling a dedicated range of newspapers, magazines, books and confectionery.
WHS Direct	24 hour Internet sales.

Smiths News, *now a separate business, comprised 44 distribution centres (or 'houses') handling newspapers and magazines for 22 000 large and small retailers.*

References

Alexander, L.D. (1985) Successfully implementing strategic decisions, Long Range Planning, 18 (3).

Chandler, A.D. (1962) *Strategy and Structure: Chapters in the History of the American Industrial Enterprise*, MIT Press.

Child, J.A. (1977) *Organization: A Guide to Problems and Practice*, Harper & Row. (A more recent edition is now available.)

Drucker, P.F. (1988) The coming of the new organization, *Harvard Business Review*, January–February.

Fayol, H. (1916) *General and Industrial Administration*, Pitman, 1949 (translation of French original).

Greiner, L.E. (1972) Evolution and revolution as organizations grow, Harvard Business Review, July–August.

Hunsicker, J.Q. (1982) The matrix in retreat, *Financial Times*, 25 October.

Lawrence, P.R. and Lorsch, J.W. (1967) *Organization and Environment*, Richard D Irwin.

Mitchell, D. (1988) Making Acquisitions Work: *Lessons from Companies' Successes and Mistakes*, Report published by Business International, Geneva.

Owen, A.A. (1982) How to implement strategy, *Management Today*, July.

Pitts, RA and Daniels, J.D. (1984) Aftermath of the matrix mania, *Columbia Journal of World Business*, Summer.

Reed, R. and Buckley, M.R. (1988) Strategy in action – techniques for implementing strategy, *Long Range Planning*, 21 (3).

Salter, M.S. (1970) Stages in corporate development, *Journal of Business Policy*, Spring.

Thompson, A.A. and Strickland, A.J. (1980) *Strategy Formulation and Implementation*, Richard D Irwin.

Chapter 15

Leading change

Learning objectives

Having read to the end of this chapter, you should be able to:

● appreciate the dynamics of strategic change, its management, its role in growth, and major forces for, and types and modes of, change (**Section 15.1**)

● explain why people frequently resist change and how resistance can be overcome (**Section 15.2**)

● identify a number of different approaches to the planned management of change (**Section 15.3**)

● assess the importance of power, how it is used in change situations, and how managers can improve their political effectiveness in organizations (**Section 15.4**).

Introduction

Organizations and managers face change on a continuous basis, especially in volatile environments, with some changes being reactions to external threats and others proactive attempts to seize opportunities and manage the environment. Organizations should seek to obtain and maintain congruence between their environment, values and resources, making changes when there are pressures from either the environment or their resources. Organizations must seek to create and sustain competitive advantage, and wherever possible innovate to improve their competitive position, implying a readiness to change and the ability to implement the proposed changes.

This chapter examines the management of change in terms of leadership, culture and power, intrapreneurship, empowerment and learning organizations.

In this race ... you run the first four laps as fast as you can – and then you gradually increase the speed.

WILLIAM WEISS, WHEN CEO, AMERITECH

15.1 Strategic change: dynamics, management, growth, forces, types and modes

Figure 15.1 illustrates the strategic change process. Driven by the strategic leader and affected markedly by the organizational culture, the organization is attempting both to manage in (reactively) and manage (proactively) its external environment. The structure, objectives and the related performance measures are determined by the mission and direction and they, in turn, guide the decisions, actions and outcomes. These outcomes can then be compared with performance expectations; the timing of change is critical; and, if things are not changed at the appropriate time, the organization is likely to be reactive and may well end up perpetually crisis fighting.

Strategies, as we have said earlier, follow life cycles and throughout a strategy's life there should be innovative, incremental improvements in the face of competition. But when industries, markets or technologies are disrupted, companies must adapt and perhaps transform themselves if they are to survive, which may be more pronounced if they have been 'betting' as opposed to 'hedging'. Betting implies having pursued a focus strategy and relied on a limited range of related products rather than having diversified to spread the risk across a number of industries, which is hedging.

Figure 15.1   The strategic change process

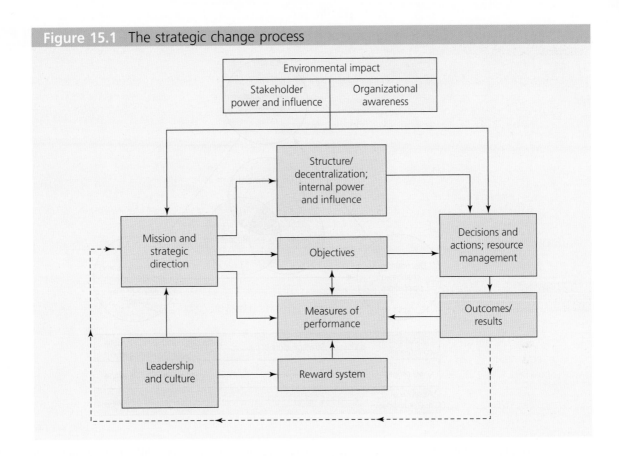

Hence effective organizations must be able to *manage change*, with managers and employees being supportive rather than resistant or hostile. When strategies change, structures and responsibilities often change too, clearly affecting people. Kotter and Schlesinger (1979) and later Waterman (1987) suggested that most companies or divisions need to make moderate organizational changes at least every year, with major changes every 4 to 5 years – a demand that has certainly not relaxed today!

While organizational changes can be reactive and forced by external change, effective strategic management requires *learning*. Managers must be aware of their environment, assessing trends and deciding in advance what should be done about perceived opportunities and threats. Planning activities and systems should ensure that the future is considered, and the resultant plans should encompass the implementation aspects of any proposed changes and the need to be flexible to accommodate unexpected changes. Moreover, innovation should be possible within the organization and managers should constantly be looking for ways of being more effective and able to proceed with appropriate changes.

Ideally, the organization will seek to develop a culture where people do not feel threatened when they are constantly asked to question and challenge existing behaviours and acknowledged ways of doing things, and change them – a culture that sees innovation and change as normal; a culture that is ideal for dealing with the competitive chaos that characterizes many industries and markets; a culture where people do not automatically ask: 'Who is already doing this?' when someone proposes an innovative change. Such a culture cannot happen without strong strategic leadership which fosters, encourages and rewards intrapreneurial and innovative contributions from managers and other employees throughout the organization.

Such a culture will frequently be based around a working atmosphere of creativity and fun; people must enjoy doing things differently and originally, actively looking for new competitive opportunities, instead of simply copying others.

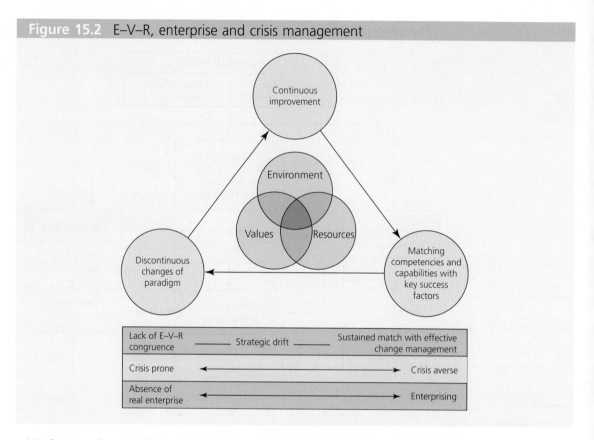

Figure 15.2 E–V–R, enterprise and crisis management

A change culture is highly desirable for many organizations but very difficult to achieve. Hence, the implementation of change requires *a perceived need for change*, which can originate with either the strategic leader or managers throughout the company who are aware of the possibilities; *the necessary resources*, involving aspects of competency as well as physical resources; and *commitment*, influenced by organizational culture, the extent to which managers are responsive and innovative.

Figure 15.2 takes the concept of E–V–R (environment–values–resources) congruence and restates the idea from the perspective of effective change management. The *environment* provides opportunities for organizations to benefit from innovation and continuous improvement; on other occasions the environment will encourage more dramatic, discontinuous change. This pressure can take the form of a threat (major environmental disturbance) or an opportunity (whereby the organization, 'seeing the future' ahead of its rivals, can shape its environment). The relative strength of the organization's *resources* is reflected in the success of existing strategies; *values* dictate the ability of the organization to manage change effectively. Strategic effectiveness demands congruency. The bottom bars confirm that an organization which enjoys E–V–R congruence is likely to be enterprising and relatively crisis averse, whereas strategic drift and lost congruence are matched with crisis proneness and a relative lack of enterprise.

The cycle of growth

Figure 15.3 is based around four stages of organizational development and growth – creativity, nurturing, 'doing' and control – which organizations must be able to accomplish, or face weakness if any is relatively over-abundant or under-achieved. Continued progression around the loop implies that an organization is managing the change agenda, whilst failing to do so implies a failure to adapt to change pressures.

The model is iterative and systematic, beginning with creativity – new ideas in a somewhat chaotic environment – followed by more passive reflection and nurturing when the idea is crafted into a real opportunity, often where a new business idea springs up. Whilst many organizations and entrepreneurs spend insufficient time carrying out this essential strategic thinking, it is equally possible to become bogged

Figure 15.3   The cycle of growth

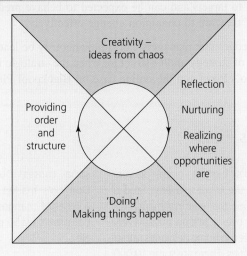

down in planning and not move on to action. Generally, this action or 'doing' phase brings about success and growth, demanding proper organization and structure in order that there can be management and control. The danger is that this control can stifle innovation through stasis and a loss of entrepreneurial drive. To ensure that the organization can continue to grow, fresh ideas – renewed creativity – is needed once more. We saw earlier in Chapter 8 (Figure 8.5) how some strategic leaders deliberately engineer a (perceived) crisis before a real one takes hold in order to drive the change process.

Ideally, an organization will progress from one stage to another and continue around the cycle; and yet many people have ideas which never become opportunities, and some entrepreneurial organizations are so involved in the doing stage that they only put in the proper structure when it becomes essential. Once systems, rules and control procedures begin to take hold, fresh creativity can easily be stifled. Naturally creative people may not seem to fit in with the more disciplined approach the organization has adopted. Most of us are capable of being creative, but we need to be working in an appropriate organization culture which encourages us to be creative. Consequently, this progression is unlikely just to happen – movement is likely to require triggers and some clear manifestation of need.

In addition, there are sub-loops in the cycle, such as creating and developing an opportunity or strategic thinking and action; while strategy and structure, as we have seen before, are also linked, while intrapreneurship is represented by a creativity-reflection-doing sub-loop within an appropriate structure.

Individuals are likely to be comfortable in one or two of these four roles and less comfortable in the others, such that strategic leaders must build management teams to make sure they secure the help they need to overcome their naturally weaker areas.

Leading strategic change

We looked at different styles of strategic leadership, at strategic issues in leadership and at intrapreneurial organizations in Chapter 10, and used the term 'meta strategy' for the leader's vision of how strategies should be created, implemented and changed.

Kotter (1990) argues that the leader must 'create and manage change', thus delineating four important differences between managers and leaders:

- Leaders work with the future in mind and do not always have to be bound by timescales (although time pressures to deliver can be important); managers are more concerned with planning and budgeting within defined time frames.

- Leaders champion organizational communications; managers work with the form of the organization.

- Managers concentrate on problem solving; leaders aim to inspire and motivate others.
- Managers work to targets and can be expected to behave predictably; leaders must at times be unpredictable if they are to champion change effectively.

Kotter acknowledges that managers can simultaneously be leaders and *vice versa*, such that we might expect changes of strategy and/or structure when the strategic leader changes – as we can see in Case 15.1 on Domino's Pizza and the online case on Blackpool Pleasure Beach.

Case 15.1   Domino's Pizza   US, Int

Domino's is the world's biggest pizza delivery company. Pizza Hut is the biggest overall; and a few years ago Papa John's took the lead in America for home deliveries. Serving well over 1 million pizzas every day, Domino's always specialized in home deliveries rather than providing restaurant facilities. There are some 10 000 company-owned and franchised outlets in 70 countries; some 500 of these are in the UK. The business model is built around speedy deliveries and consistent quality. Customers were historically offered a generous discount on any home delivery that took longer than 30 minutes. Delivery staff were required to wear trainers and to be fit enough to run between their delivery trucks (or motor cycles) and customers' houses, and to run up apartment stairs rather than wait for lifts. There were competitions between different regions for the best pizzas and fastest service. But the company had to change its promotional message after a delivery cyclist was involved in a nasty road accident whilst endeavouring to deliver a pizza within minutes of a telephone order being placed.

Entrepreneur Tom Monaghan in Ann Arbor, Michigan founded the company, in 1960. He ran the company for 38 years before selling it to a venture capitalist buy-in for $1 billion. The new CEO was David Brandon.

When the business became successful, Monaghan had taken to a 'tycoon lifestyle' with yachts, corporate jets and luxury homes. His personal office was 3000 square foot in size. The headquarters was in farmland he owned and where buffalo roamed quite freely. Yet, paradoxically perhaps, he was a committed Catholic. Later he concluded that he had allowed his personal pride to dominate his actions and he set out to change the culture and style. During the 1990s a new dress code was enforced. Men must wear dark suits and white shirts; women must wear skirts. By the time he sold the business he had divested many of the corporate 'possessions' he had bought. Since 1998 he has devoted his energies – and some of his fortune – to helping social causes. During the 1990s sales increased but Domino's market share declined. Brandon introduced a series of changes – and in 5 years managed to increase net profits by 50 per cent. Market share also recovered. He:

- abandoned the formal dress code
- set out to lower (the high) staff turnover and improve service
- freshened up the stores, refitting many of them
- added new senior managers to the existing team
- extended the bonus scheme
- strengthened top-down communications linked to a personal visible presence and availability
- became more discerning about overseas locations
- Extended the local-market toppings the company offered.

Domino's has always been an innovative business:

- It was the first pizza outlet to use fibreglass trays for dough – which simplify handling and ensure better preservation.
- It introduced the sturdy corrugated box for take-aways – the moisture and any fat from the pizzas doesn't make the box soggy and the cheese doesn't stick to the top.

- Later it introduced the 'HeatWave' delivery bags – each bag contains a heater disc to substantially reduce heat loss during delivery.
- It also developed the 'Pizza Screen' – a mesh tray which allows the base to be cooked more evenly.
- In 1999 Domino's was the first to offer online ordering.
- It pioneered 'commissaries' to provide and deliver dough to every store so staff there can focus on finishing, cooking and delivering pizzas.
- Finally Domino's has created a number of distinctive pizzas.

Prior to the credit crunch (2008) and economic recession the popularity of take-away food was predicted to continue expanding at a healthy rate.

Questions

1   Had you been Brandon would you have stuck with the 'delivery only' business model or introduced complementary restaurant facilities?
2   From your own experiences, what might give a pizza delivery company a competitive edge?

Heifetz and Linsky (2002) warn that 'dangerous' mental health problems may afflict strategic leaders because they must ask people to adapt, such that real leadership – linked to the change agenda – involves confronting people with adaptive challenges that they would often rather ignore, and may well rebel against. Some leaders erroneously assume that changes can be dealt with in a 'technical' (or managerial(ist)) way, using existing tools and capabilities, which may result in short-lived change benefits. Adaptive change is quite likely to involve restructuring and job losses … hardly popular! Sometimes certainty must be abandoned for uncertainty. Leadership frequently involves giving people news that they would rather not hear.

Meanwhile, Buchanan *et al.* (1999) suggested that leaders are courting trouble if they encourage or permit what they term 'initiative overload', which occurs when individual managers are unable to deal effectively with the uncertainty facing them thus causing them to: become cynical about any new change demands; lose motivation; become less coherent and less productive; possibly even burnout. Change is, therefore, not managed effectively in the organization and so, when there is any real likelihood of this happening, the leader's role is to clarify priorities and to help people to stay focused on what matters.

The increasing number and popularity of 'my story' books by prominent strategic leaders highlights the potential rewards from organizational success. However, strategic leaders may have to pay the price for failure since shareholders and other stakeholders will demand that they are held accountable when expectations are not met. That said, they rarely leave empty handed – golden handshakes can be very generous!

Institutional pressures can ensure that the strategic leader is seen to be responsible for their strategic decisions and the performance of the company. Three years after the stock market crash of 1987, for example, only one chief executive from the ten worst performing companies (measured by share price movements) was still in their post. Visible 'losers' included George Davies, the creator of Next. Davies, though, reinvented himself as the entrepreneurial designer he truly is; he first introduced the hugely successful George clothing range to Asda before creating the Per Una range for Marks and Spencer. Not all 'losers' are this successful and some disappear from the 'front-line' of corporate life but secure (sometimes lucrative) part-time and advisory roles. Change can be a risky business, but change remains essential. We look in greater detail at some of these issues in the next sections of this chapter.

Management of change: forces, dynamics, levels and types

Organizations face change pressures from the environment, and the significance, regularity and impact of these pressures will be determined by the complexity and volatility of the environment (see Chapter 4). Whatever the reason for change, a business has grown to a particular level and is now approaching a metaphorical fork in the road. Continuing straight on, continuing with existing products, processes and services, is not a realistic option. The business must change direction and, if it makes the appropriate decision, it can continue uphill and enjoy renewed growth, albeit with something different. If it makes an inappropriate decision, the route is downhill. The problem is that the business often reaches this fork relatively suddenly and unexpectedly. What Grove (1996) calls **strategic inflection points** are characterized by uncertainty, but for the ready and flexible organization, they can be a real new opportunity. Dealing with these change pressures is always going to be hardest for the successful, entrenched business. Grove (1996) believes it is important to be a first mover at the strategic inflection point by finding new and appropriate ways of adding value that matters to customers – not simply alternatives that are different from rival organizations – and to price at a level the customer will accept quickly. Somehow costs then have to be driven down to a level where a margin is possible. Since the timing of strategic inflection points will always be characterized by uncertainty, they must recognize just who in the organization is in the best position to be spotting trends and signals and engage them in discussion.

People who seem to be 'off-the-wall' should not be dismissed because they are 'off-line'. Cassandra foretold danger for the Trojans, but they ignored her and, complacent, they never spotted the horse in their midst! Remember the time to worry is when you are doing well. Even when he saw the 'writing on the wall' during his impious feast, it was too late for Belshazzar the king to stop the Medes and the Persians invading his city, killing him and replacing him with Darius. Organizations must somehow recognize when it is essential to give up on analysis (of largely historical data) and rely more on someone's intuition. After all, we can never predict the future with certainty unless, for example, we have the help of a divine handwriting on a wall. But we can unlock the secrets of the present if we ask the right questions, think about the answers we are being given, look at signals and triggers in the environment, think about new resource-based possibilities, properly identify problems and look for creative opportunities to make things more as we feel they should be.

At any time, managers may see opportunities and wish to adapt existing strategies. There are, therefore, several forces which encourage change, and a variety of different change situations. Change, though, affects people, their jobs and responsibilities and their existing behavioural patterns and can also change the underlying culture of the organization, making people thus wary or even hostile, which is increasingly likely if they fail to understand the reasoning behind the proposed changes and if they personally feel that they are losing rather than gaining from the changes. The various forces for change, the reasons why people resist change, and an outline framework for the effective management of change are considered in this section.

Forces for change

Major forces for change include, first, *technical obsolescence and technical improvements* due to change pressures from outside the organization in the form of new developments by competitors and the availability of new technologies which the organization might wish to harness. Internal research and development and innovatory ideas from managers can generate technical change internally – a significant issue in high-technology companies and industries, and particularly where product life cycles are becoming shorter. Some organizations follow product strategies built around short life cycles, product obsolescence (both physical and design) and persuading customers to replace the product regularly, such as with mobile telephones where handsets that once seemed state of the art are quickly an antique due to dramatic changes in design, screen size, camera mega-pixels and MP3 capacity.

Second, *political and social events*, again outside the control of the firm, will force companies to respond; for example, increased public awareness of environmental issues and government encouragement of the use of lead-free petrol (through media coverage and price advantages from lower taxation) forced car manufacturers to respond. In the first decade of the twenty-first century, one of the key pressure areas from the public on supermarkets is over the concept of 'Fairtrade' in terms of paying growers a fair price for the produce they cultivate, and the payment policies of major companies when using Third World labour in the goods produced for them. However, these concerns largely stem from guilt-ridden middle-class consumers, whereas those in relative poverty in the UK often have no alternative.

Case 15.2 (The One Foundation) describes an unusual organization that was established as a response to such change pressures.

Case 15.2   One Foundation   UK, Africa

One Foundation was established for the purpose of generating revenue to support specific needy causes. It sources and markets a limited range of consumer products – each with its own related cause.

It came about in part because Duncan Goose, who had a background in advertising and marketing, had made a connection with Play Pumps when he was on a motorbike tour of the world. *Play Pumps was explained in a short case in Chapter 4. Play Pumps itself began in South Africa with the idea of using children playing on a roundabout and having fun to pump water from underground to storage tanks. A £1000 hand pump can lift 150 litres an hour from a reasonable distance below ground. A Play Pump costs between £3000 and £5000 and by harnessing the energy from the roundabout to power a vertical drive shaft some 1400 litres can be captured every hour.*

Things happened, some 3 years later when a group of friends was talking about a variety of topics and when one of them said that around 1 billion people in the world do not have access to clean and fresh drinking water. Duncan Goose believed they could – and should – do something about this. The conversation was the actual trigger point.

One Water is bottled water from Powys in Wales, and the One Foundation has it bottled and branded and distributes it to earn money that is ploughed directly into building more Play Pumps, mainly in Africa. The business started trading in 2004. As is the case with all its products, the company has been able to secure distribution and make its products widely available – and the packaging makes clear how the surpluses generated will be used. One Water has been chosen by Virgin Atlantic for all of its flights. Vitamin enhanced water has been added to the range and this has widened the revenue generating potential.

As well as water, One Foundation also markets organic eggs to support community farming activities; hand-wash liquid soap to fund the sinking of pit latrines with associated hand-washing facilities; toilet rolls to install proper toilets in developing countries with inadequate sanitation; plasters to fund bicycle-ambulances; and condoms to help with HIV/AIDS counselling. The One Foundation also works with a micro financing agency.

There is a declared clear target customer – the 'questioning middle class who would shop in John Lewis (or somewhere similar) and pay just a tad more for a product that is ethical and environmental'. That said the products can be found in supermarkets and in Wilkinson's.

The One Foundation is different from Trade Plus Aid (*Chapter 3 Case*) in a number of ways but there is a common ethos. This is a different business and revenue model that changes perceptions on how aid might be brought to Africa and elsewhere and what can constitute the mission and purpose of an organization. In one sense the One Foundation is clearly a charity; on the other hand it is developing and marketing products that compete directly with leading brands on the market – many of which are produced by some of the world's leading consumer goods companies. We would, for example, associate bottled water with Nestlé and plasters with Johnson & Johnson.

Questions

1 Do you agree with the argument that this business was established as a reaction to a perceived Third World need?

2 What do you see as the advantages (and disadvantages) of this particular strategic approach and the organizational implications it has?

3 Once you learn about the motives for the business does it make you more (or less) interested to buy the product?

SOURCE: THIS CASE STUDY WAS PREPARED USING PRIMARILY PUBLICLY AVAILABLE SOURCES OF INFORMATION FOR THE PURPOSES OF CLASSROOM DISCUSSION; IT DOES NOT INTEND TO ILLUSTRATE EITHER EFFECTIVE OR INEFFECTIVE HANDLING OF A MANAGERIAL SITUATION.

Third, *the tendency for large organizations and markets to become increasingly global*, while again providing opportunities and new directions of growth for many organizations, have forced firms to respond to changing competitive conditions. The growing incidence of joint ventures and strategic alliances, discussed in Chapter 12, is a feature of this. Fourth, *increases in the size, complexity and specialization of organizations* create pressure for further changes, with large complex specialist organizations increasing their use of information technology (IT) in their operations, introducing automation and just-in-time (JIT) systems, which create a need for greater specialist expertise from both managers and other employees, possibly necessitating training and changes in their jobs. Effective use of these technological opportunities also requires greater co-operation and co-ordination between functions and managers, which has also led to the massive growth in outsourcing where IT based product help desks serving the UK are located in places like Bangalore in India.

Fifth, *the greater strategic awareness and skills of managers and employees* who want job satisfaction and personal challenges need opportunities for growth within the organization, which can be promotion opportunities or changes in the scope of jobs. Such changes require both strategic development and growth by the company, and appropriate styles of non-autocratic leadership, and yet many companies may pay lip service to the slogan 'our staff are our greatest asset' and all that this should mean.

The current dynamics of change

The strategic environment, especially competitive forces, determines how proactivity and change orientation make an organization more effective. Peters (1989) highlights factors that, despite industry and firm variations, require receptivity to change:

- the general dynamics and uncertainty of world economies
- time horizons, a strategic weapon in the face of uncertainty
- organization structures designed to enable decisions to be made quickly
- quality, design and service, which must be responsive to customer perceptions and competitor activities, are essential for competitive advantage.

Levels of change

Change decisions can be categorized in terms of their significance to the organization and the appropriate level of intervention (Table 15.1), with six levels forming a vertical hierarchy, enabling needs/problems to be clarified and tackled appropriately. If the problem is one of operating efficiencies, then the intervention should be at functional strategy level, which alone would be inadequate for dealing with higher order needs. As one ascends the hierarchy the challenges and difficulties increase – as shown in Chapter 7, changing the culture of the organization can be slow and problematical, and structural changes can be difficult to implement, particularly where individuals perceive themselves to be losing rather than benefiting.

In recent years, the recession-hit high street banks have introduced major changes in an attempt to protect and consolidate their profits, and these have systematically moved up to the highest level. A variety of approaches has been used to improve productivity and reduce costs, but this alone was inadequate. The services provided to customers have been reviewed, resulting, for example, in new branch interiors and the introduction of personal bankers and specialist advisers – and these changes have been linked to restructuring, the closure of some small branches, job losses and increased market segmentation of business clients. Banks rethought their corporate strategies, with concentration on core activities now being preferred. During the 1990s, the cultural focus saw a reduced emphasis on image and marketing and a return to the more productive utilization of assets, harnessing IT, to improve margins. And many customers think the banks still need to change further.

Table 15.1   Levels of change

Need	Level of change	Approaches/tactics
New mission; different ways of doing things	Values; culture, styles of management	Organizational development
New corporate perspective/strategy	Objectives; corporate strategy	Strategic planning
	Organization structure	New organization design
Improved competitive effectiveness (existing products and service)	Competitive strategies; strategic positioning; systems and management roles	Empowerment; management by objectives; performance management; job descriptions; policies
Improved efficiencies	Business processes	Business process re-engineering
	Functional strategies; activities; organization of tasks	Method study; job enrichment

Case 15.3 examines change in the UK National Health Service over a 3-year period and picks up on a number of these issues. The story of banks and the case on the NHS both flag how difficult it is to create and sustain genuine E–V–R congruence.

Case 15.3   The UK National Health Service between 2006 and 2009 UK

Implementing change

In 2006 retired corporate CEO and television presenter (Sir) Gerry Robinson spent a period of time with the NHS Trust hospital in Rotherham. The engagement was filmed for the BBC and Robinson's self-imposed task was to reduce waiting lists and waiting times.

In his endeavours he engaged with the Chief Executive and consultants and anaesthetists, hospital managers, theatre sisters and ward nurses in different parts of the hospital. Some individuals were 'up for change' whilst others were clearly feeling threatened by the thought of change. There was no real culture of change, and supporters and opponents could be found in any staff group, and were, in fact, actually found in all of them.

Essentially Robinson was trying to enable the entrepreneurs within the hospital to be given a chance.

It was clear to Robinson that he was not looking for a 'one-size-fits-all' answer – what might work was going to be different in different sections. It was, therefore, all about empowerment and local initiatives – and then about sharing the outcomes so others could learn. Interestingly, the CEO was an NHS-outsider but needed to be encouraged by Robinson to 'walk the floors', to *lead* and to speak routinely with the staff. His interventions, when they happened, clearly affected staff confidence to try out changes in their own areas.

The following is a list of different initiatives (suggested and championed by staff in various roles) that were tried, many of which, but not all, worked favourably:

- one additional patient on every consultant list for every (half-day) clinic – this improved waiting lists for children quite markedly
- switching from two (half-day but specified target hours) lists a day to one all-day list
- parallel theatre lists where two consultants and their teams could work adjacently and use capacity more effectively – moving from one procedure to another when and where it made sense
- using theatres routinely on a Friday afternoon rather than only exceptionally
- pooling patients amongst a qualified team – which was tried in endoscopy, but wouldn't be appropriate everywhere
- anaesthetists providing recovery services so that surgeons were able to move on more quickly.

The follow-up in 2007

Gerry Robinson returned to Rotherham General Hospital roughly a year after his first visit. He confirmed there had been changes, largely driven by the CEO taking more ownership.

But that did not mean everything was working effectively. He commented that it seemed to take staff forever to reach a point where they are doing what had been staring them in the face when they started talking and deliberating. The structure and systems continued to inhibit.

The following points came out of the programme:

- The NHS remains driven by government policy and initiatives and some of these are questionable. The Rotherham Primary Care Trust was investing huge amounts to build a convenient new drop-in centre in the town centre (a Polyclinic) where people could turn up for quick-and-easy treatments – but the impact would be lower utilization of some hospital resources.
- Governments appear to understand policy better than they do front-line (local) management. The issue is not so much changing policy but making existing policies work on the ground.
- There need to be *champions* of change and also a *willingness to make it happen*. There is a need for 'enablers' to influence the culture.
- Small successes 'every day' can be more influential than occasional big impacts. Linked to this, it is perhaps better to focus on making things work within existing structures rather than changing the structure.
- There will continue to be tensions and clashes between staff groups. Who runs the hospital, for example – managers, consultants or the CEO? But these can be resolved – sometimes using humour. In the first programme one frustrated manager had asked of the consultants – *How old are they behaving today?* In response the consultants had acquired T-shirts with 'Delinquent' printed on the front and 'I am acting ? years old today' on the back. In this context it is worth remembering that creativity and innovation prosper in a culture of fun and irreverence, even though the work is serious and taken seriously.

The situation in 2009

Robinson wrote an article for the *Daily Telegraph* in March 2009, where he suggested that crises in patient care (continue to) stem from 'excessive bureaucracy and poor quality leadership'. In recent years, he said, the number of people in management positions had soared and

exceeded the number of consultants tending to the sick. Their salaries had also risen substantially. The outcome: more managers but not better management. Robinson argued for better 'checks and balances' and monitoring procedures. Lines of responsibility were ineffective. The complexity was slowing down decision-making and hiding accountability.

He cited an abundance of paper checks (box ticking to document everything) but questioned whether this was ever followed up. One telling comment was that Chief Executives are apparently so tied up managing their managers they don't manage the medical staff, who then go their own way. One conclusion is that the whole system of what is centralized and what is decentralized needs revisiting.

'Until we learn to manage the NHS more effectively we will never have the health service we pay for – and deserve.'

Reference for last section

Robinson, G. (2009) 'Cure the NHS with far fewer managers', *Daily Telegraph*, 28 March.

Questions

1 What do you think are the main lessons to be learned from this case?
2 Will it ever be easy to engineer change in an institution like the NHS?
3 Does the saying 'two steps forward, one step back' explain the very best that could be hoped for?

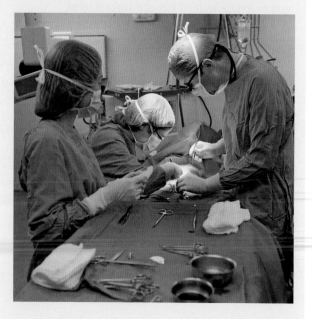

Types of change

Summarizing these points, Daft (1983) identifies the four basic types of change which affect organizations as technology, the product or service, administrative changes and people. Invariably, a change in one of these factors will place demands for change on one or more of the others. When an organization decides to launch a new product, it may also need to invest in new technology, modify its existing production plant and either acquire people with, or train existing employees in, the new skills required. Major changes in the strategic perspective, such as an acquisition, will change the organization structure, in turn necessitating changes in jobs and behaviour patterns. However necessary the changes may be, and however ready the organization might be to implement them, the outcomes may not be positive for everyone affected.

15.2 The change process and resistance to change

Change frequently disrupts normality – job security seems threatened, existing behaviour patterns and values are questioned, people are required to be more flexible and to take more risks. While the organization may be facing strong external pressures, managers and other employees are likely to query or resist the need to change, especially if individuals feel threatened, or perceive themselves to be losing out rather than benefiting or not being rewarded in some way for co-operating.

People should be encouraged to recognize the need for change, the benefits and the external threats from not changing, which can involve the engineered crisis. Managed change should be planned and evolutionary, although some organizations have attempted to become more flexible such that people not only accept change, but constantly seek new opportunities for change and improvement. Although change can be speedy and dynamic – normally when it is forced by powerful external influences – managing change positively in a growth situation, taking advantage of opportunities rather than responding to threats, requires that the process begins gradually and on a limited scale, and then spreads. Advancement needs consolidation and learning. The innovation stage, which can easily go wrong, requires that the change agents (who will not always be the strategic leader) find powerful and influential allies and supporters. Time and effort must be invested in explaining, justifying and persuading while trial and error leads to incremental learning. Early supporters should be visibly rewarded for their commitment, which will encourage others and begin to consolidate the changes. Conservative people (by temperament, not politics!) are inevitably going to be late joiners; and some older people, together with those who are set in their ways, are likely to be laggards. Because changes can be slow to take off, they often appear to be failing once the process is well under way, which will renew opposition and resistance. During the process, the environment should be continually monitored and the programme may need amendment if circumstances alter.

Remember, it is not always the man on the shop floor who opposes change. It can be the second or third tier of management who are the most reactionary.

SIR PETER GIBBINGS, EX-CHAIRMAN, ANGLIA TELEVISION

No positive changes will occur within a company unless the chief executive realizes that people are basically opposed to change. A climate for change must be created in people's minds.

Changes need to be planned and everyone must be reassured that these changes will be for the betterment of the company, its employees, customers and shareholders. Changes have therefore to be managed against a set of objectives and to a timetable.

JACQUES G. MARGRY, WHEN GROUP CHIEF EXECUTIVE, PARKER PEN LTD

People do not resist change per se … they resist loss.

HEIFETZ AND LINSKY, 2002

There are several reasons why change pressures might be resisted, and certain circumstances where the implementation of change will have to be planned carefully and the needs of people considered. First, some resistance can be expected where people have worked out ways of doing things which are beneficial to them in terms of *their* objectives and preferences and thus may see change as a threat. Similarly, when people have mastered tasks and feel in control of their jobs and responsibilities, they are likely to feel relatively safe and secure personally. Again, change may be perceived as a threat to their security, although the aim might be to ensure the security of the organization as a whole. The university sector is a particularly difficult sector in which to achieve change in part because academics are mainly rewarded for being selfish in terms of pursuing their research and getting it published, such that most if not all their energy goes into this process. As a result, they often just do not support change or anything else that would detract from their main aim – their research output – as this output often leads to increased status and financial rewards in a new institution.

Second, resistance to 'sideways change' (expanding certain activities while contracting elsewhere) is likely unless the people affected are fully aware of the reasons and implications. Third, where particular policies, behaviour patterns and ways of doing things have been established and accepted for a long time and in effect have become part of the culture of the organization, change will require careful implementation and the need for change may not be accepted readily. Fourth, people often have some fear of the unknown. Feeling comfortable with situations, policies and procedures that they know and understand is, therefore, an important aspect of change.

Fifth, the organization itself, or particular managers, may resist external pressures if the change involves considerable expense, investment in new equipment and the associated risks. This issue can be exacerbated where there has previously been substantial investment in plant and equipment which technically is still satisfactory and, although demand may be falling, there may be a reluctance to sell or close. Sixth, resistance is likely to be forthcoming where there are perceived flaws or weaknesses in the proposal. Change decisions may be made by the strategic leader and then delegated for implementation. Managers who are closer to the market may have some justified reservations if they have not been consulted during the formulation process.

The opposition may be to the change itself, or to the proposed means of implementation, and both can and must be overcome if changes are to be implemented successfully. Casualties are, however, possible and sometimes inevitable. Some people will leave because they are uncomfortable with the changes.

Kotter and Schlesinger (1979) have identified six ways of overcoming resistance to change, and these are described in Critical Reflection 15.1, suggesting that each method has both advantages and disadvantages and can be appropriate in particular circumstances. Issues raised by some of these alternatives are developed further in this chapter. Organizational development is considered as an approach to gaining support through active participation by managers on a continuous basis; manipulative approaches are discussed as a Machiavellian use of power and influence. The next section considers a number of general aspects in the management of change before specific strategies are discussed in more detail.

Argyris and Schön (1978) concluded that the most knowledgeable and experienced employees are most likely to feel inhibited and frustrated by change demands. Their sense of inhibition causes disbelief and distrust; employees lose their sense of commitment and they develop defensive routines in an attempt to either impede or prevent change, which becomes so embedded it is hard to overcome – and it cannot be defeated by force under any normal circumstances. Instead, the culture must be transformed until it reaches a state where change is welcomed by what they term 'action science', which fundamentally requires the generation of powerful, shared knowledge that is relevant to the needs of both the business and its employees with communications, understanding and trust being at the core (ibid). Effective change occurs when managers and employees modify their behaviour in a desired or desirable way, and when the important changes are lasting rather than temporary.

Lewin (1947) contends that permanent changes in behaviour involve three stages – unfreezing previous behaviour, changing and then refreezing the new patterns – which are crucial if changes in culture are required. *Unfreezing* is the readiness to acquire or learn new behaviour. People are willing to accept that existing strategies and ways of doing things could be improved and made more effective, and normally this needs a trigger such as declining sales or profits, or the threat of closure or acquisition. *Change* occurs when people who perceive the need for change try out new ideas, which could be introduced gradually or they may be more dramatic.

Critical Reflection 15.1   Six Ways of Overcoming Resistance to Change

1 Education and communication

Education and communication should help people to understand the logic and the need for change. A major drawback can be the inherent time delays and logistics when a lot of people are involved. It also requires mutual trust.

2 Participation and involvement

The contention is that people will be more supportive of the changes if they are involved in the formulation and design. Again, it can be time-consuming; and if groups are asked to deliberate and make decisions there is a risk that some decisions will be compromises leading to sub-optimization.

3 Facilitation and support

This can involve either training or counselling but there is no guarantee that any resistance will be overcome.

4 Negotiation and agreement

Negotiation and agreement are normally linked to incentives and rewards. Where the resistance stems from a perceived loss as a result of the proposed change, this can be useful, particularly where the resisting force is powerful. However, offering rewards every time changes in behaviour are desired is likely to prove impractical.

5 Manipulation and co-optation

This encompasses covert attempts to influence people, for example by the selective use of information and conscious structuring of events. Co-optation involves 'buying off' informal leaders by personal reward or status. These methods are ethically questionable, and they may well cause grievances to be stored for the future.

6 Explicit and implicit coercion

The use of threats can work in the short run but is unlikely to result in long-term commitment.

Source

Kotter, J.P. and Schlesinger, L.A. (1979) Choosing strategies for change, *Harvard Business Review*, March–April.

Choosing the appropriate change strategy once the need is clarified may involve the selection of one from a number of alternatives, and consequently there are opportunities for involving the people who are most likely to be affected. Power structures are likely to be altered and consequently resistance might be evident from certain people. Particularly where the pressures for change are significant, and the likely impact of the changes will be dramatic and felt widely throughout the organization, the change strategy will need a champion. Organizations in difficulty often appoint a new strategic leader to introduce fresh ideas and implement the changes, since newcomers are unlikely to be associated with the strategies which now need changing, or they might move general managers to different business units. *Refreezing* takes place when the new behaviour patterns are accepted and followed willingly, such that people are supportive and convinced of the wisdom of the changes. Ideally, the new approaches become established within the culture, and rewards are often influential in ensuring that refreezing does, in fact, take place.

Whilst this simple model provides an excellent outline of the basic stages in a managed change process, if we want to foster a culture which embraces perpetual change we need to be careful about refreezing new behaviour too rigidly. Throughout the change process, people should be aware of why changes are being proposed and are taking place, and that they understand the reasons. Indeed, Margerison and Smith (1989) suggest that the management of change exhibits four key features:

1 *dissatisfaction* with the present strategies and styles

2 *vision* of the better alternative – a clear picture of the desired state which can be communicated and explained to others (again emphasizing the need for a champion of the change)

3 *a strategy* for implementing the change and attaining the desired state

4 *resistance* to the proposals at some stage.

Lewin (1951) has proposed that changes result from the impact of a set of driving forces upon restraining forces, and Figure 15.4 illustrates his theme of a state of equilibrium which is always under some pressure

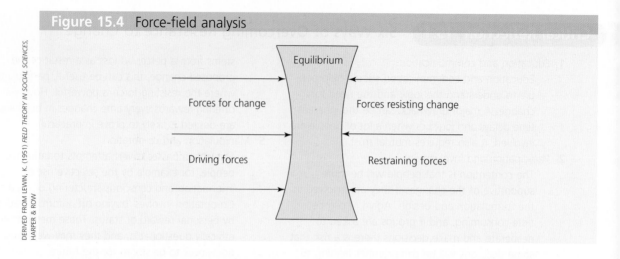

Figure 15.4 Force-field analysis

DERIVED FROM LEWIN, K. (1951) *FIELD THEORY IN SOCIAL SCIENCES,* HARPER & ROW

to change. The extent to which it does change will depend upon whether the driving forces (external or internal in origin, and likely to have economic aspects, e.g. increased sales, profitability, efficiency, etc.) or restraining forces (any resistance to change) prove to be stronger. Corporate, competitive and functional strategies may appear in need of change, but existing strategies may have people who are loyal and committed to them, who will be affected and may feel concerned, seeking to abandon or modify change proposals.

Although the driving forces will be concerned with improving organizational efficiency and effectiveness, the opposition is more likely to stem from personal concerns than from disagreement that improved efficiency and effectiveness are desirable. Lewin suggests that the driving forces are based more on logic and the restraining forces on emotion. However, people who are aware of the situation may seek to argue their opposing case in relation to the relative ability of the change proposal to achieve the required improvements. As a result, the ensuing debate concentrates on these issues and opponents may choose not to be honest and open about their personal fears, feeling that their arguments must concentrate on the economic issues – such that the decision, whatever it might be, has not encompassed important underlying behavioural issues. Effective managers of change situations will be clearly aware of both the driving forces and the real restraining forces, and will seek to strengthen the justifications by communication and explanation and diffuse opposition by exploring the likely impact with the people affected. Critical Reflection 15.2 summarizes important issues for the effective management of change.

To many, uncertainty is a shadow of the unknown, to be avoided; far better, as we are stuck with an uncertain world, is to look upon it as the spice of life.

SIR PETER HOLMES, WHEN CHAIRMAN, SHELL UK

Teach people that change is inevitable and, if embraced, can be fun.

LESLIE HILL, WHEN CHAIRMAN AND CHIEF EXECUTIVE,
CENTRAL INDEPENDENT TELEVISION PLC

15.3 Strategies for implementation and change

Implementation may be viewed as an activity which follows strategy formulation – structures and systems are changed to accommodate proposed changes in strategy. However, implementation, instead of following formulation, may be considered in depth at the same time as the proposed strategy is thought through and before final decisions are made, which is more likely to happen where several managers, especially those who will be involved in implementation, are consulted when the strategy is evaluated.

Critical Reflection 15.2   Issues in Effective Change Management

- Change programmes must be championed.
- There needs to be a clear purpose to which people can subscribe ... which can be justified and defended.
- The change proposals will not be backed by everyone.
- Managers must decide how much to communicate and when – there are dangers in both inadequate information provision and in being too open and candid.
- Senior managers must take responsibility; while empowerment is important, people still need effective leadership.
- Effective change management frequently involves well-led teams and may require process or even structural change.

- Creating and broadcasting early successes speeds up the process, especially as programmes often lose momentum part-way through.
- Setbacks must be anticipated and managed, and the momentum maintained.
- It is dangerous to claim victory too quickly; the changes must become anchored in the culture.
- The feelings of people who might be hurt by the changes must not be overlooked.

Sources

Eccles, T. (1994) *Succeeding With Change*, McGraw-Hill.
Kotter, J.P. (1995) Why transformation efforts fail, *Harvard Business Review*, March–April.

Strategies may emerge from the operation of the organization structure. Where managers are encouraged to be innovatory and make incremental changes, elements of trial and error and small change decisions are often found. Implementation and formulation operate simultaneously; the changes are contained rather than dramatic and resistance may similarly be contained. Innovatory organizations can develop change orientation as part of the culture; people expect things to change regularly and accept changes. Bourgeois and Brodwin (1984) have identified five distinct approaches to strategy implementation and strategic change.

- The strategic leader, primarily a thinker/planner rather than a doer, possibly using expert planners or enlisting planning techniques, defines changes of strategy and then hands over to senior managers for implementation.

- The strategic leader again decides on major changes of strategy and then considers the appropriate changes in structure, personnel and information and reward systems if the strategy is to be implemented effectively. Quinn (1988) contends that the strategic leader may reveal the strategy gradually and incrementally as they seek to gather support during implementation, a theme that is developed later in this section. (In both these cases, the strategic leader needs to be powerful as both involve top-down strategic change.)

- The strategic leader and senior managers (divisional heads, business unit general managers or senior functional managers) meet for lengthy discussions with a view to formulating proposed strategic changes. All of the managers are briefed and knowledgeable, and the aim is to reach decisions to which they will all be committed. Strategies agreed at the meetings are then implemented by the managers who have been instrumental in their formulation and, while this approach involves several managers, it is still primarily centralized.

- The strategic leader concentrates on establishing and communicating a clear mission and purpose for the organization through a decentralized structure by developing an appropriate organization culture and establishing an organization-wide unity of purpose. While the strategic leader will retain responsibility for changes in the strategic perspective, decisions concerning competitive and functional strategy changes are decentralized to general and functional managers who are constrained by the mission, culture, policies and financial resources established by the strategic leader.

- Managers throughout the organization are widely encouraged to be innovative and come up with new ideas for change, which are evaluated by a framework established by the strategic leader, recognizing that those which are accepted and resourced result in increased status for the managers concerned.

Ghoshal and Caulkin (1998) warn that major, dramatic change is associated with charismatic and tough strategic leaders who attract and reward ambitious high-flying managers who, like them, operate a dehumanizing style of management to drive through the changes; leading to 'a lot of change, a lot of stress and a lot of fear'. Instead, they argue, organizations need either people who can exercise power robustly but with wisdom, passion and constraint or checks to ensure that people are not forgotten in the drive for change.

Ideas for change, of course, can start at the bottom of the organization rather than always at the top with change possibly being seen as both a clearly managed process and the incremental outcome of the decisions taken in an innovative, change-orientated organization where managers are empowered. These basic approaches highlight a number of general themes and ideas, which are considered below.

Top-down strategic change

A number of approaches can be involved in drawing up organizations' strategies, but here changes in strategy are ultimately centralized decisions, which may be both popular and viable if the strategies that are selected can be implemented effectively. It was mentioned earlier that resistance can be expected if managers who are charged with carrying out changes in strategy feel that there are flaws in the proposals, and so the appropriate level of consultation must take place during formulation. Capable managers are needed throughout the organization to deal with operational issues, and the quality of the information systems which underpin the planning is a crucial issue. The approach is attractive to strategic leaders who are inclined more towards the analytical aspects of strategy than they are towards behavioural issues.

Quinn's (1988) incremental model is another primarily top-down approach, but it suggests a high degree of political skill (discussed later in the chapter) on the part of the strategic leader who appreciates the difficulties involved in implementing change. Change impacts structures and systems, culture and power relationships, and the strategic leader is either personally or ultimately responsible for the proposed changes in strategy, and for establishing the structure and processes within the organization.

Quinn's approach is as follows:

- The strategic leader will develop their own informal information and communication channels, both within and external to the organization, and will draw on this as much as using the formal systems.

- The strategic leader must generate *awareness* of the desired change with the appropriate managers within the organization. This involves communication and cultural issues.

- The strategic leader will seek to legitimize the new approach or strategy, lending it authority, if not, at this stage, credibility.

- They will then seek to gather key supporters for the approach or strategy.

- The new strategy may be floated as a minor tactical change to minimize resistance, and possibly keep the ultimate aim unclear. Alternatively, the strategy may be floated as a trial or experiment. Opposition will be removed by, for example, ensuring that supporters chair key committees, and that stubborn opponents are moved to other parts of the organization.

- The strategy will be flexible so that incremental changes can be made in the light of the trials. There will be a strong element of learning by doing, so that any unexpected resource limitations, such as a shortage of key skills, will be highlighted.

- Support for the change will harden, and proposals crystallized and focused.

- Finally, the proposed changes will be formalized and ideally accepted within the organization. This should involve honest evaluation and attempts to improve upon the original ideas. It is particularly important to look ahead and consider how the new strategy might be developed further in the future.

Quinn's approach incorporates the likely impact upon people and culture, and a pragmatic search for a better way to do things once the change decision is made.

Empowerment and change

Employees must be empowered to sustain a culture of change, but not everyone is comfortable with added responsibilities and accountability – being risk averse – and again resistance can be expected. Inevitably, change-focused organizations will be happy for such people, who are barriers to change and actively seek to prevent changes which may be essential for the future of the business, to leave. Unfortunately, many of these people are likely to have experience, knowledge and expertise which is valuable to the organization and might also be useful – at least temporarily – to a competitor, and for this reason there may be a reluctance to release them.

Empowerment cannot succeed without an appropriate supporting reward system and, while financial rewards will remain important, they are not the complete answer. People must not be rewarded simply because they are holding down a particular job or position; part of their pay must be based on their measured contribution. Outstanding performers must be rewarded for their continuing efforts and, as organizations are increasingly flattened, with fewer layers in the hierarchy, a series of promotions no longer provides the answer.

Empowered middle managers are critically important for the effective management of strategic change, but all too often they are hostile because of fear and uncertainty in a culture of blame. Mistakes are not tolerated, and people are reluctant to take risks. Such managers are portrayed as villains, when really the organizational climate is making them victims. Change and empowerment will only happen when managers are not afraid to 'unfreeze and learn'.

Organizations can benefit from developing people, building their abilities and self-confidence and then providing them with greater stimulation and challenge. Success will yield the opportunity to take on more responsibility and, initially, the organization motivates them but they become increasingly self-motivated. Part of their reward package is their enhanced reputation in a successful business, together with increased informal power and influence, and they can develop the ability to foster and champion innovation and change – strategic changes which they own.

A culture of innovation and gradual but continuous change will impact mainly on competitive and functional strategies – the lowest two levels of the hierarchy featured in Table 15.1 earlier – and clearly they also support corporate strategic changes which may themselves be emergent in nature or the outcome of either a visionary or a planning mode of strategy creation.

Organizational development and innovation

The theme of organizational development (OD) is that developing an appropriate organizational culture will generate desirable changes in strategy. Beckhard (1969) defined OD as effort which is 'planned, organization-wide, and managed from the top, designed to increase organizational effectiveness and health through planned interventions in the organization's processes, using behavioural science knowledge'.

OD is, in essence, planned cultural change. The model which has been used to provide the structure for this book shows strategic leadership and culture as being central to both strategic awareness and decision-making. The appreciation by managers of the effectiveness of the current match between resources and the environment, their ability and willingness to make adaptive changes to capitalize on environmental changes, and the formulation and implementation of major changes in corporate strategy are all influenced by the culture of the organization and the style of strategic leadership. Hence, it is crucial for the strategic leader to develop the appropriate culture for the mission and purpose that they wish to pursue. OD helps to develop a co-operative and innovative culture. OD aims to establish mechanisms encouraging managers to be more open, participative and co-operative when dealing with problems and making decisions and the specific objectives are to:

- improve organizational effectiveness and, as a result,
- ensure higher profits and better customer service (in its widest context)
- enable more effective decision-making
- enable the firm to make and manage changes more smoothly
- increase innovation
- reduce conflict and destructive political activity
- engender greater trust and collaboration between managers and business units.

Organized OD programmes involve activities such as team building and collaborative decision-making, bringing managers together and encouraging them to share and discuss problems and issues. The thinking is that when managers learn more about the problems facing the organization as a whole, and about other managers who may have different technical or functional perspectives, they become more aware of the impact of the decisions that they make. In addition, if they collaborate and share responsibilities, they are more likely to feel committed to joint decisions.

Although aiming to change the attitudes and behaviour of people in organizations, OD can also allow and encourage the same people to initiate and implement changes through their discussions. Establishing the programmes is likely to involve outside experts who can be seen as objective. OD programmes are not normally a response to specific problems but a general, longer-term approach to the management of change.

Given that one rationale for OD is collaboration and collective responsibility, a key theme is the reduction of conflict between managers, functions, business units or divisions within the organization; and it also implies a reduction in the use of manipulative styles of management, or dysfunctional political activity, whereby managers pursue personal goals in preference to the wider needs of the organization. Functional and dysfunctional political activity is explored in the last section of this chapter, which looks at the bases and uses of power by managers.

Transformational change and strategic regeneration

Powerful environmental issues such as deregulation, globalization, the *imbalance* of the factors of production (land, labour and capital are not always available when and where they could be used effectively) and economic recessions have combined to place enormous pressures on companies to survive and adapt. The significance of these issues vary annually but, in aggregate terms, the outcome is an increasingly turbulent and uncertain business environment for most organizations, private and public sector, manufacturing and service, large and small, profit-seeking and not-for-profit.

Companies have responded by seeking to manage their assets and strategic resources more efficiently and effectively – the lowest two levels of the change hierarchy – and some have restructured, while others have radically changed their processes through **business process re-engineering**. However, continuous improvement to an organization's *competitive* capabilities, though essential, will not always be sufficient to meet these pressures. Peters (1992) argues that the challenge for some companies is 'not just about a *programme* of change ... strategies and structures need to change perpetually'. Drucker (1993), agreeing, contends that 'every organization must prepare to abandon everything it does'. Both authors imply wholesale corporate renewal or reinvention, which we call **transformational change**; while the terms 'strategic regeneration' and 'discontinuous change' are synonymous.

Successful transformation requires both an external (as organizations must search for new product, new service and new market opportunities, working with suppliers, distributors and customers to redefine markets and industries) and an internal (structures, management styles and cultures capable of creating and delivering these products and services) focus. Innovation is dependent on processes and people, whilst strategic awareness, information management and change are critically important if the organization is to outperform its competitors.

Achieving this position may require *simultaneous* changes to corporate strategies and perspectives, organization structures and styles of management and, in order to implement **transformational change**, Goss *et al.* (1993) insist that companies must be able to change their context – 'the underlying assumptions and invisible premises on which their decisions and actions are based' – such that their 'inner nature or being' must be altered. Managers must learn how to think strategically, and be open to new paradigms and perspectives, and change what the company is and not simply the things that it does. Companies are being challenged with changing all the levels of the change hierarchy simultaneously – a huge and complex task for any organization.

Incremental change at the competitive and functional level, trying harder and searching for improvements, must appear to offer an easier, less painful route. The fundamental question is whether it alone is enough to meet the strategic demands of the contemporary business environment. Some of the international companies featured in this book have clearly attempted to tackle these important challenges. British Airways (BA) realized in the 1980s that, contrary to much popular opinion at the time, airline customers are willing to pay extra for service and, by defining that service and differentiating successfully, BA consequently changed its strategies, structure and culture and became one of the most profitable airlines in the world. The changes at BA have proved successful (at least over time, if not consistently), but this success has been diminished somewhat by external events and the move to a more business-orientated clientele which has also come under threat from rival airlines such as easyJet. General Electric's (GE) transformation philosophy and programme is described in Case 15.4 and, although rather historical, remains a useful and insightful story.

Case 15.4   Transformational Change at General Electric (GE)   US

John F (Jack) Welch became Chief Executive Officer at General Electric in 1981. His personal vision, style and approach are explored in a later case in Chapter 16. This case describes 'one of the most far-reaching programmes of innovation in business history'.

The programme involved three stages:

- *Awakening* – the realization of the need for change
- *Envisioning* – establishing a new vision and harnessing resources
- *Re-architecting* – the design and construction of a new organization.

Although Welch was the identified strategic leader, several committed senior managers worked together to drive through the cultural changes.

GE has been restructured, and clear progress has been made, but the process of change continues.

GE in the early 1980s – the need for change

The company had sound assets, reflected in a strong balance sheet, but it was seen as bureaucratic and heavily focused on the USA. It was not technologically advanced and it clearly needed a more international perspective.

Specific problems were diagnosed:

- Revenue growth was slow. GE's core business (electrical equipment) was particularly slow
- As a result, expensive investments were creating cash-flow problems
- Poor productivity was causing low profit margins
- Innovation was limited
- Decision-making was slow
- Negative internal politics was rife.

The transformation process

Awakening

Welch realized that his first challenge was to determine which managers offered the greatest potential as transformational leaders, agents of discontinuous change.

He then sought to clarify and articulate the extent of the need for change, focusing on the above weaknesses. Resistance took three forms:

- Technical – A reliance on existing bureaucratic systems and a fear of the unknown; a distrust of international expansion.
- Political – A desire to protect existing power bases, especially where the strategic value of the particular business was declining.

- Cultural – an unwillingness to accept competitive weaknesses – overconfidence from past successes.

Changes

- Welch forced people to benchmark competitors' performance standards and achievements, rather than rely only on internal measures and budgets.
- He also took control of external corporate communications, and
- Radically changed GE's approach to management training and development. Rigid rules and procedures about how things should be done were abolished.

Envisioning

A new vision was developed gradually during the mid-to late 1980s, and it finally became encapsulated in a matrix. Highlights of the new vision are featured in Table 15.2.

Welch saw the technical, political and cultural systems as three strands of a rope which must be changed and realigned together.

Re-architecting

At the heart of the vision is an 'organization without boundaries' and with an emphasis on internal and external linkages and architecture. Information must flow freely. People must be in a position – and willing – to act quickly. 'A large organization with the speed, flexibility and self-confidence of a small one.'

A number of boundaries had to be removed as part of the implementation process:

- vertical/hierarchical – management layers were removed. Welch introduced performance incentives for many more managers and employees; in the past GE had focused on only senior executives
- horizontal/internal walls – cross-functional project teams were created
- external – there was a new emphasis on the whole supply or added value chain; alliances were forged with suppliers; customer satisfaction levels were tracked.

Removing these boundaries clearly required radical changes to the ways in which people worked together, made decisions and carried out tasks. Welch believed that the changes must be inspired from the top and that

any senior managers who resisted the new style 'would have to go'.

Reference

Adapted from Tichy, N.M. (1993) Revolutionize your company, *Fortune*, 13 December.

Questions

1 This case has described a major programme of change and transformation, championed by an exceptional strategic leader, Jack Welch. While it has been reported extensively, and 'the world' knows what Welch has set out to do and what he has achieved, few organizations have been able to replicate his achievement. So how valuable might our insight really be?

2 Why would a programme of this scale and ambition be difficult to replicate?

GENERAL ELECTRIC **http://www.ge.com**

Table 15.2 Highlights of GE's corporate vision

	Strategy	Structure	Management style
Technical	Focus on market (segments) where the company can be no. 1 or no. 2	Decentralized Foster the sharing of best practices and pull down internal boundaries	Different reward systems for different businesses, dependent on needs Continuous training and development
Political	Prioritize high-growth industries Foster internal and external alliances to harness synergy potential	Flatter, open structure to remove power bases Cross-function and cross-business development teams. Empowerment to lowest levels of management	Flexible reward systems '360 degree evaluations' from superiors, peers and subordinates
Cultural	Speedy change to strategies	Corporate values but individual business cultures and styles	Track attitudes and values – commitment to customers and quality – and to outperforming competitors Intrapreneurial, innovative, incremental and adaptive change – as a result of – learning from upward, downward and lateral communications

Pascale *et al.* (1997) argue that effective transformation requires that people understand the organization and its businesses – the big picture – and robust straight-talking should be encouraged to tease out the existing weaknesses in the organization as well as ideas for new opportunities, such that transformation then involves 'managing from the future'. A shared purpose and direction sets the agenda, and setbacks must be harnessed in true entrepreneurial fashion. People must accept accountability but, linked to proper rewards, this should be done in an inventive way that ensures that people are engaged in the process. 'There has to be a relentless discomfort with the status quo.' Of course, success then requires attention to detail at the activity level. The little picture.

Hamel (1994) contends transformational change needs vision and perseverance, and that companies must invest resources in an attempt to set the new competitive high ground first by changing the key success factors, inevitably implying time and risk, which must be a managed and understood process. Speculative investment in the long-term must be risky because *spending precedes understanding*, as companies are heading into unknown territory, but companies which choose to avoid the risk, and rely instead on monitoring and copying competitors (such that *understanding precedes spending*), may be caught out.

Hamel cites three important barriers to effective transformational change:

1 Too many senior managers in an industry have related, often industry-specific, backgrounds, and this inhibits their creative thinking.

2 Political pressures to maintain the *status quo* emanate from managers who feel threatened personally, an issue that is looked at next.

3 The sheer difficulty of creating new competitive strategies in industries that are changing dynamically, continuously and chaotically.

Critical Reflection 15.3   Twelve Steps in Transformational Change

1 Recognize the scale of the challenge and don't ignore it.
2 Consider where the barriers to change might be strongest.
3 Build a guiding team and establish any necessary partnerships.
4 Establish a sense of urgency and bring the challenge and the issues to the attention of others.
5 Clarify a clear strategic direction or 'vision' for the transformation. This would include a defined business model, key values and drivers and recognition of the relevant strategic competencies required.
6 Communicate this vision, taking ownership and responsibility for it.
7 Seize the initiative as far as barriers to change are concerned.
8 Empower others to act on the vision. Emphasize the need for innovation, emergence and intrapreneurship. The idea is to involve people as widely as possible so the drive to change becomes systemic.
9 Seek to generate short-term wins – which can be publicized and used as a vehicle to reward the change-drivers.
10 Consolidate these short-term wins to increase and maintain the momentum.
11 Monitor and evaluate performance and achievements on an ongoing basis.
12 'Institutionalize' the changes.

References

This list of 12 steps has been developed from a number of separate sources, including:

Francis, D., Bessant, J. and Hobday, M. (2003) Managing radical organizational transformation, *Management Decision*, 41 (1).

Kotter, J.P. (1995) Why transformation efforts fail, *Harvard Business Review*, March–April.

Abrahamson (2000) implies that major change could be going out of fashion, unless, of course, it becomes essential. Companies that periodically reinvent themselves often face resistance, distress, disaffection and upheaval. All too often the desired or planned changes are not implemented effectively, prompting another programme of change. Abrahamson, therefore, recommends *'dynamic stability'* – continuous tinkering with existing businesses, alternating occasional major changes with several incremental ones – and his research suggests that:

- First, copying can prove very rewarding – there is no need always to be first. Major leaps forward can be uncomfortable and disruptive for both customers and employees and the competitors who follow when the situation has settled down again can still enjoy the benefits without incurring the risk of the pioneer. Sustained competitive advantage often comes from staying just ahead of rivals with constant innovation and leadership. It is a matter of degree.

- Second, home-grown processes are invariably more acceptable culturally than those imported from another country with an 'alien' culture.

Clearly, organizations need to ensure that they change in accordance with real external pressures and to recognize that good ideas can always be found by monitoring the world's best performers, and they need to acquire and use this knowledge to craft something that can work for them. Critical Reflection 15.3 provides a summary framework for managing transformational change.

15.4 Power and politics

The greatest leader is the one who enables people to say: 'We did it ourselves.'

CHINESE PROVERB ATTRIBUTED TO LAO-TSU

A leader can stop an organization in its tracks but he can't turn it around on his own. In a year you can change things at a superficial level, using the charismatic model, but you need five to change the culture.

MORPETH HEADMASTER, SIR ALASDAIR MACDONALD, DISCUSSING CHANGE IN SECONDARY SCHOOLS

Managing change requires that managers have the requisite power to implement decisions and that they are able to exert influence. There are several bases of power, both organizational and individual, which constitute resources for managers. The processes that they adopt for utilizing these power bases, and their styles of management, determine their success in influencing others. The ability of managers to exert power and influence is manifested in a number of ways, including budgets, rewards, organization structure and positions, promotions and management development, information systems and symbols of power and status.

Managers who regularly attempt to get things done, both with and through other people, and introduce changes, have the problem of generating agreement, consent or at least compliance with what should be done, how and when. Typically, opinions and perspectives will differ and disagreements may or may not be significant, ranging from the polite and friendly to those involving threats and coercion. Each side, quite simply, is attempting to influence the conduct of the other. In this section we consider the power resources that managers are able to use and how they might use them.

Checkland (1986) defines **organizational politics** as the process by which differing interests reach *accommodation* – a word that he chooses deliberately and in preference to consensus – and which relates to the dispositions and use of power and influence, and behaviour which is not prescribed by the policies established within the organization. As discussed later, political activity by managers in order to influence others, and ensure that their decisions and strategies are carried out, is essential. Politics can be legitimate and positive, although it can also be more negative and illegitimate (when managers are seeking to influence others in order to achieve their personal goals, often described as Machiavellianism which is discussed at the section's end). The need for change is affected by the relative power and influence of external stakeholders (powerful customers and suppliers, policy-makers) in relation to the organization, all of which may represent potential threats and demands for change. In turn, the management and implementation of change is affected by the relative power of the organization. Proposed strategies can be implemented when the organization possesses the appropriate power to acquire the resources which are needed and to generate consumer demand, but other strategies may be infeasible. At the same time, the decisions taken within organizations concerning changes of corporate, competitive and functional strategies are influenced by the disposition of relative power between functions, business units or divisions, and the ways in which managers seek to use power and influence. Internal and external sources of power are discussed further in Critical Reflection 15.4, based on the work of Mintzberg (1983).

Critical Reflection 15.4   Internal and External Sources of Power

Mintzberg (1983) contends that it is essential to consider both internal and external sources of power, and their relative significance, when assessing the demands for, and feasibility of, certain strategic changes. The organization's stakeholders will vary in terms of their relative power and the ways in which they exert influence. The interests of the owners of the firm, for example, are legally represented by the board of directors. While large institutional shareholders may exert considerable influence over certain decisions, many private shareholders will take no active part. Employees may be represented by external trade unions, who again may or may not exert influence.

The power relationships between the firm and its stakeholders are determined by the importance and scarcity of the resource in question. The more essential and limited the supply of the resource, the greater the power the resource provider has over the firm.

According to Mintzberg, these external power groups may be focused and their interests pulled together by a dominant power, or they may be fragmented.

Where there are very strong external influences, the organization may seek to establish close co-operation or mutual dependence, or attempt to reduce its dependence on the power source. The historic relationship between Marks and Spencer and many of its suppliers is a good example of mutual dependence of this nature. Marks and Spencer encouraged many of their clothing suppliers to invest in the latest technology for design and manufacturing in order that they can both succeed against international competition. Marks and Spencer have typically been the largest customer of their suppliers, buying substantial quantities as long as both demand and quality are maintained. However, it is important that their suppliers are aware of fashion changes because they bear the risk of over-production and changes in taste.

Internal power is linked to the structure of the organization. It is manifested in four ways:

- the personal control system of the strategic leadership
- rules, policies and procedures
- political activities external to these two factors
- cultural ideologies that influence decision-makers.

External and internal power sources combine to determine a dominant source of power at any time, and Mintzberg suggests six possibilities:

- *a key external source*, such as a bank or supplier, or possibly the government as, say, a key buyer of defence equipment – the objectives of the source would normally be clearly stated and understood
- *the operation of the organization structure*, and the strategies and activities of general and functional managers who are allocated the scarce resources: the relative power of business units is influenced by the market demand for their products and services, but generally external sources exert indirect rather than direct influence; functional managers can enjoy power if they are specialists and their skills are in short supply
- *strong central leadership*

- *ideologies* – certain organizations, such as charities or volunteer organizations, are often dominated by the underlying ideologies related to helping others
- *professional constraints* – accountants' and solicitors' practices, for example, have established codes of professional practice which dictate and influence behaviour. On occasions, this can raise interesting issues for decision-makers. A frequently used example is the television journalist or news editor working for the BBC or ITN and able to influence reporting strategies and policies. When assessing sensitive issues, does the person see him- or herself as a BBC or ITN employee or as a professional journalist, and do the two perspectives coincide or conflict?
- *active conflict* between power sources seeking dominance: while this can involve either or both internal and external sources, it is likely to be temporary as organizations cannot normally survive prolonged conflict.

The dominant source of power becomes a key feature of the organizational culture, and a major influence on manager behaviour and decision-making.

Reference

The source of the basic arguments is: Mintzberg, H. (1983) *Power In and Around Organizations*, Prentice-Hall.

Farrell and Petersen (1982) classify political activity in three dimensions: 'legitimate or illegitimate'; 'vertical or lateral'; and 'internal or external to the organization'. Some examples are outlined below:

A complaint or suggestion by an employee directly to a senior manager, bypassing an immediate superior, would be classified as legitimate, vertical and internal. Discussions with fellow managers from other companies within an industry would be legitimate, lateral and external, unless they involved any illegal activities such as price fixing. Informal communications and agreements between managers are again legitimate, while threats or attempts at sabotage are clearly illegitimate. Power and politics can enable managers to be proactive and to influence their environment rather than being dominated and manipulated by external events, and are key aspects of strategy implementation because they affect managers at all levels of the organization and decisions concerning both internal and external changes.

The bases of power

Seven bases of manager power were introduced and described in Chapter 7: reward, coercive, legitimate, personal, expert, information and connection, and the extent to which managers and other employees in organizations use each of these sources of power is a major determinant of corporate culture.

Reward and coercive power (the ability to sanction and punish) are two major determinants of employee motivation, and both can be very significant strategically. Thompson and Strickland (1981) argue that motivation is brought about primarily by the reward and punishment systems in the organization; and Blanchard and Johnson (1982) suggest that effective management involves establishing clear objectives for employees, and rewarding and sanctioning performance against objectives appropriately. Strategic leaders who dominate their organizations and coerce their senior managers can be effective, particularly when the organization is experiencing decline and major changes in strategy are urgently required.

Legitimate power is determined primarily by the organization structure, and consequently changes in structure will affect the power, influence and significance of different business units, functions and individual managers. *Personal power*, which can lead to the commitment of others to the power holder, can be very important in incremental changes. Managers who are supported and trusted by their colleagues and subordinates will find it easier to introduce and implement changes.

Expert power can persuade others that proposed changes in strategy are feasible and desirable. While expert power may not be real, and instead be power gained from reputation, it is unlikely that managers who genuinely lack expertise can be successful without other power bases. Moreover, expertise is job related, e.g. an expert specialized accountant may lose expert power temporarily if he or she is promoted to general manager. Consequently, an important tactic in the management of change is to ensure that those managers who are perceived to be expert in the activity or function concerned are supportive of the proposed changes. *Information* and related *connection power* are becoming increasingly significant as IT grows in importance.

These seven power bases are all visible sources plus, in addition, *invisible power* such as the way in which an issue or proposal is presented, which can influence the way it is dealt with. Managers who appreciate the objectives, perspectives and concerns of their colleagues will present their ideas in ways that are likely to generate their support rather than opposition. Membership of informal, but influential, coalitions or groups of managers can be a second source of power, particularly if the people involved feel dependent on each other. Third, information that would create opposition to a decision or change proposal might be withheld. In the same way that access to key information can be a positive power source, the ability to prevent other people obtaining information can be either a positive or a negative source of power.

Lukes (1974) has identified three further important aspects of power, namely:

- the ability to prevent a decision, or not make one
- the ability to control the issues on which decisions are to be made
- the ability to ensure that certain issues are kept off agendas.

The use of such power by individuals can inhibit changes which might in the long-term be in the best interests of the organization.

In discussing the nature of power and how it is exercised, we should consider just how the exercise of power needs to be legitimate if it is to be successful over time. Rawls (1971) outlined two principles of justice: (i) with respect to the basic structure of society regarding the basic liberties of citizens based on freedom of speech, thought, assembly, conscience and the rule of law, i.e. any exercise of power that took away any of these rights would be unfair, unjust and could be legitimately opposed and (ii) 'the distribution of income and wealth and the design of organizations that make use of the differences in authority and responsibility, or chains of command. While the distribution of wealth and income need not be equal, it must be to everyone's advantage and at the same time, positions of authority and offices of command must be accessible to all… The distribution of wealth and income must be consistent so that everyone benefits or if an unequal distribution is to everyone's advantage. Injustice, then, is simply inequalities that are not to the benefit of all.'

In the case of many businesses facing financial difficulties, a concern about justice and how justice and fairness is exercised if large financial institutions are bailed out, but then fail to lend some of that money to their customers so that everyone benefits in some way. Arguably, that would be an illegitimate exercise of power by banks, removing the cloak of fairness and justice from them, making them legitimate targets because they had failed to live up to their part of the social and economic bargain.

Political effectiveness and political ability

Hayes (1984) contends that effective managers appreciate clearly what support they need from other people if proposed changes are to be carried through, and what they will have to offer in return by reaching agreements (or accommodations) providing mutual advantages. The organization as a whole must have effective and politically competent general and functional managers to restrain personal objectives and prevent undesirable changes championed by individual managers. Problems can occur where some managers are politically effective and able to implement change, and others are relatively ineffective and reach agreements with other managers whereby their personal interests and the organization's interests are adversely affected.

Certain sources of personal power are essential for managers who are effective politically and able to influence others (Allen *et al.*, 1979; Dixon, 1982), as suggested in certain tactics for managing change featured in Table 15.3, and managers should be perceived by others to have expertise, ability and a reputation built on past successes. Depending on the relative power of outside stakeholders, such as suppliers or customers, external credibility can also prove valuable, as does having access to information and to other powerful individuals and groups of managers. A manager perceived as a radical agent of change can arouse fear and uncertainty, possibly leading to opposition. As discussed earlier, it can be valuable to implement a change of strategy gradually and incrementally, allowing people to make adaptive changes as the learning experience develops. At the same time, opposition should be brought out into the open rather than being allowed to develop without other people being aware.

Politically effective and successful managers that are able to implement their decisions and proposed changes will generally possess an appreciation and clear understanding of organizational processes and also be sensitive to the needs of others. The strategic leader ought also be an able politician and, indeed, the type and incidence of incremental changes in strategies throughout the organization will also be affected by the political ability – relating to the use of power and influence in the most appropriate way in particular circumstances – of managers with the most politically abled being instrumental in introducing changes. Where the strategic leader wishes to encourage managers to be adaptive and innovative, they should consider the political ability of the managers concerned.

MacMillan (1978) argues that introducing and implementing change frequently requires the use of power and influence, which he examines in terms of the control of situations and the ability to change people's intentions. Where a person wishes to exercise control over the behaviour of other people, either within the organization or external to it, they have two basic options: (i) to *structure the situation* so that others comply with their wishes or (ii) to communicate with other people and thus seek to change their perceptions so that they see things differently and decide to do as the manager (or leader) suggests. In other words, they succeed in *changing their intentions*, and both of these approaches are regarded to be strategies of manipulation.

Where a manager is concentrating on structuring the situation, they are using certain power bases as enabling resources and where they are attempting to change intentions they are seeking to use influence. Power, in particular personal power, is again important as a source of influence. The outcome from both the situational and intentional approaches can be either positive or negative such that, when the effect is positive, the other people feel that they are better off as a result of the changes, but the effect is negative if they feel worse off.

MacMillan (1978) identifies four tactics in relation to these points:

1 *Inducement* implies an ability to control the situation, and the outcome is perceived as beneficial by others involved. A large retail organization with several stores might require managers to be mobile as a condition of their employment, and reward them with improved status, salary increases and relocation expenses every time they move. The situation is controlled; ideally, the managers concerned feel positive about the moves.

2 *Coercion* is again a controlled situation, but the outcome is perceived negatively, and the same managers might be threatened with no further promotions unless they agreed to certain moves within the company.

3 *Persuasion* where the manager does not try to control or change the situation but argues that the other people can or will benefit by behaving in certain ways, such that the desired outcome is positive. People might be persuaded to agree to a change which is not immediately desirable by suggestions that future rewards will be forthcoming.

4 *Obligation* is another intentional tactic, but the outcome is negative, as people are persuaded to behave in a certain way by being made to feel that they have an obligation. It might be suggested

Table 15.3 Political power bases and tactics

Bases of personal power

Expertise	Particularly significant where the skill is in scarce supply
	It is possible to use mobility, and the threat of leaving, to gain support for certain changes of strategy – again dependent upon the manager's personal importance to the firm
Assessed stature	A reputation for being a winner or a manager who can obtain results. Recent successes are most relevant
Credibility	Particularly credibility with external power sources, such as suppliers or customers
Political access	Being well known around the organization and able to influence key groups of managers
Control over information	Internal and external sources
	Information can be used openly and honestly or withheld and used selectively – consequently, it is crucial to know the reliability of the source
Group support	In managing and implementing change it is essential to have the support of colleagues and fellow managers

Political tactics to obtain results

Develop liaisons	As mentioned above, it is important to develop and maintain both formal and informal contacts with other managers, functions and divisions
	Again, it is important to include those managers who are most powerful
Present a conservative image	It can be disadvantageous to be seen as too radical an agent of change
Diffuse opposition	Conflicts need to be brought out into the open and differences of opinion aired rather than kept hidden. Divide and rule can be a useful strategy tactic.
Trade-off and compromise	In any proposal or suggestion for change it is important to consider the needs of other people whose support is required
Strike while the iron is hot	Successful managers should build on successes and reputation quickly
Research	Information is always vital to justify and support proposals
Use a neutral cover	Radical changes, or those that other people might perceive as a threat to them, can sometimes be usefully disguised and initiated as minor changes. This is linked to the next point
Limit communication	A useful tactic can be to unravel change gradually in order to contain possible opposition
Withdraw strategically	If things are going wrong, and especially if the changes are not crucial, it can be a wise tactic on occasions to withdraw, at least temporarily

- Politically successful managers understand organizational processes and they are sensitive to the needs of others.
- Effective political action brings about desirable and successful changes in organizations – it is functional.
- Negative political action is dysfunctional, and can enable manipulative managers to pursue their personal objectives against the better interests of the organization.
- The strategic leader needs to be an effective politician.

Sources: Allen, R.W., Madison, D.L., Porter, L.W., Renwick, P.A. and Mayes, B.T. (1979) Organisational politics: tactics and characteristics of its actors. *California Management Review*, 22, Fall and Dixon, M (1982) The world of office politics, *Financial Times*, 10 November.

that people: (i) owe the company something for the money that has been invested in their previous, training, (ii) owe particular managers a favour for something that has happened in the past or (iii) are obligated to the group of people that they have been working with for some years and should not let them down.

Managers may or may not have a number of alternative tactics to select from, and those with positive outcomes are preferable to those causing negative feelings if both are available and likely to yield the desired results. Managers whose power bases are limited and who need speedy results may have to coerce or obligate people.

Kanter (1983) emphasizes that successful managers of change situations are able to keep their power invisible both during and after the change, since participation in the change is then perceived to stem from commitment or conviction rather than from power being exercised over people. Kanter contends that it is important for middle managers in organizations to be skilful in managing change as they implement the detailed strategies, and that strategic leaders must be able to ensure that they have support from their middle managers for the overall corporate strategy.

Culture broadly encapsulates manifest actions and behaviour and underlying beliefs, and effective cultural change must include both (see Chapter 7) with willing support for, and compliance with, the change. Without a change in beliefs, compliance will be reluctant. Strong, political managers who oppose the changes will show either covert or even overt non-compliance, their choice reflecting their style and power. Bartlett and Ghoshal (1995) argue that the radical and forced downsizing of the early 1990s left many companies with a context of 'compliance, control, contract and constraint' such that behaviour has changed, but not beliefs since elements of the old culture remain to create confusion. A challenge of creativity and innovation means that they must find ways of adding new values for competitive advantage, which will require a context of support, trust and liberation, and a willingness to accept stretching objectives, alongside appropriate control disciplines.

Organizational politics and ethics

Managers can clearly use political behaviour both for and against the best interests of the organization; at the same time, they can also behave either ethically or unethically. But positive and ethical behaviour is required to satisfy all the stakeholders effectively. Negative politics, while ethical, could imply that internal stakeholders (maybe even individual managers and functions) receive priority over external stakeholders. Positive politicking which is unethical may well appear successful in the short term, but possibly with a long-term downside risk. Where negative politics combine with unethical behaviour, there is likely to be corruption.

Machiavellianism is the term often used to describe coercive management tactics which Marriott (1908), translating Machiavelli's sixteenth century book *The Prince*, uses to cover 'the ruthless use of power, particularly coercive power, and manipulation to attain personal goals'. While coercive power can be used effectively by managers, it may not always be easy to justify, especially if other alternatives are available. Coercion may not be practical on a repeat basis, and any fear of threats not carried out quickly recedes. Jay (1967), however, contends that Machiavelli also offers much useful advice for ethical managers. Basing his arguments on Machiavelli's views on strategies and tactics for annexing and ruling nations, Jay argues that chief executive strategic leaders should concentrate their efforts outside the organization, developing and strengthening the strategic perspective and, to feel able to do this, the internal structure and systems must be sound and effective, and managers must be supportive of proposals from the top.

General and functional managers should be free to operate and feel able to make certain changes, but their overall power should be contained, and they should exercise leadership based on power which yields the freedom to decide how things should be done. Managers should avoid pursuing personal goals against the interest of the organization as a whole, and need a clear awareness of what is happening throughout the organization and with the appropriate punishment of offenders, and reward of successful managers.

Pearce and DeNisi (1983) stress that most organizations are managed partially by informal coalitions or groupings of managers superimposed upon the formal structure. Managers in key positions in the organization, those in charge of important resources or responsible for products upon which the profits or reputation of the organization depend, should be known to be committed and loyal to the strategic leader. Moreover, any informal and powerful coalitions that develop should also be supportive and the strategic leader may have to remove or switch senior managers occasionally as a reminder of his or her overall power.

This is particularly likely to happen after an acquisition, during a restructuring exercise, or on the appointment of a new strategic leader.

Strategic coalitions are a major force behind strategy formulation, especially where the overall strategic leader is relatively weak. An effective leader, therefore, seeks to use coalitions that already exist, and encourage the formation of other loyal ones. In considering the feasibility of changes and how to implement them, it is important to examine the underlying political abilities and behaviour within the firm: who has power, how it is manifested and how it is used. Without taking these factors into account, implementation is likely to prove hazardous.

Research Snapshot 15.1

Leading change has been traced back as far as the book of Job, especially considering how, in the Jungian analysis, 'the transformations of consciousness … are highly relevant to the ways that organizations and their leaders face chaotic, turbulent and/or unpredictable circumstances' (Smith and Elmes, 2002). The literature on leading change in organizations has been extensively reviewed, showing that it is 'often contradictory, mostly lacking empirical evidence and supported by unchallenged hypotheses' (By, 2005). Change leaders in the public sector can lead chaotic change, i.e. 'changes in an organization when the external and internal complexity and uncertainty is high', and they must, 'therefore[,] take better account of unpredictability, uncertainty, self-governance, emergence and other premises describing chaotic circumstances', which means that change leaders must, 'pay attention to how people form identities in organizations and avoiding design-oriented managerial interventions, as well as keeping at bay the anxiety caused by not being in managerial control' (Karpa and Helga, 2008).

Fenton and Pettigrew (2006) found that, within an engineering consultancy attempting to undertake a global strategy, leaders were opposed to change which they perceived as potentially jeopardizing their identity. Research has examined how leaders lead and can cope with change in financial services firms, specifically noting that, 'change leaders are themselves part of the process, and that the judgemental and cognitive processes which employees engage in, in their relationship with those leading change, is crucial' (Woodward and Hendry, 2004). Some classic work on change leadership has focused upon vision and the construction of coalitions (Kotter, 2005), the way in which leaders' attempts to make changes in their organizations may result in failure (Kotter, 2007), and how 'leverage points', as a response to 'pain' and 'significant emotional events', can be used to achieve change (McAllaster, 2004). On the other hand, it has been suggested that change leadership can be most effectively achieved through identifying its 'organization-specific DNA', and then 'self-organizing', 'spreading change by minimum intervention' and being able to 'read change signals correctly' (Karpa, 2006). Leaders must both choose changes but also determine the best way to implement such changes, in the case of Deutsche Lufthansa and its 'strategic change programme' (Bruch et al., 2005). Balogun (2003) further argued that middle managers are 'change intermediar[ies]' who are essential to the implementation of change by 'interpretation of the change intent' and yet such middle managers may experience 'workload issues and role conflict' as a result of these duties.

For leaders to achieve successful change, Gilley et al. (2008) observed that 'the abilities to communicate appropriately and motivate others significantly influence a leader's ability to implement change effectively and drive innovation.' Charismatic leadership has been identified to be important to enable effective innovation (and, by implication, performance) within research and development teams, given that they can engender a 'sense of team identity and commitment, and encourage team members to co-operate through the expression of ideas and participation in decisions' (Paulsen et al., 2009).

The articles below provide a deeper understanding of leading change in organizations. The further reading from this literature will help students to develop their perception and critical awareness of the topic, and also to highlight the developing thinking in relation to how change can be led within organizations.

Further Reading

Balogun, J. (2003) 'From blaming the middle to harnessing its potential: Creating change intermediaries', British Journal of Management, Vol. 14, pp. 69–83.

Bruch, H., Gerber, P. and Maier, V. (2005) 'Strategic change decisions: doing the right change right', *Journal of Change Management*, Vol. 5, No. 1, pp. 97–107.

By, R.T. (2005) 'Organisational change management: A critical review', *Journal of Change Management*, Vol. 5, No. 4, pp. 369–380.

Fenton, E. and Pettigrew, A. (2006) 'Leading change in the new professional service firm: Characterizing strategic leadership in a global context', in R. Greenwood and R. Suddaby (Eds.) *Professional Service Firms, Research in the Sociology of Organizations*, Vol. 24, Emerald Group Publishing Limited, pp. 101–137.

Gilley, A., Dixon, P. and Gilley, J. W. (2008) 'Characteristics of leadership effectiveness: Implementing change and driving innovation in organizations', *Human Resource Development Quarterly*, Vol. 19, pp. 153–169.

Karpa, T. (2006) 'Transforming organisations for organic growth: The DNA of change leadership', *Journal of Change Management*, Vol. 6, No. 1, pp. 3–20.

Karpa, T. and Helga, T.I.T. (2008) 'From change management to change leadership: Embracing chaotic change in public service organizations', *Journal of Change Management*, Vol. 8, No. 1, pp. 85–96.

Kotter, J.P. (2005) 'Leading change: Create a vision and build coalitions to bring about change', *Leadership Excellence*, Vol. 22, No. 11, pp. 5–6.

Kotter, J.P. (2007) 'Why transformation efforts fail', John P. Kotter, *Harvard Business Review*.

McAllaster, C.M. (2004) 'The 5 P's of change: Leading change by effectively utilizing leverage points within an organization', *Organizational Dynamics*, Vol. 33, No, 3, pp. 318–328.

Paulsen, N., Maldonado, D., Callan, V.J. and Ayoko, O. (2009) 'Charismatic leadership, change and innovation in an R&D organization', *Journal of Organizational Change Management*, Vol. 22, No. 5, pp. 511–523.

Smith, C. and Elmes, M. (2002) 'Leading change: insights from Jungian interpretations of The Book of Job', *Journal of Organizational Change Management*, Vol. 15, No. 5, pp. 448–460.

Woodward, S. and Hendry, C. (2004) 'Leading and coping with change', *Journal of Change Management*, Vol. 4, No. 2, pp. 155–183.

Summary

Most organizations must compete or operate in dynamic environments where change is inevitable, some of which will always be reactive, but the most effective organizations manage, as well as manage in, their environments. The strategic leader and the organization culture realistically drive the whole change process.

Effective *change management* requires a clear perception of need (dissatisfaction with the existing *status quo*), a way forward (a new direction or perceived opportunity), the capability to change (the necessary resources) and commitment (change needs managing). A four-stage cycle of change can be identified: beginning with a creative idea, an opportunity is nurtured before an action stage grows the business. Structure follows to provide control. At this time, new ideas are needed to maintain the cycle of growth.

There is a number of levels of change: the corporate culture, the organizational mission, corporate strategies, organization structures, systems and processes, competitive strategies and operational tasks and activities. As we ascend this hierarchy, the complexity and the difficulty of the challenge increases. A simple model of change management has three Lewinian stages: unfreezing existing behaviour, changing behaviour and refreezing new behaviour as common practice.

However, there is an argument that organizations should have a culture that accepts and embraces constant change, and consequently we need to be careful about the implications of refreezing.

Resistance to change is likely as people's jobs are affected and some will perceive themselves to be losing out. Change can be *continuous, innovatory* and *improvemental* – or *discontinuous and transformational*, implying simultaneous changes to strategy, structure and style.

Sometimes this is essential, but it can be very disruptive and unsettling for people.

Change management cannot be separated from power and influence, which are required to engineer and effect change – and may also be used in an attempt to stop it. There are two key dimensions: the relative power of the organization in respect of its external environment; and the relative power of different businesses, divisions, departments and individuals within the organization itself. There are seven key *power bases*: reward, coercive, legitimate, personal, expert, information and connection.

The way that individuals use power and influence is a manifestation of their political abilities. *Organizational politics* can be positive if it is used to carry through and implement decisions that are clearly in the interests of the organization. Negative politics is the tool of Machiavellian managers who pursue self-interest at the expense of other colleagues and possibly at the expense of the whole organization.

Online cases for this chapter

Online Case 15.1: Apple
Online Case 15.2: Walt Disney Corporation

Online Case 15.3: Blackpool Pleasure Beach

Questions and research assignments

1 Describe an event where you have personally experienced forces for change, and discuss any forces that were used to resist the change. What tactics were adopted on both sides?

2 Describe a strategic leader (at any level in an organization of your choice) whom you consider to be a powerful person. What types of power does he or she possess?

3 Describe a manager whom you believe is successful at using organizational politics. On what observations and experiences are you basing your decision? How might you measure political effectiveness and the elements within it?

4 As a manager, what are your personal power bases? How politically effective are you? How could you increase your overall power and improve your effectiveness?

Internet and library projects

1 Select an industry or company and ascertain the forces that have brought about changes in the last 10 years. How proactive/reactive have the companies been, and with what levels of success?

2 Analyze the news broadcasts of two rival TV networks, such as the BBC and ITN, or Sky and CNN, and evaluate whether their reporting of industrial and business news is similar or dissimilar. Are they reporting to inform or to persuade about, say, the merits or demerits of government policy? To what extent are they constrained by government?

Strategy activity

Kraft   US

Measured by value, Kraft is the second largest food company in the world, behind Nestlé. It has become best known for its processed macaroni and cheese. Its leading brands include Ritz Crackers and Dairylea cheese spread; but in the USA it is also famous for Oreo cookies, Jell-O and Kool-Aid.

At the end of the last century there were 175 plants, but soon after that time 20 had to close with the loss of 8000 jobs. There were two main reasons for this: hostility from certain consumers worried about problems of obesity, and pressure from own-label brands.

Kraft's CEO at the time, Roger Deromedi, was concerned to develop foods that were healthier. More whole grains were added to cereals and extra calcium was added to processed cheese, for example. Kraft declared it would no longer direct advertisements for junk foods to under-12s. He also concluded Kraft's marketing people were 'spending too much time planning … they need to be out with customers'.

He sought to streamline decision-making inside the organization and invited customers to suggest new product ideas. New ideas from the public – that Kraft developed – included parmesan cheese packaged with a disposable plastic cheese grater; and a microwaveable hot dog and bun.

More recently a new issue arose when the cost of milk, a major ingredient for Kraft, started rising around the world.

Questions

1 Do you agree with Deromedi's approach? How much of a strategic challenge did he face?

2 How would you evaluate the strategic logic of Kraft's successful bid to acquire Cadbury's in late 2009?

References

Abrahamson, E. (2000) Dynamic stability, *Harvard Business Review*, January–February.

Allen, R.W., Madison, D.L., Porter, L.W., Renwick, P.A. and Mayes, B.T. (1979) Organizational politics: tactics and characteristics of its actors, *California Management Review*, 22, Fall.

Argyris, C. and Schön, D. (1978) *Organization Learning: A Theory of Action Perspective*, Addison Wesley.

Bartlett, C. and Ghoshal, S. (1995) Rebuilding behavioural context: turn process re-engineering into people rejuvenation, *Sloan Management Review*, Autumn.

Beckhard, R. (1969) *Organization Development: Strategies and Models*, Addison-Wesley.

Blanchard, K. and Johnson, S. (1982) *The One Minute Manager*, Morrow.

Bourgeois, L.J. and Brodwin, D.R. (1984) Strategic implementation: five approaches to an elusive phenomenon, *Strategic Management Journal*, 5.

Buchanan, D., Clayton, T. and Doyle, M. (1999) Organization development and change – the legacy of the 90s, *Human Resource Management Journal*, 9 (2).

Checkland, P.B. (1986) The politics of practice. Paper presented at the IIASA International Roundtable 'The Art and Science of Systems Practice', November.

Daft, R.L. (1983) *Organization Theory and Design*, West.

Dixon, M. (1982) The world of office politics, *Financial Times*, 10 November.

Drucker, P. (1993) *Managing in Turbulent Times*, Butterworth-Heinemann.

Eccles, T. (1994) *Succeeding With Change*, McGraw-Hill.

Farrell, D. and Petersen, J.C. (1982) Patterns of political behaviour in organizations, *Academy of Management Review*, 7 (3).

Ghoshal, S. and Caulkin, S. (1998) An escape route from ruthlessness, *Financial Times*, 18 November.

Goss, T., Pascale, R. and Athos, A. (1993) The reinvention roller coaster: risking the present for a powerful future, *Harvard Business Review*, November–December.

Grove, A.S. (1996) Only The Paranoid Survive, Harper Collins.

Hamel, G. (1994) Competing for the Future, Economist Conference, London, June.

Hayes, J. (1984) The politically competent manager, *Journal of General Management*, 10 (1).

Heifetz, R. and Linsky, M. (2002) *Leadership On The Line*, Harvard Business School Press.

Jay, A. (1967) *Management and Machiavelli*, Holt, Rinehart & Winston.

Kanter, R.M. (1983) The middle manager as innovator. In *Strategic Management* (ed. R.G. Hamermesch), John Wiley.

Kotter, J.P. (1990) *A Force for Change: How Leadership Differs from Management*, The Free Press.

Kotter, J.P. (1995) Why transformation efforts fail, *Harvard Business Review*, March–April.

Kotter, J.P. and Schlesinger, L.A. (1979) Choosing strategies for change, *Harvard Business Review*, March–April.

Lewin, K. (1947) Frontiers in group dynamics: concept, method and reality in social science, *Human Relations*, 1.

Lewin, K. (1951) *Field Theory in Social Sciences*, Harper & Row.

Lukes, S. (1974) *Power: A Radical View*, MacMillan.

MacMillan, I.C. (1978) *Strategy Formulation: Political Concepts*, West

Margerison, C. and Smith, B. (1989) Shakespeare and management: managing change, *Management Decision*, 27 (2).

Marriott, W.K. (1908) Translation into English of *The Prince* written by N Machiavelli in the 1500s.

Mintzberg, H. (1983) *Power In and Around Organizations*, Prentice-Hall.

Pascale, R., Millemann, M. and Gioja, L. (1997) Changing the way we change, *Harvard Business Review*, November–December.

Pearce, J.A. and DeNisi, A.S. (1983) Attribution theory and strategic decision-making: an application to coalition formation, *Academy of Management Journal*, 26, March.

Peters, T. (1989) Tomorrow's companies: new products, new markets, new competition, new thinking, *The Economist*, 4 March.

Peters, T. (1992) *Liberation Management – Necessary Disorganization for the Nanosecond Nineties*, Macmillan.

Quinn, J.B. (1988) Managing strategies incrementally. In *The Strategy Process: Concepts, Contexts and Cases* (eds J.B. Quinn, H. Mintzberg and R.M. James), Prentice-Hall.

Rawls, J. (1971) *A Theory of Justice*, Oxford University Press.

Thompson, A.A. and Strickland, A.J. (1981) *Strategy and Policy: Concept and Cases*, Business Publications.

Waterman, R.H. Jr (1987) *The Renewal Factor*, Bantam.

Chapter 16

Managing strategy
in the organization

Learning objectives

Having read to the end of this chapter, you should be able to:

- describe and explain alternative approaches to, and styles of, managing strategy; and alternative corporate portfolios and control mechanisms **(Section 16.1)**

- define the terms 'heartland' and 'corporate **parenting**' and explain their significance and implications **(Section 16.2)**

- discuss resource management including general managers, human resources and allocating resources **(Section 16.3)**

- define risk, identify the risks faced by organizations and discuss how they might be approached and managed; and their relationship to crisis avoidance and crisis management **(Section 16.4)**.

Introduction

Growth is often an important objective for organizations, frequently involving diversification and acquisitions in either related or unrelated areas. In recent years the strategic logic of large, diversified conglomerates has been questioned as many organizations have instead chosen to focus on related businesses, technologies or core competencies, where they can more readily add value across the businesses and generate synergy. Whatever the strategic choice, it must be implemented successfully: for example, GE – the opening case, Case 16.1 – has become the world's leading company (by asset value) whilst remaining extensively diversified. GE is also linked to Cases 16.2 and 16.3 later in this chapter. Conglomerate, diversified businesses cannot be dismissed automatically since they can be both successful and profitable if they can find new suitable businesses to acquire, opportunities for growth with their subsidiary businesses and if their **strategic control** system is appropriate. Simply, the strategy can still be justified if it can be implemented successfully. This chapter explores alternative approaches to strategic control and applies these issues to diversified conglomerates, examining the relationship between the corporate centre and individual businesses.

Case 16.1   General Electric (GE) – *The Welch years*   US

General Electric (GE) became diversified into four 'long-cycle businesses' – power systems, aircraft engines, defence electronics and medical systems (such as brain and body scanners) – and four 'short-cycle businesses' – plastics engineering, household consumer goods, lighting and NBC Television in the USA. GE also provides financial services (through the specialist GE Finance subsidiary) – which in terms of monetary assets is effectively one of the largest banks in America.

The company is truly global – it sells more in Europe than British Aerospace, one of the UK's leading manufacturers and a direct competitor. GE, under Chief Executive Jack Welch, proved that a business does not have to be 'focused on one or two related activities' to be successful and profitable. Before he retired, Welch changed the culture, 'turned people on' and delivered results through carefully crafted incentives.

Welch delayed his planned retirement by a year whilst he attempted to acquire Honeywell, only to be thwarted by the European Competition Commission – which feared there was a conflict of interests between GE Finance (which has a huge aircraft leasing arm) and Honeywell Engines.

(Case 15.4 on transformational change at GE explained the culture change programme in more detail.)

Unlike many other diversified conglomerates, GE sought to gain 'maximum' value from its disparate activities by investing to provide a platform for growth. GE wanted to be Number One or Number Two in every market segment in which it competes. It seeks to exploit the breadth and diversity of its portfolio to find new ways for adding value and new customers.

> *Being a conglomerate makes no sense unless you can leverage the size and diversity of the company and spread learning and best practices across the company.*
>
> LARRY JOHNSTON, EX-GE EXECUTIVE

The company is decentralized and employees are encouraged to speak out and pursue ideas. External contacts and sources are constantly monitored for new leads and opportunities. 'We'll go anywhere for an idea.' Welch always believed, 'the winners of the 1990s would be those who could develop a culture that allowed them to move faster, communicate more clearly and involve everyone in a focused effort to serve ever more demanding customers.' GE has its own 'university' and brings managers of various levels in all the businesses together regularly to explain what they are doing and to share new ideas.

> *We have this incredible intellect in GE ... we are exposed to so many industries that when we [senior managers] all get together we have the opportunity to maximize our intellect. That's the advantage of a multi-business company ... we can share ideas.*
>
> WELCH

Much of this is facilitated through Management Councils – comprising people from different businesses and divisions – who meet quarterly. Every member of a council must bring to every meeting at least one idea from which other managers could learn something valuable or useful. One notable example was the idea of 'reverse mentoring' to deal with the demands of e-commerce. Older managers were encouraged to use younger and more aware managers as their mentors, even though they might be lower in the current hierarchy.

Fortune magazine declared Welch to be the 'manager of the [twentieth] century' for his achievement in turning a 'slumbering dinosaur' into a 'lean and dynamic company with a paradigm of a new management style'. Whereas Percy Barnevik redesigned the ABB structure (explained in Case 14.5), Welch transformed GE through management style. They both believed 'small is beautiful' and that innovation and intrapreneurship is critical.

When you have read both cases, you can compare outcomes. The decentralization at GE aims to, 'inject down the line the attitudes of a small fast-moving entrepreneurial business and thereby improve productivity continuously'. Integration strategies promote the sharing of ideas and best practices.

There is a developed strategy of moving managers between businesses and countries to transfer ideas and create internal synergy, together with a reliance on employee training. It has been said that 'if you sit next to any GE executive on a 'plane they will all tell the same story about where the company is going'. There is a shared and understood direction and philosophy, despite the diversity. Promotion is normally given to those managers who can prove they are 'boundary-less'.

Welch regularly attended training courses to collect opinion and feedback. 'My job is to listen to, search for, think of and spread ideas, to expose people to good ideas and role models.' GE's *'work out'* programme involves senior managers presenting GE's vision and ideas to other managers and employees, and then later reconvening to obtain responses and feedback on perceived issues and difficulties. All employees in a unit, regardless of level, are thus provided with an opportunity to review and comment upon existing systems and procedures. The check is always based on whether they add value. External advisers (such as university academics) monitor that communications are genuinely two-way. GE also developed *'Six Sigma Quality Management'* which has been adopted by companies around the world.

Managers are actively encouraged to work closely with suppliers and customers, and they have '360 degree evaluations', with inputs from superiors, peers and subordinates. 'People hear things about themselves they have never heard before.' Products and businesses should be Number One or Number Two in a market, and if they are not achieving this, their managers are expected to ask for the resources required to get there.

Welch summarized his philosophy as follows:

> *If we are to get the reflexes and speed we need, we've got to simplify and delegate more – simply trust more. We have to undo a 100-year-old concept and convince our managers that their role is not to control people and stay on top of things, but rather to guide, energize and excite. But with all this must come the intellectual tools, which will mean continuous education of every individual at every level of the company.*

Nevertheless some felt that Welch's reign spawned an emphasis on cost cutting and leaner management.

Jeffrey Immelt

It was inevitable that people would question whether GE could survive when Welch retired in 2001. His chosen successor, Jeffrey Immelt, straight away made changes – but only limited ones to the structure and style – and the company continued to thrive and prosper. Immelt had a marketing background and was promoted from Chief Executive of GE Medical Systems. After he had established himself he started to make changes to the GE strategy, but the Welch style and approach has largely remained intact.

In 2003 Vivendi Universal was merged with GE's NBC. Also in 2003 GE acquired the UK healthcare group, Amersham, which had a number of important biotechnology activities. This was followed, in 2004, by a leading airport security scanning system business. Since 9/11 airport security has been a growing business around the world.

In 2004 Immelt declared 'GE was to evolve from an industrial and financial conglomerate dedicated to the relentless pursuit of profit to an innovator bent on finding long-term growth opportunities'. Science – including nanotechnology – would be instrumental. Developments could and would be applied across the GE businesses. One significant innovation was satellite tracking systems. These were utilized by TIP, GE's recently acquired European trailer leasing business, to track any vehicles or loads that had been hijacked.

Healthcare and energy would be targeted markets. To contribute to the necessary changes a number of managerial competencies were to be stressed: namely external focus, clear thinking, imagination, inclusive leadership and confident expertise. Some critics of Welch felt his style had 'spread a fear of failure and stifled risk taking'. Reflecting his background in marketing, Immelt emphasized the need for organic growth, and there was to be a real focus on generating such growth. The percentages of revenues and profits generated outside the USA would be increased. That said, throughout 2004 GE proceeded to acquire a series of businesses to support its existing activities and priorities. Altogether some $17.5 billion was spent.

In 2005 GE's insurance business activities were sold to Swiss Re – its recent profits had been 'disappointing'. In 2006 the nuclear power units were moved into a joint venture with Hitachi. Profits were holding up but GE's stock was under-performing the main indices.

In 2007 GE paid $4.8 billion to buy the aerospace division of Smiths Industries (see Case 16.2 next on Smiths). The business makes components including computer systems, cockpit displays and landing gear. The detection and security businesses of the two groups would also be joined together in a new joint venture, Smiths GE Detection.

In early 2008 first quarter profits fell below declared projections and analysts' expectations. Maybe Immelt's investments were not paying off...however strategically logical they might appear to be. Welch went on record and said 'Immelt had a credibility issue'. At the same time he defended his successor's strategy.

In 2009 NBC/Universal became a joint venture with the cable company, Comcast. GE held a 49 per cent stake, Comcast 51 per cent.

In 2010 GE acquired the gas turbines manufacturer, Dresser, which is an American business that had spread overseas. The cost: US$3 billion. This was followed by the purchase of a British oil drilling pipe maker. There were further oil and gas acquisitions in 2011.

The main product areas had become: aviation, power generation, healthcare and transport. These were structured as GE Energy, GE Technology Infrastructure and GE Home and Business Solutions. GE Capital continued to contribute over half the total revenue.

GE had, rather inevitably, not been able to avoid the impact of the global recession. Rounding the figures, GE's global revenues amounted to US$180 billion in 2008, but they declined year-on-year to $150 billion in 2011. Net earnings for these 4 years were successively: $17 billion, $11 billion, $12 billion and $14 billion.

Questions

1 Do you think Welch's management style could be easily copied by other organizations? Why? Why not?
2 Do you agree with the changes introduced by Immelt?
3 How difficult is it to balance long-term growth and investments with the need for regular profits?

GENERAL ELECTRIC **http://www.ge.com**

SOURCE: THIS CASE STUDY WAS PREPARED USING PRIMARILY PUBLICLY AVAILABLE SOURCES OF INFORMATION FOR THE PURPOSES OF CLASSROOM DISCUSSION; IT DOES NOT INTEND TO ILLUSTRATE EITHER EFFECTIVE OR INEFFECTIVE HANDLING OF A MANAGERIAL SITUATION.

The implementation of intended strategies – and the ability of the organization to be responsive in a dynamic, competitive environment – require the organization's strategic resources to be deployed and managed both efficiently and effectively. The organization must, on the one hand, seek to be crisis averse rather than crisis prone and, on the other hand, must be able to deal with crises if and when they do occur. All of these issues are a reflection of the organization's ability to appreciate and manage risk and they are also discussed in this chapter.

This chapter includes debates, opinions and interpretations, but few clear-cut answers since both the strategy and the structure need to change but stay complementary as the business environment changes and, if straightforward and clear-cut, many organizations would be more successful than they actually are.

16.1 Managing corporate strategy and implementation

Good choices and effective implementation matter, are related but are different, as Table 16.1 shows, since decisions about what to do require competency in strategic thinking with a focus on ideas and direction. Implementation is more operational and tactical, demanding expertise in systems and management; new strategic ideas can be seen as potential new projects with a need for project management competency.

A synergistic, successful and profitable portfolio of businesses has, first, related competencies and capabilities, which can be transferred between businesses, or between each business and the corporate headquarters or the overall strategic leader. Second, it has the ability to create and build value, both individually and collectively, by the businesses and the corporate headquarters and, third, the ability to implement strategies and strategic ideas to achieve their potential – a contribution that is again individual (e.g. in the form of profit streams because of a strong competitive position) and collective, through learning, sharing and the transfer of skills and resources.

We, therefore, have brought together a number of key themes in this chapter, including the relatedness of the actual businesses in the portfolio and the management of the portfolio of activities to ensure that strategies are implemented effectively.

Figure 16.1 shows how strategy and implementation must work together harmoniously for competitive, strategic and (where relevant) financial success. Where the strategy is stretched or particularly demanding for the resources possessed by the organization, under-achievement will likely occur even where there is sound implementation. If the accompanying implementation is also weak, the organization is likely to seem fragmented and fragile. A basically sound strategy, poorly implemented, would typically suggest structural and stylistic flaws.

Many organizations face a basic dilemma of understanding why something is wrong; for example, if the strategy or the implementation is mainly to blame where performance is below expectations. Many businesses have reacted to the current very competitive and increasingly global business environment to

Table 16.1 Managing strategy and implementation

Managing corporate strategy	Strategy implementation
Need to think strategically	Tactical and operational perspective
What we call 'strategic management'	Realistically resource management
About direction	About systems and management
Focus on new ideas and options	Focus on delivery
What the organization is doing	How the organization does things
Choices concern businesses to be in or not be in – and how to be competitive	Choices relate to the management of projects and activities – operational rather than strategic

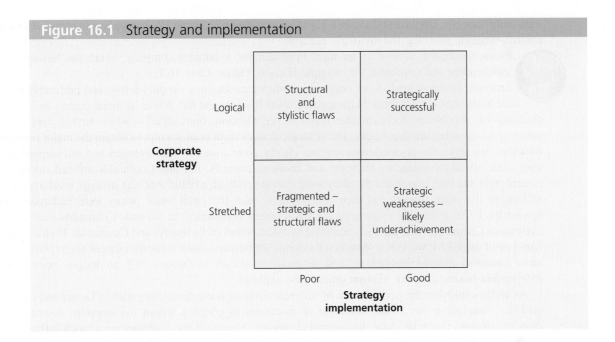

Figure 16.1   Strategy and implementation

work on both, such that strategies have typically become more focused and structures less hierarchical. Richter and Owen (1997) found evidence of refocusing and simpler structures.

Goold and Campbell (1988) have contrasted the views of Sir Hector Laing, ex-chairman of United Biscuits – who contended that it takes a number of years to build a business, and that during this period corporate headquarters should help the general managers of business units to develop their strategies – with those of Lord Hanson – who argued that it is more appropriate for head office to remain detached from operations, and instead of involvement, to set strict financial targets, given that all Hanson businesses were reputedly for sale at any time. Both approaches have been shown to work, but with different levels of overall performance and strategic growth patterns and, in essence, it is determined by the quality of management! The Hanson approach typified that of many diversified conglomerates in the 1980s, but it lost favour with investors in the 1990s. This fact alone was cause enough for many of them to refocus or break up, as the online cases on Hanson and BTR *et al.* show.

These two approaches represent two ends of a spectrum, and a third approach is a compromise between the two. However, much top-level strategy could be essentially based on the view that 'it's the management, stupid' that makes things work, whereas often failure is about the adoption of a 'me too' strategy simply because it has worked elsewhere. Figure 16.2 illustrates this spectrum and the determining variables: the extent of centralization and decentralization (which influences the nature and role of strategic planning in the organization) and the nature of key reporting systems (the extent to which they are loose and flexible or

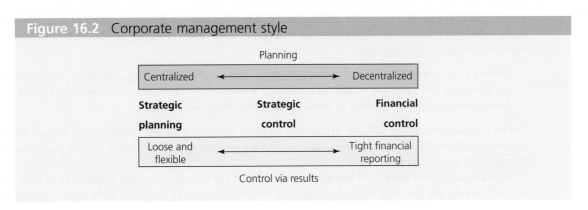

Figure 16.2   Corporate management style

tight and financial). Goold and Campbell (1988) thus categorized large UK companies in terms of financial control, strategic planning and **strategic control**.

Financial control is seen as an ideal approach for a holding company where the businesses are independent and unrelated, for example Hanson, Online Case 16.1.

Strategic planning tends to be adopted in companies focusing on only a few, and preferably related, core businesses e.g. Cadbury Schweppes, United Biscuits and BP. While financial control and strategic planning are appropriate for particular types of organization, both styles – while having very positive advantages – also feature drawbacks. The strategic control style is an attempt to obtain the major benefits of the other two styles for organizations that are clearly diversified but with linkages and interdependencies, with value added by balancing strategic and financial controls. ICI and Courtaulds utilized the strategic control style and both concluded that they were over-diversified, a belief that was strongly reinforced by the attitude of the stock market and their shareholders, such that their share prices were underperforming against the FTSE index, the average of the UK's largest companies. In the end, Courtaulds was split into Courtaulds Chemicals (subsequently acquired by Akzo Nobel of Germany) and Courtaulds Textiles (sold to Sara Lee of the USA); while ICI separated its chemicals business, with some divestment and replacement by more consumer-focused businesses, and its pharmaceuticals businesses. ICI no longer exists and an independent business, as the relevant online case explains.

As well as studying the performance of different firms in these three categories in Goold and Campbell (1988) – concluding that, while the style of management adopted within the structure determines the strategic changes that take place, the overall corporate strategy of the company very much influences the choice of style – Goold *et al.* (1993) later confirmed that financial control is ideally suited to a group of autonomous businesses in a conglomerate, but it is less suitable for a portfolio of core businesses or ones seeking to compete globally. Strategic planning continued to add value as long as corporate managers had close knowledge and experience of their core businesses.

Appreciating the specific and unique problems and opportunities faced by subsidiary businesses is particularly important for establishing fair reward systems. These reward systems, based on specific performance targets (e.g. growth in revenue, absolute profits or profitability ratios), could be based within business units categorized as having high-, medium- or low-growth potential with various factors used in evaluating their relative performances (return on assets, cash flow, strategic development programmes and increases in market share) with rewards given accordingly, which is particularly relevant where general managers were changed around to reflect their particular styles of management and the current requirements of the business unit (Stonich, 1982).

One question left unanswered concerns the extent to which the conclusions of Goold and Campbell (1988) and Goold *et al.* (1993) result from British management strengths, weaknesses and preferences given that certain Japanese companies have grown organically at impressive rates while maintaining strict financial controls and directing corporate strategic change from the centre, which is affected by legislation restricting the ability of Japanese companies to grow by acquisition and merger.

Managing the corporate portfolio

Porter (1987) argues that corporate strategy makes the corporate whole add up to more than the sum of its parts, further contending that the corporate strategies of too many companies dissipate rather than create shareholder value. He comments:

> *Moving from competitive strategy to corporate strategy is the business equivalent of passing through the Bermuda Triangle. The failure of corporate strategy reflects the fact that most diversified companies have failed to think in terms of how they really add value.*

Porter's arguments are as follows. Corporate strategy involves two key questions or issues. First, what businesses should the company choose to compete in; second, how strategically distinct businesses should be managed at the corporate level.

While synergy has been held out as the justification for strategic changes (especially if they involved diversification) and the ideas behind synergy are defensible, synergy *potential* alone cannot justify change.

Implementation matters and, realistically, synergy is frequently based on intangibles and possibilities rather than the definite. Reflecting on acquisitions that fail to deliver promised synergies, we can never be sure how much of the problem was the strategic logic and how much was implementation and hence portfolio management, backed by the analytical techniques discussed in Chapter 9, was attractive when developed by management consultants.

Portfolio management assumes that competition occurs at the business level, and is where competitive advantages are developed. Businesses should compete for centralized corporate investment resources, which should be divested if there are no further opportunities for developing new values – with a cost-effective organization structure enabling cross-fertilization between the businesses while maintaining overall control. The role of the corporate headquarters was to seek and acquire attractive (potentially highly profitable) businesses, fit them in to the organization, assess their requirements and allocate strategic resources according to their position in the relevant matrix. Of course, in reality, many low-performing businesses were retained, diluting the earnings potential and, as a consequence, shareholders sometimes became sceptical. Their belief was that they could diversify their own portfolio of investments as a hedge against risk – they did not need the businesses to do so on their behalf.

However, restructuring, which is one variant of portfolio management, requires the identification of industries and companies with the potential for restructuring and transformation with new technologies, new people and/or consolidation, such that there is no need at all for them to be related to the existing businesses in the portfolio.

The new parent intervenes to turn around the business: first, by cost-cutting and increased efficiency, and second, by adding new values to build a stronger competitive base and position. Once there are no further opportunities to add value, the business should be sold to raise money for further acquisitions. Restructuring works well when the strategic leadership can spot and acquire undervalued companies and then turn them around with sound management skills, even though they might be in unfamiliar industries. In a sense, there is an underlying belief that good managers can manage anything, and to a degree there is some truth in this assertion but whether they manage the renewal as well as the consolidation determines its success, as does having an appropriate structure and style of corporate management. Naturally, if suitable undervalued businesses cannot be found – which is typically the case when a country's economy has been tightened and weak competitors have already disappeared as closures or acquisitions – restructuring has no basis.

Another approach is sharing activities and transferring skills where, as Porter argues, there are inter-relationships between the existing and new businesses, whether tangible or intangible. Activities, know-how, customers, distributors and competitors can all be shared and their benefits must outweigh the costs involved. The outcome of sharing can be clearly tangible (such as better capacity utilization) or intangible, e.g. through learning and intelligence. While, for example, a shared salesforce is often a possibility, higher calibre people can sometimes be recruited, but different selling skills may be required for different products (some being sold on price, others on performance differences) and the attention given to certain ones may be inadequate. The greatest returns should normally be found where activities are actually shared, but alternatively transferring skills can also be beneficial where businesses must be sufficiently similar that sharing expertise is meaningful, and the potential advantage will always be greater if the capabilities involved are fresh to the new industry.

16.2   Corporate parenting and the heartland

Goold *et al.* (1994) reinforce Porter's arguments by contending that acquisitions can be justified where the corporation can add value to the business, generating either synergy or valuable emergent properties. Any business must add value to its parent corporation which, in turn, must add value to the subsidiary, it being better off with its existing parent than it would be with another parent or on its own. **Parenting** skills, therefore, relate to the ability of a head office and strategic leadership to manage a portfolio of businesses efficiently and effectively and to change the portfolio as and when necessary, such that head offices can destroy value if a subsidiary does not fit with the rest of the portfolio and is consequently held back.

Parenting skills vary between countries and cultures, such as in Japan where the most successful companies effectively secure and sustain access to government, power and influence, access investment capital, and retain skilled managers, much being facilitated by the *keiretsu*, families of companies interlinked by share ownership and characterized by intertrading, regular meetings of senior executives and sometimes geographical proximity in a single 'corporate village', with interwoven companies which can operate without any overall corporate headquarters.

Figure 16.3 builds on the arguments of Goold *et al.* (1994), drawing these points together. On one axis is strategic logic, the link between products, services, competencies and key success factors across the corporate portfolio; and on the other axis are the parenting issues, the fit between the needs of individual businesses and the corresponding capabilities of the parent organization. Where they fit together well, there is a heartland of related businesses, which is explained below. Where there is no natural synergy between the businesses, the organization can be successful to some degree if the parent company uses a *holding company* structure.

Where the parenting issues are not addressed properly, either strategic or structural flaws and the consequent under-performance will be evident and here *strategic flaws* again imply fragmented businesses with no real synergy potential but which are linked to an inappropriate structure and style, with a real likelihood of poor performance. *Structural flaws* reflect a potential for synergy but a potential that is not being realized because of structural and stylistic weaknesses.

The heartland

Goold *et al.* (1994) use the term *heartland* to describe a range of businesses to which a corporation can add value and not destroy it. A heartland might be constituted by common key success factors, related core competencies and/or strategic capabilities and/or a common or related industry or technology.

Any individual business within the heartland should be able to achieve levels of success that it would not be able to achieve as an independent business or with another parent. At the same time, the parent

Figure 16.3 Corporate parenting

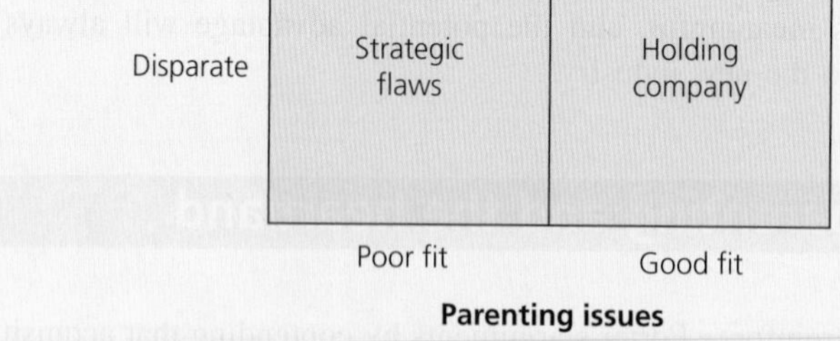

	Poor fit	Good fit
Matched	Structural flaws	Heartland
Disparate	Strategic flaws	Holding company

Strategic logic

Parenting issues

Strategic logic – Link between products, services, competencies and key success factors across the portfolio

Parenting issues – The fit between the needs of individual businesses and the capabilities of the parent organization should benefit both financially and strategically – in other words, other businesses in the portfolio benefit from the presence of the one under the spotlight – thus implying a 'win–win' situation, whereas it can easily be a 'win–lose' or even a 'lose–lose' where the fit is so poor that there is a real resource distraction. The corporate portfolio should be based around a heartland of businesses that are in some way related and any which are not, and especially where they are a potential or actual distraction, should be divested. As an organization divests in this way to refocus, it is quite normal for this to be followed by, or concurrent with, acquisitions of related businesses to strengthen the core of the new focus, as illustrated in Case 16.2 on Smiths Industries.

Case 16.2 Smiths Industries: Developing a New 'Heartland'   UK

In the 1990s Smiths Industries owned an 'apparently widespread portfolio of engineering businesses' but argued that there was a related heartland. The stock exchange categorized Smiths as an aerospace business, but it comprised:

- aerospace components
- telecommunications products
- flexible hoses for vacuum cleaners
- medical products
- electrical instruments for cars.

Structurally, there were three divisions:

- aerospace – civil, military and after-sales service
- medical – equipment and consumables
- industrial.

A chief executive, Keith Butler-Wheelhouse, was recruited from Saab and he argued the company was about 'clever engineering'. Between 1996 and summer 2000, under his leadership, there were 26 acquisitions, mainly bolt-on related businesses. The company delivered 'above average returns and profit growth from some unpromising sectors' and its share price performance was better than most engineering companies.

Butler-Wheelhouse argued that Smiths was:

- focused on niche markets and relatively small businesses
- spread across eight distinct markets such that no single business could make or break the whole organization
- able to generate a cash flow which can fund both organic growth and further acquisitions.

In 2000 Smiths acquired a 'big one'. Tube Investments, long associated with motor vehicles components, was diversified into seals (mechanical and polymer), fluid storage (cars and refrigerators) and aerospace (Dowty landing gear and general systems).

Smiths would continue to build its heartland around 'clever engineering' but the business was to be 'reinvented' as an aerospace engineering business with interests in other high-growth niche opportunities – such as medical equipment and systems for detecting explosives. Various automotive businesses were put up for sale, with mixed success. In the end those that wouldn't sell were floated off as an independent group. Polymer seals were sold in 2003 – at a loss because of an anxiety to divest this non-core activity.

Butler-Wheelhouse commented in 2003 that 'in the past year we've spent 5 minutes wondering whether we've got a balanced portfolio of businesses and the rest of the time being concerned about how to run the company and generate profits'.

In 2004 Smiths acquired the US medical equipment business, Medex, and thus became a much bigger player in this industry. The argued logic was based more on complementary products (easier to sell a larger range) than on cost saving opportunities.

In 2007 the aerospace interests were sold to General Electric for $4.8 billion. The detection interests of both companies were amalgamated as a separate joint venture company, in which Smiths had a 64 per cent controlling holding. Neither company wanted to sell their detection interests to the other or to anyone else.

One year earlier the various contributions to revenue and profits had been:

2006	% of revenue	% of operating profits
Aerospace	36	29
Detection	12	15
Medical Equipment	21	27
Specialty Engineering	31	29

Butler-Wheelhouse retired in 2008. What exactly was his successor, Philip Bowman, inheriting? Would he split the rest of the business up or keep it intact? After all, his leading investors were arguing that 'the business was worth less than the sum of its parts'.

Bowman decided to divide the group into five parts – Medical Products (which would be based in the USA), Detection (based in Watford in the UK) and three speciality engineering businesses, all to be based in America. The size of the UK headquarters was reduced substantially and more power devolved to the divisions.

Questions

1 How would you summarize the 'heartland' of Smiths Industries before and after the acquisition of Tube Investments?

2 What are your views on the 2003 quote from Keith Butler-Wheelhouse?

3 How significant (relatively) is corporate strategy and how significant is operational strategy to deliver results?

4 Do you believe that in 2009 the company has a strong heartland or is it realistically a holding company of diverse interests?

5 Were further changes either necessary or appropriate?

SMITHS INDUSTRIES **http://www.smiths-group.com**

Figure 16.4 offers a framework for assessing the strategic logic of a proposed addition to the corporate portfolio. On one axis is the extent of the linkages and synergy in the existing portfolio and on the other axis is the relationship between the competencies required to run the new business effectively and the organization's existing competencies and capabilities. Logically, we are looking for a match – the top right quadrant. Where the existing match is low but the newcomer has similar competencies to certain existing businesses, there could be a logic in going ahead and divesting non-related activities at the same time: the bottom right quadrant – which could have the effect of strengthening the portfolio. The top left quadrant of Figure 16.4 has the potential for an unrelated business to dilute value and synergy, while an unrelated business added to a non-synergistic portfolio would merely enhance the strategic problems.

Determining the heartland concerns, first, whether the parent is able to provide – and is actually providing – the services and support the individual businesses need; and, second, whether the businesses have the people and competencies to fulfil the expectations of the parent. Goold *et al.* (1994) offer the following framework as a starting point for assessing the existence of, or potential for, a heartland.

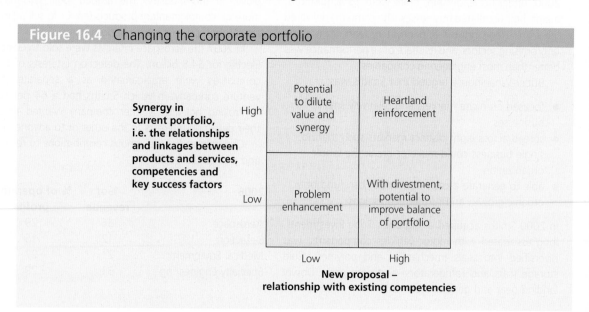

Figure 16.4   Changing the corporate portfolio

1   Mental maps (or philosophies) of the parent, incorporating issues of culture and values and broad policies for dealing with events and opportunities.

2   Issues of structure, systems and processes, incorporating the style of corporate management and including procedures for appointing, promoting and rewarding people, the relative significance of budgeting and financial reporting, strategic planning systems and capital allocation procedures.

3   Central services and resources: provided centrally or devolved.

4   Key people throughout the organization: functions, skills and competencies.

5   The nature of any decentralization 'contracts' and expectations, linked to issues of power, responsibility and accountability, reward and sanction systems; and the expectations that subsidiaries can have for the support they receive from corporate headquarters.

Typically, head offices have been larger and grander in centralized organizations but, while being reduced in size with their activities distributed to subsidiaries, they serve the global legal and financial needs of the business, and support strategy making. In general, they add and subtract businesses from the corporate portfolio, create linkages to drive synergy throughout the organization, design, support and maintain the organization structure, and provide certain key services. However, many head offices have provided a more extensive range of services, including marketing, management development and personnel, property management, centralized research and development, corporate public relations and industrial relations. Head offices clearly need to add value to the corporation and, with the recent trend for organizations to slim down the size and scope of head offices, in many cases only corporate strategy, financial reporting and control and secretarial/legal services remain centralized while some are only responsible for *policies* but not the activities.

Head offices can best add value to the business as a whole by addressing how they: (i) control and co-ordinate the constituent businesses (structure, corporate leadership and internal communications and synergy), (ii) advise the strategic leader and keep them strategically aware, (iii) drive performance and improvement through effective reward systems and (iv) decide which activities should be provided from head office (for which a fee should be levied), devolved to the individual businesses or bought in from outside specialists.

Alternative approaches include the stand-alone holding company, financial control approach; centralizing specific functions and services; controlling strategic change at the corporate level; and fostering linkages, learning and sharing good practices.

Head offices can destroy value if they: become established as *the* perceived centre for expertise in the corporation, assume that potential linkages and synergy will happen automatically, duplicate effort and costs unnecessarily, buy and sell businesses at the wrong prices and/or create or perpetuate a culture where internal competition takes precedence over the need to compete with external rivals.

16.3   Resource management

The role and skills of general managers

General managers (such as chief executives, managing directors, divisional and business unit heads) co-ordinate the work of subordinate specialist managers and are responsible for the management of strategy implementation and, in certain cases, strategy formulation, and they must match the resources they control with their particular environment effectively and thus achieve E–V–R congruence.

General managers in divisions and business units (Chapter 14) do not have full responsibility for strategy creation and implementation, and can be pressurized by corporate headquarters; and can turn to head office in their search for additional finance and other resources, which may operate differently from the external market, but justification should still be required. The relationship between general managers and head office will determine whether they are free to change their portfolios of business units and products or just adapt competitive and functional strategies, which will also be affected by performance measures and expectations. Where specific short-term objectives and targets are set, and monitored strictly, general managers are less likely to focus on corporate changes and instead will concentrate on more immediate changes which can yield faster results. Their flexibility to make changes will increase as their targets become more vague and directional and less specific. Even though the general managers of business units may not be responsible individually for the formulation of changes in the corporate strategy which will affect their sphere of influence, they will invariably be responsible for the implementation of the changes.

While effective strategic management concerns issues of formulation and implementation and strategic choices concern the nature and orientation of the organization (the strategic perspective) and the deployment of its resources (ideally to achieve and sustain competitive advantage), the strategic choice is implemented by strategic leaders who, as observed in Chapter 10, (a) exhibit different patterns of behaviour and styles of management and (b) will have different technical skills and biases as a result of their background. Arguably, alternative general managers would seek to implement basically the same strategy in different ways. The views of a number of authors concerning the relationship between general manager skills and particular strategies are discussed below.

Herbert and Deresky (1987), examining the issue of match between the general manager and the strategy, identified the important orientations and styles given below:

Strategy	*Styles and qualities required*
Development (start-up and growth)	Aggressive, competitive, innovative, creative and entrepreneurial
Stabilizing (maintaining competitive position)	Conservative, careful and analytical
Turnaround	Autonomous, risk and challenge oriented and entrepreneurial

They contend that financial skills are important for all strategies, with marketing skills being particularly important at the development stage and production and engineering skills invaluable for stabilizing strategies, thus raising three issues:

1 Which specialist functional managers might be most appropriate for promotion to general management in particular circumstances?

2 Is a change of general manager appropriate as products and businesses grow and decline and need changes in their strategies?

3 As strategies develop and change, should general managers adapt their styles of management accordingly?

Dixon (1989) suggests that *innovatory general management skills* are most required in the early and late stages of the life of a business or product in its present form and that these skills are required to establish or recreate competitive advantage and, in the case of terminal decline, to find an alternative product, service or business. These changes are often best accomplished by outsiders with fresh ideas and, correspondingly, the constant search for efficiencies and improvements while an established product or business is maturing is normally best carried out by specialists. Changes in senior management, structure or values may be involved and, since the outlook and styles of general managers are likely to be different, and their responses to different sets of expectations and performance targets will vary, this raises the issue of which managers are most appropriate for managing particular strategies.

There are similarities and differences in these various conclusions, reflecting again that there is no one best answer. The issue of match between general manager and strategy is important, such that one might expect that changes in one will lead to changes in the other. Clearly, as organizations become flatter and more decentralized skills in synthesis and integration are critically important.

Kanter (1989), researching the general management skills required to run businesses effectively in the competitive environment of the late 1980s and the 1990s, argued that large companies must be able to match corporate discipline with entrepreneurial creativity in order to become leaner and more efficient, whilst being committed to both quality and innovation. Suggesting that *process is more important than structure*, three strategies, explained in Critical Reflection 16.1, are important:

1 restructuring to improve synergy from diverse businesses

2 the development of joint ventures and strategic alliances to input new ideas

3 the encouragement of intrapreneurship within organizations.

Handy (first articulated in 1994, 1995) continues to contend that, in order for companies to remain competitive internationally, they have had to rethink their basic structures: 'Fewer key people at the heart of the organization, paid very well, producing far more value.' Handy acknowledges that it is quite feasible that corporations will continue to grow, either organically or through acquisition, but believes that either physically or behaviourally they need to be in small units, focused and closely networked to their suppliers and customers. More activities and components will be bought in from specialists than is the case at the moment; internally, they will also comprise networks characterized by subsidiarity, with the centre (as distinct from a traditional head office) doing only what the parts cannot do themselves. The real power will switch from the top of the organization to the businesses, and consequently a co-ordinating mission and purpose will be essential. Handy favours 'federalism' or reverse delegation – the centre acts on the bidding of, and on agreement with, the parts – and he is basically supporting a decentralization trend, but goes much further.

Critical Reflection 16.1 Rosabeth Moss Kanter on Competitiveness

Future success lies in the capability to change and to accomplish key tasks by using resources more efficiently and more effectively. Organizations must be innovative and, at the same time, control their costs. Sustainable competitive advantage, however, does not come from either low costs, or differentiation or innovation alone. It needs the whole organization to be *focused, fast, flexible and friendly*.

Being *focused* requires investment in core skills and competencies, together with a search for new opportunities for applying the skills. Intrapreneurship should be fostered to improve the skills constantly; and managers throughout the organization should be strategically aware and innovative. They should own the organization's mission, which, by necessity, must be communicated widely and understood.

Fast companies move at the right time, and are not caught out by competitors. New ideas and opportunities from the environment will be seized first. Ideally, they will be innovating constantly to open up and sustain a competitive gap, because gradual improvements are likely to be more popular with customers than are radical changes. However, instant success takes time – the organization culture must be appropriate.

Flexibility concerns the search for continual improvement. The implication is a learning organization where ideas are shared and collaboration between functions and divisions generates internal synergy. This, in turn, suggests that performance and effectiveness measures, and rewards, concentrate on outcomes.

Internal synergy can be achieved with cross-functional teams and special projects, and by moving people around the organization in order to spread the best practices. General Motors allows components and assembly workers, who work in separate plants in different locations, to contact each other by telephone to sort out problems and faults without relying on either written communications or messages which go 'up, across and down again'. These workers see each other as 'colleagues in the *whole* organization'. It is important that internal constraints (imposed by other functions and divisions) and which restrain performance are highlighted and confronted. To be effective requires a clear and shared vision and purpose for the organization, decentralization and empowerment.

Friendly organizations are closely linked to their suppliers and customers to generate synergy through the added value chain. Such external collaboration may be in the form of strategic alliances.

Reference

The material in this box is summarized from: Kanter, R.M. (2000) *When Giants Learn To Dance*, Touchstone.

Supported by sophisticated information technology and systems, people will become recognized as the most important strategic resource and, because their expertise and intelligence is an intangible asset, largely unquantifiable, it will become harder to value the real assets of a business. Consequently, the appropriate measures of performance must be carefully evaluated, and reward systems will have to be derived which motivate and keep those managers who are potentially the most mobile. The valuable managers will not all be at the most senior levels. Disagreeing with many strategic leaders of global organizations, Handy believes that switching jobs regularly and moving people between different parts of the organization, perhaps to other countries, can be dysfunctional. Simply, they will not be in place long enough to become known and, in the future, trust will be an essential element in management, strategic change and strategy implementation.

> *We have designed organizations based on distrust. We have designed organizations so that people will not make mistakes. And, of course, we now encourage people to make mistakes because that is how they learn.*

> HANDY

Handy's arguments imply major changes to strategies, structures and styles of management for many organizations. Where these changes are simultaneous – amounting to strategic regeneration in effect – the changes are dramatic, painful and often difficult to carry through.

Strategic resource management and planning

Figure 16.5 recapitulates how the corporate mission and purpose provide the basis from which corporate and competitive strategies are derived. The corporate portfolio provides a number of ways for the organization to pursue its mission – but each business in the portfolio will require different levels of attention and resourcing. These decisions relate to priorities linked to the potential of, and desired outcomes from, each business. The achievement of competitive advantage and success comes down, in the end, to individual contributions, and to guide and manage these, objectives, targets and milestones will be set.

Once broad or detailed intended strategies have been determined, the firm must plan their implementation, making the required resources available where and when they are needed, then *allocating* them to different managers, functions and businesses, and ensuring they are *co-ordinated* to generate synergy. Managers responsible for implementation must understand what is expected of them and be empowered and motivated to take the necessary decisions and actions. Indeed, *monitoring and control* systems are required.

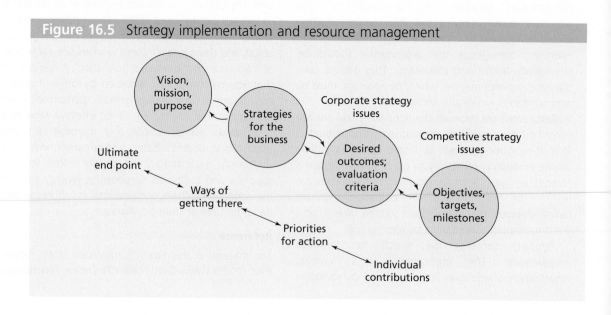

Figure 16.5   Strategy implementation and resource management

At the corporate strategy level, organizations might establish priorities for different divisions and businesses using portfolio analysis, and evaluate the strategic and financial implications of alternative investments. Decisions may be taken within the constraints of existing capital, financial and human resources; if they demand new resources, these must be obtained in an appropriate timescale. Proposed acquisitions may require an organization to raise funding externally; organic development of new products may require new skills and competencies. Resources can be switched from one part of a business to another.

At the functional level, *policies* and procedures can guide managers and other employees in the utilization of these corporate resources to add value, create competitive advantage and achieve the desired objectives. These policies can be tightly defined to maintain strong, central control, or very loose and flexible to enable people to use their initiative and be flexible. The ongoing management of the resources will then use action plans and budgets.

Action plans relate to the detailed strategies and plans for the various key functions, the activities which must be carried out if competitive and corporate strategies are to be implemented successfully while, together with *budgets*, they attempt to integrate sales, supply potential, production activities and cash flow to ensure that resources are available to produce goods and services where and when they are required. The organization would like to avoid a situation where it has requests that it would like to take, or worse, it has booked orders, but it does not have the resources to enable production or supply (i.e. over-trading and over-commitment). Both its bank and its customers can easily end up disappointed. It would also wish to avoid situations where it has idle capacity and no orders, or instances where it is producing for stock rather than for customers. This dilemma is one faced all the time by many small businesses, which endeavour to balance the resource-based perspective of strategy with the opportunity-driven approach.

This planning process then provides a useful check that the corporate and competitive strategies that have been formulated are both appropriate and feasible in the sense that they can be implemented. At the same time, this planning and budgeting must not be so rigid that the organization is unable to be responsive. Forecasts and judgements will never be completely accurate; when intended strategies are implemented, there will need to be incremental changes and revisions to plans. The plans should incorporate clear milestones – target levels of achievement against a timescale. By constant monitoring, the organization can check whether it is booking sufficient business, whether it is producing the necessary quality on time, whether it is under-producing or over-producing, whether its costs and prices are different from those that it forecast and whether it is managing the movement of cash in and out of the business to the budgeted targets.

A review of progress can highlight potential deficiencies to either resource requirements or likely outcomes. If orders are exceeding expectations, additional resources may be required if the organization is to properly satisfy the new level of demand. If these cannot be found, schedules will need to be changed and perhaps future supplies rationed. If orders are below expectations, then either new business opportunities will need targeting at short notice, possibly implying very competitive prices and low margins, or end-of-year targets revised downwards. Vigilance and pragmatism here can help to ensure that the organization does not face unexpected crises, while effective communications and management information systems are essential for planning, monitoring and control.

The allocation of resources at a corporate level is closely tied to the planning system through which priorities must be established. Portfolio analyses such as the directional policy matrix may well be used to help to determine which products and business units should receive priority for investment funding; and any new developments that are proposed will require resources.

Corporate resources may be allocated in different ways in line with the speed of growth of the organization and the degree of instability in the environment:

1 *Rapid growth.* The resource allocation process must be able to accommodate this growth and the consequent and possibly continual demand for additional resources. In all cases, the decisions should balance the potential financial gains with the strategic logic implied. While divisions or business units may be making individual requests for resources to support certain programmes, the opportunities for synergy, sharing activities and transferring skills across activities should be assessed, along with the desirability of the implications of the various proposals for the overall strategic perspective of the organization.

2 *Limited change and stability.* Resource allocation for continuing programmes could be a straightforward extrapolation of previous budgets, incorporating an allowance for inflation but a mere continuation of present strategies without evaluation and proper review may lead to ineffectiveness. Established policies, such as fixing advertising budgets at an agreed percentage of projected sales revenue or maintaining particular levels of stocks, are likely to be a key feature of this approach.

3 *Decline situations.* Some quite tough decisions often have to be taken and, where the organization as a whole is in difficulty, the strategic leader must search for new opportunities for redeploying resources. Selected business units that are experiencing decline, unless they have opportunities for turnaround, should transfer resources to activities with better growth and profit potential. Once resources are allocated to divisions, business units and functions, there will be further allocations to individual managers within each area which, to a greater or lesser extent, will be delegated to the general manager or functional manager in charge of each one (**functional** or **operational** resource planning); and interdependencies between the budget holders should be considered.

Functional resource planning raises a number of essential considerations: (i) the relative importance of each function, using perhaps the value chain, (ii) competitive advantage within functional activities along with an appreciation of key success factors and competitive opportunities to ensure strategic effectiveness, (iii) linkages between functions, which are the sources of potential synergy, should be considered such that any appropriate sharing of resources should be encouraged. Activities should be complementary and supportive, and (iv) the whole resource allocation process must take account of sequential dependencies where they exist.

In terms of both efficiency and effectiveness measures in relation to the allocation and deployment of resources, savings in time and costs (without threatening quality) lead to higher productivity, higher profits and the freeing up of resources which can be deployed elsewhere. Organizations should evaluate whether resources are being allocated to those products, services and activities which are most important for the organization as a whole and for the achievement of its objectives. This analysis is applicable at organizational, divisional and business unit level, where these resources have an opportunity cost especially where resources are finite and limited. If growth or profitability or both are important objectives, the resources should be allocated to those products and services which can best fulfil the objectives. However, sufficient resources should be allocated to development programmes that lead to growth and profits in the future.

Decisions made to alter resource allocations and concentrate them in different areas lead to issues of managing change (Chapter 15). Resource reductions in favour of alternative products may be resisted by certain managers, and their ability and willingness to resist change pressures from higher management will be related to their power bases and their ability to influence decisions, also considered in Chapter 15.

The need to measure and evaluate performance, and to make changes when necessary, applies at all levels of the organization. The attention of managers must not be focused too narrowly on only their areas of responsibility, as their contributions to other managers and their commitment to the overall interests of the organization are the sources of synergy. While these measures of individual performance are crucial, the effectiveness of all functional, competitive and corporate strategies and their abilities to achieve corporate objectives are the ultimate measures.

The effectiveness of the contribution of such activities as research and development is difficult to assess, but this aspect is no excuse for not trying.

Measurement and control

Figure 16.6 summarizes these ideas and Figure 16.7 charts several possible performance measures. Those on the right focus on efficiency and reflect a financial control culture and those on the left are crucial indicators of a commitment to service, quality and excellence. The culture of the organization will dictate which measures are given priority, but establishing such excellence measures requires a real attempt to reconcile the different expectations of the stakeholders. Where there is no common agreement, the

Figure 16.6 Monitoring and control

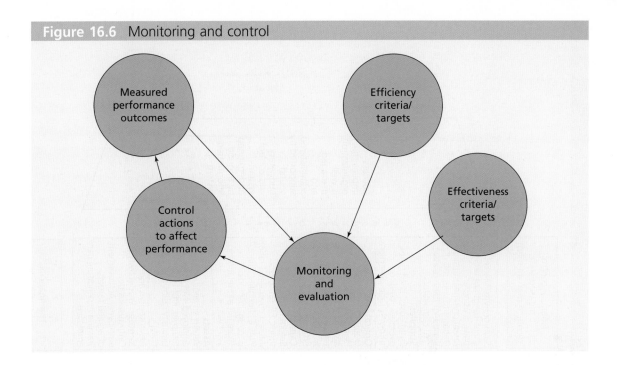

objectives and measures selected will reflect the relative power of the various stakeholders. In any case, commercial pressures invariably focus attention on resource management and efficiencies, which are easier to set and monitor. Also, because efficiency measures are possible and often straightforward, they may become elevated in significance and be seen as the foundation for the objectives: hence measurement potential, and not stakeholder satisfaction, dictates objectives.

Arguably, the central linked issues in measurement and control are (i) what is communicated to managers in terms of performance expectations, and (ii) how they are rewarded and sanctioned for their success or failure to achieve their targets. Resources should be allocated to enable managers to perform as required and, at the same time, to motivate them. Reed and Buckley (1988) argue that, when handled effectively, strategy implementation through action plans can be proactive such that strategies can be adapted in line with changes in the environment. Where these have been ill-conceived, there is likely to be more reaction to events and external threats. However, this aspect of implementation is difficult to achieve, with Wernham (1984) contending that managers benefit from appreciating 'superordinate organizational goals' and the overall strategic perspective, and that perceived internal inconsistencies between the performance expected of different managers can be demotivating. Communication and information systems should, therefore, make managers aware about where the organization is going strategically and how well it is doing. Wernham (1984) also implies that resource allocations and strategic priorities should be seen as fair and equitable, and that political activity to acquire or retain resources for the pursuit of personal objectives, or to support ineffective strategies, must be contained.

McMahon and Perrit (1973) have demonstrated that the effectiveness of managers in achieving their objectives is enhanced when the control levers are high, but Lawrence and Lorsch (1967) indicate that these controls also need to be loose and flexible if the environment is volatile.

Resources are allocated through the budgeting process, which establishes a quantitative short-term link between expectations and resources. Managers need to be aware of wider strategic issues and their attention should be focused on long-term strategies as well as short-term tactics and actions designed to bring immediate results, an approach that necessitates that managers are aware of the key success factors for their products and business units, and of how their competitive environments are changing. While they must achieve budget targets, there must also be a continuing search for new ways of creating, improving and sustaining competitive advantage. While budgeting is essential for allocating resources on a short-term basis

Figure 16.7 Some possible measures of performance

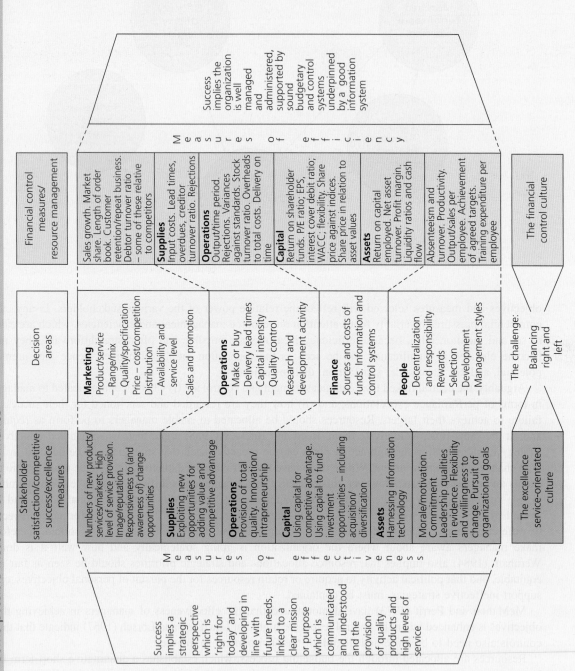

and progress against budget targets is a vital efficiency measure, organizational effectiveness also depends on longer-term flexibility. New developments and strategies, and improved ways of doing things, must also be considered. These may well involve changes in structures and policies as well as in the status of individual business units and managers. Issues in the implementation and management of change were the subject of Chapter 15.

16.4 Risk and crises

Risk taking and risk management

While risks are inherent in the choices that organizations make and (though different) strategy implementation, the key elements in any risk are the potential upside and downside from future events and the likelihood of certain things happening. Forecasting and scenario planning are uncertain, but are still important as managers exercise judgement in the decisions that they take: the greater their awareness, insight and understanding of emerging trends and opportunities, the more informed their decisions should be. Decisions and risk are linked irrevocably as the strategic decisions made by organizations and managers reflect their management of the risks they face. Organizations that manage risks effectively will be less crisis prone and in a stronger position to deal with potential crises and unexpected events when they do occur. In Case 16.3 we look at the lack of preparedness by British Airports Authority and British Airways for the opening of the new (in 2008) Heathrow Terminal 5 – and the consequent costs and risks to their business.

Case 16.3   BAA and Heathrow's Terminal 5   UK

In early 2009 the UK (Labour) government approved the construction of a third runway at the UK's leading airport, London Heathrow. Anyone who travels through this airport will know how busy and congested it can be; but a new runway would be controversial as it would affect homes (that might need demolishing), transport networks and noise levels in the area. The immediate outcome was protests by people determined to voice their opposition to the development. This happened just months after problems with the opening of the newest terminal, Terminal 5, at Heathrow. The new Coalition government intervened and by 2012 the official line was that there would not be a new runway at Heathrow. But the problem of under-capacity and stretched resources was not going away – additional runway capacity would have to be provided somewhere and somewhere ideally in the south east of England.

The new terminal 'belonged' to British Airways (BA) but the airport is controlled and managed by BAA, British Airports Authority. The terminal had been due to be fully functional in April 2008, and whilst it did open it wasn't ready. It had cost £4.3 billion and it would allow BA to move many flights from other terminals, especially Terminal 4, thus freeing up space there for other airlines – although considerable work was required to make Terminal 4 ready for other airlines to move in. Terminal 5 is some distance apart from the other four terminals and there is no dedicated inter-terminal connecting transit system.

As soon as the new Terminal 5 opened it was clear that staff were not coping. Many were finding it hard to even get to work on time because of parking problems and tight security checks once they arrived on site. This was compounded by staff shortages in key areas. Check-in queues were consequently lengthy and either flights were delayed or cancelled, or passengers missed their flights. Temporary marquees were erected outside the terminal to accommodate people who could not access the terminal building itself because of the sheer numbers of people ahead of them.

Bags were not being loaded on to planes because of systems problems in baggage handling and also because of inadequate staff training in the new procedures. This applied to both new check-ins and transfers. Simply, bags were being checked in and transferred in faster than staff could take them off the belts and route them to where they should be going for their onward flight. Thousands of cases went astray for a period of time – if not permanently. The media carried stories of enterprising business people who were buying (unseen) job lots of lost bags – hoping they were buying cases with valuables and clean clothes rather than dirty washing!

Very quickly it was announced that the opening would be cancelled and postponed until the summer. More extensive training and testing would take place. Both BA and BAA were seen as accountable in different ways. The pilots' union, BALPA, claimed BA needed a 'major management and management style shake-up'. BA's response was that it had taken a 'calculated risk' opening up in April and that things had gone wrong – BA admitted it had 'compromised on the test programme'.

BA's Chief Executive, Willie Walsh, further admitted the self-imposed problems in the first 5 opening days cost the airline £16 million. But, he said, their analysis indicated delaying the opening would have been more expensive. The problem ... the opening was subsequently delayed! Certain management staff left BA. Shortly afterwards staff also left BAA, including the person responsible for overseeing the opening of the new terminal.

Further down the line, and prior to the real opening in August 2008, came an expensive advertising campaign designed to 'restore confidence'. Some wondered whether this would only serve to remind people of the much-publicized chaos 4 months earlier.

All of these problems arose at a time when BAA was under attack for quite different reasons and facing a different type of crisis. The UK Competition Commission had been investigating BAA and concluded it was too powerful and in control of too many airports. BAA was originally in the public sector but it was one of the companies privatized by the Thatcher government in the 1980s. Much more recently it had been bought by the Spanish company Ferrovial. A substantial proportion of its revenue is earned from the rents it can obtain for the retail and catering space that it leases out.

BAA ran three airports in the London area, Heathrow, Gatwick and Stansted, three in Scotland, Glasgow, Edinburgh and Aberdeen, and also Southampton and Naples in Italy. Its powerful position was adjudged to be causing 'adverse consequences for consumers' – there was some feeling that it had become too focused on exploiting its lucrative retail and catering concessions. There had to be some reason why too many passengers and flights were being delayed.

The Commission ruled – subject to further discussion and possible appeal – that BAA should sell two London and one Scottish airport. BAA responded that the ruling was 'disproportionate' and that Heathrow would not be sold under any circumstances. BAA also owns and operates the fast rail link to Central London, the Heathrow Express. Some, though, mused whether this was appropriate when the runway decision was still pending and nowhere near resolved.

It soon emerged that others were interested in buying Gatwick. These included a consortium involving Virgin Atlantic and also Manchester Airport, which also owns East Midlands Airport. One sting in the tail is that these forced sales might have to go through during the economic recession when prices would be far lower than earlier valuations of the assets. Gatwick was sold in 2009 and Edinburgh in 2012 to Global Infrastructure Partners, which is substantially funded by GE Capital. Almost immediately after it was sold, Gatwick was closed down for 2 days because of heavy snow – and the new owners were immediately criticized for operating failures! Stansted might also have to be sold later.

Late in 2012 it was announced that the BAA name would be dropped and the company known as Heathrow Ltd – but each airport in the group would trade under its own name.

Questions

1 Do you think there is any likelihood that the tough ruling by the Competition Commission might have been influenced by BAA's involvement in the aborted opening of Terminal 5?

2 Is this an (other) situation that we might call 'good strategy and poor implementation'?

Risk can be best understood as an uncertain prediction about future behaviour in a market or industry, with a chance that the outcome of this behaviour could be detrimental to an organization. Clearly, an organization must try to manage these risks to reduce both the likelihood of a particular event and the extent of any possible downside which, in turn, demands an understanding of inherent risks in decisions.

Opportunities and strategies that involve new customers, new markets, new countries and/or new competencies all imply risk – an element of chance that something can go wrong – and the greater the potential impact (the downside) of what could go wrong, the greater the risk, thus reinforcing the value of a heartland of related businesses which, in turn, should reduce the number of risk variables involved. When a company moves away from what it knows, it increases its risk because there are more unknown uncertain future factors but, at the same time, not changing in a dynamic environment can also be very risky!

Companies must, therefore, make strategic choices, which sometimes they get wrong. But what appears to be a poorly judged choice can sometimes be turned around with appropriate changes during the implementation phase, such that risk is best managed in an organization that has a culture of flexibility and innovation and is successful at getting its people involved and committed.

Certain business environments – such as high-technology industries where there is constant innovation and technological change, or pharmaceuticals with its long pipeline to develop, test and market a new drug, or oil exploration with expensive investments in the hope of finding oil – involve higher levels of risk than others.

Four criteria are important in the decision and these are (i) the attractiveness of each option to the decision-maker, (ii) the extent to which they are prepared to accept the potential loss in each alternative, (iii) the estimated probabilities of success and failure and (iv) the degree to which the decision-maker is likely to affect the success or failure.

Risk, entrepreneurship and decision-making

Entrepreneurs are often described as risk takers, including a personal risk – it is their business, often their money and usually their reputation that is at stake – which can increase as the business becomes more successful and visible and, whilst the rewards for entrepreneurial success can be very high, the social stigma of a major failure can be traumatic.

Arguably, risk awareness and opportunity awareness should be separated since risk concerns that which can be quantified (but is unpredictable) and opportunity that which is much more judgemental. While a University Business School trained professional manager may seek to measure and evaluate the risk in the decisions that they have to take such that where there is an uncertain opportunity they may well perceive the risk to be too great, entrepreneurs are aware of both but are attracted by the opportunity.

Indeed, sometimes entrepreneurs have a feel for, or an insight into, a situation and an opportunity which may be the outcome of learning from previous experiences, i.e. they know what they are doing and in many instances they do not see themselves taking major risks – in which case, they are really *managing* the risks, even though they may not be able to quantify them and are accepting and retaining the inherent risk and going ahead. Other people, whose understanding of the situation and perception of the inherent risk is different, may be unwilling to take the same risk and hence they do not pursue the opportunity. Some successful entrepreneurs also recognize when an opportunity is beginning to disappear and they time their exit carefully, and focus their endeavours on a new opportunity: an excellent illustration of risk management, for they are seeking to avoid future risks.

Their perception of risk will change over time and with experience such that, once an entrepreneur has grown one venture successfully, they are likely to develop confidence alongside their experience – the concept of entrepreneurial learning – in which entrepreneurs (at least, some entrepreneurs) learn from their mistakes. Some entrepreneurs start with a failure, with Kets de Vries (1997) arguing that many entrepreneurs start in this way but are then determined to start all over again with a fresh risk and, convinced that 'the world' is against them ('the world' is full of people who resent other people who succeed and enjoy it when they don't succeed, and so failure can be expected), such that their challenge is to have another go, but this time to succeed. Attitudes towards risk affect the way in which managers make decisions, and Dunnette and Taylor (1975), researching industrial managers, concluded:

> *High risk takers tended to make more rapid decisions, based on less information than low risk takers, but they tended to process each piece of information more slowly ... although risk-prone decision-makers reach rapid decisions by the expedient of restricting their information search, they give careful attention to the information they acquire.*

Environmental factors may prove significant, for instance the availability and cost of finance, forecasts of market opportunities and market buoyancy, and feelings about the strengths and suitability of internal resources will all be important, whilst for other managers within the organization the overall culture and styles of leadership and the reward systems will influence their risk taking.

Managing risk

While the term 'risk management' is often associated with the idea of insurance, it is too narrow a perspective since organizations often pursue strategies that seek to manage or minimize risk. The first main step in risk management is clarifying the risks involved, which involves four elements: personal risk, opportunity risk, (business) environmental risks and resource-based risks. Table 16.2 provides a framework for evaluating the environmental and business risks.

Table 16.2   Assessing business risks

Type of risk	Example
External environmental risks	
Supply risks	Over-dependency on a supplier
	Outsourcing something which is strategically critical
Market/demand risks	Customer preference changes
Stakeholder risks	Misjudged priorities
Social responsibility and ethical issues	Failure to deal effectively with a chemical spill or a major incident
Politico-economic risks	Turbulence in an overseas market
Innovation risks	Misjudging market acceptance for a new idea
Competitive risks	Existing competitors 'out-innovate' the business
	Price competition
	Powerful new rivals enter the industry
Resource-based risks	
Materials risks	Need to handle/transport dangerous materials
Process risks	Corner-cutting to save time and money
Managerial risks	People's ability to cope with the dynamics of change in the organization
People risks	Inadequate or inappropriate training
Commitment risks	Individuals do not pull their weight, especially in a crisis
Structural risks	Inappropriate balance between centralization (for control) and decentralization (for flexibility)
	Internal barriers to co-operation
Complexity	The spread of activities is too complex and leads to fragmentation and internal conflict
Financial risks	Undercapitalization
	Cash-flow problems
Technology risks	Inadequate information systems

The second step is to select (from alternatives) what to do about the various risks: (i) *retain* the risk and prepare for possible eventualities – the risks have to be taken or an opportunity or a venture would have to be abandoned, (ii) *transfer* the risk, which could be achieved by switching it to someone else (divesting a business), diluting it (through a joint venture or strategic alliance) or insuring against it and (iii) *regulate* the risk perhaps by investing to reduce it.

Some believe that, in some instances, organizations do not take certain risks sufficiently seriously and thus place people's lives in danger, either by not appreciating the existence of a risk, or by ignoring the dangers.

Clarke and Varma (1999) argue that changes in the external business environment mean that satisfying stakeholders effectively is more risky and uncertain for organizations than it was in the past, such that risk management has become a strategic issue – yet many firms treat it tactically and piecemeal. Therefore, they are more crisis prone than ideally they should be, which is considered below.

The risk-taking organization

Birch and Clegg (1996) list a number of characteristics that will restrict risk taking by individual managers and employees:

- centralized and/or committee decision-making
- adherence to formal systems and budgets
- reliance on performance rewards based on preset (and inflexible) plans
- early evaluation of new ideas and proposals
- mistakes being sanctioned too readily (arguably making the same mistake more than once should be disciplined, of course!)
- management by fear
- a culture of caution.

They also suggest that risk taking can be encouraged by:

- decentralization and informality
- initiatives and projects which cut across organizations
- rewarding managers and employees for new initiatives which have succeeded
- providing resources to develop new ideas
- limited adherence to 'badges of office' and job titles
- encouraging and respecting learning
- trusting people and encouraging them to enjoy what they do – a culture with an element of fun.

Case 16.4 (Huawei) will allow you to consider whether this successful Chinese telecoms company is managing its various risks sufficiently robustly.

Crisis avoidance and management

Crisis management involves managing certain risks and future uncertainties, dealing with opportunities and surprises, and managing resources to cope with unexpected and unlikely events in the organization's environment: E–V–R (environment–values–resources) congruence again – strategically key, as failure to deal effectively with crises leads to losses of confidence, competitiveness, profits and market share.

Crisis management involves elements of planning (crisis prevention or avoidance, i.e. the search for potential areas of risk, and decisions about reducing the risks) and management (being able to deal with crises if and when they occur), such that how organizations deal with crises either enhances or damages their reputation since there will always be an economic cost and little logic in trying to avoid it.

SOURCE: THIS CASE STUDY WAS PREPARED USING PRIMARILY PUBLICLY AVAILABLE SOURCES OF INFORMATION FOR THE PURPOSES OF CLASSROOM DISCUSSION; IT DOES NOT INTEND TO ILLUSTRATE EITHER EFFECTIVE OR INEFFECTIVE HANDLING OF A MANAGERIAL SITUATION.

Case 16.4   Huawei

Ch

Huawei Technologies Company provides telecommunications equipment and services. Based in Shenzen, Guandong Province, it is China's leading telecoms provider – and the second largest in the world, behind Ericsson. Annual revenues exceed US$30 billion. Huawei was started in 1987 by Ren Zhengfei, a former officer in China's People's Liberation Army. It is still a private company owned by its shareholders. Ren, with less than 2 per cent, remains the company's largest shareholder; he has led the company from the outset. Its 110 000 employees give it a larger headcount than Microsoft. Of these some 46 per cent work in research and development – and their average age is under 30. Facilities have been established in Germany, India, Russia, Sweden and the USA as well as China. By early 2011 Huawei had applied for some 49 000 worldwide patents and been granted 18 000. *Fast Company* declared Huawei to be the fifth most innovative company in the world in 2010.

It began as a sales agency for network switches for an established Hong Kong company but by 1990 had established its own research and development into telephone exchanges and equipment. It first targeted hotels and small businesses. The first overseas sales for its own products were in 1997 and by 2005 international sales exceeded domestic sales – and the ratio is now 3:1. Huawei began to work with other companies around the world – British Telecom, Optus (Australia), Telus (US), Bell (Canada) and IBM – and joint ventures with companies including 3Com, Siemens and Motorola followed. It now works with 45 out of the top 50 telecoms businesses around the world. Huawei naturally migrated into mobile phone technology as this industry took off.

There are now three revenue streams in the business. Telecoms networks (60 per cent of revenue) is the largest of these and this now mainly involves network equipment for the mobile phone industry, but it also includes broadband. Global Services (20 per cent) provides equipment, services and consultancy for individual businesses, helping them to build and support what they need. Devices (the remaining 20 per cent) include modems, network cards, video-on-demand boxes and mobile handsets (both tablets and smart phones). These are seen as convergent technologies.

Why has Huawei been as successful as it clearly has been?

Blending its natural wage cost advantages with advanced technologies has made it very innovative and fast moving. Its research and development scientists and engineers are said to work some 2750 hours in a year, almost twice the norm for a similar employee in Europe. They have used their advantages to drive down costs in the industry and thus make them very price competitive. Huawei claims to have always been problem and customer focused, willing to customise solutions. Ren drives his people to be ambitious and to strive to stay ahead of rival organizations – and to work collaboratively. Video conferencing is used extensively. He shuns the hierarchical chains of command that personify many of China's large businesses. In addition a large proportion of the manufacturing is outsourced so that Huawei can remain largely focused on developing new products and services.

Huawei, though, has not grown as it has without some controversy. At various times it has been alleged that the company has engaged in patent infringements, bribery, industrial espionage and supplying organizations such as the Taliban in Afghanistan. This it has vehemently denied – just as it has the suggestion the company has always been linked to the Chinese military. Whilst there have been persistent denials and occasional settlements, none of the accusations seem to have created a major crisis for the business.

Question

Do you think the company's perception of the risks it is dealing with is different from those of some critical outsiders?

If at least some of the allegations were true why have they not become crises for Huawei?

Simplified, there are three decision areas in determining the crisis strategy:

1 Decisions concerning what can go wrong, the probability of it happening, and the impact it will have if it does happen.

2 Crises planning, which are decisions about investing in prevention in order to reduce or minimize the risk which invariably implies cost increases, such that less is often done than conceivably could be done.

3 Mechanisms for contingency management.

The decisions involve trade-offs between costs and risks to find the best balance between points 2 and 3, and successful management of crisis situations involves both awareness and the ability to deal effectively with unexpected change pressures. As an outcome of 9/11, there have been demands for armed sky marshals to travel on aircraft on certain routes, which has been standard practice on El Al (Israel's national airline) for many years, but the reaction of American airlines to this suggestion has been much more supportive than most European airlines.

The word 'crisis' covers a number of different issues and events, including a mixture of technical and managerial elements. Some incidents are clearly 'thinkable' and efforts can be made to avoid them or reduce their potential impact, while others remain more unthinkable. Fires, fraud and computer failure are typical crises that might affect any organization almost any time; and poisoning scares or contamination of food products, and oil or chemical spillages, are foreseeable crises for particular companies. Major transport accidents, when they happen, are crises for the railway, shipping company or airline involved. Sometimes, but not always, the accident will prove to have been preventable such that there is an obvious logic in making contingency plans and being prepared. In addition, organizations can sometimes be affected by natural disasters, events outside their control. Shrivastava *et al.* (1988) define a major crisis as: 'Organizationally based disasters which cause extensive damage and social disruption, involve multiple stakeholders and unfold through complex technological, organizational and social processes.'

Figure 16.8 provides a framework for categorizing different incidents, with 'thinkability' on one axis, with the horizontal axis separating the planned from the unplanned response, and the terms 'crisis management' and 'disaster management' used as a convenient form of separating the planned and unplanned response to a major event. The four examples in the diagram are the roll-on roll-off car ferry *Herald of Free Enterprise* that sank in 1987 as it was leaving Zeebrugge with the loss of 193 lives; the crush at Hillsborough football stadium in 1989 in which 96 Liverpool FC fans died and over 750 were injured; the fire at Kings Cross Underground station in 1987 in which 31 people died; and two major fires in the Channel Tunnel in 1996 and 2008 in which there were no deaths. The Hillsborough disaster is still 'news' today as the behaviour of some members of the Police force involved – both during and after the actual event – remains under scrutiny.

Strategic changes can also lead to crises of confidence, particularly amongst employees. Rumours that a firm might be taken over often imply redundancies; falling sales and profits suggest possible cutbacks or closure. Good internal communications and openness are required to minimize the potential damage, especially as competitors might see these situations as competitive opportunities. Smith (1990) explains why some crises happen when they might have been avoided:

1 A set of organizational problems making the organization crisis prone, which relate to issues of culture and power, misguided strategies and poor control systems. There might be evidence of dangerous cost-cutting or simple neglect.

2 The incident itself often provoked when particular external events clash with the organizational problems.

3 Legitimation, i.e. when the incident or crisis is investigated there is a ready willingness to apportion blame and a failure to learn properly from the experiences. Organizational change does not take place and the problems are merely reinforced, so the same type of crisis could easily happen again.

Figure 16.8 A framework for crises and disasters

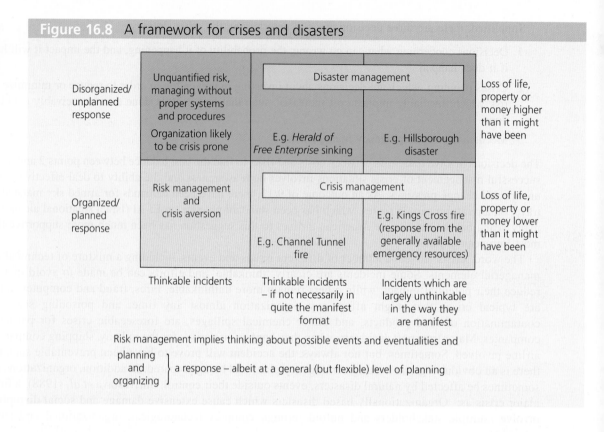

Risk management implies thinking about possible events and eventualities and planning and organizing } a response – albeit at a general (but flexible) level of planning

Many organizations are actually frail, rather than strong, and relatively crisis prone with an often over-inflated view of their strengths and competencies and too much belief in their infallibility, providing us with a 7–Cs framework for investigating crises, summarized in Table 16.3 (Smith, 1990). We tend to focus our interest on the cold factors, and by ignoring the warm ones the organization becomes more crisis prone (ibid). Strategy in Action 16.1 applies these points to the Millennium Dome.

Organizational difficulties and crises occur in several ways and take many forms. Weak strategies (which may have been strong in the past), substandard products and services, unacceptably low prices or excessive costs can often be remedied by diagnosing and acting on the problem with a hard/cold element and an external focus. They are a relative weakness because of the relative strengths of competitors, and can be observed and measured by monitoring competitor activities, tracking sales and market shares and simply talking to customers and distributors. Ineffective management practices, the softer or warmer side, have internal origins and require a different approach and may be hidden as people divert attention from them by blaming problems and crises on external competitive factors or unexpected events.

Table 16.3 The 7–Cs crisis management framework

Warm factors – people related	Culture
	Communications
Cold factors – technocratic	Configuration – issues of power and influence
	Control
	Coupling and complexity – the nature of the event itself
	Costs
	Contingency planning

Strategy in Action 16.1 The Millennium Dome – an Application of the Crisis Management Framework

The intention of the Millennium Dome was to build a lasting structure in Greenwich, London, funded by a mixture of government funding, lottery money and private sponsorship. It would be opened on the evening of 31 December 1999 to celebrate the new millennium and then used for 1 year as a special exhibition with individual zones designed and funded by the sponsors. It was not to be a theme park, but it was to be a signal to the world that Britain could manage a major and ambitious celebratory project 'as well as, if not better than, anyone else in the world'. After 2000 the Dome would be sold to a private company for a use to be determined later. The whole project was tied in to public-transport developments, notably the Jubilee Line Extension of the London Underground – for parking at the Dome was to be severely limited.

The initial outcomes

- The Dome was opened on time.
- However, many of the guests at the special opening night ceremonies had not received their tickets and had to queue for them at an underground station.
- There was hostile media criticism from the moment the Dome was opened. Many visitors commented on the lack of any 'wow' factor. Ironically, the London Eye, the viewing wheel built by British Airways, which experienced technical difficulties and a delayed start, received a better reaction and has proved very popular and lucrative.
- It quickly transpired that the sales and revenue projections were over-optimistic and were never going to be met. They were revised downwards more than once.
- Additional money from the National Lottery was provided on more than one occasion to prevent bankruptcy.
- The person appointed as chief executive of the New Millennium Experience Company (which managed the whole project), Jennie Page, was forced to resign, as was the non-executive chairman of the board, Robert Ayling of British Airways. Jennie Page was replaced by Pierre-Yves Gerbeau from Euro-Disney; Ayling by David Quarmby, chairman of the British Tourist Authority. After just a few weeks in the post,

Quarmby returned to his original non-executive role on the board. David James, an experienced 'company doctor', was recruited to rescue a rapidly deteriorating situation. James took over some of Gerbeau's responsibilities.

- After just 1 day in the post, James commented publicly that he was 'appalled' at the financial systems that he had inherited. Controls were inadequate and there was no proper register of assets. Visitor projections (already reduced substantially) were still unrealistic and yet more lottery funding was required if the Dome was to remain open until the end of 2000.
- The Conservative (opposition) party called for the Dome to be closed early and for political resignations. Both demands appeared to 'fall on deaf ears', although Prime Minister Blair acknowledged that mistakes had been made. It was also commented that the Dome 'had always been a regeneration project and not a visitor attraction'.
- Nomura (the Japanese Bank) initially agreed to buy the building, to develop theme park activities in 2001, but pulled out of negotiations when it was unable to gain access to the financial information that it needed for its planning.

Applying the crisis management framework

Culture
- Arrogant assumptions about what people (paying customers) would want.
- Arrogance about British achievements – in the event, France's lighting of the Eiffel Tower received more praise.
- There was a clear culture of blame.
- There was a failure to synthesize the political agenda of the government and private sector project management.

Communications
- Clearly fragmented.
- Lack of cohesion amongst the stakeholders.
- Some 'truths' were kept hidden.

- Arguably, the general public was never fully clear about the project and what it stood for.
- What was to be a 'triumph' has become an embarrassment linked to 'face saving' and damage limitation.
- The media generally became hostile towards the project.

Configuration

- There was a clear political agenda, driven by the early leadership of Peter Mandelson. The project had to be seen as a success.
- There was also a secondary agenda – it was to be linked with public transport developments. The Jubilee Line itself was fraught with problems and was handed over to American contractors to complete.

Control

- There was a lack of clear governance and responsibility – who actually 'owned' the project?
- Financial controls were inadequate.
- The immovable completion deadline added a new dimension with extra pressures.

Coupling and complexity

- There were too many perspectives and expectations.
- This was exacerbated by the underlying desire to demonstrate creativity, innovation and 'great achievement'.

Costs

- Poor forecasting – especially concerning paying visitors – meant that the costs and break-even projections were never realistic.
- There was a very visible need to 'beg' for more subsidy which reinforced a perception of mismanagement.

Contingency planning

- An early closure was never a realistic option for the government.
- This made cost overruns more likely and sponsorship more difficult.
- Revenue shortfalls would be allowed, but only in a culture of blame.

Final outcomes

A number of potential bidders – interested in developing both homes and leisure facilities – came forward after the Dome closed, only to either withdraw or be rejected by the Government. After protracted negotiations, a developer was found for the Dome site, which would become a 20 000 seat concert arena, one of the largest and most popular in Europe. An initial opening date of 2006 was put back to 2007, but since it opened as The O2 Arena, it has been very successful with a wide mix of concerts and events. When the Dome closed, some £800 million of public money had been sunk in to the project and there were additional maintenance costs. It was estimated the proposed developments should, over time, recoup some £550 million of this. The American private investors stood to make a great deal of money if the O2 Arena was a success.

Activity

Given these figures it is interesting to check the current events schedule at the O2 Arena – and the ticket prices – and consider the current financial returns. It is also important to factor in the wide range of restaurants, bars, shops, snack outlets and concession stands which add to the revenues. How might we evaluate the Millennium Dome project? As a second project, you might compare this story with that of the London 2012 Olympics.

Crisis fighting in organizations

Organizational environments have become increasingly dynamic and turbulent in recent years. As environments spring more and more shocks and surprises on them, organizations must develop new ways of dealing with uncertainty. Some organizations actively seek to influence and even manage their environments; others rely more heavily on their ability to react and respond quickly and they may make a virtue out of their ability to crisis fight. However, extensive crisis fighting is time-consuming, reducing the time and space available for wider strategic thinking, such that real growth opportunities may be missed.

Over a period of time no organization is successful, seen as successful and able not to be affected by crises, but most could manage their resources more efficiently and more effectively and, as a result, be less prone to crises (whether externally generated crises or self-created). As shown above, the long-term situation is made worse when an organization which has dealt with a crisis fails to learn and make itself less crisis prone for the future. Managerial competency in crisis fighting is often perceived to be both a strength and a virtue. People complain about stress levels but paradoxically enjoy the challenge of a crisis. Dealing with the problem quickly and pragmatically gives people satisfaction and a sense of achievement. Even laid-back people can find new motivation and strength. In turn, those with expertise also have to improvise on many occasions since instructions and procedures cannot predict every eventuality.

Crisis fighting in organizations takes up time, and managers are pragmatic but often not thoughtful beyond the confines of their immediate span of responsibility. Internal rivalry may well be reinforced such that people's competitive energy is focused on beating other parts of the organization (who are perceived as rivals rather than colleagues) instead of the real external competitors, thus forcing a short-term time horizon on many issues and decisions and making people frustrated and to lose confidence in their organization. Ironically, though, crisis fighting can be customer orientated as managers react to customer pressures and requests. Consequently, the long-term damage to the organization, which it is fostering through a failure to learn properly, can be hidden behind short-term successes – further reinforced by people using the short-term successes to hide and ignore the deeper problems.

In contrast, trying to eliminate the regular and ubiquitous crisis fighting and replace it with a more harmonious culture where people share information and trust and help each other may seem positively boring, but it can free up time and can foster valuable innovation. It goes further than opening up new windows of opportunity for a firm and can elevate it to a new level of (previously inaccessible) opportunity. Scenario building, contingency planning and crisis management strategies can all help with unexpected events, which to some large extent are often foreseeable but not necessarily avoidable. Well-managed innovation and new product and service developments can strengthen an organization's competitiveness and reduce its crisis proneness. Internal crises generated by complacency with current good fortune, a reluctance to change, poor decisions and weak management demand a change in culture and style. Understanding, trust and commitment must be fostered.

Crisis proneness and crisis aversion

Characteristics indicating crisis proneness in an organization are listed in Table 16.4, and organizations need to determine the extent to which they are manifest. Managers often believe that they are better at knowing what needs to be changed than actually managing and implementing the changes, which may be based on

Table 16.4 The crisis-prone organization

- Specialist functions that cannot or do not think and act holistically.
- A tendency to look inwards at the expense of looking outwards – internal-competition not external-competition focus.
- A strong, rigid belief in present (even past) competitive paradigms.
- A reluctance or inability to properly embrace the demands of a changing environment.
- Inadequate communications – e.g. vertical but not horizontal; horizontal at discrete levels but only vertical downwards.
- An inability correctly to interpret triggers and signals.
- Willingness of individuals to break rules and procedures readily for short-term results – and hide the detail, their knowledge.

personal opinion and judgement. Without openness, trust, sharing and learning, organizations may not realize what they already know and may not be able to leverage and exploit a strategic resource, their knowledge. Moreover, they may not realize what they do not know and may not fully appreciate the opportunities available to the privileged competitors in an industry.

Figures 16.9 and 16.10 summarize the important themes of this section and highlight the demands on an organization. A fragmented short-termist firm will spend too much time and waste resources in crisis fighting. If it fails to manage the soft issues involved in establishing trust and co-operation, it is likely to under-achieve as it develops longer-term strategies. If, however, it can manage the people issues more effectively it can single-loop learn and foster innovative improvements with existing products and services. Now as it develops longer-term strategies it will be better placed to take a more holistic view and improve its overall effectiveness.

> *It's not going to be one heroic act or gesture by me that's going to make the real difference; it's going to be thousands and thousands of separate actions by people in the company, every hour of the day, that will make the difference. Add all these up and the combined power is enormous.*
>
> BEVERLEY HODSON, EX-RETAIL MANAGING DIRECTOR, WH SMITH, QUOTED IN ITS
> INTERNAL MAGAZINE, *NEWSLINK*, JUNE 1997

These actions should be self-supporting to foster synergy, rather than fragmented.

Crisis avoidance

Bartha (1995) suggests that many, but not all, crises develop gradually and nobody spots their progress, but they can be prevented if organizations objectively monitor their environment and assess the emerging strategic issues. An organization can hence develop a relative aversion to crises – as opposed to being crisis prone – if it develops associated competencies in awareness, learning and stakeholder management and must do so to identify, assess and deal with potential opportunities and threats before opportunities disappear (perhaps because they have been exploited by a competitor) or threats turn into crises. Another emerging threat would be a gap between the performance level expected of the organization by its stakeholders, especially its shareholders, and the actual performance level.

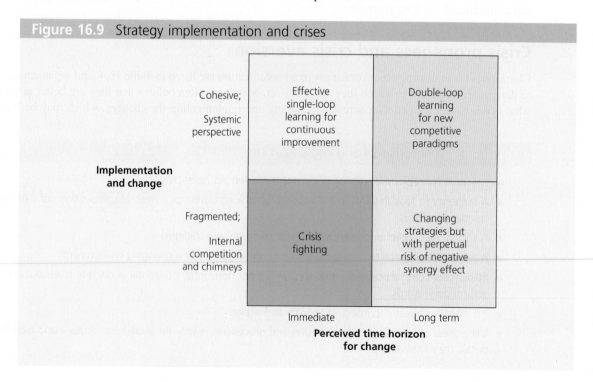

Figure 16.9   Strategy implementation and crises

Cohesive; Systemic perspective — Effective single-loop learning for continuous improvement — Double-loop learning for new competitive paradigms

Implementation and change

Fragmented; Internal competition and chimneys — Crisis fighting — Changing strategies but with perpetual risk of negative synergy effect

Immediate — Long term

Perceived time horizon for change

Figure 16.10 Strategy implementation and crisis avoidance

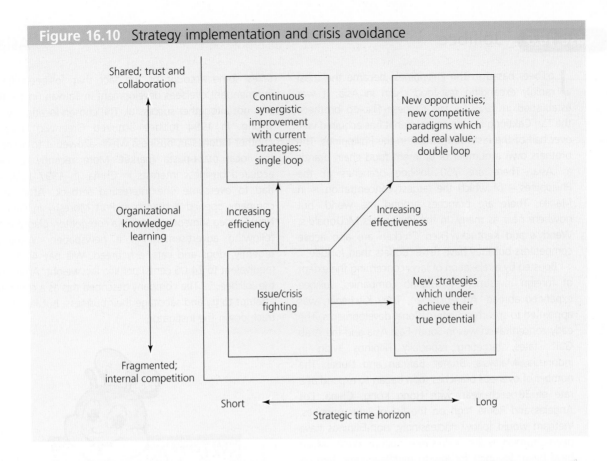

A number of elements are involved in *scanning the environment* including monitoring competitor activity, constant contact with key stakeholders, such as customers, distributors and suppliers, and awareness of pending government legislation and pressure group developments, perhaps informed by the media.

Opportunities will emerge where the organization can build upon its strengths or tactically out-manoeuvre a rival; the crisis might occur if the opportunity is missed by the organization but picked up by a competitor. A potential threat can be present in a number of ways: new legislative restrictions, a disappearing market, financial difficulties for an important supplier or distributor. Information and triggers can be received anywhere in the organization at any time; the firm must make sure that their significance is appreciated and that they are channelled to those people, functions and businesses who could benefit. Communication systems and the ability of individual managers to take an organization-wide, or holistic, perspective are crucial.

The ability of managers to act upon the information will, in turn, depend upon organizational policies and the extent of their empowerment; their willingness to act will be affected by their personality, their competencies, their motivation and the reward/sanction system practised by the organization.

Case 16.5 describes the success story behind Jollibee but highlights a number of issues the company has had to deal with. We might ask: can any organization be truly crisis averse?

Crisis management

There are a number of identifiable steps in attempting to manage crises effectively: identify the most obvious areas of risk; establish procedures and policies for ensuring that risks do not become crises by discussing possible scenarios; identify, train and prepare a crisis management team in advance; build the team; and conduct stakeholder analysis by clarifying which stakeholders are most likely to be affected by

Case 16.5   Jollibee

Asia

Jollibee, based in the Philippines, became the most rapidly expanding fast-food chain in Asia. It was established in 1978 by five Chinese–Filipino brothers, the Tan Caktiong family, since when it has acquired well over half of the fast-food market in the Philippines. The brothers own a number of different food chain brands in Asia. There are 750 Jollibee branches in the Philippines – of which the largest concentration is in Manila. There are branches around the world, but nowhere near as many. In the Philippines McDonald's, Wendy's and Kentucky Fried Chicken are also active competitors but they have fewer outlets than Jollibee.

Boosted by a relaxation of laws concerning the extent of foreign investment in Filipino companies, Jollibee expanded abroad. An Australian, Tony Kitchener, was appointed to spearhead international developments. The early concentration was in South-East Asia and the Arab Gulf states, targeting especially Filipinos living in Indonesia, Malaysia, Brunei, Bahrain and Dubai. The number of overseas branches soon began to expand at a rate of 30 each year, with Hong Kong, China, Los Angeles and Rome high on the list of later priorities. Vietnam would follow. Increasingly, non-Filipinos have been attracted by the chain's individual products, which have been designed for low-to middle-income families with a sweet tooth, and for children's parties. Prices are kept slightly below those of McDonald's. The main product is an Asian-style hamburger, distinctive because it is cooked *with* the spices rather than them being placed on top afterwards – McDonald's has countered this with its local McDough brand. In addition, there are Spaghetti Fiesta (a Chinese-type mixed chow), salads and mango pie (a locally popular dish). While the hamburger tends to be ubiquitous, different countries have separate menus. Chicken masala is the most popular product in Malaysia and the Gulf. The bulk of the beef is imported from Australia and Jollibee makes all its own bread.

Jollibee waited for critical mass before announcing that 'its burgers are THE Asian fast food'. The company has also diversified, beginning with the acquisition of a pizza chain in the Philippines in 1993.

Expansion is now with joint ventures and franchising such that capital for growth is not a big problem. A majority of the outlets are now franchised. It also takes some account of the fact that Jollibee's first independent overseas development in Taiwan (in 1988) was not altogether successful. The chosen location was wrong. In 1994 Jollibee acquired Greenwich Pizza, another Indonesian business which allowed it to access the local pizza-pasta market. More recently it has acquired business interests in China. In 1997 Jollibee had to overcome one interesting setback. After the company opened a branch in Port Moresby in Papua New Guinea someone, possibly a competitor, placed the following advertisement in a newspaper: 'Wanted urgently, dogs and cats, any breed. Will pay 40 toea (equivalent to 24 US cents) per kilo live weight. Apply to the Jollibee….' The company described this as a criminal attempt to try and sabotage their business, but failed to track down the instigator.

In 1998 and 1999 Jollibee, like many Asian businesses, had to deal with what might have been a far bigger potential crisis – the uncertainty caused by high domestic inflation and drastic falls in the value of local currencies. In the event this turned into a wonderful opportunity for Jollibee – whose growth continued unabated. Redundant, experienced executives were keen to buy franchises – in part because the demand for fast food grew. In a part of the world where eating out is normal, the lower-priced fast food outlets took business away from more expensive restaurants.

Questions

1 Can anything sensible be done to prevent an incident such as the rogue advertisement, or does it always come down to effective reaction?
2 Do you think this amounts to anything more than 'bad luck'?
3 Has the growth and success of Jollibee been influenced by an entrepreneurial, opportunistic approach during a period of inflation and uncertainty?
4 Do you think it is coincidental that McDonald's has also been targeted by activists?

particular crises – and how. After a crisis, customers either exhibit loyalty or switch to competitors, while the confidence of distributors and the banks may also prove important. The media often play a significant role and their stance is likely to influence the confidence of other stakeholders and, where stakeholder perspectives and expectations differ, they may need to deal with each group on an individual basis.

Finally, a clear communications strategy is essential since ethical issues may be involved, and the company will be expected to be co-operative, open, honest, knowledgeable and consistent. They must be seen to be in control and not attempting to cover up, since the media will want to know what has happened, why, and what the company intends to do about the situation. 'No comment' may well be interpreted as defensiveness or incompetence, such that an effective information system will be required for gathering and disseminating the salient facts.

Regester and Larkin (1997) offer the following advice to organizations:

1 Be prepared.

2 Demonstrate human concern when something happens.

3 Consider the worst possible outcomes.

4 Communicate at all times, at all levels.

5 Avoid obsequious people as spokesmen or women.

6 Do not believe that procedure manuals prevent incidents.

7 Do believe 'there is a first time for everything'.

The crisis-averse organization

Figure 16.11 highlights that, to survive, a firm must retain customers, acquire new customers, obtain employee support and commitment by motivating and rewarding them, and meet financial targets to ensure shareholder loyalty. Achieving these outcomes depends on both strategy and structure, which in turn depend upon effective strategic leadership. A sound, appropriate, communicated and shared purpose and vision should be manifested in appropriate, feasible and desirable corporate and competitive strategies which must be implemented with a high level of customer service, improved continuously, and changed to new corporate and competitive paradigms at appropriate times and opportunities.

These aspects demand environmental awareness and the ability of the organization to respond to change pressures and to external strategic disturbances. While we talk about an organization-wide response, the real challenge lies with individual managers and employees, who are closest to customers, suppliers and distributors. Innovative people drive functional-level improvements which can strengthen competitiveness; but they must be empowered and committed – issues of structure, style and implementation. The hard aspects of strategy – leadership, vision and ideas – must be supported by the soft people aspects.

Figure 16.11   The crisis-averse organization

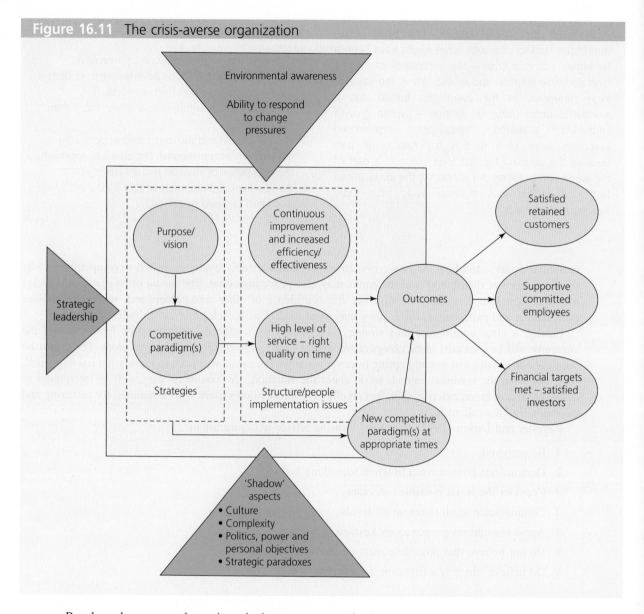

People and processes determine whether managers and other employees support and facilitate change, or inhibit the strategic changes that are necessary for survival.

Egan (1993) adopts the term 'shadow side' of organizations to embrace issues of culture, complexity, politics, power, personal objectives and the ability of the organization to deal with the range of strategic challenges discussed above; and they can be positive or negative influences. Where they are negative, the organization is likely to be more crisis prone; for the organization to be crisis averse, they must be largely positive. Organizations must find ways of empowering their employees, harnessing their commitment and promoting organizational learning if the shadow side is to make a positive contribution to strategic management and change.

The most proactive strategy for crisis management can be compared with the notion of total quality management, as the organization is looking for a culture where all employees think about the implications and risks in everything they do. Reactions when a crisis has happened can prove to be effective or ineffective, as effective management is likely to mean that confidence is maintained and that there is no long-term loss of customers, market share or share price. That is more likely to happen in an open, flexible structure than it is in one which is bureaucratic (Booth, 1990).

Figure 16.12 A crisis-management framework

Corporate reputation: the stakeholders' view of the company

- Strong / Weak (vertical axis)
- Thin high profile | Crisis avoiding
- Crisis prone | Unsung heroes

Corporate competency reflected in the company's ability to satisfy the needs and expectations of its stakeholders* effectively (Low — High horizontal axis)

*The stakeholders: customers; employees; investors; suppliers; environmentalists

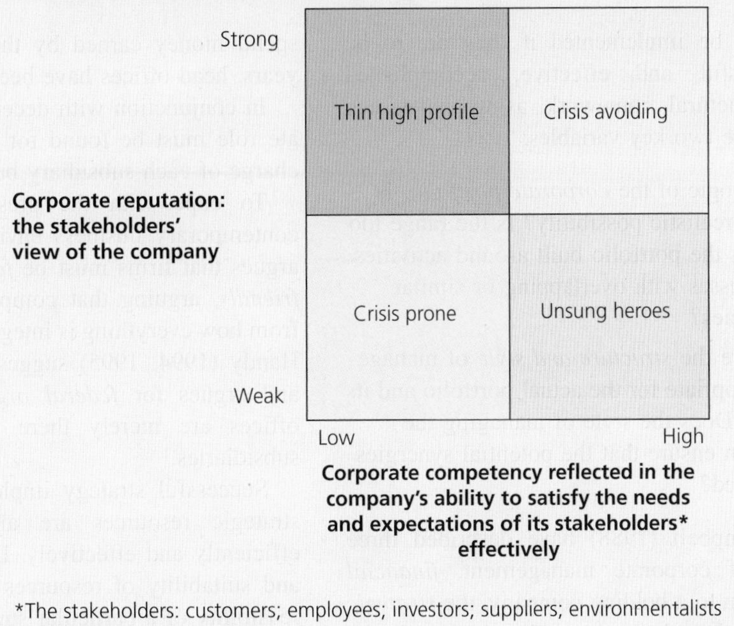

Kabak and Siomkos (1990) offer a spectrum of four reactive approaches: (i) one extreme (and normally ineffective) is *denial of responsibility*, arguing the company is an innocent victim or that no harm has been done, (ii) a better, but still ineffective, approach is *involuntary regulatory compliance,* (iii) *voluntary compliance* involves a positive company response towards meeting its responsibilities and (iv) the other extreme strategy, the *super effort*, whereby the company does everything it can, openly and honestly, and stays in constant touch with all affected stakeholders.

While there is little argument against the logic of planning ahead of a crisis, some organizations are cautious about the extent to which one should attempt to plan.

A crisis management framework

Companies succeed if they meet the needs and expectations of their stakeholders; companies which fail to meet these needs and expectations, long-term, must be in trouble and they may collapse. Perception of relative success and failure is critical. Companies that are succeeding need to be recognized for this. Companies that are not succeeding will want to cover up their weaknesses if they can. The simple matrix illustrated in Figure 16.12 is based on these premises. Companies that satisfy their stakeholders, and are seen to do so, are classified as crisis avoiders. Crisis-prone organizations fail on both counts. Companies with a strong reputation they do not wholly deserve are termed 'thin high profile' as the situation is likely to be very fragile and fluid. The fourth quadrant contains 'unsung heroes', companies whose reputation does not do justice to their real achievements.

Summary

Strategies must be implemented if they are to be judged successful and effective, accomplished through the structural framework, as we have seen earlier. There are two key variables:

- First, the logic of the *corporate portfolio*. Is synergy a realistic possibility? Is the range too diverse? Is the portfolio built around activities and businesses with overlapping or similar competencies?

- Second, are the *structure and style* of management appropriate for the actual portfolio and its diversity? Does the style of managing the corporation ensure that the potential synergies are achieved?

Goold and Campbell (1988) have described three broad styles of corporate management, *financial control style* akin to a holding company, the *strategic planning style* based on centralization and the *strategic control style* which is a sort of half-way house that attempts to build on the strengths of the other two.

Defining corporate strategy as the overall strategy for a diversified firm, Porter described four approaches to managing a corporate portfolio: *Portfolio management* is the approach whereby each business is looked at independently to assess its worth to the firm; *restructuring* is the attempt to make both an industry and a business more attractive by improving competitiveness – when an organization can no longer add any further value, the business should be divested; *sharing assets* offers the best opportunity for creating and exploiting synergy across a range of businesses; but *transferring skills* can also prove valuable. Goold *et al.* (1994) have highlighted the importance of *corporate parenting* – essentially the fit between a head office and the subsidiary businesses in an organization and the opportunities for two-way benefits. Where each business can benefit from being part of an organization, and also make a positive contribution to the whole organization, we have what Goold *et al.* call a *heartland* of related businesses. Businesses should be acquired and divested to strengthen the heartland.

The *corporate headquarters* drives the strategy of the business and provides the structural framework. The range of services which remain centralized is a reflection of the adopted style of corporate management. Head offices should add value and not merely spend money earned by the subsidiaries. In recent years, head offices have been slimmed down.

In conjunction with decentralization, an appropriate role must be found for the general managers in charge of each subsidiary business.

To cope with the pressures and demands of contemporary business environments Kanter (1989) argues that firms must be *focused, fast, flexible and friendly*, arguing that competitive advantage comes from how everything is integrated and works together. Handy (1994, 1995) suggests a more radical thesis and argues for *federal organizations*, where head offices are merely there to serve the needs of subsidiaries.

Successful strategy implementation requires that strategic resources are allocated and controlled efficiently and effectively. In reality, the availability and suitability of resources is a determinant of the feasibility of a particular strategic option. Of course, the existence of resources does not, in itself, guarantee effective implementation – resources have to be managed. In addition, resources should be flexible to allow adaptive and incremental change. We can think of *resource allocation* at two key levels:

- the allocation of *corporate resources* to particular businesses or divisions, based on perceived needs and priorities, and often linked to the growth of the business or industry in question

- the allocation of *functional* resources to build and add value in order to create and sustain competitive advantage.

Policies are designed to guide the use of resources by managers.

Budgets are used to allocate resources for particular activities and tasks. Budgets, however, are often short term in scope and the measurement of performance against budget targets may be more an evaluation of efficiency in the use of resources than of longer-term strategic effectiveness.

Resource allocation and management – and the inherent decisions – reflect the way in which the organization and its managers are dealing with the risks that they face.

The key dimensions of risk are:

- the likelihood of certain eventualities – some of which could imply a detrimental impact for the organization, and

- the extent of the downside (perhaps a loss of orders, revenues or confidence) if the particular incident in question does occur.

While there is always a personal risk for entrepreneurs and strategic leaders in corporate strategy changes, a useful framework for clarifying and analyzing risks is based on external (environmental) and internal (resource-based) factors.

Risks can be retained, transferred or regulated. The relative success or relative failure of an organization to deal with the risks that it faces determines the extent to which it is crisis prone or crisis averse. Crises can be major or minor, 'thinkable' in advance or more realistically unforeseeable. Consequently, organizations need strategies for avoiding crises in the first place and then for dealing with those crises

that do occur: handled well, a crisis can enhance the reputation of an organization; handled badly, the impact can be substantial and prolonged.

Crises and disasters contain a mixture of 'cold' (technocratic) and 'warm' (people-related) elements. All too often organizations focus their attention on the cold elements when it is the warm ones that hold the key. By not learning lessons and by apportioning blame too readily, organizations can legitimize crises and simply increase the likelihood of them happening again.

It remains a paradox that many managers are proud of their ability to crisis fight and deal with problems as they arise, which merely reinforces a reactive attitude and a short-term perspective, and can be short-sighted.

Online cases for this chapter

Online Case 16.1: Hanson
Online Case 16.2: Three Diversification Strategies – BTR, Tomkins and Williams
Online Case 16.3: ICI and Zeneca
Online Case 16.4: The AA, RAC and Green Flag
Online Case 16.5: Black Cat/Standard Fireworks

Online Case 16.6: Air France, and the Concorde Disaster
Online Case 16.7: The 2012 Olympics
Online Case 16.8: TWA and Swissair
Online Case 16.9: Perrier

Questions and research assignments

1 For which (general) corporate strategies are the financial control, strategic planning and strategic control styles of corporate management most appropriate?

2 How do you think the need for general managers might have changed as organization structures have generally been flattened and delayered?

3 Reflect on the work of Kanter and Handy in the late twentieth century – Section 16.3 in the text. What view if any has best profiled the nature of the modern organization?

4 Are you personally risk averse or perceived as a risk taker? On what evidence are you drawing this conclusion?

Internet and library projects

1 Update the material on any or all of the four conglomerate businesses discussed in the two online cases on Hanson and BTR, Tomkins and Williams.

Using this and details of the corporate strategies pursued by other large companies with which you are familiar, which of the following two statements do you most agree with?

'Conglomerate diversification has now given way to focus strategies – focus is here to stay.'

'Focus strategies cannot generate sufficient growth long-term to satisfy shareholders – diversification will make a comeback.'

2 Take any large organization with which you are familiar. How have its head office structure and roles changed in recent years?

3 For an organization with which you are familiar, ascertain the main stated policies for finance, production, personnel and marketing.

How are these policies used? How were they created? How do they rate in terms of the principles of good policies discussed in the text?

4 Ascertain the budgeted resources and targets allocated to one manager whom you are able to interview.

What measures of performance are utilized? What feedback is provided? What does the manager do with the feedback? What do you believe is the personal impact of the budget and measures of performance on the manager? Are they motivated? Rewarded or sanctioned for success or failure?

5 Either by contacting a local councillor or using the Internet, ascertain how planning and budgeting are managed in your local authority. What have been the priority areas in the past? What are the current priorities? How have the changes in priority been decided?

6 In August 2000 the Russian nuclear submarine Kursk sank in the Barents Sea after an internal explosion. The whole crew was lost and the Russian government was criticized for not calling on foreign help and expertise as quickly as it might have done. What are the lessons in risk and crisis management from this incident?

7 Use the Internet to assess the possible long-term damage to Ford Motors when it was discovered (in 2000) that the Bridgestone/Firestone tyres used on its Explorer four-wheel drive vehicles were potentially dangerous and had been the cause of a number of accidents over a period of time. How do you think both Ford and Bridgestone handled the crisis – effectively or ineffectively?

8 Perhaps using the online case on the 2012 Olympics, consider whether this was genuinely a risk worth taking. The 'feel-good' factor generated cannot be questioned – but will there have been a financial cost to the Nation, albeit partially hidden? Given the issues with security staff shortly before the games opened – and the reality that some teams insisted on providing their own security – were all the risks under control?

9 Review the causes of the Deepwater Horizon drilling rig (operated by BP) oil spillage into the Gulf of Mexico in 2011. Was this, as many commentators believe, avoidable? Was the situation handled well after it happened? Can you apply the 7–C's framework to this event?

Strategy activity

Product recalls in the toy industry

When products that have been sold through retailers have to be recalled because there is some problem or danger, then costs can be substantial and corporate reputations can be damaged. For companies, there are issues of public relations, supply chain management and crisis management. In recent years a number of toy products have been recalled and replaced. It is not the only industry where this problem occurs; and although there is a common theme to the instances related here – manufacturing in China – this is not the only reason recalls happen.

Mega Brands is a Montreal-based distributor of children's building sets – its Mega Blocks compete with Lego, for example – art materials and magnetic toys. Sales in 2006 amounted to some $500 million.

In November 2005 a toddler in Seattle died after swallowing some small magnets that had become detached from a Magnetix toy sourced from a New Jersey (US) company that Mega Brands had acquired 6 months earlier. The toys originated in China and Mega 'did everything it could' to make sure new toys coming through were safe. Products were redesigned to ensure the magnets were embedded more securely, and new production standards and inspection procedures put in place. Labelling and instructions were also made clearer. But hostile press coverage continued and eventually, in 2006, this led to a huge number of products being recalled and replaced although there did not appear to have been any further serious incidents. Continuing stories suggested, for example, that the company might have gone further. Labelling might be improved, but the basic packaging had been retained. Did it need to be changed, or not? The *perception* was that it did. In 2007 there was a second recall.

It also became apparent that in today's world of selling old toys on auction sites such as eBay, normal recall programmes may not be enough. Mega set out to buy any items it spotted being sold on in this way. Although there is still a handful of outstanding lawsuits, the number of customer complaints now seems to have died down.

In August 2007 leading toy distributor **Mattel** recalled 18 million Chinese-made toys after concerns over lead paint and magnets. These included Barbie dolls and die-cast cars. Mattel has contract manufacturing plants in China – but it emerged these had been sub-contracting the painting operations.

Two months earlier, in June 2007, **Fisher Price** recalled 1.5 million toys over lead content concerns. And just before this a New York based distributor had recalled 1.5 million Thomas the Tank Engine products – again for lead. **Toys R Us** had recalled vinyl baby bibs – yet again for lead.

Moreover, these problems were not confined to the US. Leading New Zealand distributor, **The Warehouse**, had recalled children's pyjamas containing formaldehyde – some children had been badly burned when their night-clothes accidentally caught fire.

The US Consumer Safety Commission began to argue that toys must be tested more rigorously before they left China – which would increase costs and slow down supplies. But undoubtedly a price worth paying …

It is perhaps useful to think of these issues in the context of the Chinese baby milk contamination stories that happened in 2008. Products had been contaminated with melamine to reduce production costs – over 50 000 children, most of them in China itself, became quite seriously ill and four died. The issue was taken seriously, executives charged with murder, convicted and sentenced to death.

Question

Although recalls and replacements can prove very costly, it will arguably always be tempting to look for cost reduction opportunities wherever they can be found – as these can lead to either (or both) lower prices and higher profits. But can we ever legislate for companies that either cut corners or seek to take what turn out to be inappropriate risks?

References

Bartha, P. (1995) Preventing a high-cost crisis, *Business Quarterly*, Winter.

Birch, P. and Clegg, B. (1996) *Imagination Engineering*, Pitman.

Booth, S. (1990) Dux at the crux, *Management Today*, May.

Clarke, C.J. and Varma, S. (1999) Strategic risk management – the new competitive edge, *Long Range Planning*, 32 (4).

Dixon, M. (1989) The very model of a mythical manager, *Financial Times*, 10 May.

Dunnette, M.D. and Taylor, R.N. (1975) Influence of dogmatism, risk taking propensity and intelligence on decision-making strategy for a sample of industrial managers, *Journal of Applied Psychology*, 59 (4).

Egan, G. (1993) Adding Value: A Systematic Guide to Business-driven Management and Leadership, Jossey Bass.

Friedman, M. (1979) The social responsibility of business is to increase its profits. In *Business Policy and Strategy* (eds D.J. McCarthy, R.J. Minichiello and J. R. Curran), Irwin.

Goold, M. and Campbell, A. (1988) *Strategies and Styles*, Blackwell.

Goold, M., Campbell, A. and Luchs, K. (1993) Strategies and styles revisited: strategic planning and financial control, *Long Range Planning*, 26 (5); Strategies and styles revisited: strategic control – is it tenable? *Long Range Planning*, 26 (6).

Goold, M., Campbell, A. and Alexander, M. (1994) *Corporate Level Strategy*, John Wiley.

Green, O. (1994) Quoted in *Management Today*, June.

Handy, C. (1994) *The Empty Raincoat*, Hutchinson.

Handy, C. (1995) Beyond Certainty: *The Changing Worlds of Organizations*, Hutchinson.

Herbert, T.T. and Deresky, H. (1987) Should general managers match their business strategies? *Organizational Dynamics*, 15 (3).

Jackson, T. (1995) Giant bows to colossal pressure, *Financial Times*, 22 September.

Kabak, I.W. and Siomkos, G.J. (1990) How can an industrial crisis be managed effectively? *Industrial Engineering*, June.

Kanter, R.M. (1989) *When Giants Learn to Dance*, Simon & Schuster.

Kets de Vries, M. (1997) Creative rebels with a cause, in Birley, S. and Muzyka, D., *Mastering Enterprise*, Financial Times/Pitman.

Lawrence, P.R. and Lorsch, J.W. (1967) *Organization and Environment*, Richard D Irwin.

McMahon, J.T. and Perrit, G.W. (1973) Toward a contingency theory of organizational control, *Academy of Management* Journal, 17.

Porter, M.E. (1987) From competitive advantage to corporate strategy, *Harvard Business Review*, May–June.

Reed, R. and Buckley, M.R. (1988) Strategy and action: techniques for implementing strategy, *Long Range Planning*, 21 (3).

Regester, M. and Larkin, J. (1997) *Risk Issues and Crisis Management*, Institute of Public Relations.

Richter, A. and Owen, G. (1997) The UK cut down to size, *Financial Times*, 10 March.

Shrivastava, P., Mitroff, I., Miller, D. and Miglani, M. (1988) Understanding industrial crises, *Journal of Management Studies*, 25 (4).

Smith, D. (1990) Beyond contingency planning – towards a model of crisis management, *Industrial Crisis Quarterly*, 4 (4).

Stonich, P.J. (1982) *Implementing Strategy*, Ballinger.

Wernham, R. (1984) Bridging the awful gap between strategy and action, *Long Range Planning*, 17.

Chapter 17

Final thoughts and reflections: the practice of strategy

**PART 1
Understanding strategy**

1 What is strategy and who is involved?
- Appendix

2 The business model and the revenue model

3 Strategic purpose
- Supplement: Using frameworks to analyze strategy cases

**PART 5
Strategy implementation**

14 Strategy implementation and structure

15 Leading change

16 Managing strategy in the organization

17 Final thoughts and reflections: the practice of strategy

STRATEGIC MANAGEMENT: AWARENESS AND CHANGE

**PART 2
Analysis and positioning**

4 The business environment and strategy

5 Resource-led strategy

6 The dynamics of competition

7 Introducing culture and values

**PART 4
Strategic growth issues**

11 Strategic control and measuring success

12 Issues in strategic and international growth

13 Failure, consolidation and recovery strategies

**PART 3
Strategy development**

8 Creating and formulating strategy: alternatives, evaluation and choice

9 Strategic planning

10 Strategic leadership and intrapreneurship: towards visionary leadership?

Success is never final.

WINSTON CHURCHILL

Things may come to those who wait – but only the things left by those who hustle.

ABRAHAM LINCOLN

Introduction

In these final thoughts and reflections we synthesize the main ideas from this book to reinforce them and also to address two questions: first – what is the purpose of strategy? – and second – what is strategy? Here we revisit the key issue of what 'strategy' and the practice of strategy really involves. Whittington (2001) is one author who has defined strategy and he has addressed the question of its importance; his prominence in researching 'strategy as practice' (see also Whittington, 1996) is highlighted in the Research Snapshot in Chapter 1.

Many organizations now operate or compete in dynamic, turbulent, uncertain, and chaotic financial and business environments which, in business terms, partly results from industries and markets becoming ever more global – as well as continual improvements in technology, *inter alia*, causing product, service and **strategic life cycles** to shorten. Organizations must, therefore, act, react and change more quickly, some changes being continuous and emergent, as vigilant, responsive organizations seize opportunities and innovate ahead of their rivals.

Other changes will be discontinuous and imply changes in competitive paradigms. Technology can both create and destroy industries, markets and windows of opportunity, while breakpoints – or switches to new competitive rules and agendas – happen increasingly frequently. Organizations cannot ignore this reality and the pressures that they bring, however disruptive the changes might be.

17.1 The purpose of strategy

In the simplest terms, the purpose of strategy is to enable organizations to cope with the challenges of an uncertain, dynamic and (for some) competitive 'world', to find and seize fresh opportunities and to thus deliver an acceptable and sustainable level of performance. It might seem simple! In reality, it is more complex and requires vision, attention to detail and constant vigilance and flexibility.

Famous and long-standing organizations, such as Coca-Cola, Microsoft and Walt Disney, continue to survive these breakpoints – sometimes actually creating them – and, as a result, they thrive, grow and prosper and exploit their competencies and reputation. They create E–V–R (environment–values–resources) congruency and sustain it with carefully managed change. These organizations can be many things – perhaps entrepreneurial, perhaps professional – and are exceptional. We can learn from their actions, strategies and behaviour, although it will always remain difficult to explain fully all of the reasons for their success. Simply attempting to copy their behaviour is not an adequate answer to the challenges facing organizations.

Other companies grow more steadily and uncertainly, never seeming to have the same command over their environment. Nonetheless, they do survive, partly with innovation and partly with contingent reaction. Other organizations survive for some period of time, but then decline as they lose E–V–R congruency, while others still only survive with a change of leadership, style and culture. However, some businesses disappear every year, some due to takeover or liquidation. It is, therefore, all too easy for currently successful firms to lose their edge and their competitive advantage, due to four main reasons (Miles and Snow, 1994):

- a lack of awareness and a failure to be alert to new opportunities and threats
- retaining a belief in a successful competitive paradigm for too long, which market leaders seem particularly prone to do by relying on *continuous* change to retain their leadership

- an unwillingness to accept the need for structural or cultural change, and

- poor judgement, causing a company to make poor, inappropriate decisions.

There are important lessons to be learned from their relative demise, and we can see how these four reasons relate to four key themes in strategy: strategic thinking and awareness; competition; strategy implementation; and strategic decision-making.

Two related but distinct perspectives allow us to examine strategic effectiveness, the first being about success and the second about survival. One: what reasons lie behind the relative prosperity of our most successful organizations, those which continue to add value for their customers, differentiate their products and services, and control their costs? And two: what factors distinguish a crisis averse from a crisis prone (i.e. lurching from crisis to crisis, never really managing its environment) organization? Whilst it is arguably fashionable to talk about competitiveness, competitive advantage and success, it is less fashionable but equally important and relevant to explore the issues behind crisis aversion – given that too many organizations hover on the narrow line separating survival from failure.

Organizations are systems that comprise people who are trying to act purposefully rather than thrash around without any real purpose (Checkland, 1981). However, people differ in their perspective and perceptions, and use their personal meaning systems to interpret events, actions, opportunities and threats and to decide upon responses. While their personal strengths must be captured and exploited, organizational information systems should ensure that they work within the parameters of the corporate purpose, vision and policies and that their initiatives and contributions are shared and understood.

Remember opportunity and risk: success over time requires organizations to be entrepreneurial, to find new opportunities and to manage the inherent and inevitable risks.

The new technological revolution and the increase in globalization have forced change on organizations everywhere, regardless of their type, size and sector. Few are unscathed, some have embraced change positively and willingly, and others more reluctantly. Those who have failed to change have probably been sold or liquidated, leading perhaps to a more flexible but slimmed-down workforce.

On the positive side, many managers and employees are better educated, given that they are information technology (IT) literate knowledge workers in a knowledge-based society and, indeed, some of them possess scarce skills. In some organizations, people have become less constrained and more empowered, willing to be creative and show initiative in a more open, less hierarchical firm. Finally, information often flows more horizontally and freely, enriching and speeding up decision-making.

However, many workers are now part-time and 'peripheral', as opposed to 'core'. When re-engineering their processes and changing their structures, too many companies went too far – they downsized but not 'rightsized', and important skills and competencies were lost. Indeed, strategies focusing on core activities and competencies by divesting those which are non-core have created an increasing incidence of strategic alliances and networks. Managing these networks effectively demands new capabilities, which many organizations have failed to develop fully. People today feel under greater pressure and stress, and there is more fear and insecurity. To some extent, the bounty of globalization and technology is stress. 'Hard', as distinct from 'soft', human resource strategies are practised in too many companies, and many employees, instead of committing themselves to a single company, look to switch organizations and industries as they take more control of their working lives, despite widespread managerial unemployment and insecurity.

Sadly, many large organizations, composed of very intelligent people, are still slow to respond to change pressures and, when they do, their behaviour is often ponderous. In the new world of rapid change, having the 'right' strategic leader is ever more important. Individuals can, and often do, act dynamically and entrepreneurially; yet many organizations have still to work out how to capture the intelligence and learning in order to facilitate the change process, and still do not manage their human assets well. Thus the paradox of the large organization is learning how to behave like the archetypal small business. The challenge of embracing both the 'hard' and 'soft' elements of strategic management to increase strategic awareness and manage strategic change more effectively remains a major challenge for many organizations, and is more likely to intensify than to disappear.

Hence we next identify ten key elements of strategy, review the strategic paradoxes already debated throughout the book and finish with a view on what strategy is and the practice of strategy.

17.2 Ten key elements of strategy

Figure 17.1 shows ten elements of strategy discussed at various points in the book: the first six (in the central box) being interdependent and, if interwoven effectively, the organization should be more crisis averse than crisis prone; with the remaining four impacting upon the whole process of strategy creation and implementation:

1 **Perspectives of strategy** Strategy can be about the past (emergent patterns from previous decisions), the present (strategic positions) and the future (strategic plans), or at the levels of broad purpose and narrow tactical ploys. Such perspectives are relevant to the debate about what strategy is, since its relevance varies: for the strategic leader, it is the overall corporate strategy for the whole organization; for other senior managers, competitive positions and the competitive strategies determining its competitive advantage; for lower-level middle and junior managers, activities and functional strategies, but they must understand the wider picture and the contribution that they make.

2 **Corporate strategy and synergy** As discussed towards the end of the book, whether or not there is a logical and defensible heartland of related businesses comprising the corporate portfolio determines if, in a ideal scenario, each business is individually competitive and successful in its own right, while contributing synergistically to the corporate parent and to other businesses in the portfolio – with the parent organization equally being able to contribute value to each business.

3 **Strategic positioning and competitive advantage** To be successful and achieve competitive advantage, each business or activity will need to establish, and sustain with change, a clear and strong competitive position delivering either a cost advantage (compared to rivals) or a differentiated position which customers perceive as relevant and valuable, or ideally both.

Figure 17.1 The ten key elements of strategy

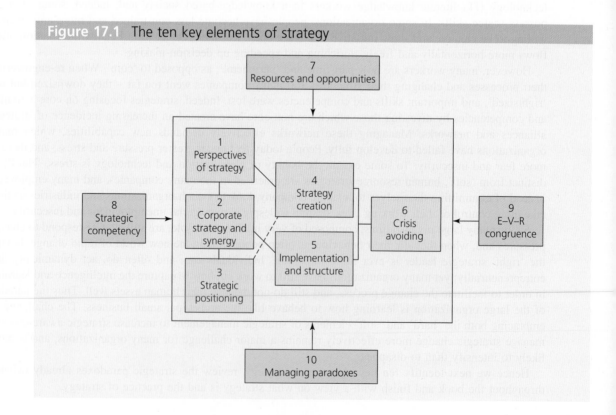

Its competitive advantage is the position itself, but comes from the activities – competencies and capabilities – creating and sustaining the position of advantage.

4   **Strategy creation** Strategy creation is about change and, consequently, the organization's approach is dictated by the strategic leader and influenced, and possibly constrained, by the culture of the organization. Three broad approaches were identified: (i) **visionary** or **entrepreneurial strategy** creation, itself a reflection of strong strategic leadership, (ii) *planned strategy*, the outcome of analysis and possibly the outcome of a planning system (which, with *visionary strategy*, reflect intended strategies) and (iii) **emergent** strategy creation, which takes two forms, incremental changes to intended strategies during the implementation phase, and adaptive strategy creation in a dynamic and turbulent environment. Organizations need to find an effective blend of the three, all of which are likely to be present to some degree. Remember the challenge of distinguishing between strategy and tactics (actions and activities) and how we explained in Strategy in Practice boxes 3.1 and 8.1 that tactical decisions can drive strategy – rather than, as is often assumed to be the case, the other way round. Strategy in Practice 17.1 revisits the theme.

Strategy in Practice 17.1   Reflections from Formula 1

Formula 1 motor racing is fast, competitive and exciting. Fractions of a second can differentiate race winners from the rest of the field. It is international and involves 'big money'. Some of the world's leading companies are involved as both competitors and sponsors. The sport's governing body places constraints on design, tyres and other operating elements to make sure there is real competition and racing. The quality of the cars (technology and design; performance and reliability), the individual drivers and the behind-the-scenes teams all affect the outcomes. But so too do luck and circumstance.

Something unfortunate can happen to any driver or their car in any race – the leader might have a puncture (foreseeable but unavoidable); they might run out of fuel (foreseeable and avoidable). This can deprive that driver of a win that seemed to be theirs; at the same time, it can also present a wonderful opportunity to any rival that might capitalize. Equally, a driver can be taken out through no fault of their own, if, say, someone drives into them. Any driver can make a mistake in a split second misjudgement. If the car ahead runs off the road momentarily, the car behind will probably have to swerve; this can be threatening but it can also be an instant window of opportunity to seize an advantage.

Now take as a potential scenario that a safety car has come out after some incident and is slowing down the race. Drivers are required to stay in race order – unless they take the opportunity to do a pit stop and change their tyres – but the gaps between the cars will close. Hard-won advantages by race leaders can easily be lost. Yet it is a typical strategy for drivers to do this if they are likely to have to take a stop at some point later in the race. Let's say the race leader – and maybe the car in second place – both opt to take pit stops (expected) but the driver in third place doesn't (unexpected). Once the race resumes, this 'third place' driver will now be at the head of the field with clear track ahead – he could surge ahead and open up a lead. If he can delay his next pit stop – or even avoid it – he could have a massive advantage. It is a huge gamble – one affected by the stage of the race and the state of their tyres and fuel – but it could pay off. Clearly, once any decisions are made, they will be known to the rival competitors who are in a position to evaluate any potential consequences. Any reactions will have to be almost instantaneous. There is, therefore, an opportunity to take one's rivals by surprise – but also the potential to be surprised.

All drivers and teams will start with a race plan, or a strategy for how they plan to race. There will be policies for how they deal with certain incidents, such as a safety car. Sometimes they will follow this plan to the letter; sometimes they will make changes. Who decides this – the driver or the team boss? And how long might they have to make up their mind? In practice, the team boss in the pits has access to detailed information about their own drivers and the position (and some of the tactics) of every other driver in the race. They have a 'big picture' that it is only available to an individual driver from the pits via communication channels. But the driver is the person who can see what is happening directly around them in real time and has to deal with it instantaneously. The two must work together.

This scenario illustrates both opportunity and risk. Experience will help with the decision – but the 'right' decision requires far more than experience.

5 **Strategy implementation and structure** Strategies must be implemented before they can be deemed successful and, while organization structures are designed to ensure that intended strategies can be implemented effectively, the very operation of the structure is the foundation for emergent strategy creation. This element is naturally connected to the relative significance of centralization and decentralization and the extent of manager empowerment.

6 **Crisis avoidance** If these first five elements are being dealt with effectively, the organization should be relatively crisis averse in a dynamic environment, but if they are not, the organization is likely to be more crisis prone.

7 **Resources and opportunities** Three approaches to the management of strategy, while different but not mutually exclusive, comprise: (i) the **opportunity-driven** approach, beginning with a scan of the external business environment to seek new opportunities to be exploited, (ii) the **resource-based** approach, simultaneously attempting to open windows of opportunity because they possess (or can obtain) the necessary strategic resources, and exploiting further their distinctive competencies and capabilities, and (iii) the **competition-based** approach, more tactical and reactive in nature, concerning the ability and willingness to deal with competitor tactics and initiatives.

8 **Strategic competency** Going beyond core (technological) competencies and strategic (process) capabilities discussed above, strategic competency embraces everything an organization must be capable of doing effectively, or at least satisfactorily, if it is to survive, grow and prosper – e.g. strategic thinking, stakeholder satisfaction, the capability to deliver consistent quality, change competencies, social responsibility and crisis avoidance (see Richardson and Thompson, 1996).

9 **E–V–R congruence** Successful organizations create and sustain congruency between the external **environment** (the source of fresh opportunities and threats), their **values** and their **resources** (competencies, capabilities and strengths) governing their ability to change continuously (incrementally) and discontinuously (occasionally to new competitive paradigms).

10 **Strategic paradoxes** Discussed in more detail in the next section.

17.3 Strategic paradoxes

Strategic paradoxes help explain the realities of strategy and the strategic challenges facing organizations; and they concern aspects about which the organization must make decisions. The answers are not clear-cut, and yet these choices – and the relatedness of the decisions taken on each of the issues – will have a marked impact upon its strategic effectiveness. This section recaps the main strategic paradoxes, which have all been previously addressed within the book.

Paradox 1: Past and future All organizations build on the past, sometimes learning from their successes or from their mistakes, and which may imply continuous improvement around the same competitive paradigm – and yet the future may require more dramatic and discontinuous change, leading to the abandonment of past and current competitive paradigms. Rather than either (i) mistakenly persisting with products whose life cycle is heading for decline or (ii) changing for the sake of change (which is disruptive and may threaten control and quality), balance is needed.

Paradox 2: Intended and emergent strategy Strategic analysis and planning plays an important role in strategy, as does the contribution of a strong and charismatic entrepreneurial leader, but plans and intentions must be seen as flexible and it is dangerous to be reliant on just one main source of ideas. In such a dynamic and competitive environment, learning and emergent strategy will always be vital, such that the challenge is again one of balance.

Paradox 3: Reactive or proactive? Some commentators argue that the real challenge for organizations is one of coping in an environment that is chaotic, unpredictable and uncertain, and that they must be able both to manage in and to manage their environments by responding to unexpected events by leading the change agenda.

Paradox 4: Resource-based or opportunity driven? As explained earlier in this chapter, both need to be adopted simultaneously but inevitably one or the other will take priority: but which, and with what emphasis?

Paradox 5: Cost or differentiation? Again, the answer is both! Organizations, in their search for competitive advantage, can never ignore costs, though we can distinguish between striving to be the cost leader (with lower costs than one's main rivals for the same product or service) and effective cost management. Organizations that look to add new values and differentiate their products and services in distinctive ways must invest (and increase their costs) to create this difference – while not pointlessly adding costs and benefits that are of little consequence to customers. The secret lies in understanding and managing the key cost drivers.

Paradox 6: Focus or diversify? Contemporary strategic logic says focus, and the era of the diversified conglomerate is over for the moment. However, a very tight focus can restrain growth and, consequently, most growth-oriented organizations will diversify in justifiably related areas. The link might be technology or markets.

Paradox 7: How big? The focus/diversify dilemma is related to growth ambitions such that a large organization may be able to claim critical mass, perhaps important in its industry, especially where it has ambitions to be a global competitor. Some very successful organizations deliberately set out to be Number one or Number two in every market segment in which they compete – but their challenge is to retain the flexibility and the innovation of the small, entrepreneurial business as they grow to ensure that they do not reach a position of stasis in the cycle of growth and perhaps have to engineer a crisis to address the need for renewed creativity. Even the largest global organizations need to be relevant locally around the world.

Paradox 8: Centralize or decentralize? Although centralization enables retention of control at the top of the organization and allows for hands-on leadership from the strategic leader, it can unfortunately make the organization slow to respond in a dynamic environment. Decentralization and empowerment can increase flexibility, in conjunction with a hands-off leadership style, but now control has to be achieved through a carefully crafted information system. Whilst balancing the two satisfactorily may seem impossible, with organizations continually swinging from one to the other, there may be minor adjustments or perhaps major structural changes.

In conclusion – what is strategy?

At this point, we recommend you revisit Figure 1.4 which illustrates that strategy in practice (and in reality) concerns who decides ... what to do ... why and how ... and when things need to change. Since strategy is about being aware and being in control of the change agenda, requiring organizations to have clear answers for key strategic questions, strategy, therefore, is:

- *Knowing where the organization is and how well it is performing*, demanding a clear understanding of strategic positioning, supported by effective performance measures.

- *Ensuring that employees know and support what the organization stands for and where it is going*, implying that strategies are value driven and that employees appreciate the role and significance of their contribution, and accomplished with a sound and shared mission, purpose and direction.

- *Knowing how the organization intends to follow this direction*, requiring intended strategies which build on, and exploit, key resources, competencies and capabilities in the context of identified opportunities.

- *Ensuring that strategies and strategic ideas are implemented, while recognizing that there is a constant need for vigilance and flexibility*, specifically an organization that can respond to environmental turbulence, competitor actions and occasional setbacks and innovate to change its strategies, in which people have some control over the work they contribute.

The appropriate performance measures concern efficiency (doings things right) and effectiveness (doing the right things). Effectiveness encompasses the interests of all key stakeholders – in particular employees, who contribute ideas and ensure that strategies are implemented, customers, for whom the value is created and built, and the shareholders who retain faith in the business and support it financially. Where these are in place, we should have an organization which can demonstrate E–V–R congruence and which will be more crisis averse than crisis prone.

In a nutshell, strategy is about what organizations do.

It is about doing the right things in the right way – and for the right reasons.

These activities are carried out by everyone in the organization. Managers 'everywhere' and at all levels affect the choices, decisions and tactics. It is, therefore, important that managers think strategically and appreciate the (holistic) impact of their decisions, choices and actions. Having read this book, you may (and should) think that strategy is not 'rocket science', but why is that not more evident?

References

Checkland, P.B. (1981) *Systems Thinking, Systems Practice*, John Wiley.

Miles, R.E. and Snow, C.C. (1994) *Fit, Failure and the Hall of Fame: How Companies Succeed or Fail*, Free Press.

Richardson, B. and Thompson, J.L. (1996) Strategic and Competitive Success: Towards a Model of the Comprehensively Competent Organization, *Management Decision*, Vol 34, No 2.

Whittington, R. (1996) 'Strategy as practice', Long Range Planning, 731–735.

Whittington, R. (2001) What is Strategy and does it matter? Second edition, Cengage Learning: Andover.

Bibliography

Abell, D. (1978) Strategic windows, *Journal of Marketing*, 42, July.

Abrahamson, E. (2000) Dynamic stability, *Harvard Business Review*, January–February.

Andrews, K.R. (1989) Ethics in practice, *Harvard Business Review*, September–October.

Atkinson, A.A., Waterhouse, J.H. and Wells, R.B. (1997) A stakeholder approach to strategic performance management, *Sloan Management Review*, Spring.

Barney, J.B. (1986) Organizational culture – can it be a source of sustainable competitive advantage?, *Academy of Management Review*, 11 (3).

Bartlett, C. and Ghoshal, S. (1987) Managing across borders – new organizational responses, *Sloan Management Review*, Fall.

Bartlett, C. and Ghoshal, S. (1994) Beyond strategy to purpose, *Harvard Business Review*, November–December.

Biggadike, R. (1979) The risky business of diversification, *Harvard Business Review*, May–June.

Bishop, J.D. (1991) The Moral Responsibility of Corporate Executives for Disasters, *Journal of Business Ethics*, 10.

Bourantes, D. and Mandes, Y. (1987) Does market share lead to profitability?, *Long Range Planning*, 20 (5).

Bourgeois, L.J. and Brodwin, D.R. (1984) Strategy implementation – five approaches to an elusive phenomenon, *Strategic Management Journal*, 5.

Brody, P. and Ehrlich, D. (1998) Can big companies become successful venture capitalists?, *McKinsey Quarterly, 2.*

Bryson, J.M. (1988) A strategic planning process for public and non-profit organizations, *Long Range Planning*, 21 (1).

Campbell, A. and Yeung, S. (1991) Creating a sense of mission, *Long Range Planning*, August.

Campbell, A. and Alexander, M. (1997) What's wrong with strategy? *Harvard Business Review*, November– December.

Caulkin, S. (1996) Focus is for wimps, *Management Today*, December.

Chan Kim, W. and Mauborgne, R. (2002) Charting your company's future, *Harvard Business Review*, May–June.

Clarke, C.J. and Gall, F. (1987) Planned divestment – a five-step approach, *Long Range Planning*, 20 (1).

Clarke, C.J. (1988) Using finance for competitive advantage, *Long Range Planning*, 21 (2).

Clarke, C.J. and Brennan, K. (1990) Building synergy in the diversified business, *Long Range Planning*, 23 (20).

Courtney, H.G., Kirkland, J. and Viguerie, S.P. (2001) Strategy under uncertainty, *Harvard Business Review*, March–April.

De Geus, A. (1997) The living company, *Harvard Business Review*, March–April.

Devlin, G. and Bleackley, M. (1988) Strategic alliances – guidelines for success, *Long Range Planning*, 21 (5).

Douglas, S. and Wind, Y. (1987) The myth of globalization, *Columbia Journal of World Business*, Winter.

Drucker, P.F. (1988) The coming of the new organization, *Harvard Business Review*, January–February.

Drucker, P.F. (1989) What business can learn from nonprofits, *Harvard Business Review*, July–August.

Eisenhardt, K.M. (1999) Strategy as strategic decision making, *Sloan Management Review*, 40, Spring.

Emery, F.E. and Trist, E.L. (1965) The causal texture of organizational environments, *Human Relations*, 18.

Ford, J.D. (1981) The management of organizational crises, *Business Horizons*, May–June.

Francis, D. *et al.* (2003) Managing radical organizational transformation, *Management Decision*, 41 (1).

Garvin, D.A. (1984) What does product quality really mean?, *Sloan Management Revue*, Fall.

Ginsberg, A. and Hay, M. (1994) Confronting the challenges of corporate entrepreneurship, *European Management Journal*, 12 (4).

Ginter, P. and Duncan, J. (1990) Macroenvironmental analysis, *Long Range Planning*, December.

Goffee, R. and Jones, G. (2000) Why should anyone be led by you?, *Harvard Business Review* September–October.

Goold, M. and Campbell, A. (1987) Managing diversity – strategy and control in diversified British companies, *Long Range Planning*, 20 (5).

Goold, M. and Campbell, A. (2002) Parenting in complex structures, *Long Range Planning*, 35.

Goss, T., Pascale, R. and Athos, A. (1993) The re-invention roller coaster – risking the present for a powerful future, *Harvard Business Review*, November– December.

Hamel, G. and Prahalad, C.K. (1989) Strategic intent, *Harvard Business Review*, May–June.

Hamel, G. and Prahalad, C.K. (1994) Seeing the future first, *Fortune*, September 5.

Hamel, G. (1996) Strategy as revolution, *Harvard Business Review*, July–August.

Hamel, G. (1999) Bringing Silicon Valley inside, *Harvard Business Review*, September–October.

Handy, C. (1989) End of the world we know, *Management Today*, April.

Hansen, M.T. (1999) What's your strategy for managing knowledge?, *Harvard Business Review*, March–April.

Harrigan, K.R. and Porter, M.E. (1983) End game strategies for declining industries, *Harvard Business Review*, July– August.

Harrison, R. (1972) Understanding your organization's character, *Harvard Business Review*, May–June. Miles, R., Snow, C., Meyer, A. and Coleman, H. (1978)

Organizational strategy structure and process, *Academy of Management Review*, July.

Haspeslagh, P. (1982) Portfolio planning – uses and limits, *Harvard Business Review*, January–February.

Hedley, B. (1977) Strategy and the 'business portfolio', *Long Range Planning*, 10.

Huffman, B. (2001) What makes a strategy brilliant?, *Business Horizons*, 44 (4).

Idenburg, P.J. (1993) Four styles of strategy development, *Long Range Planning*, 26 (6).

Kanter, R.M. (1989) The new managerial work, *Harvard Business Review*, November–December.

Kanter, R.M. (1994) Collaborative advantage: the art of alliances, *Harvard Business Review*, July–August.

Kanter, R.M. (2003) Leadership and the psychology of turnarounds, *Harvard Business Review*, May–June.

Kaplan, R.S. and Norton, D.P. (1992) The balanced storecard – measures that drive performance, *Harvard Business Review*, January–February.

Kaplan, R.S. and Norton, D.P. (1996) Using the balanced scorecard as a strategic management system, *Harvard Business Review*, January–February.

Kaplan, R.S. and Norton, D.P. (2000) Having trouble with your strategy? Then map it, *Harvard Business Review*, September–October.

Kets de Vries, M. (1994) CEOs also have the blues, *European Journal of Management*, September.

Kets de Vries, M. (1996) Leaders who make a difference, *European Management Journal*, 14 (5).

Kotter, J.P. (1995) Why transformation efforts fail, *Harvard Business Review*, March–April.

Levitt, T. (1983) The globalization of markets, *Harvard Business Review*, May-June.

McFarlane, F.W. (1984) Information technology changes the way you compete, *Harvard Business Review*, May–June.

Maccoby, M. (2000) Narcissistic leaders, *Harvard Business Review*, January–February.

Markides, C. (1997) To diversify or not to diversify, *Harvard Business Review*, November–December.

Markides, C.C. (1999) A dynamic view of strategy, *Sloan Management Review*, 40, Spring.

Miller, D. (1992) The Icarus paradox – how exceptional companies bring about their own downfall, *Business Horizons*, January–February.

Mintzberg, H. and Waters, J.A. (1985) Of strategies deliberate and emergent, *Strategic Management Journal*, 6.

Mintzberg, H. (1987) Crafting strategy, *Harvard Business Review*, July–August.

Mintzberg, H. (1991) The effective organization – forces and forms, *Sloan Management Review*, Winter.

Mintzberg, H. (1999) Reflecting on the strategy process, *Sloan Management Review*, 40, Spring.

Morris, E. (1988) Vision and strategy – a focus for the future, *Journal of Business Strategy*, 8 (2).

Pascale, R., Millemann, M. and Gioja, L. (1997) Changing the way we change, *Harvard Business Review*, November–December.

Pearson, E.A. (1994) Tough minded ways to get innovative, *Harvard Business Review*, May–June.

Peters, T.J. (1980) Putting excellence into management, *Business Week*, July 21.

Peters, T.J. and Waterman, R.H. Jr (1982) *In Search of Excellence: Lessons from America's Best Run Companies*, Harper & Row – includes details of The McKinsey 7-S framework, which is useful for resource analysis.

Peters, T. (1993) The transformation of positively everything, *Director*, March.

Pitts, R.A. and Daniels, J.D. (1984) Aftermath of the matrix mania, *Columbia Journal of World Business*, Summer.

Porter, M.E. (1979) How competitive forces shape strategy, *Harvard Business Review*, March–April.

Porter, M.E. (1987) From competitive advantage to corporate strategy, *Harvard Business Review*, May–June.

Porter, M.E. (1990) *The Competitive Advantage of Nations*, The Free Press.

Porter, M.E. (1996) What is strategy?, *Harvard Business Review*, November–December.

Porter, M.E. (2001) Strategy and the Internet, *Harvard Business Review*, March–April.

Quinn, J. (1980) Managing strategic change, *Sloan Management Review*, Summer.

Rayport, J.F. and Sviokla, J.J. (1995) Exploiting the virtual value chain, *Harvard Business Review*, November–December.

Richardson, W.A. (1994) Comprehensive approach to strategic management – leading across the strategic management domain, *Management Decision*, 32 (8).

Richardson, W. (1988) Towards a profile of the visionary leader, *Small Business Enterprise and Development*, 1 (1).

Ringbakk, K.A. (1971) Why planning fails, *European Business*, Spring.

Salancik, G.R. and Pfeffer, J. (1977) Who gets power – and how they hold on to it: a strategic-contingency model of power, *Organizational Dynamics*, Winter.

Sahlman, W.A. (1997) How to write a great business plan, *Harvard Business Review*, July–August.

Schein, E.H. (1984) Coming to a new awareness of culture, *Sloan Management Review*, 25 (2).

Senge, P. (1990) The leader's new work – building learning organizations, *Sloan Management Review*, Fall.

Simon, H.A. (1964) On the concept of organizational goal, *Administrative Science Quarterly*, 9 (1).

Stacey, R. (1993) Strategy as order emerging from chaos, *Long Range Planning*, 26 (1).

Stalk, G. (1988) Time – the next source of competitive advantage, *Harvard Business Review*, July–August.

Stopford, J.M. and Baden-Fuller, C. (1990) Corporate rejuvenation, *Journal of Management Studies*, July.

Tichy, N. (1996) Simultaneous transformation and CEO succession – key to global competitiveness, *Organizational Dynamics*, Summer.

Tilles, S. (1963) How to evaluate corporate strategy, *Harvard Business Review*, July–August.

Waterman, R., Peters, T. and Phillips, J. (1980) Structure is not organization, *Business Horizons*, June.

Weinshall, T.D. and Vickery, L. (1987) Entrepreneurs: a balanced view of their role in innovation and growth, *European Management Journal*, 5 (4).

Whipple, W. (1989) Evaluating alternative strategies using scenarios, *Long Range Planning*, 22 (3).

Williamson, P.J. (1999) Strategy as options on the future, *Sloan Management Review*, 40, Spring.

Zack, M.H. (1999) Developing a knowledge strategy, *California Management Review*, 41 (3).

Glossary

acquisition—the purchase of one company by another, for either cash or equity in the parent. Sometimes the word *takeover* is preferred when the acquisition is hostile, and resisted by the company being bought. Similarly, *mergers* are when two companies simply *agree* to come together as one.

activities—those things – acts and tasks – undertaken by an organization which, when aggregated, dictate the strength of a *strategic position*.

adaptive strategic change—strategies that emerge and develop on an ongoing basis as companies learn of new environmental opportunities and threats and adapt (or respond) to competitive pressures.

adding value—technically, the difference between the value of a firm's outputs and its inputs; the additional value is added through the deployment and effort of the organization's resources. Successful organizations will seek to add value to create outputs which are perceived as important by their customers. The *added value* or *supply chain* is the sequential set of activities from suppliers, through manufacturers and distributors, which is required to bring products and services to the marketplace.

alliance (strategic alliance)—an agreement, preferably formalized, with another organization. The alliance might be with an important supplier, with a major distributor, or possibly with a competitor, say for joint research and development.

appropriability—the ability of an organization to ensure that at least some of the benefits earned from the value that it creates and adds comes back to the organization, rather than only benefiting others, such as suppliers, customers or even competitors.

architecture—a relational network involving either or both external linkages (*see alliance*) or internal linkages between managers in a company or businesses in a conglomerate. The supply chain is one such network. The main benefits concern information exchanges for the mutual gain of those involved, and *synergies* (see below) from interdependencies. Sometimes linked with reputation and innovation as key strategic resources for an organization.

backward (vertical) integration—the process by which a manufacturer acquires direct control over its inputs, such that it makes what it previously bought in. See also *vertical integration*.

benchmarking—a process of comparative evaluation – of products, services and the performance of equipment and personnel. Sometimes companies attempt to benchmark their competitors; on other occasions they will benchmark those organizations which are seen as high performers.

Blue Ocean Strategy—is where organizations discover radical new opportunities for competitive advantage and thus reduce the likelihood of damage from aggressive price competition.

branding—the additional value and reassurance provided to customers through the reputation of the business, represented by the strength and visibility of its brand name.

break-even—the level of activity where the total costs incurred in producing and selling a product or service – or pursuing a particular strategy – are equal to the total revenues generated.

business environment—*see environment*.

business ethics—the principles, standards and conduct that an organization practises – and sometimes states formally – and the way in which it deals with its people, its external stakeholders and environmental issues that arise.

business model—a concise summary of the organization and its strategy which answers three questions – what, for whom and why? What products and business activities the organization will engage in – and what it will not, who the target market is for each product or business and what their compelling reason to buy is – the why element.

business process re-engineering—the analysis and redesign of workflows and processes within organizations and between them (i.e. along the supply chain).

combination strategies—term used where more than one discrete strategic alternative is pursued at the same time. Particularly relevant for a mixture of market penetration, market development and product development strategies; and invariably implies innovation.

competitive advantage—the ability of an organization to add more value for its customers than its rivals, and thus attain a position of relative advantage. The challenge is to sustain any advantage once achieved.

competitive logic—linked to *competitive advantage*, competitive logic concerns the robustness and viability of the competitive strategy for a product, service or business.

competitive platforms—the important bases of competition in an industry and for an individual competitor.

competitive strategy—the means by which organizations seek to achieve and sustain competitive advantage. Usually the result of distinctive *functional strategies*. There should be a competitive strategy for every product and service produced by the company.

competitor gap analysis—a comparison of the organization with its leading competitors in terms of their respective ability to satisfy key success factors. Ideally, this will involve an input from relevant customers.

competitor-influenced strategy—strategies and tactics that arise from a need to compete in an industry or environment – for both markets and resources. When an organization introduces changes, competitors are likely to react, forcing further incremental changes. At the same time, competitors introduce new strategic ideas that vigilant organizations will respond to.

concentration ratio—normally the degree to which added value and/or turnover and/or assets in an industry are concentrated in the hands of a few suppliers. High concentration is reflected in monopoly and oligopoly industry structures. Sometimes measured in terms of aggregate output controlled by the largest companies in a country.

controls—means by which progress against stated objectives and targets is measured and monitored, and changed as necessary.

core competencies—distinctive skills, normally related to a product, service or technology, which can be used to create a competitive advantage. See also *strategic capability*. Together, they form key resources that assist an organization in being different from (and ideally superior to) its competitors.

corporate governance—the selection, role and responsibilities of the strategic leadership of the organization, their conduct and their relationships with internal and external stakeholders. Sometimes responsibility for overall strategy and ongoing operations will be separated.

corporate strategy—the overall strategy for a diversified or multi-product/multi-service organization. Refers to the overall scope of the business in terms of products, services and geography.

cost leadership—the lowest cost producer in a market, after adjustments for quality differences. An important source of competitive advantage in either a market or a segment of a market. Specifically, the cost leader is the company that enjoys a cost advantage over its rivals through the management of its resources, and not simply because it produces the lowest quality.

cost of capital—the cost of capital employed to fund strategic initiatives, combining the rate of interest on debt and the cost of equity. The typical formula used is the weighted average cost of capital which encompasses the relative proportions of debt and equity. Should normally be lower than the discounted rate of return from the investment or initiative – *see discounted cash flow*.

credit crunch—a term used to explain a shortage of credit in an economy. The impact is felt by organizations which experience difficulties in borrowing money to invest and expand.

crisis management—how the organization (a) seeks to reduce the likelihood of, and (b) manages in the event of, a major disturbance which has the potential to damage the organization's assets or reputation. Some crises are the result of mismanagement or inadequate controls; others begin outside the organization and may be unavoidable.

critical mass—relates to the actual and relative size of an organization in terms of its ability to be influential and powerful in its industry or environment.

critical success factors—*see key success factors*.

culture—the values and norms of an organization, which determine its corporate behaviour and the behaviour of people within the organization.

decentralization/centralization—the extent to which authority, responsibility and accountability are devolved throughout the organization. Centralization should yield tight control; decentralization motivates managers and allows for speedier reactions to environmental change pressures.

delayering—the flattening of an organization structure by removing layers of management and administration.

differentiation—products and services are differentiated when customers perceive them to have distinctive properties that set them apart from their competitors.

directional policy matrix—a planning technique used to compare and contrast the relative competitive strengths of a portfolio of products and services produced by an organization. Used to help in evaluating their relative worth and investment potential.

discounted cash flow (DCF)—the sum of the projected cash returns or flows over a period of years from a strategic investment or initiative. Future figures are reduced (specifically, inflation is removed) to bring them in line with present values.

diversification—the extent of the differences between the various products and services in a company's portfolio (its range of activities). The products and services may be *related* through, say, marketing or technology, or *unrelated*, which normally implies that they require different management skills.

divestment—term used when an organization sells or spins off (or maybe even closes) a business or activity. Usually linked to a strategy of increased focus.

divisionalization—a form of organization structure whereby activities are divided and separated on the basis of different products or services, or geographical territories.

dot.com companies—organizations that have emerged as the power and potential of the Internet has been realized and exploited. dot.com companies will normally trade over the Internet, but some are essentially service providers.

double-loop learning—an assessment of the continuing appropriateness and value of existing competitive positions and paradigms and the ability to create new competitive positions, ideally ahead of competitors. See also *single-loop learning*.

downsizing—sometimes associated with business process re-engineering, downsizing occurs when organizations rationalize their product/service ranges and streamline their processes. People, in particular layers of management, are removed. See also *rightsizing*.

e-commerce—short for electronic commerce, and meaning trading over the Internet.

economies of scale—cost savings accrued with high volume production, which enables lower unit production costs.

effectiveness—the ability of an organization to meet the demands and expectations of its various stakeholders, those individuals or groups with influence over the business. Sometimes known as 'doing the right things'.

efficiency—the sound management of resources to maximize the returns from them. Known as 'doing things right'.

emergent strategy—term used to describe and explain strategies which emerge over time and often with an element of trial and error. Detailed implementation is not prescribed in advance. Some emergent strategies are *incremental changes* with learning as intended strategies are implemented. Other *adaptive strategies* are responses to new environmental opportunities and threats.

empowerment—freeing people from a rigid regime of rules, controls and directives and allowing them to take responsibility for their own decisions and actions.

entrepreneur—someone who perpetually creates and innovates to build something of recognized value around perceived opportunities.

entrepreneurial/visionary strategies—strategies created by strong, visionary strategic leaders. Their successful implementation relies on an ability to persuade others of their merit.

environment—everything and everyone outside the organization or organizational boundary – including competitors, customers, financiers, suppliers and government.

E–V–R (environment–values–resources) congruence—the effective matching of an organization's resources (R) with the demands of its environment (E). A successful and sustained match has to be managed and frequently requires change; successfully achieving this depends on the organization's culture and values (V).

experience curve—the relationship between (reducing) unit costs and the total number of units ever produced of a product. Usually plotted as a graph, and often with a straight-line relationship on logarithmic axes. The percentage unit cost reduction holds steady every time output is doubled.

financial control—term used to describe the form of control normally found in a *holding company* structure. Strategy creation is decentralized to independent business units which are required to meet agreed financial targets.

focus strategy—concentration on one or a limited number of market segments or niches.

forward (vertical) integration—when an organization takes control of aspects of its distribution, transport or direct selling. See also *vertical integration*.

functional strategies—the strategies for the various functions carried out by an organization, including marketing, production, financial management, information management, research and development and human resource management. One or more functional strategies will typically be responsible for any distinctive competitive edge enjoyed by the company.

functional structure—a structure based around individual functions, such as production, sales and finance, all of which report to an identifiable managing director/chief executive.

generic strategies—the basic competitive strategies – based on cost leadership, differentiation and focus – which are open to any competitor in an industry, and which can be a source of competitive advantage.

global strategies—strategies for companies which manufacture and market in several countries and/or continents. Issues concern, for example, the location of manufacturing units and the extent to which control is centralized at a home base or decentralized on a local basis.

governance—the location of power and responsibility at the head of an organization. See also *corporate governance*.

heartland—term used to describe a cluster of businesses (in a multi-business organization) which can be justifiably related and integrated to generate synergies.

holding company—a structure where the various businesses are seen as largely independent of each other and managed accordingly.

horizontal integration—the acquisition or merger of firms at the same stage in the supply chain. Such firms may be direct competitors or focus on different market segments.

implementation—see *strategy implementation*.

innovation—changes to products, processes and services in an attempt to sharpen their competitiveness – through either cost reduction or improved distinctiveness. Strategically, it can apply to any part of a business.

intangible resources—resources which have no physical presence, but which can add real value for the organization. Reputation and technical knowledge would be typical examples.

intellectual capital—the hidden value (and capital) tied up in an organization's people which can set it apart from its competitors and be a valuable source of competitive advantage and future earnings. Difficult to quantify and value for the balance sheet. Linked to *knowledge*.

intended strategies—prescribed strategies the organization intends to implement, albeit with incremental changes. Sometimes the result of (formal) strategic planning; sometimes the stated intent of the strategic leader. May be described alternatively as *prescriptive strategies*.

intrapreneurship—the process of internal entrepreneurship. Occurs when managers or other employees accept responsibility and actively champion new initiatives aimed at making a real difference.

joint venture—a form of strategic alliance where each partner takes a financial stake. This could be a shareholding in the other partner or the establishment of a separate, jointly owned, business.

just-in-time (JIT)—systems or processes for ensuring that stocks or components are delivered just when and where they are needed, reducing the need for inventory.

key (or critical) success factors—environmentally based factors which are crucial for competitive success. Simply, the things that an organization must be able to do well if it is to succeed.

knowledge—an amalgamation of experience, values, information, insight and strategic awareness – which goes beyond the notions of data and information. Retained, managed and exploited, it can be a valuable source of competitive difference and advantage. See also *intellectual capital*.

leadership—see *strategic leader*.

learning organization—one which is capable of harnessing and spreading best practices, and where employees can learn from each other and from other organizations. The secret lies in open and effective communications networks.

leverage—the exploitation by an organization of its resources to their full extent. Often linked to the idea of *stretching resources*.

life cycle—see *strategic life cycle*.

liquidation—the closing down of a business, normally because it has failed. Typically a last resort, when a rescue or sale has either not been possible or not successful.

logical incrementalism—term adopted by John B. Quinn to explain strategy creation in small, logical, incremental steps.

long tail—relates to an extended product life cycle, especially for products (or services) whose popularity rises and falls rapidly due to 'fashion'. Through e-commerce, products (such as CD titles and books) can remain available without normal distribution channels needing to carry expensive inventory.

Machiavellianism—where individuals use power and influence to structure situations and events, and bring about outcomes, which are more in their own personal interests than those of the organization. Linked to *organizational politics*.

market development—continuing with existing products and services but, and possibly with modifications and additions, seeking new market and new market segment opportunities.

market-driven strategy—alternative term for *opportunity-driven strategy*.

market penetration—persisting with existing products/services and existing customers and markets but accepting that continuous, incremental improvement is possible to strengthen the relevant strategic position. The assumption is that sales and revenue can be increased.

market segment(ation)—the use of particular marketing strategies to target identified and defined groups of customers.

merger—see *acquisition*.

milestones—interim targets which act as indicators or measures of progress in the pursuit of objectives and the implementation of strategies.

military strategy—strategy and planning in the context of warfare through the ages. Strategy has its origins in warfare and consequently a study of military strategy can provide valuable insights into corporate behaviour.

mission—a statement of the organization's present main activities.

mission statement—a summary of the essential aim or purpose of the organization; its essential reason for being in business.

monopoly power—the relative power of an individual company in an industry. It does not follow that a dominant competitor will act against the best interests of customers and consumers, but it could be in a position to do so.

monopoly structure—term for an industry with a dominant and very powerful competitor. Originally based on the idea of total control, competitive authorities around the world now consider a 25 per cent market or asset share to be a basis for possible monopoly power.

multinational company—a company operating in several countries. See *global strategies*.

niche marketing—concentration on a small, identifiable market segment with the aim of achieving dominance of the segment.

not-for-profit organization—term used to describe an organization (such as a charity) that does not have profit as a fundamental objective. Such organizations will, however, have to achieve a cash surplus to survive.

objectives—short-term targets or milestones with defined measurable achievements. A desired state and hoped-for level of success.

oligopoly—(structure) an industry dominated by a small group of competitors.

opportunity-driven strategy—strategy creation and development that begins with an analysis of external environmental threats and opportunities. See also *resource-based strategy*.

organizational politics—the process by which individuals and groups utilize power and influence to obtain results. Politics can be used legitimately in the best interests of the organization, or illegitimately by people who put their own interests above those of the organization.

outsource/outsourcing—procuring products and services from independent suppliers rather than producing them within the organization. Often linked to strategies of focusing on core competencies and capabilities.

paradigm—a recipe or model for linking together the component strands of a theory and identifying the inherent relationships, a competitive paradigm explains the underpinning logic of a competitive strategy or position.

parenting—the skills and capabilities used by a head office to manage and control a group of subsidiary businesses. The head office should be able to add value for the businesses, while the businesses should, in turn, be able to add value for the whole organization.

performance indicators or measures—quantifiable measures and subjective indicators of strategic and competitive success.

PEST analysis—an analysis of the *political, economic, social* and *technological* factors in the external environment of an organization, which can affect its activities and performance.

plan—a statement of intent, generally linked to a programme of tactics for strategy implementation.

planning—see *strategic planning*.

planning gap—a planning technique which enables organizations to evaluate the potential for, and risk involved in, seeking to attain particular growth targets.

policies—guidelines relating to decisions and approaches which support organizational efforts to achieve stated (intended) objectives. Can be at any level in the organization, and can range from mandatory regulations to recommended courses of action. They may or may not be written down formally.

portfolio analysis—techniques for evaluating the appropriate strategies for a range of (possibly diverse) business activities in a single organization. See *directional policy matrix*.

power—the potential or ability to do something or make something happen. Externally, it refers to the ability of an organization to influence and affect the actions of its external stakeholders. Internally, it concerns the relationships between people.

prescriptive strategies—see *intended strategies*.

private equity funds—venture capital funds whereby professional investors secure funds to invest in organizations, sometimes parachuting in a new management team when they take ownership. The funders are usually looking to sell or float the business in a relatively short timescale to recover their funds and at the same time make a healthy return.

product development—developing additional and normally related products and services to enhance the range available to existing customers and markets, and thereby increase sales and revenue.

profit—the difference between total revenues and total costs. Often profit is a fundamental objective of a manufacturing or service business.

profitability—financial ratios which look at profits generated in relation to the capital that has been employed to generate them. Two different ratios relate (a) trading profit (or profit before interest and tax) to total capital employed (known as the return on capital employed) and (b) profit after interest and tax to shareholders' funds (known as the return on shareholders' funds).

public sector organizations—organizations controlled directly or indirectly by government and/or dependent on government for a substantial proportion of their revenue. Includes local authorities, the National Health Service in the UK and the emergency services.

quality—strategically, quality is concerned with the ability of an organization to 'do things right – first time and every time' for each customer. This includes internal customers (other departments in an organization) as well as external customers. *Total quality management* is the spreading of quality consciousness throughout the whole organization.

reputation—the strategic standing of an organization in the eyes of its customers and suppliers.

resource-based strategy—strategy creation built around the further exploitation of core competencies and strategic capabilities.

retrenchment—strategy followed when an organization is experiencing difficulties and needs to cut costs and consolidate its resources before seeking new ways to create and add value. Sometimes involves asset reduction (perhaps the sale of a business) and job losses.

revenue model—linked directly to the Business Model, the revenue model illustrates why and how a product, service or business is profitable.

rightsizing—linked to downsizing, implies the reduction in staffing is at a level from which the organization can grow effectively. On occasions, downsizing can mean that strategically important skills and competencies are lost; rightsizing implies this is not the case.

risk management—the understanding where and how things can and might go wrong, appreciating the extent of any downside if things do go wrong, and putting in place strategies to deal with the risks either before or after their occurrence.

scenarios—conceptual possibilities of future events and circumstances. Scenario planning involves using these to explore what might happen in order to help prepare managers for a wide range of eventualities and uncertainties in an unpredictable future environment.

single-loop learning—the ability to improve a competitive position on an ongoing and continuous basis, acknowledging there is always the possibility of improvement. Sometimes the competitive paradigm itself has to be changed – see *double-loop learning*.

small- and medium-sized enterprises (SMEs)—term used to embrace new and growing businesses, and those which (for any number of reasons) do not grow beyond a certain size.

social responsibility—strategies and actions that can be seen to be in the wide and best interests of society in general and the environment. Sometimes associated with the notion of mutual self-interest.

spheres of influence—building an arsenal of products and services that enable real influence across a wide range of critical interests. Routes to growth around a key *heartland*. Also related to protecting existing interests in the face of competition.

squirrel approach—to strategic management resembles a squirrel climbing a tree, cautiously moving upwards from the trunk. The squirrel has limited options and makes many small well informed decisions. This approach is viewed as less risky, as the squirrel is on familiar territory.

stakeholders—any individual or group capable of affecting (and being affected by) the actions and performance of an organization.

strategic alliance—see *alliance*.

strategic architecture—see *architecture*.

strategic awareness—appreciating the strategic position and relative success of the organization. Knowing how well it is doing, why and how – relative to its competitors – and appreciating the nature of the external environment and the extent of any need to change things.

strategic business unit—a discrete grouping within an organization with delegated responsibility for strategically managing a product, a service or a particular group of products or services.

strategic capability—process skills used to add value and create competitive advantage.

strategic change—changes that take place over time to the strategies and objectives of the organization. Change can be gradual, emergent and evolutionary, or discontinuous, dramatic and revolutionary.

strategic changes—changes to intended (possibly planned) strategies as they are implemented. Result from ongoing learning and from changes in the environment or to forecast assumptions.

strategic control—a style of corporate control whereby the organization attempts to enjoy the benefits of delegation and decentralization with a portfolio of activities which, while diverse, is interdependent and capable of yielding synergies from co-operation.

strategic inflection points—introducing important changes at the right moment – related to both competition and customer expectations. Can act as a transformation point in the history of an industry.

strategic issues—current and forthcoming developments inside and outside the organization which will impact upon the ability of the organization to pursue its mission and achieve its objectives.

strategic leader—generic term used to describe a manager who is responsible for changes in the corporate strategy.

strategic life cycle—the notion that strategies (like products and services) have finite lives. After some period of time they will need improving, changing or replacing.

strategic management—the process by which an organization establishes its objectives, formulates actions (strategies) designed to meet these objectives in the desired timescale, implements the actions and assesses progress and results.

strategic planning—*in strategy creation*: the systematic and formal creation of strategies – to be found in many organizations, and capable of making a very significant contribution in large, multi-activity organizations. *In strategic control*: centralized control, most ideal where there is a limited range of core businesses.

strategic positioning—the chosen or realized relationship between the organization and its market. Clearly linked to competitive strategies and competitive advantage. The position itself is not a source of advantage, but the activities that underpin the position are.

strategic regeneration (or renewal)—major and simultaneous changes to strategies, structures and styles of management. See also *transformational change*.

strategic thinking—the ability of the organization (and its managers) to (a) synthesize the lessons from past experiences and to share the learning, (b) be aware of current positions, strengths and competencies and (c) clarify the way forward for the future.

strategy—the means by which organizations achieve (and seek to achieve) their objectives and purpose. There can be a strategy for each product and service, and for the organization as a whole.

strategy creation—umbrella term for the formulation and choice of new strategies. Encapsulates direction from the strategic leader (or an entrepreneur), strategic planning, and emergent strategy. See: *emergent strategy; entrepreneurial strategies; strategic planning.*

strategy implementation—the processes through which the organization's chosen and intended strategies are made to happen.

stretching resources—the creative use of resources to add extra value for customers – through innovation and improved productivity.

supply chain—the linkage between an organization, its suppliers, its distributors and its customers.

sustainable competitive advantage—a sustained edge over competitors in an industry, usually achieved by first creating a valuable difference and then sustaining it with improvement and change.

SWOT analysis—an analysis of an organization's *strengths* and *weaknesses* alongside the *opportunities* and *threats* present in the external environment.

synergy—term used for the added value or additional benefits which ideally accrue from the linkage or fusion of two businesses, or from increased co-operation either between different parts of the same organization or between a company and its suppliers, distributors and customers. Internal co-operation may represent linkages between either different divisions or different functions.

tactics—specific actions that follow on from intended strategies but which can also form a foundation for emergent strategy.

tangible resources—the organization's physical resources, such as plant and equipment.

transfer price—associated with the transfer of products, components or services between businesses in the same organization. A particularly important issue where there are considerable interdependencies between businesses. The (corporately) imposed or agreed transfer price can be of markedly different attractiveness to the buying and selling businesses and can be a source of friction.

transformational change—major and simultaneous changes to strategies, structures and styles of management. See also *strategic regeneration*.

turnaround strategy—an attempt to find a new competitive position for a company in difficulty.

values—the underpinning attitudes and manifest behaviours (perhaps desired as well as actual) that an organization wishes to have and to demonstrate.

value chain—framework for identifying (a) where value is added and (b) where costs are incurred. There is an internal value chain and one that embraces the complete supply chain. Internally, it embraces the key functions and activities.

vertical integration—where firms directly enter those parts of the added value chain served by their suppliers or distributors, the term used is vertical integration. To achieve the potential benefits of vertical integration (specifically synergy from co-operation) without acquiring a business which normally requires specialist and different skills, firms will look to establish strong alliances and networks.

vision—a statement or picture of the future standing of an organization. Linked to the mission or purpose, it embraces key values.

Index

Credits

Images

The publisher would like to thank the following sources for permission to reproduce their copyright protected imagery:

Alamy – pp 17br (Justin Kase z12z), 36br (David Stock), 148br (TJP), 156br (Benjamin Stansall), 173tr (Saverio Maria Gallotti), 189br (Jeff Greenberg "0 people images"), 213br (jvphoto), 229br (Silicon-ValleyStock), 269br (ZUMA Wire Service), 317br (Indiapix), 357br (AlamyCelebrity), 368tr (Dan Lamont), 427br (Peter Forsberg/CR), 439tr (Daniel Swee), 458br (James Davies), 466br (Jeffrey Blackler), 582br (Richard Handley); **Shutterstock** – pp 13br (Hank Shiffman), 32tr (Pavel L Photo and Video), 54br (Yuri Arcurs), 61br (chaoss), 78br (saddako), 87br (Lucian Coman), 90br (Michal Ninger), 115bl (SARIN KUNTHONG), 120br (Raia), 135br (Mike Flippo), 161br (Netfalls - Remy Musser), 163br (Steve Mann), 204br (Rainer Plendl), 233br (Tomas Skopal), 253br (Valeriy Lebedev), 273br (Dieter H), 280br (Fulcanelli), 314br (kurhan), 325tr (M. Khebra), 327tr (Julien_N), 352br (Rob Bayer), 397tr (Dmitriy Kalinin), 395br (ifong), 397br (spirit of america), 419br (Verdateo), 423tr (Uros Zunic), 462br (Moreno Soppelsa), 472br (joannawnuk), 495br (Shawn Kashou), 496br (Amanda Koehler), 501br (Jun Mu), 508br (fuyu liu), 520br (Lyudmila Suvorova), 523br (africa924), 566br (Franck Boston), 536br (Andrew F. Kazmierski), 570br (michaeljung), 574br (Bernhard Classen), 578br (Ziggy Folkmanis), 596tr (brave rabbit); **Glasses Direct** – pp 56br (Courtesy of Glasses Direct); **Kungka's Can Cook** – pp 247tr and 247br (Courtesy of Kungka's Can Cook); **soleRebels** – pp 264br (Courtesy of soleRebels); **Innocent** – pp 344br (Courtesy of Innocent)

Text and figures

Whittington, R. (1993), *What is Strategy – and does it matter?*, Cengage Learning, in 'Critical Reflection 1.1: Directions of strategic thought'; Ansoff, H.I. (1987), *Corporate Strategy*, Revised edition, Penguin, in 'Figure 9.2: Ansoff's growth vector'.